LEAVING CERTIFICATE MATHS

HIGHER LEVEL

Power of Maths

PAPER 1

Tony Kelly and
Kieran Mills

PUBLISHED BY:
Educate.ie
Walsh Educational Books Ltd
Castleisland, Co. Kerry, Ireland
www.educate.ie

EDITORS:
Finola McLaughlin, Fiona McPolin and Antoinette Walker

DESIGN:
Kieran O'Donoghue

COVER DESIGN:
Kieran O'Donoghue

LAYOUT:
Compuscript

PROOFREADER:
Ciara McNee

PRINTED AND BOUND BY:
Walsh Colour Print, Castleisland,
Co. Kerry, Ireland

PHOTOGRAPHS AND ILLUSTRATIONS:
Artistashmita/Dreamstime.com; Dreamstime.com; Gil C/Shutterstock.com; iStockphoto.com; Jason and Bonnie Grower/ Shutterstock.com; Martin Green/ Dreamstime.com; Shutterstock.com; Thinkstock.com; Wikicommons (public domain)

The authors and publisher have made every effort to trace all copyright holders. If any have been overlooked we would be happy to make the necessary arrangements at the first opportunity.

ISBN: 978-1-910052-96-9

ACKNOWLEDGEMENTS

The authors would like to thank Pat Saville for her invaluable assistance in writing this book. We would also like to thank Ian Wilkinson and Owen Wardell for providing additional mathematical expertise.

Contents

Introduction

Power of Maths is the first new Leaving Certificate Higher Level series since the full implementation and examination of the new Maths syllabus. The new syllabus encourages teachers and students to engage deeply with mathematical content. *Power of Maths* promotes this engagement by developing students' mathematical knowledge and problem-solving skills.

The *Power of Maths Higher Level* package includes two textbooks (with free ebooks), two Activity Books, step-by-step instructional videos and fully worked-out solutions. *Power of Maths* introduces content in a staged and graded manner and ensures that the principles of Maths are firmly established before students are guided through more complex material. Students who use the *Power of Maths* series will be fully prepared for the demands of the most recent Leaving Certificate exam papers.

Content covered in *Power of Maths Paper 1* and *Power of Maths Paper 2*:

Power of Maths Paper 1 Higher Level has been divided into 10 major sections: Number, Algebraic Expressions, Algebraic Equations, Sequences and Series, Financial Maths, Complex Numbers, Functions, Differentiation, Integration, and Mathematical Induction. This reflects the content that can be examined in the Higher Level Leaving Certificate Paper 1 examination.

Geometry, Mensuration, Trigonometry, Co-ordinate Geometry, Probability, and Statistics are covered in *Power of Maths Paper 2 Higher Level*. This reflects the content that can be examined in the Higher Level Leaving Certificate Paper 2 examination.

The first three sections of *Power of Maths Paper 1* and *Power of Maths Paper 2* provide the foundations for the rest of the course. We recommend completing Sections 1, 2 and 3 of *Power of Maths Paper 1* first, followed by Sections 1, 2 and 3 of *Power of Maths Paper 2*. Sections can then be completed sequentially, alternating between *Power of Maths Paper 1* and *Power of Maths Paper 2*, as you please.

Key features of *Power of Maths Paper 1*:

Learning outcomes

- Each chapter begins with a set of learning outcomes to guide students through the content.

Tips and key terms

- Tip and key term boxes appear throughout to aid understanding.

Examples

- *Power of Maths* is packed with examples. **Worked Examples** explain the reasoning behind a given approach to solving a problem. These examples underpin the philosophy behind the new approach to learning Maths.
- **Numbered Examples** apply the principles learnt to all types of situations. They utilise the more traditional approach to teaching Maths.
- **Short Examples** appear throughout the text and are indicated by a green arrow. These examples give students short and snappy explanations, helping them to undertake the exercises that follow.

Exercises

- Exercises appear at **regular intervals** in the text so that students can carry out questions with a minimum amount of teaching.
- **Questions in the exercises are graded**. Earlier questions provide plenty of practice and rigour to allow students to become totally familiar with the techniques required for carrying out a particular mathematical procedure. Gradually students are asked to use these techniques and **apply them to real-life situations**.

Activity boxes

- Activity boxes in the margin direct students to optional extra activities in the Activity Book.

Digital icons

- Digital icons link to step-by-step instructional videos and other digital resources on **www.educateplus.ie**.

Revision questions

- Revision questions at the end of each section provide plenty of practice of the type of questions examined in the Leaving Certificate examination.

Revision summaries

- Revision summaries at the end of each section reinforce and embed learning.

Activity Book

Power of Maths Paper 1 Higher Level comes with an Activity Book. The optional activities are signposted in the margin of this textbook and are designed to allow students to discover mathematical concepts on their own and to acquire a deep understanding of the material. This enhances the enjoyment of the subject, allowing students to learn complex material as effortlessly as possible.

Digital resources

Digital icons in the Algebraic Expressions, Algebraic Equations, and Differentiation sections in this textbook link to step-by-step instructional videos. Students can access the videos by clicking on the icon in the ebook or by visiting **www.educateplus.ie**.

These step-by-step instructional videos are designed to make the learning of difficult concepts as easy as possible. They also provide further exercises to complement the material in the textbook and Activity Book.

Students and teachers also receive a **free ebook** with the textbook. It can be downloaded using the redeem code on the inside front cover of this textbook.

Additional teachers' resources

Fully worked-out solutions for all of the exercises are available for teachers on **www.educateplus.ie**.

Finally, enjoy the experience of learning a beautiful subject.

Tony Kelly and Kieran Mills

SECTION 1

Number

'Mathematics is the queen of sciences and number theory is the queen of mathematics' – Carl Friedrich Gauss.

This section introduces the different types of numbers that we use today. Arithmetic is a set of rules for manipulating these numbers.

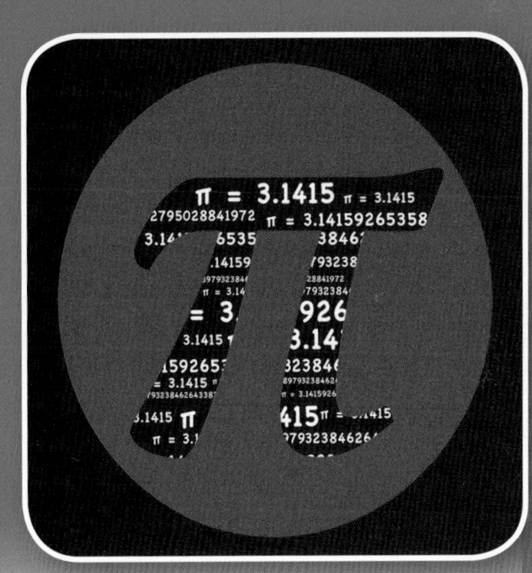

Number Systems

Learning Outcomes

- To understand that the set of natural numbers is made up of composite and prime numbers.
- To understand that the set of integers includes natural numbers as well as zero and whole negative numbers.
- To understand that the set of rational numbers are fractions which are the ratio of integers. Rationals can be written as either terminating or recurring decimals.
- To understand the idea of an irrational number and that the set of real numbers is the union of rational and irrational numbers.
- To understand, at this stage, that there is a set of complex numbers (imaginary numbers). All the other number sets are subsets of this set. (The set of complex numbers is so important a whole section is devoted to it later in the book.)
- To understand what is meant by the absolute value or modulus of a number.

Our present system of numbers was developed by dealing with progressively more difficult problems as they arose throughout the history of humankind.

1.1 Natural numbers

The natural numbers are the counting numbers. The set of **whole positive numbers** is called the set of natural numbers. This set is denoted by $\mathbb{N}$.

$\mathbb{N} = \{1, 2, 3, 4, 5, \ldots\}$

TIP

Zero (0) is not a natural number.

Prime numbers and composite numbers

The set of natural numbers can be divided into the following subsets:

Prime Numbers	*and*	**Composite Numbers**	*and*	**1**

Every natural number is a prime number, a composite number or 1.

KEY TERM

A **prime number** is a natural number greater than 1, which can be divided only by itself and 1.

All other natural numbers are composite numbers or 1.

17 is a prime number because its only divisors are 1 and 17.

18 is not a prime number as its divisors are 1, 2, 3, 6, 9, 18. So 18 is a composite number.

KEY TERM

The **factors** of a natural number are its whole positive number divisors.

WORKED EXAMPLE

Factors tell you whether a number is a prime or a composite number

Consider the number 14. The factors of 14 are: 1, 2, 7, 14, so 14 is a composite number.

Consider the number 19. The factors of 19 are: 1, 19. These are the only factors of 19. So 19 is a prime number.

Prime numbers are extremely important as they are the building blocks from which **all natural numbers** greater than 1 can be built. Every composite number can be expressed as a product of prime numbers.

ACTIVITY 1

ACTION
Identifying composite and prime numbers

OBJECTIVE
To investigate whether numbers are composite or prime

EXAMPLE 1

State whether the following numbers are prime or composite.

(a) 22

(b) 24

(c) 2^{10}

(d) 1023

(e) 29

Solution

(a) $22 = 2 \times 11$ is composite.

Prime Prime

(b) $24 = 2 \times 12 = 2 \times 2 \times 2 \times 3$ is composite.

(c) $2^{10} = 2 \times 2 \times 2 \times 2 \times 2 \times 2 \times 2 \times 2 \times 2 \times 2$ is composite.

(d) $1023 = 3 \times 341 = 3 \times 11 \times 31$ is composite.

(e) 29 is prime.

WORKED EXAMPLE

Is the number 1457 a prime number?

Divide the prime numbers in order into 1457 until one of them divides in exactly. If no prime number divides in exactly, then the number is itself a prime number.

Prime factor	N = 1457
2	1457 = 2 × 728 + 1
3	1457 = 3 × 485 + 2
5	1457 = 5 × 291 + 2
7	1457 = 7 × 208 + 1
11	1457 = 11 × 132 + 5
13	1457 = 13 × 112 + 1
17	1457 = 17 × 85 + 12
19	1457 = 19 × 76 + 13
23	1457 = 23 × 63 + 8
29	1457 = 29 × 50 + 7
31	1457 = 31 × 47
37	Stop

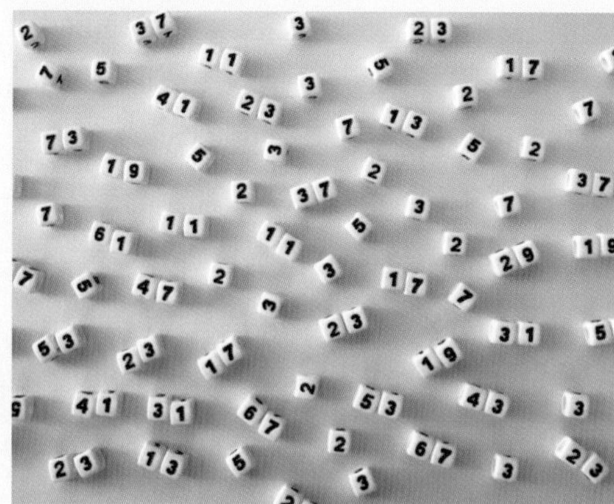

$\therefore$ 1457 = 31 × 47

1457 is composite number.

There are a few tests you can apply to a number to see whether or not it is a prime number.

Techniques for testing for primes

Test 1

With the exception of the number 2, all numbers with a last digit of 2, 4, 6 or 8 are composite. Why?

169 471 468 214 is a composite number.

TIP

2 is the only even prime number.

Test 2

With the exception of 5, all numbers with a last digit of 0 or 5 are composite numbers. Why?

52 745 is a composite number because 52 745 = 5 × 10 549.

62 150 is a composite number because 62 150 = 5 × 12 430.

Test 3

With the exception of the number 3, all numbers whose digits add to a multiple of 3 are divisible by 3 and so are composite.

12 356 781 = 3 × 4 118 927 because the digits 12 356 781 add up to 33.

Test 4

Eratosthenes, an Ancient Greek librarian at Alexandria, showed that a natural number is prime, if and only if, it is not divisible by any prime number which is less than or equal to the square root of the natural number.

Eratosthenes' technique: Divide the number you are testing by all primes up to, and including, the square root of the number. If none of these divide in exactly, the number is prime.

For example, to show if 1457 is a composite number:

- Find the square root of the number: $\sqrt{1457} = 38{\cdot}17$
- Divide all primes less than or equal to 38 into 1457.

ACTIVITY 2

ACTION
Deciding which numbers are prime

OBJECTIVE
To pick out the prime numbers from the first 100 natural numbers

EXAMPLE 2

Is 569 a prime number?

Solution

$\sqrt{569} = 23{\cdot}8$ [**Test 4**]

Possible prime factors < 23·8 are:

2, 3, 5, 7, 11, 13, 17, 19, 23

Prime factor	N = 569
3	$569 = 3 \times 189 + 2$
7	$569 = 7 \times 81 + 2$
11	$569 = 11 \times 51 + 8$
13	$569 = 13 \times 43 + 10$
17	$569 = 17 \times 33 + 8$
19	$569 = 19 \times 29 + 18$
23	$569 = 23 \times 24 + 17$

5	6	9

Therefore, 569 is a prime number because it has no prime factors less than 23·8.

Why did we not test 2 and 5?

ACTIVITY 3

ACTION
Working with prime factors

OBJECTIVE
To draw factor trees in order to work out prime factors

How many prime numbers are there?

You will meet the idea of proof by contradiction a number of times in this book. It is central to the idea of **proof** in mathematics. Here is a gem of a proof **by contradiction** due to the mathematician Euclid.

Theorem: There are infinitely many prime numbers.

Proof: Assume on the contrary that there is a finite number n of prime numbers $P_1, P_2, \ldots, P_n$ (and that is the lot).

Consider the number: $N = P_1 \times P_2 \times \ldots\ldots\ldots\ldots \times P_n + 1$

N is either prime or composite.

$$N = P_1 \times P_2 \times \ldots\ldots\ldots\ldots \times P_n + 1$$

$$\Rightarrow \frac{N}{P_i} \text{ gives a remainder of 1 for } i = 1, 2 \ldots n$$

Therefore, N cannot be composite since none of $P_1, \ldots, P_n$ divide into it exactly.

Therefore, N is a prime number which is not one of $P_1, \ldots, P_n$.

This contradicts that all primes are in the list $P_1 \ldots P_n$. Our assumption must be wrong.

Therefore, there is an infinite number of primes.

EXERCISE 1

1. Say which number is prime, composite or neither. Find the prime factors of the composite numbers.

   (a) 18 **(f)** 85

   (b) 45 **(g)** 62

   (c) 11 **(h)** 79

   (d) 28 **(i)** 51

   (e) 90 **(j)** 47

2. Which of the following natural numbers are prime?

   27, 38, 47, 91, 80, 1, 123, 465, 530

3. Is 413 625 914 856 a prime number? Why?

4. Is 32 794 221 a prime number? Why? Check it on your calculator.

5. **(a)** Is 2^{2013} a prime number? Why?

   (b) Is 5^{27} a prime number? Why?

6. Use Eratosthenes' technique to show that:

   (a) 799 is composite,

   (b) 797 is prime.

7. There are 36 students in a class. The numbers of boys and girls are both prime numbers. If there are two more boys than girls in the class, how many of each is there?

8. 'Every number between 1 and 100 can be written as a sum of two primes.' Give a simple example to show that this is not true.

9. **(a)** Write out the first 10 even natural numbers.

   (b) If n is the nth natural number, express the nth even natural number in terms of n.

   (c) Is an even natural number multiplied by an even natural number always even?

   (d) Prove the result in part **(c)** by multiplying the nth and kth even natural numbers.

10. **(a)** Write out the first 10 odd natural numbers.

    (b) If n is the nth natural number, what is the nth odd natural number?

    (c) Is an odd number multiplied by an odd number always odd?

    (d) Prove the result in part **(c)** by multiplying the nth and kth odd natural numbers.

11. When sending sensitive information like bank details over the internet, we want the information to be secure. This means that only the intended receiver gets the information. To do this, a system of encryption that cannot be hacked is necessary. Today encryption is called public key cryptography, or RSA encryption after its inventors.

    It is based on the fact that **it is easy** to generate two very large prime numbers p and q that multiply to give a very large composite number N. But, it is very difficult to factorise a very large composite number N into its prime factors in a finite amount of time.

    (a) $p = 34\,537$ and $q = 99\,991$ are prime. Find $N = pq$.

    (b) $N = 3\,763\,913$ is a composite number. Find its prime factors p and q, if $p = 2111$.

12. There is no formula for generating primes. However, a certain class of primes, called Mersenne primes, can be generated from the formula: $M = 2^p - 1$, which states that if $2^p - 1$ is prime for p prime, then M is a Mersenne prime.

For $p = 2, 3, 5, 7, 11, 13, 17$ and 19, find the Mersenne primes.

13. A cicada is a shy locust that only emerges to mate every 13 years (some of the species only emerge every 17 years). Why does this give the cicada a better chance of survival? Consider this from the point of view of predators with reproductive cycles of 2 or 4 or 6 years.

1.2 Integers

Why do we need even more numbers?

Consider the equations:

$x + 3 = 3$

with the solution $x = 3 - 3 = 0$

and

$x + 5 = 2$

with the solution $x = 2 - 5 = -3$

These equations have no solutions in the set of natural numbers $\mathbb{N}$, as 0 (zero) and negative numbers do not exist in this set. In order to solve such equations, the set of natural numbers must be extended to include 0 and negative numbers. This new set is called the set of **integers** and is denoted by $\mathbb{Z}$.

$\mathbb{Z} = \{\ldots -3, -2, -1, 0, 1, 2, 3\ldots\}$ can be shown on the number line as follows:

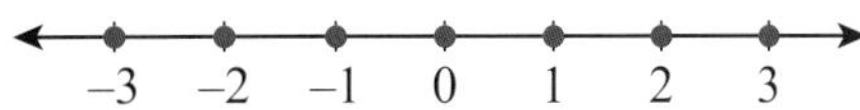

The set of natural numbers $\mathbb{N}$ is a subset of the set of integers $\mathbb{Z}$. This is written mathematically as $\mathbb{N} \subset \mathbb{Z}$.

Consecutive integers

Consecutive integers are whole numbers in which the difference between one integer and the previous one is 1 when written in ascending order of magnitude.

$-74, -73, -72$ are three consecutive integers because $-73 - (-74) = -72 - (-73) = 1$.

If a is an integer: $a, a + 1, a + 2$ and $a - 1, a, a + 1$ are consecutive integers.

EXERCISE 2

1. The melting point of mercury is −39 °C. The freezing point of ethanol is −114 °C. How much hotter is the melting point of mercury than the freezing point of ethanol?

2. Write down three consecutive integers in ascending order starting at −27.

3. The Roman Empire started in 27 BC and ended in AD 476. How long did the Roman Empire last?

4. The mean temperature in a city falls from 4 °C on the first day of the month by 1 °C for the next 9 days and then rises by 2 °C for the next 2 days. What is the mean temperature on the 12th day?

5. An investment is in the red by € 10 000 on 31 December 2012. It increases by € 3000 every month on the first of the month, starting on 1 January 2013. What is its value on 31 December 2013?

6. A very high temperature of 54 °C was once recorded in the Middle East. A very low temperature of −71 °C was once recorded in Siberia. What was the difference in temperature from highest to lowest?

7. The highest temperature reading on a thermometer is 212 °F and the lowest temperature reading is 32 °F. What is the temperature range of this thermometer?

8. A group of 100 integers alternates between −2 and 4 as shown: −2, 4, −2, 4… Find the sum of this group of numbers.

9. Evaluate:
   (a) $(-1)^3$
   (b) $(-1)^{105}$
   (c) $(-1)^{2014}$
   (d) $(-1)^n$, $n \in \mathbb{N}$, n even
   (e) $(-1)^n + (-1)^{n+1}$, $n \in \mathbb{N}$
   (f) $(-1)^{2n+1}$, $n \in \mathbb{N}$

10. Three consecutive integers add to −24. What are they?

11. Write out the sets:
    (a) $\mathbb{Z} \setminus \mathbb{N}$
    (b) $\mathbb{Z} \cap \mathbb{N}$

    Is $\mathbb{Z} \cup \mathbb{N} = \mathbb{Z}$?

1.3 Rational numbers

Why do we need even more numbers?

The equation $3x = 7$ cannot be solved using the set of integers.

$$3x = 7$$

$$x = \frac{7}{3}$$

The fraction $\frac{7}{3}$ is not an integer. It is not a whole number. In order to solve such equations, the set of integers must be extended to include positive and negative fractions. This new set is called the set of rational numbers. It is denoted by $\mathbb{Q}$.

KEY TERM

A **rational number** (fraction) is a number of the form $\frac{a}{b}$, where a and b are both integers.

In other words, a rational number is a ratio of two integers. Some examples of rational numbers are:

$$-\frac{48}{53}, \frac{79}{23}, -\frac{5}{1}, \frac{-5}{-2}, \frac{0}{1}$$

All integers themselves are rational as every integer can be written as a ratio of the integer and 1:

$6 = \frac{6}{1}, -42 = -\frac{42}{1}, -7 = -\frac{7}{1}$

There are infinitely many rational numbers between any two integers:

$1, \ldots, \frac{1}{4}, \ldots, \frac{1}{2}, \ldots, \frac{3}{4}, \ldots, 2.$

The set of integers $\mathbb{Z}$ is a subset of the set of rationals $\mathbb{Q}$. This is written mathematically as $\mathbb{Z} \subset \mathbb{Q}$.

Equivalence of fractions

If a number is multiplied by 1, its value remains the same. The number 1 can be written in many equivalent ways:

$1 = \frac{1}{1} = \frac{2}{2} = \frac{3}{3} = \frac{4}{4} = \frac{-3}{-3} = \frac{p}{p}$

Multiplying the numerator and denominator of a rational number by the same number produces equivalent fractions, as they all have the same value.

$\frac{2}{3} \times \frac{2}{2} = \frac{4}{6}$

$\frac{2}{3} \times \frac{3}{3} = \frac{6}{9}$

$\frac{2}{3} \times \frac{4}{4} = \frac{8}{12}$

$\therefore \frac{4}{6} = \frac{6}{9} = \frac{8}{12}$

This is an important idea in simplifying 'double-decker' fractions. A double-decker fraction is simply one fraction divided by another fraction.

$\dfrac{\frac{7}{6}}{\frac{3}{2}}$ and $\dfrac{-5}{\frac{2}{3}}$ are examples of double-decker fractions.

To simplify a double-decker fraction, multiply the top fraction and the bottom fraction by the lowest common denominator (LCD) of the denominators of both fractions.

EXAMPLE 3

Simplify the following:

(a) $\dfrac{\frac{7}{6}}{\frac{3}{2}}$ **(b)** $\dfrac{-\frac{7}{2}}{3}$

Solution

(a) LCD of 6 and 2 is 6.

$$\dfrac{\frac{7}{6}}{\frac{3}{2}} = \dfrac{\frac{7}{6} \times \frac{6}{1}}{\frac{3}{2} \times \frac{6}{1}} = \dfrac{\frac{42}{6}}{\frac{18}{2}} = \frac{7}{9}$$

(b) $$\dfrac{-\frac{7}{2}}{3} = \dfrac{-\frac{7}{2}}{\frac{3}{1}} = \dfrac{-\frac{7}{2} \times 2}{\frac{3}{1} \times 2} = -\frac{7}{6}$$

Cancelling fractions

Conversely, if a fraction is divided by 1, its value does not change.

$\therefore \frac{3}{9} = \frac{3}{9} \div \frac{3}{3} = \frac{3 \div 3}{9 \div 3} = \frac{1}{3}$

This is called cancelling and can be used to reduce fractions to their simplest form.

- $\frac{27}{18}$ is simplified by dividing the numerator and denominator by the same number 9.

$$\frac{27}{18} = \frac{{}^{3}\cancel{27}}{{}_{2}\cancel{18}} = \frac{3}{2}$$

Your calculator simplifies fractions automatically.

Rationals and decimals

Every rational number can be expressed as a decimal.

WORKED EXAMPLE

Terminating and recurring decimals

$\frac{3}{8} = 0{\cdot}375$ is called a terminating decimal as it has a finite number of digits. This result can be obtained by dividing 8 into 3·000 by long division.

However, $\frac{11}{9} = 1{\cdot}22222...$ Similarly, this result can be obtained by long division. The digit 2 recurs. Decimals such as 1·222... are called non-terminating (never-ending), recurring decimals.

$1{\cdot}22222... = 1{\cdot}\dot{2}$ for short. The dot over the 2 indicates it is to be repeated forever (*ad infinitum*).

$1{\cdot}3\dot{7} = 1{\cdot}37777777...$

$0{\cdot}\dot{5}\dot{2} = 0{\cdot}525252...$

Every rational number can be expressed either as a terminating decimal or a non-terminating, recurring decimal.

$\frac{4}{5} = 0{\cdot}8$ [Terminating decimal]

$\frac{2}{3} = 0{\cdot}\dot{6}$ [Recurring decimal]

WORKED EXAMPLE

Converting a recurring decimal into a rational

Convert $0{\cdot}6\dot{3}$ into a rational number.

Step 1: Let $N = 0{\cdot}63333...$ **(1)**

Step 2: Multiply both sides by 10^1 since there is **one** repeated digit.

$10N = 6{\cdot}3333...$ **(2)**

Step 3: Subtract **(1)** from **(2)**

$$10N = 6{\cdot}3333...\ \textbf{(1)}$$
$$N = 0{\cdot}6333...\ \textbf{(2)}$$
$$9N = 5{\cdot}7000$$
$$N = \frac{5{\cdot}7}{9} = \frac{57}{90} = \frac{19}{30}$$

Check this result on your calculator.

ACTIVITY 4

ACTION
Working with rationals

OBJECTIVE
To write numbers in decimal form as rationals

EXAMPLE 

Convert $2{\cdot}\dot{5}\dot{7}$ into a rational.

Solution

$2{\cdot}57 = 2{\cdot}575757...$ has two repeated digits.

$$N = 2{\cdot}575757...$$
$$100N = 257{\cdot}5757...$$
$$N = 2{\cdot}5757...$$
$$99N = 255$$
$$N = \frac{255}{99} = \frac{85}{33}$$

EXERCISE 3

1. Copy the Venn diagram below.

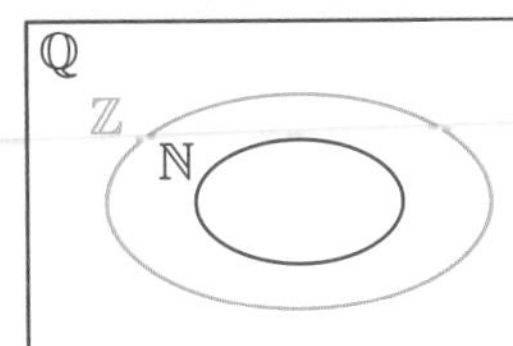

$\mathbb{Q}$ = Set of rational numbers

$\mathbb{Z}$ = Set of integers

$\mathbb{N}$ = Set of natural numbers

(a) Fill the following numbers into the appropriate region of the Venn diagram:

$-3, 0, \frac{1}{2}, \frac{70}{5}, 27, -\frac{3}{2}, 1$

(b) **(i)** Is $\mathbb{Q} \cap \mathbb{Z} = \mathbb{Z}$? Why?

(ii) Is $\mathbb{Q} \cap \mathbb{N} = \mathbb{N}$? Why?

(c) Shade in $\mathbb{Q} \setminus \mathbb{Z}$. How would you describe this set in words?

2. 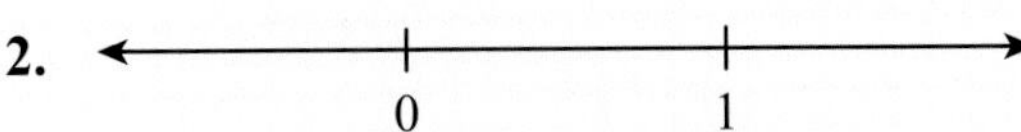

(a) How many rational numbers are greater than 0 and less than 1?

(b) If x is one of these rational numbers, describe x using mathematical symbols.

3. Simplify:

(a) $\dfrac{\frac{1}{2}}{\frac{1}{4}}$ **(c)** $-\dfrac{2}{\frac{7}{2}}$

(b) $\dfrac{\frac{7}{6}}{\frac{3}{5}}$ **(d)** $\dfrac{\frac{1}{2}}{2}$

4. Find the rationals for the following non-terminating, recurring decimals.

(a) $0{\cdot}\dot{2}$ **(c)** $4{\cdot}\dot{1}\dot{3}$

(b) $0{\cdot}\dot{3}\dot{7}$ **(d)** $4{\cdot}5\dot{2}$

5. a, b are positive whole numbers.

(a) Solve $x + 7 = 9$.

What set of numbers do you need to solve $x + a = b$, if $b > a$?

(b) Solve $x + 7 = 2$.

What set of numbers do you need to solve $x + a = b$, if $b < a$?

(c) Solve $5x = -2$.

What set of numbers do you need to solve $ax = b$?

1.4 Real numbers

Irrational numbers

To solve the equation $x^2 = 4$, you need to find two identical numbers which, when multiplied together, give 4. Clearly, $x = \pm 2$ or $\pm\sqrt{4}$. The answers are rational numbers. But how about $x^2 = 2$?

$x^2 = 2 \Rightarrow x = \pm\sqrt{2}$, where $\sqrt{2}$ is a positive number, which when multiplied by itself gives 2.

This number is hard to think of but it does exist. It represents a real measurement. Remember Pythagoras:

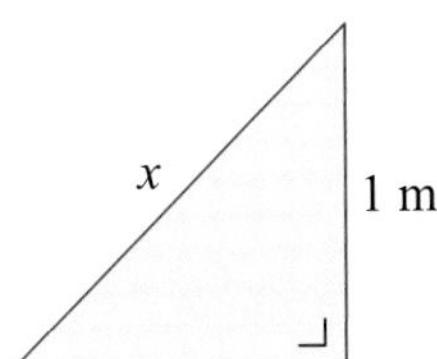

$x^2 = 1^2 + 1^2$

$x^2 = 2$

$x = \sqrt{2}$ m

The distance $\sqrt{2}$ m does exist.

The calculator gives $\sqrt{2} = 1{\cdot}41421356237$.
It stops at 11 decimal places because no more digits can fit onto the screen of the calculator.

The number goes on forever (non-terminating) with no repeated pattern (non-recurring). This is unlike a rational number and it cannot be written as a rational. It is called an irrational number.

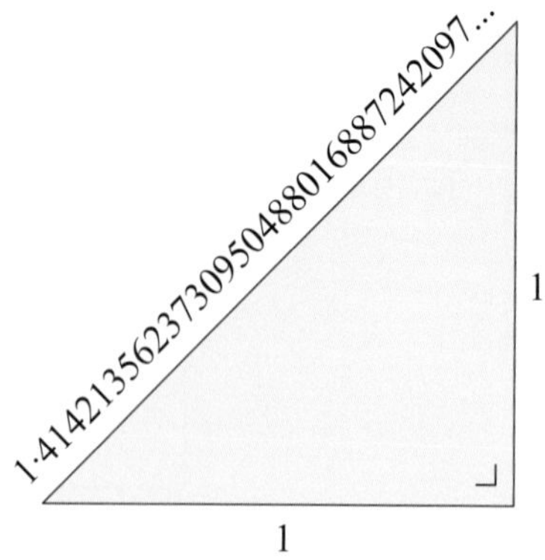

KEY TERM

An **irrational number** is a number that cannot be written as a terminating decimal nor as a non-terminating, recurring decimal.

Mathematical murder: A student of Pythagoras called Hippasus recognised these numbers. Pythagoras could not accept the idea that there were numbers which were not rational, so he allegedly killed Hippasus!

Pythagoras

The square roots of all rational numbers $\frac{a}{b}$ are irrational, unless a and b are perfect squares. There is an infinite number of irrationals.

$\sqrt{\frac{81}{16}} = \frac{9}{4}$ is rational but the following are irrational:

$\sqrt{\frac{1}{2}} = \frac{1}{\sqrt{2}}, \sqrt{\frac{3}{16}} = \frac{\sqrt{3}}{4}, -\sqrt{3} = -1{\cdot}732050808...,$

$\pi = 3{\cdot}14159265358979323846264..., e = 2{\cdot}71828182845904...,$

$\sqrt[3]{6} = 1{\cdot}817120593...$

The set of real numbers $\mathbb{R}$ is the union of the set of rational numbers and the irrational numbers. This set can be represented on the number line as follows:

$-\sqrt{3}$ $\quad \frac{1}{2}$ $\quad \sqrt{2}$ $\quad \pi$

$-2 \quad -1 \quad 0 \quad 1 \quad 2 \quad 3 \quad 4$

EXAMPLE 5

Show that $\sqrt{2}$ lies between 1·41 and 1·42 using your calculator.

Solution

$1{\cdot}41^2 = 1{\cdot}9881$

$1{\cdot}42^2 = 2{\cdot}0164$

$(\sqrt{2})^2 = 2$

$\therefore 1{\cdot}41 < \sqrt{2} < 1{\cdot}42$

EXAMPLE 6

Use your calculator to evaluate $\sqrt[3]{4}$. Is it rational? Why?

Solution

$\sqrt[3]{4}$ means can you think of three identical numbers which, when multiplied together, give 4.

$\sqrt[3]{4} = 1{\cdot}587401052...$ is a non-terminating, non-recurring decimal. Therefore, it is irrational.

The set of natural numbers is a subset of the set of integers, which is a subset of the set of rationals, which is a subset of the set of real numbers. This is represented mathematically as $\mathbb{N} \subset \mathbb{Z} \subset \mathbb{Q} \subset \mathbb{R}$.

ACTIVITY 5

ACTION
Working with number systems

OBJECTIVE
To understand to which set a particular number belongs

ACTIVITY 6

ACTION
Constructing lines of length root 2 and root 3

OBJECTIVE
To learn how to use your compass and set square to draw lines with irrational lengths

Constructing $\sqrt{2}$ and $\sqrt{3}$

(a) $\sqrt{2}$

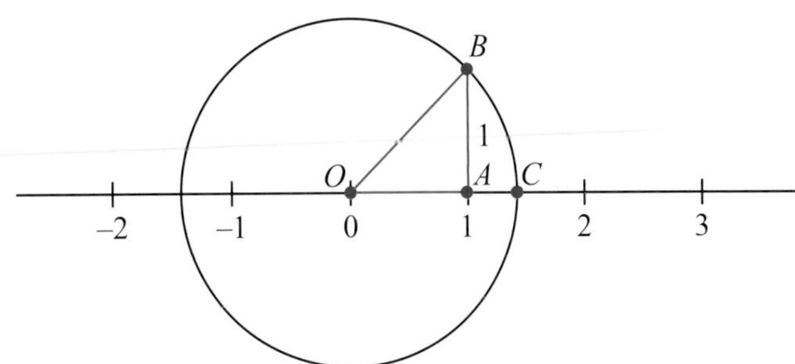

Method

1. Draw a line $[OA]$ of length 1 unit on the number line.
2. Draw line $[AB]$ perpendicular to $[OA]$ of length 1 unit at A.
3. Join O to B.
4. Draw circle of centre O and radius $|OB| = \sqrt{2}$.
5. Mark where the circle cuts the number line on the positive side as C.
6. $|OC| = |OB| = \sqrt{2}$.

(b) $\sqrt{3}$

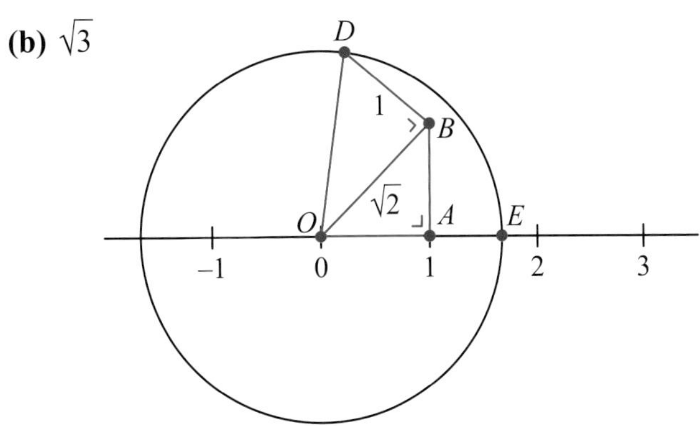

Method

1. Draw line $[OA]$ of length 1 unit on the number line.
2. Draw a line segment $[AB]$ perpendicular to $[OA]$ of length 1 unit at A.
3. Join O to B.
4. Draw a line segment $[BD]$ perpendicular to $[OB]$ of length 1 unit. Join D to O.
5. Draw a circle of centre O and radius $|OD| = \sqrt{3}$.
6. Find where the circle cuts the positive number line at E.
7. $|OE| = |OD| = \sqrt{3}$

To prove $\sqrt{2}$ is not rational

If $\sqrt{2}$ is rational, it can be expressed as a fraction $\frac{m}{n}$ in its lowest terms (where m and n have no common factors other than 1).

An example of such a fraction is $\frac{7}{3}$.

Proof

$\sqrt{2} = \frac{m}{n}$, $m, n \in \mathbb{Z}$, where m and n have no common factors other than 1.

$\Rightarrow \frac{m}{n} \times \frac{m}{n} = 2$

$\Rightarrow \frac{m \times m}{n \times n} = 2$, which means $n \times n$ and $m \times m$ have a common factor other than 1.

This is impossible because m and n themselves have no common factors other than 1.

Therefore, $\sqrt{2}$ cannot be rational. This is another example of proof by contradiction.

1.5 Complex numbers

You might think that all equations can be solved using the set of real numbers $\mathbb{R}$. This is not the case. Compare the following equations:

$x^2 = 1 \Rightarrow x = \pm\sqrt{1} = \pm 1$

$x^2 = -1 \Rightarrow x = \pm\sqrt{-1}$

But what is $\sqrt{-1}$?

In other words, can you think of two **identical numbers**, which when multiplied together give –1? It seems impossible! Don't be put off by this minor inconvenience. Imagine, like the mathematician Euler did, that $\sqrt{-1}$ does exist and call it i. Therefore, $i = \sqrt{-1}$. i is called an **imaginary number**. Equations such as $x^2 = -1$ can be solved using a set of numbers known as the set of complex numbers. This set of complex numbers is denoted by $\mathbb{C}$.

- $\sqrt{-9} = \sqrt{9 \times (-1)}$
  $= \sqrt{9}\sqrt{-1}$
  $= 3 \times i$
  $= 3i$
  $= 0 + 3i$

- $1 + \sqrt{-9} = 1 + 3i$

A complex number z is a number of the form $z = a + bi$, where $a, b \in \mathbb{R}$ and $i = \sqrt{-1}$.

Examples of complex numbers

(a) $3 = 3 + 0i$

(b) $-\frac{2}{3} = -\frac{2}{3} + 0i$

(c) $3 - 5i$

(d) $\sqrt{2} = \sqrt{2} + 0i$

(e) $-\frac{1}{\sqrt{2}} + 3i$

All numbers can be written as complex numbers. The set of natural numbers is a subset of the set of integers, which is a subset of the set of rationals, which is a subset of the set of real numbers, which is a subset of the set of complex numbers. This is represented mathematically as $\mathbb{N} \subset \mathbb{Z} \subset \mathbb{Q} \subset \mathbb{R} \subset \mathbb{C}$.

The various number systems can be represented by the Venn diagram below:

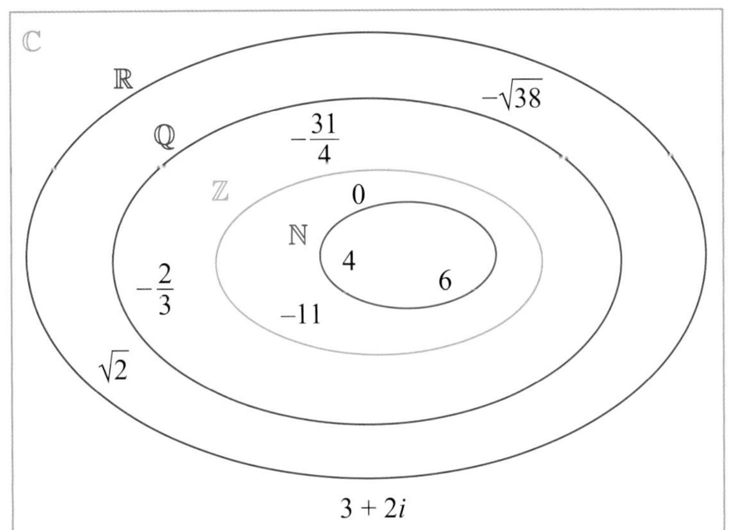

Complex numbers are so important that a whole section will be devoted to them later in the book.

1.6 Absolute value

ACTIVITY 7

ACTION
Working with absolute values

OBJECTIVE
To position various numbers on the number line

The absolute value or modulus $|x|$ of a real number x is simply its distance to the origin.

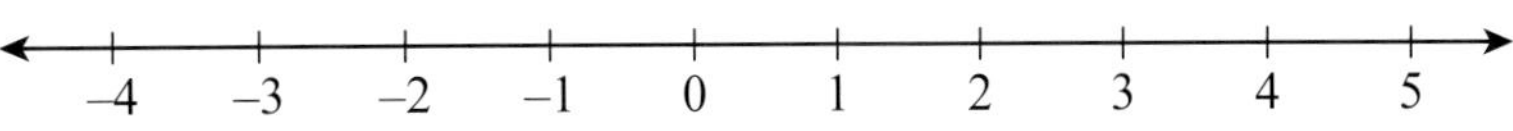

- $|-3| = 3$ [The distance of –3 to 0.]
- $|3| = 3$ [The distance of 3 to 0.]
- $\left|-\frac{1}{2}\right| = \frac{1}{2}$ [The distance of $-\frac{1}{2}$ to 0.]
- $|\sqrt{2}| = \sqrt{2}$
- $|-7{\cdot}35| = 7{\cdot}35$

The modulus is never negative as it is a distance.

- $|7 - 3| = |4| = 4$
- $|3 - 7| = |-4| = 4$

This means $|a - b| = |b - a|$

EXERCISE 4

1. Evaluate:

(a) $|-72|$

(b) $\left|-\frac{69}{4}\right|$

(c) $|1{\cdot}72|$

(d) $\left|\frac{1}{\sqrt{2}}\right|$

(e) $\left|-\frac{3\sqrt{2}}{4}\right|$

(f) $|0|$

(g) $|-\pi|$

(h) $\left|\frac{5}{6}\right|$

2. Evaluate:

(a) $|3 - 5|$

(b) $|5 - 3|$

(c) $|\sqrt{2} - 1|$

(d) $|\pi - 3|$

(e) $|3 - \pi|$

(f) $|\sqrt{2} - \sqrt{3}|$

(g) $|a - b|, a > b$

(h) $|a - b|, b > a$

CHAPTER 2 Arithmetic

Learning Outcomes

- To be able to do all kinds of calculations involving percentages.
- To be able to manipulate numbers written in scientific notation and to use these numbers to make estimates based on order of magnitude.
- To appreciate the importance of tolerance levels and errors.
- To be able to round off numbers and hence estimate and approximate the values of expressions involving such numbers.
- To be familiar with the concept of quantities changing with time, including speed and acceleration.
- To understand how quantities can be directly and inversely proportional to each other.

2.1 Percentages

ACTIVITY 8

ACTION
Working with fractions, decimals and percentages

OBJECTIVE
To work with fractions, decimals and percentages and, when presented with various shapes, to write down the shaded area as a fraction, decimal and percentage

Percentages play an important part in our daily lives. You often hear statements like 'The footballer gave 110%' or 'House prices are up by 7%'. A percentage just means part of 100.

- $\frac{1}{2} = \frac{4}{8} = \frac{50}{100}$ = 50 parts of 100 = 50 per cent = 50%
- $0{\cdot}37 = \frac{37}{100}$ = 37 parts of 100 = 37%

A percentage is simply a fraction in which the denominator is 100. Per cent is represented by %.

$57\% = \frac{57}{100} = 0{\cdot}57$

$100\% = \frac{100}{100} = 1$

Techniques for working with percentages

1. To convert a number written as a rational or a decimal into a percentage, multiply it by 100.

- $\frac{3}{4} = \left(\frac{3}{4} \times 100\right)\% = 75\%$
- $0{\cdot}62 = (0{\cdot}62 \times 100)\% = 62\%$
- $3{\cdot}25 = (3{\cdot}25 \times 100)\% = 325\%$

2. To convert a number written as a percentage into a rational number or a decimal, divide the number by 100.

- $67\% = \frac{67}{100} = 0{\cdot}67$ [Move the decimal point two places to the left.]
- $27{\cdot}5\% = 0{\cdot}275$

3. To express one quantity as a percentage of another, write the first quantity as a fraction of the second and then multiply by 100%. [See Example 1.]

4. To find a percentage of a quantity, multiply the quantity by the decimal equivalent of the percentage.

- 25% of €230 $= \frac{25}{100} \times$ €230 $= 0{\cdot}25 \times$ €230 $=$ €57·50

5. To increase a quantity by $r\%$, multiply it by $\left(1 + \frac{r}{100}\right)$.

- Increase 800 by 20%: $800 + 800 \times 0{\cdot}2 = 800(1 + 0{\cdot}2) = 800 \times 1{\cdot}2 = 960$

6. To decrease a quantity by $r\%$, multiply it by $\left(1 - \frac{r}{100}\right)$. [See Example 2.]

7. To find a quantity which has been increased by $r\%$ to a given value, divide this given value by $\left(1 + \frac{r}{100}\right)$ to get the original value. [See Example 3.]

8. To find a quantity which has been decreased by $r\%$ to a given value, divide this given value by $\left(1 - \frac{r}{100}\right)$ to get the original value. [See Example 4.]

EXAMPLE 1

32 litres (l) of oil leaked from a tank containing 160 l. What percentage of the oil leaked?

Solution

32 l out of 160 l: $\frac{32}{160} = \frac{1}{5} = \frac{1}{5} \times 100\% = 20\%$

EXAMPLE 2

A piece of skirting board of length 1·2 m has to be reduced by 15% to fit. What is the required length?

Solution

$15\% = 0{\cdot}15$

New length $l = 1{\cdot}2 - 1{\cdot}2 \times 0{\cdot}15$

$= 1{\cdot}2(1 - 0{\cdot}15)$

$= 1{\cdot}2(0{\cdot}85) = 1{\cdot}02$ m

EXAMPLE 3

The number of students that sat the Physics exam in 2013 was 8400. This was an increase of 5% on the number that sat the Physics exam in 2012. How many students sat the Physics exam in 2012?

Solution

$$1 + \frac{r}{100} = 1 + \frac{5}{100} = 1{\cdot}05$$

N is the number of students that sat the Physics exam in 2012:

$$1{\cdot}05N = 8400$$

$$N = \frac{8400}{1{\cdot}05} = 8000$$

EXAMPLE 4

The price of a house in 2013 was 43% less than its price in 2008. If the price in 2013 was €342 000, what was the price in 2008?

Solution

$$1 - \frac{r}{100} = 1 - \frac{43}{100} = 0{\cdot}57$$

p was the price in 2008:

$$0{\cdot}57p = 342\,000$$

$$p = \frac{342\,000}{0{\cdot}57} = €600\,000$$

EXERCISE 5

1. **(a)** Joe's team played 20 games in a season. They won 18 of them. What percentage of the games did Joe's team win?

(b) The political party Fianna Fáil received 9562 votes out of 26 500 in a constituency. What was its percentage share of the vote, correct to the nearest whole number?

(c) There are 45 crew members on a ship. Eighteen of them are officers. What percentage of the crew are officers?

(d) A metal bar has a mass of 23 g. If 21·3 g is pure silver, what percentage of the metal bar, correct to one decimal place, is pure silver?

(e) There are 32 students in a class. Eight of the students are female. What percentage of the students are male?

2. **(a)** Mary got 80% of the questions in a Maths test right. How many questions did she get right if there were 40 questions in all?

(b) There are 166 Dáil deputies in Dáil Éireann. 28·3% of them are from Dublin. How many Dublin deputies are there in Dáil Éireann?

(c) A meal for five in a restaurant costs €152. If the waiter was given a tip of 15% of the cost of the meal, how much did he get?

(d) If 16% of 62 000 students took the Higher Level Maths exam in 2013, how many students took this exam?

(e) A woman put €10 000 into a saving account for one year. The rate of interest for one year was 3·2%. How much interest did she get at the end of the year?

3. **(a)** A sitting-room suite cost €2453 plus 15% delivery charge. What was the total cost?

(b) A laptop is reduced by 22% in a sale. If the presale price was €530, what is the sale price?

(c) In 1800, the land area of the USA was 867 980 square miles. In 1803, after the Louisiana Purchase, the land area increased by 95%. What was the land area of the USA after the purchase?

(d) Cheap Air increased its number of daily flights to Spain by 20% on 1 June. If the number of daily flights to Spain on 31 May was 15, what was the number on 1 June?

(e) A pharmaceutical company reduces the price of a packet of statins by 28% from €40 per packet. What is the new price of a packet of statins?

4. (a) A clothes shop reduced the price of a brand of jeans by 15%. If the reduced price is €35·70, what was the original price?

(b) The number of deaths on Irish roads in 2011 was 186. This was a 12·26% decrease on the number of deaths in 2010. How many people died on Irish roads in 2010?

(c) Between 1990 and 2000, the population of the USA increased by 13%. If the population in 2000 was 281 million, what was the population in 1990, correct to two decimal places?

(d) The price of a television was €688·80, including tax at 23%. What was the price before tax was applied?

(e) The political party Fine Gael won 76 seats in the 2011 general election. This was an increase of 49% over their 2007 election result. How many seats did Fine Gael win in the 2007 election?

2.2 Scientific notation

Some numbers are very big. For example, the radius of the Earth is 6 400 000 m. Other numbers are very, very small. For example, the charge on the electron is 0·00000000000000000016 Coulombs (C).

There is a much better way to write such numbers. It is known as **scientific notation**.

Writing numbers in scientific notation

Every time you multiply a number by 10, the decimal point moves one place to the right.

- $326{\cdot}475 \times 10^1 = 3264{\cdot}75$

  $326{\cdot}475 \times 10^2 = 326{\cdot}475 \times 10^1 \times 10^1 = 3264{\cdot}75 \times 10^1 = 32\,647{\cdot}5$

Every time you divide a number by 10, the decimal point moves one place to the left.

- $\dfrac{4678{\cdot}253}{10^2} = \dfrac{4678{\cdot}253}{10^1 \times 10^1} = \dfrac{467{\cdot}8253}{10^1} = 46{\cdot}7825$

  Technique for writing large numbers in scientific notation: You can balance the left movement of the decimal point by multiplying by 10 to a positive power.

- $563{\cdot}875 = \dfrac{563{\cdot}875}{1} = \dfrac{563{\cdot}875}{1} \times \dfrac{10^2}{10^2} = \dfrac{563{\cdot}875}{100} \times 10^2$

  $\therefore\ 563{\cdot}875 = 5{\cdot}63875 \times 10^2$

  If you move a decimal point two places to the **left**, you have to multiply by 10^{+2} so that its value is unchanged.

Technique for writing small numbers in scientific notation: You can balance the right movement of the decimal point by multiplying by 10 to a negative power.

- $0{\cdot}00735 = \dfrac{0{\cdot}00735}{1} = \dfrac{0{\cdot}00735}{1} \times \dfrac{10^3}{10^3}$

$= \dfrac{0{\cdot}00735 \times 10^3}{10^3} = \dfrac{7{\cdot}35}{10^3} = 7{\cdot}35 \times 10^{-3}$

$\therefore\ 0{\cdot}00735 = 7{\cdot}35 \times 10^{-3}$

If you move a decimal point three places to the **right**, you have to multiply by 10^{-3} so that its value is unchanged.

- $5623{\cdot}4 = 5{\cdot}6234 \times 10^{+3}$
- $0{\cdot}0000053 = 5{\cdot}3 \times 10^{-6}$

To write a number in scientific notation it must be written in the form $a \times 10^n$, where $1 \leq a < 10$ and $n \in \mathbb{Z}$. This means you must move the decimal point so that there is **exactly one digit** to the left of the decimal point.

In general:

- If you move a decimal point n places to the **left**, you must multiply the new number by 10^{+n}.
- If you move a decimal point n places to the **right**, you must multiply the new number by 10^{-n}.

EXAMPLE 5

Write the following numbers in scientific notation:

(a) 3425

(b) 6 400 000 m

(c) 0·0000516

(d) −457·2

(e) 0·00000000000000000016 C

Solution

(a) $3425 = 3425{\cdot}0 = 3{\cdot}425 \times 10^3$

(b) $6\,400\,000 \text{ m} = 6{\cdot}4 \times 10^6 \text{ m}$

(c) $0{\cdot}0000516 = 5{\cdot}16 \times 10^{-5}$

(d) $-457{\cdot}2 = -4{\cdot}572 \times 10^2$

(e) $0{\cdot}00000000000000000016 \text{ C} = 1{\cdot}6 \times 10^{-19} \text{ C}$

ACTIVITY 9

ACTION
Using scientific notation

OBJECTIVE
To carry out a number of calculations in your head on numbers in scientific notation

Carrying out scientific notation calculations

If numbers are given in scientific notation and the number in front of the power of 10 is a whole number, you can add, subtract, multiply and divide quickly in your head. Otherwise, use your calculator.

1. Multiplying and dividing numbers in scientific notation:

- $4 \times 10^3 \times 2 \times 10^4 = 8 \times 10^7$ [Add the powers.]
- $4 \times 10^{-5} \times 3 \times 10^7 = 12 \times 10^2 = 1{\cdot}2 \times 10^3$
- $\dfrac{9 \times 10^{27}}{(3 \times 10^8)^2} = \dfrac{9 \times 10^{27}}{9 \times 10^{16}} = 1 \times 10^{11}$ [Subtract the powers.]

2. Adding and subtracting numbers in scientific notation:
   - $\underline{5} \times 10^4 + \underline{2} \times 10^4 = 7 \times 10^4$ [(5 apples) + (2 apples) = 7 apples]

   Technique: You can only add (subtract) numbers in scientific notation with the same power of 10.
   - $3 \times 10^4 + 2 \times 10^3 = 3 \times 10^4 + 0{\cdot}2 \times 10^4 = 3{\cdot}2 \times 10^4$

   Technique: Always change the number with the smaller power of 10 to a number with the bigger power of 10 before adding or subtracting.

ACTIVITY 10

ACTION
Finding orders of magnitude

OBJECTIVE
To write down the orders of magnitude of given numbers

Order of magnitude estimation

In carrying out rough calculations, estimates or comparisons, numbers are often rounded off to the nearest power of 10. A number rounded to the nearest power of 10 is called its **order of magnitude**.

Finding the order of magnitude estimate of a number

1. Write the number in scientific notation, i.e. in the form $a \times 10^n$, where $1 \leq a < 10$.
2. If $a < 5$, the order of magnitude is n. If $a > 5$, add 1 to n to get the order of magnitude.
   - The order of magnitude of $1{\cdot}6 \times 10^3$ is 3. [3 is the power of 10.]
   - The order of magnitude of 9×10^{-3} is –2. [–2 is the power of 10 plus 1.]
3. Since orders of magnitude are just powers of 10, they can be combined by the rules of powers.
   - The order of magnitude of $2 \times 10^4 \times 6 \times 10^3$ is $4 + 4 = 8$.
   - The order of magnitude of $\dfrac{3 \times 10^{-4}}{2 \times 10^{-5}}$ is $-4 - (-5) = 1$.

EXAMPLE 6

The number of hairs on a human head is between 100 000 and 150 000. What is the order of magnitude of the number of hairs on a human head?

Solution

$100\,000 = 1 \times 10^5$

$150\,000 = 1{\cdot}5 \times 10^5$

1×10^5 to $1{\cdot}5 \times 10^5$: Order of magnitude of 5

EXAMPLE 7

The radius of the Earth is 6 400 000 m and the radius of the Sun is 696 342 000 m. Find an order of magnitude comparison of the radius of the Sun to the radius of the Earth.

Solution

Radius of Sun = 696 342 000 m = $6{\cdot}96342 \times 10^8$
Order of magnitude = 9

Radius of Earth = 6 400 000 m = $6{\cdot}4 \times 10^6$
Order of magnitude = 7

$$\therefore \frac{\text{Radius of Sun}}{\text{Radius of Earth}} = \frac{10^9}{10^7} = 10^2$$

Order of magnitude = 9 – 7 = 2

Radius of Sun $\simeq$ 100 × Radius of Earth

EXERCISE 6

1. Write the following numbers, which are written in scientific notation, in standard decimal form:
   - **(a)** $3{\cdot}0 \times 10^{-2}$
   - **(b)** $4{\cdot}12 \times 10^{-4}$
   - **(c)** $3{\cdot}57 \times 10^{5}$
   - **(d)** 2×10^{6}
   - **(e)** $5{\cdot}6 \times 10^{-7}$
   - **(f)** 6×10^{-5}
   - **(g)** 1×10^{-4}
   - **(h)** 1×10^{5}
   - **(i)** $3{\cdot}3 \times 10^{0}$
   - **(j)** $7{\cdot}8 \times 10^{8}$

2. **(a)** A quadrillion is 1 000 000 000 000 000. What is its order of magnitude?

   (b) A googol is 10^{100}. What is its order of magnitude?

3. **(a)** Using $E = mc^2$, find the order of magnitude of E, if $m = 7{\cdot}2 \times 10^{-27}$ kg and $c = 3 \times 10^{8}$ m s^{-1}.

   (b) Using $f = \frac{E}{h}$, find the order of magnitude of f, if $E = 6{\cdot}4 \times 10^{-19}$ J and $h = 6{\cdot}6 \times 10^{-34}$ J s.

   (c) The mass of the Earth is $5{\cdot}98 \times 10^{24}$ kg. The mass of the Great Pyramid of Giza is $5{\cdot}9 \times 10^{9}$ kg. Compare the mass of the Earth to that of the Great Pyramid of Giza using their orders of magnitude as estimates.

4. **(a) (i)** Which is 4357 nearer to: 1000 or 10 000?

   (ii) Estimate the order of magnitude of 4357.

   (iii) What is the order of magnitude of 270 134?

   (b) Mary wants to convert 4357 km into miles. The conversion factor is 1 km = 0·62 miles.

   When she does the calculation, she gets 270 134 miles. She knows this is wrong.

   (i) State, using the order of magnitude of each number, how she knows that she is wrong.

   (ii) Evaluate $4357 \times 0{\cdot}62$ on your calculator. How do you think Mary got 270 134 miles?

   (iii) What is 4357 km in miles?

5. The probability of being dealt a royal flush in poker is 649 739 to 1. What is the order of magnitude of this probability?

6. Estimate the number of €20 notes that fill a container with dimensions 2 m × 2 m × 2 m, if the dimensions of a €20 note are $13{\cdot}3$ cm $\times$ $7{\cdot}2$ cm $\times$ 10^{-2} cm. Use an order of magnitude estimation.

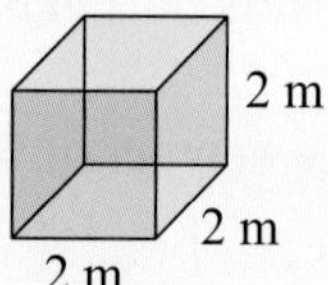

2.3 Errors

No physical measurement is ever exact. The accuracy of a measurement is always determined by the sensitivity and accuracy of the apparatus and the skill of the observer. The accuracy of a measurement is how close the result of the measurement is to the true or accepted value.

Tolerance level (margin of error)

A machine requires steel rods of length ($2{\cdot}3 \pm 0{\cdot}1$) cm. This means that any rod of length in the range ($2{\cdot}3 - 0{\cdot}1$) cm to ($2{\cdot}3 + 0{\cdot}1$) cm is acceptable, i.e. all values from 2·2 cm to 2·4 cm.

The range of values of quantity that is acceptable (allowed/permitted/tolerated) is known as its **tolerance level**.

KEY TERM

The **tolerance level** is the greatest range of variation in the values of a quantity that is acceptable.

- Quality Food only accepts bananas from their growers with a tolerance level of (160 ± 8) g for the mass of a banana. This means the maximum acceptable mass is 168 g and the minimum acceptable mass is 152 g.
- For safety reasons, an acceptable bolt for a car part must have a diameter between 45·8 mm and 46·2 mm. What is the tolerance level for the diameter of the bolt?

  The midvalue $= \dfrac{45{\cdot}8 + 46{\cdot}2}{2} = \dfrac{92{\cdot}0}{2} = 46$

  $\therefore$ Tolerance level = ($46 \pm 0{\cdot}2$) mm

Since no measurement is exact, a measurement is quoted with a tolerance level that gives the range within which the true value lies. The temperature of a boiling liquid was measured as ($78{\cdot}6 \pm 0{\cdot}2$) °C. This means that the true value lies between 78·4 °C and 78·8 °C.

ACTIVITY 11

ACTION
Understanding errors

OBJECTIVE
To understand how errors accumulate when results are added and subtracted

Experimental results and the accumulation of errors

When the results of a measurement are added or subtracted, their errors always **accumulate** (add).

- A metre stick is used to measure the length of a wooden plank. The plank is longer than 1 m so that two measurements must be made.

  The first measured length is ($96{\cdot}0 \pm 0{\cdot}1$) cm and the remaining length is ($13{\cdot}0 \pm 0{\cdot}1$) cm. The total length of the plank is ($109 \pm 0{\cdot}2$) cm.

Even when you subtract two measurements, their errors add.

EXAMPLE 8

A weighing scales can measure the mass of objects to an accuracy of $\pm 0{\cdot}002$ g. The mass of a beaker is measured as 42·056 g. The mass of the beaker with a copper sulfate solution is measured as 42·863 g. What is the possible range of values of the mass of the copper sulfate solution?

Solution

Mass of beaker = ($42{\cdot}056 \pm 0{\cdot}002$) g

Mass of beaker plus copper sulfate solution = ($42{\cdot}863 \pm 0{\cdot}002$) g

Mass of copper sulfate solution = ($0{\cdot}807 \pm 0{\cdot}004$) g

The true value of the mass of copper sulfate solution lies in the range = 0·803 g to 0·811 g.

Absolute and percentage error

WORKED EXAMPLE

Understanding absolute and percentage errors

A 750 g box of cornflakes in a consignment of food is weighed by Customs. It is found to have a mass of 820 g.

Accepted mass of the box of cornflakes = 750 g

Measured mass = 820 g

Absolute error = |820 g – 750 g| = 70 g

Percentage error $= \dfrac{70 \text{ g}}{750 \text{ g}} \times 100\% = 9\tfrac{1}{3}\%$

Do you think that Customs will suspect that the box of cornflakes is concealing something?

Absolute error in a quantity = |Measured value of quantity – Accepted value of quantity|

Percentage error in a quantity $= \dfrac{\text{Absolute error in quantity}}{\text{Accepted value of quantity}} \times 100\%$

EXAMPLE 9

A piece of metal piping used in a washing machine has an accepted length of 21·00 cm. A percentage error of 7% is permitted. If a machinist starts with a pipe of length 30 cm, what is:

(a) the maximum length,

(b) the minimum length

that he can cut off to produce a pipe which can be used?

Solution

Maximum permitted length = 21 × 1·07 = 22·47 cm

Minimum permitted length = 21 × 0·93 = 19·53 cm

(a) Maximum length of cut-off = 30 – 19·53
= 10·47 cm

(b) Minimum length of cut-off = 30 – 22·47
= 7·53 cm

EXERCISE 7

1. **(a)** The recommended retail price (RRP) of a certain model of calculator is €(13 ± 5%). What is the maximum price the retailer should charge?

(b) The resistance of a resistor in a washing machine must have a value between 3·5 Ω and 3·9 Ω. What tolerance level is written on the resistor?

(c) The maximum value of the diameter of a battery that can fit into a slot in a phone is 4·2 mm. The minimum diameter that can fit is 3·8 mm. What is its tolerance level?

(d) The maximum value of the area of the square cover for a book is 16 cm^2 and the minimum value is 12·96 cm^2. Find the tolerance level of the side of the square in the picture.

(e) In the square shown, the tolerance level of the side of the square is (2·4 ± 0·3) cm. What is the tolerance level of the area?

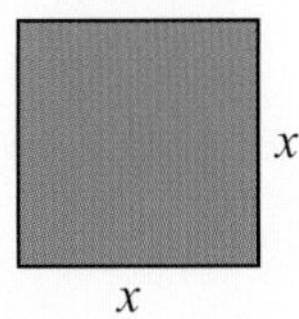

(f) The tolerance level of a bottle of washing-up liquid is (550 ± 10) ml. What is:

(i) the maximum volume,

(ii) the minimum volume of liquid a bottle could contain?

2. **(a)** A scientist gave the density of mercury as (13 600 ± 4%) kg/m^3. Quote her result with an absolute error.

(b) A 400 g tin of beans is weighed at the airport. It is found to have a mass of 480 g. Find:

(i) the absolute error,

(ii) the percentage error.

(c) A man was weighed accurately in a gym. His mass was recorded as 80 kg. When he weighed himself at home, the scales recorded 74 kg. What is the percentage error in the home scales' reading? When his wife weighed herself at home, the scales read 62 kg. What was her true mass, correct to the nearest kilogram?

2.4 Approximation and estimation

Technique for rounding off decimals

- Write 16·1238732 correct to three decimal places.

  Go to the **fourth** digit after the decimal point. If this digit is greater than or equal to 5, increase the digit in the third place after the decimal point by 1:

  16·123**8**732 is 116·124 correct to three decimal places.

- Round 7·62 off to the nearest integer (whole number).

  As the first digit after the decimal point is greater than 5, round up the whole number in front of the decimal point by 1.

  7·**6**2 is rounded up to 8.

EXAMPLE 10

If $M = 6 \times 10^{24}$, $R = 6{\cdot}4 \times 10^6$ and $G = 6{\cdot}7 \times 10^{-11}$, find g correct to one decimal place, if $g = \dfrac{GM}{R^2}$.

Solution

Put brackets around each letter.

$$g = \frac{(G)(M)}{(R)^2}$$

$$g = \frac{(6{\cdot}7 \times 10^{-11}) \times (6 \times 10^{24})}{(6{\cdot}4 \times 10^6)^2} = 9{\cdot}8$$

Significant figures

Whenever a measurement is given, it is assumed the measurement is accurate to the last written digit. A length of 57·8 m indicates that this measurement can be made accurate to one-tenth of a metre.

The digits in a number that indicate the accuracy of the number are called its significant figures.

Rounding to significant figures: To round off a number to a given number of significant figures, change the number into scientific notation ($a \times 10^n$) first. The number of digits in a corresponds to the specified number of significant figures.

ACTIVITY 12

ACTION
Using approximation and estimation

OBJECTIVE
To round off a variety of numbers to a certain number of decimals or significant figures

Technique for writing numbers to a certain number of significant figures

Write the following to three significant figures:

- $1472 = 1{\cdot}472 \times 10^3$ [Three significant figures means three digits in a.]
  $\therefore 1472 = 1{\cdot}47 \times 10^3 = 1470$ to three significant figures
- $56\,321 = 5{\cdot}6321 \times 10^4$ [Three significant figures means three digits in a.]
  $\therefore 56\,321 = 5{\cdot}63 \times 10^4 = 56\,300$
- $0{\cdot}03256 = 3{\cdot}256 \times 10^{-2}$
  $\therefore 0{\cdot}03256 = 3{\cdot}26 \times 10^{-2} = 0{\cdot}0326$

Estimation

A quick estimate of a quantity can be made by rounding up or rounding down the numbers that make up the quantity. This allows you to do the calculation in your head.

EXAMPLE 11

Estimate the value of $\dfrac{3{\cdot}8 \times 10^4 \times 6{\cdot}2 \times 10^4}{2{\cdot}95 \times 10^{-3} \times 2{\cdot}1 \times 10^9}$ as a whole number.

Solution

$$\text{Estimate} = \frac{4 \times 10^4 \times 6 \times 10^4}{3 \times 10^{-3} \times 2 \times 10^9} = \frac{24 \times 10^8}{6 \times 10^6}$$

$$= 4 \times 10^2 = 400$$

EXAMPLE 12

Estimate the volume of a sphere of radius 21·5 cm in cm^3, if the volume is given by $V = \frac{4}{3}\pi r^3$ and $\pi = 3{\cdot}14$. Give your answer as a whole number.

Solution

$$V \approx \tfrac{4}{3}(\pi)(r)^3 \approx \tfrac{4}{3}(3)(20)^3 = 4 \times 8000 = 32\,000 \text{ cm}^3$$

EXAMPLE 13

A student buys 5 pens at 58c each, a newspaper at €2·00, a writing pad for €2·89 and a can of cola for 90c. Make a quick estimate to see if he has enough money in a €10 note to buy all the items.

Solution

Estimate = €(5 × 0·6 + 2 + 3 + 1) = €9

EXERCISE 8

1. **(a)** If $A = \pi r^2$, find A correct to one decimal place, given $r = 3{\cdot}7$ cm.

   (b) If $u = \dfrac{vf}{v-f}$, find u correct to two decimal places, given $f = 23{\cdot}4$ and $v = 43{\cdot}8$.

   (c) If $f = \dfrac{1}{2l}\sqrt{\dfrac{T}{\mu}}$, find f correct to two decimal places, given $l = 0{\cdot}503$, $T = 9{\cdot}8$ and $\mu = 0{\cdot}00032$.

   (d) If $x = y^3$, find y correct to three decimal places, given $x = 27{\cdot}32$.

   (e) If $A = \pi r^2 + 2\pi rh$, find A correct to one decimal place, given $r = 5{\cdot}2$ and $h = 11{\cdot}47$.

2. Round off the following:

   (a) 479 357 correct to four significant figures

   (b) 1·3274 correct to three significant figures

   (c) 57·321 correct to four significant figures

   (d) 6·023 correct to two significant figures

   (e) 0·0005734 correct to three significant figures

3. If $T = 2\pi\sqrt{\dfrac{k}{g}}$, estimate the value of T, given $\pi = 3{\cdot}14$, $g = 9{\cdot}8$ and $k = 38{\cdot}6$ by rounding each number off to the nearest whole number.

4. The approximation 60×50 was used for the calculation 61×49. Find the percentage error in the approximation to two decimal places.

2.5 Average rate of change (with respect to time)

WORKED EXAMPLE Explaining average rate of change

LeBron James played in a basketball match and scored 6 points after 18 minutes, 20 points after 30 minutes, 28 points after 42 minutes, and 39 points after 48 minutes. This information is set out in the table and represented graphically, as shown.

Time in minutes (t)	0	18	30	42	48
Number of points (N)	0	6	20	28	39

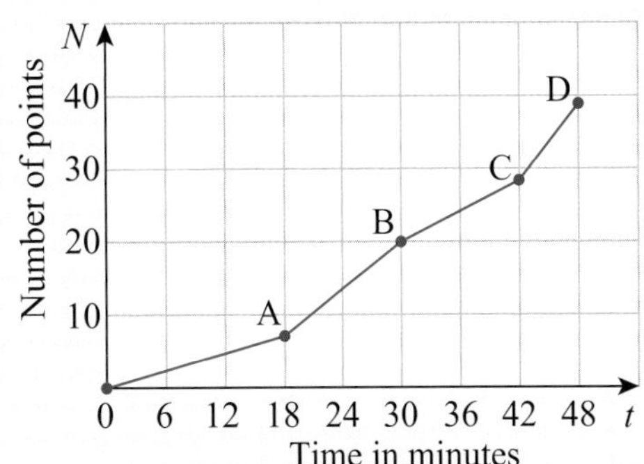

His average scoring rate in the first 18 minutes

$= \dfrac{6-0}{18} = \dfrac{1}{3}$ points per minute.

His average scoring rate in the last 6 minutes

$= \dfrac{39-28}{48-42} = \dfrac{11}{6}$ points per minute.

His average scoring rate for the whole match

$= \dfrac{39-0}{48-0} = \dfrac{39}{48}$ points per minute.

KEY TERM

If Q_1 is the value of a quantity Q at time t_1 and Q_2 is the value of the quantity Q at time t_2, the **average rate of change** of Q with respect to $t = \dfrac{Q_2 - Q_1}{t_2 - t_1}$.

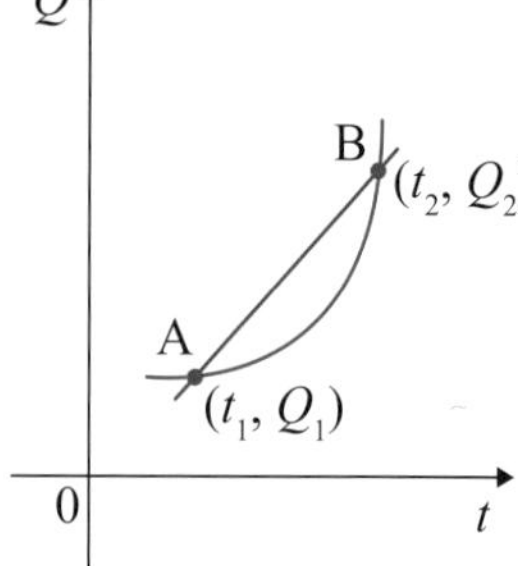

Average rate of change between times t_1 and $t_2 = \dfrac{Q_2 - Q_1}{t_2 - t_1}$ = slope of the line AB.

EXAMPLE 14

If $Q = t^2 + 2t - 1$, find the average rate of change of Q from $t = 2$ to $t = 5$.

Solution

$Q = t^2 + 2t - 1$

$\mathbf{t_1 = 2:}\ Q_1 = 2^2 + 4 - 1 = 7$

$\mathbf{t_2 = 5:}\ Q_2 = 5^2 + 10 - 1 = 34$

Average rate of change of $Q = \dfrac{34 - 7}{5 - 2} = \dfrac{27}{3} = 9$

Speed and acceleration

Speed: When the quantity Q is distance s, the average rate of change is speed v.

Speed: $v = \dfrac{s_2 - s_1}{t_2 - t_1} = \dfrac{\text{Change in distance}}{\text{Change in time}}$

Acceleration: When the quantity Q is speed v, the average rate of change is acceleration a.

Acceleration: $a = \dfrac{v_2 - v_1}{t_2 - t_1} = \dfrac{\text{Change in speed}}{\text{Change in time}}$

EXAMPLE 15

The first 10 minutes of a warm-up cycle by a racing cyclist is shown on a distance–time graph.

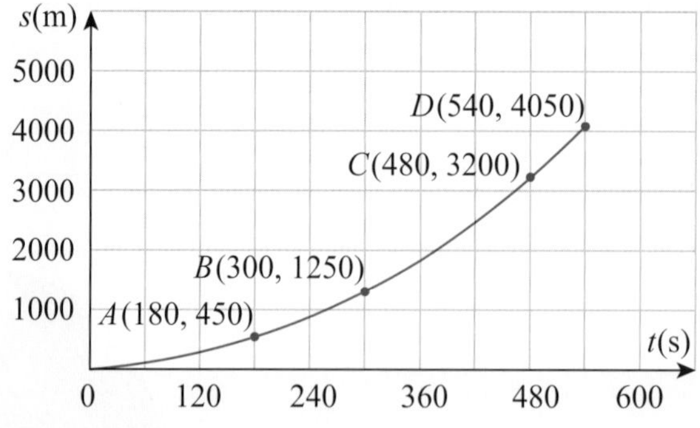

Find the average speed:

(a) between the third minute and eighth minute,

(b) between the fifth minute and ninth minute.

Solution

(a) Between the third minute and eighth minute:

Slope of line AC: $v = \dfrac{3200 - 450}{480 - 180}$

$= \dfrac{2750}{300}$

$= 9{\cdot}17$ m/s

(b) Between the fifth minute and ninth minute:

Slope of line BD: $v = \dfrac{4050 - 1250}{540 - 300}$

$= \dfrac{2800}{240}$

$= 11{\cdot}67$ m/s

EXERCISE 9

1. A scuba diver is 8 m below the surface of the water 10 seconds after entering the water, and 32 m below the surface after 45 seconds. What is her average rate of descent, correct to two decimal places?

2. The population P of a city in millions is given by $P = (0{\cdot}00006)t^2 + (0{\cdot}01)t + 1$, where t is the number of years after the year 2000. Find the average rate of change of the population from 2005 to 2010.

3. If $T = 32 \times 2^{-t}$, find the average rate of change of temperature T (°C) from $t = 2$ to $t = 4$, where t is the time in hours.

4. The table below shows the split times of athlete Usain Bolt in his 2009 world record run in Berlin.

Distance s(m)	0	20	40	60	80	100
Time t(s)	0	2·89	4·64	6·31	7·92	9·58

Find his average speed, giving your answer correct to two decimal places:

(a) over the first 20 m, **(b)** over the last 20 m, **(c)** over the whole race.

5. An oil tank is being emptied. The volume V in litres of oil remaining in the tank after time t, in hours, is given by $V = 80(30 - t)^2$, $0 \le t \le 30$.

Find the average rate of change of volume:

(a) during the first 10 hours, **(b)** during the last 10 hours, **(c)** over the whole 30 hours.

6. If $V = t^3 - 3t^2 + 5t - 2$, find the average rate of change of V from $t = 1$ to $t = 3$, if V is volume in cm^3 and t is time in seconds.

2.6 Direct proportion

Proportion

KEY TERM

A **proportion** is an equation that states that two ratios are equal.

- $4:8 = 1:2$

  $\therefore \frac{4}{8} = \frac{1}{2}$

- $a:b = 3:2$

  $\therefore \frac{a}{b} = \frac{3}{2}$

WORKED EXAMPLE

Explaining direct proportion

The table shows the cost y in € of a number x of Yorkie bars:

x	1	2	3	4	5
y	0·9	1·80	2·70	3·6	4·5

The table shows that if the value of x is doubled, the value of y is doubled, and if the value of x is tripled, the value of y is tripled, and so on. This is the meaning of direct proportion.

A variable y is directly proportional to a variable x (and vice versa), if when x is multiplied by any number, then y is multiplied by the same number.

The symbol for 'directly proportional' is $\propto$.

$y \propto x$ means that y is directly proportional to x.

From the above table, for every pair of values (x, y), $\frac{y}{x} = 0{\cdot}9 =$ constant. This is a consequence of the directly proportional relationship between x and y.

$\frac{y}{x} = 0{\cdot}9 \Rightarrow y = 0{\cdot}9x$

0·9 is called the **constant of proportionality**.

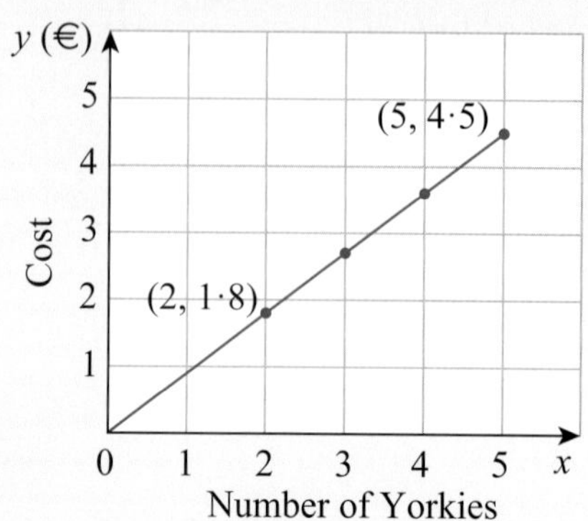

In general, $y \propto x \Leftrightarrow \frac{y}{x} = k \Leftrightarrow y = kx$, where k is a constant.

If you plot y (cost) against x (number of Yorkie bars), you get a straight line through the origin. The slope of the straight line is k, the constant of proportionality.

$$\text{Slope} = \frac{4{\cdot}5 - 1{\cdot}8}{5 - 2} = 0{\cdot}9 = k$$

For every directly proportional relationship $y = kx$, the graph of y against x is always a straight line through the origin of slope k.

ACTIVITY 13

ACTION
Understanding direct proportion

OBJECTIVE
To draw a graph from a table of results and to answer questions that involve direct proportionality

EXAMPLE 16

If w is directly proportional to t:

(a) Write down an equation relating w to t.

(b) Find the constant of proportionality if $t = 20$, when $w = 60$.

(c) Find t, when $w = 57$.

Solution

(a) $w = kt$

(b) $\boldsymbol{t = 20, w = 60}$:

$60 = 20k$

$k = 3$ [The constant of proportionality]

$w = 3t$

(c) $\boldsymbol{w = 57}$: $57 = 3t$

$t = 19$

EXAMPLE 17

The graph below shows the speed of a snowball t seconds after falling from rest from the top of a building. The graph is a straight line.

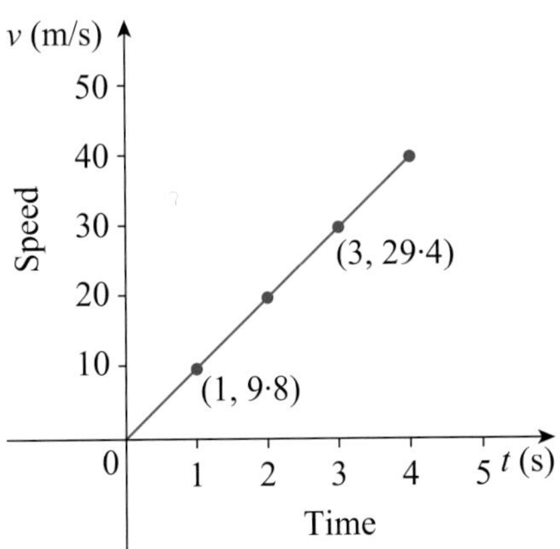

(a) Use the graph to find the constant of proportionality k between the variables. Hence, write an equation linking v to t.

(b) Use the equation to find the speed of the snowball after 2·5 s.

Solution

(a) This is a straight line through the origin

$\therefore\ v \propto t \Rightarrow v = kt$

$$\text{Slope} = \frac{29{\cdot}4 - 9{\cdot}8}{3 - 1} = 9{\cdot}8 = k$$

$v = 9{\cdot}8t$

(b) $\boldsymbol{t = 2{\cdot}5}$ s: $v = 9{\cdot}8 \times 2{\cdot}5$

Speed = 24·5 m/s

WORKED EXAMPLE Looking at another type of direct proportion

Consider the following table of results linking x and y.

x	1	2	3	4	5
y	3	12	27	48	75

Clearly $\frac{y}{x}$ is **not** the same for all (x, y) in this table. However, if the x values are squared, the situation changes.

x^2	1	4	9	16	25
y	3	12	27	48	75

$\frac{y}{x^2} = 3$ (a constant) $\Rightarrow y = 3(x^2)$

We say that y is directly proportional to x^2: $y \propto x^2$

A graph of y against (x^2) gives a straight line through the origin.

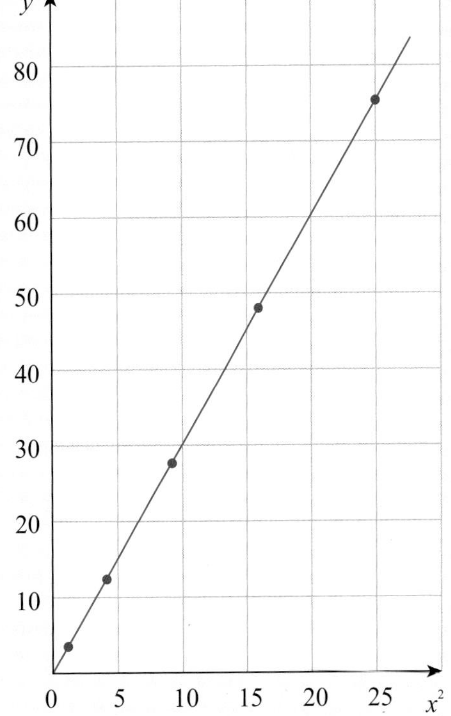

EXERCISE 10

1. A car travels 216 km on 15 litres (l) of petrol. How many kilometres will the car travel using 25 l of petrol, assuming a directly proportional relationship between distance travelled and petrol consumption?

2. y is directly proportional to x and $y = 50$ when $x = 20$. Find an equation relating y to x.
   - **(a)** Find y when $x = 25$.
   - **(b)** Find x when $y = 30$.

3. The force F on a mass is directly proportional to its acceleration a. If $a = 100$ when $F = 400$, write down a formula relating F to a. Find a when $F = 560$.

4. The current I in a resistor is directly proportional to the voltage V across the resistor. If $I = 2$ when $V = 6$, write down a formula relating I to V. If $V = 10$, find I.

5. The graph of y against x is a straight line through the origin.

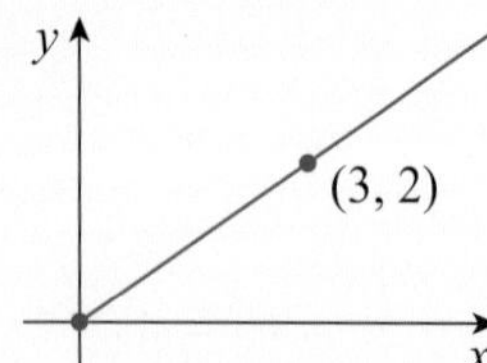

   - **(a)** Write down a formula relating y to x.
   - **(b)** What is the constant of proportionality?
   - **(c)** If $x = 900$, find y.
   - **(d)** If (a, b) and (c, d) are on the straight line, show that $\frac{a}{b} = \frac{c}{d}$.

6. Hooke's law states that the tension force F (N) in a spring is directly proportional to its extension x (m).
   - **(a)** Write down this statement using mathematical symbols.
   - **(b)** If k is the constant of proportionality, write down the law using F, k and x.
   - **(c)** Find k if $F = 4$ N when $x = 0{\cdot}005$ m.
   - **(d)** Find F when $x = 3{\cdot}7$ cm.
   - **(e)** Draw a graph to illustrate the relationship between F and x.

7. If $y \propto x$, find the constant of proportionality if $y = 35$ when $x = 7$. Find x when $y = 72$.

8. If in each case $y \propto x$, find u, v and w.

(a)

x	2	4	6
y	6	12	w

(b)

x	1	3	w	8
y	u	9	15	24

(c)

x	9	12	u	17
y	w	60	75	v

9.

x	2	3	4	5
y	15	22·5	30	37·5

   - **(a)** Is $y \propto x$? Why?
   - **(b)** What is the constant of proportionality?
   - **(c)** Write down an equation relating y to x.
   - **(d)** Draw a graph of y against x.
   - **(e)** What is its slope?

10. In each of the following, state whether the relationship between y and x is directly proportional or not. State a reason for your answer.
   - **(a)** $y = 2x$
   - **(b)** $3x - y = 0$
   - **(c)** $y = x + 1$
   - **(d)** $y = \frac{x}{2}$
   - **(e)** $y = x^2$

2.7 Inverse proportion

- A man driving a 1990 Fiesta completed a journey in 2 hours at 40 km/h. A woman driving a 2014 Ferrari completed the same journey in 1 hour at 80 km/h.
- A single pump can fill a swimming pool in 24 hours. If three pumps of the same power as the single pump are used, it only takes 8 hours to fill the pool.

These are examples of **inverse proportion**.

The value of one variable y decreases at the same rate as the value of the other variable x increases. In other words: If x is halved, y is doubled, or if x is quadrupled, y is quartered, and so on.

WORKED EXAMPLE Explaining inverse proportion

A table of results linking variables x and y is shown.

x	2	3	4	5	6
y	6	4	3	2·4	2

As x increases from 2 to 4 (doubles), y decreases from 6 to 3 (halves).

For every pair (x, y) of variables, $xy = 12 =$ constant.

$y = \frac{12}{x} \Rightarrow y \propto \frac{1}{x}$

This is expressed as 'y is directly proportional to one over x (the inverse of x)'

or

'y is inversely proportional to x'.

In general, if $y = \frac{k}{x}$, then y is inversely proportional to x and vice versa. k is called the constant of proportionality. A graph of y against $\frac{1}{x}$ is a straight line through the origin of slope k.

$y \propto \frac{1}{x} \Leftrightarrow y = \frac{k}{x} \Leftrightarrow xy = k$

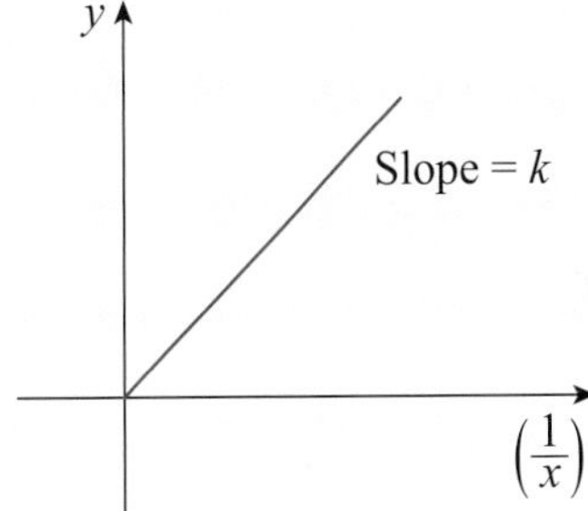

The product xy is constant.

ACTIVITY 14

ACTION
Understanding inverse proportion

OBJECTIVE
To draw a graph from a table of results and to answer questions that involve inverse proportionality

EXAMPLE 18

If p is inversely proportional to s, find an expression relating p to s.

If $p = 6$ when $s = 15$:

(a) find the constant of proportionality,

(b) find s when $p = 20$,

(c) find p when $s = 12$.

Solution

$p \propto \frac{1}{s} \Rightarrow p = \frac{k}{s}$

(a) $\boldsymbol{p = 6, s = 15}$: $6 = \frac{k}{15}$

$k = 90$

$p = \frac{90}{s}$

(b) $\boldsymbol{p = 20}$: $s = \frac{90}{20} = 4{\cdot}5$

(c) $\boldsymbol{s = 12}$: $p = \frac{90}{12} = 7{\cdot}5$

EXAMPLE 19

Five computers process a certain amount of information in 12 hours. How long will it take 18 computers to process the same information?

Solution

Clearly, as the number of computers N increases, the processing time t decreases.

$$\therefore t \propto \frac{1}{N} \Rightarrow t = \frac{k}{N}$$

$$\mathbf{N = 5, t = 12:}\ 12 = \frac{k}{5}$$

$$k = 60$$

$$\therefore t = \frac{60}{N}$$

$$\mathbf{N = 18:}\ t = \frac{60}{18} = \frac{10}{3} = 3\tfrac{1}{3} \text{ hours} = 3 \text{ hours } 20 \text{ minutes}$$

EXERCISE 11

1. If $y \propto \frac{1}{x}$ and $y = 20$ when $x = 5$, find the constant of proportionality.

(a) Find x when $y = 25$.

(b) Find y when $x = 40$.

2. The time t to be served in a restaurant is inversely proportional to the number N of waiters working.

(a) Write down a formula relating t to N.

(b) If it takes 30 minutes to be served by 10 waiters, find the constant of proportionality.

(c) How long does it take to be served by 12 waiters?

3. A bus journey takes 40 minutes at an average speed of 60 km/h.

(a) Is the relation between the time of a journey t (minutes) and speed v (km/h) a directly or an inversely proportional relation?

(b) Write down a formula relating t to v.

(c) How fast must the bus go to cover the same journey in 30 minutes?

4. Boyle's law states that the pressure P in a gas is inversely proportional to the volume V of the gas, at constant temperature.

(a) Explain what this means by stating what happens to the pressure as the volume increases.

(b) Write down a formula relating P to V.

(c) If, when the volume is V_1, the pressure is P_1 and when the volume is V_2, the pressure is P_2, show that $P_1V_1 = P_2V_2$.

P_1 V_1	→	P_2 V_2

(d) If $V = 0{\cdot}01\ \text{m}^3$ when $P = 5\ \text{N m}^{-2}$, find V when $P = 3{\cdot}2\ \text{N m}^{-2}$, correct to four decimal places.

5. If x men can complete a job in t days, write down a relationship between x and t. Find the constant of proportionality if 30 men can complete the job in 20 days. How many men are needed to complete the job in 24 days?

6. If it takes 5 pumps to empty a swimming pool in 8 hours, how many pumps will it take to empty the pool in $2\frac{1}{2}$ hours?

7. There is enough food in a refugee camp to feed 300 people for 14 days. If 200 more refugees arrive at that instant, how long will the food last?

8. The frequency of vibration of a violin string varies inversely with the length l of the string. A violin string of length 0·254 m vibrates at 512 Hz. Find the frequency of a 0·2 m string.

9. The graph of v (km/h) of a ball against $\frac{1}{m}$ (kg^{-1}) is a straight line through the origin, where v is the speed of a ball of mass m (kg).

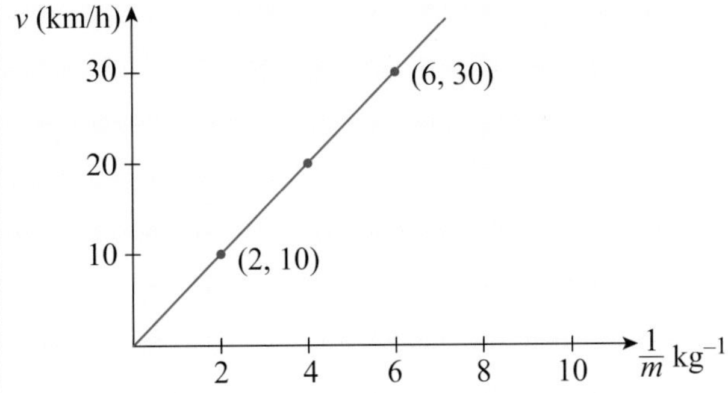

(a) Find the slope of the graph.

(b) Write down an equation relating v to m. Find v when $m = 0{\cdot}2$ kg.

10. The acceleration due to gravity g (m/s^2) is inversely proportional to the square of the distance r (m) from the centre of the Earth.

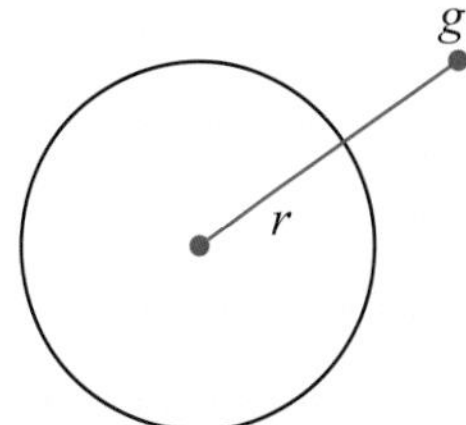

(a) Write down an equation connecting g and r.

(b) If $g = 9{\cdot}8$ m/s^2 when $r = 6{\cdot}4 \times 10^6$ m, find g when $r = 3{\cdot}2 \times 10^7$ m.

REVISION QUESTIONS

1. $\mathbb{R}^+$ is the set of positive real numbers.

(a) Show $\mathbb{R}^+$ on the number line.

(b) Copy the Venn diagram below. Place the following numbers in the Venn diagram: $10, 0, -3, \frac{1}{2}, -\frac{2}{3}, \sqrt{2}, 1$

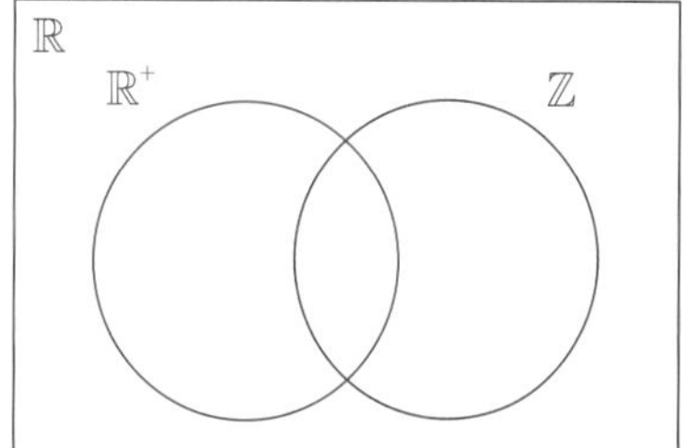

(c) What set is $\mathbb{R}^+ \cap \mathbb{Z}$?

(d) Describe in words the set $A = \{x \mid x < 0,\ x \in \mathbb{R}\}$.

2. **(a)** Why are all prime numbers, except 2, odd?

(b) For $n \in \mathbb{N}$, Joe claims there is always at least one prime number between n and $2n$ inclusive. Investigate this claim for $n = 1, 2, 3, 4, 5$, by copying and completing the table:

n	Primes	$2n$
1		
2		
3		
4		
5		

(c) If k and l are two prime numbers with $l > 2$ and $k > l$, show that $k^2 - l^2$ can never be prime.

3. **(a)** Show that 123 is not divisible by 7 or 11 or 13, but that 123 123 is divisible by 7 and 11 and 13.

(b) Show that 347 347 is divisible by 7 and 11 and 13.

(c) Evaluate the following:

(i) $7 \times 11 \times 13$

(ii) $579 \times 7 \times 11 \times 13$

(d) If abc is a three-digit number, show that $abc \times 7 \times 11 \times 13$ is a six-digit number $abcabc$. (Hint: $1001 = 1000 + 1$)

4. **(a)** Write the following in order of increasing size in the form $a \times 10^n$, $1 \le a < 10$:

$215{\cdot}7 \times 10^2,\ 22{\cdot}5 \times 10^3,\ 0{\cdot}032 \times 10^5,\ 2{\cdot}5 \times 10^4$

(b) **(i)** By rounding off each number to the nearest whole number, estimate the value of:

$$Q = \frac{132{\cdot}3 - 1{\cdot}74 \times \sqrt{0{\cdot}64}}{35{\cdot}3 - (5{\cdot}2)^2},$$

as a whole number.

(ii) Evaluate Q correct to three significant figures, using your calculator.

(c) A man measures the length l of a rectangular room with a metre stick. He needs to use the metre stick four times, as shown. The error in each measurement is $\pm\, 0{\cdot}1$ cm.

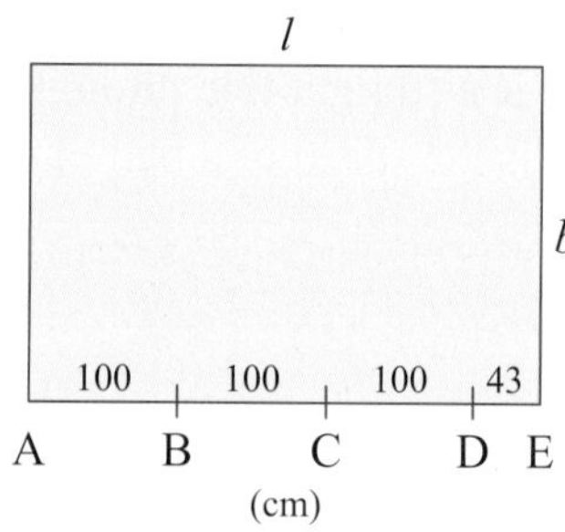

(i) What is the maximum value of l?

(ii) What is the minimum value of l?

Before he measures the width, his friend points out that a tape measure might be useful. Using the tape measure, he measures the width b to a value $(254 \pm 0{\cdot}1)$ cm. Find the maximum and minimum areas of the room in m^2, correct to three decimal places.

5. **(a)** Write $0{\cdot}0000016$ in the form $a \times 10^n$, $1 < a \le 10$.

(b) The force F in Newtons between two charges $q_1 = 0{\cdot}0000016$ C and $q_2 = 0{\cdot}0000016$ C is given by

$$F = \frac{9 \times 10^9 \times q_1 \times q_1}{r^2}.$$

If $r = 1{\cdot}6 \times 10^{-1}$ m, evaluate F without using your calculator. Show your work clearly.

(c) (i) Estimate $Q = \dfrac{5{\cdot}9 \times \sqrt{16{\cdot}2}}{3{\cdot}2}$, by rounding each number to the nearest whole number.

(ii) Using your calculator, find the exact value of Q correct to one decimal place.

(iii) Find the percentage error in the estimate correct to one decimal place.

6. (a) Light travels at $2{\cdot}9 \times 10^5$ km/s. How many kilometres will light travel in 10 minutes? Give your answer in the form $a \times 10^n$, $1 \leq a < 10$.

(b) (i) By rounding each number to the nearest whole number, estimate the value of:

$$Q = \left(\frac{5{\cdot}8 + \sqrt[3]{27{\cdot}1}}{3{\cdot}12}\right)^2$$, as a whole number.

(ii) Use your calculator to evaluate Q, correct to two decimal places.

(c) Koola produces cans of cola with a tolerance level of (330 ± 5) ml. If a girl drinks three cans of Koola on a particular day, what is:

(i) the maximum possible volume of Koola she consumes,

(ii) the minimum possible volume of Koola she consumes?

If there is 0·11 g of sugar in 1 ml of Koola, what is the maximum amount of sugar in grams the girl gets from Koola on that day?

7. (a) If $a = 3 \times 10^{-2}$ and $b = 8 \times 10^{-3}$, find $a + 4b$ in the form $a \times 10^n$, $1 \leq a < 10$, without using your calculator. Show your work clearly.

(b) The tolerance level of the area A of a square plastic cover for a mobile phone is $(1{\cdot}97 \pm 0{\cdot}28)$ cm^2.

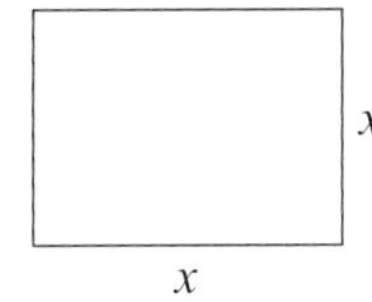

(i) What is the tolerance level of each side?

(ii) If adjacent sides have the minimum and maximum allowed lengths, respectively, what would be the area of the rectangle?

(c) A lunch bill for Joe and Mary is shown.

Joe		Mary	
Soup	€3·95	Salad	€4·10
Salad	€4·10	Beef	€12·95
Salmon	€9·85	Ice cream	€3·10
Apple pie	€5·10		

(i) Make a quick estimate of the bill, giving your answer as a whole number.

(ii) Calculate the exact value on your calculator.

(iii) Find the percentage error in the quick estimate, correct to two decimal places.

8. (a) (i) Arrange the following numbers in ascending order:

$2200,\ 2{\cdot}4 \times 10^3,\ 2{\cdot}4,\ 10^3,\ 2{\cdot}4 \times 10^{-3}$

(ii) Evaluate $7 \times 10^{11} + 9 \times 10^{11} + 8 \times 10^{10}$, giving your answer in the form $a \times 10^n$, $1 \leq a < 10$, without using your calculator.

(b) The specific gravity of diesel oil has a tolerance level $(0{\cdot}89 \pm 0{\cdot}07)$. Crude oil has a specific gravity of 0·79. What is the least percentage change that the specific gravity of the crude oil must undergo to become diesel oil, correct to one decimal place?

(c) On a certain map, 25 km is represented by 2 cm. If two cities on the map are:

(i) 7 cm apart,

(ii) 12·5 cm apart,

find the actual distance between them.

(d) The current I in amps in an electrical circuit varies inversely as the resistance R of the circuit.

(i) Write down a formula connecting I and R.

(ii) If the current is 8 amps when the resistance is 24 ohms, find the current when the resistance is 30 ohms.

9. **(a)** Plot a graph of y against x using the table of results shown.

x	5	10	15
y	2	4	6

(i) Explain why y is directly proportional to x.

(ii) Find the constant of proportionality.

(iii) Write down a formula connecting y and x.

(iv) Find x when $y = 32{\cdot}5$.

(b) The distance s in metres of a body from a fixed point after t seconds is given by $s = 3t^2$.

Find the average rate of change between $t = 2$ and $t = 6$.

(c) A car with an average speed of r km/h takes t hours to complete a journey.

(i) If r is inversely proportional to t, write down a formula connecting r and t.

(ii) If the car takes 3 hours to complete a journey at an average speed of 75 km/h, how long would it take to complete the journey at an average speed of 85 km/h, correct to two decimal places?

10. **(a)** In a normal deck of cards, what percentage of the cards are:

(i) face cards, correct to two decimal places,

(ii) diamonds,

(iii) diamonds or queens, correct to two decimal places?

(b) Express $\frac{7}{371}$ as a decimal, correct to three significant figures.

(c) **(i)** If $y = x^2$, find the average rate of change of y from $x = -4$ and $x = -1$.

(ii) At a speed of 75 mph, the fuel efficiency of a Subaru is 30 miles/gallon. If the driver slows down to a speed of 60 mph, the fuel efficiency is 35 miles/gallon. What is the average rate of change of the fuel efficiency as the speed drops from 75 mph to 60 mph?

(d) To balance a see-saw the distance in metres a person is from the pivot P is inversely proportional to his mass in kg. Eamon, whose mass is 60 kg, is sitting 2 m from the pivot. Emma's mass is 48 kg. How far from the pivot must Emma sit so that the see-saw is balanced?

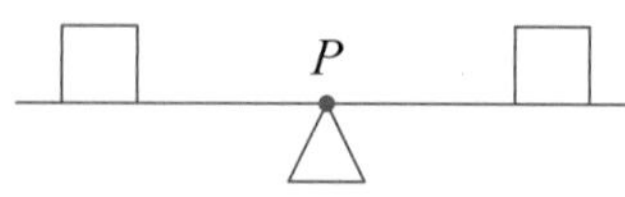

SUMMARY

Number Systems

1. Natural numbers:

$\mathbb{N} = \{1, 2, 3, \ldots\}$

A prime number is a natural number greater than 1, which can only be divided by itself and 1.

2. Integers:

$\mathbb{Z} = \{\ldots, -3, -2, -1, 0, 1, 2, 3, \ldots\}$

Consecutive integers can be written as:

$a, a + 1, a + 2, \ldots$

or

$a - 1, a, a + 1, \ldots$

3. Rational numbers:

$\mathbb{Q} = \left\{\ldots, -15, \ldots, -\frac{2}{3}, \ldots, 0, \ldots, \frac{1}{2}, \ldots, \frac{11}{3}, \ldots, 10, \ldots\right\}$

Every rational number can be expressed as a terminating decimal or a non-terminating, recurring decimal.

4. Real numbers:

$\mathbb{R} = \left\{\ldots, -\pi, \ldots, -\sqrt{3}, \ldots, -\frac{2}{3}, \ldots, 0, \ldots, \sqrt{2}, \ldots, 2\pi, \ldots\right\}$

5. Complex numbers:

Complex numbers are denoted by $\mathbb{C}$.

$i = \sqrt{-1}$

$z = a + bi,\ a, b \in R,\ i = \sqrt{-1}$

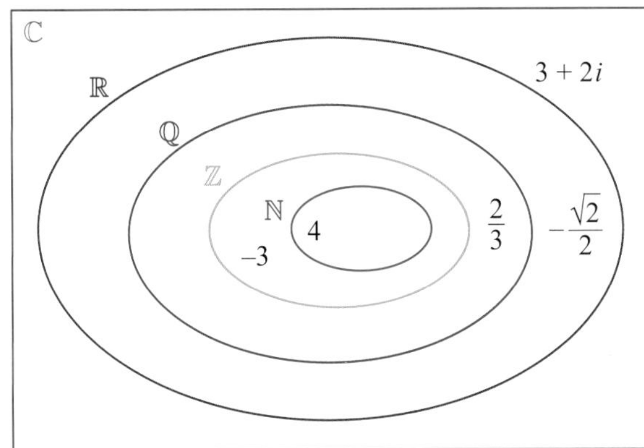

$\mathbb{N} \subset \mathbb{Z} \subset \mathbb{Q} \subset \mathbb{R} \subset \mathbb{C}$

6. Absolute value (modulus) of a number:
|Number| = Positive value of the number

Arithmetic

1. Percentages:

(a) A percentage is a fraction expressed as part of 100: $r\% = \frac{r}{100}$

(b) To increase a quantity by $r\%$, multiply it by $\left(1 + \frac{r}{100}\right)$.

(c) To decrease a quantity by $r\%$, multiply it by $\left(1 - \frac{r}{100}\right)$.

2. Scientific notation: $a \times 10^n$, $n \in \mathbb{Z}$ and $1 \le a < 10$

3. The order of magnitude of $a \times 10^n$, $1 \le a \le 10$, is n if $a < 5$, and is $n + 1$ if $a \ge 5$.

4. The tolerance level of a measurement is the greatest range of variation in the measurement that is allowable.

5. **(a)** Absolute error in a quantity = |Measured value of the quantity – Accepted value of the quantity|

(b) Percentage error in a quantity

$$= \frac{\text{Absolute error in the quantity}}{\text{Accepted value of the quantity}} \times 100\%$$

6. Significant figures: Write the number in the form $a \times 10^n$, $1 \le a < 10$ and give the required number of digits in a.

7. **(a)** Average rate of change of Q with respect to

$t = \frac{Q_2 - Q_1}{t_2 - t_1}$

= slope of line AB

(b) Speed $v = \frac{s_2 - s_1}{t_2 - t_1} = \frac{\text{Change in distance}}{\text{Change in time}}$

Acceleration $a = \frac{v_2 - v_1}{t_2 - t_1} = \frac{\text{Change in speed}}{\text{Change in time}}$

8. Direct and inverse proportion:

Direct: $y \propto x \Rightarrow y = kx,\ k \in \mathbb{R}$

Inverse: $y \propto \frac{1}{x} \Rightarrow y = \frac{k}{x},\ k \in \mathbb{R}$

SECTION 2

Algebraic Expressions

Algebra is the gateway to problem-solving. Being able to express a problem in the symbolic language of algebra enables you to develop abstract reasoning skills. Algebra is the language of mathematics.

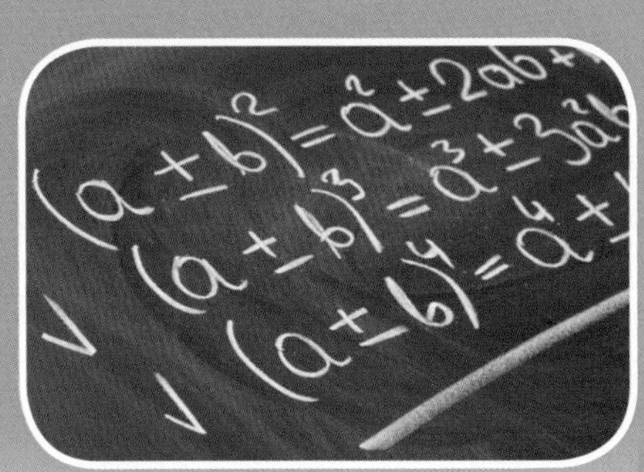

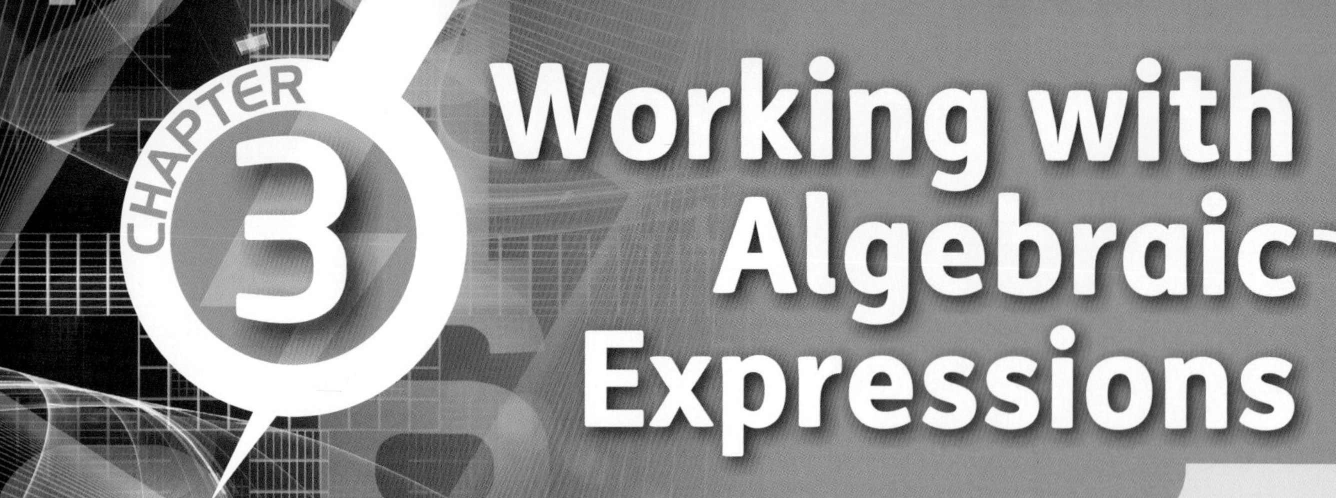

Working with Algebraic Expressions

Learning Outcomes

- To understand the basics of adding and multiplying algebraic expressions.
- To find the value of an algebraic expression by substituting the values of its variables.
- To use the binomial theorem to expand binomials raised to a power.
- To pick out particular terms in a binomial expansion.
- To use various techniques of factorisation to turn algebraic expressions into their factors.
- To apply your knowledge to modelling problems.

3.1 Algebraic basics

ACTIVITY 1

ACTION
Writing out the terms and coefficients in algebraic expressions

OBJECTIVE
To recognise the terms and coefficients in algebraic expressions

Key terms

It is important that you understand the language of algebra.

KEY TERM

A **variable** is a symbol (letter) that can take on a range of values. The symbols used are usually letters such as x and y, but there is nothing wrong with boxes (□), circles (○) or brackets ( ).

KEY TERM

A **term** is a number (constant) multiplied by one or more variables, or just a number on its own.

Examples of terms: $5x$, $-6xy$, $3x^2y$, $-5(2x + 3)$, -7

KEY TERM

An **expression** is made up of a number of terms separated by + or – signs.

- The expression $3x^2 + 2y - x(y - 1)$ has three terms.
- The expression $-2y^2 + 3xy^2 - \frac{1}{2}x + 4$ has four terms.

ACTIVITY 2

ACTION
Understanding the meanings of algebraic expressions

OBJECTIVE
To write an algebraic expression in its simplest form

KEY TERM

The **coefficient** of a variable or a group of variables is the number (constant) multiplying them.

- In the expression $4x - 3y + 5x^2y - 2$, the coefficient of x is +4, the coefficient of y is −3, the coefficient of x^2y is +5 and the constant (numerical) coefficient is −2.

Multiplication of algebraic terms

ACTIVITY 3

ACTION
Multiplying algebraic terms

OBJECTIVE
To understand the processes involved in multiplying algebraic terms, including commutativity and associativity

1. Commutative property for multiplication:
- $x \times y = y \times x$
  You can switch the order of multiplication.

2. Associative property for multiplication:
- $3xy = (3x)y = 3(xy)$
  When you multiply three or more objects, you can group any two together to multiply.
- $2 \times x \times x = 2 \times (x \times x) = 2x^2$
- $3 \times x \times 2 \times y = (3 \times 2) \times (x \times y)$
  $= 6 \times (xy)$
  $= 6xy$

3. Distributive property for multiplication:
- $-3x(x - 2y) = -3x^2 + 6xy$
  You multiply **all terms** in a bracket by an object (number or variable) outside the bracket.

Combining like terms

You can only combine like terms in an expression. In an expression, like terms are terms that have exactly the same variable (letters) composition.

- $5x^2y + 2yx^2 = 7x^2y$

You cannot make an expression such as $2x + 3y$ any simpler, as you cannot combine unlike terms.

ACTIVITY 4

ACTION
Combining terms using magic squares

OBJECTIVE
To use magic squares to combine terms in algebraic expressions

EXAMPLE 1

Simplify the following:

(a) $4x - 3y + 5z$

(b) $4x^2y + 5xy - 6yx^2 + 1 - 2xy$

Solution

(a) $4x - 3y + 5z = 4x - 3y + 5z$ [There are no like terms, so leave the expression as it is.]

(b) $4x^2y + 5xy - 6yx^2 + 1 - 2xy$
$= 4x^2y - 6x^2y + 5xy - 2xy + 1$ $[yx^2 = x^2y]$
$= -2x^2y + 3xy + 1$ [Gather up like terms]

ACTIVITY 5

ACTION
Expanding brackets and combining like terms

OBJECTIVE
To multiply out brackets term by term and then combine terms

Multiplying out (expanding) brackets and combining like terms

- $3x + 2y(4x - 1)$ [Always get rid of the brackets first].
  $= 3x + 8xy - 2y$
- $-4x + 3y - 2 - 3(2y - 5x + 9)$
  $= -4x + 3y - 2 - 6y + 15x - 27$
  $= 11x - 3y - 29$
  Make sure you combine terms **after** the brackets have been removed.

WORKED EXAMPLE

Expanding brackets of the type $(x + a)(y + b)$

Multiply out $(x + a)(y + b)$. [Each bracket has two terms.]

$(x + a)(y + b) = x(y + b) + a(y + b)$

$= xy + xb + ay + ab$

The same result is obtained by multiplying out term by term. Every term in the first bracket is multiplied by every term in the second bracket.

$(x + a)(y + b) = xy + xb + ay + ab$

Observe the following:
To obtain the first term in the answer, multiply the first terms of the two brackets: $x \times y = xy$

$(\mathbf{x} + a)(\mathbf{y} + b) = \mathbf{xy} + xb + ay + ab$ [First × First = First]

To obtain the last term of the answer, multiply the last terms of the two brackets: $a \times b = ab$

$(x + \mathbf{a})(y + \mathbf{b}) = xy + xb + ay + \mathbf{ab}$ [Last × Last = Last]

To get the middle terms, multiply the first term of one bracket by the last term of the second bracket. Do this for both brackets: $x \times b = xb$ and $y \times a = ya$
Call these middle terms the mixtures. Now you have all the terms in the answer.

$(x + a)(y + b) = xy + \mathbf{xb} + \mathbf{ay} + ab$

When you multiply out two brackets with two terms in each bracket, the answers can have four terms, three terms or two terms.

1. Four terms

$(2x - 1)(4y - 3) = 8xy - 6x - 4y + 3$ (four terms)

or

2. Three terms

$(4x - y)(x + 2y) = 4x^2 + 8xy - xy - 2y^2$

$= 4x^2 + 7xy - 2y^2$ (three terms)

There are three terms in this answer because the mixtures combine into a single term.
An expression with three terms is also called a **trinomial**.

or

3. Two terms

$(2x - 3y)(2x + 3y) = 4x^2 + 6xy - 6xy - 9y^2$

$= 4x^2 - 9y^2$ (two terms)

There are two terms in this answer because the mixtures cancel. The two terms in this answer are also called the **difference of two squares**.

More multiplication of brackets

1. Difference of two squares

A difference of two squares expression is obtained by the multiplication of two brackets of the type:

(Difference of two terms) × (Sum of the same two terms)

- $(3x - 5y)(3x + 5y) = 9x^2 + 15xy - 15xy - 25y^2 = 9x^2 - 25y^2 = (3x)^2 - (5y)^2$
- $(ax + by)(ax - by) = (ax)^2 - (by)^2 = a^2x^2 - b^2y^2$

TIP

Remember as:

(First – Second)(First + Second) = $(\text{First})^2 - (\text{Second})^2$

2. Perfect squares

A perfect square consists of two identical brackets.

- $(3x - 2y)^2 = (3x - 2y)(3x - 2y) = 9x^2 - 6xy - 6yx + 4y^2 = 9x^2 - 12xy + 4y^2$

  The quick way to do a perfect square is to remember the following:

TIP

Remember as:
$(\text{First term} + \text{Second term})^2$
$= (\text{First term})^2 + 2(\text{First term})(\text{Second term}) + (\text{Second term})^2$

- $(2x - 1)(2x - 1) = (2x)^2 + 2(2x)(-1) + (-1)^2 = 4x^2 - 4x + 1$

3. Harder multiplication

Use the following steps for multiplying three brackets:

1. Multiply two first (choose which two carefully to make it easier).
2. Tidy up your answer and then multiply by the remaining bracket.

- $(x - 1)(x + 1)(y - 2)$ [Multiply the first two first as it gives the difference of two squares.]

  $= (x^2 - 1)(y - 2)$

  $= x^2y - 2x^2 - y + 2$

ACTIVITY 6

ACTION
Finding the value of an algebraic expression

OBJECTIVE
To find the value of an expression when given a value of a variable

Finding the value of an algebraic expression

To find the value of an algebraic expression, simply fill in the given value(s) of the variable(s).

Method

1. Put a bracket around each variable.
2. Fill in the value of each variable.
3. Simplify each term – always calculate the brackets first.
4. Combine the terms.

EXAMPLE 2

Evaluate $4x^2y - 2xy^2 + 5xy - 7$, if $x = 2$ and $y = -3$.

Solution

$4x^2y - 2xy^2 + 5xy - 7$ [This is a two-variable expression. Put brackets around the variables first.]

$= 4(x)^2(y) - 2(x)(y)^2 + 5(x)(y) - 7$

Substituting in $\mathbf{x = 2}$ and $\mathbf{y = -3}$ gives:

$4(2)^2(-3) - 2(2)(-3)^2 + 5(2)(-3) - 7$

$= -48 - 36 - 30 - 7$

$= -121$

EXERCISE 1

1. Multiply out and simplify the following:

(a) $(x + 2)(x + 5)$

(b) $(3x + 7)(2x + 3)$

(c) $(y + 5)(y + 8)$

(d) $(3x - 5)(2x - 1)$

(e) $x(x - 3)(2x + 4)$

(f) $(2x^2 + x + 1)(x + 1)$

(g) $(x^2 - x + 5)(x - 3)$

(h) $(x - 1)(3x^2 + 5x - 7)$

(i) $(-2x^2 + 5x - 6)(1 - x)$

2. Multiply out the following. The answers are a difference of two squares expression, which simplifies the process.

(a) $(x + 2)(x - 2)$

(b) $(2x - 1)(2x + 1)$

(c) $(4x - 1)(4x + 1)$

(d) $(x^2 + 1)(x^2 - 1)$

(e) $(3x - 2)(3x + 2)$

(f) $(4x - 3y)(4x + 3y)$

(g) $(x^2 - 5)(x^2 + 5)$

(h) $(x^n - 3)(x^n + 3)$

3. Multiply out the following perfect squares:

(a) $(x + 2)^2$

(b) $(3x + 2)^2$

(c) $(x - 4)^2$

(d) $(5x - 4)^2$

(e) $(x^2 - 11)^2$

(f) $(4y - 5)^2$

(g) $(ax - b)^2$

(h) $(a + 1)^2 - (a - 1)^2$

4. Multiply out and simplify the following:

(a) $(x - 2)(x + 1)(x + 2)$

(b) $(2x - 1)(x + 3)(2x + 1)$

(c) $(2x + 3)(3x - 1)(2x - 3)$

(d) $(x + 1)^3$ [Hint: $(x + 1)^2(x + 1)$]

(e) $(2x - 1)^3$ [Hint: $(2x - 1)^2(2x - 1)$]

(f) $(x - 2)(2x + 1)(x - 3)$

5. (a) If $a = x - 3$ and $b = 2x + 5$, find the following, in terms of x:

(i) $a + b$ **(iv)** b^2

(ii) $a - b$ **(v)** ab

(iii) a^2 **(vi)** a^2b

(b) If $p = x^2 - x + 1$ and $q = 2x^2 + 3x - 2$, find the following, in terms of x:

(i) $p + q$ **(iii)** $p + 2q$

(ii) $p - q$ **(iv)** $2q - 3p$

(c) If $p = 2x^2 + 5x - 1$ and $q = 4x^3 - 2x^2 + 5x - 1$, find the following, in terms of x:

(i) $p + q$ (iii) $3p - 2q$

(ii) $q - p$ (iv) $q - xp$

6. Find the values of the following expressions:

(a) $3x + 11y$ if $x = -2$ and $y = 3{\cdot}5$

(b) $4x - 3y + 8$ if $x = -1, y = -6$

(c) $5x^2$ if $x = -3$

(d) $-5x^2$ if $x = -3$

(e) $(5x)^2$ if $x = 3$

(f) $x^2 - 3y^2$ if $x = 3$ and $y = -2$

(g) $2x^2 + 5x - 7$ if $x = 5$

(h) $-5x^2 + 7x - 3$ if $x = -2$

(i) $(2x + 3y)^2$ if $x = -3$ and $y = 4$

(j) $2x^2y - 3xy^2 - 7$ if $x = 3$ and $y = -2$

(k) $3x^2y^2 - 5x + 7(x - y)^2$ if $x = -2$ and $y = 0{\cdot}5$

3.2 Binomial theorem

ACTIVITY 7

ACTION
Working with the binomial theorem

OBJECTIVE
To explore every aspect of the binomial theorem

KEY TERM

An expression with two terms is called a **binomial**. The **binomial theorem** is a quick way to multiply out (expand) binomials raised to a power.

Examples of binomials raised to a power:

$(a + b)^4$, $(a - b)^7$, $(2a + 5)^4$, $(1 + 2x)^9$, $\left(5x - \frac{3}{y}\right)^6$, $\left(2a + \frac{1}{5}\right)^{20}$

In general, to expand out expressions of the form $(x + y)^n$, where $n \in \mathbb{N}$, you use the binomial theorem.

THE BINOMIAL THEOREM

$$(x + y)^n = {}^nC_0(x)^n(y)^0 + {}^nC_1(x)^{n-1}(y)^1 + {}^nC_2(x)^{n-2}(y)^2 + \dots + {}^nC_n(x)^0(y)^n$$

ACTIVITY 8

ACTION
Expanding binomials

OBJECTIVE
To apply the binomial theorem to expand a number of binomials raised to a certain power

${}^nC_0$, ${}^nC_1$, ${}^nC_2$ ... are known as binomial coefficients.

How ${}^nC_r$ is calculated

${}^nC_r = \dfrac{n!}{r!(n-r)!}$, where $n! = n(n-1)(n-2) \dots 1$

▸ $${}^5C_3 = \frac{5!}{3!(5-3)!} = \frac{5!}{3!2!} = \frac{5 \times 4 \times 3 \times 2 \times 1}{3 \times 2 \times 1 \times 2 \times 1} = 10$$

You can do this calculation on a calculator using the **nCr** button.

WORKED EXAMPLE

Expanding $(x + y)^5$

Follow the pattern in the formula by letting $n = 5$.

$$(x + y)^n = {}^nC_0(x)^n(y)^0 + {}^nC_1(x)^{n-1}(y)^1 + {}^nC_2(x)^{n-2}(y)^2 + \dots + {}^nC_n(x)^0(y)^n$$

$$(x + y)^5 = {}^5C_0(x)^5(y)^0 + {}^5C_1(x)^4(y)^1 + {}^5C_2(x)^3(y)^2 + {}^5C_3(x)^2(y)^3 + {}^5C_4(x)^1(y)^4 + {}^5C_5(x)^0(y)^5$$

$$\therefore (x + y)^5 = x^5 + 5x^4y + 10x^3y^2 + 10x^2y^3 + 5xy^4 + y^5$$

Some observations of this binomial expansion.

1. The powers of x decrease in steps of 1 from 5 to 0 reading from left to right.
2. The powers of y increase in steps of 1 from 0 to 5 reading from left to right.
3. The sum of the powers in every term is 5.

There are six term.s in the expansion. The number of terms is always one greater than n.

First term: ${}^5C_0(x)^5(y)^0$ | Fourth term: ${}^5C_3(x)^2(y)^3$

Second term: ${}^5C_1(x)^4(y)^1$ | Fifth term: ${}^5C_4(x)^1(y)^4$

Third term: ${}^5C_2(x)^3(y)^2$ | Sixth term: ${}^5C_5(x)^0(y)^5$

[Notice, in each case, the subscript in the binomial coefficient is one less than the number of the term.]

General term: ${}^nC_r(x)^{n-r}(y)^r$ which is the $(r + 1)$st term.

- $(p+q)^4 = {}^4C_0(p)^4(q)^0 + {}^4C_1(p)^3(q)^1 + {}^4C_2(p)^2(q)^2 + {}^4C_3(p)^1(q)^3 + {}^4C_4(p)^0(q)^4$
  $= p^4 + 4p^3q + 6p^2q^2 + 4pq^3 + q^4$
- $(3x-2)^3 = {}^3C_0(3x)^3(-2)^0 + {}^3C_1(3x)^2(-2)^1 + {}^3C_2(3x)^1(-2)^2 + {}^3C_3(3x)^0(-2)^3$
  $= 27x^3 - 54x^2 + 36x - 8$
- The fifth term in $(p-q)^7$ has a binomial coefficient of ${}^7C_4$.
  Fifth term $= {}^7C_4(p)^3(-q)^4 = 35p^3q^4$
- The fourth term in $(2x+y)^8$ has a binomial coefficient of ${}^8C_3$.
  Fourth term $= {}^8C_3(2x)^5(y)^3 = 56(32x^5)y^3 = 1792x^5y^3$

ACTIVITY 9

ACTION
Picking out terms in a binomial expansion

OBJECTIVE
To show you understand the binomial by picking out individual terms in the expansion

Picking out terms in a binomial expansion

EXAMPLE 3

In the expansion of $(p+q)^7$, what is the term with q^5?

Solution

q^5 means p must be to the power 2 [Powers add up to 7.]

Term with q^5: ${}^7C_5(p)^2(q)^5 = 21p^2q^5$

EXAMPLE 4

What is the term with a^4 in the expansion of $(a-2b)^9$?

Solution

a^4 means $(-2b)$ must be to the power 5.

$$\text{Term} = {}^9C_5\, a^4\, (-2b)^5$$
$$= -126a^4 \times 32b^5$$
$$= -4032a^4b^5$$

EXAMPLE 5

In $\left(2x + \frac{y}{4}\right)^8$, what is the term with y^3?

Solution

$$\text{Term} = {}^8C_3(2x)^{8-3}\left(\frac{y}{4}\right)^3$$
$$= {}^8C_3(2x)^5\left(\frac{y}{4}\right)^3$$
$$= 56 \times 32x^5 \times \frac{y^3}{64}$$
$$= 28x^5y^3$$

EXERCISE 2

1. Use your calculator to evaluate:
$^5C_0$, $^{10}C_0$, $^{18}C_0$, $^6C_0$, $^8C_0$. What is $^nC_0$?

2. Use your calculator to evaluate:
$^5C_5$, $^{10}C_{10}$, $^{18}C_{18}$, $^6C_6$, $^8C_8$ and hence evaluate ^nC_n

3. Using your calculator show:
   (a) $^5C_2 = {}^5C_3$
   (b) $^{10}C_4 = {}^{10}C_6$
   (c) $^7C_3 = {}^7C_4$
   (d) $^{18}C_5 = {}^{18}C_{13}$

   Make a conclusion.

4. Expand out the following:
   (a) $(x + 1)^4$
   (b) $(p + q)^8$
   (c) $(q + p)^5$
   (d) $(x - 2y)^4$
   (e) $(2x + 3y)^3$
   (f) $(0{\cdot}6 + 0{\cdot}4)^6$
   (g) $(0{\cdot}8 + 0{\cdot}2)^4$

5. (a) Find the fifth term in $(p + q)^8$.
   (b) Find the fourth term in $(x + y)^7$.
   (c) Find the third term in $(2x + y)^6$.
   (d) Find the sixth term in $(p - q)^7$.

6. Find the term with:
   (a) p^3 in the expansion of $(p + q)^7$
   (b) q^5 in the expansion of $(p + q)^8$
   (c) $(0{\cdot}6)^4$ in the expansion of $(0{\cdot}4 + 0{\cdot}6)^{12}$
   (d) $(0{\cdot}85)^5$ in the expansion of $(0{\cdot}85 + 0{\cdot}15)^9$
   (e) p^6 in the expansion of $(p + q)^{10}$
   (f) q^3 in the expansion of $(p + q)^8$

3.3 Factorisation (working backwards)

KEY TERM

Factorisation means splitting up an algebraic expression into factors that multiply together to give the expression.

ACTIVITY 10

ACTION
Factorising algebraic expressions

OBJECTIVE
To use your techniques to revise factorising

Factorisation technique 1

Highest common factor (HCF)

- $5x + 10y + 15$ [5 is the HCF of $5x + 10y + 15$ as it is the largest object that divides into all three terms.]

  $= 5 \times x + 5 \times 2y + 5 \times 3 = 5(x + 2y + 3)$
- $5x^2y^2 - 10xy = 5xy(xy - 2)$
- $7x(x - 2y) - 3y(x - 2y) = (x - 2y)(7x - 3y)$

Factorisation technique 2

Grouping

To factorise an expression with four (or more) terms with no highest common factor, group the terms into pairs that each have a highest common factor.

WORKED EXAMPLE

How grouping works

The terms in the expression $6xy + 3xz + 2wy + zw$ have no highest common factor (HCF) but the first pair of terms has a HCF and the second pair of terms has a HCF.

$6xy + 3xz + 2wy + zw$

$= (6xy + 3xz) + (2wy + zw)$

$= 3x(2y + z) + w(2y + z)$

Four terms have been combined into two terms. These two terms have a HCF of $(2y + z)$.

$3x(2y + z) + w(2y + z)$

$= (2y + z)(3x + w)$

- $2x^2 - bx + 4ax - 2ab = (2x^2 - bx) + (4ax - 2ab)$

  $= x(2x - b) + 2a(2x - b)$

  $= (2x - b)(x + 2a)$

- $ax - bx - ay + by + a - b$

  $= (ax - bx) + (-ay + by) + (a - b)$

  $= x(a - b) - y(a - b) + 1(a - b)$ [Do not forget the 1.]

  $= (a - b)(x - y + 1)$

Factorisation technique 3

Trinomials

A trinomial is an expression with three terms such as $6x^2 + 19xy + 10y^2$.

You multiply $(3x + 2y)(2x + 5y)$ together in order to get $6x^2 + 19xy + 10y^2$.

It is tricky to work backwards from $6x^2 + 19xy + 10y^2$ to get its factors of $(3x + 2y)$ and $(2x + 5y)$ because when you multiply these brackets the middle terms are combined into the single term $19xy$ in the final expression.

WORKED EXAMPLE

Technique for factorising trinomials 1

Factorise $4x^2 - 4x - 15$.

Step 1: Write down two terms that multiply together to give $4x^2$. [$4x \times x = 4x^2$ or $2x \times 2x = 4x^2$]

Step 2: Write down two terms that multiply together to give 15. [$1 \times 15 = 15$ or $3 \times 5 = 15$]

It will take some trial and error to get the right combination of the cross products. The combination that works is shown:

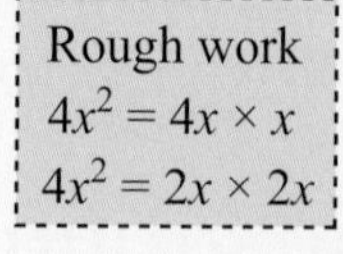

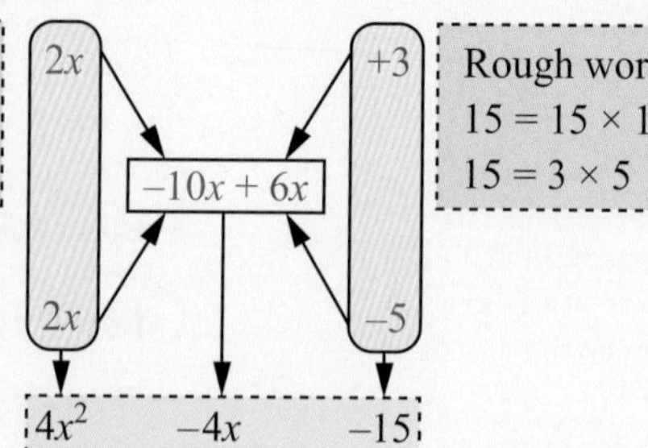

Step 3: The cross products are $6x$ and $10x$. By putting the appropriate signs on the cross products, can you combine them to get the middle term of $-4x$? Obviously, $+ 6x - 10x = -4x$ works.

Step 4: Read straight across on each side to get the factors of $(2x + 3)$ and $(2x - 5)$.

$\therefore 4x^2 - 4x - 15 = (2x + 3)(2x - 5)$

WORKED EXAMPLE Technique for factorising trinomials 2

Factorise $14y^2 + 3xy - 2x^2$.

Step 1: Write down two terms that multiply together to give $14y^2$. $[14y \times y = 14y^2$ or $7y \times 2y = 14y^2]$

Step 2: Write down two terms that multiply together to give $2x^2$. $[2x \times x = 2x^2]$

Step 3: The cross products are $7xy$ and $4xy$. By putting the appropriate signs on the cross products, can you combine them to get the middle term of $+3xy$? Obviously, $+7xy - 4xy = +3xy$ works.

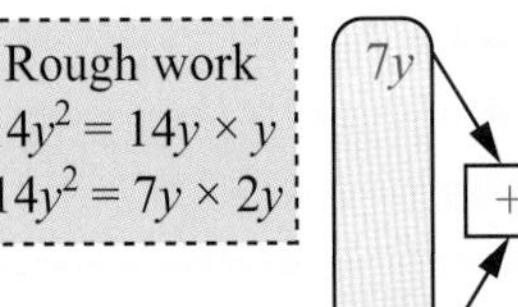

Rough work
$14y^2 = 14y \times y$
$14y^2 = 7y \times 2y$

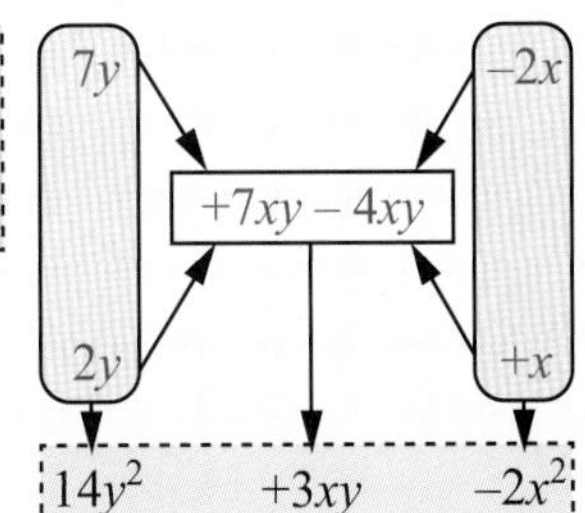

Step 4: Read straight across on each side to get the factors of $(7y - 2x)$ and $(2y + x)$.

$\therefore 14y^2 + 3xy - 2x^2 = (7y - 2x)(2y + x)$.

Factorisation technique 4

Difference of two squares

$(x - y)(x + y) = x^2 + xy - xy - y^2 = x^2 - y^2$

$$x^2 - y^2 = (x - y)(x + y)$$

TIP

Remember as:

(First)^2 – (Second)^2 = (First – Second)(First + Second)

- $400x^2 - 49y^2 = (20x)^2 - (7y)^2 = (20x - 7y)(20x + 7y)$
- $(x + y)^2 - (z)^2 = ((x + y) - z)((x + y) + z) = (x + y - z)(x + y + z)$

Factorisation technique 5

Sum and difference of two cubes

The following are the factors for the sum and difference of two cubes:

$$a^3 + b^3 = (a + b)(a^2 - ab + b^2)$$
$$a^3 - b^3 = (a - b)(a^2 + ab + b^2)$$

Multiply out the factors on the right-hand side to show that you get the expression on the left-hand side.

TIP

Remember as:

1. (First)^3 + (Second)^3 = (First + Second) ((First)^2 – (First) × (Second) + (Second)^2)
2. (First)^3 – (Second)^3 = (First – Second) ((First)^2 + (First) × (Second) + (Second)^2)

ACTIVITY 11

ACTION
Factorising the difference of two cubes using a geometrical approach

OBJECTIVE
To arrive at the formula for the difference of two cubes by a geometric approach

- $x^3 + 8y^3 = (x)^3 + (2y)^3 = (x + 2y)(x^2 - 2xy + 4y^2)$
- $10y^3 - 270x^3 = 10(y^3 - 27x^3) = 10[(y)^3 - (3x)^3]$ [Always take out the HCF first.]

  $= 10(y - 3x)(y^2 + 3xy + 9x^2)$
- $(a - 1)^3 + (a + 1)^3 = [(a - 1) + (a + 1)][(a - 1)^2 - (a - 1)(a + 1) + (a + 1)^2]$

  $= (2a)[a^2 - 2a + 1 - a^2 + 1 + a^2 + 2a + 1]$

  $= (2a)(a^2 + 3)$

Factorisation technique 6

Harder factors

Sometimes an expression with four terms cannot be factorised by grouping into two pairs. If this is the case, try a three and one grouping.

- $x^2 + 2xy + y^2 - 1$

  $= (x^2 + 2xy + y^2) - 1$

  $= (x + y)(x + y) - 1$

  $= (x + y)^2 - 1^2$

  $= (x + y - 1)(x + y + 1)$
- $9a^2 - 12ab + 4b^2 - 25c^2$

  $= (9a^2 - 12ab + 4b^2) - (5c)^2$

  $= (3a - 2b)^2 - (5c)^2$

  $= (3a - 2b - 5c)(3a - 2b + 5c)$

Steps for factorisation

1. If you can, take out a highest common factor (HCF) first. There is not always a HCF.

2. Look at what is left inside the bracket and apply one of the following methods to this:

(i) grouping

(ii) trinomial

(iii) difference of two squares

(iv) sum of two cubes and difference of two cubes

(v) there are no factors

EXAMPLE 6

Factorise the following fully:

(a) $1 - 3x - 4x^2$

(b) $7x^2 - 28y^2$

(c) $2a^2 + 6ac - 4ab - 12bc$

(d) $154x^2 - 50x + 4$

(e) $(x + 2y)^2 - (x - 2y)^2$

(f) $15a^3 + 120a^3b^3$

Solution

(a) $1 - 3x - 4x^2$ [−1 is the HCF]
$= -1(4x^2 + 3x - 1)$
$= -1(4x - 1)(x + 1)$

(b) $7x^2 - 28y^2$ [7 is the HCF]
$= 7(x^2 - 4y^2)$
$= 7(x - 2y)(x + 2y)$

(c) $2a^2 + 6ac - 4ab - 12bc$
$= 2(a^2 + 3ac - 2ab - 6bc)$
$= 2\{a(a + 3c) - 2b(a + 3c)\}$
$= 2(a + 3c)(a - 2b)$

(d) $154x^2 - 50x + 4$
$= 2(77x^2 - 25x + 2)$
$= 2(7x - 1)(11x - 2)$

(e) $(x + 2y)^2 - (x - 2y)^2$
$= \{(x + 2y) - (x - 2y)\}\{(x + 2y) + (x - 2y)\}$
$= (4y)(2x)$
$= 8xy$

(f) $15a^3 + 120a^3b^3$
$= 15a^3(1 + 8b^3)$
$= 15a^3(1 + 2b)(1 - 2b + 4b^2)$

EXERCISE 3

1. Factorise the following by taking out the highest common factor:
   (a) $3x^2 + 9x - 18$
   (b) $8a^2 - 16a^2b^2$
   (c) $7x^2y^2 - 14x^2y$
   (d) $3(x - 2y) - 5x(x - 2y)$
   (e) $m(a + b) - 3n(a + b)$

2. Factorise the following by grouping:
   (a) $ax^2 + 2ax + x + 2$
   (b) $ax - bx + ay - by$
   (c) $2x - 6 - bx + 3b$
   (d) $x^2z - 2x^2 - 2y^2 + y^2z$
   (e) $3x - 8y - 2 + 12xy$
   (f) $21 - 3ax^2 - 14by^2 + 2abx^2y^2$

3. Factorise the following trinomials:
   (a) $x^2 + 5xy - 14y^2$
   (b) $10x^2 + 13x - 3$
   (c) $7x^2 - 22xy + 3y^2$
   (d) $2a^2 + ab - 3b^2$
   (e) $(a - 1)^2 + 2(a - 1) - 15$
   (f) $30x^2 - 17x + 2$
   (g) $b^2x^2 + 2bxc + c^2$
   (h) $4p^2 - 4p + 1$

4. Factorise the following difference of two squares and simplify:
   (a) $4x^2 - 1$
   (b) $25x^2 - y^2$
   (c) $x^2 - a^2b^2$
   (d) $4m^2 - 81n^2$
   (e) $(x + y)^2 - z^2$
   (f) $(2x - y)^2 - (x + y)^2$
   (g) $(x + 1)^2 - z^2$
   (h) $(\text{Yoke})^2 - (\text{Thing})^2$
   (i) $(3a + 2b)^2 - (2a - 3b)^2$
   (j) $504^2 - 496^2$

5. Factorise the following sums and differences of two cubes:
   (a) $x^3 + 64$
   (b) $x^3 + 27y^3$
   (c) $8x^3 - 27$
   (d) $1000 - 27y^3$
   (e) $a^3b^3 + c^3$
   (f) $125x^3 - 64a^3b^3$
   (g) $(x - 2)^3 + 8$
   (h) $(x - 2)^3 + (x + 2)^3$
   (i) $x^3 - (1 - y)^3$
   (j) $(\text{Thing})^3 - (\text{Yoke})^3$

6. Factorise the following fully:
   (a) $2x^2 - 8$
   (b) $18a^2 - 8b^2$
   (c) $36x^2 + 15xy - 9y^2$

(d) $x^2y + 2x^2 - y - 2$

(e) $28 - 7x^2$

(f) $4x^2 - 24xy + 36y^2$

(g) $-2x^2 + 4xy - 2y^2$

(h) $(a + 1)^2 - 9$

(i) $16(x - 1)^2 - 4$

(j) $2a^2 - 578$

(k) $3x^3 - 24$

(l) $x^2y^3 - 27x^2$

(m) $a^2b^4 - 8a^2b$

(n) $-2x^3 - 54$

(o) $\cos^3\theta + \sin^3\theta$

7. Factorise the following fully:

(a) $x^2 + 2xy + y^2 - 81$

(b) $a^2 + 6a + 9 - b^2$

(c) $a^2 + 8ab + 16b^2 - c^2$

(d) $a^2 - 2ab + b^2 - 16c^2$

(e) $x^4 - y^4$

(f) $x^6 - y^6$

(g) $a^2 - 2ab + b^2 - a + b$

(h) $x^3 + x - 2x^2$

(i) $x^4 + 2x^2 + 1$

(j) $a^4 - a + ba^3 - b$

8. (a) Derive $x^3 - y^3 = (x - y)(x^2 + xy + y^2)$ from $x^3 + y^3 = (x + y)(x^2 - xy + y^2)$.

(b) Expand out $(a - 4b)(a + b) + 3ab$ and hence factorise this expression.

(c) Expand out $(2x + 1)^2 + (x - 1)^2 - 2(7x - 1)$ and hence factorise this expression.

(d) A is the square $PQRS$ of side x. B is the square shown of side y.

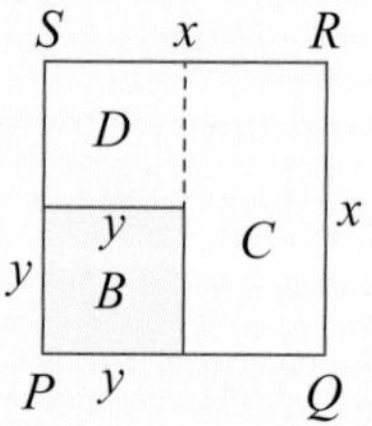

Using Area A – Area B = Area C + Area D, show that $x^2 - y^2 = (x - y)(x + y)$.

3.4 Algebraic modelling

KEY TERM

Algebraic modelling means translating a problem, stated in words, into an algebraic expression.

WORKED EXAMPLE Modelling a problem

1. A rugby out-half scores two tries, one conversion and three penalties in a match. How many points does he score in total? (1 try = 5 points, 1 conversion = 2 points, 1 penalty = 3 points)

Number of points = $2 \times 5 + 1 \times 2 + 3 \times 3 = 10 + 2 + 9 = 21$

2. A rugby out-half scores x tries, y conversions and three penalties in a match. Write down an expression for the total number of points he scores.

	Tries	Conversions	Penalties
Number of scores	x	y	3
Points per score	5	2	3
Number of points	$5x$	$2y$	9

$\therefore$ Total number of points = $5x + 2y + 9$

ACTIVITY 12

ACTION
Algebraic modelling

OBJECTIVE
To warm up with some solid basics before getting down to the business of algebraic modelling

EXAMPLE 7

The breadth of a rectangular field is 20 m longer than its length x.

Write down an expression, in terms of x, for:

(a) the breadth b, **(b)** the perimeter P, **(c)** the area A.

Solution

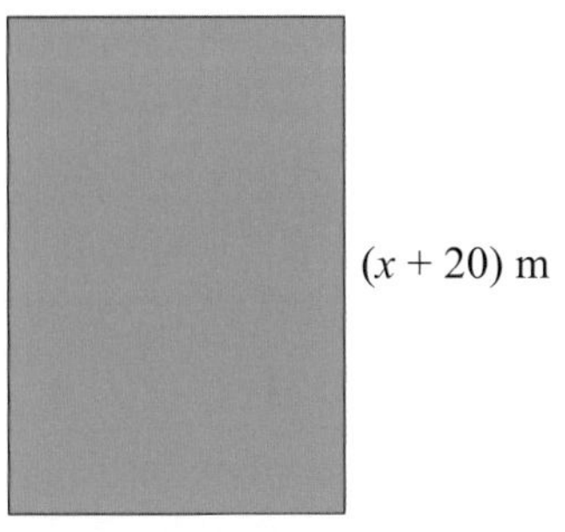

(a) $b = x + 20$

(b) $P = x + (x + 20) + x + (x + 20)$
$= x + x + 20 + x + x + 20$
$= 4x + 40$

(c) $A = x(x + 20)$
$= x^2 + 20x$

Guidelines for modelling

1. Identify the quantity to be modelled (cost, price, area, length, etc.) and give it a symbol.
2. Draw a diagram if appropriate (unless given).
3. Identify the number of variables (one or more) and if appropriate put them on the diagram.
4. Write the quantity to be modelled in terms of this (these) variable(s).

EXAMPLE 8

A running track has two straights and two semicircular ends, as shown.

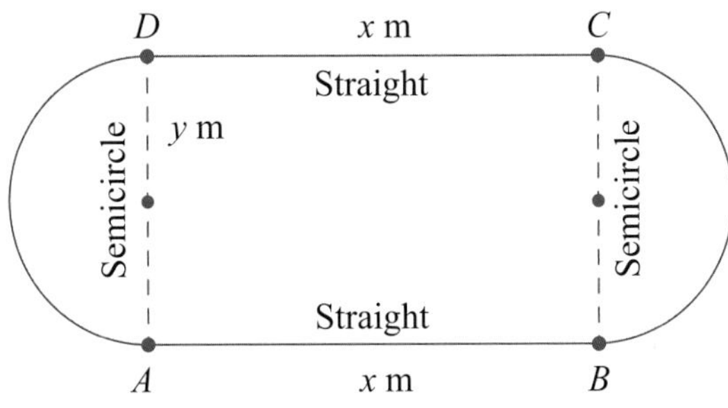

If x m is the length of each straight and y m the radius of each semicircular end,

(a) find an expression in terms of x and y for:

(i) the perimeter P,

(ii) the area A_1 of the rectangular region $ABCD$,

(iii) the total area A_2.

(b) If $x = 100$ m and $y = 31{\cdot}85$ m, find the perimeter to the nearest metre. Use $\pi = 3{\cdot}14$.

(c) If a runner has an average speed of 30 km/h, how long does it take the runner to complete one full circuit of the track?

Solution

(a)

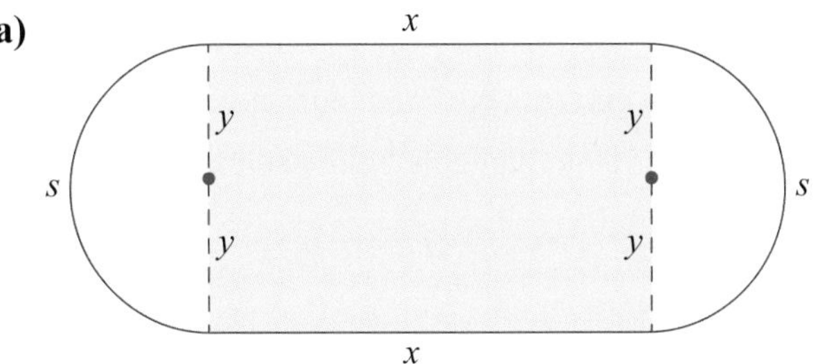

(i) $P = 2x + 2s$
$= 2x + 2(\pi y)$
$= 2x + 2\pi y$

(ii) Area $A_1 = x \times 2y = 2xy$

(iii) $A_2 = 2xy + \pi y^2$

(b) $P = 2(x) + 2\pi(y)$

Filling in $x = 100$ and $y = 31{\cdot}85$ gives:

$P = 2(100) + 2\pi(31{\cdot}85)$

$= 400$ m

(c) Speed $= 30$ km/h $= \dfrac{30 \times 1000\text{ m}}{3600\text{ s}} = \dfrac{25}{3}$ m/s

$$\text{Time} = \frac{\text{Distance}}{\text{Speed}}$$

$$= \frac{400}{\frac{25}{3}}$$

$$= 48\text{ s}$$

EXERCISE 4

1. An entrepreneur bought x phones at €30 each and sold y of them at €98 each. By completing the table, find the entrepreneur's net profit, in terms of x and y.

	Sold	Bought
Number of phones		
Price/unit		
Total		

2. An L-shaped flowerbed is shown with $|DC| = x$ m and $|CB| = y$ m. If $[AB]$ is 1 m longer than $[CD]$ and $[ED]$ is 2 m longer than $[CB]$, find expressions for:

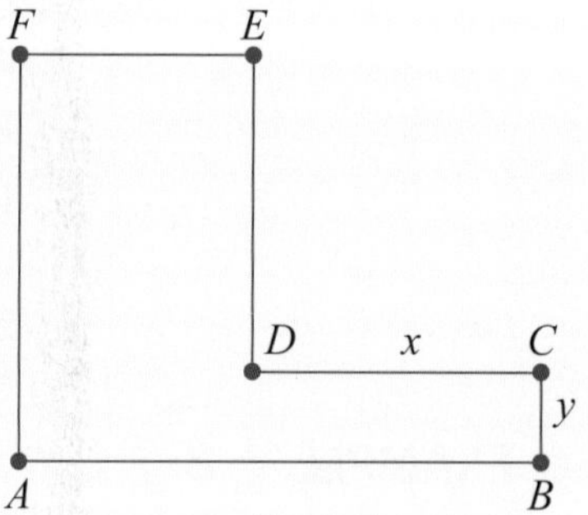

(a) the perimeter P,

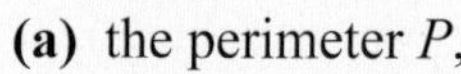

(b) the area A of the flowerbed, in terms of x and y.

3. The product of a number x and the square of another number y is greater than the product of the number x squared and the number y. Find an expression for D, the difference between the bigger number and the smaller number, in terms of x and y.

4. A petty cash box contains $10x$ one cent coins, $10x$ two cent coins, $5x$ five cent coins, $20x$ ten cent coins, $15x$ twenty cent coins, $7x$ fifty cent coins, $5x$ one euro coins and $3x$ two euro coins. It also contains $2y$ five euro notes, $3y$ ten euro notes and one 20 euro note.

Complete the table below and find an expression for the total amount A of cash in the box in cents.

Cash type	1c	2c	5c	10c	20c	50c	1€	2€	5€	10€	20€
Number											
Value in cents											

5. **(a)** For the rectangle shown, find an expression in terms of x and y:

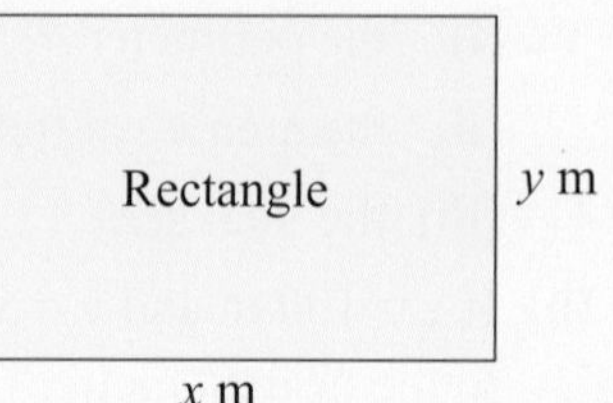

(i) for the perimeter P of the rectangle,

(ii) for the area A of the rectangle.

(b) If $x = 20$ and $y = 30$, what is the length of the perimeter? What is the area of the rectangle?

6. A farmer constructs a fence around a field in the shape of a trapezium $ABCD$ with $[AD]$ parallel to $[BC]$ and $[AB]$ perpendicular to $[BC]$.

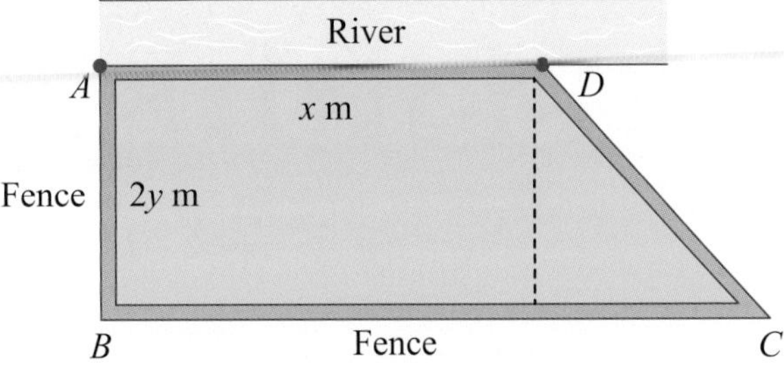

(a) If $|BC|$ is 4 m longer than $|AD|$ and $|DC|$ is 2 m longer than $|AB|$, find an expression for the length L of fencing in terms of x and y.

(b) Find an expression for the area A enclosed by the fence in terms of x and y.

(c) Find y.

7. (a) If x is a whole number, find an expression in terms of x and y for:

(i) the next whole number,

(ii) the sum of these two consecutive whole numbers.

(b) Find the values of the sum of two consecutive whole numbers if x is the first number by copying and completing the following:

	Sum of two consecutive whole numbers
$x = 1$	$1 + 2 = 3$
$x = 2$	
$x = 3$	
$x = 4$	
$x = 5$	
$x = 6$	
$x = 7$	

What conclusion can you make?

8. r is the radius of a circle, centre O, inscribed in a square $ABCD$.

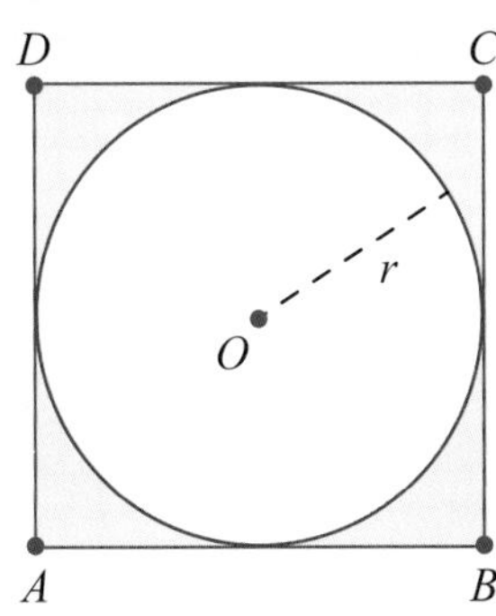

Find an expression in terms of r for:

(a) the circumference of the circle,

(b) the perimeter of the square,

(c) the area of the circle,

(d) the area of the square,

(e) the area of the shaded region.

9. (a) A man can swim at 2 m/s and walk at 1·5 m/s. If he takes x seconds to swim from A to B and y seconds to walk from B to D, find an expression for the length of the journey $ABCD$, in terms of x and y.

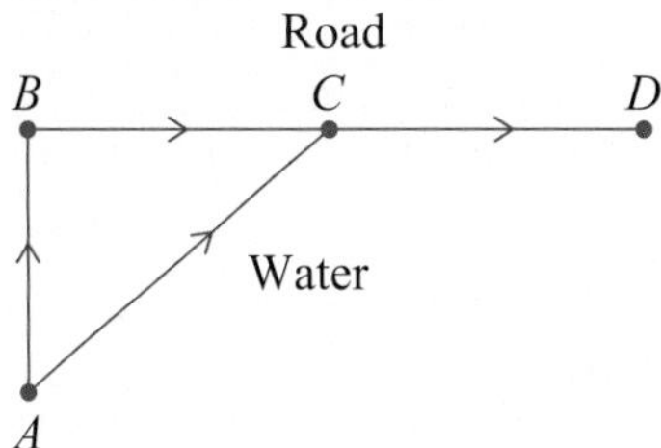

(b) A woman can swim at 1·8 m/s and walk at 1·3 m/s. If she takes $(x + 30)$ seconds to swim from A to C and $(y - 10)$ seconds to walk from C to D, find an expression for the length of the journey ACD, in terms of x and y.

10. $ABCD$ is a rectangular frame with a picture inside, as shown.

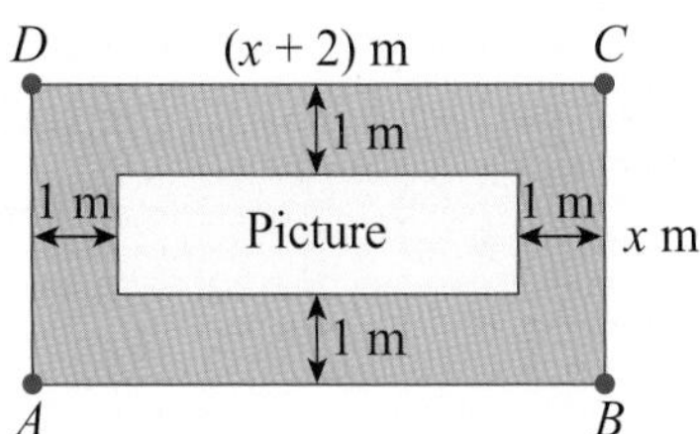

Find an expression in terms of x for the area of:

(a) rectangle $ABCD$,

(b) the picture,

(c) the border.

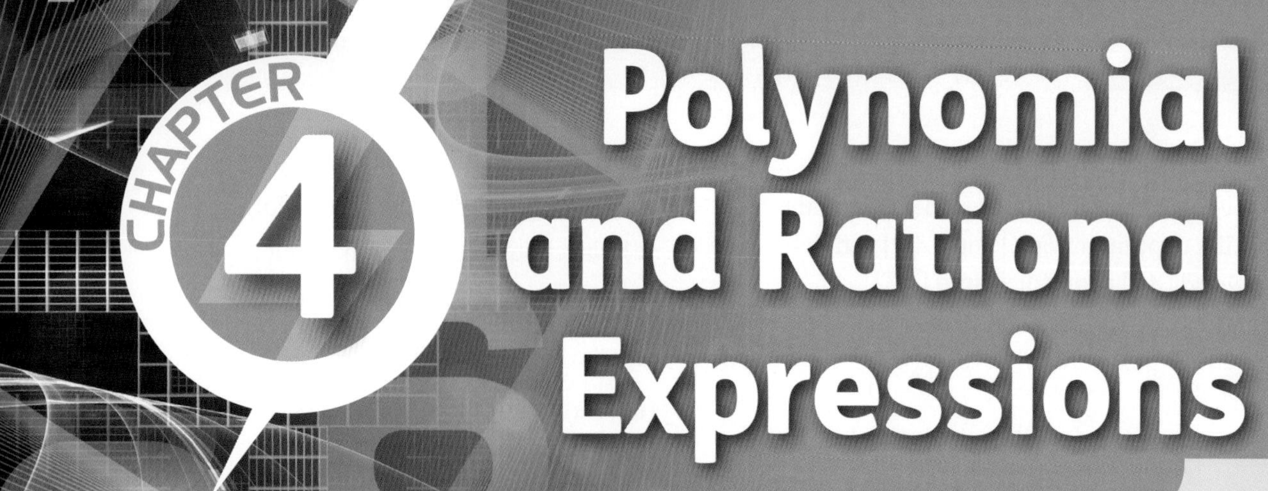

Chapter 4 Polynomial and Rational Expressions

Learning Outcomes

- To recognise linear, quadratic and cubic expressions as polynomial expressions and to understand how they combine.
- To be able to carry out operations on rational expressions.

4.1 Polynomial expressions

ACTIVITY 13

ACTION
Recognising the different types of polynomial expressions from their equations and graphs

OBJECTIVE
To explore linear, quadratic and cubic equations and graphs

Expressions such as x, $3x$, $3x - 7$, x^2, $5x^2$, $6x^2 - 5x + 3$, x^3, $2x^3$ and $3x^3 - 5x^2 + 7x - 11$ are all examples of polynomial expressions. These expressions consist of terms of whole number powers of the variable in descending order multiplied by a constant. They are classified according to the highest power of the variables as follows:

1. A polynomial of degree 1 has highest power 1.
   Examples: x^1, $3x^1 - 7$, $-2x^1 + 3$, $ax + b$
   These are also called linear expressions because of the x^1 term.
2. A polynomial of degree 2 has highest power 2.
   Examples: x^2, $\frac{1}{2}x^2$, $-2x^2 + x$, $4x^2 - 9x + 1$, $ax^2 + bx + c$
   These are also called quadratic expressions because of the x^2 term.
3. A polynomial of degree 3 has highest power 3.
   Examples: x^3, $-3x^3$, $2x^3 + 5x^2 - 7$, $\frac{1}{2}x^3 - 5x^2 + 11x - 3$, $ax^3 + bx^2 + cx + d$
   These are also called cubic expressions because of the x^3 term.

Multiplying polynomials

Your understanding of algebra will be greatly improved if you can recognise patterns and predict results based on the type of polynomials involved in any operation.

1. If you multiply a **linear** expression by a **linear** expression you get a quadratic expression.
   $(2x - 3)(4x + 1) = 8x^2 + 2x - 12x - 3 = 8x^2 - 10x - 3$
   A quadratic expression is obtained when you multiply two linear expressions.

   Linear × Linear = Quadratic

ACTIVITY 14

ACTION
A modelling approach involving the multiplication of terms

OBJECTIVE
To use a practical problem involving the multiplication and combination of algebraic terms

2. If you multiply a **linear** expression by a **quadratic** expression you get a cubic expression.

$$(2x - 5)(x^2 - 3x + 5) = 2x^3 - 6x^2 + 10x - 5x^2 + 15x - 25$$
$$= 2x^3 - 11x^2 + 25x - 25$$

A cubic expression is obtained when you multiply a linear and a quadratic expression.

Linear × Quadratic = Cubic

3. If you multiply a **linear** expression by a **linear** expression by a **linear** expression you get a cubic expression.

$$(2x + 7)(-5x + 2)(x - 1) = (-10x^2 + 4x - 35x + 14)(x - 1)$$
$$= (-10x^2 - 31x + 14)(x - 1)$$
$$= -10x^3 + 10x^2 - 31x^2 + 31x + 14x - 14$$
$$= -10x^3 - 21x^2 + 45x - 14$$

A cubic expression is obtained when you multiply three linear expressions.

Linear × Linear × Linear = Cubic

ACTIVITY 15

ACTION
Recognising patterns when multiplying brackets

OBJECTIVE
To understand that when each bracket has its terms lined up in descending powers, multiplying the first terms by the first terms yields the first term in the answer. The same idea applies to the last terms.

There is another important observation that we can make. It was discussed in the previous chapter.

Looking at the examples above:

Multiplying the first term by the first term in each bracket will give the highest power in the product as the first term.

$(2x + 7)(-5x + 2)(x - 1) = -10x^3 - 21x^2 + 45x - 14$

Multiplying the last term by the last term in each bracket will give the constant term in the product as the last term.

$(2x - 5)(x^2 - 3x + 5) = 2x^3 - 11x^2 + 25x - 25$

These observations only hold if each polynomial is written in order of descending powers.

When tidying up products of brackets, always write your answers in the following form:

Linear: $ax + b$

Quadratic: $ax^2 + bx + c$

Cubic: $ax^3 + bx^2 + cx + d$

EXAMPLE 1

Multiply out the following:

(a) $(-3x + k)(4x + l)$

(b) $(2x^2 - kx + 3)(x + l)$

Solution

(a) $(-3x + k)(4x + l) = -12x^2 - 3xl + 4kx + kl$
$= -12x^2 + (-3l + 4k)x + kl$

(b) $(2x^2 - kx + 3)(x + l) = 2x^3 + 2lx^2 - kx^2 - kxl + 3x + 3l$
$= 2x^3 + (2l - k)x^2 + (-kl + 3)x + 3l$

Factorisation of polynomials

A quadratic expression has either no factors or it has two linear factors.

A cubic expression has a linear and a quadratic factor. The quadratic factor may sometimes be further factorised into two linear factors, giving three linear factors.

- $3x^3 + x^2 - 2x$ [Cubic]
  $= x(3x^2 + x - 2)$ [Linear × Quadratic]
  $= x(3x - 2)(x + 1)$ [Linear × Linear × Linear]

It is important to remember that factorisation is just another way of writing the original expression.

This means that when you multiply out factors, you must get all of the terms **identical** to the original expression.

EXAMPLE 2

If $10x^2 - 9x + 2 = (5x - k)(2x - 1)$, find k.

Solution

Multiply out the brackets and line up the terms.

$10x^2 - 9x + 2 = (5x - k)(2x - 1)$

$= 10x^2 - 5x - 2kx + k$

$= 10x^2 + (-5 - 2k)x + k$

Lining up the x term gives:

$-5 - 2k = -9$

$4 = 2k$

$k = 2$

or

Lining up the constant term gives:

$k = 2$

or

$-k \times -1 = 2$ [Last × Last = Last]

$k = 2$

Identities

Factors are **identities**. This means they are true for **all** values of the variable x.

$x^2 - 5x + 6 = (x - 3)(x - 2)$ is true for **all values** of x.

Try some:

$\mathbf{x = 2}$**:** $2^2 - 10 + 6 = (2 - 3)(2 - 2)$

$0 = 0$

$\mathbf{x = -3}$**:** $(-3)^2 + 15 + 6 = (-6)(-5)$

$30 = 30$

You can use this idea to your advantage.

EXAMPLE 3

If $x^3 + 2x^2 + kx + 2 = (x - 1)(x^2 + ax - 2)$, find k and a.

Solution

Method 1 (Lining up)

$x^3 + 2x^2 + kx + 2 = (x - 1)(x^2 + ax - 2)$

$= x^3 + ax^2 - 2x - x^2 - ax + 2$

$= x^3 + (a - 1)x^2 + (-2 - a)x + 2$

Lining up the x^2 term gives:

$a - 1 = 2$

$a = 3$

Lining up the x term gives:

$-2 - a = k$

$k = -5$

Method 2 (Choosing values)

Choose any two values you like for x in:

$x^3 + 2x^2 + kx + 2 = (x - 1)(x^2 + ax - 2)$

$\mathbf{x = 1}$**:** $1 + 2 + k + 2 = 0$

$k = -5$

$\mathbf{x = -1}$**:** $-1 + 2 - k + 2 = (-2)(1 - a - 2)$

$3 - k = 2a + 2$

$8 = 2a + 2$

$6 = 2a$

$a = 3$

EXAMPLE 4

If $3x^2 + 5x - 1$ is a factor of $3x^3 + 11x^2 + 9x - 2$, find the other factor.

Solution

$3x^3 + 11x^2 + 9x - 2 = (3x^2 + 5x - 1) \times \text{(Linear)}$

$3x^3 + 11x^2 + 9x - 2 = (3x^2 + 5x - 1)(x + 2)$

The linear factor is easy to find because the first terms in the brackets on the right must multiply to give $3x^3$ and the last terms must multiply to give –2.

EXAMPLE 5

If $2x - 1$ and $x + 2$ are factors of $6x^3 + x^2 - 18x + 8$, find the other factor.

Solution

$6x^3 + x^2 - 18x + 8 = (2x - 1)(x + 2) \times \text{(Linear)}$

$6x^3 + x^2 - 18x + 8 = (2x - 1)(x + 2)(3x - 4)$

The linear factor is easy to find because the first terms in the brackets on the right must multiply to give $6x^3$ and the last terms must multiply to give +8.

EXAMPLE 6

If $3x + 2$ is a factor of $9x^3 - 19x - 10$, find the quadratic factor.

Solution

$9x^3 + 0x^2 - 19x - 10 = (3x + 2) \times \text{(Quadratic)}$

A quadratic is made up of three terms. You can find the first and last term by inspection. Call the middle term kx.

$9x^3 + 0x^2 - 19x - 10 = (3x + 2)(3x^2 + kx - 5)$

To find k, multiply out the brackets on the right and line up.

$9x^3 + 0x^2 - 19x - 10 = 9x^3 + 3kx^2 - 15x + 6x^2 + 2kx - 10$

$= 9x^3 + (3k + 6)x^2 + (-15 + 2k)x - 10$

$3k + 6 = 0$ *or* $-15 + 2k = -19$

$3k = -6$ $2k = -4$

$k = -2$ $k = -2$

Quadratic factor: $3x^2 - 2x - 5$

EXAMPLE 7

If $x^2 + px - q$ is a factor of $2x^3 + px^2 - 3x + q^2$, find the values of p and q.

Solution

A cubic expression is made up of a quadratic factor multiplied by a linear factor.

$2x^3 + px^2 - 3x + q^2 = (x^2 + px - q)(2x - q)$

[First × First = First and Last × Last = Last]

$2x^3 + px^2 - 3x + q^2$

$= 2x^3 + (2p - q)x^2 + (-pq - 2q)x + q^2$

Lining up the coefficients of x^2:

$p = 2p - q$

$q = p$

Lining up the coefficients of x:

$-3 = -pq - 2q$ [Put $q = p$]

$p^2 + 2p - 3 = 0$

$(p - 1)(p + 3) = 0$

$\therefore p = -3, 1$ and $q = -3, 1$

EXAMPLE 8

If $(2x - 1)$ is a factor of $2x^3 + ax^2 - bx + 1$, show that $a = (2b - 5)$.

Solution

A cubic expression is made up of a quadratic factor multiplied by a linear factor. A quadratic expression has three terms. The middle term of the quadratic expression is unknown – call it px.

$2x^3 + ax^2 - bx + 1 = (2x - 1)(x^2 + px - 1)$

$2x^3 + ax^2 - bx + 1 = 2x^3 + (2p - 1)x^2 + (-p - 2)x + 1$

Lining up the coefficients of x^2:

$a = 2p - 1$ **(1)**

Lining up the coefficients of x:

$b = p + 2$ **(2)**

$a = 2p - 1$

$-2b = -2p - 4$ **(2)** × (−2)

$a - 2b = -5$

$\therefore a = 2b - 5$

EXERCISE 5

1. Simplify the following and give your answer in descending powers of x:

(a) $2x - 5 + x - 2$

(b) $5x^2 - 7x - 6 - x^2 + 1$

(c) $3x^2 + 2x^3 - 5x + 7x^3 - 5x^2 + 1$

(d) $2 - 3x + 5x^2 - 8x^3 + 7x - 3$

(e) $-x^3 + 5x^2 - 2x + 3x^3 - 2x^2 + 7x$

2. Multiply out the following and give your answer in order of descending powers of x:

(a) $(x + 1)(x + k)$

(b) $(2x + 1)(kx + 1)$

(c) $(x - 1)(kx + 2)$

(d) $(1 - 2x)(x - k)$

(e) $(x^2 + x)(x + k)$

(f) $(x^2 - x + 1)(x - k)$

(g) $(2x^2 - 1)(kx - 5)$

(h) $(3x - 1)(x^2 + kx - 2)$

(i) $(2x + 1)(3x^2 + kx - 3)$

(j) $(x - c)(x^2 + kx + d)$

3. **(a)** If $x - 1$ is a factor of $x^2 - kx + 3$, find k.

(b) If $x + 3$ is a factor of $kx^2 + 4x - 6$, find k.

(c) If $2x - 1$ and $3x + 2$ are factors of $ax^2 + bx + c$, find a, b and c.

(d) If $2x - 3$ is a factor of $4x^2 - 4x - 3$, find the other factor.

(e) If $4x - 1$ is a factor of $8x^2 + kx + 7$, find the other factor and k.

(f) If $ax^2 + bx + 8 = (3x - 1)(5x - k)$, find k, a and b.

(g) Find the quadratic polynomial with factors:

(i) $5x - 1$ and $2x - 3$

(ii) $10x - 2$ and $2x - 3$

(iii) $5x - 1$ and $4x - 6$

(h) Find the quadratic polynomial with factors:

(i) $x+\sqrt{2}, x-\sqrt{2}$

(ii) $x+\sqrt{3}-1, x-\sqrt{3}+1$

(iii) $2x+\sqrt{3}, x-2\sqrt{3}$

4. (a) If x^2+x+2 is a factor of x^3+kx^2+lx+2, find the other factor and k and l.

(b) If $2x^2+bx-5$ is a factor of $2x^3-x^2+kx+10$, find the other factor and b and k.

(c) ax^2+2 is a factor of $18x^3+kx^2+6x-2$. Find k and a and the other factor.

(d) If $x-1$ is a factor of x^3+2x^2-kx+4, find $k \in \mathbb{R}$ and the other factors.

(e) If $x-2$ is a factor of $P(x)=x^3-2x^2-3x-k$, find k and the quadratic factor of $P(x)$.

(f) If $(x+1)$ and $(x-3)$ are both factors of kx^3-6x^2+bx-6, find k, $b \in \mathbb{R}$ and the other factor.

5. (a) If $(x-p)^2$ is a factor of x^3+qx+r, show: **(i)** $r=2p^3$, **(ii)** $q=-3p^2$.

(b) If $(x-1)$ is a factor of $x^3+ax^2-(a+1)^2+12$, $a>0$, find $a \in \mathbb{R}$.

(c) If x^2-px+q is a factor of $x^3+3px^2+3qx+r$, show:

(i) $q=-2p^2$,

(ii) $r=-8p^3$.

(d) If x^2-a^2 is a factor of $f(x)=x^3+x^2+px+q$:

(i) show $p=q=-a^2$,

(ii) write $f(x)$ in form $(x^2-a^2)(x+r)$.

(e) If $3-x$ is a factor of $P(x)=6+x-4x^2+x^3$, find the other factors of $P(x)$.

(f) If $x-a$ is a factor of x^3-c, show $c=a^3$.

(g) If x^2-px+1 is a factor of ax^3+bx+c, show $c^2=a(a-b)$.

(h) If $(x-1)^2$ is a factor of ax^3+bx^2+1, find a and b.

(i) If $(x-a)^2$ is a factor of $x^3+3rx+q$, show:

(i) $r=-a^2$

(ii) $q=2a^3$

(j) If x^2+ax+b is a factor of x^3+qx^2+rx+s show:

(i) $r=b+a(q-a)$

(ii) $s=b(q-a)$

ACTIVITY 16

ACTION
Dividing polynomials

OBJECTIVE
To follow the procedure step by step for dividing polynomials

Division of polynomials

Dividing polynomials 1: Factorise the numerator and denominator and cancel.

$$\frac{12x^2-x-6}{4x-3}=\frac{(3x+2)(4x-3)}{(4x-3)}=3x+2$$

Dividing polynomials 2: If you cannot factorise the denominator, do long division. Long division of polynomials is done in much the same way as long division of numbers.

WORKED EXAMPLE

Explaining the long division process

Carry out, by long division, a cubic expression divided by a linear expression:

$$\frac{4x^3-4x^2-x+1}{2x+1}=?$$

$(2x+1)$ is called the divisor. $(4x^3-4x^2-x+1)$ is the polynomial expression into which you are dividing. The answer you will obtain is called the quotient.

So, divide the polynomial by the divisor to get the quotient.

Method

1. Divide the highest power of x in the divisor into the highest power of x in the polynomial.

$$\begin{array}{r|l} & 2x^2 \\ \hline 2x+1 & 4x^3 - 4x^2 - x + 1 \end{array}$$

2. Multiply the whole divisor $(2x + 1)$ by x and subtract these terms from the terms of the polynomial by changing their sign and adding.

$$\begin{array}{r|l} & 2x^2 \\ \hline 2x+1 & 4x^3 - 4x^2 - x + 1 \\ & \mp 4x^3 \mp 2x^2 \\ \hline & \quad - 6x^2 - x + 1 \end{array}$$

3. Repeat steps 1 and 2 until you cannot divide any more.

$$\begin{array}{r|l} & 2x^2 - 3x + 1 \\ \hline 2x+1 & 4x^3 - 4x^2 - x + 1 \\ & \mp 4x^3 \mp 2x^2 \\ \hline & \quad - 6x^2 - x + 1 \\ & \quad \pm 6x^2 \pm 3x \\ \hline & \qquad + 2x + 1 \\ & \qquad \mp 2x \mp 1 \\ \hline & \qquad\quad 0 \end{array}$$

4. You should end up with no remainder.

$$\therefore \frac{4x^3 - 4x^2 - x + 1}{2x + 1} = 2x^2 - 3x + 1$$

or

By factorisation:

$4x^3 - 4x^2 - x + 1 = (2x + 1)(2x^2 + kx + 1)$

$= 4x^3 + 2kx^2 + 2x + 2x^2 + kx + 1$

$= 4x^3 + x^2(2k + 2) + x(k + 2) + 1$

Equating coefficients of x: $k + 2 = -1$

$k = -3$

$\therefore 4x^3 - 4x^2 - x + 1 = (2x + 1)(2x^2 - 3x + 1)$

Remember: $\frac{\text{Cubic}}{\text{Quadratic}} = \text{Linear}$, $\frac{\text{Cubic}}{\text{Linear}} = \text{Quadratic}$, $\frac{\text{Quadratic}}{\text{Linear}} = \text{Linear}$

Always factorise first if you can.

$$\frac{x^3 - 8}{x - 2} = \frac{\cancel{(x-2)}(x^2 + 2x + 4)}{\cancel{(x-2)}}$$

[$x^3 - 8$ can be factorised as it is the difference of two cubes.]

$$= x^2 + 2x + 4$$

EXERCISE 6

1. Simplify the following:

(a) $\dfrac{x-2}{2-x}$

(b) $\dfrac{x^2-2x}{2-x}$

(c) $\dfrac{5x^2+15x}{5x}$

(d) $\dfrac{x^3+x}{x^2+1}$

(e) $\dfrac{x^3+x^2}{x+1}$

(f) $\dfrac{15x^2+11x-14}{3x-2}$

(g) $\dfrac{3x^3-24}{3x-6}$

(h) $\dfrac{3+3x^3}{3x^2-3x+3}$

(i) $\dfrac{16x^3-28x^2+6x}{8x-2}$

(j) $\dfrac{-4x^2+36}{x-3}$

2. Simplify the following:

(a) $\dfrac{x^3+7x^2+14x+8}{x+2}$

(b) $\dfrac{x^3-4x^2+5}{x+1}$

(c) $\dfrac{4x^3-11x+3}{2x-3}$

(d) $\dfrac{10x^3-31x^2+27x-30}{2x-5}$

(e) $\dfrac{x^3-25x}{x-5}$

(f) $\dfrac{-6x^3-7x^2+x-3}{3x^2-x+1}$

(g) $\dfrac{x^3+x^2-x-1}{x+1}$

(h) $\dfrac{6x^3+x^2-2x}{2x-1}$

(i) $\dfrac{27x^3-1}{3x-1}$

(j) $\dfrac{x^3-7x+6}{x^2+2x-3}$

3. The volume of the box shown is given by $V = 2x^3 + 7x^2 + 7x + 2$.

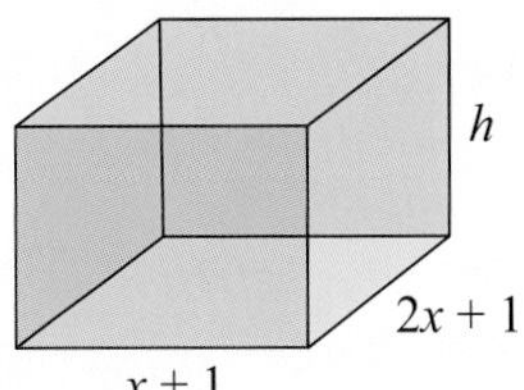

Find: **(a)** h in terms of x, **(b)** the surface area A, in terms of x.

4. If $x - 1$ is a factor of $x^3 + kx^2 - 4x + 1$, show that $k = 2$.

5. If $x - 2$ is a factor of $x^3 + ax^2 + bx + 6$, show that $b + 2a = -7$.

6. If $x^2 - 5x + 11$ is a factor of $x^3 - 2x^2 + ax + 33$, show that $a = -4$.

4.2 Rational expressions

ACTIVITY 17

ACTION
Adding algebraic fractions

OBJECTIVE
To follow the procedure of finding a lowest common denominator (LCD) and simplifying algebraic expressions

KEY TERM

A **rational expression** is one expression divided by another.

Examples: $\dfrac{x}{2x-1}, \dfrac{5x^2-2}{2x^2+7x^2-1}, \dfrac{2^x}{\sqrt{x-1}}$

Addition and subtraction

To add or subtract rational expressions, find the lowest common denominator (LCD).

$$\frac{1}{x} + \frac{1}{x^2y} = \frac{xy+1}{x^2y}$$

Always factorise the denominator, if possible, to find the LCD and put brackets around all expressions with more than one term.

EXAMPLE 9

Simplify $\frac{3}{x-5}+\frac{2}{5-x}$.

Solution

$$\frac{3}{x-5}+\frac{2}{5-x}$$
$$=\frac{3}{(x-5)}+\frac{2}{-1(x-5)}$$
$$=\frac{(-1\times 3)+(1\times 2)}{-1(x-5)}$$
$$=\frac{-1}{-(x-5)}$$
$$=\frac{1}{(x-5)}$$

EXAMPLE 10

Simplify $\frac{4}{x^2-1}-\frac{7}{2x^2-3x-5}$.

Solution

$$\frac{4}{x^2-1}-\frac{7}{2x^2-3x-5}$$
$$=\frac{4}{(x-1)(x+1)}-\frac{7}{(2x-5)(x+1)}$$
$$=\frac{4(2x-5)-7(x-1)}{(x+1)(x-1)(2x-5)}$$
$$=\frac{8x-20-7x+7}{(x+1)(x-1)(2x-5)}$$
$$=\frac{x-13}{(x+1)(x-1)(2x-5)}$$

[Do not multiply out the brackets on the bottom unless asked to do so.]

Multiplication of rational expressions

Multiply the tops and multiply the bottoms and/or cancel.

- $\frac{-3ab^2}{5b^3c}\times\frac{15b^2c^2}{-9a^2b}=\frac{ab^4c^2}{a^2b^4c}=\frac{c}{a}$

Put brackets around expressions with more than two terms and factorise, if possible.

ACTIVITY 18

ACTION
Multiplying and dividing algebraic fractions

OBJECTIVE
To factorise and cancel brackets in order to simplify fractions that are multiplied and divided

EXAMPLE 11

Simplify $\frac{a^2-b^2}{ab+a^2}\times\frac{ab}{a-b}$.

Solution

$$\frac{a^2-b^2}{ab+a^2}\times\frac{ab}{a-b}$$
$$=\frac{(a^2-b^2)}{(ab+a^2)}\times\frac{ab}{(a-b)}$$
$$=\frac{(a-b)(a+b)}{a(b+a)}\times\frac{ab}{(a-b)}=\frac{ab}{a}$$
$$=b$$

Multiply out brackets by multiplying each term in one bracket by each term in the other bracket.

ACTIVITY 19

ACTION
Reducing algebraic fractions to their lowest form

OBJECTIVE
To reduce algebraic fractions by factorising and cancelling

EXAMPLE 12

Simplify $\left(\frac{2}{x}+\frac{x^3}{2}\right)\left(\frac{x}{2}\quad\frac{4}{x^3}\right)$.

Solution

$$\left(\frac{2}{x}+\frac{x^3}{2}\right)\left(\frac{x}{2}-\frac{4}{x^3}\right)$$

$$=\frac{2}{x}\times\frac{x}{2}-\frac{2}{x}\times\frac{4}{x^3}+\frac{x^3}{2}\times\frac{x}{2}-\frac{x^3}{2}\times\frac{4}{x^3}$$

$$=1-\frac{8}{x^4}+\frac{x^4}{4}-2$$

$$=-1-\frac{8}{x^4}+\frac{x^4}{4}$$

- $\left(\frac{x}{y}-\frac{1}{2}\right)\left(\frac{x}{y}+\frac{1}{2}\right)=\left(\frac{x}{y}\right)^2-\left(\frac{1}{2}\right)^2=\frac{x^2}{y^2}-\frac{1}{4}$ [Difference of two squares]
- $\left(x+\frac{1}{x}\right)^2=x^2+2(x)\left(\frac{1}{x}\right)+\left(\frac{1}{x}\right)^2=x^2+2+\frac{1}{x^2}$ [Perfect square]

Reducing fractions to their lowest form

To reduce rational expressions to their lowest form, factorise the top and the bottom if possible, and cancel.

- $\frac{(12-6x-6x^2)}{(12x-3x^3)}=\frac{-6(x^2+x-2)}{-3x(x^2-4)}=\frac{-6(x-1)\cancel{(x+2)}}{-3x(x-2)\cancel{(x+2)}}=\frac{2(x-1)}{x(x-2)}$
- $\frac{x^3-1}{x^2+x+1}=\frac{(x^3-1)}{(x^2+x+1)}=\frac{(x-1)\cancel{(x^2+x+1)}}{\cancel{(x^2+x+1)}}=x-1$

Division (double-decker fractions)

ACTIVITY 20

ACTION
Simplifying double-decker fractions

OBJECTIVE
To simplify more complicated fractions called double-deckers

To divide rational expressions, invert the divisor and multiply and/or cancel.

- $\dfrac{\frac{x^2-1}{y^3}}{\frac{x+1}{y^2}}=\frac{(x^2-1)}{y^3}\times\frac{y^2}{(x+1)}=\frac{(x-1)(x+1)}{y^3}\times\frac{y^2}{(x+1)}=\frac{x-1}{y}$

Or

Multiply above and below by the LCD of all fractions.

- $\dfrac{10+\frac{9}{x}-\frac{7}{x^2}}{2+\frac{3}{x}-\frac{2}{x^2}}=\dfrac{\left(10+\frac{9}{x}-\frac{7}{x^2}\right)\times x^2}{\left(2+\frac{3}{x}-\frac{2}{x^2}\right)\times x^2}$

$$=\frac{10x^2+9x-7}{2x^2+3x-2}=\frac{(5x+7)\cancel{(2x-1)}}{\cancel{(2x-1)}(x+2)}=\frac{5x+7}{x+2}$$

EXERCISE 7

1. Simplify the following:

(a) $\frac{4}{p-2}+\frac{2p}{2-p}$

(b) $\frac{x}{2}-\frac{1}{x}$

(c) $\frac{x}{x-1}-\frac{x+1}{x-2}$

(d) $\frac{\alpha}{\beta}-\frac{\beta}{\alpha}$

(e) $\frac{1}{9}+\frac{x-3}{18x}-\frac{4x-1}{24x}$

(f) $m-\frac{1}{m}$

(g) $\frac{1-n}{2+2n}-\frac{1+n}{2-2n}+\frac{2n}{1-n^2}$

(h) $\frac{a+1}{4a+8}-\frac{a-1}{5a-10}+\frac{2a}{5a^2-20}$

(i) $\frac{3x}{x^2-1}+\frac{x-2}{x^2+x}-\frac{4}{x+1}$

(j) $\frac{7}{x^2+13x+30}+\frac{1}{x^2+5x+6}$

2. Simplify the following:

(a) $\frac{2a^2}{35b^2}\times\frac{28b^2}{4ab}$

(b) $\frac{3x-1}{3-9x}$

(c) $\frac{3ab}{3a^2-6ab}\times\frac{4b^2-2ab}{8ab}$

(d) $\frac{a^2+8a+15}{a^2-9}\times\frac{a^2-3a}{ab+5b}$

(e) $\frac{3x^2-11x+10}{x^2-4}\times\frac{x+2}{3x-5}$

(f) $\frac{2x^2-11x+12}{2x^2+11x-21}\times\frac{x^2+6x-7}{x^2-5x+4}$

(g) $\frac{y^3+27}{y^3-9y}\times\frac{y^2+3y}{y+3}$

(h) $\left(\frac{3}{a}-2\right)\left(\frac{3}{a}+2\right)$

(i) $\left(\frac{a}{3}-\frac{b}{2}\right)^2$

(j) $\left(\frac{2}{x}+\frac{3}{y}\right)\left(\frac{x}{2}-4y\right)$

(k) $\left(\frac{x}{2}-1\right)\left(\frac{x}{2}+1\right)(4x-8)$

3. Simplify the following:

(a) $\frac{4x^2}{2x}$

(b) $\frac{2x}{4x^2}$

(c) $\frac{6x-18}{15-5x}$

(d) $\frac{6a^2+2a}{3a^2+a}$

(e) $\frac{-5a^2+17a-6}{3-a}$

(f) $\frac{6b^2-51b-27}{b-9}$

(g) $\frac{4x^2+x-3}{4x^2-7x+3}$

(h) $\frac{x^4-y^4}{x^2-y^2}$

(i) $\frac{x^6-y^6}{(x^3-y^3)(x^2-xy+y^2)}$

(j) $\frac{6x^3-7x^2+2x}{2x^2-x}$

4. Simplify the following:

(a) $\frac{\frac{3}{x}}{\frac{x}{2}}$

(b) $\frac{3x}{\frac{2}{x}}$

(c) $\frac{\frac{x}{2}}{3x}$

(d) $\frac{x-\frac{1}{x}}{\frac{x-1}{x}}$

(e) $\frac{2+\frac{1}{x}}{2-\frac{1}{x}}$

(f) $\frac{1-\frac{3}{x}+\frac{10}{x^2}}{-1+\frac{2}{x}+\frac{15}{x^2}}$

(g) $\frac{at-at^2}{\frac{a}{t}-\frac{a}{t^2}}$

Exponentials and Logs

Learning Outcomes

- To apply the rules for carrying out operations on exponentials (powers).
- To understand how to manipulate surd expressions.
- To apply the rules for carrying out operations on logs.

5.1 Exponential expressions (powers)

ACTIVITY 21

ACTION
Learning the multiplication rule for exponentials

OBJECTIVE
To understand that when numbers to the same base are multiplied, you add their powers

You already know that $2^3 = 2 \times 2 \times 2$ and $y^4 = y \times y \times y \times y$. But what do $2^{\frac{1}{3}}, 3^{\frac{2}{5}}, 3^{-\frac{1}{2}}$ mean? These are all exponential expressions.

KEY TERM

An **exponential expression** can be written in the form a^p where, $p \in \mathbb{R}$.

a is called the **base** of the expression.
p is called the **power**, the **index** or the **exponent** of the expression.

- $\left(\frac{3}{2}\right)^3 = \left(\frac{3}{2}\right) \times \left(\frac{3}{2}\right) \times \left(\frac{3}{2}\right) = \frac{27}{8}$
- $\left(-2\frac{1}{4}\right)^2 = \left(-\frac{9}{4}\right)^2 = \left(-\frac{9}{4}\right) \times \left(-\frac{9}{4}\right) = \frac{81}{16}$

Rules of exponential expressions

1. The multiplication rule

WORKED EXAMPLE The multiplication rule for powers

$y^2 \times y^3 = y \times y \times y \times y \times y = y^5$

When you multiply two exponential expressions with the **same base**, you add the powers.

In general: $a^p \times a^q = a^{p+q}$

- $10^5 \times 10^3 = 10^8$
- $3^{\frac{1}{2}} \times 3^{\frac{2}{3}} = 3^{\frac{7}{6}}$
- $(a + 2b)^7 \times (a + 2b)^4 = (a + 2b)^{11}$
- $x^{-7} \times x^{-5} = x^{-12}$
- $e^{2-x} \times e^{-3+2x} = e^{x-1}$

2. The division rule

ACTIVITY 22

ACTION
Learning the division rule for exponentials

OBJECTIVE
To understand that when numbers to the same base are divided, you subtract their powers

WORKED EXAMPLE The division rule for powers

$$\frac{y^5}{y^3} = \frac{\cancel{y} \times \cancel{y} \times \cancel{y} \times y \times y}{\cancel{y} \times \cancel{y} \times \cancel{y}} = y^2$$

When you divide exponential expressions with the **same base**, you subtract the power on the bottom from the power on the top.

In general: $\boxed{\frac{a^p}{a^q} = a^{p-q}}$

- $\frac{10^{23}}{10^{19}} = 10^4$
- $\frac{2^{3x}}{2^x} = 2^{2x}$
- $\frac{3^{\frac{2}{3}}}{3^{\frac{1}{2}}} = 3^{\frac{1}{6}}$
- $\frac{(a^2 - 2b)^8}{(a^2 - 2b)^5} = (a^2 - 2b)^3$
- $\frac{x^5}{x^{-3}} = x^{5-(-3)} = x^8$
- $\frac{7^{-2}}{7^{-3}} = 7^{-2-(-3)} = 7^1$
- $\frac{e^{5-3x}}{e^{2+4x}} = e^{(5-3x)-(2+4x)} = e^{3-7x}$

3. The one rule

WORKED EXAMPLE The one rule for powers

$$\frac{y^4}{y^4} = \frac{\cancel{y} \times \cancel{y} \times \cancel{y} \times \cancel{y}}{\cancel{y} \times \cancel{y} \times \cancel{y} \times \cancel{y}} = 1 = y^{4-4} = y^0$$

$(\text{Anything})^0 = 1$ (Except 0^0)

In general: $\boxed{a^0 = 1}$

- $2^0 = 1$
- $\left(\frac{1}{2}\right)^0 = 1$
- $(-3)^0 = 1$
- $(x^2)^0 = 1$
- $\left(\frac{x^2}{y}\right)^0 = 1$
- $e^0 = 1$

4. The power of a power rule

ACTIVITY 23

ACTION
Learning the power of a power rule

OBJECTIVE
To understand that when numbers to a power are raised to a power, you multiply their powers

WORKED EXAMPLE Power of powers

$(y^2)^3 = y^2 \times y^2 \times y^2 = y^6$

When you put an exponential expression to a power, you multiply the two powers.

In general: $\boxed{(a^p)^q = a^{pq}}$

- $(10^3)^5 = 10^{15}$
- $(3^{\frac{1}{2}})^{\frac{2}{3}} = 3^{\frac{1}{3}}$
- $(x^{-3})^{-2} = x^6$
- $(e^{x-2})^4 = e^{4x-8}$
- $(2^{2x})^{-3} = 2^{-6x}$

5. Powers of products and quotients

ACTIVITY 24

ACTION
Learning about powers of products and quotients

OBJECTIVE
To manipulate more complicated expressions raised to a power

WORKED EXAMPLE Powers of products and quotients

$(2y)^4 = 2y \times 2y \times 2y \times 2y$
$= 2 \times 2 \times 2 \times 2 \times y \times y \times y \times y$
$= 2^4y^4 = 8y^4$

$\left(\frac{y}{2}\right)^3 = \frac{y}{2} \times \frac{y}{2} \times \frac{y}{2} = \frac{y \times y \times y}{2 \times 2 \times 2} = \frac{y^3}{2^3} = \frac{y^2}{8}$

When products and quotients are raised to a power, put each factor to the power.

In general: $(ab)^p = a^pb^p$ and $\left(\frac{a}{b}\right)^p = \frac{a^p}{b^p}$

- $\left(\frac{a^2}{b}\right)^3 = \frac{a^6}{b^3}$
- $\left(\frac{xy}{2z}\right)^4 = \frac{x^4y^4}{2^4z^4} = \frac{x^4y^4}{16z^4}$
- $\left(\frac{3x^{-2}}{4y^2}\right)^2 = \frac{3^2 \times x^{-4}}{4^2y^4} = \frac{9x^{-4}}{16y^4}$
- $(5e^x)^{\frac{1}{2}} = 5^{\frac{1}{2}}e^{\frac{1}{2}x}$

WARNING
Be careful. Never apply this rule to a sum of terms raised to a power.
$(a + b)^p \neq a^p + b^p$, except for $p = 1$.
$(a + b)^2 \neq a^2 + b^2$ because $(a + b)^2 = a^2 + 2ab + b^2$

6. Working with negative powers

ACTIVITY 25

ACTION
Working with negative powers

OBJECTIVE
To learn how to work with negative powers and the procedure for turning them into positive powers

WORKED EXAMPLE Negative powers

What does y^{-2} mean?

$y^{-2} = \frac{y^{-2}}{1} = \frac{y^{-2}}{1} \times \frac{y^2}{y^2} = \frac{y^{-2} \times y^2}{1 \times y^2} = \frac{y^0}{y^2} = \frac{1}{y^2}$

$\therefore y^{-2} = \frac{1}{y^2}$

- $3^{-2} = \frac{1}{3^2} = \frac{1}{9}$

$\frac{1}{y^{-3}} = \frac{1}{y^{-3}} \times \frac{y^3}{y^3} = \frac{1 \times y^3}{y^{-3} \times y^3}$

$= \frac{y^3}{y^0} = \frac{y^3}{1} = y^3$

- $\frac{1}{2^{-3}} = 2^3 = 8$

Therefore, if you have an exponential expression with a negative power, you can move the base with the negative power up or down. This leaves you with the same base with the sign of the power changed.

In general: $a^{-p} = \frac{1}{a^p}$ and $\frac{1}{a^{-p}} = a^p$

- $5^{-4} = \frac{1}{5^4} = \frac{1}{625}$
- $\frac{2^{-3}}{3^{-2}} = \frac{3^2}{2^3} = \frac{9}{8}$

- $\frac{4^{-1}}{5^2} = \frac{1}{5^2 \times 4^1} = \frac{1}{100}$
- $\frac{3x^{-2}}{zy^{-3}} = \frac{3y^3}{zx^2}$
- $\frac{3y^{-2}}{4} = \frac{3}{4y^2}$
- $(ab)^{-2} = a^{-2}b^{-2} = \frac{1}{a^2b^2}$

The flipping trick:

$$\left(\frac{a}{b}\right)^{-p} = \frac{a^{-p}}{b^{-p}} = \frac{b^p}{a^p} = \left(\frac{b}{a}\right)^p$$

- $\left(-\frac{5}{4}\right)^{-2} = \left(-\frac{4}{5}\right)^2 = \frac{4^2}{5^2} = \frac{16}{25}$
- $\left(\frac{3x}{2y^2}\right)^{-3} = \left(\frac{2y^2}{3x}\right)^3 = \frac{2^3y^6}{3^3x^3} = \frac{8y^6}{27x^3}$

7. Non-whole number powers

What do $8^{\frac{2}{3}}$, $16^{\frac{1}{2}}$, $25^{-\frac{3}{2}}$ mean?

ACTIVITY 26

ACTION
Working with fractional powers

OBJECTIVE
To follow the procedure for working step by step with fractional powers

WORKED EXAMPLE

Explaining fractional powers

Both of these statements are true:

$2 \times 2 \times 2 = 8$ and $8^{\frac{1}{3}} \times 8^{\frac{1}{3}} \times 8^{\frac{1}{3}} = 8^1$

So, if you want to think of three identical numbers that multiply to give 8, the answer is $8^{\frac{1}{3}}$ or 2.

Each of these numbers is known as the cube root of 8 or $\sqrt[3]{8}$.

$\therefore \sqrt[3]{8} = 8^{\frac{1}{3}} = 2$

A fractional power is a root.

In general: $a^{\frac{1}{q}} = \sqrt[q]{a}$

- $16^{\frac{1}{4}} = \sqrt[4]{16} = 2$ [$\sqrt[4]{16}$ means the positive 4th root]
- $(-27)^{\frac{1}{3}} = \sqrt[3]{-27} = -3$

What about other fractions?

$8^{\frac{2}{3}} = (8^{\frac{1}{3}})^2 = 2^2 = 4$ *or*

$8^{\frac{2}{3}} = (8^2)^{\frac{1}{3}} = (64)^{\frac{1}{3}} = \sqrt[3]{64} = 4$

In general:

$$a^{\frac{p}{q}} = \sqrt[q]{a^p} = (a^p)^{\frac{1}{q}} = (a^{\frac{1}{q}})^p$$

The best way to evaluate $a^{\frac{p}{q}}$ is to evaluate the root before the power (do the q before the p).

- $16^{\frac{3}{4}} = (16^{\frac{1}{4}})^3 = (2)^3 = 8$
- $\sqrt[4]{16} = (16)^{\frac{1}{4}} = 2$
- $\sqrt[3]{8^2} = (8^2)^{\frac{1}{3}} = (8^{\frac{1}{3}})^2 = (2)^2 = 4$
- $\sqrt[3]{x^2y} = (x^2y)^{\frac{1}{3}} = x^{\frac{2}{3}}y^{\frac{1}{3}} = \sqrt[3]{x^2}\sqrt[3]{y}$
- $\sqrt[n]{a^{\frac{n}{2}}b^{\frac{n}{3}}} = (a^{\frac{n}{2}}b^{\frac{n}{3}})^{\frac{1}{n}} = a^{\frac{1}{2}}b^{\frac{1}{3}} = \sqrt{a}\sqrt[3]{b}$

EXAMPLE 1

Simplify **(a)** $\dfrac{8^{-\frac{2}{3}}}{4^{-\frac{1}{2}}}$, **(b)** $\dfrac{(-5)^2 \times 25^{\frac{1}{2}}}{5^{-3} \times (25)^3}$.

Solution

(a) $\dfrac{8^{-\frac{2}{3}}}{4^{-\frac{1}{2}}} = \dfrac{4^{\frac{1}{2}}}{8^{\frac{2}{3}}}$ [Get rid of negative powers.]

$= \dfrac{(2^2)^{\frac{1}{2}}}{(2^3)^{\frac{2}{3}}} = \dfrac{2^1}{2^2} = \dfrac{2}{4} = \dfrac{1}{2}$

(b) $\dfrac{(-5)^2 \times 25^{\frac{1}{2}}}{5^{-3} \times (25)^3} = \dfrac{25 \times 5^3 \times 25^{\frac{1}{2}}}{(25)^3}$

$= \dfrac{25 \times 125 \times 5}{25 \times 25 \times 25} = 1$

EXAMPLE 2

Write $\dfrac{(3^2)^{-3} \times \sqrt{3} \times (-3)^4}{(27)^{\frac{1}{3}} \times 9^{-\frac{3}{2}}}$ in the form 3^p, where $p > 0$.

Solution

$\dfrac{(3^2)^{-3} \times \sqrt{3} \times (-3)^4}{(27)^{\frac{1}{3}} \times 9^{-\frac{3}{2}}}$

$= \dfrac{3^{-6} \times 3^{\frac{1}{2}} \times 3^4}{(3^3)^{\frac{1}{3}} (3^2)^{-\frac{3}{2}}}$

$= \dfrac{3^{-\frac{3}{2}}}{3^1 \times 3^{-3}}$

$= \dfrac{3^{-\frac{3}{2}}}{3^{-2}}$

$= 3^{-\frac{3}{2}+2} = 3^{\frac{1}{2}} = \sqrt{3}$

EXAMPLE 3

Simplify $\dfrac{(e^x)^2 \times (e^{2x-1})^{-2}}{\sqrt{e^{4x-2}} \times (e^{x+1})^{-3}}$, giving your answer in the form e^{ax+b}.

Solution

$\dfrac{(e^x)^2 \times (e^{2x-1})^{-2}}{\sqrt{e^{4x-2}} \times (e^{x+1})^{-3}}$ $\left[\sqrt{e^{4x-2}} = (e^{4x-2})^{\frac{1}{2}}\right]$

$= \dfrac{e^{2x} \times e^{-4x+2}}{e^{2x-1} \times e^{-3x-3}}$

$= \dfrac{e^{-2x+2}}{e^{-x-4}} = e^{(-2x+2)-(-x-4)}$

$= e^{-x+6}$

EXAMPLE 4

The population P of yeast cells after t hours is given by $P = 10^6 \times (\sqrt{2})^t$.

(a) Show that $P = 10^6 \times 2^{\frac{t}{2}}$.

(b) Find the population P_1 after n hours.

(c) Find the population P_2 after $(n+2)$ hours.

(d) Find the percentage change in population from n hours to $(n+2)$ hours.

Solution

(a) $P = 10^6 \times \left(2^{\frac{1}{2}}\right)^t = 10^6 \times 2^{\frac{t}{2}}$

(b) $P_1 = 10^6 \times 2^{\frac{n}{2}}$

(c) $P_2 = 10^6 \times 2^{\frac{(n+2)}{2}}$

(d) Percentage change in the yeast population

$$= \frac{\left|10^6 \times 2^{\frac{(n+2)}{2}} - 10^6 \times 2^{\frac{n}{2}}\right|}{10^6 \times 2^{\frac{n}{2}} \times 100\%}$$

$$= \frac{10^6 \left|2^{\frac{n}{2}} \times 2^1 - 2^{\frac{n}{2}}\right|}{10^6 \times 2^{\frac{n}{2}}} \times 100\%$$

$$= \frac{10^6 \times 2^{\frac{n}{2}} \left|2 - 1\right|}{10^6 \times 2^{\frac{n}{2}}} \times 100\%$$

$= 100\%$

EXERCISE 8

1. Evaluate the following without using your calculator:

(a) 3^3 **(b)** 2^5 **(c)** 5^4 **(d)** 10^8 **(e)** 1^{2013} **(f)** $(-1)^4$ **(g)** $(-1)^{21}$ **(h)** $(-2)^4$ **(i)** $(-3)^5$ **(j)** $\left(\frac{1}{2}\right)^2$ **(k)** $\left(\frac{2}{3}\right)^2$ **(l)** $\left(-\frac{1}{2}\right)^3$ **(m)** $\left(-\frac{4}{5}\right)^2$ **(n)** $\left(3\frac{1}{2}\right)^2$ **(o)** $\left(2\frac{3}{4}\right)^2$ **(p)** $\left(-2\frac{1}{2}\right)^3$

2. Evaluate the following without using your calculator:

(a) 2^{-1} **(b)** 3^{-2} **(c)** 4^{-3} **(d)** 5^{-2} **(e)** 2^{-4} **(f)** $(3{\cdot}6)^{-1}$ **(g)** $\left(\frac{3}{4}\right)^{-1}$ **(h)** $2^{-1} \times 3$ **(i)** 2×3^{-1} **(j)** $\frac{2}{3^{-1}}$ **(k)** $\frac{3^{-1}}{2}$ **(l)** $\frac{1}{3^{-1} \times 2^{-1}}$ **(m)** $(-8)^{-2}$ **(n)** $(-3)^{-3}$ **(o)** $(3 \times 2^{-1})^{-3}$

3. Evaluate the following exactly without using your calculator:

(a) $9^{\frac{3}{2}}$ **(b)** $25^{\frac{1}{2}}$ **(c)** $25^{\frac{3}{2}}$ **(d)** $8^{\frac{4}{3}}$ **(e)** $36^{-\frac{1}{2}}$ **(f)** $64^{-\frac{1}{3}}$ **(g)** $6 \times 36^{-\frac{1}{2}}$ **(h)** $2 \times 16^{\frac{1}{2}}$ **(i)** $6 \times 100^{-\frac{3}{2}}$ **(j)** $4 \times 49^{\frac{1}{2}}$ **(k)** $3 \times 4^{-\frac{1}{2}}$ **(l)** $\left(\frac{1}{9}\right)^{\frac{1}{2}}$ **(m)** $(100\,000\,000)^{\frac{3}{4}}$ **(n)** $(-8)^{\frac{5}{3}}$ **(o)** $100^{-\frac{1}{2}}$ **(p)** $\left(\frac{4}{9}\right)^{-\frac{1}{2}}$ **(q)** $\left(\frac{8}{27}\right)^{\frac{1}{3}}$ **(r)** $\left(-\frac{8}{27}\right)^{\frac{1}{3}}$ **(s)** $\left(-\frac{8}{27}\right)^{-\frac{1}{3}}$ **(t)** 8^0 **(u)** $\left(\frac{1}{27}\right)^{-\frac{1}{3}}$ **(v)** $\left(-\frac{1}{27}\right)^{-\frac{1}{3}}$ **(w)** $\left(2\frac{1}{4}\right)^{-\frac{1}{2}}$ **(x)** $\left(\frac{25}{16}\right)^{-\frac{1}{2}}\left(\frac{3}{2}\right)^2$ **(y)** $\left(-\frac{1}{2}\right)^0 \times \left(\frac{16}{9}\right)^{-\frac{3}{2}}$

4. Write:

(a) $8\sqrt{2}$ in the form $2^p, p > 0$

(b) $\dfrac{27\sqrt{3}}{3}$ in the form $3^p, p > 0$

(c) $\dfrac{4\sqrt{2}}{32}$ in the form $\dfrac{1}{2^p}, p > 0$

(d) $\dfrac{49\sqrt{7}}{\sqrt[3]{7}}$ in the form $7^p, p > 0$

(e) $\dfrac{125^{\frac{2}{3}} \times 5^2}{25 \times \sqrt{5}}$ in the form $5^p, p > 0$

(f) $\dfrac{10^{23} \times 2 \times 10^{15}}{2 \times 10^{19} \times (10^{-2})^4}$ in the form $10^p, p > 0$

(g) $\left(\dfrac{3}{2}\right)^4 \times 2 \times \dfrac{1}{3^{-2}}$ in the form $\dfrac{3^p}{2^q}, p > 0, q > 0$

(h) $\dfrac{16\sqrt{2}}{\sqrt{8}}$ in the form $2^p, p > 0$

(i) $\dfrac{27^{\frac{2}{3}} \times 3^2}{9\sqrt{3}}$ in the form $3^p, p > 0$

(j) $\left(\dfrac{5}{3}\right)^{-1} \times \dfrac{(25)^3}{3^{-2}} \times \dfrac{9^{-\frac{3}{2}}}{125^{\frac{2}{3}}}$ in the form $5^p, p > 0$

5. Write in the form a^p or $\dfrac{1}{a^p}$, where $p \in \mathbb{R}, p > 0$:

(a) $a^7 \times a^2$

(b) $(a^7)^3$

(c) $a^7 \times a^{-3}$

(d) $\dfrac{a^7}{a^3}$

(e) $\sqrt[3]{a}$

(f) $a\sqrt{a}$

(g) $(a\sqrt[3]{a})^3$

(h) $\dfrac{a^{14}}{a^2}$

(i) $\dfrac{a}{a^3}$

(j) $\dfrac{a^2}{\sqrt{a}}$

(k) $\dfrac{a^2}{a^{-3}}$

(l) $\sqrt[3]{a^2}$

(m) $\dfrac{\sqrt{a} \times (a^2)^3}{a^{-2} \times (a^3)^{-1}}$

(n) $\dfrac{(a^{-2})^{\frac{1}{2}} \times (a^3)^{-\frac{1}{2}}}{\sqrt{a}}$

(o) $\dfrac{\sqrt{a^3} \times (a^{-2})^{\frac{3}{2}}}{(a^{-2})^2 \times a^{-1}}$

6. Simplify the following, giving all your answers with positive powers:

(a) $\dfrac{x^2 \times (xy)^2}{y}$

(b) $\dfrac{5x^3 \times 6x^4}{15x^2}$

(c) $\dfrac{28x^4}{7x^3}$

(d) $\dfrac{36x^3}{72x^5}$

(e) $\dfrac{42x^5}{7x^2 \times 3x^3}$

(f) $\dfrac{70x^3(xy)^4}{5xy \times 7xy^2}$

(g) $\dfrac{2^x \times 2^{3x}}{2^{2x}}$

(h) $\dfrac{x^4 \times 2^{5x}}{2^x \times x^3}$

(i) $\dfrac{(3xy)^2 \times 2xy}{9(x^2y)^3}$

(j) $\left(\dfrac{x^2y}{3z^3}\right)^4$

(k) $\dfrac{7y^2 \times 25y^2}{5xy^3 \times 14xy}$

(l) $\dfrac{(a+3b)^2(a+3b)^6}{(a+3b)^3}$

(m) $\dfrac{xyab^2}{abx^2y^2}$

(n) $\dfrac{(2^x)^2 \times (3^x)^3}{2 \times 2^{2x} \times 3 \times 3^x}$

(o) $\dfrac{a^{-2}}{2y^2}$

(p) $\dfrac{2a^2}{y^{-2}}$

(q) $\dfrac{4x^{\frac{3}{2}}}{2x^{\frac{1}{2}}}$

(r) $\dfrac{25y^{-3}}{5y^{-2}}$

(s) $\dfrac{8x^{\frac{4}{3}}y^{\frac{5}{2}}}{4x^{\frac{1}{3}} \times 2y^{\frac{3}{2}}}$

(t) $\dfrac{16(x^2y)^{\frac{3}{2}}}{8\sqrt{y}x}$

7. The population P of a certain strain of bacteria is given by $P = 1500 \times 3^t$, where t is the time in hours.

(a) Find the population P_1 after 4 hours.

(b) Find the population P_2 after 10 hours.

(c) Compare these populations by dividing P_2 by P_1.

8. The mass M of a radioactive material in grams (g) left after t hours is given by $M = \dfrac{20}{16^t}$.

(a) Show that $M = 20 \times 2^{-4t}$.

(b) Compare the mass M_2 left after $(x + 7)$ hours with the mass M_1 left after $(x + 6)$ hours by dividing M_2 by M_1.

9. The mass M of a drug in milligrams (mg) in a person's body after t hours is given by

$$M = \sqrt[3]{\frac{8000}{8^{3t}}}.$$

(a) Show that $M = 20 \times 2^{-3t}$.

(b) Find M after 1 hour.

(c) Find the percentage change in M between t and $(t + 1)$.

10. The value V in € of an investment after t years is given by $V = 5000(1{\cdot}08)^t$.

(a) Compare the amount V_2 after $(t + 3)$ years with the amount V_1 after t years, giving your answer to four decimal places.

(b) Find the value of the investment after five years, correct to the nearest euro.

(c) Find the value of the investment after eight years, correct to the nearest euro.

5.2 Surds

ACTIVITY 27

ACTION
Recognising surds

OBJECTIVE
To identify whether numbers are surds or rational numbers

ACTIVITY 28

ACTION
Simplifying surds

OBJECTIVE
To break surds down into their simplest form

ACTIVITY 29

ACTION
Adding surds

OBJECTIVE
To combine surds into their simplest form

KEY TERM

A **surd expression** is an expression involving square roots of variable(s) or numbers that cannot be simplified into a rational expression.

$\sqrt{2}$, $3\sqrt{2}$, $2 + \sqrt{2}$, $\sqrt{x}$, $\sqrt{3} + \sqrt{x}$, $\sqrt{x} + 3\sqrt{y}$ are all surd expressions.

TIP

Remember: $\sqrt{a} = a^{\frac{1}{2}}$

The rules of exponents apply to surds.

Simplifying surds

To simplify surds you need two important results:

1. $\sqrt{ab} = (ab)^{\frac{1}{2}} = a^{\frac{1}{2}} b^{\frac{1}{2}} = \sqrt{a} \times \sqrt{b}$
2. $\sqrt{\frac{a}{b}} = \left(\frac{a}{b}\right)^{\frac{1}{2}} = \frac{a^{\frac{1}{2}}}{b^{\frac{1}{2}}} = \frac{\sqrt{a}}{\sqrt{b}}$

- $\sqrt{45} = \sqrt{9 \times 5} = \sqrt{9} \times \sqrt{5} = 3\sqrt{5}$
- $\sqrt{16 - 4x} = \sqrt{4(4 - x)} = \sqrt{4} \times \sqrt{4 - x} = 2\sqrt{4 - x}$
- $\sqrt{4x^3} = \sqrt{4 \times x^2 \times x} = 2x\sqrt{x}$
- $\sqrt{9x^2 + 36y^2} = \sqrt{9(x^2 + 4y^2)} = \sqrt{9}\,\sqrt{x^2 + 4y^2} = 3\sqrt{x^2 + 4y^2}$
- $\sqrt{2\frac{1}{4}} = \sqrt{\frac{9}{4}} = \frac{\sqrt{9}}{\sqrt{4}} = \frac{3}{2}$

WARNING

Remember: $\sqrt{a^2 + b^2} \neq a + b$

Adding and subtracting surds

As usual, you can add and subtract like terms only.

You cannot combine $\sqrt{2} + \sqrt{3}$ into a single surd,

but $2\sqrt{2} + 5\sqrt{2} + 7\sqrt{2} = 14\sqrt{2}$. [Just as $2a + 5a + 7a = 14a$.]

- $3 + \sqrt{5} + 6 - 2\sqrt{5} + 5\sqrt{5} = 9 + 4\sqrt{5}$
- $\frac{2\sqrt{7}}{3} + \frac{3}{2} - \frac{\sqrt{7}}{6} + \frac{5}{6} = \frac{4\sqrt{7} + 9 - \sqrt{7} + 5}{6}$

  $= \frac{3\sqrt{7} + 14}{6} = \frac{14}{6} + \frac{3\sqrt{7}}{6} = \frac{7}{3} + \frac{\sqrt{7}}{2}$
- $2\sqrt{5} + \sqrt{45} - 3\sqrt{20}$

  $= 2\sqrt{5} + \sqrt{9 \times 5} - 3\sqrt{4 \times 5} = 2\sqrt{5} + 3\sqrt{5} - 3 \times 2\sqrt{5}$

  $= 2\sqrt{5} + 3\sqrt{5} - 6\sqrt{5} = -\sqrt{5}$
- $2\sqrt{x} + \sqrt{x^3} = 2\sqrt{x} + \sqrt{x^2 \times x} = 2\sqrt{x} + \sqrt{x^2} \times \sqrt{x}$

  $= 2\sqrt{x} + x\sqrt{x} = \sqrt{x}(2 + x)$

ACTIVITY 30

ACTION
Multiplying surds

OBJECTIVE
To multiply and break down surds to their simplest form

Multiplication of surds

To multiply out brackets with surds, multiply each term in one bracket by each term in the other bracket and combine like terms.

TIP

Remember: $\sqrt{a} \times \sqrt{b} = a^{\frac{1}{2}} \times b^{\frac{1}{2}} = (ab)^{\frac{1}{2}} = \sqrt{ab}$

- $2(\sqrt{3} + 4\sqrt{2}) = 2\sqrt{3} + 8\sqrt{2}$
- $\sqrt{x}(\sqrt{x} + 3) = \sqrt{x^2} + 3\sqrt{x} = x + 3\sqrt{x}$
- $(3 + \sqrt{2})(4 - 5\sqrt{2}) = 12 - 15\sqrt{2} + 4\sqrt{2} - 5\sqrt{4}$

  $= 12 - 11\sqrt{2} - 10 = 2 - 11\sqrt{2}$
- $(\sqrt{x} - 2\sqrt{y})(\sqrt{y} + 3\sqrt{x}) = \sqrt{xy} + 3\sqrt{x^2} - 2\sqrt{y^2} - 6\sqrt{x}\sqrt{y} = 3x - 2y - 5\sqrt{xy}$

Perfect squares

- $(\sqrt{a} + \sqrt{b})^2 = (\sqrt{a} + \sqrt{b})(\sqrt{a} + \sqrt{b}) = \sqrt{a^2} + \sqrt{ab} + \sqrt{ba} + \sqrt{b^2} = a + 2\sqrt{ab} + b$
- $(\sqrt{3} + \sqrt{2})^2 = (\sqrt{3})^2 + 2(\sqrt{3})(\sqrt{2}) + (\sqrt{2})^2 = 3 + 2\sqrt{6} + 2 = 5 + 2\sqrt{6}$
- $(3\sqrt{x} - y)^2 = (3\sqrt{x})^2 + 2(3\sqrt{x})(-y) + (-y)^2 = 9x - 6y\sqrt{x} + y^2$

Difference of two squares

- $(\sqrt{a} + \sqrt{b})(\sqrt{a} - \sqrt{b}) = \sqrt{a^2} - \cancel{\sqrt{ab}} + \cancel{\sqrt{ba}} - \sqrt{b^2} = \sqrt{a^2} - \sqrt{b^2} = a - b$

  [The surds above are called **conjugate surds**. This is a really important result for dealing with the division of surds.]
- $(3\sqrt{2} - 5)(3\sqrt{2} + 5) = (3\sqrt{2})^2 - (5)^2 = 18 - 25 = -7$
- $(\sqrt{n+1} - \sqrt{n})(\sqrt{n+1} + \sqrt{n}) = (\sqrt{n+1})^2 - (\sqrt{n})^2 = (n + 1) - n = 1$

Division (rationalising the denominator)

When you divide surds, the answer should never have a surd in the denominator. This process of getting rid of surds on the bottom is called rationalising the denominator.

ACTIVITY 31

ACTION
Rationalising the denominators of surds

OBJECTIVE
To rationalise by multiplying above and below by the conjugate of the denominator

1. Simple denominators

$$\frac{3}{\sqrt{2}} = \frac{3}{\sqrt{2}} \times \frac{\sqrt{2}}{\sqrt{2}} = \frac{3\sqrt{2}}{2}$$

To rationalise a surd with a denominator of the form $a\sqrt{b}$, multiply above and below by $\sqrt{b}$.

- $\frac{\sqrt{5}}{\sqrt{7}} = \frac{\sqrt{5}}{\sqrt{7}} \times \frac{\sqrt{7}}{\sqrt{7}} = \frac{\sqrt{35}}{7}$
- $\frac{4+\sqrt{3}}{\sqrt{2}} = \frac{4+\sqrt{3}}{\sqrt{2}} \times \frac{\sqrt{2}}{\sqrt{2}} = \frac{4\sqrt{2}+\sqrt{6}}{2}$

2. Compound denominators

To rationalise a surd with a denominator of the form $a + b\sqrt{c}$ or $a\sqrt{b} + c\sqrt{d}$, multiply above and below by the conjugate surd of the denominator.

$$\frac{2}{3\sqrt{2}+2} = \frac{2}{3\sqrt{2}+2} \times \frac{(3\sqrt{2}-2)}{(3\sqrt{2}-2)} = \frac{2(3\sqrt{2}-7)}{(3\sqrt{2})^2-(2)^2} = \frac{2(3\sqrt{2}-2)}{18-4}$$

$$= \frac{2(3\sqrt{2}-2)}{14} = \frac{(3\sqrt{2}-2)}{7}$$

EXAMPLE 5

Rationalise the denominators of the following:

(a) $\frac{5}{\sqrt{3}-\sqrt{2}}$, **(b)** $\frac{\sqrt{x}+\sqrt{y}}{\sqrt{x}-\sqrt{y}}$.

Solution

(a) $\frac{5}{\sqrt{3}-\sqrt{2}} = \frac{5}{\sqrt{3}-\sqrt{2}} \times \frac{(\sqrt{3}+\sqrt{2})}{(\sqrt{3}+\sqrt{2})}$

$$= \frac{5(\sqrt{3}+\sqrt{2})}{(\sqrt{3})^2-(\sqrt{2})^2} = \frac{5(\sqrt{3}+\sqrt{2})}{1} = 5(\sqrt{3}+\sqrt{2})$$

(b) $\frac{\sqrt{x}+\sqrt{y}}{\sqrt{x}-\sqrt{y}} = \frac{(\sqrt{x}+\sqrt{y})}{(\sqrt{x}-\sqrt{y})} \times \frac{(\sqrt{x}+\sqrt{y})}{(\sqrt{x}+\sqrt{y})}$

$$= \frac{x+\sqrt{xy}+\sqrt{xy}+y}{x-y}$$

$$= \frac{x+2\sqrt{xy}+y}{x-y}$$

EXERCISE 9

1. Write the following surds in their simplest form:

(a) $\sqrt{12}$

(b) $\sqrt{27}$

(c) $\sqrt{1210}$

(d) $\sqrt{512}$

(e) $\sqrt{\frac{8}{9}}$

(f) $\sqrt{\frac{18}{25}}$

(g) $\sqrt{\frac{147}{100}}$

(h) $\sqrt{4x^3}$

(i) $\sqrt{8x^2y^3}$

(j) $\sqrt{\frac{12x^3}{y^2}}$

(k) $\sqrt{\frac{16z^{61}}{9x^2y^2}}$

2. Simplify the following surds:

(a) $\sqrt{11} - 2\sqrt{11} + 4\sqrt{11}$

(b) $5 + 7\sqrt{3} - 9 + 8\sqrt{3}$

(c) $x + \sqrt{y} - 3\sqrt{y} + 2x - 5\sqrt{y}$

(d) $\sqrt{28} + \sqrt{63} - \sqrt{175}$

(e) $\sqrt{125} - 2\sqrt{180} + \sqrt{245}$

(f) $\sqrt{8} + \sqrt{12} + \sqrt{18} + \sqrt{27}$

(g) $\sqrt{75} - 3\sqrt{48} + \sqrt{147}$

(h) $\sqrt{x} + x\sqrt{x} - \sqrt{x^3}$

(i) $a\sqrt{ay^3} + y\sqrt{a^3y} + \sqrt{a^3y^3}$

(j) $\sqrt{x-3} - \sqrt{4x-12} + 2\sqrt{x-3} - \sqrt{25x-75}$

3. Multiply out and simplify the following surds:

(a) $(\sqrt{2})^3$

(b) $\sqrt{2} \times \sqrt{3}$

(c) $2\sqrt{6} \times 5\sqrt{18}$

(d) $\sqrt{6}(3\sqrt{2} + 2\sqrt{3} + \sqrt{6})$

(e) $(\sqrt{3} + 1)^2$

(f) $(\sqrt{3} - 1)(\sqrt{3} + 1)$

(g) $\sqrt{ab}(a\sqrt{b} + b\sqrt{a})$

(h) $(\sqrt{7} + \sqrt{13})^2$

(i) $(\sqrt{7} + \sqrt{13})(\sqrt{7} - \sqrt{13})$

(j) $(2\sqrt{x} + 3\sqrt{y})^2$

(k) $(\sqrt{x+2} + \sqrt{x+1})(\sqrt{x+2} - \sqrt{x+1})$

(l) $\sqrt{x}(2\sqrt{x} - 3) + 5(\sqrt{x} - x)$

(m) $\frac{1}{2}(\sqrt{a+x} - \sqrt{a-x})^2$

(n) $(x + \sqrt{2})(x - 1)(x - \sqrt{2})$

(o) $(x^{\frac{1}{2}} + 1)(x^{\frac{1}{2}} - 1)$

(p) $\left(\frac{1}{\sqrt{x}} - 1\right)\left(\frac{1}{\sqrt{x}} + 1\right)$

(q) $\left(4\sqrt{y} + \frac{3}{\sqrt{y}}\right)\left(4\sqrt{y} - \frac{3}{\sqrt{y}}\right)$

(r) $\left(\sqrt{x} + \frac{2}{\sqrt{x}}\right)^2$

(s) $\left(\frac{\sqrt{x}}{y} - \frac{y}{\sqrt{x}}\right)^2$

4. Rationalise each denominator:

(a) $\frac{1}{\sqrt{5}}$

(b) $-\frac{1}{\sqrt{2}}$

(c) $\frac{2}{\sqrt{3}}$

(d) $\frac{4}{5\sqrt{2}}$

(e) $\frac{-3}{2\sqrt{3}}$

(f) $\frac{\sqrt{6}}{2\sqrt{7}}$

(g) $\frac{x}{\sqrt{y}}$

(h) $\frac{\sqrt{x}}{\sqrt{y}}$

(i) $\frac{1}{\sqrt{2}+1}$

(j) $\frac{1}{3-2\sqrt{2}}$

(k) $\frac{6}{3\sqrt{2} - 2\sqrt{3}}$

(l) $\frac{\sqrt{5}+1}{\sqrt{5}-1}$

(m) $\frac{5\sqrt{x}}{3 - 2\sqrt{x}}$

(n) $\frac{\sqrt{3}+\sqrt{2}}{\sqrt{3}-\sqrt{2}}$

(o) $\frac{x}{\sqrt{a} - \sqrt{a-x}}$

5. If $y = 2 - \sqrt{3}$, evaluate $y^2 - 4y + 1$.

6. BCD is an isosceles triangle.

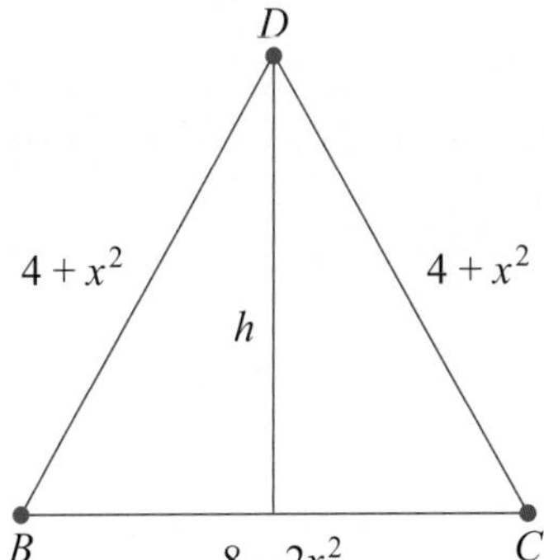

Find:

(a) the height h in terms of x,

(b) the area of the triangle in terms of x.

7. If $x = \sqrt{3} + \sqrt{2}$ and $y = \sqrt{3} - \sqrt{2}$, find $x^2 + xy + y^2$.

8. Show $\sqrt{1 - \frac{x^2}{y^2}} = \frac{\sqrt{y^2 - x^2}}{y}$.

9. If $V = 20h^2\sqrt{\frac{1}{25h^2} - 0{\cdot}05}$, show that V can be written as $V = 2h\sqrt{4 - 5h^2}$.

10. Kepler showed that the periodic time P for a satellite to make a complete orbit around a planet of mass M at a distance r from the centre of the planet is given by $P = 2\pi\sqrt{\frac{r^3}{GM}}$, where G is a constant.

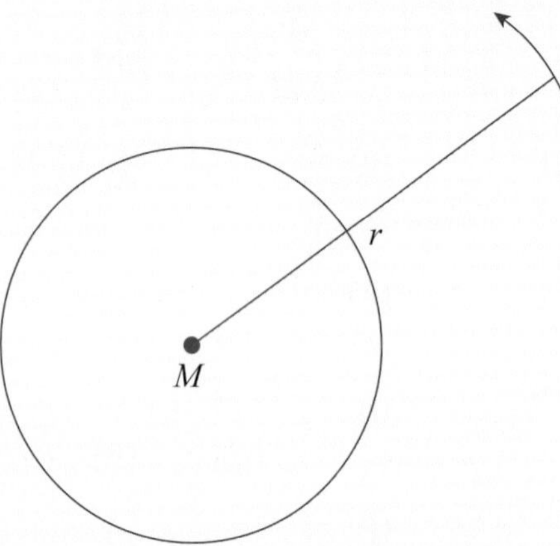

(a) Write down the periodic times:

(i) P_1 for a satellite at $r = R$,

(ii) P_2 for a satellite at $r = 4R$.

(b) Show that $\frac{P_1}{P_2} = \frac{1}{8}$.

11. If x, y and z are consecutive terms in a geometric sequence, then $\frac{y}{x} = \frac{z}{y}$. Show that the following numbers are consecutively in a geometric sequence:

(a) $5, \sqrt{35}, 7$ **(b)** $a, \sqrt{ab}, b$

12. The mass M of an object moving at a speed v is given by $M = \frac{M_0}{\sqrt{1 - \frac{v^2}{c^2}}}$, where M_0 is the mass at rest and c is the speed of light.

(a) Show that M can be written as

$$M = \frac{M_0 c\sqrt{c^2 - v^2}}{c^2 - v^2}.$$

(b) If $v = \frac{4c}{5}$, show that $M = \frac{5M_0}{3}$.

13. A simple pendulum consists of a mass M on the end of a string of length L moving back and forth as shown.

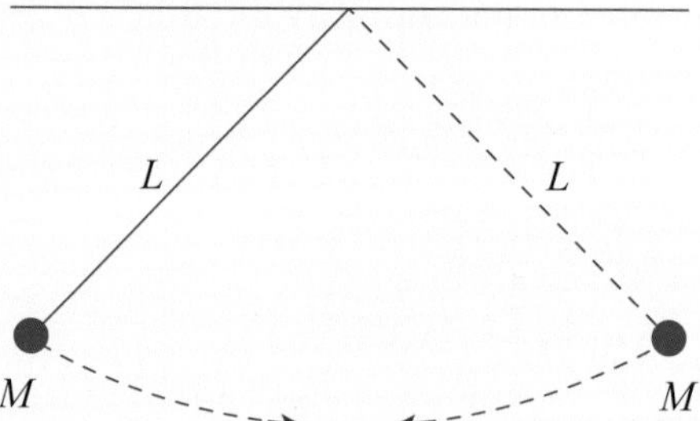

The time to swing from right to left and back again is given by $T = 2\pi\sqrt{\frac{L}{g}}$, where g is a constant.

(a) Write down the time T_1 if $L = d$.

(b) Write down the time T_2 if $L = \frac{d}{4}$.

(c) Show that $\frac{T_1}{T_2} = 2$.

5.3 Logs

What is a log?

$\log_3 9$ is read as log 9 to base 3. But what does it mean? It simply means the **power** to which you must put the **base** 3 to get 9. In other words, it asks you to find the power p where $3^p = 9$.

In general, $\log_a x$ is the **power** to which you must put the **base** a to get x.

KEY TERM

The **log** of a number to a given base is the power to which the base must be raised to give the number.

A log is a power.

ACTIVITY 32

ACTION
Understanding logs

OBJECTIVE
To develop a deeper understanding of logs

- $\log_2 8 = 3$ [The power to which you put 2 to get 8: $2^3 = 8$]
- $\log_4 8 = \frac{3}{2}$ [The power to which you put 4 to get 8: $4^{\frac{3}{2}} = 8$]
- $\log_5 1 = 0$ [The power to which you put 5 to get 1: $5^0 = 1$]
- $\log_3(-9) = ?$ [The power to which you put 3 to get -9 does not exist: $3^? = -9$]
  There is no such number. **You cannot have the log of a negative number.**
- $\log_4\left(\frac{1}{16}\right) = -2$ $\left[\text{The power to which you put 4 to get } \frac{1}{16}: 4^{-2} = \frac{1}{4^2} = \frac{1}{16}\right]$
- $\log_7 7 = 1$ [The power to which you put 7 to get 7: $7^1 = 7$]

Properties of logs with a positive base

1. $\log_a 1 = 0$, where a is any base (because $a^0 = 1$ for all $a \neq 0$).
2. $\log_a$ (negative number) does not exist where a is any base.
3. $\log_a b =$ negative number, if $0 < b < 1$ and $a > 1$, $a, b \in \mathbb{R}$.
   Example: $\log_2\left(\frac{1}{4}\right) = -2$ [$\log_a$ (positive proper fraction) = negative number]
4. $\log_a a = 1$, where a is any base (because $a^1 = a$).

ACTIVITY 33

ACTION
Getting out of logs ('hooshing')

OBJECTIVE
To learn how to effortlessly turn logs into their exponential expressions

Getting out of logs

Remember a log is just a **power**.

There are two different ways of asking the question: To what power do you put 3 in order to get 9?

$\log_3 9 = \square$ This is the log form of the question.	*or*	$9 = 3^{\square}$ This is the power form of the question.

So a log statement has an equivalent power statement and vice versa.

$\log_3 9 = 2$	$\Leftrightarrow$	$9 = 3^2$
Log statement	and its equivalent	Power statement

In general: $\log_a y = x \Leftrightarrow y = a^x$

$\log_a y$ is a shorthand notation for asking a simple question: To what power do you raise a to get y?

Going from the log statement to the power statement is called 'getting out of logs'. For the example above, the process involves moving the 3 to the right, pushing the 2 up above it and crossing out the log, leaving the 9 behind. This process is unofficially called '**hooshing**'.

$\log_3 9 = 2$ *hoosh* $\Rightarrow 9 = 3^2$	and	$9 = 3^2$ $\Rightarrow \log_3 9 = 2$

- $\log_2 16 = 4 \Leftrightarrow 16 = 2^4$
- $\log_4 \frac{1}{2} = -2 \Leftrightarrow \frac{1}{2} = 4^{-2}$

ACTIVITY 34

ACTION
Adding logs

OBJECTIVE
To apply the rules of logs to simplify the addition of logs to the same base

The rules for manipulating logs

1. Addition

$\log_2 16 + \log_2 4 = 4 + 2 = 6 = \log_2 64$

This seems to indicate that $\log_2 16 + \log_2 4 = \log_2 (16 \times 4)$.

$$\log_a x + \log_a y = \log_a(xy)$$

TIP
You can only add logs with the same base when applying this rule.

The rule can be extended to the addition of many logs:

$\log_a x_1 + \log_a x_2 + \log_a x_3 + \cdots + \log_a x_n = \log_a(x_1 \times x_2 \times \cdots \times x_n)$

- $\log_3 4 + \log_3 \frac{1}{2} + \log_2 3 = \log_2(4 \times \frac{1}{2} \times 3) = \log_2 6$
- $\log_a y + \log_a y^2 + \log_a x + \log_a 2 = \log_a (2xy^3)$

EXAMPLE 6

Simplify $\log_7\left(\frac{1}{2}\right) + \log_7\left(\frac{2}{x-1}\right) + \log_7(7x-7)$.

Solution

$\log_7\left(\frac{1}{2}\right) + \log_7\left(\frac{2}{x-1}\right) + \log_7(7x-7)$

$= \log_7\left(\frac{1}{2} \times \frac{2}{x-1} \times 7x - 7\right)$

$= \log_7\left(\frac{1}{2} \times \frac{2}{(x-1)} \times 7(x-1)\right)$

$= \log_7 7$

$= 1$

ACTIVITY 35

ACTION
Subtracting logs

OBJECTIVE
To apply the rules of logs to simplify the subtraction of logs to the same base

2. Subtraction

$\log_2 16 - \log_2 8 = 4 - 3 = 1 = \log_2 2$

This seems to indicate $\log_2 16 - \log_2 8 = \log_2\left(\frac{16}{8}\right)$.

$$\log_a x - \log_a y = \log_a\left(\frac{x}{y}\right)$$

TIP
You can only subtract logs with the same base when applying this rule.

- $\log_6 18 - \log_6\left(\frac{1}{2}\right) = \log_6\left(\frac{18}{\frac{1}{2}}\right) = \log_6 36 = 2$
- $\log_k 6(x+2)^3 - \log_k 3(x+2)^4 = \log_k\left(\frac{6(x+2)^3}{3(x+2)^4}\right) = \log_k\left(\frac{2}{x+2}\right)$
- $\log_b x - \log_b y - \log_b z = \log_b\left(\frac{x}{y}\right) - \log_b z = \log_b\left(\frac{\frac{x}{y}}{z}\right) = \log_b\left(\frac{x}{yz}\right)$

ACTIVITY 36

ACTION
Multiplying logs by a number

OBJECTIVE
To apply the rules of logs to simplify logs that have been multiplied by a number

3. Multiplication by a number

$3\log_2 4 = 3 \times 2 = 6 = \log_2 64$

This seems to indicate $3\log_2 4 = \log_2 (4)^3$.

$$k\log_a x = \log_a (x)^k$$

- $4\log_2 5 = \log_2 (5)^4 = \log_2 625$
- $-\frac{1}{2}\log_3 7 = \log_3 (7)^{-\frac{1}{2}} = \log_3\left(\frac{1}{\sqrt{7}}\right)$
- $x\log_e 2 = \log_e (2)^x = \log_e 2^x$
- $\frac{1}{2}\log_7 (x^2+1) = \log_7 (x^2+1)^{\frac{1}{2}} = \log_7 \sqrt{x^2+1}$

ACTIVITY 37

ACTION
Changing the base of logs

OBJECTIVE
To learn how to go quickly from the log of one base to another

4. Change of base

When you convert a measurable quantity from one set of units to another, you have to multiply by a conversion factor.

For example: 1 inch = 2·54 cm = 2·54 × 1 cm. 2·54 is the conversion factor.

To investigate how to convert a log in one base to a log in another base, it is worthwhile comparing the log of the same expression in different bases.

- $\dfrac{\log_2 16}{\log_2 4} = \dfrac{4}{2} = 2 = \log_4 16$
- $\dfrac{\log_9 27}{\log_9 3} = \dfrac{\frac{3}{2}}{\frac{1}{2}} = 3 = \log_3 27$

Can you see the pattern?

- $\dfrac{\log_b x}{\log_b a} = \log_a x.$

$$\log_a x = \frac{\log_b x}{\log_b a}$$

This is known as the change of base property.

It changes $\log_a x$ to $\log_b x$ by multiplying $\log_b x$ by the conversion factor of $\dfrac{1}{\log_b a}$.

A special case: If $x = b$, $\log_a b = \dfrac{\log_b b}{\log_b a} = \dfrac{1}{\log_b a}$

$$\log_a b = \frac{1}{\log_b a}$$

TIP

If you invert a log, you interchange the base with the expression inside the log.

- $\log_3 (x-1) = \dfrac{\log_2 (x-1)}{\log_2 3}$ [Changing base 3 to base 2]
- $\log_a x = \dfrac{\log_e x}{\log_e a} = \log_e x \times \log_a e$ [Changing base a to base e and invert]
- $\log_{16} 8 = \dfrac{1}{\log_8 16}$ [Invert]
- $\dfrac{1}{\log_x 15} = \log_{15} x$ [Invert]

5. All the log rules together

1. Breaking down the log of a complicated expression into a string of individual logs

Remember:

(a) Multiplication → (+) logs (addition)

(b) Division → (−) logs (subtraction)

(c) Power → Multiplies logs

- $\log_4\left(\dfrac{3x^2}{4y}\right) = \log_4 3 + \log_4 x^2 - \log_4 4 - \log_4 y = \log_4 3 + 2\log_4 x - 1 - \log_4 y$

- $\log_2\left(\dfrac{\sqrt{1-x^2}}{(4+x^3)^5}\right) = \log_2(1-x^2)^{\frac{1}{2}} - \log_2(4+x^3)^5 = \dfrac{1}{2}\log_2(1-x^2) - 5\log_2(4+x^3)$

- $\log_3\left\{\dfrac{2x-1}{(4x+1)(x-2)}\right\}^{\frac{3}{2}} = \dfrac{3}{2}\log_3\left(\dfrac{2x-1}{(4x+1)(x-2)}\right)$

  $= \dfrac{3}{2}\{\log_3(2x-1) - \log_3(4x+1) - \log_3(x-2)\}$

EXAMPLE 7

The magnitude M of an earthquake on the Richter scale is given by $M = \log_{10}\left(\dfrac{E}{E_0}\right)^{\frac{2}{3}}$, where E is the energy, in joules, released in the earthquake and $E_0 = 10^{4\cdot 4}$ J.

(a) Show that $M = \frac{2}{3}[\log_{10} E - \log_{10} E_0]$.

(b) Evaluate $\log_{10} E_0$.

(c) The 1906 San Francisco earthquake released 6×10^{16} J of energy. What was its magnitude on the Richter scale, if $\log_{10} 6 = 0\cdot778$?

Solution

(a) $M = \log_{10}\left(\dfrac{E}{E_0}\right)^{\frac{2}{3}} \Rightarrow M = \dfrac{2}{3}\log_{10}\left(\dfrac{E}{E_0}\right)$

$= \frac{2}{3}[\log_{10} E - \log_{10} E_0]$

(b) $\log_{10} E_0 = \log_{10} 10^{4\cdot 4} = 4\cdot 4\log_{10} 10 = 4\cdot 4$

(c) $M = \frac{2}{3}[\log_{10}(6 \times 10^{16}) - 4\cdot 4]$

$= \frac{2}{3}[\log_{10} 6 + \log_{10} 10^{16} - 4\cdot 4]$

$= \frac{2}{3}[0\cdot 778 + 16 - 4\cdot 4]$

$= \frac{2}{3}(12\cdot 378) = 8\cdot 252$

2. Combining a string of individual logs into a single log

Remember:

(a) (+) Logs → Multiply together on the top

(b) (−) Logs → Multiply together on the bottom

(c) A number multiplying a log moves into the log as a power

- $2\log_2 x - 3\log_2 y = \log_2 x^2 - \log_2 y^3 = \log_2\left(\dfrac{x^2}{y^3}\right)$

- $\log_4 8(x^2-1) - \log_4(x+1) - \log_4(x-1) = \log_4\left\{\dfrac{8(x^2-1)}{(x+1)(x-1)}\right\}$

  $= \log_4\left\{\dfrac{8(x-1)(x+1)}{(x+1)(x-1)}\right\}$

  $= \log_4 8 = \frac{3}{2}$

3. Two log tricks

(a) $\log_a x = y \Leftrightarrow x = a^y = a^{\log_a x}$

$\therefore a^{\log_a x} = x$

(b) $\log_a(a^x) = x\log_a a = x$

$\therefore \log_a(a^x) = x$

- $2^{\log_2 5} = 5$
- $e^{\log_e 7} = 7$
- $\log_8 8^{\frac{1}{2}} = \frac{1}{2}$
- $\log_e e^{2x} = 2x$

EXERCISE 10

1. Evaluate the following exactly:

(a) $\log_{10} 100$

(b) $\log_{10}(10^{-5})$

(c) $\log_{10}\left(\frac{1}{10}\right)$

(d) $\log_e \sqrt{e}$

(e) $\log_k\left(\frac{1}{k}\right)$

(f) $\log_p\left(\frac{1}{p^2}\right)$

(g) $\log_5 \sqrt[3]{25}$

(h) $\log_{\frac{1}{2}} 16$

(i) $\log_{\sqrt{2}} 4$

(j) $\log_{\frac{1}{9}} 27$

2. Write the following logs in exponential (power) form:

(a) $\log_{17} 289 = 2$

(b) $\log_4 16 = 2$

(c) $\log_4\left(\frac{1}{16}\right) = -2$

(d) $\log_{16} 4 = \frac{1}{2}$

(e) $\log_{16}\left(\frac{1}{4}\right) = -\frac{1}{2}$

(f) $\log_3 3 = 1$

(g) $\log_a 1 = 0$

(h) $\log_b a = c$

(i) $\log_8 16 = \frac{4}{3}$

(j) $\log_{16} 8 = \frac{3}{4}$

3. Write the following as a single log (in the form $\log_a x$) and simplify, where possible:

(a) $\log_2 3 + \log_2 5$

(b) $\log_3 a + \log_3 4a$

(c) $\log_e(1-x) + \log_e(1+x)$

(d) $\log_5 7 + \log_5 \frac{1}{7}$

(e) $\log_5 \sqrt{y} + \log_5 \sqrt{y}$

(f) $\log_4(x-1) + \log_4(x^2+x+1)$

(g) $\log_3 e^x + \log_3 e^{2x-1}$

(h) $\log_x\left(\frac{x^4}{y}\right) + \log_x\left(\frac{y}{x^3}\right)$

(i) $\log_k(x^2-1) + \log_k\left(\frac{1}{x+1}\right)$

(j) $\log_x 2^x + \log_x 2^{-x}$

4. Write the following as a single log (in the form $\log_a x$):

(a) $\log_2 6 - \log_2 3$

(b) $\log_3 3a - \log_3 a$

(c) $\log_e(x^2-1) - \log_e(x+1)$

(d) $\log_5 7 - \log_5\left(\frac{1}{7}\right)$

(e) $\log_4(x^3-1) - \log_4(x^2+x+1)$

(f) $\log_3 e^{x+1} - \log_3 e^{x-1}$

(g) $\log_9(3x+6) - \log_9(x+2)$

(h) $\log_b(ba+b^2) - \log_b(a+b)$

(i) $\log_{\sqrt{x}} \sqrt{xy} - \log_{\sqrt{x}} \sqrt{y}$

(j) $\log_a x - \log_a\left(\frac{1}{x}\right)$

5. Write the following as a single log (in the form $\log_a x$):

(a) $3\log_2 5$

(b) $-2\log_3 7$

(c) $\frac{1}{2}\log_4 25$

(d) $-\frac{3}{2}\log_2 36$

(e) $2\log_k y$

(f) $2\log_5\sqrt{1+x^2}$

(g) $-\frac{1}{2}\log_3 z^2y^2$

(h) $\frac{2}{3}\log_7 8y^{\frac{3}{2}}$

(i) $x\log_e 2$

(j) $\frac{1}{2}\log_5\left(\frac{1}{y^2}\right)$

6. (a) Write $\log_3 5$ in base 2.
   (b) Write $\log_7 4$ in base 5.
   (c) Write $\log_a y$ in base b.
   (d) Write $\log_5(x-2)$ in base 7.
   (e) Write $\log_{10} a$ in base e.
   (f) Write $\log_5 3$ in base 3.
   (g) Write $\log_4 x$ in base x.
   (h) Write $\log_x 5$in base 5.
   (i) Write $\dfrac{1}{\log_2 x}$ in base x.
   (j) Write $\dfrac{1}{\log_e x}$ in base x.

7. (a) Write the following as a string of logs:
   (i) $\log_a x^2\sqrt{y}$
   (ii) $\log_2(u^2v^3)$
   (iii) $\log_5\left(\dfrac{3\sqrt{x}}{p^2q^3}\right)$
   (iv) $\log_3\left(\dfrac{27x^3}{3y^6}\right)$
   (v) $\log_a\left(\dfrac{1}{a^2}\right)$
   (vi) $\log_k(x+3)^2(2x-1)^3$
   (vii) $\log_2\left(\dfrac{(x+7)^7}{4\sqrt{2x-3}}\right)$
   (viii) $\log_5\left(\dfrac{x-1}{x+1}\right)^{\frac{1}{2}}$

   (b) If $a=\log_{10}2$ and $b=\log_{10}3$, express the following in terms of a and b:
   (i) $\log_{10}6$
   (ii) $\log_{10}24$
   (iii) $\log_{10}\left(\dfrac{9}{8}\right)$
   (iv) $\log_{10}60$
   (v) $\log_{10}30$
   (vi) $\log_{10}81$
   (vii) $\log_{10}\left(\dfrac{16}{27}\right)$
   (viii) $\log_{10}\left(\dfrac{400}{27}\right)$
   (ix) $\log_{10}48$
   (x) $\log_3 12$

8. (a) Write the following as a single log and hence, evaluate exactly, where possible:
   (i) $\log_{10}25+\log_{10}4$
   (ii) $\log_3 21-\log_3 7$
   (iii) $\frac{1}{2}\log_{10}4+\log_{10}35-\log_{10}7$
   (iv) $\log_3 2+2\log_3 3-\log_3 18$

   (b) Write the following as a single log:
   (i) $2\log_5 x+\log_5 y$
   (ii) $3\log_k x+2\log_k y-\frac{1}{4}\log_k z$
   (iii) $\frac{1}{2}\log_3(x-1)-\frac{3}{2}\log_3(x+1)$
   (iv) $7\{\log_3(x+5)+\log_3 2-3\log_3(4x-1)\}$
   (v) $\log_4 a^2+\log_4\frac{1}{a}+\log_4\sqrt{a}$
   (vi) $\frac{1}{4}\log_a(x^2+3x+2)+\frac{1}{4}\log_a\left(\dfrac{x+1}{x+2}\right)$
   (vii) $\frac{1}{2}\{\log_e 9-3\log_e(x^2+1)+2\log_e(3x+2)\}$
   (viii) $x\log_e x-\frac{1}{2}\log_e x+e\log_e x$

9. If $\log_2 y=\log_2 x+2$, show that $y=4x$.

10. If $\log_e A+2\log_e y=3\log_e y+D$, show that $y=Ae^{-D}$.

11. If $f(x)=\log_a x$, show that
$$\frac{f(x+h)-f(x)}{(x+h)-x}=\log_a\left(1+\frac{h}{x}\right)^{\frac{1}{h}}.$$

12. If $\log_5 y=2\log_5 x-\log_5(x+1)+c$, show that $y=\dfrac{x^2}{x+1}5^c$.

13. Use the rules of logs to show that:

(a) $\log_a a^x = x$

(b) $a^{\log_a x} = x$

14. Simplify the following:

(a) $\log_3 3^7$

(b) $3^{\log_3 4}$

(c) $\log_5 \sqrt{5}$

(d) $10^{\log_{10} 3}$

(e) $\log_x (x^8)$

(f) $e^{\frac{1}{2}\log_e x}$

Check the answers to **(a)**, **(b)**, **(c)** and **(d)** on your calculator.

15. **(a)** Using $\log_b a = \dfrac{\log_c a}{\log_c b}$, solve for $\log_c a$.

Hence, simplify:

$\log_2 3 \times \log_3 4 \times \log_4 5 \times \log_5 6 \times \log_6 7 \times \log_7 8$

(b) Simplify:

$\log_2 2 \times \log_2 4 \times \log_2 8 \times \ldots \times \log_2 2^n$

16. Show that:

(a) $\log_a (x + \sqrt{x^2 - 1}) + \log_a (x - \sqrt{x^2 - 1}) = 0$

(b) $\log_b (\sqrt{x} + \sqrt{x - 1}) + \log_b (\sqrt{x} - \sqrt{x - 1}) = 0$

17. The loudness L of a sound in decibels is given by $L = 10 \log_{10} \left(\dfrac{I}{I_0}\right)$, where I is the intensity of the sound in W m^{-2} and $I_0 = 10^{-12}$ W m^{-2}.

(a) Find:

(i) the loudness in decibels of normal conversation which has an intensity of $I = 10^{-7}$ W m^{-1},

(ii) the loudness of amplified rock music which has an intensity of 10^{-1} W m^{-2}.

(b) If a sound has a loudness L_1 for intensity I_1 and loudness L_2 for intensity $1000I_1$, show that $L_2 - L_1 = 30$.

18. Show that $\dfrac{1}{\log_2 x} + \dfrac{1}{\log_3 x} + \dfrac{1}{\log_4 x} + \dfrac{1}{\log_5 x} + \dfrac{1}{\log_6 x} = \dfrac{1}{\log_{720} x}$.

19. Evaluate the following exactly:

(a) $\log_3 3^{54}$

(b) $3^{\log_3 5 - \log_3 2}$

(c) $10^{2 - \log_{10} 2}$

(d) $\log_3 8 \times \log_8 9$

20. If $\log_{10} x = (1 + p)$ and $\log_{10} y = (1 - p)$, show that $xy = 100$.

REVISION QUESTIONS

1. **(a)** Express $\dfrac{3-\sqrt{5}}{3+\sqrt{5}}$ in the form $\dfrac{a-b\sqrt{5}}{2}$, $a, b \in \mathbb{N}$.
   (b) If $2x-1$ is a factor of $2x^3+x^2+kx+6$, $k \in \mathbb{Z}$, find k and the other factors.
   (c) If $ax+b$ is a factor of $2ax^2+(2b-a)x+c$, find the second factor and show that $b=-c$.

2. **(a)** If $x=1-\sqrt{3}$ and $y=1+\sqrt{3}$, express $\dfrac{y-x}{xy}$ in the form $a\sqrt{b}$, $a \in \mathbb{Z}$, $b \in \mathbb{N}$.
   (b) Simplify $\dfrac{4}{x^2+12x+20}-\dfrac{3}{x^2+14x+40}$.
   (c) If $\dfrac{a}{b}=\dfrac{c}{d}$, show that $\dfrac{a^2-b^2}{a^2+b^2}=\dfrac{c^2-d^2}{c^2+d^2}$.

3. **(a)** If $5x^2-20x+8=a(x+b)^2+c$ for all x, find $a, b, c \in \mathbb{Z}$.
   (b) If $\dfrac{ax}{b-c}=\dfrac{by}{2(c-a)}=\dfrac{cz}{3(a-b)}$, show that $6ax+3by+2cz=0$.
   (c) Express $\left(x^2+\sqrt{2}+\dfrac{1}{x^2}\right)\left(x^2-\sqrt{2}+\dfrac{1}{x^2}\right)$ in the form $x^n+\dfrac{1}{x^n}$, where $n \in \mathbb{N}$.

4. **(a)** Show that $\dfrac{3x-5}{x-2}+\dfrac{1}{2-x}$, $x \neq 2$, simplifies to a constant.
   (b) Express $\dfrac{\sqrt{x}}{\sqrt{x}-1}+\dfrac{\sqrt{x}}{\sqrt{x}+1}$ as a single fraction.
   (c) (i) If $a-b(c-x)^2=6x-7-x^2$ for all $x \in \mathbb{R}$. Find $a, b, c \in \mathbb{N}$.
   (ii) If x^2+x+1 is a factor of $2x^3+ax^2-x+b$, find $a, b \in \mathbb{Z}$.

5. **(a)** Expand $(p+q)^3$.
   (b) What is the term with q^3 in the expansion of $(p+q)^7$?
   (c) Show that $p^3+q^3-(p+q)^3=-3pq(p+q)$.

6. **(a)** Show that $\dfrac{3}{1+x^p}+\dfrac{3}{1+x^{-p}}$ simplifies to a constant.
   (b) (i) Express $\dfrac{6y}{x(x+4y)}-\dfrac{3}{2x}$ as a single fraction.
   (ii) If $2x-\sqrt{3}$ is a factor of $4x^2-kx+\sqrt{3}$, find the other factor and $k \in \mathbb{R}$.
   (c) If x^2-ax-3 is a factor of x^3-5x^2+bx+9, find $a, b \in \mathbb{N}$.

7. **(a)** If $x=999\,999\,999\,999$, evaluate $\dfrac{x^2-4}{x-2}$ exactly.
   (b) (i) Evaluate $\dfrac{\sqrt{10^{2009}}}{\sqrt{10^{2011}}-\sqrt{10^{2007}}}$ exactly.
   (ii) Simplify $\left(1+\sqrt{2x^2}\right)^2-\sqrt{8x^2}$.
   (c) Show: **(i)** $2^{n+1}+2^n=3\times 2^n$
   (ii) $\dfrac{3^{2008}+3^{2011}}{3^{2009}+3^{2010}}=\dfrac{7}{3}$
   (iii) $\dfrac{5\times 2^x-8\times 2^{x-2}}{2^x-2^{x-1}}=6$

8. The number of phones produced by a factory per week is given by $N_1=50x^{\frac{1}{2}}y^{\frac{3}{2}}$, where x is the average number of workers that attend per week and y is the average number of hours worked by each worker per week.
   (a) Find the number of phones produced in a week in which the average attendance is 256 workers and the average number of hours worked is 36.
   (b) For another factory producing the same phone $N_2=20x^{\frac{3}{2}}y^{\frac{1}{2}}$. Find the number of phones produced by this factory in a week in which the average attendance is 256 workers and the average number of hours worked is 36.
   (c) Show that $\dfrac{N_1}{N_2}=\dfrac{5y}{2x}$.
   (d) Show that for a 40-hour week in each factory, an attendance of 100 workers in each will produce the same number of phones per week.

9. The stopping distances in metres (m) of a car travelling at v km/h is given by $S_1=\dfrac{v^{\frac{5}{3}}}{20}$ for a wet road and $S_2=\dfrac{v^{\frac{4}{3}}}{6}$ for a dry road.
   (a) Copy and complete the table below. Give the values in the last two columns, correct to two decimal places, and make a conclusion.

v km/h	$v^{\frac{5}{3}}$	$v^{\frac{4}{3}}$	S_1	S_2
27				
64				
125				

   (b) Show that $\dfrac{S_1}{S_2}=\dfrac{3\sqrt[3]{v}}{10}$.

(c) If the speed of a car is 74·088 km/h, compare its stopping distance on a wet road to that on a dry road.

(d) At $v = \frac{1000}{27}$ km/h, show that $S_1 = S_2$.

10. **(a)** Show that $\dfrac{\log_{10} x^6 - \log_{10} x^3}{\log_{10} x^2 - \log_{10} x} = 3$.

(b) If $\dfrac{\log_2 a}{p} = \dfrac{\log_2 b}{2p} = \dfrac{\log_2 c}{3p} = \log_2 x$,

show that $\dfrac{b^2}{ac} = 1$.

(c) If $x^2 + y^2 = 14xy$, show that $(x + y)^2 = 16xy$.

Hence, show that $\dfrac{\log_a x + \log_a y}{2} = \log_a\left(\dfrac{x+y}{4}\right)$.

11. The power P of a lens is given by $P = \frac{1}{f}$ where f is its focal length in metres (m).

(a) The focal length of lens A is x m. Write down an expression for its power, in terms of x.

Lens A

(b) Lens B has a focal length of $-(x + 2)$ m. Write down an expression for the power of lens B, in terms of x.

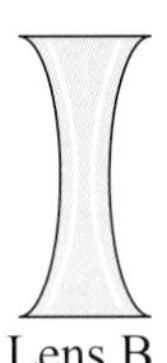
Lens B

(c) When lens A and B are combined, the power of the combination is obtained by adding their powers together. Find an expression for the power of the combination as a single fraction, in terms of x.

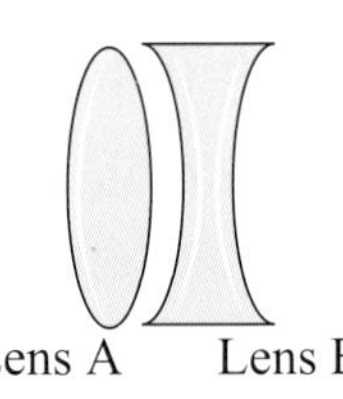
Lens A Lens B

(d) If $x = \frac{1}{2}$, find the power of this combination as a fraction. If the focal length of the combination is one divided by the power, find this focal length as a fraction.

12. **(a)** A boy rows downstream for 2 km at a speed of $(x - 2)$ km/h from a point A to point B. Write down an expression for the time of the journey in terms of x, $x > 0$.

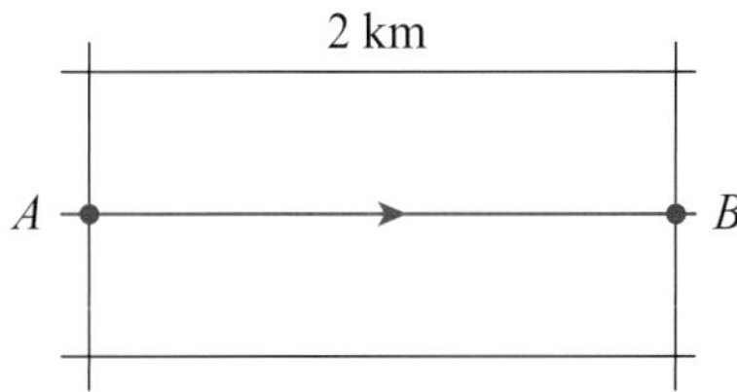

(b) A man rows the same journey at a speed of $(x + 2)$ km/h. Write down an expression for the time he takes.

(c) Which one takes the shorter time? Why?

(d) Write down an expression for the difference in times. Give your answer as a single fraction in the form $\dfrac{a}{x^2 - b^2}$.

(e) If $x = 12$, find this difference to the nearest second.

13. **(a)** The number of bacteria in a sample A after t minutes is given by $50 \times 2^{t+6}$.

Express this number in the form $a \times 2^t$. Find the number of bacteria initially in the sample.

(b) The number of bacteria in a sample B after t minutes is given by the expression 100×4^t.

Write this expression in the form $b \times 2^{2t}$. Find the number of bacteria initially in this sample.

(c) Find the ratio of the number of bacteria in sample B to that in sample A after t minutes in the form 2^p. What is this ratio after:

(i) 2 minutes,

(ii) 5 minutes,

(iii) 10 minutes?

(d) Make a conclusion.

SUMMARY

1. Combining terms:

   Multiply out brackets term by term and combine like terms.

   Difference of two squares: $(a - b)(a + b) = (a)^2 - (b)^2$

   Perfect square: $(a + b)^2 = (a)^2 + 2(a)(b) + (b)^2$

2. Evaluating algebraic expressions:

   Put brackets around the variables and then substitute the given values.

3. Binomial theorem:

   (a) $(x + y)^n = {}^nC_0(x)^n(y)^0 + {}^nC_1(x)^{n-1}(y)^1 + {}^nC_2(x)^{n-2}(y)^2 + \ldots + {}^nC_n(x)^0(y)^n$

   (b) In $(p + 2q)^7$ the fifth term is given by ${}^7C_4(p)^{(7-4)}(2q)^4$

4. Factorisation:

   Steps: **(a)** Take out the HCF.

   (b) Factorise what is left by one of the following methods:

   (i) grouping

   (ii) trinomials

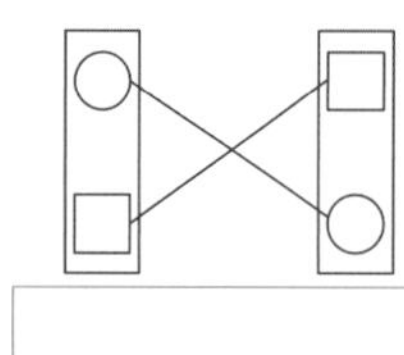

   (iii) difference of two squares: $(a)^2 - (b)^2 = ((a) - (b))((a) + (b))$

   (iv) sum of two cubes: $(a)^3 + (b)^3 = ((a) + (b))((a)^2 - (a)(b) + (b)^2)$

   (v) difference of two cubes: $(a)^3 - (b)^3 = ((a) - (b))\,((a)^2 + (a)(b) + (b)^2)$

5. Polynomials:

   (a) Types

   (i) Linear $ax + b$ (L)

   (ii) Quadratic $ax^2 + bx + c$ (Q)

   (iii) Cubic $ax^3 + bx^2 + cx + d$ (C)

   (b) Multiplication

   (i) $\text{L} \times \text{L} = \text{Q}$

   (ii) $\text{L} \times \text{L} \times \text{L} = \text{C}$

   (iii) $\text{L} \times \text{Q} = \text{C}$

   (c) Division

   (i) $\frac{\text{Q}}{\text{L}} = \text{L}$

   (ii) $\frac{\text{C}}{\text{Q}} = \text{L}$

   (iii) $\frac{\text{C}}{\text{L}} = \text{Q}$

   Division can be done by the division process or by factorisation with lining up.

6. Rational expressions:

   (a) Addition and subtraction: common denominator

   (b) Multiplication: multiply the tops and multiply the bottoms (cancel)

   (c) Division: invert the divisor and multiply or multiply above and below by the common denominator of all fractions

7. Exponential expressions:

(a) $a^p a^q = a^{p+q}$

(b) $\dfrac{a^p}{a^q} = a^{p-q}$

(c) $(a^p)^q = a^{pq}$

(d) $a^0 = 1$

(e) $a^{-p} = \dfrac{1}{a^p}$

(f) $a^{\frac{1}{q}} = \sqrt[q]{a}$

(g) $a^{\frac{p}{q}} = \sqrt[q]{a^p} = (\sqrt[q]{a})^p$

(h) $(ab)^p = a^p b^p$

(i) $\left(\dfrac{a}{b}\right)^p = \dfrac{a^p}{b^p}$

8. Surds:

(a) Addition and subtraction: add and subtract like terms

(b) Multiplication

(i) $\sqrt{a} \times \sqrt{b} = \sqrt{ab}$

(ii) Conjugate surds

$(\sqrt{a}-\sqrt{b})(\sqrt{a}+\sqrt{b})=a-b$

(c) Division: $\dfrac{\sqrt{a}}{\sqrt{b}} = \sqrt{\dfrac{a}{b}}$

(d) Rationalising the denominator – multiply above and below by the conjugate of the denominator

(e) Properties of surds

(i) $(\sqrt{a})^p = \sqrt{a^p} = a^{\frac{p}{2}}$

(ii) $(\sqrt{a})^2 = a$

(iii) $a\sqrt{a} = \sqrt{a^2} \times \sqrt{a} = \sqrt{a^3}$

9. Logs:

(a) Definition: $\log_a y = x \Leftrightarrow y = a^x$

(b) Properties of logs

(i) $\log_a (xy) = \log_a x + \log_a y$

(ii) $\log_a \left(\dfrac{x}{y}\right) = \log_a x - \log_a y$

(iii) $\log_a (x^q) = q \log_a x$

(iv) $\log_a 1 = 0$

(v) $\log_a \left(\dfrac{1}{x}\right) = \log_a 1 - \log_a x = -\log_a x$

(vi) $\log_a (a^x) = x \log_a a = x$

(vii) $a^{\log_a x} = x$

(viii) $\log_a b = \dfrac{1}{\log_b a}$

(ix) $\log_b a = \dfrac{\log_c a}{\log_c b}$

Algebraic Equations

Modelling a problem mathematically means expressing words in the form of equations that are true statements involving the unknown quantities. The golden rule of equations: Do unto one side of the equation what you do to the other side.

Chapter 6 Polynomial Equations

Learning Outcomes

- To solve linear equations.
- To solve quadratic equations by factorisation, completing the square and using the quadratic formula.
- To solve cubic equations.
- To model and solve word problems leading to linear, quadratic and cubic equations.

Introducing equations

An equation is a mathematical statement with two sides. An equation consists of a left-hand side (LHS) and a right-hand side (RHS) with an equality sign (=) between them.

Equation: LHS = RHS

Solving an equation means finding the values of the unknown quantity (variable) which make the statement true.

Example: $\underbrace{3x + 2}_{\text{LHS}} = \underbrace{5}_{\text{RHS}}$

The value of 1 for the unknown value x makes this statement true. The value 1 for x that makes the statement true is known as a solution or root of the equation. The process of finding the solutions of an equation is known as solving the equation.

➲ An equation behaves like a balance. Whatever you do to one side, you must do to the other side to maintain equilibrium.

When you solve an equation, you should substitute the values obtained back into the original equation to check whether or not they make the statement true. Only those values that satisfy the original equation are acceptable solutions (roots).

The basic technique for solving all equations: Whatever operation you do to one side of an equation, you must do exactly the same operation to the other side of the equation.

Polynomial equations

Polynomial equations are equations of the form:

$a_n x^n + a_{n-1}x^{n-1} + a_{n-2}x^{n-2} + \ldots + a_0 = 0$, where $n \in \mathbb{N}$ and $a_n, a_{n-1}, \ldots, a_0$ are constants.

The fundamental theorem of algebra states that a polynomial equation of degree n has exactly n roots. Therefore:

(i) A quadratic equation $ax^2 + bx + c = 0$ has exactly two roots and

(ii) A cubic equation $ax^3 + bx^2 + cx + d = 0$ has exactly three roots.

However, it is important to state that all the roots may not be real roots. Some, or all, of the roots may be complex.

6.1 Linear equations

ACTIVITY 1

ACTION
Interpreting linear equations

OBJECTIVE
To write linear equations in the form $y = ax + b$ and hence find the x and y intercepts

A linear equation is an equation that can be written in the form $ax^1 + b = 0$, where $a \neq 0$, b are fixed numbers.

a is called the coefficient of x.

b is called the constant term.

The equation is linear because the highest power of the variable x in the equation is 1.

Method of solution

$$ax + b = 0$$
$$ax = -b$$
$$x = -\frac{b}{a}$$

This is the one, and only one, solution (root) of a linear equation. Every linear equation has one and only one root.

▸ $3x + 2 = 0$
$$3x = -2$$
$$x = -\frac{2}{3}$$

WORKED EXAMPLE Graphical solution of a linear equation

(a) $y = f(x) = ax + b$ is the equation of a straight line.

(b) $y = 0$ is the equation of the x-axis.

The solution of $ax + b = 0$ is the value of x at which the straight line crosses the x-axis. Its value is $x = -\frac{b}{a}$.

▸ Find where $y = 4x - 8$ crosses the x-axis:

$4x - 8 = 0$

$x = 2$

Therefore, $y = 4x - 8$ crosses the x-axis at (2, 0).

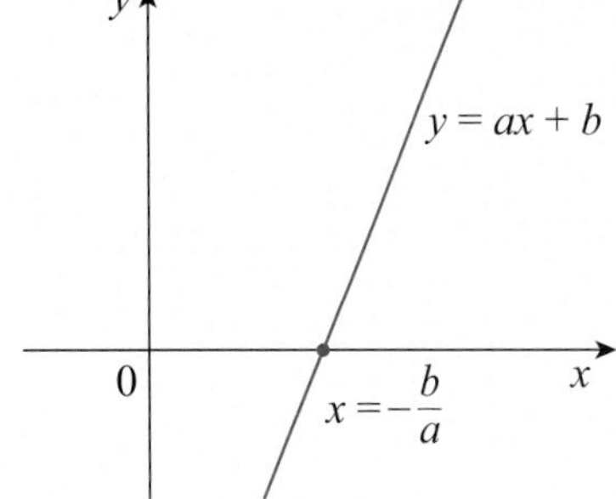

In general, finding the points at which a curve $y = f(x)$ crosses the x-axis means exactly the same thing as solving the equation $f(x) = 0$ or finding the roots of the equation $f(x) = 0$.

Steps for solving linear equations

1. Clear all fractions by multiplying all terms on each side by the common denominator of all terms.
2. Multiply out all brackets.
3. Tidy up each side by combining like terms.
4. Get the variables (usually x) on one side and the numbers on the other side.
5. Solve for the variable (usually x).

EXAMPLE 1

Solve for x: $\frac{x-8}{7} - \frac{x-3}{3} = \frac{5}{21}$

Solution

$\frac{(x-8)}{7} - \frac{(x-3)}{3} = \frac{(5)}{21}$ [Put brackets around terms on top before multiplying by 21.]

$\frac{21(x-8)}{7} - \frac{21(x-3)}{3} = \frac{21(5)}{21}$

$3(x-8) - 7(x-3) = (5)$

$3x - 24 - 7x + 21 = 5$

$-4x - 3 = 5$

$-4x = 5 + 3$

$-4x = 8$

$x = \frac{8}{-4}$

$x = -2$

Checking a solution

To show that a value is a solution of an equation, substitute it back into the original equation.

EXAMPLE 2

Investigate if $g = \frac{1}{2}$ is a solution of $\frac{2g-2}{4} - \frac{g}{4} = 1$.

Solution

LHS	RHS
$\frac{(2g-2)}{4} - \frac{(g)}{4}$	1
$\boldsymbol{g = \frac{1}{2}}$: $\frac{2\left(\frac{1}{2}\right) - 2}{4} - \frac{\left(\frac{1}{2}\right)}{4}$	
$= -\frac{3}{8}$	

LHS ≠ RHS. It is not a solution.

Mathematical modelling (word problems)

WORKED EXAMPLE

Modelling a linear problem

A pipe 55 cm in length is cut into three pieces: a long piece, a short piece and an intermediate-length piece. The short piece is 20 cm shorter than the long piece. The long piece is twice as long as the intermediate piece. What are the lengths of all three pieces?

This is an example of a mathematical problem that is stated in words (a word problem). Mathematical modelling is the technique of translating these words into a mathematical equation and hence solving it.

1. Read the problem carefully and draw a diagram, if appropriate.
2. Assign a variable to one of the quantities to be found and hence assign variables to the other quantities.

   Let x = length of the intermediate piece

Long	Intermediate	Short
$2x$	x	$(2x - 20)$

3. Translate the word problem into an equation:

   $2x + x + (2x - 20) = 55$

   [All of the pieces add up to the total length.]
4. Solve the equation:

$$2x + x + 2x - 20 = 55$$
$$5x - 20 = 55$$
$$5x = 75$$
$$x = 15$$

5. List all answers:

Long	Intermediate	Short
30 cm	15 cm	10 cm

ACTIVITY 2

ACTION
Learning techniques for modelling linear problems

OBJECTIVE
To learn some basic techniques to aid the modelling of linear problems

EXAMPLE 3

Four consecutive integers add to –38. What are they?

Solution

1. Consecutive integers mean adding 1 to one of them gives the next one.
2. Let x = smallest integer

   The four consecutive integers are: (x), $(x + 1)$, $(x + 2)$, $(x + 3)$.
3. $x + (x + 1) + (x + 2) + (x + 3) = -38$ [They add to –38.]
4. $x + x + 1 + x + 2 + x + 3 = -38$

$$4x + 6 = -38$$
$$4x = -44$$
$$x = -11$$

5. The integers are –11, –10, –9, –8.

EXAMPLE 4

Part of €3000 was invested at 6% per annum (p.a.) and the remainder was invested at 5% per annum. If the total interest earned at the end of the first year was €167, find the amount invested at each rate.

Solution

1. $6\% = 0{\cdot}06 = \dfrac{6}{100}$

   $5\% = 0{\cdot}05 = \dfrac{5}{100}$
2. Let x = amount invested at 6%

   $(3000 - x)$ = amount invested at 5%
3. $x \times 0{\cdot}06 + (3000 - x) \times 0{\cdot}05 = 167$
4. $\dfrac{6x}{100} + \dfrac{(3000 - x)5}{100} = 167$

$$6x + 5(3000 - x) = 16\,700$$
$$6x + 15\,000 - 5x = 16\,700$$
$$x + 15\,000 = 16\,700$$
$$x = 16\,700 - 15\,000$$
$$x = 1700$$

5. €1700 at 6% p.a.

   €1300 at 5% p.a.

EXAMPLE 5

Eimear wants to get an A1 mark as an average for four Maths tests. To do this, her average mark must be 90 or more. In her first three tests, she scored 86, 91 and 94, respectively. What is the lowest mark she can get on the final test to get an A1?

Solution

1. Her total marks over four tests must be at least 360.
2. Let x = mark in the final test
3. $x + 86 + 91 + 94 = 360$
4. $x + 271 = 360$

   $x = 89$
5. The lowest mark is 89.

EXERCISE 1

Solve the following equations:

1. (a) $5 - 4(x - 3) = x - 2(x - 1)$

   (b) $0{\cdot}2(4 + 2f) - 0{\cdot}1(f + 2) = 2$

   (c) $2\left(x - \frac{3}{2}\right) - 6x = 3(x - 12) - 23$

   (d) $4 - 2\left(3x - \frac{7}{2}\right) = 3\left(2x - \frac{2}{3}\right) - 2\left(\frac{1}{2} - x\right)$

   (e) $3x - 2(x + 1) = -4(x - 2) - (1 - x)$

2. (a) $\frac{x}{2} = 1$

   (b) $\frac{1}{6x} = -\frac{2}{3}$

   (c) $\frac{1}{2}(x + 2) = 8$

   (d) $\frac{x + 3}{2} = 5$

   (e) $\frac{1}{3}(x - 4) = 1$

   (f) $\frac{x}{2} + \frac{x}{3} = \frac{5}{2}$

   (g) $\frac{3x}{4} - \frac{1}{2} = \frac{5x}{8}$

3. (a) $\frac{x - 8}{7} + \frac{x - 3}{3} = \frac{5}{21}$

   (b) $\frac{x + 3}{2} + \frac{2(2 - x)}{3} = \frac{3x + 1}{4} - 2$

   (c) $\frac{3}{2}(x - 1) - \frac{1}{4}(x - 19) = \frac{2}{3}(x + 2)$

   (d) $\frac{2(x - 2)}{5} - 2(x - 2) = \frac{4(1 - 2x)}{3}$

4. (a) Show that $x = 5$ is a solution of the equation $\frac{x}{2} + \frac{2x - 1}{6} = 4$.

   (b) Show that $x = 2$ is not a solution of $\frac{x + 4}{2} + x = 4$.

   (c) Investigate if $x = 1 - \sqrt{2}$ is a solution of $x(1 + \sqrt{2}) = -1$.

   (d) Find k, if $x = 1$ is a solution of $\frac{kx + 3}{4} - \frac{kx + 2}{3} = \frac{1}{2}$.

5. Solve the following:

   (a) A piece of rope, 92 cm long, is cut into two pieces so that the longest piece is three times the length of the shorter piece. How long are the two pieces?

   (b) The ratio of the length to breadth of a rectangle is 5:3. If the perimeter is 44 m, find the length, breadth and area of the rectangle.

   (c) A ribbon, 60 cm long, is cut into three pieces such that each piece is 5 cm longer than the next piece. Find the length of each piece.

   (d) The sum of two numbers is 20. If the difference between the bigger number and half the smaller number is 8, find the numbers.

   (e) If the sum of three consecutive even numbers is 48, find them.

   (f) If Sandra is two years older than Anna and the sum of half of Sandra's age and one-third of Anna's age is 11, what is the age of each girl?

   (g) The sum of three consecutive natural numbers, each of which is divisible by 3, is 72. Find the numbers.

(h) Polly and her **twin** brother will have a total age of 38 in four years' time. What are their present ages?

(i) Of 25 plants purchased, some cost €1·50 each and some cost €1 each. If the total cost was €33, how many of each were purchased?

(j) An electricity supply company has a fixed charge of €42 for every two months and 9·5c per unit of electricity used. If the Wilson family got a bill of €76·20 for the last two months, how many units of electricity did they use?

(k) The average of five consecutive natural numbers is 9. What are they?

(l) A car covers part of a 100 km journey at 60 km/h and the remainder at 80 km/h. If the total time for the journey was 1 hour 20 min, find the distance travelled at 80 km/h.

(m) Josh deposits €10 per week in a bank after an initial deposit of €500. His brother Noah deposits €6 per week after an initial deposit of €980. If they made their initial deposits at the same time, after how many weeks will they have the same amount of money in their accounts?

(n) The difference between half a number and one-third of the same number is 69. What is the number?

(o) A man is twice as old as his son now. If he was three times as old as his son 10 years ago, how old is each now?

6.2 Quadratic equations

A quadratic equation is an equation that can be written in the form $ax^2 + bx + c = 0$, where a, b, c are constants and $a \neq 0$.

a is called the coefficient to x^2 and must not be zero. (Why?)

b is called the coefficient of x.

c is called the constant term.

If the highest power of the variable in an equation is 2, the equation is a quadratic equation.

Methods of solution

There are three methods of solving quadratic equations:

1. Factorisation
2. Completing the square
3. The quadratic formula

1. Factorisation

Factorisation is the fastest way of solving quadratic equations. However, it does not always work. It depends on a fundamental idea in mathematics called the zero factor property, which states that if $pq = 0$, then $p = 0$ or $q = 0$, or both are equal to zero.

WORKED EXAMPLE Solving a quadratic by factorisation

Solve $6x^2 - x - 2 = 0$. This is a sum of three terms. Convert it into a product of two linear factors:

$(3x - 2)(2x + 1) = 0$

$\quad p \qquad\quad q$

By the zero factor property: $3x - 2 = 0$ *or* $2x + 1 = 0$

$3x = 2$	$2x = -1$
$x = \frac{2}{3}$	$x = -\frac{1}{2}$

1. These are the solutions or roots of the equation $6x^2 - x - 2 = 0$. They are the **only** numbers in the universe for which $6x^2 - x - 2 = 0$.
2. They are the points at which the curve $y = 6x^2 - x - 2$ crosses the x-axis.
3. You can check your solution by substituting them back into the LHS of the original expression:

   $6(x)^2 - (x) - 2$

   $\boldsymbol{x = \frac{2}{3}}$: $6\left(\frac{2}{3}\right)^2 - \left(\frac{2}{3}\right) - 2 = 6 \times \frac{4}{9} - \frac{2}{3} - 2 = 0$

   $\boldsymbol{x = -\frac{1}{2}}$: $6\left(-\frac{1}{2}\right)^2 - \left(-\frac{1}{2}\right) - 2 = 6 \times \frac{1}{4} + \frac{1}{2} - 2 = 0$

Summary of the process (Equation, Factors, Roots):
Equation: $6x^2 - x - 2 = 0$
Factors: $(3x - 2)(2x + 1) = 0$
Roots: $\frac{2}{3}, -\frac{1}{2}$

- Equation: $6x^2 - 3x = 0$
  Factors: $3x(2x - 1) = 0$ [Always take out the HCF first.]
  Roots: $0, \frac{1}{2}$

EXAMPLE 6

A variable current I in amps in an electric circuit after t seconds is given by $I = t^2 - 12t + 25$.

Find the times at which the current is 5 amps.

Solution

$I = t^2 - 12t + 25 = 5$

Equation: $t^2 - 12t + 20 = 0$

Factors: $(t - 2)(t - 10) = 0$

Roots:

$t - 2 = 0$	$t - 10 = 0$
$t = 2$	$t = 10$

Therefore, the current is 5 amps after 2 seconds and 10 seconds.

EXAMPLE 7

If $g = -3$ is a solution of the quadratic equation $kg^2 - 2kg - 60 = 0$, find $k \in \mathbb{R}$.

Solution

$kg^2 - 2kg - 60 = 0$

Since $g = -3$ is a solution of the equation, when you substitute in this value, it makes the equation true.

$k(g)^2 - 2k(g) - 60 = 0$

$\boldsymbol{g = -3}$: $k(-3)^2 - 2k(-3) - 60 = 0$

$9k + 6k - 60 = 0$

$15k = 60$

$k = 4$

2. Completing the square

You know how to square out a bracket in your head.

$(x + 3)^2 = x^2 + 6x + 9 \quad [(\text{First})^2 + 2(\text{First})(\text{Second}) + (\text{Second})^2]$

Expand the following bracket:

$$\left(x + \frac{k}{2}\right)^2 = x^2 + 2(x)\left(\frac{k}{2}\right) + \left(\frac{k}{2}\right)^2$$

$$\left(x + \frac{k}{2}\right)^2 = x^2 + kx + \frac{k^2}{4}$$

$$(x^2 + kx) = \left(x + \frac{k}{2}\right)^2 - \left(\frac{k}{2}\right)^2$$

$$(x^2 + kx) = \left(x + \frac{\text{coefficient of } x}{2}\right)^2 - \left(\frac{\text{coefficient of } x}{2}\right)^2$$

This result is the basis of the technique known as completing the square.

- $(x^2 + 12x) = \left(x + \frac{12}{2}\right)^2 - \left(\frac{12}{2}\right)^2 = (x + 6)^2 - 6^2$

If the coefficient of x^2 is not 1, just factorise out this coefficient first.

- $3x^2 - 15x = 3[(x^2 - 5x)] = 3\left[\left(x - \frac{5}{2}\right)^2 - \frac{25}{4}\right] = 3\left(x - \frac{5}{2}\right)^2 - \frac{75}{4}$

The technique for completing the square can be used to write every quadratic expression $ax^2 + bx + c$ in the form $p(x + q)^2 + r$.

- $x^2 + 8x - 7 = [(x^2 + 8x)] - 7 = [(x + 4)^2 - 16] - 7 = (x + 4)^2 - 23$

ACTIVITY 3

ACTION
Completing the square

OBJECTIVE
To bring you through the steps for completing the square on a variety of quadratics

Steps for completing the square on $ax^2 + bx + c$:

1. Take out the coefficient of x^2 as a factor.
2. Group the x^2 and x term in a bracket as $(x^2 + kx)$.
3. Write $(x^2 + kx) = \left(x + \frac{k}{2}\right)^2 - \left(\frac{k}{2}\right)^2$.
4. Combine the numbers.
5. Multiply back in by the coefficient of x^2.

EXAMPLE 8

Write $-2x^2 + 9x - 4$ in the form $p(x + q)^2 + r$.

Solution

$-2x^2 + 9x - 4$

1. $-2x^2 + 9x - 4 = -2\left[x^2 - \frac{9x}{2} + 2\right]$
2. $-2x^2 + 9x - 4 = -2\left[\left(x^2 - \frac{9x}{2}\right) + 2\right]$
3. $-2x^2 + 9x - 4 = -2\left[\left(x - \frac{9}{4}\right)^2 - \frac{81}{16} + 2\right]$
4. $-2x^2 + 9x - 4 = -2\left[\left(x - \frac{9}{4}\right)^2 - \frac{49}{16}\right]$
5. $-2x^2 + 9x - 4 = \frac{49}{8} - 2\left(x - \frac{9}{4}\right)^2$

EXAMPLE 9

(a) Solve $5x^2 - 6x - 2 = 0$.

(b) Solve $ax^2 + bx + c = 0$.

Solution

(a)

$$5x^2 - 6x - 2 = 0$$

$$\left(x^2 - \frac{6}{5}x\right) - \frac{2}{5} = 0 \quad \text{[Dividing by 5.]}$$

$$\left[\left(x - \frac{3}{5}\right)^2 - \frac{9}{25}\right] - \frac{2}{5} = 0$$

$$\left(x - \frac{3}{5}\right)^2 = \frac{19}{25}$$

$$x - \frac{3}{5} = \pm\frac{\sqrt{19}}{5}$$

$$x = \frac{3}{5} \pm \frac{\sqrt{19}}{5}$$

(b) This technique works every time and for all quadratic equations. It leads to the quadratic formula for the solution of $ax^2 + bx + c = 0$.

$$ax^2 + bx + c = 0$$

$$\left(x^2 + \frac{b}{a}x\right) + \frac{c}{a} = 0 \quad \text{[Dividing by } a.\text{]}$$

$$\left[\left(x + \frac{b}{2a}\right)^2 - \frac{b^2}{4a^2}\right] + \frac{c}{a} = 0$$

$$\left(x + \frac{b}{2a}\right)^2 = \frac{b^2}{4a^2} - \frac{c}{a}$$

$$\left(x + \frac{b}{2a}\right)^2 = \frac{b^2 - 4ac}{4a^2}$$

$$x + \frac{b}{2a} = \pm\frac{\sqrt{b^2 - 4ac}}{2a}$$

$$x = \frac{-b \pm \sqrt{b^2 - 4ac}}{2a}$$

The result in Example 9(b) is the famous quadratic formula which solves any and all quadratic equations. It is a summary of the completing the square technique.

ACTIVITY 4

ACTION
Using the quadratic formula

OBJECTIVE
To practise using the quadratic formula by solving a number of equations

3. The quadratic formula (magic formula)

It is impossible to solve $x^2 - 2x - 2 = 0$ by factorisation as it does not factorise obviously. The quadratic formula can be used to solve all quadratic equations whether they can be factorised or not.

It states: The solutions (roots) of the quadratic equations $ax^2 + bx + c = 0$, where a, b, c are constants and $a \neq 0$, are given by:

$$x = \frac{-b \pm \sqrt{b^2 - 4ac}}{2a}$$

EXAMPLE 10

Solve $x^2 - 2x - 2 = 0$.

Solution

$$x^2 - 2x - 2 = 0$$

$$a = 1, b = -2, c = -2$$

$$x = \frac{-(-2) \pm \sqrt{(-2)^2 - 4(1)(-2)}}{2(1)}$$

$$x = \frac{2 \pm \sqrt{4 + 8}}{2}$$

$$x = \frac{2 \pm \sqrt{12}}{2}$$

$$x = 1 + \sqrt{3},\ 1 - \sqrt{3}$$

The two roots of the equation $x^2 - 2x - 2 = 0$ are $1 + \sqrt{3}$, $1 - \sqrt{3}$.

EXAMPLE 11

The height h in metres of a ball t seconds after it is thrown up into the air at 14 m/s is given by $h = 14t - 4{\cdot}9t^2$. Find the time at which the height of the ball is 5 m, correct to one decimal place.

Solution

$h = 14t - 4{\cdot}9t^2$

$h = 5$: $5 = 14t - 4{\cdot}9t^2$

$4{\cdot}9t^2 - 14t + 5 = 0$

$a = 4{\cdot}9,\ b = -14,\ c = 5$

$$t = \frac{-(-14) \pm \sqrt{(-14)^2 - 4(4{\cdot}9)(5)}}{2(4{\cdot}9)}$$

$$t = \frac{14 \pm \sqrt{98}}{9{\cdot}8}$$

$t = 0{\cdot}4$ s and $t = 2{\cdot}4$ s. What do these two answers mean?

Properties of the quadratic formula

$$x = \frac{-(b) \pm \sqrt{(b)^2 - 4(a)(c)}}{2(a)}$$

The quantity $(b^2 - 4ac)$ under the square root is known as the **discriminant** because it discriminates between different types of roots. For $a, b, c \in \mathbb{R}$:

1. If $(b^2 - 4ac) > 0$, you always get two **different**, real roots.
2. If $(b^2 - 4ac) = 0$, you always get two **equal**, real roots.
3. If $(b^2 - 4ac) < 0$, there are no solutions. The roots are complex.

WORKED EXAMPLE Exploring the roots of quadratics

1. If $(b^2 - 4ac) > 0$, you always get two **different**, real roots.

   $2x^2 - 7x + 4 = 0$

   $a = 2,\ b = -7,\ c = 4$

   $(b^2 - 4ac) = (-7)^2 - 4(2)(4) = 49 - 32 = 17 > 0$

   $$x = \frac{7 \pm \sqrt{17}}{4} = 0{\cdot}72,\ 2{\cdot}78$$

2. If $(b^2 - 4ac) = 0$, you always get two **equal**, real roots.

   $16x^2 - 248x + 961 = 0$

   $a = 16,\ b = -248,\ c = 961$

   $(b^2 - 4ac) = (-248)^2 - 4(16)(961) = 0$

   $$x = \frac{248 \pm \sqrt{0}}{2(16)} = 7{\cdot}75,\ 7{\cdot}75$$

   In this case, the expression $ax^2 + bx + c$ is always a perfect square and can be written in the form $(px + q)^2$.

   $16x^2 - 248x + 961 = (4x - 31)^2$

3. If $(b^2 - 4ac) < 0$, there are no solutions. The roots are complex because
$\sqrt{b^2 - 4ac} = \sqrt{\text{Negative number}}$ for which there are no solutions.
$(b^2 - 4ac) < 0$ means that the quadratic equation has no **real** roots. It has complex roots which will be dealt with later.
Consider the equation: $x^2 - 2x + 5 = 0$
$a = 1, b = -2, c = 5$
$(b^2 - 4ac) = (-2)^2 - 4(1)(5) = -16 < 0$
$$x = \frac{2 \pm \sqrt{-16}}{2}$$
$x^2 - 2x + 5 = 0$ has no solutions.

The equation $ax^2 + bx + c = 0$, $a, b, c \in \mathbb{R}$, has:

1. Two different real roots if $b^2 > 4ac$.
2. Two equal real roots if $b^2 = 4ac$.
3. No real roots if $b^2 < 4ac$.
4. Real roots if $b^2 \geq 4ac$.

EXAMPLE 12

If $2x^2 - kx + x + 2 = 0$ has equal roots, find k.

Solution

$2x^2 - kx + x + 2 = 0$
$2x^2 + (1 - k)x + 2 = 0$
$a = 2, b = (1 - k), c = 2$
Equal roots: $b^2 = 4ac$

$(1 - k)^2 = 4(2)(2)$
$(1 - k)^2 = 16$
$1 - k = \pm 4$
$k = -3, 5$

Graphical solutions of quadratic equations

$y = ax^2 + bx + c$ is the equation of the quadratic function. The general shape of the graph of such a function is either:

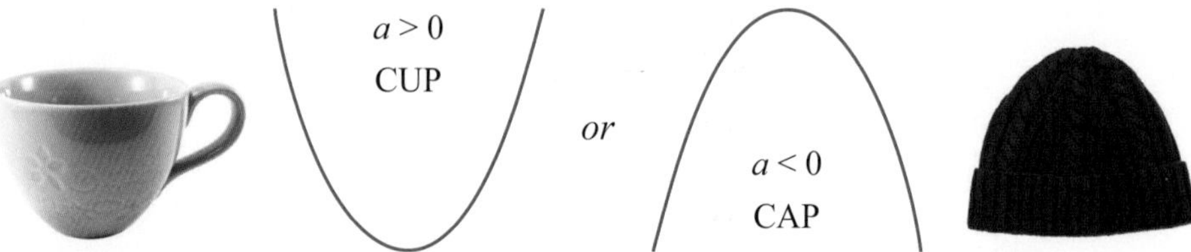

This general shape is known as a **parabola**. $y = 0$ is the equation of the x-axis. Therefore, the solutions of $ax^2 + bx + c = 0$ are the values of x at which the parabola crosses the x-axis.

EXAMPLE 13

Find the points at which the curve $y = 3x^2 - 5x + 1$ crosses the x-axis. Give your answers correct to two decimal places. Draw a rough sketch of its graph.

Solution

$3x^2 - 5x + 1 = 0$

$a = 3, b = -5, c = 1$

$$x = \frac{5 \pm \sqrt{(-5)^2 - 4(3)(1)}}{2(3)}$$

$$x = \frac{5 \pm \sqrt{13}}{6} = 0{\cdot}23,\ 1{\cdot}43$$

x-intercepts: $(0{\cdot}23, 0)$, $(1{\cdot}43, 0)$

Rough sketch: $a > 0 \Rightarrow \cup$ is the shape.

It crosses the y-axis when $x = 0 : y = 1$

$(0, 1)$ is the y-intercept.

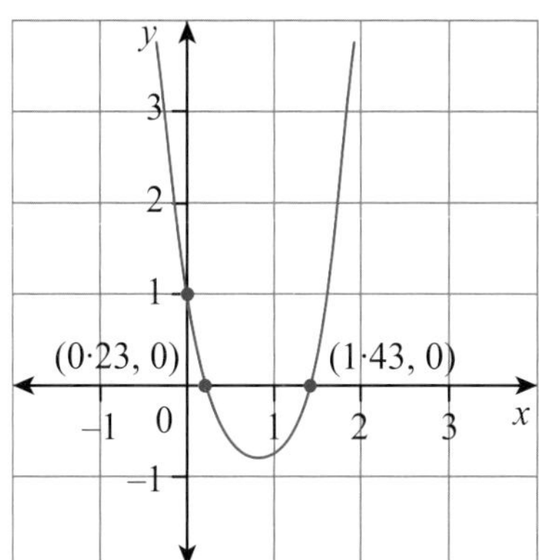

EXAMPLE 14

A tunnel in the shape of a parabola is described by the equation $y = -x^2 + 11x - 21{\cdot}25$, where x is in metres. Find $|SL|$, the maximum width of the tunnel.

Solution

S and L are the points where the curve crosses the x-axis.

$-x^2 + 11x - 21{\cdot}25 = 0$

$a = -1, b = 11, c = -21{\cdot}25$

$$x = \frac{-11 \pm \sqrt{(11)^2 - 4(-1)(-21{\cdot}25)}}{2(-1)} = 2{\cdot}5,\ 8{\cdot}5$$

$S\,(2{\cdot}5, 0)$, $L\,(8{\cdot}5, 0)$

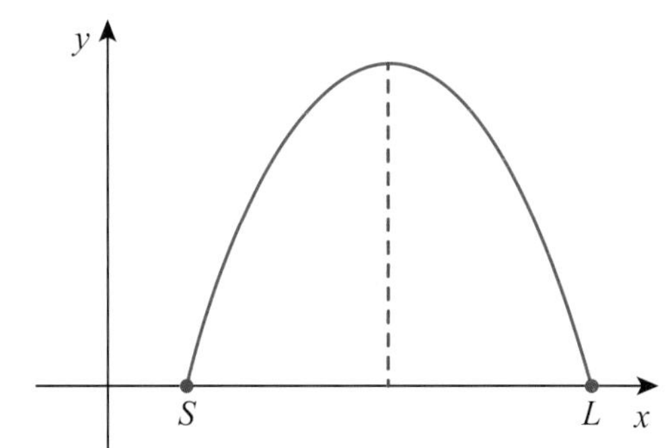

$|SL| = 8{\cdot}5 - 2{\cdot}5 = 6$ m

Finding the quadratic equation from its roots (working backwards)

WORKED EXAMPLE Finding a quadratic from its roots

Given the equation $12x^2 + x - 6 = 0$, the roots can be found as follows:

Equation: $12x^2 + x - 6 = 0$

Factors: $(3x - 2)(4x + 3) = 0$

Roots: $x = \frac{2}{3}, x = -\frac{3}{4}$

The equation can be found from the roots by reversing the process. Given the roots $x = -\frac{3}{5}, x = \frac{4}{3}$ of a quadratic equation, the equation can be found as follows:

Roots: $x = -\frac{3}{5}, x = \frac{4}{3}$

Factors: $(5x + 3)(3x - 4) = 0$

Equation: $15x^2 - 11x - 12 = 0$

If $\frac{q}{p}$ and $\frac{r}{s}$ are the roots of a quadratic equation, the equation is $(px - q)(sx - r) = 0$.

- Roots: $x = -5, x = \frac{1}{3}$
  Factors: $(x + 5)(3x - 1) = 0$
  Equation: $3x^2 + 14x - 5 = 0$

There is a trick for doing this reverse process all in one go and it simplifies harder questions.

A quadratic equation can be written as $x^2 - Sx + P = 0$, where S is the sum of the roots and P is the product of the roots.

- Roots: = 2, 5
  $S = 2 + 5 = 7, P = 2 \times 5 = 10$
  Equation: $x^2 - 7x + 10 = 0$
- Roots = $4 + 2\sqrt{3}, 4 - 2\sqrt{3}$
  $S = 8, P = 4$
  Equation: $x^2 - 8x + 4 = 0$

General strategy for solving quadratic equations

Steps for solving quadratic equations:

1. Factorise all denominators.
2. Multiply all terms by the lowest common denominator (LCD).
3. Multiply out all brackets.
4. Get all terms on one side in the form $ax^2 + bx + c = 0$.
5. Take out the highest common factor (HCF).
6. Solve by factorisation or by using the quadratic formula.
7. Check your solutions.

EXAMPLE 15

Solve $\frac{-x^2}{6x^2 + 11x + 4} = \frac{1}{2x + 1} + \frac{2}{3x + 4}$.

Solution

$\frac{-x^2}{(6x^2 + 11x + 4)} = \frac{1}{(2x + 1)} + \frac{2}{(3x + 4)}$ [Factorise all denominators.]

$\frac{-x^2}{(3x + 4)(2x + 1)} = \frac{1}{(2x + 1)} + \frac{2}{(3x + 4)}$ [Multiply across by LCD: $(3x + 4)(2x + 1)$]

	Check:	LHS	RHS
$-x^2 = (3x + 4) + 2(2x + 1)$			
$-x^2 = 3x + 4 + 4x + 2$			
$x^2 + 7x + 6 = 0$	$x = -1$:	$\frac{-(-1)^2}{6(-1)^2 + 11(-1) + 4} = \frac{-1}{-1} - 1$	$\frac{1}{-1} + \frac{2}{1} = 1$
$(x + 1)(x + 6) = 0$			
$x = -1, -6$	$x = -6$:	$\frac{-(-6)^2}{6(-6)^2 + 11(-6) + 4} = \frac{-36}{154} = -\frac{18}{77}$	$\frac{1}{-11} + \frac{2}{-14} = -\frac{18}{77}$

Using quadratics to solve other equations

The equations $3x^2 + 5x - 1 = 0$, $3g^2 + 5g - 1 = 0$ and $3(\text{yoke})^2 + 5(\text{yoke}) - 1 = 0$ all have the same solutions for **their** variable because they have the same coefficients:

$a = 3, b = 5, c = -1$

$$\left.\begin{matrix} x \\ g \\ \text{yoke} \end{matrix}\right\} = \frac{-5 \pm \sqrt{(5)^2 - 4(3)(-1)}}{6} = \frac{-5 \pm \sqrt{37}}{6}$$

ACTIVITY 5

ACTION

Using techniques for modelling quadratic problems

OBJECTIVE

To learn some basic techniques to aid the modelling of quadratic problems

EXAMPLE 16

Solve $x^2 + 3x - 54 = 0$.

Hence, solve $\left(t + \frac{8}{t}\right)^2 + 3\left(t + \frac{8}{t}\right) - 54 = 0$ for $t \neq 0$.

Solution

These two equations have the same coefficients: $a = 1$, $b = 3$, $c = -54$. Hence, they have the same solutions for their variable.

$x^2 + 3x - 54 = 0$

$(x - 6)(x + 9) = 0$

$x = 6, -9$

$t + \frac{8}{t} = 6$	$t + \frac{8}{t} = -9$
$t^2 + 8 = 6t$	$t^2 + 8 = -9t$
$t^2 - 6t + 8 = 0$	$t^2 + 9t + 8 = 0$
$(t - 4)(t - 2) = 0$	$(t + 8)(t + 1) = 0$
$t = 4, 2$	$t = -8, -1$

Mathematical modelling (word problems)

Steps for modelling problems:

The steps used for modelling problems leading to quadratic equations are the same as those used for modelling problems leading to linear equations.

1. Read the problem carefully and draw a diagram, if appropriate.
2. Assign a variable to one of the quantities to be found and hence assign variables to the other quantities.
3. Translate the word problem into an equation.
4. Solve the equation.
5. List all answers.

EXAMPLE 17

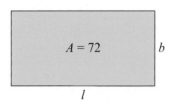

The perimeter of a rectangular garden is 36 m. If its area is 72 m^2, find the length and breadth of the garden.

Solution

1. Area = Length × Breadth

$A = 72$ b l

2. Let l = length of the garden

   $l + b = 18$

   $b = (18 - l)$

3. $A = l \times b$

   $A = l(18 - l) = 72$

4. $18l - l^2 = 72$

   $l^2 - 18l + 72 = 0$

   $(l - 6)(l - 12) = 0$

   $l = 6, 12$

5. $l = 6$, $b = 12$ | $l = 12$, $b = 6$

   Answer: 12 m and 6 m

EXAMPLE 18

A rectangular metal frame has an area of metal of 76 cm^2. If the dimensions of the glass on the inside of the frame are 10 cm × 5 cm, find the uniform width of the frame.

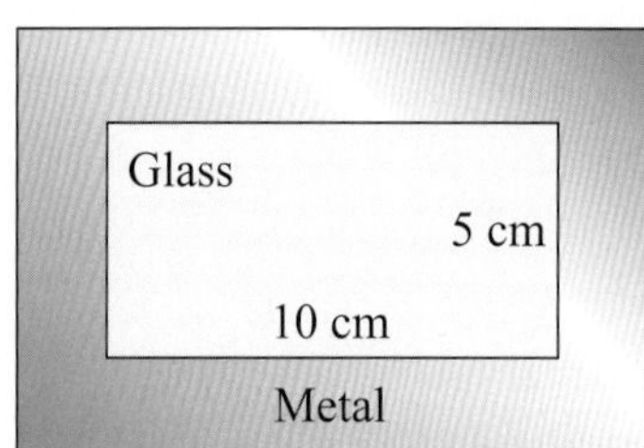

Solution

1. The area A of the metal region = 76 cm^2
2. Let x = width of the frame
3. Metal area A = area of frame – area of glass

   $A = (10 + 2x)(5 + 2x) - 10 \times 5$

   $76 = 4x^2 + 30x$

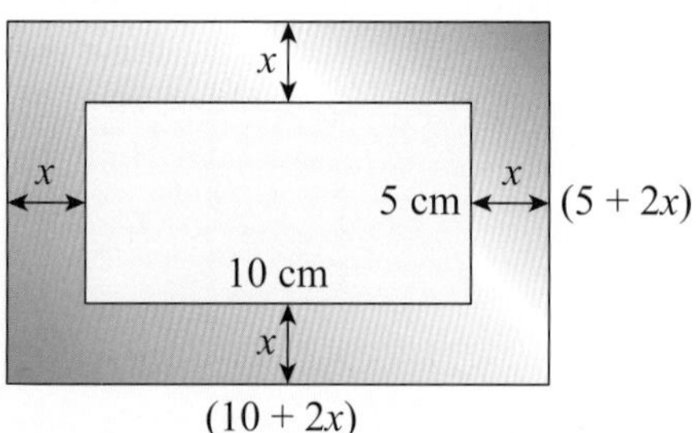

4. $4x^2 + 30x - 76 = 0$

   $2x^2 + 15x - 38 = 0$

   $(x - 2)(2x + 19) = 0$

   $x - 2 = 0$ | $2x + 19 = 0$

   $x = 2$ | $x = -\frac{19}{2}$ [Reject this solution as you cannot have negative widths.]

   Answer: $x = 2$ cm

EXAMPLE 19

The profit P in euro per week of a local newspaper is given by $P = -0{\cdot}0025x^2 + 10x - 6000$, $0 \le x \le 2500$, where x is the number of newspapers sold per week.

Find:

(a) the break-even point (the value of x for which there is no profit),

(b) the number of newspapers that must be sold to give a profit of €2400 per week.

Solution

$P = -0{\cdot}0025x^2 + 10x - 6000$

(a) Break-even point:

$P = 0$: $-0{\cdot}0025x^2 + 10x - 6000 = 0$

$0{\cdot}0025x^2 - 10x + 6000 = 0$

$$x = \frac{10 \pm \sqrt{(-10)^2 - 4(0{\cdot}0025)(6000)}}{2(0{\cdot}0025)}$$

$x = 3264{\cdot}9,\ 735{\cdot}09$

Reject 3264·9 because it is not in the domain.

Answer: 735 newspapers

(b) $P = €2400$: $-0{\cdot}0025x^2 + 10x - 6000 = 2400$

$-0{\cdot}0025x^2 + 10x - 8400 = 0$

$0{\cdot}0025x^2 - 10x + 8400 = 0$

$$x = \frac{10 \pm \sqrt{(-10)^2 - 4(0{\cdot}0025)(8400)}}{2(0{\cdot}0025)}$$

$= 2800,\ 1200$

Answer: 1200 [2800 is not in the domain.]

EXAMPLE 20

Two cars P and Q left a shopping centre at the same time. P headed due north and Q headed due east. After a certain time P had travelled 10 km further than Q. If at this time they were 30 km apart as the crow flies, find how far each had travelled from the shopping centre, correct to one decimal place.

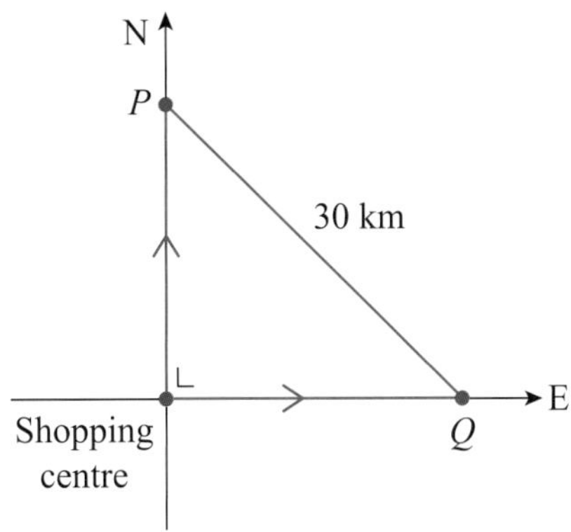

Solution

If Q travelled x km, P travelled $(x + 10)$ km.
A right-angled triangle means that Pythagoras' theorem can be used.

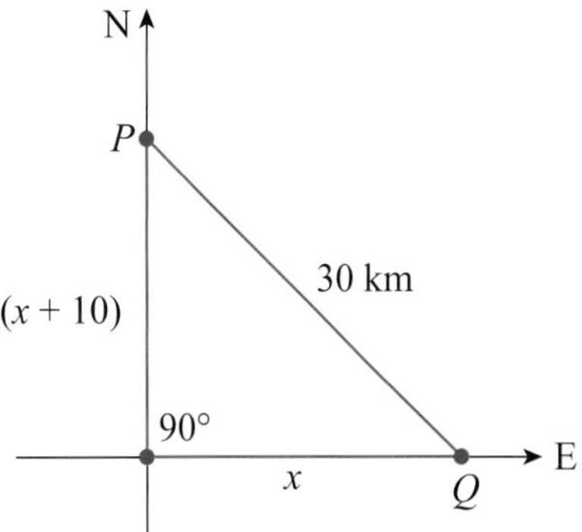

Pythagoras: $x^2 + (x + 10)^2 = 30^2$

$x^2 + x^2 + 20x + 100 = 900$

$2x^2 + 20x - 800 = 0$

$x^2 + 10x - 400 = 0$

$$x = \frac{-10 \pm \sqrt{(10)^2 - 4(1)(-400)}}{2} = 15{\cdot}6,\ -25{\cdot}6$$

[Reject the negative solution.]

Q was 15·6 km from the shopping centre and P was 25·6 km from the centre.

EXAMPLE 21

A missile is launched from a silo at S. It follows the trajectory described by the equation $y = -0{\cdot}0014x^2 + 0{\cdot}6x + 20$, where x is in metres. If it lands at L, find $|SL|$, correct to the nearest metre.

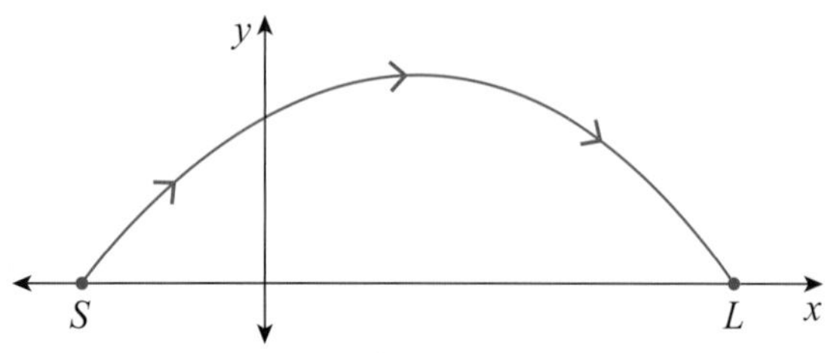

Solution

The points at which the curve crosses the x-axis are the solutions of $-0{\cdot}0014x^2 + 0{\cdot}6x + 20 = 0$.

$a = -0{\cdot}0014$, $b = 0{\cdot}6$, $c = 20$

$$x = \frac{-(0{\cdot}6) \pm \sqrt{(0{\cdot}6)^2 - 4(-0{\cdot}0014)(20)}}{2(-0{\cdot}0014)}$$

$x = -31, 460$ m

$S(-31, 0)$, $L(460, 0)$

$\therefore |SL| = 31 + 460 = 491$ m

EXAMPLE 22

The fixed cost for a company, which produces x units per week, is €1000. The variable cost is €$(4 - 0{\cdot}2x)$ per unit. If the selling price is €5 per unit, for a weekly output of x units, find an expression for:

(a) the total cost C per week,

(b) the total revenue R per week,

(c) the total profit P per week if $P = R - C$.

Hence, find:

(d) the break-even point correct to the nearest whole number (the point at which $P = 0$),

(e) the output x which gives a weekly profit of €2000.

Solution

The output is x items per week.

(a) $C = 1000 + (4 - 0{\cdot}2x)x = 1000 + 4x - 0{\cdot}2x^2$

(b) $R = 5x$

(c) $P = R - C = 5x - 1000 - 4x + 0{\cdot}2x^2$

$P = 0{\cdot}2x^2 + x - 1000$

(d) $\boldsymbol{P = 0}$: $0{\cdot}2x^2 + x - 1000 = 0$

$$x = \frac{-1 \pm \sqrt{(1)^2 - 4(0{\cdot}2)(-1000)}}{2(0{\cdot}2)} = 68{\cdot}25, -73{\cdot}25$$ [Reject the negative solution.]

Answer: 68 units

(e) $\boldsymbol{P = 2000}$:

$0{\cdot}2x^2 + x - 1000 = 2000$

$0{\cdot}2x^2 + x - 3000 = 0$

$$x = \frac{-1 \pm \sqrt{(1)^2 - 4(0{\cdot}2)(-3000)}}{2(0{\cdot}2)} = 120, -125$$ [Reject the negative solution.]

Answer: 120 units

EXAMPLE 23

A river cruiser goes 12 km upstream and then back again over 3 hours in total. The speed of the river is 3 km/h. Find the speed that the boat can move in still water.

Upstream — Downstream $\rightarrow$ 3 km/h

Q ← P

Solution

$$\text{Speed} = \frac{\text{Distance}}{\text{Time}} \Rightarrow \text{Time} = \frac{\text{Distance}}{\text{Speed}}$$

Let x = speed of the boat in still water

$|PQ| = 12$

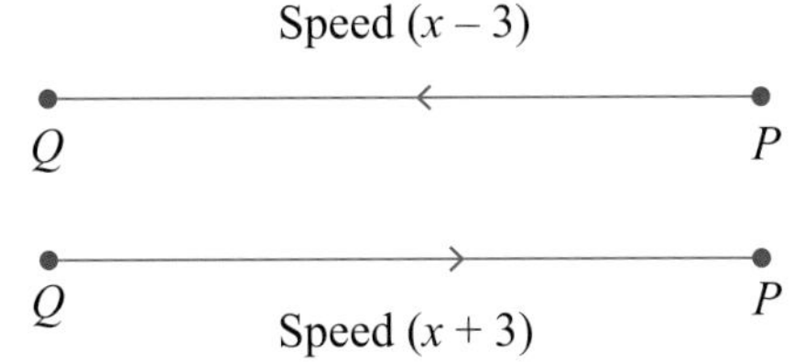

Time to go upstream $= \dfrac{12}{x-3}$

Time to go downstream $= \dfrac{12}{x+3}$

$$\therefore \frac{12}{x-3} + \frac{12}{x+3} = 3$$

$$12(x+3) + 12(x-3) = 3(x-3)(x+3)$$

$$12x + 36 + 12x - 36 = 3(x^2 - 9)$$

$$24x = 3x^2 - 27$$

$$3x^2 - 24x - 27 = 0$$

$$x^2 - 8x - 9 = 0$$

$$(x+1)(x-9) = 0$$

$x = -1, 9$ [Reject the negative solution.]

Answer: 9 km/h

EXERCISE 2

1. Solve the following quadratic equations:
   - **(a)** $(x+2)(x-1) = 0$
   - **(b)** $(x-3)(2x+1) = 0$
   - **(c)** $(2x-7)^2 = 0$
   - **(d)** $x(x-3) = 0$
   - **(e)** $2x(3x-7) = 0$
   - **(f)** $x^2 - 2x = 0$
   - **(g)** $5x^2 - 15x = 0$
   - **(h)** $x^2 - \dfrac{x}{9} = 0$
   - **(i)** $3x^2 - 27 = 0$
   - **(j)** $4x^2 - x = 0$

2. Solve the following quadratic equations by factorisation:
   - **(a)** $x^2 - 25 = 0$
   - **(b)** $3x^2 - 12 = 0$
   - **(c)** $x^2 - 2x - 15 = 0$
   - **(d)** $3x^2 + 24x - 99 = 0$
   - **(e)** $2x^2 + 3x + 1 = 0$
   - **(f)** $12x^2 - 23x + 10 = 0$
   - **(g)** $3x^2 + 16x - 12 = 0$
   - **(h)** $21x^2 + 3x - 24 = 0$
   - **(i)** $-4x^2 + 20x - 24 = 0$
   - **(j)** $16x^2 - \frac{1}{64} = 0$

3. Simplify the following and solve the resulting quadratics:

(a) $x(x + 24) = 25$

(b) $(x + 3)(x + 5) = 3 + x$

(c) $2x - 2(x - 1) = x(x - 1)$

(d) $5(2x^2 - 3x - 2) = 3(x^2 - 6x - 2)$

(e) $(2x - 1)^2 - (x + 2)^2 = 0$

4. **(a)** If -2 is a root of the quadratic equation $kx^2 - 4x - 2 = 0$, find $k \in \mathbb{R}$.

(b) Show that $1 + \sqrt{2}$ is a solution of the equation $x^2 - 2x - 1 = 0$.

(c) Investigate if $-\frac{3}{2}$ is a solution of the equation $2x^2 + 5x + 3 = 0$.

(d) If 2 and -3 are roots of the equation $px^2 + qx - 18 = 0$, find $p,\ q \in \mathbb{R}$.

(e) If $(x + 1)$ and $(x + 2)$ are factors of $px^2 + qx + 10 = 0$, find $p,\ q \in \mathbb{R}$.

5. Solve the following quadratic equations by completing the square:

(a) $x^2 - 4x + 2 = 0$

(b) $x^2 - 2x - 7 = 0$

(c) $x^2 + 2x - 4 = 0$

(d) $2x^2 - 2x - 1 = 0$

(e) $4x^2 + 8x - 1 = 0$

(f) $3x^2 - 7x - 1 = 0$

(g) $-x^2 + 5x - 2 = 0$

(h) $-4x^2 + 8x - 3 = 0$

(i) $x^2 - 5x + 6 = 0$

(j) $2x^2 - 3x - 7 = 0$

6. Solve the following quadratic equations by using the quadratic formula, giving your answers in surd form and then as decimals, correct to two decimal places:

(a) $x^2 - 2x - 30 = 0$

(b) $x^2 = 2x + 9$

(c) $4x^2 - 19x + 1 = 0$

(d) $6x^2 + x = 2$

(e) $6x^2 - 15x - 18 = 0$

(f) $3x^2 - 8x - 2 = 0$

(g) $7x^2 + 8x = 2$

(h) $(3x - 2)(2x + 4) - 4x^2 + 5 = 0$

(i) $x^2 - 3 = 0$

(j) $4x^2 - 32 = 0$

7. **(a)** By calculating $b^2 - 4ac$, state the nature of the roots of the following quadratic equations. State whether the roots are real and different, real and equal, or complex. In the case of different real roots, state if they are rational or irrational.

(i) $x^2 - 5x + 6 = 0$

(ii) $x^2 - 6x = -9$

(iii) $(3x - 2)^2 = 0$

(iv) $x(x + 1) = 2x^2 - 7$

(v) $x^2 - 2x + 10 = 0$

(vi) $4x^2 - 12x + 13 = 0$

(vii) $x^2 - 2\sqrt{3}x + 3 = 0$

(viii) $2\sqrt{2}x^2 - 5x + \sqrt{2} = 0$

(b) Find k if the roots of the following quadratic equations are equal:

(i) $kx^2 + kx + 1 = 0,\ k \neq 0$

(ii) $kx^2 - x^2 - 12x - 3 = 0$

(c) **(i)** Show that $x^2 + kx + k - 1 = 0$ has two real, different roots for all $k \in \mathbb{R}$, $k \neq 2$, by solving the equation.

(ii) Show that $x^2 - 2kx + 2x + k^2 - 2k + 1 = 0$ has equal, real roots for all $k \in \mathbb{R}$.

8. If $y = ax^2 - 6x$ is the equation of the curve below, find a.

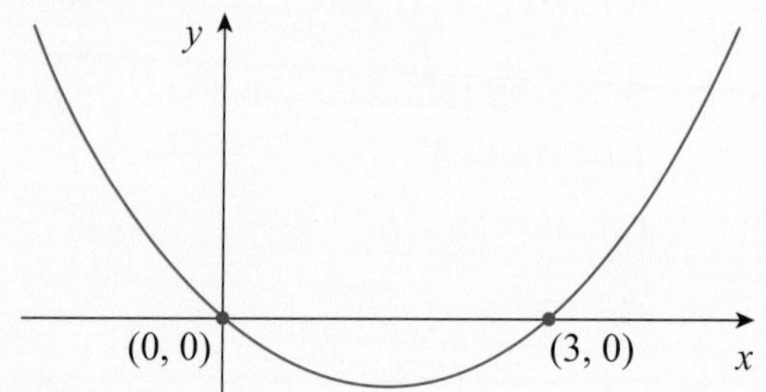

9. If $y = ax^2 + bx + 8$ is the equation of the graph below, find a and b.

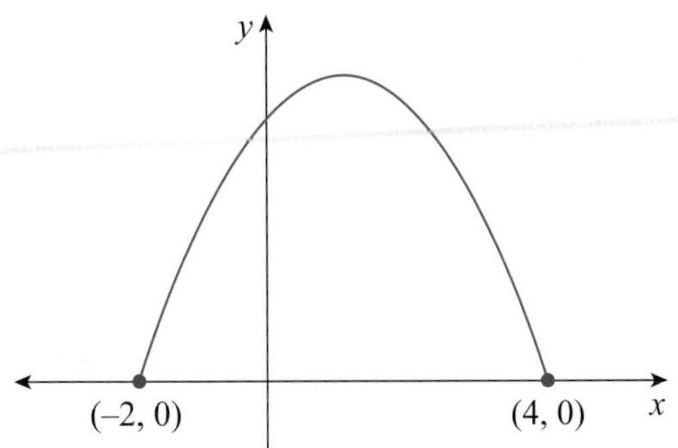

10. If $y = ax^2 + bx + 15$ is the equation of the graph below, find a and b.

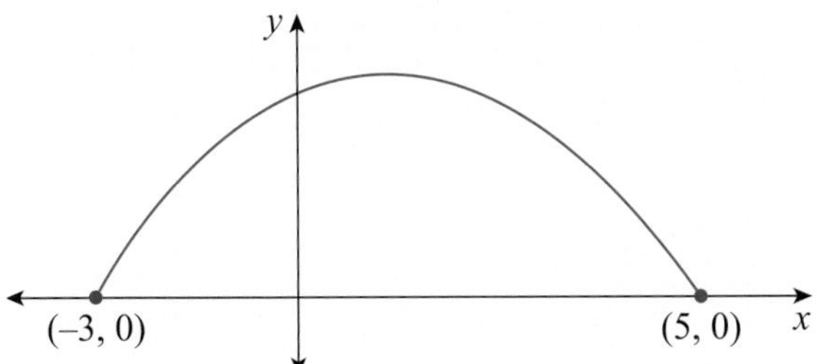

11. Form the quadratic equations with the following roots:

(a) $1, 2$
(b) $3, 3$
(c) $-1, -2$
(d) $5, -6$
(e) $\sqrt{2}, -\sqrt{2}$
(f) $\frac{1}{2}, \frac{3}{2}$
(g) $\frac{2}{3}, -\frac{1}{5}$
(h) $2 + \sqrt{3}, 2 - \sqrt{3}$
(i) $-4 + 3\sqrt{5}, -4 - 3\sqrt{5}$
(j) α, β

12. Solve the following equations:

(a) $x^2 = \dfrac{13x + 5}{6}$

(b) $\dfrac{3}{x} + \dfrac{5}{x + 2} = 2$

(c) $\dfrac{4}{(x + 6)(x + 4)} + 7 = \dfrac{2}{x + 4}$

(d) $\dfrac{1}{16x^2 + 8x - 3} + \dfrac{1}{12} = \dfrac{-1}{4(4x + 3)}$

(e) $\dfrac{6 - 4x}{x^2 - 9} + \dfrac{3}{x + 3} + \dfrac{2x}{x - 3} = 0$

(f) $\dfrac{x(x - 7)}{x - 5} + \dfrac{10}{x - 5} = \dfrac{x}{3}$

(g) $\dfrac{3x}{x - 2} + \dfrac{6}{x^2 - 5x + 6} = \dfrac{4}{x - 3}$

(h) $\dfrac{1}{x + 1} - \dfrac{1}{3} = \dfrac{1}{x + 2}$, correct to one decimal place

(i) $\dfrac{1}{x^2 - x - 6} = \dfrac{1}{2x^2 + 4x} + \dfrac{1}{4x + 8}$

(j) $\dfrac{1}{4x^2 - 1} - \dfrac{x}{2x + 1} = 0, x \neq -\dfrac{1}{2}$

13. Solve the following equations:

(a) $x^2 - 7x + 10 = 0$ for x and hence $(y - 2)^2 - 7(y - 2) + 10 = 0$ for y

(b) $6x^2 - 11x - 10 = 0$ for x and hence $6(t - 1)^2 - 11(t - 1) - 10 = 0$ for t

(c) $3x^2 - 7x + 4 = 0$ for x and hence $3\left(\dfrac{y}{3} - 1\right)^2 - 7\left(\dfrac{y}{3} - 1\right) + 4 = 0$ for y

(d) $x^2 - 10x + 21 = 0$ for x and hence $\left(x - \dfrac{18}{x}\right)^2 - 10\left(x - \dfrac{18}{x}\right) + 21 = 0$ for x

(e) $5x^2 - 23x + 12 = 0$ for x and hence $(y - 2)^2 - 4{\cdot}6(y - 2) = -2{\cdot}4$ for y

(f) $3x^2 - 19x + 20 = 0$ for x and hence $3x - 19\sqrt{x} + 20 = 0$ for x

(g) $x^2 + x - 20 = 0$ for x and hence $2^{2t} + 2^t - 20 = 0$ for t

(h) $x^2 - 11x + 30 = 0$ for x and hence $(t^2 + t) - 11(t^2 + t) + 30 = 0$ for t

14. (a) In a round-robin hockey tournament, each team is paired with every other team once. If there are x teams, the number N of games that are played is given by $N = \dfrac{x^2 - x}{2}$. If 66 games are played, how many teams entered?

(b) Find three consecutive even natural numbers such that the sum of their products in pairs is equal to 104.

(c) When tickets for a rock concert cost €40, the average attendance was 600. For each €1 increase in cost, the attendance decreased by 60. At what ticket price would the total income be €13 500? (Hint: For an increase in ticket price of €x, the attendance is $(600 - 60x)$ and the ticket price is $(40 + x)$.)

(d) When the sum of 6 and twice a natural number is subtracted from the square of the number, the result is 2. Find this number.

(e) The profit P in € made by selling x computers is modelled by the equation $P = -5x^2 + 1200x + 6000$. How many computers must be sold to make a profit of €53 500?

(f) The total resistance R of two resistors in parallel is given by $\frac{1}{R} = \frac{1}{r} + \frac{1}{r+3}$.

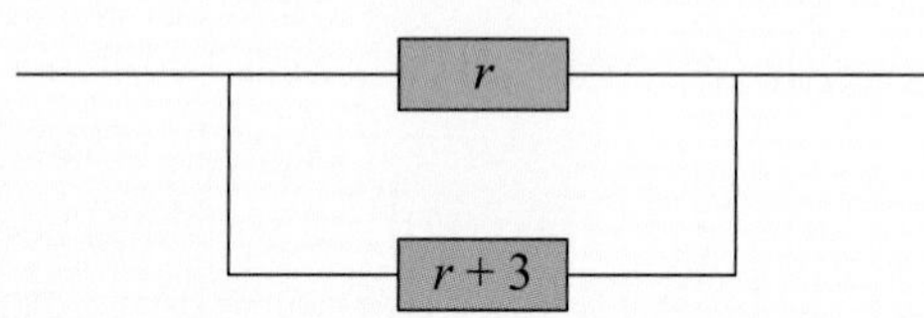

If $R = 2$ ohms, find r in ohms.

(g) Bill and Ben can paint a room together in 2 hours and 24 minutes. Bill can paint the room on his own 2 hours faster than Ben. How long would each take on his own to paint the room? (Hint: If Bill can paint a room in x hours, he can paint $\frac{1}{x}$ of the room in 1 hour.)

(h) A golf ball is thrown up on the moon. The equation of the ball's height h(m) above the lunar surface t seconds after launch is given by $h = 12{\cdot}8t - 0{\cdot}8t^2$. Find when it is 22·4 m above the surface.

(i) Mr Whippy drove 120 km from Dublin to Newry. On the return trip, he drove 10 km/h slower than on the outward trip. If the return journey was 10 minutes longer, find his outward and inward speeds.

(j) Two ships P and Q leave port O at the same time. Ship P travels along the line OP and ship Q travels along the line OQ. After a certain time, Q has travelled 10 km further than P and their distance apart is $10\sqrt{7}$ km.

Find $|OP|$ and $|OQ|$.
(Hint:
$|PQ|^2 = |OQ|^2 + |OP|^2 - 2|OP||OQ| \cos 60°$)

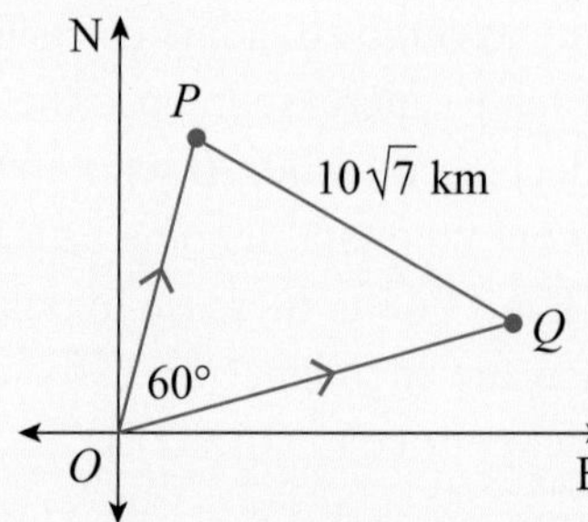

Note: You can leave this question until you have studied the cosine rule in the trigonometry section.

(k) A regulation tennis court for a doubles match is laid out so that its length is 1·85 m longer than twice its width. The area of the doubles court is 267 m². Find the length and breadth of a doubles court, correct to one decimal place.

Anyone for tennis?

(l) A flowerbed is laid out in a garden in an L shape, as shown. If 8 m of edging is used, show that the area of the bed is given by $A = 4x - x^2$ if $|PQ| = |RQ|$. Find x if the area is 2·56 m².

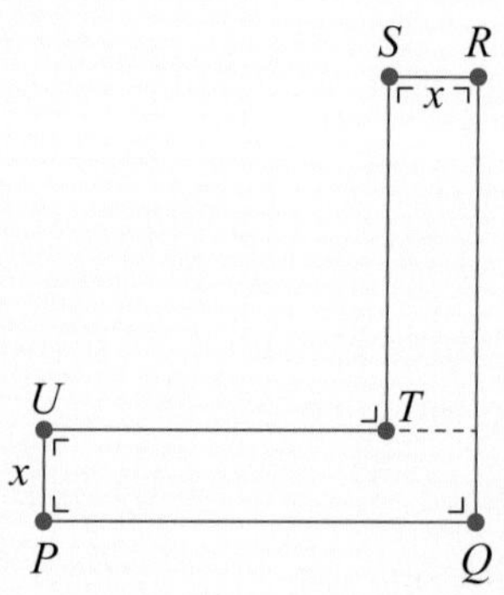

(m) A frog is sitting 1·5 m to the left of the edge of a rock at O. He notices a juicy fly to the right of the rock on a flower. The frog leaps over the rock and catches the fly. His height h(m) above the ground in his parabolic path is given by the equation $h = -4x^2 + 4x + 3$, where x is his distance relative to O in metres. Find how far the fly is from the frog before he leaps.

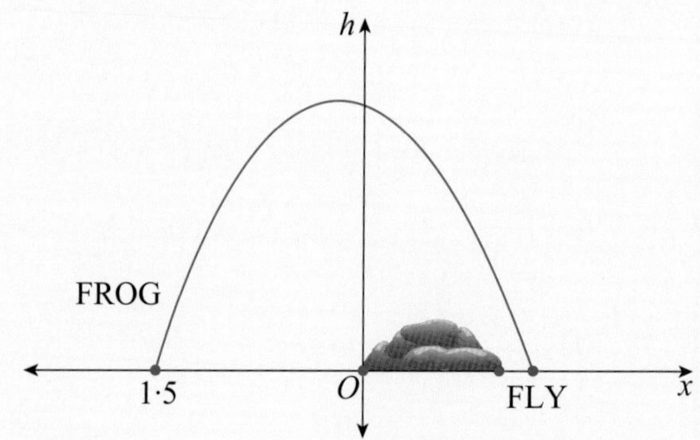

(n) The total surface area of a solid cylinder of height 6 cm is 110π cm^2. Find the radius of its base.

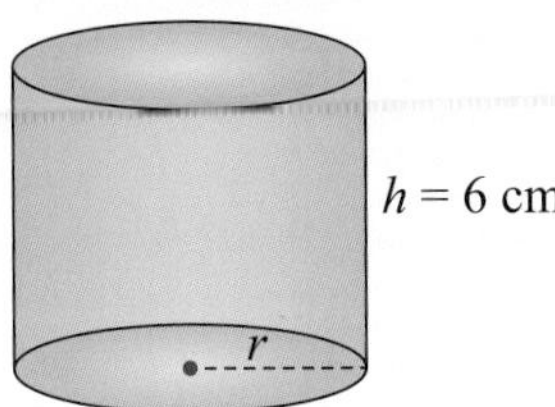

(o) A house owner wants to build an extension in the shape of a cuboid so that the length l is 3 m longer than the width. Find l in terms of w.

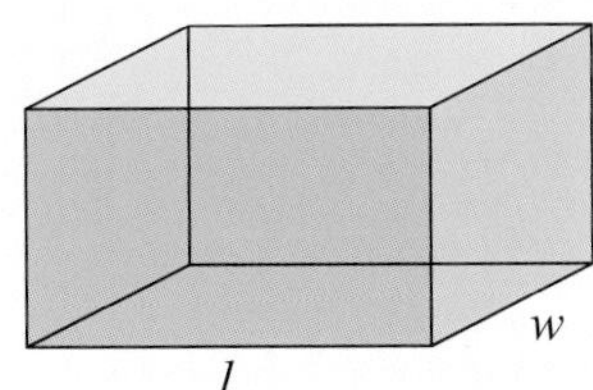

The planning regulations state that the area of the floor space occupied by the extension must not exceed 50% of the floor space of the house to which it is attached. The floor space of the house is 14 m by 12 m. Show that $w^2 + 3w - 84 = 0$, if the largest extension is built. Find l and w, correct to one decimal place.

(p) Simone walks 17 m diagonally across a rectangular field from P to R and returns along the outside in the direction $R \rightarrow Q \rightarrow P$. If the total distance she travels is 40 m, find $|PQ|$ and $|QR|$.

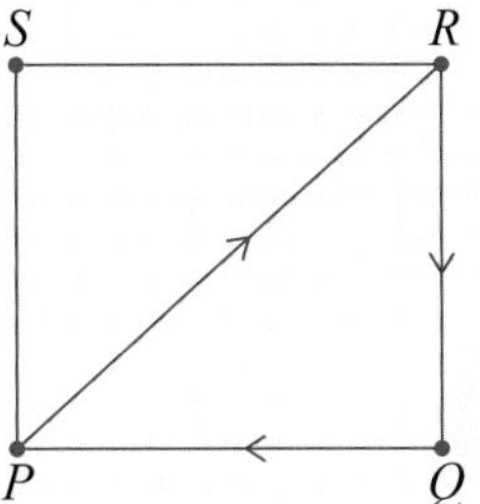

6.3 Cubic equations

ACTION
Working with cubic equations

OBJECTIVE
To learn the techniques needed to solve cubic equations

A cubic equation is an equation which can be written in the form $ax^3 + bx^2 + cx + d = 0$, where a, b, c, d are constants and $a \neq 0$.

a is the coefficient of x^3 and must not be zero. (Why?)

b is the coefficient of x^2.

c is the coefficient of x.

d is the constant term.

The power 3 in x^3 makes the equation cubic. If the highest power of the variable in a polynomial equation is 3, the equation is cubic.

Method of solution

There is no simple formula for solving a cubic equation. It is solved using the **factor theorem** followed by factorisation or division.

The factor theorem

The factor theorem states the obvious:

THE FACTOR THEOREM

If k is a root of a polynomial equation $P(x) = 0$, then $(x - k)$ is a factor of $P(x)$ and vice versa.

or

For a polynomial $P(x)$, $P(k) = 0 \Leftrightarrow P(k) = (x - k)Q(x)$, where $Q(x)$ is a polynomial of degree one less than $P(x)$.

This theorem can be applied to all polynomial equations.

EXAMPLE 24

Show that –3 is a root of $2x^2 - x - 21 = 0$. Find the other factor and the other root.

Solution

$P(x) = 2x^2 - x - 21$ is a quadratic expression.

$P(-3) = 2(-3)^2 - (-3) - 21 = 18 + 3 - 21 = 0$

$\therefore -3$ is a solution (root) of $2x^2 - x - 21 = 0$

By the factor theorem, $(x + 3)$ is a factor of $2x^2 - x - 21$.

$(2x^2 - x - 21) = (x + 3)(2x - 7) = 0$

[Quadratic = Linear × Linear]

$x = -3, \frac{7}{2}$

EXAMPLE 25

(a) If $x - 1$ is a factor of $P(x) = x^3 + 2x^2 - 3kx + 4$, find $k \in \mathbb{R}$.

(b) If $(x + 1)$ and $(x + 3)$ are factors of $P(x) = kx^3 - 6x^2 + lx - 6$, find $k, l \in \mathbb{R}$.

Solution

(a) $(x - 1)$ is a factor of $P(x)$

$\Rightarrow 1$ is a root of $x^3 + 2x^2 - 3kx + 4 = 0$.

$P(1) = (1)^3 + 2(1)^2 - 3k(1) + 4 = 0$

$1 + 2 - 3k + 4 = 0$

$7 = 3k$

$k = \frac{7}{3}$

(b) $(x + 1)$ is a factor of $P(x)$

$\Rightarrow -1$ is a root of $kx^3 - 6x^2 + lx - 6 = 0$.

$P(-1) = k(-1)^3 - 6(-1)^2 + l(-1) - 6 = 0$

$-k - 6 - l - 6 = 0$

$k + l = -12$ ... **(1)**

$(x + 3)$ is a factor of $P(x)$

$\Rightarrow -3$ is a root of $kx^3 - 6x^2 + lx - 6 = 0$.

$P(-3) = k(-3)^3 - 6(-3)^2 + l(-3) - 6 = 0$

$-27k - 54 - 3l - 6 = 0$

$27k + 3l = -60$

$9k + l = -20$ ... **(2)**

Equation **(2)** – **(1)**: $8k = -8$

$k = -1$

Substituting into **(1)**: $l = -11$

EXAMPLE 26

Show that –2 is a root of the cubic equation $3x^3 + 11x^2 + 4x - 12 = 0$. Find the other factor(s) and hence solve the equation.

Solution

$P(x) = 3x^3 + 11x^2 + 4x - 12 = 0$

$\mathbf{x = -2}$: $P(-2) = 3(-2)^3 + 11(-2)^2 + 4(-2) - 12$

$= -24 + 44 - 8 - 12 = 0$

$\therefore (x + 2)$ is a linear factor.

The other factor is a quadratic factor. It can be found in two ways:

1. Factorisation and lining up:

$3x^3 + \underline{11}x^2 + 4x - 12 = (x + 2)(3x^2 + px - 6)$

$= 3x^3 + 6x^2 + px^2 + 2px - 6x - 12$

$= 3x^3 + \underline{(6 + p)}x^2 + (2p - 6)x - 12$

Lining up x^2: $11 = 6 + p$ [The coefficients on the LHS must match the coefficients on the RHS.]

$p = 5$

$\therefore 3x^2 + 11x^2 + 4x - 12 = (x + 2)(3x^2 + 5x - 6)$

2. Long division:

$$
\begin{array}{r|l}
 & 3x^2 + 5x - 6 \\
x+2 & 3x^3 + 11x^2 + 4x - 12 \\
 & \mp 3x^3 \mp 6x^2 \\
\hline
 & 5x^2 + 4x - 12 \\
 & \mp 5x^2 \mp 10x \\
\hline
 & -6x - 12 \\
 & \pm 6x \pm 12 \\
\hline
 & 0
\end{array}
$$

$\therefore 3x^3 + 11x^2 + 4x - 12 = (x + 2)(3x^2 + 5x - 6)$

By the zero factor property:

$x + 2 = 0 \Rightarrow x = -2$

$3x^2 + 5x - 6 = 0$

$$x = \frac{-5 \pm \sqrt{(5)^2 - 4(3)(-6)}}{6}$$

$$= \frac{-5 \pm \sqrt{97}}{6}$$

The roots are $-2, \frac{-5 - \sqrt{97}}{6}, \frac{-5 + \sqrt{97}}{6}$.

Steps for solving cubic equations with at least one integer root:

1. Guess an integer root k of $ax^3 + bx^2 + cx + d = 0$ by testing integer factors of the constant term d.
2. From this root, form a linear factor $(x - k)$.
3. Factorise the cubic into a linear $(x - k)$ factor and a quadratic factor $Q(x)$ by lining up or by long division.
4. Solve the equation $(x - k)Q(x) = 0$.
   $Q(x) = 0$ can be solved by factorisation or by the quadratic formula.

WORKED EXAMPLE Solving cubic equations

Solve $x^3 - 7x^2 + 10x + 6 = 0$ if it has an integer root.

1. $P(x) = x^3 - 7x^2 + 10x + 6$

   The only possible integer roots are integer factors of 6. Do you know why? The integer factors of 6 are $\pm 1, \pm 2, \pm 3$.

   $P(1) = 1 - 7 + 10 + 6 = 10 \neq 0$

   $P(-1) = -1 - 7 - 10 + 6 = -12 \neq 0$

   $P(2) = 8 - 28 + 20 + 6 = 6 \neq 0$

   $P(-2) = -8 - 28 - 20 + 6 = -50 \neq 0$

   $P(3) = 27 - 63 + 30 + 6 = 0$ [Breakthrough]

   $\therefore$ 3 is a root.

2. $(x - 3)$ is a linear factor.
3. Lining up:

   $$x^3 - \underline{7}x^2 + 10x + 6 = (x - 3)(x^2 + px - 2)$$
   $$= x^3 - 3x^2 + px^2 - 3px - 2x + 6$$
   $$= x^3 + \underline{(p - 3)}x^2 + (-3p - 2)x + 6$$

   Lining up $\mathbf{x^2}$: $p - 3 = -7$

   $p = -4$

   $\therefore x^3 - 7x^2 + 10x + 6 = (x - 3)(x^2 - 4x - 2)$

Long division:

$$\begin{array}{r} x^2 - 4x - 2 \\ x-3\,\overline{)\,x^3 - 7x^2 + 10x + 6} \\ \mp x^3 \pm 3x^2 \\ \hline -4x^2 + 10x + 6 \\ \pm 4x^2 \mp 12x \\ \hline -2x + 6 \\ \pm 2x \mp 6 \\ \hline 0 \end{array}$$

$\therefore x^3 - 7x^2 + 10x - 6 = (x - 3)(x^2 - 4x - 2)$

4. $(x - 3)(x^2 - 4x - 2) = 0$

$(x - 3) = 0 \Rightarrow x = 3$

$x^2 - 4x - 2 = 0 \Rightarrow x = \dfrac{4 \pm \sqrt{16 + 8}}{2} = \dfrac{4 \pm 2\sqrt{6}}{2} = 2 \pm \sqrt{6}$

The three roots are $3, 2 + \sqrt{6}, 2 - \sqrt{6}$.

Graphical solutions of cubic equations

1. The general shapes of cubic functions $y = ax^3 + bx^2 + cx + d$ are:

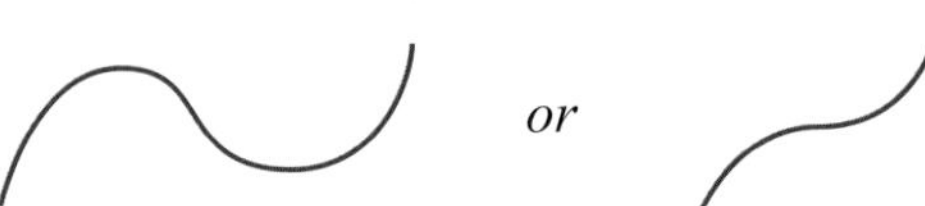

2. The solutions of $ax^3 + bx^2 + cx + d = 0$ are the values of x at which these curves cross the x-axis.

EXAMPLE 27

The graph of $y = 6x^3 - 13x^2 + 4$ is shown below. Find the co-ordinates of the points U, V and W.

Solution

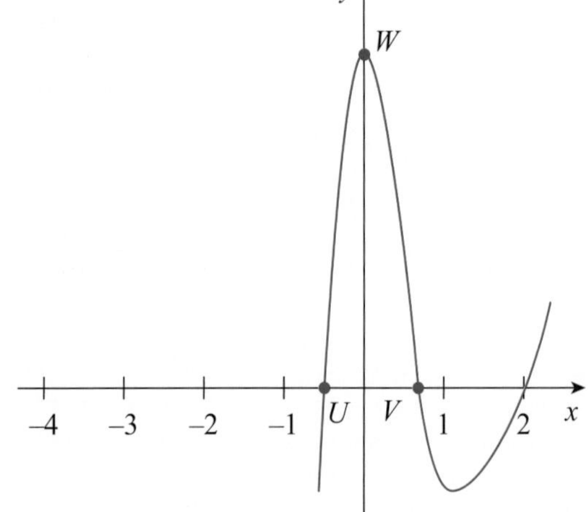

1. 2 is a root.

2. $(x - 2)$ is a factor.

3. $6x^3 - \underline{13}x^2 + 0x + 4 = (x - 2)(6x^2 + rx - 2)$

$= 6x^3 - 12x^2 + rx^2 - 2rx - 2x + 4$

$= 6x^3 + \underline{(r - 12)}x^2 + (-2r - 2)x + 4$

Lining up x^2: $r - 12 = -13$

$r = -1$

$\therefore 6x^3 - 13x^2 + 4 = (x - 2)(6x^2 - x - 2)$

or

Long division:

$$\begin{array}{r} 6x^2 - x - 2 \\ x-2\,\overline{)\,6x^3 - 13x^3 + 0x + 4} \\ \underline{\mp 6x^3 \pm 12x^2} \\ -x^2 + 0x + 4 \\ \underline{\pm x^2 \pm 2x} \\ -2x + 4 \\ \underline{\pm 2x \pm 4} \\ 0 \end{array}$$

$\therefore\ 6x^3 - 13x^2 + 4 = (x - 2)(6x^2 - x - 2)$

4. $(x - 2)(6x^2 - x - 2) = 0$

$x - 2 = 0$

$x = 2$

$6x^2 - x - 2 = 0$

$(3x - 2)(2x + 1) = 0$

$x = \frac{2}{3}, -\frac{1}{2}$

$-\frac{1}{2}, \frac{2}{3}, 2$ are the roots.

$U\left(-\frac{1}{2}, 0\right), V\left(\frac{2}{3}, 0\right)$

W is where the curve crosses the y-axis ($x = 0$).

$\boldsymbol{x = 0}$: $y = 0 - 0 + 4 = 4$

$W(0, 4)$ is the y-intercept.

Forming a cubic equation from its roots

By the factor theorem, if –3, 2, 1 are the three roots of a cubic equation, $(x + 3)$, $(x – 2)$, $(x – 1)$ are the three linear factors and so $(x + 3)(x – 2)(x – 1) = 0$ is the cubic equation. This cubic equation expands out to $x^3 – 7x + 6 = 0$.

EXAMPLE 28

Form the cubic equation with roots of $-\frac{2}{3}, \frac{1}{2}$ and 1.

Solution

Roots: $-\frac{2}{3}, \frac{1}{2}, 1$

Factors: $(3x + 2)(2x – 1)(x – 1) = 0$

Equation: $(3x + 2)(2x – 1)(x – 1) = 0$

$6x^3 – 5x^2 – 3x + 2 = 0$

Another method to obtain a cubic equation from its roots is to form a quadratic factor from two roots first, as follows:

1. Find:

   S = sum of the roots

   P = product of the roots
2. Form the quadratic factor: $(x^2 – Sx + P)$
3. Multiply the quadratic factor by the linear factor obtained from the third root and put equal to zero.

EXAMPLE 29

Form the cubic equation with roots $-2, 2 - \sqrt{3}, 2 + \sqrt{3}$.

Solution

Form a quadratic factor from $2 - \sqrt{3}, 2 + \sqrt{3}$.

Roots: $2 - \sqrt{3}, 2 + \sqrt{3}$

Sum $S = 4$, Product $P = 1$

Quadratic factor: $(x^2 – 4x + 1)$

Cubic equation: $(x^2 – 4x + 1)(x + 2) = 0$

$x^3 – 2x^2 – 7x + 2 = 0$

EXAMPLE 30

If $-5+\sqrt{3}$ and $-5-\sqrt{3}$ are roots of the cubic equation $x^3+7x^2+kx-66=0$. Find the other root and $k \in \mathbb{R}$.

Solution

Roots: $-5+\sqrt{3}, -5-\sqrt{3}$

Sum $S=-10$, Product $P=22$

Quadratic factor: $(x^2+10x+22)$

$x^3+7x^2+kx-66$

$=(x^2+10x+22)(x-3)=0 \quad [-66=22\times -3]$

The other root: $x-3=0 \Rightarrow x=3$

Multiply out the RHS:

$x^3+7x^2+\underline{kx}-66=x^3+7x^2-\underline{8x}-66$

Lining up the coefficients of x gives $k=-8$.

Mathematical modelling (word problems)

The steps are the same as those used in modelling problems involving linear and quadratic equations.

EXAMPLE 31

A cone is inscribed in a sphere with centre O and with radius 5, as shown. If x is the distance from the centre of the sphere to the centre of the base of the cone, show that the volume V of the cone is given by $V=\frac{1}{3}\pi(125+25x-5x^2-x^3)$.

If the volume of the cone is $\frac{128}{3}\pi$ cm^3, find x.

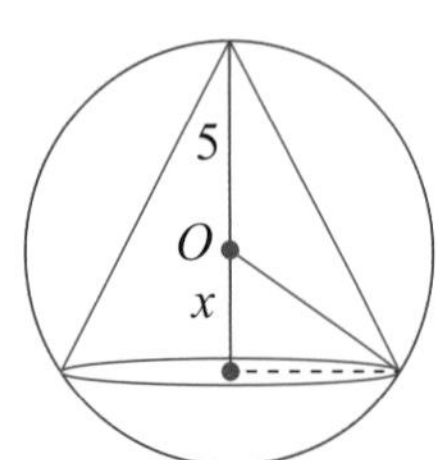

Solution

Volume of a cone $V=\frac{1}{3}\pi r^2 h$

$|AB|=h=(5+x)$

$r=\sqrt{(25-x^2)}$

$V=\frac{1}{3}\pi r^2 h=\frac{1}{3}\pi(25-x^2)(5+x)$

$V=\frac{1}{3}\pi(125+25x-5x^2-x^3)$

$\frac{1}{3}\pi(125+25x-5x^2-x^3)=\frac{128}{3}\pi$

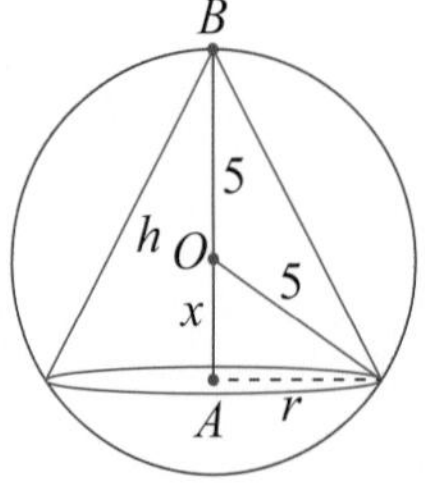

$125+25x-5x^2-x^3=128$

$x^3+5x^2-25x+3=0$

$P(x)=x^3+5x^2-25x+3$

$P(1)=1+5-25+3=-16\neq 0$

$P(2)=8+20-50+3=-19\neq 0$

$P(3)=27+45-75+3=0$

3 is a root $\Leftrightarrow (x-3)$ is a factor:

$x^3+\underline{5}x^2-25x+3=(x-3)(x^2+kx-1)$

$=x^3+\underline{(k-3)}x^2+(-3k-1)x+3$

Lining up: x^2: $k-3=5$

$k=8$

$x^3+5x^2-25x+3=(x-3)(x^2+8x-1)=0$

$x-3=0$

$x=3$

$x^2+8x-1=0$

$x=\dfrac{-8\pm\sqrt{64+4}}{2}=-4\pm\sqrt{17}$

$=0{\cdot}12, -8{\cdot}12$ [Reject negative solution.]

Answers: 3 cm or 0·12 cm

EXERCISE 3

1. **(a)** Is $(x - 2)$ a factor of $x^3 - 5x^2 + 7x - 2$?
   (b) Is $(2x + 1)$ a factor of $x^3 + 7x^2 - 9x - 6$?
   (c) Is $(x - a)$ a factor of $x^3 - 2ax^2 + 3a^2x - 2a^3$?
   (d) If $(x - 1)$ is a factor of $x^3 - 7x^2 + 11kx - 16$, find k.
   (e) $ax^3 - 2x^2 + 3x - 27$ is divisible by $(2x - 3)$. Find a.
   (f) If $(x - k)$ is a factor of $kx^3 - k^2x^2 + kx - 4$, find $k > 0$.
   (g) If $x^3 - ax^2 + 9x - b$ is divisible by $(x - 1)$ and $(x + 2)$, find a and b.
   (h) If $ax^3 + 4x^2 + bx - 8$ is divisible by $(2x - 1)$ and $(x + 1)$, find a and b.

2. Show, by substitution, that the given value of x is a root of the equation. Hence, find the other roots:
   (a) $x = 0$ of $2x^3 - 3x^2 - 5x = 0$
   (b) $x = -2$ of $x^3 + 9x^2 + 14x = 0$
   (c) $x = 3$ of $x^3 - 2x^2 - 5x + 6 = 0$
   (d) $x = \frac{2}{3}$ of $3x^3 - 2x^2 - 3x + 2 = 0$
   (e) $x = -\frac{1}{2}$ of $6x^3 + 7x^2 - 1 = 0$

3. Find the roots of the cubic equation given that an integer root exists:
   (a) $2x^3 + x^2 - 13x + 6 = 0$
   (b) $12x^3 - 11x^2 - 2x + 1 = 0$
   (c) $6x^3 + 25x^2 + 32x + 12 = 0$
   (d) $4x^3 - 16x^2 + 9x + 9 = 0$
   (e) $4x^3 - 9x^2 - 16x + 21$

4. **(a)** Show that $x + 2$ is a factor of $x^3 + 4x^2 - 11x - 30 = 0$. Hence, solve the equation $x^3 + 4x^2 - 11x - 30 = 0$.
   (b) Show that $2x^3 - 3x^2 - 4x - 1 = 0$ is divisible by $2x + 1$ and hence solve the equation $2x^3 - 3x^2 - 4x - 1 = 0$.
   (c) Solve the equation $x^3 - 16x^2 + 79x - 124 = 0$, if 4 is a root.
   (d) Find k if $x^3 - kx^2 + 21x - 9$ is divisible by $x - 3$ and solve the equation $x^3 - kx^2 + 21x - 9 = 0$.
   (e) $P(x) = 6 - 5x - x^2 + x^3$. Show that $2 - x$ is a factor and hence solve $P(x) = 0$.

5. For the cubic functions described by the curves below, find the points U, V, W and Z.
   (a) $y = (2x + 3)(2x - 1)(2x - 7)$

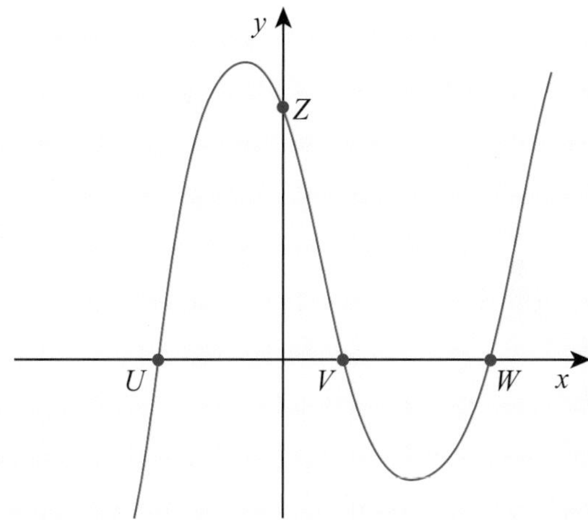

   (b) $y = (2x - 5)(x - 2)^2$

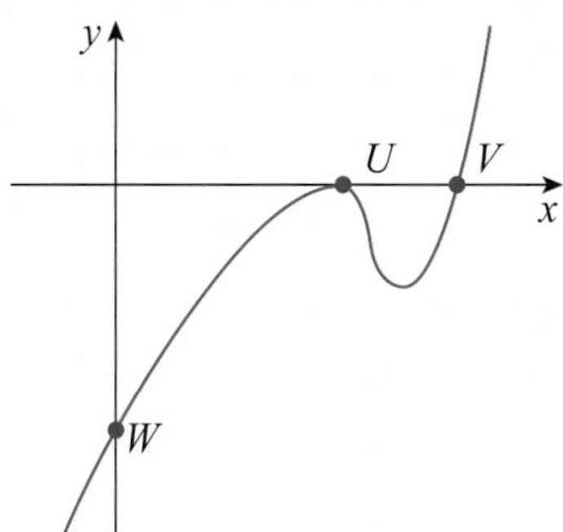

   (c) $y = (x - 3)(x^2 - 2x - 1)$

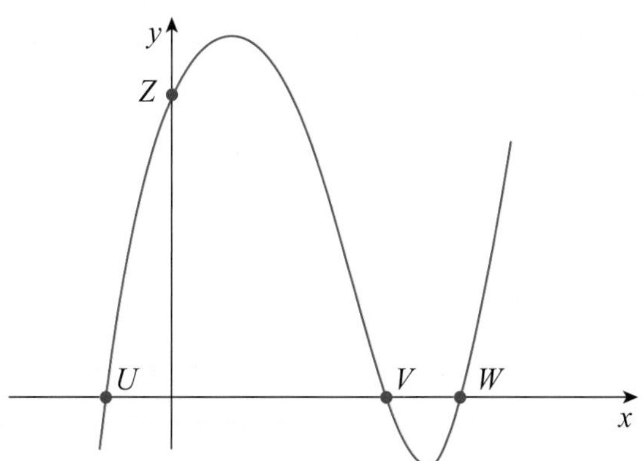

(d) $y = 3x^3 - 2x^2 - x$

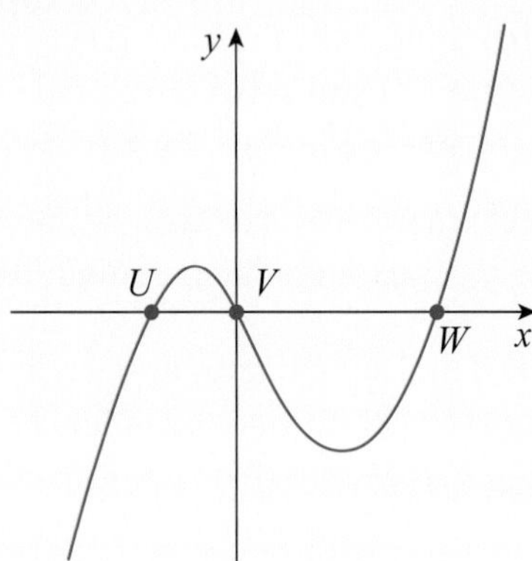

(e) $y = 2x^3 - 3x^2 - 3x + 2$

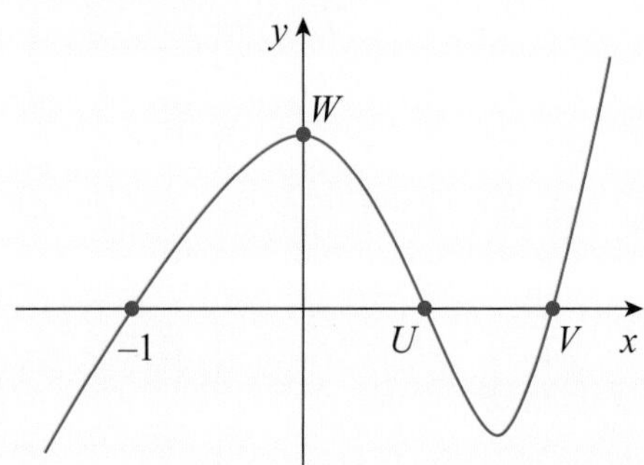

(f) $y = x^3 - 2x^2 + 1$

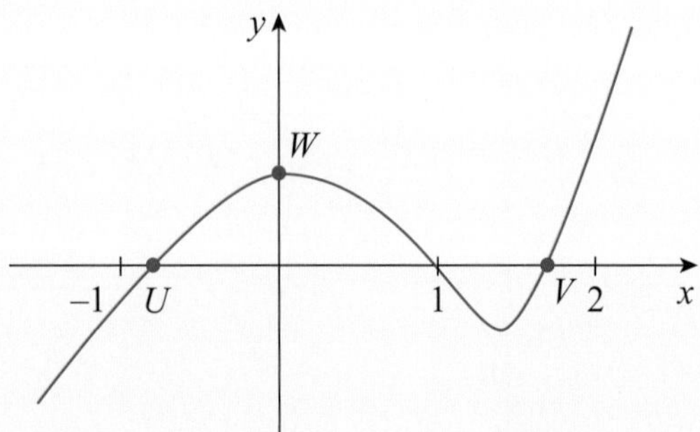

6. From the roots given, form the cubic equation:

(a) $-1, -2, 4$

(b) $2, 2, 2$

(c) $\frac{1}{2}, 2, -3$

(d) $a, -a, c$

(e) $2 + \sqrt{3}, 2 - \sqrt{3}, 5$

(f) $\sqrt{3}, -\sqrt{3}, 7$

7. If $3 - \sqrt{7}$, $3 + \sqrt{7}$ are two of the roots of the equation $x^3 - 9x^2 + 20x - 6 = 0$, find the other root.

8. A shed consists of a cube of sides x, x and x, where x is in metres, with a triangular prism as a roof. Show that the volume V of the shed is given by $V = \frac{x^3}{2} + \frac{3x^2}{2}$.

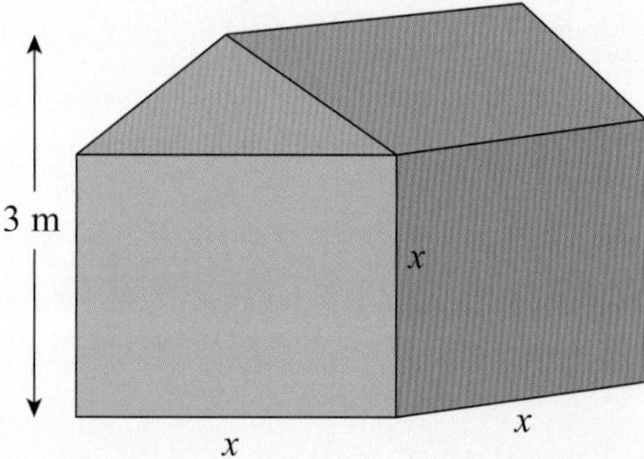

Find x if the volume of the shed is 10 m^3 and $x \in \mathbb{N}$.

9. If the area of the right-angled triangle shown is $\sqrt{5}$, show that $2x^3 + x^2 - 20 = 0$ and hence find $x \in \mathbb{N}$ and the lengths of all sides.

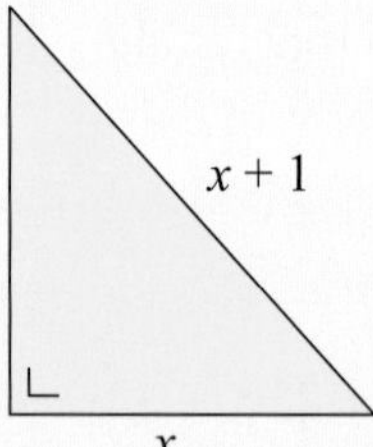

10. A body moves in a straight line from a fixed point O. Its distance s in metres after t seconds from O is given by $s = 3t^3 - 2t^2 - 3t + 2$. Find the times at which it is at O, given that one of these times is a whole positive number.

11. An observatory consists of a hemispherical dome on a cylindrical base. Show that $x^3 + 15x^2 - 162 = 0$ if the volume is 108π m^3 and x is in metres. Find x if $x \in \mathbb{N}$.

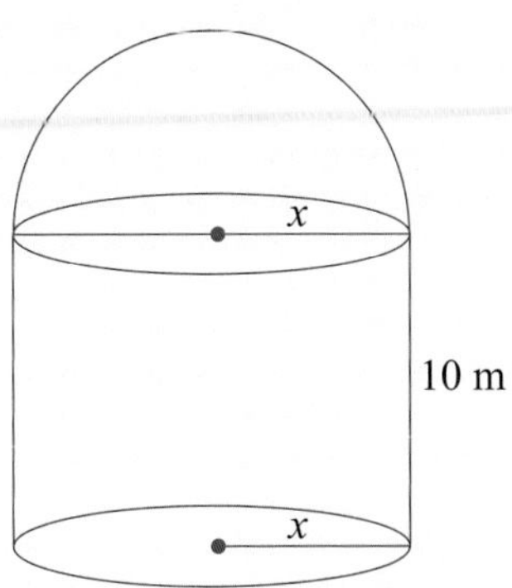

12. A rectangular sheet of metal 80 cm by 50 cm is used to form an open box by removing squares of side x cm from each corner, as shown, and folding up the flaps along the dotted lines. Show that the volume V of the box is given by $V = 4x^3 - 260x^2 + 4000x$. Find x if $V = 9768$ cm^3. Give answers to two decimal places if required.

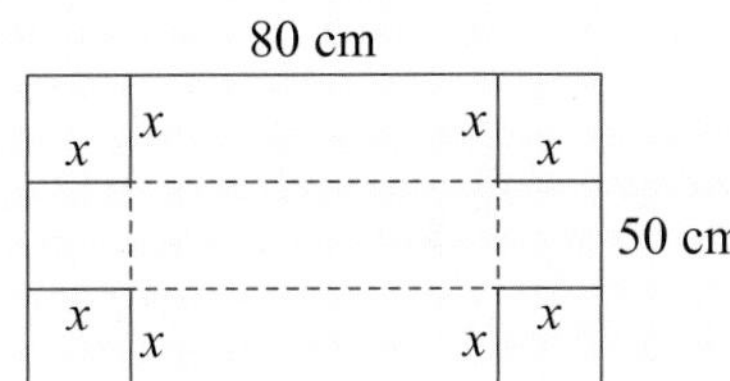

Other Types of Equations

Learning Outcomes

- To solve surd equations (equations with square roots).
- To solve literal equations where a given variable is isolated and written in terms of the other variables.
- To solve exponential or power equations.
- To solve log equations.
- To solve modulus equations.

7.1 Surd equations

A surd equation is an equation with one or more square roots.

ACTIVITY 7

ACTION
Working with surd equations

OBJECTIVE
To learn the techniques needed to solve surd equations

EXAMPLE 1

Solve $\sqrt{3x+7} - x = 1$.

Solution

$\sqrt{3x+7} - x = 1$ [If there is one square root, isolate it.]

$\sqrt{3x+7} = (x+1)$ [Put a bracket around $(x+1)$ in order to square it.]

$3x + 7 = (x+1)^2$

$3x + 7 = x^2 + 2x + 1$

$0 = x^2 - x - 6$ [Solve for x.]

$0 = (x+2)(x-3)$

$x = -2, 3$

Check your answer(s):

$\boldsymbol{x = -2}$: $\sqrt{-6+7} + 2 = \sqrt{1} + 2$
$= 3$ [Wrong]

$\boldsymbol{x = 3}$: $\sqrt{9+7} - 3 = \sqrt{16} - 3 = 4 - 3$
$= 1$ [Correct]

$x = 3$ is the only acceptable answer.

EXAMPLE 2

Solve $\sqrt{2x+7} - \sqrt{x} = 2$.

Solution

$\sqrt{2x+7} - \sqrt{x} = 2$ [If there are two square roots, get them on opposite sides of the equation first.]

$\sqrt{2x+7} = (\sqrt{x} + 2)$

$2x + 7 = (\sqrt{x} + 2)^2$

$2x + 7 = x + 4\sqrt{x} + 4$ [Isolate the square root.]

$(x + 3) = 4\sqrt{x}$ [Square both sides.]

$x^2 + 6x + 9 = 16x$

$x^2 - 10x + 9 = 0$ [Solve for x.]

$(x - 1)(x - 9) = 0$

$x = 1, 9$

Check your answer(s):

$x = 1$: $\sqrt{9} - \sqrt{1} = 3 - 1 = 2$ [Correct]

$x = 9$: $\sqrt{25} - \sqrt{9} = 5 - 3 = 2$ [Correct]

$x = 1, 9$ are both acceptable answers.

Solving equations with rational powers

To solve equations of the form $f[(x)]^{\frac{p}{q}} = a$, where $p, q \in \mathbb{R}$:

Put both sides to the power $\frac{q}{p}$ to give:

$f(x) = a^{\frac{q}{p}}$ if p is odd,

$f(x) = \pm (a)^{\frac{q}{p}}$ if p is even.

EXAMPLE 3

Solve:

(a) $x^5 = 32$ **(b)** $x^{-\frac{2}{3}} = 4$ **(c)** $(2x+1)^{\frac{3}{5}} = 27$

Solution

(a) $x^5 = 32$

$x = 32^{\frac{1}{5}}$

$x = 2$

(b) $x^{-\frac{2}{3}} = 4$

$x = \pm (4)^{-\frac{3}{2}}$

$x = \pm (2^{-3})$

$x = \pm \frac{1}{8}$

(c) $(2x+1)^{\frac{3}{5}} = 27$

$2x + 1 = 27^{\frac{5}{3}}$

$2x + 1 = 243$

$x = 121$

EXERCISE 4

1. Solve the following for x:
   - **(a)** $\sqrt{x} = \frac{1}{10}$
   - **(b)** $\sqrt{x} = 5 \times 10^4$
   - **(c)** $\sqrt{x+2} - 5 = 0$
   - **(d)** $\frac{5}{\sqrt{2x-3}} = \frac{1}{2}$
   - **(e)** $\sqrt{\frac{x}{x+1}} = \frac{2}{3}$
   - **(f)** $\sqrt{x(2x-1)} = 6$
   - **(g)** $3 + \sqrt{3x+1} = x$
   - **(h)** $x - 5 = \sqrt{7-x}$
   - **(i)** $\sqrt{x^2-7} = 7 - x$

(j) $2x - \sqrt{2x-1} = x + 2$

(k) $\sqrt{2x} = 1 + \sqrt{x+1}$

(l) $\sqrt{2x-1} + \sqrt{3x+1} = 7$

2. (a) If $P = r + \dfrac{n}{\sqrt{Z}}$, show that $Z = \dfrac{n^2}{(P-r)^2}$.

(b) If $A = r + \sqrt{r^2 + h^2}$, show that $h = \sqrt{A^2 - 2Ar}$.

(c) If $T = 2\pi\sqrt{\dfrac{r^3}{GM}}$, show that $r = \sqrt[3]{\dfrac{GMT^2}{4\pi^2}}$.

(d) If $p = r\left(\sqrt{\dfrac{x+y}{x-y}} - 1\right)$, show that $\dfrac{x}{y} = \dfrac{(p+r)^2 + r^2}{(p+r)^2 - r^2}$.

3. The geometric mean of two numbers, x and $2x + 1$, is the square root of their product. Find x, if their geometric mean is 6.

4. The periodic time T of a simple pendulum is given by $T = 2\pi\sqrt{\dfrac{l}{9{\cdot}8}}$, where l is its length in metres and T is in seconds. Find the length of a pendulum in centimetres with periodic time 1 second, correct to one decimal place.

5. When the square root of a real number is added to the square root of the number after it has been increased by 1, the answer is 5. Find this number.

6. If the volume of the rectangular box shown is 36 cm^3, find x and the lengths of the sides of the base.

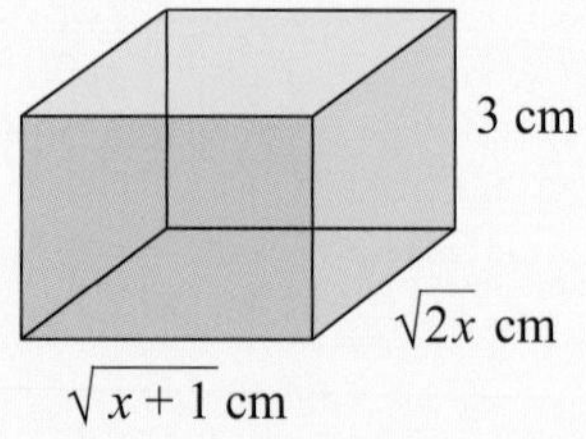

7. If the length of the diagonal of the rectangle shown is 4 cm and the area of the rectangle is 7·68 cm^2, find the dimensions of the rectangle.

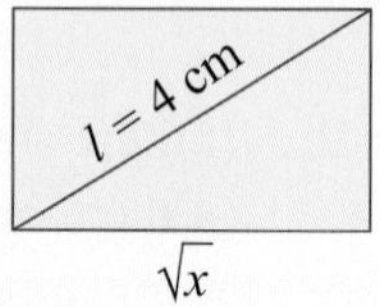

8. (a) Evaluate $(1 + \sqrt{2})^2$. Hence, show $1 + \sqrt{2} = \sqrt{3 + 2\sqrt{2}}$.

(b) Find A, the point of intersection of $y = 2\sqrt{x}, x \geq 0$ and $y = x - 1$. Use the answer to verify $1 + \sqrt{2} = \sqrt{3 + 2\sqrt{2}}$.

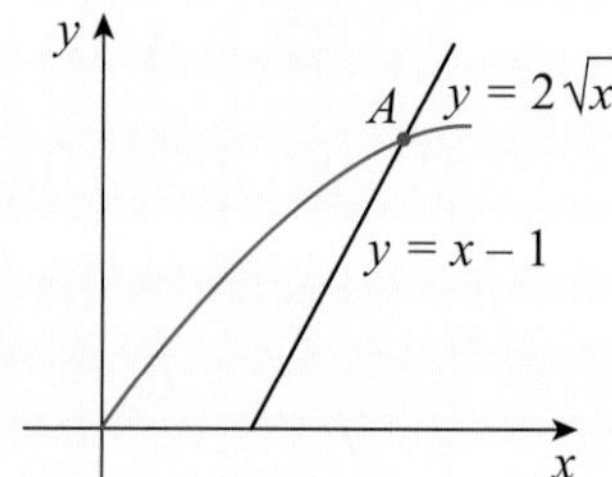

9. Solve the following:

(a) $x^{\frac{2}{5}} = 16$

(b) $(x + 1)^4 = 16$

(c) $(2x - 1)^3 = 8$

(d) $x^{\frac{4}{5}} = 81$

(e) $x^{\frac{5}{3}} = 9 \times 3^3$

(f) $x^{\frac{6}{5}} = 2^3 \times 8$

7.2 Literal equations

A literal equation is an equation with more than one unknown variable (letter).

- $S = ut$ (3 letters)
- $F = x + \dfrac{3}{x}$ (2 letters)
- $\dfrac{h}{p} = \sqrt{\dfrac{p}{z} + \dfrac{x}{3}}$ (4 letters)

ACTIVITY 8

ACTION
Working with literal equations

OBJECTIVE
To learn the techniques needed to solve literal equations

Steps for solving literal equations

Follow the steps outlined below to solve for a stated letter in terms of the other(s):

1. Get rid of fractions by multiplying both sides by the common denominator of all fractions.
2. Multiply out all brackets.
3. Get rid of square roots by isolating them and squaring.
4. Bring all terms containing the required letter to one side of the equation.
5. Take out the required letter as a factor (if necessary).
6. Solve for the letter.

(For literal equations involving exponentials and logs, see these sections on equations in this chapter.)

Note: Sometimes Steps 2 and 3 are easier to do before Step 1.

In the following examples, the letter in red is to be written in terms of the other letters:

- $b = u + t$
  $b - u = t$
  $\therefore t = b - u$

- $V = IR$
  $\frac{V}{I} = R$

- $x + \frac{tz}{y} = z$ [Get rid of the fractions. Multiply across by y.]
  $xy + tz = zy$ [Move all terms with y to right.]
  $tz = zy - xy$ [Take out a factor of y on right.]
  $tz = y(z - x)$ [Solve for y.]
  $\frac{tz}{z - x} = y$
  $\therefore y = \frac{tz}{z - x}$

- $A - \sqrt{r^2 + h^2} = 0$
  $A = \sqrt{r^2 + h^2}$ [Isolate the square root.]
  $A^2 = r^2 + h^2$
  $A^2 - h^2 = r^2$
  $\therefore r = \pm\sqrt{A^2 - h^2}$

EXAMPLE 4

The amount of energy E in joules released in a nuclear reaction is given by $E = mc^2$, where m is the mass of Uranium-235 in kg and c is the speed of light in m/s. Solve for c and find c if $m = 3$ g and $E = 2{\cdot}7 \times 10^{14}$ J.

Solution

$E = mc^2$

$\frac{E}{m} = c^2$

$\sqrt{\frac{E}{m}} = c$

$c = \sqrt{\frac{2{\cdot}7 \times 10^{14}}{3 \times 10^{-3}}} = 3 \times 10^8$ m/s

EXAMPLE 5

The concentration C of a certain drug in the bloodstream in mg/l after t hours is given by $C = \frac{4t}{t+2}$. Solve for t and find the time for the concentration to become 2 mg/l.

Solution

$$C = \frac{4t}{(t+2)}$$

$$C(t+2) = 4t$$

$$Ct + 2C = 4t$$

$$2C = 4t - Ct$$

$$2C = t(4 - C)$$

$$t = \frac{2C}{4 - C}$$

$\mathbf{C = 2:}$ $t = \frac{2 \times 2}{4 - 2} = 2$ hours

EXAMPLE 6

The distance of an image v from a mirror is given by $\frac{1}{u} + \frac{1}{v} = \frac{1}{f}$ where u is the distance of the object from the mirror and f is the focal length of the mirror. u, v and f are all measured in centimetres. Express v in term of u and f. If $u = 30$ cm and $f = 20$ cm, find v.

Solution

$\frac{1}{u} + \frac{1}{v} = \frac{1}{f}$ [Multiply all terms by uvf.]

$$vf + uf = uv$$

$$uf = uv - vf$$

$$uf = v(u - f)$$

$$\frac{uf}{u - f} = v$$

$\mathbf{u = 30}$ **and** $\mathbf{f = 20:}$ $v = \frac{30 \times 20}{30 - 20} = 60$ cm

EXERCISE 5

1. Solve the following for the letter within the bracket:

   (a) $\frac{h}{q} = 1 + st \quad (q)$

   (b) $E = \frac{1}{2}(v^2 - u^2)m \quad (u)$

   (c) $\frac{P_1V_1}{T_1} = \frac{P_2V_2}{T_2} \quad (T_1)$

   (d) $a = \frac{m_1 g}{m_1 + m_2} \quad (m_1)$

   (e) $\frac{T}{W} = \frac{t}{W + 2s} \quad (W)$

   (f) $E = \frac{(R - a)W}{2RP} \quad (R)$

   (g) $P = \frac{f(R^2 - D^2)}{(R^2 + D^2)} \quad (R)$

   (h) $q^2 + \frac{Rq}{L} + \frac{1}{LC} = 0 \quad (C)$

   (i) $A = \pi r^2 + 2\pi rh \quad (h)$

   (j) $p = q + \sqrt{3q^2 + 5h^2} \quad (h)$

2. The surface area A of a right circular cone is given by $A = \pi rl + \pi r^2$.

   Show that $A = \pi r^2 + \pi r\sqrt{r^2 + h^2}$.

   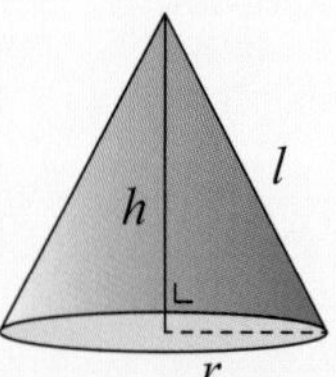

   Hence, show that $h = \frac{\sqrt{A(A - 2\pi r^2)}}{\pi r}$.

   If $A = 3\pi r^2$, show that $h = \sqrt{3}r$.

3. The cost C in euro of cleaning up a polluted area is given by $C = 80d\sqrt{A} + s$, where s is a fixed cost in euro, A is the area of the polluted region in m^2 and d is a constant which depends on the type of waste. Express A in terms of C, d and s. Find the area of an oil-polluted region that could be cleaned up for a cost of €70 000, given a fixed cost of €10 000 and $d = 15$ €/m.

4. In the special theory of relativity, the mass m in kg of a particle travelling at v m/s is given by $m = \frac{m_0}{\sqrt{1 - \frac{v^2}{c^2}}}$, where m_0 is the mass of the particle at rest in kg and c is the speed of light. Show that $v = \frac{c}{m}\sqrt{m^2 - m_0^2}$.

If $c = 3 \times 10^8$ m/s, find v when $m = 2m_0$, correct to one decimal place.

7.3 Exponential equations (power equations)

ACTIVITY 9

ACTION
Working with exponential equations

OBJECTIVE
To learn the techniques needed to solve exponential equations

Exponential equations are equations in which the unknown quantity is a power. They can be written in the form $a^{f(x)} = c$, where $f(x)$ is a function of x, and a and c are constants.

Steps for solving exponential equations

1. Get both sides to the same base raised to a single power using the rules of powers.
2. Equate the powers to solve for the unknown quantity.

▸
$$2^x = 32$$
$$2^x = 2^5$$
$$x = 5$$

▸
$$3 \times 3^{x+1} = 81 \times 3^{2x-5}$$
$$\frac{3^{x+1}}{3^{2x-5}} = \frac{81}{3}$$
$$3^{-x+6} = 27$$
$$3^{-x+6} = 3^3$$
$$-x + 6 = 3$$
$$x = 3$$

EXAMPLE 7

Solve $2^{x^2} = 8^{x - \frac{2}{3}}$.

Solution

$$2^{x^2} = 8^{x - \frac{2}{3}}$$
$$2^{x^2} = (2^3)^{x - \frac{2}{3}}$$
$$2^{x^2} = 2^{3x - 2}$$
$$x^2 - 3x + 2 = 0$$
$$(x - 1)(x - 2) = 0$$
$$x = 1, 2$$

If you cannot get the same base, isolate the base with the variable power on one side and then take the common log (log to base 10) instead of equating the powers.

EXAMPLE 8

Solve:

(a) $7^x = 23$ **(b)** $5^{x-1} = 4 \times 5^{2x-1}$

Solution

(a) $7^x = 23$

$$\log_{10} 7^x = \log_{10} 23$$

$$x \log_{10} 7 = \log_{10} 23$$

$$x = \frac{\log_{10} 23}{\log_{10} 7} = \log_7 23 \approx 1{\cdot}61$$

(b) $5^{x-1} = 4 \times 5^{2x-1}$

$$\frac{5^{x-1}}{5^{2x-1}} = 4$$

$$5^{-x} = 4$$

$$\log_{10} 5^{-x} = \log_{10} 4$$

$$-x \log_{10} 5 = \log_{10} 4$$

$$x = -\frac{\log_{10} 4}{\log_{10} 5} = -\log_5 4 \approx -0{\cdot}86$$

A special base *e*

ACTIVITY 10

ACTION
Understanding e

OBJECTIVE
To understand the nature of base e

The base *e* occurs in many places in Maths, Physics and the natural world.

Consider the value of $\left(1 + \frac{1}{n}\right)^n$ as n gets bigger and bigger. The table shows the results of $\left(1 + \frac{1}{n}\right)^n$ for higher and higher values of n.

n	$\left(1 + \frac{1}{n}\right)^n$
1	2·00000000
10	2·59374246
100	2·70481383
1000	2·71692393
10 000	2·71814593
100 000	2·71826824
1 000 000	2·71828047
10 000 000	2·71828169
100 000 000	2·71828181
1 000 000 000	2·71828183

Clearly, as $n \to \infty$, $\left(1 + \frac{1}{n}\right)^n \to 2{\cdot}71828$. This number is e.

$e \approx 2{\cdot}71828$ is the value of $\left(1 + \frac{1}{n}\right)^n$ as $n \to \infty$.

Press e on your calculator to get its value.

- $e^2 = 7{\cdot}389$ correct to three decimal places.

  It is such an important base that the log of an expression to base e is known as the natural log and has its own notation (ln).

- $\log_e 3 = \ln 3$ [This is the power to which you put e to get 3.]
- $\log_e x = \ln x$
- $\log_e (x^2 + 3x - 2) = \ln(x^2 + 3x - 2)$

WORKED EXAMPLE

Solving exponentials to base *e*

Solve $e^x = 2$

There are two ways to do this:

Method 1

$e^x = 2$ [Take common log of both sides.]

$\log_{10} e^x = \log_{10} 2$

$x \log_{10} e = \log_{10} 2$

$$x = \frac{\log_{10} 2}{\log_{10} e} = \log_e 2 = \ln 2$$

Method 2

$e^x = 2$ [Take natural log of both sides.]

$\ln e^x = \ln 2$

$x \ln e = \ln 2$

$x = \ln 2$ [$\ln e = \log_e e = 1$]

EXAMPLE 9

Solve $5e^{x+1} = 7e^{2x+3}$.

Solution

$5e^{x+1} = 7e^{2x+3}$

$$\frac{5}{7} = \frac{e^{2x+3}}{e^{x+1}}$$

$$\frac{5}{7} = e^{x+2}$$

$$\ln\left(\frac{5}{7}\right) = \ln e^{(x+2)}$$

$$\ln\left(\frac{5}{7}\right) = (x+2)\ln e$$

$$\ln\left(\frac{5}{7}\right) = x+2$$

$$x = \ln\left(\frac{5}{7}\right) - 2 \simeq -2{\cdot}336$$

A very important trick (*e*–ln trick)

Remember that $\log_a a^{f(x)} = f(x)$ and $a^{\log_a f(x)} = f(x)$.

The *e*–ln trick states: $\ln e^{f(x)} = f(x)$ and $e^{\ln f(x)} = f(x)$.

- $\ln e^2 = 2$
- $e^{\ln \cos x} = \cos x$
- $\ln e^{x+2} = x+2$
- $e^{\frac{1}{2}\ln x} = e^{\ln x^{\frac{1}{2}}} = x^{\frac{1}{2}}$

When *e* and ln come together, they cancel each other out because they are inverse functions of each other.

EXERCISE 6

1. Write the following in the form 2^k:

(a) $8^{\frac{2}{3}}$ **(b)** $16^{\frac{1}{2}}$ **(c)** $\dfrac{1}{8^{-\frac{4}{3}}}$

(d) $\dfrac{2^{-2}}{4^{-1}}$ **(e)** $\dfrac{\sqrt{8}}{32}$ **(f)** $\dfrac{4^2 \times 16^{\frac{1}{2}}}{64^{\frac{2}{3}} \times 4^3}$

(g) $\dfrac{16\sqrt{2}}{32}$ **(h)** $\dfrac{64 \times 32}{128^{\frac{2}{3}} \times 16^2}$ **(i)** $\sqrt[3]{4}$

2. Write the following in the form 3^p:

(a) 9 **(b)** 9^4 **(c)** $\dfrac{1}{9^1}$

(d) $\dfrac{1}{9^{-3}}$ **(e)** $\dfrac{1}{9^{-\frac{3}{2}}}$ **(f)** $(3\sqrt{3})^4$

(g) $\left(\dfrac{\sqrt{27}}{3}\right)^3$ **(h)** $\left(\dfrac{3\sqrt{3}}{9}\right)^{-2}$ **(i)** $\dfrac{3^{\frac{1}{4}} \times 3 \times 3^{\frac{1}{6}}}{\sqrt{3}}$

3. Write the following in the form $2^{f(x)}$:

(a) 4^x (b) 8^{x+1} (c) $\frac{1}{2^x}$ (d) 2×8^x (e) $\frac{8^x}{2}$ (f) $\frac{2}{8^x}$

(g) 16^{1-x} (h) $\frac{16}{2^x}$ (i) $\frac{32^x}{2}$ (j) $(4^x)^2$ (k) $\frac{4^{x+3}}{2^x}$

(l) $2 \times (8)^{(x+1)}$ (m) $\left(\frac{16^x}{\sqrt{2}}\right)^2$ (n) $\frac{2^x}{2^{3x}}$ (o) $\frac{2^{-2x}}{2^{-4x}}$

4. Write the following in the form $3^{f(x)}$:

(a) 9^x (b) $\frac{1}{9^x}$ (c) $\frac{3^x}{9^x}$ (d) $\frac{3^{3x+7}}{3^{2x}}$ (e) $\frac{3^{2x+1}}{3^{1-x}}$

(f) $\frac{9^{x+1}}{3}$ (g) 27^{1-x} (h) $\frac{9}{3^{x+2}}$ (i) $27^x \times 3$ (j) $(3^x)^2 \times 3$ (k) $\left(\frac{3^x}{9}\right)^2$

(l) $\frac{81^x}{3^{x-2}}$ (m) $\frac{\sqrt{27}}{9^x}$ (n) $\left(\frac{3^x}{3^{2x-1}}\right)^2$ (o) $\frac{9^x}{3^{-x}}$

5. Solve the following for x:

(a) $4^x = 16$ (b) $4^x = \frac{1}{16}$ (c) $4^x = 16^2$ (d) $\frac{1}{4^x} = 16$ (e) $8^x = 16$ (f) $4^x = 8$ (g) $25^x = 125$ (h) $9^x = \frac{1}{27}$ (i) $3^{x+1} = 81$ (j) $8^{x+2} = 4^{x-1}$

(k) $2^x = \sqrt{8}$ (l) $9^{x-1} = 3^{x+2}$ (m) $27 \times 9^{x-1} = 3 \times 3^{x-2}$ (n) $(2 \times 3^x)^2 = 36$ (o) $(3 \times 8^x)^2 \times 64 = 144$ (p) $2^{x^2} \times 2^{2x} = 8$ (q) $\frac{3^{x^2}}{3^{4x}} = 243$ (r) $4^{x^2} \times (2^2)^{-7x} = \frac{1}{2^{24}}$ (s) $\frac{3}{9^x} = \frac{\sqrt{3}}{27}$

6. (a) Express $\frac{\sqrt{8}}{32}$ in the form 2^k.

Hence, solve $\left(\frac{\sqrt{8}}{32}\right)^4 = 2^{2x+1}$.

(b) Express $27 \times \sqrt[3]{81}$ in the form 3^k.

Hence, solve $(27 \times \sqrt[3]{81})^{3x} = 3^{x-2}$.

(c) Express $\frac{64}{\sqrt{32}}$ in the form 2^k.

Hence, solve $\left(\frac{64}{\sqrt{32}}\right)^{2x+1} = 8^{x+2}$.

(d) Express $\frac{5 \times 25^3}{\sqrt{125}}$ in the form 5^p.

Hence, solve $\left(\frac{5 \times 25^3}{\sqrt{125}}\right)^2 = 5^{3x-1}$.

7. If $2^x = 16^6$ and $2^y = 64^4$, show that $x = y$.

8. An insect population P increases according to the law $P = 153 \times 9^{2t-1}$, where P is the number of insects in the colony t years after the population is first observed. Find:

(a) the initial population,

(b) when the population is 12 393.

9. Another insect population P increases according to the formula $P = 17 \times 3^{3t+1}$, where P is the number of insects in the sample t minutes after the observation begins. Find:

(a) the initial population,

(b) when the number of insects in the colony is 37 179.

10. If the two populations in Questions 9 and 10 are observed beginning at the same time, when will they be equal?

11. The percentage P of light transmitted by n sheets of plastic is given by $P = 25 \times 2^{2-n}$.

(a) What percentage is transmitted by zero sheets?

(b) What percentage of light is transmitted by four sheets?

(c) How many sheets transmit 0·78125% of light?

12. **(a)** Solve $e^{x^2} = \frac{e^{3x}}{e^2}$.

(b) If $4e^{x+1} = 8$, show that $x = \ln 2 - 1$.

(c) If $5^x = 3$, show:

(i) $x = \frac{\ln 3}{\ln 5}$ **(ii)** $x = \frac{\log_{10} 3}{\log_{10} 5}$

Can you give your answer in another form? Compare the answers using your calculator.

(d) If $N = N_0 e^{-kt}$, show that $t = \frac{1}{k}\ln\left(\frac{N_0}{N}\right)$.

(e) If $y = A(1 - e^{mx})$, show that $x = \frac{1}{m}\ln\left(\frac{A-y}{A}\right)$.

(f) A model for the world population growth is given by $P = P_0 e^{\frac{rt}{100}}$, where P is the population after t years, P_0 is the initial population and r is the annual percentage growth rate. Show that $t = \frac{100}{r}\ln\left(\frac{P}{P_0}\right)$.

If $r = 3$, find the time for the population to double, correct to the nearest year.

(g) If $5^{x+1} = 3^{2x-1}$, show $x = \frac{\ln 15}{\ln(1{\cdot}8)}$.

(h) The current I in a certain electrical circuit at time t is given by $I = \frac{V}{R}(1 - e^{-\frac{Rt}{L}})$, where V is the voltage, R is the resistance and L is the inductance. Show that $t = \frac{L}{R}\ln\left(\frac{V}{V-IR}\right)$.

7.4 Log equations

ACTIVITY 11

ACTION
Working with log equations

OBJECTIVE
To learn the technique needed to solve log equations

Log equations are equations that can be written in the form $\log_a f(x) = c$, where $f(x)$ is a function of x, and c and a are constants.

Steps for solving log equations

1. Get the same base. There are two ways to do this:

   (a) $\log_b a = \frac{1}{\log_a b}$ [Swap the letters when you move a log up or down.]

   (b) $\log_b a = \frac{\log_c a}{\log_c b}$ [Change of base.]

2. Get all the logs on one side.
3. Get a single log.
4. Get out of logs. [Hoosh]

▸ $\log_2 x = 4$
$x = 2^4$ [Hoosh]
$x = 16$

EXAMPLE 10

Solve $\log_5(7x+4) = -\log_5(3x-4) + 3$.

Solution

$\log_5(7x+4) = -\log_5(3x-4) + 3$. [The base is the same: base 5.]

$\log_5(7x+4) + \log_5(3x-4) = 3$ [Get the logs on one side.]

$\log_5(7x+4)(3x-4) = 3$ [Get a single log.]

$(7x+4)(3x-4) = 5^3$ [Get out of logs.]

$21x^2 - 16x - 16 = 125$

$21x^2 - 16x - 141 = 0$

$(21x+47)(x-3) = 0$

$x = -\frac{47}{21}, x = 3$ [$-\frac{47}{21}$ is not allowed as this would give the log of a negative number.]

EXAMPLE 11

Solve $\log_3 x + 3\log_x 3 = 4$.

Solution

$\log_3 x + 3\log_x 3 = 4$ [Get all logs in the same base.]

$\log_3 x + \dfrac{3}{\log_3 x} = 4$ [Multiply across by $\log_3 x$.]

$(\log_3 x)^2 + 3 = 4\log_3 x$ [Quadratic equation in $\log_3 x$]

$(\log_3 x)^2 - 4\log_3 x + 3 = 0$

$(\log_3 x - 3)(\log_3 x - 1) = 0$

$\log_3 x - 3 = 0$

$\log_3 x = 3$

$x = 3^3$

$x = 27$

$\log_3 x - 1 = 0$

$\log_3 x = 1$

$x = 3^1$

$x = 3$

EXAMPLE 12

Solve $\log_2 x \times \log_4 x = \frac{9}{2}$.

Solution

$\log_2 x \times \log_4 x = \frac{9}{2}$

Get the same base by changing $\log_4 x$ to base 2:

$\log_4 x = \dfrac{\log_2 x}{\log_2 4} = \dfrac{\log_2 x}{2}$

$\log_2 x \times \dfrac{\log_2 x}{2} = \dfrac{9}{2}$

$(\log_2 x)^2 = 9$

$\log_2 x = \pm 3$

$\log_2 x = 3$

$x = 2^3$

$x = 8$

$\log_2 x = -3$

$x = 2^{-3}$

$x = \frac{1}{8}$

EXAMPLE 13

Solve $\log_e p = \log_e 4 + 2h$ for p.

Solution

$\log_e p - \log_e 4 = 2h$

$\log_e\left(\dfrac{p}{4}\right) = 2h$

$\dfrac{p}{4} = e^{2h}$

$p = 4e^{2h}$

EXAMPLE 14

Solve $\frac{1}{2}\ln(y+1) = \ln(x+2) + \ln(A) + B$ for y.

Solution

$\frac{1}{2}\ln(y+1) = \ln(x+2) + \ln(A) + B$

$\frac{1}{2}\ln(y+1) - \ln(x+2) - \ln A = B$

$\ln\left(\dfrac{\sqrt{y+1}}{A(x+2)}\right) = B$

$\dfrac{\sqrt{y+1}}{A(x+2)} = e^B$

$\sqrt{y+1} = A(x+2)e^B$

$y + 1 = A^2(x+2)^2e^{2B}$

$y = A^2(x+2)^2e^{2B} - 1$

EXAMPLE 15

The decibel level D (dB) of a sound is given by $D = 10\log_{10}(I) - 10\log_{10}(I_0)$, where I is the intensity of sound in W/m^2 and $I_0 = 10^{-12}$ W/m^2. Solve for I. Find I when $D = 80$ dB, the decibel level of normal talk.

Solution

$D = 10\log_{10}(I) - 10\log_{10}(I_0)$

$\frac{D}{10} = \log_{10}\left(\frac{I}{I_0}\right)$

$10^{\frac{1}{10}D} = \frac{I}{I_0}$

$I = I_0 \times 10^{\frac{1}{10}D}$

$\boldsymbol{D = 80, I_0 = 10^{-12}}$: $I = 10^{-12} \times 10^{\frac{80}{10}} = 10^{-12} \times 10^8 = 10^{-4}$ W/m^2

EXERCISE 7

1. Solve the following for x:
   (a) $\log_2 x = 3$
   (b) $\log_3 x^2 = 2$
   (c) $\log_{10}\sqrt{x} = 4$
   (d) $\log_7(x - 1) = 2$
   (e) $\log_2(x^2 - 5x + 2) = 3$
   (f) $\log_{10}\left(\frac{x-2}{3}\right) = 2$
   (g) $\log_3\left(\frac{6x^2 + 14x - 4}{x}\right) = 2$
   (h) $\log_k x = b$
   (i) $\log_e\sqrt{x-1} = -1{\cdot}4$
   (j) $\log_e(x^2 - 3) = 2{\cdot}3, x > 0$, correct to one decimal place

2. Solve the following for x:
   (a) $2\log_x 64 = 3$
   (b) $\log_x 2 + \log_x 32 = 2, x > 0$
   (c) $1 + \log_2(3x + 1) = \log_2(2x + 1)$
   (d) $\log_5 x = 1 - \log_5(x - 4)$
   (e) $\log_{10}(5x + 1) = 2 + \log_{10}(2x - 3)$
   (f) $\log_3(x^2 + 4) - \log_3(x + 2) = 2 + \log_3(x - 2)$
   (g) $2\log_5 x = 2\log_5 3 + \log_5(x - 2)$
   (h) $\log_5 x = 1 + \log_5 3 - \log_5(2x + 1)$
   (i) $\log_a(x + 1) = \log_a(3x - 1) - \log_a x$
   (j) $2\log_3(x + 4) - 2 = \log_3 9$
   (k) $\log_2(x + 1) + \log_2(x - 1) = 3$
   (l) $2\log_3(x + 3) = \log_3(4x + 3) + 1$
   (m) $2\log_9 x = \frac{1}{2} + \log_9(5x + 18)$

3. Solve for x:
   (a) $(\log_2 x)^2 - 5\log_2 x + 6 = 0$
   (b) $\frac{6}{\log_x 4} + \frac{6}{\log_4 x} = 13$
   (c) $2\log_3 x + 2\log_x 3 = 5$
   (d) $\log_9\left(\frac{x}{3}\right) = \log_9 x \times \log_x 3$
   (e) $3\log_8(x + 19) = \log_2(18x + 2)$
   (f) $\log_2 x - \log_x 2 = \log_4 x + \frac{1}{2}$

4. (a) If $\log_e y = x + \log_e c$, show that $y = ce^x$.
   (b) If $\log_e y - \log_e x - ax = \log_e c$, show that $y = cxe^{ax}$.
   (c) If $\frac{1}{2}\ln y - \ln(x - 1) = \ln c$, show that $y = c^2(x - 1)^2$.
   (d) If $2{\cdot}5\log_{10}L_0 + M = 6 + 2{\cdot}5\log_{10}L$, show that $L = L_0 \times 10^{\frac{2m-12}{5}}$.
   (e) If $n = \frac{\ln p - \ln q}{\ln(1 - r)}$, show that $p = q(1 - r)^n$.
   (f) If $\ln y - \frac{1}{2}\ln x + \ln(x + 1) = x$, show that $y = \frac{\sqrt{x}\, e^x}{x+1}$.
   (g) $\ln(y + 5) - \ln x = 2 + \ln(y + 3)$, show that $y = \frac{3e^2x - 5}{1 - e^2x}$.

(h) If $\ln(1+x) - \ln(1-x) = 2y$, show that $x = \dfrac{e^{2y}-1}{e^{2y}+1}$.

(i) If $\ln(2x+1) = \ln\left(\dfrac{y}{2}\right) - A$ and $x = 0$ when $y = 2e$, find A. Hence, show that $y = 2e(2x+1)$.

(j) If $\ln e^{y} + e^{\ln x} = e^{2\ln x}$, show that $y = x(x-1)$.

5. The formula connecting the number N of objects sold as a function of its selling price p is given by the formula $\log_2 N = \log_2 F - b\log_2 p$.

(a) If $N = 512$ for $p = 8$ and $N = 2048$ for $p = 4$, find F and b.

(b) For $p = 16$, find N.

(c) Express p in terms of N.

(d) For $N = 4096$, find p.

6. In certain parts of the world, the area A (km^2) affected by an earthquake is related to the magnitude M of the quake by the formula $M = 2\log_{10}(A+4000) - 5$.

(a) For $A = 6000\ \text{km}^2$, find M.

(b) Find A in terms of M.

(c) Find the area affected by an earthquake of magnitude 5.

7. For children aged between 5 and 12 years, an experimental model relating their weight W (kg) to their height h (m) is given by $\log_3 W = \log_3 2{\cdot}5 + 1{\cdot}8h$.

(a) Show that $W = 2{\cdot}5 \times 3^{1\cdot8h}$.

(b) Find the predicted weight of a child of height 1 m, correct to one decimal place.

(c) Show that $h = \log_3\left(\dfrac{W}{2{\cdot}5}\right)^{\frac{1}{1\cdot8}}$ and find the predicted height of a 50 kg child, correct to two decimal places.

7.5 Absolute value (modulus) equations

ACTIVITY 12

ACTION
Working with absolute values

OBJECTIVE
To calculate the absolute values of various numbers using the number line

The absolute value of a real number is simply its distance to the origin.

Notation: $|x|$ is read as the modulus or absolute value of the real number x.

- $|-3|$ = distance of -3 to 0.

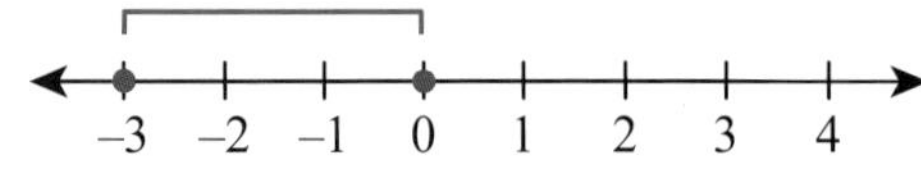

$\therefore |-3| = 3$

- $|4| = 4$

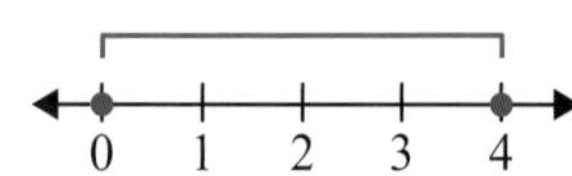

$$|x| = \begin{cases} x \text{ if } x \geq 0, x \in \mathbb{R} \\ -x \text{ if } x < 0, x \in \mathbb{R} \end{cases}$$

Therefore:

- $|\pi - 3| = \pi - 3$ [Since $\pi - 3 > 0$]
  but $|3 - \pi| = -(3 - \pi) = \pi - 3$ [Since $3 - \pi < 0$]

Note: $|x_1 - x_2| = |x_2 - x_1|$ always. (Can you say why?)

ACTIVITY 13

ACTION
Working with absolute value equations

OBJECTIVE
To learn the techniques needed to solve absolute value equations

Solving modulus equations of the form $|ax + b| = c$ or $|ax + b| = |cx + d|$

Technique: To solve $|x| = 3$, you need to find numbers x such that the distance of x from the origin is 3.

Clearly, this means $x = \pm 3$.

$|x| = 3 \Rightarrow x = \pm 3$

This gives us a clue as to how to solve equations of the type $|ax + b| = c$ or $|ax + b| = |cx + d|$.

Simply remove all vertical bars and put ± around the expression on one side or the other of the equation.

ACTIVITY 14

ACTION
Plotting graphs with absolute value functions

OBJECTIVE
To draw graphs of absolute value functions and write down the linear equations

EXAMPLE 16

Solve $|2x - 7| = 11$.

Solution

$|2x - 7| = 11$

$2x - 7 = \pm 11$

$2x - 7 = 11$	$2x - 7 = -11$
$2x = 18$	$2x = -4$
$x = 9$	$x = -2$

$x = -2, 9$

Check the solutions:

$x = -2$: $|2(-2) - 7| = 11$ [Correct]

$x = 9$: $|2(9) - 7| = 11$ [Correct]

EXAMPLE 17

Solve $|4x - 7| = |2x + 1|$.

Solution

$|4x - 7| = |2x + 1|$

$(4x - 7) = \pm(2x + 1)$

It is not necessary to have ± on both sides as this would give you four options, two of which are the same.

$4x - 7 = 2x + 1$	$4x - 7 = -2x - 1$
$2x = 8$	$6x = 6$
$x = 4$	$x = 1$

$x = 1, 4$

Check the solutions:

$x = 1$: $|4(1) - 7| = |2(1) + 1|$ [Correct]

$x = 4$: $|4(4) - 7| = |2(4) + 1|$ [Correct]

Plotting a graph of an absolute value function of the form $y = |ax + b|$ in the x–y plane

WORKED EXAMPLE Plotting graphs of absolute value functions

Method 1

Plot $y = |2x - 3|$.

Choose some values of x as follows:

x	$\frac{1}{2}$	1	$\frac{3}{2}$	2	$\frac{5}{2}$
$2x$	1	2	3	4	5
$2x - 3$	–2	–1	0	1	2
$y = \|2x - 3\|$	2	1	0	1	2

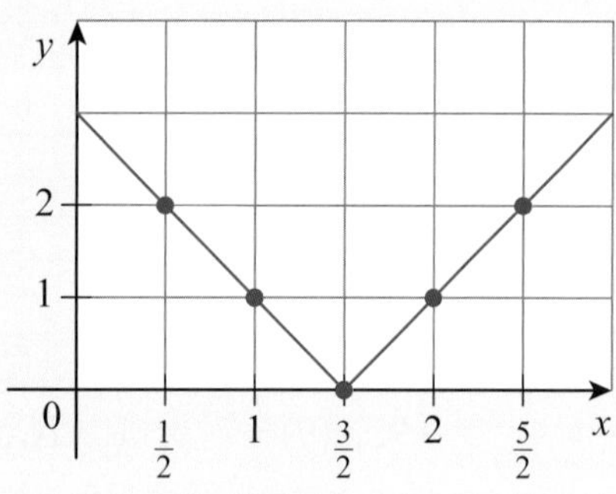

The resulting graph is V-shaped.

Method 2

Plot $y = |x - 4|$.

$y = |x - 4| \Rightarrow y = \pm(x - 4)$

This gives two straight lines: $y = x - 4$ and $y = 4 - x$.

$\boldsymbol{y = x - 4}$**:** Points (4, 0), (6, 2)

$\boldsymbol{y = 4 - x}$**:** Points (4, 0), (2, 2)

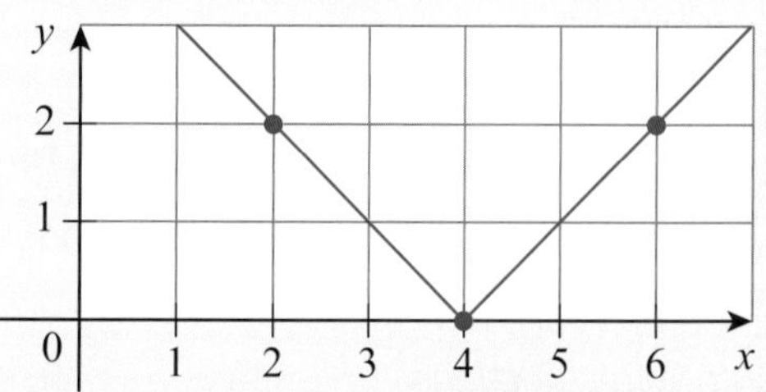

The resulting graph is also V-shaped.

Graphs of $y = |ax + b|$ can never go below the x-axis.

EXAMPLE 18

Solve $|2x + 1| = 5$ by plotting $y = |2x + 1|$ and $y = 5$.

Solution

$y = |2x + 1| \Rightarrow y = \pm(2x + 1)$ [The equations are straight lines.]

$\boldsymbol{y = 2x + 1}$**:** Points (0, 1), $\left(-\frac{1}{2}, 0\right)$

$\boldsymbol{y = -2x - 1}$**:** Points (–1, 1), $\left(-\frac{1}{2}, 0\right)$

$y = 5$ is also a straight line.

Graphically, the lines $y = -2x - 1$ and $y = 2x + 1$ intersect the line $y = 5$ at $x = -3$ (Point A) and $x = 2$ (Point B).

$\therefore$ The solutions are $x = -3, 2$.

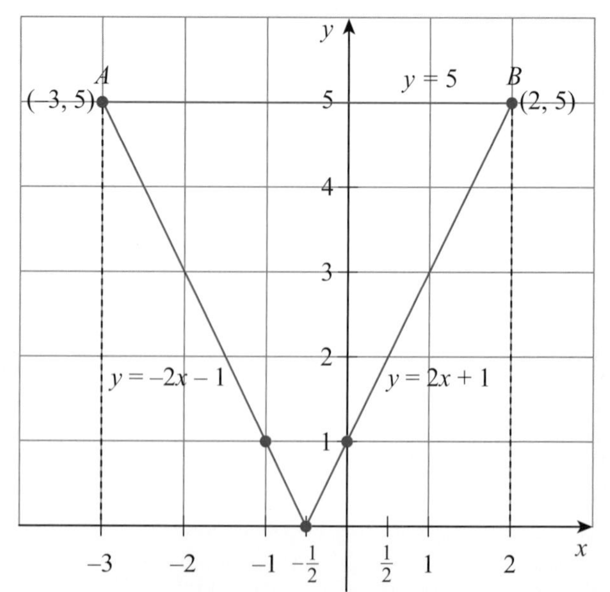

Algebraically:

$$|2x+1| = 5$$

$$2x + 1 = \pm 5$$

$2x + 1 = 5$	$2x + 1 = -5$
$2x = 4$	$2x = -6$
$x = 2$	$x = -3$

$$x = -3, 2$$

EXERCISE 8

1. Evaluate the following:

(a) $|-5|$

(b) $|5|$

(c) $|\sqrt{5}|$

(d) $\left|-\frac{1}{\sqrt{5}}\right|$

(e) $|e|$

(f) $|3-\sqrt{3}|$

(g) $|\sqrt{2}-2|$

(h) $|2\pi - 7|$

(i) $|t^2+1|, t \in \mathbb{R}$

(j) $|e^x + 1|, x \in \mathbb{R}$

(k) $|2^x|, x \in \mathbb{R}$

(l) $|a-b|, b > a$

2. Solve:

(a) $|x| = 7$

(b) $|x+7| = 8$

(c) $|4x-1| = 9$

(d) $|3x+2| = 5$

(e) $|3x-1| = |2x+3|$

(f) $|\sqrt{x+1}| = 5$

(g) $|\sqrt{17-2x}| = x-1$

(h) $\left|\frac{1}{x}\right| = 2$

3. Plot the following in the x–y plane:

(a) $y = |x|$

(b) $y = |x+1|$

(c) $y = |x-1|$

(d) $y = |x|+2$

(e) $y = |2x+5|$

4. **(a)** Plot $y = |x-3|$ and $y = 4$. Hence, solve $|x-3| = 4$.

(b) Plot $y = |2x-1|$ and $y = x$. Hence, solve $|2x-1| = x$.

5. Using $a = -8$ and $b = 4$, show that:

(a) $|ab| = |a||b|$

(b) $\left|\frac{a}{b}\right| = \frac{|a|}{|b|}$

(c) $|a+b| < |a|+|b|$

(d) $|a-b| > |a|-|b|$

6. **(a)** Is $|ab| = |a||b|$ for all $a, b \in \mathbb{R}$?

(b) Is $\left|\frac{a}{b}\right| = \frac{|a|}{|b|}$ for all $a, b \in \mathbb{R}$?

(c) Is $|a+b| < |a|+|b|$ for all $a, b \in \mathbb{R}$? Give a counter example (i.e. an example that disproves this result).

(d) Is $|a-b| > |a|-|b|$ for all $a, b \in \mathbb{R}$? Give a counter example.

7. If x is 3 units from 2, write down an equation for x. Hence find x.

8. Is $|x|^2 = x^2 = |x^2|$ always? Why?

Systems of Simultaneous Equations

Learning Outcomes

- To solve simultaneous linear equations in two unknowns.
- To solve simultaneous equations involving linear equations and equations of order two in two unknowns.
- To solve simultaneous linear equations in three unknowns.
- To model and solve word problems involving simultaneous equations.

Systems of simultaneous equations

A system of simultaneous equations consists of two or more equations in two or more unknowns.

$2x + 3y = 7$

$3x - 5y = 1$

This set of two equations has two unknowns, x and y. The solution of this system of simultaneous equations is the values of x and y that make both equations true at the same time (simultaneously). There are three different types to be considered.

8.1 Linear equations in two unknowns 

ACTIVITY 15

ACTION
Working with equivalent equations

OBJECTIVE
To learn the techniques needed to solve linear simultaneous equations

These are simultaneous equations of the form: $ax + by = d$
$ex + fy = g$

1. The unknowns are x and y in this case.
2. The coefficients of x and y are a, e and b, f, respectively. The constants are d and g.
3. They are called linear equations because if you plot y against x for each equation, you get a straight line.

The method of solution is called **elimination by addition**.

WORKED EXAMPLE Solving linear equations in two unknowns

Solve $2x + 3y = 7$ and $3x - 5y = 1$ by elimination by addition.

Step 1: Write the x term under the x term, the y term under the y term, and the constant under the constant. Decide which letter to eliminate by looking at the coefficients of x or y.

$2x + 3y = 7 \ldots \textbf{(1)}$

$3x - 5y = 1 \ldots \textbf{(2)}$

Step 2: Multiply equation (**1**) by 3 and equation (**2**) by –2. Their x coefficients will then both become –6. Remember that when you multiply an equation by a number, you must multiply **all** terms in the equation. Add both equivalent equations so that the terms in x are eliminated. Solve for y.

$$\begin{aligned} 6x + 9y &= 21 \ldots \textbf{(1)} \ (\times 3) \\ -6x + 10y &= -2 \ldots \textbf{(2)} \ (\times -2) \\ \hline 19y &= 19 \\ y &= 1 \end{aligned}$$

Step 3: Find the value of x by substituting $y = 1$ back into any of the previous equations. Putting $y = 1$ into equation (**1**):

$$\begin{aligned} 2x + 3(1) &= 7 \\ 2x &= 4 \\ x &= 2 \end{aligned}$$

Step 4: Present your answer in the form $(x, y) = (2, 1)$. This is the point of intersection of the two lines $2x + 3y = 7$ and $3x - 5y = 1$ when plotted on co-ordinated rectangular axes.

Eliminate fractions by multiplying by the LCD and then multiply out the brackets.

EXAMPLE 1

Solve: $\dfrac{(x+2)}{3} + \dfrac{(y-3)}{2} = 6$

$\dfrac{(x-2)}{5} - \dfrac{(y+3)}{6} = -1$

Solution

$\dfrac{(x+2)}{3} + \dfrac{(y-3)}{2} = 6 \ (\times 6)$ [Get rid of fractions first.]

$$\begin{aligned} 2(x+2) + 3(y-3) &= 36 \\ 2x + 4 + 3y - 9 &= 36 \\ 2x + 3y &= 41 \ldots \textbf{(1)} \end{aligned}$$

$$\frac{(x-2)}{5} - \frac{(y+3)}{6} = -1 \ (\times 30)$$

$$\begin{aligned} 6(x-2) - 5(y+3) &= -30 \\ 6x - 12 - 5y - 15 &= -30 \\ 6x - 5y &= -3 \ldots \textbf{(2)} \end{aligned}$$

Step 1: Eliminate x.

$2x + 3y = 41 \ldots \textbf{(1)}$

$6x - 5y = -3 \ldots \textbf{(2)}$

Step 2: Solve for y.

$$\begin{aligned} -6x - 9y &= -123 \ \ldots \textbf{(1)} \ (\times -3) \\ 6x - 5y &= -3 \ \ \ \ldots \textbf{(2)} \\ \hline -14y &= -126 \\ y &= 9 \end{aligned}$$

Step 3: Solve for x.

Using (2):

$$\begin{aligned} \boldsymbol{y = 9}: \quad 6x - 5(9) &= -3 \\ 6x &= 42 \\ x &= 7 \end{aligned}$$

Step 4: $(x, y) = (7, 9)$

EXAMPLE 2

Solve: $\log_2 x - \log_3 y = 4$

$3\log_2 x + \log_3 y = 0$

Solution

$\log_2 x - \log_3 y = 4 \ldots (1)$

$3\log_2 x + \log_3 y = 0 \ldots (2)$

$4\log_2 x = 4$

$\log_2 x = 1$

$x = 2^1 = 2$

Using (1):

$x = 2$: $\log_2 2 - \log_3 y = 4 \ldots (1)$

$1 - \log_3 y = 4$

$\log_3 y = -3$

$y = 3^{-3} = \frac{1}{27}$

$(x, y) = \left(2, \frac{1}{27}\right)$

Word problems using two simultaneous linear equations in two unknowns

To illustrate the approach to modelling a problem with two variables using simultaneous equations, consider the following example.

WORKED EXAMPLE Modelling a simultaneous equation problem

Some 800 tickets were sold for a basketball match. An adult ticket cost €13·50 and a child ticket cost €8. A total of €10 140 was collected from selling all tickets. How many adult tickets were sold and how many child tickets were sold?

Solution

1. Always let x and y be the answers to the questions asked and be absolutely clear what they represent. There are two unknowns, x and y, so you need two equations.

   Let x be the number of adult tickets sold and y the number of child tickets sold.

2. Translate the words in the problem into two linear equations:

   (a) The total number of tickets was 800: $x + y = 800$

   (b) The total amount of money collected was €10 140.

   The money collected from selling x adult tickets at €13·50 per ticket = $13{\cdot}5x$

   The money collected from selling y child tickets at €8 per ticket = $8y$

   $13{\cdot}5x + 8y = 10\,140$

3. Now solve the equations using the elimination by addition method:

$x + y = 800 \quad \ldots (1)$

$13{\cdot}5x + 8y = 10\,140 \quad \ldots (2)$

$-8x - 8y = -6400 \quad \ldots (1)\ (\times -8)$

$13{\cdot}5x + 8y = 10\,140 \quad \ldots (2)$

$5{\cdot}5x = 3740$

$x = 680$

Using (1):

$x = 680$: $680 + y = 800$

$y = 120$

Answer: 680 adult tickets and 120 child tickets.

Type 1: Numbers

EXAMPLE 3

Five times a number and three times a second number add to 27. Twice the second number and three times the first add to 17. Find these numbers.

Solution

Let x = first number

Let y = second number

$5x + 3y = 27$ ... **(1)**

$3x + 2y = 17$ ... **(2)**

$10x + 6y = 54$ ... **(1)** $(\times 2)$

$-9x - 6y = -51$ ... **(2)** $(\times -3)$

$x = 3$

Using (2):

$3(3) + 2y = 17$

$2y = 8$

$y = 4$

Answer: The two numbers are 3 and 4.

Type 2: Geometry

EXAMPLE 4

The perimeter of a rectangle is 82 m. The length is 8 m longer than twice the breadth. Find the length, the breadth and the area of the rectangle.

Solution

Let x = length

Let y = breadth

Perimeter $= 2x + 2y = 82$ ... **(1)**

Length = 2 (Breadth) + 8:

$x = 2y + 8$

$x - 2y = 8$ ... **(2)**

$2x + 2y = 82$ ... **(1)**

$x - 2y = 8$ ... **(2)**

$3x = 90$

$x = 30$

Using (2):

$\boldsymbol{x = 30}$: $(30) - 2y = 8$

$22 = 2y$

$y = 11$

Length = 30 m

Breadth = 11 m

Area $= 30 \times 11 = 330\ \text{m}^2$

Type 3: Business and finance

EXAMPLE 5

Enda has more money than Mícheál. If Enda gave Mícheál €55 000, they would have the same amount. However, if Mícheál gave Enda €8000, Enda would have twice as much as Mícheál. How much money does each have?

Solution

Let x = amount of Enda's money

Let y = amount of Mícheál's money

$x - 55\,000 = y + 55\,000$

$x - y = 110\,000$ ... **(1)**

$(x + 8000) = 2(y - 8000)$

$x + 8000 = 2y - 16\,000$

$x - 2y = -24\,000$ ... **(2)**

$x - y = 110\,000$ ... **(1)**

$x - 2y = -24\,000$ ... **(2)**

$x - y = 110\,000$ ... **(1)**

$-x + 2y = 24\,000$ ... **(2)** $(\times -1)$

$y = 134\,000$

Using (1):

$\boldsymbol{y = 134\,000}$**:** $x - (134\,000) = 110\,000$

$x = 244\,000$

Answer: Enda has €244 000 and Mícheál has €134 000.

Type 4: Mixtures

A solution of one substance in another is simply a mixture of the two. If you are told that a 20% solution of sugar in water is made up, this simply means that 1 litre of a mixture of water and sugar has 0·2 litres of sugar and 0·8 litres of water. So x litres of such a solution would have $0{\cdot}2x$ litres of sugar and $0{\cdot}8x$ litres of water.

EXAMPLE 6

Twenty litres of a 15% solution of a disinfectant in water is made up of two solutions. One solution is made up of 22% of the disinfectant in water and the other solution is made up of 8% of the disinfectant in water. How many litres of each solution are there?

Solution

Let x = number of litres of 22% solution

Let y = number of litres of 8% solution

The total number of litres is 20 litres.
$x + y = 20$ ... **(1)**

The total amount of disinfectant in the 20 litres:
$0{\cdot}15 \times 20 = 3$ litres

$0{\cdot}22x + 0{\cdot}08y = 3$ ... **(2)**

$x + y = 20$ ... **(1)**

$0{\cdot}22x + 0{\cdot}08y = 3$ ... **(2)**

$-0{\cdot}22x - 0{\cdot}22y = -4{\cdot}4$ ... **(1)** $(\times -0{\cdot}22)$

$0{\cdot}22x + 0{\cdot}08y = 3$ ... **(2)**

$-0{\cdot}14y = -1{\cdot}4$

$y = 10$

Using (1):

$\boldsymbol{y = 10}$**:** $x + (10) = 20$

$x = 10$ litres

$x = 10$ l, $y = 10$ l

Type 5: Speed, distance and time problems

Remember: Speed $= \dfrac{\text{Distance}}{\text{Time}}$

For a river: A boat travelling downstream is moving with the current, which adds to the boat's cruising speed, making it go faster. A boat travelling upstream goes against the current, which subtracts from the boat's cruising speed, slowing it down.

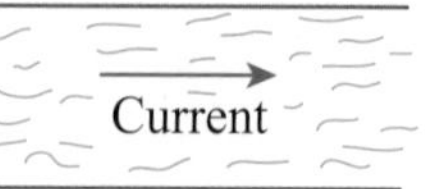

For an aeroplane:

A tailwind adds to the aeroplane's cruising speed, but a headwind subtracts from the aeroplane's cruising speed, slowing it down.

EXAMPLE 7

It takes 15 minutes for a man to swim 0·5 km upstream. The return trip takes 5 minutes. Find the speed of the man and the speed of the current in km/h.

Solution

Journey upstream

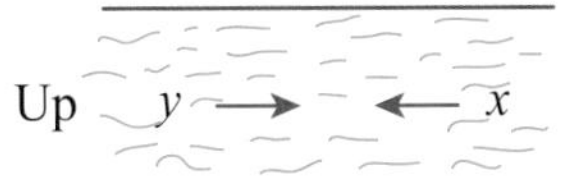

Journey downstream

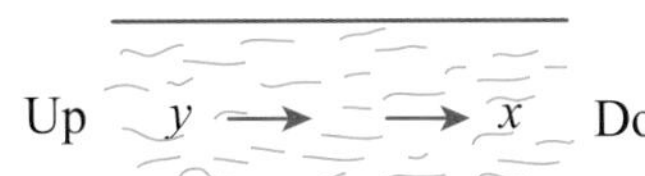

Let x = speed of man in still water

Let y = speed of the current

To swim upstream: Net speed $= x - y = \dfrac{\text{Distance}}{\text{Time}}$

$$x - y = \frac{0{\cdot}5}{0{\cdot}25} = 2$$

$$x - y = 2 \ldots \textbf{(1)}$$

To swim downstream: Net speed $= x + y = \dfrac{\text{Distance}}{\text{Time}}$

$$= \frac{0{\cdot}5}{\frac{1}{12}} = 6$$

$$x + y = 6 \ldots \textbf{(2)}$$

$$x - y = 2 \ldots \textbf{(1)}$$
$$x + y = 6 \ldots \textbf{(2)}$$
$$2x = 8$$
$$x = 4$$

Using (2):

$\boldsymbol{x = 4}$: $(4) + y = 6$

$y = 2$ km/h

Speed of man = 4 km/h

Speed of current = 2 km/h

EXERCISE 9

(A) CONCEPTS AND SKILLS

Solve the following pairs of linear simultaneous equations:

1. $2x - 5y = 3$
$x - 3y = 1$

2. $3x - 5y = 44$
$5x + 7y = 12$

3. $2x - 3y = 24$
$\dfrac{5x}{3} - \dfrac{y}{2} = 12$

4. $\dfrac{x}{2} + \dfrac{y}{5} = 4$
$\dfrac{x}{4} + \dfrac{y}{2} = 6$

5. $4x + 11 = 3y$
$3(x - 2) - 7y = 0$

6. $5x - 2y = 7 = 9x - 5y$

7. $7 - 6(x - 3y) = 4$
$3(x + 2y) + 6 = 5x + 10y$

8. $2(x - 1) + \dfrac{y - 1}{4} = 3$
$\dfrac{x}{2} + \dfrac{y}{5} = 2$

9. $\dfrac{3(x + 2)}{4} - \dfrac{(y + 3)}{2} = 1$
$\dfrac{5(x - y + 2)}{6} = \dfrac{5}{2}$

10. $\dfrac{2}{3} - x = \dfrac{y}{6} - 3$
$2x - 3y = -6$

11. $\dfrac{1}{x} + \dfrac{1}{y} = 3$
$\dfrac{1}{x} - \dfrac{1}{y} = 1$

12. $\dfrac{4}{x} + \dfrac{3}{y} = -5$
$\dfrac{3}{x} - \dfrac{2}{y} = \dfrac{19}{4}$

13. Solve the following for x and y:

(a) $27^x = 9,\ 2^{x-y} = 64$

(b) $2^x = 8^{y+1},\ (3^2)^y = 3^{x-9}$

(c) $a^{4x} \times a^y = a^3,\ \dfrac{b^{2x}}{b^y} = 1$

(d) $2^{x+1} = 16,\ x^y = 81$

(e) $4^{x+y} = 8,\ 4^{x-y} = 16$

(f) $x^{\frac{3}{2}} = 125,\ x^{y+1} = 5$

(g) $2^{x+y} = 8,\ 5^{2x-y} = 1$

14. $3\log_4 y + 2\log_5 x = 3$

$\log_5 x + \log_4 y = 1$

15. $2\log_3 x + \log_2 y = 10$

$4\log_3 x - 3\log_2 y = 0$

16. $\log_3 x - \log_3 y = 4$

$\log_2(x - 33y) = 4$

(B) CONTEXTS AND APPLICATIONS

Numbers

1. The sum of two numbers is 135. Their difference is 7. Find them.
2. The difference of two numbers is 3. If three times the larger number less twice the smaller one is 13, find them.
3. Three times a number and twice a second number add to –1. If twice the first number added to three times the second number is –9, find these numbers.
4. The difference between two numbers is 5. If three times the larger number plus five times the smaller number is 111, find them.
5. One half of the sum of two numbers is equal to their difference. What are the numbers if their sum is 96?
6. Two numbers add to 12. If one of these is subtracted from three times the other, the answer is also 12. Find them.

Geometry

7. The perimeter of a rectangular field is 114 m. The length is 7 m greater than the breadth. Find the length, the breadth and the area of the rectangle.

8. The lengths of the rectangle shown are all in centimetres.

(a) Find x and y.

(b) Find the perimeter and area of the rectangle.

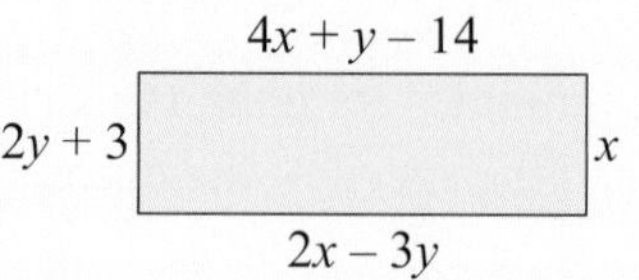

9. The lengths of the sides of the equilateral triangle shown are given in centimetres.

(a) Find x and y.

(b) Find the perimeter and area of the triangle.

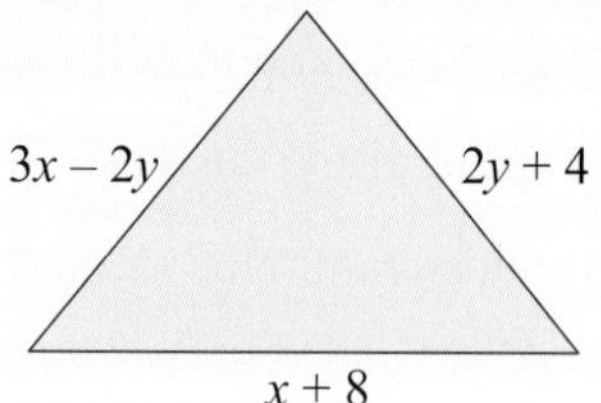

10. The shortest side of the isosceles triangle ACB is $[AC]$. If the perimeter is 17 cm and $|AC|$ is 4 cm shorter than $|AB|$, find the length of all sides.

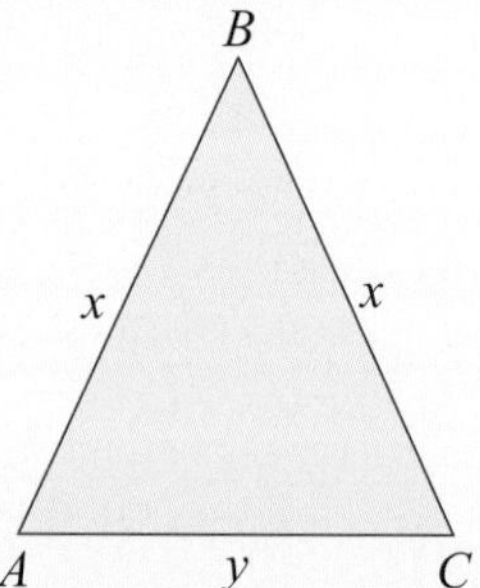

Business and finance

11. Peter invested €20 000. Part of his money was invested at 2% per annum and the rest at 3% per annum. If the interest at the end of a year was €450, find how much was invested at each rate.

12. Mr Nolan bought 100 shares in Bankwin and 50 shares in Academic Enterprise. The total cost of all 150 shares was €790.

Mrs Harvey bought 40 shares in Bankwin and 110 shares in Academic Enterprise. The total cost of all 150 shares was €874.

Find the price of a Bankwin share and of an Academic Enterprise share.

Mixtures

13. A man has €2·25 in his pocket, consisting of 5 cent and 10 cent coins only. If the total number of coins in his pocket is 41, find the number of each coin is his possession.

14. A test consists of 13 questions. There are 5-mark questions and 12-mark questions. If the test is worth 100 marks in total, how many of each type of question are there?

15. A parking lot has 162 spaces in total. It has twice as many spaces for cars as it has for trucks. How many spaces has the lot for cars? How many spaces has it for trucks?

16. How many litres of a 30% alcohol solution and how many litres of a 50% alcohol solution must be mixed to produce 20 litres of a 40% alcohol solution?

17. A goldsmith uses two gold alloys. The first alloy is 90% gold and the second is 80% gold. How many grams of each should she mix together to produce 53·1 g of an alloy that is 87% gold?

Time

18. A boat made a trip of 6 km upstream (against the current) in 15 minutes. The return trip (with the current) took 12 minutes. Find the speed of the current and the speed of the boat in still water.

19. An aeroplane travels 1920 km in 2 hours with a tailwind. The return trip with a headwind takes $2\frac{1}{2}$ hours. Find the cruising speed of the aeroplane and the wind speed.

20. A rowing team competes in a competition with two legs. The first leg covers 9·6 km in the direction of the current. The second leg covers the same 9·6 km against the current. It takes 24 minutes to complete the first leg and 36 minutes to complete the second leg. Find the speed of the current and the speed of the boat in still water.

Miscellaneous

21. Two computer processors, A and B, carry out two consecutive algorithms. For the first algorithm, processor A is in service for 2 seconds and processor B is in service for 3 seconds. The total number of computations for this algorithm is 2 000 000. The processors work in parallel. For the second algorithm, processor A is in service for 3 seconds and processor B is in service for 2 seconds. The total number of computations for this algorithm is 15 000 000. The processors work in parallel. Find the processing rate (the number of computations per second) for each processor.

22. An alloy is a mixture of metals. One alloy is made up of a concentration of 25% copper and 75% tin. Another alloy is made up of 80% copper and 20% tin. The two alloys are melted together and give a mixture of 50% copper and 50% tin, which weighs in total 330 g. Find the masses of the original alloys.

23. A photovoltaic (solar) array is a linked collection of solar panels. The perimeter of such an array is 142 cm, the breadth being 2 cm longer than half the length. Find the length, the breadth and the area of the array.

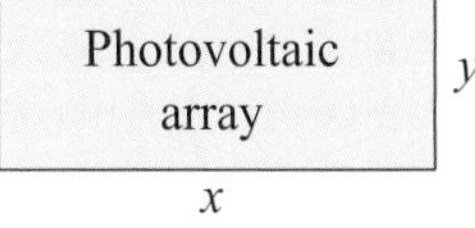

8.2 One linear equation and one equation of order two in two unknowns

An equation of order two is an equation in which in at least one term the powers of the variables add to exactly 2 and in no term the powers of the variables add to more than 2.

Examples: $x^2 + y^2 = 4, x^2 - y = 7x, \ xy + x^2 = 2y^2$

We use **substitution** for solving one linear equation and one equation of order two.

ACTIVITY 16

ACTION
Using simultaneous equations involving a linear and an equation of order two

OBJECTIVE
To learn the techniques needed to solve linear and order two simultaneous equations

WORKED EXAMPLE

Solving linear and order two simultaneous equations

Solve $x - y = -3$ and $x^2 + xy = -1$ simultaneously.

Step 1: Start with the linear equation $x - y = -3$ and solve for x or y. Choose cleverly.

$y = (x + 3) \ldots$ **(1)**

Put a bracket around the terms on the right-hand side.

Step 2: Substitute this expression for y into $x^2 + x(y) = 1 \ldots$ **(2)**

$x^2 + x(x + 3) = -1$

Multiply out the brackets:

$x^2 + x^2 + 3x = -1$

$2x^2 + 3x + 1 = 0$ [This is a quadratic in x.]

Step 3: Solve the quadratic by factorisation or by using the magic formula:

$(2x + 1)(x + 1) = 0$

$x = -\frac{1}{2}, x = -1$

Step 4: Get the corresponding values for y using equation (**1**).

$\boldsymbol{x = -\frac{1}{2}}$**:** $y = (-\frac{1}{2} + 3) = \frac{5}{2}$

$\boldsymbol{x = -1}$**:** $y = (-1 + 3) = 2$

$\left(-\frac{1}{2}, \frac{5}{2}\right)$ and $(-1, 2)$ are the solutions.

What do these solutions mean?

They are the points of intersection of the straight line with equation $x - y = -3$ and the curve with equation $x^2 + xy = -1$.

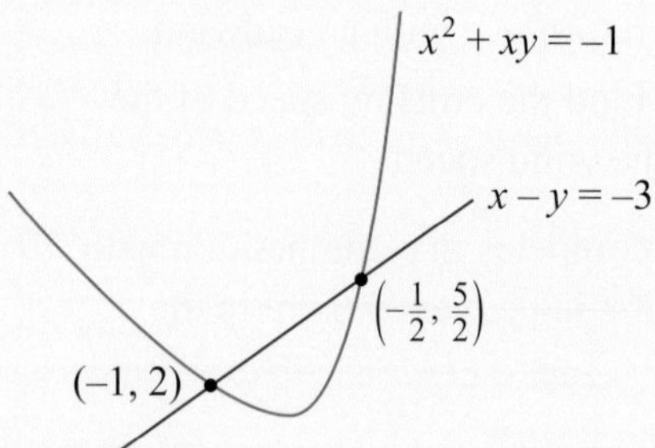

EXAMPLE 8

Solve $y^2 + 4xy + 35 = 0$ and $2x + 3y = 5$ simultaneously.

Solution

Step 1: $2x + 3y = 5$

$$2x = (5 - 3y)$$

$$x = \left(\frac{5 - 3y}{2}\right) \ldots \textbf{(1)}$$

Step 2: $y^2 + 4(x)y + 35 = 0$ ... **(2)**

$$y^2 + \frac{4y(5-3y)}{2} + 35 = 0$$ [Multiply each term by 2.]

$$2y^2 + 4y(5-3y) + 70 = 0$$

$$2y^2 + 20y - 12y^2 + 70 = 0$$

$$10y^2 - 20y - 70 = 0$$

$$y^2 - 2y - 7 = 0$$

Step 3: $y = \frac{2 \pm \sqrt{4+28}}{2} = \frac{2 \pm \sqrt{32}}{2}$

$$y = 1 \pm 2\sqrt{2}$$

Step 4: $\boldsymbol{y = 1 + 2\sqrt{2}}$**:** $x = \frac{5 - 3(1+2\sqrt{2})}{2}$

$$= 1 - 3\sqrt{2}$$

$\boldsymbol{y = 1 - 2\sqrt{2}}$**:** $x = \frac{5 - 3(1-2\sqrt{2})}{2}$

$$= 1 + 3\sqrt{2}$$

The solutions are

$(1 - 3\sqrt{2}, 1 + 2\sqrt{2}), (1 + 3\sqrt{2}, 1 - 2\sqrt{2})$.

Word problems involving one linear equation and one equation of order two

The strategy is much the same as for two linear equations word problems. Always let x and y be the answers to the questions asked and be absolutely clear what they represent.

EXAMPLE 9

The sum of two numbers is 3 and the sum of their squares is 65. What are the numbers?

Solution

Let x = one number

Let y = the other number

$$x + y = 3 \quad \dots \textbf{(1)}$$

$$x^2 + y^2 = 65 \quad \dots \textbf{(2)}$$

$$x + y = 3 \quad \dots \textbf{(1)}$$

$$y = (3 - x)$$

Into (2): $x^2 + (3-x)^2 = 65$

$$x^2 + 9 - 6x + x^2 = 65$$

$$2x^2 - 6x - 56 = 0$$

$$x^2 - 3x - 28 = 0$$

$$(x+4)(x-7) = 0$$

$$x = -4, 7$$

$\boldsymbol{x = -4}$**:** $y = (3 - x) = (3 - (-4)) = 7$

$\boldsymbol{x = 7}$**:** $y = (3 - x) = (3 - (7)) = -4$

The numbers are -4 and 7.

EXAMPLE 10

A television screen has diagonals of length 100 cm. If the perimeter of the screen is 280 cm, find the length, breadth and area of the screen.

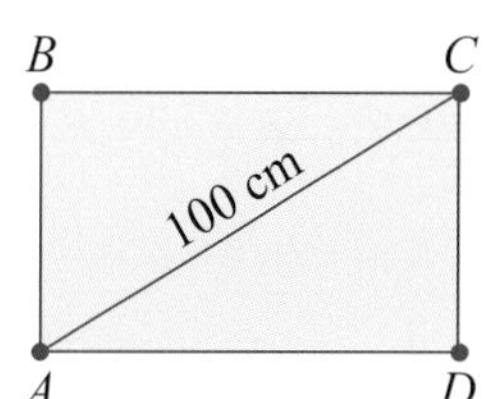

Solution

Let x = length of screen

Let y = breadth of screen

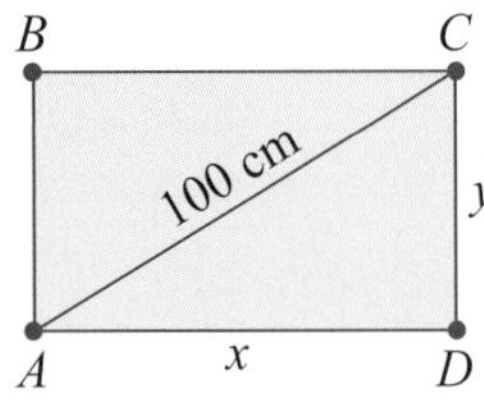

Perimeter: $2x + 2y = 280$

$$x + y = 140 \quad \ldots \textbf{(1)}$$

Diagonals: $x^2 + y^2 = 10\,000 \quad \ldots \textbf{(2)}$

$$x + y = 140$$

$$y = (140 - x)$$

Into (2): $x^2 + (140 - x)^2 = 10\,000$

$$x^2 + 19\,600 - 280x + x^2 = 10\,000$$

$$2x^2 - 280x - 9600 = 0$$

$$x^2 - 140x - 4800 = 0$$

$$(x - 80)(x - 60) = 0$$

$$x = 80, 60$$

$x = 80$: $y = (140 - x) = (140 - 80) = 60$

$x = 60$: $y = (140 - x) = (140 - 60) = 80$

Answers: length = 80 cm, breadth = 60 cm *or* length = 60 cm, breadth = 80 cm

Area = $80 \times 60 = 4800$ cm^2

EXAMPLE 11

Bus A leaves Dublin and travels due west to Galway. Bus B leaves Dublin 12 minutes later and travels the same route. Bus B overtakes Bus A 156 km from Dublin. If the average speed of Bus B is 5 km/h greater than the average speed of Bus A, find these average speeds.

Solution

Let x = average speed of Bus A

Let y = average speed of Bus B

Speed: $y = x + 5$

$$x = (y - 5) \ldots \textbf{(1)}$$

Time for Bus A to travel 156 km $= \dfrac{156}{x}$

Time for Bus B to travel 156 km $= \dfrac{156}{y}$

$\dfrac{156}{x} - \dfrac{156}{y} = \dfrac{12}{60} = \dfrac{1}{5}$ [Multiply across by $5xy$.]

$780y - 780x = xy \ldots$ **(2)**

Substitute equation **(1)** into **(2):**

$$780y - 780(y - 5) = y(y - 5)$$

$$3900 = y(y - 5)$$

$$y^2 - 5y - 3900 = 0$$

$$(y + 60)(y - 65) = 0$$

$$y = -60, 65$$

$y = -60$: $x = y - 5 = (-60) - 5 = -65$ [Not allowed.]

$y = 65$: $x = y - 5 = (65) - 5 = 60$

Answers: Bus A travels at 60 km/h and Bus B travels at 65 km/h.

EXERCISE 10

(A) CONCEPTS AND SKILLS

Solve the following for x and y:

1. $x + y = 7$
   $xy = 12$
2. $x - y = 1$
   $xy = 42$
3. $x + y = 3$
   $x^2 + y^2 = 5$
4. $x - y - 1 = 0$
   $x^2 + y^2 = 13$
5. $x^2 + xy + y^2 = 52$
   $x + y = 8$

6. (a) $x + y - 6 = 0$
$x^2 + 2y^2 - 24 = 0$

(b) What can you conclude about $x + y - 6 = 0$ in terms of its intersection with the curve $x^2 + 2y^2 - 24 = 0$?

7. $3x + y = 10$
$2x^2 + y^2 = 19$

8. $2x + y + 1 = 0$
$4x^2 + y^2 = 25$

9. $2x - y = 5$
$xy = 0$

10. $2x + y = 1$
$y = x^2 - 4x - 2$

11. $2x + 3y = -1$
$x^2 + y^2 = 25$

12. $2x + 3y = 4$
$x^2 + 2xy = 5$

13. $5x - 3y = -1$
$x^2 + y^2 = 5$

14. $3x - 2y = 1$
$x^2 + y^2 + 6x - 2y = 6$

15. $3x + 4y = 1$
$x^2 + y^2 - 2x + 2y - 3 = 0$

16. $x + y = 3$
$\frac{2}{x} + \frac{4}{y} = 4$

(B) CONTEXTS AND APPLICATIONS

1. The difference of two numbers is 3. The sum of their squares is 185. Find two pairs of such numbers.

2. The sum of two numbers is 42. The difference of their squares is 168. Find the pair of such numbers.

3. The product of two positive numbers is 120. Their difference is 7. If x is the larger and y the smaller of the numbers, find x and y.

4. Find two numbers such that their sum is 3 and their product is 1.

5. The area of a rectangular section of a field for playing sports is 3600 m^2. If the perimeter is 250 m, find the length and breadth of the field.

6. The equation of the circle s is $x^2 + y^2 = 34$. The equation of the line l is $2x - y = -1$. Find the co-ordinates of the points of intersection of the line and the circle.

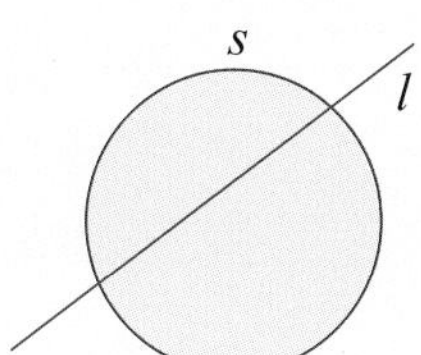

7. The lengths of all sides of the rectangle shown are in centimetres. Find x and y, the length, breadth and area of the rectangle.

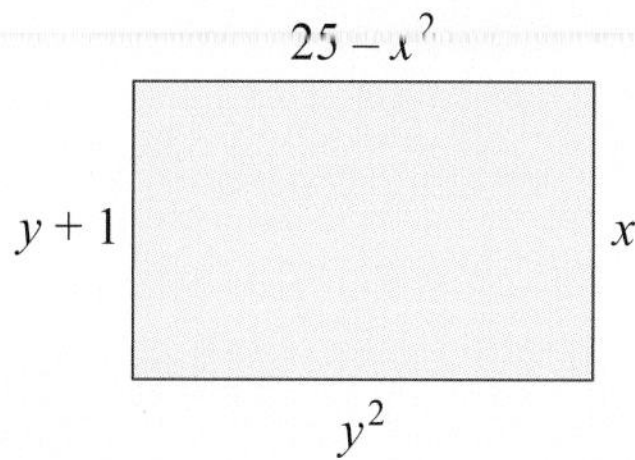

8. A fish tank with no lid has a total area of 1·88 m^2. If the sum of the length, the breadth and the height is 1·9 m, find x, y and the volume of the tank.

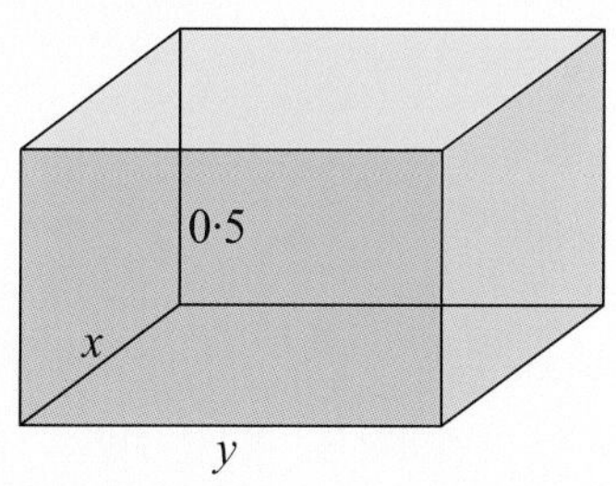

9. Two ferries run by Irish Ferries leave every day from Dublin Port to Holyhead by exactly the same route. The distance of the trip is 148 km. The average speed of the *Jonathan Swift* is 34 km/h greater than the average speed of the slower *Ulysses* ferry. As a result, the *Jonathan Swift* arrives 1 hour 42 minutes ahead of the *Ulysses*. Find the average speed of each ferry.

10. The ellipse has the formula $x^2 + 9y^2 = 9$. Find where the line $x - y = 3$ intersects the ellipse.

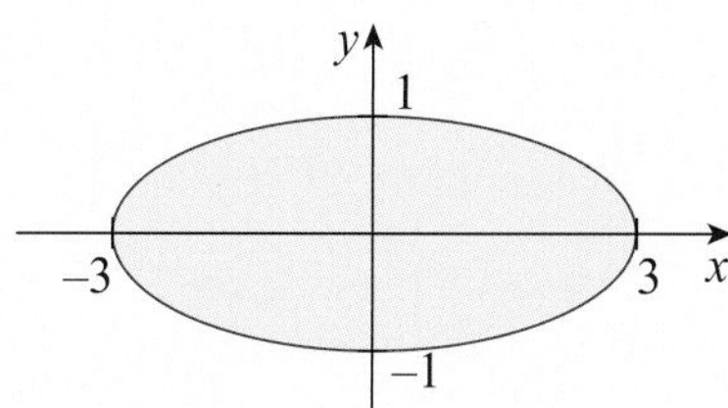

8.3 Three linear simultaneous equations in three unknowns

The technique for solving a system of three simultaneous linear equations in three unknowns is to reduce them to two equations in two unknowns. This is done by eliminating one unknown from a pair of the equations and then eliminating the same unknown from a different pair of equations.

WORKED EXAMPLE Solving three linear simultaneous equations

Solve

$x - 2y + 3z = 4$

$2x + y - 4z = 3$

$3x - 4y + z = 2$

for x, y, z.

Step 1: Label each equation and write the x's under the x's, the y's under the y's, the z's under the z's and the constants under the constants.

$x - 2y + 3z = 4 \ldots$ **(1)**

$2x + y - 4z = 3 \ldots$ **(2)**

$3x - 4y + z = 2 \ldots$ **(3)**

Step 2: Eliminate z from equations **(1)** and **(3)** and z from equations **(2)** and **(3)**.

(1): $x - 2y + 3z = 4$

(3) × −3: $-9x + 12y - 3z = -6$

$-8x + 10y = -2 \ldots$ **(4)**

(2): $2x + y - 4z = 3$

(3) × 4: $12x - 16y + 4z = 8$

$14x - 15y = 11 \ldots$ **(5)**

Step 3: Solve equations **(4)** and **(5)** in two unknowns by elimination.

Eliminating y gives:

(4) × 3: $-24x + 30y = -6$

(5) × 2: $28x - 30y = 22$

$4x = 16$

$x = 4$

Step 4: Find y by substituting the value of x into equation **(4)** or **(5)**.

(4): $-8 \times 4 + 10y = -2$

$10y = 30$

$y = 3$

Get z by substituting the values of x and y into equations **(1)** or **(2)** or **(3)**.

(1): $4 - 2 \times 3 + 3z = 4$

$3z = 6$

$z = 2$

Present your answer as $(x, y, z) = (4, 3, 2)$.

What is the meaning of this answer? Geometrically, each original equation represents a plane in 3D space. The solution represents the point of intersection of three planes in 3D space.

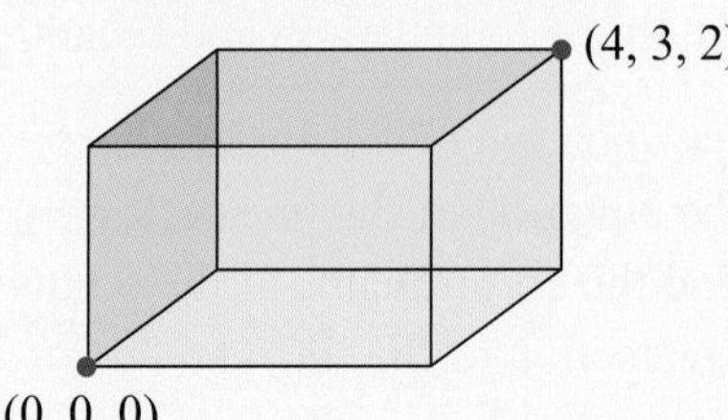

EXAMPLE 12

Solve

$$\frac{x-z}{4}-\frac{(x-y)}{3}=0$$

$$\frac{x-2}{5}+\frac{y+3}{7}=\frac{x+y}{6}$$

$$\left(\frac{x}{2}-\frac{y}{3}\right)=1+\frac{y}{6}-\frac{z}{5}$$

for x, y, z.

Solution

The first thing to do here is to get rid of fractions in each equation and then remove the brackets.

$$\frac{(x-z)}{4}-\frac{(x-y)}{3}=0\ (\times 12)$$

$3(x-z)-4(x-y)=0$

$3x-3z-4x+4y=0$

$-x+4y-3z=0$ … **(1)**

$$\frac{(x-2)}{5}+\frac{(y+3)}{7}=\frac{(x+y)}{6}\ (\times 210)$$

$42(x-2)+30(y+3)=35(x+y)$

$42x-84+30y+90=35x+35y$

$7x-5y=-6$ … **(2)**

$$\left(\frac{x}{2}-\frac{y}{3}\right)=\left(1+\frac{y}{6}-\frac{z}{5}\right)(\times 30)$$

$$30\left(\frac{x}{2}-\frac{y}{3}\right)=30\left(1+\frac{y}{6}-\frac{z}{5}\right)$$

$15x-10y=30+5y-6z$

$15x-15y+6z=30$ … **(3)**

Solve the simultaneous equations.

Step 1: $-x+4y-3z=0$ … **(1)**

$7x-5y+0z=-6$ … **(2)**

$15x-15y+6z=30$ … **(3)**

Step 2: Eliminating z from equations **(1)** and **(3)** will give an equation in x and y.

(1) $\times 2$: $-2x+8y-6z=0$

(3): $15x-15y+6z=30$

$13x-7y=30$ … **(4)**

Step 3: Eliminate y from equations **(2)** and **(4)**.

(2) $\times 7$: $49x-35y=-42$

(4) $\times -5$: $-65x+35y=-150$

$-16x=-192$

$x=12$

Step 4: Substitute the value of x into equation **(2)**.

$84-5y=-6$

$5y=90$

$y=18$

Substitute the value of x and y into equation **(1)**.

$-12+72-3z=0$

$3z=60$

$z=20$

$(x, y, z)=(12, 18, 20)$

Word problems involving three simultaneous equations in three unknowns

The strategy is much the same as for the previous types of simultaneous equations. Always let x, y and z be the answers to the questions asked and be absolutely clear what they represent.

EXAMPLE 13

Three solutions contain sulphuric acid. The first contains 30% acid, the second 20% acid and the third 50% acid. A student wishes to use all three solutions to obtain a mixture of 60 litres of 28% acid using three times as much of the 20% solution as the 50% solution. How many litres of each solution should he use?

Solution

Let x = number of litres of 30% acid

Let y = number of litres of 20% acid

Let z = number of litres of 50% acid

Total volume of 60 litres: $x + y + z = 60$ … (**1**)

Concentration of acid:

$0{\cdot}3x + 0{\cdot}2y + 0{\cdot}5z = 0{\cdot}28 \times 60$

$3x + 2y + 5z = 168$ … (**2**)

Use three times as much of the 20% solution as the 50% solution: $y = 3z$

$y - 3z = 0$ … (**3**)

Solve the simultaneous equations:

(**1**) × 3: $3x + 3y + 3z = 180$

(**2**) × −1: $-3x - 2y - 5z = -168$

$y - 2z = 12$ … (**4**)

(**3**) × −1: $-y + 3z = 0$

$z = 12$

Into (3):

z = 12: $y = 3(12) = 36$

Substituting back into equation (**1**):
$x = 60 - 12 - 36 = 12$

Answers: 12 litres of 30% acid, 36 litres of 20% acid, 12 litres of 20% acid

EXAMPLE 14

A dietician in a school is asked to design a menu using three basic foodstuffs: L, M and N. However, the menu must have exactly 52 units of vitamin C, 17 units of vitamin E and 27 units of vitamin B_3, respectively. The number of units per gram of each vitamin for each foodstuff is shown in the table below.

	Units per gram		
Vitamin	**L**	**M**	**N**
C	0·5	0·8	0·4
E	0·1	0·3	0·2
B_3	0·4	0·3	0·1

How many grams of each foodstuff must be used?

Solution

Let x = number of grams of L

Let y = number of grams of M

Let z = number of grams of N

Vitamin C: $0{\cdot}5x + 0{\cdot}8y + 0{\cdot}4z = 52$

$5x + 8y + 4z = 520$ … (**1**)

Vitamin E: $0{\cdot}1x + 0{\cdot}3y + 0{\cdot}2z = 17$

$x + 3y + 2z = 170$ … (**2**)

Vitamin B_3: $0{\cdot}4x + 0{\cdot}3y + 0{\cdot}1z = 27$

$4x + 3y + z = 270$ ... (**3**)

Solve the simultaneous equations:

(**1**): $5x + 8y + 4z = 520$

(**2**) × −2: $-2x - 6y - 4z = -340$

$x + 2y = 180$ … (**4**)

(**2**): $x + 3y + 2z = 170$

(**3**) × −2: $-8x - 6y - 2z = -540$

$-7x - 3y = -370$ … (**5**)

(4) × 3: $9x + 6y = 540$

(5) × 2: $-14x - 6y = -740$

$-5x = -200$

$x = 40$

Substitute x into equation (**4**): $120 + 2y = 180$

$y = 30$

Substitute x and y into equation (**1**):

$200 + 240 + 4z = 520$

$z = 20$

Answers: 40 g of L, 30 g of M, 20 g of N

EXERCISE 11

(A) CONCEPTS AND SKILLS

Solve the following simultaneous equations:

1. For x, y, z:
$x + y + z = 6$
$2x - y - z = -3$
$x - 3y + 2z = 1$

2. For a, b, c:
$3a + b + 2c = 6$
$a + b + 4c = 3$
$2a + 3b + 2c = 2$

3. For g, f, c:
$2g + f + c = 8$
$5g - 3f + 2c = 3$
$7g + f + 3c = 20$

4. For x, y, z:
$2x - y - z = 1$
$2x - 3y - 4z = 0$
$x + y - z = 4$

5. For x, y, z:
$x - 2y - 3z = 3$
$x + y + z = 2$
$2x - 3y - 5z = 5$

6. For x, y, z:
$x + 3y - 2z = 6$
$2x + y + 3z = 18$
$3x - y = 6$

7. For x, y, z:
$3x + 2z = 2$
$4y + z = 6$
$2x + 3y = 10$

8. For x, y, z:
$x + 2y = z + 1$
$x + \frac{y}{3} + \frac{z}{6} = 3$
$2x - 3y = 2z - 19$

9. For x, y, z:
$\frac{1}{x} = \frac{2}{3}$
$\frac{1}{x+y} = \frac{2}{5}$
$\frac{1}{x+y+z} = 1$

10. For x, y, z:
$\frac{1}{x} = 1\frac{1}{4}$
$\frac{1}{x} + \frac{1}{y} = 2\frac{1}{3}$
$\frac{1}{x} + \frac{1}{y} + \frac{1}{z} = 3\frac{1}{2}$

11. For x, y, z:
$\frac{x}{5} - \frac{y}{3} + \frac{z}{2} = -2$
$\frac{2x}{3} + \frac{y}{2} + z = \frac{5}{6}$
$x + y - \frac{z}{2} = 10$

12. For x, y, z:
$2x + y - z = 12$
$3x - 2z = 19$
$x + 5z = -5$

(B) CONTEXTS AND APPLICATIONS

1. Kirchhoff's laws are used to solve electrical circuits. The currents in each arm x, y, z are shown.

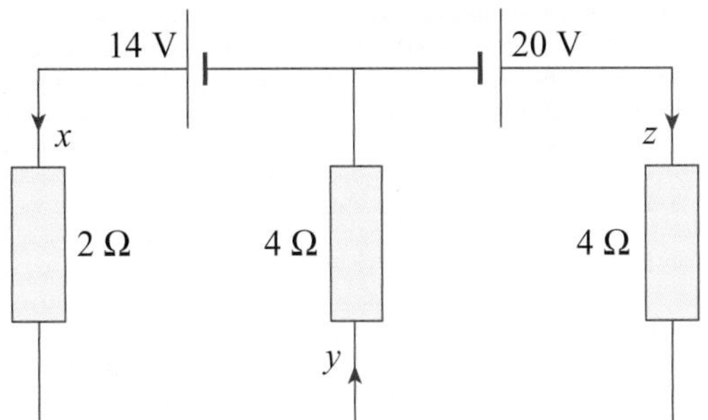

The three Kirchhoff's equations for this circuit are:

(1) $y = x + z$

(2) $14 = 2x + 4y$

(3) $4z + 4y = 20$

Find the current in each arm in amps (A).

2. The equation of a curve is given by $y = ax^2 + bx + c$. Three points $A(-1, 12)$, $B(1, 6)$, $C(2, 9)$ are on the curve. Find a, b, c.

3. A stable population of 42 000 birds lives on three islands. Although there is migration between the islands each year, the population on each island is constant. Every year 20% of the birds on A migrate to B, 10% of the birds on B migrate to C and 40% of the birds on C migrate to A.

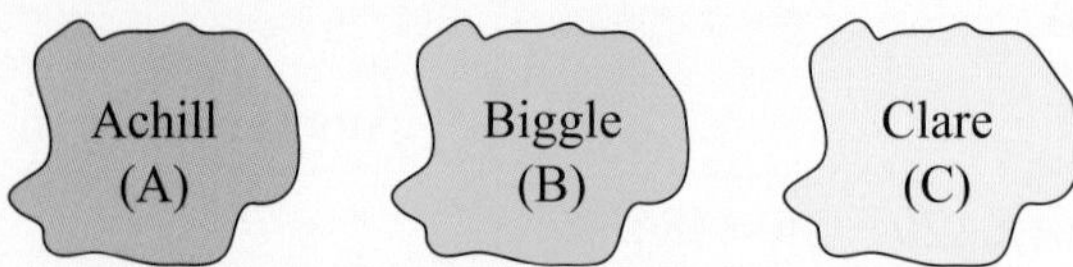

Write down three equations and find the number of birds on each island.

4. A tent company makes three types of tent: a one-person tent, a two-person tent and a four-person tent.
The manufacturing process has three stages: cutting, assembling and packaging. The maximum number of hours available per week for each of these processes is as follows:

Cutting: 380 hours

Assembling: 313 hours

Packaging: 107 hours

The table below shows the number of hours required to do each of these jobs.

	One-person tent	Two-person tent	Four-person tent
Cutting	0·6 h	1 h	1·2 h
Assembling	0·5 h	0·8 h	1 h
Packaging	0·1 h	0·2 h	0·4 h

How many tents of each type must be produced per week for the company to operate at maximum capacity?

Inequalities

Learning Outcomes

- To understand the rules for dealing with inequalities.
- To solve linear inequalities and plot the solutions to inequalities on a number line.
- To solve quadratic, rational and modulus inequalities and plot the solutions.
- To prove inequalities.

The previous chapters examined mathematical statements in which one side is equal to (=) the other side. Inequalities involve mathematical statements where one side is not equal to the other side.

- $5 > 2$ [5 is greater than 2]
- $2 < 4$ [2 is less than 4]
- $x \leq -4$ [x is less than or equal to -4]
- $y \geq 3$ [y is greater than or equal to 3]

9.1 Techniques for handling inequalities

Inequalities are tricky to handle. If you see an inequality, take your time and think about it. To illustrate the rules of inequalities, consider the following numerical example:

ACTIVITY 17

ACTION
Understanding basic inequality operations

OBJECTIVE
To learn the techniques needed to carry out basic inequality operations

WORKED EXAMPLE Understanding inequalities

Start with $8 > 4$.

Add +5 to both sides: $13 > 9$ [This is a true statement.]

Subtract 5 from both sides: $3 > -1$ [This is a true statement.]

Move all terms to the left: $8 - 4 > 0$ [This is a true statement.]

Move all terms to the right: $0 > 4 - 8$ [This is a true statement.]

Switch sides: $-4 > -8$ [This is a true statement.]

Multiply both sides by +2: $16 > 8$ [This is a true statement.]

Divide both sides by +2: $4 > 2$ [This is a true statement.]

But

Multiply both sides by –2: $-16 > -8$ [This is a false statement.]

Divide both sides by –2: $-4 > -2$ [This is a false statement.]

It seems that you can do the same operations to inequalities as you can do to equations, except multiply or divide by a negative number.

There are a couple of other operations you should watch out for:

1. Squaring:

$4 > 2$

Square both sides: $16 > 4$ [This is a true statement.]

But

$4 > -8$

Square both sides: $16 > 64$ [This is a false statement.]

2. Inverting:

$4 > 2$

Invert both sides: $\frac{1}{4} > \frac{1}{2}$ [This is a false statement.]

But

$4 > -2$

Invert both sides: $\frac{1}{4} > -\frac{1}{2}$ [This is a true statement.]

Rules of inequalities

The same operations for inequalities as equalities can be carried out, except:

1. Multiplying and dividing by a negative number:

Never multiply or divide both sides of an inequality by a negative number.

You do not have to multiply or divide inequalities by negative numbers because you can just switch sides to get rid of the minus in front of the unknown (variable).

- $-2x > 8$

  $-8 > 2x$

  $-4 > x$

  $x < -4$

2. Inverting:

Never invert both sides of an inequality.

You do not have to invert inequalities as you can multiply or divide both sides by a positive number.

- $\frac{1}{2} > -2$ [Multiply both sides by +2.]

  $1 > -4$
- $\frac{3}{n} > \frac{1}{6}, n \in \mathbb{N}$ [Multiply both sides by $6n$.]

  $18 > n$

3. Squaring:

Square both sides only if you are certain both sides of the inequality are positive.

- $7 > 5$

  $7^2 > 5^2$ [This is a true statement.]
- $a > b, a, b > 0$

  $a^2 > b^2$

  But
- $-5 > -7$

  $25 > 49$ [This is a false statement.]

WARNING

If you do multiply both sides of an inequality by a negative number, you must also reverse the inequality sign.

Reading an inequality

$8 > 4$ can be read as '8 is greater than 4' as you read from left to right. It can be rewritten as $4 < 8$, which reads as '4 is less than 8'. So $7 > x$ can be rewritten as $x < 7$.

TIP

The smaller number is always at the tip of the arrow of the inequality sign.

$-6 \leq x \Leftrightarrow x \geq -6$ [−6 stays at the tip of the inequality sign whichever way you write the inequality.]

9.2 Solving inequalities

ACTIVITY 18

ACTION
Working with linear inequalities

OBJECTIVE
To learn the techniques needed to solve linear inequalities

An inequality can be solved graphically or algebraically. Algebraically is always quicker. There are four types of inequalities to be treated:

1. Linear
2. Quadratic
3. Rational
4. Modulus

1. Linear inequalities

These are inequalities involving linear functions of a variable of the form $ax + b$.

EXAMPLE 1

Solve $\frac{5-7x}{3} \geq \frac{7-3x}{5}$, $x \in \mathbb{R}$ and show your answer on the number line.

Solution

$\frac{(5-7x)}{3} \geq \frac{(7-3x)}{5}$ [Multiply across by 15.]

$5(5-7x) \geq 3(7-3x)$

$25 - 35x \geq 21 - 9x$

$-35x + 9x \geq 21 - 25$

$-26x \geq -4$

$4 \geq 26x$

$\frac{2}{13} \geq x, x \in \mathbb{R}$ *or* $x \leq \frac{2}{13}, x \in \mathbb{R}$

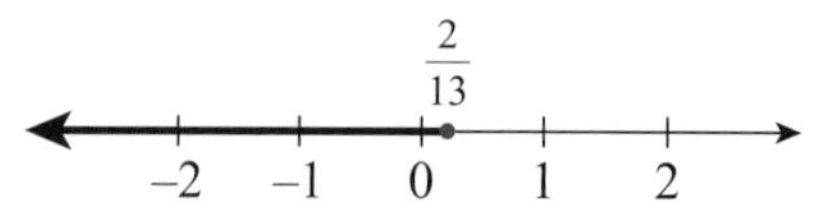

2. Quadratic inequalities

These are inequalities involving quadratic functions of a variable of the form $ax^2 + bx + c$.

WORKED EXAMPLE Solving quadratic inequalities

Solve $x^2 + 2 < x + 8, x \in \mathbb{R}$.

Step 1: Get all terms on one side so that the sign of the number in front of the x^2 variable is positive. This inequality is called the test box.

$\boxed{x^2 - x - 6 < 0}$ … Test box

Step 2: Solve the equality to get the roots.

$x^2 - x - 6 = 0$

$(x + 2)(x - 3) = 0$

Roots: –2, 3

Step 3: These roots divide the inequality into three distinct regions. Arrange the roots in ascending order from left to right. Choose any number in each region and put it into the test box to see if the inequality holds (✓) or does not hold (×) in that region. This is the **region test**.

⟵ (left of –2)	–2 ⟷ +3	+3 ⟶
$x^2 - x - 6 < 0$	$x^2 - x - 6 < 0$	$x^2 - x - 6 < 0$
$-3: 9 + 3 - 6 < 0$	$0: 0 - 0 - 6 < 0$	$4: 16 - 4 - 6 < 0$
$6 < 0$	$-6 < 0$	$6 < 0$
×	✓	×
	↓	
	$-2 < x < 3, x \in \mathbb{R}$	

Step 4: Write the solution: $-2 < x < 3, x \in \mathbb{R}$

This region test can be illustrated graphically by plotting $y = x^2 - x - 6, x \in \mathbb{R}$.

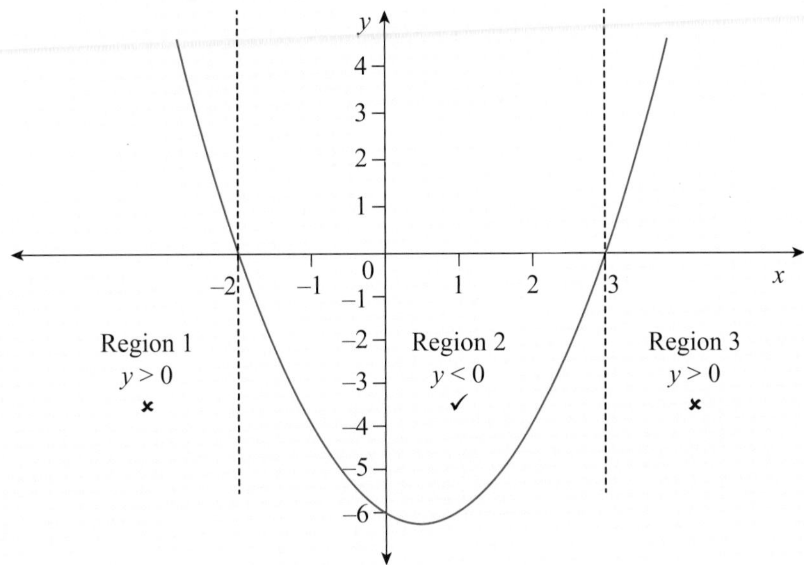

EXAMPLE 2

Solve $2x^2 - 7x - 3 \geq 0, x \in \mathbb{R}$.

Solution

Step 1: $\boxed{2x^2 - 7x - 3 \geq 0}$ ... Test box

Step 2: Solve the equality.

$$x = \frac{7 \pm \sqrt{(-7)^2 - 4(2)(-3)}}{2(2)} = \frac{7 \pm \sqrt{73}}{4}$$

Step 3: Apply the region test.

$$\longleftarrow \boxed{\frac{7 - \sqrt{73}}{4} \approx -0{\cdot}39} \longleftrightarrow \boxed{\frac{7 + \sqrt{73}}{4} \approx 3{\cdot}89} \longrightarrow$$

$2x^2 - 7x - 3 \geq 0$	$2x^2 - 7x - 3 \geq 0$	$2x^2 - 7x - 3 \geq 0$
$-1: 2 + 7 - 3 \geq 0$	$0: 0 - 0 - 3 \geq 0$	$4: 32 - 28 - 3 \geq 0$
$6 \geq 0$	$-3 \geq 0$	$1 \geq 0$
✓	×	✓
↓		↓
$x \leq \frac{7 - \sqrt{73}}{4}$		$x \geq \frac{7 + \sqrt{73}}{4}$

Step 4: Write the solution: $x \leq \frac{7 - \sqrt{73}}{4}, x \geq \frac{7 + \sqrt{73}}{4}, x \in \mathbb{R}$

3. Rational inequalities

These are inequalities involving a ratio of two linear functions of the same variable of the form $\frac{ax+b}{cx+d}$.

> The trick here is to multiply both sides by the square of the linear function on the bottom unless you are certain it is positive.

In $\frac{3x-1}{2x-5}$, $x \in \mathbb{R}$, the linear function $(2x - 5)$ will be positive or negative depending on the value of x.

In $\frac{3x-1}{4x+3}$, $x > 0$, $x \in \mathbb{R}$, the linear function $(4x + 3)$ is always positive.

EXAMPLE 3

Solve $\frac{(x-8)}{(x+2)} > -1, x \neq -2, x \in \mathbb{R}$.

Solution

$\frac{(x-8)}{(x+2)} > -1$ [Multiply both sides by $(x+2)^2$ because it is always positive.]

$(x-8)(x+2) > -1(x+2)^2$ [Move all terms to the left.]

$(x-8)(x+2) + (x+2)^2 > 0$ [Take out the HCF.]

$(x+2)[(x-8)+(x+2)] > 0$

$\boxed{(x+2)(2x-6) > 0}$ … Test box

Solve the equality: $(x+2)(2x-6) = 0$

$x = -2, 3$

Carry out the region test:

← (below −2)	↔ (between −2 and 3)	→ (above 3)
$(x+2)(2x-6) > 0$	$(x+2)(2x-6) > 0$	$(x+2)(2x-6) > 0$
$-3: (-1)(-9) > 0$	$0: (2)(-6) > 0$	$4: (6)(2) > 0$
✓	✗	✓

Solution: $x < -2, x > 3, x \in \mathbb{R}$

4. Modulus inequalities

These are inequalities involving the absolute value of linear functions of a variable of the form $|ax + b|$.

EXAMPLE 4

Solve $|2x-3| \leq 5, x \in \mathbb{R}$.

Solution

$\boxed{|2x-3| \leq 5}$ … Test box

Solve the equality: $|2x-3| = 5$

$2x - 3 = \pm 5$

$x = -1, 4$

Carry out the region test:

← (below −1)	↔ (between −1 and 4)	→ (above 4)
$\lvert 2x-3\rvert \leq 5$	$\lvert 2x-3\rvert \leq 5$	$\lvert 2x-3\rvert \leq 5$
$-2: \lvert -7\rvert \leq 5$	$0: \lvert -3\rvert \leq 5$	$5: \lvert 7\rvert \leq 5$
$7 \leq 5$	$3 \leq 5$	$7 \leq 5$
✗	✓	✗

Solution: $-1 < x < 4, x \in \mathbb{R}$

EXAMPLE 5

Normal human body temperature is 36·8 °C. A temperature x that differs from the normal by at least 1·0 °C is considered unhealthy. Write down a formula satisfied by x and find the range of unhealthy body temperatures. Is 35·9 °C a healthy body temperature?

Solution

Let x = body temperature

$\therefore \boxed{|x - 36{\cdot}8| \geq 1{\cdot}0}$ ... Test box [x represents an unhealthy body temperature.]

Solve the equality: $x - 36{\cdot}8 = \pm 1{\cdot}0$

$x = 35{\cdot}8,\ 37{\cdot}8$

Carry out the region test:

← 35·8	↔	37·8 →
$\lvert x - 36{\cdot}8\rvert \geq 1{\cdot}0$	$\lvert x - 36{\cdot}8\rvert \geq 1{\cdot}0$	$\lvert x - 36{\cdot}8\rvert \geq 1{\cdot}0$
34·8: $\lvert 34{\cdot}8 - 36{\cdot}8\rvert \geq 1{\cdot}0$	36·0: $\lvert 36{\cdot}0 - 36{\cdot}8\rvert \geq 1{\cdot}0$	38·8: $\lvert 38{\cdot}8 - 36{\cdot}8\rvert \geq 1{\cdot}0$
$\lvert 2\rvert \geq 1{\cdot}0$	$\lvert 0{\cdot}8\rvert \geq 1{\cdot}0$	$\lvert 2\rvert \geq 1{\cdot}0$
✓	✗	✓

Solution: $x \leq 35{\cdot}8$ °C, $x \geq 37{\cdot}8$ °C, $x \in \mathbb{R}$, are unhealthy body temperatures.

35·9 °C is not unhealthy as it is not within this range.

Using the graph of $y = |ax + b|$ to solve a modulus inequality

EXAMPLE 6

Solve $|2x - 1| < 5$ graphically.

Solution

Plot $y = |2x - 1|$.

$y = |2x - 1|$

$y = \pm(2x - 1)$

This gives two straight lines: $y = 2x - 1$, $y = -2x + 1$.

Rewrite these lines and call them k and l.

k: $2x - y = 1$

l: $2x + y = 1$

Solve the lines simultaneously to find out where they intersect.

k: $2x - y = 1$ ... **(1)**

l: $2x + y = 1$ ... **(2)**

$4x = 2$

$x = \frac{1}{2}$

Using (2):

$\boldsymbol{x = \frac{1}{2}}$: $1 + y = 1 \Rightarrow y = 0$

$\therefore \left(\frac{1}{2}, 0\right)$ is the point of intersection of k and l.

Find where k and l intersect $y = 5$:

k: $2x - y = 1$

$\boldsymbol{y = 5}$: $2x - 5 = 1$

$x = 3$

Point of intersection is (3, 5).

l: $2x + y = 1$

$\boldsymbol{y = 5}$: $2x + 5 = 1$

$x = -2$

Point of intersection is (–2, 5).

Plot k, l and $y = 5$.

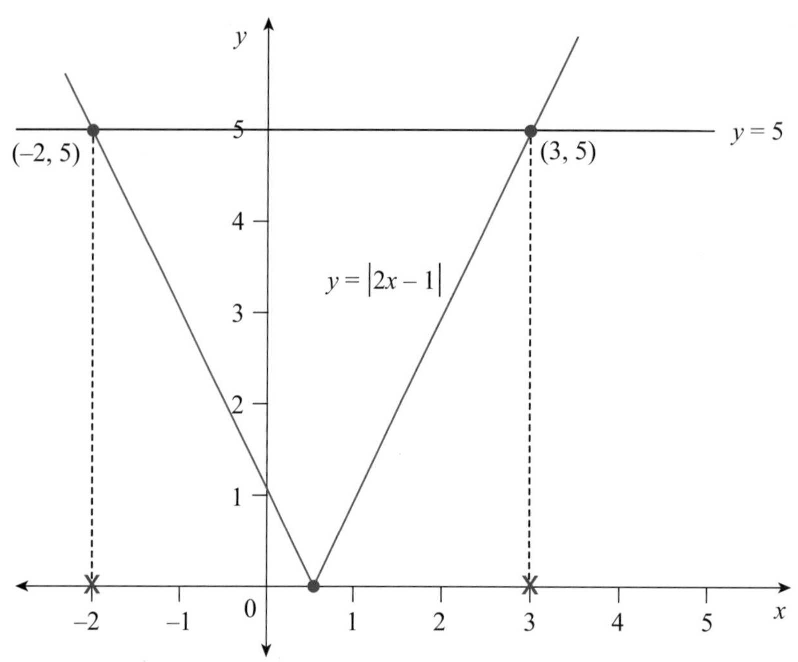

$\therefore |2x - 1| < 5$ is the set of points on $y = |2x - 1|$ below $y = 5$.

Solution: $-2 < x < 3$

EXERCISE 12

1. Solve the following for $x \in \mathbb{R}$ and plot the solution set on the number line:
   (a) $-3x < 6$
   (b) $5 - 2x \geq -7$
   (c) $x - 2 \leq 4x - 7$
   (d) $4 - 3(1 - x) \geq 10$
   (e) $\frac{x}{3} \geq 2 + \frac{x}{5}$
   (f) $\frac{x-4}{5} < \frac{2x+1}{7}$

2. Solve the following for $x \in \mathbb{R}$:
   (a) $x^2 + 3x - 10 > 0$
   (b) $x^2 - 4x - 77 < 0$
   (c) $2x^2 + 5x \geq 3$
   (d) $3x^2 \leq -7x - 2$
   (e) $-6 - 2x^2 \geq -7x$
   (f) $4x^2 > 1$

3. Solve the following for $x \in \mathbb{R}$:
   (a) $\frac{x-2}{x+1} > 3, x \neq -1$
   (b) $\frac{x-5}{x+2} < 2, x \neq -2$
   (c) $\frac{2x+3}{x} > 2, x \neq 0$
   (d) $\frac{3x-4}{x+2} < 1, x \neq -2$
   (e) $\frac{2x-3}{3x-4} > 1, x \neq \frac{4}{3}$

4. Solve the following for $x \in \mathbb{R}$:
   (a) $|x| < 4$
   (b) $|x - 1| > 5$
   (c) $|2x + 1| \leq 7$
   (d) $|3x - 11| \geq 10$
   (e) $\frac{1}{5}|3x - 7| < 1$
   (f) $2|5 - 2x| - 10 \geq 10$

5. Solve the following graphically:
   (a) $|x - 1| < 4$
   (b) $|2x + 3| \leq 7$
   (c) $|4x - 3| \geq 15$
   (d) $|2 - x| > 4$

6. **(a)** The normal household voltage in Ireland is 220 V. It is acceptable for the actual voltage x to differ from the normal by at most 8 V. Write down a modulus inequality to describe this. Show that:
   (i) 215 V is acceptable, but
   (ii) 208 V is unacceptable.

   (b) Joe's IQ score is more than 13 points away from Pita's. If Pita scored 112, in what range is Joe's score?

(c) The water temperature in a certain industrial process should be 70 °C. However, the process works fine if the actual temperature x is less than or equal to 7 °C away from the ideal. Find the acceptable range of temperatures. Is a temperature of 76·8 °C acceptable?

(d) The difference between John's age and his brother's age is less than 3 years. If John's age is 16, what is the range of possible ages of his brother?

7. (a) Find the range of values of k for which $x^2 - kx + 1 = 0$ has real roots.

(b) Find the range of values of k for which $x^2 + (3k - 1)x + k = 0$ has real roots.

9.3 Proving inequalities

The easiest way to prove an inequality is to assume that the complete opposite of the inequality stated is true and to disprove this by contradiction.

EXAMPLE 7

Prove that $x + \frac{1}{x} \geq 2$ for all $x > 0, x \in \mathbb{R}$.

Solution

Prove that $x + \frac{1}{x} \geq 2$ for all $x > 0, x \in \mathbb{R}$.

Assume that $x + \frac{1}{x} < 2$ for all $x > 0, x \in \mathbb{R}$.

$x^2 + 1 < 2x$

$x^2 - 2x + 1 < 0$

$(x - 1)^2 < 0$

This is clearly untrue, so $x + \frac{1}{x} < 2$ for all $x > 0, x \in \mathbb{R}$ is not true.

$\therefore x + \frac{1}{x} \geq 2$ for all $x > 0, x \in \mathbb{R}$.

EXERCISE 13

1. Prove that $a^2 + b^2 \geq 2ab$ for all $a, b \in \mathbb{R}$.

2. Prove that $\frac{2ab}{a + b} \leq \sqrt{ab}$ for all positive a and b.

3. Prove that $\frac{x^4}{1 + x^4} \leq \frac{1}{2}$ for all $x \in \mathbb{R}$.

4. Prove that $(a + b)\left(\frac{1}{a} + \frac{1}{b}\right) \geq 4$ for all positive a and b.

REVISION QUESTIONS

1. **(a)** Solve $\frac{4^{3+x}}{8^{10x}} = \frac{2^{10-2x}}{64^{3x}}$.

(b) Solve:

(i) $\sqrt{3x+4} = 2 + \sqrt{x}$

(ii) $\log_4(6x+1) - 2 = 2\log_4 x$

(c) Solve $\frac{x-1}{x-2} > 3, x \neq 2, x \in \mathbb{R}$.

2. **(a)** Solve:

$2x - y + 3z = 20$

$7x + y + z = 23$

$3x + y - z = 3$

(b) Solve:

$x^2 - 2 = 2y^2$

$3x = y + 7$

(c) **(i)** Solve $|x - 3| > 2$.

(ii) Show that $ax^2 + 2x - (a-2) = 0$ has real roots for all $a \in \mathbb{R}$.

3. **(a)** The quadratic equation $x^2 + (b+4)x + (1+4b) = 0$ has equal roots.

(i) Show that $b^2 - 8b + 12 = 0$.

(ii) Find b.

(b) Show that $(x-2)$ is a factor of $P(x) = x^3 + x^2 - 10x + 8$. Hence, express $P(x)$ as the product of three linear factors. Draw a rough sketch of $y = x^3 + x^2 - 10x + 8$.

(c) Show that k is a root of $x^3 - 6kx^2 + 11k^2x - 6k^3 = 0$ and find the other roots in terms of k.

4. **(a)** Solve:

$\frac{1}{x} + \frac{1}{y} = \frac{1}{2}$

$\frac{2}{x} = \frac{3}{y} - 2$

(b) The graph of the quadratic function $y = x^2 + bx + c$ is shown. Find b, c and the point E.

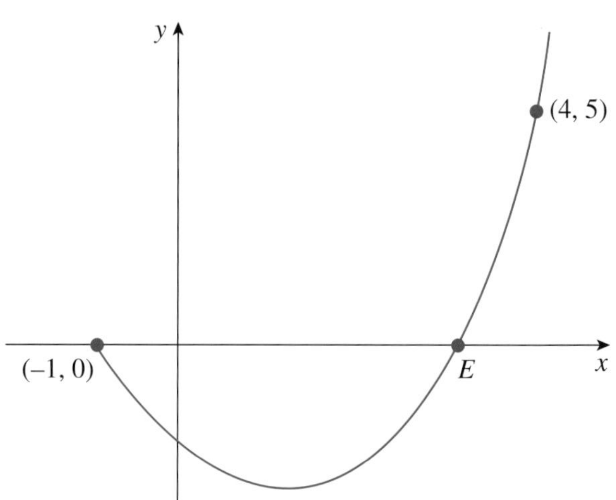

(c) Two vertical posts, AD and BC, are a distance l apart. A chain of length d is hung between D and C, as shown. The length of the vertical sag in the middle of the chain is S and is given by $S = \sqrt{\frac{l(d-l)}{3}}$.

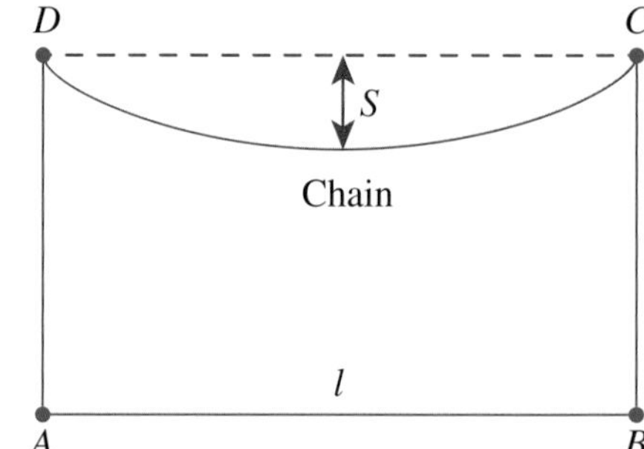

Show that $l^2 - dl + 3S^2 = 0$ and find l in terms of d and S. For $d = 4$ and $S = 1$, find l.

5. **(a)** The mass m(g) of a radioactive isotope decreases with time t in years, according to the formula $m = 40 \times 2^{-\frac{1}{3}t}$. Find t:

(i) when $m = 10$ g,

(ii) when $m = 2$ g.

Give answers to the nearest year.

(b) The distance s in metres of a body from a fixed point O after t seconds is given by $s = 8t - t^2 + 12$. Find when it is 24 m from O. By writing $8t - t^2 + 12$ in the form $a - (t-b)^2$, find the maximum distance of the body from O.

(c) In a group of tennis players in a tournament, each player must play either singles or mixed doubles (a man and a woman as a pair), but not both. Half of the women and one-third of the men play mixed doubles. What percentage of the group play mixed doubles?

(Hint: A mixed double means the number of men and woman participating in these teams must be the same.)

6. (a) The intensity of light I emerging from a liquid of concentration c is given by $\log_{10} I = 1 - (c - 1)\log_{10} 2$, $c > 0$. Show that $I = \frac{20}{2^c}$. Find I when $c = 4$.

(b) The line l has equation $x - y + 1 = 0$. If d is the distance from any point (x, y) on l to the point $(2, 1)$, show that $d^2 = 2x^2 - 4x + 4$. By writing $2x^2 - 4x + 4$ in the form $p + a(x - k)^2$, find the minimum value of d and the point (x, y).

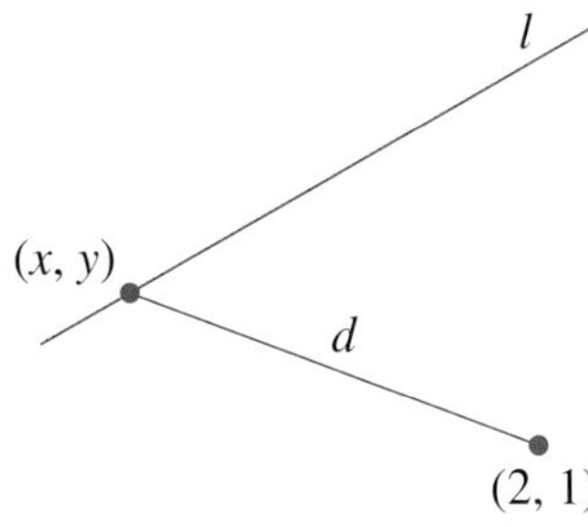

7. (a) Sparky Electrical states that it can rewire a school in 12 days. Volta Electrical states that it can rewire the same school in 15 days. If the board of management of the school hired both companies to do the rewiring, how long will it take both to complete the job working together?

(b) (i) Solve $x^2 - 2x \leq 4$, $x \in \mathbb{R}$.

(ii) Solve $x^2 > 4$, $x \in \mathbb{R}$.

(iii) Joe's last Maths mark is more than 8 marks away from Joan's last mark. If Joan's last mark was 82, what is the range of Joe's score?

(c) Prove $\frac{a}{b^2} + \frac{b}{a^2} \geq \frac{1}{a} + \frac{1}{b}$ for all positive a and b.

(d) There are three categories of ticket prices for a concert: €40, €60 and €90. The concert hall can hold 420 people. The total receipts for a full house are €26 200. The number of €90 tickets available is half the number of all other tickets. Find the number of each category of ticket.

8. (a) Solve $|7 + x| = 2$, $x \in \mathbb{Z}$.

(b) Find the points of intersection of the line $l: 3x - 4y = 0$ and the ellipse $s: \frac{x^2}{32} + \frac{y^2}{18} = 1$

Find also the points at which the ellipse crosses the axes.

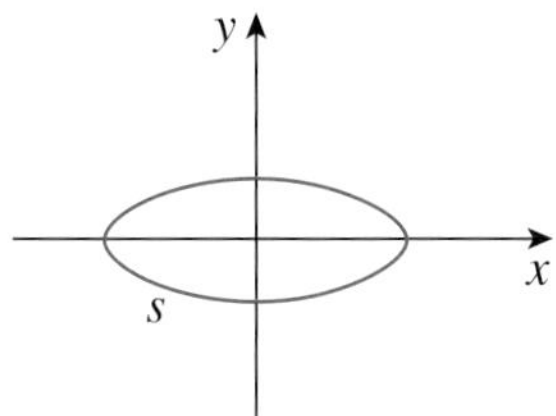

(c) (i) Solve $4e^x - 1 = 0$.

(ii) Solve $e^{\ln x} + \ln e^x = 8$.

(iii) If $u = \log_3 x$, write $a^2 \log_3 x = \log_x 3 - a$ as a quadratic in u. Solve u in terms of a.

9. (a) Solve $a^2x^2 + abx - 6b^2 = 0$.

(b) Solve $x^2 - 7x + 12 = 0$ for x and hence solve $(\log_2 t)^2 - 7(\log_2 t) + 12 = 0$ for t.

(c) Show that $x^2 - (k + 3)x + (k + 2) = 0$ has real roots for all $k \in \mathbb{R}$.

10. (a) If –2 and 3 are roots of $ax^2 + bx + 6 = 0$, find a and b.

(b) If $x - 1$ and $x - 2$ are both factors of $x^3 + bx^2 + cx - 6$, find b and c and solve $x^3 + bx^2 + cx - 6 = 0$.

(c) Solve:

(i) $\log_2 x + 12\log_x 2 = 7$

(ii) $27^x = 81$

$2^{x-y} = 32$

SUMMARY

1. Linear equations: $ax + b = 0 \Rightarrow x = -\frac{b}{a}$

2. Quadratic equations: $ax^2 + bx + c = 0$

   (a) Solution:

   (i) By factorisation

   (ii) By completing the square

   (iii) By using the quadratic formula:

   $$x = \frac{-b \pm \sqrt{b^2 - 4ac}}{2a}$$

   (b) Properties of quadratics:

   (i) $b^2 > 4ac$ or $b^2 - 4ac > 0$ gives two different, real roots:

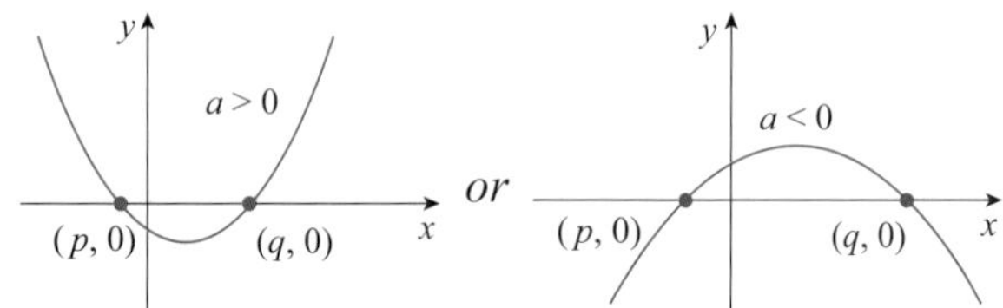

   (ii) $b^2 = 4ac$ or $b^2 - 4ac = 0$ gives two equal, real roots:

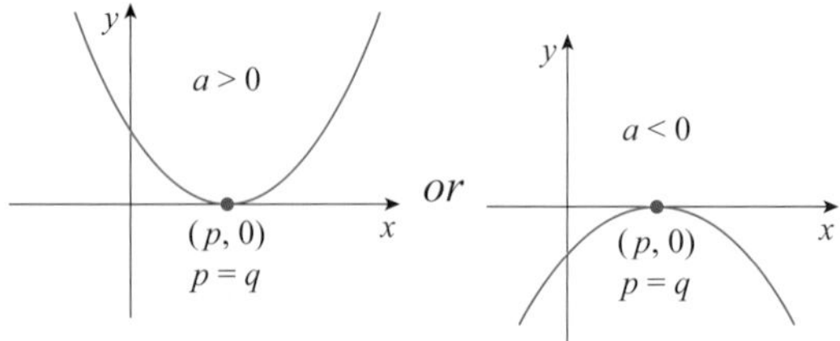

   (iii) $b^2 < 4ac$ or $b^2 - 4ac < 0$ gives complex roots:

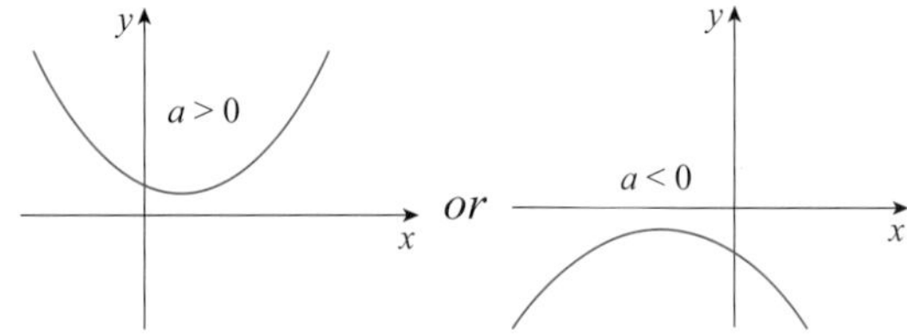

   (iv) Forming a quadratic equation from its roots $\frac{q}{p}, \frac{r}{s}$: $(px - q)(sx - r) = 0$

   or

   $x^2 - Sx + P = 0$, where S is the sum of the roots and P the product of the roots.

3. Cubic equations: $ax^3 + bx^2 + cx + d = 0$

   (a) Solution: Given an integer root k, form a linear factor $(x - k)$ and solve the equation by division or factorisation.

   (b) Forming a cubic equation from its roots:

   (Linear)(Quadratic) = 0

4. Square root equations: Isolate the square root and square both sides.

5. Literal equations: Isolate the unknown variable.

6. Exponential equations:

   Get the same base and find the solutions by equating the powers $a^f = a^g \Rightarrow f = g$.

   or

   Take the log of both sides after getting the base with the unknown power on one side:

   $a^y = c \Rightarrow \log_a a^y = \log_a c \Rightarrow y = \log_a c$

7. Log equations:

   Steps for solution:

   (a) Get the same base.

   (b) Get all logs on one side.

   (c) Get a single log.

   (d) Get out of logs (Hoosh): $\log_b y = c \Rightarrow y = b^c$

8. Modulus equations:

   $|ax + b| = cx + d \Rightarrow ax + b = \pm(cx + d)$

9. Simultaneous equations:

   Types:

   (a) Two linear equations in two unknowns: Solve by elimination by addition.

   (b) One linear equation and one equation of order two: Solve by substitution.

   (c) Three linear equations in three unknowns: Solve by elimination by addition.

10. Word problems:

Write down:

(a) One equation for one unknown

(b) Two equations for two unknowns

(c) Three equations for three unknowns

Solve the equations.

11. Inequalities:

(a) Linear inequalities: $ax + b \geq 0 \Rightarrow x \geq -\frac{b}{a}$ once $a > 0$.

(b) Quadratic/rational/modulus inequalities: Find the roots of the equality and do the region test using the test box.

(c) Proofs: Disprove the opposite by contradiction.

SECTION 4

Sequences and Series

Seeing and understanding patterns is important for many reasons.

- Patterns enable you to make order out of apparent chaos.
- Patterns enable you to make accurate predictions.
- Patterns enable you to see mathematical relationships and hence to take short cuts.

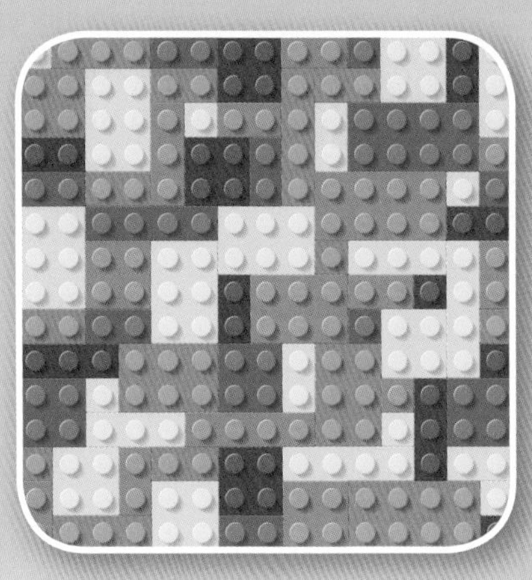

CHAPTER 10 Patterns

Learning Outcome

- To recognise patterns of numbers, shapes and objects and to construct a formula connecting the value of the nth term T_n in a pattern with its place number n in the pattern.

ACTIVITY 1

ACTION
Completing the pattern

OBJECTIVE
To recognise patterns and to fill in the missing terms in the sequence

It is very important to be able to recognise patterns in symbols, numbers and shapes and to be able to predict the next symbol, number or shape in a pattern.

It is even better if you can predict **any** symbol, number or shape using a rule (formula) as then you really do understand the underlying connection between them.

One of the most famous patterns in maths is the Fibonacci sequence (pattern). This was discovered in 1202 by Leonardo of Pisa, who was nicknamed Fibonacci (meaning 'the good-natured son').

Fibonacci in nature (spirals)

The sequence is 1, 1, 2, 3, 5, 8, 13, 21, 34, …

It is an **infinite** sequence as it never ends. The first nine terms of the sequence are listed. Can you predict the 10th term?

Of course, it is 21 + 34 = 55.

This sequence occurs in nature in modelling the population growth of rabbits and describing the spiral in a snail's shell.

10.1 What is a sequence?

KEY TERM

A **sequence** is a set of objects (symbols, numbers or shapes) listed in order from left to right with commas between the objects.

- 7, 29, 133, ...
- 0·9, 0·99, 0·999, ...
- Δ, δ, Ω, Δ, δ, Ω, ...

An individual object in a sequence is known as a term of the sequence. Each term is assigned a label which specifies its position in the list.

ACTIVITY 2

ACTION
Writing down terms from sequences

OBJECTIVE
To write down specified terms from given sequences

WORKED EXAMPLE

Infinite and finite sequences

Consider the following list of numbers: 1, 3, 5, 7, 9, …

This is the sequence of the odd natural numbers.

It is an **infinite** sequence as it does not end. The … (three dots) means that it goes on forever.

Each object in order is called a term.

1, 3, 5, 7, 9, …

1 is the first term, 3 is the second term, 5 is the third term, 7 is the fourth term …

Now look at the following list of numbers: 57, 48, 39, 30, 21, 12, 3.

This sequence is a **finite** sequence as it ends at 3.

The first term is 57. We use T_1 (T for term, 1 for first) to label this term.

The second term is labelled as T_2 and its value is 48.

T_5 is the value of the object in fifth place in the list reading from left to right. So $T_5 = 21$.

WORKED EXAMPLE

Recognising patterns from shapes

Triangular numbers are made by forming triangular patterns with circular discs, as shown.

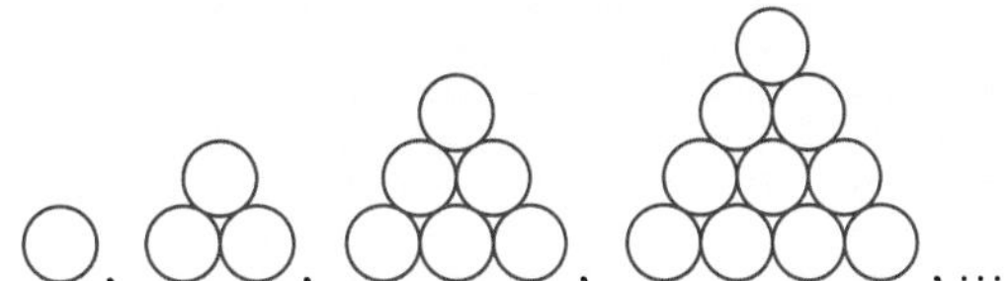

The number of discs in each shape generates the 'triangular numbers'.

Shape number	Number of discs
1	1
2	3
3	6
4	10

The sequence of the number of discs is: 1, 3, 6, 10, …

Can you predict the number of discs in the fifth shape? It is 15, of course.

Sometimes it is easy to see patterns.

- In the sequence M, T, W, T, ... the next term is F.

This is a sequence of the first letters of the days of the week starting on Monday (M).

Sometimes it is difficult to see patterns.

- In the sequence 10, 1, 11, 1, 12, 1, 1, ... the next term is 1.

This sequence is the number of strikes of a clock bell every half-hour starting at 10.

WORKED EXAMPLE Fibonacci's rabbits

If you start out with a pair of baby rabbits (B), after one month, they turn into a pair of adult rabbits (A). Assuming every month after they become adult rabbits, each pair of adults has a pair of babies, the table below shows the growth of this population of rabbits.

Start					B				Number of pairs of rabbits
Start					B				1
1 Month					A				1
2 Months					AB				2
3 Months				AB	A				3
4 Months				AB	A	AB			5
5 Months			AB	A	AB	AB	A		8
6 Months	AB	A	AB	AB	A	AB	A	AB	13

This is the Fibonacci sequence: 1, 1, 2, 3, 5, 8, 13, …

$T_1 = 1$, $T_2 = 1$, $T_3 = 2 = 1 + 1$, $T_4 = 3 = 2 + 1$, $T_5 = 5 = 3 + 2$

Can you predict T_8?

$T_8 = T_7 + T_6 = 13 + 8 = 21$

What about T_{31}?

10.2 Rule of a sequence

A sequence usually has a rule. This is a way of finding the value of any specified term in the sequence.

ACTIVITY 3

ACTION
Generating a rule from a sequence

OBJECTIVE
To recognise patterns in sequences and to write down a rule for the sequence

WORKED EXAMPLE Finding the rule of a sequence

The sequence 3, 8, 13, 18, 23, … starts at 3 and jumps by 5 from term to term.

The statement above is a rule of sorts but it does not really help you to find the 58th term in a simple and quick way. If you had a formula that related the value (T_n) of the nth term to its position (n) in the list, then you could find any specified term.

The rule above gives you a clue for finding a formula for T_n.

$T_1 = 3$

$T_2 = 8 = 3 + (1 \text{ jump of } 5) = 3 + 1 \times 5$

$T_3 = 13 = 3 + (2 \text{ jumps of } 5) = 3 + 2 \times 5$

$T_4 = 18 = 3 + (3 \text{ jumps of } 5) = 3 + 3 \times 5$

$\therefore T_n = 3 + ((n - 1) \text{ jumps of } 5) = 3 + (n - 1)5 = 5n - 2$

Another way to look at this sequence is to try to relate the value of any term T_n to its place number n in the list. In a table, the sequence is as follows:

Number of the term	Value of the term
$n = 1$	$3 = T_1 = 5 \times 1 - 2$
$n = 2$	$8 = T_2 = 5 \times 2 - 2$
$n = 3$	$13 = T_3 = 5 \times 3 - 2$
$n = 4$	$18 = T_4 = 5 \times 4 - 2$
$n = 5$	$23 = T_5 = 5 \times 5 - 2$

$\therefore T_n = 5 \times n - 2 = 5n - 2$

$T_n = 5n - 2$ is the value of the nth term of the sequence and is known as the **general term**.

This is a very powerful formula for a sequence as it enables you to:

1. **Find the value of any term in the list.**

   To find the value of a term, simply replace n by the number of the term.

   To find the value of the 37th term in the sequence, replacing n with 37 in $T_n = 5n - 2$ gives:

   $T_{37} = 5 \times 37 - 2 = 183$

   The 37th term is 183.

2. **Find the position of a term in the list, given its value.**

   Using the sequence above, find which term has a value of 158. Since 158 is some term in the list, it must have a name (label). Call it T_n.

   $T_n = 158 = 5n - 2$

   $5n = 160$

   $n = 32$

   The 32nd term in the list has a value of 158.

In general, it is very difficult to find a general term T_n for a sequence when given its first few terms.

ACTIVITY 4

ACTION
Using the Fibonacci sequence

OBJECTIVE
To learn to construct the Fibonacci sequence and to generate its general term

WORKED EXAMPLE

Finding the general term T_n of a sequence is not always easy

Find T_n for the sequence 5, 13, 35, 97, … , given that $5 = 2^1 + 3^1$.

Number of the term	Value of the term
$n = 1$	$T_1 = 5 = 2^1 + 3^1$
$n = 2$	$T_2 = 13 = 2^2 + 3^2$
$n = 3$	$T_3 = 35 = 2^3 + 3^3$
$n = 4$	$T_4 = 97 = 2^4 + 3^4$

$\therefore T_n = 2^n + 3^n$

This would have been extremely difficult to find without the hint.

However, given T_n for a sequence, it is very easy to find any specified term because you simply replace n, wherever it appears, by the specified value.

EXAMPLE 1

For a sequence $T_n = n^2 - 1$, find:

(a) the first four terms

(b) the eighth term

(c) which term has a value of 195

(d) T_{n+1}

(e) T_{n-1}

(f) T_{n+2}

Solution

$T_n = (n)^2 - 1$

(a) $T_1 = (1)^2 - 1 = 0$

$T_2 = (2)^2 - 1 = 3$

$T_3 = (3)^2 - 1 = 8$

$T_4 = (4)^2 - 1 = 15$

(b) $T_8 = (8)^2 - 1 = 63$

(c) $T_n = 195 \Rightarrow n^2 - 1 = 195$

$n^2 = 196$

$n = 14$

(d) $T_{n+1} = (n+1)^2 - 1$

$= n^2 + 2n + 1 - 1$

$= n^2 + 2n$

(e) $T_{n-1} = (n-1)^2 - 1$

$= n^2 - 2n + 1 - 1$

$= n^2 - 2n$

(f) $T_{n+2} = (n+2)^2 - 1$

$= n^2 + 4n + 4 - 1$

$= n^2 + 4n + 3$

EXERCISE 1

1. For the sequence −8, −3, 2, 7, ...

(a) find T_1,

(b) find $T_4 - T_3$,

(c) write down a rule, in words, for this sequence,

(d) using your rule, find the values of the following terms: T_7, T_8, T_9, T_{10},

(e) show that $T_8 - T_7 = T_{10} - T_9$,

(f) complete $T_n = -8 + (\quad) \times 5$,

(g) find T_{34},

(h) state if it is a finite or an infinite sequence.

2. For the sequence 11, 14, 17, 20, 23, 26, ...

(a) copy and complete the table:

Number of the term	Value of the term
$n = 1$	$11 = T_1 = 3 \times 1 + 8$
$n = 2$	$14 = T_2 = 3 \times 2 + 8$
$n = 3$	$17 = T_3 =$
$n = 4$	$20 = T_4 =$
$n = 5$	$23 = T_5 =$
$n = 6$	$26 = T_6 =$

(b) write down a formula T_n for this sequence,

(c) using this formula, find:

(i) T_{37}

(ii) T_{100}

(iii) T_{101}

(d) show that $T_{101} - T_{100} = 3$.

3. For the sequence 1, 8, 27, 64, ...

(a) copy and complete the table:

Number of the term	Value of the term
$n = 1$	$1 = T_1 = 1^3$
$n = 2$	$8 = T_2 = 2^3$
$n = 3$	
$n = 4$	

(b) find a possible formula for T_n,

(c) use your calculator to find T_{22}.

4. For the sequence 6, 18, 54, 162, ...

(a) complete the statement: Any term divided by the previous one = ______

(b) copy and complete the table:

Number of the term	Value of the term
$n = 1$	$6 = T_1 = 2 \times 3^1$
$n = 2$	$18 = T_2 = 2 \times 3^2$
$n = 3$	$54 = T_3 =$
$n = 4$	$162 = T_4 =$

(c) write down a formula for T_n,

(d) using the formula in part **(c)**, find $\frac{T_{100}}{T_{99}}$ without using your calculator.

5. The formula for the general term of a sequence is $T_n = 3n - 2$.

(a) Find:

(i) T_1

(ii) T_2

(iii) T_7

(iv) T_{11}

(b) Which term has a value of 94?

(c) Show that $T_{n+1} - T_n = 3$.

(d) Make a conclusion about the sequence.

6. For a sequence $T_n = n^2 + 2n$:

(a) find the first five terms,

(b) which term has a value of 120?

(c) find $T_{n+1} - T_n$,

(d) make a conclusion about the sequence.

7. For a sequence $T_n = \frac{n}{2n+1}$:

(a) find the first five terms,

(b) which term has a value of $\frac{25}{51}$?

(c) show that $T_{n+1} - T_n = \frac{1}{(2n+3)(2n+1)}$,

(d) make a conclusion about the sequence.

8. The general term for a sequence is $T_n = \frac{4}{2^n}$.

(a) Write out the first five terms.

(b) Which term has a value of $\frac{1}{128}$?

(c) Show that $\frac{T_{15}}{T_{14}} = \frac{1}{2}$.

(d) Show that $\frac{T_{n+1}}{T_n} = \frac{1}{2}$.

9. The general term of a sequence is $T_n = \log_{10} n$.

(a) Find:

(i) T_1

(ii) T_{100}

(iii) T_{n+1}

(b) Express $T_{n+1} - T_n$ as a single log function.

10. The general term of a sequence is $T_n = \frac{100}{5^{3n-1}}$.

(a) Find:

(i) T_1 **(ii)** T_2 **(iii)** T_{n+1}

(b) Show that $\frac{T_{n+1}}{T_n} = \frac{1}{125}$.

(c) Make a conclusion about this sequence.

11. A fence is constructed by starting with a five-bar section consisting of two vertical bars and three horizontal bars.

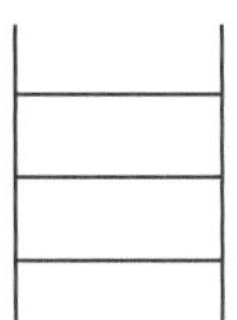

Four-bar sections are then added.

The first few stages in the construction are shown.

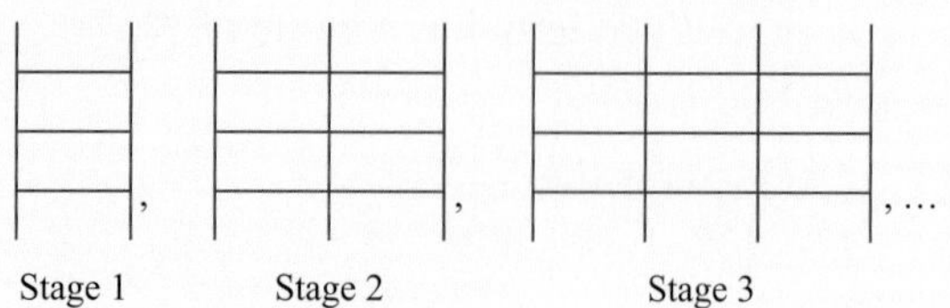

(a) Draw the fourth pattern.

(b) Write a sequence to show the number of bars in each stage.

(c) Complete the table:

Stage number n	Number of bars T_n
1	
2	
3	
4	

(d) Find a formula for T_n.

(e) How many bars are there in the 10th stage?

(f) Which stage has 61 bars?

12. (a) For the polygons below:

(i) copy and complete the table:

Polygon	Number of sides	Sum of interior angles
Triangle	3	180°
Quadrilateral		
Pentagon	5	540°
Hexagon		

(ii) hence, copy and complete the table:

Number of sides of a polygon N	Sum of interior angles T_n
3	180° = 180° × 1 = 180° × (3 − 2)
4	
5	540° = 180° × 3 = 180° × (5 − 2)
6	

(iii) write down a formula for T_n.

(b) what is the sum of the interior angles of a decagon (a 10-sided figure)?

(c) how many sides does a polygon have if the sum of the interior angles is 3780°?

13. (a) Write out the number of diagonals of the given polygons.

(i) 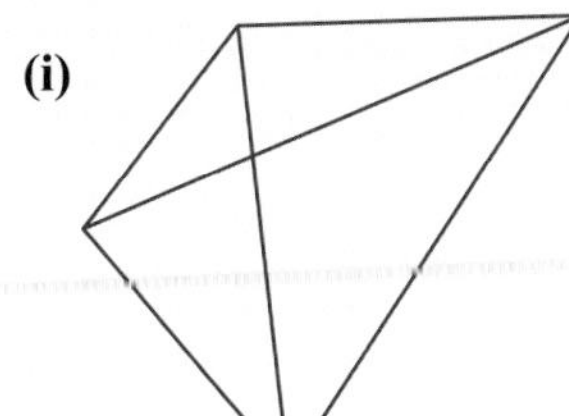

(ii) 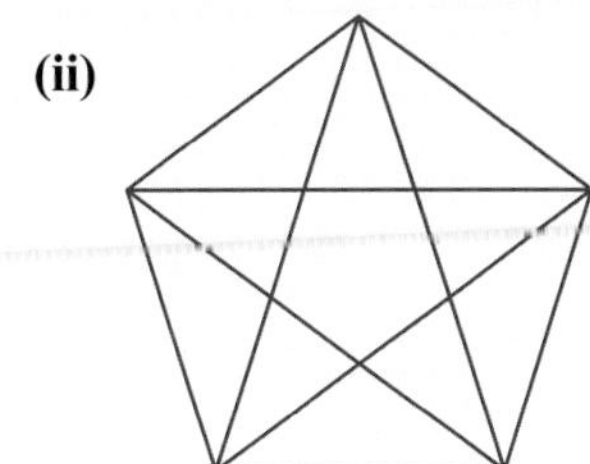

(iii) 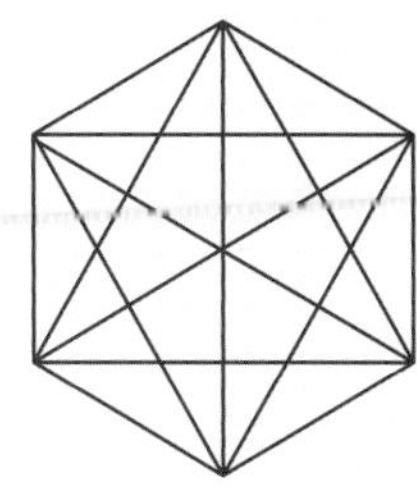

(b) Write a sequence to show the number of diagonals in polygons with 4, 5, 6, 7 and 8 sides.

(c) The general term of this sequence is given by $T_n = \dfrac{n(n-3)}{2}$. Verify it is true for a pentagon and a hexagon.

(d) Use the general term to find the number of diagonals of a 15-sided polygon.

(e) If a polygon has 135 diagonals, how many sides does it have?

14. (a) Copy and complete the table below:

Pattern number n	Shape	Number of small squares T_n
1		$T_1 = 2 \times (2) + (1) = 5$
2		$T_2 = 3 \times (\ ) + (\ ) =$
3		$T_3 = 4 \times (\ ) + (\ ) =$
4		$T_4 =$

(b) Find a formula for T_n. Because T_n is a quadratic expression, the sequence T_1, T_2, T_3, ... is known as a quadratic sequence.

(c) Write down the sequences of differences of consecutive terms in part **(a)**.

(d) What do you notice about the sequence in part **(c)**?

Analysing Sequences and Series

Learning Outcomes

- To understand the concept of the limit of a sequence.
- To find the limits of sequences.
- To understand the meaning of a series and to use the sigma (Σ) notation.

11.1 Convergence of a sequence

Idea of a limit

The flea hop

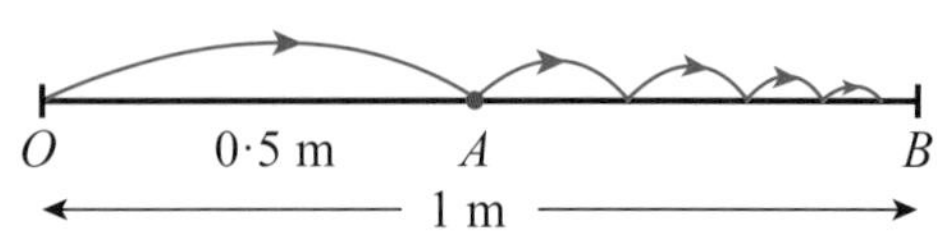

A flea wants to hop from O to B, a distance of 1 m. Its first hop is $\frac{1}{2}$ m. However, it gets tired and it finds it can only hop half of the remaining distance on each subsequent hop. The flea's distance in metres from B after each hop is:

Hop 1,	Hop 2,	Hop 3,	Hop 4 ...
↓	↓	↓	↓
$\frac{1}{2}$,	$\frac{1}{4}$,	$\frac{1}{8}$,	$\frac{1}{16}$ ...

Clearly, the more hops the flea makes, the distance it is from B gets smaller and smaller and it gets closer and closer to 0 m from B. However, the flea never actually gets to B.

As the number of hops increases, the distance the flea is from B gets closer and closer to 0 m.

This is the idea of a limit.

WORKED EXAMPLE

Exploring the limits of sequences

- Consider the sequence 2, 4, 6, 8, 10, … , $2n$, …

$$\begin{array}{cccccc} 2, & 4, & 6, & 8, & 10, \ldots, & 2n, \ldots \\ \downarrow & \downarrow & \downarrow & \downarrow & \downarrow & \downarrow \\ T_1, & T_2, & T_3, & T_4, & T_5, \ldots, & T_n, \ldots \end{array}$$

As you go further and further along the list, the value of each term gets bigger and bigger and will eventually become enormous (infinitely large).

As the number n of the term gets bigger, the value of each term is increasing without any limit to its value.

As $n \to \infty$ (n goes to infinity), $T_n \to \infty$ (T_n goes to infinity)

or

$\lim\limits_{n\to\infty} T_n = \infty$ [The limiting (lim) value of T_n as n gets bigger and bigger is infinity (unlimited).]

- Consider the sequence 0·9, 0·99, 0·999, 0·9999, …

Clearly, as you go further and further along the list, the value of each term is getting closer and closer to 1 (is increasing to a limiting value).

As n gets bigger and bigger, T_n gets closer and closer to 1.

As $n \to \infty$, $T_n \to 1$

or

$\lim\limits_{n\to\infty} T_n = 1$ [The limiting value (lim) of T_n as n gets bigger and bigger is 1 (limited).]

- Finally, consider the alternating sequence 3, −2, 3, −2, 3, −2, …

This sequence is going nowhere.

You simply cannot work out the value of T_n as n gets bigger and bigger. It has no limit.

In conclusion, there are three possibilities for the limit of a sequence:

1. $\lim\limits_{n\to\infty} T_n = \infty =$ infinity
2. $\lim\limits_{n\to\infty} T_n =$ finite number
3. $\lim\limits_{n\to\infty} T_n =$ does not exist

ACTIVITY 5

ACTION
Examining convergent and divergent sequences

OBJECTIVE
To examine a number of sequences and to state whether they converge to a particular value or diverge

KEY TERM
A sequence with an infinite limit or no limit is known as a **divergent sequence**.

KEY TERM
A sequence with a finite limit is known as a **convergent sequence**.

- −3, 2, 7, 12, … is divergent because $\lim\limits_{n\to\infty} T_n = \infty$.
- 0·3, 0·33, 0·333, 0·3333, … is convergent because $\lim\limits_{n\to\infty} T_n = \frac{1}{3}$.
- 1, −1, 1, −1, … is divergent because $\lim\limits_{n\to\infty} T_n$ does not exist.
- $1, 1\frac{1}{2}, 1\frac{3}{4}, 1\frac{4}{5}, 1\frac{5}{6}, \ldots$ is convergent because $\lim\limits_{n\to\infty} T_n = 2$.

Evaluating a limit

A question might ask you to evaluate $\lim_{x \to 1}(3x + 2)$.

This means that you have to find the value of $(3x + 2)$ as x gets closer and closer to 1. The table below illustrates this:

x	0·9	0·99	0·999	0·9999	$\to 1$
$3x + 2$	4·7	4·97	4·997	4·9997	$\to 5$

$\therefore \lim_{x \to 1}(3x + 2) = 5 = 3(1) + 2$

You could just substitute 1 for x into $3x + 2$. This works most of the time.

ACTIVITY 6

ACTION
Working with limits

OBJECTIVE
To evaluate a limit (using a calculator)

Important limits

Infinity limits are limits in which the variable approaches infinity.

1. $\lim_{n \to \infty}\left(\frac{1}{n}\right)$

n	100	1000	10 000	100 000	1 000 000	$\to \infty$
$\frac{1}{n}$	0·01	0·001	0·0001	0·00001	0·000001	$\to 0$

$\therefore \lim_{n \to \infty}\frac{1}{n} = 0$ (because $\frac{1}{\infty} = 0$)

This is intuitively obvious because as n becomes enormous, $\frac{1}{n}$ becomes $\left(\frac{1}{\text{huge number}}\right)$, which equates to a tiny number.

2. $\lim_{n \to \infty} r^n$

n	1	2	4	8	10	$\to \infty$
2^n	2	4	16	256	1024	$\to \infty$
$\left(\frac{1}{2}\right)^n$	$\frac{1}{2}$	$\frac{1}{4}$	$\frac{1}{16}$	$\frac{1}{256}$	$\frac{1}{1024}$	$\to 0$

$\therefore \lim_{n \to \infty} 2^n = \infty$ but $\lim_{n \to \infty}\left(\frac{1}{2}\right)^n = 0$

- $\lim_{n \to \infty}\left(\frac{3}{2}\right)^n = \left(\frac{3}{2}\right)^\infty = \infty$ [The limit is infinity as $r = \frac{3}{2}$.]
- $\lim_{n \to \infty}\left(\frac{4}{5}\right)^n = \left(\frac{4}{5}\right)^\infty = 0$ [The limit is zero as $r = \frac{4}{5}$.]
- $\lim_{n \to \infty}(-3)^n = (-3)^\infty = \infty$ [The limit is infinity as $r = -3$.]
- $\lim_{n \to \infty}\left(-\frac{1}{3}\right)^n = 0$ [The limit is zero as $r = -\frac{1}{3}$.]

$$\lim_{n \to \infty} r^n = \begin{cases} 0 \text{ if } -1 < r < 1 \\ \infty \text{ if } r < -1,\ r > 1 \end{cases}$$

Rules of limits

There are four rules for taking limits. These rules are stated for functions of a variable x:

1. Sum rule: $\lim_{x \to a}\{f(x) + g(x)\} = \lim_{x \to a} f(x) + \lim_{x \to a} g(x)$

- $\lim_{n \to 2}(n - n^2) = \lim_{n \to 2} n - \lim_{n \to 2} n^2 = 2 - 4 = -2$ [n is the variable]

2. **Multiplication by a constant rule:** $\lim_{x\to a} cf(x) = c\lim_{x\to a} f(x)$, c constant

- $\lim_{n\to -2}\left(\frac{n^3}{2}\right) = \frac{1}{2}\lim_{n\to -2} n^3 = \frac{1}{2}(-8) = -4$
- $\lim_{n\to \frac{1}{2}} (3n^2 - 2n) = 3\lim_{n\to \frac{1}{2}} n^2 - 2\lim_{n\to \frac{1}{2}} n = 3 \times \frac{1}{4} - 2 \times \frac{1}{2} = \frac{3}{4} - 1 = -\frac{1}{4}$

3. **Product rule:** $\lim_{x\to a} \{f(x) \times g(x)\} = \lim_{x\to a} f(x) \times \lim_{x\to a} g(x)$

- $\lim_{x\to \frac{3}{2}} x(2x+3) = \lim_{x\to \frac{3}{2}} x \times \lim_{x\to \frac{3}{2}}(2x+3) = \frac{3}{2} \times (6) = 9$

4. **Quotient rule:** $\lim_{x\to a}\left\{\frac{f(x)}{g(x)}\right\} = \frac{\lim_{x\to a} f(x)}{\lim_{x\to a} g(x)}$

- $\lim_{x\to -3} \frac{3x^2}{x+1} = \frac{\lim_{x\to -3} 3x^2}{\lim_{x\to -3}(x+1)} = \frac{27}{-2} = -\frac{27}{2}$

These rules enable you to substitute the value of the variable directly into the function. If you get a well-defined answer, this is the value of the limit.

Evaluating infinity limits

An infinity limit is the limit of a function as the variable tends to ∞: $\lim_{x\to\infty} f(x)$.

It is easy to take an infinity limit in most cases. You just substitute ∞ for the variable in the function.

- $\lim_{x\to\infty} (4x^2 + 7) = 4(\infty)^2 + 7 = \infty$
- $\lim_{n\to\infty} \frac{5}{n+1} = \frac{5}{\infty + 1} = \frac{5}{\infty} = 0$
- $\lim_{n\to\infty} \frac{n}{n+1} = \frac{\infty}{\infty}$

$\lim_{n\to\infty} \frac{n}{n+1}$ is troublesome as $\frac{\infty}{\infty}$ is not defined. This does not mean that the limit does not exist, it is just that you are having difficulty determining it.

WORKED EXAMPLE

Determining limits that give $\frac{\infty}{\infty}$

Technique for evaluating limits of this type:

1. Take out a factor of the variable in the numerator and the denominator.
2. Cancel the takeout factors.
3. Take the limit.

- $\lim_{n\to\infty} \frac{n}{n+1} = \frac{\infty}{\infty}$ [This is not defined.]

$$\lim_{n\to\infty} \frac{n}{n+1} = \lim_{n\to\infty} \frac{n(1)}{n\left(1+\frac{1}{n}\right)} = \lim_{n\to\infty} \frac{1}{\left(1+\frac{1}{n}\right)} = \frac{1}{1+\frac{1}{\infty}} = \frac{1}{1+0} = 1$$

- $\lim_{x\to\infty} \frac{2x+3}{3x-2} = \left(\frac{\infty}{\infty}\right)$ [This is not defined.]

$$\lim_{x\to\infty} \frac{2x+3}{3x-2} = \lim_{x\to\infty} \frac{x\left(2+\frac{3}{x}\right)}{x\left(3-\frac{2}{x}\right)} = \lim_{x\to\infty} \frac{\left(2+\frac{3}{x}\right)}{\left(3-\frac{2}{x}\right)} = \frac{\left(2+\frac{3}{\infty}\right)}{\left(3-\frac{2}{\infty}\right)} = \frac{2+0}{3-0} = \frac{2}{3}$$

Testing a sequence for convergence or divergence given a formula for its general term T_n

To test a sequence for convergence or divergence given its general term T_n, evaluate $\lim_{n\to\infty} T_n$.

1. If this limit is ∞ or undefined, the sequence is divergent.
2. If this limit is a finite number L, this sequence is convergent to L.

EXAMPLE 1

Test the sequences below for convergence or divergence and, if convergent, state to what number the sequence is convergent:

(a) $T_n = 2n + 1$ **(b)** $T_n = \dfrac{1}{2^n}$ **(c)** $T_n = \dfrac{3n}{2n+5}$

Solution

(a) $T_n = 2n + 1$

$$\lim_{n\to\infty} T_n = \lim_{n\to\infty}(2n+1)$$
$$= 2(\infty) + 1 = \infty$$

The sequence is divergent.

(b) $T_n = \dfrac{1}{2^n}$

$$\lim_{n\to\infty} T_n = \lim_{n\to\infty}\frac{1}{2^n} = \frac{1}{2^\infty} = \frac{1}{\infty} = 0$$

The sequence is convergent to 0.

(c) $T_n = \dfrac{3n}{2n+5}$

$$\lim_{n\to\infty} T_n = \lim_{n\to\infty}\frac{3n}{2n+5} = \left(\frac{\infty}{\infty}\right)$$ [This is not defined. Follow the three steps.]

$$\lim_{n\to\infty} T_n = \lim_{n\to\infty}\frac{3n}{2n+5} = \lim_{n\to\infty}\frac{n(3)}{n\left(2+\frac{5}{n}\right)} = \lim_{n\to\infty}\frac{3}{\left(2+\frac{5}{n}\right)}$$

$$= \frac{3}{\left(2+\frac{5}{\infty}\right)} = \frac{3}{2+0} = \frac{3}{2}$$

The sequence is convergent to $\frac{3}{2}$.

EXERCISE 2

1. Write down $\lim_{n\to\infty} T_n$ for the following sequences and state if they are convergent or divergent. Use your calculator if necessary.

   (a) $\frac{1}{1}, \frac{1}{4}, \frac{1}{9}, \frac{1}{16}, \dots$

   (b) $\frac{5}{2}, \frac{3}{2}, \frac{1}{2}, -\frac{1}{2}, -\frac{3}{2}, \dots$

   (c) $\frac{3}{10}, \frac{33}{100}, \frac{333}{1000}, \frac{3333}{10\,000}, \dots$

   (d) $\frac{1}{3}, \frac{1}{9}, \frac{1}{27}, \frac{1}{81}, \dots$

   (e) $10, 100, 1000, 10\,000, \dots$

   (f) $0{\cdot}6, 0{\cdot}66, 0{\cdot}666, 0{\cdot}6666, \dots$

   (g) $\frac{1}{2}, \frac{2}{3}, \frac{3}{4}, \frac{4}{5}, \dots$

   (h) $7, -3, 8, -2, 7, -3, 8, -2, \dots$

   (i) $\left(2-\frac{1}{2}\right), \left(2-\frac{1}{3}\right), \left(2-\frac{1}{4}\right), \dots$

   (j) $0{\cdot}09, 0{\cdot}099, 0{\cdot}0999, \dots$

2. Evaluate the following limits:

   (a) $\lim_{x\to 2}(5x+1)x$

   (b) $\lim_{x\to 3}(3x+5x^2)$

   (c) $\lim_{x\to -2}\left(\frac{3x}{2} - \frac{7}{x}\right)$

   (d) $\lim_{x\to -1}\frac{2x^2-1}{3x+2}$

   (e) $\lim_{n\to\infty} 3n$

   (f) $\lim_{n\to\infty}\frac{2}{n+1}$

   (g) $\lim_{n\to\infty} 3\left(\frac{1}{2}\right)^n$

   (h) $\lim_{n\to\infty} 2(3)^n$

   (i) $\lim_{n\to\infty}\left\{3\left(\frac{2}{3}\right)^n + \frac{1}{n} + 7\right\}$

   (j) $\lim_{x\to\infty}\left(\frac{3}{x^2+1}\right)$

3. Evaluate the following limits:

(a) $\lim_{n\to\infty} \frac{n}{3n+1}$

(b) $\lim_{n\to\infty} \frac{2n+1}{3n}$

(c) $\lim_{n\to\infty} \frac{2n-1}{2n+1}$

(d) $\lim_{n\to\infty} \frac{3-2n}{4+n}$

(e) $\lim_{n\to\infty} \frac{5}{n^2}$

(f) $\lim_{n\to\infty} \frac{3}{2n^2+1}$

(g) $\lim_{n\to\infty} \frac{n^2-1}{n+1}$

(h) $\lim_{n\to\infty} \frac{n+2}{n^2-4}$

(i) $\lim_{n\to\infty} \frac{2^n+1}{4^n}$

(j) $\lim_{n\to\infty} \frac{\frac{1}{2}n+7}{\frac{4}{3}n+5}$

4. Given the general term T_n, test the following sequences for convergence or divergence:

(a) $T_n = \frac{2}{n}$

(b) $T_n = \frac{3}{2^n}$

(c) $T_n = \frac{1}{n^2}$

(d) $T_n = \frac{n-1}{n+1}$

(e) $T_n = \frac{3n-6}{4-5n}$

(f) $T_n = 2\left(\frac{3}{5}\right)^n$

(g) $T_n = \frac{1}{2} - \frac{n}{n+1}$

(h) $T_n = \left(\frac{x}{x+1}\right)^n$, where $x > 0, x \in \mathbb{R}$

11.2 Examining series

KEY TERM

A **series** is the **sum** of the individual terms of a sequence.

ACTIVITY 7

ACTION
Working with sequences and series

OBJECTIVE
To write the corresponding series when presented with a sequence

Given the sequence: 3, 8, 18, 38, … , its corresponding series is: 3 + 8 + 18 + 38 + …

The first term of a series is the same as the first term of the corresponding sequence, the second term of a series is the same as the second term of the corresponding sequence, and so on. The individual terms in both are exactly the same (the commas have just been replaced by + signs).

This means that the general term of a sequence and its corresponding series is exactly the same.

For the sequence $\frac{2}{3}, \frac{2}{5}, \frac{2}{7}, \ldots,$

$T_1 = \frac{2}{3}, T_2 = \frac{2}{5}, T_n = \frac{2}{2n+1}.$

For the corresponding series $\frac{2}{3} + \frac{2}{5} + \frac{2}{7} + \ldots,$

$T_1 = \frac{2}{3}, T_2 = \frac{2}{5}, T_n = \frac{2}{2n+1}.$

If the general term of a sequence is $T_n = \frac{n}{n+1}$, the corresponding series is

$T_1 + T_2 + T_3 + \ldots = \frac{1}{2} + \frac{2}{3} + \frac{3}{4} + \ldots$

As with a sequence, a **finite** series stops, but an **infinite** series goes on forever.

ACTIVITY 8

ACTION
Exploring partial sums of series

OBJECTIVE
To calculate the partial sums of a number of series

The sum and partial sums of a series

The sum of a finite series is obtained by adding up all of its terms.

- The sum of the series $-2 + 1 + 4 + 7 + 10 + 13$ is given by $S = 33$.

  It has six terms. This sum is called S_6.

  $S_6 = T_1 + T_2 + T_3 + T_4 + T_5 + T_6$

The partial sums of a series can be found as follows:

$S_1 = T_1 =$ sum of the first term

$S_2 = T_1 + T_2 =$ sum of the first two terms

$S_3 = T_1 + T_2 + T_3 =$ sum of the first three terms

$\therefore S_n = T_1 + T_2 + T_3 + \ldots + T_n =$ sum of the first n terms

- For the series $-9 + 23 - 41 + 87 - 169 + \ldots$

  $S_1 = -9 = T_1 = -9$

  $S_2 = -9 + 23 = T_1 + T_2 = 14$

  $S_5 = -9 + 23 - 41 + 87 - 169 = -109$

- For a series, if the sum of the first n terms is given by $S_n = n^3 - 2n$:

  $S_1 = 1^3 - 2 \times 1 = -1 = T_1$

  $S_2 = 2^3 - 2 \times 2 = 4 = T_1 + T_2$

  $T_2 = 4 - T_1 = 4 + 1 = 5$

  $S_3 = 3^3 - 6 = 21 = T_1 + T_2 + T_3$

  $T_3 = 21 - 4 = 17$

  This means the sequence from which this series came is: $-1, 5, 17$

EXAMPLE 2

For a series $S_n = 2n^2 - 3n$, find S_1, S_2, S_3 and S_4. Hence, find T_1, T_2, T_3 and T_4.

Solution

$S_n = 2n^2 - 3n$

$S_1 = 2(1)^2 - 3(1) = -1$

$S_2 = 2(2)^2 - 3(2) = 2$

$S_3 = 2(3)^2 - 3(3) = 9$

$S_4 = 2(4)^2 - 3(4) = 20$

$T_1 = S_1 = -1$

$T_1 + T_2 = S_2 = 2 \Rightarrow T_2 = 2 - (-1) = 3$

$T_3 = S_3 - S_2 = 9 - 2 = 7$

$T_4 = S_4 - S_3 = 20 - 9 = 11$

Finding T_n from S_n

If you subtract the sum of the first 47 terms of a series from the sum of the first 48 terms you get:

$$\begin{array}{l} S_{48} = \cancel{T_1} + \cancel{T_2} + \cdots + \cancel{T_{47}} + T_{48} \\ S_{47} = \cancel{T_1} + \cancel{T_2} + \cdots + \cancel{T_{47}} \\ \hline S_{48} - S_{47} = T_{48} \end{array}$$

All this says is that the difference between the sum of the first 48 terms and the sum of the first 47 terms is the extra term T_{48}.

In general, for all sequences and series: $S_n - S_{n-1} = T_n$ for all $n \geq 2, n \in \mathbb{N}$.

EXAMPLE 3

For a series $S_n - 2^n - 1$, show that $T_n = 2^{n-1}$. Show that $T_1 = S_1$.

Solution

$T_1 = S_n - S_{n-1} \Rightarrow 2^n - 1 - (2^{n-1} - 1)$

$= 2^n - 1 - 2^{n-1} + 1$

$= 2^n - 2^{n-1}$

$= 2^{n-1}(2 - 1)$

$= 2^{n-1}$

$T_1 = 2^{(1)-1} = 2^0 = 1$

$S_1 = 2^{(1)} - 1 = 2 - 1 = 1$

$\therefore T_1 = S_1$

The Σ (sigma) notation – a shorthand method for writing a series

A series can be written in one of two ways:

1. List: $\frac{1}{1^2} + \frac{1}{2^2} + \frac{1}{3^2} + \frac{1}{4^2} + \cdots + \frac{1}{105^2}$.

Or

2. $\sum$ notation: $\sum_{n=1}^{105} \frac{1}{n^2}$

ACTIVITY 9

ACTION
Working with $\sum$

OBJECTIVE
To practise using the $\sum$ notation

Understanding the Σ notation

A series can be written in the form $\sum_{\text{Start value}}^{\text{End value}} T_n$ where T_n is the general term.

It is important to understand the following:

1. The sigma $\sum$ sign stands for 'add up'.

2. The symbol beside the $\sum$ sign is the general term T_n of the series.

3. $\sum_{\text{Start value}}^{\text{End value}} T_n$ means add up all of the values of T from T_{Start} to T_{End}.

To convert the $\sum$ notation into list form, fill the value of the variable into the general term beginning at the start value and stopping at the end value. Increase the value of the variable by 1 each time and put + signs between each term.

$$\sum_{n=1}^{3}(4n-1)^2 = (4 \times 1 - 1)^2 + (4 \times 2 - 1)^2 + (4 \times 3 - 1)^2$$

$$\downarrow \qquad \downarrow \qquad \downarrow \qquad \downarrow$$

$$T_n \qquad T_1 \qquad T_2 \qquad T_3$$

This is S_3 as it adds up the first three terms of a series.

- $\sum_{r=1}^{5}(2r+1)$ [This is S_5 as it adds up the first five terms of a series.]

  $S_5 = \sum_{r=1}^{5}(2r+1) = (2\times1+1)+(2\times2+1)+(2\times3+1)+(2\times4+1)+(2\times5+1)$

  $= T_1 + T_2 + T_3 + T_4 + T_5$

  In this case, $T_r = 2r + 1$. The variable used here is r and so the general term is called T_r.

- $\sum_{n=1}^{\infty}\frac{2}{3n+1} = S_\infty = \frac{2}{4}+\frac{2}{7}+\frac{2}{10}+\frac{2}{13}+\frac{2}{16}+\ldots$

  General term: $T_n = \frac{2}{3n+1}$

- $\sum_{p=1}^{n}2^p = S_n = 2^1 + 2^2 + \ldots + 2^n$

  General term: $T_p = 2^p$

EXAMPLE 4

For a series $\sum_{n=1}^{n}(n^2 - n)$,

(a) find T_n,

(b) show that $T_1 = S_1$,

(c) find S_3 and S_4 and show that $S_4 - S_3 = T_4$.

Solution

(a) $\sum_{n=1}^{n}(n^2 - n) = S_n = (1^2 - 1) + (2^2 - 2) + \ldots + (n^2 - n)$

$\therefore\ T_n = n^2 - n$

(b) $S_1 = \sum_{n=1}^{1}(n^2 - n) = (1^2 - 1) = 1$

$T_1 = (1)^2 - (1) = 1$

(c) $S_4 = \sum_{n=1}^{4}(n^2 - n) = (1^2 - 1) + (2^2 - 2) + (3^2 - 3) + (4^2 - 4) = 1 + 2 + 6 + 12 = 21$

$S_3 = \sum_{n=1}^{3}(n^2 - n) = (1^2 - 1) + (2^2 - 2) + (3^2 - 3) = 1 + 2 + 6 = 9$

$T_4 = (4)^2 - 4 = 16 - 4 = 12$

$S_4 - S_3 = 21 - 9 = 12 = T_4$

The $\sum$ rules

There are three rules for $\sum$.

1. **Split rule:** You can split the sigma of the general term that is expressed as a sum into individual sigmas of each component of the general term.

$$\sum_{n=1}^{4}(n^2+n) = (1^2+1)+(2^2+2)+(3^2+3)+(4^2+4)$$
$$= (1^2+2^2+3^2+4^2)+(1+2+3+4)$$
$$\therefore \sum_{n=1}^{4}(n^2+n) = \sum_{n=1}^{4}n^2 + \sum_{n=1}^{4}n$$

2. **Constant factor rule:** You can take a constant factor out of sigmas.

$$\sum_{n=1}^{5}3n^2 = 3\times1^2+3\times2^2+3\times3^2+3\times4^2+3\times5^2$$
$$= 3(1^2+2^2+3^2+4^2+5^2)$$
$$\therefore \sum_{n=1}^{5}3n^2 = 3\sum_{n=1}^{5}n^2$$

3. **The one rule:** $\sum_{n=1}^{n}1$ means add 1 to itself n times.

$$S_n = \sum_{n=1}^{n}1 = \sum_{n=1}^{n}n^0 = 1^0+2^0+3^0+\ldots n^0 = 1+1+1+\ldots+1 = n$$

All the rules together:

$$\sum_{n=1}^{18}(3n-2) = \sum_{n=1}^{18}3n - \sum_{n=1}^{18}2 = 3\sum_{n=1}^{18}n - 2\sum_{n=1}^{18}1 = 3\sum_{n=1}^{18}n - 2\times18 = 3\sum_{n=1}^{18}n - 36 = S_{18}$$

$$\sum_{n=1}^{n}(n+1)^2 = \sum_{n=1}^{n}(n^2+2n+1) = \sum_{n=1}^{n}n^2 + 2\sum_{n=1}^{n}n + \sum_{n=1}^{n}1 = S_n$$

EXERCISE 3

1. **(a)** A series has a general term given by $T_n = 2n - 1, n \in \mathbb{N}$.
   (i) Write out the first five terms in list form.
   (ii) Find S_5 and S_4.
   (iii) Show that $S_5 - S_4 = T_5$.

   (b) The general term of a series is given by $T_n = \dfrac{n+1}{2n+3}, n \in \mathbb{N}$.
   (i) Write out the first six terms in list form.
   (ii) Find S_4, S_3 and S_2.
   (iii) Show that $S_4 - S_3 = T_4$ and $S_3 - S_2 = T_3$.

   (c) The general term of a series is given by $T_n = \dfrac{n^2+1}{4}, n \in \mathbb{N}$.
   (i) Write out the first seven terms in list form.
   (ii) Show that $S_7 - S_6 = T_7$.

   (d) The general term of a series is given by $T_n = \dfrac{3}{n+1}$.
   (i) Find T_1, T_2, T_3, T_4 and T_5.
   (ii) Find S_1, S_2, S_3, S_4 and S_5.
   (iii) Show that $S_2 - S_1 = T_2$.

2. **(a)** The sum of the first n terms of a series is given by $S_n = n^2 + 5n$. Find:
   (i) S_1 **(iv)** T_1
   (ii) S_2 **(v)** T_2
   (iii) S_3 **(vi)** T_3
   (vii) Write out the first three terms of the series in list form.

(b) The sum of the first n terms of a series is given by $S_n = 3^n - 1$. Find:

(i) S_1 **(v)** T_1

(ii) S_2 **(vi)** T_2

(iii) S_3 **(vii)** T_3

(iv) S_4 **(viii)** T_4

(ix) Write out the first four terms of the series in list form.

(c) The sum of the first n terms of a series is given by $S_n = \left[\frac{n(n+1)}{2}\right]^2$. Find:

(i) S_1 **(vi)** T_1

(ii) S_2 **(vii)** T_2

(iii) S_3 **(viii)** T_3

(iv) S_4 **(ix)** T_4

(v) S_5 **(x)** T_5

(xi) Write out the first five terms of the series in list form.

(xii) Can you write down a possible general term T_n for this series?

3. **(a)** The sum of the first 32 terms of a series is 427. The sum of the first 31 terms is 402. Find the 32nd term.

(b) The sum of the first 47 terms of a series is −138. The 48th term is 4. What is the sum of the first 48 terms?

(c) For a series, $S_7 = 18$ and $S_8 = 22$. Find T_8.

(d) For a series, $S_{50} = 4293$ and $T_{51} = 41$. Find S_{51}.

(e) For a series, $S_n = n^2 - n$. Find S_{n-1}, T_n, T_1 and T_{20}.

(f) For a series, $S_n = \frac{n}{2}(n+1)$. Find S_{n-1}, T_n, T_1 and T_{38}.

(g) For a series, $S_n = \frac{n}{6}(n+1)(2n+1)$. Find S_{n-1}, T_n, T_1 and T_{20}.

4. Write out the following in list notation:

(a) all terms in $\sum_{n=1}^{10}(n-2)^2$,

(b) all terms in $\sum_{r=1}^{7}(2r+5)$,

(c) the first three terms in $\sum_{r=1}^{\infty}\left(\frac{3}{2}\right)^r$,

(d) all terms in $\sum_{n=1}^{8}\frac{n-1}{n+2}$,

(e) all terms in $\sum_{r=1}^{5}\left(\frac{1}{2}\right)^r - 2r$,

(f) the first two and the last two terms in $\sum_{l=1}^{n}\left(\frac{3}{4}\right)^l$,

(g) the first two and the last two terms in $\sum_{n=1}^{n+4}\frac{1}{2^{n-1}}$,

(h) the first two and the last two terms in $\sum_{n=1}^{n+3}\frac{1}{n}$,

(i) all terms in $\sum_{r=1}^{8}(2r^2+r+1)$,

(j) the first two and the last two terms in $\sum_{n=1}^{n} n!$

5. For each series in Question 4, write down the general term and say how many terms are in each sum.

6. Write the following series in $\sum$ form by finding the general term first:

(a) $1^2 + 2^2 + \cdots + 20^2$

(b) $\frac{1}{1} + \frac{1}{2} + \frac{1}{3} + \frac{1}{4} + \cdots + \frac{1}{35}$

(c) $2 + 4 + 6 + 8 + \cdots + 100$

(d) $3 + 5 + 7 + \cdots + (2r+1) + \cdots + 35$

(e) $\frac{1}{6} + \frac{1}{18} + \frac{1}{54} + \cdots \frac{1}{2 \times 3^n} + \cdots$

(f) $\frac{1}{3 \times 5} + \frac{1}{4 \times 6} + \cdots + \frac{1}{(n+2)(n+4)} + \cdots + \frac{1}{20 \times 22}$

(g) $4 + 5 + 6 + \cdots + (r+3) + \cdots + 48$

(h) $\frac{1}{4} + \frac{1}{8} + \frac{1}{16} + \cdots \frac{1}{2^{n+1}} + \cdots$

Arithmetic Sequences and Series

Learning Outcomes

- To solve problems involving arithmetic sequences and series.
- To model word problems that are arithmetic in nature.

12.1 Defining an arithmetic sequence

ACTIVITY 10

ACTION
Understanding an arithmetic sequence

OBJECTIVE
To understand an arithmetic sequence

WORKED EXAMPLE Arithmetic sequence 1

As dry air moves up in the atmosphere, it cools down. In fact, it cools by 3 °C for every 300 m rise. If the ground temperature is 20 °C, the temperature of the air at heights of 300 m, 600 m, 900 m, 1200 m and 1500 m above the surface of the ground are shown in the table below.

Height (m)	300	600	900	1200	1500
Temperature (°C)	17	14	11	8	5

The sequence of temperatures in °C is 17, 14, 11, 8, 5.

The first term T_1 is 17 °C and it decreases at a constant rate of 3 °C.

This means that the difference between any term and the previous term is a constant equal to −3. Therefore, this sequence is arithmetic.

WORKED EXAMPLE Arithmetic sequence 2

For the sequence $\frac{3}{2}, \frac{7}{4}, 2, \frac{9}{4}, \frac{5}{2}, \dots,$

$T_1 = \frac{3}{2}, T_2 = \frac{7}{4}, T_2 - T_1 = \frac{7}{4} - \frac{3}{2} = \frac{1}{4}$

$T_4 = \frac{9}{4}, T_5 = \frac{5}{2}, T_5 - T_4 = \frac{5}{2} - \frac{9}{4} = \frac{1}{4}$

The difference between any two terms appears to give the same constant number. This sequence is arithmetic.

ACTIVITY 11

ACTION
Working with arithmetic sequences (1)

OBJECTIVE
To write down the first term and common difference of a number of arithmetic sequences

KEY TERM

An **arithmetic sequence** or **progression** is a list of terms that starts with any object (number, symbol, shape, function) and keeps on adding the same constant to each term to get the next term.

- Start with −2 and keep on adding 5:

  −2, 3, 8, 13, 18, …

  +5 +5 +5 +5

- Start with x^2 and keep on adding y: $x^2, x^2 + y, x^2 + 2y, x^2 + 3y, \ldots$

It is important to note the following:

1. Every arithmetic sequence has a starting term T_1 (the first term).
2. Any term minus the previous term is the same constant d (the common difference).
3. If you know the first term T_1 and the constant d, you can generate the whole sequence.
   - If the first term T_1 of an arithmetic sequence is 50 and the constant d that is to be added to each term is −4, the sequence is 50, 46, 42, 38, 34, …
   - In the arithmetic sequence 4, 7, 10, … , $T_1 = 4$ and $d = T_2 - T_1 = 7 - 4 = 3$.

12.2 General term T_n of an arithmetic sequence

ACTIVITY 12

ACTION
Working with arithmetic sequences (2)

OBJECTIVE
To explore various arithmetic sequences and to gain an understanding of how these sequences operate

If you start with the first term $T_1 = a$ and keep on adding the constant d you generate the general arithmetic sequence:

$a, \quad a + d, \quad a + 2d, \quad a + 3d, \ldots$

$\uparrow \quad \uparrow \quad \uparrow \quad \uparrow$

$T_1, \quad T_2, \quad T_3, \quad T_4, \ldots$

$T_1 = a =$ the first term

$T_2 = a + 1d$

$T_3 = a + 2d$

$T_4 = a + 3d$

$T_{57} = a + 56d$

TIP

If you are told that the 57th term of an arithmetic sequence is −82, you can write $a + 56d = -82$.

The general term T_n of any arithmetic sequence is given by:

$$T_n = a + (n - 1)d.$$

- For the arithmetic sequence: 15, 18, 21, … ,

  $a = 15$ = first term = T_1

  d = any term − previous term = 18 − 15 = 3

  $T_{38} = a + 37d = 15 + 37 \times 3 = 15 + 111 = 126$

As already stated, for all arithmetic sequences:

1. $T_1 = a$ = first term.
2. d = common difference = any term − previous one.
3. If you know a and d, you can find every other term in the sequence.

EXAMPLE 1

A cyclist freewheels downhill travelling 1·2 m in the first second and, in each succeeding second, 1·5 m more than in the previous second. Write out, as a sequence, the distances travelled in the first 4 seconds. Find the distance travelled in the 12th second.

Solution

1st Second	2nd Second	3rd Second	4th Second
1·2 m	2·7 m	4·2 m	5·7 m

Arithmetic sequence: 1·2, 2·7, 4·2, 5·7, …

$\therefore a = 1{\cdot}2, d = 1{\cdot}5$

$T_{12} = a + 11d = 1{\cdot}2 + 11 \times 1{\cdot}5 = 17{\cdot}7$ m.

EXAMPLE 2

If 3, x, y, 24 are consecutive terms of an arithmetic sequence, find x and y and the general term of the sequence.

Solution

Arithmetic sequence: 3, x, y, 24

Write down the terms you know.

$T_1 = a = 3$ **(1)**

$T_4 = a + 3d = 24$ **(2)**

(2) − (1): $3d = 21$

$d = 7$

The arithmetic sequence is: 3, 10, 17, 24, …

$\therefore x = 10, y = 17$

$T_n = a + (n - 1)d = 3 + (n - 1)7 = 7n - 4$

EXAMPLE 3

A carpentry firm wishes to construct a 12-rung ladder where the lengths of the rungs decrease uniformly. The length of the third rung must be 85 cm and the length of the eighth rung must be 60 cm. Find the lengths of the first rung and the last rung. Write out the lengths of the first five rungs.

Solution

$T_3 = 85 = a + 2d$ **(1)**

$T_8 = 60 = a + 7d$ **(2)**

$\therefore$ **(2) − (1):** $-25 = 5d$

$d = -5$

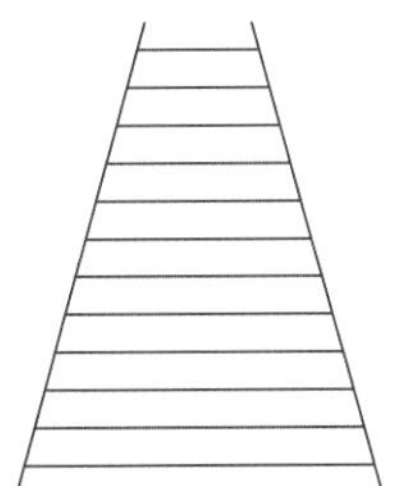

(1): $a - 10 = 85 \Rightarrow a = 95$

$T_{12} = a + 11d = 95 + 11 \times (-5) = 40$ cm

Lengths of first five rungs:

95 cm, 90 cm, 85 cm, 80 cm, 75 cm

Given the general term of an arithmetic sequence, you can find any specified term.

- For an arithmetic sequence $T_n = 5 - 2n$

  $a = T_1 = 5 - 2 \times 1 = 3$

  $T_2 = 5 - 2 \times 2 = 1$

  $d = T_2 - T_1 = 1 - 3 = -2$

  Arithmetic sequence: 3, 1, −1, −3, …

EXAMPLE 4

How many terms are in the finite arithmetic sequence 7, 3, −1, −5, −9, … , −129?

Solution

Arithmetic sequence: 7, 3, −1, −5, −9, … , −129.

$T_1 = a = 7, d = -4$

$T_n = a + (n-1)d = 7 + (n-1)(-4) = 11 - 4n$

Call the last term T_n: $T_n = 11 - 4n = -129$

$4n = 140$

$n = 35$

There are 35 terms in the sequence.

−129 is the 35th term.

EXAMPLE 5

For the arithmetic sequence −4, −1, 2, 5, …

(a) find T_n,

(b) what term in the sequence has a value of 152?

(c) is 117 a term in the sequence?

(d) plot a graph of T_n against n,

(e) find the slope of the graph,

(f) what can you conclude about the slope of the graph in relation to the arithmetic sequence?

Solution

Arithmetic sequence: −4, −1, 2, 5, …

(a) $a = -4, d = 3$

$T_n = a + (n-1)d = -4 + (n-1)3$

$T_n = 3n - 7$

(b) If you know T_n, you can find the position of any term in the sequence.

$T_n = 3n - 7 = 152$

$3n = 159$

$n = 53$

152 is the 53rd term.

(c) Remember in all sequences $n \in \mathbb{N}$.
If 117 is a term in the sequence, you should be able to find its position n in the list.

$T_n = 3n - 7 = 117$

$3n = 124$

$n = 41\frac{1}{3}$

Therefore, 117 is not a term in the sequence as n must be a natural number.

(d)

n	1	2	3	4
T_n	−4	−1	2	5

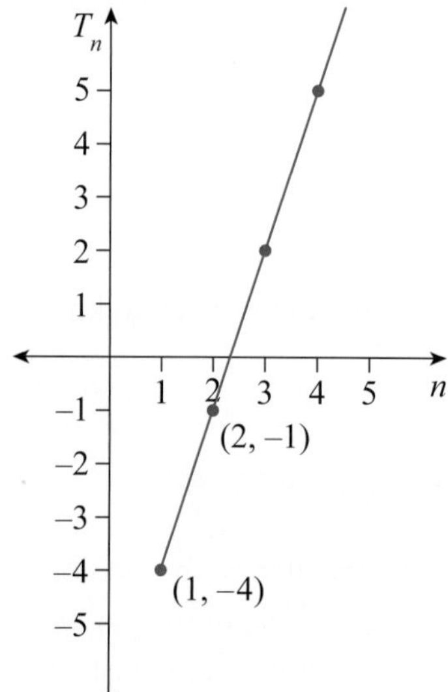

The general term $T_n = 3n - 7$ is the equation of the straight line.

(e) This graph is a straight line.

Choose two points on this line: (1, −4), (2, −1)

$\therefore$ Slope $m = \dfrac{-4 + 1}{1 - 2} = 3$

(f) Slope = 3 = d = common difference

Test for an arithmetic sequence

The crucial test for an arithmetic sequence is:

Any term − Previous one = Constant for all terms

or in symbols

$T_{n+1} - T_n = d(\text{constant})$ for all $n \in \mathbb{N}$

EXAMPLE 6

Show that the sequence with $T_n = \frac{3n}{2} + 5$ is an arithmetic sequence.
Find d, a and T_{34}.

Solution

$T_n = \frac{3}{2}n + 5$

$T_{n+1} = \frac{3}{2}(n+1) + 5 = \frac{3}{2}n + \frac{13}{2}$ **(1)**

$T_n = \frac{3}{2}n + 5$ **(2)**

(2) − (1): $T_{n+1} - T_n = \frac{3}{2}$ = constant for all n

Therefore, this sequence is an arithmetic sequence.

$d = \frac{3}{2}$ = common difference

$a = T_1 = \frac{3}{2} + 5 = \frac{13}{2}$

$T_{34} = \frac{3}{2}(34) + 5 = 56$ [Given the general term, you can find any specified term.]

EXAMPLE 7

Show that the sequence with the general term $n(2n+1)$ is not an arithmetic sequence.

Solution

$T_n = n(2n+1)$

$T_{n+1} = (n+1)(2(n+1)+1) = (n+1)(2n+3)$

$T_{n+1} = 2n^2 + 5n + 3$

$T_n = 2n^2 + n$

$T_{n+1} - T_n = 4n + 3 \neq$ constant

Therefore, this sequence is not an arithmetic sequence.

12.3 Consecutive terms of an arithmetic sequence

You are regularly asked to deal with **three consecutive** terms of an arithmetic sequence.

It is important to note the following:

1. If you are given the freedom to choose your own three consecutive terms of an arithmetic sequence, the best choice is $a - d, a, a + d$.

ACTIVITY 13

ACTION
Exploring consecutive terms in an arithmetic sequence

OBJECTIVE
To practise a number of problems involving three consecutive terms in an arithmetic sequence

2. If you are told that three numbers a, c, b are consecutively in an arithmetic sequence, then write:

$c - a = b - c$

$2c = a + b$

$c = \frac{a+b}{2}$ [The middle one is the mean of the other two.]

3. Given two numbers a, b, the **arithmetic mean** c of them is a number between a and b such that the three numbers a, c, b are consecutive terms of an arithmetic sequence. So, if c is the arithmetic mean of a and b, then a, c, b are consecutive terms of an arithmetic sequence.

$\therefore c = \frac{a+b}{2}$ [The **arithmetic mean** is just the average of a and b.]

- The arithmetic mean of 4 and 8 is $\frac{4+8}{2} = 6$.
- The arithmetic mean of −7 and 11 is $\frac{-7+11}{2} = 2$.

EXAMPLE 8

If three consecutive terms of an arithmetic sequence add to 9, find them if their product is −120.

Solution

Let the numbers be $a - d, a, a + d$.

Sum: $(a - d) + a + (a + d) = 9$

$3a = 9$

$a = 3$

Product: $(3 - d)(3)(3 + d) = -120$

$9 - d^2 = -40$

$d^2 = 49$

$d = \pm 7$

$\boldsymbol{d = +7}$ **gives:** −4, 3, 10

$\boldsymbol{d = -7}$ **gives:** 10, 3, −4

You get the same three numbers.

EXAMPLE 9

(a) If $2x - 3, x^2, x + 2$ are three consecutive terms of an arithmetic sequence, find x.

(b) If $\frac{1}{b+c}, \frac{1}{a+c}, \frac{1}{a+b}$ are consecutive terms of an arithmetic sequence, show that $b^2 - a^2 = c^2 - b^2$.

Solution

(a) Arithmetic sequence: $2x - 3, x^2, x + 2$

$x^2 = \frac{(2x-3)+(x+2)}{2}$

$2x^2 = 3x - 1$

$2x^2 - 3x + 1 = 0$

$(2x - 1)(x - 1)$

$x = \frac{1}{2}, 1$

(b) Three consecutive terms means:

$\frac{1}{(a+c)} - \frac{1}{(b+c)} = \frac{1}{(a+b)} - \frac{1}{(a+c)}$

$\frac{(b+c)-(a+c)}{(a+c)(b+c)} = \frac{(a+c)-(a+b)}{(a+b)(a+c)}$

$\frac{(b-a)}{(b+c)} = \frac{(c-b)}{(a+b)}$

$(b - a)(a + b) = (c - b)(b + c)$

$b^2 - a^2 = c^2 - b^2$

This result means that a^2, b^2, c^2 are also consecutive terms of an arithmetic sequence.

EXAMPLE 10

The arithmetic mean of two numbers is $23\frac{1}{2}$. Their product is 510. Find the numbers.

Solution

Let the numbers be a and b:

$$\frac{a+b}{2} = 23\frac{1}{2} \quad \textbf{(1)}$$

$$a + b = 47$$

$$ab = 510 \quad \textbf{(2)}$$

From **(1)**: $b = (47 - a)$

Substitute into **(2)**: $a(47 - a) = 510$

$47a - a^2 = 510$

$a^2 - 47a + 510 = 0$

$(a - 17)(a - 30) = 0$

$a = 17, b = 30$ or $a = 30, b = 17$

EXERCISE 4

1. **(a)** An arithmetic sequence has $a = 4$ and $d = 5$. Find T_1, T_2, T_3, T_5, T_{11} and T_{122}.

   (b) For the arithmetic sequence 4, 2, 0, … , find T_1, T_2, T_3, T_{55} and T_{105}.

   (c) For an arithmetic sequence, $a = 5$ and $d = \frac{1}{2}$. Find T_1, T_7, T_9, T_{50} and T_{73}.

   (d) Find the fifth, eighth and 22nd terms of the arithmetic sequence 3, 6, 9, 12, … .

   (e) A baker receives a delivery of 520 kg of flour. He uses no flour on the day it is delivered (day 1). He uses 20 kg every day after that. How much flour will he have left at the end of the 18th day?

   (f) Joe walks 2 km on the first day of his fitness programme and increases the distance by 550 m every day after that. How far does he walk on the 14th day?

   (g) At the start of 1 April, Mary has 192 sweets left over from Easter. She eats six sweets per day starting on 1 April until they are finished. How many sweets will she have at the start of 15 April?

   (h) A coin collection is valued at €24 000 in 2002. Its value increases by €3000 annually.

   (i) Write out, as a sequence, the value of the collection from 2002 to 2006 inclusive.

   (ii) Is the sequence arithmetic? Why?

   (iii) Find a and d.

   (iv) How much would the collection be worth in 2041?

2. **(a)** Find the 22nd term in the arithmetic sequence 2, 8, 14, … .

   (b) The second term of an arithmetic sequence is 4 and the sixth term is 16. Find the first four terms.

   (c) In an arithmetic sequence, the third term is 9 and the eighth term is 44. Find the first five terms.

   (d) The sixth term of an arithmetic sequence is 30 and the 11th term is 45. Find the first term and the common difference.

   (e) The eighth term of an arithmetic sequence is −22 and the 13th term is −42. Find the first four terms.

   (f) The third term of an arithmetic sequence is 92 and the ninth term is 68. Find the first term and the common difference.

   (g) In an arithmetic sequence, the sixth term is eight times the second term and the fourth term is 18. Find the arithmetic sequence.

   (h) In an arithmetic sequence, the 19th term is seven times the second term and the eighth term is 53. Find a and d.

(i) The difference between the 12th term of an arithmetic sequence and the seventh term of an arithmetic sequence is 30. The 13th term is seven times the second term. Find a and d.

(j) Peter climbs up the Eiffel Tower. He climbs a certain number of steps in the first minute and after that continues at a steady pace. If he climbs 54 steps in 2 minutes and 262 steps in total in 10 minutes, find the number of steps he climbs per minute after the first minute.

(k) On the first day of the month, a baker receives a delivery of flour and uses the same amount of flour every day after that. At the end of the fifth day of the month, the baker has 728 kg remaining and at the end of the 13th day she has 504 kg remaining. How much flour does she use per day? How much flour was delivered on the first day of the month?

(l) The seats in a cinema are arranged so that each row accommodates three more people than the previous row. If the first row has 24 seats, how many seats are there in the 11th row?

3. Find a, d and the general term (T_n) for the following arithmetic sequences and hence the specified term in the bracket:

(a) $2, 4, 6, \ldots\ (T_{20})$

(b) $-1, 2, 5, \ldots\ (T_{15})$

(c) $\frac{3}{2}, 2, \frac{5}{2}, \ldots\ (T_{11})$

(d) $-3, -5, -7, \ldots\ (T_{27})$

(e) $1, \frac{1}{2}, 0, \ldots\ (T_{30})$

(f) $p, p-1, p-2, \ldots\ (T_9)$

(g) $2b-3, 2b+1, 2b+5, \ldots\ (T_{14})$

(h) $\log_3 2, \log_3 2 + \log_3 4, \log_3 2 + 2\log_3 4, \ldots\ (T_9)$

(i) $\sqrt{3}, \sqrt{3}+\sqrt{2}, \sqrt{3}+2\sqrt{2}, \ldots\ (T_{20})$

(j) $\sin 15°, \sin 15° - x, \sin 15° - 2x, \ldots\ (T_{10})$

4. A walker walks 4 km per day. On 1 September, she increases the distance by 0·1 km and decides to increase it by 0·1 km every day from then on.

(a) What distance does she walk on 8 September?

(b) Write down the general term of the sequence of distances on consecutive days.

5. Calculate the first term a and the common difference d for the following arithmetic sequences given their general term T_n. Hence, write down the first five terms of each sequence.

(a) $T_n = 3n$

(b) $T_n = n + 1$

(c) $T_n = 2n - 1$

(d) $T_n = 5n + 2$

(e) $T_n = 8n - 13$

(f) $T_n = 6 - 3n$

(g) $T_n = \frac{1}{2}(5n - 1)$

(h) $T_n = \frac{1}{3} - \frac{5n}{3}$

6. **(a)** Which term is 342 in the arithmetic sequence 12, 67, 122, …?

(b) Which term is 249 in the arithmetic sequence 2, 15, 28, …?

(c) Which term is −112 in the arithmetic sequence 5, −8, −21, …?

(d) Find T_n for the arithmetic sequence 12, 8, 4, …. For what value of n is $T_n = -96$?

(e) Is 124 a term of the arithmetic sequence 5, 8, 11, …?

(f) Is 27 a term of the arithmetic sequence $2, 4\frac{1}{2}, 7, \ldots$?

(g) At the start of 9 June, Meg has 220 sweets in a box. She eats seven sweets per day starting on 9 June. On what date will she have 87 sweets left at the end of the day?

(h) How many terms are there in the following arithmetic sequence: $10, 6\frac{1}{2}, 3, \ldots, -21\frac{1}{2}$?

(i) A new car was valued at €27 000 on 1 January 2000. It depreciated by the same amount every year. On 1 January 2012 it had no value (€0). Show that the value of the car from 1 January 2000 to 1 January 2012 could be an arithmetic sequence. How many terms are in this arithmetic sequence? By how much did the car depreciate each year?

7. **(a)** The straight line shown is a graph of T_n against n, for an arithmetic sequence.

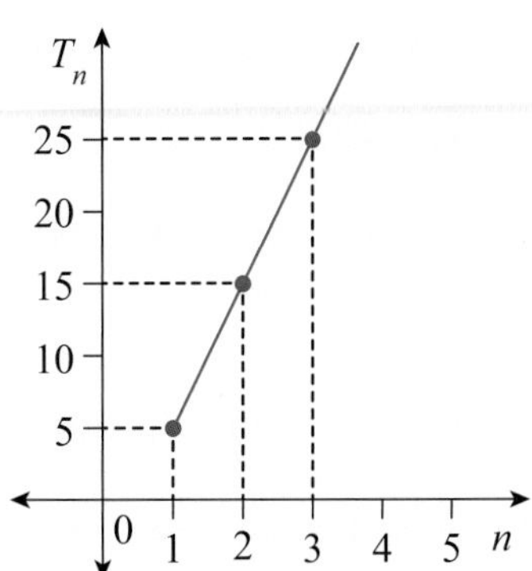

(i) What sort of sequence is described by this graph? Why?

(ii) Find the slope of this graph.

(iii) Find the first term T_1.

(iv) Find the equation of this graph.

(v) Find T_4 and T_5.

(b) The straight line shown is a graph of T_n against n, for an arithmetic sequence.

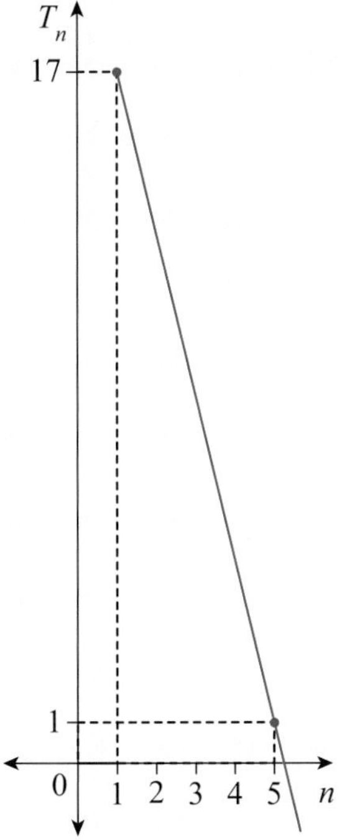

(i) Is the sequence increasing or decreasing? Why?

(ii) Find the slope of this graph.

(iii) Find T_1 and the common difference.

(iv) Find the equation of this graph.

(v) Find T_{33}.

8. Test the sequences with the given general term T_n to see if they are arithmetic sequences. In the case of those that are arithmetic sequences, find a and d.

(a) $T_n = 3n + 5$

(b) $T_n = \frac{3n}{4} - 8$

(c) $T_n = n^2 + 3n$

(d) $T_n = 3 \times 5^n$

(e) $T_n = \frac{n(n+1)}{2}$

9. **(a)** If $4, x, y, -32$ are consecutive terms of an arithmetic sequence, find x and y.

(b) If $5\frac{1}{4}, x, y, 12\frac{3}{4}$ are consecutive terms of an arithmetic sequence, find x and y.

(c) If $3k, 5k + 2, 8k - 1$ are the first three terms of an arithmetic sequence, find k and the 12th term.

(d) If $x, 5, y, 19$ are the first four terms of an arithmetic sequence, find x, y and T_{18}.

(e) If $2, x - y, 2x + y + 7, x - 3y$ are the first four terms of an arithmetic sequence, find x and y.

(f) The sum of three consecutive numbers in an arithmetic sequence is 3. If the sum of their squares is 35, find the numbers.

(g) If $2a + 1, 3a - 2, 5a + 7$ are three consecutive terms of an arithmetic sequence, find a and the three numbers.

(h) If $x + 1, x^2 - 2, 3x + 1$ are three consecutive terms of an arithmetic sequence, find x and the three numbers if $x > 0$.

(i) If $\frac{1}{3a+1}, \frac{1}{4a}, \frac{1}{3a}$ are three consecutive terms of an arithmetic sequence, find a.

10. **(a)** The sum of three consecutive terms of an arithmetic sequence is -6. Their product is 10. Find the three terms.

(b) The sum of three consecutive terms of an arithmetic sequence is 24. If the sum of their squares is 242, find the terms.

(c) The sum of three consecutive terms in an arithmetic sequence is 21. The product of the first and third numbers is 45. Find the three terms.

(d) The sum of three consecutive numbers in an arithmetic sequence is 6. Their product is −24. Find the numbers.

11. (a) Find the arithmetic mean of the following numbers:

(i) 4, 6

(ii) −7, 18

(iii) $2x - 1, 3x + 7$

(iv) $x - 1, x + 1$

(v) $\frac{1}{2}, \frac{2}{5}$

(vi) a^2, b^2

(b) (i) The arithmetic mean of two numbers is 5. Their product is 21. Find the two numbers.

(ii) The arithmetic mean of two numbers is 3. Their product is −7. Find the two numbers.

12.4 Arithmetic series

Carl Friedrich Gauss

An arithmetic series is obtained by adding up the individual terms of an arithmetic sequence.

The sum S_n of the first n terms of an arithmetic series

A famous mathematician named Gauss examined the problem of adding up the first 100 natural numbers.

$$1 + 2 + 3 + 4 + \ldots + 97 + 98 + 99 + 100$$

Gauss thought of an ingenious method.

He added the first and last numbers: $1 + 100 = 101$. He then added the second and second last numbers: $2 + 99 = 101$, and so on.

Gauss got 101 as an answer every time. Since there are 50 pairs of such numbers, he concluded that:

$$1 + 2 + 3 + \ldots + 99 + 100 = 101 \times 50 = 5050 = (1 + 100) \times \frac{100}{2}$$

He generalised this result to add up the first n natural numbers as:

$$1 + 2 + 3 + \ldots + n = (1 + n) \times \frac{n}{2} = \frac{n(n+1)}{2}$$ and concluded:

Sum of the first n natural numbers: $1 + 2 + 3 + \ldots + n = \frac{n(n+1)}{2}$

ACTIVITY 14

ACTION
Finding the sum of the first n natural numbers

OBJECTIVE
To verify Gauss' formula by adding up the first 10 natural numbers

▸ Evaluate $1 + 2 + 3 + \ldots + 213 + 214$.

$$1 + 2 + 3 + \ldots + 213 + 214 = \frac{214(215)}{2} = 23\,005$$

You can apply this idea to add up the first n terms of any arithmetic series:

WORKED EXAMPLE

Finding the sum of n terms of an arithmetic series

First term = a

Common difference = d

Add n terms of this arithmetic series. Call S_n the sum of the first n terms of this sequence.

$S_n = a + (a + d) + (a + 2d) + \ldots + [a + (n - 1)d]$ [There are a total of n terms.]

$S_n = \{a + a + a + \ldots + a\} + d\{1 + 2 + 3 + \ldots + (n - 1)\}$

$\therefore S_n = na + d \times \dfrac{(n-1)n}{2}$ [using Gauss' formula]

$S_n = \dfrac{2na + d(n-1)n}{2} = \dfrac{n}{2}[2a + (n-1)d]$

The sum S_n of the first n terms of any arithmetic series with first term a and common difference d is given by:

$$S_n = \frac{n}{2}[2a + (n-1)d]$$

It is important to remember the following about this formula:

1. S_n = the sum of the first n terms of an arithmetic series.

   $S_1 = T_1 = a$

   $S_2 = T_1 + T_2$

   $S_n = T_1 + T_2 + \ldots + T_n$
2. n = the number of terms to be added.
3. $a = T_1$ = first term.
4. d = common difference = any term − previous one.

Mathematical patterns are found in nature with the Fibonacci sequence and Golden ratio making numerous appearances. The designs in these flowers are produced from such patterns.

EXAMPLE 11

For the arithmetic series $-3 + 10 + 23 + 36 + \ldots$, find:

(a) S_1,

(b) the common difference d,

(c) the 38th term,

(d) the sum of the first 38 terms,

(e) the general term T_n,

(f) the general summing formula S_n.

Solution

(a) $S_1 = T_1 = -3 = a$

(b) $d = T_2 - T_1 = 10 - (-3) = 13$

(c) $T_{38} = a + 37d = -3 + 37(13) = 478$

(d) $S_{38} = \frac{38}{2}[2(-3) + (38 - 1)(13)]$

$= 19[-6 + (37)(13)] = 9025$

(e) $T_n = a + (n - 1)d$

$= -3 + (n - 1)13 = 13n - 16$

(f) $S_n = \frac{n}{2}[2a + (n - 1)d]$

$= \frac{n}{2}[2(-3) + (n - 1)13]$

$= \frac{n}{2}[13n - 19] = \frac{13}{2}n^2 - \frac{19}{2}n$

TIP
For an arithmetic series, S_n is always a quadratic expression.

Given S_n, you can work backwards to get n.

EXAMPLE 12

Mr O'Brien repays a loan over n months. His monthly repayments form an arithmetic sequence.

He repays €139 in the first month, €135 in the second month, €131 in the third month, and so on.

(a) Find the amount Mr O'Brien pays in the 15th month.

(b) Over n months he repays a total of €2020. Form an equation in n and show it may be written as $2n^2 - 141n + 2020 = 0$. Solve for n and find how many months it takes Mr O'Brien to repay this loan.

Solution

Arithmetic sequence: 139, 135, 131, …

$a = 139,\ d = -4$

(a) $T_{15} = a + 14d = 139 + 14(-4) = 139 - 56 = 83$

Mr O'Brien pays €83 in the 15th month.

(b) $S_n = \frac{n}{2}[2 \times (139) + (n-1)(-4)] = 2020$

$$\frac{n}{2}[278 - 4n + 4] = 2020$$

$$2n^2 - 141n + 2020 = 0$$

$$(2n - 101)(n - 20) = 0$$

$$\therefore n = 20$$

It takes Mr O'Brien 20 months to pay back €2020.

EXAMPLE 13

Find the sum of all natural numbers that are divisible by 3 from 78 to 453 inclusive.

Solution

These numbers form the arithmetic series: $78 + 81 + 84 + \ldots + 453$.

$a = 78,\ d = 3$

How many numbers are there in this list (what is n)? To find n, let $T_n = 453 =$ last term.

$$78 + (n-1)3 = 453$$

$$(n-1)3 = 375$$

$$n - 1 = 125$$

$$n = 126 \quad \text{[There are 126 terms.]}$$

$$S_{126} = \frac{126}{2}[2 \times 78 + 125 \times 3]$$

$$= 63[531]$$

$$= 33\,453$$

EXAMPLE 14

Find the least number of terms of the arithmetic series $3 + 7 + 11 + \ldots$ that must be added to give a sum greater than 405.

Solution

Arithmetic series: $3 + 7 + 11 + \ldots$

$a = 3,\ d = 4$

Solve $S_n > 405$ [The number of terms that must be added to give a sum greater than 405.]

Solve the equality $S_n = 405$ first.

$$S_n = \frac{n}{2}[2(3) + (n-1)4] = 405$$

$$3n + 2n^2 - 2n = 405$$

$$2n^2 + n - 405 = 0$$

$$n = \frac{-1 \pm \sqrt{1 + 3240}}{4} = \frac{-1 \pm \sqrt{3241}}{4} = 13{\cdot}98$$

Therefore, 14 terms will give a sum greater than 405.

EXERCISE 5

1. Find the given sums for each of the following arithmetic series:
   (a) $3 + 5 + 7 + 9 + \dots$ S_n and S_{12}
   (b) $7 + 5 + 3 + 1, \dots$ S_n and S_{15}
   (c) $3 + 2\frac{1}{2} + 2 + \dots$ S_n and S_{20}
   (d) $0 + -\frac{3}{4} + -\frac{3}{2} + \dots$ S_n and S_{26}
   (e) $-8 - 5 - 2 + 1 + \dots$ S_n and S_{54}
   (f) $\frac{2}{\sqrt{2}} + 2\sqrt{2} + 3\sqrt{2} + \dots$ S_n and S_{10}
   (g) $\frac{1}{4} + \frac{7}{12} + \frac{11}{12} + \dots$ S_n and S_{40}

2. (a) Michael saves €80 in the first week and increases this by €10 per week every week for the next 14 weeks. How much will Michael have saved after 15 weeks?
   (b) Fiona's starting salary is €32 000. It increases incrementally every year by €800. What are her gross earnings if she retires after 40 years? What is Fiona's final salary?
   (c) Mr Phillips buys a new car every two years. The first car he bought in 1990 cost €22 000. If the price of each new car is €3500 more than the previous one, how much did Mr Phillips spend on cars between 1990 and 2008 inclusive?
   (d) Gemma got a new mobile phone on 1 September. She sent five texts on the day she got the phone. Every day after that, she sent two more texts per day than the previous day. How many texts did Gemma send on 30 September? How many texts in all did she send during September?
   (e) In an arena there are 120 seats in the front row, 115 in the second row, 110 in the third row, and so on. This pattern continues until the last row which has 55 seats. How many rows are there and what is the total number of seats in the arena?
   (f) A dressmaker uses 60 buttons on her first day of business. As business gets better, the number of buttons she uses increases by 12 each day after that. If the dressmaker works 22 days in the month, how many buttons will she have used in the month?

3. (a) How many terms of the arithmetic sequence 3, 7, 11, … must be added to give a total of 990?
   (b) How many terms of the arithmetic series $4 + 7 + 10 + \dots$ must be added to give a total of 714?
   (c) Find the least number of terms of the arithmetic sequence 17, 14, 11, … that must be added to give a negative sum.
   (d) The sum of the first n terms of an arithmetic series is -185. Find n, if the first term is -50 and the common difference is 7.
   (e) A water tank contains 352 litres of water. On a particular day it develops a leak and leaks 7 litres on that day. As the leak gets worse, the tank leaks 5 litres more each day than the previous day. Find how many days it will take for the tank to empty.

4. (a) Find the sum of all even numbers less than 247.
   (b) Find the sum of all even numbers from 76 to 248 inclusive.
   (c) Find the sum of all odd numbers from 77 to 235 inclusive.
   (d) Find the sum of all natural numbers from 21 to 371 inclusive that are divisible by 7.

5. (a) The first term of an arithmetic series is 5. The sum of the first 20 terms is 240. Find the common difference.
   (b) The ninth term of an arithmetic series is -2 and the sum of the first nine terms is -90. Find the first term and the common difference. Write out the first three terms of the arithmetic sequence.
   (c) Find the first term and the common difference for an arithmetic series with $S_{15} = 585$ and $S_7 = 105$.

(d) Find the first term and the common difference and write out the first three terms for an arithmetic series with $T_{12} = 10$ and $S_{20} = -100$.

(e) The fifth term of an arithmetic series is $\frac{23}{2}$ and the sum of the first five terms is $\frac{65}{2}$. Find the first term and the common difference.

(f) The sum of the first 10 terms of an arithmetic series is -140 and the sum of the first 21 terms is -2604. Find the first term and the common difference.

(g) A man has initial savings on 1 January of a particular year. He increases his savings by the same amount on 1 January each year. After the 30th year, his total savings amounted to €62 100. In the sixth year he saved €1500. Find the man's initial savings and the amount he increased his savings by each year.

6. **(a)** The general term for a sequence is $3n + 7$. Show that it is an arithmetic series. Find a, d and S_n.

(b) The sum of the first 21 terms of an arithmetic series is zero. Find the sum of the second 21 terms, in terms of the first term a.

(c) If S is the sum of the first n terms of an arithmetic series with first term a and common difference d, show that $n^2d - n(d - 2a) - 2S = 0$.

(d) Prove for an arithmetic series $S_{2n-1} = (2n - 1)T_n$ and find S_{25} if $T_{13} = 5$.

(e) The sum of the first n terms of an arithmetic series is given by $S_n = n^2 - 16n$, find:

(i) S_1, T_1, S_2 and T_2

(ii) a and d

(iii) T_n

(iv) n if $S_n = -63$

(f) Prove Gauss' formula for the sum of the first n natural numbers: $1 + 2 + 3 + \ldots + n = \frac{n}{2}(n + 1)$ using S_n for an arithmetic series.

(g) If $S_n = 0$ for an arithmetic series, show that $n = 1 - \frac{2a}{d}$. For $a = 50$ and $d = -5$, find n.

12.5 Arithmetic series using the $\sum$ notation

Remember that the $\sum$ notation is just a shorthand way of writing a series.

You can find the sum of an arithmetic series that is given in the $\sum$ notation in two ways:

1. By using the formula: $S_n = \frac{n}{2}[2a + (n - 1)d]$

or

2. By using the $\sum$ rules and Gauss' formula: $\sum_{n=1}^{n} n = 1 + 2 + \ldots + n = \frac{n}{2}(n + 1)$.

EXAMPLE 15

Evaluate the given sum of the arithmetic series $\sum_{n=1}^{35}(2n - 3)$.

Solution

Method 1

$$\sum_{n=1}^{35}(2n - 3) = S_{35}$$

$$T_n = 2n - 3$$

$$T_1 = 2 - 3 = -1 = a$$

$$T_2 = 4 - 3 = 1$$

$$d = T_2 - T_1 = 2$$

$$S_{35} = \frac{35}{2}[2 \times (-1) + 34 \times 2]$$

$$= 1155$$

Method 2

$\sum_{n=1}^{35}(2n-3) = S_{35}$ [Do S_n first using the $\sum$ rules.]

$S_n = \sum_{n=1}^{n}(2n-3) = \sum_{n=1}^{n} 2n - \sum_{n=1}^{n} 3 = 2\sum_{n=1}^{n} n - 3\sum_{n=1}^{n} 1$

$= \frac{2n}{2}(n+1) - 3n$

$= n(n+1) - 3n$

$= n^2 - 2n$

$= n(n-2)$

$S_{35} = 35(33) = 1155$

EXAMPLE 16

If $\sum_{n=1}^{n}(3n-7) = 605$ for an arithmetic series, find n.

Solution

$\sum_{n=1}^{n}(3n-7) = 605$

$3\sum_{n=1}^{n} n - 7\sum_{n=1}^{n} 1 = 605$

$\frac{3n}{2}(n+1) - 7n = 605$

$3n^2 + 3n - 14n = 1210$

$3n^2 - 11n - 1210 = 0$

$(3n+55)(n-22) = 0$

$n = 22$

EXERCISE 6

1. Given the sums of the following arithmetic series:
   - **(i)** find T_n
   - **(ii)** find T_1 and T_2
   - **(iii)** find a and d
   - **(iv)** state how many terms are in each series and evaluate all finite sums

   (a) $S_{12} = \sum_{n=1}^{12}(n+1)$

   (b) $S_\infty = \sum_{n=1}^{\infty}(3-n)$

   (c) $S_n = \sum_{n=1}^{n}(2+3n)$

   (d) $S_n = \sum_{n=1}^{25}(5-n)$

   (e) $S_n = \sum_{n=1}^{n}\left(3 - \frac{n}{2}\right)$

2. Evaluate the given sums for the following arithmetic series:

   (a) $\sum_{n=1}^{30}(4-n)$

   (b) $\sum_{n=1}^{n}(2+5n)$

   (c) $\sum_{n=1}^{58}\left(\frac{5n}{2} - \frac{1}{2}\right)$

   (d) $\sum_{n=1}^{15}\frac{3n+1}{2}$

   (e) $\sum_{n=1}^{36}\frac{4n-7}{3}$

3. Find n for the following arithmetic series:

   (a) $\sum_{n=1}^{n}(n+3) = 114$

   (b) $\sum_{n=1}^{n}(3-2n) = -99$

   (c) $\sum_{n=1}^{n}\left(\frac{n}{2} - 4\right) = 124$

   (d) $\sum_{n=1}^{n}\left(\frac{3n}{4} - 1\right) = 184$

Geometric Sequences and Series

Learning Outcomes

- To solve problems involving geometric sequences and series.
- To model word problems that are geometric in nature.

13.1 Defining a geometric sequence

ACTIVITY 15

ACTION
Understanding a geometric sequence

OBJECTIVE
To gain an understanding of a geometric sequence

WORKED EXAMPLE Geometric sequence 1

Joe saves €2·50 in the first month of his new job and doubles the amount he saves the next month. He continues this pattern of saving twice the amount he saved the previous month.

Month 1	Month 2	Month 3	Month 4	Month 5	Month 6	Month 7	Month 8
2·5	5	10	20	40	80	160	320

The sequence shown in the table is 2·5, 5, 10, 20, 40, 80, 160, 320.

The first term T_1 of the sequence is 2·5. Each term is then multiplied by a **constant** of 2 to get the next term. This means that any term divided by the previous term is constant and equal to 2.

WORKED EXAMPLE Geometric sequence 2

A rubber ball is dropped from a height of 40 m. It rebounds to $\frac{3}{5}$ of the height it has fallen from after each bounce.

After the first bounce, the ball ascends to a height of $40 \times \frac{3}{5} = 24$ m.

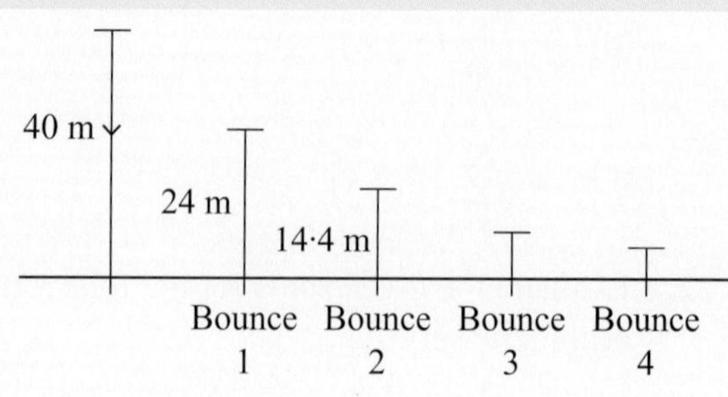

The maximum height of the ball above the ground on the first bounce is 24 m.

The maximum height of each subsequent bounce is $\frac{3}{5}$ of the height of the previous bounce.

The sequence of maximum heights is: 24 m, 14·4 m, 8·64 m, 5·184 m, 3·1104 m.

This again means that any term divided by the previous term is a constant equal to 0·6.

$$\frac{T_2}{T_1} = \frac{14{\cdot}4}{24} = \frac{T_3}{T_2} = \frac{8{\cdot}64}{14{\cdot}4} = \frac{T_4}{T_3} = \frac{5{\cdot}184}{8{\cdot}64} = \frac{3}{5}$$

ACTIVITY 16

ACTION
Working with geometric sequences (1)

OBJECTIVE
To write down the first term and common difference of a number of geometric sequences

ACTIVITY 17

ACTION
Working with geometric sequences (2)

OBJECTIVE
To explore various geometric sequences and to gain an understanding of how these sequences operate

KEY TERM

A **geometric sequence** is a list of terms that starts with any object (number, symbol, function) and keeps on multiplying each term by the same constant to get the next term.

- Start with 2 and keep on multiplying by 3:

2, 6, 18, 54, 162, ...

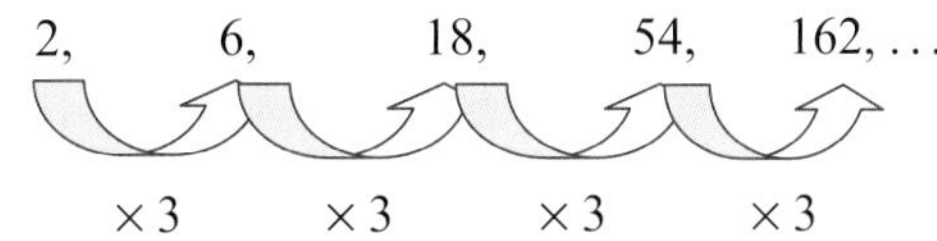

- Start with −3 and keep on multiplying by $\frac{1}{2}$:
  Geometric sequence: $-3, -\frac{3}{2}, -\frac{3}{4}, -\frac{3}{8}, \dots$
- Start with y^2 and keep on multiplying by $\log_2 x$:
  Geometric sequence: $y^2, y^2 \log_2 x, y^2 (\log_2 x)^2, y^2 (\log_2 x)^3, \dots$

It is important to note the following:

1. Every geometric sequence has a starting term T_1 (the first term).
2. Any term divided by the previous term is the same constant called r (common ratio).
3. If you know the first term and the constant r, you can generate the whole sequence.
   - If the first term of a geometric sequence is $\frac{1}{2}$ and the constant that multiplies each term is 6, the first five terms of the sequence are $\frac{1}{2}$, 3, 18, 108, 648 ....
   - In the geometric sequence 81, 54, 36, ... ,
     $T_1 = 81,\ r = \frac{T_2}{T_1} = \frac{54}{81} = \frac{2}{3}$.

13.2 The general term T_n of a geometric sequence

If you start with the first term $T_1 = a$ and keep on multiplying by the constant r, you generate the general geometric sequence:

$$\begin{matrix} a, & ar, & ar^2, & ar^3, \dots \\ \uparrow & \uparrow & \uparrow & \uparrow \\ T_1, & T_2, & T_3, & T_4, \dots \end{matrix}$$

$T_5 = a(r)^4$ [It is a good idea to put brackets around r.]

$T_{59} = a(r)^{58} = ar^{58}$

TIP

If you are told the 59th term of a geometric sequence is 97, you can write $ar^{58} = 97$.

The general term of any geometric sequence with first term a and common ratio r is given by:

$$T_n = a(r)^{n-1}$$

- For a geometric sequence: 4, 6, 9, …

  $a = 4$

  $r = \dfrac{\text{any term}}{\text{previous one}} = \dfrac{6}{4} = \dfrac{3}{2}$

  $T_{20} = a(r)^{19} = 4\left(\dfrac{3}{2}\right)^{19}$

As already stated, for all geometric sequences:

1. $T_1 = a$ = first term.
2. r = common ratio $= \dfrac{\text{any term}}{\text{previous one}}$.
3. If you know a and r, you can find every other term in the sequence.

EXAMPLE 1

A rocket travels 500 m in the first second of its motion. The distance it covers increases in each subsequent second by 4% over the distance covered in the previous second. Find the distances travelled in each of the first 4 seconds and the distance travelled in the 12th second, correct to three decimal places.

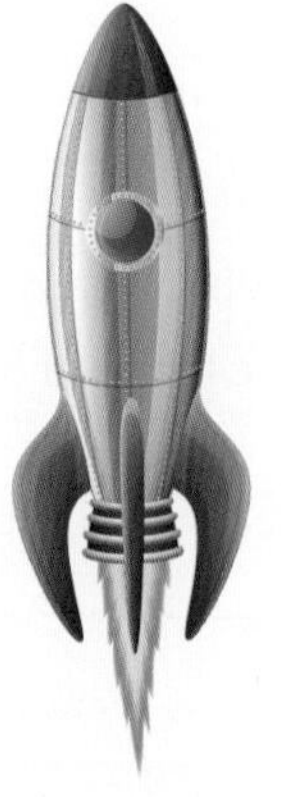

Solution

The rocket travels 500 × 1·04 = 520 m.

1st second	2nd second	3rd second	4th second
500 m	520 m	540·8 m	562·432 m

$a = 500$, $r = 1{\cdot}04$

$T_{12} = ar^{11} = 500(1{\cdot}04)^{11} = 769{\cdot}727$ m

EXAMPLE 2

If $-2, x, y, \frac{27}{4}$, are consecutive terms of a geometric sequence, find x and y and the general term of the sequence.

Solution

Geometric sequence: $-2, x, y, \frac{27}{4}$

Write down the terms you know:

$T_1 = a = -2$ **(1)**

$T_4 = ar^3 = \frac{27}{4}$ **(2)**

$\dfrac{ar^3}{a} = \dfrac{27}{4} \times -\dfrac{1}{2}$ [Divide equation **(2)** by equation **(1)**.]

$r^3 = -\frac{27}{8}$

$r = -\frac{3}{2}$

The geometric sequence is $-2, 3, -\frac{9}{2}, \frac{27}{4}$

$\therefore x = 3, y = -\frac{9}{2}$

$T_n = a(r)^{n-1} = (-2)\left(-\frac{3}{2}\right)^{n-1}$

EXAMPLE 3

A seaplane makes a landing on water. During any second, the distance it travels decreases by the same percentage of the distance travelled during the previous second.

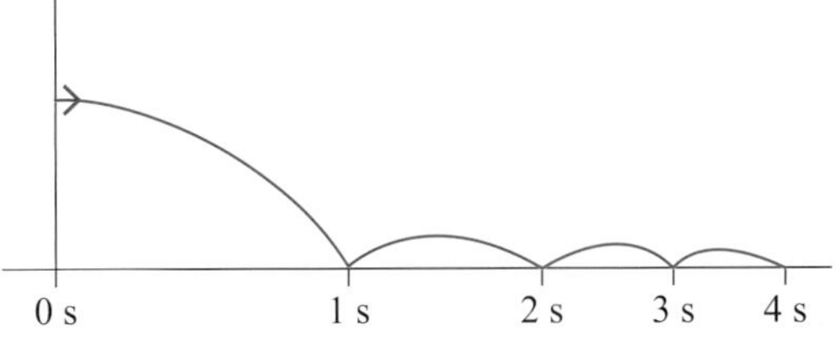

In the 2nd second the plane travelled 320 m and in the fifth second it travelled 163·84 m.

(a) Find the percentage decrease in distance from 1 second to the next,

(b) Find the distance travelled in the first second.

(c) Find the distance travelled in the 20th second, correct to two decimal places.

(d) Write out the distances travelled by the seaplane in the first 5 seconds.

Solution

$T_2 = 320 = ar$ **(1)**

$T_5 = 163 \cdot 84 = ar^4$ **(2)**

(a) $r^3 = \dfrac{64}{125}$ [Divide equation (**2**) by equation (**1**).]

$r = \dfrac{4}{5} = 0 \cdot 8 = 80\%$

(b) $ar = 320$

$a = \dfrac{320}{0 \cdot 8} = 400$

The plane travels 400 m in the first second.

(c) $T_{20} = a(r)^{19} = 400 \times (0 \cdot 8)^{19} = 5 \cdot 76$ m

(d) Distances travelled:

400 m, 320 m, 256 m, 204·8 m, 163·84 m

If you know the value of the nth term of a geometric sequence, you can find its position in the sequence (the number of the term).

EXAMPLE 4

For the geometric sequence 5, 10, 20, …

(a) find T_n,

(b) which term has a value of 163 840?

(c) is 7200 a term in this sequence?

Solution

Geometric sequence: 5, 10, 20, …

Write down what you know: $a = 5$, $r = 2$

(a) $T_n = ar^{n-1} = 5 \times 2^{n-1}$

(b) If you know T_n you can find the position of any term in the sequence.

$5 \times 2^{n-1} = 163\,840$

$2^{n-1} = 32\,768$ [Take the log to base 10 of both sides.]

$\log_{10} 2^{n-1} = \log_{10} 32\,768$

$(n-1)\log_{10} 2 = \log_{10} 32\,768$

$n - 1 = \dfrac{\log_{10} 32\,768}{\log_{10} 2}$

$n - 1 = 15$

$n = 16$

The 16th term in the sequence has a value of 163 840.

(c) If 7200 is a term in the sequence, you should be able to find its position n in the list.

$T_n = 5 \times 2^{n-1} = 7200$

$2^{n-1} = 1440$

$n - 1 = \dfrac{\log_{10} 1440}{\log_{10} 2} = 10 \cdot 5$

$n = 11 \cdot 5$

Therefore, 7200 is not in the sequence. Remember, in all sequences $n \in \mathbb{N}$.

EXAMPLE 5

How many terms are there in the finite geometric sequence: 81, 108, 144, … $\frac{65\,536}{81}$?

Solution

Geometric sequence: 81, 108, 144, … $\frac{65\,536}{81}$.

$T_1 = a = 81,\ r = \frac{108}{81} = \frac{4}{3}$

$T_n = a(r)^{n-1} = 81\left(\frac{4}{3}\right)^{n-1}$

Call the last term T_n.

$$T_n = 81\left(\frac{4}{3}\right)^{n-1} = \frac{65\,536}{81}$$

$$\left(\frac{4}{3}\right)^{n-1} = \frac{65\,536}{6561}$$

$$\log_{10}\left(\frac{4}{3}\right)^{n-1} = \log_{10}\left(\frac{65\,536}{6561}\right)$$

$$(n-1)\log_{10}\left(\frac{4}{3}\right) = \log_{10}\left(\frac{65\,536}{6561}\right)$$

$$n - 1 = \frac{\log_{10}\left(\frac{65\,536}{6561}\right)}{\log_{10}\left(\frac{4}{3}\right)}$$

$$n - 1 = 8$$

$$n = 9$$

Therefore, 256 is the value of the ninth term. There are nine terms in the sequence.

Test for a geometric sequence

The crucial test for a geometric sequence is that:

$$\frac{\text{Any term}}{\text{Previous term}} = \text{Constant for all terms}$$

or in symbols

$$\frac{T_{n+1}}{T_n} = r\text{, constant for all } n \in \mathbb{N}$$

EXAMPLE 6

Show that the sequence with the general term $T_n = \frac{5}{2^{n+1}}$ is a geometric sequence. Find a, r and T_{12}.

Solution

$T_n = \frac{5}{2^{n+1}}$

$T_{n+1} = \frac{5}{2^{n+2}}$

$\frac{T_{n+1}}{T_n} = \frac{5}{2^{n+2}} \times \frac{2^{n+1}}{5} = \frac{1}{2}$ = constant for all $n \in \mathbb{N}$.

Therefore, this sequence is a geometric sequence.

$a = T_1 = \frac{5}{2^2} = \frac{5}{4}$

$r = \frac{T_{n+1}}{T_n} = \frac{1}{2}$

$T_{12} = a(r)^{11} = \frac{5}{4}\left(\frac{1}{2}\right)^{11} = \frac{5}{2^{13}}$

13.3 Consecutive terms of a geometric sequence

You are regularly asked to deal with **three consecutive** terms of a geometric sequence.

It is important to note the following:

1. If you are given the freedom to choose your own three consecutive terms of a geometric sequence, the best choice for these is $\frac{a}{r}$, a, ar.

2. If you are told that three numbers a, c, b are consecutively in a geometric sequence, then write:

$$\frac{c}{a} = \frac{b}{c}$$

$$c^2 = ab$$

$c = \sqrt{ab}$ [The middle term is the square root of the product of the other two.]

3. Given two numbers a, b, the **geometric mean** c of them is a number between a and b such that the three numbers a, c, b are consecutive terms of a geometric sequence. So, if c is the geometric mean of a and b, then a, c, b are consecutive terms of a geometric sequence.

$\therefore c = \sqrt{ab}$ [The **geometric mean** of two numbers is the square root of their product.]

- The geometric mean of the numbers 6 and 12 is $\sqrt{6 \times 12} = \sqrt{72} = 6\sqrt{2}$.

ACTIVITY 18

ACTION
Exploring consecutive terms in a geometric sequence

OBJECTIVE
To practise a number of problems involving three consecutive terms in a geometric sequence

EXAMPLE 7

The lengths of the sides of a triangle are three consecutive terms of a geometric sequence. The shortest side is 3 cm long. If the perimeter is 21 cm, find the lengths of the other two sides.

Solution

Let the lengths of the sides be $\frac{a}{r}$, a, ar.

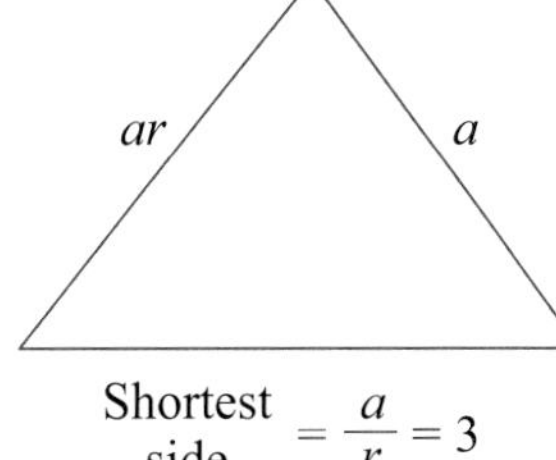

Shortest side $= \frac{a}{r} = 3$

Shortest side: $\frac{a}{r} = 3$

$$a = 3r$$

$$ar = 3r^2$$

$$\text{Perimeter} = 3 + 3r + 3r^2 = 21$$

$$r^2 + r + 1 = 7$$

$$r^2 + r - 6 = 0$$

$$(r - 2)(r + 3) = 0$$

$$r = 2$$

The length of the other two sides are 6 cm and 12 cm.

EXAMPLE 8

If $x + 1$, $2x$, $2x + 3$, … are three consecutive terms of a geometric sequence, find x and the three terms.

Solution

Geometric sequence: $x + 1$, $2x$, $2x + 3$, …

Consecutive terms of a geometric sequence:

$$\frac{2x}{x+1} = \frac{2x+3}{2x}$$

$$4x^2 = 2x^2 + 5x + 3$$

$$2x^2 - 5x - 3 = 0$$

$$(2x + 1)(x - 3) = 0$$

$$x = -\frac{1}{2}, 3$$

$\boldsymbol{x = -\frac{1}{2}}$**:** $\frac{1}{2}$, -1, 2

$\boldsymbol{x = 3}$**:** 4, 6, 9

EXAMPLE 9

The arithmetic mean of two numbers x and y is 6·5. Their geometric mean is 6. Find x and y.

Solution

Numbers: x, y

Arithmetic mean: $\frac{x+y}{2} = 6\cdot5$

$x + y = 13$ **(1)**

Geometric mean: $\sqrt{xy} = 6$

$xy = 36$ **(2)**

(1): $y = (13 - x)$

Substituting into equation **(2):** $x(13 - x) = 36$

$x^2 - 13x + 36 = 0$

$(x - 4)(x - 9) = 0$

$x = 4, 9$

$y = 9, 4$

The two numbers are 4 and 9.

EXERCISE 7

1. (a) Find a and r and the general term T_n for the following geometric sequences:

(i) 16, 8, 4, …

(ii) 8, 12, 18, 27, …

(iii) 48, 36, 27, …

(iv) 2, −6, 18, −54, …

(v) $1, \frac{1}{3}, \frac{1}{9}, \frac{1}{27}, \dots$

(vi) $xy, x^2y, x^3y, \dots$

(b) The first term of a geometric sequence is 6 and the common ratio is 3. Find the general term T_n.

(c) Find the first term, common ratio, 10th term and the general term of the geometric sequence: 1, −7, 49, … .

(d) Find the general term and hence the specified term in brackets, of the following geometric sequences:

(i) $1, 2, 4, \dots (T_6)$

(ii) $\frac{3}{4}, \frac{3}{2}, 3, \dots (T_{18})$

(iii) $1, 5, 25, \dots (T_{31})$

(iv) $7, \sqrt{42}, 6, \dots (T_{21})$

(v) $2\tan x, 6\tan^2 x, 18\tan^3 x, \dots (T_{15})$

(vi) $2\log_2 3, 4(\log_2 3)^2, 8(\log_2 3)^3, \dots (T_{17})$

(vii) $b^5, b^5c, b^4c^2, \dots (T_{51})$

(viii) $\left(\frac{c}{2}\right), \frac{cb}{6}, \frac{cb^2}{18}, \dots (T_{12})$

2. Find the first term and common ratio of the following geometric sequences and write down the first five terms.

(a) $T_n = 2^n$

(b) $T_n = 3 \times 2^{n-2}$

(c) $T_n = x^n y^{n-1}$

(d) $T_n = \left(\frac{a}{b}\right)^{n+1}$

(e) $T_n = 5^n$

(f) $T_n = \frac{4^{n-2}}{8}$

(g) $T_n = 2\sin^n x$

(h) $T_n = 3(\sqrt{3})^{n+2}$

3. The curve below is a graph of T_n against n for a geometric sequence.

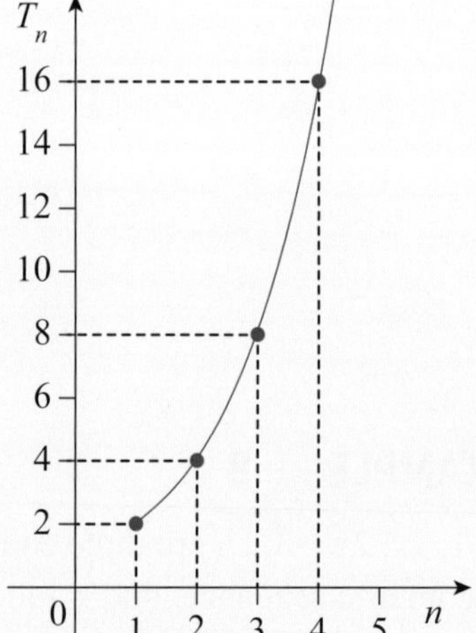

Find:

(a) T_1

(b) T_2

(c) a, r

(d) the general term T_n

(e) T_{20}

4. (a) Which term has a value of $\frac{1}{2^{23}}$ in the geometric sequence 8, 4, 2, …?

(b) Which term has a value of 2187 in the geometric sequence 1, 3, 9, …?

(c) Which term has a value of $\frac{64}{243}$ in the geometric sequence $2, \frac{4}{3}, \frac{8}{9}, \ldots$?

(d) Is -2^{12} a term in the geometric sequence −4, 8, −16, …?

(e) Is $\frac{3^4}{2^8}$ a term in the geometric sequence $\frac{2}{3}, \frac{1}{2}, \frac{3}{8}, \ldots$?

(f) An insect population halves its size from 5 000 000 every day according to the data in the table below:

End of day	1	2	…	?
Population	5 000 000	2 500 000		78 125

At the end of what day is the insect population 78 125?

(g) A business hopes to grow by 50% every year. If its value in 2013 is €5120, in what year will its value be €196 830?

5. How many terms are there in the following geometric sequences?

(a) 3, 9, 27, … , 729

(b) $8, 4, 2, \ldots, \frac{1}{128}$

(c) $\frac{3}{2}, -3, 6, \ldots, -192$

(d) $144, 72, 36, \ldots, 2\frac{1}{4}$

(e) $1, x, x^2, \ldots, x^p$

(f) $b^2, b^4, \ldots, b^{2p+2}$

(g) 81, 108, … , 256

(h) −3, 6, −12, … , 384

6. Test the following sequences to see if they are geometric sequences. In the case of a geometric sequence, find a and r.

(a) $T_n = n - 1$

(b) $T_n = \left(\frac{3}{2}\right)^{n-1}$

(c) $T_n = 2\left(\frac{1}{2}\right)^{n+1}$

(d) $T_n = \frac{7^n}{7^{2n-1}}$

(e) $T_n = \frac{1}{2}(3)^{n-2}$

(f) $T_n = \frac{(-5)^{n+1}}{3}$

7. A ball is dropped from 16 m. It bounces to 50% of its previous height on each bounce as it rebounds. List as a sequence the heights the ball bounces on the first, second, third, fourth and fifth bounces.

Copy the grid shown and draw a graph of these heights versus the number of the bounce.

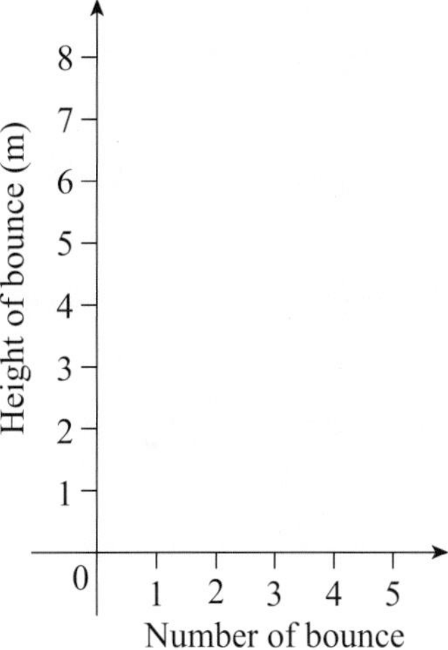

8. (a) Show that when you increase €1000 by 3% it is the same as multiplying €1000 by 1·03.

(b) €1000 is invested at 3% p.a. compound interest on 1 January 2014. The interest is added on 31 December every year.

Write down the value of the investment at the end of the following years by copying and filling in the table below:

Year 1	Year 2	Year 3	Year 4

(c) Find a and r for the geometric sequence.

(d) What is the value of the investment at the end of Year 10, correct to the nearest euro?

9. When a coin is tossed once, there are two possible outcomes, as shown in the diagram.

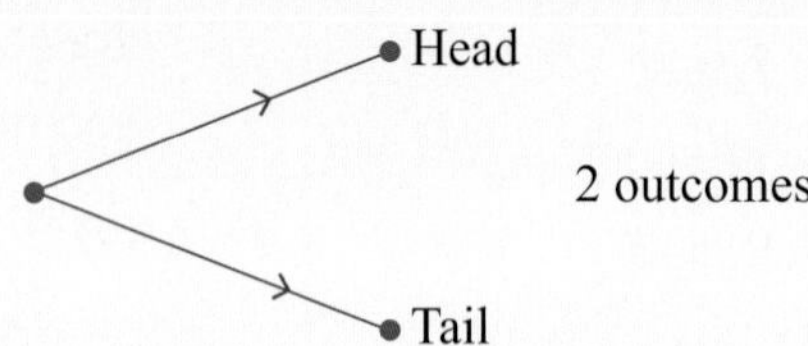

(a) Copy and complete the tree diagram below to find the number of outcomes when a coin is tossed twice.

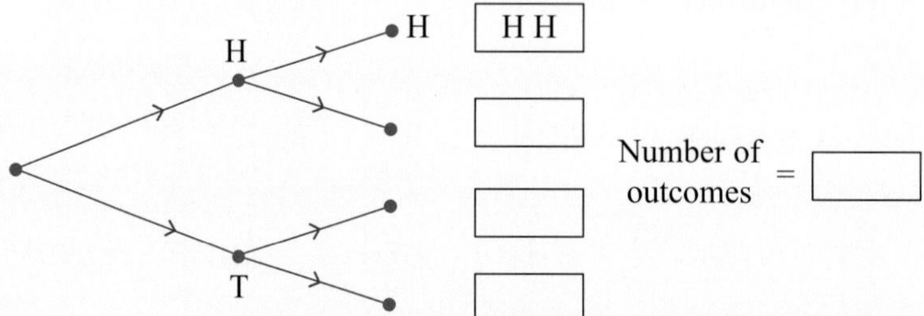

(b) Copy and complete the tree diagram below to find the number of outcomes when a coin is tossed three times.

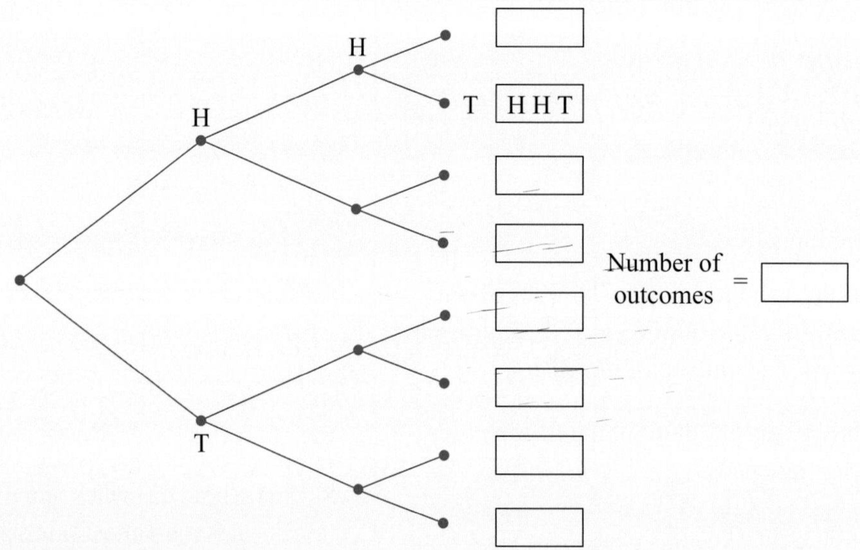

(c) Copy and complete the table below:

Number of tosses	1	2	3	4	5	6	7
Number of outcomes	2^1						

(d) Is the sequence of number of outcomes a geometric sequence? Why? If it is a geometric sequence, what is the number of outcomes if a coin is tossed 14 times?

10. (a) A die is thrown once. How many outcomes are there?

(b) If a die is thrown twice, how many outcomes are there?

(c) If a die is thrown 10 times, how many outcomes are there?

(d) Find the probability of throwing a triple if a die is thrown three times.

11. The number of pupils in a school increases by 6% per annum. When the school opened, there were 150 pupils on the roll. How many pupils will there be in the school on the eighth anniversary of the opening? Copy and fill in the table below to help you answer the question. Give each answer to the nearest whole number.

Year 1	Year 2	Year 3	...	Year 8
150				

12. (a) The value of a car depreciates at an annual rate of 8%. If the car cost €22 000 find:

(i) its value at the end of one year,

(ii) its value at the end of six years, correct to the nearest euro.

(b) A sample of a radioactive isotope has 6 000 000 radioactive nuclei in it. Its half-life is 15 seconds. This means that half of the atoms are left after 15 seconds. Find the number of radioactive isotopes left after 105 seconds.

(c) An equilateral triangle has side 24 cm. Its midpoints D, E, F are joined to form a new equilateral triangle. This pattern is repeated ad infinitum.

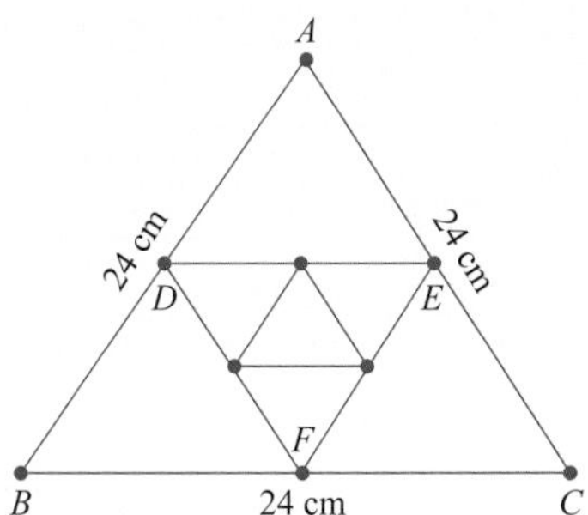

Find the length of the perimeter of the eighth triangle in the sequence.

(d) There are 2048 football teams. How many matches must be played in the seventh round if the winner of each match moves on to the next round and there are no replays?

(e) An environmental protection council estimated that there were 15 000 rats in the sewers of a small town. They decided to set a target of eliminating 2% of the rats that existed at the start of each day by the end of that day. If the council achieves its target:

(i) how many rats will be eliminated by the end of the first day?

(ii) how many rats will remain at the end of the first day?

(iii) how many rats will remain at the end of the seventh day, to the nearest whole number?

13. (a) What is the 20th term of the geometric sequence 1, −2, 4, −8, …?

(b) Find the common ratio and the first term of the geometric sequences that have a fourth term 4 and an eighth term 324. Write down the first four terms of the geometric sequences.

(c) The 32nd term of a geometric sequence is 4 and the 37th term is 128. Find r and a and the first four terms.

(d) The first term of a geometric sequence is $\frac{2}{5}$ and the fifth term is $\frac{81}{40}$. Find a, $r > 0$ and T_7.

(e) Joan knows that her salary increases by the same percentage at the start of each year. Her salary at the start of 2010 was €32 000 and at the start of 2013 was €37 044. Find this percentage increase per annum. What will Joan's salary be at the start of 2015, correct to the nearest euro?

(f) A heat pump decreases the temperature of a room by the same percentage every hour over 24 hours starting at 13:00 hours. The temperature of the room at 16:00 hours was 24 °C and 12·288 °C at 19:00 hours. What was the percentage decrease per hour and the temperature at 13:00 hours?

14. (a) 2, x, y, z, 162 are consecutive terms of a geometric sequence. Find x, y and z.

(b) If −5, x, y, −320 are consecutive terms of a geometric sequence, find x and y.

(c) There are four employees in a firm. The salaries of the four employees form a geometric sequence. If the lowest salary is €26 000 and the highest salary is €57 122, find the salaries of the other two employees.

15. (a) Three consecutive terms of a geometric sequence add to 21. If their product is 216, find the terms.

(b) 18 is the middle term of three consecutive terms in a geometric sequence. If their sum is 78, find the terms.

16. (a) If $x + 9, x - 6, 4$ are consecutive terms of a geometric sequence, find x and the three terms.

(b) If $\frac{1}{x+1}, \frac{3}{3x-1}, \frac{9}{5x+1}$ are three consecutive terms of a geometric sequence, find x and the three terms.

(c) $b, b + 5, b + 15$ are three consecutive terms of a geometric sequence. Find b. If b is the first term, find the eighth term.

17. (a) Find the geometric mean of the following numbers:

(i) 36 and 9

(ii) 1 and 1·21

(iii) a and ar^4

(iv) $(x + y)^2$ and $(x - y)^2$

(b) (i) The geometric mean of x^2 and 4 is 6. Find x.

(ii) The sum of two numbers is 10 and their geometric mean is 4. Find the numbers.

(iii) The difference of two numbers is 6. Their geometric mean is $3\sqrt{3}$. Find the numbers.

13.4 Geometric series

A geometric series is obtained by adding up the individual terms of a geometric sequence.

The worked example that follows is an interesting way of adding up the terms of a finite geometric series.

ACTIVITY 19

ACTION
Working with a geometric series

OBJECTIVE
To add the terms in a geometric series and to come to an understanding of how a summing formula simplifies the task

WORKED EXAMPLE

A technique for adding up the terms of a geometric sequence

$3 + 6 + 12 + 24 + 48$ is a geometric series with five terms.

$a = 3, r = 2$

$S_5 = 3 + 6 + 12 + 24 + 48$

Multiply S_5 by the common ratio $r = 2$, move each number one place to the right and subtract from S_5:

$$S_5 = 3 + 6 + 12 + 24 + 48 \qquad \textbf{(1)}$$

$$2S_5 = \quad 6 + 12 + 24 + 48 + 96 \qquad \textbf{(2)}$$

$$S_5 - 2S_5 = 3 \qquad -96 \qquad \textbf{(1)} - \textbf{(2)}$$

$$S_5 = 93$$

You can check this by doing S_5 in the conventional way: $S_5 = 3 + 6 + 12 + 24 + 48 = 93$

Now apply this trick to any geometric series.

$$S_n = a + ar + ar^2 + \cdots + ar^{n-1} \quad \textbf{(1)}$$

$$rS_n = \quad ar + ar^2 + \cdots ar^{n-1} + ar^n \quad \textbf{(2)}$$

$$S_n - rS_n = a - ar^n \quad \textbf{(1) – (2)}$$

$$S_n(1 - r) = a(1 - r^n)$$

$$S_n = \frac{a(1 - r^n)}{1 - r}$$

The sum S_n of the first n terms of any geometric series with first term a and common ratio r is given by:

$$S_n = \frac{a(1 - (r)^n)}{(1 - r)}$$

This is a very useful technique as it will add up any partial sum of any geometric series.

It is important to note the following about this formula:

1. S_n = Sum of the first n terms of a geometric series.

$S_1 = T_1 = a$

$S_2 = T_1 + T_2$

$S_n = T_1 + T_2 + \cdots + T_n$

2. n is the number of terms to be added.

3. $a = T_1$ = first term.

4. $r = \text{common ratio} = \dfrac{\text{any term}}{\text{previous one}}$.

EXAMPLE 10

For the geometric series $\frac{4}{9} + \frac{4}{3} + 4 + 12 + \ldots$, find:

(a) S_1,

(b) the common ratio r,

(c) the fifteenth term T_{15},

(d) the sum of the first 15 terms S_{15},

(e) the general term T_n,

(f) the general summing formula S_n.

Solution

(a) $S_1 = T_1 = \frac{4}{9} = a$

(b) $r = \frac{12}{4} = 3$

(c) $T_{15} = ar^{14} = \frac{4}{9}(3)^{14} = 4 \times 3^{12}$

(d) $S_{15} = \dfrac{\frac{4}{9}(1 - (3)^{15})}{1 - 3} = \dfrac{\frac{4}{9}(3^{15} - 1)}{2} = \frac{2}{9}(3^{15} - 1)$

(e) $T_n = \frac{4}{9}(3)^{n-1}$

(f) $S_n = \dfrac{\frac{4}{9}(1 - 3^n)}{1 - 3} = \frac{2}{9}(3^n - 1)$

EXAMPLE 11

A spacecraft increases the distance it travels in successive seconds by 2%. If it travels 100 m in the first second, find the total distance the spacecraft travels in the first 20 seconds of its flight, correct to the nearest metre.

Solution

Number of seconds	1	2	3
Distance in metres	100	102	104·04

Distance travelled in the first 20 seconds
= 100 + 102 + 104·04 + … to 20 terms.

This is the sum of the first 20 terms of a geometric series with $a = 100$ and $r = 1{\cdot}02$.

$$S_{20} = \frac{100(1-(1{\cdot}02)^{20})}{1-1{\cdot}02} = 2429{\cdot}74$$

Distance = 2430 m

EXAMPLE 12

A builder is drilling a hole in a wall 72·05 cm thick. In the first second, he drills 31·25 cm and every second after that, he drills $\frac{3}{5}$ of the distance he drilled the previous second. How long will it take the builder to drill the hole?

Solution

The successive distances form the geometric series $31{\cdot}25 + 18{\cdot}75 + \cdots$

$a = 31{\cdot}25,\ r = 0{\cdot}6$

$$S_n = 72{\cdot}05 = \frac{31{\cdot}25(1-(0{\cdot}6)^n)}{1-0{\cdot}6}$$

$$\frac{2882}{3125} = 1-(0{\cdot}6)^n$$

$$(0{\cdot}6)^n = \frac{243}{3125}$$

Take the log of both sides.

$$\log_{10}(0{\cdot}6)^n = \log_{10}\left(\frac{243}{3125}\right)$$

$$n\log_{10}(0{\cdot}6) = \log_{10}\left(\frac{243}{3125}\right)$$

$$\therefore\ n = \frac{\log_{10}\left(\frac{243}{3125}\right)}{\log_{10}(0{\cdot}6)} = 5$$

Answer: 5 seconds

EXAMPLE 13

Find the least number of terms of the geometric sequence 2, 6, 18, … that must be added to give a sum greater than 2000.

Solution

Geometric sequence: 2, 6, 18, …

$a = 2,\ r = 3$

Solve $S_n = 2000$ first

$$S_n = \frac{2(1-(3)^n)}{1-3} = 2000$$

$$3^n - 1 = 2000$$

$$3^n = 2001$$

$$\log_{10} 3^n = \log_{10} 2001$$

$$n\log_{10} 3 = \log_{10} 2001$$

$$n = \frac{\log_{10} 2001}{\log_{10} 3} = 6{\cdot}9$$

Therefore, seven terms must be added to give a sum greater than 2000.

EXAMPLE 14

The sum of the first ten terms of a geometric series is 472 384. If the common ratio is 3, find the first term and the value of the 15th term.

Solution

$S_{10} = 472\,384,\ r = 3$

$\dfrac{a(1-3^{10})}{1-3} = 472\,384$

$a = \dfrac{472\,384 \times 2}{(3^{10}-1)} = 16$

$T_{15} = ar^{14} = 16 \times 3^{14}$

13.5 The sum to infinity (S_∞) of a geometric series

WORKED EXAMPLE Summing a geometric series to infinity

If you compare the two geometric series:

(a) $1 + \frac{1}{2} + \frac{1}{4} + \frac{1}{8} + \frac{1}{16} + \frac{1}{32} + \cdots$ and

Forming the partial sums gives:

$S_1 = 1$

$S_2 = 1 + \frac{1}{2} = 1\frac{1}{2}$

$S_3 = 1 + \frac{1}{2} + \frac{1}{4} = 1\frac{3}{4}$

$S_4 = 1 + \frac{1}{2} + \frac{1}{4} + \frac{1}{8} = 1\frac{7}{8}$

$S_5 = 1 + \frac{1}{2} + \frac{1}{4} + \frac{1}{8} + \frac{1}{16} = 1\frac{15}{16}$

$S_6 = 1 + \frac{1}{2} + \frac{1}{4} + \frac{1}{8} + \frac{1}{16} + \frac{1}{32} = 1\frac{31}{32}$

Although the partial sums are getting bigger, they are not getting out of control.

In fact, they are getting closer and closer to 2.

Written mathematically: $\lim_{n\to\infty} S_n = 2$

The sum to infinity (S_∞) of this geometric series is 2.

$\therefore S_\infty = 2$

(b) $1 + 2 + 4 + 8 + 16 + 32 + \cdots$

$S_1 = 1$

$S_2 = 1 + 2 = 3$

$S_3 = 1 + 2 + 4 = 7$

$S_4 = 1 + 2 + 4 + 8 = 15$

$S_5 = 1 + 2 + 4 + 8 + 16 = 31$

$S_6 = 1 + 2 + 4 + 8 + 16 + 32 = 63$

The partial sums are getting bigger and indeed out of control. They are approaching infinity.

Written mathematically:

$\lim_{n\to\infty} S_n = \infty$

The sum to infinity of this geometric series is ∞.

$\therefore S_\infty = \infty$

So, it seems some infinite geometric series have finite sums to infinity and others have infinite sums to infinity. What is the condition for a geometric series to have a finite sum to infinity?

$$\lim_{n\to\infty} S_n = \frac{a(1-r^\infty)}{1-r} = \begin{cases} \dfrac{a(1-0)}{1-r} = \dfrac{a}{1-r}, \text{ if } -1 < r < 1 \\[2ex] \dfrac{a(1-\infty)}{1-r} = \infty, \text{ if } r > 1, r < -1 \end{cases}$$

This is because: $\lim_{n\to\infty} r^n = \begin{cases} 0 \text{ if } -1 < r < 1 \\ \infty \text{ if } r > 1, r < -1 \end{cases}$

Conclusion

1. If the common ratio r of a geometric series is a fraction between -1 and 1, it has a finite sum to infinity given by $S_\infty = \frac{a}{1-r}$.
2. If the common ratio r of a geometric series is not between -1 and 1, it has an infinite sum to infinity.

You might ask why we did not look at the sum to infinity of an arithmetic series. The answer is that their sum to infinity is always infinite.

- For the geometric sequence $4, \frac{8}{3}, \frac{16}{9}, \dots$

  $a = 4, r = \frac{2}{3}$

  $S_\infty = \frac{a}{1-r} = \frac{4}{1-\frac{2}{3}} = 12$

- For the geometric series $1 + \cos^2 x + \cos^4 x + \cdots$

  $a = 1, r = \cos^2 x$

  $S_\infty = \frac{a}{1-r} = \frac{1}{1-\cos^2 x} = \frac{1}{\sin^2 x}$

  When $x = 30°$: $S_\infty = \frac{1}{\sin^2 30°} = 4$

EXAMPLE 15

A ball is thrown from a window. It hits the ground 1 m from the base of the window and continues to bounce along the ground. The horizontal length of each bounce is e times the length of the previous bounce length.

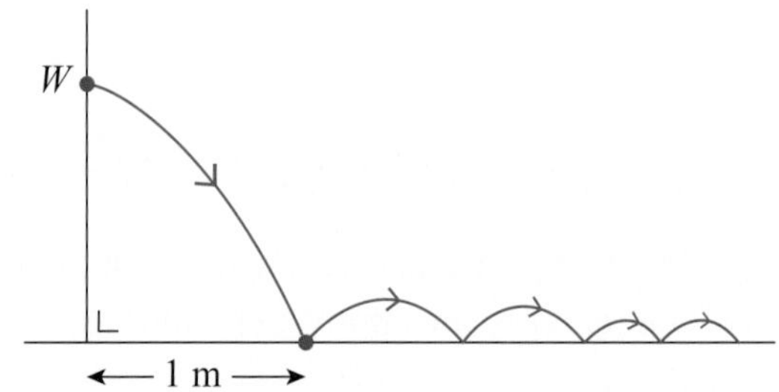

Find:

(a) the total horizontal distance travelled by the ball in coming to rest if $0 < e < 1$,

(b) the total horizontal distance travelled by the ball in coming to rest if $e = \frac{3}{4}$.

Solution

(a) Geometric series: $1 + e + e^2 + \cdots$

$a = 1, r = e$

$S_\infty = \frac{a}{1-r} = \frac{1}{1-e}$ m

(b) $e = \frac{3}{4}$: $S_\infty = \frac{1}{1-\frac{3}{4}} = 4$ m

EXAMPLE 16

If the sum to infinity of a geometric series is 8 and the first term is 2, find its common ratio.

Solution

$S_\infty = 8, a = 2$

$S_\infty = \frac{2}{1-r} = 8$

$1 - r = \frac{1}{4}$

$r = \frac{3}{4}$

The following is an example of the economics multiplier effect.

EXAMPLE 17

A new company opens in a small town. It pays €680 000 per year in salaries. If 40% of this is spent in the town and 40% of the spent money is also kept in the community and this process continues ad infinitum, how much money is generated for the town per year from the salaries of the employees?

Solution

Geometric sequence: 680 000, 272 000, 108 800, …

$a = 680\,000$, $r = 0{\cdot}4$

$$S_\infty = \frac{a}{1-r} = \frac{680\,000}{1-0{\cdot}4} = 1\,133\,333$$

Answer: €1 133 333 is generated in the town per year.

EXAMPLE 18

Find the least number of terms n of the geometric sequence 8, 4, 2, 1, … that must be added so that the difference between the sum of these terms and the sum to infinity is less than 0·05.

Solution

Geometric sequence: 8, 4, 2, 1, …

$$a = 8, r = \tfrac{1}{2}$$

$$S_n = \frac{a(1-(r)^n)}{1-r} = \frac{8\left(1-\left(\frac{1}{2}\right)^n\right)}{1-\frac{1}{2}} = 16\left(1-\left(\frac{1}{2}\right)^n\right)$$

$$S_\infty = \frac{a}{1-r} = \frac{8}{1-\frac{1}{2}} = 16$$

You want to solve $S_\infty - S_n < 0{\cdot}05$.

Solve $S_\infty - S_n = 0{\cdot}05$ first.

$$16 - 16\left(1-\left(\frac{1}{2}\right)^n\right) = 0{\cdot}05$$

$$16 \times \left(\tfrac{1}{2}\right)^n = 0{\cdot}05$$

$$\frac{16}{2^n} = 0{\cdot}05$$

$$2^n = 320$$

$$n = \frac{\log_{10}320}{\log_{10}2} = 8{\cdot}32$$

Therefore, nine terms are the least number of terms needed so that $S_\infty - S_n < 0{\cdot}05$.

Recurring, non-terminating decimals

The formula $S_\infty = \dfrac{a}{1-r}$ can be used to write non-terminating recurring decimals as rationals.

- $0{\cdot}2\dot{7} = 0{\cdot}27777\ldots = \dfrac{2}{10} + \left(\dfrac{7}{100} + \dfrac{7}{1000} + \ldots\right)$

  The expression in the brackets is S_∞ for a geometric series with

  $a = \frac{7}{100}$ and $r = \frac{1}{10}$.

  $$S_\infty = \frac{a}{1-r} = \frac{\frac{7}{100}}{1-\frac{1}{10}} = \frac{7}{90}$$

  $$\therefore 0{\cdot}2\dot{7} = \frac{2}{10} + \frac{7}{90} = \frac{5}{18}$$ [Check this answer on your calculator.]

- $0{\cdot}636\,363\ldots = \dfrac{63}{100} + \dfrac{63}{10\,000} + \ldots$

  This is S_∞ for a geometric series with $a = \frac{63}{100}$ and $r = \frac{1}{100}$.

  $$S_\infty = \frac{a}{1-r} = \frac{\frac{63}{100}}{1-\frac{1}{100}} = \frac{63}{99} = \frac{7}{11}$$

13.6 Geometric series using the Σ notation

A geometric series is often written in the $\sum$ notation. It is very easy to recognise a geometric series in the $\sum$ notation. Just look at the general term T_n. The series is a geometric series if there is a constant base to a variable power in the general term.

- $\sum_{p=1}^{12}\left(\frac{1}{2}\right)^p$ [This series is geometric as there is a constant base of a $\frac{1}{2}$ to a variable power p.]

EXAMPLE 19

Evaluate $\sum_{n=1}^{\infty} p^n q^{n-1}$, $p, q < 1$.

Solution

Writing $\sum_{n=1}^{\infty} p^n q^{n-1}$ as a list gives

$S_\infty = p + p^2q + p^3q^2 + \dots$.

This is S_∞ for a geometric series with $a = p$, $r = pq$.

$$S_\infty = \frac{p}{1 - pq}$$

EXAMPLE 20

Find the least value of $n \in \mathbb{N}$ for which

$\sum_{n=1}^{n}(1{\cdot}02)^{n-1} > 500.$

Solution

$\sum_{n=1}^{n}(1{\cdot}02)^{n-1}$ is S_n for a geometric series.

$\sum_{n=1}^{n}(1{\cdot}02)^{n-1} = 1 + (1{\cdot}02)^1 + (1{\cdot}02)^2 + \dots + (1{\cdot}02)^{n-1}$

$a = 1$, $r = (1{\cdot}02)$

$$S_n = \frac{1(1-(1{\cdot}02)^n)}{1-1{\cdot}02} = 500$$

$$(1{\cdot}02)^n - 1 = 10$$

$$(1{\cdot}02)^n = 11$$

$$n = \frac{\log_{10}11}{\log_{10}1{\cdot}02} = 121{\cdot}089$$

Therefore, $n = 122$.

To find the first term a, the common ratio r and the number of terms for a geometric series written in the $\sum$ notation, write out the first three terms and look at the subscripts and superscripts.

ACTIVITY 20

ACTION
Working with the Σ notation

OBJECTIVE
To become familiar with how the Σ notation works

EXAMPLE 21

Evaluate $\sum_{n=0}^{12}\left(\frac{2}{3}\right)^{n+1}$.

Solution

$\sum_{n=0}^{12}\left(\frac{2}{3}\right)^{n+1}$ is S_{13} of a geometric series.

$$S_{13} = \frac{2}{3} + \frac{4}{9} + \frac{8}{27} + \dots + \left(\frac{2}{3}\right)^{13}$$

This series is a geometric series with $a = \frac{2}{3}$ and $r = \frac{2}{3}$ and 13 terms ($n = 0$ to $n = 12$).

$$S_{13} = \frac{\frac{2}{3}\left(1-\left(\frac{2}{3}\right)^{13}\right)}{1-\frac{2}{3}} = 2\left(1-\left(\frac{2}{3}\right)^{13}\right)$$

EXERCISE 8

1. For each of the following geometric series (or sequences), find the given sums:

   (a) $4 + 6 + 9 + \cdots$ (S_n and S_{12})

   (b) $1, \frac{1}{2}, \frac{1}{4}, \ldots$ (S_n and S_6)

   (c) $3, -6, 12, \ldots$ (S_n and S_8)

   (d) $x, x^2, x^3, \ldots$ (S_n and S_{15})

   (e) $2, -\sqrt{2}, 1, \ldots$ (S_n and S_{22})

   (f) $\frac{1}{b^2} + \frac{1}{b^4} + \frac{1}{b^6} + \cdots$ (S_n and S_{20})

   (g) $2 + 2\sqrt{3} + 6 + \cdots$ (S_n and S_{40})

   (h) $\frac{3}{4}, \frac{3}{2}, 3, \ldots$ (S_n and S_{11})

2. **(a) (i)** Find the sum of the first five powers of 2.

   (ii) Find the sum of the first ten powers of 2.

   (iii) Using parts **(i)** and **(ii)**, find the sum of the second five powers of 2.

   (b) Find the sum of the eighth to the 15th terms inclusive of the geometric series $64 + 32 + 16 + \cdots$.

   (c) How many terms are in the finite geometric series $\frac{1}{16} + \frac{1}{8} + \frac{1}{4} + \cdots + 256$? Find the sum of this series.

   (d) A man invests €200 on 1 January 2013 and leaves it in the bank until 31 December 2017. The investment pays 3% per annum compound interest.

   (i) How much money will the man get on 31 December 2017?

   (ii) If the man invests €200 at the start of every year starting on 1 January 2013 for five years at 3% per annum compound interest, how much money will he have accumulated on 31 December 2017?

   (e) The cost of laying a pipe decreases by 20% for each successive 100 m of pipe laid. If the first 100 m costs €4000 to lay, find the total cost of laying 1 km of pipes.

   (f) 10 000 children were born in a country in the year 2008. If this figure increases by 5% per annum, find:

   (i) how many children were born in 2015?

   (ii) how many children in total were born between 2008 and 2015, inclusive?

   (g) $\dfrac{3\left(1-\left(\frac{1}{2}\right)^n\right)}{1-\frac{1}{2}} = \dfrac{3\left(\left(\frac{1}{2}\right)^n - 1\right)}{\frac{1}{2}-1}$? Why?

   (h) A chessboard has 64 squares. A one cent coin is placed on the first square, 2 one cent coins are placed on the second square, 4 one cent coins are placed on the third square, and so on. Find:

   (i) how many one cent coins will be on the 64th square,

   (ii) the total amount of money on all 64 squares.

   (i) A certain drug has a half-life of 3 hours. This means that half of the dose remains in the bloodstream after 3 hours. The drug is administered in doses of D mg every 6 hours for up to 18 hours. Find, in terms of D, the number of milligrams in the bloodstream 18 hours after D mg have been administered.

3. **(a)** How many terms of the geometric series 9, 6, 4, … must be added to give a sum of $\frac{211}{9}$?

(b) If $P(1\cdot06)^1 + P(1\cdot06)^2 + \cdots + P(1\cdot06)^{10} = 1500$, find P, to the nearest whole number.

(c) How many terms of the geometric sequence 8, 24, 72, must be added to give 968?

(d) How many terms of the geometric sequence 4, 12, 36, … must be added to give 1456?

(e) What is the least number of terms of the geometric sequence 2, 8, 32, … that must be added to give a sum greater than 1000?

(f) A student lives 2 km from her college. She cycles 500 m in the first minute of her journey to the college and in each subsequent minute she cycles 80% of the distance cycled in the previous minute. Estimate the time, in minutes, it takes the student to reach her college, correct to one decimal place.

4. **(a)** The first term of a geometric series is 16. The fourth term is 54. Find the sum of the first five terms.

(b) Find the least number of terms n such that S_n for the geometric series $1 + \frac{1}{3} + \frac{1}{9} + \cdots$ differs from $1\cdot5$ by less than $0\cdot001$?

(c) The first term of a geometric series is 16 and the seventh is $\frac{1}{4}$. Find $r > 0$. Find S_7 for this geometric series.

(d) The first term of a geometric sequence is 5. The sum of the first three terms is 285. Find the common ratio.

(e) Show that $\log_3 x$, $\log_9 x$, $\log_{81} x$ are three consecutive terms of a geometric sequence. Find S_{12} for the series $\log_3 x + \log_9 x + \log_{81} x$.

5. **(a)** The nth term of a series is $T_n = 3 \times 2^{n-1}$. Show that it is a geometric series. Find S_n.

(b) The nth term of a series is $T_n = \frac{2}{3^n}$. Show that it is a geometric series. Find a, r and S_n.

(c) If S is the sum of the first n terms of the geometric series $a, ar, ar^2, \ldots$ and P is the sum of the first n terms of the geometric series $\frac{1}{a}, \frac{1}{ar}, \frac{1}{ar^2}, \ldots$, show that $S = a^2 r^{n-1} P$.

6. Find the sum to infinity for the following geometric series:

(a) $1, \frac{2}{7}, \frac{4}{49}, \ldots$

(b) $2, \frac{8}{5}, \frac{32}{25}, \ldots$

(c) $1, -\frac{1}{2}, \frac{1}{4}, \ldots$

(d) $8, 2, \frac{1}{2}, \ldots$

(e) $\frac{1}{x}, \frac{1}{x^2}, \frac{1}{x^3}, \ldots \ (x > 1)$

(f) $1, \sin^2 x, \sin^4 x, \ldots$ when $x = 45°$

(g) $8, 6, \frac{9}{2}, \ldots$

(h) $\left(\frac{3}{5}\right), \left(\frac{3}{5}\right)^2, \left(\frac{3}{5}\right)^3, \ldots$

7. **(a)** The first term of a geometric sequence is 50 and the third term is 2. Find the sum to infinity.

(b) The first term of a geometric sequence is 96 and its sum to infinity is 128. Find the first four terms of the geometric sequence.

(c) The second term of a geometric series is 5 and its sum to infinity is $\frac{80}{3}$. Find the first term and the common ratio.

(d) The second term of a geometric series is 6 and the fifth term is $\frac{3}{4}$. Find the sum to infinity.

8. **(a)** Find the sum to infinity of the geometric sequence $1, -\tan^2 x, \tan^4 x, \ldots$ for $0 < x < 45°$ and find its value when $x = 30°$.

(b) Find the least number of terms of the geometric series $12 + 6 + 3 + \cdots$ that must be added to differ from the sum to infinity by less than $0{\cdot}02$.

(c) A student starts with a right-angled triangular piece of cardboard 100 cm in height and base 60 cm. Using different colours, he places smaller triangles on top of the bigger one, ad infinitum. The lengths of the sides of all successive triangles are exactly half the length of each previous triangle. Find the total area of all the triangles.

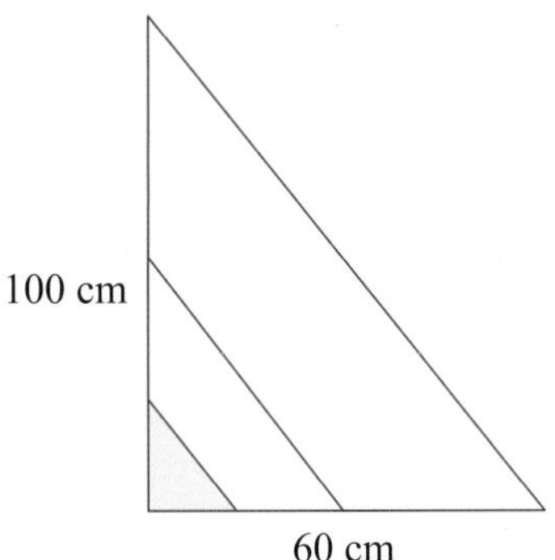

(d) The sum to infinity of the geometric series $b, bp, bp^2, \ldots$ is 6. The sum to infinity of the geometric series $b^2, b^2p^2, b^2p^4, \ldots$ is $\frac{36}{5}$. Find b and p.

9. Write each non-terminating, recurring decimal below in the form $\frac{a}{b}$, $a, b \in \mathbb{N}$:

(a) $0{\cdot}1\dot{6}$

(b) $0{\cdot}\dot{2}\dot{3}$

(c) $6{\cdot}\dot{3}$

(d) $1{\cdot}\dot{1}\dot{9}$

(e) $2{\cdot}\dot{4}\dot{2}$

(f) $0{\cdot}4\dot{2}\dot{1}$

10. Evaluate the following:

(a) $\sum_{n=1}^{5} 3^n$

(b) $\sum_{n=1}^{6} 4^{n-1}$

(c) $\sum_{r=1}^{7} \left[3\left(\frac{1}{2}\right)^r\right]$

(d) $\sum_{p=1}^{\infty} 2\left(\frac{1}{3}\right)^p$

(e) $\sum_{n=0}^{\infty} \sin^{2n} x$

REVISION QUESTIONS

1. **(a)** What is the common ratio of the geometric series $\sum_{n=0}^{\infty}\left(\frac{\sqrt{3}}{6}\right)^n$? Evaluate this sum in the form $\frac{a}{b}(c+\sqrt{3})$, $a, b, c \in \mathbb{N}$.

(b) How many terms are there in the geometric series $\sum_{r=6}^{16}\left(\frac{1}{4}\right)^r$? Evaluate this sum.

(c) Find k, correct to the nearest whole number, if $\sum_{r=1}^{25} k(1{\cdot}032)^{1-r} = 1000$.

(d) Find the least value of $n \in \mathbb{N}$ for which $\sum_{r=1}^{\infty}\left(\frac{1}{3}\right)^r - \sum_{r=1}^{n}\left(\frac{1}{3}\right)^r < 0{\cdot}001$.

(e) Write $0{\cdot}\dot{3}\dot{7}$ as an infinite geometric series and hence express it as a rational.

(f) The sum to infinity of a geometric series is $5\frac{1}{3}$ and the common ratio is $-\frac{1}{2}$. Find:

(i) the first term

(ii) the 20th term

(iii) the sum of the first 20 terms

2. **(a)** Given the geometric sequence 27, 9, 3, … ,

(i) find the nth term T_n,

(ii) say why the sum to infinity S_∞ exists for this sequence,

(iii) find S_n,

(iv) find S_∞,

(v) find the least number of terms n such that $S_\infty - S_n < 0{\cdot}01$.

(b) 20 water tanks are decreasing in size so that the volume of each tank is half the volume of the previous one.

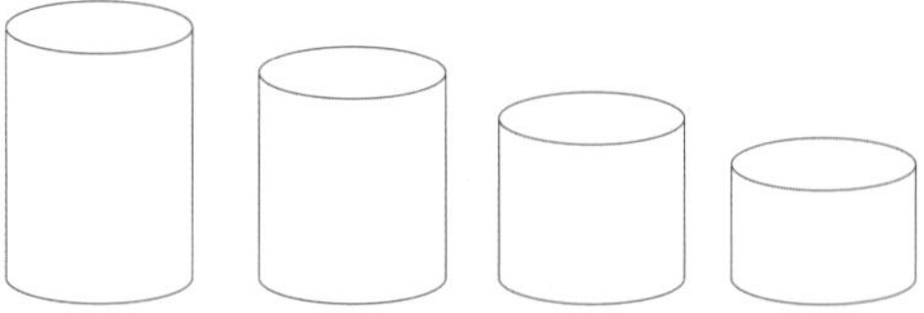

The first tank is empty, but the remaining 19 tanks are full of water. Investigate if it is possible for the first tank to hold all of the water from the other 19 tanks.

3. Peter has matchsticks all of the same length. He arranges them in squares in rows, as shown.

Row 1:

Row 2:

Row 3:

(a) Find an expression for the number N of matchsticks required to make n squares in row n.

(b) Find the total number of matchsticks needed to complete 10 rows.

(c) If Peter had 2500 matchsticks at the beginning, he could complete k rows. Find k.

4. **(a)** The first complete swing of a pendulum is 12 cm. Each subsequent swing is 0·92 of the length of the previous swing. How far does the pendulum travel before coming to rest?

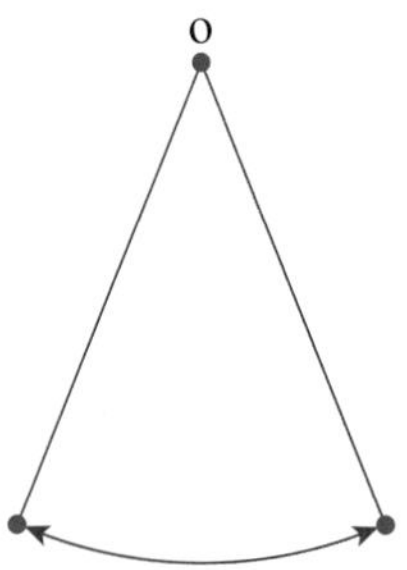

(b) Evaluate $\sum_{n=0}^{\infty}\left(\frac{x}{1+x}\right)^n$, $x > 0$.

(c) A piece of paper is 0·1 mm thick. Imagine that you can fold it as many times as you like. After one fold the paper is 0·2 mm thick and after two folds it is 0·4 mm thick, and so on.

(i) How thick is the paper after eight folds?

(ii) How many times should it be folded to be 2 m or more thick?

(iii) How many times should it be folded for its thickness to reach the moon, which is 4×10^8 m away?

5. (a) How many terms of the arithmetic sequence $-2, 2, 6, 10, \dots$ add up to 798?

(b) How many terms of the geometric sequence $4, 12, 36, \dots$ add up to 118 096?

(c) The sum to infinity of the geometric series $a, ar, ar^2, \dots$ is 13·5. The sum to infinity of the geometric series $a^2, a^2r^2, a^2r^4, \dots$ is $\frac{729}{8}$. Find a and r.

6. (a) By writing $0{\cdot}1\dot{7}$ as a geometric series, express it in the form $\frac{p}{q}, p, q \in \mathbb{N}$.

(b) In a geometric sequence, the sum of the first and third terms is 52. The sum of the second and fourth terms is 78. Find the first term.

(c) The shortest side a of a triangle is 6 cm. If all three sides are consecutively in a geometric sequence, find the length of each side if the perimeter is 28·5 cm.

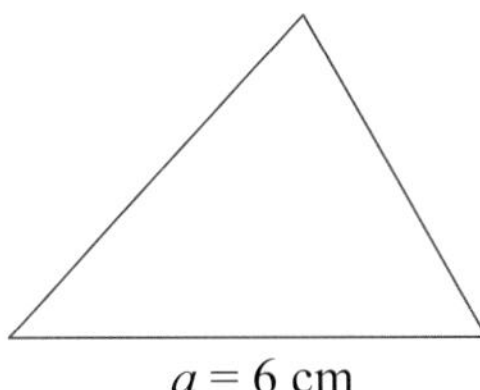

7. (a) The first three terms of an arithmetic sequence are $\log_a p^2, 2\log_a pq, 2\log_a pq^2$. If $pq^2 = a$, find the sum S_5 of the first five terms.

(b) 100 g of a volatile liquid is left to evaporate. Each day it loses $\frac{1}{10}$ of its mass at the beginning of that day. On what day will the mass left become less that 50 g?

(c) 120° is the largest angle in a triangle. The length of the longest side is $3l$. The lengths of the sides form an arithmetic sequence. Use the cosine rule to find the length of each side. [Note: You can leave this question until trigonometry has been covered.]

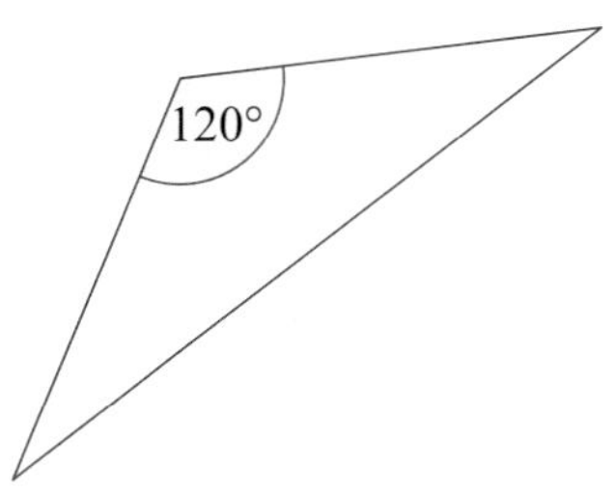

8. (a) Mr Thrifty invests €500 per year at the start of each year for 10 years at 3% p.a. compound interest. What is his total investment worth at the end of the 10th year, correct to the nearest euro?

(b) The concentration of a drug in the bloodstream reduces by half every 2 hours. If a dose d is administered every 4 hours, find the concentration of the drug in the bloodstream after the nth dose is administered. If a concentration of more than 600 mg in the bloodstream is considered dangerous, find the largest dose that can be given for a treatment of four doses, correct to two decimal places.

(c) (i) For the geometric series $a, ar, ar^2, \dots$, find S_{2n}.

(ii) For another geometric series $b, br^2, br^4, \dots$, find S_n.

(iii) If $S_{2n} = S_n$, show that $r = \frac{b}{a} - 1$.

9. (a) Find the least number of terms of the geometric sequence $5, \frac{5}{2}, \frac{5}{4}, \dots$ that must be added so that its sum differs from its sum to infinity by less than 0·01.

(b) Find three consecutive terms of an arithmetic sequence whose sum is 3 and whose product is -8.

(c) The arithmetic mean of x and y is 10. Their geometric mean is $4\sqrt{6}$. Find x and y.

10. (a) A geometric series is given by:

$e^{3x} + 3e^{x} + 9e^{-x} + \dots$.

Find the sum to infinity when $x = \ln 2$.

(b) All the terms of a geometric sequence are positive. The first term is k and the second term is $k^2 - k$. Find the range of values of k for which the series converges. If $k = \frac{4}{3}$, find S_∞.

(c) The general term of a quadratic sequence is given by $T_n = an^2 + bn + c$.

(i) Show that $t_n = T_{n+1} - T_n = 2an + a + b$.

(ii) Show that $t_{n+1} - t_n = 2a$. What can you conclude about the sequence $t_1, t_2, \dots$?

SUMMARY

1. Convergence of a sequence with general term T_n: $\lim_{n\to\infty} T_n = L$

   The sequence is convergent if L is finite, but is divergent if L is infinite or does not exist.

2. Series:

   (a) A series is the sum of the terms of a sequence:

   $$S_n = \sum_{n=1}^{n} T_n$$

   (b) The $\sum$ rules:

   (i) $\sum_{n=1}^{n} (u_n + v_n) = \sum_{n=1}^{n} u_n + \sum_{n=1}^{n} v_n$

   (ii) $\sum_{n=1}^{n} ku_n = k\sum_{n=1}^{n} u_n$ where $k \in \mathbb{R}$

   (iii) $\sum_{n=1}^{n} 1 = n$

3. Arithmetic sequences and series:

   (a) The general term: $T_n = a + (n - 1)d$

   Example: $T_{57} = a + 56d$

   (b) The sum S_n of the first n terms:

   $S_n = \frac{n}{2}[2a + (n - 1)d]$

   (c) Test for an arithmetic sequence:

   $T_{n+1} - T_n = d =$ constant for all $n \in \mathbb{N}$

   (d) Notation

   $T_1 = S_1 = a =$ first term

   $n =$ place number of a term

   $d =$ common difference $=$ any term $-$ previous one

   $T_n =$ value of the term in the nth place

   $S_n =$ sum of the first n terms

   (e) Three consecutive terms in an arithmetic sequence: choose $a - d, a, a + d$

   (f) The arithmetic mean c of two numbers a and b is given by: $c = \frac{a+b}{2}$

4. Geometric sequences and series:

   (a) The general term $T_n = a(r)^{n-1}$

   Example: $T_{25} = ar^{24}$

   (b) The sum S_n of the first n terms:

   $$S_n = \frac{a(1 - (r)^n)}{1 - r}$$

   (c) The sum to infinity $S_\infty = \frac{a}{1 - r}$ if $-1 < r < 1$

   (d) Test for a geometric sequence:

   $\frac{T_{n+1}}{T_n} = r =$ constant for all $n \in \mathbb{N}$

   (e) Notation

   $T_1 = S_1 = a =$ first term

   $n =$ place number of a term

   $r =$ common ratio $= \frac{\text{any term}}{\text{previous one}}$

   $T_n =$ value of the term in the nth place

   $S_n =$ sum of the first n terms

   (f) Three consecutive terms in a geometric sequence: choose $\frac{a}{r}, a, ar$

   (g) The geometric mean c of two numbers a and b is given by $c = \sqrt{ab}$

   (h) Recurring decimals: use $S_\infty = \frac{a}{1 - r}$

5. $\sum$ notation

   (a) Arithmetic series: $S_n = \sum_{n=1}^{n} a + (n - 1)d$

   (b) Geometric series: $S_n = \sum_{r=1}^{n} a(r)^{n-1}$

Financial Maths

Understanding how money works is an essential part of living your life and planning for your future. 'I think the whole issue of a debt ceiling makes no sense to me whatsoever. Anybody who is remotely adroit at arithmetic doesn't need a debt ceiling to tell you where you are.' – Alan Greenspan, former chairman of the US Federal Reserve.

Financial Maths 1

Learning Outcomes

- To calculate unit rates.
- To convert from one system of units to another.
- To use exchange rates.
- To calculate value added tax (VAT).
- To calculate income tax, PRSI and USC.
- To understand cost price, selling price, profit and loss, and profit margin.

14.1 Unit rates

ACTIVITY 1

ACTION
Working with unit rates

OBJECTIVE
To understand the idea of solving problems by finding the unit value first

Have you ever looked at two products side by side on a supermarket shelf and asked yourself which is better value? Crunchy Peanuts are priced at €3·70 for 250 g. Beside them on the shelf are Munchy Peanuts priced at €3·90 for 300 g. To decide which is the better value, you need to find the price of each product per gram.

Crunchy	**Munchy**
250 g costs 370 c	300 g costs 390 c
1 g costs $\frac{370}{250}$ c = 1·48 c	1 g costs $\frac{390}{300}$ c = 1·3 c
Cost: 1·48 c/g	Cost: 1·3 c/g

This is the unit rate for each product and compares like with like. The Munchy Peanuts are better value for money.

EXAMPLE 1

35 kg of coal is priced at €17·15. How much will 80 kg of coal cost you?

Solution

35 kg costs €17·15.

1 kg costs $\frac{€17·15}{35}$ = €0·49

80 kg costs €0·49 × 80 = €39·20

ACTIVITY 2

ACTION
Converting to different units

OBJECTIVE
To understand the idea of solving problems by converting to different units

Conversion factors

For everyday measurement of length, area, volume, mass and time, most countries use the **metric system** of units. A few countries, notably the UK and the US, use an older system of units to measure these quantities. This older system is called the **imperial system**. For example, the Square Mile is the financial district in London. Scientists in every part of the world use the metric system.

Quantity	Metric system	Imperial system
Length	Centimetre (cm), metre (m), kilometre (km)	Inch, foot, yard, mile
Area	cm^2, m^2, km^2	Square inch, square foot, square yard, square mile
Volume	cm^3, m^3, litre (l)	Fluid ounce, pint, gallon
Mass	Gram (g), kilogram (kg), tonne	Ounce, pound, stone, ton
Time	Second (s), minute, hour	Second, minute, hour

You can convert between units in the same system and between units in different systems. All you need to know is the **conversion factor**.

1. Metric to metric

TIP
Bracket a unit before you convert it.

- If 1 km = 10^3 m, what is 5 km^2 in m^2?
  $5\text{ km}^2 = 5 \times (1\text{ km})^2 = 5 \times (10^3\text{ m})^2 = 5 \times 10^6\text{ m}^2$ $[(10^3)^2 = 10^6]$
- If 1 cm = 10^{-2} m, what is 25·6 cm^3 in m^3?
  $25{\cdot}6\text{ cm}^3 = 25{\cdot}6 \times (1\text{ cm})^3 = 25{\cdot}6 \times (10^{-2}\text{ m})^3 = 25{\cdot}6 \times 10^{-6}\text{ m}^3$
  $= 2{\cdot}56 \times 10^{-5}\text{ m}^3$ [You can use your calculator at any point in the calculation.]

EXAMPLE 2

Convert 1 litre (l) to m^3 if 1 cm = 10^{-2} m and 1 litre (l) = 10^3 cm^3.

Solution

$1\text{ l} = 1 \times (1\text{ l}) = 1 \times (10^3\text{ cm}^3)$

$= 1 \times 10^3 \times (1\text{ cm})^3$

$= 1 \times 10^3 \times (10^{-2}\text{ m})^3$

$= 1 \times 10^3 \times 10^{-6}\text{ m}^3$ [Add the powers]

$1\text{ l} = 1 \times 10^{-3}\text{ m}^3$

EXAMPLE 3

(a) If 1 km = 10^3 m and 1 hour = 3600 s, convert 90 km/h to m/s if 1 km = 10^3 m and 1 h = 3600 s.

(b) Convert 6 m/s to km/h.

Solution

(a) $90\text{ km/h} = 90 \times \dfrac{(1\text{ km})}{(1\text{ h})}$

$= 90 \times \dfrac{(10^3\text{ m})}{(3600\text{ s})} = \dfrac{90\text{ m}}{3{\cdot}6\text{ s}} = 25\text{ m/s}$

(b) $6\text{ m/s} = 6 \times \dfrac{(1\text{ m})}{(1\text{ s})}$

$= 6 \times \dfrac{(10^{-3}\text{ km})}{\left(\dfrac{1}{3600}\text{ h}\right)} = 6\text{ km} \times 3{\cdot}6\text{ h} = 21{\cdot}6\text{ km/h}$

2. Metric to imperial and vice versa

- If 1 inch = 2·54 cm, what is 12 inches or 1 foot in cm?

  1 inch = 2·54 cm

  12 inches = 12 × 2·54 cm = 30·48 cm

  12 inches = 1 foot

  ∴ 1 foot = 30·48 cm

EXAMPLE 4

(a) A driver from the Republic of Ireland crosses the border into Northern Ireland. The speed limits in the Republic are in kilometres per hour (km/h). Speed is measured in Northern Ireland in miles per hour (mph). What is 120 km/h in mph if 1 km = 0·62137 miles?

(b) A quick method to convert a speed in km/h to a speed in mph is to multiply the speed in km/h by $\frac{5}{8}$. Find the percentage error this gives when converting 120 km/h to mph, correct to one decimal place.

Solution

(a) $120\text{ km/h} = 120 \times \frac{(1\text{ km})}{(1\text{ h})}$

$= 120 \times \frac{(0{\cdot}62137\text{ miles})}{(1\text{ h})}$

$= 74{\cdot}5644$ mph

(b) 120 km/h = 74·5644 mph

Quick method: $120\text{ km/h} = 120 \times \frac{5}{8}\text{ mph} = 75\text{ mph}$

Percentage error in quick answer $= \frac{(75 - 74{\cdot}5644)}{74{\cdot}5644} \times 100\%$

$= 0{\cdot}6\%$

EXERCISE 1

1. **(a)** A car travels 251·2 km in 4 hours. Its average speed is how far it travels in 1 hour. What is its average speed?

(b) A shop has an offer of six cans of cola for the price of five. If the price of one individual can is €1·08, how much do you pay for six cans? How much are you paying per can?

(c) A shop has a 'special offer' on a large 200 g jar of coffee for €6·50. A smaller 100 g jar costs €3·00. Is this a 'special offer'?

(d) A 160-page refill pad costs €2·50. A 200-page 'jumbo' refill pad costs €3·60. Which is the better value?

(e) An 870 ml bottle of washing-up liquid costs €2·99. The 530 ml bottle of the same liquid costs €2·22 and the 433 ml costs €1·51. Which is the best value?

(f) 60% of a building site has area 312 m^2. What is the area of 80% of the site?

(g) Forty cars occupy 58% of a parking lot. What percentage of the lot is occupied by 25 cars?

(h) In a cinema 120 patrons means the cinema is half-full. What fraction of the seats in the cinema is filled by 160 patrons?

2. Convert the following, giving your answer in standard form $a \times 10^n$, $1 \le a < 10$.

(a) 5 cm to m

(b) 2·7 m to km

(c) 5·4 km^2 to m^2

(d) 2·6 cm^2 to m^2

(e) $680\ cm^3$ to m^3

(f) 5 tonne to kg

(g) $5·6\ cm^3$ to m^3

(h) 5 l to cm^3

(i) 5 l to m^3

3. Convert the following:

(a) 72 km/h to m/s

(b) 108 km/h to m/s

(c) 100 km/h to m/s

(d) 45 km/h to m/s

(e) 10 m/s to km/h

(f) 15·6 m/s to km/h

(g) 3 m/s to km/h

(h) 25 m/s to km/h

(i) 75 km/h to m/s

(j) 9 m/s to km/h

4. The capacity of a family saloon petrol tank is 49·2 l. How many gallons is this correct to the nearest gallon? (1 gallon = 3·785 l)

5. The River Nile is 4160 miles long. How long is the Nile in km? (1 mile = 1·61 km)

6. Mount Everest is 29 029 feet high. What is its height in metres, correct to one decimal place? (1 metre = 3·281 feet)

7. The mean density of the Earth is $5·515\ g/cm^3$. Compare this density to the mean density of Jupiter, which is $1326\ kg/m^3$, correct to two decimal places.

8. Javier Sotomayor set a world high jump record at 8·02 feet in 1993 in Salamanca, Spain. What is this height in metres? Javier's height is 1·95 m. How many feet can he jump above his height? Give both answers correct to two decimal places. (1 foot = 0·3048 m)

9. A building site measures 125 m by 420 m.

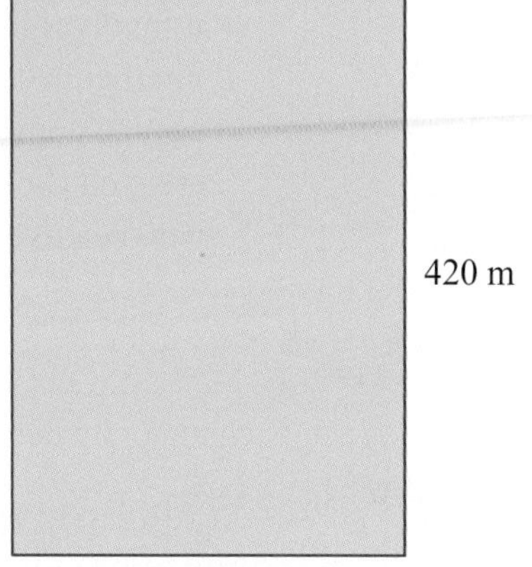

What is its area in:

(a) m^2,

(b) km^2,

(c) hectares
(1 hectare = 100 m × 100 m = $10^4\ m^2$),

(d) acres, to the nearest acre?
(1 hectare = 2·471 acres)

10. A house is built on a rectangular plot with an area of 3 acres. Its length is 121 yards. What is its breadth? (1 acre = 4840 square yards)

11. The speed of light is 3×10^8 m/s. What is this speed in:

(a) km/h,

(b) mph, correct to two significant figures?
(1 mile = 1·61 km)

Currency exchange

Currency exchange is exactly the same as converting units of measurement except it involves money. If you visit a country outside the eurozone or buy goods on the internet from another country, you normally use the currency of that country. It is easy to convert from one currency to another once you are given the **exchange rate** and you can work out unit rates. The exchange rate is simply the conversion factor between two currencies.

EXAMPLE 5

On a certain day the exchange rate between the euro and the dollar is €1 = $1·32.

(a) How many dollars will you get for €500?

(b) How many euro will you need to get $594? (Assume there is no commission charged.)

Solution

(a) €1 = $1·32

€500 = $500 × 1·32 = $660

(b) $1·32 = €1

$$\$1 = €\frac{1}{1{\cdot}32}$$

$$\$594 = €\frac{594}{1{\cdot}32} = €450$$

Most banks and foreign exchange companies charge a commission on transactions. They take a slice of the money you wish to convert *before* they convert it.

EXAMPLE 6

Peter wants to change €600 into roubles as he is travelling to St Petersburg. The bank charges a fixed commission of 1·5% on all foreign exchange transactions. If the exchange rate is €1 = 47·32 roubles, how many roubles does he get?

Solution

A commission of 1·5% means Peter has only 98·5% of €600 to convert to roubles.

98·5% of €600 = 0·985 × 600 = €591

€1 = 47·32 roubles

€591 = 591 × 47·32 = 27 966·12 roubles

Have you ever noticed when you walk into a bank there is a foreign exchange board that looks like the table below?

	Country	Currency	Buys	Sells
1	USA	Dollar	**1·3949**	**1·3266**
2	UK	Pound	0·8394	0·7983
3	UAE	Dirham	5·2061	4·8093
4	Canada	Dollar	1·5702	1·4505
5	South Africa	Rand	15·7342	14·5349

Banks are currency traders. They make a profit on all foreign exchange transactions. The table above gives the conversion rate for €1. On a particular day, the table shows that the bank will buy dollars at a rate of €1 = $**1·3949**, but will sell dollars at a rate of €1 = $**1·3266**.

EXAMPLE 7

(a) A man returning from a trip to the USA has \$556 left. He goes to the bank on his way home from the airport to convert this money. According to the foreign exchange board, how many euro does he get? (Assume there is no commission.)

(b) When the man arrives home his son says he is off to New York the following day. His father gives him €398·59 and tells him to go to the bank to convert it to dollars. According to the foreign exchange board, how many dollars does he get? (Assume there is no commission.)

Solution

(a) The bank is buying the man's dollars, so he gets the 'buy rate'.

€1 = \$1·3949

$\$1 = €\frac{1}{1{\cdot}3949}$

$\$556 = €\frac{556}{1{\cdot}3949} = €398{\cdot}59$

(b) The bank is selling dollars, so the son gets the 'sell rate'.

€1 = \$1·3266

€398·59 = \$528·77

The bank makes a nice profit!

EXERCISE 2

1. Change €800 into the stated currency with the given exchange rate.
   (a) Pounds sterling (£): rate €1 = £0·8242
   (b) US dollars (\$): rate €1 = \$1·364
   (c) Canadian dollars (CAD\$): rate €1 = CAD\$1·521
   (d) South African rand (R): rate €1 = R15·31
   Give all answers correct to two decimal places.

2. Change the following, giving all answers correct to two decimal places:
   (a) \$500 into euro if €1 = \$1·364
   (b) £650 into euro if €1 = £0·8242
   (c) 70 000 roubles into euro if €1 = 48·03 roubles
   (d) 553 000 yen (¥) into US dollars (\$) if ¥1 = \$0·009776
   (e) \$200 into pounds (£) if £1= \$1·655
   (f) 95 Malaysian ringgit into Indian rupees if 1 Indian rupee = 0·05326 ringgits

3. Joanne went on a Christmas trip to New York.
   (a) She changed €1200 into US dollars (\$) at an exchange rate of €1= \$1·364. How many dollars did she receive if a commission of 1% was charged on the €1200?
   (b) In New York, she bought a coat for \$230 and Christmas presents for \$482. She spent \$220 on other expenses. She changed the dollars she had left at JFK Airport in New York at a rate of €1 = \$1·34 and no commission. How many euro did she have when she arrived home?

4. The table below shows the exchange rates between three currencies: euro (€), Thai bahts (THB) and Hong Kong dollars (HKD).

	€	THB	HKD
€	1	44·96	10·60

   (a) Convert 3000 THB into **(i)** €, **(ii)** HKD.
   (b) How many THB can you get for €50?
   (c) How many THB can you get for 600 HKD?

5. A foreign exchange office exchanges €1 for US dollars with the buy rate of $1·3949 and the sell rate of $1·3266.
   (a) If Seán walks into the office with $900 to exchange, how many euro will he get?

   (b) Ten minutes later, Michael walks into the office looking for $900. How many euro will he have to pay for these?
   (c) What profit does the office make on these two transactions?

6. The graph shows the relationship between euro (€) and pounds sterling (£) over a particular period of time.

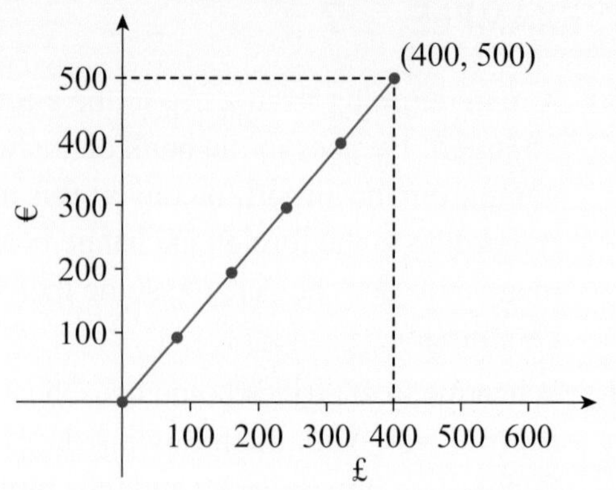

Use the graph to find:
   (a) the slope of the straight line,
   (b) the equation of the straight line,
   (c) how many euro you get for £200,
   (d) how many pounds you get for €300,
   (e) the exchange rate from euro to pounds (how many pounds you get for €1).

What does the slope tell you about the relationship between € and £ over this period of time?

14.2 Tax

VAT

Value added tax (VAT) is a government tax on consumer spending. Everyone who pays for goods and services pays VAT. Usually the VAT is built into the price of the goods or services. For example, the price of *The Irish Times* newspaper is €2 (including VAT). This means that you pay €2 for the paper, but the Government gets a cut of the €2.

Rates of VAT

The rates of VAT vary from country to country in the EU and from year to year. In 2015 in Ireland, the **standard rate** of VAT was 23%. This rate applies to all goods and services that do not fall into the reduced rate categories of 13·5% and 9%. Some goods and services are VAT exempt. This means they have a zero rating (0%) of VAT. The table below shows the VAT rates in Ireland in 2015.

Standard rate	23%	Cars/televisions/paper/food/consultancy services
Reduced rate	13·5%	Fuel/electricity/building services
Reduced rate	9%	Restaurants/cinemas/newspapers
Zero rate	0%	Bread/milk/educational services

TIP

Always assume the price of goods or services excluding VAT is 100%.

EXAMPLE 8

A laptop as advertised on television costs €420, excluding VAT. If the VAT rate is 23%, what is the actual cost to the buyer?

Solution

Cost without VAT = 100% = €420

Actual cost = 123% = €420 × 1·23 = €516·60

EXAMPLE 9

A restaurant bill comes to €59·95 including VAT at 9%. If eating in restaurants was VAT exempt, what would the bill have cost?

Solution

Bill with VAT = 109% = €59·95

Bill without VAT = 100% = $€\frac{59 \cdot 95}{109} \times 100 = €55$

EXAMPLE 10

Mary buys a pair of shoes in Spain at a bargain price of €48 (VAT included). The sales assistant tells her that the price would have been €40 if the VAT had not been included.

(a) What is the VAT rate on shoes in Spain?

(b) What would she have paid in Ireland for a pair of shoes that cost €40, excluding VAT of 23%?

Solution

(a) Rate of VAT = $\frac{(48 - 40)}{40} \times 100 = 20\%$

(b) Cost excluding VAT = €40

Cost including VAT = €40 × 1·23 = €49·20

EXAMPLE 11

The Kennys decide to redecorate their kitchen. They sit down to calculate the cost and set out their estimates as follows:

1. **Measurements:**
   - **(a)** Area of floor to be tiled = 13 m^2
   - **(b)** Area of walls to be tiled = 7·7 m^2
2. **Raw material costs:**
   - **(a)** Cost of floor tiles = €60 per m^2
   - **(b)** Cost of wall tiles = €42 per m^2
   - **(c)** Cost of paint = €88
     Costs all include VAT.
3. **Labour costs:**
   The tiler charges €45 per hour excluding VAT at 13·5%.
4. **Other:**
   The cost of grout and adhesive is €44 excluding VAT at 23%.
   What is the Kenny's estimate, assuming the tiler takes 20 hours to complete the job?

Solution

Cost of floor tiles	€60 × 13	= €780
Cost of wall tiles	€42 × 7·7	= €323·40
Cost of paint		= €88
Cost of grout and adhesive	€44 × 1·23	= €54·12
Labour costs	€45 × 20 × 1·135	= €1021·50
Estimated cost		= €2267·02

ACTIVITY 3

ACTION
Calculating tax on earnings

OBJECTIVE
To calculate the tax to be paid on a single person's and married person's salary

Taxes on earnings

The total amount of money (gross income) you earn in a year is subject to various taxes. What you see at the top of your payslip is not what you get. The Government takes its cut of your earnings.

1. PRSI and USC

PRSI (Pay Related Social Insurance) and USC (Universal Social Charge) are taxes on your gross income. A person on a gross yearly salary of €42 000 would pay PRSI of €1680 and USC of €1603·06 in 2016.

Most employees pay PRSI at a rate of 4%. USC is levied in bands. The first €12 012 is levied at 1%, the next €6656 is levied at 3%, the next €51 376 at 5·5%, and the remainder at 8%.

2. Income tax

Income tax is applied to your gross income at two rates:

- The **standard rate** of 20% is applied to the first €33 800 of your salary.
- The **higher rate** of 40% is applied to the remainder of your salary.

EXAMPLE 12

A person has a gross yearly salary of €46 000. What is their gross yearly income tax if the first €33 800 is taxed at 20% and the remainder is taxed at 40%?

Solution

Gross income = €46 000

20% of €33 800 = €6760

40% of €12 200 = €4880

Gross income tax = €6760 + €4880 = €11 640

To reduce their income tax every person is given **tax credits**.

3. Tax credits

A tax credit is an amount of money which is used to reduce your gross income tax. The amount depends on personal circumstances. For most single workers it is €3300 per year.

So after all of this, how do you calculate your yearly take-home (net) pay?

Steps to calculate your net yearly income:

1. Calculate your gross income tax and then reduce this by your tax credits to get your net income tax deduction.
2. Calculate your PRSI and USC deductions on your gross income.
3. Subtract your PRSI, USC and net income tax deductions from your gross income to get your net income.

EXAMPLE 13

An IT worker has a gross salary of €52 000 per year.

(a) Calculate his gross income tax per year if the first €33 800 is taxed at 20% and the remainder is taxed at 40%.

(b) Calculate his net income tax per year if his tax credits amount to €3300 per year.

(c) Calculate his total deductions if his PRSI and USC deductions amount to €4233·06.

(d) Calculate his net yearly income.

Solution

Gross yearly income = €52 000

(a) Gross income tax:
€33 800 at 20% = €6760
€18 200 at 40% = 7280
Gross income tax = €6760 + €7280 = €14 040

(b) Net income tax = €14 040 – €3300 = €10 740

(c) Net income tax = €10 740
USC/PRSI = €4233·06
Total deductions = €10 740 + €4233·06
= €14 973·06

(d) Gross yearly income = €52 000
Total deductions = €14 973·06
Net yearly income = €52 000 – €14 973·06
= €37 026·94

EXAMPLE 14

A teacher has a gross yearly income of €47 000. Her yearly tax credits are €3300.

(a) Find her gross yearly income tax if the first €33 800 is taxed at 20% and the remainder at 40%.

(b) Find her net income tax per year.

(c) Find her USC and PRSI deductions if her net yearly income is €34 502.

Solution

Gross yearly income = € 47 000

(a) € 33 800 at 20% = €6760
€13 200 at 40% = €5280
Gross income tax = €6760 + €5280 = €12 040

(b) Net income tax = €12 040 – €3300 = €8740

(c) Net income = €34 502
Total deductions = €47 000 – €34 502 = €12 498
PRSI and USC deductions = €12 498 – €8740
= €3758

EXERCISE 3

1. A jacket costs €220 before VAT is applied at 23%. How much does the customer pay for the jacket?
2. A camera costs £289 before VAT is applied at 20%. What price does the buyer pay for the camera?
3. A gaming console in listed online at US $250 excluding VAT. If Seamus in Dublin wants to buy this console, he will have to pay VAT at 23% on the price in euro. How much will he actually pay for the console if the exchange rate applied is $1 = €0·714?
4. An LED TV costs €357 including VAT. What price does the customer pay?
5. A laptop costs €458 including VAT at 21% in Spain. What is the cost of the laptop before VAT?
6. A meal in a restaurant in Cork costs €68 including VAT at 9%. What is the cost of the meal before VAT is applied?
7. A tourist to Ireland buys silver costing €325·47 including VAT at 23%. She is told by the sales assistant that she will get a refund of the amount of VAT paid if she presents her receipt at Dublin Airport. How much of a refund is she due?

8. The price of a car is €33 000 excluding VAT. The table below shows the VAT rates in all 19 eurozone countries:

Country	Standard VAT rate (%)
Austria	20
Belgium	21
Cyprus	19
Estonia	20
Finland	24
France	20
Germany	19
Greece	23
Ireland	23
Italy	22
Latvia	21
Lithuania	21
Luxembourg	17
Malta	18
The Netherlands	21
Portugal	23
Slovakia	20
Slovenia	22
Spain	21

(a) What is the lowest price you could pay for this car?

(b) What is the highest price you could pay for this car?

9. A car dealership in a European country has VAT at 18% included in its car prices. If the price of a Sports Spitfire is €42 000, find the price of the car excluding VAT. In the Budget, the VAT rate was increased to 20%. What is the price of the car to the consumer after the Budget?

10. The O'Connors get an extension to their house costing €17 700 before VAT. VAT on labour is 13·5% and VAT on materials is 23%. How much will the extension cost if the labour costs were €7600 excluding VAT?

11. A woman has a salary of €30 000 per year. She pays income tax at 20% on all of her salary. What is her gross income tax? If her tax credits are €3300, find her net income tax.

12. AJ pays income tax, USC and PRSI on his income. His gross weekly wages are €500.

(a) He pays income tax at 20% on all of his wages. He has a weekly tax credit of €63. How much income tax does he pay?

(b) He pays USC at 1% on the first €231, 3% on the next €128 and 5·5% on the remainder of his gross weekly wages. What are his USC deductions?

(c) He also pays PRSI at a rate of 4% on his gross weekly wages. How much PRSI does he pay?

(d) What are his total weekly deductions?

(e) What is his net weekly wage?

13. Sarah's gross yearly salary is €56 000.

(a) Her PRSI is 4% of her gross salary. What is her PRSI?

(b) Her USC is 1% on the first €12 012, 3% on the next €6656 and 5·5% on the remainder. How much USC is deducted?

(c) Her income tax is 20% on the first €33 800 of her salary and 40% on the remainder. Her yearly tax credits are €3370. Find her net income tax.

(d) Find her net yearly salary and her net monthly take-home pay.

14. A man pays PRSI at 4% of his gross yearly income. If his PRSI amounts to €1920, find his gross yearly income. If USC is applied to the first €12 012 of his gross yearly income at 1%, the next €6656 at 3% and the remainder at 5·5%, find his total USC deductions.

15. A man pays tax on the first €33 800 of his gross yearly income at 20% and the remainder at 40%. Find his gross yearly income if his tax credits are €3300 and his net income tax is €12 936.

16. A computer programmer pays USC at 1% on the first €12 012 of his gross yearly income, 3% on the next €6656 and 5·5% on the remainder. If his total USC deductions are €3068·48, find:

(a) his gross yearly income,

(b) his PRSI contributions at 4% of his gross income,

(c) his net yearly income if the first €33 800 is taxed at 20% and the remainder at 40%, given his tax credits are €3300 per annum.

14.3 Buying and selling

Profit and loss

1. Profit

WORKED EXAMPLE Understanding profit and loss

A man buys a painting in an auction for €150. He sells it three years later for €450.

The price at which you buy something is known as the **cost price** (CP).

The cost price of the painting: CP = €150

The price at which you sell something is known as the **selling price** (SP).

The selling price of the painting: SP = €450

The man has made a **profit** (P) of €300.

His profit: P = SP – CP = €450 – €150 = €300

He has made this profit on a purchase price of €150.

His **percentage profit**: $(\%P) = \frac{300}{150} \times 100\% = 200\%$

$$\text{Percentage profit } (\%P) = \frac{\text{Profit}}{\text{Cost price}} \times 100\%$$

Percentage profit is also known as **percentage mark-up**.

The **profit margin** is the percentage of the selling price that is turned into profit.

The profit margin on the painting $= \frac{300}{450} \times 100\%$
$= 66\frac{2}{3}\%$

Profit (P) = Selling price (SP) – Cost price (CP)

$$\text{Percentage profit} = \frac{\text{Profit}}{\text{Cost price}} \times 100\%$$

$$\text{Profit margin} = \frac{\text{Profit}}{\text{Selling price}} \times 100\%$$

2. Loss

WORKED EXAMPLE

Calculating percentage loss

NAMA bought a hotel for €540 000 in 2010 and sold it in 2013 for €400 000.

NAMA has made a loss (L) = €540 000 – €400 000 = €140 000

The loss L = CP – SP = €140 000

Percentage loss $= \frac{140\,000}{540\,000} \times 100\% = 25{\cdot}9\%$

This **percentage loss** is also known as **percentage discount**.

Loss (L) = Cost price (CP) – Selling price (SP)

Percentage loss $= \frac{\text{Loss}}{\text{Cost price}} \times 100\%$

EXAMPLE 15

A shop gives a discount of 40% on the original price of a bicycle in a sale. If the sale price is €168, find the original price.

Solution

SP = €168 = 60% of CP

$\text{CP} = \frac{€168}{0{\cdot}6} = €280$

EXAMPLE 16

A retail games store buys game consoles from a wholesaler for €180 each. The store marks up the price by 62%. What is the selling price of a console?

Solution

Cost price = €180

SP = 162% of CP = €180 × 1·62 = €291·60

EXAMPLE 17

A furniture store has a New Year's sale in which there is a 20% discount on all items less than €1000 and a discount of 30% on all items that are priced at €1000 or more. Ms Rice buys a table for €700, a bed for €1200 and a sideboard for €1000. How much does she pay for all three items?

Solution

Cost of table = €700 × 0·8 = €560

Cost of bed = €1200 × 0·7 = €840

Cost of sideboard = €1000 × 0·7 = €700

Total spend = €560 + €840 + €700 = €2100

EXERCISE 4

1. Copy and complete the following tables:

(a)

Cost price	Selling price	Profit	% Profit	Profit margin
€100	€150			
	€300	€120		
€250			25%	
	€72			30%
€72		€88		

(b)

Cost price	Selling price	Loss	% Loss
€100	€75		
€172		€85	
	€100	€70	

2. (a) What percentage is €137·52 of €687·60?

   (b) A ring is bought for €852 and sold for a profit of 26%. What is the selling price?

3. Bucket Electronics wants to decrease the price of a laptop from €560 to €480. What percentage discount must they advertise, correct to one decimal place?

4. A man goes to Northern Ireland to buy a television set priced at £420. During a sale there is a discount on this price of 15%. How many euro must the man change into pounds sterling to cover the cost of the television in the sales if €1 = £0·80?

5. A retailer bought 150 games for Christmas at €23·50 each. She sold 90 at €45 each and the remainder at a 20% discount.

   (a) What was the value of her total sales?

   (b) What was her percentage profit correct to one decimal place?

   (c) What was her profit margin correct to one decimal place?

6. PC Universe bought 100 external hard drives at €78 each and 58 USB cables at €12 each. It made a 55% profit on the sale of each hard drive. All items were sold. If the total amount of sales was €12 925·20, find the percentage profit on the USB cables.

7. The selling price S in euro of a car after t years can be expressed as follows:

   $S = 30\,000(0{\cdot}87)^t$

   (a) What is the current selling price?

   (b) What will the selling price be in 3 years?

Financial Maths 2

Learning Outcomes

- To distinguish between simple interest and compound interest and to solve problems involving both.
- To understand AER and APR.
- To solve problems on depreciation by the reducing balance method.
- To understand the time value of money and its implications when borrowing and saving.
- To be able to perform calculations involving mortgages, bonds, lotteries and pensions using a geometric series.

15.1 Calculating interest

When individuals or financial institutions lend money they expect the original amount of money to be repaid in full. In addition, they expect the borrower to pay them a charge for the privilege of using their money.

The original amount of money is called the **principal** P and the charge for the privilege of using the money is called the **interest** I.

- Mr O'Brien repaid a loan of €12 000 (principal) with interest of €1585. This means for the privilege of using the €12 000, he has to pay an extra €1585.
- Mrs Brown invested €5000 in a building society for a year. At the end of the year she withdrew her investment, which amounted to €5250. Therefore, the building society paid her interest of €250 for using her money.

ACTIVITY 4

ACTION
Working with simple interest

OBJECTIVE
To go through the steps to calculate the simple interest on a sum of money

The **interest** on an investment or a loan can be calculated in two ways: simple interest or compound interest.

Simple interest

Simple interest is the interest applied to an investment or a loan by calculating the interest on the **original principal only** at the end of each period of interest (usually per year).

In simple interest, only the original principal earns interest.

WORKED EXAMPLE

How simple interest is calculated

€1200 is invested for 3 years at 4% per annum simple interest.

Note: Per annum (p.a.) means per year.

The interest after 1 year = 4% of €1200 = €1200 × 0·04 = €48

The value of the investment after 1 year is €1248.

During the second year, the interest is applied to the original principal of €1200 only, and not on €1248.

The interest for the second year is also €48.

After 2 years, the total interest = 2 × €48 = €96.

After 3 years, the total interest = 3 × €48 = €144.

The interest on €1200 invested for **3 years** at simple interest of 4% p.a. is given by:

$I = €1200 \times 0{\cdot}04 \times 3 = €1200 \times \frac{4}{100} \times 3 = €144$

This idea can be generalised into the simple interest formula:

$$I = \frac{P \times r \times t}{100}$$

where:

I = simple interest

P = principal (the amount borrowed or lent)

r = percentage rate (per year)

t = duration or term of the loan or investment (in years)

EXAMPLE 1

Calculate the simple interest on a loan of €22 000 at a rate of 6·5% p.a. over 2 years and 6 months.

Solution

$P = €22\,000$

$r = 6{\cdot}5\%$

$t = 2{\cdot}5$ years

$I = \frac{P \times r \times t}{100} = \frac{22\,000 \times 6{\cdot}5 \times 2{\cdot}5}{100} = €3575$

EXAMPLE 2

What interest rate per annum must I get so that €10 000 will earn €1260 simple interest in 3 years?

Solution

$P = €10\,000$

$I = €1260$

$t = 3$ years

$r = ?$

$I = \frac{P \times r \times t}{100}$

$r = \frac{100I}{Pt}$

$r = \frac{100 \times 1260}{10\,000 \times 3} = 4{\cdot}2$

$r = 4{\cdot}2\%$

Simple interest repayments

Normally loans are repaid in regular equal amounts over the term of the loan rather than at the end of the term. The principal and the interest must be repaid in full by the end of the term. For simple interest loans, it is easy to work out the amount of each repayment using the formula:

$$\text{Amount of each repayment} = \frac{\text{Total amount to be repaid}}{\text{Number of repayments}}$$

EXAMPLE 3

Calculate the monthly repayments on a car loan of €18 000 at a simple interest rate of 7·2% p.a. over 5 years.

Solution

$P = €18\,000$

$r = 7·2\%$

$t = 5$ years

$I = \frac{18\,000 \times 7·2 \times 5}{100} = €6480$

Total repayment = €18 000 + €6480 = €24 480

Amount of each monthly payment $= \frac{€24\,480}{5 \times 12} = €408$

ACTIVITY 5

ACTION
Mastering the compound interest formula

OBJECTIVE
To go through the steps to calculate the compound interest on a sum of money

Compound interest

When compound interest is applied to a loan or an investment, the principal at the start of a period of interest is the sum of the principal and interest at the end of the preceding period. €50 interest on a principal of €1000 invested at compound interest at the end of a year gives a principal of €1050 at the start of the second year.

> In compound interest, both the interest and the principal earn interest for the second period and all future periods.

You earn interest when you put your money into a savings account. The rate r tells you how much interest you earn. The final value (also called future value) F of the money at the end of the saving period will be greater than the present value or principal P of the money when you start saving.

WORKED EXAMPLE

Understanding the compound interest formula

Calculate the interest earned on €100 invested at an annual rate of 4·5%.

Annual rate (percentage) $r = 4·5\%$

i is the annual rate of interest expressed as a fraction or decimal.

Annual rate of interest $i = \frac{4·5}{100} = 0·045$

Interest earned = €100 × 0·045 = €4·50

If you add this interest to the original principal or present amount P, you have the final sum or future value F of money in the bank.

$F = €100 + €4·50 = €104·50$

This can be done in one go, as follows:

$F = €100(1 + 0·045) = €100(1·045) = €104·50$

Your money is invested for 3 years at compound interest. How much is it worth after this time?

Year 1: $F = €100(1·045) = €104·50$

Year 2: $F = €104·50(1·045) = €109·2025$

Year 3: $F = €109·2025(1·045)$
$= €114·1166125 \approx €114·12$

There is obviously a quicker way to do this calculation:

$F = €100(1·045)^3 = €114·12$

The present value is €100. The future value after 3 years is €114·12.

There is a general formula given in the *Formulae and Tables* book for calculating compound interest:

$$F = P(1 + i)^t$$

where:

F = final sum (future value)

P = principal (present value)

t = time (years)

i = (annual) rate of interest as a decimal or fraction

EXAMPLE 4

€850 is invested for 6 years at an annual interest rate of 4·5%. Calculate the final amount and the interest earned.

Solution

$i = 0{\cdot}045$

$P = €850$

$t = 6$ years

$F = ?$

$I = ?$

$F = P(1+i)^t$

$F = 850(1{\cdot}045)^6 = €1106{\cdot}92$

$I = F - P$

$= €1106{\cdot}92 - €850$

$= €256{\cdot}92$

EXAMPLE 5

€8500 is invested for 7 years at a certain annual interest rate, yielding €12 201·62. What was the annual interest rate?

Solution

$P = €8500$

$F = €12\,201{\cdot}62$

$t = 7$ years

$i = ?$

$F = P(1+i)^t$

$12\,201{\cdot}62 = 8500(1+i)^7$

$\frac{12\,201{\cdot}62}{8500} = (1+i)^7$

$\left(\frac{12\,201{\cdot}62}{8500}\right)^{\frac{1}{7}} = 1+i$

$i = \left(\frac{12\,201{\cdot}62}{8500}\right)^{\frac{1}{7}} - 1$

$= 0{\cdot}0529999$

$r = 5{\cdot}3\%$

EXAMPLE 6

€4950 is invested for a certain time at an annual interest rate of 3·6%, yielding €6120·17. How long was the money invested?

Solution

$P = €4950$

$i = 0{\cdot}036$

$F = €6120{\cdot}17$

$t = ?$

$F = P(1+i)^t$

$6120{\cdot}17 = 4950(1{\cdot}036)^t$

$\frac{6120{\cdot}17}{4950} = 1{\cdot}036^t$

$\log_{10}\left(\frac{6120{\cdot}17}{4950}\right) = \log_{10}1{\cdot}036^t$

$\log_{10}\left(\frac{6120{\cdot}17}{4950}\right) = t\log_{10}1{\cdot}036$

$t = \frac{\log_{10}\left(\frac{6120{\cdot}17}{4950}\right)}{\log_{10}1{\cdot}036} = 6\text{ years}$

EXAMPLE 7

A sum of money is invested for 10 years at an annual rate of 4·25%, yielding €1243·30. What was the original sum invested?

Solution

$i = 0{\cdot}0425$

$F = €1243{\cdot}30$

$t = 10$ years

$P = ?$

$F = P(1+i)^t$

$P = \frac{F}{(1+i)^t}$

$= \frac{1243{\cdot}30}{1{\cdot}0425^{10}}$

$= €820$

Annual equivalent rate (AER)

Various financial institutions offer their financial products in a variety of ways. You may be told that you can double your money in 10 years or you will receive a monthly interest rate of 0·75%. It is difficult to compare all of these products to see which will yield you the greatest amount of interest.

To simplify the process, these institutions are legally obliged to tell you the **annual equivalent rate** (AER) of the product you are being offered.

WORKED EXAMPLE Calculating the annual equivalent rate (AER)

You have €5000 to put into a savings account. Bank A is offering a financial product which promises you that your money will increase its value by 20% after 5 years. Bank B tells you that your money will earn interest annually at 4%. Which product should you choose?

AER of Bank A: ?

AER of Bank B: 4%

Calculate the sum of money in your account in Bank A after 5 years.

$F = 5000(1{\cdot}2) = €6000$

Now work out the interest rate that yields the same sum of money (€6000) compounded annually for 5 years.

$P = €5000$

$F = €6000$

$t = 5$ years

$i = ?$

$F = P(1 + i)^t$

$6000 = 5000(1 + i)^5$

$1{\cdot}2 = (1 + i)^5$

$1{\cdot}2^{\frac{1}{5}} = 1 + i$

$\therefore i = 1{\cdot}2^{\frac{1}{5}} - 1 = 0{\cdot}0371$

$\therefore r = 3{\cdot}7\%$

Choose Bank B's product as it is offering a slightly higher AER.

In general, work out the AER as follows:

What is the AER of receiving a 20% increase after 5 years on your investment?

Given rate: $F = P(1{\cdot}2)$

AER: $F = P(1 + i)^5$

$\therefore P(1{\cdot}2) = P(1 + i)^5$

$(1{\cdot}2)^{\frac{1}{5}} = (1 + i)$

$\therefore i = 1{\cdot}2^{\frac{1}{5}} - 1 = 0{\cdot}0371$

$\therefore r = 3{\cdot}7\%$

EXAMPLE 8

A sum of money is invested for 8 years at a certain annual rate, giving a percentage increase in the original sum of 42·2%. What is the annual interest rate (AER), correct to one decimal place?

Solution

$P(1{\cdot}422) = P(1 + i)^8$

$(1 + i) = 1{\cdot}422^{\frac{1}{8}}$

$i = 1{\cdot}422^{\frac{1}{8}} - 1 = 0{\cdot}045$

$r = 4{\cdot}5\%$

EXAMPLE 9

The annual interest rate is 6·5%. What is the monthly interest rate? What is the weekly interest rate? Calculate each percentage rate to three decimal places. €3500 is invested for 2 years. Find the final amount by compounding annually, monthly and weekly, using the appropriate interest rate for each period.

Solution

$r = 6{\cdot}5\%$ (annual interest rate)

$i = 0{\cdot}065$ (annual interest)

Monthly rate	Weekly rate
$P(1 + i)^{12} = P(1{\cdot}065)^1$	$P(1 + i)^{52} = P(1{\cdot}065)^1$
$(1 + i)^{12} = 1{\cdot}065$	$(1 + i)^{52} = 1{\cdot}065$
$i = 1{\cdot}065^{\frac{1}{12}} - 1 = 0{\cdot}00526$	$i = 1{\cdot}065^{\frac{1}{52}} - 1 = 0{\cdot}00121$
$r = 0{\cdot}526\%$	$r = 0{\cdot}121\%$

When you use the annual interest rate, the time needs to be in years, in this case 2 years.

Annually: $F = P(1 + i)^t = 3500(1{\cdot}065)^2 = €3969{\cdot}79$

When you use the monthly interest rate, the time needs to be in months, in this case 24 months.

Monthly: $F = P(1 + i)^t = 3500(1{\cdot}00526)^{24} = €3969{\cdot}63$

When you use the weekly interest rate, the time needs to be in weeks, in this case 104 weeks.

Weekly: $F = P(1 + i)^t = 3500(1{\cdot}00121)^{104} = €3969{\cdot}05$

As you can see, the answers are slightly different due to rounding errors.

Using the formula:

If t is in years, use the annual interest rate.

If t is in months, use the monthly interest rate.

Whatever the time period is, use the interest rate for that time period.

i is the annual interest rate (AER).

The monthly interest rate i_M: $(1 + i_M) = (1 + i)^{\frac{1}{12}} \Rightarrow i_M = (1 + i)^{\frac{1}{12}} - 1$

The weekly interest rate i_W: $(1 + i_W) = (1 + i)^{\frac{1}{52}} \Rightarrow i_W = (1 + i)^{\frac{1}{52}} - 1$

EXAMPLE 10

(a) A company advertises an investment where your money is compounded monthly at a monthly rate of 0·55%. If you invest €2500 in this investment scheme, how much is your money worth after 18 months?

(b) All investment products are legally obliged to give the annual equivalent rate (AER). What is the AER for this product, correct to one decimal place?

(c) Using the AER, calculate the worth of the investment after 18 months.

Solution

(a) $r = 0{\cdot}55$ (monthly rate)

$i = 0{\cdot}0055$ (monthly interest)

$P = €2500$

$t = 18$ months

$F = ?$

The time is in months when the monthly interest rate is used.

$F = P(1 + i)^t = 2500(1{\cdot}0055)^{18} = €2759{\cdot}42$

(b) $P(1 + i)^1 = P(1{\cdot}0055)^{12}$

$1 + i = 1{\cdot}0055^{12}$

$i = 1{\cdot}0055^{12} - 1 = 0{\cdot}068$

$r = 6{\cdot}8\%$

(c) $i = 0{\cdot}068$ (annual rate)

$P = €2500$

$t = \frac{18}{12}$ years

$F = ?$

The time is in years when the yearly interest rate is used.

$F = P(1 + i)^t = 2500(1{\cdot}068)^{\frac{18}{12}} = €2759{\cdot}29$

Note: It makes no difference to the future value of your investment whether you compound annually or monthly provided you use the appropriate interest for the period in question.

Depreciation

The value of most assets decreases for many reasons as time passes. They become unfashionable, they may suffer wear and tear, or they become inefficient. However, some items increase in price over time, like gold or antiques. Their value appreciates.

One method for calculating depreciation is called the **reducing balance method**. In this method, the value of an item is decreased by the same fixed percentage every year.

WORKED EXAMPLE

Calculating depreciation

A car bought for €26 000 depreciates by 18% every year. What is its value after 3 years?

At the end of the first year, the value = 82% of €26 000 = €26 000 × 0·82 = €21 320

At the end of the second year, the value = 82% of €21 320 = €21 320 × 0·82

= €26 000 × (0·82) × (0·82) = €26 000 × $(0{\cdot}82)^2$

= €17 482·40

At the end of the third year, the value = 82% of €17 482·40

= €17 482·40 × (0·82)

= €26 000 × $(0{\cdot}82)^2 \times 0{\cdot}82$

= €26 000 × $(0{\cdot}82)^3$ = €14 335·57

In general, the final value F of an item, which depreciates at r% per depreciation period, is given by:

$F = P\left(1 - \frac{r}{100}\right)^t$, where P is the initial value of the item and t is the time in years.

The depreciation formula can also be written as:

$F = P(1 - i)^t$, where $i = \frac{r}{100}$ is the decimal rate of depreciation.

The general formula for calculating depreciation is given in the *Formulae and Tables* book:

$$F = P(1 - i)^t$$

F = final value (future value)

P = principal (present value)

t = time (years)

i = (annual) rate of interest as a decimal or fraction

EXAMPLE 11

A washing machine is bought for €580. It depreciates at 15% p.a. What is its value after 5 years? By how much has it depreciated in 5 years?

Solution

P = €580

$t = 5$ years

$r = 15\%$

$i = 0{\cdot}15$

$F = P(1 - i)^t = 580(1 - 0{\cdot}15)^5 = 580(0{\cdot}85)^5$

F = €257·35

It has depreciated by €580 – €257·35 = €322·65.

EXAMPLE 12

Joe bought a scooter for €1500. After 3 years he estimated its value at €768. Calculate the percentage rate of depreciation p.a. using the reducing balance method.

Solution

F = €768

P = €1500

$t = 3$ years

$F = P(1 - i)^t \Rightarrow 768 = 1500(1 - i)^3$

$\frac{768}{1500} = \frac{64}{125} = (1 - i)^3$

$1 - i = \left(\frac{64}{125}\right)^{\frac{1}{3}} = \frac{4}{5}$

$i = 1 - \frac{4}{5} = \frac{1}{5} = 0{\cdot}2$

$\therefore r = 20\%$

EXAMPLE 13

A company purchases an asset for €25 000. The asset has a useful lifetime of 4 years before it is scrapped. The scrap value is estimated to be €4000. The asset is estimated to depreciate at 36·75% p.a. The accountant has two methods available to her for calculating depreciation on this asset: the reducing balance method and the straight line method. Carry out the calculations for each method showing the value of the asset after each year and the amount by which the asset has depreciated. Comment on which method should be used.

Solution

Reducing balance method:
Use the formula $F = P(1 - i)^t$:

$P = €25\,000$

$r = 36·75$

$i = 0·3675$

Year 1: $F = 25\,000(1 - 0·3675)^1 = €15\,812·50$

Loss in value = €25 000 – €15 812·50 = €9187·50

Year 2: $F = €25\,000(1 - 0·3675)^2 = €10\,001·41$

Loss in value = €25 000 – €10 001·41 = €14 998·59

Year	Value	Depreciation
0	€25 000·00	0
1	€15 812·50	€9187·50
2	€10 001·41	€14 998·59
3	€6325·89	€18 674·11
4	€4001·13	€20 998·87

Straight line method:
The formula for this method is in the *Formulae and Tables* book:

$$A = \frac{P - S}{t}$$

A = annual depreciation amount

P = initial value

S = scrap value

t = useful economic life

In this example, $P = €25\,000$, $S = €4000$, $t = 4$ years

$$A = \frac{P - S}{t} = \frac{25\,000 - 4000}{4} = €5250$$

Year	Value	Depreciation
0	€25 000	0
1	€19 750	€5250
2	€14 500	€10 500
3	€9250	€15 750
4	€4000	€21 000

One major difference between the two methods is that in the reducing balance method the asset has lost much more of its value in the first year compared to the straight line method. The reducing balance method gives you a truer value of your asset. For example, most of the value of a new car is lost the second you drive it out of the salesroom.

Although the reducing balance depreciation formula, $F = P(1 - i)^t$, is normally applied to monetary problems, it can be used for any item that depreciates.

EXAMPLE 14

Michael goes on a diet. His goal is to decrease his body weight in kg by 1% per week. If he achieves this goal, what will his weight be after 6 weeks if his initial weight is 80 kg? Give this weight correct to one decimal place. What is his percentage change in weight after 6 weeks, correct to one decimal place?

Solution

$P = 80$ kg

$i = 0·01$

$t = 6$ weeks

$F = 80(1 - 0·01)^6 = 80(0·99)^6 = 75·3$ kg

His percentage change in weight $= \frac{\text{Change in weight}}{\text{Original weight}} \times 100\% = \frac{(80 - 75·3)}{80} \times 100\% = 5·9\%$

EXERCISE 5

1. **(a)** Calculate the simple interest on a loan of €15 500 at a rate of 5·5% p.a. over 2 years and 6 months.

   (b) Calculate the simple interest on a loan of €675 at a rate of 8·75% p.a. over 3·5 years.

   (c) What interest rate per annum must I get so that €12 000 will yield €1500 in 3 years using simple interest? Give your answer correct to one decimal place.

   (d) What interest rate per annum must I get so that €875 will yield €1200 in 4 years using simple interest? Give your answer correct to one decimal place.

   (e) Calculate the monthly repayments on a car loan of €12 700 at a simple interest rate of 6·2% p.a. over 5 years.

2. A suite of furniture has a total purchase price of €4200. John buys the suite on the following terms: 10% deposit with the balance plus simple interest paid monthly at 8% p.a. over 4 years.

   (a) Calculate the amount of the deposit.

   (b) What is the balance owing after the initial deposit?

   (c) Calculate the interest payable.

   (d) What is the total amount to be repaid?

   (e) Find the amount of each monthly repayment.

3. Michelle wants to buy a used car that has a cash price of €13 500. The dealer offers terms of 10% deposit and monthly repayments of €372·94 for 3 years.

   (a) Calculate the amount of the deposit.

   (b) Calculate the total amount to be paid in monthly repayments.

   (c) What is the total amount Michelle pays for the car?

   (d) How much more than the cash price of the car does Michelle pay?

   (e) What is simple interest per annum charged by the dealer? Give your answer correct to two decimal places.

4. Jack wants to purchase a car. He has saved €1500 as a deposit but the cost of the car is €5000. Jack takes out a loan from the bank to cover the balance of the car plus €1150 to cover his insurance costs.

   (a) How much will Jack need to borrow from the bank?

   (b) Jack takes the loan out over 3 years at 7·5% p.a. simple interest. How much interest will Jack pay?

   (c) What are Jack's monthly repayments?

   (d) What is the total cost of the car after paying off the loan, including the insurance costs?

5. Lara borrows €15 000 over 4 years from the bank. The loan is charged at 7·4% p.a. simple interest. The loan is to be repaid in equal monthly instalments. Calculate the amount of each monthly repayment.

6. **(a)** How much does €10 000 amount to at 3% p.a. compound interest after:

   (i) 1 year,

   (ii) 2 years,

   (iii) 3 years?

   (b) How much does €25 000 amount to at 2·5% p.a. compound interest after:

   (i) 1 year,

   (ii) 2 years,

   (iii) 3 years?

7. **(a)** How much does €10 000 amount to in 2 years at an AER of 1·5%?

   (b) How much does €22 000 amount to in 3 years at an AER of 2·4%?

8. Paula invests €6000 for 5 years at 9% p.a. simple interest. Eoin also invests €6000 for 5 years, but his interest rate is 7·6% p.a. with interest compounded annually.

   (a) Calculate the value of Paula's investment on maturity.

(b) Calculate the value of Eoin's investment on maturity. Give your answer to the nearest euro.

(c) Which investment is more profitable and by how much?

9. (a) What principal must be invested to amount to €21 500 in 2 years at an AER of 2%?

(b) What principal must be invested to amount to €15 600 in 3 years at an AER of 3·4%?

(c) What sum of money invested at an AER of 4·5% will amount to €22 823·32 in 3 years?

10. (a) What is the AER if €12 600 amounts to €13 000 in 2 years? Give your answer correct to two decimal places.

(b) What is the AER if €28 400 amounts to €30 500 in 3 years? Give your answer correct to one decimal place.

11. (a) €7500 is invested for a certain length of time at an annual compound interest rate of 3·2%, yielding €8507·07. How long was the money invested?

(b) €4525 is invested for a certain length of time at an annual compound interest rate of 4·25%, giving interest of €1657·85. How long was the money invested?

12. Saving accounts

(a) Bank of Ireland offered a 9-month fixed term account, paying 2·5% on maturity. Find the total value of €10 000 after 9 months.

(b) An Post offers a savings bond giving a gross annual interest of 4% for 3 years. What is the total value of €15 500 at the end of 3 years?

(c) An Post savings bonds give a gross amount of €12 480 on an investment of €12 000 after 3 years. What is the gross percentage interest rate?

(d) An Post savings bonds give an AER of 1·32%. What does an investment of €26 500 amount to in 5 years?

(e) A savings bond amounts to €36 404·38 on an investment of €35 000 in 3 years. What is the AER, correct to two decimal places?

13. Susan inherits €15 000. She wants to invest it in a high-risk fund to double her inheritance in 2 years. What must the AER of the fund be, correct to one decimal place?

14. A double-your-interest account earns 2% interest in the first year and 4% in the second year. The interest is added to the account at the end of each year. If a person invests €25 000 in this account, how much will they have in this account at the end of 2 years? How much more interest can be earned by investing the money in an account for 2 years at 3% AER?

15. €P was invested at r% compound interest. The interest for the first year was €125. The interest for the second year was €131·25. Find r and P.

16. A man borrows €10 000 from a bank for 3 years at an annual percentage rate (APR) of 4·5%. He is given two options to repay the loan.

Option 1: To repay the total principal and interest in 3 years.

Option 2: To repay the loan monthly, using the following loan repayments table.

The APR table shows the monthly repayments on each €1000 borrowed for a loan at a fixed APR for a fixed term.

Number of payments	4%	4·5%	5%
12	85·15	83·38	85·61
24	43·43	43·65	43·87
36	29·50	29·75	29·97
48	22·60	22·80	23·03
60	18·42	18·64	18·87

Find the total cost of repayment:

(a) using option 1,

(b) using option 2 (use the APR repayment table).

Which option is better?

17. A sum of money is invested for 10 years at a certain annual rate giving a percentage increase on the original sum of 36·5%. What is the annual interest rate, correct to two decimal places?

18. An annual interest rate is 4·25%. What is the monthly interest rate? What is the weekly interest rate? Calculate each percentage rate to three decimal places. €2800 is invested for 3 years. Find the final amount by compounding annually, monthly and weekly.

19. A motorcycle which cost €4700 depreciates at a rate of 18% p.a. Find its value after 4 years to the nearest euro using the reducing balance method.

20. A 4 × 4 vehicle depreciated to €20 410 in 5 years at a rate of 15% p.a. Find its original value using the reducing balance method to the nearest euro.

21. A photocopier bought at €24 000 depreciated to €12 288 in 3 years. Find the rate of depreciation using the reducing balance method.

22. A car rental company paid €32 000 for a car. The company expects to rent it out for 3 years and then sell it.

(a) If it depreciates at 25% p.a., find its value after 3 years by the reducing balance method.

(b) If the company sells it at a percentage loss of 10% on its depreciated value, how much does the company get for the car from its sale?

23. The current value of a car is €22 500. It depreciates by 25% p.a. by the reducing balance method. Find the percentage change in value after 2 years.

24. A company purchases an asset for €25 000. The asset has a useful lifetime of 5 years before it is scrapped. The scrap value is estimated to be €7500. The asset is estimated to depreciate at 21·4% p.a. The accountant has two methods available to her for calculating depreciation on this asset: the reducing balance method and the straight line method. Carry out the calculations for each method showing the value of the asset after each year and the amount by which the asset has depreciated.

25. An asset is purchased for €32 500 and has a lifetime of 5 years. After this time, the asset is replaced. Its scrap value is estimated to be €3500.

(a) Using the straight line method of depreciation, calculate the loss in value of the asset each year.

(b) The accountant thinks it is preferable to apply the reducing balance method for depreciation. What percentage rate of depreciation per annum should be applied to the asset to the nearest whole number?

26. A company director buys a new printing press for €650 000. The press depreciates at the rate of 12% p.a. and is written off when its value falls below €120 000. After how many years, to the nearest whole number, should the press be written off?

27. Paul has a computer valued at €P. The value of the computer depreciates by r% annually over a period of 6 years. At the end of the 6 years, the value of the computer has been reduced to one-tenth of its original value. Find the value of r correct to one decimal place.

15.2 Using a geometric series for financial calculations

1. Saving

In a savings account, deposits are often put into the account at regular intervals. For example, you may make a deposit at the beginning of every week or at the beginning of every month.

Each deposit will earn interest for a different period of time. This makes calculating the interest at the end of the saving period quite complicated. The individual deposits form a geometric series.

WORKED EXAMPLE Savings accounts

You are saving money every month in an account. How much is it worth at the end of the saving period? For example, €100 is put into a savings account at the beginning of each month at an annual rate of 5·5%. How much is in the account after 5 years?

There are 60 months in 5 years. The first €100 is invested for 60 months. The second €100 is invested for 59 months. The third €100 is invested for 58 months, and so on. The last €100 is invested for 1 month. What about the interest rate? You need to use the monthly interest rate.

$(1 + i_M) = (1 + i)^{\frac{1}{12}} = (1{\cdot}055)^{\frac{1}{12}}$

The final amount F is calculated as follows:

$$F = 100(1{\cdot}055^{\frac{1}{12}})^{60} + 100(1{\cdot}055^{\frac{1}{12}})^{59} + 100(1{\cdot}055^{\frac{1}{12}})^{58} + \ldots + 100(1{\cdot}055^{\frac{1}{12}})^{1}$$

$$\therefore F = 100(1{\cdot}055)^{\frac{60}{12}} + 100(1{\cdot}055)^{\frac{59}{12}} + 100(1{\cdot}055)^{\frac{58}{12}} + \ldots + 100(1{\cdot}055)^{\frac{1}{12}}$$

This is a geometric series. Rewrite it as follows:

$$F = 100[1{\cdot}055^{\frac{1}{12}} + 1{\cdot}055^{\frac{2}{12}} + \ldots + 1{\cdot}055^{\frac{58}{12}} + 1{\cdot}055^{\frac{59}{12}} + 1{\cdot}055^{\frac{60}{12}}]$$

$$S_n = \frac{a(1 - r^n)}{1 - r}$$

$a = 1{\cdot}055^{\frac{1}{12}}$, $r = 1{\cdot}055^{\frac{1}{12}}$, $n = 60$

$$F = 100 \times \frac{1{\cdot}055^{\frac{1}{12}}(1 - 1{\cdot}055^{\frac{60}{12}})}{1 - 1{\cdot}055^{\frac{1}{12}}} = €6895{\cdot}20$$

You will have €6895·20 in your savings account at the end of 5 years.

Ask the question in reverse. What sum of money would I have to save each month in order to have €10 000 in my account after 5 years at an annual rate of 5·5%? Call the amount of your monthly savings x.

$$F = x(1{\cdot}055)^{\frac{60}{12}} + x(1{\cdot}055)^{\frac{59}{12}} + x(1{\cdot}055)^{\frac{58}{12}} + \ldots + x(1{\cdot}055)^{\frac{1}{12}} = 10\,000$$

$$x[1{\cdot}055^{\frac{1}{12}} + 1{\cdot}055^{\frac{2}{12}} + \ldots + 1{\cdot}055^{\frac{58}{12}} + 1{\cdot}055^{\frac{59}{12}} + 1{\cdot}055^{\frac{60}{12}}] = 10\,000$$

$a = 1{\cdot}055^{\frac{1}{12}}$, $r = 1{\cdot}055^{\frac{1}{12}}$, $n = 60$

$$x \times \frac{1{\cdot}055^{\frac{1}{12}}(1 - 1{\cdot}055^{\frac{60}{12}})}{1 - 1{\cdot}055^{\frac{1}{12}}} = 10\,000$$

$$\therefore x = \frac{10\,000(1 - 1{\cdot}055^{\frac{1}{12}})}{1{\cdot}055^{\frac{1}{12}}(1 - 1{\cdot}055^{\frac{60}{12}})} = €145{\cdot}03$$

You need to save €145·03 every month for 5 years in order to have €10 000 in your account at the end of the saving period.

TIP

Saving monthly: There are 12 saving periods per annum. Each saving amount is multiplied by $(1 + i)^{\frac{1}{12}}$ where i is the annual interest rate.

Saving weekly: There are 52 saving periods per annum. Each saving amount is multiplied by $(1 + i)^{\frac{1}{52}}$ where i is the annual interest rate.

EXAMPLE 15

Brian wishes to have €12 500 in his savings account after 4 years, putting a certain sum of money into his account at the beginning of each month. If the annual interest rate is 6·3%, how much does he invest (save) each month?

Solution

There are 48 months in 4 years. If the first payment is invested at the beginning of the first month, it will be in the account for 48 months. The second payment will be there for 47 months. The last payment will be in the account for 1 month.

$$F = x(1{\cdot}063)^{\frac{48}{12}} + x(1{\cdot}063)^{\frac{47}{12}} + x(1{\cdot}063)^{\frac{46}{12}} + \ldots + x(1{\cdot}063)^{\frac{1}{12}} = 12\,500$$

$$x[1{\cdot}063^{\frac{1}{12}} + 1{\cdot}063^{\frac{2}{12}} + \ldots + 1{\cdot}063^{\frac{46}{12}} + 1{\cdot}063^{\frac{47}{12}} + 1{\cdot}63^{\frac{48}{12}}] = 12\,500$$

$$a = 1{\cdot}063^{\frac{1}{12}},\ r = 1{\cdot}063^{\frac{1}{12}},\ n = 48$$

$$x \times \frac{1{\cdot}063^{\frac{1}{12}}(1 - 1{\cdot}063^{\frac{48}{12}})}{1 - 1{\cdot}063^{\frac{1}{12}}} = 12\,500$$

$$S_n = \frac{a(1 - r^n)}{1 - r}$$

$$\therefore x = \frac{12\,500(1 - 1{\cdot}063^{\frac{1}{12}})}{1{\cdot}063^{\frac{1}{12}}(1 - 1{\cdot}063^{\frac{48}{12}})} = €229{\cdot}31$$

2. Borrowing

Normally when you borrow money from a lender, you pay back the debt in instalments. Trying to calculate how much you should pay back can be a tricky process. The repayments form a geometric series.

APR (annual percentage rate) on loans

Personal loans are used to finance house purchases, college fees, cars, etc. When you take out a loan, it is for a fixed length of time (the term) and the interest charged by the lender is known as the APR (annual percentage rate) and is compound interest.

The interest can be fixed or variable. A fixed rate does not change over the term. For example, a fixed rate of 3·7% for 5 years will be applied for the full term of the loan. The variable rate can change over the term depending on domestic and/or global economic conditions.

Loans are normally repaid monthly on the **reducing balance** of the loan because the loan decreases as repayments are made. This makes it difficult to work out monthly repayments.

The principal P is also called the present value of your money. The final amount F is also called the future value of your money. Remember that money has a time value.

The present value of €100 today is worth €105 in a year's time based on an annual interest rate of 5%. If I left the €100 under the mattress, its value in a year's time would be €95·24. So the present value P of €100 in a year's time is €95·24. How is this calculation carried out?

$F = 100$

$P = ?$ [What sum of money today is worth €100 in a year's time?]

$i = 0{\cdot}05$

$F = P(1 + i)^t$

$\therefore\ P = \dfrac{F}{(1+i)^t} = \dfrac{100}{1{\cdot}05} = €95{\cdot}24$

There is a general formula given in the *Formulae and Tables* book:

$$P = \frac{F}{(1+i)^t}$$

F = final (future) value

P = principal (present value)

t = time (years)

i = annual rate of interest as a decimal or fraction

When regular payments are being used to pay off a loan, then we are usually interested in calculating their present values (value right now). This is the basis upon which the loan repayments and/or the APR are calculated.

When regular payments are being used for investment, we may instead be interested in their future values (value at some time in the future). This tells us how much we can expect to have when the investment matures.

ACTION
Proving the amortisation formula

OBJECTIVE
To use the amortisation formula to calculate the amount of annual repayments

Amortisation

Amortisation is the paying off of a debt in regular instalments. A mortgage is an example of an amortised loan.

WORKED EXAMPLE

Explaining amortisation

You take out a loan of €5000 for 5 years at an annual interest rate of 5%. If you had to pay the entire amount owed after 5 years, the amount due to the lender would be $€5000 \times 1{\cdot}05^5 = €6381{\cdot}41$. This would equate to an average annual repayment of €1276·28.

However, you are usually required to pay off loans in regular instalments (amortisation). By paying regular amounts over the term of the loan, your average annual payments will be less than €1276·28.

You want to repay the loan in five equal annual repayments. What is the amount A of each repayment?

The present value of making your first repayment after 1 year is $\frac{A}{1{\cdot}05}$.

The present value of making your second repayment after 2 years is $\frac{A}{1{\cdot}05^2}$.

The present value of making your third repayment after 3 years is $\frac{A}{1{\cdot}05^3}$.

The present value of making your fourth repayment after 4 years is $\frac{A}{1{\cdot}05^4}$.

The present value of making your fifth repayment after 5 years is $\frac{A}{1{\cdot}05^5}$.

The sum of all five present repayments is equal to the sum borrowed.

$$\frac{A}{1{\cdot}05} + \frac{A}{1{\cdot}05^2} + \frac{A}{1{\cdot}05^3} + \frac{A}{1{\cdot}05^4} + \frac{A}{1{\cdot}05^5} = 5000$$

$$A\left[\frac{1}{1{\cdot}05} + \frac{1}{1{\cdot}05^2} + \frac{1}{1{\cdot}05^3} + \frac{1}{1{\cdot}05^4} + \frac{1}{1{\cdot}05^5}\right] = 5000$$

$$a = \frac{1}{1{\cdot}05},\ r = \frac{1}{1{\cdot}05},\ n = 5$$

$$A \times \frac{\frac{1}{1{\cdot}05}\left(1 - \frac{1}{1{\cdot}05^5}\right)}{1 - \frac{1}{1{\cdot}05}} = 5000 \qquad \boxed{S_n = \frac{a(1-r^n)}{1-r}}$$

$$A = 5000 \times \frac{1 - \frac{1}{1{\cdot}05}}{\frac{1}{1{\cdot}05}\left(1 - \frac{1}{1{\cdot}05^5}\right)} = €1154{\cdot}87$$

There is a formula for working out the monthly repayments:

$$\boxed{A = P\frac{i(1+i)^t}{(1+i)^t - 1}}$$

A = annual repayment amount

P = principal (amount of the loan)

t = time (years)

i = annual interest rate

Annual:

$P = €5000$

$i = 0{\cdot}05$ $\qquad A = P\frac{i(1+i)^t}{(1+i)^t - 1}$

$t = 5$ years

$A = ?$

$$= 5000 \times \frac{0{\cdot}05(1{\cdot}05)^5}{1{\cdot}05^5 - 1} = €1154{\cdot}87$$

This formula should only be used for loans. A table setting out the annual repayments shows that you will pay €5774·35 on a €5000 loan.

Year	Annual repayment	Present values of repayments
1	€1154·87	€1099·88
2	€1154·87	€1047·50
3	€1154·87	€997·62
4	€1154·87	€950·11
5	€1154·87	€904·87
Total	€5774·35	€4999·98

WORKED EXAMPLE

Explaining mortgages

A woman needs to borrow €250 000 to buy a house. She takes the loan out over 20 years at a fixed mortgage rate of 4·2%. What are her monthly repayments? She gets the full €250 000 now. If she paid it back in one go after 20 years, she would have to pay $€250\,000 \times 1{\cdot}042^{20} = €569\,238{\cdot}66$.

She pays it off by making monthly repayments over 20 years. In order for her to plan financially for the future, she will make the same monthly repayment throughout the 20 years. Call this monthly repayment €x. She has 240 repayments to make (20×12 months $= 240$ months).

If you use 4·2% as the rate, leave the time period in years. Let A be the amount of each repayment.

The present value of making her first repayment after 1 month is $\dfrac{A}{1{\cdot}042^{\frac{1}{12}}}$.

The present value of making her second repayment after 2 months is $\dfrac{A}{1{\cdot}042^{\frac{2}{12}}}$.

The present value of making her last repayment after 240 months is $\dfrac{A}{1{\cdot}042^{\frac{240}{12}}}$.

The sum of all 240 present repayments is equal to the sum borrowed.

$$\frac{A}{1{\cdot}042^{\frac{1}{12}}} + \frac{A}{1{\cdot}042^{\frac{2}{12}}} + \dots + \frac{A}{1{\cdot}042^{\frac{240}{12}}} = 250\,000$$

$$A\left[\frac{1}{1{\cdot}042^{\frac{1}{12}}} + \frac{1}{1{\cdot}042^{\frac{2}{12}}} + \dots + \frac{1}{1{\cdot}042^{\frac{240}{12}}}\right] = 250\,000$$

$$a = \frac{1}{1{\cdot}042^{\frac{1}{12}}},\ r = \frac{1}{1{\cdot}042^{\frac{1}{12}}},\ n = 240$$

$$A \times \frac{\frac{1}{1{\cdot}042^{\frac{1}{12}}}\left(1 - \frac{1}{1{\cdot}042^{\frac{240}{12}}}\right)}{1 - \frac{1}{1{\cdot}042^{\frac{1}{12}}}} = 250\,000$$

$$A = 250\,000 \times \frac{\left(1 - \frac{1}{1{\cdot}042^{\frac{1}{12}}}\right)}{\frac{1}{1{\cdot}042^{\frac{1}{12}}}\left(1 - \frac{1}{1{\cdot}042^{\frac{240}{12}}}\right)} = €1530{\cdot}97$$

Use the amortisation formula to work out the monthly repayments. To do this, you need to change the annual interest rate to a monthly interest rate and put the time in months.

Annual		Monthly
$P = €250\,000$	$P(1+i)^t$ (monthly) $= P(1+i)^t$ (yearly)	$P = €250\,000$
$i = 0{\cdot}042$	$(1+i)^{12} = 1{\cdot}042^1$	$i = 0{\cdot}0034344$
$t = 20$ years	$\therefore i = 1{\cdot}042^{\frac{1}{12}} - 1 = 0{\cdot}0034344$	$t = 240$ months
$A = ?$		$A = ?$

$$A = P\frac{i(1+i)^t}{(1+i)^t - 1}$$

$$A = 250\,000\frac{0{\cdot}0034344(1{\cdot}0034344)^{240}}{(1{\cdot}0034344)^{240} - 1} = €1530{\cdot}98$$

EXAMPLE 16

A businessman is setting up an export business. He borrows €200 000 over 10 years from the bank at an interest rate of 6·2% per annum. He agrees to pay off the debt in 10 equal annual repayments, with the first repayment 1 year after he takes out the loan.

(a) Calculate his annual repayment amount.

(b) Make a payment schedule showing the annual fixed repayments, the annual interest on the outstanding balance, the portion of the repayment contributing towards reducing the debt, and the outstanding balance for each year.

(c) Draw a graph of the interest and debt repayments for each year.

Solution

(a) Use the amortisation formula to calculate the annual repayment amount.

Annual:

$P = €200\,000$

$i = 0{\cdot}062$

$t = 10$ years

$A = ?$

$$A = P\frac{i(1+i)^t}{(1+i)^t - 1}$$

$$A = 200\,000 \times \frac{0{\cdot}062(1{\cdot}062)^{10}}{(1{\cdot}062)^{10} - 1} = €27\,431{\cdot}66$$

(b) Make a repayment schedule.

You borrow the money at the beginning of the year so your outstanding balance is €200 000. You will make annual fixed repayments of €27 431·66.

Payment 1: You make your first repayment at the end of the year. The interest that you owe at the end of the year is €200 000 × 0·062 = €12 400.

This means the amount of debt you pay off is €27 431·66 – €12 400 = €15 031·66. Therefore, the balance of what you owe is €200 000 – €15 031·66 = 184 968·34.

Payment 2: You make your second repayment at the end of the second year. The interest that you owe at the end of the year is €184 968·34 × 0·062 = €11 468·04.

This means the amount of debt you pay off is €27 431·66 – €11 468·04 = €15 963·62. Therefore, the balance of what you owe is €184 968·34 – €15 963·62 = 169 004·72.

Repayment number	Fixed repayment	Interest	Debt repayment	Balance
0	€0			€200 000·00
1	€27 431·66	€12 400.00	€15 031·66	€184 968·34
2	€27 431·66	€11 468·04	€15 963·62	€169 004·72
3	€27 431·66	€10 478·29	€16 953·37	€152 051·35
4	€27 431·66	€9427·18	€18 004·48	€134 046·87
5	€27 431·66	€8310·91	€19 120·75	€114 926·12
6	€27 431·66	€7125·42	€20 306·24	€94 619·88
7	€27 431·66	€5866·43	€21 565·23	€73 054·65
8	€27 431·66	€4529·39	€22 902·27	€50 152·38
9	€27 431·66	€3109·45	€24 322·21	€25 830·17
10	€27 431·66	€1601·47	€25 830·19	€0

ACTIVITY 7

ACTION

Compiling a repayment schedule

OBJECTIVE

To use the amortisation formula to compile a repayment schedule and draw a graph to illustrate the debt and interest portions of the repayments over time

(c) Mark in the debt and interest portions of each annual repayment.

Early on in the repayment schedule a large proportion of the annual repayment is paying off the interest. As time goes on, more and more of your annual repayments go towards paying off the debt.

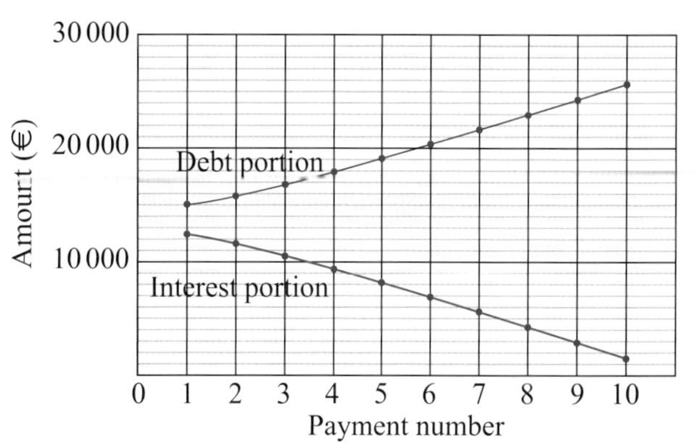

Pensions

Pensions are tricky to calculate. Firstly, you need to decide how much you want to draw down each month or year when you retire. Secondly, you need to calculate how much you save or invest each month before you retire in order to make this happen.

WORKED EXAMPLE

Calculating a pension

When you retire you want to receive €28 000 at the beginning of each year for 25 years. What sum of money do you need to have saved for retirement? Assume that money can be invested at an annually adjusted annual rate of 3·4%.

You may think you need €700 000 in your retirement fund when you retire (€28 000 × 25). However, as you are not receiving your retirement fund in a lump sum, you just need the present value of €700 000 paid out annually over 25 years.

On your retirement, you will receive €28 000 as your first payment. Your second payment is not due for a year. So in your retirement fund, you need the present value of €28 000 paid in 1 year.

This is $\frac{€28\,000}{1{\cdot}034} = €27\,079{\cdot}30$.

$$\text{Fund} = 28\,000 + \frac{28\,000}{1{\cdot}034} + \frac{28\,000}{1{\cdot}034^2} + \frac{28\,000}{1{\cdot}034^3} + \dots + \frac{28\,000}{1{\cdot}034^{24}}$$

$$= 28\,000\left[1 + \frac{1}{1{\cdot}034} + \frac{1}{1{\cdot}034^2} + \frac{1}{1{\cdot}034^3} + \dots + \frac{1}{1{\cdot}034^{24}}\right]$$

$$a = 1,\ r = \frac{1}{1{\cdot}034},\ n = 25$$

$$\text{Fund} = 28\,000 \times \frac{1\left(1 - \frac{1}{1{\cdot}034^{25}}\right)}{1 - \frac{1}{1{\cdot}034}} = €482\,393{\cdot}60$$

$$S_n = \frac{a(1 - r^n)}{1 - r}$$

You need €482 393·60 in your retirement fund. You now have to work out each month how much you need to pay into your pension to have €482 393·60 in your retirement fund. For example, say that you have 40 years until retirement. You need to put €x into your fund at the start of each month.

40 years = 40 × 12 months = 480 months

$$F = x(1{\cdot}034)^{\frac{480}{12}} + x(1{\cdot}034)^{\frac{479}{12}} + x(1{\cdot}034)^{\frac{478}{12}} + \ldots + x(1{\cdot}034)^{\frac{1}{12}} = 482\,393{\cdot}60$$

$$x\left[1{\cdot}034^{\frac{1}{12}} + 1{\cdot}034^{\frac{2}{12}} + \ldots + 1{\cdot}034^{\frac{478}{12}} + 1{\cdot}034^{\frac{479}{12}} + 1{\cdot}034^{\frac{480}{12}}\right] = 482\,393{\cdot}60$$

$$a = 1{\cdot}034^{\frac{1}{12}},\ r = 1{\cdot}034^{\frac{1}{12}},\ n = 480$$

$$x \times \frac{1{\cdot}034^{\frac{1}{12}}\left(1 - 1{\cdot}034^{\frac{480}{12}}\right)}{1 - 1{\cdot}034^{\frac{1}{12}}} = 482\,393{\cdot}60$$

$$S_n = \frac{a(1 - r^n)}{1 - r}$$

$$\therefore x \times \frac{482\,393{\cdot}60\left(1 - 1{\cdot}034^{\frac{1}{12}}\right)}{1{\cdot}034^{\frac{1}{12}}\left(1 - 1{\cdot}034^{\frac{480}{12}}\right)} = €477{\cdot}80$$

Therefore, you need to save €477·80 every month for 40 years in order to receive €28 000 annually on retirement for 25 years.

People are always encouraged to start saving for their pensions as early as possible. Say you did not start your pension until 15 years later, leaving you now with 25 years of contributions. What would your monthly contributions to your pension fund now have to be?

25 years = 25 × 12 months = 300 months

$$F = x(1{\cdot}034)^{\frac{300}{12}} + x(1{\cdot}034)^{\frac{299}{12}} + x(1{\cdot}034)^{\frac{298}{12}} + \ldots + x(1{\cdot}034)^{\frac{1}{12}} = 482\,393{\cdot}60$$

$$x\left[1{\cdot}034^{\frac{1}{12}} + 1{\cdot}034^{\frac{2}{12}} + \ldots + 1{\cdot}034^{\frac{298}{12}} + 1{\cdot}034^{\frac{299}{12}} + 1{\cdot}034^{\frac{300}{12}}\right] = 482\,393{\cdot}60$$

$$a = 1{\cdot}034^{\frac{1}{12}},\ r = 1{\cdot}034^{\frac{1}{12}},\ n = 300$$

$$x \times \frac{1{\cdot}034^{\frac{1}{12}}\left(1 - 1{\cdot}034^{\frac{300}{12}}\right)}{1 - 1{\cdot}034^{\frac{1}{12}}} = 482\,393{\cdot}60$$

$$\therefore x = \frac{482\,393{\cdot}60\left(1 - 1{\cdot}034^{\frac{1}{12}}\right)}{1{\cdot}034^{\frac{1}{12}}\left(1 - 1{\cdot}034^{\frac{300}{12}}\right)} = €1027{\cdot}07$$

Bonds

Companies raise money by selling bonds. When you purchase a bond, you receive an annual payment plus a lump sum when the bond matures. Calculations involve trying to work out a fair market value for the purchase of the bond.

EXAMPLE 17

A company wishes to raise money by issuing 10-year bonds which pay out €250 at the end of each year plus a lump sum of €3000 when the bond matures. Given an annual interest rate of 3·8%, calculate a fair market value for the bond.

Solution

Calculate the present value of €3000 in 10 years' time.

$$P = \frac{F}{(1+i)^t} = \frac{3000}{1{\cdot}038^{10}} = €2066{\cdot}08$$

Calculate the present value of ten €250 payments at the end of each year.

$$P = \frac{250}{1{\cdot}038^1} + \frac{250}{1{\cdot}038^2} + \ldots + \frac{250}{1{\cdot}038^{10}}$$

$$= 250\left[\frac{1}{1{\cdot}038^1} + \frac{1}{1{\cdot}038^2} + \ldots + \frac{1}{1{\cdot}038^{10}}\right]$$

$$a = \frac{1}{1{\cdot}038}, r = \frac{1}{1{\cdot}038}, n = 10$$

$$P = 250 \times \frac{\frac{1}{1{\cdot}038}\left(1 - \frac{1}{1{\cdot}038^{10}}\right)}{1 - \frac{1}{1{\cdot}038}}$$

$$S_n = \frac{a(1-r^n)}{1-r}$$

$$= €2048{\cdot}06$$

Fair payment for the bond
$= €2066{\cdot}08 + €2048{\cdot}06 = €4114{\cdot}14$

Lotteries

EXAMPLE 18

Most lottery games in the USA allow winners of the jackpot prize to choose between two forms of the prize: an annual-payments option or a cash-value option. In the case of the New York Lottery, there are 26 annual payments in the annual-payments option, with the first payment immediately and the last payment in 25 years' time. The payments increase by 3·5% each year. The amount advertised as the jackpot prize is the total amount of these 26 payments. The cash-value option pays a smaller amount than this.

(a) Find, correct to the nearest dollar, the value of the first annual payment A that corresponds to an advertised jackpot prize of $18·5 million. What is the value of the last annual payment, correct to the nearest dollar?

(b) A winner who chooses the cash-value option immediately receives the total of the present values of the 26 annual payments. The interest rate used for the present-value calculations is 4·65%. Find the amount of prize money payable under the cash-value option. That is, find the total of the present values of the 26 annual payments. Give your answer in millions of dollars, correct to one decimal place.

Solution

(a) Annual-payments option:

$$18\,500\,000 = A + A \times 1{\cdot}04 + A \times 1{\cdot}04^2 + A \times 1{\cdot}04^3 + \ldots + A \times 1{\cdot}04^{25}$$

$$= A[1 + 1{\cdot}04 + 1{\cdot}04^2 + 1{\cdot}04^3 + \ldots + 1{\cdot}04^{25}]$$

$$a = 1, r = 1{\cdot}04, n = 26$$

$$18\,500\,000 = \frac{A \times 1(1 - 1{\cdot}035^{26})}{1 - 1{\cdot}035}$$

$$S_n = \frac{a(1-r^n)}{1-r}$$

$$\therefore A = \frac{18\,500\,000(1 - 1{\cdot}035)}{(1 - 1{\cdot}035^{26})} = \$447\,800$$

The lotto winner receives $447 800 as their first annual payment.

The value of their last annual payment is $\$447\,800 \times 1{\cdot}035^{26} = \$1\,095\,300$

(b) Cash-value option:

First payment = \$447 800

$$\text{Second payment} = \frac{\$447\,800 \times 1{\cdot}035}{1{\cdot}0465} = \$442\,879$$

$$\text{Third payment} = \frac{\$447\,800 \times 1{\cdot}035^2}{1{\cdot}0465^2} = \$438\,012$$

$$\text{Jackpot} = 447\,800 + \frac{447\,800 \times 1{\cdot}035}{1{\cdot}0465} + \frac{447\,800 \times 1{\cdot}035^2}{1{\cdot}0465^2} + \ldots + \frac{447\,800 \times 1{\cdot}035^{25}}{1{\cdot}0465^{25}}$$

$$= 447\,800\left[1 + \frac{1{\cdot}035}{1{\cdot}0465} + \left(\frac{1{\cdot}035}{1{\cdot}0465}\right)^2 + \ldots + \left(\frac{1{\cdot}035}{1{\cdot}0465}\right)^{25}\right]$$

$$a = 1,\ r = \left(\frac{1{\cdot}035}{1{\cdot}0465}\right),\ n = 26$$

$$\text{Jackpot} = \frac{447\,800 \times 1\left[1 - \left(\frac{1{\cdot}035}{1{\cdot}0465}\right)^{26}\right]}{1 - \left(\frac{1{\cdot}035}{1{\cdot}0465}\right)} = \$10{\cdot}2 \text{ million}$$

$$S_n = \frac{a(1 - r^n)}{1 - r}$$

Continuous compounding

For a given rate of interest (AER), we usually take the compounding period per year. Some investment products decide to add the interest to your money after 6 months or 1 month or every day. If your money is compounded every 6 months, the interest rate is halved and the time period doubled. Would you get a greater return if you could compound your money every second?

WORKED EXAMPLE Continuous compounding

Invest €1 at an AER of 100% compounded annually. The value of your money at the end of the year is: $F = P(1 + i)^t = 1(1 + 1)^1 = €2$

Now say your money was compounded every 6 months. The interest rate for 6 months would now be 50%. The value of your money at the end of the year: $F = 1(1 + 0{\cdot}5)^2 = €2{\cdot}25$

This process continues as shown in the table below:

Compounding period	Final value
Yearly	$F = 1(1 + 1)^1 = €2$
6 months	$F = 1\left(1 + \frac{1}{2}\right)^2 = €2{\cdot}25$
1 month	$F = 1\left(1 + \frac{1}{12}\right)^{12} = €2{\cdot}61303529$
1 week	$F = 1\left(1 + \frac{1}{52}\right)^{52} = €2{\cdot}692596954$
1 day	$F = 1\left(1 + \frac{1}{365}\right)^{365} = €2{\cdot}714567482$

1 hour	$F = 1\left(1 + \frac{1}{365 \times 24}\right)^{365 \times 24} = €2{\cdot}718126692$
1 minute	$F = 1\left(1 + \frac{1}{365 \times 24 \times 60}\right)^{365 \times 24 \times 60} = €2{\cdot}71827923$
1 second	$F = 1\left(1 + \frac{1}{365 \times 24 \times 60 \times 60}\right)^{365 \times 24 \times 60 \times 60} = €2{\cdot}718281615$

No matter how often the euro is compounded, it seems to be getting closer to €2·718. This number looks familiar – it is e. We have already seen that e is the following limit: $\lim_{x \to \infty}\left(1 + \frac{1}{n}\right)^n = 2{\cdot}718 = e$

Check it out on your calculator by substituting bigger and bigger values for n into $\left(1 + \frac{1}{n}\right)^n$.

The following formula is used for continuous compounding where your money is compounded over infinitesimal (very, very small) time periods:

$$F = Pe^{it}$$

F = final value

P = principal

i = annual interest rate expressed as a decimal

t = time in years

EXAMPLE 19

€5000 is invested where interest is compounded continuously at an annual interest rate of 2·4%. Calculate the final value of this investment after 2 years.

Solution

$P = €5000$

$t = 2$ years

$i = 0{\cdot}024$

$F = ?$

$F = Pe^{it}$

$= 5000e^{0{\cdot}024 \times 2}$

$= €5245{\cdot}85$

Understanding APR and AER

The term APR is generally used only for borrowings and AER is generally used for savings and investments. APR (annual percentage rate) is the annual rate of interest payable on mortgages, loans, credit cards and other credit products. It is generally used to allow borrowers to compare different credit offers because it not only includes the relevant interest rate, but also any charges involved, such as arrangement fees. This means, for example, a mortgage with an interest rate of 5% could have an APR of 5·2% once the other costs are taken into account.

AER (annual equivalent rate) is generally used in savings accounts. It explains what rate of interest you will earn depending on how often interest is added to your account. For example, an account that accumulates interest monthly will have a lower interest rate than one that pays annually because the monthly account will benefit from compound interest more quickly. However, they might both have the same AER. In this way, AER allows comparison between savings accounts that pay interest at different intervals in the same way that APR allows comparison between loans with different interest rates and charges.

AER does not include costs and charges simply because there generally are not any associated with savings accounts. Because of this lack of fees, savings accounts often quote their interest rate as APR. For example, a savings account that pays 6% interest a year also has an APR of 6%. This is the interest rate plus any fees/charges (none) that need to be included. It also has an AER of 6% because interest is paid annually.

EXERCISE 6

1. **(a)** €1500 is put into an investment account at the beginning of the year at an AER of 5·75%. How much is the investment worth after 10 years? How much interest will be earned?

   (b) €2200 is put into a savings account at the beginning of the year at an AER of 6·5%. How much is in the account after 5 years? How much interest will be earned?

   (c) €225 is put into a savings account at the beginning of each month for 3 years at an AER of 3·25%. How much is in the account after 3 years? How much interest will be earned?

   (d) €60 is put into a savings account at the beginning of each week at an AER of 4·4%. How much is in the account after 2 years? How much interest will be earned?

   (e) €75 is saved weekly for 2 years with an AER of 3·4% applied to the savings. How much will be in the account after 2 years? How much interest will be earned?

2. €5000 is deposited in a savings account at the beginning of 2015. €1500 is then put into the account at the beginning of every year from 2016 to 2020. How much is in the account at the end of 2020, if an AER of 4·85% is applied to the account throughout the saving period?

3. €155 is put into a savings account at the beginning of each month for 4 years. The AER is 3·25%. How much is in the account after 4 years?

4. You put €250 into a savings account at the beginning of each month for 2 years. Your saving per month is increased to €300 for the next 2 years. The AER is 4·5%. How much is in your account after 4 years? How much interest did you earn?

5. You are saving your money every week for 3 years in order to purchase a car. €100 is put into the savings account at the beginning of each week for 1 year and 3 months. Your saving per week decreases to €75 for the remaining time. The AER is 3·2%. How much is in your account after 3 years?

6. Money is deposited monthly in a regular savings account with a variable interest rate. €250 is deposited at the beginning of the month for 5 years. The AER for the first 2 years is 3·6%, decreasing to 3·2% for the final 3 years. How much is in the account on maturation?

7. What sum of money must you save each month in order to have €5000 in your account after 3 years at an annual rate of 4·25%?

8. What sum of money must you save each month in order to have €10 800 in your account after 4 years at an annual rate of 3·75%? How much must you save weekly to receive the same amount?

9. Seán wants to have €8500 in his saving account after 3·5 years, putting a certain sum of money into his account at the beginning of each month. If the annual interest rate is 5·8%, how much does he invest (save) each month?

10. A loan of €9500 is taken out from a bank at a fixed annual rate of 6·4%. The loan is to be repaid after 4 years with equal repayments made at the end of each month. What is the monthly repayment needed to repay the loan?

11. €12 500 is borrowed from a lending institution at a fixed annual rate of 5·75%. The loan is to be repaid after 5 years with equal repayments made at the end of each month. What is the monthly repayment needed to repay the loan? The borrower has an option from the lending institution to extend the loan to 6 years. What would be the monthly repayments for the longer loan period? How much more does the borrower pay by availing of the longer loan period?

12. €15 000 is borrowed from a car finance company to purchase a car. The fixed annual rate offered is 4·8%. The loan is to be repaid after 5 years with equal repayments made at the end of each month. What is the monthly repayment needed to repay the loan? The borrower has an option from the finance company to make equal weekly repayments. What would be the weekly repayments? How much less does the borrower pay by availing of weekly repayments?

13. Joan needs to borrow €350 000 to buy a house. She takes the loan out over 20 years at a fixed mortgage rate of 3·8%. What are her monthly repayments?

14. A couple needs to borrow €420 000 to buy a house. They take the loan out over 25 years at a fixed mortgage rate of 3·2%. What are their monthly repayments?

15. A loan of €18 000 is taken out by a company from a bank at a fixed annual rate of 7·2%. The loan is to be repaid after 6 years with equal repayments made at the end of each year. Calculate the annual repayments. Copy and complete the following table:

Year	Annual repayment	Present values of repayments
1		
2		
3		
4		
5		
6		
Total		

16. (a) When you retire, you want to receive €45 000 at the beginning of each year for 30 years. What sum of money do you need to have saved for retirement? Assume that money can be invested at an annually adjusted annual rate of 3·4%.

(b) How much do you have to save each month to reach your retirement fund, given that you are 30 years from retirement and the annual rate of interest is 3·4%?

17. (a) When you retire, you want to receive €32 000 at the beginning of each year for 25 years. What sum of money do you need to have saved for retirement? Assume that money can be invested at an annually adjusted annual rate of 3·6%.

(b) How much do you have to save each month to reach your retirement fund, given that you are 35 years from retirement and the annual rate of interest is 3.6%?

(c) Say you did not start your pension until 10 years later. What would your monthly contributions to your pension fund now be?

18. A company wishes to raise money by issuing 10-year bonds that pay out €350 at the end of each year plus a lump sum of €3500 when the bond matures. Given an annual interest rate of 3·4%, calculate a fair market value for the bond.

19. A charity wishes to raise money by issuing 5-year bonds that pay out €100 at the end of each year plus a lump sum of €2000 when the bond matures. Given an annual interest rate of 2·8%, calculate a fair market value for the bond.

20. A lottery game has a jackpot prize of €12·5 million. You can receive the full value of the jackpot only if you receive your payments spread over 20 years. If you want all your prize money now, you will receive a reduced cash-value option. The winner decides on an annual-payments option. There are 20 annual payments, with the first payment immediately and the last payment in 20 years' time. The payments increase by 3·8% each year. The amount advertised as the jackpot prize is the total amount of these 20 payments.

Find, correct to the nearest euro, the value of the first annual payment that corresponds to an advertised jackpot prize of €12·5 million. What is the value of the last annual payment, correct to the nearest euro?

21. €4600 is invested where interest is compounded continuously at an annual interest rate of 2·8%. Calculate the final value of this investment after 3 years.

22. €525 is invested where interest is compounded continuously at an annual interest rate of 3·36%. Calculate the final value of this investment after 2 years.

23. €10 000 is invested in a savings account for 5 years at an AER of 3·2%.

(a) What is the value of the investment after 5 years?

(b) What is the value of the investment after 5 years if your sum of money was compounded monthly?

(c) What is the value of the investment after 5 years if your sum of money was compounded continuously?

REVISION QUESTIONS

1. Laura purchased a new car valued at €28 000. She paid a 15% deposit and was told she could have 5 years to pay off the balance of the car price plus simple interest. Another scheme was also offered to her. It involved paying off the balance of the car price plus simple interest in 8 years. If she chose the longer period to repay the loan, she would end up paying €7140 more. The simple interest rate for the 8-year loan period was 1·5% more per annum than for the 5-year scheme.

(a) How much deposit did she pay?

(b) What was the balance to be paid on the car?

(c) Find the interest rate for each of the two schemes.

(d) Find the total amount paid for the car for each of the schemes.

(e) What were the monthly repayments for each of the schemes?

2. €10 000 is invested for 3 years at compound interest. The AER for the first year was 3% and the AER for the second year was 2%.

(a) Find the amount of the investment at the end of the second year.

(b) At the beginning of the third year, a further €5000 was invested. The AER for the third year was r%. The total investment at the end of the third year was €15 893·65. Find r.

3. Paul wants to borrow €22 500 at an annual percentage rate of 6·2%. He wants to repay the loan in seven equal instalments over 7 years, with the first payment 1 year after he takes out the loan. Each annual repayment will be €A.

(a) Write out, in terms of A, the sum P of the present values of his repayments as a geometric series.

(b) Using the geometric series formula for summing terms, write out an expression for this series and hence calculate A.

(c) Use the amortisation formula, $A = P\frac{i(1+i)^t}{(1+i)^t - 1}$, where i is the annual interest rate written as a decimal and t is the time in years, to also calculate A.

(d) Paul decides he wants to make monthly repayments rather than annual repayments. Calculate the monthly rate of interest correct to four decimal places.

(e) Using the amortisation formula, calculate the monthly repayments.

(f) How much does Paul save by making monthly repayments over the repayment period?

4. A school play was staged by the second-year students in a secondary school to raise money for a school bus. The ticket pricing was as follows:

Category	Price
Children under 12 years	€5·00
Children between 12 and 18 years	€7·50
Adults	€10·00
Senior citizens	€8·00

On the night of the show, the attendance was 60 adults, 20 senior citizens, 80 children aged between 12 and 18 years, and 40 children under 12 years.

(a) Find the total ticket sales.

(b) During the interval refreshments were sold. If the cost of the refreshments was €78 and the income from them was €228, find the percentage profit from refreshments, to the nearest whole number.

(c) The parents association added €34 290 to the net takings of the play and refreshments. If the total amount was invested at an AER of 2·5% for 3 years, what was its total value at the end of this period?

(d) The bus was priced at €42 000 excluding VAT at 23%. What is the price of the bus when VAT is included?

(e) What percentage discount must the motor dealer give to the school in order that its investment will pay for the bus, correct to the nearest whole number?

5. The spreadsheet below gives details of the hours worked and the rates of pay for three employees of a supermarket.

	A	B	C	D	E
1	Employee	Weekday hourly rate in €	Weekday hours worked	Weekend hours worked	Gross weekly pay in €
2	Felicity	9	25		297
3	Noah	13·20	24	6	
4	Ciara		40	0	852

The weekend hourly rate is double the weekday hourly rate.

(a) Fill in these cells: **(i)** D2, **(ii)** E3, **(iii)** B4.

(b) What is Ciara's gross weekly salary?

(c) If tax is levied at 20% on the first €650 and 40% on the remainder of Ciara's salary, find her gross tax.

(d) Find her net tax if Ciara's weekly tax credit is €63.

(e) Find Ciara's PRSI deduction if PRSI is levied at 4% on her gross salary.

(f) Find Ciara's USC deduction if the first €231 is levied at 1%, the next €128 at 3%, and the remainder at 5·5%.

(g) Find Ciara's net weekly take-home pay, if net pay = gross pay – net tax – PRSI – USC.

6. **(a)** The loan amount P is the sum of the present values of all the repayments, assuming repayment is made at the end of each repayment period. If A is the periodic repayment amount, t is the number of repayment periods, and i is the interest rate for the repayment period expressed as a decimal or fraction, write out P as a sum of t terms.

(b) Hence, show that $A = P\dfrac{i(1+i)^t}{(1+i)^t - 1}$.

7. **(a)** A company's turnover in 2012 was €325 475. It increased its turnover in 2013 by 3·5%. What was the company's turnover in 2013?

(b) A holiday complex offers three different types of holiday homes, as shown in the table.

Holiday home type	Number of homes	Maximum occupancy	Weekly rent in July per home
A	10	5	€500
B	12	6	€600
C	18	8	€800

If during one week in July, all holiday homes were fully occupied, find:

(i) the total number of people staying at the complex during that week,

(ii) the total rental income for that week,

(iii) the percentage profit margin for that week if the total costs C for cleaning, maintenance, wages, administration, mortgages, etc. are given by $C = €(50n + 3000)$, where n is the number of occupants. Give your answer correct to one decimal place.

(iv) During September a discount of 30% is given on each home. Find the rental income in a week in September in which six type A, eight type B and three type C homes were occupied.

8. The metric body mass index (BMI) formula is $\text{BMI} = \dfrac{\text{mass}}{(\text{height})^2}$, where mass is in kilograms (kg) and height is in metres (m).

(a) On 1 January, Joe's mass was 100 kg and his height was 1·7 m. Find his BMI correct to one decimal place.

(b) Over 3 months, Joe loses 6% of his mass each month. Find his BMI on 1 April, correct to one decimal place.

(c) What was the percentage change in his BMI between 1 January and 1 April, correct to one decimal place?
The imperial BMI formula is:
$\text{BMI} = 703 \times \frac{\text{mass}}{(\text{height})^2}$, where mass is in pounds and height is in inches.

(d) If 1 kg = 2·20463 pounds and 1 inch = 0·0254 m, find Joe's mass in pounds and height in inches on 1 April, correct to one decimal place.

(e) Show the imperial BMI gives the same value as the metric BMI for Joe on 1 April.

9. John returns from a weekend in London with £550. At the airport, Hibernian Bank's currency exchange board displays the exchange rate for €1.

Country	Currency	Buys	Sells
USA	Dollar ($)	1·3494	1·3266
UK	Pound (£)	0·8394	0·7983
Canada	Dollar (CAD)	1·5702	1·4505
South Africa	Rand (R)	15·7342	14·5349

(a) What rate will John get to change his £ into €?

(b) How many euro will John get for his £550?

John decides to hang on to his £550. When he gets home his sister Mary tells him she is going shopping in Belfast the next day. She says she is going to convert €670 to £.

(c) What rate will Mary get in the Hibernian Bank?

(d) How many pounds sterling will she get for her €670?

(e) John and Mary decide to do a deal. John gives Mary his £550 for her €670. Explain why both save money from this transaction.

10. (a) Find the compound interest on €6000 invested at 2·3% AER for 4 years.

(b) A loan of €40 000 is to be repaid by a single repayment of €45 369, 2 years from now. Find the APR of this loan.

(c) Before going on a holiday to Paris, Joan meets up with two friends, Mia from the USA and Kylie from Australia. Mia changes $100 into pounds sterling and her remaining $1000 into euro. Kylie changes AUS $150 into pounds sterling and her remaining AUS $1100 into euro. Joan changes £800 into euro.

Use the exchange rates below to find the total number of euro the three friends bring to Paris, correct to the nearest euro.
£1 = $1·67
£1 = AUS $1·85
£1 = €1·22

11. The value V of a car depreciates according to the straight line graph shown (using the straight line method of depreciation). $t = 0$ is 1 January 2010.

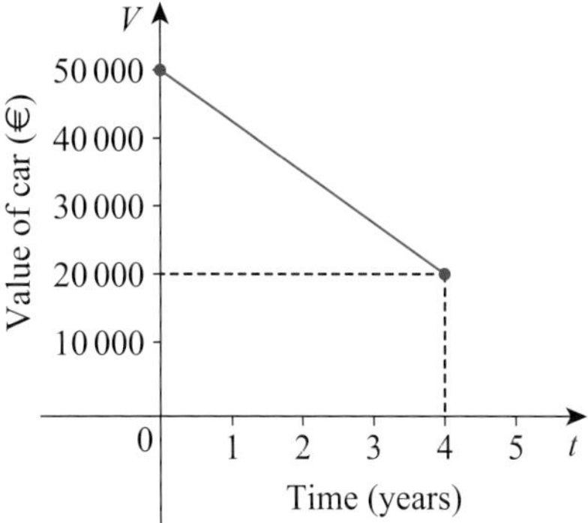

(a) Find the value of the car in:
(i) January 2010, and
(ii) January 2014 from the graph.

(b) Find the slope of the graph.

(c) Find the equation of the straight line.

(d) Use the equation of the straight line to find when the value of the car will be zero.

(e) Find the rate of depreciation per annum by the reduced balanced method that gives the same depreciation from 1 January 2010 to 1 January 2014. Give your answer correct to one decimal place.

12. The length of a kitchen wall is 4·32 m and its height is 1·9 m. It is to be tiled with tiles of dimensions 15 cm × 15 cm.

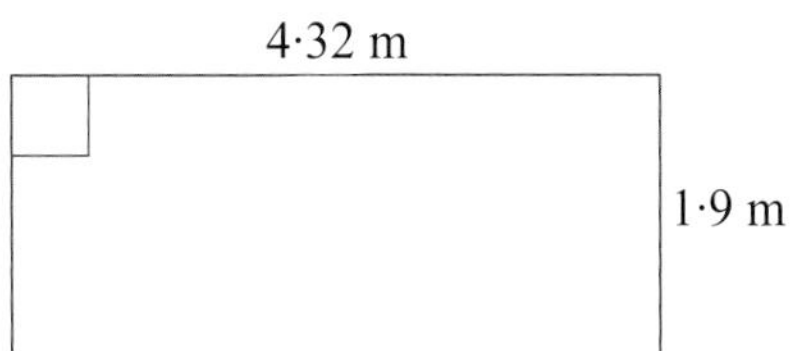

Find:

(a) the area of the wall,

(b) the total number of tiles required,

(c) the percentage wastage, correct to one decimal place.

The tiles come in boxes of 40.

(d) How many boxes are required for the job?

(e) How many spare tiles are left over?

(f) If each box costs €85 excluding VAT at 23%, find the total cost of the tiles.

13. A businessman sets up a printing company. He borrows €250 000 over 8 years from the bank at an interest rate of 5·4% per annum. He agrees to pay off the debt in eight equal annual repayments, with the first repayment 1 year after he takes out the loan.

(a) Calculate his annual repayment amount.

(b) Make a repayment schedule showing the annual fixed repayments, the annual interest on the outstanding balance, the portion of the repayment contributing towards reducing the debt, and the outstanding balance for each year.

(c) Draw a graph of the interest and debt repayments for each year.

14. Most lottery games in the USA allow winners of the jackpot prize to choose between two forms of the prize: an annual-payments option or a cash-value option. In the case of one lottery, there are 15 annual payments in the annual-payments option, with the first payment immediately and the last payment in 15 years' time. The payments increase by 2·8% each year. The amount advertised as the jackpot prize is the total amount of these 15 payments. The cash-value option pays a smaller amount than this.

(a) Find, correct to the nearest dollar, the value of the first annual payment A that corresponds to an advertised jackpot prize of \$21·6 million. What is the value of the last annual payment, correct to the nearest dollar?

(b) A winner who chooses the cash-value option immediately receives the total of the present values of the 15 annual payments. The interest rate used for the present-value calculations is 3·65%. Find the amount of prize money payable under the cash-value option. That is, find the total of the present values of the 15 annual payments. Give your answer in millions, correct to one decimal place.

SUMMARY

1. Unit rates:

   5 objects cost €20.

   1 object costs €4.

   7 objects cost €28.

2. Value added tax (VAT) can be included or not included in a cost price.

3. Income tax and deductions:

   (a) Pay Related Social Insurance (PRSI) is calculated as a percentage of gross income.

   (b) Tax on income:

   (i) Gross tax:

   20% on the first €33 800 of gross income.

   40% on the remainder.

   (ii) Net tax = gross tax – tax credits

   (c) Universal Social Charge (USC): There are different rates for different bands of income.

4. Profit (P) = Selling price (SP) – Cost price (CP):

   $$\text{Percentage profit} = \frac{\text{Profit}}{\text{Cost price}} \times 100\%$$

   $$\text{Profit margin} = \frac{\text{Profit}}{\text{Selling price}} \times 100\%$$

5. Loss (L) = Cost price (CP) – Selling price (SP):

   $$\text{Percentage loss} = \frac{\text{Loss}}{\text{Cost price}} \times 100\%$$

6. Simple interest:

   $$I = \frac{P \times r \times t}{100}$$

   I = interest

   P = principal

   r = percentage rate per year (p.a.)

   t = time in years

7. Compound interest:

   $$F = P\left(1 + \frac{r}{100}\right)^t = P(1+i)^t$$

   F = final amount after t periods

   P = principal

   r = percentage rate per interest period

   t = number of interest periods in the term

   i = annual rate of compound interest expressed as a decimal or fraction

8. Depreciation by the reducing balance method:

   $$F = P\left(1 - \frac{r}{100}\right)^t = P(1-i)^t$$

   F = value after t periods

   P = principal

   r = percentage rate per depreciation period

   t = number of depreciation periods

   i = annual rate of depreciation expressed as a decimal or fraction

9. Saving:

   When saving regular amounts in a savings account or paying back regular amounts to clear a loan, the payments form a geometric series where the sum of n terms S_n is given by:

   $$S_n = \frac{a(1-r^n)}{1-r}$$

   a = the first term

   r = the common ratio

10. Amortisation (mortgages and loans):

    Equal repayments at equal intervals:

    $$A = P\frac{i(1+i)^t}{(1+i)^t - 1}$$

    A = annual repayment amount

    P = principal

    i = annual rate of interest expressed as a decimal or fraction

    t = time in years

11. Continuous compounding:

    $$F = Pe^{it}$$

    F = final value

    P = principal

    i = annual rate of interest expressed as a decimal or fraction

    t = time in years

SECTION 6

Complex Numbers

Complex numbers may appear strange at first but with a bit of practice they really are easy. Complex numbers have important applications in areas such as electronics and relativity.

Chapter 16 Complex Numbers 1

Learning Outcomes

- To understand the idea of imaginary and complex numbers.
- To plot complex numbers on the Argand diagram.
- To perform the following operations on complex numbers: addition, subtraction, multiplication by a scalar, modulus, conjugate, multiplication, division, argument.
- To interpret addition, multiplication, multiplication by a scaler and division geometrically.

16.1 Why imaginary numbers are needed

ACTIVITY 1

ACTION
Asking: Is it real or imaginary?

OBJECTIVE
To recognise whether numbers are real or imaginary

Leonhard Euler

To solve the equation $x^2 = 4$ or $x \times x = 4$, you have to find two identical numbers which, when multiplied together, give 4.

No problem: $(+2) \times (+2) = 4$ and $(-2) \times (-2) = 4$

$\therefore x = \pm 2$

But now try to solve $x^2 = -1$ or $x \times x = -1$. You have to think of two identical numbers which, when multiplied together, give -1.

$\therefore x = \pm \sqrt{-1}$

Like the great mathematician Euler (pronounced *oiler*), imagine that $\sqrt{-1}$ does exist and give it a name *i*. From now on *imagine* $i = \sqrt{-1}$.

Hundreds of years ago, Euler imagined $\sqrt{-1}$ did exist and called it *i* (*iota*). Based on this 'imaginary number', a new system of numbers called complex numbers was developed. These complex numbers have enormous applications in physics, engineering, science and IT.

Imaginary numbers are as normal as every other number. They are a tool to describe the world in the same way that 0 and negative numbers were invented to deal with problems that arose in the development of mathematics.

Square roots of positive and negative integers

$$i = \sqrt{-1} \Rightarrow i^2 = -1$$

- $\sqrt{-9} = \sqrt{9 \times -1} = \sqrt{9} \times \sqrt{-1} = 3 \times i = 3i$
- $-\sqrt{-12} = -\sqrt{12 \times -1} = -\sqrt{4 \times 3 \times -1}$
  $= -\sqrt{4} \times \sqrt{3} \times \sqrt{-1} = -2\sqrt{3}i$
- $\sqrt{-4} + \sqrt{-16} = \sqrt{4 \times -1} + \sqrt{16 \times -1}$
  $= \sqrt{4} \times \sqrt{-1} + \sqrt{16} \times \sqrt{-1} = 2i + 4i = 6i$

KEY TERM

Numbers of the form bi, with $b \in \mathbb{R}$ and $i = \sqrt{-1}$, are called **imaginary numbers.**

If $b = 0$, the number bi is both real and imaginary.

Examples: $\sqrt{3}i, -4i, -\frac{2}{3}i, -7{\cdot}2i, 3\sqrt{2}i$ are all imaginary numbers.

If there is no i in a number, the number is a real number.

ACTIVITY 2

ACTION
Exploring powers of i

OBJECTIVE
To write various powers of i in their simplest form

Whole number powers of i

Higher natural number powers of i can be broken down into multiples of i and i^2 using $i^2 = -1$.

$i^3 = i^2 \times i = -1 \times i = -i$

$i^4 = i^2 \times i^2 = -1 \times -1 = +1$

$i^5 = i^2 \times i^2 \times i = -1 \times -1 \times i = i$

$i^6 = i^2 \times i^2 \times i^2 = -1 \times -1 \times -1 = -1$

i	$= i$
i^2	$= -1$
i^3	$= -i$
i^4	$= 1$
i^5	$= i$

Any whole number power of i has one of the four values: $1, i, -1, -i$.

- $3i^3 = 3 \times i^2 \times i = 3 \times (-1) \times i = -3i$
- $4i^2 + 2i^4 = 4(-1) + 2(i^2)(i^2) = 4(-1) + 2(-1)(-1)$
  $= -4 + 2 = -2$

TIP

Since $i^4 = 1$, any power of i that is a multiple of 4 is also 1.

- $i^{32} = (i^4)^8 = (1)^8 = i$

To simplify very high natural number powers of i, just divide the power by 4 and work out i to the power of the remainder.

- $i^{27} = (i^4)^6 \times i^3 = (1)^6 \times i^3 = i^3 = -i$

or

TIP

Divide the power by 4 and put i to the power of the remainder.

- $i^{27} = i^3 = -i$ [27 ÷ 4 = 6 remainder 3]
- $i^{78} = i^2 = -1$ [78 ÷ 4 = 19 remainder 2]
- $(3i^{14})^3 = 3^3 \times i^{42} = 27 \times i^2 = -27$
- $(-\sqrt{2}i^3)^3 = (-\sqrt{2})^3 \times i^9 = -2\sqrt{2}i$

EXERCISE 1

1. Simplify the following and say if the number is real or imaginary:

(a) $\sqrt{16}$

(b) $-\sqrt{49}$

(c) $-\sqrt{18}$

(d) $\sqrt{-16}$

(e) $\sqrt{-49}$

(f) $-\sqrt{-25}$

(g) $\sqrt{-3}$

(h) $\sqrt{-2}$

(i) $\sqrt{\frac{-9}{16}}$

(j) $4\sqrt{-100}$

(k) $-3\sqrt{-144}$

2. Simplify the following and say if the number is real or imaginary:

(a) $\sqrt{16} + \sqrt{9}$

(b) $-\sqrt{16} - \sqrt{25}$

(c) $\sqrt{-16} + \sqrt{-9}$

(d) $-\sqrt{-16} - \sqrt{-25}$

(e) $3\sqrt{-16} + 4\sqrt{-25} - 2\sqrt{-4}$

(f) $3\sqrt{-2} - 4\sqrt{-8}$

(g) $\sqrt{-18} + 2\sqrt{-2}$

(h) $4\sqrt{-4} + 2\sqrt{-16} - 5\sqrt{-9}$

3. Simplify the following:

(a) i^7

(b) i^8

(c) i^9

(d) i^{10}

(e) $3i^4$

(f) $2i^{13}$

(g) $-3i^{11}$

(h) $-4i^3$

(i) $3i^8 + 4i^2$

(j) $5i^3 - 6i$

(k) $i \times 3i^2 \times 6i^{12}$

(l) $3i^5 + 2i^7$

(m) $i - i^3$

(n) $(2i)^5$

(o) $(-2i)^6$

(p) $(-\sqrt{2}i)^6$

(q) $(3i^2)^7$

(r) $(-\sqrt{2}i^2)^3$

(s) $i^{200\,000}$

(t) $i^{200\,003}$

4. **(a)** Is bi always imaginary if $b \in \mathbb{R}$ and $i = \sqrt{-1}$, $b \neq 0$?

(b) Is bi^2 imaginary if $b \in \mathbb{R}$, $b \neq 0$ and $i = \sqrt{-1}$?

(c) Is $\sqrt{-4}i$ an imaginary number if $i = \sqrt{-1}$?

16.2 What is a complex number?

ACTIVITY 3

ACTION
Understanding complex numbers

OBJECTIVE
To examine statements about complex numbers and to decide if they are true or false

Real numbers such as 2 and imaginary numbers such as $2i$ exist, but can a number be both real and imaginary at the same time? This question leads to the idea of a **complex number**.

KEY TERM

A **complex number** z is a number that can be written in the form $z = a + bi$, where $a, b \in \mathbb{R}$ and $i = \sqrt{-1}$.

Examples of complex numbers

- $z = 3 + 2i = 3 + 2 \times i$ [$a = 3 \in \mathbb{R}$, $b = 2 \in \mathbb{R}$ and $i = \sqrt{-1}$]
- $z = -\frac{1}{2} + \sqrt{3}i$
- $z = -7 = -7 + 0i$ [A purely real complex number]
- $z = -4i = 0 - 4i$ [A purely imaginary complex number]
- $z = 0 = 0 + 0i$

It is important to note the following:

1. a and b can be any real numbers.
2. a is called the real part (Re) of the complex number z.
3. b is called the imaginary part (Im) of the complex number z.
4. $a + bi$ is often written as $a + ib$.

ACTIVITY 4

ACTION
Working with real and imaginary numbers

OBJECTIVE
To pick out the real and the imaginary parts of complex numbers and to put them into sets

Standard form of a complex number

You must get used to putting every complex number in the standard form:

z = (Real part) + (Imaginary part)i = Re + Imi

So, $z = -6 + 2i$ is fine. It is in standard form. But $w = -2i + 6$ is not in standard form. Rewrite it as $w = 6 - 2i$ before doing anything else.

- $z = -3 + 2i$

  [Re = –3, Im = +2]
- $z = \frac{2}{3} - \sqrt{5}i$

  [Re = $\frac{2}{3}$, Im = $-\sqrt{5}$]
- $z = -8 \Rightarrow z = -8 + 0i$

  [Re = –8, Im = 0]
- $z = xi + 5 - 7i + 3q,\ x, q \in \mathbb{R}$

  $z = (5 + 3q) + (x - 7)i$

  [Re = $5 + 3q$, Im = $x - 7$]

All real numbers are complex numbers as are all imaginary numbers.

0 is the complex number $0 + 0i$: $0 = 0 + 0i$.

EXERCISE 2

Find the real and the imaginary parts of the complex numbers below by writing each one in standard form: $a + bi$ = Re + Imi, where $a, b \in \mathbb{R}$, $i = \sqrt{-1}$.

1. $5 + 2i$
2. $-2i + 5$
3. $\sqrt{2} + i$
4. -6
5. $3i$
6. $\frac{1}{2}i - \frac{2}{3}$
7. $\frac{\sqrt{2}}{7} - 7i$
8. $-\frac{1}{\sqrt{3}}i + \frac{7}{2}$
9. $x + y - i^5 + 7$
10. $3x + 5yi - 2pi + 3q$
11. $2i - 3 - ki + 1,\ k \in \mathbb{R}$
12. $2 + 3i - 5ki + k,\ k \in \mathbb{R}$

16.3 The Argand diagram

Complex numbers can be plotted as points on a two-dimensional (2D), rectangular, co-ordinated diagram known as the Argand diagram.

The real part (Re) is plotted on the real axis (x-axis) and the imaginary part (Im) is plotted on the imaginary axis (y-axis).

ACTION
Drawing Argand diagrams

OBJECTIVE
To plot complex numbers on Argand diagrams and to explore the properties of these numbers

The complex number $z = 2 + 3i$ with Re = 2 and Im = 3 is plotted as shown:

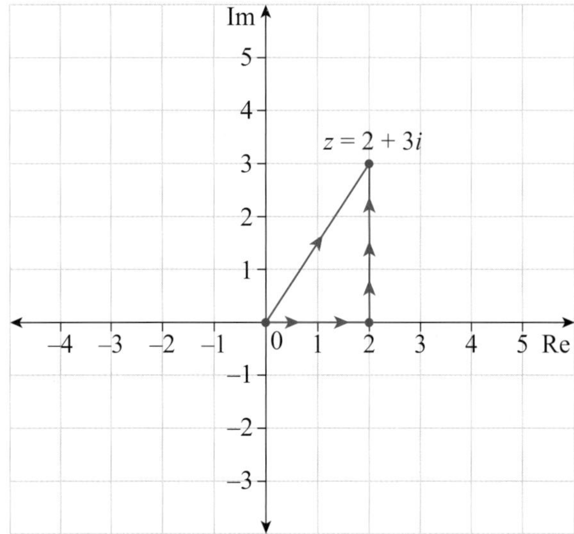

Note: The same scale is used on both axes.

Starting at 0, go +2 units along the real (Re) axis. Then go +3 units up parallel to the imaginary (Im) axis, to reach the point (2, 3).

In general, $z = x + yi$ with Re $= x$ and Im $= y$ is represented by the point (x, y) on the Argand diagram.

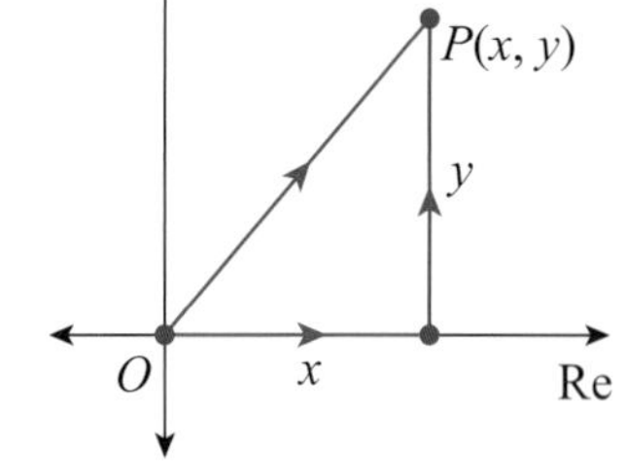

The point $P(x, y)$ represents the complex number $z = x + yi$. The point $O(0, 0)$ represents the complex number $0 = 0 + 0i$.

Every complex number can be represented by a point in 2D space. Complex numbers are 2D in the sense they have one foot in the real dimension and one foot in the imaginary dimension. It is this 2D behaviour that makes them useful. They can be used to store two pieces of information simultaneously. Operations involving complex numbers can be used to process data on two different quantities simultaneously.

WORKED EXAMPLE

Plotting complex numbers on the Argand diagram

Plot the following complex numbers on an Argand diagram.

Complex number		Corresponding point	Complex number		Corresponding point
$z_1 = 0 + 1i$	↔	(0, 1)	$z_5 = 0 - 3i$	↔	(0, −3)
$z_2 = 1 + i$	↔	(1, 1)	$z_6 = -2 + 4i$	↔	(−2, 4)
$z_3 = -4 + 0i$	↔	(−4, 0)	$z_7 = 4 - 3i$	↔	(4, −3)
$z_4 = -2 - 5i$	↔	(−2, −5)	$z_8 = 6 + 0i$	↔	(6, 0)

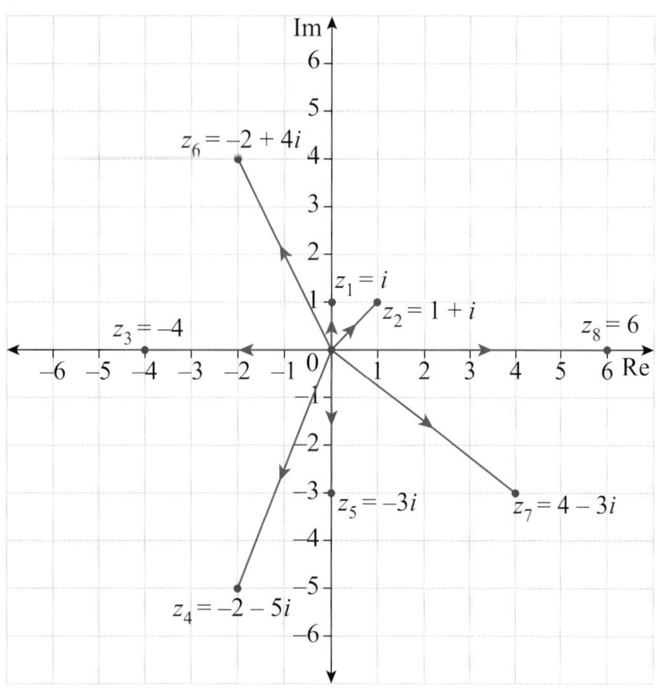

When using the Argand diagram, think of the complex number $z = x + yi$ as represented by the point $P(x, y)$.

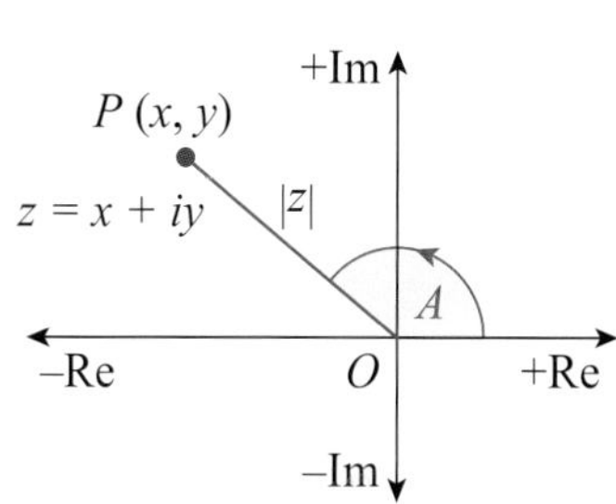

When you plot a complex number on the Argand diagram, the distance from $O(0, 0)$ to $P(x, y)$ is written as $|z|$.

$|z|$ is called the modulus of z.

The angle A, measured anticlockwise from the +Re axis to $[OP]$, is known as the argument of z or just arg z.

EXERCISE 3

1. Write down the points P on an Argand diagram corresponding to the following complex numbers:

(a) $2 + 7i$

(b) $3 + 18i$

(c) $17 + 52i$

(d) $11 - 5i$

(e) $-3 + 7i$

(f) $-7 - 6i$

(g) $\frac{1}{2} + \frac{3}{2}i$

(h) $\sqrt{2} - \frac{7}{2}i$

(i) $-5i + 6$

(j) $-11i - 8$

(k) $x + 1 - 2i, x \in \mathbb{R}$

(l) $yi + 3i - 2, y \in \mathbb{R}$

2. Write down the complex numbers z corresponding to the given points on an Argand diagram:

(a) $(1, 0)$

(b) $(-3, 0)$

(c) $(0, 5)$

(d) $(-5, 6)$

(e) $(-7, -2)$

(f) $\left(\frac{1}{2}, \sqrt{2}\right)$

(g) $\left(-\frac{2}{3}, 1\right)$

(h) $\left(5, -\frac{11}{3}\right)$

(i) $\left(4, \frac{3}{\sqrt{2}}\right)$

(j) $\left(\frac{1}{\sqrt{2}}, \frac{1}{\sqrt{2}}\right)$

(k) $(y - 1, 2)$

(l) $(-3, a - 2), a \in \mathbb{R}$

3. Plot the following complex numbers on the same Argand diagram:

(a) $z_1 = 5$

(b) $z_2 = 2 + 3i$

(c) $z_3 = 4i$

(d) $z_4 = -3 + 5i$

(e) $z_5 = -5$

(f) $z_6 = -4 - 2i$

(g) $z_7 = -2i$

(h) $z_8 = 4 + i$

4. Plot $z = 3 + 4i$ on an Argand diagram.

(a) What point P represents z?

(b) Find the slope of $[OP]$, where $O(0, 0)$.

(c) Find the distance $|OP| = |z|$ using the distance formula.

5. The point P on an Argand diagram represents a complex number z. The origin is $O(0, 0)$.

(a) Find:

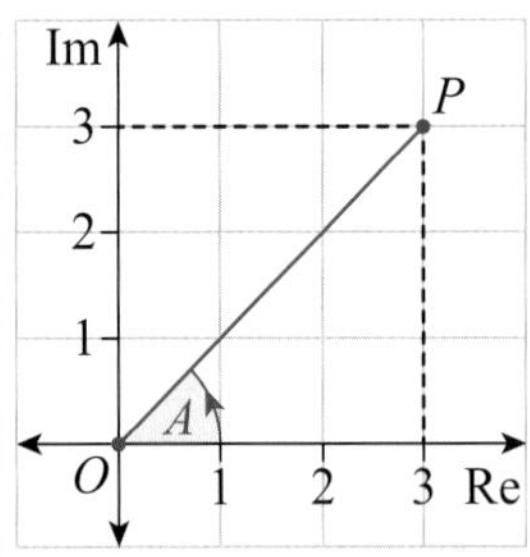

(i) z in the form $a + bi$, $a, b \in \mathbb{R}$

(ii) the slope of OP

(iii) $\tan A$

(iv) $|OP| = |z|$

(b) If $z = x + 4i$ and $\tan A = \frac{4}{5}$, find $x \in \mathbb{R}$ and $|z|$.

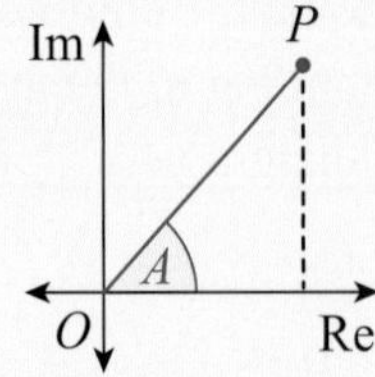

(c) If $z = -3 + yi$ and $|z| = 5$, find $y \in \mathbb{R}$. Find the slope of $[OP]$.

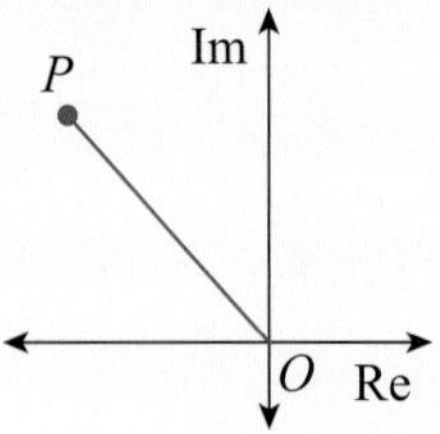

(d) If $z = -5 + yi$ and $|z| = 5\sqrt{2}$, find $y \in \mathbb{R}$.

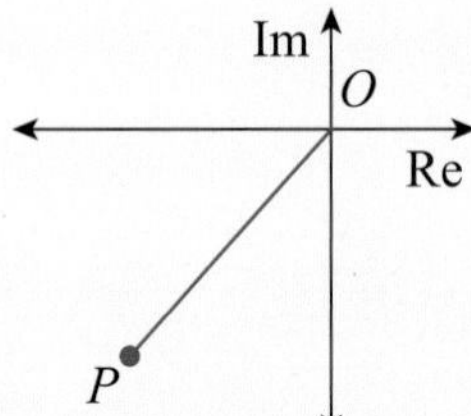

(e) If $|z| = \sqrt{58}$ and the slope of OP is $\frac{3}{7}$, find $x, y \in \mathbb{R}$, if $z = x + yi$.

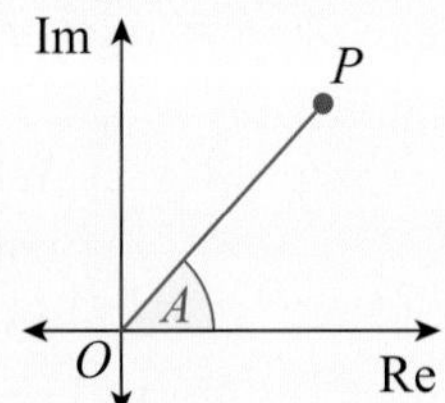

6. z_1 is plotted as point P on the Argand diagram, as shown, with origin $O(0, 0)$.

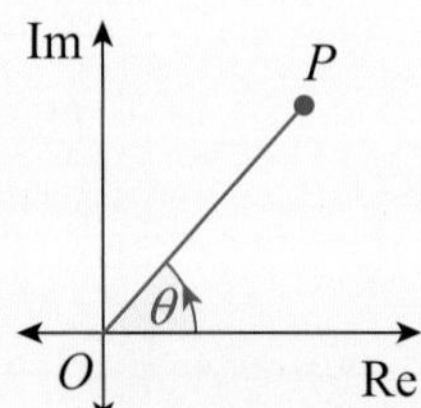

(a) If $z_1 = x + yi$, find the slope of OP and $|z_1|$.

(b) If $z_2 = -x + yi$, find the slope of the line joining O to z_2 and $|z_2|$. Find the angle that the line joining O to z_2 makes with the +Re axis, in terms of θ.

(c) Repeat **(b)** for $z_3 = -x - yi$ and $z_4 = x - yi$.

16.4 Addition and subtraction

ACTIVITY 6

ACTION
Adding and subtracting complex numbers

OBJECTIVE
To carry out the operations and to explore their geometric meaning

To add or subtract complex numbers, combine their real parts and combine their imaginary parts giving your answer in the form $a + bi$.

- $3 - 2i + 8 + 4i = 11 + 2i$ [Add the real parts and add the imaginary parts.]
- $5 - 7i - 4 - 3i = 1 - 10i$

EXAMPLE 1

If $z = 5 + 7i$ and $w = 3 + 2i$, find:

(a) $z + w$ **(b)** $z - w$

Solution

(a) $z + w = (5 + 7i) + (3 + 2i)$
$= (5 + 3) + (7 + 2)i$
$= 8 + 9i$

(b) $z - w = (5 + 7i) - (3 + 2i)$
$= (5 - 3) + (7 - 2)i$
$= 2 + 5i$

EXAMPLE 2

If $z_1 = 2 - \frac{i}{3}$, $z_2 = -\frac{1}{2} - 5i$, $z_3 = \frac{10i}{3} - \frac{3}{2}$, find $z_1 + z_2 + z_3$.

Solution

$z_1 + z_2 + z_3 = 2 - \frac{1i}{3} - \frac{1}{2} - 5i - \frac{3}{2} + \frac{10}{3}i = 0 - 2i$ (Remember $i = 1i$)

WORKED EXAMPLE Geometric meaning of adding complex numbers

1. For $z_1 = -3$ and $w = -1 + i$, draw the line joining z_1 to $z_1 + w$ on the Argand diagram.

$z_1 = -3 + 0i$, $w = -1 + i$

$\Rightarrow z_1 + w = -3 + 0i + (-1 + i) = -4 + 1i$

In terms of the Argand diagram, $z_1 = -3 + 0i$ can be represented by the point $(-3, 0)$ and $z_1 + w$ by the point $(-4, 1)$.

$z_1 \rightarrow z_1 + w$ means $(-3, 0) \rightarrow (-4, 1)$. This is the translation obtained by adding -1 to the x co-ordinate and $+1$ to the y co-ordinate.

2. For $z_2 = -2i$ and $w = -1 + i$, draw the line joining z_2 to $z_2 + w$ on the Argand diagram.

$z_2 + w = -2i + (-1 + i) = -1 - i$

$\therefore z_2 \rightarrow z_2 + w$

$\Rightarrow (0, -2) \rightarrow (-1, -1)$

Add -1 Add $+1$

This is the same translation as before.

3. For $z_3 = 2 + 4i$ and $w = -1 + i$, draw the line joining z_3 to $z_3 + w$ on the Argand diagram.

$z_3 + w = 2 + 4i + (-1 + i) = 1 + 5i$

$\therefore z_3 \rightarrow z_3 + w$

$\Rightarrow (2, 4) \rightarrow (1, 5)$

Add -1 Add $+1$

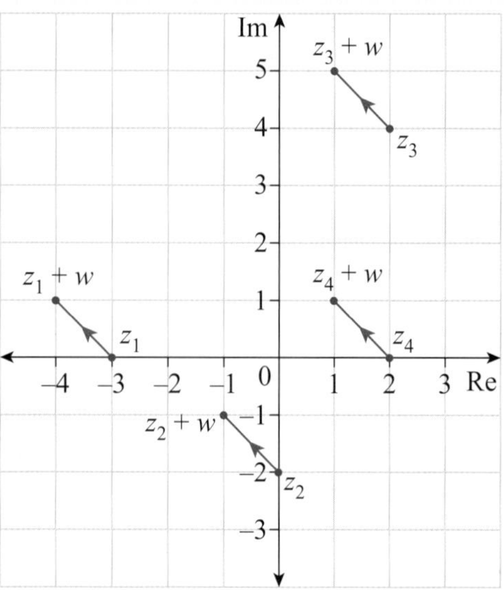

4. For $z_4 = 2$ and $w = -1 + i$, draw the line joining z_4 to $z_4 + w$ on the Argand diagram.

$z_4 + w = 2 + 0i + (-1 + i) = 1 + i$

$\therefore z_4 \rightarrow z_4 + w$

$\Rightarrow (2, 0) \rightarrow (1, +1)$

Add -1 Add $+1$

In geometrical terms, adding a complex number w to a given complex number z, translates the given number z by w.

$\therefore z \rightarrow z + w$ under the translation $0 \rightarrow w$ (where $0 = 0 + 0i$).

If $z = x + yi$ and $w = u + vi$

$z + w = x + yi + u + vi = (x + u) + (y + v)i$

$\therefore z \rightarrow z + w$

$\Rightarrow (x, y) \rightarrow (x + u, y + v)$

Add u Add v

This is the translation $(0, 0) \rightarrow (u, v)$.

Subtracting a complex number w from a given complex number z simply translates z by w under the translation $0 \rightarrow -w$.

EXAMPLE 3

(a) If $z = 5 - 7i$, what translation brings z to $8 - 11i$? What is w if $z + w = 8 - 11i$?

(b) If $z = a + bi$, $a, b \in \mathbb{R}$, what translation brings **(i)** z to $0 + 0i$, **(ii)** z to $a - bi$?

Solution

(a) $z \rightarrow 8 - 11i$

$\Rightarrow (5, -7) \rightarrow (8, -11)$

Add $+3$ Add -4

The translation is:

$(0, 0) \rightarrow (3, -4)$

$\therefore w = 3 - 4i$

(b) (i) $a + bi + w = 0 + 0i$

$w = -a - bi$

$\therefore (0, 0) \rightarrow (-a, -b)$

(ii) $a + bi + w = a - bi$

$w = 0 - 2bi$

$\therefore (0, 0) \rightarrow (0, -2b)$

WORKED EXAMPLE The parallelogram law

Add $z = 3 + i$ and $w = 2 + 3i$.

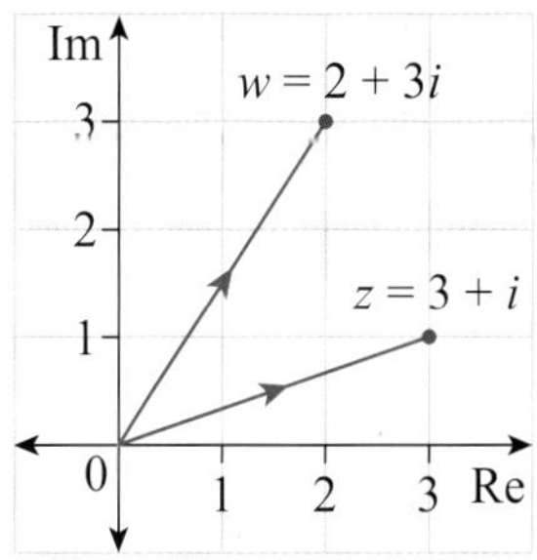

Translate the point that represents $z = 3 + i$ by the translation $0 \rightarrow w$.

$(0, 0) \rightarrow (2, 3)$

$(3, 1) \rightarrow (5, 4)$

To arrive at (5, 4), complete the parallelogram with vertices corresponding to the complex numbers 0, z, w and draw the diagonal from 0. The fourth vertex represents the complex number $z + w$.

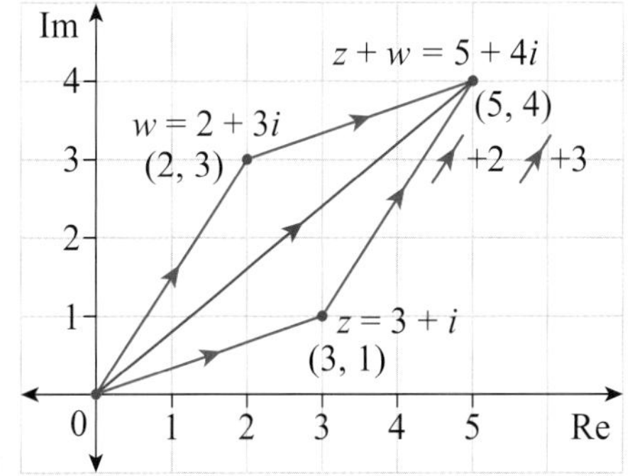

Parallelogram law

To find $z + w$, complete the parallelogram with sides joining 0 to z and 0 to w and draw the diagonal from 0 to the fourth vertex to locate $z + w$, where $0 = 0 + 0i$.

EXERCISE 4

1. Simplify the following giving your answer in the form $a + bi$, $a, b \in \mathbb{R}$:

(a) $2 + 5i + 7 + 4i$

(b) $3 + 5i + 11 + 7i$

(c) $6i + 7 + 2i + 7$

(d) $(5 + 2i) + (8 + 18i)$

(e) $3i + 2 + 9i + 1$

(f) $3 + 11i + 5 + 7i$

(g) $(4 + 12i) + (15 + 5i)$

(h) $6 + 7 + 3i$

(i) $5i + 2 + 9i$

(j) $a + 3i + b + 2i$

2. Find $z + w$ and $z - w$ for the following giving your answer in the form $a + bi$, $a, b \in \mathbb{R}$:

(a) $z = 3 + i$, $w = 6 + 7i$

(b) $z = 4$, $w = 5i$

(c) $z = 5 - 7i$, $w = 2 - i$

(d) $z = 11 + 4i$, $w = 12 + 2i$

(e) $z = 5i$, $w = \frac{1}{2} + 2i$

(f) $z = \sqrt{3} + 2i$, $w = \sqrt{3} + 2i$

(g) $z = x + 2i$, $w = x - 4i$, $x \in \mathbb{R}$

(h) $z = 5 + xi$, $w = 4 + 3xi$, $x \in \mathbb{R}$

(i) $z = x + yi$, $w = 2x + 3yi$, $x, y \in \mathbb{R}$

(j) $z = x + yi$, $w = -3y + 2xi$, $x, y \in \mathbb{R}$

3. Find $z_1 + z_2 + z_3$ if:

(a) $z_1 = 2 + 3i$, $z_2 = 3 + i$, $z_3 = 5 + 3i$

(b) $z_1 = -1 + 4i$, $z_2 = 5 - 3i$, $z_3 = -2i + 7$

(c) $z_1 = -5 - 5i$, $z_2 = 3i - 6$, $z_3 = \frac{1}{2} - 4i$

(d) $z_1 = 7$, $z_2 = -3i$, $z_3 = 5 + i$

(e) $z_1 = x - 2i$, $z_2 = 4i - x$, $z_3 = y + 3i$ $(x, y \in \mathbb{R})$

4. Simplify the following:

(a) $\sqrt{-4} - 2i + \sqrt{4} + 2$

(b) $5 - \sqrt{-8} + 7 - \sqrt{2}i$

(c) $(3 - 2i) - (8 + 5i) + 7 - 6i$

(d) $(\sqrt{8} + 4i) + (\sqrt{50} - i)$

(e) $(2\sqrt{45} - \sqrt{5}i) - (\sqrt{-45} + 3\sqrt{5})$

5. (a) If $z = -5 + 2i$ and $z + w = 8 + 6i$, find w.

   (b) If $z = -3 + 7i$, what translation maps z to $-5 + 15i$? What is w if $z + w = -5 + 15i$?

   (c) If $z = 3 + 7i$, what translation maps z to $10 - 6i$? What is w if $z - w = 10 - 6i$?

   (d) If $z_1 + w = -1 - i$ and $z_2 + w = 8 + 3i$, find $z_1 - z_2$.

6. Copy and complete the parallelogram with lines joining 0 to z and 0 to w as sides, where $0 = 0 + 0i$, and read off $z + w$.

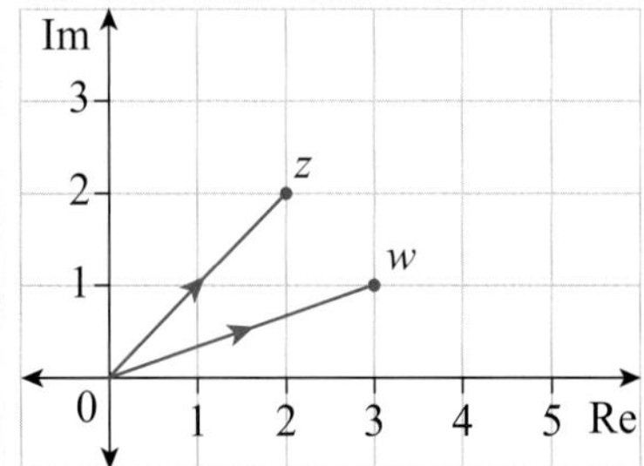

7. Copy the diagram and construct $z + w$.

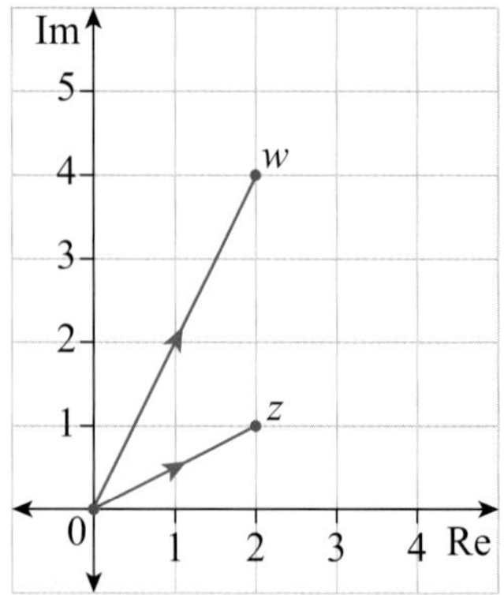

Read off:

(a) z

(b) w

(c) $z + w$

8. If $z = 1 + 2i$ and $w = 1 - 2i$, find $z + w$ and $z - w$. Plot z, w, $z + w$ and $z - w$ on the Argand diagram.

16.5 Multiplication by a scalar

KEY TERM

A **scalar** is any real number.

For example, 3, −2, $\frac{1}{2}$ and $\sqrt{3}$ are all scalars.

Therefore, a number $k + 0i = k$, $k \in \mathbb{R}$ is a scalar.

To multiply a complex number $a + bi$ by a scalar k, multiply the real part by k and the imaginary part by k.

- $-2(5 - 2i) = -10 + 4i$
- $-\frac{1}{2}\left(4 - \frac{3}{2}i\right) = -2 + \frac{3}{4}i$
- $k(a + bi) = ka + kbi, k \in \mathbb{R}$

EXAMPLE 4

If $z = 3 + 7i$ and $w = 4 - 3i$, find:

(a) $3z + 2w$ **(b)** $2z - 3w$

Solution

(a) $3z + 2w = 3(3 + 7i) + 2(4 - 3i)$

$= 9 + 21i + 8 - 6i = 17 + 15i$

(b) $2z - 3w = 2(3 + 7i) - 3(4 - 3i)$

$= 6 + 14i - 12 + 9i = -6 + 23i$

ACTIVITY 7

ACTION
Multiplying a complex number by a scalar

OBJECTIVE
To investigate the effect of multiplying complex numbers by scalars (real numbers)

WORKED EXAMPLE Geometrical meaning of multiplication by a scalar

For the complex number $z = 2 + 4i$:

1. Plot $z_1 = 2z$ and z on the same Argand diagram.
Represent z by P, z_1 by Q and the origin by O.

$z = 2 + 4i \Rightarrow z_1 = 2z = 2(2 + 4i) = 4 + 8i$

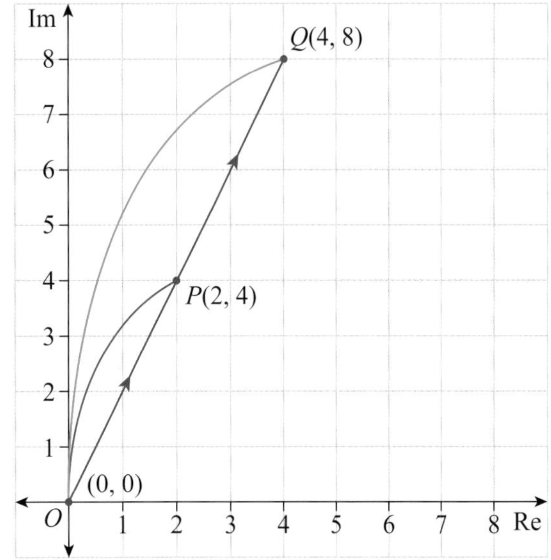

Slope of $OP = \frac{4}{2} = 2$

Slope of $OQ = \frac{8}{4} = 2$

This means that 0, z and z_1 are collinear.

Using the distance formula: $|OP| = |z| = \sqrt{(2-0)^2 + (4-0)^2} = 2\sqrt{5}$

$|OQ| = |z_1| = \sqrt{(4-0)^2 + (8-0)^2} = 4\sqrt{5}$

$\therefore |OQ| = 2|OP|$ or $|z_1| = 2|z|$

2. Plot $z_2 = -\frac{1}{2}z$ and z on the same Argand diagram.
Represent z by P, z_2 by R and the origin by O.

$z = 2 + 4i \Rightarrow z_2 = -\frac{1}{2}z = -\frac{1}{2}(2 + 4i) = -1 - 2i$

You can see that 0, z and z_2 are collinear because the slopes of OP and OQ are equal.

Slope of $OP = \frac{4}{2} = 2$

Slope of $OR = \frac{2}{1} = 2$

$|OP| = |z| = \sqrt{(2-0)^2 + (4-0)^2} = 2\sqrt{5}$

$|OR| = |z_2| = \sqrt{(-1-0)^2 + (-2-0)^2} = \sqrt{5}$

$\therefore\ |OR| = \frac{1}{2}|OP|$ or $z_2 = \frac{1}{2}|z|$

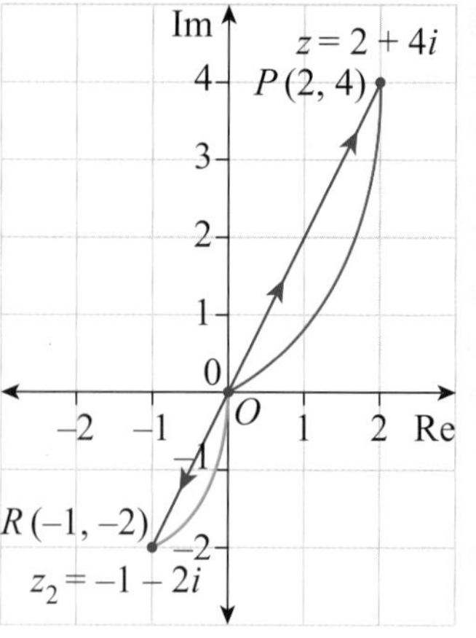

Conclusion

Multiplying a complex number z by a scalar k gives a new complex number $w = kz$, such that $0 = 0 + 0i$, w and z are on the same straight line and the distance from 0 to w is k times the distance from 0 to z.

$\therefore |w| = k|z|$

If $k > 0$, the line joining 0 to w is in the same direction as the line joining 0 to z.

If $k < 0$, the line joining 0 to w is in the opposite direction to the line joining 0 to z.

- $w = -\frac{1}{3}z$ means that 0, w and z are collinear but the line joining 0 to w is in the opposite direction to the line joining 0 to z and $|w| = \frac{1}{3}|z|$.

EXERCISE 5

1. Simplify the following giving your answer in the form $a + bi$, $a, b \in \mathbb{R}$:

(a) $4(3 + 2i)$

(b) $7(6 + 2i)$

(c) $3(8 - 2i)$

(d) $-5(-4 - 2i)$

(e) $\frac{1}{2}(-2 - 8i)$

(f) $\frac{2}{3}(5 + 18i)$

(g) $\sqrt{2}\left(\sqrt{2} + \frac{3}{\sqrt{2}}i\right)$

(h) $5(a + bi)$, $a, b \in \mathbb{R}$

(i) $k(a + bi)$, $k, a, b \in \mathbb{R}$

(j) $3(5 - i) - 7(2 + i)$

(k) $2i + 3(1 - i) - 6i$

(l) $5(2 - i) - 6(5 + 7i) - 3(4 + i)$

(m) $k(3 + 2i) + l(4 + 2i)$, $k, l \in \mathbb{R}$

(n) $k(a + bi) + l(c + di)$, $k, l, a, b, c, d \in \mathbb{R}$

2. If $z = 4 + 6i$ and $w = -5 - 3i$, evaluate the following in the form $a + bi$, $a, b \in \mathbb{R}$:

(a) $z + 2w$

(b) $2z - w$

(c) $3z + 2w$

(d) $-z - w$

(e) $-2z + 4w$

(f) $\frac{1}{2}z - 3w$

(g) $-\frac{1}{2}z + \frac{1}{2}w$

(h) $3z - w$

(i) $\frac{3}{2}z + w$

(j) $\frac{z - w}{3}$

3. $z = -5 + 12i$ is a complex number and $0 = 0 + 0i$.

(a) Find the distance from 0 to z.

(b) Write down $2z$ and the distance from 0 to $2z$.

(c) Write down $-4z$ and the distance from 0 to $-4z$.

(d) Write down $-\frac{1}{2}z$ and the distance from 0 to $-\frac{1}{2}z$.

(e) Write down $\frac{1}{13}z$ and the distance from 0 to $\frac{1}{13}z$.

4. $z = -4 - 2i$ is a complex number.

(a) Draw $z, -z, 2z, \frac{1}{2}z, \frac{5}{2}z$ on an Argand diagram.

(b) Write down the points corresponding to each complex number in part **(a)**.

(c) Find the slope of the line joining $O(0, 0)$ to each point in part **(a)** and write down the distance from $O(0, 0)$ to each point.

5. Copy the diagram and using your ruler:

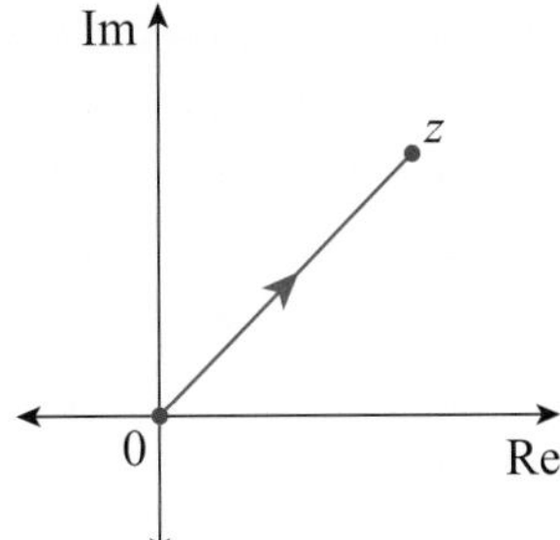

(a) mark u on the Argand diagram if $u = 2z$,

(b) mark v on the Argand diagram if $v = \frac{1}{2}z$,

(c) mark w on the Argand diagram if $w = -\frac{3}{2}z$.

6. If $z = a + bi$, $a, b \in \mathbb{R}$:

(a) find $|z|$,

(b) find $w = kz$, $k \in \mathbb{R}$,

(c) show that $|w| = k|z|$.

7. If $z = 2 - 3i$ and $w = -3 + i$, find:

(a) (i) $3z$

(ii) $2w$

(iii) $3z + 2w$

(b) Plot z, w, $3z$, $2w$ and $3z + 2w$ on an Argand diagram.

(c) Show $3z + 2w$ on the Argand diagram by completing the parallelogram with sides joining 0 to $3z$ and 0 to $2w$, if $0 = 0 + 0i$.

16.6 Modulus

How big is a complex number? Is $5 + 2i$ bigger or smaller than $2 + 5i$?

The concept of the magnitude (size) of a complex number is based on the same concept as for real numbers. The number 8 is a bigger number than 4, in the sense that it is further away from 0 than 4.

KEY TERM

The **modulus** of a complex number z is its distance to the origin $O(0, 0)$.

The modulus of a complex number is denoted by $|z|$ (read as 'mod z').

WORKED EXAMPLE

Modulus of a complex number

Find $|2 + 5i|$.

This is the distance of $2 + 5i$ from $O(0, 0)$ or the distance of $(2, 5)$ from $(0, 0)$.

$|2 + 5i| = \sqrt{(2-0)^2 + (5-0)^2} = \sqrt{(2)^2 + (5)^2} = \sqrt{29}$

Find $|w|$ if $w = 4 + i$.

$|4 + 1i| = \sqrt{(4-0)^2 + (1-0)^2} = \sqrt{16 + 1} = \sqrt{17}$

It is clear from the calculation and from the Argand diagram that $|z| > |w|$.

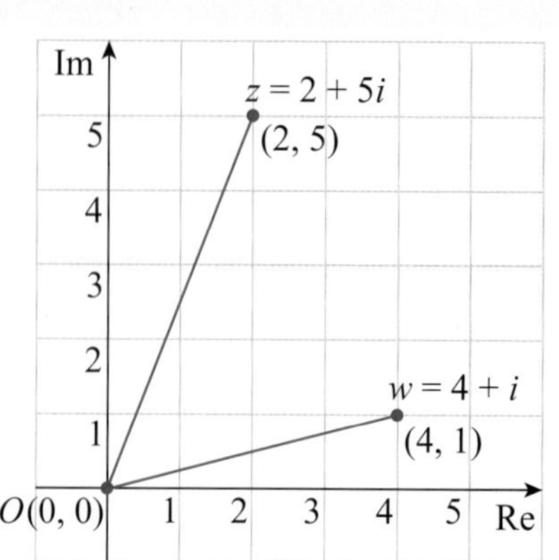

In general, for $z = a + bi$:

$|z| = \sqrt{a^2 + b^2}$

$= \sqrt{(\text{Real part})^2 + (\text{Imaginary part})^2}$

$= \sqrt{(\text{Re})^2 + (\text{Im})^2} = |OP|$

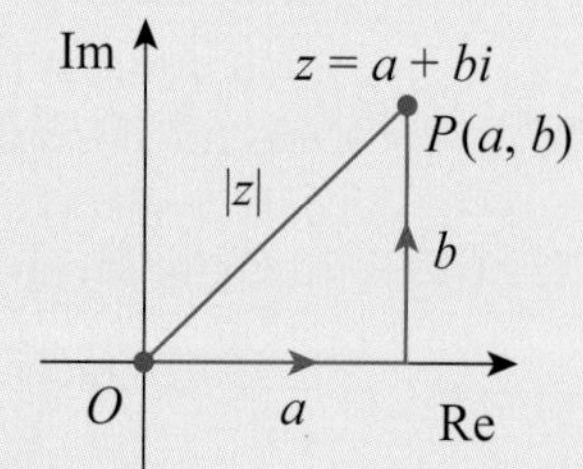

TIP

Before 'taking a modulus', always write the complex number in the form $z = a + bi = \text{Re} + \text{Im}i$.

It is important to note the following:

1. $|z|$ is always positive.
2. $|z|$ is always real because it is a distance.
3. $|i| = |0 + 1i| = \sqrt{0^2 + 1^2} = 1$

- $z = 2 + 0i$: $|z| = \sqrt{(2)^2 + (0)^2} = \sqrt{4} = 2$
- $z = 0 + 3i$: $|z| = \sqrt{(0)^2 + (3)^2} = \sqrt{9} = 3$
- $z = -1 + 1i$: $|z| = \sqrt{(-1)^2 + (1)^2} = \sqrt{2}$
- $z = 3 - 2i$: $|z| = \sqrt{(3)^2 + (-2)^2}$
  $= \sqrt{9 + 4} = \sqrt{13}$ [$z = 3 - 2i$ is $\sqrt{13}$ units from $(0, 0)$]

ACTIVITY 8

ACTION
Exploring the modulus of a complex number

OBJECTIVE
To find the moduli of complex numbers and see the effects by graphing on an Argand diagram

Steps for finding the modulus of a complex number z

1. Tidy up z into a single complex number in the form $z = a + bi$.
2. Find $|z|$ from: $|z| = \sqrt{(a)^2 + (b)^2}$.

EXAMPLE 5

Show that $|z| = |w|$, if $z = 3 - 4i$ and $w = -3 + 4i$.

Solution

$z = 3 - 4i$: $|z| = \sqrt{(3)^2 + (-4)^2} = \sqrt{9 + 16} = \sqrt{25} = 5$

$w = -3 + 4i$: $|w| = \sqrt{(-3)^2 + (4)^2} = \sqrt{9 + 16} = \sqrt{25} = 5$

$\therefore |z| = |w|$

EXAMPLE 6

If $z = 3 - 4i$ and $w = 15 + 8i$, find:

(a) $|z|$ **(d)** $|2w|$ **(f)** $|3z + w|$

(b) $|w|$ **(e)** $2|w|$ **(g)** $|z| + |w|$

(c) $|z + w|$

Solution

$z = 3 - 4i$, $w = 15 + 8i$

(a) $|z| = \sqrt{(3)^2 + (-4)^2} = \sqrt{9 + 16} = \sqrt{25} = 5$

(b) $|w| = \sqrt{(15)^2 + (8)^2} = \sqrt{225 + 64} = \sqrt{289} = 17$

(c) $|z + w| = |3 - 4i + 15 + 8i| = |18 + 4i|$
$= \sqrt{(18)^2 + (4)^2} = 2\sqrt{85}$

(d) $|2w| = |2(15 + 8i)| = |30 + 16i|$
$= \sqrt{(30)^2 + (16)^2} = 34$

(e) $2|w| = 2(17) = 34$

(f) $|3z + w| = |3(3 - 4i) + (15 + 8i)| = |9 - 12i + 15 + 8i|$
$= |24 - 4i| = \sqrt{(24)^2 + (-4)^2} = 4\sqrt{37}$

(g) $|z| + |w| = 5 + 17 = 22$

In general, the following results can be deduced from Example 6:

1. $|z + w| \neq |z| + |w|$
2. $|kz| = k|z|, k \in \mathbb{R}$

EXAMPLE 7

Find $|x + yi - 2 - 3i|$, $x, y \in \mathbb{R}$.

Solution

$|x + yi - 2 - 3i| = |(x - 2) + (y - 3)i|$
$= \sqrt{(x - 2)^2 + (y - 3)^2}$

EXAMPLE 8

If $|x + 3i| = \sqrt{13}$, find $x \in \mathbb{R}$.

Solution

$|x + 3i| = \sqrt{13} \Rightarrow \sqrt{x^2 + 9} = \sqrt{13}$

$x^2 + 9 = 13$

$x^2 = 4$

$x = \pm 2$

EXERCISE 6

1. Find $|z|$ for the following complex numbers:

(a) $z = 3 + 4i$

(b) $z = 1 + 2i$

(c) $z = 4 + 5i$

(d) $z = 2 + 5i$

(e) $z = 6i + 2$

(f) $z = 1 - i$

(g) $z = -1 + 24i$

(h) $z = -2 - 3i$

(i) $z = -\sqrt{2} + \sqrt{2}i$

(j) $z = -\frac{1}{3} + \frac{2}{3}i$

(k) $z = \frac{\sqrt{3}}{2} - \frac{1}{2}i$

(l) $z = \frac{1}{2} + \frac{1}{4}i$

2. Show that if $z = a + bi$ and $w = a - bi$, $|z| = |w|$ if $a, b \in \mathbb{R}$.

3. If $z = 3 + 4i$ and $w = 5 - 12i$, find $|z|$ and $|w|$ and then calculate each of the following:

(a) $|z + w|$ and $|z| + |w|$

(b) $|z - w|$ and $|z| - |w|$

(c) $|2z|$ and $2|z|$

(d) $|z + 3|$ and $|z| + 3$

(e) $|w + i|$ and $|w| + |i|$

(f) $|2z - w|$ and $2|z| - |w|$

(g) $\left|\frac{z}{5}\right|$ and $\frac{1}{5}|z|$

(h) $\frac{1}{13}|w|$ and $\left|\frac{w}{13}\right|$

4. Plot $0 = 0 + 0i$, $z = 3 + 4i$ and $w = 4 - 3i$ on the same Argand diagram as points O, A and B, respectively.

(a) Show that the triangle formed by these points is right-angled.

(b) Find the length of side $[AB]$ and the area of ΔOAB.

5. Copy the diagram and fill in the spaces.

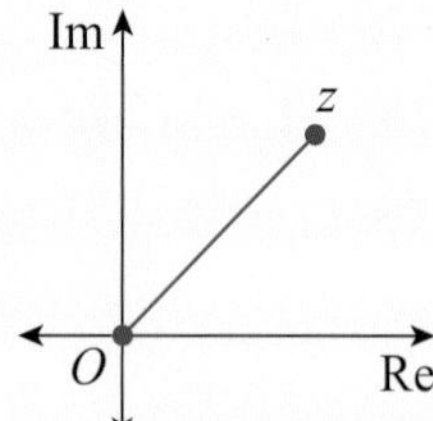

There is an _______ number of complex numbers with the same modulus as z. They all lie on a _______ with centre _______ and radius _______.

6. If a complex number z is rotated anticlockwise through 30° about the origin 0 to w, find $|w|$.

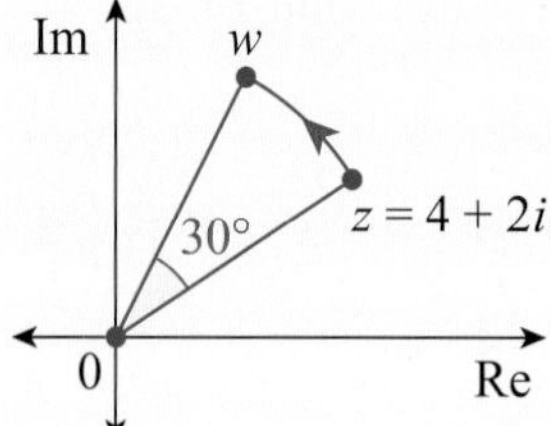

7. Plot the following complex numbers on an Argand diagram: $z_1 = 4 + 8i$, $z_2 = -4 + 8i$, $z_3 = -4 - 8i$ and $z_4 = 4 - 8i$. Label these numbers with points A, B, C and D, respectively.

(a) Show that all of these numbers have the same modulus.

(b) What is the radius of the circle with centre (0, 0) that circumscribes the rectangle $CDAB$?

(c) Find the area of this rectangle.

8. If z is a complex number, write down three other complex numbers with the same modulus as z in terms of a, b and i if $z = a + bi$, where $a, b \in \mathbb{R}$ and $i = \sqrt{-1}$.

9. **(a)** If $z = 3i + 7 - xi + y$, $x, y \in \mathbb{R}$, find $|z|$.

(b) If $z = x + yi - 2i + 3$, $x, y \in \mathbb{R}$, find $|z|$.

(c) If $z = x + yi$, find the equation and centre of the circle given by $|z| = 5$, $x, y \in \mathbb{R}$.

(d) If $z = -yi + 7 - 5i + x$, find the equation and centre of the circle given by $|z| = \sqrt{6}$, $x, y \in \mathbb{R}$.

10. Solve the following for $k \in \mathbb{R}$:

(a) $|k + 7i| = 25$

(b) $|2 + ki| = \sqrt{13}$

(c) $|2k - 3i| = 3\sqrt{5}$

(d) $|5\sqrt{3} - 3ki| = 10$

16.7 Argument

All complex numbers with the same modulus lie on a circle with centre $O(0, 0)$ and radius $r = |z|$.

$|z_1| = |z_2| = \ldots = |z_n| = \ldots = r$

You can locate a specified complex number such as z_5 by measuring out the angle to z_5 from the positive Re axis along the circle of radius r.

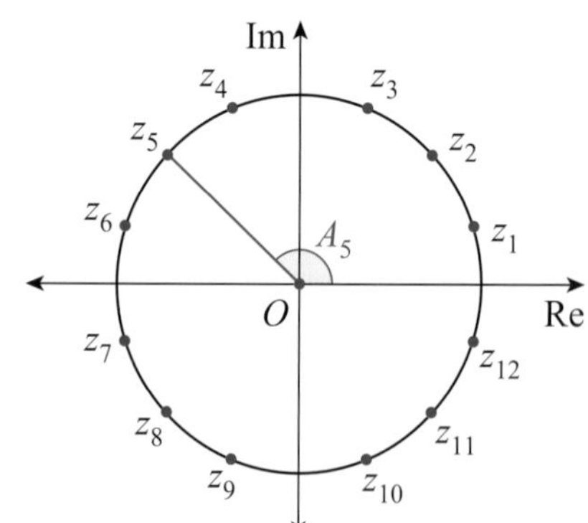

ACTIVITY 9

ACTION
Exploring the argument of a complex number

OBJECTIVE
To find the argument of complex numbers in degrees and radians

To locate z_5, you must measure out the angle in an anticlockwise direction from the positive Re axis.

This angle is known as the argument (arg for short) of the complex number: $\arg z_5 = A_5$.

KEY TERM

The **argument** ($\arg z$) of a complex number z is the angle between the line joining (0, 0) to z and the +Re axis where this angle is measured in an anticlockwise direction from the +Re axis.

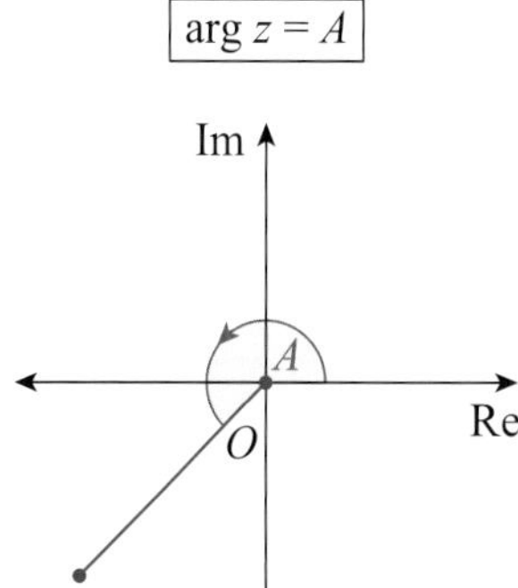

TIP

Remember, angles measured anticlockwise from the +Re axis are positive angles and angles measured clockwise from the +Re axis are negative angles.

ACTIVITY 10

ACTION
Finding the argument and modulus of z (1)

OBJECTIVE
To find the argument and the modulus of a complex number in the first quadrant

EXAMPLE 9

Find arg $(3 + 4i)$ in degrees, correct to two decimal places, and in radians, correct to three decimal places.

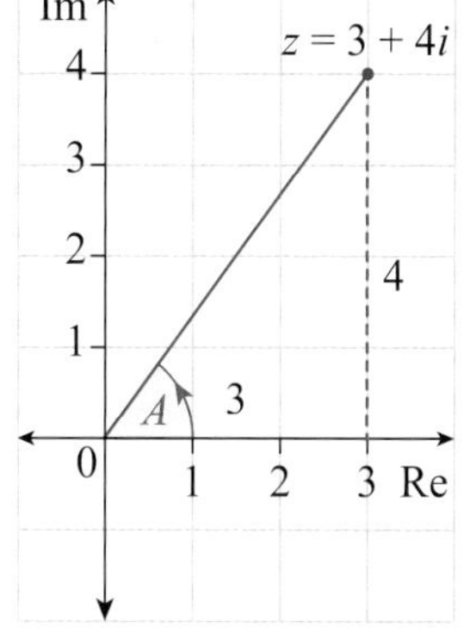

Solution

$z = 3 + 4i$

$\tan A = \frac{4}{3}$

$A = \tan^{-1}\frac{4}{3} = 53{\cdot}13° = 0{\cdot}927$ rad

$\arg z = A = 53{\cdot}13° = 0{\cdot}927$ rad

It is easy to find arg z for a complex number z in the first quadrant. For $z = a + bi$:

$\tan A = \left(\frac{b}{a}\right) \Rightarrow A = \arg z = \tan^{-1}\left(\frac{b}{a}\right) = \tan^{-1}\left(\frac{\text{Im}}{\text{Re}}\right)$

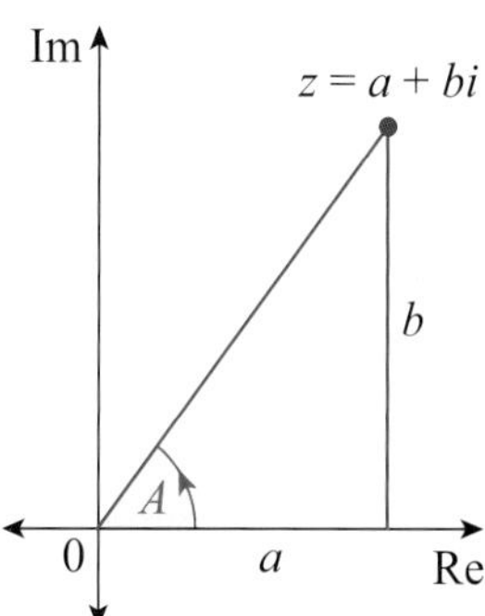

- $z = 5 + 7i$ (this number is in the first quadrant)

  $\arg z = \tan^{-1}\left(\frac{\text{Im}}{\text{Re}}\right) = \tan^{-1}\left(\frac{7}{5}\right) = 54{\cdot}46°$

What if the complex number is not in the first quadrant?

The trick here is to realise that the arguments of complex numbers in the other quadrants can be related to an angle θ in the first quadrant.

If $z_1 = a + bi$, where a and b are both positive, the arguments of z_2, z_3 and z_4 can be calculated by finding $\theta = \arg z_1 = \tan^{-1}\frac{b}{a}$ where θ is in the first quadrant.

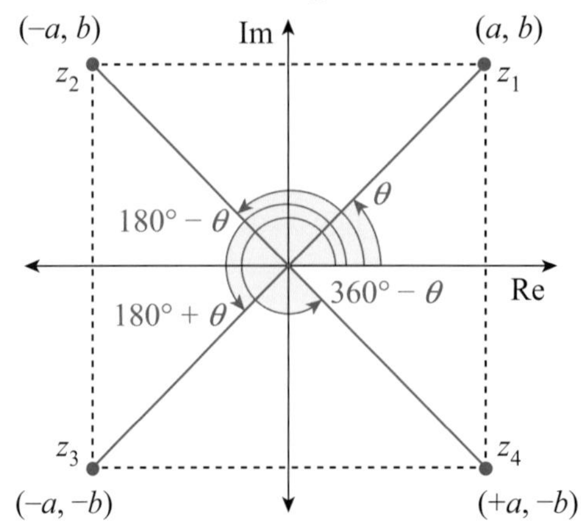

	Second Quadrant	First Quadrant
Degrees	$180° - \theta$	θ
Radians	$\pi - \theta$	θ
	Third Quadrant	**Fourth Quadrant**
Degrees	$180° + \theta$	$360° - \theta$
Radians	$\pi + \theta$	$2\pi - \theta$

Steps for finding arg *z*, where *z* is not in the first quadrant:

1. Plot the complex number z roughly to find out in which quadrant it is located and draw the angle A anticlockwise from the +Re axis to the line joining 0 to z.
2. Find the corresponding angle $\theta = \tan^{-1}\left|\frac{\text{Im}}{\text{Re}}\right|$ in the first quadrant.
3. Find A from: $A = \arg z = \begin{cases} 180° - \theta \,|\, \pi - \theta \text{ (Second)} \\ 180° + \theta \,|\, \pi + \theta \text{ (Third)} \\ 360° - \theta \,|\, 2\pi - \theta \text{ (Fourth)} \end{cases}$
   depending on the quadrant where A is located.

EXAMPLE 10

Find arg $(-5 + 3i)$ in degrees, correct to two decimal places.

Solution

$z = -5 + 3i$ is in the second quadrant.

Step 1: Draw a diagram.

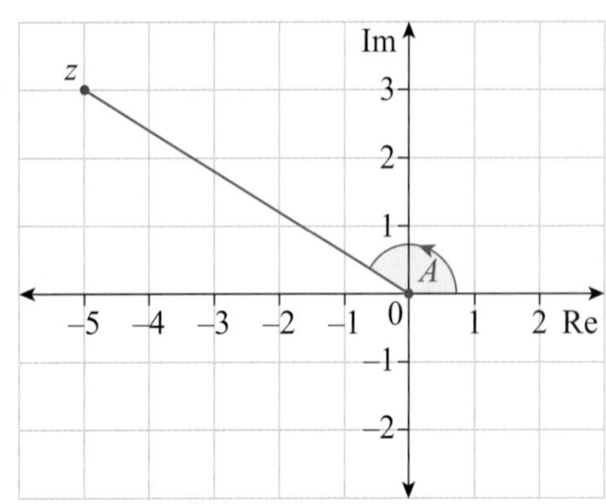

Step 2: $\theta = \tan^{-1}\left|\frac{+3}{-5}\right| = \tan^{-1}\left(\frac{3}{5}\right) = 30{\cdot}96°$

Step 3: A is in the second quadrant:
$A = 180° - 30{\cdot}96 = 149{\cdot}04°$

ACTIVITY 11

ACTION
Finding the argument and modulus of z (2)

OBJECTIVE
To find the argument and modulus of a complex number in the second quadrant

EXAMPLE 11

If $z = -\frac{\sqrt{3}}{2} - \frac{1}{2}i$, find arg z in radians.

Solution

$z = -\frac{\sqrt{3}}{2} - \frac{1}{2}i$ is in the third quadrant.

Step 1: Draw a diagram.

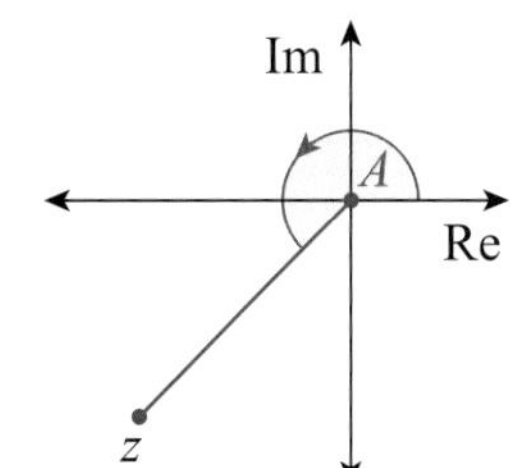

Step 2: $\theta = \tan^{-1}\left|\frac{-\frac{1}{2}}{-\frac{\sqrt{3}}{2}}\right|$

$= \tan^{-1}\left(\frac{1}{\sqrt{3}}\right) = \frac{\pi}{6}$ rads

Step 3: A is in the third quadrant:

$A = \pi + \frac{\pi}{6} = \frac{7\pi}{6}$ rad

EXAMPLE 12

Find arg $(3 - 3i)$ in degrees.

Solution

$3 - 3i$ is in the fourth quadrant.

Step 1: Draw a diagram.

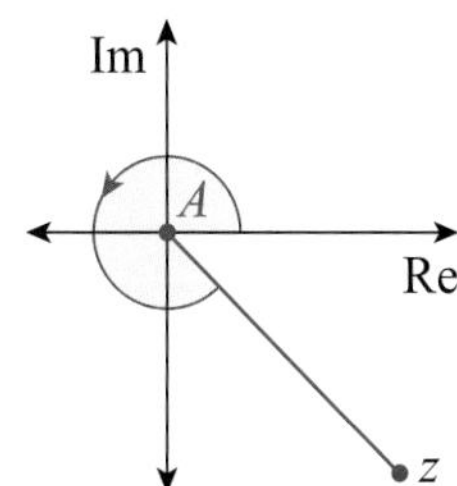

Step 2: $\theta = \tan^{-1}\left|\frac{-3}{3}\right| = \tan^{-1} 1 = 45°$

Step 3: A is in the fourth quadrant:
$A = 360° - 45° = 315°$

EXAMPLE 13

Plot the complex number z with $|z| = 3$ and arg $z = 120°$.

Solution

Draw a circle of radius 3 units, centre (0, 0).

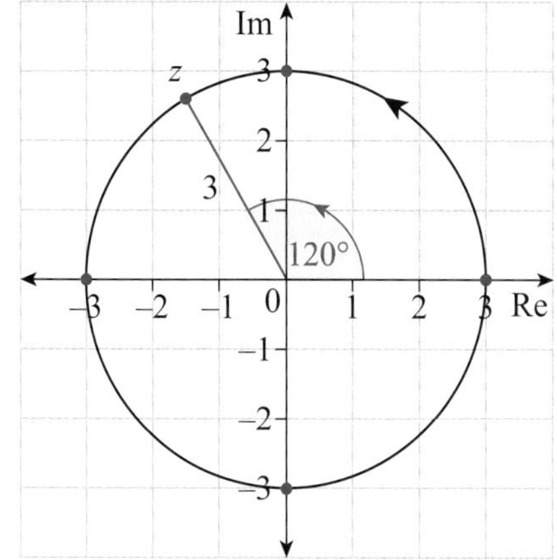

Starting at (3, 0), trace out an angle of 120° using your protractor in an anticlockwise direction to get z.

EXERCISE 7

1. For each of the following complex numbers z, plot z roughly on the Argand diagram and find $|z|$ and arg z (in radians):

(a) $z = \sqrt{3} + i$

(b) $z = -\sqrt{3} + i$

(c) $z = -\sqrt{3} - i$

(d) $z = \sqrt{3} - 1$

(e) $z = \frac{1}{2} - \frac{\sqrt{3}}{2}i$

(f) $z = -\frac{1}{\sqrt{2}} - \frac{1}{\sqrt{2}}i$

(g) $z = i$

(h) $z = -4$

(i) $z = -8i$

(j) $z = -4 - 4i$

2. Plot the following complex numbers z on graph paper using your ruler and protractor:

(a) $\arg z = 60°, |z| = 5$

(b) $\arg z = 150°, |z| = 3$

(c) $\arg z = \frac{5\pi}{3}, |z| = 1$

(d) $\arg z = \frac{5\pi}{4}, |z| = 2$

3. Find $|z|$ and $\arg z$ for the following if:

(a) $z = x + yi, x, y \in \mathbb{R}$

(b) $z = x + 3 - yi + 2i, x, y \in \mathbb{R}$

(c) $z = 3 - i + x - yi, x, y \in \mathbb{R}$

(d) $z = x - yi + c, x, y, c \in \mathbb{R}$

(e) $z = x - 3 + 2x - 3yi, x, y \in \mathbb{R}$

(f) $z = 2 - i - x - yi, x, y \in \mathbb{R}$

(g) $z = x + yi + a - bi, x, y, a, b \in \mathbb{R}$

4. Plot the curve described by the following on the Argand diagram if $x, y \in \mathbb{R}$:

(a) $\arg z = \frac{\pi}{4}$ if $z = x + yi$

(b) $\arg (z - i) = \frac{\pi}{4}$ if $z = x + yi$

(c) $\arg (z + 2 - i) = \frac{3\pi}{4}$ if $z = x + yi$

(d) $\arg (z + 4) = \frac{5\pi}{4}$ if $z = x + yi$.

5. Find x and y and hence $z = x + yi, x, y \in \mathbb{R}$, for the complex numbers on the following Argand diagrams:

(a)

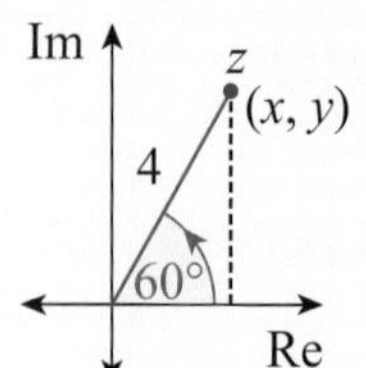

(b)

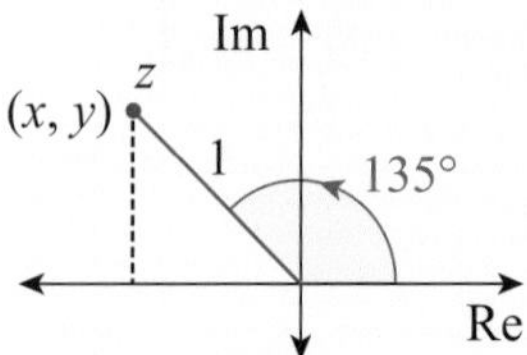

(c)

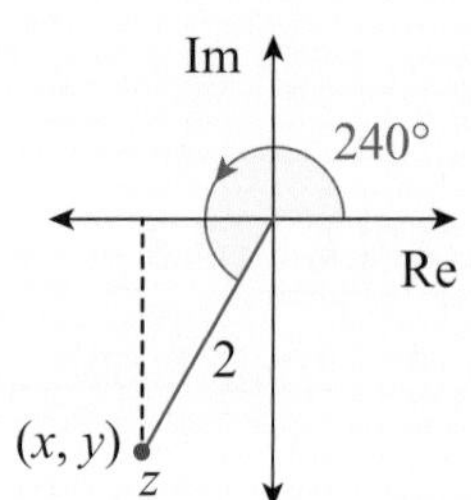

6. **(a)** Find $|z|$ and $\arg z$ if $z = \frac{1}{\sqrt{2}} + \frac{1}{\sqrt{2}}i$.

(b) Find $|w|$ and $\arg w$ if $w = 1 + 0i$.

Plot z, w and $z + w$ on an Argand diagram.

Hence, prove $\tan\left(\frac{\pi}{8}\right) = \sqrt{2} - 1$.

7. Sketch the straight line described by $\arg (z - 3 + 2i) = \frac{\pi}{4}$, if $z = x + yi$.

16.8 Conjugate

In order to divide two complex numbers, you need to understand the idea of the conjugate of a complex number.

KEY TERM

The **conjugate** $\bar{z}$ ('z bar') of a complex number z is obtained by changing the sign of the imaginary part of z.

$$z = a + bi \Rightarrow \bar{z} = a - bi \quad [+bi \text{ changes to } -bi.]$$

- $z = 3 - 2i \Rightarrow \bar{z} = \overline{3 - 2i} = 3 + 2i$
- $z = -\sqrt{3} + \frac{1}{2}i \Rightarrow \bar{z} = \overline{-\sqrt{3} + \frac{1}{2}i} = -\sqrt{3} - \frac{1}{2}i$

ACTIVITY 12

ACTION
Exploring the conjugate of a complex number

OBJECTIVE
To find the conjugate of complex numbers and to deduce some general results

TIP
Make sure the complex number is in the form $a + bi$ before you take its conjugate.

- $\overline{7i - 2} = \overline{-2 + 7i} = -2 - 7i$
- $\overline{3} = \overline{3 + 0i} = 3 - 0i = 3$ [The conjugate of a purely real number is the number itself.]
- $\overline{2i} = \overline{0 + 2i} = 0 - 2i = -2i$ [The conjugate of a purely imaginary number is the negative of the number.]
- $z = x + iy - 2i + 3, x, y \in \mathbb{R}$
  $\bar{z} = (x + 3) - i(y - 2)$
- $z = -2 - i$
  $\Rightarrow 3\bar{z} = 3(\bar{z}) = 3(\overline{-2 - i}) = 3(-2 + i) = -6 + 3i$

ACTIVITY 13

ACTION
Proving properties of conjugates

OBJECTIVE
To prove certain conjugate properties by showing the left-hand side (LHS) is equal to the right-hand side (RHS)

EXAMPLE 14

If $z = 3 - 2i$ and $w = 2 + 4i$, find the following in the form $a + bi$:

(a) $z + \bar{z}$
(b) $z - \bar{z}$
(c) $\bar{\bar{z}}$
(d) $3\bar{z} - \bar{i}$
(e) $\overline{z + w}$
(f) $\bar{z} + \bar{w}$
(g) $\overline{3z + 2w}$
(h) $3\bar{z} + 2\bar{w}$
(i) $|z|$
(j) $\bar{z}$

Solution

$z = 3 - 2i, w = 2 + 4i$

(a) $z + \bar{z} = 3 - 2i + \overline{3 - 2i}$
$= 3 - 2i + 3 + 2i = 6 + 0i = 6$

(b) $z - \bar{z} = 3 - 2i - (\overline{3 - 2i})$
$= 3 - 2i - (3 + 2i) = 3 - 3 - 2i - 2i = 0 - 4i = -4i$

(c) $\bar{\bar{z}} = \overline{\overline{3 - 2i}} = \overline{3 + 2i} = 3 - 2i \quad [\bar{\bar{z}} = z]$

(d) $3\bar{z} - \bar{i} = 3(\overline{3 - 2i}) - \bar{i}$
$= 3\ (3 + 2i) + i = 9 + 6i + i = 9 + 7i$

(e) $\overline{z + w} = \overline{3 - 2i + 2 + 4i}$
$= \overline{5 + 2i} = 5 - 2i$

(f) $\bar{z} + \bar{w} = \overline{3 - 2i} + \overline{2 + 4i}$
$= 3 + 2i + 2 - 4i = 5 - 2i$

(g) $\overline{3z + 2w} = \overline{3(z) + 2(w)} = \overline{3(3 - 2i) + 2(2 + 4i)}$
$= \overline{9 - 6i + 4 + 8i} = \overline{13 + 2i} = 13 - 2i$

(h) $3\bar{z} + 2\bar{w} = 3(\overline{3 - 2i}) + 2(\overline{2 + 4i})$
$= 3(3 + 2i) + 2(2 - 4i) = 9 + 6i + 4 - 8i = 13 - 2i$

(i) $|z| = |3 - 2i| = \sqrt{(3)^2 + (-2)^2} = \sqrt{9 + 4} = \sqrt{13}$

(j) $|\bar{z}| = |3 + 2i| = \sqrt{(3)^2 + (2)^2} = \sqrt{9 + 4} = \sqrt{13}$

ACTIVITY 14

ACTION
Proving modulus and conjugate properties

OBJECTIVE
To prove certain modulus and conjugate properties by showing the left-hand side (LHS) is equal to the right-hand side (RHS)

In general, the following results can be deduced from Example 14:

1. $\overline{z+w} = \bar{z} + \bar{w}$
2. $\overline{z-w} = \bar{z} - \bar{w}$
3. $\bar{\bar{z}} = z$
4. $\overline{kz + lw} = k\bar{z} + l\bar{w},\ k, l \in \mathbb{R}$
5. $|\bar{z}| = |z|$

EXERCISE 8

1. Find $\bar{z}$ for the following in form $a + bi$:

(a) $z = 3$
(b) $z = -2$
(c) $z = 5i$
(d) $z = -7i$
(e) $z = 3i - 2$
(f) $z = 5i - 1$
(g) $z = -6i + \sqrt{3}$
(h) $z = 5 - 1i + 3 - 2i$
(i) $z = x + 2i - 7, x \in \mathbb{R}$
(j) $z = 3 + x - yi, x, y \in \mathbb{R}$
(k) $z = 4x - 3i + y - 2,$ $x, y \in \mathbb{R}$

2. If $z = 5 + 7i$ and $w = -2 - 8i$, find the following:

(a) $3\bar{z}$
(b) $4\bar{w}$
(c) $\overline{3z + 4w}$
(d) $2\bar{z} - \bar{w}$
(e) $\overline{\frac{w}{2} + z}$
(f) $2\bar{z} + w$
(g) $\overline{z + \bar{w}}$
(h) $\overline{3\bar{z} - \bar{w}}$
(i) $8\bar{z} + 7\bar{w}$
(j) $3\bar{\bar{z}} + \bar{w}$

3. **(a)** If $z_1 = 3 + 4i$, find $\bar{z}_1$.

(i) Plot z_1 and $\bar{z}_1$ on an Argand diagram.

(ii) Join z_1 and $\bar{z}_1$ with a line segment and an arrow from z_1 to $\bar{z}_1$.

Repeat the process in parts **(i)** and **(ii)** above for the following and plot all complex numbers and their conjugates on the same Argand diagram:

(b) $z_2 = -3 - 2i$
(c) $z_3 = 1 - 3i$
(d) $z_4 = -2 + i$
(e) Make a conclusion regarding z and $\bar{z}$ in geometric terms.

4. **(a)** If $z = -15 + 8i$, find $\bar{z}$. Show that $|z| = |\bar{z}|$.

(b) If $z = \sqrt{3} + i$, find $\bar{z}$. Show that $|z| = |\bar{z}|$.

(c) If $z = \frac{3}{5} - \frac{4}{5}i$, find $\bar{z}$. Show that $|z| = |\bar{z}|$.

(d) If $z = -5 + 12i$, find $-z$, $\bar{z}$ and $-\bar{z}$. Show that $|z| = |-z| = |\bar{z}| = |-\bar{z}|$.

5. If z is any complex number, write down three other complex numbers with the same modulus as z, in terms of z, the minus sign and the conjugate symbol.

6. If $z = a + bi$ and $w = c + di$, $a, b, c, d \in \mathbb{R}$, show that:

(a) $\bar{\bar{z}} = z$
(b) $\overline{z + w} = \bar{z} + \bar{w}$
(c) $\overline{z - w} = \bar{z} - \bar{w}$
(d) $\overline{kz + lw} = k\bar{z} + l\bar{w},\ k, l \in \mathbb{R}$
(e) $z + \bar{z} = 2a$
(f) $w - \bar{w} = 2di$
(g) $|z| = |\bar{z}|$

16.9 Multiplication

To multiply complex numbers, multiply out the brackets term by term and put $i^2 = -1$ when it occurs.

$$(4 - 2i)(5 + 3i) = 4 \times 5 + 4 \times 3i - 2i \times 5 - 2i \times 3i$$
$$= 20 + 12i - 10i - 6i^2 = 20 + 2i + 6 = 26 + 2i$$

EXAMPLE 15

If $z = 2 + 3i$, $w = 5 - 4i$ and $u = -1 - 2i$, find the following:

(a) zw	**(c)** u^2	**(e)** $\overline{zw}$	**(g)** $\lvert zw \rvert$	**(i)** $u(zw)$
(b) uz	**(d)** $z\bar{z}$	**(f)** $\bar{z}\,\bar{w}$	**(h)** $\lvert z \rvert \lvert w \rvert$	**(j)** $(uz)w$

Solution

(a) $zw = (2 + 3i)(5 - 4i)$

$= 10 - 8i + 15i - 12i^2 = 10 + 7i + 12 = 22 + 7i$

(b) $uz = (-1 - 2i)(2 + 3i)$

$= -2 - 3i - 4i - 6i^2 = -2 - 7i + 6 = 4 - 7i$

(c) $u^2 = (-1 - 2i)(-1 - 2i)$

$= 1 + 2i + 2i + 4i^2 = 1 + 4i - 4 = -3 + 4i$

(d) $z\bar{z} = (2 + 3i)(2 - 3i)$

$= 4 - 6i + 6i - 9i^2 = 4 + 9 = (2)^2 + (3)^2 = 13$

(e) $\overline{zw} = \overline{22 + 7i} = 22 - 7i$

(f) $\bar{z}\,\bar{w} = \overline{2 + 3i}\;\overline{5 - 4i}$

$= (2 - 3i)(5 + 4i) = 10 + 8i - 15i - 12i^2$

$= 10 - 7i + 12 = 22 - 7i$ [In general, $\overline{zw} = \bar{z}\,\bar{w}$.]

(g) $|zw| = |22 + 7i| = \sqrt{22^2 + 7^2} = \sqrt{533}$

(h) $|z||w| = |2 + 3i||5 - 4i| = \sqrt{2^2 + 3^2}\,\sqrt{5^2 + (-4)^2} = \sqrt{13}\sqrt{41} = \sqrt{533}$ [In general, $|zw| = |z||w|$.]

(i) $u(zw) = (-1 - 2i)(22 + 7i) = -22 - 7i - 44i - 14i^2 = -8 - 51i$

(j) $(uz)w = (4 - 7i)(5 - 4i) = 20 - 16i - 35i + 28i^2 = -8 - 51i = u(zw)$

In general, the following results can be deduced from Example 15:

1. $\overline{zw} = \bar{z}\,\bar{w}$ **2.** $|zw| = |z||w|$ **3.** $uzw = u(zw) = (uz)w$.

TIP

Conjugate Multiplication Trick

If you multiply a complex number by its conjugate, you get: (Positive value of Re)^2 + (Positive value of Im)^2.

- $(4 - 11i)(4 + 11i) = 16 + 44i - 44i - 121i^2$
  $= 16 - 121i^2 = 16 + 121 = (4)^2 + (11)^2 = 137$
- $(a + bi)\overline{(a + bi)} = (a + bi)(a - bi) = (a)^2 + (b)^2 = a^2 + b^2$ [Check it out.]
- $(\sqrt{2} + \sqrt{3}i)(\sqrt{2} - \sqrt{3}i) = (\sqrt{2})^2 + (\sqrt{3})^2 = 2 + 3 = 5$

EXAMPLE 16

Simplify $(1 - i)(2 - 3i)(1 + i)$.

Solution

$(1 - i)(2 - 3i)(1 + i)$ [Rearrange]

$= (1 - i)(1 + i)(2 - 3i)$ [Use the conjugate multiplication trick for the first two brackets.]

$= (1^2 + 1^2)(2 - 3i)$

$= 2(2 - 3i)$

$= 4 - 6i$

Powers of complex numbers

To find a power of a complex number, multiply out the brackets.

EXAMPLE 17

Expand the following:

(a) $(3 - 2i)^2$

(b) $(2 - i)^3$

(c) $(1 + i)^4$

Solution

(a) $(3 - 2i)^2 = (3 - 2i)(3 - 2i)$
$= 9 - 6i - 6i + 4i^2 = 9 - 12i - 4 = 5 - 12i$

(b) $(2 - i)^3 = (2 - i)(2 - i)(2 - i)$
$= (4 - 2i - 2i + i^2)(2 - i)$
$= (3 - 4i)(2 - i) = 6 - 3i - 8i + 4i^2 = 2 - 11i$

(c) $(1 + i)^4 = (1 + i)(1 + i)(1 + i)(1 + i)$
$= (1 + 2i + i^2)(1 + 2i + i^2)$
$= (2i)(2i) = 4i^2 = -4$

You can also expand brackets to powers using the binomial theorem.

EXAMPLE 18

Expand $(2 + 3i)^4$.

Solution

$(2 + 3i)^4 = {}^4C_0(2)^4(3i)^0 + {}^4C_1(2)^3(3i)^1 + {}^4C_2(2)^2(3i)^2 + {}^4C_3(2)^1(3i)^3 + {}^4C_4(2)^0(3i)^4$

$= 1 \times 16 \times 1 + 4 \times 8 \times 3i + 6 \times 4 \times 9i^2 + 4 \times 2 \times 27i^3 + 1 \times 1 \times 81i^4$

$= 16 + 96i - 216 - 216i + 81$

$= -119 - 120i$

De Moivre's theorem is needed for higher powers (see later in this book).

Geometric interpretation of complex number multiplication

ACTIVITY 15

ACTION
Exploring the geometric effect of multiplying numbers by powers of i (1)

OBJECTIVE
To explore the effects of multiplying numbers by powers of i

ACTIVITY 16

ACTION
Exploring the geometric effect of multiplying numbers by powers of i (2)

OBJECTIVE
To explore more difficult examples of the effects of multiplying numbers by powers of i

WORKED EXAMPLE

The geometric effect of multiplying a complex number by powers of i

Consider the complex number $z = 4 + 3i$.

$iz = i(4 + 3i) = 4i + 3i^2 = -3 + 4i$

$i^2z = -1(4 + 3i) = -4 - 3i$

$i^3z = -i(4 + 3i) = -4 - 3i^2 = 3 - 4i$

$i^4z = 1(4 + 3i) = 4 + 3i$

On the Argand diagram, z, iz, i^2z, i^3z and i^4z are represented by the points A, B, C, D and E, respectively, and O is (0, 0).

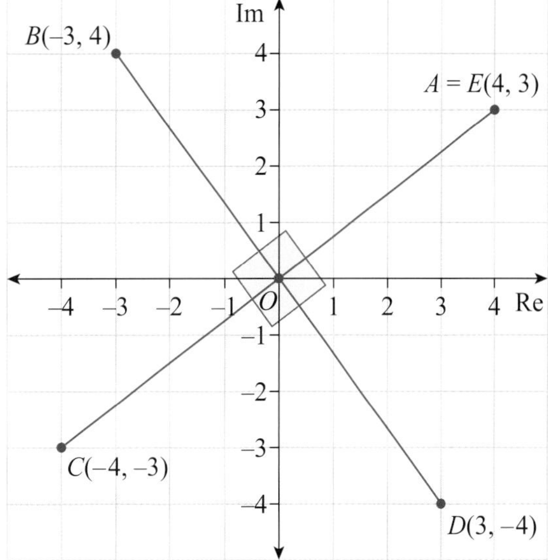

Calculate the slopes of the lines OA, OB, OC, OD and OE and the moduli of the complex numbers corresponding to the points A, B, C, D and E.

Slope of $OA = \frac{3}{4}$; $|OA| = |z| = \sqrt{4^2 + 3^2} = 5$

Slope of $OB = \frac{4}{-3} = -\frac{4}{3}$; $|OB| = |iz| = \sqrt{(-3)^2 + 4^2} = 5$

Slope of $OC = \frac{-3}{-4} = \frac{3}{4}$; $|OC| = |i^2z| = \sqrt{(-4)^2 + (-3)^2} = 5$

Slope of $OD = \frac{-4}{3} = -\frac{4}{3}$; $|OD| = |i^3z| = \sqrt{3^2 + (-4)^2} = 5$

Slope of $OE = \frac{3}{4}$; $|OE| = |i^4z| = \sqrt{4^2 + 3^2} = 5$

All of the moduli are the same.

(Slope of OA) × (Slope of OB) $= \frac{3}{4} \times \frac{4}{-3} = -1 \Rightarrow OA \perp OB$

$\therefore |\angle AOB| = 90°$

Similarly, it can be shown that $OB \perp OC$, $OC \perp OD$ and $OD \perp OE$.

Conclusion

Multiplying a complex number z by i rotates it in an anticlockwise direction about $O(0, 0)$ by 90° but leaves its modulus unchanged.

Multiplying a complex number z by i^2 rotates it in an anticlockwise direction about $O(0, 0)$ by 180° but leaves its modulus unchanged.

Multiplying a complex number z by i^3 rotates it in an anticlockwise direction about $O(0, 0)$ by 270° but leaves its modulus unchanged.

Multiplying a complex number z by i^4 rotates it in an anticlockwise direction about $O(0, 0)$ by 360° but leaves its modulus unchanged.

The multiplication of a complex number z:

By	Anticlockwise rotation of the line from 0 to z through	$\|z\|$
i	90°	unchanged
i^2	180°	unchanged
i^3	270°	unchanged
i^4	360°	unchanged

WORKED EXAMPLE

The geometric effect of multiplying two complex numbers

Consider the complex numbers $z = 2 + i$ and $w = 1 + i$.

$z = 2 + i \Rightarrow |z| = \sqrt{(2)^2 + (1)^2} = \sqrt{5}$

$\tan A = \frac{1}{2} \Rightarrow \arg z = A = 26{\cdot}57°$

$w = 1 + i \Rightarrow |w| = \sqrt{(1)^2 + (1)^2} = \sqrt{2}$

$\tan B = \frac{1}{1} \Rightarrow \arg w = B = 45°$

$z \times w = (2 + i)(1 + i) = 2 + 2i + i + i^2 = 1 + 3i$

$|zw| = \sqrt{1 + 9} = \sqrt{10} = \sqrt{2} \times \sqrt{5} = |z| \times |w|$

$\arg (zw) = \tan^{-1}\frac{3}{1} = 71{\cdot}57° = 26{\cdot}57° + 45° = \arg (z) + \arg (w)$

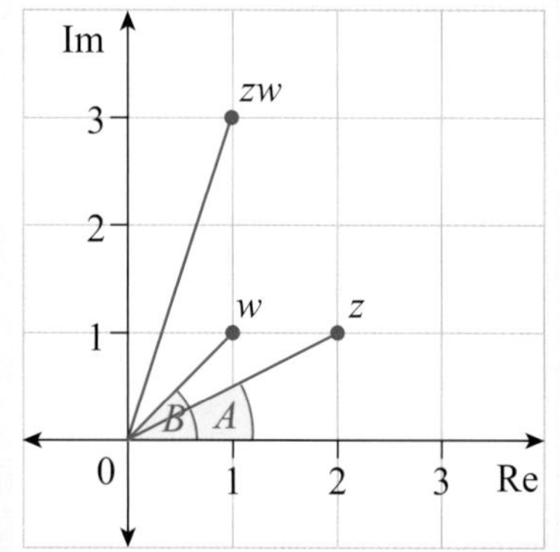

ACTIVITY 17

ACTION
Exploring the geometric effect of multiplying complex numbers

OBJECTIVE
To explore the effects of multiplying complex numbers by each other

Conclusion

When a complex number z is multiplied by a complex number w, z is rotated anticlockwise about $O(0, 0)$ by the angle w makes with the +Re axis. Its modulus is multiplied (stretched or shrunk) by the modulus of w.

EXAMPLE 19

(a) If $w = 1 + i$, find arg w.

(b) A ship is travelling along the line joining 0 to z, where $z = 2 + i$ and $0 = 0 + 0i$. The captain wants to change the heading by 45° in an anticlockwise direction. Find the new heading.

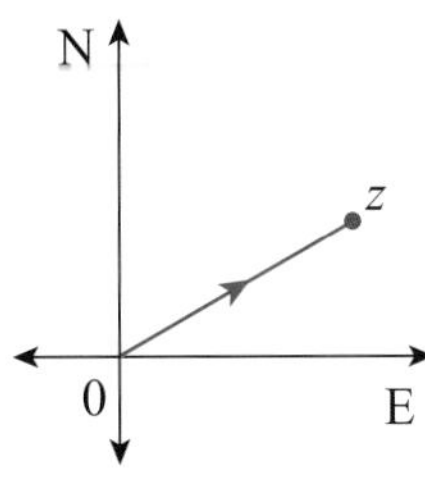

Solution

(a)

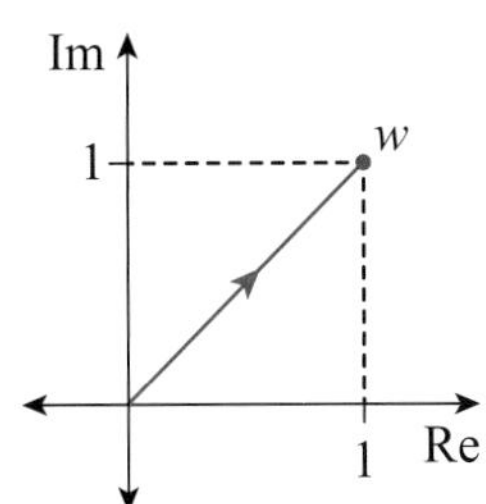

$w = 1 + i \Rightarrow \arg w = \tan^{-1}\frac{1}{1} = 45°$

(b) To rotate $z = 2 + i$ by 45°, multiply z by $w = 1 + i$.

$zw = (2 + i)(1 + i) = 2 + 2i + i + i^2$

$= 2 + 3i - 1 = 1 + 3i$

New heading:

$\tan C = \frac{3}{1} = 3 \Rightarrow C = \tan^{-1} 3 = 71{\cdot}6°$

Answer: E 71·6° N

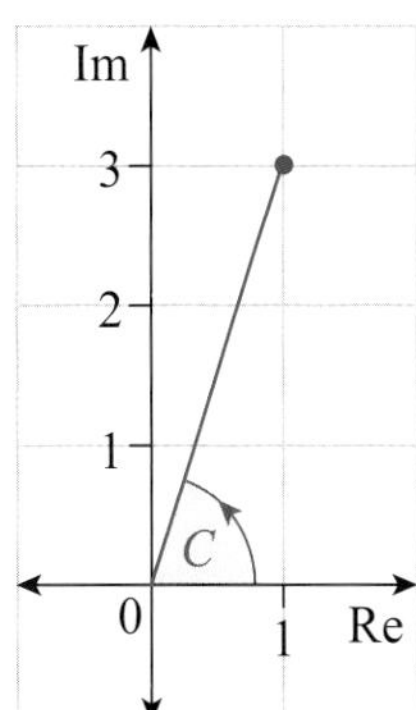

EXERCISE 9

1. Simplify the following giving your answer in the form $a + bi$, $a, b \in \mathbb{R}$:

 (a) $2i(3 + 2i)$

 (b) $(2 + i)(3 + i)$

 (c) $(3 + 2i)(4 + 3i)$

 (d) $(-2 + 3i)(5 + i)$

 (e) $(-2 - i)(-i + 2)$

 (f) $(5 + 3i)(2 - 3i)$

 (g) $(-1 - i)(-5 - 3i)$

 (h) $\left(\frac{1}{2} + i\right)\left(\frac{3}{2} - 2i\right)$

 (i) $(\sqrt{2} + 3i)(2\sqrt{2} + i)$

 (j) $(i^2 + i^3)(i^8 - i^7)$

 (k) $3i + 2(5 - 2i) - i(1 + i)$

 (l) $i^3 - i(1 + i) + i^2$

 (m) $(3 - i)(i^4 + i^7)$

2. If $z = 3 + 5i$, $w = 2 - 4i$ and $u = -5 - 3i$, find the following in the form $a + bi$, $a, b \in \mathbb{R}$:

 (a) zw **(e)** $\bar{z}\,\bar{w}$ **(i)** $uw\bar{z}$

 (b) uz **(f)** $\overline{uz}$ **(j)** $w\bar{u}z$

 (c) $\bar{z}w$ **(g)** $\bar{w}\,\bar{u}$

 (d) $\overline{zw}$ **(h)** uwz

3. Write down the answers to the following products of conjugates:

 (a) $(1 - i)(1 + i)$

 (b) $(2 + 3i)(2 - 3i)$

 (c) $(5 - 2i)(5 + 2i)$

 (d) $(6 - 3i)(6 + 3i)$

 (e) $(1 - 2i)(1 + 2i)$

 (f) $\left(\frac{1}{2} - \frac{1}{2}i\right)\left(\frac{1}{2} + \frac{1}{2}i\right)$

 (g) $(\sqrt{3} - 4i)(\sqrt{3} + 4i)$

(h) $(\sqrt{3} - \sqrt{7}i)(\sqrt{3} + \sqrt{7}i)$

(i) $(x + 2i)(x - 2i), x \in \mathbb{R}$

(j) $(x + yi)(x - yi), x, y \in \mathbb{R}$

4. Write down the answers to the following:

(a) $5(2 - i)(2 + i)$

(b) $(3 - i)(3 + i)(1 - i)$

(c) $(2 - 3i)(1 + i)(2 + 3i)$

(d) $(1 + i)(1 - i) - (2 - i)(2 + i)$

5. Simplify the following giving your answer in the form $a + bi$:

(a) $(5 + 6i)^2$

(b) $(1 - i)^3$

(c) $(1 - i)^4$

(d) $(2 + i)^2 - (2 - i)^2$

(e) $(3 + i)^2 - (3 - i)^2$

(f) $(1 + i)^4 - (1 - i)^4$

6. **(a)** Multiply $-8 + 6i$ by i.

(b) Plot $-8 + 6i$ and $i(-8 + 6i)$ on an Argand diagram.

(c) Calculate $|i(-8 + 6i)|$ and $|-8 + 6i|$.

(d) What was the effect on $-8 + 6i$ of multiplication by i?

7. **(a)** Plot $2 + 4i$ on an Argand diagram.

(b) Multiply $-i$ by $2 + 4i$.

(c) Plot $-i(2 + 4i)$ on the same Argand diagram.

(d) Calculate $|2 + 4i|$ and $|-i(2 + 4i)|$

(e) What was the effect of multiplication by $-i$ on $2 + 4i$?

8. Copy and complete the following statements: When a complex number:

(a) z is multiplied by 3 it is rotated ________ by ________ degrees and its modulus is multiplied by ________.

(b) z is multiplied by i it is rotated ________ by ________ degrees and its modulus is multiplied by ________.

(c) z is multiplied by $\frac{1}{2}i^2$ it is rotated ________ by ________ degrees and its modulus is multiplied by ________.

(d) z is multiplied by $3i^3$ it is rotated ________ by ________ degrees and its modulus is multiplied by________.

9. If $z = 1 + \sqrt{3}i$ and $w = \sqrt{3} + i$, find:

(a) $|z|$, arg z

(b) $|w|$, arg w

(c) $|zw|$, arg zw

(d) Show that $|zw| = |z| \times |w|$ and arg (zw) = arg z + arg w.

10. **(a)** Plot $z = -3 + 6i$ and $w = 1 - 2i$ on an Argand diagram.

(b) Find $|z|$. Find arg z in degrees, correct to two decimal places.

(c) Find $|w|$. Find arg w in degrees, correct to two decimal places.

(d) Evaluate zw and plot it on the Argand diagram.

(e) Find $|zw|$. Find arg zw in degrees, correct to two decimal places.

(f) Show that $|zw| = |z||w|$ and arg zw = arg z + arg w.

11. Complete the statement: If a complex number z is multiplied by w it is rotated ________ by ________ and its modulus is ________.

12. **(a)** Plot $1 + i$ on an Argand diagram.
    (b) Calculate $|1 + i|$.
    (c) What angle does the line segment joining $1 + i$ to the origin make with the positive sense of the Re axis?
    (d) Using what you know about multiplication of one complex number by another, state what will happen to $1 + i$ if it is multiplied by $1 + i$?
    (e) Knowing the modulus of $1 + i$ and the angle it makes with the real axis, use this information to work out $(1 + i)(1 + i)$.
    (f) Now calculate $(1 + i)(1 + i)$ by multiplying them out normally.
    (g) Was your prediction in part **(d)** correct?

13. Plot $z = 2 + 3i$ and its conjugate $\bar{z}$ on the Argand diagram.
    (a) Show that $|z| = |\bar{z}|$.
    (b) What angle do you expect $z\,\bar{z}$ to make with $+x$-axis?
    (c) Multiply out $z\,\bar{z}$ and plot it on the same Argand diagram as z.
    (d) Show $z\bar{z} = |z|^2$.
    (e) Complete the statement: Multiplying a complex number z by its conjugate $\bar{z}$ will always result in mapping z to a number on ________ with a modulus equal to ________.

16.10 Division

To divide one complex number by another complex number, multiply above and below by the conjugate of the number on the bottom.

EXAMPLE 20

Simplify $\dfrac{3+2i}{5+3i}$.

Solution

$\dfrac{3+2i}{5+3i} = \dfrac{(3+2i)}{(5+3i)} \times \dfrac{(5-3i)}{(5-3i)}$ [Multiply above and below by the conjugate of $(5 + 3i)$.]

$= \dfrac{(3+2i)(5-3i)}{(5+3i)(5-3i)}$ [$(5 + 3i)(5 - 3i) = 5^2 + 3^2 = (\text{Re})^2 + (\text{Im})^2$ (Conjugate multiplication trick)]

$= \dfrac{15 - 9i + 10i - 6i^2}{25+9} = \dfrac{21 + 1i}{34}$

$= \dfrac{21}{34} + \dfrac{1}{34}i$ [Write your answer in the form $a + bi$.]

Some nice results

1. $\dfrac{1}{i} = \dfrac{(1)}{(i)} \times \dfrac{(-i)}{(-i)} = \dfrac{-i}{1^2} = -i = 0 - i$

TIP

$\dfrac{1}{i} = -i$: Division by i is the same as multiplication by $-i$.

2. $\frac{1}{-i} = i$

▸ $\frac{2-3i}{i} = (2-3i)(-i) = -2i + 3i^2 = -3 - 2i$

Division is sometimes called the multiplicative inverse.

EXAMPLE 21

Simplify the following:

(a) $\frac{3-6i}{3i}$

(b) $\frac{\overline{3-2i}}{4+i}$

(c) $\frac{3}{2-i}$

(d) $\frac{1}{\cos A + i\sin A}$

Solution

(a) $\frac{3-6i}{3i} = \frac{(3-6i)}{3} \times \frac{(-i)}{1} = \frac{(-6-3i)}{3} = -2 - i$

(b) $\frac{\overline{3-2i}}{4+i} = \frac{3+2i}{4+i} = \frac{(3+2i)}{(4+i)} \times \frac{(4-i)}{(4-i)}$

$= \frac{12 - 3i + 8i - 2i^2}{17} = \frac{14+5i}{17} = \frac{14}{17} + \frac{5}{17}i$

(c) $\frac{3}{2-i} = \frac{(3)}{(2-i)} \times \frac{(2+i)}{(2+i)} = \frac{6+3i}{5} = \frac{6}{5} + \frac{3}{5}i$

(d) $\frac{1}{\cos A + i\sin A} = \frac{1}{(\cos A + i\sin A)} \times \frac{(\cos A - i\sin A)}{(\cos A - i\sin A)}$

$= \frac{\cos A - i\sin A}{\cos^2 A + \sin^2 A} = \frac{\cos A - i\sin A}{1} = \cos A - i\sin A$

EXAMPLE 22

If $z = 3 + i$ and $w = 2 - i$, find:

(a) $|z|$

(b) $|w|$

(c) $\bar{z}$

(d) $\bar{w}$

(e) $\frac{z}{w}$

(f) $\overline{\left(\frac{z}{w}\right)}$

(g) $\frac{\bar{z}}{\bar{w}}$

(h) $\left|\frac{z}{w}\right|$

(i) $\frac{|z|}{|w|}$

Solution

(a) $|z| = |3+i| = \sqrt{(3)^2 + (1)^2} = \sqrt{9+1} = \sqrt{10}$

(b) $|w| = 2 - i = \sqrt{(2)^2 + (-1)^2} = \sqrt{4+1} = \sqrt{5}$

(c) $\bar{z} = \overline{3+i} = 3 - i$

(d) $\bar{w} = \overline{2-i} = 2 + i$

(e) $\frac{z}{w} = \frac{3+i}{2-i} = \frac{(3+i)}{(2-i)} \times \frac{(2+i)}{(2+i)}$

$= \frac{6 + 3i + 2i + i^2}{4+1} = \frac{6+5i-1}{5} = \frac{5+5i}{5}$

$= \frac{5(1+i)}{5} = 1 + i$

(f) $\overline{\left(\frac{z}{w}\right)} = \overline{1+i} = 1 - i$

(g) $\frac{\bar{z}}{\bar{w}} = \frac{3-i}{2+i} = \frac{(3-i)}{(2+i)} \times \frac{(2-i)}{(2-i)}$

$= \frac{6 - 3i - 2i + i^2}{4+1} = \frac{6-5i-1}{5}$

$= \frac{5-5i}{5} = \frac{5(1-i)}{5} = 1 - i$

(h) $\left|\frac{z}{w}\right| = |1+i| = \sqrt{1^2 + 1^2} = \sqrt{2}$

(i) $\frac{|z|}{|w|} = \frac{\sqrt{10}}{\sqrt{5}} = \sqrt{2}$

In general, the following results can be deduced from Example 22:

1. $\overline{\left(\frac{z}{w}\right)} = \frac{\bar{z}}{\bar{w}}$

2. $\left|\frac{z}{w}\right| = \frac{|z|}{|w|}$

ACTIVITY 18

ACTION
Exploring the geometric effect of dividing complex numbers (1)

OBJECTIVE
To explore the geometric effects of dividing complex numbers by each other

Geometric interpretation of complex number division

Division of a complex number z by powers of i

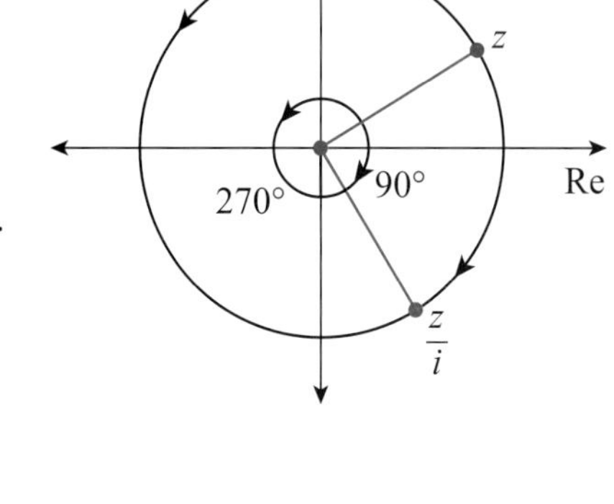

Since $\frac{z}{i} = -iz = i^3 z$, the division of a complex number z by i means an anticlockwise rotation of 270° about the origin. This is the same as a clockwise rotation of 90° about (0, 0).

Also, $\left|\frac{z}{i}\right| = |-iz| = |-i| \times |z| = |z|$

means dividing a complex number by i but leaves its modulus unchanged.

The division of a complex number z:

By	Clockwise rotation of the line joining 0 to z through	$\lvert z\rvert$
i	90°	unchanged
i^2	180°	unchanged
i^3	270°	unchanged
i^4	360°	unchanged

EXAMPLE 23

(a) Plot $z = 2 - 4i$ on the Argand diagram. Represent this point by P.

(b) Evaluate $w = \frac{z}{2i}$ and plot w on the same Argand diagram as z. Represent this point by Q.

(c) Show that $|w| = \frac{|z|}{2}$.

(d) Find the slope of $[OP]$ and the slope of $[OQ]$ where O is (0, 0).

What conclusion can be drawn from these results?

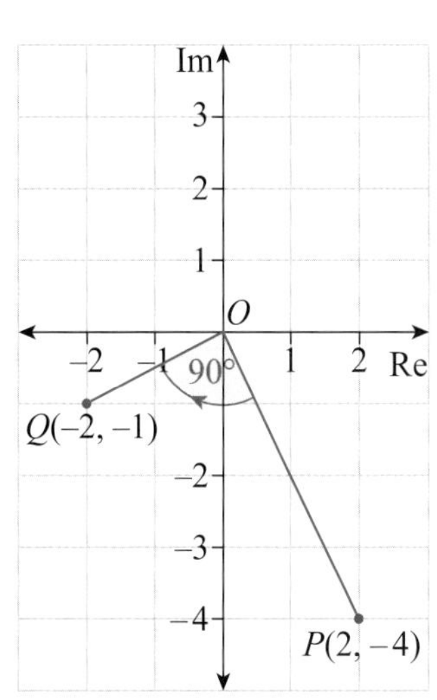

Solution

(a) $z = 2 - 4i \Rightarrow P(2, -4)$

(b) $w = \frac{2-4i}{2i} = -\frac{i}{2}(2-4i) = -i(1-2i)$

$= -2 - i \Rightarrow Q(-2, -1)$

(c) $|w| = \sqrt{(-2)^2 + (-1)^2} = \sqrt{5}$

$\frac{|z|}{2} = \frac{\sqrt{(2)^2 + (-4)^2}}{2} = \frac{\sqrt{20}}{2} = \sqrt{5}$

$\therefore |w| = \frac{|z|}{2}$

(d) Slope of $OP = \frac{-4}{2} = -2$

Slope of $OQ = \frac{1}{2}$

Slope of $OP \times$ Slope of $OQ = -2 \times \frac{1}{2} = -1$

Clearly, dividing a complex number z by $2i$ rotates it by 90° in a clockwise direction and divides its modulus by 2.

ACTIVITY 19

ACTION
Exploring the geometric effect of dividing complex numbers (2)

OBJECTIVE
To explore more difficult examples of the geometric effects of dividing complex numbers by each other

WORKED EXAMPLE

Geometrical effect of dividing complex numbers

Divide $z = 2 + 4i$ by $w = 3 + i$.

Represent z by the point P and w by the point Q. Represent the result of the division by R.

$$\frac{z}{w} = \frac{2+4i}{3+i} = \frac{(2+4i)}{(3+i)} \times \frac{(3-i)}{(3-i)} = \frac{6 - 2i + 12i - 4i^2}{9+1} = \frac{10+10i}{10} = 1 + i$$

Points: $P(2, 4)$, $Q(3, 1)$, $R(1, 1)$

$\arg z = A = \tan^{-1} 2 = 63{\cdot}43°$

$\arg w = B = \tan^{-1} \frac{1}{3} = 18{\cdot}43°$

$\arg\left(\frac{z}{w}\right) = C = \tan^{-1} 1 = 45°$

$\therefore C = A - B$ [$63{\cdot}43° - 18{\cdot}43° = 45°$]

[OP] has been rotated clockwise by the angle [OQ] makes with the +Re axis (by $\arg w$).

$\therefore \arg\left(\frac{z}{w}\right) = \arg z - \arg w$

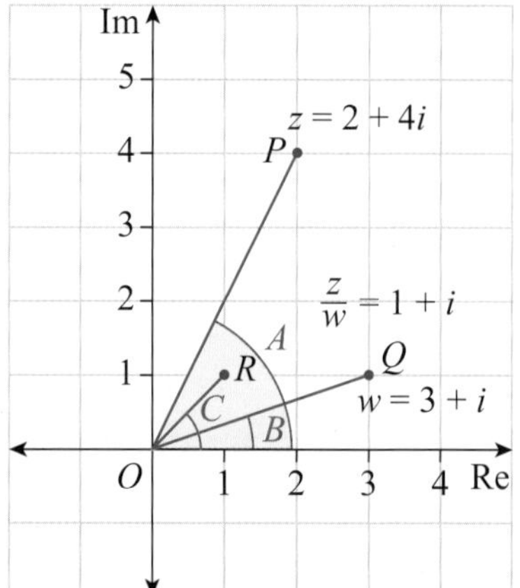

$|z| = \sqrt{2^2 + 4^2} = \sqrt{20} = |OP|$

$|w| = \sqrt{3^2 + 1^2} = \sqrt{10} = |OQ|$

$\left|\frac{z}{w}\right| = \sqrt{1^2 + 1^2} = \sqrt{2} = |OR|$

$\therefore |OR| = \frac{|OP|}{|OQ|}$

The length of $|OP|$ has been divided by the length of $|OQ|$.

Conclusion

When a complex number z is divided by a complex number w, z is rotated clockwise about (0, 0) by the angle the line joining 0 to w makes with the +Re axis and its modulus is divided by the modulus of w.

EXERCISE 10

1. Simplify the following giving your answer in the form $a + bi$, $a, b \in \mathbb{R}$:

(a) $\frac{3}{i}$

(b) $\frac{-7}{i}$

(c) $\frac{5}{-i}$

(d) $\frac{2}{3i}$

(e) $\frac{3}{2-i}$

(f) $\frac{4}{7+3i}$

(g) $\frac{-5}{2-3i}$

(h) $\frac{1+i}{2+i}$

(i) $\frac{3+i}{4+3i}$

(j) $\frac{1-2i}{3-2i}$

(k) $\frac{-4+3i}{-2+i}$

(l) $\frac{-3-5i}{-4+3i}$

(m) $\frac{3+2i}{-i}$

(n) $\frac{4+8i}{-2i}$

(o) $\frac{a+bi}{i}$

(p) $\frac{1+\sqrt{3}i}{1-\sqrt{3}i}$

2. If $z = 2 + 5i$ and $w = 3 - 4i$, find the following in the form $a + bi$, $a, b \in \mathbb{R}$:

(a) $\frac{z}{w}$

(b) $\frac{w}{z}$

(c) $\frac{1}{z}$

(d) $\frac{z}{\bar{z}}$

(e) $\frac{w}{\bar{w}}$

(f) $\frac{z}{\bar{w}}$

(g) $\frac{w}{\bar{z}}$

(h) $\frac{\bar{z}}{\bar{w}}$

(i) $\frac{\bar{w}}{\bar{z}}$

(j) $\overline{\left(\frac{z}{\bar{w}}\right)}$

(k) $\left|\frac{z}{w}\right|$

(l) $\frac{|z|}{|w|}$

(m) $\left|\frac{1}{z}\right|$

3. Simplify the following writing your answer in the form $a + bi$, $a, b \in \mathbb{R}$:

(a) $\overline{\left(\frac{1-i}{1+2i}\right)}$

(b) $(9-i) \times \frac{3+i}{2-i}$

(c) $\frac{3-7i}{-i} \times i^2$

(d) $i^3 \times \frac{\overline{(3-i)}}{2-5i}$

(e) $\frac{\frac{3}{i}+i}{\frac{3}{i}-i}$

(f) $\frac{\frac{5}{2+i}+\frac{5}{2-i}}{\frac{1}{i}}$

(g) $\frac{2+i}{2-i} - \frac{2-i}{2+i}$

4. For each z given below, its point on the Argand diagram is represented by P. Write down $|z|$ and the angle OP makes with the +Re axis, where $O(0, 0)$. For each u, represent its point on the Argand diagram by Q. Write down $|u|$ and the angle OQ makes with the +Re axis, where $O(0, 0)$. Give all angles correct to the nearest degree.

(a) $z = 3$, $u = \frac{z}{i}$

(b) $z = -9i$, $u = \frac{z}{i^3}$

(c) $z = -8$, $u = \frac{z}{2i^2}$

(d) $z = 12$, $u = \frac{z}{3i^3}$

(e) $z = 1 - i$, $u = \frac{z}{\sqrt{2}i}$

(f) $z = 4 - 3i$, $u = \frac{z}{5i^3}$

5. If $z = 4 - 4\sqrt{3}i$ and $w = -\sqrt{3} - i$:

(a) find $\frac{z}{w}$, $\left|\frac{z}{w}\right|$, $\arg\left(\frac{z}{w}\right)$,

(b) find $|z|$, $\arg z$,

(c) find $|w|$, $\arg w$,

(d) show: $\left|\frac{z}{w}\right| = \frac{|z|}{|w|}$ and $\arg\left(\frac{z}{w}\right) = \arg z - \arg w$,

(e) what is the effect on z of dividing it by w?

6. $z = \sqrt{3} + i$, $w = 1 + i$ and $0 = 0 + 0i$.

(a) Find $|z|$ and the angle the line joining 0 to z makes with the +Re axis.

(b) Find $|w|$ and the angle the line joining 0 to w makes with the +Re axis.

(c) Find $u = \frac{z}{w}$. Find $|u|$ and the angle the line joining 0 to u makes with the +Re axis.

7. z and w have moduli 6 and $\frac{3}{2}$ and arguments 120° and 45°, respectively.

(a) State the modulus and argument of:

(i) zw **(ii)** $\frac{z}{w}$

(b) Explain why w^2 is purely imaginary. Hence, find w^2.

Complex Numbers 2

Learning Outcomes

- To solve simple complex number equations.
- To solve quadratic and cubic equations with complex roots.
- To convert complex numbers in Cartesian form to polar form and vice versa.
- To use de Moivre's theorem to find powers and roots of complex numbers and to prove certain trigonometric identities.

17.1 Equality

ACTIVITY 20

ACTION
Exploring the equality of complex numbers

OBJECTIVE
To work with some simple examples involving the equality of complex numbers

Two complex numbers are equal if they have the same co-ordinates on the Argand diagram.

$a + bi = c + di$ means:

1. $a = c$ (x co-ordinates are equal) and $b = d$ (y co-ordinates are equal).

Or

2. Re = Re (the real parts are equal) and Im = Im (the imaginary parts are equal).

- $x + yi = 3 + 2i,\ x, y \in \mathbb{R}$

  Re = Re $\Rightarrow x = 3$, Im = Im $\Rightarrow y = 2$

- $x - yi + 2 - 3i = 2 + i,\ x, y \in \mathbb{R}$

  $(x + 2) + i(-y - 3) = 2 + 1i$

  $x + 2 = 2 \qquad -y - 3 = 1$

  $x = 0 \qquad y = -4$

- $(x - 2) + yi = 0,\ x, y \in \mathbb{R}$

  $(x - 2) + yi = 0 + 0i$ [Remember $0 = 0 + 0i$]

  $x - 2 = 0 \qquad y = 0$

  $x = 2$

EXAMPLE 1

Solve $(x - yi)(2i - 7) = 16 + 3i,\ x, y \in \mathbb{R}$.

Solution

$$(x - yi)(2i - 7) = 16 + 3i$$
$$2xi - 7x - 2yi^2 + 7yi = 16 + 3i$$
$$2xi - 7x + 2y + 7yi = 16 + 3i$$
$$(-7x + 2y) + i(2x + 7y) = 16 + 3i$$

$-7x + 2y = 16$ **(1)** [Re = Re]

$2x + 7y = 3$ **(2)** [Im = Im]

$-14x + 4y = 32$ **(1)** × 2

$14x + 49y = 21$ **(2)** × 7

$53y = 53$

$y = 1$

Into (1): $-7x + 2 = 16$

$-7x = 14$

$x = -2$

EXAMPLE 2

Solve $\dfrac{x + yi}{3 - 2i} = 5 + i,\ x, y \in \mathbb{R}$.

Solution

$$x + yi = (5 + i)(3 - 2i)$$
$$x + yi = 15 - 10i + 3i - 2i^2$$
$$x + yi = 15 - 10i + 3i + 2$$
$$x + yi = 17 - 7i$$
$$x = 17 \text{ and } y = -7$$

EXERCISE 11

1. Solve the following for $x, y \in \mathbb{R}$:

(a) $x + yi = 2 + 3i$

(b) $x + 7yi = -3 + 21i$

(c) $2x - 3yi = -8 - 9i$

(d) $x + 3 - yi = 4 + 6i$

(e) $x + 3(x - yi) - 2yi = 6 + 10i$

(f) $x - 2i + i(y - 2x) = 3 + 2yi$

(g) $x + yi - 2(xi + 3y) = 4 + 14i$

(h) $4x - 3i(x + 2y) = y + 9$

(i) $3(x + yi) - 2(y - xi) = 6 + 17i$

(j) $-5x - 2yi + 4(xi + y - 3) = 0$

2. **(a)** Solve $(x + yi)(3 + 2i) = -1 + 8i$ for $x, y \in \mathbb{R}$.

(b) Solve $\dfrac{x + yi}{1 + i} = 5 + i,$ for $x, y \in \mathbb{R}$.

(c) If $w + \dfrac{2}{w} = x + yi$, find $x, y \in \mathbb{R}$ if $w = 1 + i$.

(d) Solve for $x, y \in \mathbb{R}$ if $\dfrac{2}{z} + \dfrac{5}{w} = x + yi$, where $z = -1 + i$ and $w = 2 + i$.

(e) Solve for $x, y \in \mathbb{R}$ if $\dfrac{13}{w} - 5 + 4i = x + yi$, if $w = 3 + 2i$.

3. Solve the following for $x, y \in \mathbb{R}$ if $z = x + yi$. (Hint: Isolate z first and then put $z = x + yi$.)

(a) $\dfrac{1}{z} = 2 - i$

(b) $\dfrac{3}{z} = 1 + i$

(c) $\dfrac{3}{z - 1} = i - 3$

(d) $\dfrac{3 - i}{z + i} = 2 - i$

17.2 Quadratic and cubic equations

ACTIVITY 21

ACTION
Solving quadratic equations with complex numbers

OBJECTIVE
To solve a variety of quadratic equations using the magic formula

Quadratic equations

The quadratic equation $az^2 + bz + c = 0$ can always be solved using the quadratic formula $z = \frac{-b \pm \sqrt{b^2 - 4ac}}{2a}$, whether the coefficients a, b, c are real or complex. The solutions for z can also be real or complex.

- $z^2 - (4 + i)z + (4 + 2i) = 0 \quad [a = 1, b = -(4 + i), c = (4 + 2i)]$

$$z = \frac{(4 + i) \pm \sqrt{(4 + i)^2 - 4(4 + 2i)}}{2} = \frac{(4 + i) \pm \sqrt{16 + 8i + i^2 - 16 - 8i}}{2}$$
$$= \frac{(4 + i) \pm \sqrt{-1}}{2} = \frac{(4 + i) \pm i}{2} = 2, 2 + i$$

All of the coefficients are not real and one root is complex and the other is real.

Is there any way to predict whether the roots are real and/or complex from the coefficients?

ACTIVITY 22

ACTION
Forming quadratic equations given the roots

OBJECTIVE
To write down a quadratic equation given a variety of roots

Forming a quadratic equation from its roots

Remember that you can form a quadratic equation given its roots by using $z^2 - Sz + P = 0$, where S = the sum of the roots and P = the product of the roots. Four possibilities arise:

- Roots: –3 and 8 [Roots are both real.]
  $S = 5, P = -24$
  Equation: $z^2 - 5z - 24 = 0$ [All coefficients are real.]
- Roots: $-4, 1 + i$ [One root is real and one is complex.]
  $S = (-3 + i), P = -4 - 4i$
  Equation: $z^2 - (-3 + i)z - 4 - 4i = 0$ [All coefficients are not real.]
- Roots: $2 - i, 3 + 2i$ [Both roots are complex.]
  $S = 5 + i, P = (2 - i)(3 + 2i) = 6 + 4i - 3i - 2i^2 = 8 + i$
  Equation: $z^2 - (5 + i)z + (8 + i) = 0$ [All coefficients are not real.]
- Roots: $4 - 2i, 4 + 2i$ [Both roots are complex but are the conjugates of each other.]
  $S = 8, P = 4^2 + 2^2 = 20$
  Equation: $z^2 - 8z + 20 = 0$ [All coefficients are real.]

These examples lead to the **conjugate root theorem**.

Conjugate root theorem (CRT)

CRT FOR QUADRATICS

If **all** the coefficients of a quadratic equation are real, then the roots are both real or are complex conjugates of each other, and vice versa.

It is important to note the following:

1. If you are told that −3 is a root of a quadratic equation with all real coefficients, then the other root must also be real.
2. If you are told that $(-3 - 5i)$ is a root of a quadratic equation with all real coefficients, then the other root is its complex conjugate $(-3 + 5i)$.
3. If $az^2 + bz + c = 0$ has all real coefficients, $z = \dfrac{-b \pm \sqrt{b^2 - 4ac}}{2a}$ gives two real roots if $b^2 - 4ac \geq 0$, but two complex conjugate roots if $b^2 - 4ac < 0$.

▸ $3z^2 - 2z + 7 = 0 \quad [a = 3, b = -2, c = 7]$ (The coefficients are all real.)

$b^2 - 4ac = 4 - 84 = -80 < 0$.

Therefore, the roots are complex conjugates of each other.

EXAMPLE 3

$-2 + 5i$ is a root of a quadratic equation with all real coefficients. Find this equation.

Solution

CRT states that the roots are $-2 + 5i$ and $-2 - 5i$.
[You can apply CRT as you are told all coefficients are real.]

$S = -2 + 5i + (-2 - 5i) = -4$

$P = (-2 + 5i)(-2 - 5i)$

$= 2^2 + 5^2 = 29$

Equation: $z^2 + 4z + 29 = 0$ using $z^2 - Sz + P = 0$

EXAMPLE 4

If $3 - 4i$ is a solution (root) of $z^2 + bz + c = 0$, find $b, c \in \mathbb{R}$.

Solution

$b, c \in \mathbb{R}$ means that all coefficients are real.

Roots: $3 - 4i$, $3 + 4i$

$S = 6$, $P = 25$

$z^2 + bz + c = z^2 - 6z + 25 = 0$

$b = -6$, $c = 25$

EXAMPLE 5

Show that $3 - 2i$ is a root of the equation $z^2 - 5(1 - i)z - 13i = 0$. Find the other root.

Solution

If $3 - 2i$ is a root of the equation, it satisfies the quadratic equation. Substituting $3 - 2i$ for z:

$(3 - 2i)^2 - 5(1 - i)(3 - 2i) - 13i$

$= 9 - 12i + 4i^2 - 5(3 - 2i - 3i + 2i^2) - 13i$

$= 9 - 12i - 4 - 5(1 - 5i) - 13i$

$= 5 - 25i - 5 + 25i = 0$

$\therefore$ $3 - 2i$ is a root.

Let the other root of the equation $z^2 - Sz + P = 0$ be α.

Sum of roots: $S = 5(1 - i) = \alpha + 3 - 2i$

$\Rightarrow \alpha = 5 - 5i - 3 + 2i = 2 - 3i$

Cubic equations

Since every cubic equation $az^3 + bz^2 + cz + d = 0$ has three roots, we can form this cubic equation by forming a quadratic factor from any two roots $(z^2 - Sz + P)$ and a linear factor from the other root.

$C = Q \times L = 0$

C (cubic) = Q (quadratic) × L (linear) = 0

Clearly, if all three roots are real, then all the coefficients a, b, c, d will also be real as the quadratic factor and the linear factor will have real coefficients.

EXAMPLE 6

Form the cubic equation with roots 3, 2, –1.

Solution

Roots: 3, 2, –1

Form a quadratic factor using roots 3 and 2 and a linear factor from the –1 root.

Quadratic factor: $z^2 - Sz + P = z^2 - 5z + 6$

$$Q \times L = 0$$

$$(z^2 - 5z + 6)(z + 1) = 0$$

$$\therefore z^3 - 4z^2 + z + 6 = 0$$

However, if two roots are complex conjugates of each other and the other root is real, the quadratic formed from the conjugate roots will have all real coefficients as will the linear factor formed from the real root. This means the cubic equation will have all real coefficients.

EXAMPLE 7

Form the cubic equation with roots $3 - i$, $3 + i$ and 5.

Solution

Form a quadratic factor from the conjugate roots $(3 - i)$ and $(3 + i)$ using $z^2 - Sz + P$ and a linear factor from the root 5.

$S = 6, P = 10 \Rightarrow Q = z^2 - 6z + 10$

$Q \times L = (z^2 - 6z + 10)(z - 5) = 0$

$z^3 - 11z^2 + 40z - 50 = 0$

This leads to the CRT for cubics.

CRT FOR CUBICS

If all the coefficients of a cubic equation are real, then the roots are all real or two of them are complex conjugates and the other is real, and vice versa.

EXAMPLE 8

If $1 + 2i$ and 3 are two of the roots of a cubic equation with all real coefficients, find this equation.

Solution

If $1 + 2i$ is a root, $1 - 2i$ is also a root [CRT].

Roots: $1 + 2i$, $1 - 2i$, 3

$Q \times L = 0 \Rightarrow (z^2 - 2z + 5)(z - 3) = 0$

$z^3 - 5z^2 + 11z - 15 = 0$

EXAMPLE 9

Solve $z^3 - 5z^2 + 8z - 6 = 0$, if $1 - i$ is a root.

Solution

$z^3 - 5z^2 + 8z - 6 = 0$ has all real coefficients. Therefore, CRT applies.

Roots: $1 - i, 1 + i, \alpha$

$C = Q \times L = 0$

$z^3 - 5z^2 + 8z - 6 = (z^2 - 2z + 2)(z - \alpha) = 0$

$\Rightarrow -2\alpha = -6$ [Last × Last = Last]

$\alpha = 3$

Roots are $1 - i, 1 + i, 3$

EXAMPLE 10

If $5 - 3i$ is a root of $z^3 - kz^2 + 24z + 34 = 0$, find all the roots and $k \in \mathbb{R}$.

Solution

$z^3 - kz^2 + 24z + 34 = 0$

$k \in \mathbb{R}$ means the CRT can be used.

Roots: $5 - 3i, 5 + 3i, \alpha$

$z^3 - kz^2 + 24z + 34 = (z^2 - 10z + 34)(z - \alpha) = 0$

$\Rightarrow -34\alpha = 34$ [Last × Last = Last]

$\alpha = -1$

$z^3 - kz^2 + 24z + 34 = (z^2 - 10z + 34)(z + 1) = 0$

Multiplying out:

$z^3 - kz^2 + 24z + 34 = z^2 - 9z^2 + 24z - 34 = 0$

Lining up z^2: $-k = -9$

$k = 9$

EXERCISE 12

1. Form the quadratic equations with the following roots:
   - **(a)** $4, 5$
   - **(b)** $-4, -5$
   - **(c)** $-\frac{2}{3}, \frac{1}{4}$
   - **(d)** $2 - \sqrt{3}, 2 + \sqrt{3}$
   - **(e)** $m, \frac{1}{m}$
   - **(f)** $-2 + 5i, -2 - 5i$
   - **(g)** $-\sqrt{3} + 2i, -\sqrt{3} - 2i$
   - **(h)** $a + bi, a - bi, a, b \in \mathbb{R}$
   - **(i)** $-\frac{\sqrt{3}}{2} + \frac{1}{2}i, -\frac{\sqrt{3}}{2} - \frac{1}{2}i$
   - **(j)** $-5i, 5i$

2. Solve the following quadratic equations:
   - **(a)** $z^2 - 9 = 0$
   - **(b)** $z^2 + 9 = 0$
   - **(c)** $z^2 + 4z + 29 = 0$
   - **(d)** $z^2 - 2z + 7 = 0$
   - **(e)** $z^2 - 8z + 25 = 0$
   - **(f)** $2z^2 + 10z + 13 = 0$
   - **(g)** $z^2 + 11z + 24 = 0$
   - **(h)** $12z^2 + 11z - 5 = 0$
   - **(i)** $36z^2 - 36z + 13 = 0$
   - **(j)** $z^2 + z + 1 = 0$

3. Form the quadratic equation with all real coefficients given one root:
   - **(a)** $1 - 2i$
   - **(b)** $-3 + 2i$
   - **(c)** $\frac{2 - 3i}{2}$
   - **(d)** $-3 - \sqrt{2}i$
   - **(e)** $\sqrt{5}i$
   - **(f)** $-7 - 2i$
   - **(g)** $\frac{2}{3 - i}$
   - **(h)** $\frac{3 - 4i}{1 + i}$

4. For each of the following, evaluate $b^2 - 4ac$, and state whether the roots are real and different, real and equal or complex:

(a) $z^2 - 10z + 24 = 0$ **(f)** $6z^2 - 2z + 1 = 0$

(b) $z^2 - 6z + 9 = 0$ **(g)** $25z^2 - 30z + 7 = 0$

(c) $z^2 - 2z + 2 = 0$ **(h)** $z^2 - 2\sqrt{3}z + 3 = 0$

(d) $9z^2 - 7 = 0$ **(i)** $3z^2 + 14z - 5 = 0$

(e) $z^2 + 4 = 0$ **(j)** $\dfrac{5}{3-z} = z$

5. **(a)** If i is a root of $z^2 - az + b = 0$, find $a, b \in \mathbb{R}$.

(b) If $3 - i$ is a root of $z^2 + bz + c = 0$, find $b, c \in \mathbb{R}$.

(c) If $-5 - 2i$ is a root of a quadratic equation with all real coefficients, find the equation.

(d) If $2 - \sqrt{3}i$ is a root of $z^2 - kz + c = 0$, find $k, c \in \mathbb{R}$.

(e) If $a + 2i$ is a root of $z^2 - 2z + b = 0$, find $a, b \in \mathbb{R}$.

(f) If $a + bi$ is a root of $z^2 - 4z + 13 = 0$, find $a, b \in \mathbb{R}$.

(g) If i is a root of $2z^2 - 5z + k = 0$, find k.

6. Prove that if $z = a + bi$ and $w = x$, $a, b, x \in \mathbb{R}$, $b \neq 0$, the sum of z and w is always complex (not purely real) and the product of z and w can be complex or real.

7. Prove that if $z = a + bi$ and $w = c + di$, $a, b \neq 0$, $c, d \neq 0 \in \mathbb{R}$, if the sum and the product of these are both real, z and w must be complex conjugates of each other.

8. Form the cubic equation with the following roots:

(a) $1, -3, 5$ **(d)** $1 + \sqrt{3}i, 1 - \sqrt{3}i, -1$

(b) $1 + i, 1 - i, 3$ **(e)** $3 - 4i, 3 + 4i, -2$

(c) $2i, -3, 2$ **(f)** $2 + 3i, 2 - 3i, 4$

9. Solve the following cubic equations:

(a) $z^3 - 5z^2 + 8z - 6 = 0$, if $1 - i$ is a root

(b) $z^3 - 3z + 52 = 0$, if $2 + 3i$ is a root

(c) $z^3 - 3z^2 + 9z - 27 = 0$, if $-3i$ is a root

(d) $z^3 - (2 + i)z^2 + (5 + 2i)z - 5i = 0$, if i is a root

(e) $z^3 - iz^2 + 9z - 9i = 0$, if i is a root

(f) $z^3 - (2a + 1)z^2 + (2a + a^2 + b^2)z - (a^2 + b^2) = 0$, if $a + bi$ is a root $a, b \in \mathbb{R}$

10. Find $k \in \mathbb{R}$ for the following if:

(a) $2 - 3i$ is a root of $z^3 - 3z + k = 0$

(b) $2 - 3i$ is a root of $z^3 - kz^2 + z + 39 = 0$

(c) $1 + 3i$ is a root of $z^3 - 6z^2 + kz - 40 = 0$

(d) $3 - 2i$ is a root of $kz^3 - 19z^2 + 45z - 13 = 0$

17.3 Polar form

ACTIVITY 23

ACTION
Working in polar form

OBJECTIVE
To write down the modulus and argument of complex numbers written in polar form

You can locate a complex number z in the Argand diagram (2D) with two pieces of information in two different ways.

1. Cartesian form: By giving the rectangular co-ordinates, x and y, of the complex number z.

$z = x + yi$ is represented by the point $P(x, y)$.

This method was devised by René Descartes and (x, y) are known as the Cartesian co-ordinates of z.

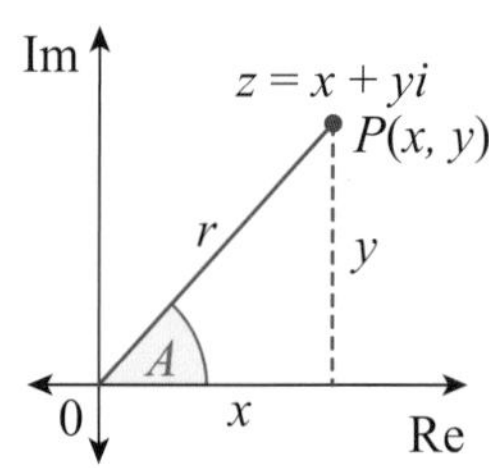

ACTIVITY 24

ACTION
Writing complex numbers in polar and Cartesian form

OBJECTIVE
To write complex numbers in polar and Cartesian form given the modulus and argument

2. **Polar form:** By measuring an angle A (arg z) anticlockwise from the +Re axis, drawing a line through the origin $O(0, 0)$ at this angle and measuring out a distance $r = |z|$ along this line to reach z.

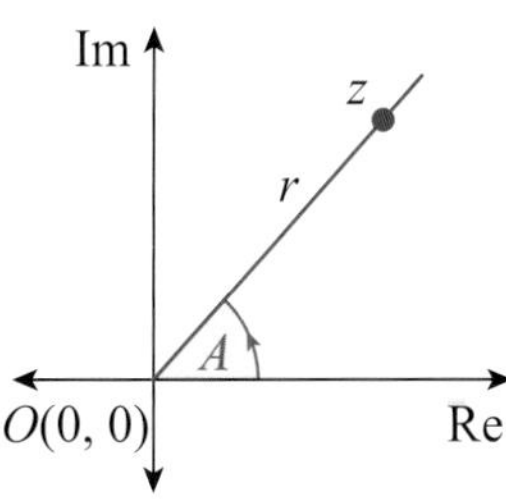

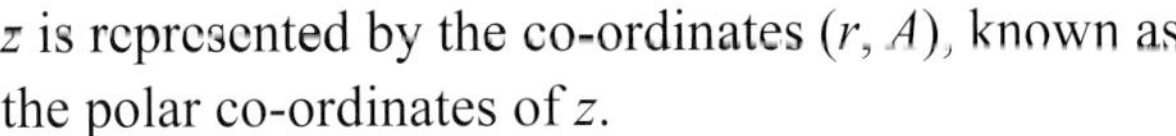
z is represented by the co-ordinates (r, A), known as the polar co-ordinates of z.

The relationship between polar and Cartesian co-ordinates

Cartesian form: $z = x + yi$

$$\cos A = \frac{x}{r} \Rightarrow x = r\cos A$$

$$\sin A = \frac{y}{r} \Rightarrow y = r\sin A$$

$$\therefore\ z = x + yi = r\cos A + i\,r\sin A$$

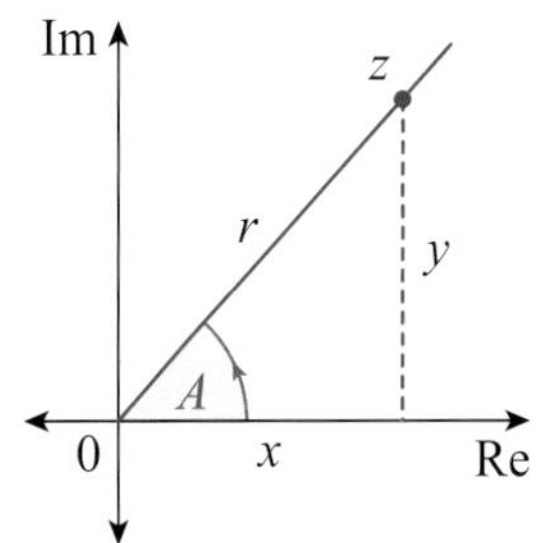

$\Rightarrow z = r(\cos A + i\sin A)$: **polar form**

It is important to note the following:

1. Remember, polar form and Cartesian form are just different forms of the **same** complex number.
2. $r = |z| = \sqrt{\text{Re}^2 + \text{Im}^2} = \sqrt{x^2 + y^2}$
3. $\tan A = \dfrac{y}{x} \Rightarrow A = \arg z = \tan^{-1}\left(\dfrac{\text{Im}}{\text{Re}}\right) = \tan^{-1}\left(\dfrac{y}{x}\right)$
4. Polar form is always written as $r(\cos A + i\sin A)$ where $\text{Re} = r\cos A$ and $\text{Im} = r\sin A$.

Converting from polars to Cartesians

EXAMPLE 11

For the complex number z shown on the Argand diagram, find:

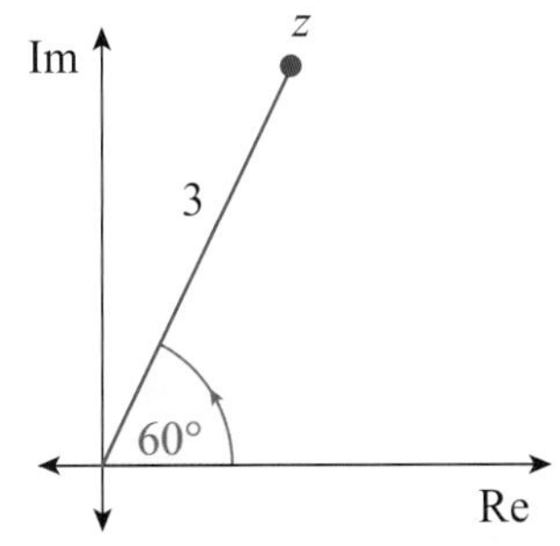

(a) $|z|$
(b) $\arg z$
(c) z in polar form
(d) z in Cartesian form

Solution

(a) $r = 3 = |z|$

(b) $A = 60° = \arg z$

(c) Polar form: $z = r(\cos A + i\sin A)$
$= 3(\cos 60° + i\sin 60°)$

(d) Cartesian form: $z = 3(\cos 60° + i\sin 60°)$
$$= 3\left(\frac{1}{2} + \frac{\sqrt{3}}{2}i\right) = \frac{3}{2} + \frac{3\sqrt{3}}{2}i$$

EXAMPLE 12

A complex number z has $|z| = 5$ and $\arg z = 132°$.

(a) Plot z on an Argand diagram.

(b) Write z in polar form.

(c) Write z in Cartesian form, correct to two decimal places.

Solution

(a) $|z| = 5 \Rightarrow r = 5$

$\arg z = 132° \Rightarrow A = 132°$

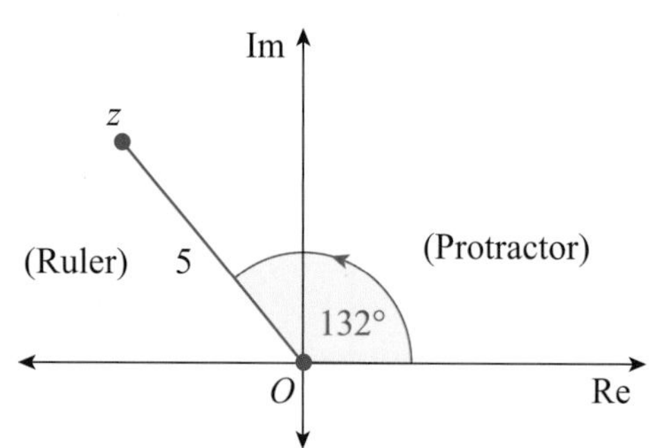

(b) $z = 5(\cos 132° + i\sin 132°)$ **Polar form**

(c) $z = 5(\cos 132° + i\sin 132°)$

$= 5(-0{\cdot}669 + i\,0{\cdot}7431)$

$= -3{\cdot}35 + 3{\cdot}72i$ **Cartesian form**

EXAMPLE 13

For $z = 2\left(\cos\frac{5\pi}{3} + i\sin\frac{5\pi}{3}\right)$, find $|z|$ and $\arg z$ and write it in Cartesian form.

Solution

$r = 2 = |z|$

$A = \frac{5\pi}{3} = 300° = \arg z$

$$z = 2\left(\cos\frac{5\pi}{3} + i\sin\frac{5\pi}{3}\right) = 2\left(\frac{1}{2} - \frac{\sqrt{3}}{2}i\right) = 1 - \sqrt{3}i$$

EXAMPLE 14

A ship is travelling at a speed of 30 km/h with a bearing N 60° E, as shown.

Write its velocity v

(a) in polar form and

(b) in Cartesian form.

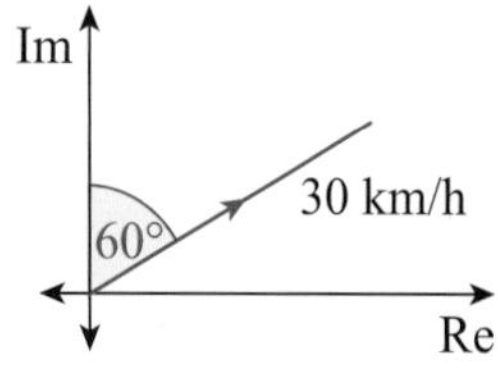

Solution

$r = |v| = 30$

$A = \arg v = 30°$

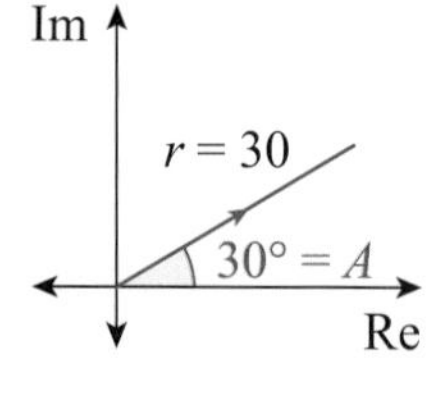

(a)  $v = 30(\cos 30° + i\sin 30°)$

(b) 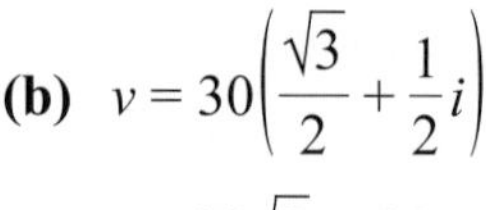 $v = 30\left(\frac{\sqrt{3}}{2} + \frac{1}{2}i\right)$

$= 15\sqrt{3} + 15i$

ACTIVITY 25

ACTION
Exploring the reference angles of complex numbers

OBJECTIVE
To explore the relationship between four different complex numbers

Converting from Cartesians to polars

This is much more difficult than converting from polars to Cartesians as it is difficult to find the angle A.

Trigonometry review

If $\tan A = -1$, find A.

The minus sign for $\tan A$ means that A is either in the second or the fourth quadrants.

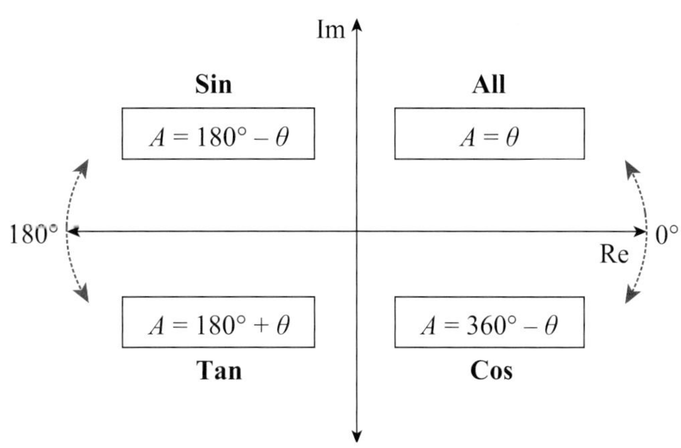

The reference angle θ in the first quadrant is the angle whose tan is the same as the modulus of $\tan A$.

$\tan \theta = |\tan A| = 1$, θ in first quadrant.

$\Rightarrow \theta = 45°$

$A = 180° - \theta = 180° - 45° = 135°$ [Second quadrant]

or

$A = 360° - \theta = 360° - 45° = 315°$ [Fourth quadrant]

[This is covered extensively in the Trigonometry section in *Power of Maths – Paper* 2.]

Steps for changing from Cartesians to polars

To change from Cartesians to polars, you need to find r and A (that is $|z|$ and $\arg z$).

ACTIVITY 26

ACTION
Writing the polar form of complex numbers given in Cartesian form

OBJECTIVE
To consider situations where you are given complex numbers in Cartesian form and are asked to write them in their polar form

1. Find $r = |z| = \sqrt{(\text{Re})^2 + (\text{Im})^2}$.
2. Draw a rough Argand diagram and state the quadrant in which z is located.

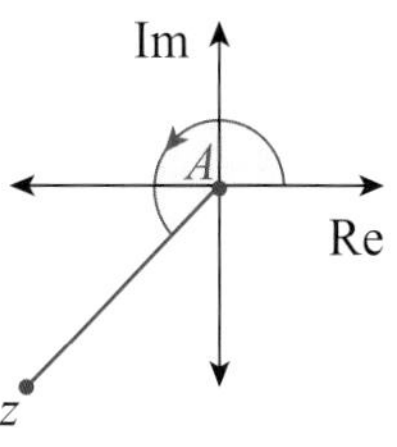

3. Find $|\tan A| = \left|\frac{\text{Im}}{\text{Re}}\right| =$ and hence $\theta = \tan^{-1} = \left|\frac{\text{Im}}{\text{Re}}\right| =$ in the first quadrant.
   Hence, find A.

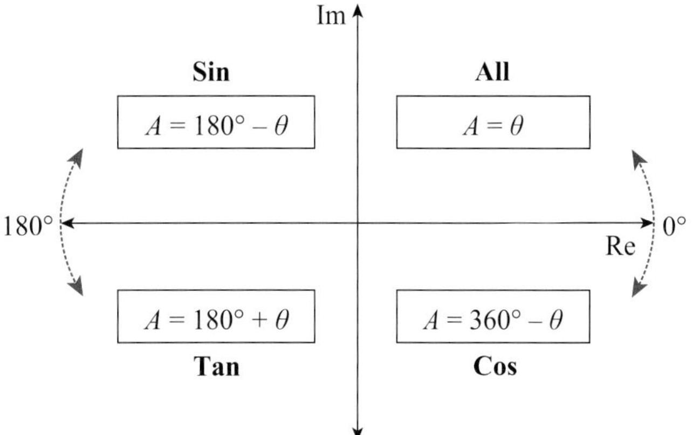

4. Fill r and A into $z = r(\cos A + i \sin A)$.

EXAMPLE 15

Plot $z = -2 + 2i$ on an Argand diagram.

Find $|z|$ and $\arg z$ and hence write z in polar form.

Solution

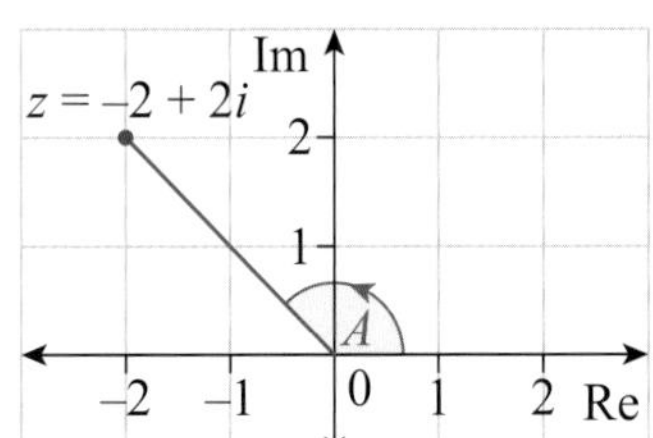

$r = |z| = \sqrt{(-2)^2 + (2)^2} = \sqrt{8} = 2\sqrt{2}$

z is in the second quadrant: $\tan A = \frac{\text{Im}}{\text{Re}} = \frac{+2}{-2} = -1$

$\therefore\ |\tan A| = \left|\frac{\text{Im}}{\text{Re}}\right| = 1.$

The related angle θ in the first quadrant has $\tan\theta = 1$

$\therefore\ \theta = \tan^{-1} 1 = 45°$

$A = 180° - 45° = 135°$

$z = r(\cos A + i\sin A) = 2\sqrt{2}(\cos 135° + i\sin 135°)$

$z = 2\sqrt{2}\left(\cos\frac{3\pi}{4} + i\sin\frac{3\pi}{4}\right)$

EXAMPLE 16

Write $z = \frac{\sqrt{3}}{2} + \frac{1}{2}i$ in polar form.

Solution

$r = |z| = \sqrt{\left(\frac{\sqrt{3}}{2}\right)^2 + \left(\frac{1}{2}\right)^2} = 1$

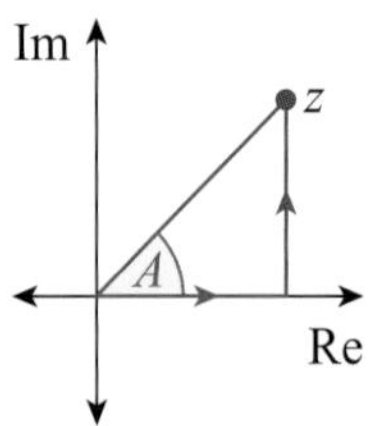

A is in the first quadrant.

$|\tan A| = \left|\frac{\frac{1}{2}}{\frac{\sqrt{3}}{2}}\right| = \frac{1}{\sqrt{3}} \Rightarrow \theta = \tan^{-1}\left(\frac{1}{\sqrt{3}}\right) = 30°$

A in the first quadrant $\Rightarrow A = \theta = 30°$

$z = 1(\cos 30° + i\sin 30°) = 1\left(\cos\frac{\pi}{6} + i\sin\frac{\pi}{6}\right)$

EXAMPLE 17

Write $z = -2 + 6i$ in polar form, giving the angle in degrees, correct to two decimal places.

Solution

$r = |z| = \sqrt{(-2)^2 + (6)^2} = \sqrt{4 + 36} = 2\sqrt{10}$

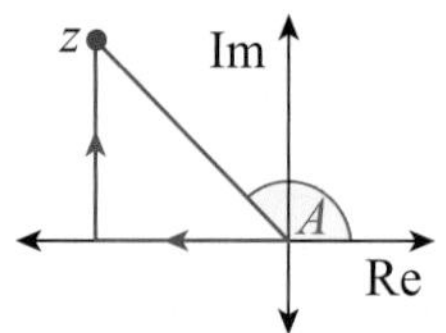

A is in the second quadrant.

$|\tan A| = \left|\frac{6}{-2}\right| = 3 \Rightarrow \theta = \tan^{-1} 3 = 71{\cdot}57°$

A in the second quadrant $\Rightarrow A = 180° - 71{\cdot}57°$
$= 108{\cdot}43°$

$\therefore\ z = 2\sqrt{10}(\cos 108{\cdot}43° + i\sin 108{\cdot}43°)$

TIP

If A is a borderline angle (that is if z is on one of the axes), you need to do steps **1** and **2** only.

EXAMPLE 18

Write $z = -2i$ in polar form.

Solution

$z = 0 - 2i$

$r = |z| = \sqrt{(0)^2 + (-2)^2} = 2$

$A = 270° = \frac{3\pi}{2}$ rad

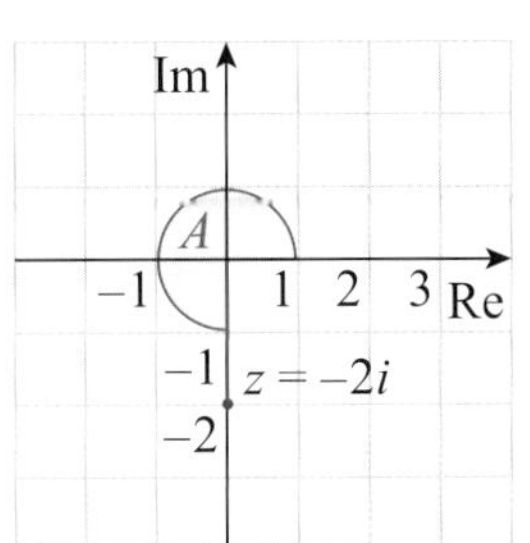

$\therefore z = 2(\cos 270° + i\sin 270°)$

$= 2\left(\cos\frac{3\pi}{2} + i\sin\frac{3\pi}{2}\right)$

General polar form

ACTIVITY 27

ACTION
Changing complex numbers to general polar form

OBJECTIVE
To change complex numbers to general polar form by adding $2n\pi, n \in \mathbb{N}_0$, to the angle

Consider a complex number with $r = 2$ and $A = 30°$. The corresponding point in the Argand diagram is P, as shown. However, complex numbers with the same modulus of 2 and arguments of $30° + 360°$, $30° + 720°$, … are represented by the same point.

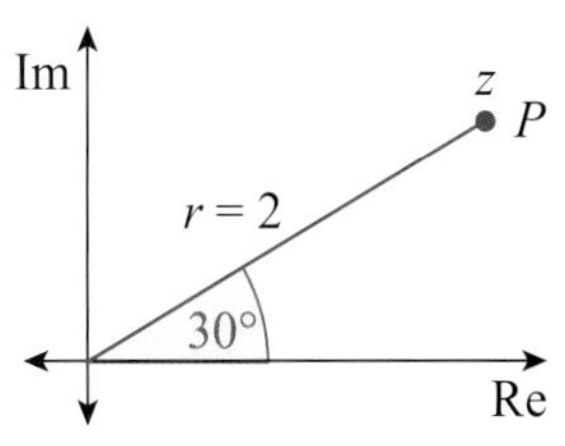

For $|z| = r$ and $\arg z = A$, there is an infinite number of complex numbers represented by the same point in the Argand diagram corresponding to angles: $A, A + 360°, A + 720°, A + 1080°, \ldots$ in degrees.

or

$A, A + 2\pi, A + 4\pi, A + 6\pi, \ldots$ in radians

This set of angles in radians can be generalised by the angle $A + 2n\pi$, $n \in \mathbb{N}_0 = \{0, 1, 2, 3, \ldots\}$

> The general polar form for a complex number with $|z| = r$ and $\arg z = A$ is given by $z = r\{\cos(A + 2n\pi) + i\sin(A + 2n\pi)\}, n \in \mathbb{N}_0$.

To write a complex number in general polar form, follow the same procedure as for polar form but in **Step 4** add $2n\pi$ to the angle A.

EXAMPLE 19

Write $z = 3 - \sqrt{3}i$ in general polar form.

Solution

$z = 3 - \sqrt{3}i$

$r = |z| = \sqrt{(3)^2 + (-\sqrt{3})^2} = 2\sqrt{3}$

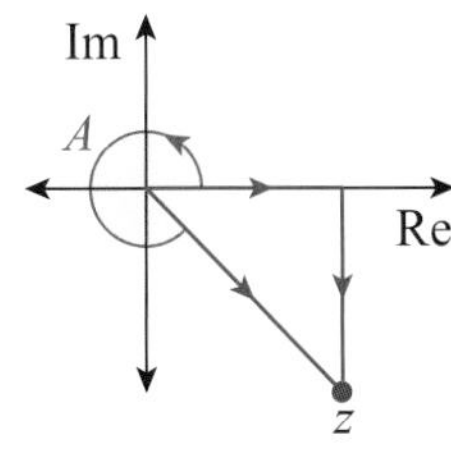

A is in the fourth quadrant.

$|\tan A| = \left|\frac{-\sqrt{3}}{3}\right| = \frac{1}{\sqrt{3}} \Rightarrow \theta = \tan^{-1}\frac{1}{\sqrt{3}} = 30°$

$A = 360° - 30° = 330° = \frac{11\pi}{6}$ rad

In general polar form:

$z = 2\sqrt{3}\left\{\cos\left(\frac{11\pi}{6} + 2n\pi\right) + i\sin\left(\frac{11\pi}{6} + 2n\pi\right)\right\}$

$= 2\sqrt{3}\left\{\cos\left(\frac{11\pi + 12n\pi}{6}\right) + i\sin\left(\frac{11\pi + 12n\pi}{6}\right)\right\}$

EXERCISE 13

1. Write z in Cartesian form for the following:
   (a) $z = 2(\cos 30° + i\sin 30°)$
   (b) $z = \sqrt{2}(\cos 315° + i\sin 315°)$
   (c) $z = 1\left(\cos\frac{5\pi}{3} + i\sin\frac{5\pi}{3}\right)$
   (d) $z = 6\left(\cos\frac{5\pi}{4} + i\sin\frac{5\pi}{4}\right)$
   (e) $z = \sqrt{3}\left(\cos\left(-\frac{\pi}{3}\right) + i\sin\left(-\frac{\pi}{3}\right)\right)$
   (f) $z = 4(\cos 2n\pi + i\sin 2n\pi),\ n \in \mathbb{N}_0$
   (g) $|z| = 2$ and $\arg z = 240°$
   (h)

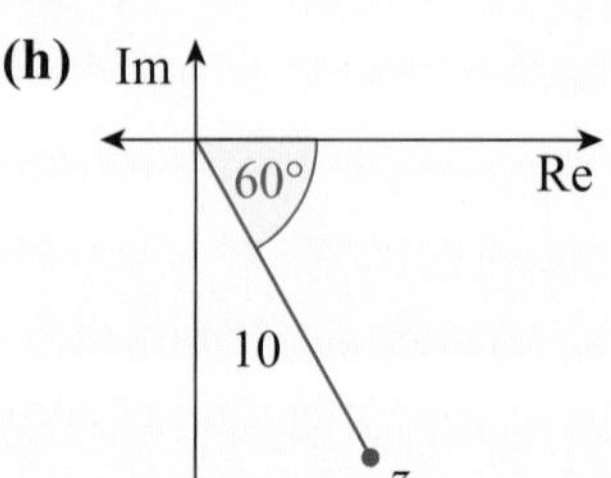

   (i)

Im
Re
–8
z

   (j) Give your answer correct to three decimal places.

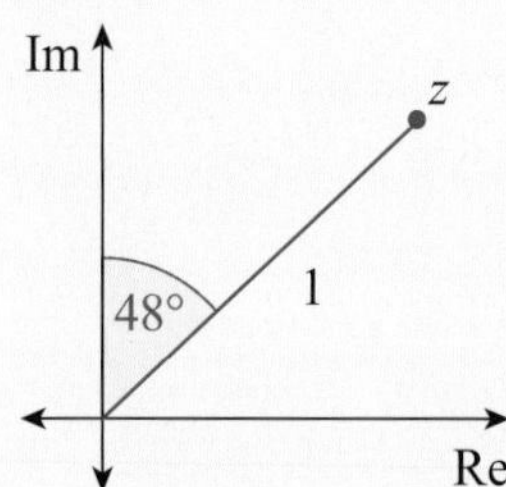

2. Plot the following on an Argand diagram:
   (a) $z = 2(\cos 60° + i\sin 60°)$
   (b) $z = 3\left(\cos\frac{2\pi}{3} + i\sin\frac{2\pi}{3}\right)$
   (c) z if $|z| = 8$, $\arg z = 200°$
   (d) z if $|z| = 4$, $\arg z = \frac{11\pi}{6}$

3. Given $|z|$ and $\arg z$, write z in the form $a + bi$, $a, b \in \mathbb{R}$:
   (a) $|z| = 3$, $\arg z = \frac{\pi}{3}$
   (b) $|z| = 1$, $\arg z = \frac{3\pi}{4}$
   (c) $|z| = \frac{1}{2}$, $\arg z = \frac{11\pi}{6}$
   (d) $|z| = 2$, $\arg z = -\frac{\pi}{4}$
   (e) $|z| = 3$, $\arg z = 210°$
   (f) $|z| = 2$, $\arg z = -150°$

4. Write the following in polar form, giving all angles in radians:
   (a) $z = 3 + 3i$
   (b) $z = -\sqrt{2} + \sqrt{2}\,i$
   (c) $z = -\frac{1}{2} + \frac{\sqrt{3}}{2}i$
   (d) $z = 8(-1 + \sqrt{3}i)$
   (e) $z = 4i + 4$
   (f) $z = -\sqrt{3} - i$
   (g) $z = \frac{5}{3} - \frac{5}{3}i$
   (h) $z = -i$
   (i) $z = -3 - 2i$ (correct to two decimal places)
   (j) $z = -\frac{4}{\sqrt{2}} - 2i$

5. Write the following in general polar form giving the angles in radians:
   (a) $z = 3$
   (b) $z = 2i$
   (c) $z = 2 + 2i$
   (d) $z = -3 + \sqrt{3}i$
   (e) $z = \frac{1}{\sqrt{2}} - \frac{1}{\sqrt{2}}i$
   (f) $z = 8(1 - \sqrt{3}i)$
   (g) $z = \frac{1}{1 - i}$
   (h) $z = -5$
   (i) $z = -6i$
   (j) $z = \frac{-2}{i}$

6. A ship at O is travelling along the line OP where $O(0, 0)$ and P represents the complex number $z = 4 + 3i$. By multiplying by a complex number, show how to change the direction by 60° in an anticlockwise direction and find the new bearing, to the nearest degree.

17.4 De Moivre's theorem

Abraham de Moivre

The French mathematician de Moivre devised a theorem concerning objects of the form $\cos A + i\sin A$. An object written in this form is known as a de Moivre Object (DMO).

There are four tricks for manipulating DMOs.

DMO 1: Multiplication trick

If you multiply two DMOs, you just add the angles.

$(\cos A \oplus i\sin A)(\cos B \oplus i\sin B)$

$= (\cos A\cos B - \sin A\sin B) + i(\sin A\cos B + \cos A\sin B)$

$= \cos(A + B) + i\sin(A + B)$

$$(\cos A \oplus i\sin A)(\cos B \oplus i\sin B) = \cos(A + B) \oplus i\sin(A + B)$$

$$\left(\cos\frac{\pi}{3} + i\sin\frac{\pi}{3}\right)\left(\cos\frac{\pi}{6} + i\sin\frac{\pi}{6}\right) = \cos\left(\frac{\pi}{3} + \frac{\pi}{6}\right) + i\sin\left(\frac{\pi}{3} + \frac{\pi}{6}\right)$$

$$= \cos\frac{\pi}{2} + i\sin\frac{\pi}{2} = 0 + i = i$$

DMO 2: Inversion trick

If you move a DMO from top to bottom, or vice versa, you change the sign between cos and sin.

$$\frac{1}{\cos A \oplus i\sin A} = \frac{1}{\cos A + i\sin A} \times \frac{\cos A - i\sin A}{\cos A - i\sin A}$$

$$= \frac{\cos A - i\sin A}{\cos^2 A + \sin^2 A} = \cos A - i\sin A$$

$$\frac{1}{\cos A \pm i\sin A} = \cos A \mp i\sin A$$

$$z\left(\cos\frac{\pi}{4} + i\sin\frac{\pi}{4}\right) = 1 \Rightarrow z = \frac{1}{\left(\cos\frac{\pi}{4} + i\sin\frac{\pi}{4}\right)} = \cos\frac{\pi}{4} - i\sin\frac{\pi}{4} = \frac{1}{\sqrt{2}} - \frac{1}{\sqrt{2}}i$$

ACTIVITY 28

ACTION
Working with de Moivre Objects (DMOs)

OBJECTIVE
To apply your knowledge of DMOs to simplify all types of complex numbers

DMO 3: Division trick

If you divide two DMOs, you subtract their angles.

$$\frac{\cos A \oplus i\sin A}{\cos B \oplus i\sin B} = (\cos A + i\sin A)(\cos B - i\sin B) \quad \textbf{[DMO 2]}$$

$$= (\cos A\cos B + \sin A\sin B) + i(\sin A\cos B - \cos A\sin B)$$

$$= \cos(A - B) + i\sin(A - B)$$

$$\frac{\cos A \oplus i\sin A}{\cos B \oplus i\sin B} = \cos(A - B) \oplus i\sin(A - B)$$

$$\frac{\cos\frac{\pi}{3} + i\sin\frac{\pi}{3}}{\cos\frac{\pi}{6} + i\sin\frac{\pi}{6}} = \cos\left(\frac{\pi}{3} - \frac{\pi}{6}\right) + i\sin\left(\frac{\pi}{3} - \frac{\pi}{6}\right) = \cos\left(\frac{\pi}{6}\right) + i\sin\left(\frac{\pi}{6}\right) = \frac{\sqrt{3}}{2} + \frac{1}{2}i$$

DMO 4: Power trick

If you raise a DMO to a power $n \in \mathbb{N}$, you multiply the angle by the power n.

$$(\cos A + i\sin A)^n = (\cos A + i\sin A)(\cos A + i\sin A) \ldots (\cos A + i\sin A) \quad [n \text{ brackets}]$$
$$= (\cos 2A + i\sin 2A)(\cos A + i\sin A) \ldots (\cos A + i\sin A) \quad [\textbf{DMO 1}]$$
$$= (\cos 3A + i\sin 3A) \ldots (\cos A + i\sin A)$$
$$= \cos nA + i\sin nA$$

$\therefore (\cos A + i\sin A)^n = \cos nA + i\sin nA$

It is also true that $(\cos A - i\sin A)^n = \cos nA - i\sin nA$.

Can you deduce it?

$$\boxed{(\cos A \oplus i\sin A)^n = (\cos nA \oplus i\sin nA)}$$

This result is an example of de Moivre's theorem.

▸ $\left(\cos\frac{5\pi}{3} + i\sin\frac{5\pi}{3}\right)^{12} = \cos\left(12 \times \frac{5\pi}{3}\right) + i\sin\left(12 \times \frac{5\pi}{3}\right)$

$= \cos 20\pi + i\sin 20\pi = 1$

EXAMPLE 20

Simplify $\frac{zw^2}{v}$ if $z = 3\left(\cos\frac{2\pi}{3} - i\sin\frac{2\pi}{3}\right)$, $w = 4\left(\cos\frac{\pi}{6} + i\sin\frac{\pi}{6}\right)$ and $v = 2\left(\cos\frac{\pi}{6} - i\sin\frac{\pi}{6}\right)$.

Solution

$$\frac{zw^2}{v} = \frac{3\left(\cos\frac{2\pi}{3} - i\sin\frac{2\pi}{3}\right) 4^2\left(\cos\frac{\pi}{6} + i\sin\frac{\pi}{6}\right)^2}{2\left(\cos\frac{\pi}{6} - i\sin\frac{\pi}{6}\right)}$$

$$= \frac{24\left(\cos\frac{2\pi}{3} - i\sin\frac{2\pi}{3}\right)\left(\cos\frac{\pi}{3} + i\sin\frac{\pi}{3}\right)}{\left(\cos\frac{\pi}{6} - i\sin\frac{\pi}{6}\right)}$$

$$= \frac{24\left(\cos\frac{\pi}{3} + i\sin\frac{\pi}{3}\right)\left(\cos\frac{\pi}{6} + i\sin\frac{\pi}{6}\right)}{\left(\cos\frac{2\pi}{3} + i\sin\frac{2\pi}{3}\right)}$$

$$= \frac{24\left(\cos\frac{\pi}{2} + i\sin\frac{\pi}{2}\right)}{\left(\cos\frac{2\pi}{3} + i\sin\frac{2\pi}{3}\right)}$$

$$= 24\left\{\cos\left(-\frac{\pi}{6}\right) + i\sin\left(-\frac{\pi}{6}\right)\right\}$$

$$= 24\left\{\frac{\sqrt{3}}{2} - \frac{1}{2}i\right\}$$

$$= 12\sqrt{3} - 12i$$

EXAMPLE 21

Simplify $\frac{(\cos A - i\sin A)^3(\cos 2A + i\sin 2A)^2}{(\cos 3A - i\sin 3A)^2}$, giving your answer in the form $\cos\theta + i\sin\theta$.

Solution

$$\frac{(\cos A - i\sin A)^3(\cos 2A + i\sin 2A)^2}{(\cos 3A - i\sin 3A)^2}$$

$$= \frac{(\cos 3A - i\sin 3A)(\cos 4A + i\sin 4A)}{(\cos 6A - i\sin 6A)}$$

$$= \frac{(\cos 6A + i\sin 6A)(\cos 4A + i\sin 4A)}{(\cos 3A + i\sin 3A)}$$

$$= \frac{\cos 10A + i\sin 10A}{\cos 3A + i\sin 3A}$$

$$= \cos 7A + i\sin 7A$$

The theorem

It has already been shown that $(\cos A \pm i\sin A)^n = \cos nA \pm i\sin nA$ for $n \in \mathbb{N}$. This is the basis of de Moivre's theorem for $n \in \mathbb{N}$. (The proof by induction is for $n \in \mathbb{N}$.) However, the theorem is more general than this and states that:

DE MOIVRE'S THEOREM

$[r(\cos A + i\sin A)]^p = r^p(\cos A + i\sin A)^p = r^p(\cos pA + i\sin pA)$ for all $p \in \mathbb{R}$.

Uses of de Moivre's theorem

Use 1: To find whole number powers of complex numbers

ACTIVITY 29

ACTION
Using de Moivre's theorem to work out powers of complex numbers

OBJECTIVE
To use de Moivre's theorem to work out powers of complex numbers and to solve equations

Steps

1. Write the complex number inside the bracket in polar form.
2. Apply de Moivre's theorem.
3. Use your calculator, giving your answer in Cartesian form.

EXAMPLE 22

Use de Moivre's theorem to evaluate $(-1 - i)^{20}$.

Solution

For $z = -1 - i$: $|z| = \sqrt{2}$, $\arg z = A = \frac{5\pi}{4}$.

1. $z = (-1 - i) = \sqrt{2}\left\{\cos\frac{5\pi}{4} + i\sin\frac{5\pi}{4}\right\}$ in polar form
2. $z^{20} = (\sqrt{2})^{20}\left\{\cos\frac{5\pi}{4} + i\sin\frac{5\pi}{4}\right\}^{20} = 2^{10}\{\cos 25\pi + i\sin 25\pi\}$
3. $z^{20} = 2^{10}\{-1 + 0i\} = -2^{10}$

EXAMPLE 23

Use de Moivre's theorem to evaluate $\left(-\frac{\sqrt{3}}{2} + \frac{1}{2}i\right)^{-7}$.

Solution

1. $z = -\frac{\sqrt{3}}{2} + \frac{1}{2}i = 1\left\{\cos\frac{5\pi}{6} + i\sin\frac{5\pi}{6}\right\}$ in polar form
2. $z^{-7} = 1^{-7}\left\{\cos\frac{5\pi}{6} + i\sin\frac{5\pi}{6}\right\}^{-7} = \left\{\cos\left(\frac{-35\pi}{6}\right) + i\sin\left(\frac{-35\pi}{6}\right)\right\} = \cos\frac{35\pi}{6} - i\sin\frac{35\pi}{6}$
3. $z^{-7} = \frac{\sqrt{3}}{2} - \frac{1}{2}i$

Use 2: To find roots of complex numbers

De Moivre's theorem can be used to find fractional powers of complex numbers.

Steps

1. Write the complex number in the bracket in **general** polar form.
2. Apply de Moivre's theorem.

3. List all of the roots (starting at $n = 0$ until you have them all).

TIP

1. There are two square roots, three cube roots, four fourth roots, etc.
2. Change to Cartesian form if your calculator gives non-decimal answers, otherwise leave in polar form.

EXAMPLE 24

Use de Moivre's theorem to find the three cube roots of $1 - i$.

Solution

1. For $z = 1 - i$: $|z| = \sqrt{2}$, $\arg z = A = \frac{7\pi}{4}$.

$$1 - i = \sqrt{2}\left\{\cos\left(\frac{7\pi}{4} + 2n\pi\right) + i\sin\left(\frac{7\pi}{4} + 2n\pi\right)\right\}, n \in \mathbb{N}_0$$

$$= \sqrt{2}\left\{\cos\left(\frac{7\pi + 8n\pi}{4}\right) + i\sin\left(\frac{7\pi + 8n\pi}{4}\right)\right\}$$

in general polar form

If you do not add $2n\pi$, you will not get all of the roots.

2. $$z^{\frac{1}{3}} = (\sqrt{2})^{\frac{1}{3}}\left\{\cos\left(\frac{7\pi + 8n\pi}{4}\right) + i\sin\left(\frac{7\pi + 8n\pi}{4}\right)\right\}^{\frac{1}{3}}$$

$$= (\sqrt{2})^{\frac{1}{3}}\left\{\cos\left(\frac{7\pi + 8n\pi}{12}\right) + i\sin\left(\frac{7\pi + 8n\pi}{12}\right)\right\}$$

3. Listing the roots, $n \in \mathbb{N}_0$.

$$n = 0: z_1 = 2^{\frac{1}{6}}\left(\cos\frac{7\pi}{12} + i\sin\frac{7\pi}{12}\right)$$

$$n = 1: z_2 = 2^{\frac{1}{6}}\left\{\cos\frac{15\pi}{12} + i\sin\frac{15\pi}{12}\right\}$$

$$= 2^{\frac{1}{6}}\left\{-\frac{1}{\sqrt{2}} - \frac{1}{\sqrt{2}}i\right\}$$

$$n = 2: z_3 = 2^{\frac{1}{6}}\left\{\cos\frac{23\pi}{12} + i\sin\frac{23\pi}{12}\right\}$$

Now you have your three cube roots. If you continue, you will see that the roots repeat.

EXAMPLE 25

Use de Moivre's theorem to solve $z^4 + 16i = 0$. Plot the solutions on an Argand diagram.

Solution

$z^4 + 16i = 0 \Rightarrow z^4 = -16i$

$z = (-16i)^{\frac{1}{4}} = (0 - 16i)^{\frac{1}{4}}$

1. $0 - 16i$

$$= 16\left\{\cos\left(\frac{3\pi + 4n\pi}{2}\right) + i\sin\left(\frac{3\pi + 4n\pi}{2}\right)\right\}$$ in general polar form

2. $$(-16i)^{\frac{1}{4}} = 16^{\frac{1}{4}}\left\{\cos\left(\frac{3\pi + 4n\pi}{2}\right) + i\sin\left(\frac{3\pi + 4n\pi}{2}\right)\right\}^{\frac{1}{4}}$$

$$= 2\left\{\cos\left(\frac{3\pi + 4n\pi}{8}\right) + i\sin\left(\frac{3\pi + 4n\pi}{8}\right)\right\}$$

3. $$n = 0: z_1 = 2\left\{\cos\frac{3\pi}{8} + i\sin\frac{3\pi}{8}\right\}$$

$$n = 1: z_2 = 2\left\{\cos\frac{7\pi}{8} + i\sin\frac{7\pi}{8}\right\}$$

$$n = 2: z_3 = 2\left\{\cos\frac{11\pi}{8} + i\sin\frac{11\pi}{8}\right\}$$

$$n = 3: z_4 = 2\left\{\cos\frac{15\pi}{8} + i\sin\frac{15\pi}{8}\right\}$$

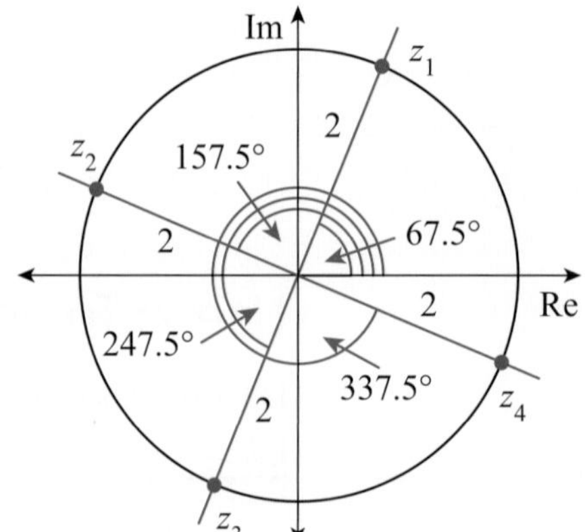

EXAMPLE 26

Show that $z = \cos\frac{4\pi}{3} + i\sin\frac{4\pi}{3}$ is one of the roots of $z^6 = 1$.

Solution

You do not have to find all six roots. You just have to show that the given z satisfies the equation $z^6 = 1$.

Substituting in for z: $\left(\cos\frac{4\pi}{3} + i\sin\frac{4\pi}{3}\right)^6 = \cos 8\pi + i\sin 8\pi = \cos 0 + i\sin 0 = 1$.

Therefore, it is a root.

ACTIVITY 30

ACTION
Proving trigonometric identities using de Moivre's theorem

OBJECTIVE
To use de Moivre's theorem to prove trigonometric identities

Use 3: To prove certain trigonometric results

There are many trigonometric identities involving cosines and sines of multiple angles written in terms of sines and cosines of single angles.

Examples: $\cos 2A = \cos^2 A - \sin^2 A$ and $\sin 3A = 3\sin A - 4\sin^3 A$.

You can prove these results using de Moivre's theorem in conjunction with the binomial theorem.

- $(\cos A + i\sin A)^2 = \cos 2A + i\sin 2A$ is de Moivre's theorem for $n = 2$.
- $(\cos A + i\sin A)^3 = \cos 3A + i\sin 3A$ is de Moivre's theorem for $n = 3$.
- $(\cos A + i\sin A)^4 = \cos 4A + i\sin 4A$ is de Moivre's theorem for $n = 4$.

Remember: The binomial coefficients for $(x + y)^3$ are 1, 3, 3, 1 and for $(x + y)^4$ are 1, 4, 6, 4, 1.

EXAMPLE 27

Use de Moivre's theorem to prove $\cos 2A = \cos^2 A - \sin^2 A$.

Solution

Write down de Moivre's theorem for $n = 2$.

$(\cos A + i\sin A)^2 = \cos 2A + i\sin 2A$

Expanding out the bracket on the left-hand side gives:

$\cos^2 A + 2i\cos A\sin A + (i\sin A)^2 = \cos 2A + i\sin 2A$

$(\cos^2 A - \sin^2 A) + 2i\cos A\sin A = \cos 2A + i\sin 2A$

This is an equation.

Re = Re gives: $\cos^2 A - \sin^2 A = \cos 2A$

$\therefore \cos 2A = \cos^2 A - \sin^2 A$

EXAMPLE 28

Use de Moivre's theorem to prove that $\sin 3A = 3\sin A - 4\sin^3 A$.

Solution

Write down de Moivre's theorem for $n = 3$: $(\cos A + i\sin A)^3 = \cos 3A + i\sin 3A$.

Expanding the bracket on the left-hand side using the binomial theorem gives:

$(\cos A)^3 + 3(\cos A)^2(i\sin A) + 3(\cos A)(i\sin A)^2 + (i\sin A)^3 = \cos 3A + i\sin 3A$

$\cos^3 A + 3i\cos^2 A\sin A - 3\cos A\sin^2 A - i\sin^3 A = \cos 3A + i\sin 3A$

$(\cos^3 A - 3\cos A\sin^2 A) + i(3\cos^2 A\sin A - \sin^3 A) = \cos 3A + i\sin 3A$

Im = Im: $3\cos^2 A\sin A - \sin^3 A = \sin 3A$

$3(1 - \sin^2 A)\sin A - \sin^3 A = \sin 3A$

$\therefore\ 3\sin A - 4\sin^3 A = \sin 3A$

EXERCISE 14

1. Plot the following on the same Argand diagram:
   (a) $z_1 = 4\left\{\cos\frac{\pi}{3} + i\sin\frac{\pi}{3}\right\}$
   (b) $z_2 = 2\left\{\cos\frac{\pi}{6} + i\sin\frac{\pi}{6}\right\}$
   (c) $z_3 = z_1 z_2$
   (d) $z_4 = \frac{z_1}{z_2}$

2. Evaluate the following in the form $a + bi$, $a, b \in \mathbb{R}$:
   (a) $\left(\cos\frac{4\pi}{3} + i\sin\frac{4\pi}{3}\right)^6$
   (b) $\left(\cos\frac{11\pi}{6} + i\sin\frac{11\pi}{6}\right)^2$
   (c) $\left[3\left(\cos\frac{5\pi}{3} + i\sin\frac{5\pi}{3}\right)\right]^4$
   (d) $[2(\cos 20^0 - i\sin 20^0)]^3$
   (e) $\left[\sqrt{2}\left(\cos\frac{7\pi}{4} + i\sin\frac{7\pi}{4}\right)\right]^{20}$

3. Evaluate the following in the form $a + bi$, $a, b \in \mathbb{R}$:
   (a) $\left(\cos\frac{\pi}{3} + i\sin\frac{\pi}{3}\right)\left(\cos\frac{2\pi}{3} + i\sin\frac{2\pi}{3}\right)$
   (b) $\dfrac{6\left(\cos\frac{\pi}{3} + i\sin\frac{\pi}{3}\right)}{3\left(\cos\frac{\pi}{6} + i\sin\frac{\pi}{6}\right)}$
   (c) $\dfrac{6\left(\cos\frac{\pi}{12} + i\sin\frac{\pi}{12}\right)^6}{3\left(\cos\frac{\pi}{6} + i\sin\frac{\pi}{6}\right)}$
   (d) $\dfrac{12\left(\cos\frac{\pi}{3} + i\sin\frac{\pi}{3}\right)}{6\left(\cos\frac{\pi}{6} - i\sin\frac{\pi}{6}\right)}$
   (e) $\dfrac{8\left(\cos\frac{\pi}{4} + i\sin\frac{\pi}{4}\right)}{16\left(\cos\frac{\pi}{2} - i\sin\frac{\pi}{2}\right)}$

4. (a) If $z = \dfrac{1}{\left(\cos\frac{\pi}{3} + i\sin\frac{\pi}{3}\right)}$, find z in the form $a + bi$.
   (b) If $z = \left(\cos\frac{\pi}{6} - i\sin\frac{\pi}{6}\right)^{-1}$, find z in the form $a + bi$.
   (c) If $z = \dfrac{1}{\left(\cos\frac{3\pi}{4} + i\sin\frac{3\pi}{4}\right)}$, find z in the form $a + bi$.
   (d) If $z = \cos A + i\sin A$ and $z - \left(\cos\frac{\pi}{6} + i\sin\frac{\pi}{6}\right)\bar{z} = 0$, find A, $0 \le A \le \pi$.

(e) If $z = \cos A + i\sin A$ and $z - \left(\cos\frac{\pi}{2} + i\sin\frac{\pi}{2}\right)\bar{z} = 0$, find z in the form $a + bi$, $a, b > 0$, $a, b \in \mathbb{R}$.

5. Write the following in the form $\cos\theta \pm i\sin\theta$:

(a) $\dfrac{\cos A + i\sin A}{\cos A - i\sin A}$

(b) $\dfrac{\cos 3A + i\sin 3A}{\cos 2A - i\sin 2A}$

(c) $\dfrac{\cos 4A - i\sin 4A}{\cos 4A + i\sin 4A}$

(d) $\dfrac{(\cos 3A + i\sin 3A)(\cos 2A - i\sin 2A)}{(\cos 4A - i\sin 4A)(\cos A + i\sin A)}$

(e) $\dfrac{(1 + i\tan A)^3}{(1 - i\tan A)^3}$

6. (a) Evaluate the following in the form $a + bi$, $a, b \in \mathbb{R}$, using de Moivre's theorem:

(i) $(1 + i)^{32}$

(ii) $(1 - i)^{26}$

(iii) $\left(\frac{\sqrt{3}}{2} + \frac{1}{2}i\right)^{100}$

(iv) $(-1 + i)^{15}$

(v) $(-1 - \sqrt{3}i)^{-20}$

(vi) $\left(-\frac{1}{2} + \frac{\sqrt{3}}{2}i\right)^{-30}$

(b) Evaluate the following using de Moivre's theorem, giving all roots:

(i) $1^{\frac{1}{3}}$

(ii) $(-16)^{\frac{1}{4}}$

(iii) $(-i)^{\frac{1}{3}}$

(iv) $(1 - i)^{\frac{1}{4}}$

(v) $\left(-\frac{\sqrt{3}}{2} + \frac{1}{2}i\right)^{\frac{1}{2}}$

(vi) $(-3i - \sqrt{3})^{\frac{1}{3}}$

(c) Solve the following using de Moivre's theorem:

(i) $z^6 + 64i = 0$

(ii) $z^5 = i$

(iii) $z^3 = \frac{\sqrt{3}}{2} + \frac{1}{2}i$

(iv) $2z^2 = -1 - \sqrt{3}i$

(d) In each case below, show that the given value of z is a root of the given equation:

(i) $z = \cos\frac{2\pi}{3} + i\sin\frac{2\pi}{3}$ of $z^6 = 1$

(ii) $z = \sqrt{3}\left\{\cos\frac{\pi}{5} + i\sin\frac{\pi}{5}\right\}$ of $z^{10} = 243$

(iii) $z = 2\cos\left\{\frac{\pi}{12} + i\sin\frac{\pi}{12}\right\}$ of $z^4 = 8 + 8\sqrt{3}i$

(iv) $z = \frac{1}{\sqrt{2}} - \frac{1}{\sqrt{2}}i$ of $z^4 = -1$

(e) (i) Use de Moivre's theorem to prove that $\cos 2A = \cos^2 A - \sin^2 A$ and $\sin 2A = 2\sin A\cos A$. Deduce that $\tan 2A = \dfrac{2\tan A}{1 - \tan^2 A}$.

(ii) Use de Moivre's theorem to prove that $\cos 3A = 4\cos^3 A - 3\cos A$.

(iii) Use de Moivre's theorem to prove that $\cos 4A = 8\cos^4 A - 8\cos^2 A + 1$.

REVISION QUESTIONS

1. $z = -\sqrt{3} + i$, where $i = \sqrt{-1}$.

(a) Show that $\frac{z}{\bar{z}} = \frac{1}{2} - \frac{\sqrt{3}}{2}i$.

(b) Find $|z|$, $|\bar{z}|$, $\left|\frac{z}{\bar{z}}\right|$.

(c) Draw z, $\bar{z}$ and $\frac{z}{\bar{z}}$ on the same Argand diagram by finding $\arg z$, $\arg \bar{z}$, $\arg\left(\frac{z}{\bar{z}}\right)$

(d) Verify that $\arg\left(\frac{z}{\bar{z}}\right) = \arg z - \arg \bar{z}$.

(e) Find the quadratic equation with roots z and $\bar{z}$ in the form $ax^2 + bx + c = 0$. What can you say about the coefficients a, b and c?

2. **(a)** With the use of computers you can generate beautiful art from complex numbers. These designs are called fractals. Fractals are generated by the iteration of complex numbers using equations of the form $z_{n+1} = (z_n)^2 - z_n + 1$, $n \in \{0, 1, 2, \dots\}$.

Using $z_0 = 1 + i$, find the next five complex numbers generated.

(b) A ship travels along the line joining 0 to z, where $0 = 0 + 0i$ and $z = 4 + 3i$.

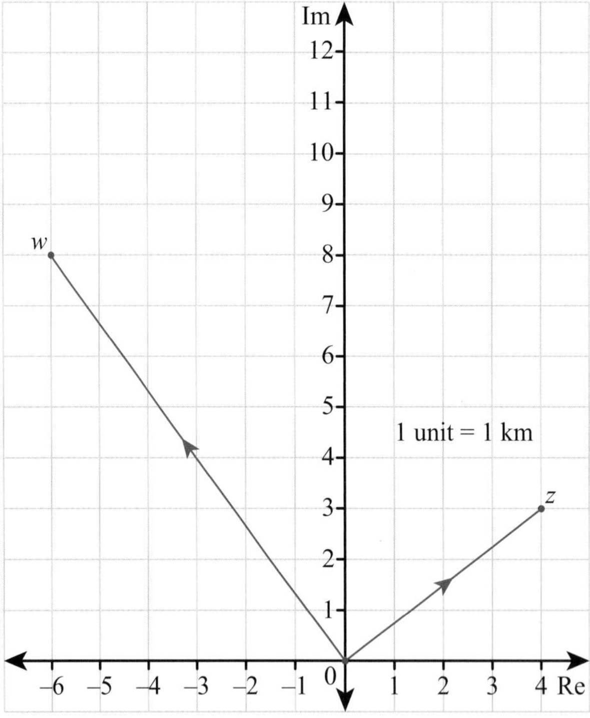

(i) Find $|z|$.

(ii) If the time it takes to get from 0 to z is 1 hour, find the ship's speed.

(iii) One hour after starting from 0, the ship changes direction by turning anticlockwise through 90° and doubles its speed. The ship's new path is parallel to the line joining 0 to w, where $|w|$ is the distance travelled by the ship in another hour.

Using the parallelogram law, show on the diagram the final position u of the ship, relative to the origin, after the 2 hours.

(iv) Write u as a complex number and find how far it is from 0.

3. (a) If $i = \sqrt{-1}$:

(i) evaluate i^{99}

(ii) simplify $\left(\frac{-1+\sqrt{3}i}{\sqrt{3}+i}\right)$

(iii) simplify $\left(\frac{-1+\sqrt{3}i}{\sqrt{3}+i}\right)^{99}$

(b) Express the following complex numbers in the form $a + bi$, $a, b \in \mathbb{R}$:

(i) z with $|z| = 2$ and $\arg z = \frac{\pi}{3}$

(ii) w with $|w| = 4$ and $\arg w = \frac{5\pi}{6}$

(iii) zw (iv) $\frac{w}{z}$

4. (a) If $z = \frac{2+3i}{1+i}$, find $z + \frac{1}{z}$ in the form $a + bi$, $a, b \in \mathbb{R}$.

(b) If $z = a + bi$ and $w = c + di$, $a, b, c, d \in \mathbb{R}$, show that $z\overline{w} + w\overline{z} = 2 \times \text{Re}(z\overline{w})$.

(c) Write down de Moivre's theorem for $n = 3$. Use this result and the binomial theorem to prove that $\sin 3A = 3 \sin A - 4 \sin^3 A$.

5. (a) If $z = 1 - \sqrt{3}i$, find z^2. Find $k \in \mathbb{R}$ if $z^2 + kz$ is real.

(b) $z = 2 + 4i$ is plotted on the Argand diagram.

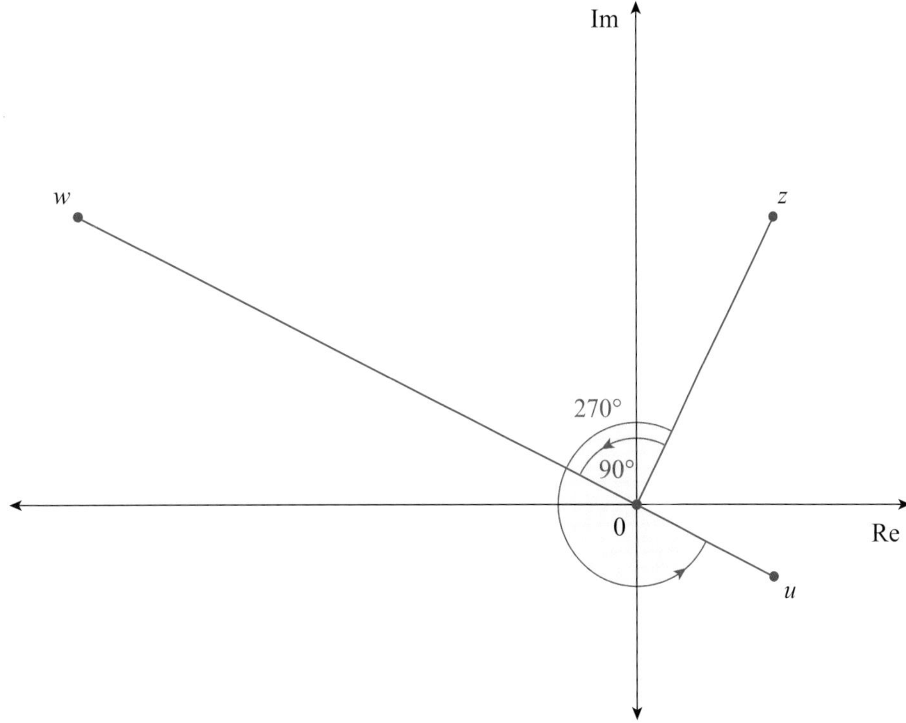

If $0 = 0 + 0i$,

(i) find w such that $|w| = 2|z|$ if an angle between the line joining 0 to w and the line joining 0 to z is 90°,

(ii) find u such that $|u| = \frac{1}{2}|z|$ if an angle between the line joining 0 to u and the line joining 0 to z is 270°,

(iii) plot v such that $|v| = 2|z|$ and v, 0 and z are collinear.

(c) Write $z = 3\sqrt{2} - 3\sqrt{6}i$ in polar form. Use de Moivre's theorem to evaluate z^{10}, in the form $k(a + bi)$, $a, b, k \in \mathbb{R}$.

6. **(a)** Solve $z^2 - 2z + 5 = 0$, giving your answer in the form $a + bi$, $a, b \in \mathbb{R}$.

(b) State the conjugate root theorem.

If $2 - 3i$ is a root of $z^3 + pz^2 + qz + 65 = 0$, $p, q \in \mathbb{R}$, find p, q and the other roots.

(c) Write $z = 5 + 12i$ in general polar form, giving the angles in radians, correct to three decimal places. Use de Moivre's theorem to evaluate $\sqrt{5 + 12i}$ in the form $a + bi$, $a, b \in \mathbb{Z}$. Verify your answers.

7. **(a)** Express the following in polar form:

(i) $u = 1 + i$

(ii) $v = \sqrt{3} + i$

(iii) $z = \dfrac{1+i}{\sqrt{3}+i}$

Find z^n, $n \in \mathbb{N}$, using de Moivre's theorem. Find the least non-zero value of n for which z^n is real.

(b) Plot the following on the same Argand diagram:

(i) A, the set of complex numbers $z = x + yi$, $x, y \in \mathbb{R}$, such that $|z - 3| = 3$

(ii) B, the set of complex numbers $z = x + yi$, $x, y \in \mathbb{R}$, such that $|z| = |z - 2|$

Find $A \cap B$.

8. **(a)** Simplify $(4 + 5i)(3 + 2i)$ in the form $a + bi$, $a, b \in \mathbb{R}$. Hence, find:

(i) $(4 - 5i)(3 - 2i)$ in the same form

(ii) the prime factors of 533 [**Hint:** $533 = 2^2 + 23^2$]

(b) The roots of $z^2 + az + b = 0$ are $4 + 3i$ and i. Find a and b.

(c) If $1 + i$ is a root of $z^2 + (p + 2i)z + 5 + qi = 0$, find $p, q \in \mathbb{R}$.

9. **(a)** **(i)** If $z = x + yi$, find $z\bar{z}$.

(ii) Solve $z\bar{z} + 2iz = 12 + 6i$ for $x, y \in \mathbb{R}$, if $z = x + yi$.

(b) If $|z| = 6$, $\arg z = 240°$, $|w| = 4$ and $\arg w = 45°$, find:

(i) $|zw|$

(ii) $\arg(zw)$

(iii) $\left|\frac{z}{w}\right|$

(iv) $\arg\left(\frac{z}{w}\right)$

(c) Explain why w^2 is purely imaginary. Hence, find w^2.

(d) What can be said about z^3? Find z^3.

10. **(a)** By factorising $z^3 - 1$, solve $z^3 - 1 = 0$, giving one real and two imaginary roots.

(b) Write $1 + 0i$ in general polar form. Find the three cube roots of 1 using de Moivre's theorem.

(c) If $w (w \neq 1)$ is one of the complex roots, show that the other is w^2.

(d) Show that:

(i) $1 + w + w^2 = 0$

(ii) $(1 + w)^3 = -1$

(iii) $(2 + 2w + 3w^2)^3 = 1$

11. **(a)** If $z = \cos\frac{\pi}{3} + i\sin\frac{\pi}{3}$, find $|z + 1|$.

(b) **(i)** Evaluate $\dfrac{1}{\cos\frac{3\pi}{4} - i\sin\frac{3\pi}{4}}$ in the form $a + bi$.

(ii) Express $\dfrac{1 + i\tan A}{1 - i\tan A}$ in the form $\cos\theta + i\sin\theta$. Hence, write $\left(\dfrac{1 + i\tan A}{1 - i\tan A}\right)^7$ in the same form.

(iii) Express $\dfrac{(\cos A + i\sin A)^4}{(\cos A - i\sin A)^3}$ in the form $\cos\theta + i\sin\theta$.

(c) If $z = \cos A + i\sin A$, show that:

(i) $z^n + z^{-n} = 2\cos nA$

(ii) $z^n - z^{-n} = 2i\sin nA$

(iii) $z^{2n} - 2z^n\cos nA + 1 = 0$

SUMMARY

1. Imaginary numbers:

   (a) $i = \sqrt{-1} \Rightarrow i^2 = -1$

   (b) $i^n = \begin{cases} 1 \\ i \\ -1 \\ -i \end{cases}, n \in \mathbb{N}_0 = \{0, 1, 2, 3, \ldots\}$

   (c) $i^n = i^R$, where R is the remainder when n is divided by 4

2. Complex number definition: $z = a + bi$, where $a, b \in \mathbb{R}$, $i = \sqrt{-1}$

   a is the real part (Re) of z

   b is the imaginary part (Im) of z

3. The Argand diagram:

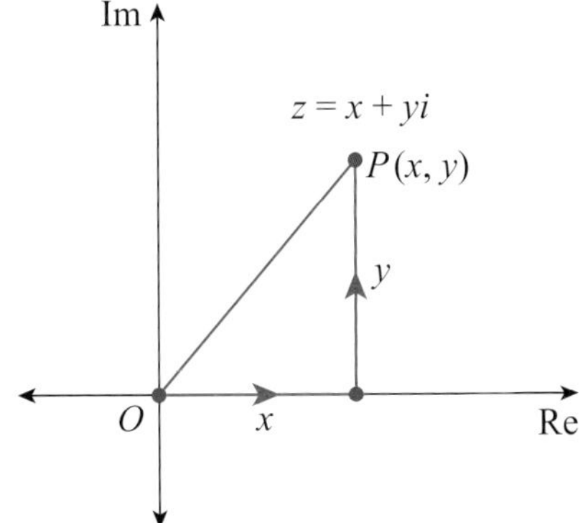

4. Addition of complex numbers:

   $(a + bi) + (c + di) = (a + c) + (b + d)i$

   Add the real parts and add the imaginary parts.

5. Multiplication of a complex number by a scalar $k \in \mathbb{R}$

   $k(a + bi) = ka + kbi$

6. The modulus of a complex number $z = a + bi$:

   $|z| = \sqrt{a^2 + b^2} = \sqrt{(\text{Re})^2 + (\text{Im})^2}$

7. The argument of a complex number $z = a + bi$:

   $\arg z = \tan^{-1}\left(\frac{b}{a}\right) = \tan^{-1}\left(\frac{\text{Im}}{\text{Re}}\right)$

8. The conjugate of a complex number $z = a + bi$:

   $\bar{z} = a - bi$

   Change the sign between Re and Im.

9. Multiplication of complex numbers:

   $(a + bi)(c + di) = (ac - bd) + (bc + ad)i$

   Multiply out the brackets and put $i^2 = -1$.

   Conjugate multiplication: $(a + bi)\overline{(a + bi)}$
   $= (a + bi)(a - bi) = (a)^2 + (b)^2$

10. Division of complex numbers:

    $\frac{a + bi}{c + di} = \frac{(a + bi)(c - di)}{(c + di)(c - di)}$

    Multiply above and below by the conjugate of the complex number on the bottom.

11. Powers of complex numbers: multiply out the brackets

12. Equality of complex numbers:

    $a + bi = c + di \Rightarrow a = c$ and $b = d$

    Remember: $0 = 0 + 0i$

13. Quadratic equations:

    (a) Solution: $z = \frac{-b \pm \sqrt{b^2 - 4ac}}{2a}$

    (b) Forming a quadratic equation from its roots: $z^2 - Sz + P = 0$

    (c) Conjugate root theorem:

    If all the coefficients of a polynomial equation (quadratic/cubic) are real, then if $p + qi$ is a root so is $p - qi$, and vice versa.

14. Cubic equations:

    Cubic = Quadratic × Linear

15. Polar form:

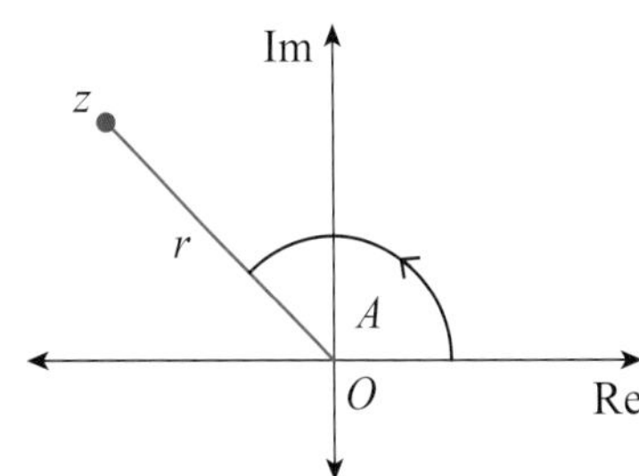

$z = x + yi \Rightarrow r = |z| = \sqrt{x^2 + y^2} = \sqrt{(\text{Re})^2 + (\text{Im})^2}$

$|\tan A| = \left|\frac{\text{Im}}{\text{Re}}\right| = \tan\theta \Rightarrow \theta = \tan^{-1}\left|\frac{\text{Im}}{\text{Re}}\right|$

Polar form:

$z = r(\cos A + i\sin A)$

General polar form:

$z = r(\cos(A + 2n\pi) + i\sin(A + 2n\pi)),\ n \in \mathbb{N}_0$

16. DMO tricks:

(a) $(\cos A \oplus i\sin A)(\cos B \oplus i\sin B) = \cos(A+B) \oplus i\sin(A+B)$

(b) $\dfrac{1}{\cos A \pm i\sin A} = \cos A \mp i\sin A$

(c) $\dfrac{\cos A \oplus i\sin A}{\cos B \oplus i\sin B} = \cos(A-B) \oplus i\sin(A-B)$

(d) $(\cos A \pm i\sin A)^n = \cos nA \mp i\sin nA$

De Moivre's Theorem (DMT):

$[r(\cos A + i\sin A)]^p = r^p(\cos A + i\sin A)^p = r^p(\cos pA + i\sin pA), p \in \mathbb{R}$

DMT Applications:

(a) Powers – polar form

(b) Roots – general polar form

(c) Trigonometric identities – binomial theorem

17. Geometrical interpretation

(a) Multiplication: If you multiply a complex number z by w, z is rotated anticlockwise about $O(0, 0)$ through arg w and its modulus is multiplied by $|w|$.

(b) Division: If you divide a complex number z by w, z is rotated clockwise about $O(0, 0)$ through arg w and its modulus is divided by $|w|$.

SECTION 7

Functions

Functions are the engines of mathematics. They relate different variables using mathematical equations and are used extensively in science, engineering, business and finance.

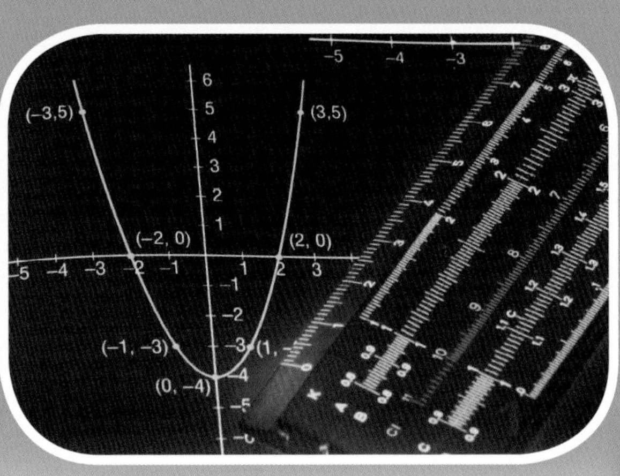

Relations and Functions

Learning Outcomes

- To understand when a relation is a function.
- To understand function notation.
- To understand the difference between injective, surjective and bijective functions.
- To find the inverse of a function.
- To understand the composition of functions.
- To understand the concept of continuity of functions.

Introduction

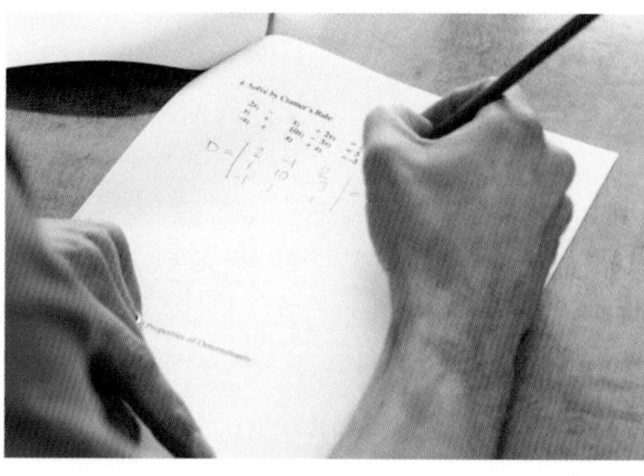

Five students sit a test where the grades that can be awarded are A, B, C, D, E and F. The results of the test are as follows:

Anne (B)

John (C)

Mary (A)

Paul (B)

Sandra (D)

There is a relation between the student and the grade received. A set S of ordered pairs can be used to represent this relation.

$S = \{(\text{Anne, B}), (\text{John, C}), (\text{Mary, A}), (\text{Paul, B}), (\text{Sandra, D})\}$

This relation can be mapped as shown:

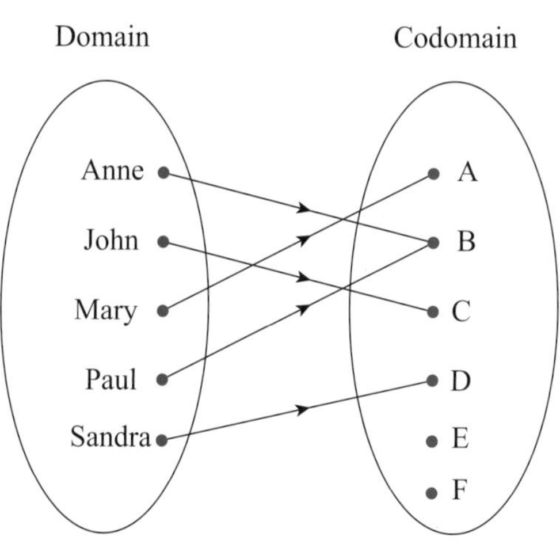

The five students form the elements of the domain. The grades that they can receive form the elements of the codomain. The range is the set of grades received by the students. The range is a subset of the codomain.

Domain = {Anne, John, Mary, Paul, Sandra}

Codomain = {A, B, C, D, E, F}

Range = {A, B, C, D}

This relation is known as a function because each element of the domain maps onto one and only one value in the codomain. This makes sense as every student who sits the test receives only one grade. It would not make sense if a student got a grade B and a grade D in the test!

18.1 What is a relation?

There are many situations in which one quantity is linked to another. Here are some examples:

- The mileage obtained per litre of fuel is linked to engine size.
- The amount of tax you pay is linked to income earned.
- Your weight is linked to the amount of food consumed.

When the value of one variable is related to the value of a second variable, there is a **relation** between them.

KEY TERM

A **relation** is a correspondence between two sets.

If x is an element of one set and y an element of another set and if a relation exists between x and y, then we say that 'y depends on x' or $x \to y$.

WORKED EXAMPLE

Mapping relations

In the relation shown in the diagram, Clare (x) corresponds to 4 (y).

County Clare has four deputies in the Dáil.

A set S of ordered pairs (x, y) can be used to represent the relation $x \to y$.

S = {(Clare, 4), (Mayo, 5), (Meath, 6), (Tipperary, 6)}

A diagram with arrows between two sets that shows a relation is known as a mapping.

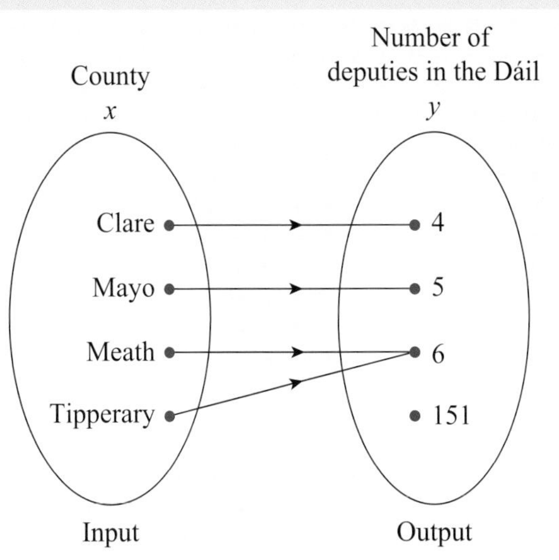

A relation between two variables x and y can also be illustrated by a graph in the Cartesian plane.

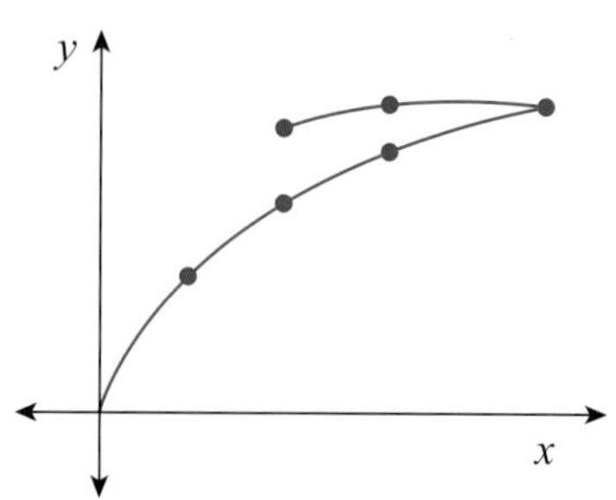

This graph represents the path of a ball which bounces off a wall.

A relation is **any** set of points in the Cartesian plane.

A relation is usually expressed in the form of an equation that connects the variables x and y.

- $y = 2x$

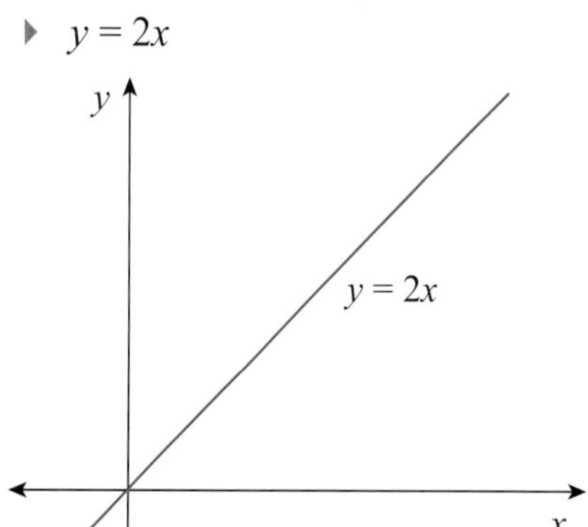

- $y^2 = 25 - x^2$

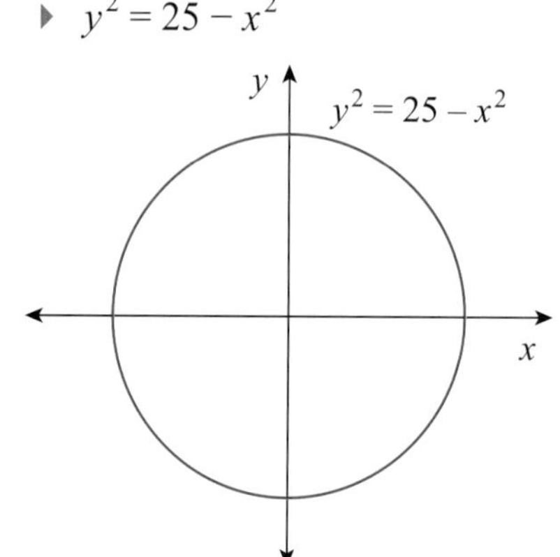

- $y = x^2$

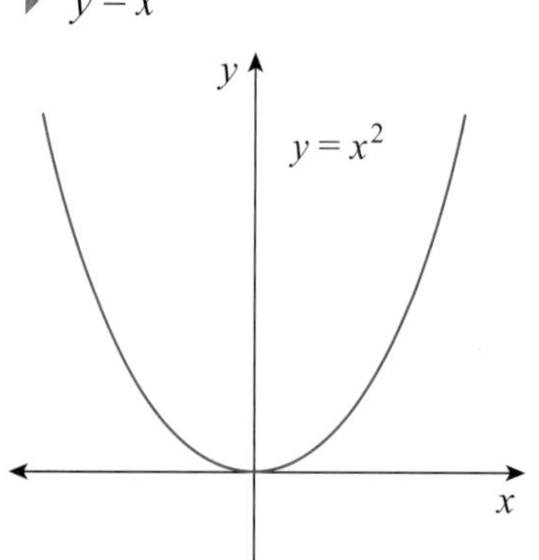

- $y = x^3$

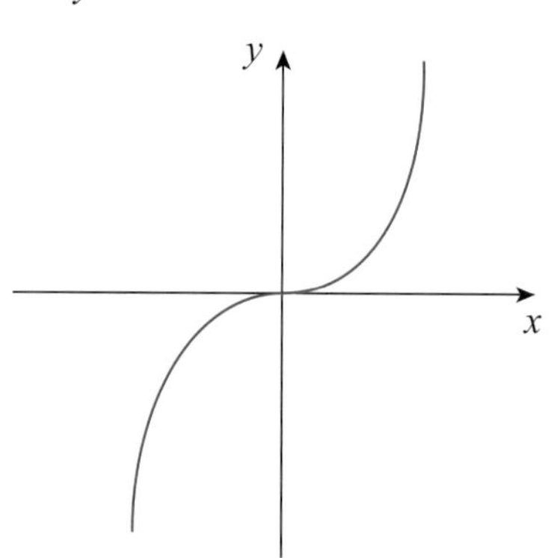

As already mentioned, the set of values which is mapped by a relation is known as the **domain** of the relation and the set of values that they are mapped onto is known as the **codomain**.

Sometimes the set of images of the domain is a subset of the set onto which the elements of the domain are mapped. The set of images is known as the **range** of the relation, and is always a subset of the codomain.

WORKED EXAMPLE Domains, codomains and ranges

Consider the relation 'every natural number is doubled'.

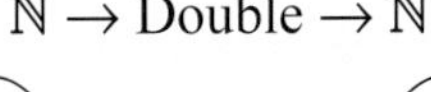

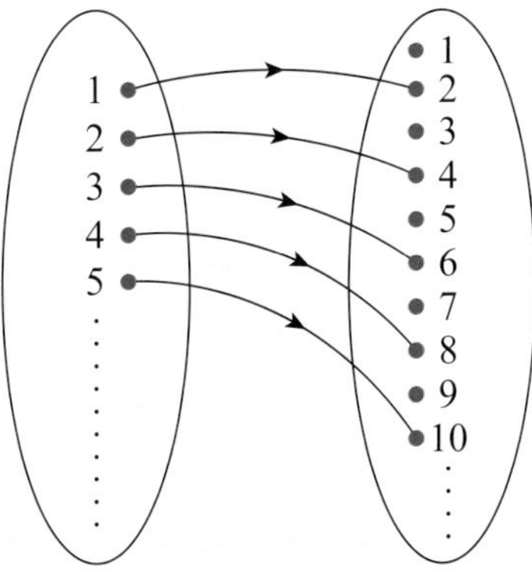

Domain = ℕ = {1, 2, 3, 4, …}

The set into which the elements of the domain is mapped is the codomain.

Codomain = ℕ = {1, 2, 3, 4, …}

The set of images or the range is the set of even natural numbers.

Range = {2, 4, 6, 8, …}

TIPS

The domain is the set of elements at the start of the arrow.

The codomain is the receiver set into which the domain is mapped.

The range is the set of elements at the ends of the arrows.

18.2 What is a function?

A function from one set (x values) to another set (y values) is a relation that associates with each x value **one and only one** value of y.

WORKED EXAMPLE Is it a function?

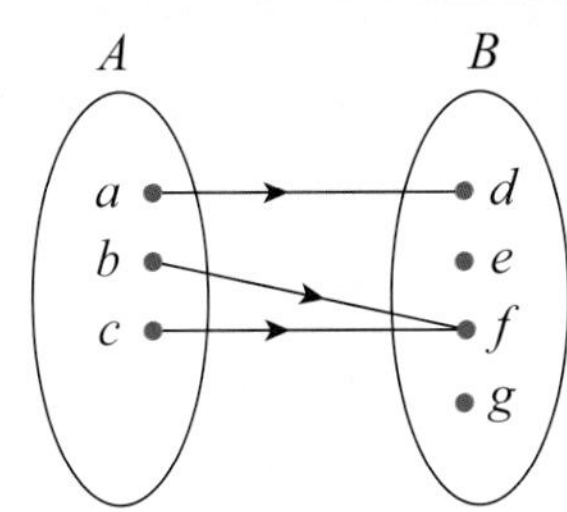

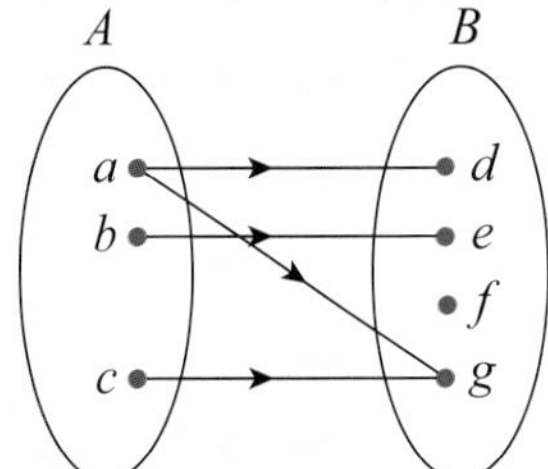

This is a function, *but* this is not a function as a has two values of y in B associated with it.

- $S = \{(-2, 3), (5, 7), (4, 11)\}$ is a function, *but*
- $S = \{(-2, 3), (-2, 7), (4, 11)\}$ is not a function as two numbers have -2 as their x value.

KEY TERM

A **function** is a relation in which no two ordered pairs (x, y) have the same x value.

ACTIVITY 1

ACTION
Determining if curves are functions

OBJECTIVE
To use the vertical line test to determine if curves are functions

Testing for a function

Test 1: Substitute test

Given a relation between x and y defined by an equation, if when you substitute a value of x you get more than one value of y, then the relation is not a function.

- Consider the relation between x and y that is defined by the equation $y^2 = x$, $x \geq 0$, $x \in \mathbb{R}$.

  Choose any value of x like $x = 9$

  $y^2 = 9$

  $y = \pm 3$

  $x = 9$ gives two values of y.

  This is not a function.

- $y = 4x + 5$, $x \in \mathbb{R}$, is a function as each value of x gives **one and only one** value of y.

ACTIVITY 2

ACTION
Working with domains, ranges and functions

OBJECTIVE
To write down the domains and ranges and state if the relation is a function

Test 2: Vertical line test

For a relation between x and y given by a graph, if when you draw all possible vertical lines in the domain on the graph and each line intersects the graph **once and only once**, then the relation is a function.

TIP
If any vertical line in the domain cuts the graph more than once, the relation is not a function.

- $y = x^2$, $x \in \mathbb{R}$, is a function:

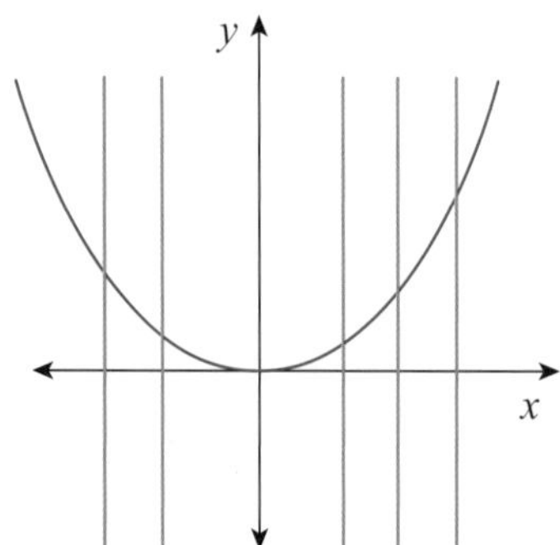

- $y^2 = 25 - x^2$, $-5 \leq x \leq 5$, $x \in \mathbb{R}$, is not a function:

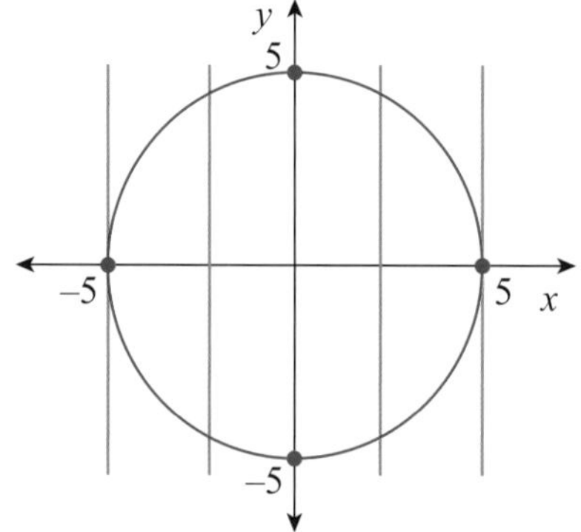

EXAMPLE 1

A particle oscillates back and forth between A and B for 4 seconds. At time t in seconds it is a distance s metres from a fixed point O.

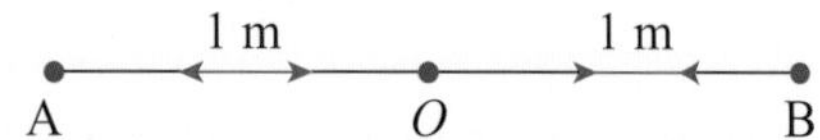

A graph of t against s is shown, $0 \leq s \leq 1$, $s \in \mathbb{R}$.

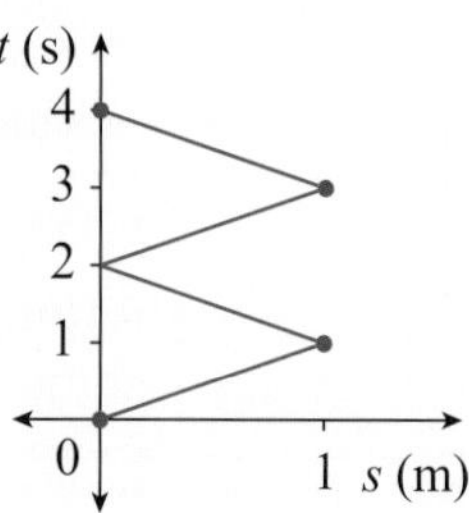

Is this a function?

Solution

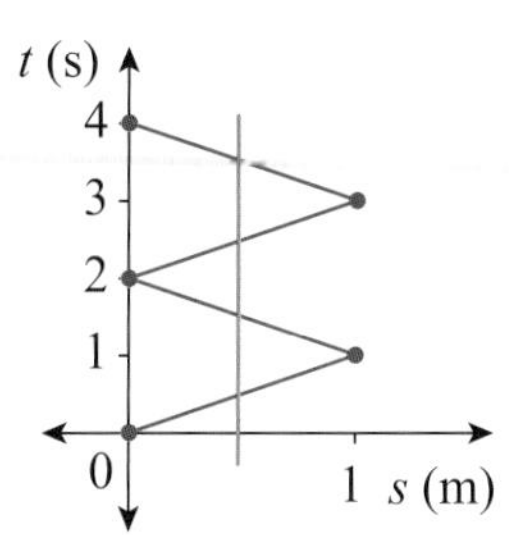

This is not a function, as a vertical line can be drawn from the domain which intersects the graph in more than one place.

The function machine

1. Evaluating functions

A function f can be visualised as a machine that takes a variable (or number), does an operation on it and spits out a new variable (number).

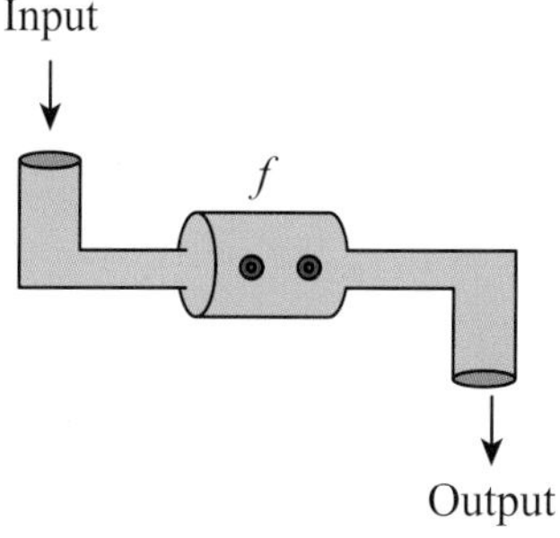

For example, in the function machine below the outputs are obtained by 'squaring' the inputs.

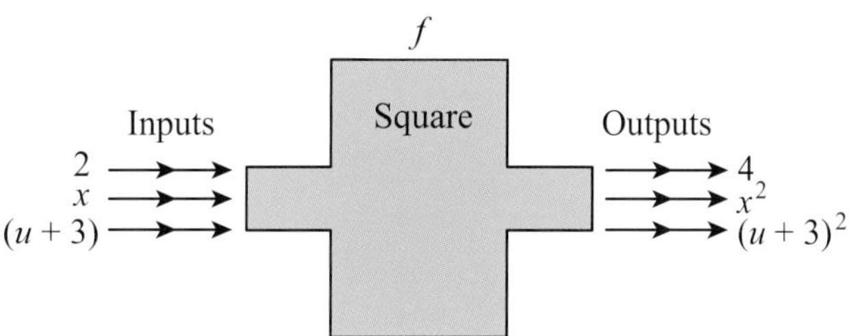

2. Domain and range

The domain of a function is the set of permissible values of the inputs (the set of values to be mapped). The range of a function is the set of values of the outputs or images (the set of results of the mapping of the elements of the domain).

EXAMPLE 2

Find the domain and the range of the function that cubes each value of $x \in \{-2, -1, 0, 1, 2\}$.

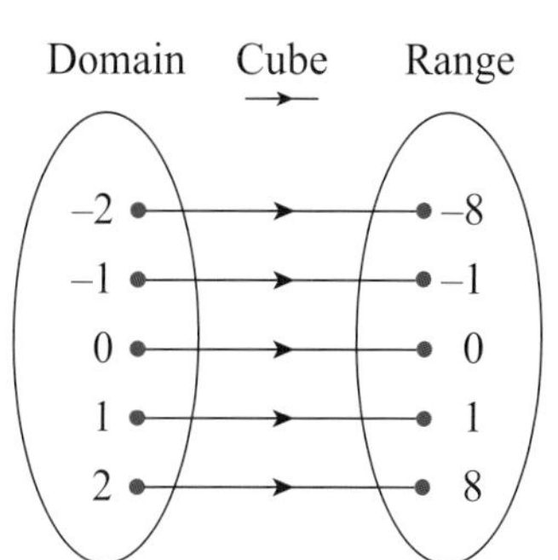

Solution

The set of values that are allowed (inputs) = domain = $\{-2, -1, 0, 1, 2\}$.

The set of images = range = $\{-8, -1, 0, 1, 8\}$.

EXERCISE 1

1. **(a)** Write down the relations described by the diagrams below as a set of ordered pairs S.

   (b) Write down the domain D and range I of each relation.

   (c) Say whether or not the relation is a function.

   (i)

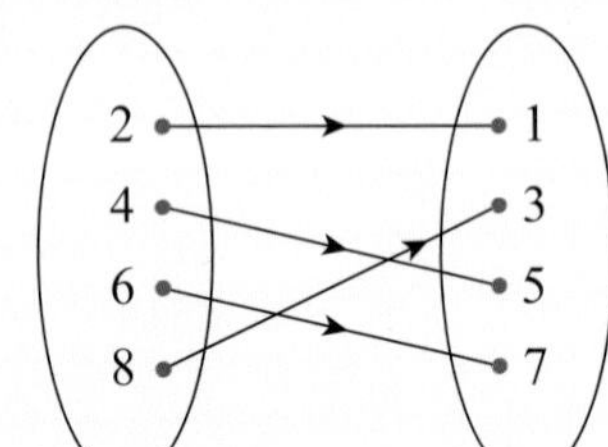

   (ii)

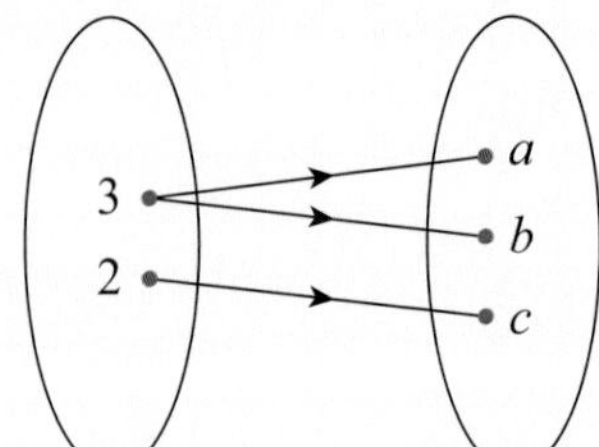

   (iii)

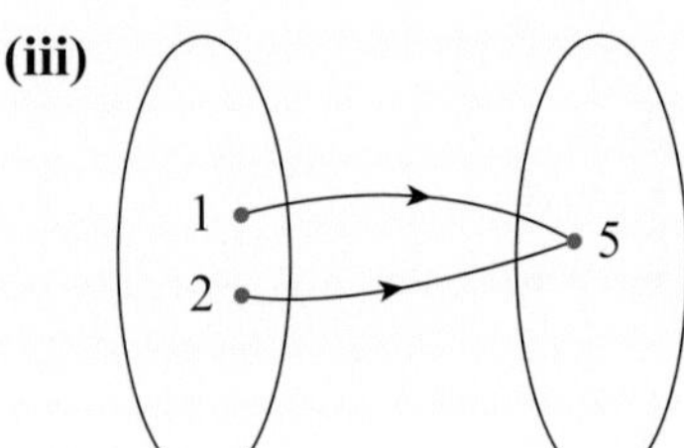

   (iv)

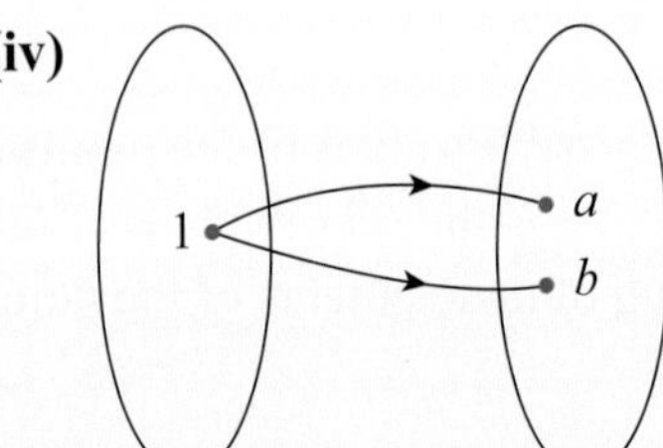

   (v)

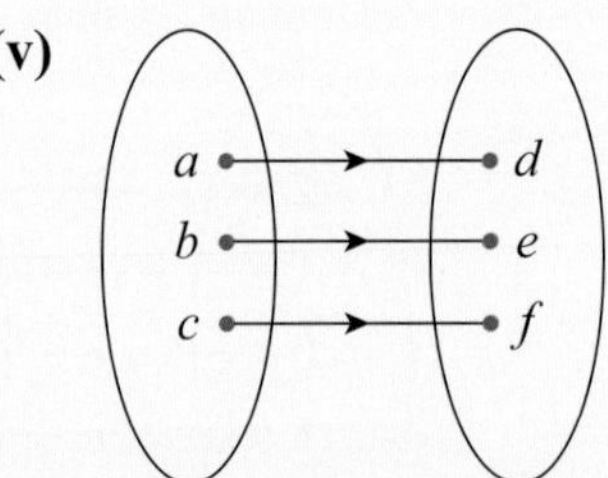

2. State if the following relations S are functions, giving a reason for your answer. Write down the domain D and range I of the relation in each case:

   (a) $S = \{(a, 1), (b, 1)\ (c, 1)\}$

   (b) $S = \{(1, a), (1, b), (2, a)\}$

   (c) $S = \{(1, 1), (2, 4), (3, 9), (4, 16)\}$

   (d) $S = \{(1, 1), (1, -1), (4, 2), (4, -2)\}$

   (e) $S = \{(1, 0), (2, 0), (3, 0), (4, 0)\}$

3. State if the relation described by the graphs below are functions. Write down the range of each relation given its domain:

   (a)

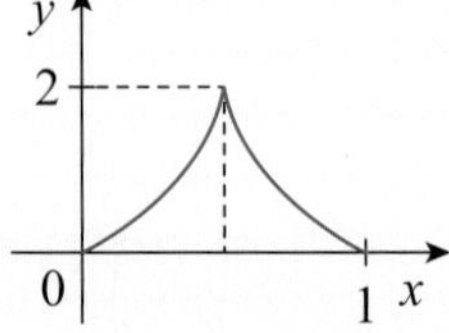

   Domain: $0 \leq x \leq 1, x \in \mathbb{R}$

   (b)

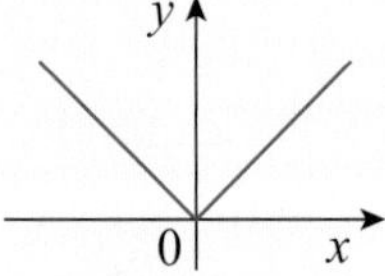

   Domain: $x \in \mathbb{R}$

   (c)

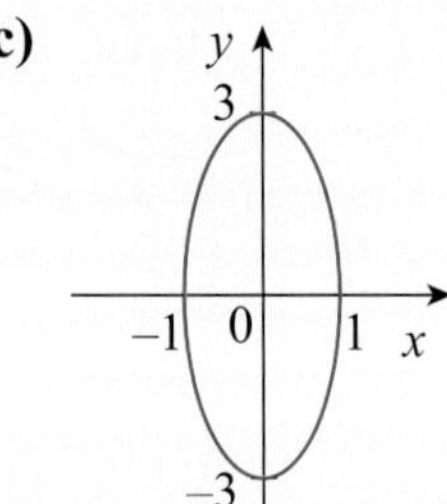

   Domain: $-1 \leq x \leq 1, x \in \mathbb{R}$

   (d)

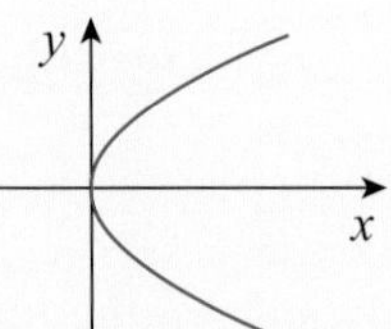

   Domain: $x \geq 0, x \in \mathbb{R}$

   (e)

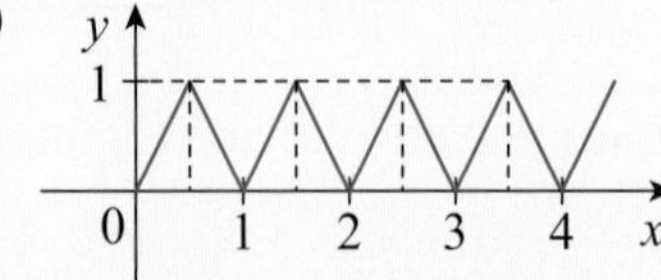

   Domain: $x \geq 0, x \in \mathbb{R}$

   (f)

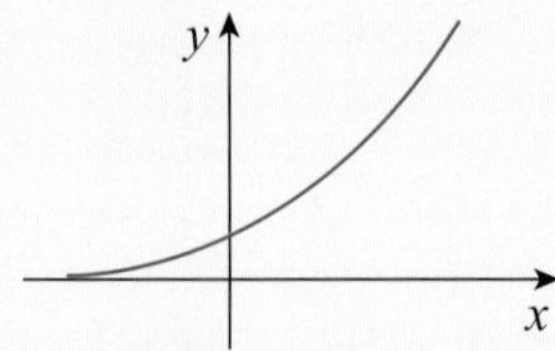

   Domain: $x \in \mathbb{R}$

18.3 Function notation

You can be asked to find the image of a variable x in four ways.

1. Bracket notation

$f(x) = 3x - 2$ [Read as f of x.]

This means the function f takes the variable x, multiplies it by 3 and subtracts 2.

EXAMPLE 3

If $f(x) = 2x^2 + 1, x \in \mathbb{R}$, find $f(-1), f(7), f(u), f(3p - 2)$.

Solution

TIP
Put a bracket around the variable x on the right-hand side first.

$f(x) = 2(x)^2 + 1$

Just replace the variable x on the right by whatever you see inside f to get the image $f(x)$.

$f(-1) = 2(-1)^2 + 1 = 3$

$f(7) = 2(7)^2 + 1 = 99$

$f(u) = 2(u)^2 + 1 = 2u^2 + 1$

$$
\begin{aligned}
f(3p - 2) &= 2(3p - 2)^2 + 1 \\
&= 2(9p^2 - 12p + 4) + 1 \\
&= 18p^2 - 24p + 8 + 1 \\
&= 18p^2 - 24p + 9
\end{aligned}
$$

2. Double-dot notation

$f: x \rightarrow \dfrac{x+5}{2}, x \in \mathbb{N}$ [This means that f sends x to $\dfrac{x+5}{2}, x \in \mathbb{N}$.]

$f: 1 \rightarrow \dfrac{1+5}{2} = 3$

The best way to deal with double dots is to change them into bracket notation immediately.

$$f(x) = \frac{(x)+5}{2}, x \in \mathbb{N}$$

EXAMPLE 4

Write down the domain and range of the following function:

$$f : x = \begin{cases} 1, x \text{ even} \\ 2, x \text{ odd} \end{cases}, x \in \mathbb{N}$$

Solution

$$f(x) = \begin{cases} 1, x \text{ even} \\ 2, x \text{ odd} \end{cases}, x \in \mathbb{N}$$

The domain $\mathbb{N} = \{1, 2, 3, \ldots\}$

$f(1) = 2$

$f(2) = 1$

$f(3) = 2$

$f(4) = 1$

The range is $\{1, 2\}$.

3. Co-ordinate notation

y is often used instead of $f(x)$ to facilitate the drawing of the graph of a function.

$y = f(x) = x^2 - 2x + 5, x \in \mathbb{R}$.

So $y = f(x)$ is the y co-ordinate corresponding to any given x co-ordinate.

EXAMPLE 5

For the function $y = f(x) = x^2 - 2x + 5, x \in \mathbb{R}$, find $f(-1)$, $f(0)$, $f(1)$, $f(2)$ and $f(3)$. Plot a graph of the function.

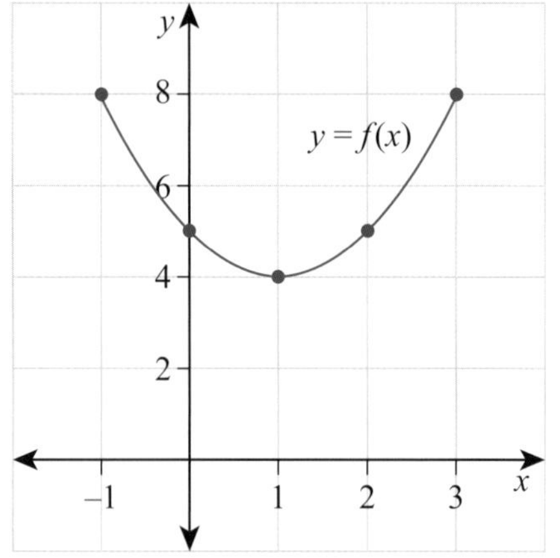

Solution

$y = f(x) = (x)^2 - 2(x) + 5$

$f(-1) = (-1)^2 - 2(-1) + 5 = 8 \therefore (-1, 8)$

$f(0) = (0)^2 - 2(0) + 5 = 5 \therefore (0, 5)$

$f(1) = (1)^2 - 2(1) + 5 = 4 \therefore (1, 4)$

$f(2) = (2)^2 - 2(2) + 5 = 5 \therefore (2, 5)$

$f(3) = (3)^2 - 2(3) + 5 = 8 \therefore (3, 8)$

If you plot the points $(x, y) = (x, f(x))$, you generate the graph of the function $y = f(x)$.

4. Graphical approach

A function $y = f(x)$ can be plotted as a graph with the values in the domain on the x-axis and the values in the range (the images) on the y-axis.

EXAMPLE 6

Using the graph shown of $y = f(x)$, find the values for $f(-1)$ and $f(0{\cdot}5)$.

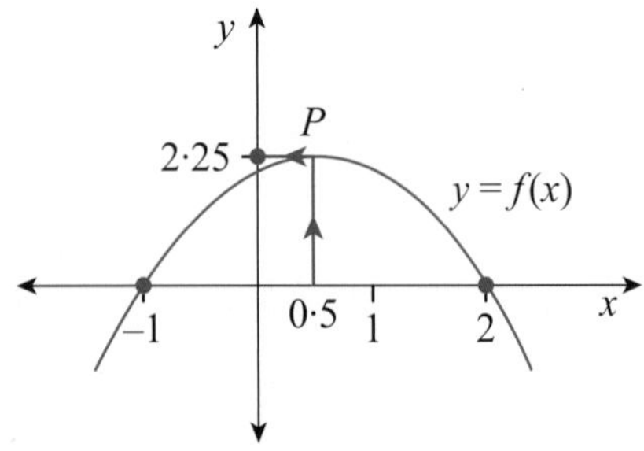

Solution

$f(-1)$ = the value of the y co-ordinate when $x = -1$.

$f(-1) = 0$

$f(0{\cdot}5)$ = the value of the y co-ordinate when x is $0{\cdot}5$.

This can be read off the graph by drawing the line $x = 0{\cdot}5$ to intersect the graph at the point P and reading off the y co-ordinate of this point from the y-axis.

$f(0{\cdot}5) = 2{\cdot}25$

Note: The letters x and $y = f(x)$ are generally used for functions. However, other letters can be used.

For example: $h(t) = t^3 - 3t^2 + 5t - 1$

EXERCISE 2

1. Evaluate the following functions at the given value of the variable:

(a) $f(x) = 3x + 2$, at $x = 5$

(b) $f(x) = \dfrac{x-8}{3}$, at $x = -4$

(c) $g(2)$, if $g(x) = \dfrac{3}{x^2 - 2}$

(d) $h(1)$, if $h(s) = 2s^2 - 3s + 4$

(e) $f(\sqrt{2})$, if $f(x) = 3x^2 - \dfrac{1}{x^2}$

(f) $g(-2)$, if $g(p) = (p - 1)(p + 3)$

(g) $h(0{\cdot}5)$, if $h(t) = t + \dfrac{1}{t}$

(h) $g\left(\dfrac{2}{3}\right)$, if $g(x) = 9x^2 - 6x + 1$

2. **(a)** If $f: x \to 2x - 1, x \in \mathbb{R}$, find $f(3)$, $f(5)$, $f\left(-\frac{3}{2}\right)$.

(b) If $h: s \to \frac{1}{s}, s \in \mathbb{R}$, find $h(1)$, $h(2)$, $h\left(\frac{1}{2}\right)$ and $h\left(-\frac{1}{3}\right)$.

(c) Find $g(3)$, $g(2)$ and $g(8) + g(1)$, if

$$g(n) = \begin{cases} 2^n, n \text{ odd}, n \in \mathbb{N} \\ \frac{1}{n}, n \text{ even}, n \in \mathbb{N}. \end{cases}$$

(d) If $y = 2x^2 - 5x + 11$, find the value of y when **(i)** $x = -3$ and **(ii)** $x = \frac{1}{2}$.

(e) Find $f(-3)$, $f(2)$ and $f(0)$ for the function described by the graph below:

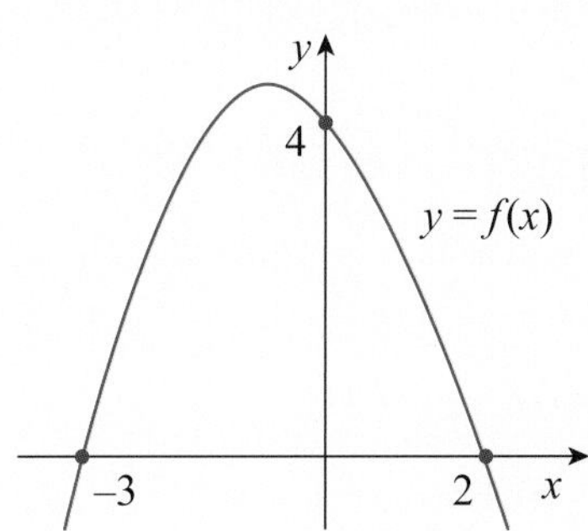

(f) If $g: s \to \frac{s^2}{3s+5}, s \in \mathbb{R}$, find $g\left(\frac{1}{3}\right)$, $g(-2)$.

(g) If $h(x)$ is described by the graph below, find $h\left(\frac{1}{2}\right)$, $h(1)$, $h(2{\cdot}5)$ and $h(3)$.

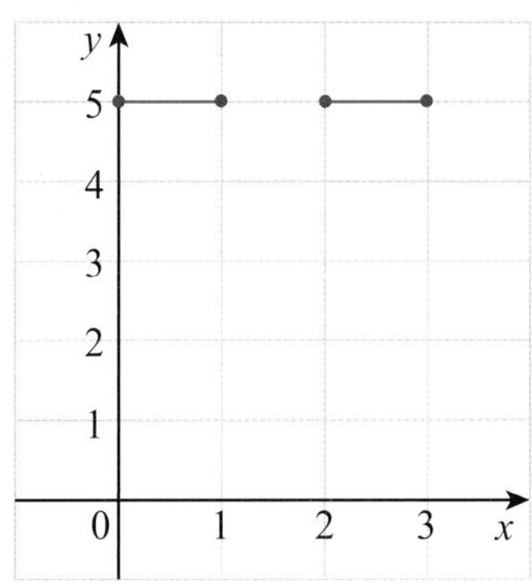

(h) If $f(x) = 3^{x-1}$, find $f(1)$ and $f(2)$.

3. **(a)** If $f(x) = 2x + 7$, find $f(2)$, $f(x + 1)$, $f(3 - 2x)$.

(b) If $g(t) = 4 - t^2$, find $g(-2)$, $g(2t)$.

(c) If $h(s) = \frac{3}{s+1}$, find $h(2)$, $h(x + 3)$.

(d) If $h(s) = s^2 + 4$, find $h(-3)$, $h(\sqrt{s})$, $h(s - 1)$.

(e) If $f(x) = 3x^2 - 2x + 1$, find $f\left(\frac{1}{2}\right)$, $f(1 - 2p)$.

(f) If $g(p) = 3 \times 2^p$, find $g(2)$, $g(3x - 1)$.

(g) If $q(x) = \sin^2 x$, find $q(30°)$, $q(4x)$.

(h) If $f(x) = \cos x$, find $f(0)$, $f(90°)$, $f(90° - p)$.

(i) If $f(x) = \log_2 x$, find $f(4)$, $f\left(\frac{1}{x}\right)$.

(j) If $h(t) = \log_{10}(t^2 + 19)$, find $h(9)$, $h(\sqrt{x - 19})$.

4. **(a)** If $f(x) = 2x + 1$, find x when $f(x) = 3$.

(b) If $h(t) = \frac{4}{5}t - 3$, find t when $h(t) = 9$.

(c) If $g(x) = x^2 - 7x + 2$, find the values of x for which $g(x) = -4$.

(d) If $f(n) = 2^n$, find the value of n for which $f(n) = 16$.

(e) If $g(x) = 3 - kx$ and $g(-4) = 19$, find $k \in \mathbb{R}$.

(f) If $f(x) = \sqrt{x} + 1$, find x when $f(x) = 3$.

(g) If $f(x) = 2x^2 + 4x - 9$, find x when $f(x) = 7$.

(h) If $h(t) = t^3 + t^2 - 2t - 10$, find t when $h(t) = -10$.

(i) If $f(x) = \log_2 x$, find x when $f(x) = -2$.

(j) If $f(x) = \log_{10}\sqrt{x}$, find x when $f(x) = 2$.

5. **(a)** If $f(x) = 4x + k$, find k if $f(5) = 0, k \in \mathbb{R}$.

(b) If $f(x) = 5 + 4x$ and $g(x) = 3x + 2$, find t if $g(t) = f(t)$.

(c) If $f(x) = 3x + 5$, for what value of x is $f(x + 1) = f(2x - 3)$?

(d) If $f(x) = x^2 + 4x$ and $g(x) = 2x + 3$, for what values of x is $f(x) = g(x)$?

(e) If $f(x) = x^2 + ax + k$, find a and $k \in \mathbb{R}$, if $f(2) = 0$ and $f(-2) = f(3)$.

(f) If $f(x) = x^3 + ax^2 + bx - 8$, find $a, b \in \mathbb{R}$, if $f(-2) = 0$ and $f(1) = 0$.

18.4 Injective, surjective and bijective functions

The words injective, surjective and bijective are properties of functions that describe their behaviour in more detail.

1. Injective functions

KEY TERM

An **injective** function from a set A to a set B is a function in which **every** value of x in A has a **different** value of y in B.

No two values of x can have the same value of y if the function is injective.

If $f(x)$ is an injective function from A to B, it follows that $f(x_1) = f(x_2) \Leftrightarrow x_1 = x_2$. The set A is the domain of the function and the set B is called the codomain. The codomain does not have to be the range.

Graphical test for an injective function

If every horizontal line in the codomain cuts the graph of $y = f(x)$ at **most once**, the function is injective.

TIP

At **most once** means not at all or once.

WORKED EXAMPLE Exploring injective functions 1

$y = f(x) = x^3$, $f: \mathbb{R} \to \mathbb{R}$ is described by the graph shown. Every element $x \in \mathbb{R}$ has a different image $y \in \mathbb{R}$.

The function is injective because each horizontal line cuts this graph once.

In this example, $f: \mathbb{R} \to \mathbb{R}$ means $\mathbb{R}$ is the domain and $\mathbb{R}$ is the codomain.

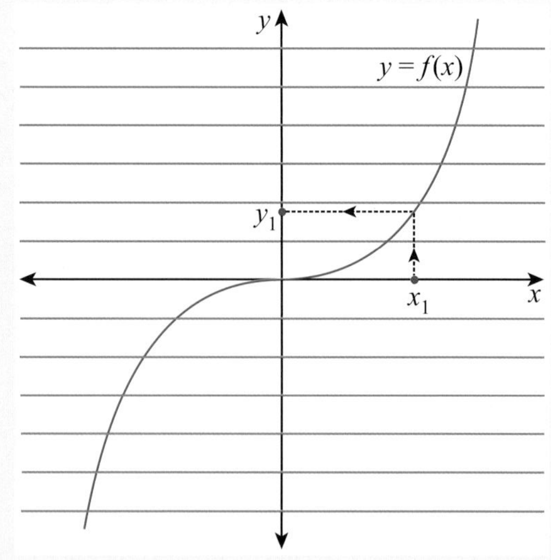

An element in the codomain B does not need to have a corresponding element in the domain A.

WORKED EXAMPLE

Exploring injective functions 2

$y = f(x), f: \mathbb{R} \to \mathbb{R}$ is described by the graph shown. $\mathbb{R}$ is the domain and $\mathbb{R}$ is the codomain. This function is injective, even though y_1 has no matching x value.

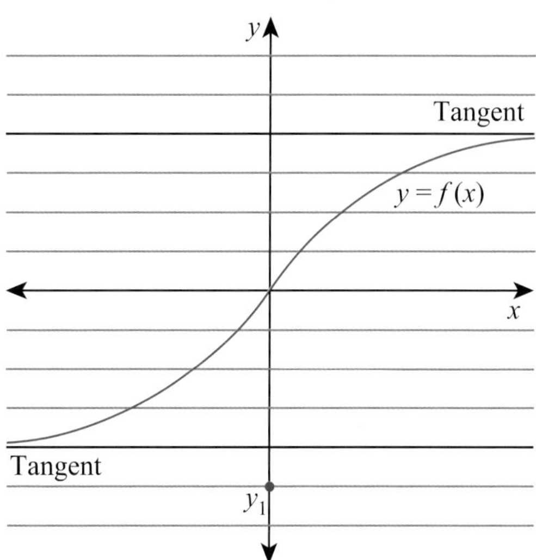

TIP

Take note of the graphical test. All horizontal lines in the codomain must cut the graph at most once. This means the horizontal lines can cut the graph once or not at all.

WORKED EXAMPLE

Exploring injective functions 3

$y = f(x) = x^2, f: \mathbb{R} \to \mathbb{R}$ is described by the graph shown. $\mathbb{R}$ is the domain and $\mathbb{R}$ is the codomain.

$y = f(x) = x^2$ is not injective as $f(-2) = f(2) = 4$.

Each x value does not have a different y value. -2 and 2 have the same y value of 4. The graphical test shows that this is not an injective function.

Some horizontal lines cut the graph in two places.

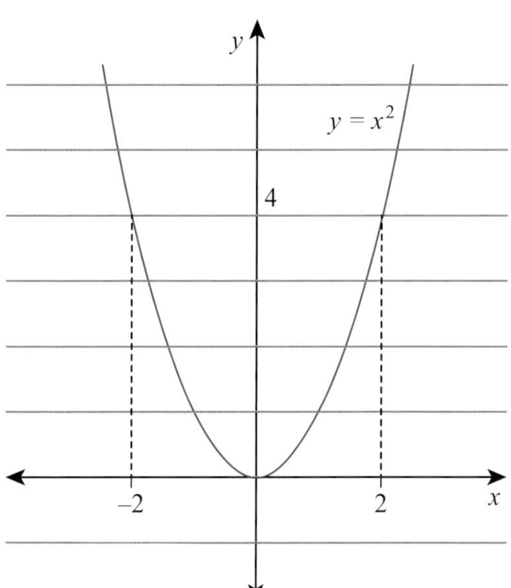

2. Surjective functions

KEY TERM

A **surjective** function from a set A to a set B is a function in which for **every** value of y in B there is at **least one** corresponding value of x in A.

Graphical test for a surjective function

A function $y = f(x)$ is surjective if every horizontal line in the codomain cuts the graph of $y = f(x)$ **at least once**.

WORKED EXAMPLE

Exploring surjective functions 1

$y = f(x), f: \mathbb{R} \to \mathbb{R}$ is described by the graph shown. $\mathbb{R}$ is the domain and $\mathbb{R}$ is the codomain.

$y = f(x)$ is surjective but not injective. Every element $y \in \mathbb{R}$ has at least one corresponding element $x \in \mathbb{R}$.

The horizontal blue lines cut the graph at least once.

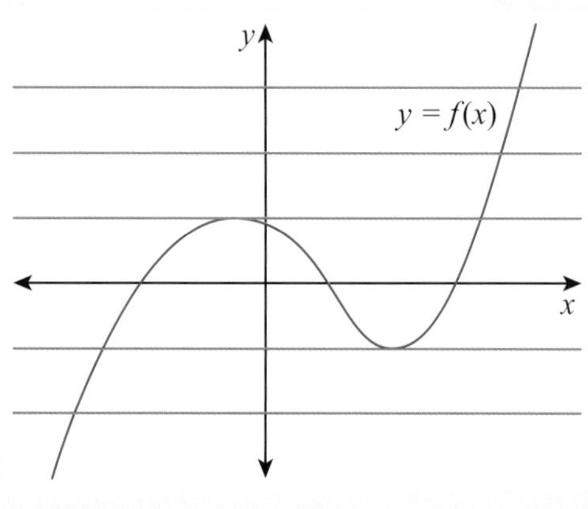

TIP

If it is possible to draw any horizontal line in the codomain across the graph of a function without making contact with the curve, then the function is not surjective.

TIP

At **least once** means once, twice, three times, etc.

WORKED EXAMPLE

Exploring surjective functions 2

$y = f(x) = x^2 - 4x, f: \mathbb{R} \to \mathbb{R}$ is described by the graph shown. $\mathbb{R}$ is the domain and $\mathbb{R}$ is the codomain.

$y = f(x) = x^2 - 4x$ is neither surjective nor injective.

The function is not surjective, as there are horizontal lines which fail to cut the graph, and it is not injective, as some horizontal lines cut the graph twice.

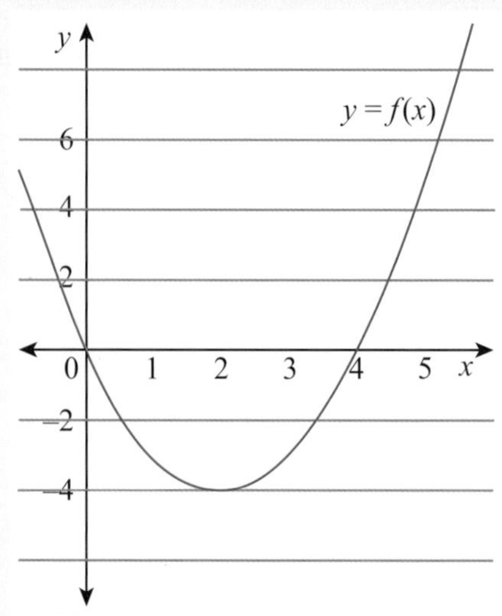

3. Bijective functions

KEY TERM

A **bijective** function from a set A to a set B is a function in which for **every** value y in B there is a different value of x in A.

Graphical test for a bijective function

A function $y = f(x)$ is bijective if every horizontal line in the codomain cuts the curve of the function **once and only once**.

WORKED EXAMPLE Exploring bijective functions

$y = f(x) = x^3 - 3x^2 + 3x + 1$, $f: \mathbb{R} \to \mathbb{R}$ is described by the graph shown. $\mathbb{R}$ is the domain and $\mathbb{R}$ is the codomain.

$y = f(x) = x^3 - 3x^2 + 3x + 1$ is bijective, as for each y value there is exactly one different x value. All bijective functions are both injective and surjective and there is an exact one-to-one correspondence between values of x and y.

The horizontal blue lines cut the graph once and only once.

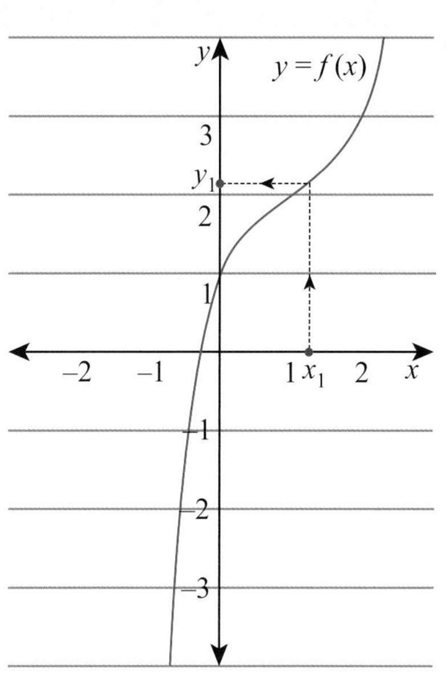

WORKED EXAMPLE Knowing your codomain

When deciding if a function is injective, surjective or bijective, make sure you know the codomain of the function before applying the horizontal line test.

For example, the function $f(x) = e^x$, $\mathbb{R} \to \mathbb{R}^+ = \{x > 0, x \in \mathbb{R}\}$ is injective and surjective from $\mathbb{R}$ to $\mathbb{R}^+$. Therefore, it is bijective from $\mathbb{R}$ to $\mathbb{R}^+$.

All horizontal lines in the codomain $\mathbb{R}^+$ intersect the curve exactly once.

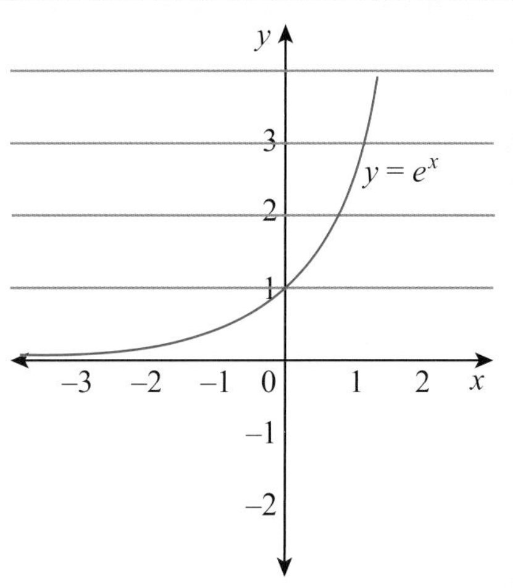

However, the function $f(x) = e^x$, $\mathbb{R} \to \mathbb{R}$, is injective but **not** surjective from $\mathbb{R}$ to $\mathbb{R}$. Therefore, it is **not** bijective from $\mathbb{R}$ to $\mathbb{R}$.

The line $y = -1$ in the codomain does not intersect the curve.

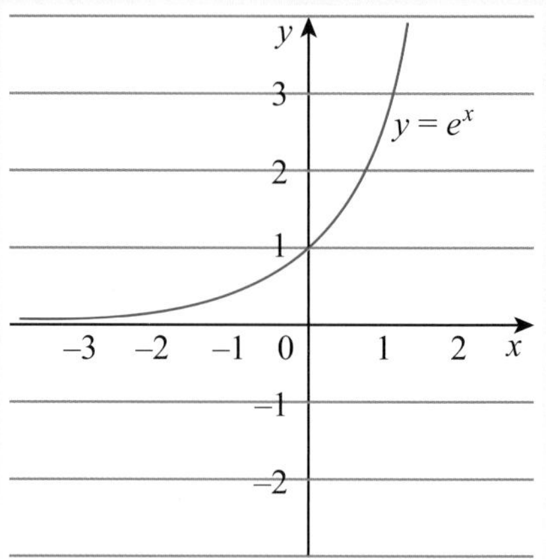

WORKED EXAMPLE

A function that is injective but not surjective

$f(x) = 2x$, $\mathbb{Z} \to \mathbb{Z}$, is graphed as shown. It consists of discrete points.

Every horizontal line from the codomain $\mathbb{Z}$ intersects the dots of the function at most once. Therefore, the function is injective. Some lines do not intersect a dot at all. Therefore, the function is not surjective because a surjective function demands that each horizontal line cuts the graph at least once. For example, the line through 3 on the y-axis does not pass through a dot.

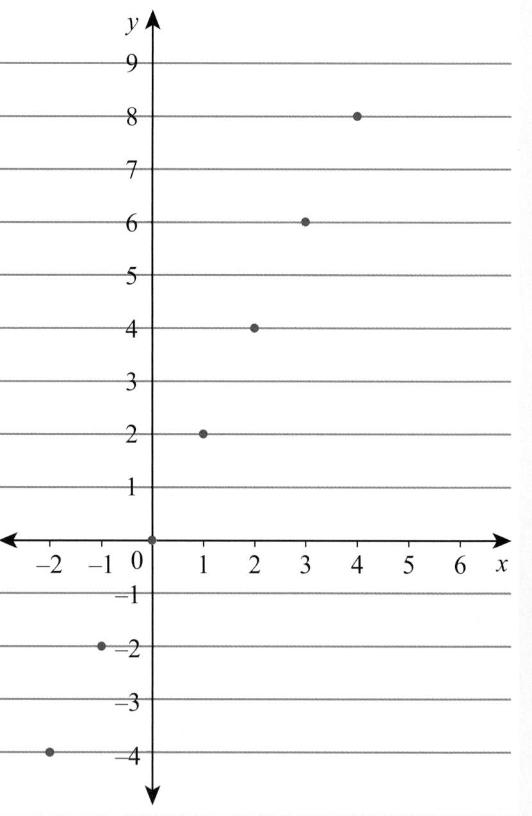

EXAMPLE 7

State why the following functions are bijective:

(a) $y = f(x) = x + 1, f: \mathbb{R} \to \mathbb{R}$

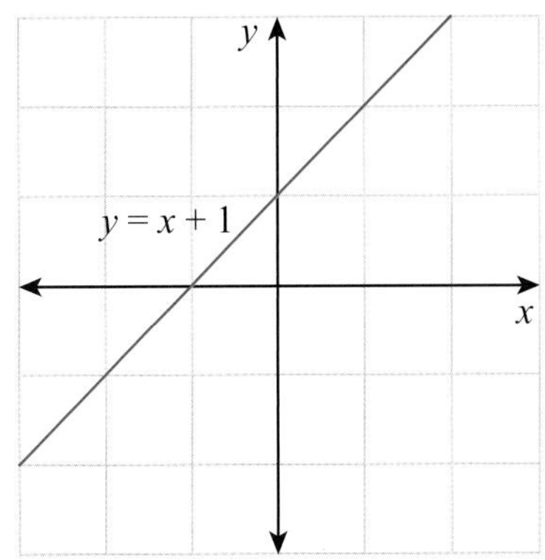

(b) $y = f(x) = 3^x, f: \mathbb{R} \to \mathbb{R}^+$

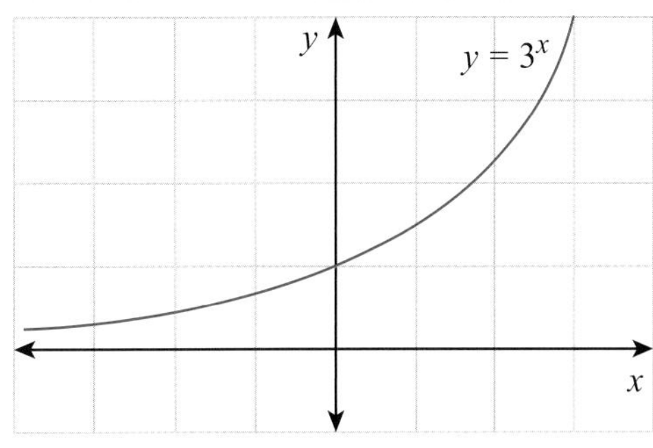

Solution

(a) This function is bijective as for every real number on the y-axis in the codomain there is a different real value on the x-axis. All horizontal lines cut the graph once and only once.

(b) This function is bijective as for every real number on the y-axis in the codomain there is a different real value on the x-axis. All horizontal lines above the x-axis cut the graph once and only once.

TIP

$\mathbb{R}^+$ is the set of real numbers greater than zero, i.e. $\mathbb{R}^+ = \{x > 0, x \in \mathbb{R}\}$.

If Example 7(b) were changed as follows: $y = f(x) = 3^x, f: \mathbb{R} \to \mathbb{R}$, the function would no longer be bijective but would be injective.

ACTIVITY 3

ACTION
Knowing the type of function

OBJECTIVE
To decide what type of function is present for given mappings of functions

EXAMPLE 8

Consider the following relations of mappings A to B, where A is the domain and B the codomain. First, state if they are a function and, if so, state if it is injective, surjective or bijective. Give reasons for your answers.

(a)

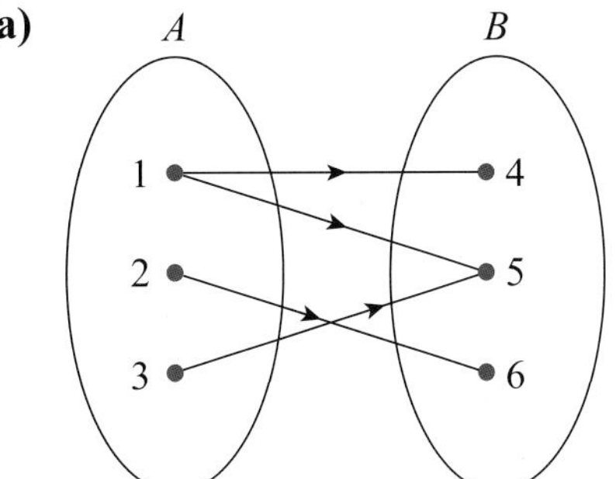

(b)

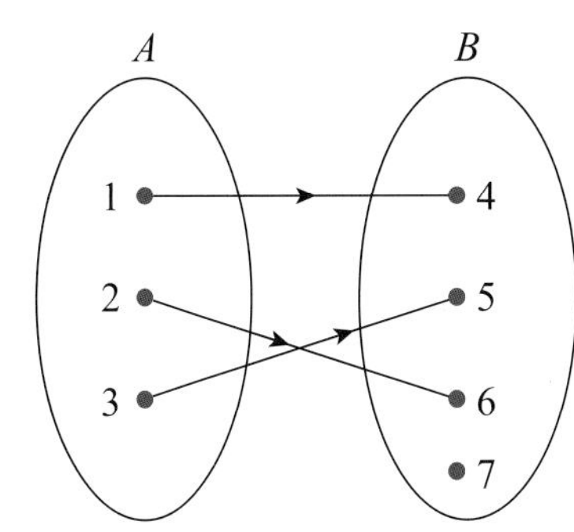

(c)

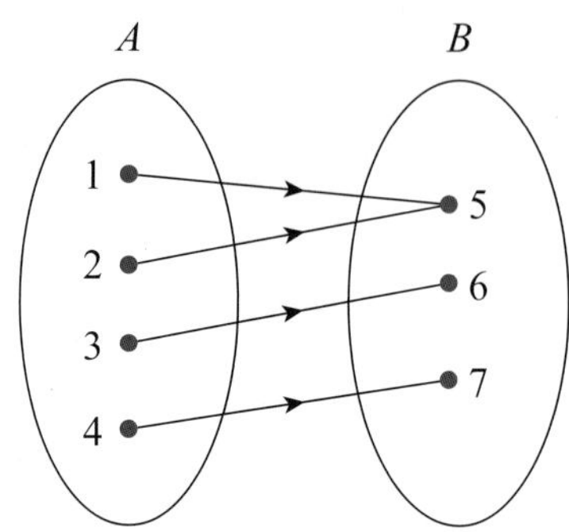

(d)

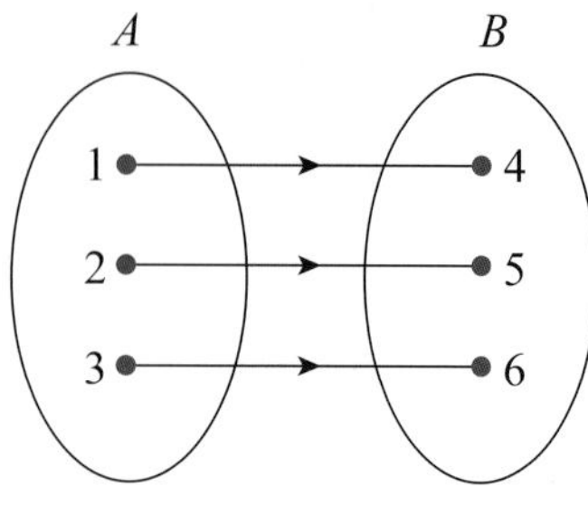

Solution

(a) This is not a function as a value in the domain maps onto two values in the codomain.

(b) This is a function as each value in the domain maps onto exactly one value in the codomain. It is an injective function as each value in the domain has a different value in the codomain. It is not surjective.

(c) This is a function as each value in the domain maps onto exactly one value in the codomain. It is a surjective function as every value in the codomain corresponds to at least one value in the domain. It is not injective.

(d) This is a function as each value in the domain maps onto exactly one value in the codomain. It is a bijective function because every value in the codomain has a different value in the domain.

EXERCISE 3

1. Determine if the following functions are injective, surjective, bijective or none of these, where $A = \{a, b\}$ and $B = \{5, 8\}$.

(a)

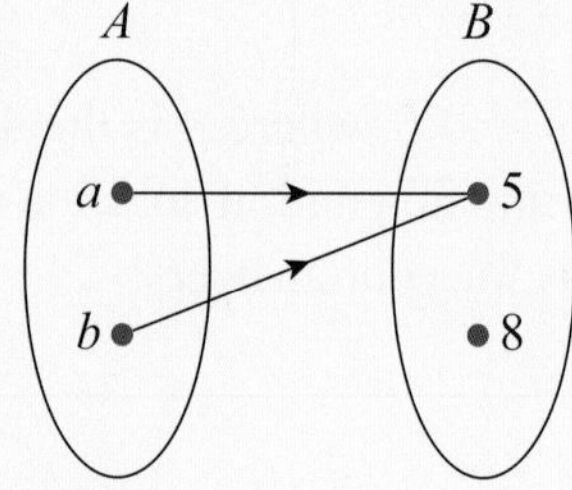

(b)

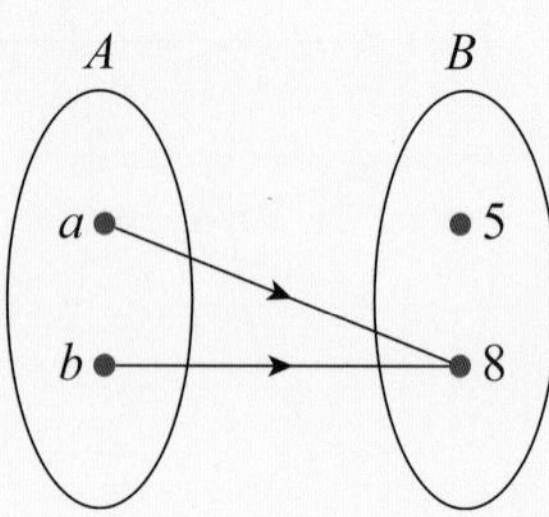

(c)

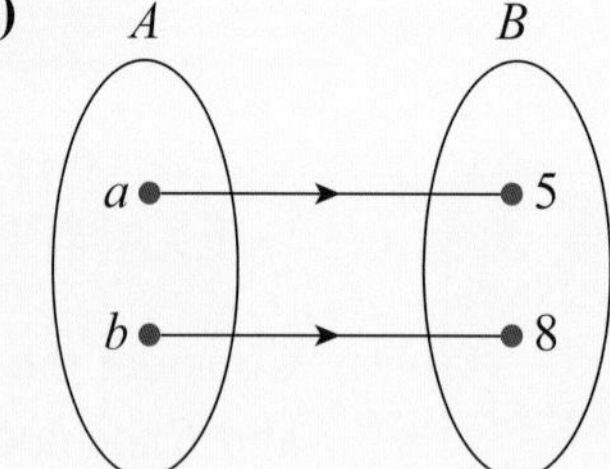

(d)

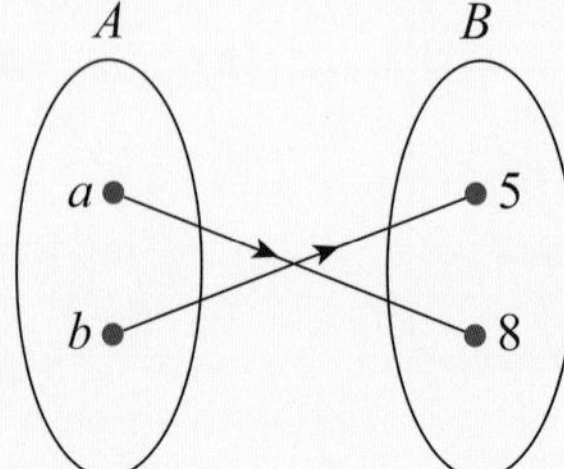

2. Determine if the following functions are injective, surjective, bijective or none of these, where $A = \{a, b, c\}$ and $B = \{5, 8\}$.

(a)

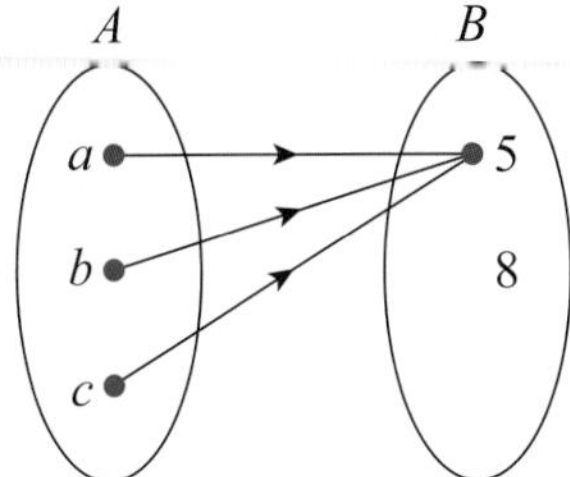

(b)

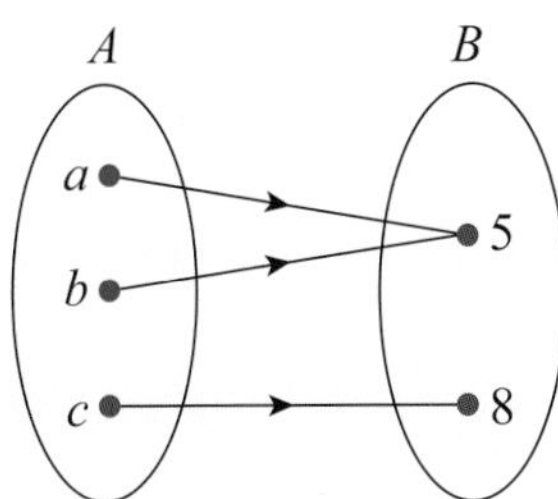

(c)

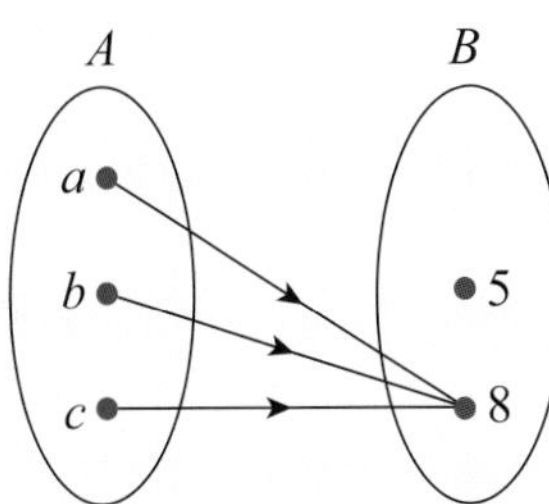

3. Determine if the following functions are injective, surjective, bijective or none of these, where $A = \{a, b\}$ and $B = \{5, 8, 9\}$.

(a)

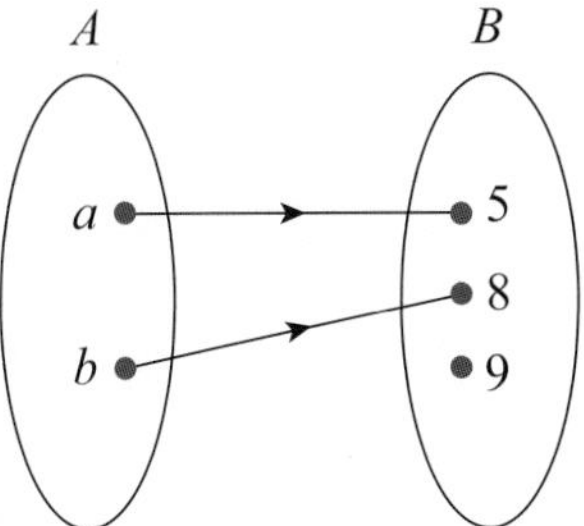

(b)

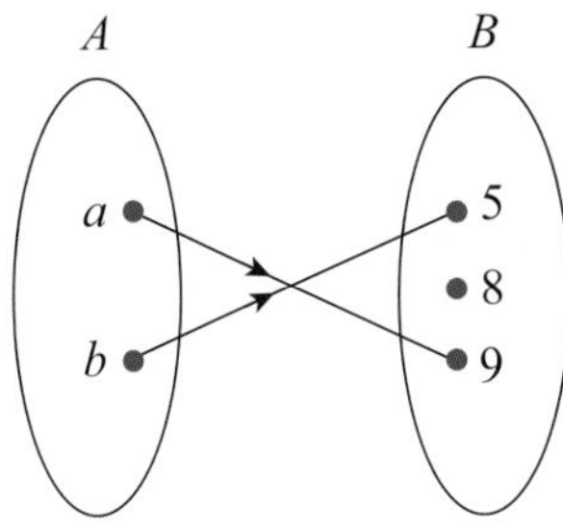

(c)

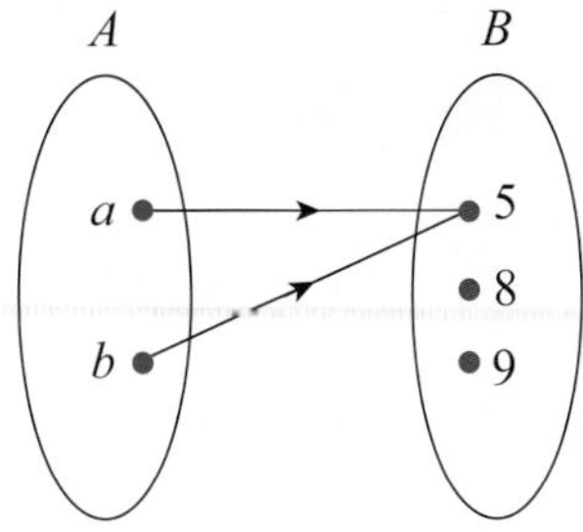

4. Set A is a set of pigeons and set B is a set of pigeon holes.

(a) In the function $f: A \to B$, two pigeons have to fly into the same pigeon hole. What does this say about the function f? Is f injective, surjective or bijective? Why?

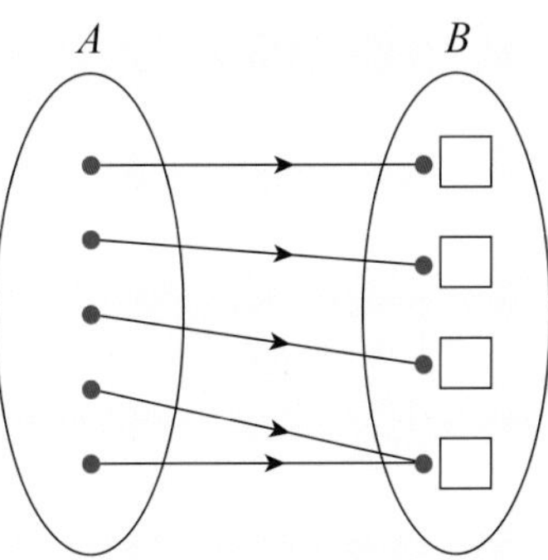

(b) In the function $f: A \to B$, each pigeon has its own pigeon hole. What does this say about the function f? Is f injective, surjective or bijective? Why?

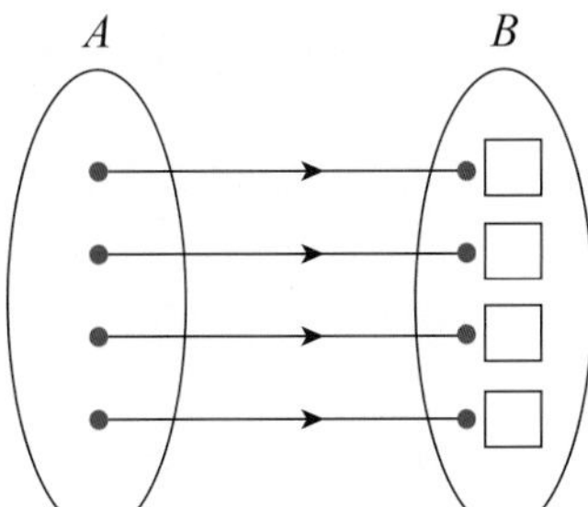

5. State if the function described by the graphs below on the given sets are injective, surjective and/or bijective or none of these.

(a) $y = f(x) = x, f: \mathbb{R} \rightarrow \mathbb{R}$

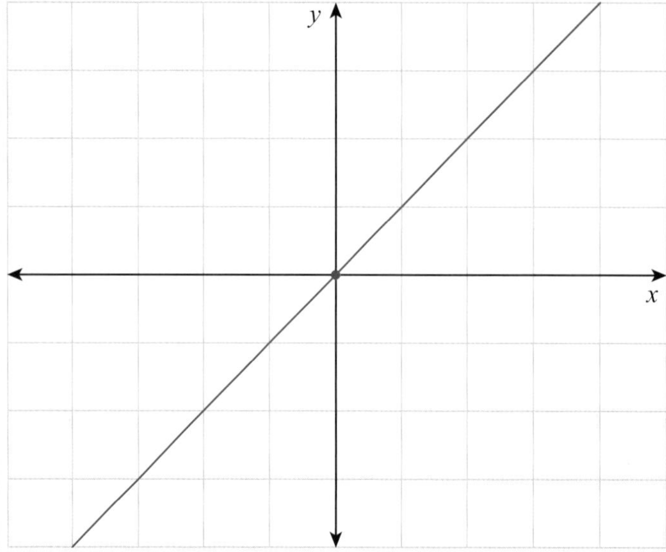

(b) $y = |x - 1| = f(x), f: \mathbb{R} \rightarrow \mathbb{R}$

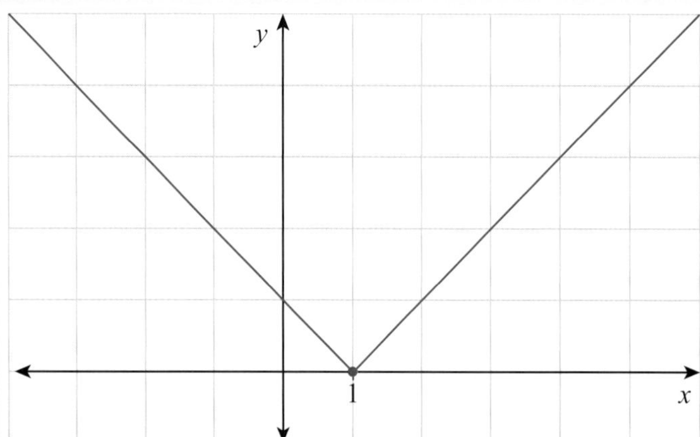

(c) $y = f(x) = x(6 - x), f: \mathbb{R} \rightarrow \mathbb{R}$

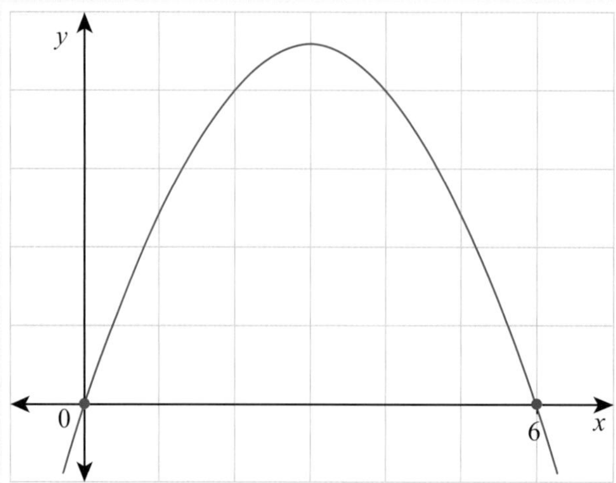

(d) $y = f(x) = x^3 - 3x + 2, f: \mathbb{R} \to \mathbb{R}$

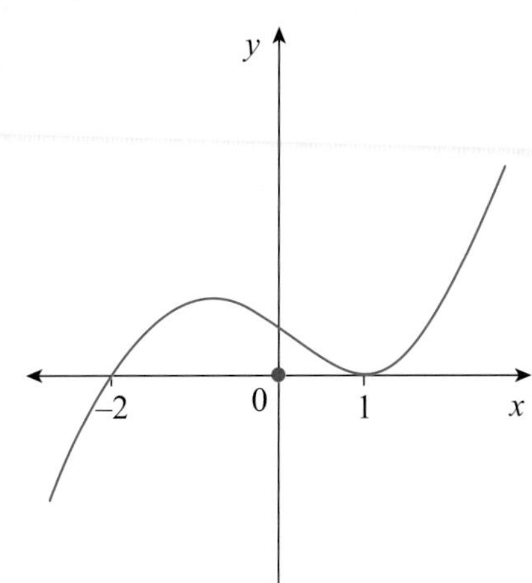

(e) $y = f(x) = 2^x, f: \mathbb{R} \to \mathbb{R}$

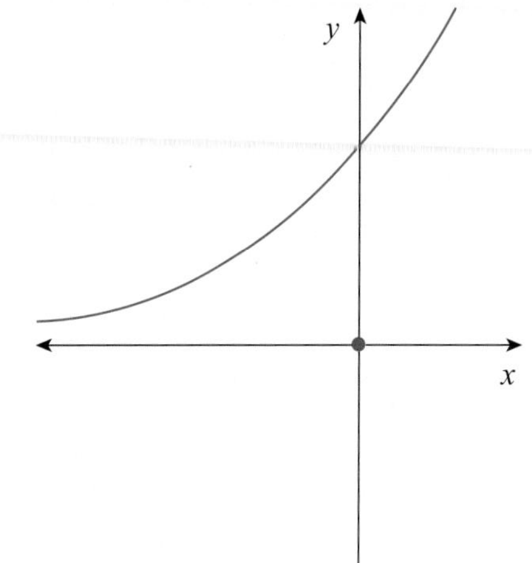

(f) $y = \log_2 x, f: \mathbb{R}^+ \to \mathbb{R}$, where $\mathbb{R}^+$ is the set of all real numbers greater than 0

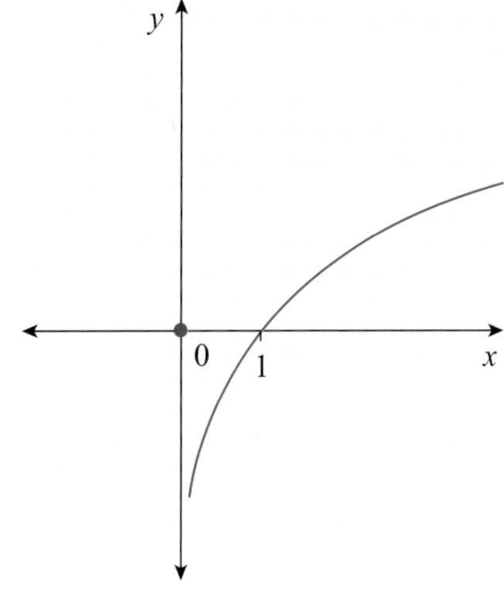

---

6. Draw a graph of a function $y = f(x), f: A \to B$, where A and B are sets of your choice:

(a) which is injective but not surjective,

(b) which is surjective but not injective,

(c) which is bijective.

7. If $y = 0{\cdot}5$, what is the value of x?
If $y = -0{\cdot}5$, what is the value of x?
If $y = 1{\cdot}5$, what is the value of x?
Explain why the function shown $y = f(x)$, $f: \mathbb{R} \to \mathbb{R}$ is injective but not bijective.

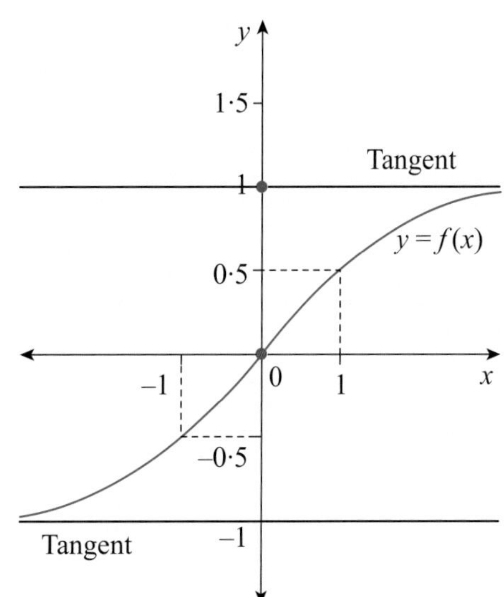

18.5 Inverse functions

The formula, $F = \frac{9}{5}C + 32$, is the formula for converting degrees Celsius C to degrees Fahrenheit F. The formula that converts degrees Fahrenheit to degrees Celsius is found as follows:

$F = \frac{9}{5}C + 32$

$F - 32 = \frac{9}{5}C$

$5(F - 32) = 9C$

$C = \frac{5}{9}(F - 32)$

This is an example of finding an inverse function.

The inverse function $f^{-1}(x)$ of a function $y = f(x)$

The idea: If a function $y = f(x)$ maps x values from a set A (domain) to y values in a set B (codomain), the inverse of $f(x)$ is the **function** that maps the y values back to the x values.

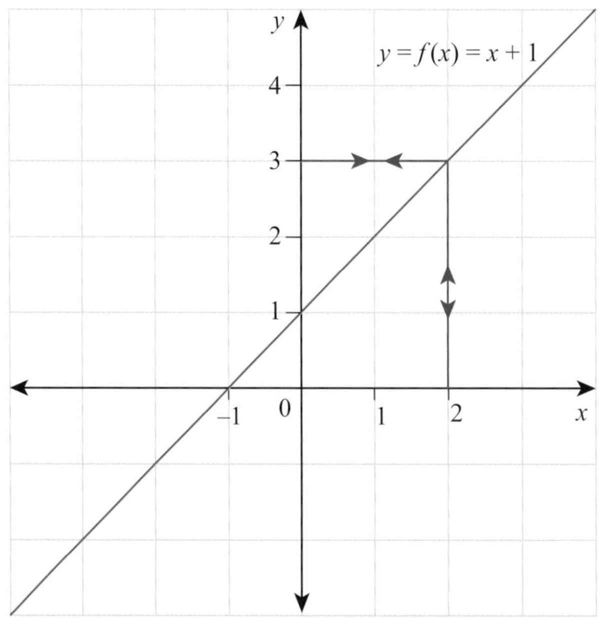

In the function shown $f(2) = 3$.

The inverse is the map f^{-1} which sends 3 back to 2 is given by $f^{-1}(3) = 2$.

The function $f(x)$ must be bijective in order for an inverse function $f^{-1}(x)$ to exist, because $f^{-1}(x)$ must be a function just like $f(x)$ above.

This means that each x value in the domain of $f(x)$ must give a different y value in the codomain and each y value in the codomain (domain of $f^{-1}(x)$) must give a different value of x in the domain of x.

WORKED EXAMPLE

Only bijective functions give you inverse functions

$f(x) = x^3$, $x \in \mathbb{R}$, $y \in \mathbb{R}$, is graphed as shown.

$f(x)$ must be bijective in order to find its inverse function. In other words, vertical and horizontal lines must intersect the curve at one and only one point.

> You can find the inverse function of a bijective function only.

When you are finding inverse functions, the domain and codomain must be specified.

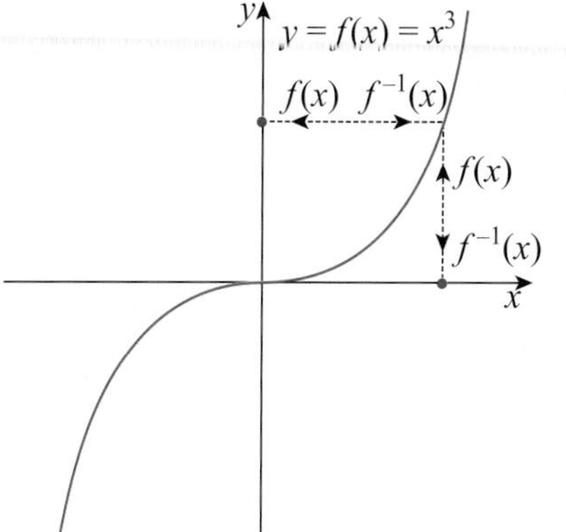

WORKED EXAMPLE

Finding the inverse of bijective functions

Find the inverse of $y = f(x) = 2^x$, $f: \mathbb{R} \to \mathbb{R}^+$. The function is bijective and so $f^{-1}(x)$ exists from $\mathbb{R}^+ \to \mathbb{R}$.

To find $f^{-1}(x)$, solve $y = 2^x$ for x.

$y = 2^x$

$\log_2 y = x$

$x = \log_2 y = g(y)$ is the inverse function which maps the y values back to the x values.

If y is replaced by x in the equation $x = \log_2 y$, we get the inverse function as a function of x, which is how functions are normally written. So, the inverse function of $y = f(x) = 2^x$ is $f^{-1}(x) = \log_2 x$.

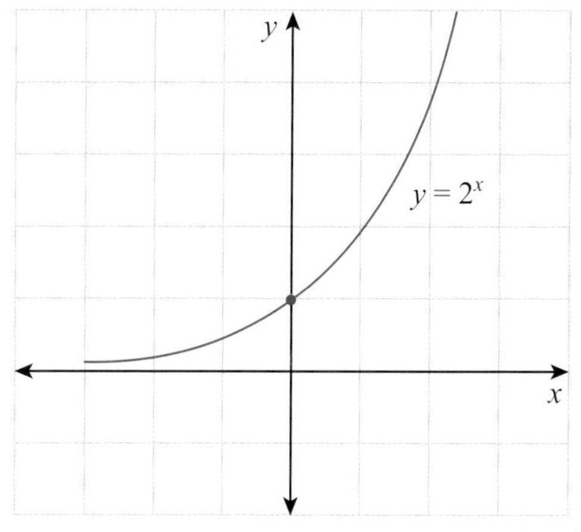

Method to find the inverse of a bijective function $y = f(x)$

1. Algebraically (solve then swap): Solve for x in terms of y and replace y by x to get $f^{-1}(x)$.

   or

2. Graphically (swap then solve): When you reflect a point $P(x, y)$ in the line $y = x$, you get the point $Q(y, x)$. In other words, the x and y co-ordinates of the point P get switched. So swap the x and y co-ordinates first and then solve y to get $f^{-1}(x)$.

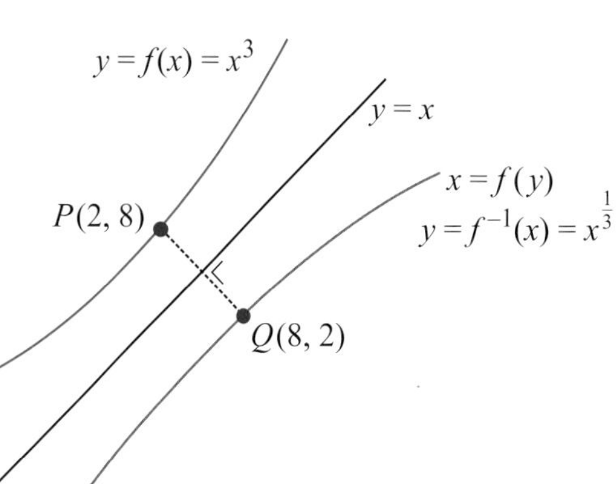

TIP

Always use the same scale on both axes when finding the inverse of a function by drawing.

EXAMPLE 9

Find the inverse functions for:

(a) $y = f(x) = 2x - 1,\ f: \mathbb{R} \to \mathbb{R}$

(b) $y = f(x) = x^3,\ f: \mathbb{R} \to \mathbb{R}$

Solution

(a) $y = f(x) = 2x - 1,\ f: \mathbb{R} \to \mathbb{R}$

Solve for x: $y = 2x - 1 \Rightarrow x = \dfrac{y+1}{2}$

Swap x and y (replace y by x):

$y = f^{-1}(x) = \dfrac{x+1}{2}$

(b) $y = f(x) = x^3, f: \mathbb{R} \to \mathbb{R}$

Solve for x: $y = x^3 \Rightarrow x = y^{\frac{1}{3}}$

Swap x and y (replace y by x):

$y = f^{-1}(x) = x^{\frac{1}{3}}$

Under reflection in the line $y = x$, a function $f(x)$ is mapped to its inverse function $f^{-1}(x)$.

ACTIVITY 4

ACTION
Drawing inverse functions

OBJECTIVE
To find inverse functions graphically

WORKED EXAMPLE Finding the inverse function graphically

The graph of the function $f(x) = 3^x$, $f: \mathbb{R} \to \mathbb{R}^+$, is shown below. By reflecting this function in the line $y = x$, draw the inverse function $f^{-1}(x)$ from $\mathbb{R}^+ \to \mathbb{R}$. What is $f^{-1}(x)$?

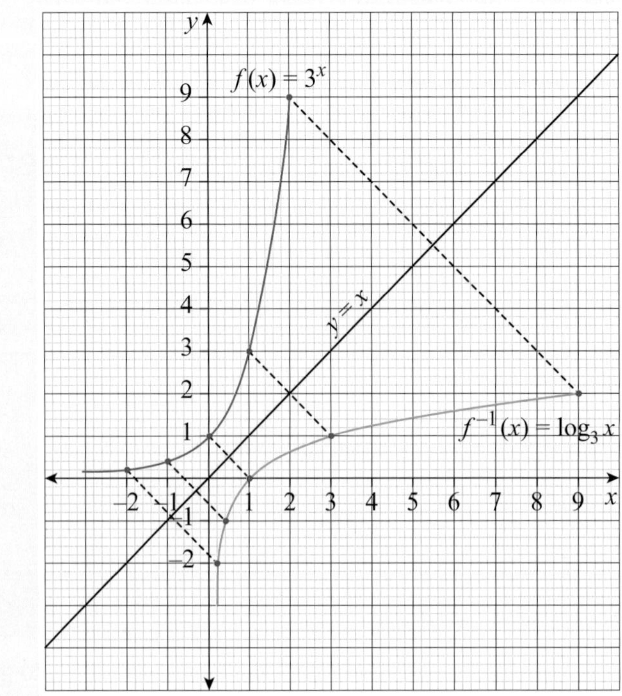

EXERCISE 4

1. If $f(x) = 2x + 1, x \in \mathbb{R}$, find:

   (a) $f(2)$ (c) $f^{-1}(5)$

   (b) $f(4)$ (d) $f^{-1}(9)$

2. If $f(x) = x^2, f: \mathbb{R} \to \mathbb{R}^+$, what is the codomain of x? Find:

   (a) $f(-3)$ (c) $f(-1)$ (e) $f(3)$

   (b) $f(-2)$ (d) $f(0)$ (f) $f(2)$

   Explain why $f^{-1}: \mathbb{R}^+ \to \mathbb{R}$ does not exist?

3. For each bijective function $f(x)$, find $f^{-1}(x)$ and state the domain and codomain of $f^{-1}(x)$:

   (a) $f(x) = 3x + 2, f: \mathbb{R} \to \mathbb{R}$

   (b) $f(x) = \dfrac{x+1}{2}, f: \mathbb{R} \to \mathbb{R}$

   (c) $f(x) = \dfrac{1}{x}, f: \mathbb{R}^+ \to \mathbb{R}^+$

   (d) $f(x) = \left(\dfrac{1}{2}\right)^x, f: \mathbb{R} \to \mathbb{R}^+$

   (e) $f(x) = \log_5 x, f: \mathbb{R}^+ \to \mathbb{R}$

   (f) $f(x) = (x + 1)^3, f: \mathbb{R} \to \mathbb{R}$

4. State if $f(x)$ has an inverse by considering the graphs of their functions $f(x)$ given below:

   (a) $f: \mathbb{R} \to \mathbb{R}$

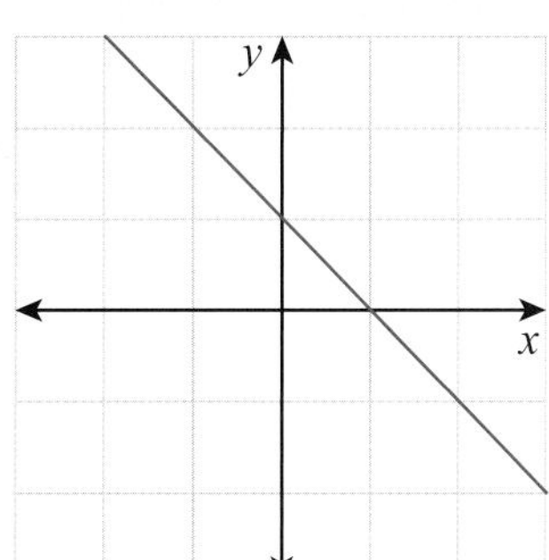

   (b) $f: \mathbb{R}^+ \to \mathbb{R}^+$

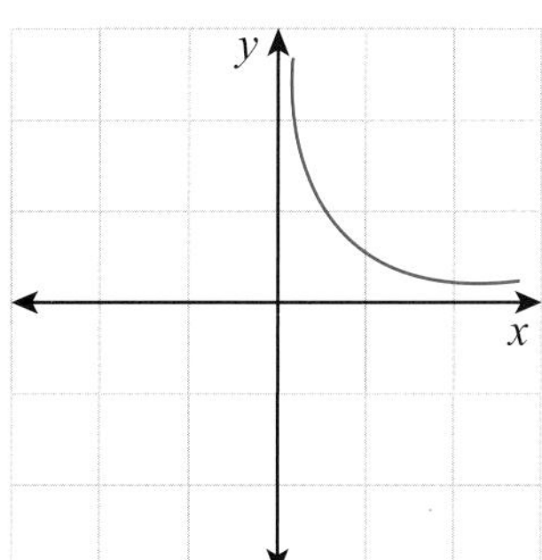

   (c) $f: \mathbb{R} \to \mathbb{R}^+$

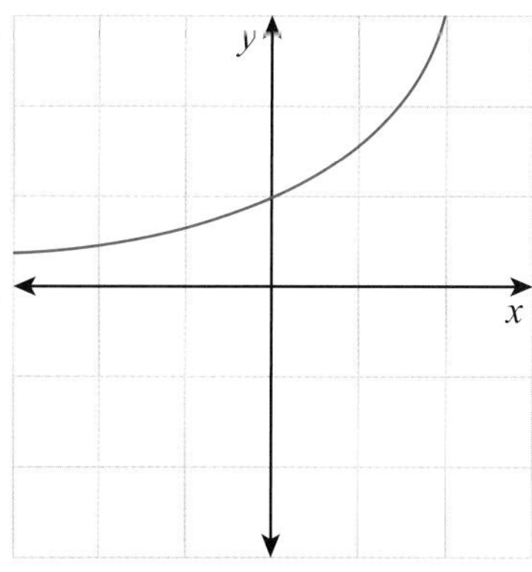

   (d) $f: \mathbb{R} \to \mathbb{R}$

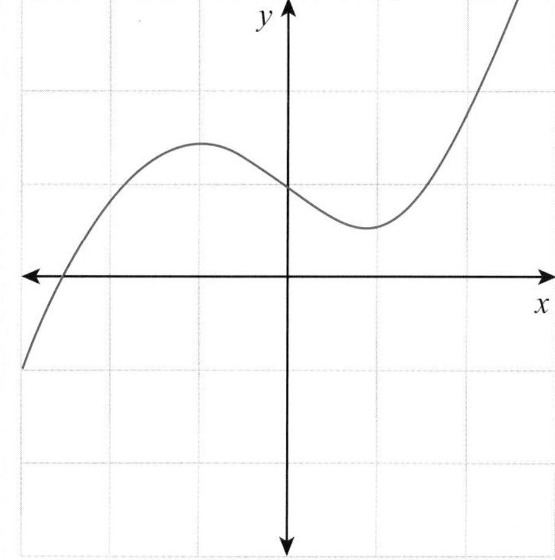

5. Show that $c = \dfrac{a+b}{2}$. Hence, show that the point Q has co-ordinates (b, a) if $|QR| = |RP|$.

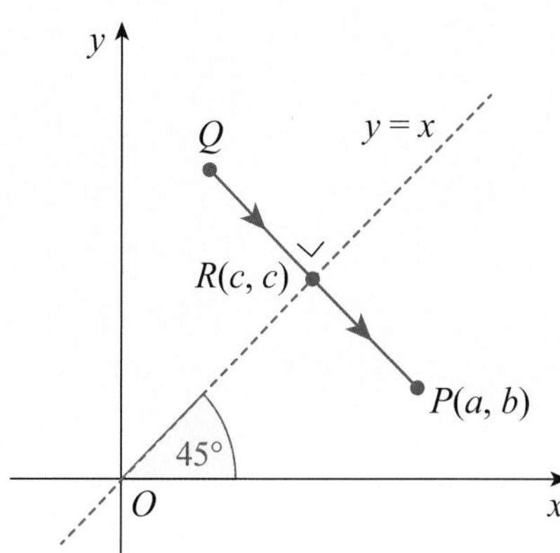

18.6 Composition of functions

Consider an oil rig that is leaking oil into the North Sea. The leaked oil spreads out as a circle on the surface of the sea. The radius $r(t)$, t minutes after the slick is spotted, is given by $r(t) = 3t + 2$, where r is in metres. r is a function of time and the area $A(r) = \pi r^2$ of the slick is a function of r. To find the area of the slick after 5 minutes, r is first found at $t = 5$ **and then** the area A is computed after r has been found.

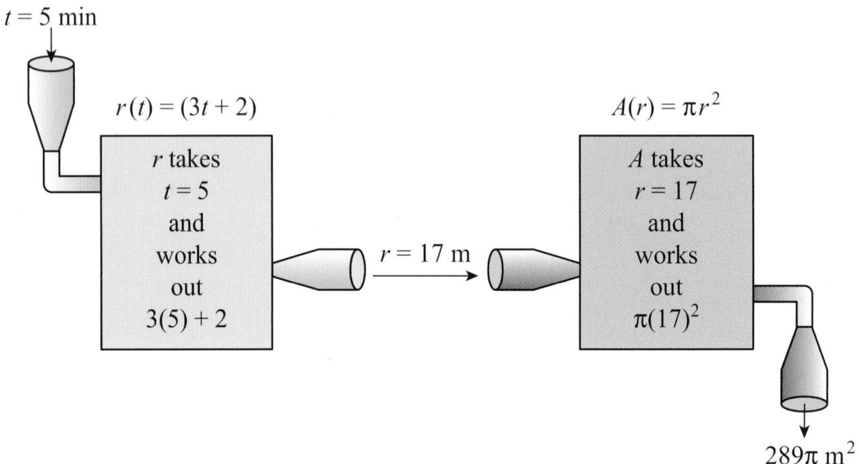

Mathematically, 'A after' r is written as $(A \text{ o } r)(t)$ *or* $A(r(t))$.

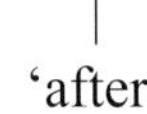

In general:

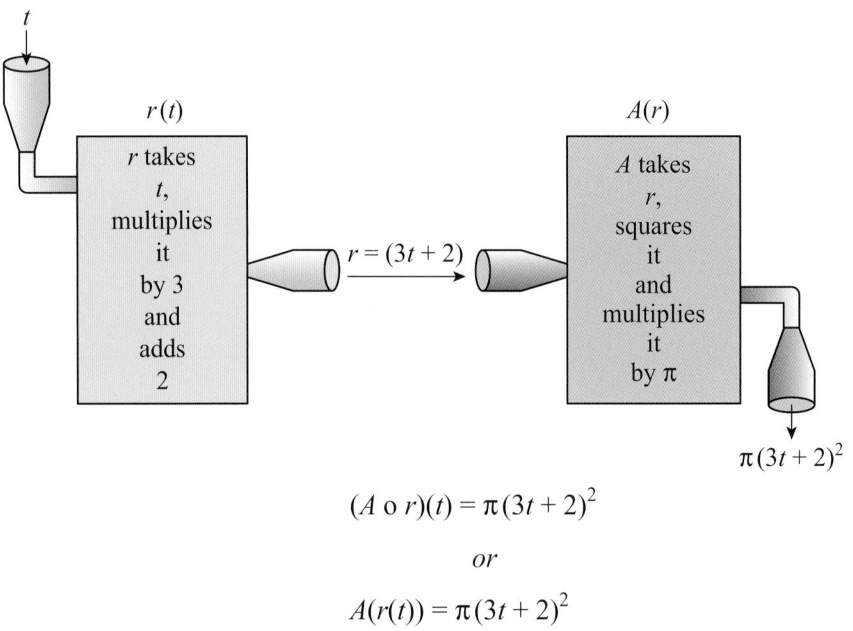

$$(A \text{ o } r)(t) = \pi(3t + 2)^2$$

or

$$A(r(t)) = \pi(3t + 2)^2$$

Method for finding the composition of functions

To find $(f \circ g)(x)$ *or* $f(g(x))$:

1. First evaluate $g(x)$ for the value of x and call the answer u.
2. Evaluate f at the value $g(x) = u$.

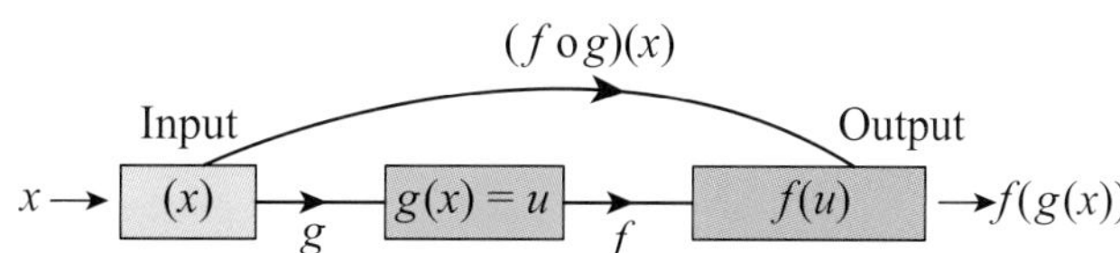

3. Write $f(u)$ in terms of x.

EXAMPLE 10

If $f(x) = 2^x$, $g(x) = x + 1$ and $h(x) = x^2$, find:

(a) $f(g(x))$ **(c)** $g(h(x))$

(b) $(h \circ f)(x)$ **(d)** $(f \circ (g \circ h))(x)$

TIP
Always do the function on the extreme right first.

Solution

(a) $g(x) = (x + 1) = u$

$f(g(x)) = f(u) = 2^u = 2^{x+1}$

(b) $f(x) = (2^x) = u$

$h(f(x)) = h(u) = u^2 = (2^x)^2 = 2^{2x}$

(c) $h(x) = x^2 = u$

$g(h(x)) = g(u) = (u) + 1 = x^2 + 1$

(d) $h(x) = x^2 = u$

$g(h(x)) = g(u) = u + 1 = v$

$fg(h(x)) = f(v) = 2^v = 2^{(u)+1} = 2^{x^2+1}$

EXERCISE 5

1. If $f(x) = 2x - 1$ and $g(x) = 3x + 2$, find:

(a) $f(g(2))$ (c) $(f \circ f)\left(\frac{1}{2}\right)$

(b) $g(f(-1))$ (d) $(g \circ g)\left(-\frac{2}{3}\right)$

2. Find $f(g(x))$ and $g(f(x))$ for the following:

(a) $f(x) = 1 - x^2$, $g(x) = 2x + 3$

(b) $f(x) = 4x$, $g(x) = \sqrt{2x + 4}$

(c) $f(x) = \frac{1}{x}$, $g(x) = 2x + 5$

(d) $f(x) = 3^x$, $g(x) = \sqrt{x}$

(e) $f(x) = \frac{x - 1}{3}$, $g(x) = x^2$

(f) $f(x) = \sin x$, $g(x) = 3x$

(g) $f(x) = x^3$, $g(x) = \frac{1}{x}$

(h) $f(x) = \sqrt{x}$, $g(x) = x^2$

3. **(a)** If $f(x) = 3x + 2$ and $g(x) = ax + 4$, find a, if $(f \circ g)(-1) = 3$.

(b) If $f(x) = x^2 - 2x$, find k, b, if $g(x) = kx + b$, $k > 0$ and $(f \circ g)(x) = 4x^2 + 8x + 3$ for all $x \in \mathbb{R}$.

(c) If $f(x) = 3x + 2$, find:

(i) $f^{-1}(x)$

(ii) $f(f^{-1}(x))$

(iii) $(f^{-1} \circ f)(x)$

4. If $f(x) = 3^x$ for all $x \in \mathbb{R}$, $g(x) = x - 2$ and $h(x) = 1 - x^2$, find:

(a) $f(g(x))$ **(f)** $(h \circ h)(x)$

(b) $g(h(x))$ **(g)** $(g \circ g)(x)$

(c) $f(h(x))$ **(h)** $f(g(h(x)))$

(d) $(h \circ g)(x)$ **(i)** $((f \circ g) \circ h)(x)$

(e) $(g \circ f)(x)$ **(j)** $(f \circ (g \circ h))(x)$

18.7 Continuity of functions

When the speed of a chemical reaction is plotted against time, the data points are connected by an unbroken curve (continuous).

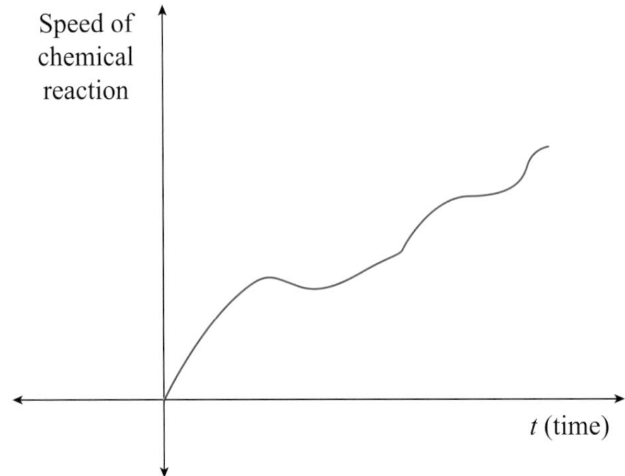

This assumes that the speed varies continuously with time and does not jump from one value to the next one without taking on the values in between.

However, the step function shown below is a discontinuous function. It is a graph of the cost of posting a parcel against its weight in grams.

The cost of posting a parcel less than or equal to 100 grams is €2·40.

The cost of posting a parcel greater than 100 grams but less than or equal to 250 grams is €3.

The cost of posting a parcel greater than 250 grams but less than or equal to 500 grams is €4.

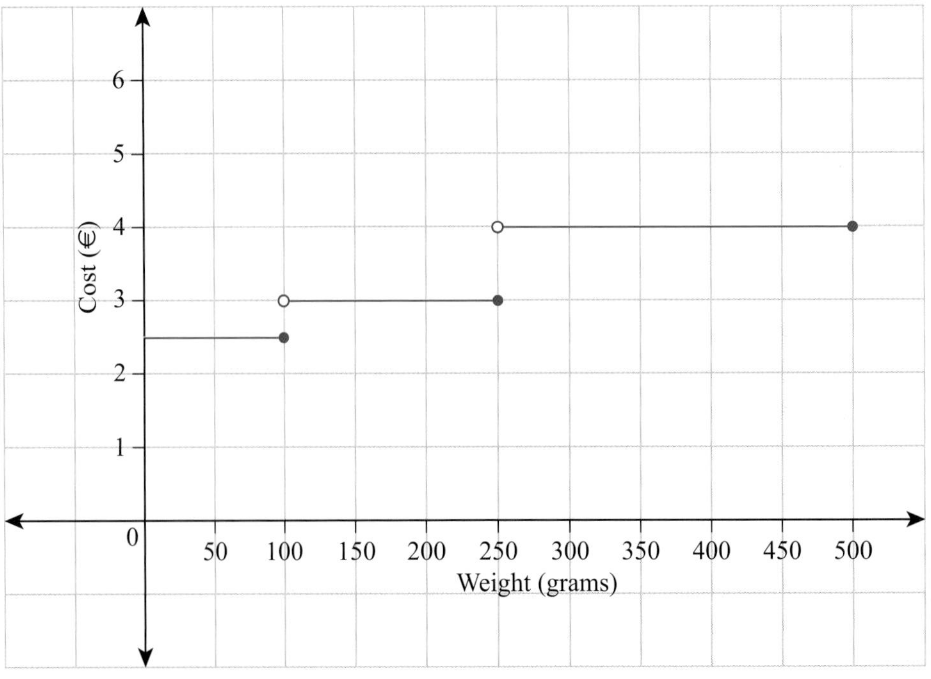

Discontinuous functions play an important role in computer science, statistics and physics.

Explaining the idea

Some functions are defined for **all values** of x in an interval (domain or part of a domain). This means their graphs have no breaks in the interval. These are called continuous functions.

- $y = f(x) = 2x + 1$ is continuous for all $x \in \mathbb{R}$.

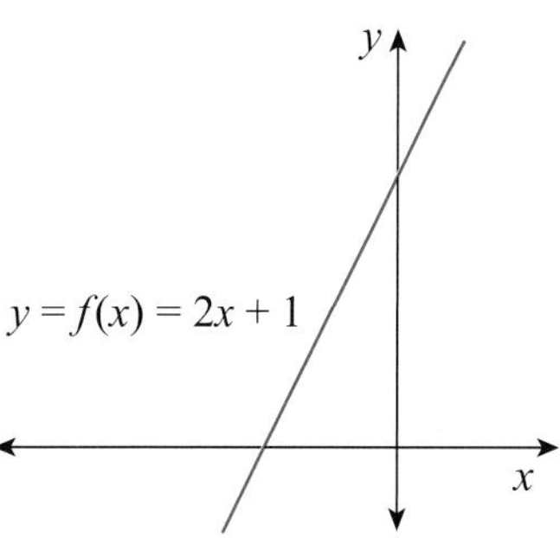

- Other functions have gaps in them. These are discontinuous functions.

  $f(x) = \dfrac{2x+1}{x-3}$ is not continuous for all $x \in \mathbb{R}$.

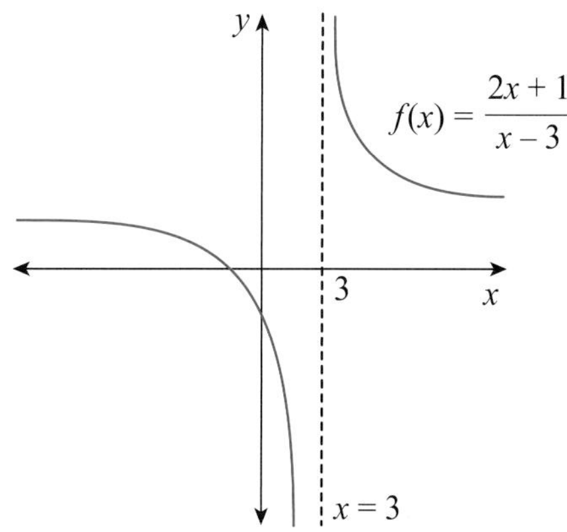

There is a break in the function at $x = 3$.

Test for continuity of functions

1. The drawing test

A function is continuous on an interval if its graph can be drawn without having to lift the pencil in the interval.

- $y = f(x)$ is continuous on $\mathbb{R}$, where $f(x) = x(x - 2)$, $x \in \mathbb{R}$.

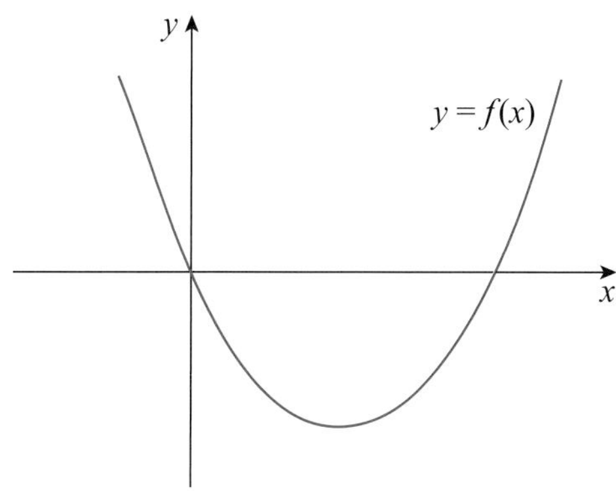

- The function $y = f(x)$ shown below is discontinuous on the interval [0, 4]. There is a break in it. It is described by the function:

$$f(x) = \begin{cases} -x + 1, 0 \le x < 1, x \in \mathbb{R} \\ \dfrac{x}{3} + \dfrac{2}{3}, 1 \le x \le 4, x \in \mathbb{R} \end{cases}$$

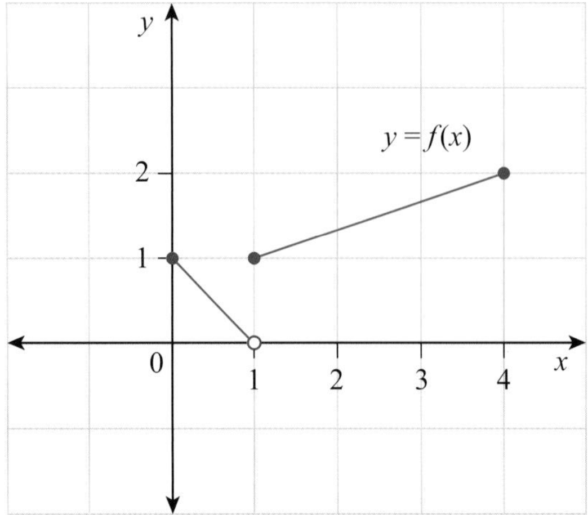

TIP

The interval $[a, b]$ means all values greater than or equal to a and less than or equal to b.

2. The limit test

A function is said to be continuous at a **point** if its values at places near the **point** are close to the value at the point. If this is not the case, the function is discontinuous at the point. This is expressed mathematically as:

> A function $f(x)$ is continuous at a point $x = a$ if $\lim_{x \to a} f(x) = f(a)$, where $f(a)$ exists and is finite.

If $f(x)$ is continuous at **all points** of an interval, then it is continuous over the interval.

EXAMPLE 11

Is the function $f(x) = \begin{cases} 4x - 6, x \ne 1 \\ 2, \quad x = 1 \end{cases}$

continuous or discontinuous for all $x \in \mathbb{R}$?

Solution

$\lim_{x \to 1} f(x) = \lim_{x \to 1} (4x - 6) = 4 - 6 = -2$

$f(1) = 2$

$\lim_{x \to 1} f(x) \ne f(1)$

Therefore, this function is not continuous because it is discontinuous at $x = 1$.

EXAMPLE 12

The speed v of a train in m/s is given by:

$$v = \begin{cases} \dfrac{6t^2}{5}, 0 \le t < 5 \\ 30, t \ge 5 \end{cases}$$

where t is in seconds. Show that this function is continuous and plot it.

Solution

$\lim_{t \to 5} v = \dfrac{6 \times 25}{5} = 30$

The value of v at $t = 5$ is 30. Therefore, this function is continuous.

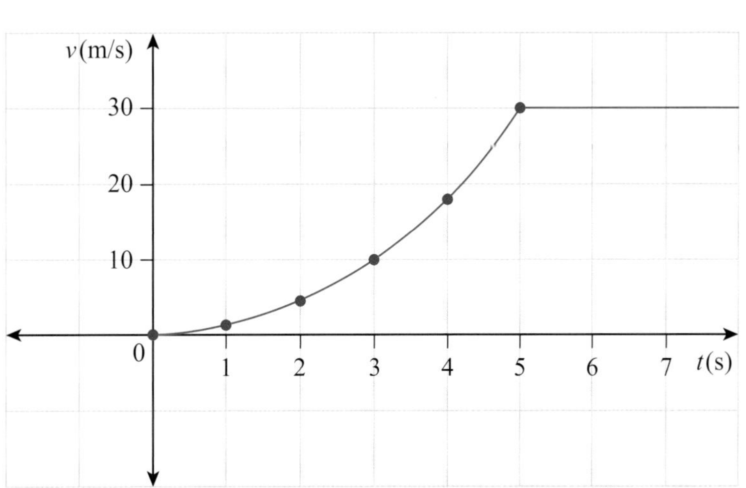

EXERCISE 6

1. State whether or not the functions described by the following graphs are continuous. State where the discontinuity occurs.

(a) $y = \begin{cases} x+1, x \leq 2, x \in \mathbb{R} \\ x^2, \quad x > 2, x \in \mathbb{R} \end{cases}$

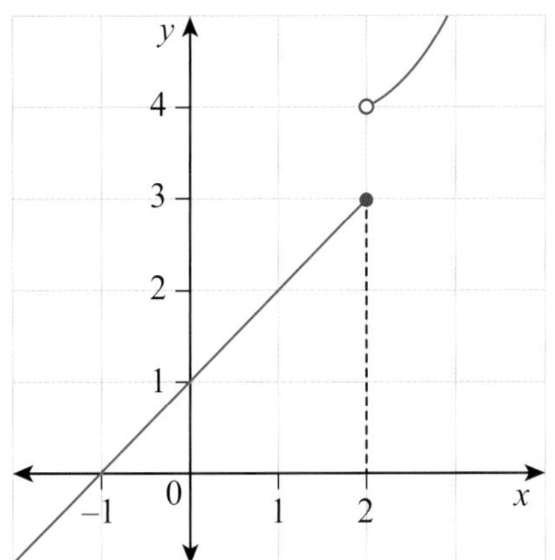

(b) $g(x) = \begin{cases} x^2, x < 0, x \in \mathbb{R} \\ 2x, x \geq 0, x \in \mathbb{R} \end{cases}$

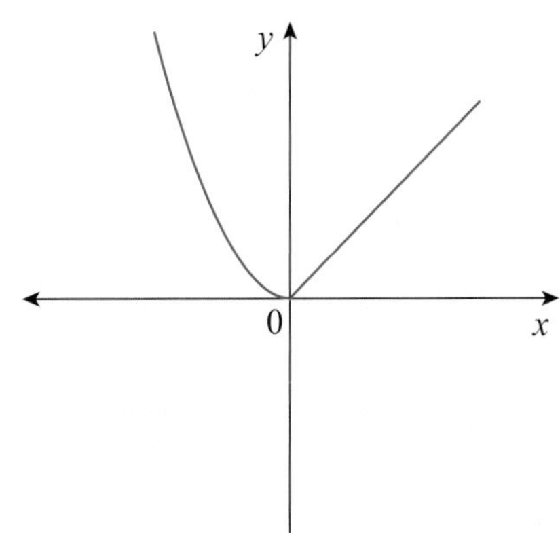

(c) $y = x + \frac{1}{x}, x \in \mathbb{R}$

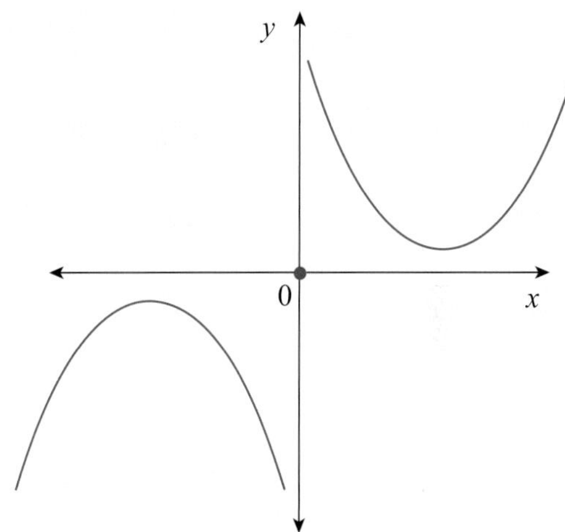

(d) $y = f(x)$

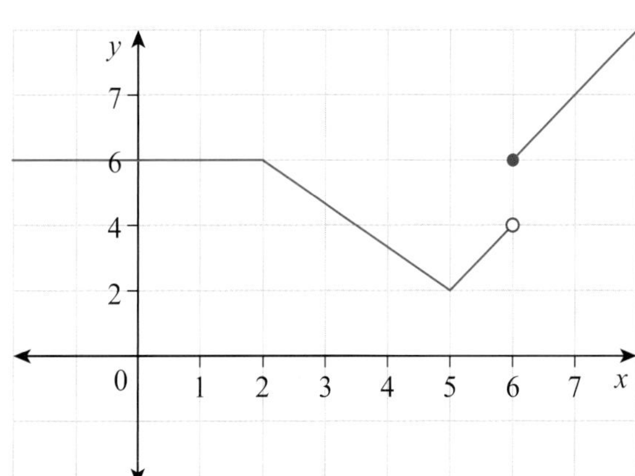

(e) $y = \begin{cases} x^2, x < 2, x \in \mathbb{R} \\ 4 - x, x \geq 2, x \in \mathbb{R} \end{cases}$

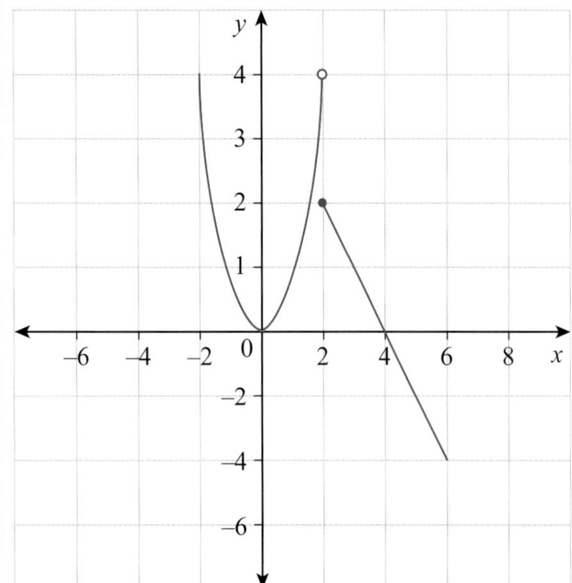

2. Describe the graph of the discontinuous function below in algebraic form.

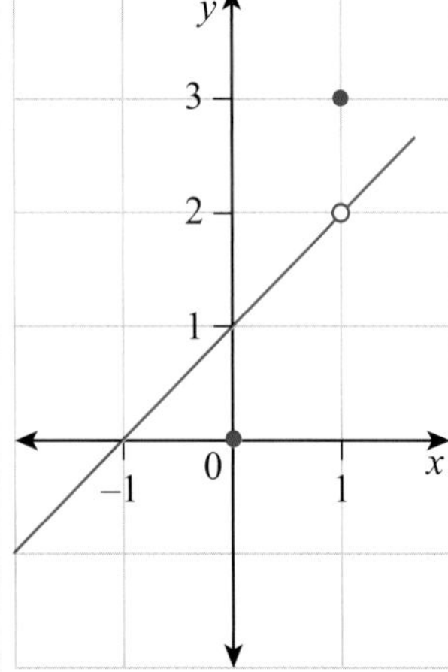

3. Test the following functions for continuity:

(a) $f(x) = \begin{cases} 2x, & x \geq 0, x \in \mathbb{R} \\ -2x + 1, & x < 0, x \in \mathbb{R} \end{cases}$

(b) $f(x) = \begin{cases} (x-4)^2 - 9, & x < 7, x \in \mathbb{R} \\ x - 7, & x \geq 7, x \in \mathbb{R} \end{cases}$

(c) $f(x) = \begin{cases} x^2 + 2x, & x \leq -2, x \in \mathbb{R} \\ x^3 - 6x, & x > -2, x \in \mathbb{R} \end{cases}$

(d) $f(x) = \begin{cases} \dfrac{x-6}{x-3}, & x < 0, x \in \mathbb{R} \\ 2, & x = 0 \\ \sqrt{4 + x^2}, & x > 0, x \in \mathbb{R} \end{cases}$

4. (a) Determine if $f(x) = \dfrac{x^2+1}{x^3+1}$, $x \in \mathbb{R}$, is continuous at $x = -1$.

(b) Find all values of a if:

$$f(x) = \begin{cases} a^2x - a, & x > 3 \\ 4, & x \leq 3 \end{cases}$$

is continuous for all $x \in \mathbb{R}$.

(c) Find all values of k and l if:

$$f(x) = \begin{cases} kx - l, & x \leq -1 \\ 2x^2 + 3kx + l, & -1 < x < 1 \\ 4, & x \geq 1 \end{cases}$$

is continuous for all $x \in \mathbb{R}$.

Linear Functions

Learning Outcomes

- To recognise a linear function.
- To be able to use both forms of an equation of a straight line: $y = mx + c$ and $(y - y_1) = m(x - x_1)$.
- To be able to find the equation of a straight line from its graph.
- To be able to find the intercepts of a straight line on the axes.
- To recognise the equations of straight lines that are parallel to the axes.
- To plot intersecting linear functions, finding where they intersect both graphically and algebraically.
- To use linear functions to solve real-life problems.

19.1 What is a linear function?

A linear function is a relationship between two variables x and y that can be written in the form $y = f(x) = mx^1 + c$ or $y = f(x) = ax + b$, where $m, c, a, b \in \mathbb{R}$ are constant real numbers. These equations are both forms of the equation of a straight line and so the graph of y against x is a straight-line graph.

m (or a) is called the coefficient of x.

c (or b) is called the constant term.

EXAMPLE 1

Write the following in the form $y = mx + c$ and hence write down the values of m and c:

(a) $3y = 7x - 11$

(b) $2x + y = 0$

Solution

(a) $3y = 7x - 11$

$y = \frac{7}{3}x - \frac{11}{3}$

$m = \frac{7}{3}, c = -\frac{11}{3}$

(b) $2x + y = 0$

$y = -2x + 0$

$\Rightarrow m = -2, c = 0$

m is the slope of the line and c is its intercept on the y-axis.

19.2 Plotting graphs of linear functions

Because graphs of linear functions are straight lines, you only need **two points** to plot a straight line.

ACTIVITY 5

ACTION
Plotting linear functions

OBJECTIVE
To plot a number of linear functions in a given domain

EXAMPLE 2

Plot the graph of $2y = 3x - 2$, $-2 \leq x \leq 4, x \in \mathbb{R}$.

Solution

$2y = 3x - 2$

$y = \frac{3}{2}x - 1$

Take the extreme values of $x = -2$ and $x = 4$ in the domain to evaluate the corresponding y values.

x	-2	4
y	-4	5

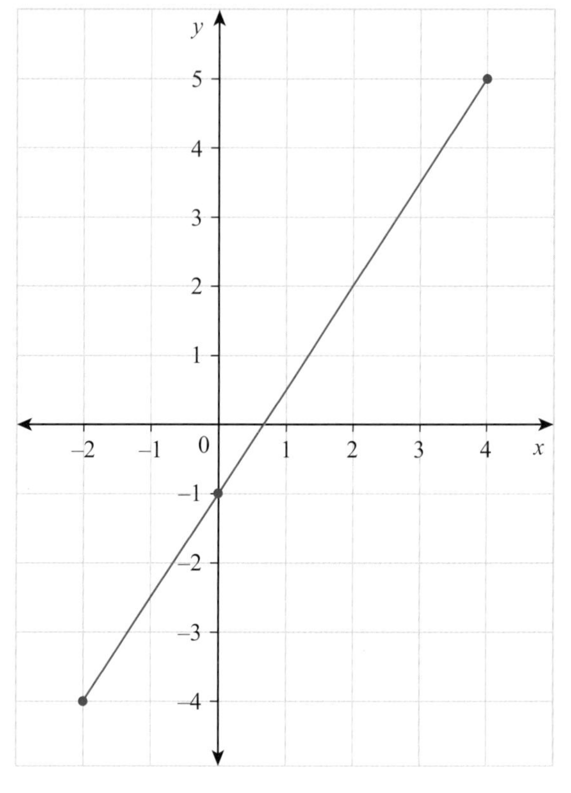

In the expression $y = mx + c$, x is known as the independent variable and y is known as the dependent variable.

19.3 Finding the equation of a straight line from its graph

Method

1. Find the slope $m = \frac{y_2 - y_1}{x_2 - x_1}$ using two points (x_1, y_1), (x_2, y_2) on the straight line.
2. Find the equation from the equation of a line formula:

   $(y - y_1) = m(x - x_1)$

   or

   $y = mx + c$, where c is the y-intercept.

EXAMPLE 3

Find the equation of the straight line l shown below.

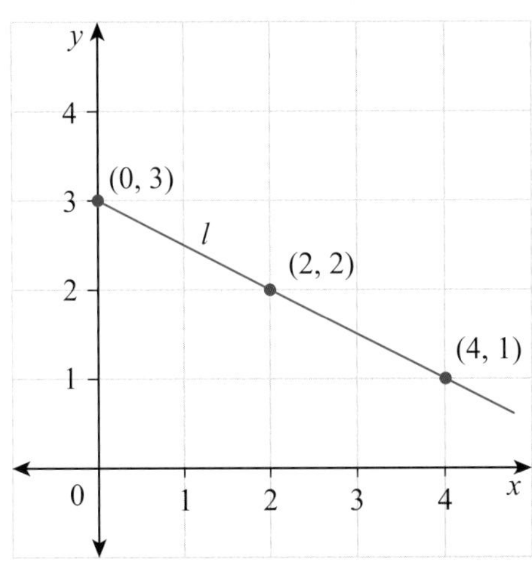

Solution

Find the slope using any two points on the line, say (2, 2) and (4, 1).

Slope $m = \frac{2-1}{2-4} = -\frac{1}{2}$

Using the slope and any point, find the equation of the line using $(y - y_1) = m(x - x_1)$.

Point: $(x_1, y_1) = (2, 2)$

$$y - 2 = -\frac{1}{2}(x - 2)$$

$$y - 2 = -\frac{x}{2} + 1$$

$$y = -\frac{1}{2}x + 3$$

or

Using the slope and the y-intercept, find the equation of the line using $y = mx + c$.

Slope $m = -\frac{1}{2}$

y-intercept: $c = 3$

$\therefore y = -\frac{1}{2}x + 3$

This is the equation of the line l. All points on this line satisfy this equation.

19.4 Properties of linear functions

1. Lines parallel to the axes

(a) Parallel to the x-axis

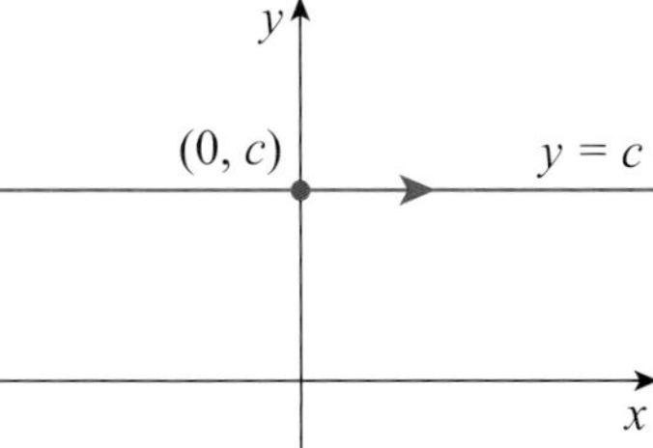

- A line parallel to the x-axis has a slope of 0. $m = 0$: $y = mx + c \Rightarrow y = c$ (constant) for all values of x.
- Every point on this line has the same y co-ordinate.
- $y = c$ is the equation of a line parallel to the x-axis through $(0, c)$.
- Therefore, the equation of the x-axis is $y = 0$ as it passes through $(0, 0)$.

(b) Parallel to the y-axis

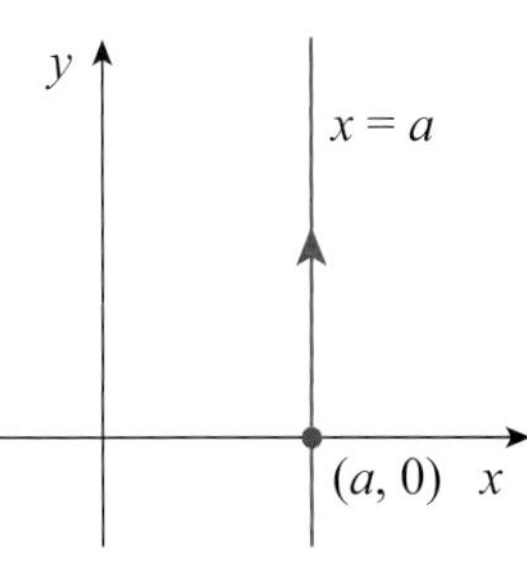

- A line parallel to the y-axis has a slope of infinity (∞).
- Every point on this line has the same x co-ordinate.
- $x = a$ is the equation of a line parallel to the y-axis through $(a, 0)$.
- Therefore, the equation of the y-axis is $x = 0$ as it passes through $(0, 0)$.

EXAMPLE 4

Write down the equations of the lines h, k, l, x, y.

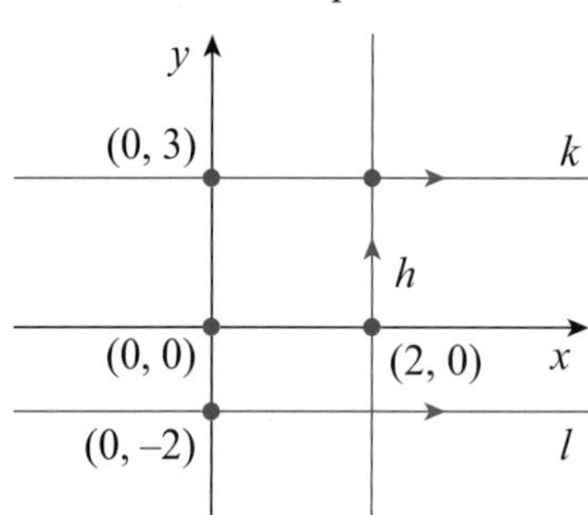

Solution

$h: x = 2$

$k: y = 3$

$l: y = -2$

$x: y = 0$

$y: x = 0$

2. Crossing the axes

(a) The x-axis has equation $y = 0$

Putting $y = 0$ in $y = mx + c$:

$$x = -\frac{c}{m}$$

If $m \neq 0$, every linear function crosses the x-axis at exactly one point, $P\left(-\frac{c}{m}, 0\right)$.

(b) The y-axis has equation $x = 0$

Putting $x = 0$ in $y = mx + c$:

$y = c$

Therefore, every linear function crosses the y-axis at exactly one point $Q(0, c)$.

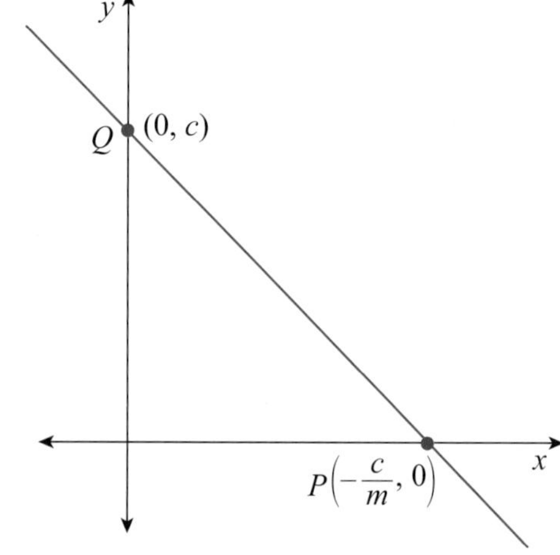

EXAMPLE 5

Find where $y = 3x - 4$ crosses the axes.

Solution

x-axis: $y = 0$

$3x - 4 = 0$

$x = \frac{4}{3}$

The line crosses the x-axis at $\left(\frac{4}{3}, 0\right)$.

y-axis: $x = 0$

$y = -4$

The line crosses the y-axis at $(0, -4)$.

19.5 Intersecting linear functions

ACTIVITY 6

ACTION
Intersecting linear functions

OBJECTIVE
To plot two linear functions and find their point of intersection both graphically and algebraically

EXAMPLE 6

Using the same grid, graph the linear functions $f(x) = x + 1$ and $g(x) = 2x - 3$ in the domain $-1 \le x \le 5$. Use the graph to solve the $f(x) = g(x)$. Verify your answer algebraically.

Solution

As the functions are linear, you just need to get two points on each line. Choose the extreme x values of the domain.

x	-1	5
$f(x)$	0	6
$g(x)$	-5	7

Graph: $f(x) = g(x)$ at $x = 4$

Algebra:

$f(x) = g(x)$

$x + 1 = 2x - 3$

$1 + 3 = 2x - x$

$4 = x$

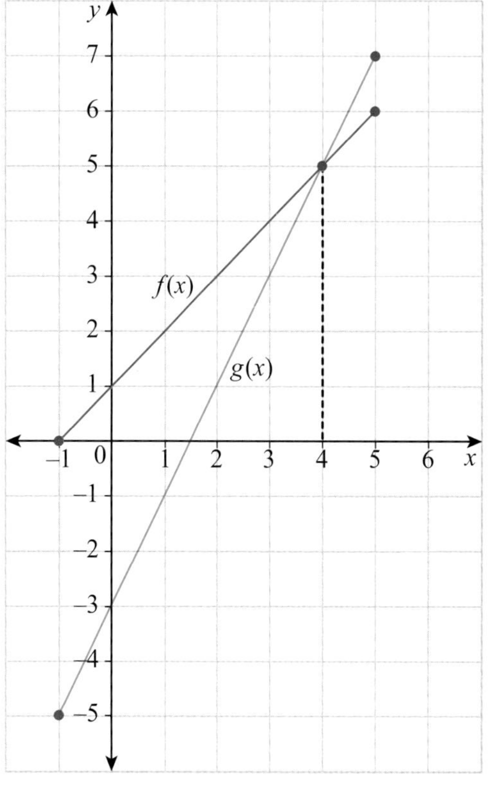

EXERCISE 7

1. Draw the following linear functions on graph paper in the given domain where $x \in \mathbb{R}$:

   Note: This is also Activity 5. The activity supplies you with the appropriate grids.

   (a) $f(x) = x + 1, -1 \le x \le 5$
   (b) $f(x) = x - 3, -2 \le x \le 6$
   (c) $f(x) = 2x + 1, -2 \le x \le 4$
   (d) $f(x) = 4x - 3, -1 \le x \le 3$
   (e) $f(x) = \frac{1}{2}x + 3, -2 \le x \le 5$

2. Write the following in the form $y = mx + c$:

   (a) $3(x + y) = 7$
   (b) $4x - 3y = 9$
   (c) $y - 0{\cdot}2 = 7(x - 0{\cdot}1)$
   (d) $y = 5$
   (e) $x + y = 8$

3. Say which functions are linear. If they are linear, write them in the form $y = mx + c$, using the given variable as x:

(a) $f(x) = \dfrac{-1 - 2x}{3}$

(b) $h(x) = \frac{3}{5}x + 4$

(c) $C(x) = 2\pi x$

(d) $f(x) = 3x^2 - 7$

(e) $F(x) = 13 - \left(\dfrac{2^{-3}}{8}\right)x$

4. Write in the form $y = mx + c$ equations for the linear functions with the following properties:

(a) Slope 3, y-intercept -2

(b) Slope -2, x-intercept 5

(c) Slope $-\frac{2}{5}$, through the point (2, 3)

(d) $f(1) = 2$, $f(-2) = 3$, where $y = f(x)$

(e) Passing through (1, 4) and (2, −3)

5. For the linear functions described by the tables and graphs below, express the dependent variable as a function of the independent variable.

(a)

Time t in years	0	1	2
Value V of computer in €	500	320	140

t is the independent variable.

(b)

Temperature T (°C)	0	5	20
Temperature θ (°F)	32	41	68

T is the independent variable.

(c)

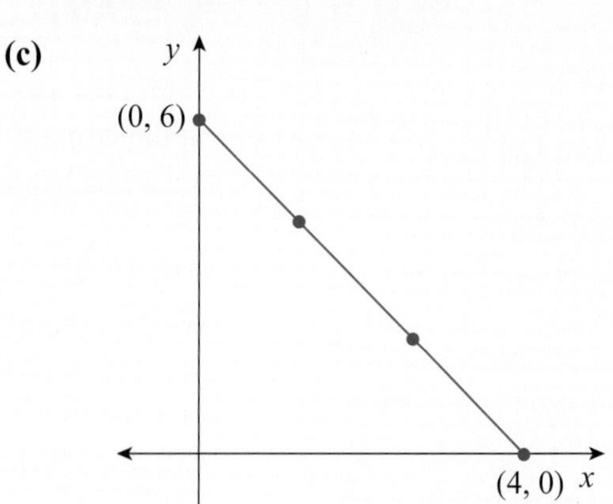

(d)

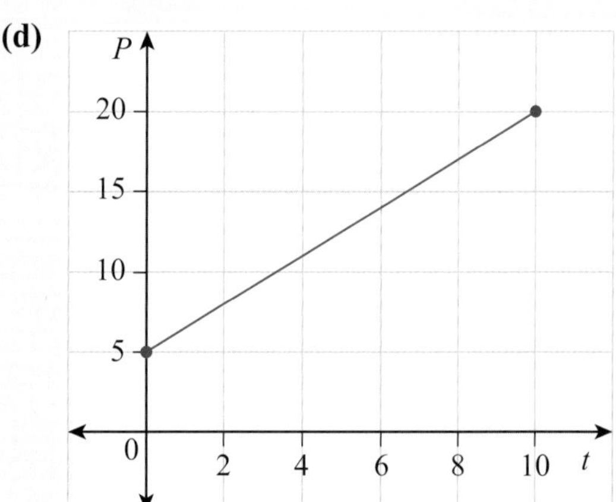

6. Using the same grid, graph the following linear functions in the given domain for $x \in \mathbb{R}$. Use the graph to solve $f(x) = g(x)$. Verify your answer algebraically.

> **Note:** This is also Activity 6. The activity supplies you with the appropriate grids.

(a) $f(x) = x + 1$ and $g(x) = 3x - 2$, $-2 \le x \le 2$, $x \in \mathbb{R}$

(b) $f(x) = 3x + 1$ and $g(x) = 3 - x$, $-2 \le x \le 4$, $x \in \mathbb{R}$

(c) $f(x) = 3$ and $g(x) = \frac{1}{2}x + 2$, $-2 \le x \le 3$, $x \in \mathbb{R}$

(d) $f(x) = 4x + 1$ and $g(x) = 3x - 2$, $-4 \le x \le 1$, $x \in \mathbb{R}$

19.6 Contexts and applications

EXAMPLE 7

The price P in euro of a stock t months after its launch on the stock market is described by the linear function on the graph shown. The launch price is €1·50.

Find a formula relating P to t and use it to find P when $t = 3{\cdot}5$ months.

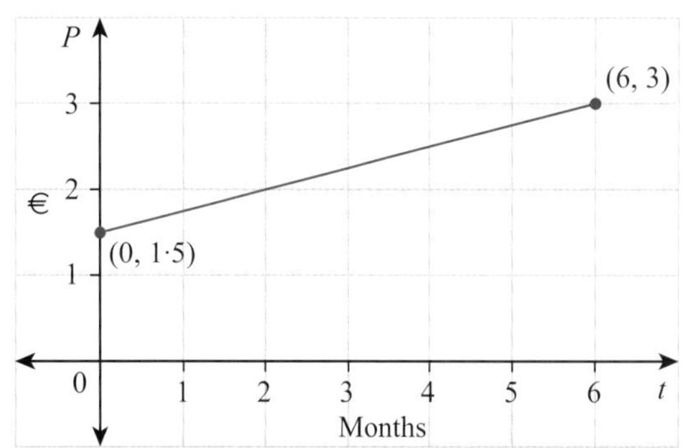

Solution

Two points on the line: (0, 1·5), (6, 3)

$y = mx + c$

Slope $m = \dfrac{3 - 1{\cdot}5}{6 - 0} = \dfrac{1{\cdot}5}{6} = \dfrac{1}{4}$

The equation: $P = \frac{1}{4}t + 1{\cdot}5 \quad [y = mx + c]$

When $t = 3{\cdot}5$: $P = \dfrac{3{\cdot}5}{4} + 1{\cdot}5 = €\,2{\cdot}375$

EXAMPLE 8

As a diver descends in the ocean, the pressure P in Pascals (Pa) increases linearly with depth h in metres (m) from its pressure at the surface. If the pressure at the surface is 1×10^5 Pa and is $1{\cdot}98 \times 10^5$ Pa at a depth of 10 m, find the equation of the straight line connecting P and h.

(a) Find the pressure at a depth of 20 m.

(b) The safe depth to which a diver can descend is the depth at which the pressure is $3{\cdot}75 \times 10^5$ Pa. What is this depth correct to two decimal places?

Solution

Surface $P = 1 \times 10^5$ Pa

$h = 10$ m

$P = 1{\cdot}98 \times 10^5$ Pa

A graph of $P(\times 10^5 \text{ Pa})$ against $h(\text{m})$ is shown.

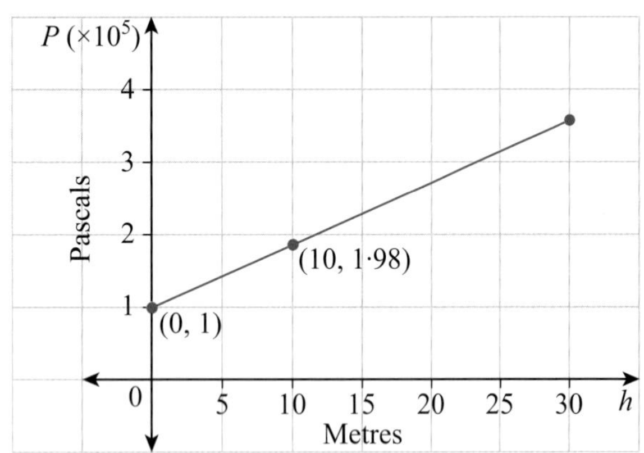

The slope m of the straight line is

$$m = \frac{(1{\cdot}98 - 1) \times 10^5}{10 - 0} = 0{\cdot}98 \times 10^4 = 9800$$

The y-intercept is $c = 1 \times 10^5$.

The equation of the straight line is

$P = 9800h + 1 \times 10^5 \quad [y = mx + c]$

(a) The pressure at a depth of 20 m is:

$P = 9800 \times 20 + 1 \times 10^5 = 2{\cdot}96 \times 10^5$ Pa

(b) The safe depth to which a diver can descend is the depth at which the pressure is $3{\cdot}75 \times 10^5$ Pa. The depth at which this occurs is given by:

$3{\cdot}75 \times 10^5 = 9800h + 1 \times 10^5$

$2{\cdot}75 \times 10^5 = 9800h$

$$h = \frac{2{\cdot}75 \times 10^5}{9800} = 28{\cdot}06 \text{ m}$$

The point of intersection of two linear functions can be found graphically or by solving their equations simultaneously.

EXAMPLE  9

Two companies, Awed and Bliss, produce wedding invitations. The cost equations for their invitations are set out below:

Awed: $C = 60 + 0{\cdot}8x$

Bliss: $C = 1{\cdot}2x$

x is the number of invitations and C is the cost in euro. Plot graphs of these two functions on the same diagram. Use your graphs to find the number of invitations for which the price charged by the two companies is the same, and what that price is. Verify your answers algebraically.

Solution

To plot the graphs of these, you need two points on each graph.

Awed: $x = 0 \Rightarrow C = 60$: $(0, 60)$

$x = 150 \Rightarrow C = 180$: $(150, 180)$

Bliss: $x = 0 \Rightarrow C = 0$: $(0, 0)$

$x = 200 \Rightarrow C = 240$: $(200, 240)$

The graphs are plotted below:

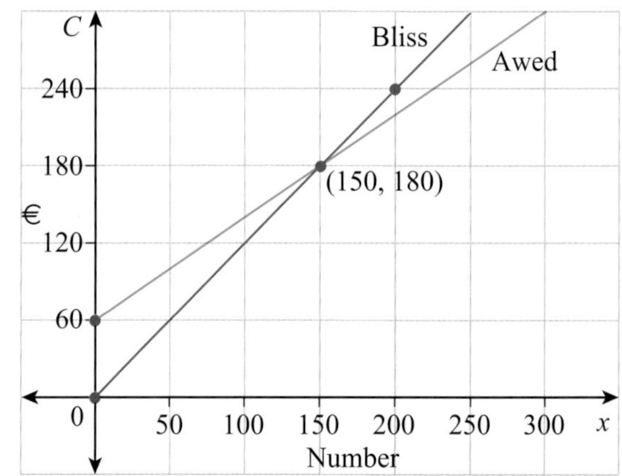

For $x > 150$, Awed is cheaper than Bliss.

They are equally expensive for $x = 150$.

You can verify this by solving the equations simultaneously:

$60 + 0{\cdot}8x = 1{\cdot}2x$

$60 = 0{\cdot}4x$

$x = 150$ and $C = 1{\cdot}2 \times 150 = 180$

EXERCISE 8

1. The value V of a car t years after its purchase is shown by the linear graph below:

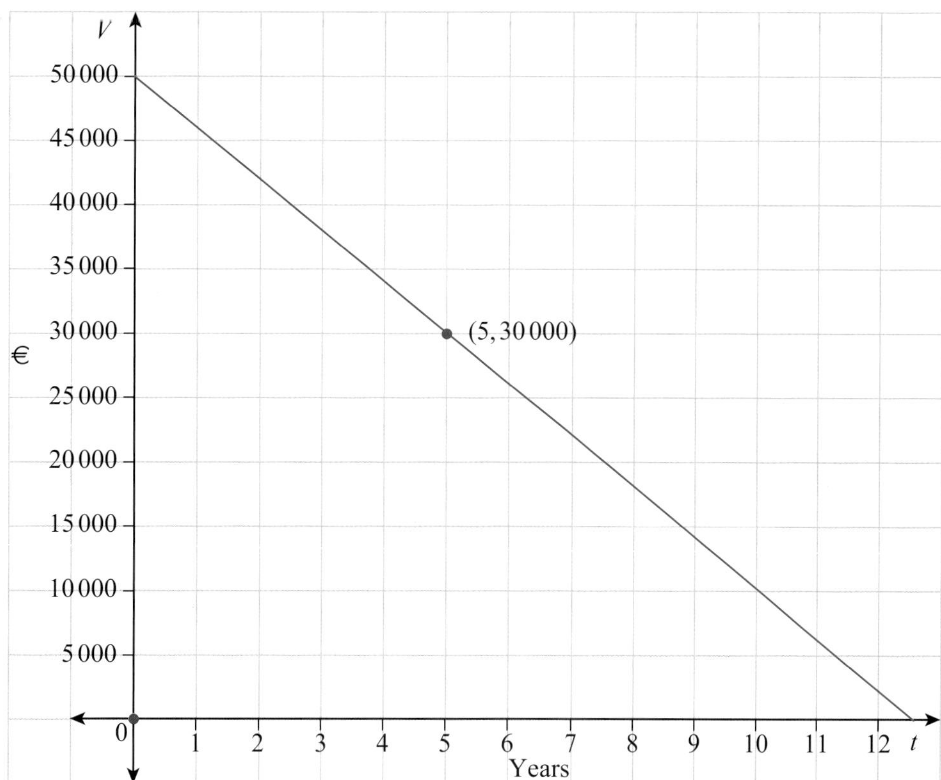

If the car cost €50 000 new and its value after 5 years was €30 000, find:

(a) the relationship between V and t,

(b) when its value was € 20 000,

(c) when its value was €0.

2. A cable car starts its journey at 6000 m above the ground. It descends at 300 m per minute. Find an expression for its distance s in metres above the ground after t minutes. Use this expression to find how long it takes to reach the ground.

3. For the points (x, y) given in the table below, investigate if y is a linear function of x.

x	−8	−4	0	4	8
y	0	0·5	1	1·5	2

If it is linear, find a formula for this relationship.

4. The populations of two countries A and B in millions from 1950 to 2000 are shown in the table below.

	1950	1960	1970	1980	1990	2000
A	8·2	9·9	12·8	16·2	18·3	24·9
B	7·6	10·0	12·4	14·8	17·2	19·6

One country experienced linear growth from 1950 to 2000.

(a) Which country was this?

(b) For the country which experienced linear growth:

(i) write down a formula relating its population P to the time t years after 1950,

(ii) find the population of this country in 2020.

(c) For the non-linear growth country, find the average rate of change of its population from 1950 to 2000.

5. In a golf club a fixed fee is paid for membership and then each round of golf is charged on top of the fixed fee. Twenty rounds of golf cost €850 and 32 rounds of golf cost €1210.

(a) Find the membership fee and the cost per round.

(b) Write down a formula for the cost C in euro of playing golf in terms of the number n of rounds played.

(c) Find the cost for 50 rounds.

(d) How many rounds of golf can a member get for €1000?

6. The number N of cases of a flu epidemic in a country t days after the discovery of its outbreak was given by $N = 80 + 30t$.

(a) Plot a graph of N against t for $0 \leq t \leq 4$.

(b) Find the number of cases of the epidemic two weeks after the outbreak if no action was taken.

(c) If after 4 days, a massive inoculation programme was initiated so that the number of cases n decreased at a steady rate of five cases per day, find a formula for n, in terms of t, for $t > 4$. How long, after the start of the inoculation programme, does it take for the epidemic to be eradicated?

Quadratic Functions

Learning Outcomes

- To recognise a quadratic function: $y = f(x) = ax^2 + bx + c$.
- To be able to plot a graph of a quadratic function.
- To be able to find properties of quadratic functions (crossing axes, vertices, axis of symmetry).
- To be able to find the equation of a quadratic function from its graph.
- To work with intersecting graphs.
- To use quadratic functions to solve real-life problems.

20.1 What is a quadratic function?

A quadratic function is a relationship between two variables x and y that can be written in the form $y = f(x) = ax^2 + bx + c$, where a, b, c are constant real numbers, $a \neq 0$.

a is called the coefficient of x^2.

b is called the coefficient of x.

c is called the constant term.

They have many applications in areas such as architecture (arches), economics, engineering, mechanics and physics.

- The trajectory (path) of a javelin is described by a quadratic function, as shown:

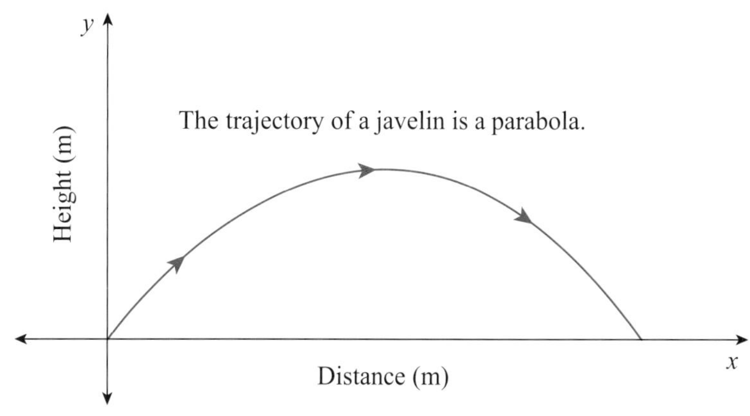

EXAMPLE 1

(a) If $y = 2x^2 - 5x + 7$, find y when $x = -2$.

(b) If $f(x) = -3x^2 + 7x - 1$, find $f\left(\frac{1}{2}\right)$.

Solution

(a) $x = -2$:

$y = 2(-2)^2 - 5(-2) + 7 = 25$

(b) $f\left(\frac{1}{2}\right) = -3\left(\frac{1}{2}\right)^2 + 7\left(\frac{1}{2}\right) - 1 = \frac{7}{4}$

20.2 Plotting graphs of quadratic functions

ACTIVITY 7

ACTION
Plotting quadratic graphs

OBJECTIVE
To draw a number of quadratic functions. (Calculator instructions are provided for generating the function values.)

Method

To plot a graph of a quadratic function:

1. Isolate y on one side of the equation.
2. Substitute the values of x in the domain to find the corresponding values of y.
3. Plot the y (dependent variable) values on the vertical axis against the x (independent variable) values on the horizontal axis.

EXAMPLE 2

Plot $y = 2x^2 - 3x - 12$ in the domain $-3 \leq x \leq 3$, $x \in \mathbb{R}$.

Solution

$y = 2x^2 - 3x - 12$

$x = -3$: $y = 2(-3)^2 - 3(-3) - 12 = 15$

$x = -2$: $y = 2(-2)^2 - 3(-2) - 12 = 2$

$x = -1$: $y = 2(-1)^2 - 3(-1) - 12 = -7$

$x = 0$: $y = 2(0)^2 - 3(0) - 12 = -12$

$x = 1$: $y = 2(1)^2 - 3(1) - 12 = -13$

$x = 2$: $y = 2(2)^2 - 3(2) - 12 = -10$

$x = 3$: $y = 2(3)^2 - 3(3) - 12 = -3$

x	-3	-2	-1	0	1	2	3
y	15	2	-7	-12	-13	-10	-3

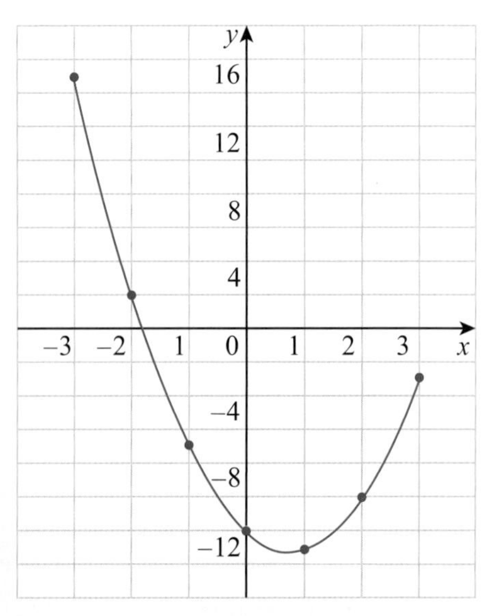

EXAMPLE 3

A rocket is launched into the air. Its height h above the ground is given by $h = 8x - 2x^2$, where h is its height in hundreds of metres and x is its distance horizontally from the launch site in hundreds of metres. Plot h against x in the domain $0 \leq x \leq 4, x \in \mathbb{R}$.

Solution

$h = 8x - 2x^2$

x	0	1	2	3	4
h	0	6	8	6	0

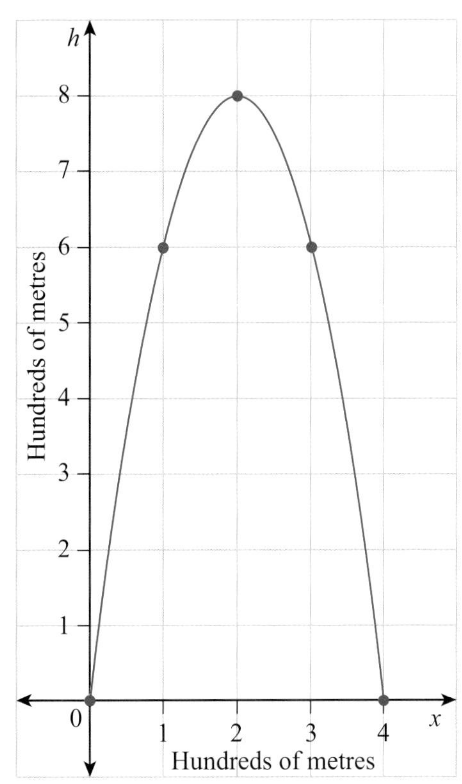

General shape of quadratic functions

The general shape of all quadratic functions, $y = ax^2 + bx + c$, is either:

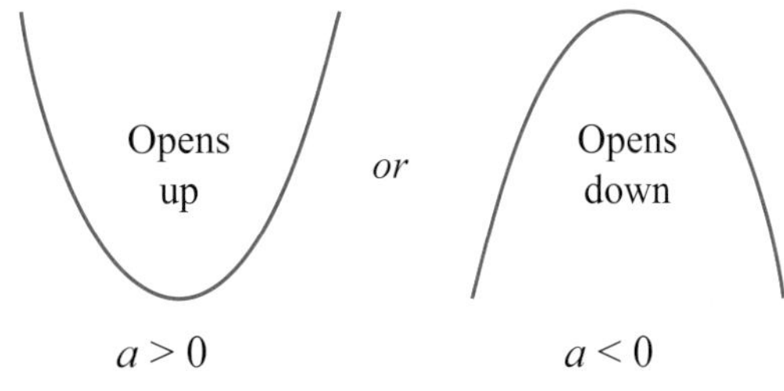

If $a > 0$, the curve opens up (Cup) like a cup.

- $y = 4x^2 - x$ has a $\cup$ shape.

If $a < 0$, the curve opens down (Cap) like a cap.

- $y = -\frac{1}{2}x^2 + 5x - 57$ has a $\cap$ shape.

You will see why quadratic functions have this shape in Section 8 Differentiation.

20.3 Properties of quadratic functions

In general, if you want to find where a quadratic function intersects a straight line, solve the equation of the quadratic function $y = f(x) = ax^2 + bx + c$ with the equation of the straight line l.

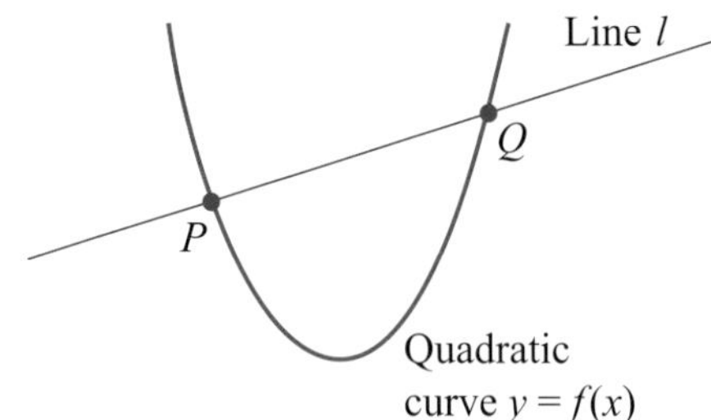

1. Finding where a quadratic function crosses the axes

(a) The y-axis

The equation of the y-axis is $x = 0$.

The equation of the quadratic function is $y = ax^2 + bx + c$.

Solving simultaneously: $y = a(0)^2 + b(0) + c = c$

$$y = c$$

The graph of the quadratic function crosses the y-axis at $(0, c)$.

(b) The x-axis

The equation of the x-axis is $y = 0$.

The equation of the quadratic function is $y = ax^2 + bx + c$.

Solving simultaneously: $ax^2 + bx + c = 0$

The point(s) where the graph of the quadratic function crosses the x-axis are the solutions of the quadratic equation $ax^2 + bx + c = 0$.

These solutions are given by: $x = \dfrac{-b \pm \sqrt{b^2 - 4ac}}{2a}$

Three situations arise:

(i) $b^2 - 4ac > 0 \Rightarrow b^2 > 4ac$

(ii) $b^2 - 4ac = 0 \Rightarrow b^2 = 4ac$

(iii) $b^2 - 4ac < 0 \Rightarrow b^2 < 4ac$

(i) $b^2 - 4ac > 0 \Rightarrow b^2 > 4ac$

This means there are **two different roots**. As a result, the graph of $y = ax^2 + bx + c$ crosses the x-axis at two different points.

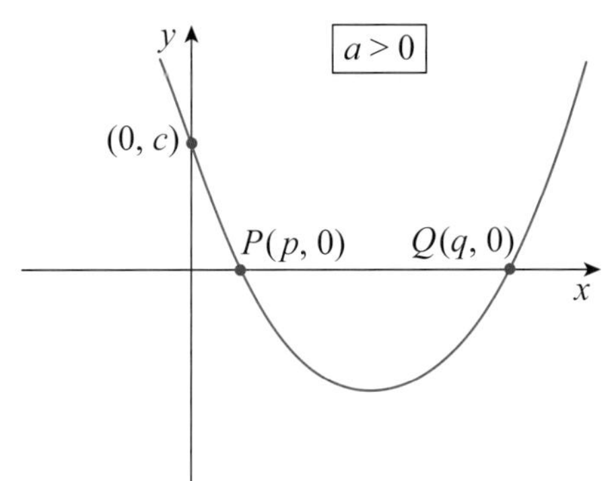

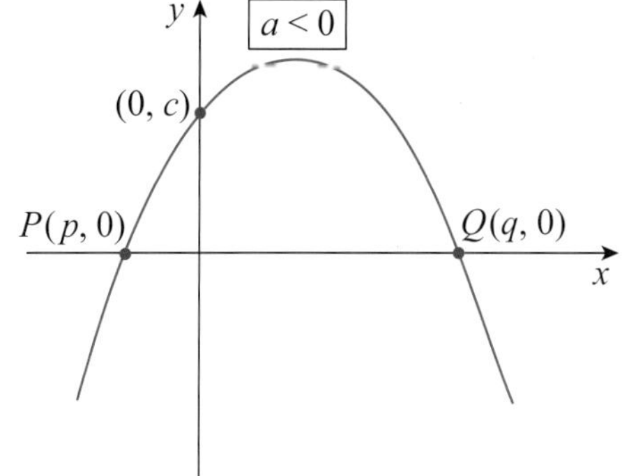

EXAMPLE 4

Find where $y = 2x^2 - x - 2$ crosses the axes.

Solution

$y = 2x^2 - x - 2$

$b^2 - 4ac = 1 + 16 = 17 > 0$

$\therefore b^2 > 4ac$ [Two different roots]

Crosses y-axis: $x = 0$

$y = -2$

It crosses the y-axis at $(0, -2)$.

Crosses x-axis: $y = 0$

$2x^2 - x - 2 = 0$

$x = \frac{1 \pm \sqrt{17}}{4} = -0{\cdot}78,\ 1{\cdot}28$

It crosses the x-axis at $P(-0{\cdot}78, 0)$ and $Q(1{\cdot}28, 0)$.

(ii) $b^2 - 4ac = 0 \Rightarrow b^2 = 4ac$

This means there are **two equal roots**. As a result, the graph of $y = ax^2 + bx + c$ crosses the x-axis at only one point P.

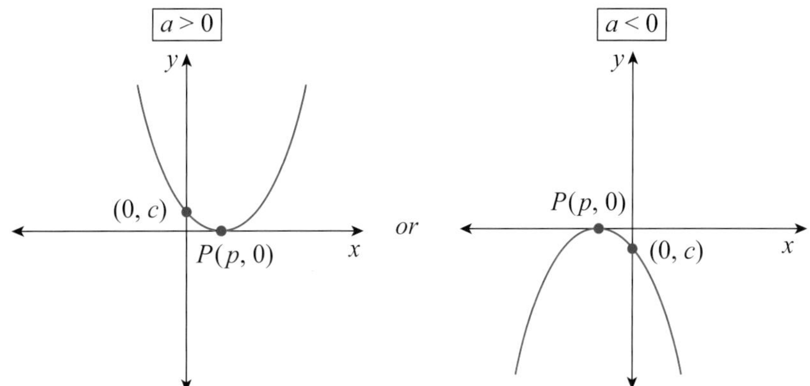

$$b^2 - 4ac = 0 \Rightarrow x = \frac{-b \pm \sqrt{0}}{2a} = \frac{-b}{2a}$$

The quadratic equation will **always** factorise into two identical factors.

$$\left(x + \frac{b}{2a}\right)\left(x + \frac{b}{2a}\right) = \left(x + \frac{b}{2a}\right)^2 = 0$$

ACTIVITY 8

ACTION
Sketching graphs given quadratic functions

OBJECTIVE
To draw a quadratic graph by looking at the equation

EXAMPLE 5

Find the points where the quadratic function $y = 3x^2 + 12x + 12$ crosses the axes.

Solution

$y = 3x^2 + 12x + 12$

$b^2 - 4ac = 144 - 144 = 0 \Rightarrow b^2 = 4ac$

Crosses *y*-axis: $x = 0$

$y = 12$

It crosses the y-axis at (0, 12).

Crosses *x*-axis: $y = 0$

$3x^2 + 12x + 12 = 0$

$x^2 + 4x + 4 = 0$

$(x + 2)(x + 2) = 0$

$x = -2, -2$

It crosses the x-axis at $P(-2, 0)$.

(iii) $b^2 - 4ac < 0 \Rightarrow b^2 < 4ac$

This means there are **no real roots** of $y = 0$. (They are complex.) The graph of $y = ax^2 + bx + c$ does **not** cross the x-axis at any point.

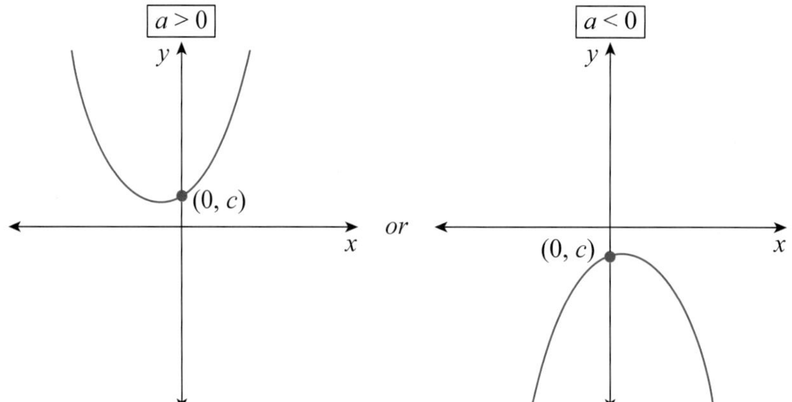

EXAMPLE 6

Find the points where $y = x^2 - 2x + 8$ crosses the axes.

Solution

$y = x^2 - 2x + 8$

$b^2 - 4ac = -28 < 0 \Rightarrow b^2 < 4ac$ [No real roots]

Crosses *y*-axis: $x = 0$

$y = 8$

It crosses the y-axis at (0, 8).

Crosses *x*-axis: $y = 0$

$x^2 - 2x + 8 = 0$

There are no real values of x.

Therefore, the curve does not cross the x-axis.

EXAMPLE 7

An underground geyser at $x = 0$ projects a jet of hot water along a path described by the equation $y = \frac{(8-x)(x-2)}{8}$, where x and y are in tens of metres and $y = 0$ is the horizontal ground.

(a) Find the depth of the source of the geyser below the ground.

(b) Find the points where the waterjet hits the ground.

(c) Plot its trajectory for $0 \le x \le 8$.

Solution

$y = \frac{1}{8}(8-x)(x-2)$

(a) $\boldsymbol{x = 0}$: $y = \frac{1}{8}(8)(-2) = -2$

It crosses the y-axis at $(0, -2) \Rightarrow -2$ is the y-intercept.

This is 20 m below the ground.

(b) $\boldsymbol{y = 0}$: $\frac{1}{8}(8-x)(x-2) = 0$

$x = 8, 2$

It crosses the x-axis at (8, 0) and (2, 0). This means the x-intercepts are at 20 m and 80 m from $x = 0$.

(c)

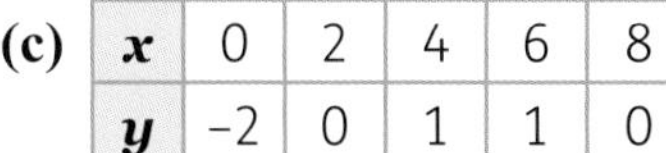

x	0	2	4	6	8
y	−2	0	1	1	0

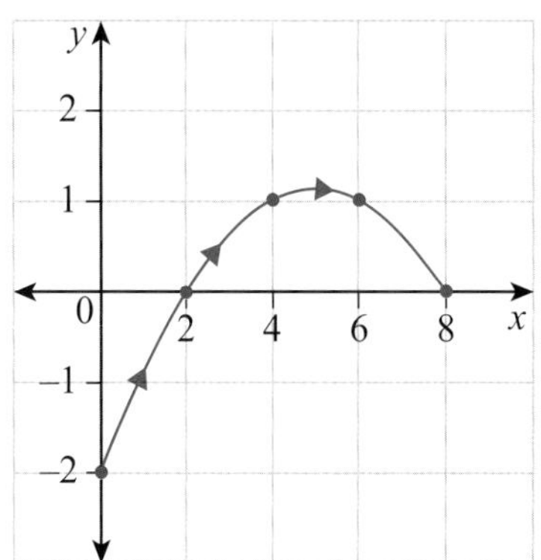

2. Finding the maximum and minimum points (vertices or turning points) of a quadratic function

Given the quadratic function $y = ax^2 + bx + c$, the maximum or minimum values of the function occur at $x = -\frac{b}{2a}$. You will see why this is the case in Section 8 Differentiation.

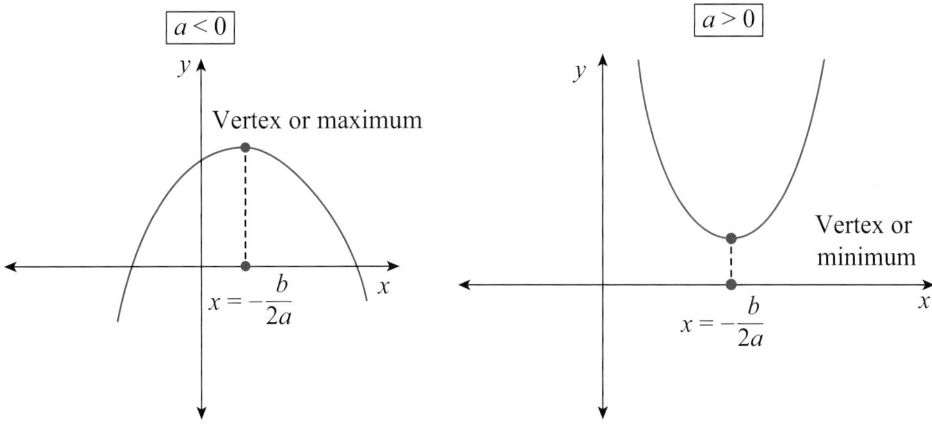

The vertex is the most important point on a quadratic graph.

EXAMPLE 8

Find the co-ordinates of the point V which gives $y = 3x^2 - 12x + 5$ its minimum value.

Solution

$y = 3x^2 - 12x + 5$

$a = 3, b = -12, c = 5$

As $a > 0$, the quadratic graph is cup-shaped and so the vertex is the point at which the minimum value of the function occurs.

At the vertex: $x = -\frac{b}{2a} = \frac{-(-12)}{6} = 2$

$\mathbf{x = 2:}\ y = 3(2)^2 - 12(2) + 5 = -7$

Therefore, the co-ordinates of the vertex are $V(2, -7)$. The minimum value of the function is -7.

EXAMPLE 9

Find the co-ordinates of the point V which gives $y = -2x^2 - x + 7$ its maximum value.

Solution

$y = -2x^2 - x + 7$

$a = -2, b = -1, c = 7$

As $a < 0$, the quadratic graph is cap-shaped and so the vertex is the point at which the maximum value of the function occurs.

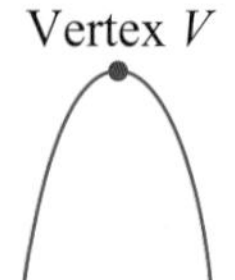

At the vertex: $x = -\frac{b}{2a} = -\frac{-(-1)}{2(-2)} = -\frac{1}{4}$

$\mathbf{x = -\frac{1}{4}:}\ y = -2\left(-\frac{1}{4}\right)^2 - \left(-\frac{1}{4}\right) + 7 = \frac{57}{8}$

Therefore, the co-ordinates of the vertex are $V\left(-\frac{1}{4}, \frac{57}{8}\right)$. The maximum value of the function is $\frac{57}{8}$.

EXAMPLE 10

A ball is projected vertically upwards from the top of a 20 m high cliff. The ball's height h, in metres above the ground, t seconds after it is thrown is given by: $h = -9{\cdot}8t^2 + 19{\cdot}6t + 20$.

(a) Find its maximum height above the ground.

(b) Find when it hits the ground, correct to two decimal places.

Solution

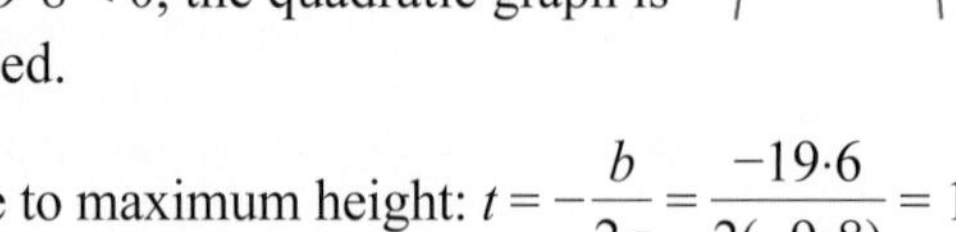

$h = -9{\cdot}8t^2 + 19{\cdot}6t + 20$

$a = -9{\cdot}8, b = 19{\cdot}6, c = 20$

As $a = -9{\cdot}8 < 0$, the quadratic graph is cap-shaped.

(a) Time to maximum height: $t = -\frac{b}{2a} = \frac{-19{\cdot}6}{2(-9{\cdot}8)} = 1$

$\mathbf{t = 1:}\ h = (-9{\cdot}8)(1)^2 + 19{\cdot}6(1) + 20 = 29{\cdot}8$ m

(b) $\mathbf{h = 0:}\ -9{\cdot}8t^2 + 19{\cdot}6t + 20 = 0$

$9{\cdot}8t^2 - 19{\cdot}6t - 20 = 0$

$t = \frac{19{\cdot}6 \pm \sqrt{19{\cdot}6^2 + 4 \times 9{\cdot}8 \times 20}}{19{\cdot}6}$

$= 2{\cdot}74$ *or* $-0{\cdot}74$ [Reject the negative value.]

$t = 2{\cdot}74$ s

It hits the ground after $2{\cdot}74$ s.

3. Finding the axis of symmetry

The axis of symmetry of a quadratic function $y = ax^2 + bx + c$ is the line through the vertex V parallel to the y-axis.

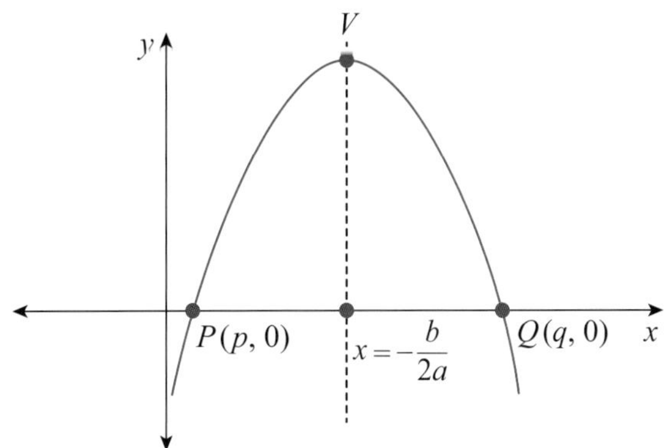

The equation of the axis of symmetry is $x = -\dfrac{b}{2a}$.

This means the roots of $ax^2 + bx + c = 0$ are symmetrical about $x = -\dfrac{b}{2a}$.

$P(p, 0)$ $\qquad$ V $\qquad$ $Q(q, 0)$

$$p = \frac{-b - \sqrt{b^2 - 4ac}}{2a} \qquad -\frac{b}{2a} \qquad q = \frac{-b + \sqrt{b^2 - 4ac}}{2a}$$

$V\left(-\dfrac{b}{2a}, 0\right)$ is the midpoint of $P(p, 0)$ and $Q(q, 0)$.

EXAMPLE 11

For the quadratic function $y = x^2 - 2x - 8$, find the point V which gives the function its minimum value. Find the roots of $x^2 - 2x - 8 = 0$ and show they are symmetrical about the x co-ordinate of V.

Solution

$y = x^2 - 2x - 8$

$a = 1, b = -2, c = -8$

Vertex V: $x = \dfrac{-b}{2a} = \dfrac{2}{2} = 1$

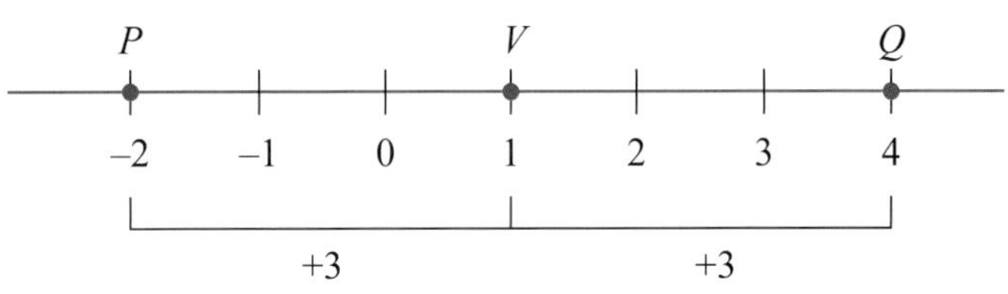

The x co-ordinate of V is 1.

$x = 1$: $y = (1)^2 - 2(1) - 8 = -9$

Therefore, the co-ordinates of the vertex are $V(1, -9)$.

Roots: $x^2 - 2x - 8 = 0$

$(x + 2)(x - 4) = 0$

$x = -2, 4$

1 is the midpoint of the roots.

EXAMPLE 12

For the function $y = -2x^2 + 5x + 3, -1 \le x \le 3, x \in \mathbb{R}$, find where it crosses the axes. Find the co-ordinates of its vertex and the equation of the axis of symmetry.

Solution

$y = -2x^2 + 5x + 3, -1 \le x \le 3, x \in \mathbb{R}$

$a = -2, b = 5, c = 3$

Crosses y-axis: $x = 0$

$y = 3$

It crosses the y-axis at $(0, 3)$.

Crosses x-axis: $y = 0$

$-2x^2 + 5x + 3 = 0$

$2x^2 - 5x - 3 = 0$

$(2x + 1)(x - 3) = 0$

$x = -\frac{1}{2}, 3$

It crosses the x-axis at $\left(-\frac{1}{2}, 0\right)$ and $(3, 0)$.

Vertex V: $x = \dfrac{3 + \left(-\frac{1}{2}\right)}{2} = \dfrac{5}{4} = 1\frac{1}{4}$ [Midpoint of the roots]

or

$x = -\dfrac{b}{2a} = -\dfrac{5}{2(-2)} = \dfrac{5}{4}$

$x = \frac{5}{4}$ is the equation of the axis of symmetry.

$\mathbf{x = \frac{5}{4}}$**:** $y = -2\left(\frac{5}{4}\right)^2 + 5\left(\frac{5}{4}\right) + 3 = \dfrac{49}{8} = 6\frac{1}{8}$

Co-ordinates of the vertex: $V\left(\dfrac{5}{4}, \dfrac{49}{8}\right)$

EXAMPLE 13

Show that the function $y = x^2 - 2x + 5 = 0, x \in \mathbb{R}$, does not cross the x-axis. Plot it by finding its vertex and where it crosses the y-axis.

Solution

$y = x^2 - 2x + 5$

$a = 1, b = -2, c = 5$

Crosses x-axis: $b^2 - 4ac = -16 < 0$

Therefore, the graph does not cross the x-axis.

Vertex V: $x = -\dfrac{b}{2a} = \dfrac{2}{2} = 1$

$x = 1$: $y = 1 - 2 + 5 = 4$

Co-ordinates of vertex : $V(1, 4)$

Crosses y-axis: $x = 0 \Rightarrow y = 5$

It crosses the y-axis at $(0, 5)$.

The axis of symmetry is $x = 1$.

Find two points to the left and to the right of the axis of symmetry.

	←			→	
x	-1	0	1	2	3
y	8	5	4	5	8

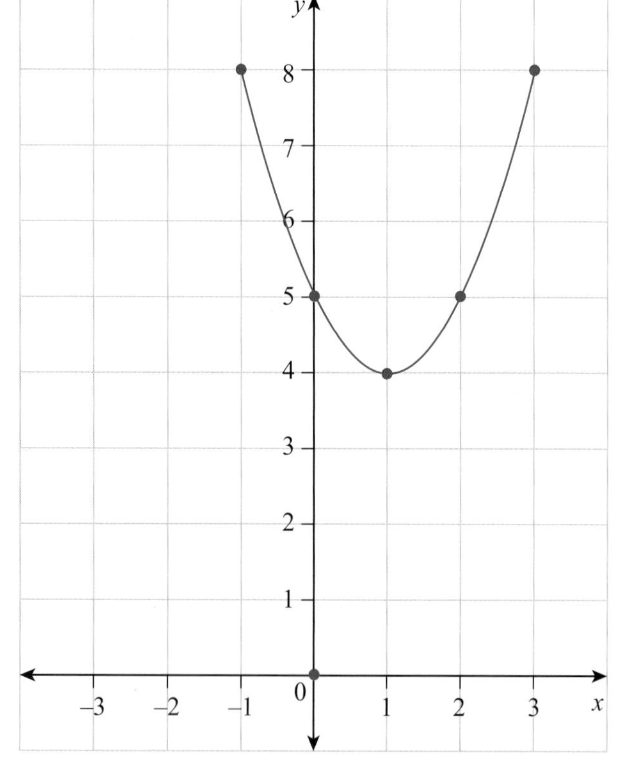

4. Finding the vertex by completing the square

Completing the square on the right-hand side of $y = ax^2 + bx + c$:

$$y = a\left(x^2 + \frac{b}{a}x + \frac{c}{a}\right)$$

$$= a\left\{\left(x + \frac{b}{2a}\right)^2 - \frac{b^2}{4a^2} + \frac{c}{a}\right\}$$

$$= a\left(x + \frac{b}{2a}\right)^2 + \left(c - \frac{b^2}{4a}\right) \quad \left[c - \frac{b^2}{4a} \text{ is constant.}\right]$$

1. For $a > 0$ (cup-shaped), $a\left(x + \frac{b}{2a}\right)^2 \geq 0$ for all $x \in \mathbb{R}$.

Therefore, the minimum value of y occurs when $\left(x + \frac{b}{2a}\right) = 0$, i.e. at $x = -\frac{b}{2a}$.

The minimum value of y is given by $y = c - \frac{b^2}{4a}$.

The co-ordinates of the vertex V are $\left(-\frac{b}{2a}, c - \frac{b^2}{4a}\right)$.

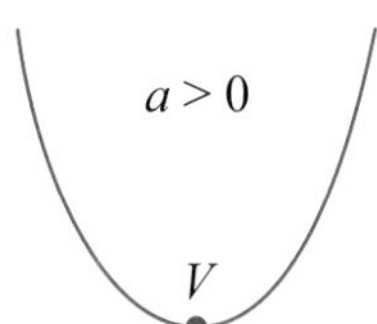

2. For $a < 0$ (cap-shaped), $a\left(x + \frac{b}{2a}\right)^2 \leq 0$ for all $x \in \mathbb{R}$.

Therefore, the maximum value of y occurs when $\left(x + \frac{b}{2a}\right) = 0$, i.e. at $x = -\frac{b}{2a}$.

The maximum value of y is given by $y = c - \frac{b^2}{4a}$.

The co-ordinates of the vertex V are $\left(-\frac{b}{2a}, c - \frac{b^2}{4a}\right)$.

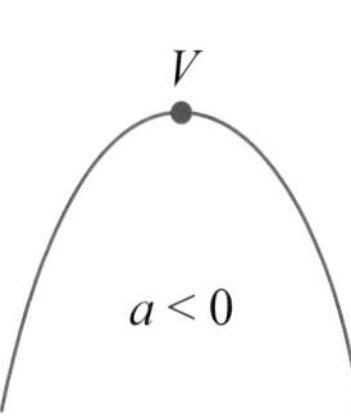

EXAMPLE 14

By completing the square, find the maximum or minimum values of:

(a) $y = 2x^2 - 6x + 1$ **(b)** $y = -3x^2 + 5x - 1$

Solution

(a) $y = 2x^2 - 6x + 1$

$$= 2\left(x^2 - 3x + \frac{1}{2}\right)$$

$$= 2\left\{\left(x - \frac{3}{2}\right)^2 - \frac{9}{4} + \frac{1}{2}\right\}$$

$$= 2\left\{\left(x - \frac{3}{2}\right)^2 - \frac{7}{4}\right\}$$

$$= 2\left(x - \frac{3}{2}\right)^2 - \frac{7}{2}$$

Now, $2\left(x - \frac{3}{2}\right)^2 \geq 0$ for all $x \in \mathbb{R}$.

Therefore, the minimum value of y occurs when $\left(x - \frac{3}{2}\right)^2 = 0 \Rightarrow x = \frac{3}{2}$.

The minimum value of $y = -\frac{7}{2}$.

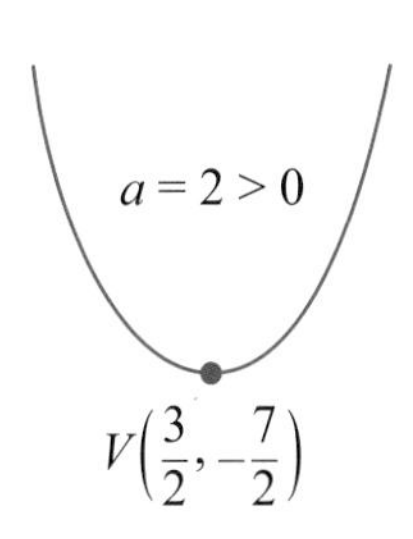

(b) $y = -3x^2 + 5x - 1$

$$y = -3\left\{x^2 - \frac{5}{3}x + \frac{1}{3}\right\}$$
$$= -3\left\{\left(x - \frac{5}{6}\right)^2 - \frac{25}{36} + \frac{1}{3}\right\}$$
$$= -3\left\{\left(x - \frac{5}{6}\right)^2 - \frac{13}{36}\right\}$$
$$= \frac{13}{12} - 3\left(x - \frac{5}{6}\right)^2$$

Now, $-3\left(x - \frac{5}{6}\right)^2 \leq 0$ for all $x \in \mathbb{R}$.

The maximum value of y occurs when $\left(x - \frac{5}{6}\right)^2 = 0 \Rightarrow x = \frac{5}{6}$.

The maximum value of $y = \frac{13}{12}$.

$V\left(\frac{5}{6}, \frac{13}{12}\right)$

$a = -3$
< 0

20.4 Finding the equation of a quadratic function from its graph

1. No roots: $b^2 - 4ac < 0$

ACTIVITY 9

ACTION
Writing the equation of a quadratic function from its graph

OBJECTIVE
To write the equation of a function by looking at its graph

EXAMPLE 15

If the quadratic curve shown has vertex (2, 3) and crosses the y-axis at (0, 6), find its equation in the form $y = ax^2 + bx + c$.

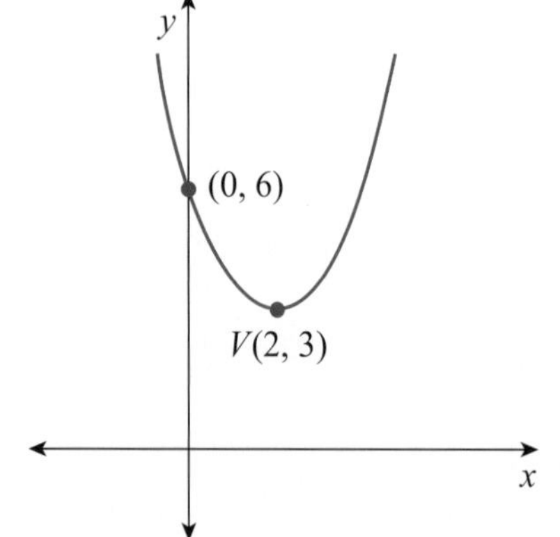

Solution

Crosses y-axis:

$x = 0 \Rightarrow y = c = 6$

Vertex V: $(2, 3) \Rightarrow x = -\frac{b}{2a} = 2$

$\therefore b = -4a$

(2, 3) is on the curve: $y = ax^2 - 4ax + 6$

$3 = 4a - 8a + 6$

$4a = 3$

$a = \frac{3}{4}$

$y = \frac{3}{4}x^2 - 3x + 6$

2. Two roots: $b^2 - 4ac \geq 0$

There are many quadratic equations which have the same two roots.

- $x^2 - 3x + 2 = 0$
- $4(x^2 - 3x + 2) = 0$
- $3x^2 - 9x + 6 = 0$
- $k(x^2 - 3x + 2) = 0$

All of the above equations have roots equal to 1 and 2.

To form a quadratic function from its roots, multiply $(x^2 - Sx + P)$ by a constant k.

$y = k(x^2 - Sx + P)$, $k \in \mathbb{R}$, is the equation of a quadratic function where S is the sum of its roots and P is the product of its roots.

EXAMPLE 16

Form the quadratic function $y = ax^2 + bx + c$ from its graph, as shown. Find the co-ordinates of the vertex V.

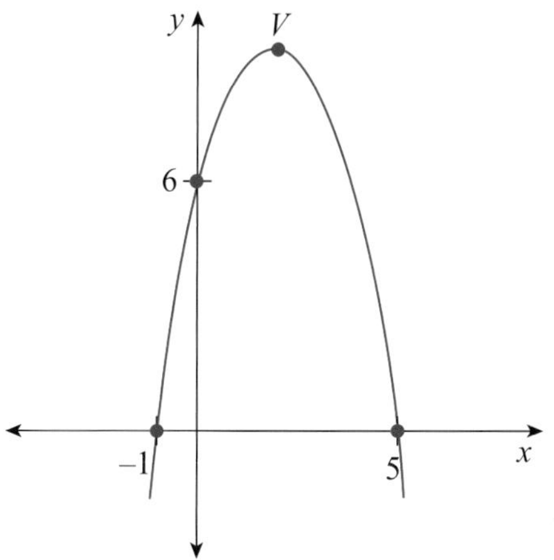

Solution

$y = k(x^2 - Sx + P)$

Roots: $-1, 5$

$S = -1 + 5 = 4$, $P = -1 \times 5 = -5$

$\therefore y = k(x^2 - 4x - 5)$

$(0, 6)$ is on the curve.

$6 = k(-5)$

$k = -\frac{6}{5}$

$y = -\frac{6}{5}x^2 + \frac{24}{5}x + 6$

Vertex V: $x = -\frac{b}{2a} \Rightarrow x = -\frac{24}{2 \times 5} \times -\frac{5}{6} = \frac{4}{2} = 2$ *or* halfway between the roots (-1 and 5).

$y = -\frac{6}{5}(4) + \frac{24}{5}(2) + 6 = \frac{54}{5}$

Co-ordinates of V: $\left(2, \frac{54}{5}\right)$

EXAMPLE 17

Form the quadratic function $y = ax^2 + bx + c$ from its graph, as shown, if $x = -1$ is the x co-ordinate of its vertex.

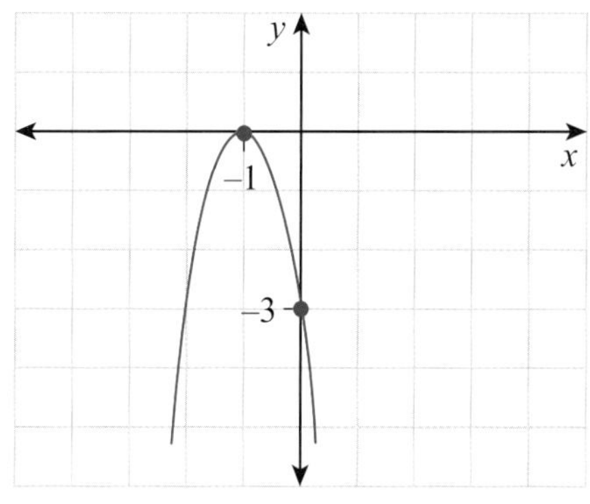

Solution

The vertex V is on the x-axis. Therefore, there are two equal roots: $-1, -1$.

$S = -2$, $P = 1$

$\therefore y = k(x^2 + 2x + 1)$

$(0, -3)$ is on the curve.

$-3 = k(1)$

$k = -3$

$y = -3x^2 - 6x - 3$

EXERCISE 9

1. Draw the following quadratic functions on graph paper in the given domain, $x \in \mathbb{R}$:

> **Note:** This is also Activity 7. The activity supplies you with the appropriate grids.

(a) $f(x) = 2x^2 - 5x + 1, -1 \leq x \leq 3$

(b) $f(x) = -2x^2 + 3x + 4, -2{\cdot}5 \leq x \leq 3$

(c) $f(x) = x^2 - 2x + 1, -1 \leq x \leq 3$

(d) $f(x) = -4x^2 + 4x - 1, -1 \leq x \leq 1$

(e) $f(x) = 2x^2 + 3x + 2, -2{\cdot}5 \leq x \leq 1$

(f) $f(x) = -x^2 + 2x - 3, -1 \leq x \leq 3$

2. Find the points at which the following quadratic functions cross the axes. Give all answers as rational or irrational numbers. If the curve does not cross the x-axis, say so.

(a) $y = x^2 - 1$ **(f)** $y = -3x^2 + 8x - 4$

(b) $y = 3x^2 + 1$ **(g)** $y = 4 - (x - 1)^2$

(c) $y = x^2 - 5x + 6$ **(h)** $y = 4(x - 2)^2 - 9$

(d) $y = (2 - x)(x - 1)$ **(i)** $y = -x^2 - 5x + 7$

(e) $y = 2(2x - 1)^2$ **(j)** $y = 2x^2 + 7x - 11$

3. For all the functions in Question 2, find the co-ordinates of the maximum or minimum value of the quadratic function and write down the equation of the axis of symmetry of each curve.

4. By calculating $b^2 - 4ac$, state for each quadratic function, $y = ax^2 + bx + c$, whether the function crosses the x-axis at:

(i) no points,

(ii) one point, or

(iii) two different points.

(a) $y = x^2 - 5$ **(f)** $y = 4(3x - 2)^2$

(b) $y = 3x^2 + 7$ **(g)** $y = 4x^2 - 1$

(c) $y = x^2 - 7x + 12$ **(h)** $y = 4x^2 - 7x - 1$

(d) $y = 5x^2 - 2x + 3$ **(i)** $y = (2x - 1)(3x + 5)$

(e) $y = 15 + 14x - 8x^2$ **(j)** $y = 3(2 - 3x)^2$

5. By completing the square for each quadratic function, find the co-ordinates of the vertex V:

(a) $y = x^2 + 2x - 11$

(b) $y = 2x^2 + 8x - 3$

(c) $y = -x^2 - 5x + 3$

(d) $y = -3x^2 + 7x - 9$

6. Find b and c, if:

(a) $y = -4x^2 + bx + c$ has a vertex at $(1, 3)$

(b) $y = 3x^2 + bx + c$ has a vertex at $(-2, 0)$

(c) $y = (2x + b)^2$ has a vertex at $x = -1$

(d) $y = \dfrac{x^2}{2} - bx + c$ has a vertex at $(4, 2)$

7. Write an equation in the form $y = ax^2 + bx + c$ for the functions graphed below:

(a)

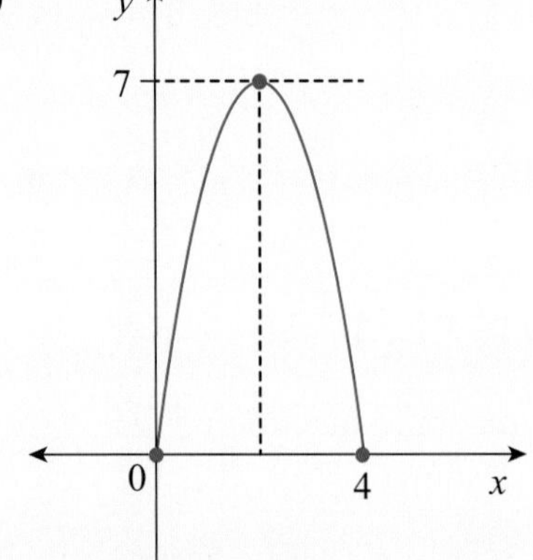

(b)

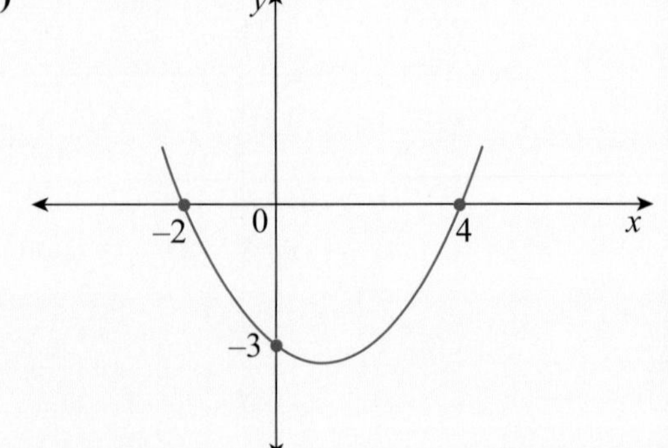

(c)

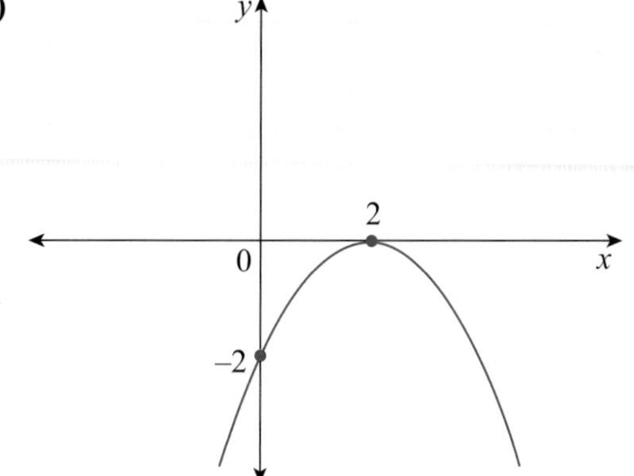

(d)

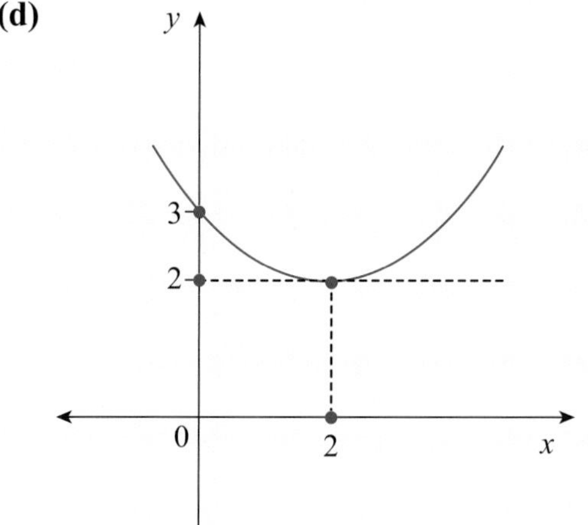

(e)

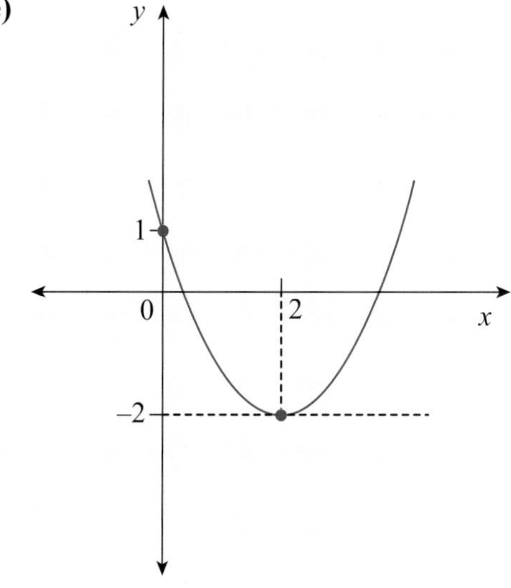

(f)

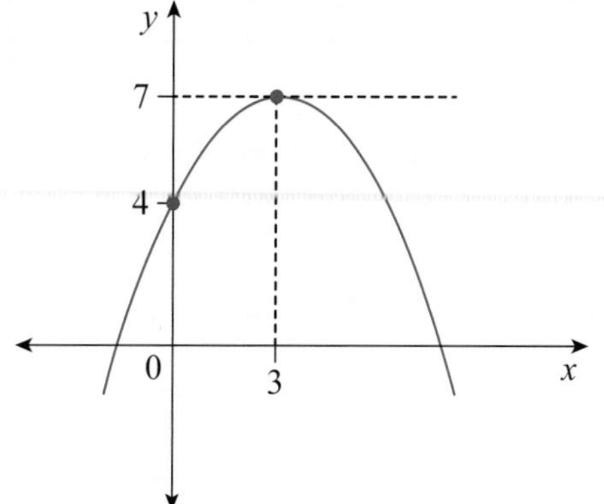

(g)

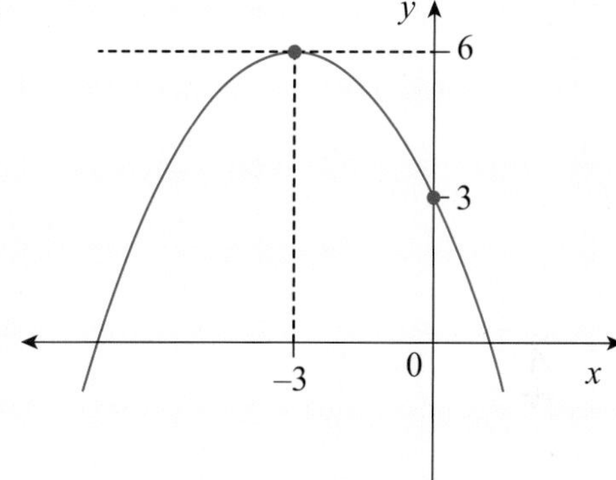

(h)

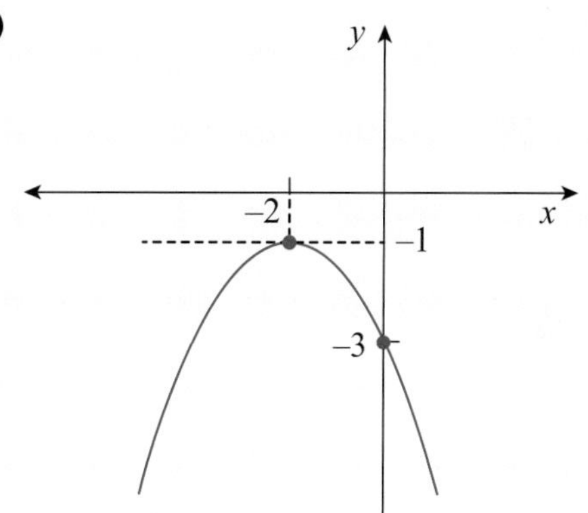

8. Write the equation of the quadratic function $y = ax^2 + bx + c$ with the following features:

(a) points where the graph cuts the x-axis: (–5, 0) and (2, 0), point where the graph cuts the y-axis: (0, 3)

(b) vertex (–3, 0), point where the graph cuts the y-axis: (0, 2)

(c) vertex (–3, –4), point where the graph cuts the y-axis: (0, –1)

(d) vertex (–2, 5), passing through (3, –2)

20.5 Intersecting quadratic functions

In general, to find where two functions f and g intersect, equate their y co-ordinates and solve. Alternatively, plot the functions on the same diagram and read off their points of intersection.

Finding the points(s) of intersection

1. Algebraically: Equate the y co-ordinates and solve the resulting equation.
2. Graphically: Plot the functions on the same graph paper and read off their points of intersection.

ACTIVITY 10

ACTION
Intersecting quadratic functions

OBJECTIVE
To plot two functions (either a linear and quadratic or two quadratics) and find their points of intersection both graphically and algebraically

EXAMPLE 18

A road with equation $y = f(x) = x^2 - 5x + 7$ is passing through a town. The road that bypasses the town is a motorway with equation $y = g(x) = x + 2$. Find the points where the road intersects the motorway. If all of the distances are in kilometres (km), find the least time a car can travel between these points if the speed limit is 120 km/h. Put the answer in minutes to one decimal place.

Solution

$y = g(x) = x + 2$

$y = f(x) = x^2 - 5x + 7$

$x + 2 = x^2 - 5x + 7$

$x^2 - 6x + 5 = 0$

$(x - 1)(x - 5) = 0$

$x = 1, 5$

Substituting into g: $y = 3, 7$

$\therefore A(1, 3)\ B(5, 7)$

$|AB| = \sqrt{16 + 16} = \sqrt{32}$ km

$v = \frac{s}{t} \Rightarrow t = \frac{s}{v} = \frac{\sqrt{32}}{120} = \frac{\sqrt{2}}{30}$ s

$t = \frac{\sqrt{2}}{30} \times 60$ minutes

$= 2\sqrt{2}$ minutes

$= 2{\cdot}8$ minutes

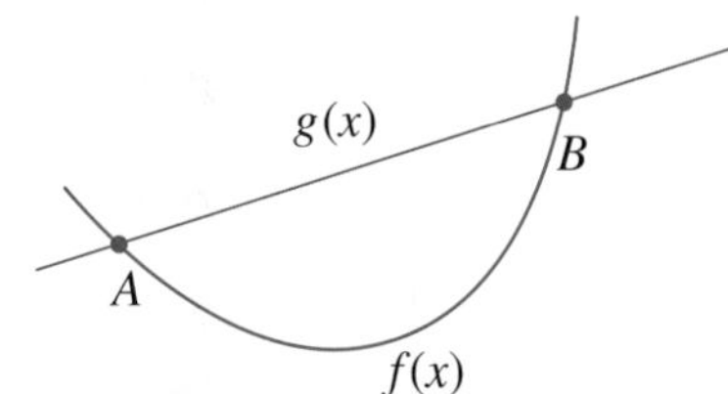

EXAMPLE 19

Plot the graph of $f(x) = x^2 - x - 6$, $-3 \le x \le 4$, $x \in \mathbb{R}$.

(a) Use the graph to solve $f(x) = 0$ and to find its y-intercept. Verify the results algebraically.

(b) Use the graph to solve $f(x) = 2$. Verify the results algebraically.

Give all answers correct to one decimal place.

Solution

x	-3	-2	-1	0	1	2	3	4
f	6	0	-4	-6	-6	-4	0	6

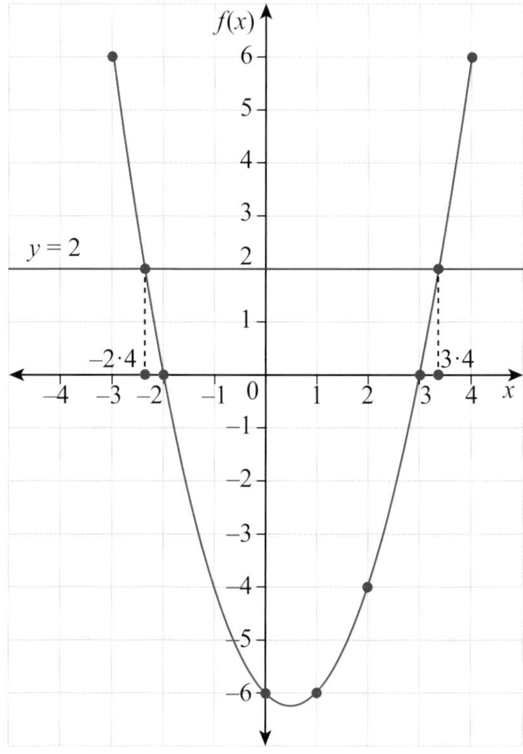

(a) Graph: $y = 0$: $x = -2, 3$

[The roots are where the graph cuts the x-axis.]

y-intercept: $y = -6$

Algebra: $f(x) = 0$:

$x^2 - x - 6 = 0$

$(x + 2)(x - 3) = 0$

$x = -2, 3$

y-intercept: $f(0) = (0)^2 - (0) - 6 = -6$

$y = -6$

(b) Draw the line $y = 2$.

Graph: $f(x) = 2$:

$x = -2{\cdot}4, 3{\cdot}4$

Algebra: $f(x) = 2$:

$x^2 - x - 6 = 2$

$x^2 - x - 8 = 0$

Use the quadratic formula: $a = 1, b = -1, c = -8$

$$x = \frac{-(-1) \pm \sqrt{(-1)^2 - 4(1)(-8)}}{2(1)}$$

$$= \frac{1 \pm \sqrt{1 + 32}}{2}$$

$$= \frac{1 \pm \sqrt{33}}{2}$$

$$= -2{\cdot}4, 3{\cdot}4$$

EXAMPLE 20

Using the table below, plot graphs of f and g on the same diagram for $-2 \le x \le 4$, $x \in \mathbb{R}$, where $f(x) = x^2 - 2x - 7$ and $g(x) = x - 6$.

x	-2	-1	0	1	2	3	4
f							
g							

(a) Use your graphs to solve $x^2 - 3x - 1 = 0$, correct to one decimal place.

(b) Solve $x^2 - 3x - 1 = 0$ algebraically, correct to one decimal place.

Solution

x	-2	-1	0	1	2	3	4
f	1	-4	-7	-8	-7	-4	1
g	-8	-7	-6	-5	-4	-3	-2

(a) $f(x) = g(x)$

$x^2 - 2x - 7 = x - 6$

$x^2 - 3x - 1 = 0$

$x = -0{\cdot}3, 3{\cdot}3$

(b) $x^2 - 3x - 1 = 0$

Use the quadratic formula: $a = 1, b = -3, c = -1$

$$x = \frac{-b \pm \sqrt{b^2 - 4ac}}{2a}$$

$$= \frac{-(-3) \pm \sqrt{(-3)^2 - 4(1)(-1)}}{2(1)}$$

$$= \frac{3 \pm \sqrt{9+4}}{2} = \frac{3 \pm \sqrt{13}}{2}$$

$= -0{\cdot}3, 3{\cdot}3$

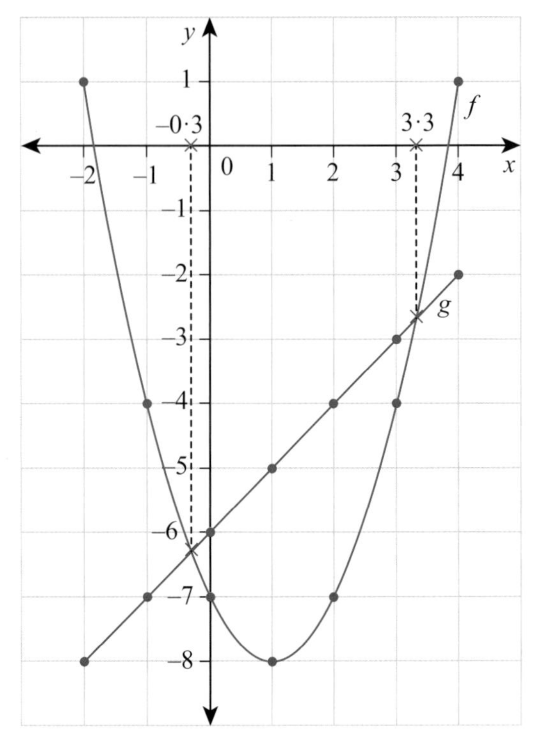

EXAMPLE 21

A plane flying along the curve $y = f(x) = x^2, x \geq 0, x \in \mathbb{R}$, is struck by a bird flying along the curve $y = g(x) = 9 - x^2, x \geq 0, x \in \mathbb{R}$. Plot the functions f and g on the same diagram and use it to estimate their point of intersection. By solving $f(x) = g(x)$, verify your estimate.

Solution

x	0	1	2	3
f	0	1	4	9
g	9	8	5	0

Graph: Co-ordinates of P: $x = 2{\cdot}1, y = 4{\cdot}5$

Algebra: $x^2 = 9 - x^2$

$2x^2 = 9$

$x^2 = \frac{9}{2}$

$x = \pm\frac{3}{\sqrt{2}} = \pm\frac{3\sqrt{2}}{2}$

$y = \frac{9}{2}$

Co-ordinates of $P\left(\frac{3\sqrt{2}}{2}, \frac{9}{2}\right) = (2{\cdot}1, 4{\cdot}5)$ on your calculator.

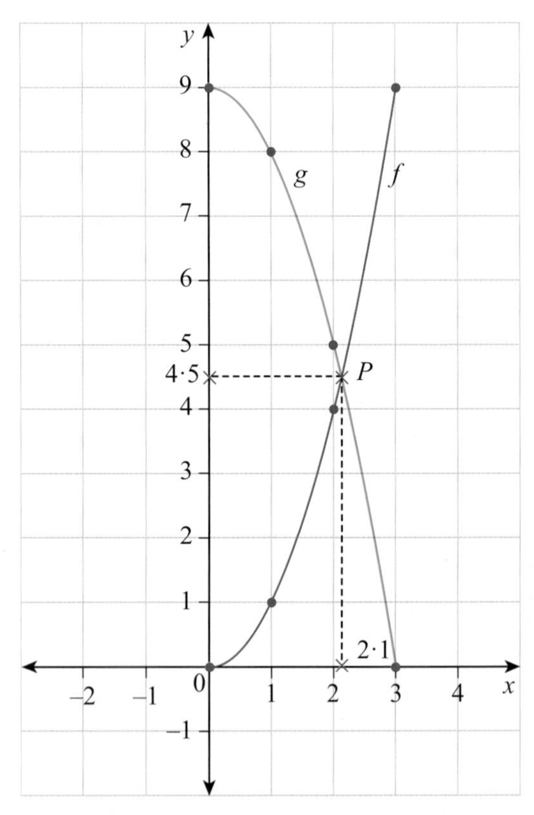

EXERCISE 10

1. Using the same grid, graph the following functions in the given domain for $x \in \mathbb{R}$. Use the graphs to solve $f(x) = g(x)$ for x, correct to one decimal place. Verify your answer algebraically.

> **Note:** This is also Activity 10.
> The activity supplies you with the appropriate grids.

(a) $f(x) = 2x^2 + 3x - 2$ and $g(x) = 2$, $-3 \le x \le 1$

(b) $f(x) = -x^2 + 2x + 5$ and $g(x) = -1$, $-2 \le x \le 4$

(c) $f(x) = -x^2 - 2x + 2$ and $g(x) = x + 1$, $-4 \le x \le 1$

(d) $f(x) = 3x^2 - 7x - 1$ and $g(x) = -2x + 3$, $-1 \le x \le 3$

(e) $f(x) = x^2 - 6$ and $g(x) = -x^2 + 4x + 5$, $-4 \le x \le 1$

(f) $f(x) = x^2 + 3$ and $g(x) = 3x^2 - x$, $-1{\cdot}5 \le x \le 2$

2. Given $f(x) = 2x^2 + 5x - 3$, $x \in \mathbb{R}$:

(a) Find:

(i) the co-ordinates of the point where f crosses the y-axis,

(ii) the co-ordinates of the points where f crosses the x-axis,

(iii) the minimum point of f.

(b) Plot f roughly on graph paper.

3. Temperatures T in degrees Celsius (°C) are recorded over a 6-hour period. The table below shows the temperature T at various times t in hours.

Time t (hours)	0	1	2	3	4	5	6
Temperature T (°C)	7	2	−1	−2	−1	2	7

(a) Plot a graph of T against t on graph paper.

(b) Use the graph to estimate:

(i) the temperature when $t = 3{\cdot}5$ hours, correct to one decimal place,

(ii) the difference between the highest and lowest temperatures for $0 \le t \le 6$,

(iii) how long in hours, correct to one decimal place, the temperature was above 2·5 °C,

(iv) when in hours the temperature is 0 °C, correct to one decimal place.

(c) If $T = at^2 + bt + c$, use the results in the table to find a, b, c.

4. The path of a jet of water from a hose is given by $h = -\frac{2}{25}(x - 20)^2 + 50$, $0 \le x \le 40$, $x \in \mathbb{R}$, where h is the height above the ground in centimetres and x is the horizontal distance from the nozzle in centimetres.

(a) Plot a graph of h against x using the table below.

x (cm)	0	10	20	30	40
h (cm)					

(b) Use your graph to find:

(i) the height of the jet when $x = 25$ cm,

(ii) the horizontal distances the jet is from the nozzle when its height is 35 cm,

(iii) the maximum height of the jet.

Give all answers correct to the nearest whole number.

5. The height h in metres of a model rocket in flight can be approximated by $h = -5t^2 + 24t + 1$, $0 \le t \le 4$, where t is the time in seconds.

(a) By copying and completing the table below, plot a graph of h against t on graph paper.

t (s)	0	1	2	3	4
h (m)					

(b) Use your graph to find:

(i) the height of the rocket after 3·5 s, correct to the nearest metre,

(ii) when the rocket is at 18 m, correct to one decimal place,

(iii) the maximum height of the rocket, correct to the nearest metre.

(c) If the exact equation for the height is $h = -4{\cdot}9t^2 + 24t + 1$, calculate the maximum height exactly.

(d) Find the percentage error in the maximum height read off the graph as a percentage of the exact value, correct to one decimal place.

6. A hang glider takes off from a point above horizontal ground. Its height f in hundreds of metres is given by $f(x) = -\frac{2}{9}x^2 + \frac{4}{3}x + 4, x \in \mathbb{R}$, where x is its horizontal distance in hundreds of metres from its starting point.
It lands on sloping ground with equation $y = g(x) = \frac{1}{5}x, x \in \mathbb{R}$.

(a) Copy and complete the table below, giving all answers correct to two significant figures.

x	0	1	2	3	4	5	6	7	8
f									
g									

(b) Plot graphs of f and g on the same diagram.

(c) Use the graphs to find:

(i) the maximum height in metres of the hang glider above horizontal ground,

(ii) its height in metres above the ground when it lands on the sloping ground.

Give both answers correct to two significant figures.

7. The price P_1 in euro per share of a banking stock varies over a 12-year period, according to the equation $P_1 = -x^2 + 15x + 12$. The price P_2 in euro per share of another banking stock varied over the same period, according to the equation $P_2 = 3x + 32$. x is the number of years after the year 2000.

(a) For what values of x are the two stock prices the same?

(b) For what values of x is $P_1 > P_2$?

8. The demand d for an item is given by $d = 125 - 5x$, where €x is the selling price of the item.

(a) Write down an inequality satisfied by x.

(b) The revenue R in euro for a selling price of €x per item is given by $R = x(125 - 5x)$. Copy and complete the table by plotting R and d against x on the same graph for $0 \le x \le 25, x \in \mathbb{R}$.

x	0	5	10	15	20	25
R						
d						

(c) Use your graphs to find:

(i) the maximum revenue, correct to two significant figures,

(ii) the value of x that gives this maximum revenue, correct to one decimal place,

(iii) x when $R = 600$, correct to the nearest whole number,

(iv) d when $R = 500$, correct to the nearest whole number.

(d) Calculate the maximum value of R.

9. Find the points of intersection of $f(x) = x^2 - x + 6$ and $g(x) = 2x^2 - 4x + 2$.

10. The paths of two asteroids, Frog f and Grog g, are mapped on a computer screen. The equations of their paths are given by: $f(x) = -x^2 + 4x + 8$ and $g(x) = x^2 - 8x + 26$. Show that their paths intersect at one point and find this point.

11. An athlete runs along a straight road. His distance s in metres from a fixed point B on the road is measured at different times t in seconds. s and t are related by the equation $s = at^2 + bt + c$. The distances are recorded as follows:

t	1	2	3	4	5	6
s	16	9	4	1	p	q

(a) Find a, b, c.

(b) Find p and q.

(c) Plot s against t on graph paper.

(d) Find how far the athlete is from B at $t = 8$.

(e) Why is the athlete moving towards B when $t < 5$ but moving away when $t > 5$?

12. (a) (i) Express $x^2 - 4x + 11$ in the form $(x - p)^2 + q$.

(ii) Hence, or otherwise, find the co-ordinates of the vertex of the curve $y = x^2 - 4x + 11, x \in \mathbb{R}$.

(iii) Is this vertex a minimum or a maximum? Why?

(b) The line g has equation $g(x) = 2x + 18$ and the curve f has equation $f(x) = x^2 - 4x + 11$. Find the points of intersection of f and g.

13. The graphs of $f(x) = px^2 + qx + r$ and $g(x) = -2x + 6$ are sketched below. (1, 12) are the co-ordinates of the maximum value of f. g crosses the x-axis at B.

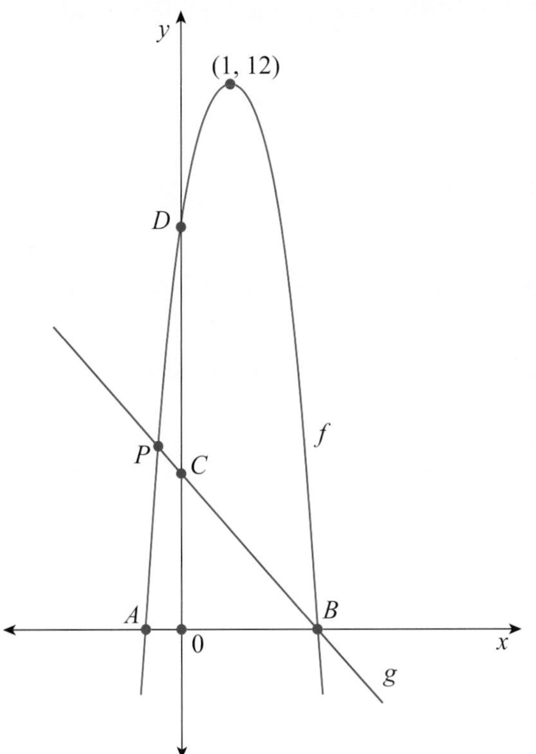

(a) Find B.

(b) Find C.

(c) Find A.

(d) Find p, q and r.

(e) Find D.

(f) Find P.

Cubic Functions

Learning Outcomes

- To recognise a cubic function: $y = f(x) = ax^3 + bx^2 + cx + d$.
- To be able to plot a graph of a cubic function and recognise the various shapes of cubic graphs.
- To be able to find properties of cubic functions (crossing axes).
- To work with intersecting graphs.
- To understand how to transform functions.
- To use cubic functions to solve real-life problems.

21.1 What is a cubic function?

A cubic function is a relationship between two variables x and y which can be written in the form $y = f(x) = ax^3 + bx^2 + cx + d$, where a, b, c, d are constant real numbers, $a \neq 0$.

a is called the coefficient of x^3.

b is called the coefficient of x^2.

c is called the coefficient of x.

d is called the constant term.

EXAMPLE 1

(a) If $y = 2x^3 - 5x^2 + 7x - 1$, find y when $x = 2$.

(b) If $f(x) = -3x^3 + 5x^2 - x - 3$, find $f(-3)$.

Solution

(a) $x = 2$: $y = 2(2)^3 - 5(2)^2 + 7(2) - 1 = 9$

(b) $f(-3) = -3(-3)^3 + 5(-3)^2 - (-3) - 3 = 126$

21.2 Plotting graphs of cubic functions

Method

To plot a graph of a cubic function:

1. Isolate y on one side of the equation.
2. Substitute the values of x in the domain to find the corresponding values of y.
3. Plot the y values on the vertical axis against the x values on the horizontal axis.

EXAMPLE 2

Plot $y = x^3 + 4x^2 + x - 6$ in the domain $-4 \le x \le 2$, $x \in \mathbb{R}$.

Solution

x	−4	−3	−2	−1	0	1	2
y	−10	0	0	−4	−6	0	20

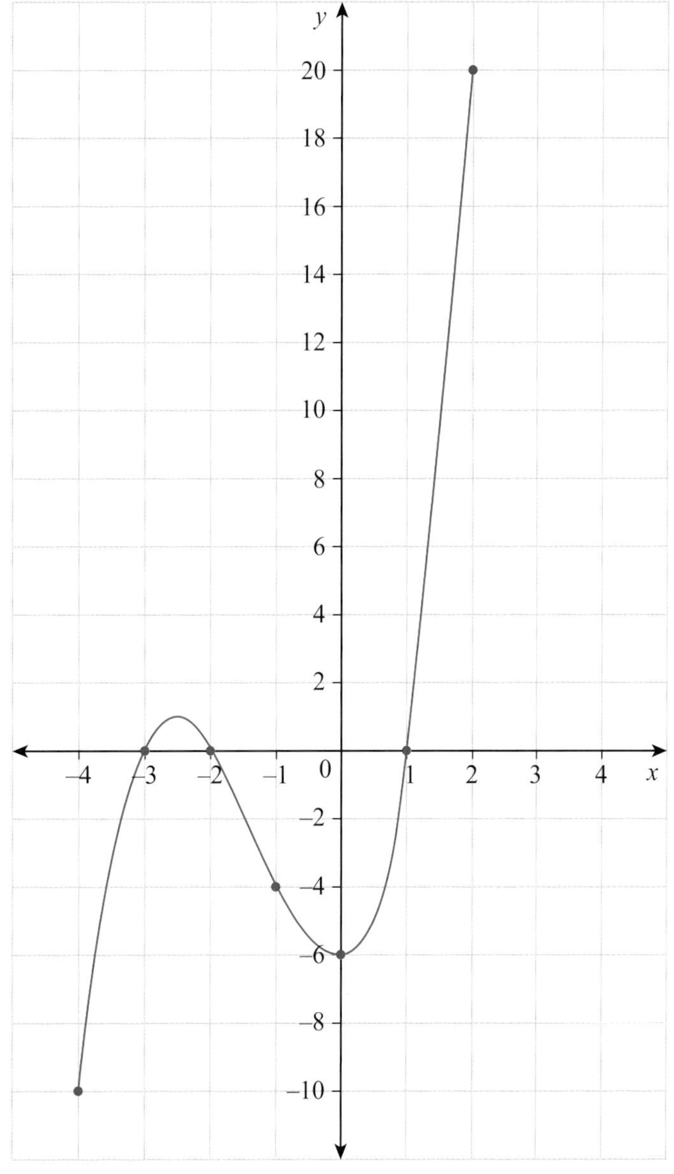

ACTIVITY 11

ACTION
Plotting cubic functions

OBJECTIVE
To draw a number of cubic functions

General shape of cubic functions

The general shape of a cubic function $y = ax^3 + bx^2 + cx + d$ depends on the sign of a, the coefficient of x^3.

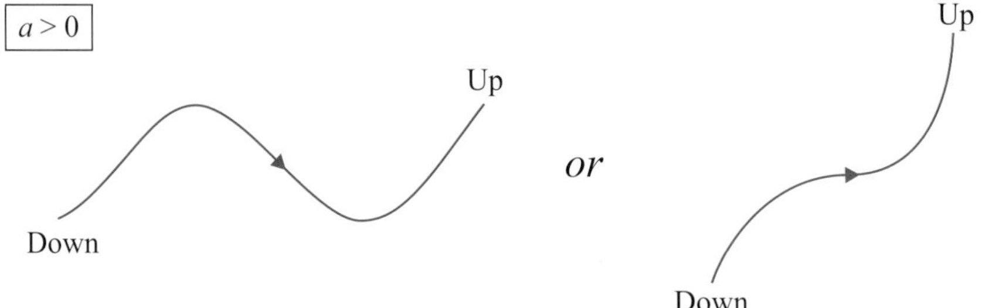

- The cubic function $y = 4x^3 - 9x^2 + 11x - 2$ has the above shape as $a = 4 > 0$.

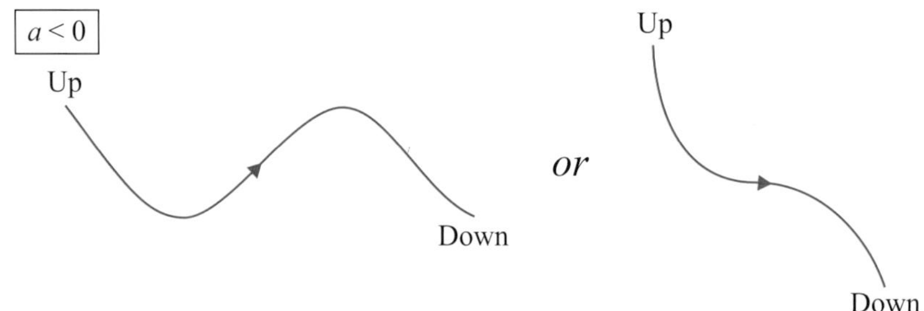

- The cubic function $y = -x^3 + 7x^2 - 5$ has the above shape as $a = -1 < 0$.

21.3 Properties of cubic functions

1. Finding where a cubic function crosses the y-axis

Solving the equation of the y-axis ($x = 0$) with the equation of the cubic function $y = ax^3 + bx^2 + cx + d$ gives $y = d$.

The graph of the cubic function crosses the y-axis at $(0, d)$.

- $y = -2x^3 + 3x^2 - 5x - 7$ crosses the x-axis at $(0, -7)$.
- $y = x^3 + 11x^2 - 3x + 4$ crosses the x-axis at $(0, 4)$.

2. Finding where a cubic function crosses the x-axis

Solving the equation of the x-axis ($y = 0$) with the equation of the cubic function $y = ax^3 + bx^2 + cx + d$ gives $ax^3 + bx^2 + cx + d = 0$.

The point(s) where the graph crosses the x-axis are the solutions of the cubic equation $ax^3 + bx^2 + cx + d = 0$.

Three situations arise:

(a) Three different real roots p, q, r

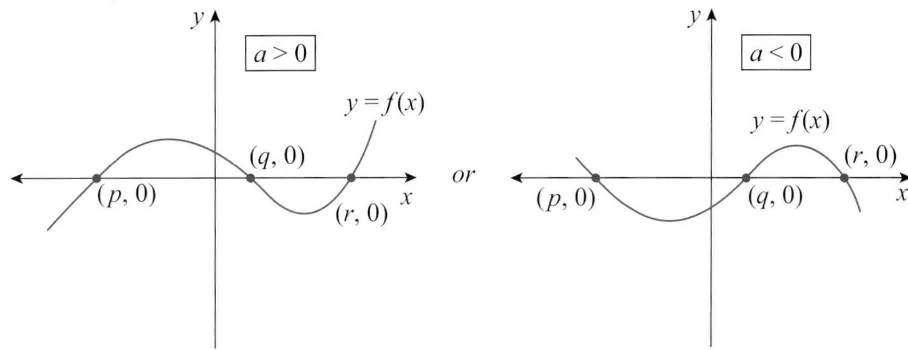

The cubic function is given by $y = k(x - p)(x - q)(x - r)$.

(b) Three roots, two of which are the same p, q, q

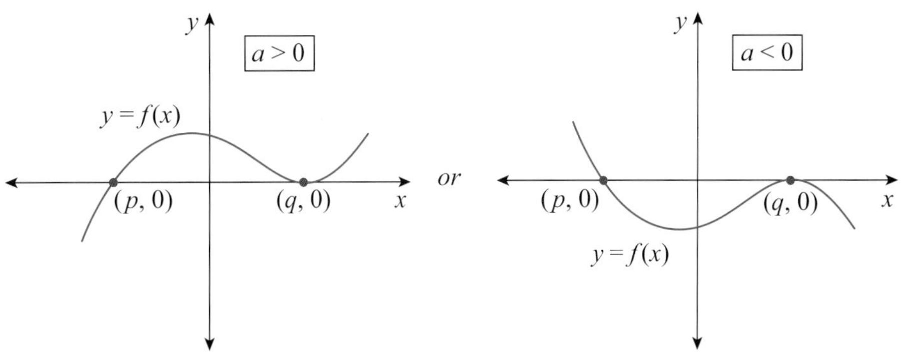

The cubic function is given by $y = k(x - p)(x - q)(x - q)$.

$y = k(x - p)(x - q)^2$

The double root is q.

(c) Only one real root

(i)

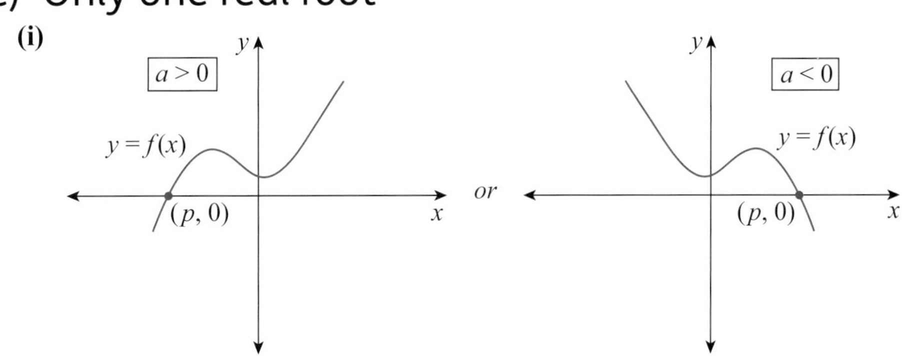

(ii)

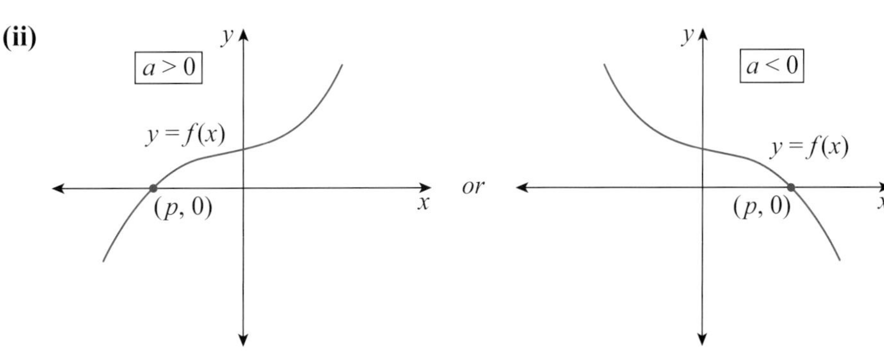

The cubic function is $y = k(x - p) \times$ (Quadratic expression).

EXAMPLE 3

Draw a sketch of $y = (2x + 1)(x - 3)(x - 1)$, $x \in \mathbb{R}$, by finding where it crosses the axes.

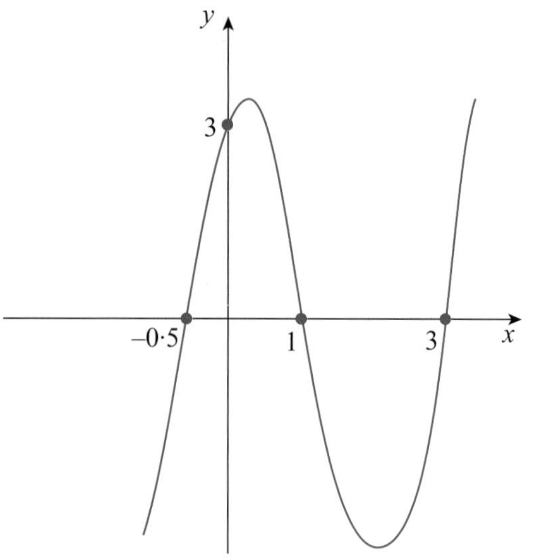

Solution

$y = (2x + 1)(x - 3)(x - 1)$

Crosses x-axis: $y = 0$: $(2x + 1)(x - 3)(x - 1) = 0$

$x = -\frac{1}{2}, 1, 3$

It crosses the x-axis at $(-\frac{1}{2}, 0)$, $(1, 0)$ and $(3, 0)$

Crosses y-axis: $x = 0$: $y = (+1)(-3)(-1) = +3$

It crosses the y-axis at $(0, 3)$.

If you multiply out the brackets, you get $+2x^3$ as the first term in the cubic function.

$a = +2 > 0$ [This gives us the general shape.]

EXAMPLE  4

Find the cubic function described by the graph shown in the form $y = ax^3 + bx^2 + cx + d$.

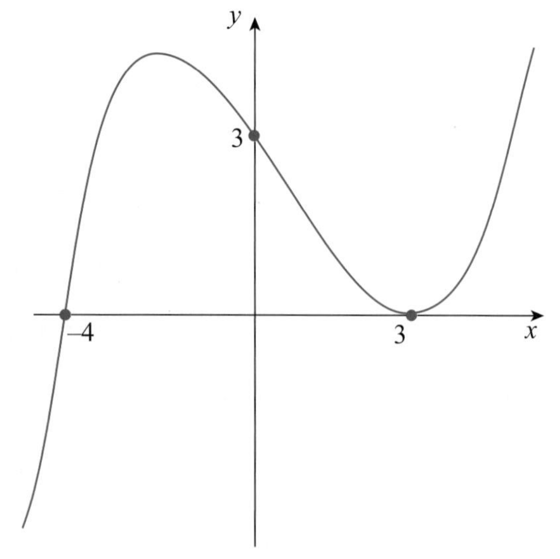

Solution

The roots are −4, 3 and 3.

$y = k(x - 3)^2(x + 4)$

$(0, 3)$ on the curve: $3 = k(-3)^2(4)$

$3 = 36k$

$k = \frac{1}{12}$

$y = \frac{1}{12}(x + 4)(x^2 - 6x + 9)$

$$y = \frac{x^3}{12} - \frac{x^2}{6} - \frac{5x}{4} + 3$$

21.4 Intersecting cubic functions

To find where two functions intersect, equate their y co-ordinates and solve the resulting equation. Alternatively, plot them on the same diagram and read off their points of intersection.

ACTIVITY 12

ACTION
Intersecting cubic functions

OBJECTIVE
To plot two functions (where at least one is cubic) and find their points of intersection

EXAMPLE 5

Plot $y = f(x) = x^3 + x^2 - 6x$ and $y = g(x) = -2x + 2$, $-3 \leq x \leq 2$, $x \in \mathbb{R}$, on the same diagram. Use your graphs to solve $x^3 + x^2 - 4x - 2 = 0$, correct to one decimal place.

Solution

x	-3	-2	-1	0	1	2
$f(x)$	0	8	6	0	-4	0
$g(x)$	8	6	4	2	0	-2

Solving: $f(x) = g(x)$

$x^3 + x^2 - 6x = -2x + 2$

$x^3 + x^2 - 4x - 2 = 0$

The points of intersection of the functions are the solutions of $x^3 + x^2 - 4x - 2 = 0$.

Solutions: $x = -2{\cdot}3, -0{\cdot}5, 1{\cdot}8$

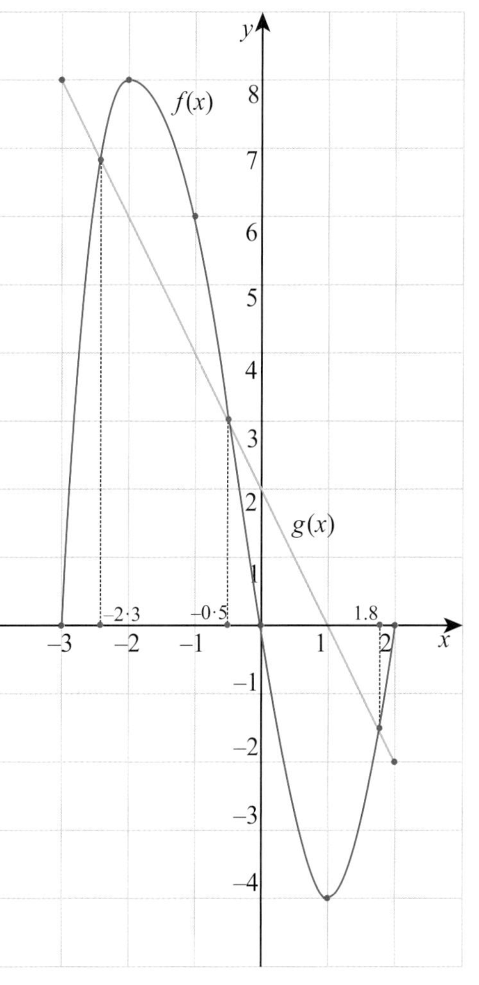

EXAMPLE 6

Plot $f(x) = -x^3 + 4x^2 + x - 4$ and $g(x) = x^2 - 2x - 3$, $-1 \leq x \leq 4$, $x \in \mathbb{R}$, on the same diagram. Use your graphs to solve $x^3 - 3x^2 - 3x + 1 = 0$, correct to one decimal place.

Solution

x	-1	0	1	2	3	4
$f(x)$	0	-4	0	6	8	0
$g(x)$	0	-3	-4	-3	0	5

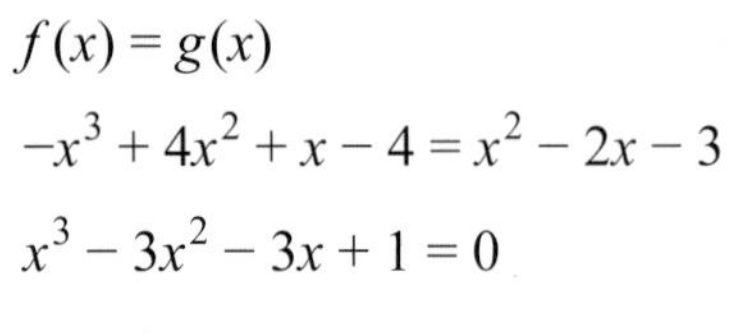

$f(x) = g(x)$

$-x^3 + 4x^2 + x - 4 = x^2 - 2x - 3$

$x^3 - 3x^2 - 3x + 1 = 0$

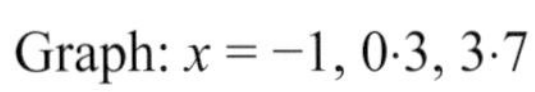

Graph: $x = -1, 0{\cdot}3, 3{\cdot}7$

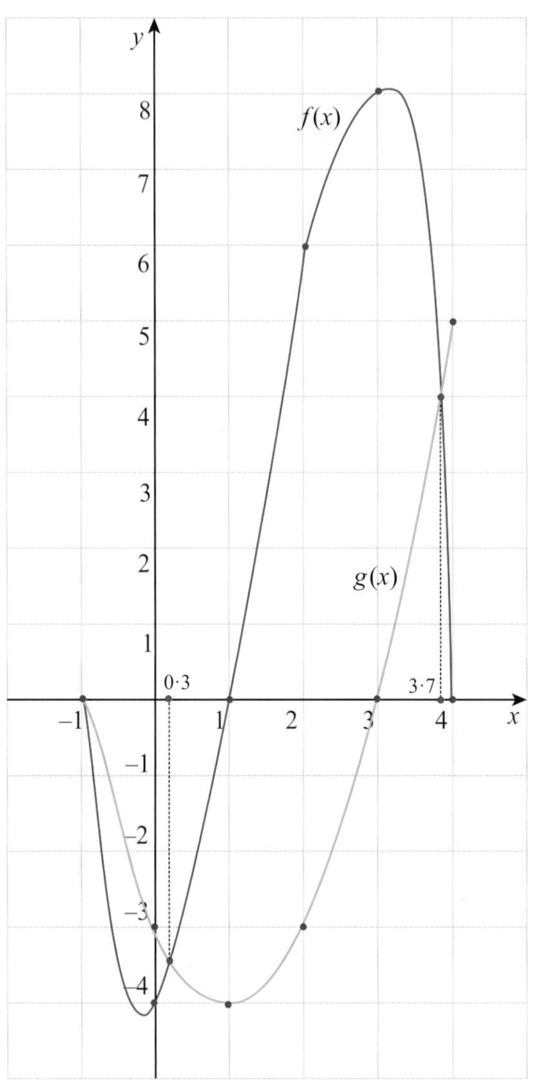

EXERCISE 11

1. Draw the following cubic functions on graph paper in the given domain for $x \in \mathbb{R}$. In each case, write down the roots correct to one decimal place and the point at which the curve crosses the y-axis:

> **Note:** This is also Activity 11. The activity supplies you with the appropriate grids.

(a) $f(x) = x^3 - 4x - 1, -2{\cdot}5 \le x \le 2{\cdot}5$

(b) $f(x) = -x^3 - 5x^2 - x + 8, -5 \le x \le 1{\cdot}5$

(c) $f(x) = x^3 - 3x - 2, -2 \le x \le 2{\cdot}5$

(d) $f(x) = -x^3 - x^2 + 5x - 3, -3 \le x \le 2$

(e) $f(x) = x^3 - 2x^2 - x - 2, -1{\cdot}5 \le x \le 3$

(f) $f(x) = x^3 - 3x^2 + 3x - 1, -1 \le x \le 2$

(g) $f(x) = -x^3 - x^2 - x - 1, -2 \le x \le 1{\cdot}5$

2. Plot the following cubic functions in the given domain for $x \in \mathbb{R}$ and state how many real roots exist for $y = 0$:

   (a) $y = -x^3 + 2x^2 - x + 2, \quad 1 \le x \le 3$

   (b) $y = (x + 3)^2(x - 2), -4 \le x \le 2$

   (c) $y = x^3 - 2x^2 - 5x + 6, -3 \le x \le 4$

   (d) $y = x^3 - 2x^2 + 3, -1 \le x \le 3$

3. Find the co-ordinates of the points at which the following cubic functions cross the axes:

   (a) $y = (x + 2)(x - 1)(x - 2)$

   (b) $y = -3x(2x - 1)(x + 2)$

   (c) $y = x(x - 1)^2$

   (d) $y = 3x(x^2 + 1)$

   (e) $y = 2(x - 2)(x^2 - 3x - 1)$

   (f) $y = (4 - x)(x^2 - 5x + 6)$

   (g) $y = (3x^2 - 2)(x + 1)$

   (h) $y = x^2(3x - 2)$

   (i) $y = (4x - 3)(x + 1)(5x - 2)$

   (j) $y = -2(x + 5)(4x^2 - x + 1)$

4. Write down the equations of the following cubic functions:

   (a)

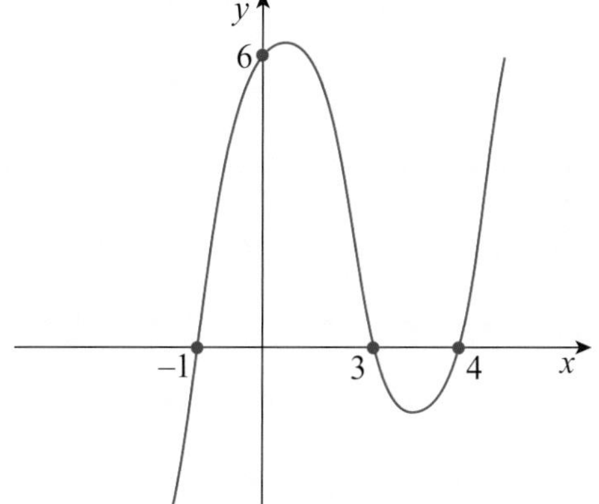

   (b)

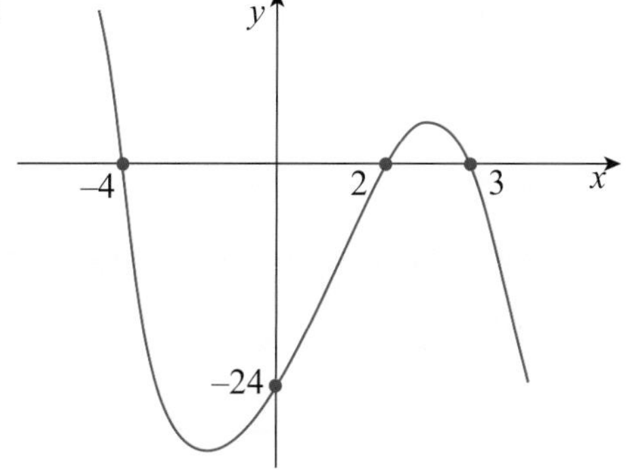

   (c)

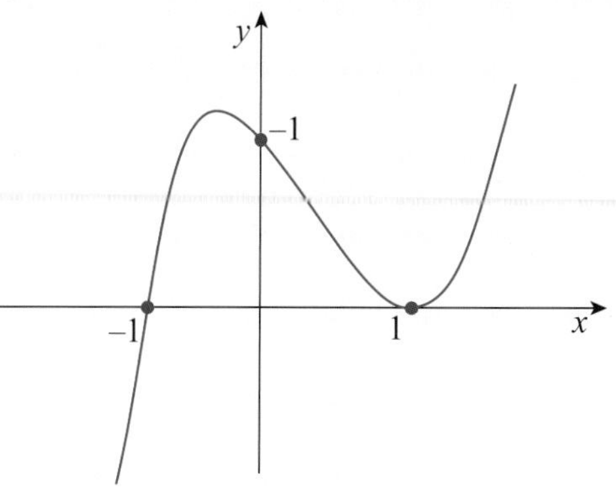

   (d)

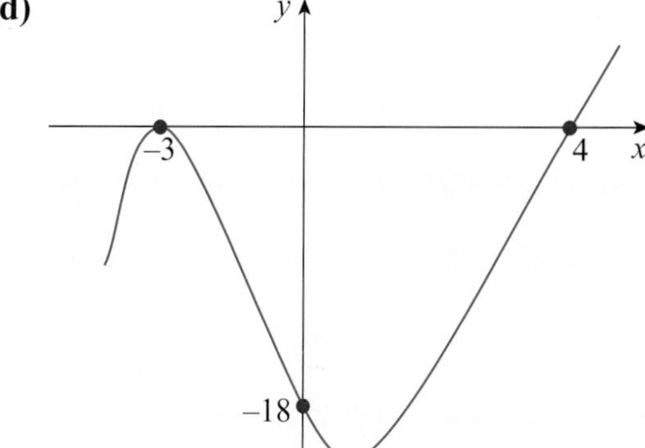

   (e)

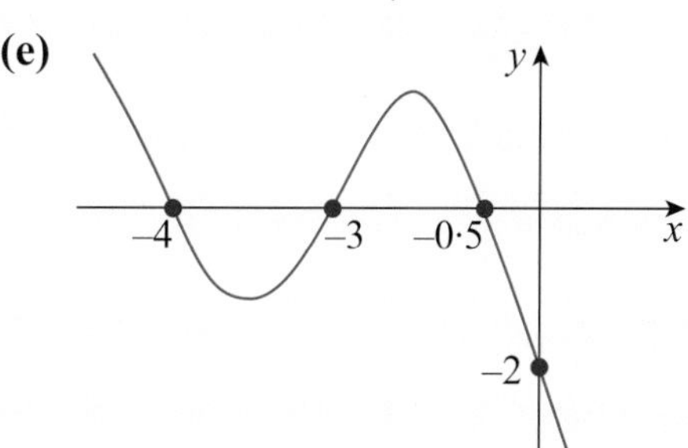

   (f)

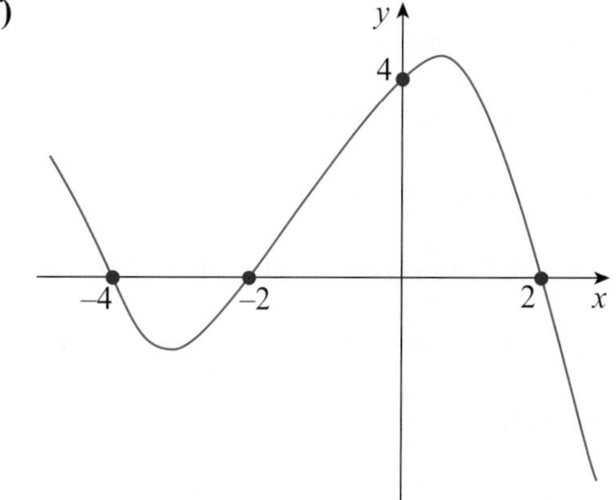

5. Find the cubic function in the form $y = ax^3 + bx^2 + cx + d$, which has the following features:

   (a) crosses the x-axis at $x = -2$, $x = 1$ and $x = 3$ and the y-axis at $(0, -4)$,

   (b) crosses the y-axis at $(0, 6)$ and the x-axis at $x = -2$, and $x = 3$, $x = 5$,

(c) touches the x-axis at $x = -2$, crosses the x-axis at $x = 1$ and crosses the y-axis at $(0, -2)$,

(d) touches the x-axis at $x = 3$, crosses the x-axis at $x = -2$ and the y-axis at $(0, 5)$.

6. The annual number N of arrests for crime per 100 000 juveniles, between 10 and 17 years, can be modelled by the function $N = -0{\cdot}36t^3 + 9{\cdot}4t^2 - 52t + 360$, where t is the number of years after 1990.

(a) Using the table below, plot a graph of N against t.

t (years)	0	5	10	15	20
N					

(b) Use your graph to find:

(i) in what years were the number of arrests 400,

(ii) the number of arrests in 1997, correct to two significant figures,

(iii) the lowest and highest number of arrests, correct to two significant figures.

7. The number M of tonnes of household waste recycled in a city t years after 2000 is given by $M = 3{\cdot}2t^3 - 19{\cdot}2t^2 + d$.

(a) If the number of tonnes recycled in 2000 was 800, find d.

(b) Use the table below to plot a graph of M against t, giving the value of M to the nearest 10 tonnes.

t (years)	0	2	4	6	8	10
M (tonnes)						

(c) Use your graph to find:

(i) the mass recycled in 2009 correct to two significant figures,

(ii) the year in which the minimum number of tonnes was recycled,

(iii) during what year the mass recycled exceeded 1000 tonnes.

8. Using the same grid, graph the following functions in the given domain, $x \in \mathbb{R}$. Use the graph to solve $f(x) = g(x)$ for $x \in \mathbb{R}$, correct to one decimal place.

Note: This is also Activity 12. The activity supplies you with the appropriate grids.

(a) $f(x) = 2x^3 + 5x^2 - 1$ and $g(x) = 2$, $-3 \leq x \leq 1$

(b) $f(x) = -x^3 + 3x^2 + 2x - 1$ and $g(x) = -2$, $-1 \leq x \leq 4$

(c) $f(x) = -x^3 + 2x^2 + 2x$ and $g(x) = -2x$, $-1{\cdot}5 \leq x \leq 3{\cdot}5$

(d) $f(x) = x^3 - 4x^2 - x + 3$ and $g(x) = x + 1$, $-1{\cdot}5 \leq x \leq 4{\cdot}5$

(e) $f(x) = x^3 + 2x^2 - 5x - 6$ and $g(x) = x^2 - 4$, $-4 \leq x \leq 3$

(f) $f(x) = -x^3 - 3x^2 + 2$ and $g(x) = x^2 + 3x - 3$, $-4 \leq x \leq 2$

(g) $f(x) = x^3 + x^2 - 5x$ and $g(x) = x^2 + x - 2$, $-4 \leq x \leq 3$

9. The graph below represents the functions $f(x) = px^3 + qx - 2$ and $g(x) = x - 2$.

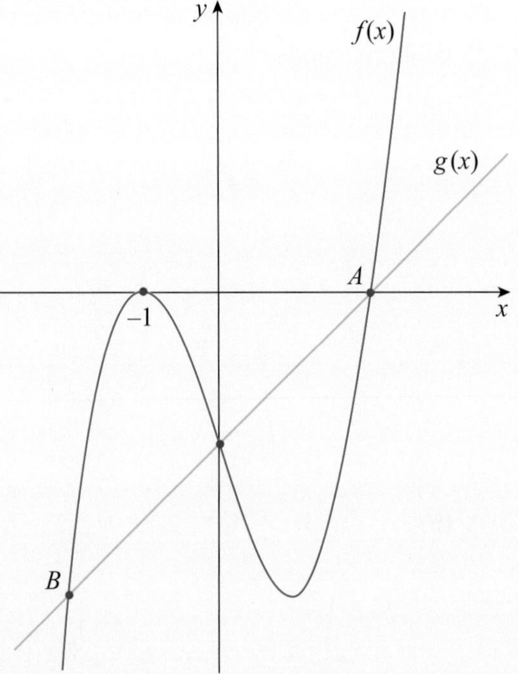

(a) Find the co-ordinates of the point A.

(b) Find p, q.

(c) Find B.

10. $f: x \to x^3 - 9x^2 + 24x - 18$ and $g: x \to 2 - \frac{2}{3}x$ are two functions defined for $x \in \mathbb{R}$.

(a) Copy and complete the table below and use it to draw the graph of $f(x) = x^3 - 9x^2 + 24x - 18$ in the domain $1 \le x \le 5$.

x	1	2	3	4	5
$f(x)$	−2				2

(b) By finding where $g(x) = 2 - \frac{2}{3}x$ crosses the axes, plot it on the same diagram as $f(x)$.

(c) Use your graphs to solve $f(x) = g(x)$, correct to one decimal place.

11. Two functions f and g are defined for $x \in \mathbb{R}$ as follows:

$f: x \to -x^3 + 2x^2 - x + 2$

$g: x \to 3 - x$

(a) Copy and complete the table below and use it to draw the graphs of f and g for $-1 \le x \le 2$, giving all answers correct to one decimal place.

x	−1	−0·5	0	0·5	1	1·5	2
$f(x)$							
$g(x)$							

(b) Use your graphs to estimate the values for which $x^3 - 2x^2 + 1 = 0$, correct to one decimal place.

12. Two functions f and g are defined for $x \in \mathbb{R}$ as follows:

$f: x \to x^3$

$g: x \to 3 - 3x^2$

(a) Copy and complete the table below and use it to draw the graphs of f and g for $-1{\cdot}5 \le x \le 1{\cdot}5$, giving all answers correct to one decimal place.

x	−1·5	−1	−0·5	0	0·5	1	1·5
$f(x)$							
$g(x)$							

(b) Use your graphs to estimate the values for which $x^3 + 3x^2 = 3$, correct to one decimal place.

(c) Write down the value of the maximum value of $g(x)$.

21.5 Transformations of functions (vertical and horizontal shifts)

Vertical shift

If a constant v is added to each y co-ordinate of a graph, the effect is to shift the whole graph vertically up or down by v units.

ACTIVITY 13

ACTION
Transforming functions

OBJECTIVE
To transform (shift) various functions

WORKED EXAMPLE Vertical shift

Consider the functions $f(x) = x^2$ and $f(x) + 2$, $-2 \le x \le 2$, $x \in \mathbb{R}$.

x	−2	−1	0	1	2
$f(x) = x^2$	4	1	0	1	4
$f(x) + 2 = x^2 + 2$	6	3	2	3	6

The shape of the graph remains unchanged but the whole graph has been translated **vertically upwards** by 2 units.

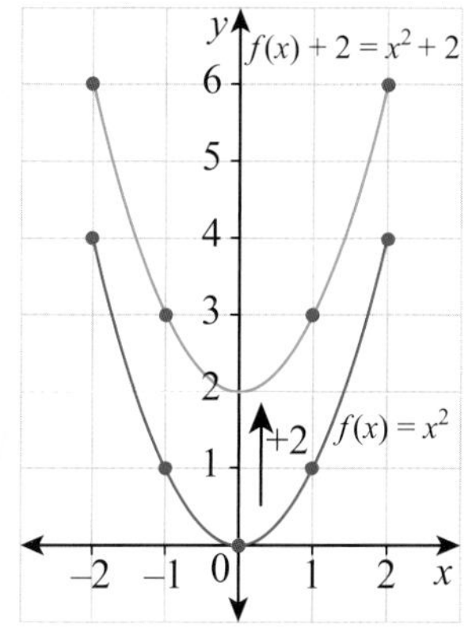

Horizontal shift

If a constant h is added to each x co-ordinate of a graph, the effect is to shift the whole graph horizontally left or right by a factor of h.

WORKED EXAMPLE Horizontal shift

Consider $f(x) = x^2$, $-2 \le x \le 2$, and $f(x + 2)$, $-4 \le x \le 0$, $x \in \mathbb{R}$.

x	−2	−1	0	1	2
$f(x) = x^2$	4	1	0	1	4

x	−4	−3	−2	−1	0
$f(x + 2) = (x + 2)^2$	4	1	0	1	4

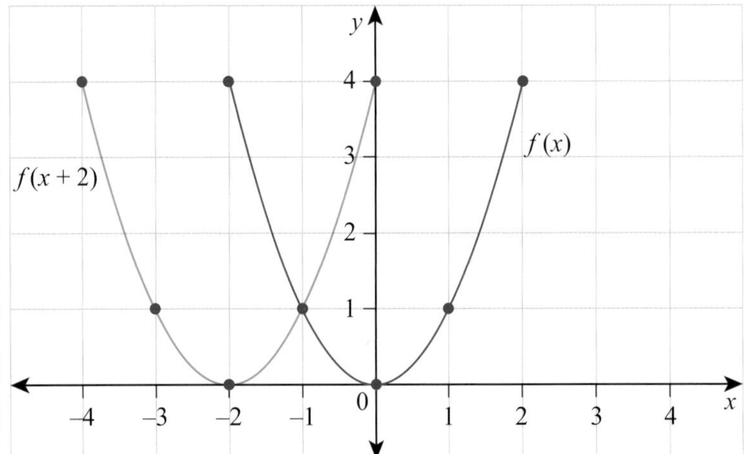

The shape of the graph remains unchanged but the whole graph has been translated **backwards** (to the left) by 2 units.

Vertical and horizontal shifts

If $y = f(x)$, then:

1. $f(x) + v$ shifts $f(x)$ vertically up by v units, if $v > 0$.
2. $f(x) - v$ shifts $f(x)$ vertically down by v units, if $v > 0$.
3. $f(x + h)$ shifts $f(x)$ horizontally left by h units, if $h > 0$.
4. $f(x - h)$ shifts $f(x)$ horizontally right by h units, if $h > 0$.

EXAMPLE 7

Plot $y = f(x) = x^2$, $x \in \mathbb{R}$, using the values $-3 \le x \le 3$. Hence, plot $y = (x - 3)^2 + 1$, $x \in \mathbb{R}$, on the same diagram.

Solution

x	−3	−2	−1	0	1	2	3
$f(x) = x^2$	9	4	1	0	1	4	9

$(x - 3)^2 + 1$ shifts the graphs of $y = x^2$ by 3 units to the right and 1 unit up.

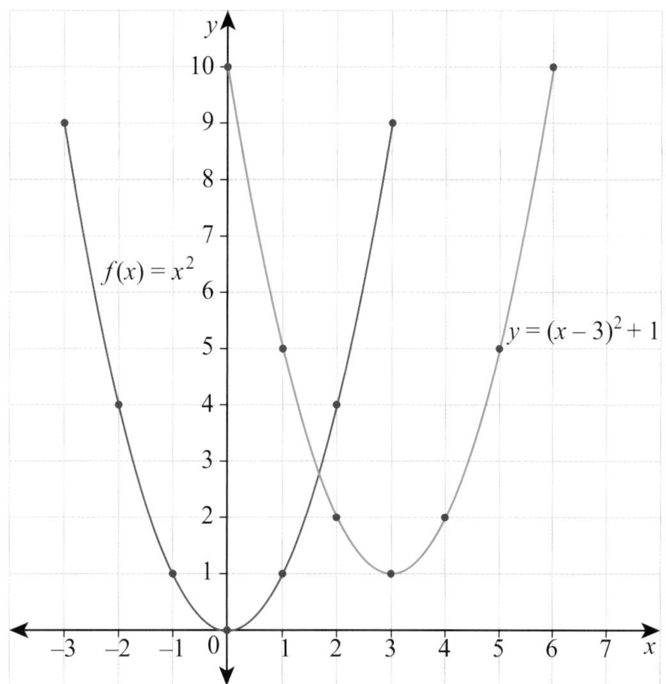

In general for $y = f(x)$:

1. $y = f(x + h) + v$ shifts $y = f(x)$ horizontally and vertically.
2. $h > 0$ results in a left horizontal shift of h units.
3. $h < 0$ results in a right horizontal shift of h units.
4. $v > 0$ results in an upwards vertical shift of v units.
5. $v < 0$ results in a downwards vertical shift of v units.

EXAMPLE 8

The path of an arrow A is shown below. Its trajectory is described by the equation $H(x) = x(8 - x)$. Another arrow B is fired from $P(2, 8)$. It has an identically shaped trajectory as A. Find the equation of the trajectory of B and how far from (0, 0) it hits the ground. x is in metres (m).

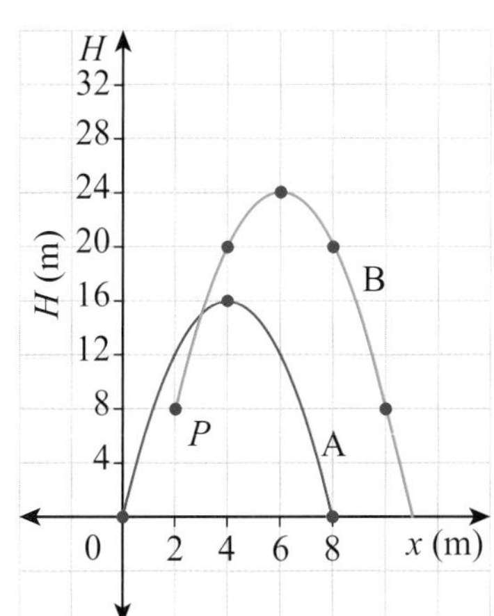

Solution

The trajectory of B is the curve A shifted to the right by 2 units and shifted up by 8 units.

$y = H(x - 2) + 8$

$y = (x - 2)(8 - (x - 2)) + 8$

$y = (x - 2)(10 - x) + 8$

$y = -x^2 + 12x - 12$

$\mathbf{y = 0}$**:** $x^2 - 12x + 12 = 0$

$x = \dfrac{12 \pm \sqrt{96}}{2}$

$x = 6 \pm 2\sqrt{6}$

The arrow hits the ground $(6 + 2\sqrt{6})$ m from (0, 0).

EXERCISE 12

1. The green-coloured graph is a transformation of the red-coloured graph whose equation is shown. Write down the equation of the transformed graph:

(a)

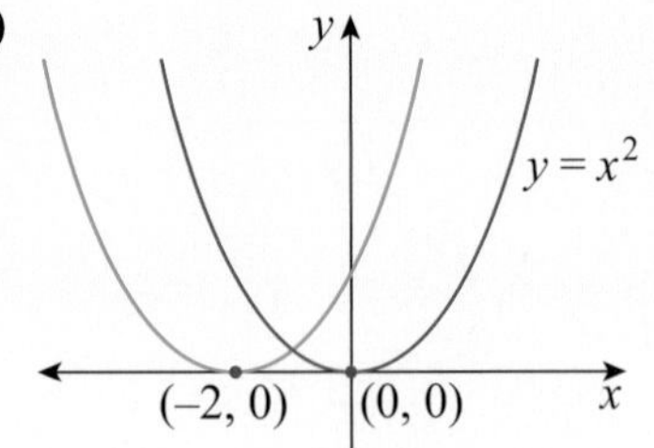

(b)

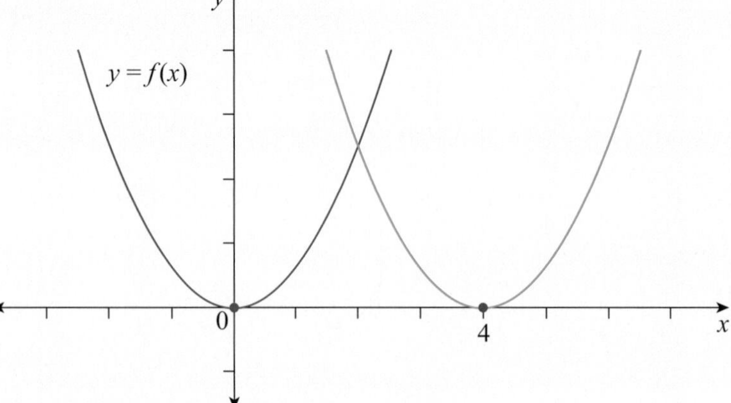

(c)

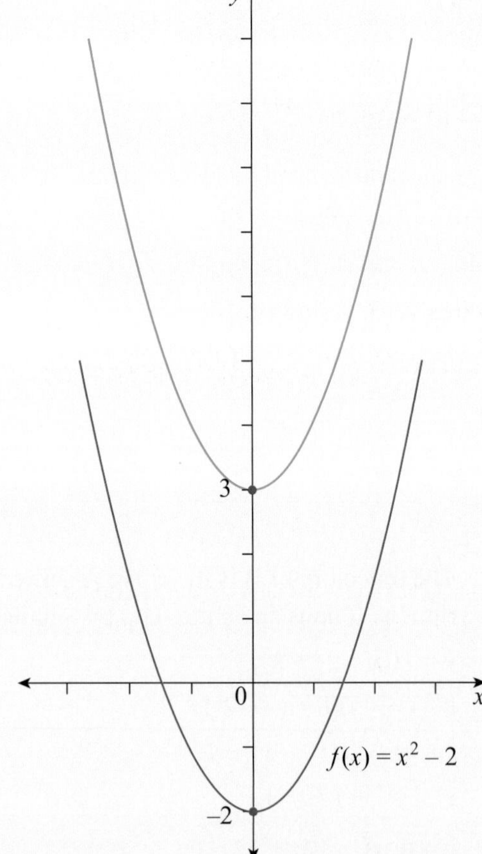

(d)

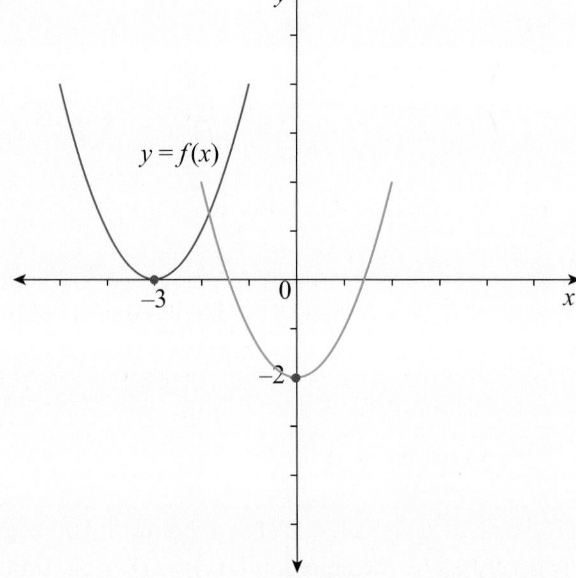

2. The diagram shows part of the curve with equation $y = f(x)$. The co-ordinates of the maximum point of this curve are (2, 4). Write down the coordinates of the maximum point of the curve with the following equations:

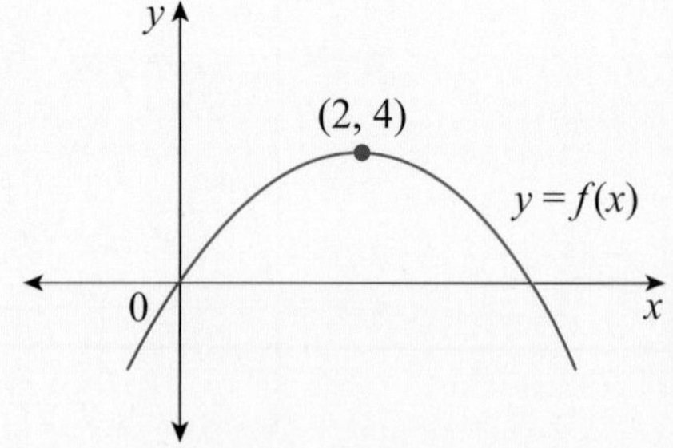

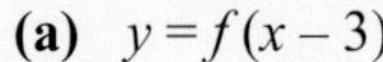

(a) $y = f(x - 3)$

(b) $y = f(x + 5)$

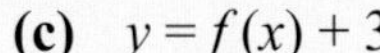

(c) $y = f(x) + 3$

(d) $y = f(x) - 5$

(e) $y = f(x + 5) - 6$

Exponential and Logarithmic Functions

Learning Outcomes

- To recognise an exponential function: $y = ka^{bx}$.
- To be able to plot a graph of an exponential function.
- To know the properties of exponential functions of the type $y = ka^{bx}$.
- To work with problems of intersecting functions involving an exponential function.
- To recognise log functions $y = k\log_a(x)$ and understand they are the inverse of exponential functions.
- To be able to plot a graph of a log function.
- To know the properties of log functions.
- To use exponential and log functions to solve real-life problems.

22.1 What is an exponential function?

ACTION
Plotting exponential functions

OBJECTIVE
To draw a number of exponential functions

The mathematics of uncontrolled growth (decay) is frightening. A single bacterium such as an *E. coli* cell can multiply rapidly (exponentially) under favourable circumstances.

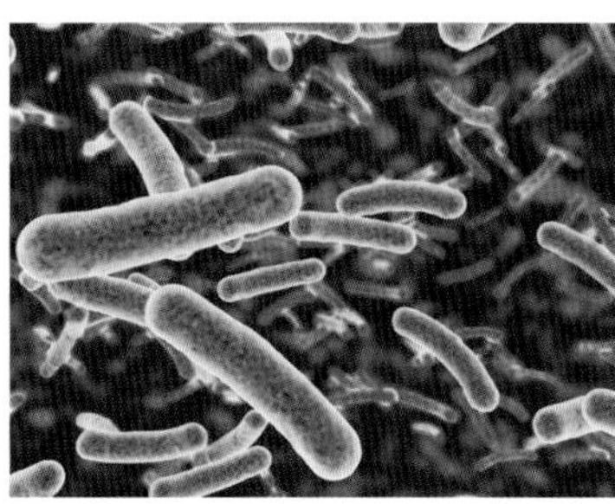

An exponential function is a relation between two variables, x and y, which can be written in the form $y = ka^{bx}$, where k, a, b are constants with $k, a, b \in \mathbb{R}$, $a > 0$.

- $y = 3 \times 2^{4x}$: $k = 3$, $a = 2$, $b = 4$

The rules of powers can be applied as normal.

EXAMPLE 1

Show that $y = 3^{-\frac{1}{2}x + 5}$ can be written in the form $y = ka^{bx}$.

Solution

$y = 3^{-\frac{1}{2}x + 5} = 3^{-\frac{1}{2}x} \times 3^5 = 243 \times 3^{-\frac{1}{2}x}$

$\therefore k = 243,\ a = 3,\ b = -\frac{1}{2}$

22.2 Plotting graphs of exponential functions

Method

Substitute the values in the domain for x and calculate the corresponding values of y.

EXAMPLE 2

Plot $y = 2^x$, $-2 \leq x \leq 3$, $x \in \mathbb{R}$.

Solution

x	-2	-1	0	1	2	3
y	$\frac{1}{4}$	$\frac{1}{2}$	1	2	4	8

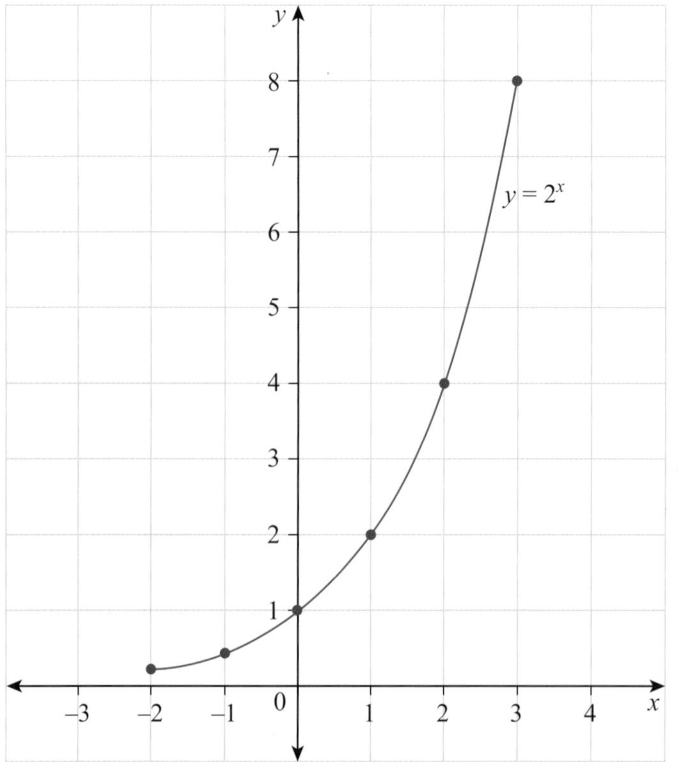

EXAMPLE 3

Show that $2(\sqrt{3})^x$ can be written as $2 \times 3^{\frac{1}{2}x}$ and hence plot $y = 2(\sqrt{3})^x$ in the domain $-2 \le x \le 2, x \in \mathbb{R}$.

Solution

$2(\sqrt{3})^x = 2\,(3^{\frac{1}{2}})^x = 2 \times 3^{\frac{1}{2}x}$

$y = 2(\sqrt{3})^x = 2 \times 3^{\frac{1}{2}x}$

x	−2	−1	0	1	2
y	$\frac{2}{3}$	1·2	2	3·5	6

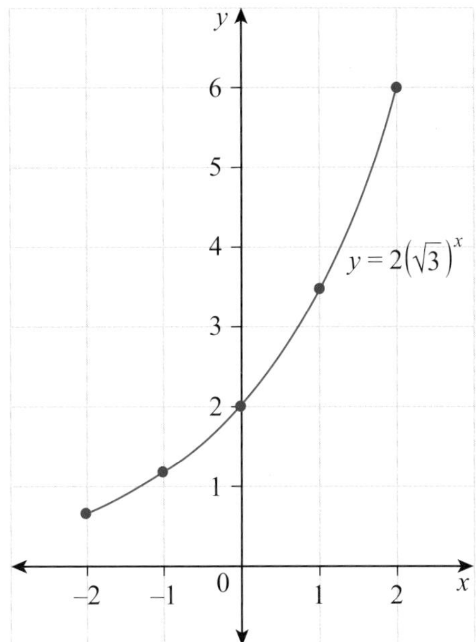

EXAMPLE 4

Plot $y = 3\left(\frac{1}{2}\right)^x, -2 \le x \le 2, x \in \mathbb{R}$.

Solution

$y = 3\left(\frac{1}{2}\right)^x = 3 \times (2^{-1})^x = 3 \times 2^{-x}$

x	−2	−1	0	1	2
y	12	6	3	1·5	0·75

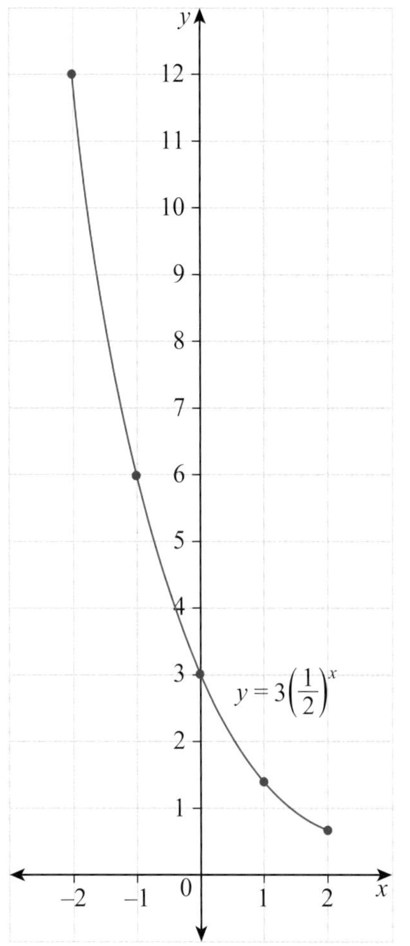

EXAMPLE 5

Show that $y = -\frac{3}{2}(\sqrt{3})^x$ can be written as $y = -1{\cdot}5 \times 3^{\frac{1}{2}x}$, and hence plot the graph in the domain $-2 \le x \le 2, x \in \mathbb{R}$.

Solution

$y = -\frac{3}{2}(\sqrt{3})^x = -1{\cdot}5 \times \left(3^{\frac{1}{2}}\right)^x = -1{\cdot}5 \times \left(3^{\frac{1}{2}x}\right) = -1{\cdot}5 \times 3^{\frac{1}{2}x}$

x	−2	−1	0	1	2
y	−0·5	−0·9	−1·5	−2·6	−4·5

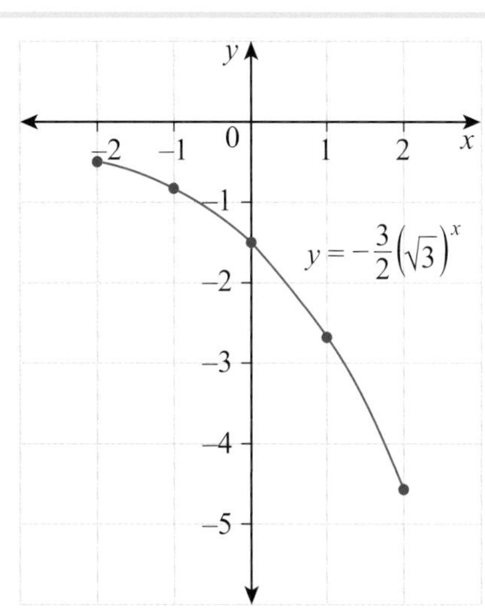

22.3 Properties of exponential functions

We are dealing with exponential functions of the form $y = ka^{bx}$, where k, a, b are constants with $k, a, b \in \mathbb{R}$, $a > 0$ and x, y are variables.

1. Exponential curves of this form never cross the x-axis. They have no real roots.
2. They always cross the y-axis ($x = 0$).

   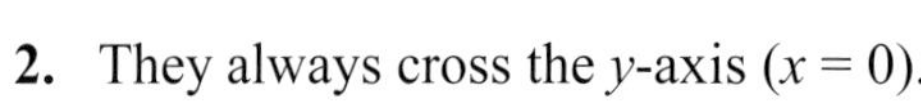

   $x = 0$: $y = ka^0 = k$

   $\therefore$ $(0, k)$ is the point at which such curves cross the y-axis.

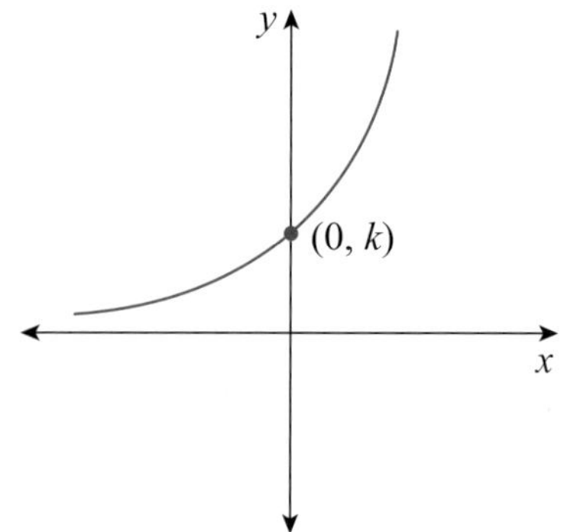

3. 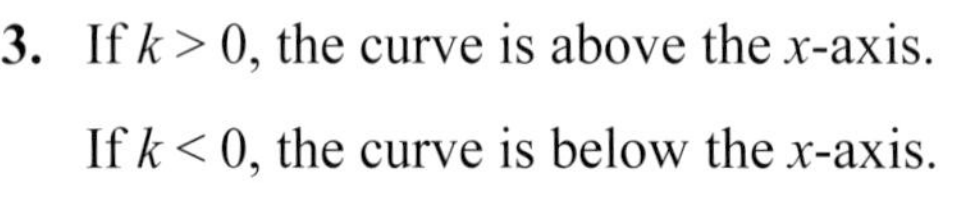

   If $k > 0$, the curve is above the x-axis.

   If $k < 0$, the curve is below the x-axis.
4. 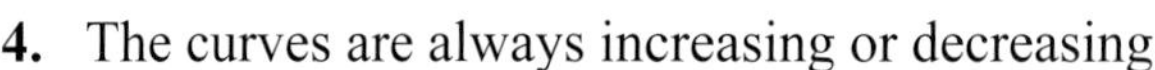

   The curves are always increasing or decreasing.

For $y = ka^{bx} + c$, the curve is just shifted vertically by a factor of c and so can cross the x-axis if $c < 0$.

EXERCISE 13

1. **(a)** Copy and complete the table below and draw the graph of the curve $y = 2^x$ in the domain $-2 \leq x \leq 2$, $x \in \mathbb{R}$:

x	−2	−1	0	1	2
y					

   (b) Use the graph to solve $2^x = 3$, correct to one decimal place.

   (c) Use the graph to find $2^{0 \cdot 5}$ correct to one decimal place.

2. The diagram shows the graph of $y = ka^x$. Find k and a, $a > 0$.

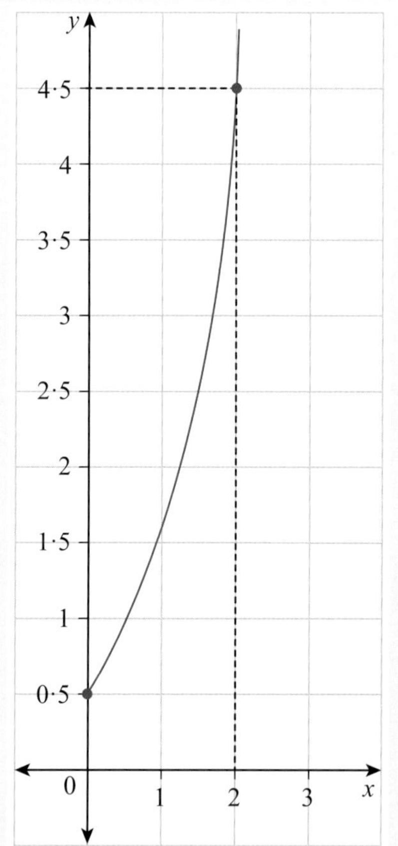

3. The population P of bees in a hive, t days after it was established, is given by $P = 20\,000(1{\cdot}15)^t$.

(a) How many bees were initially in the hive?

(b) How many bees were in the hive, correct to three significant figures:

(i) after 10 days?

(ii) after 20 days?

(c) Using the table below, plot a graph of P against t on graph paper. Give all answers in the table correct to three significant figures.

t	0	5	10	15	20
P					

(d) Use your graph to estimate when the population becomes 120 000, correct to the nearest day.

4. The number N of bacteria in a sample, t hours after starting an experiment, is given by $N = 60(3)^{0{\cdot}04t}$.

(a) Find the number of bacteria in the sample at the start of the experiment.

(b) Find the number of bacteria in the sample 3 hours after starting the experiment.

(c) Plot a graph of N against t on graph paper using the table below, giving each answer correct to three significant figures.

t	0	4	8	12	16	20	24
N							

(d) Use your graph to estimate when $N = 100$, correct to one decimal place.

(e) Find t when $N = 100$, using $N = 60(3)^{0{\cdot}04t}$. Hence, find the percentage error in your graphical estimate to the nearest percentage.

5. The value V in euro of a mobile phone after t years is given by

$V = k\left(\frac{1}{2}\right)^t$, k is a constant.

(a) Find k if the mobile phone is worth €80 after 4 years.

(b) Find its value after 5 years.

(c) After how many years is it worth €5?

6. Let $f(x) = 2^{-x} - 4$, $x \in \mathbb{R}$.

(a) Find where $f(x)$ crosses the x-axis.

(b) Find where $f(x)$ crosses the y-axis.

(c) Sketch $f(x)$ in the domain $-3 \leq x \leq 2$ using the table below. Give all answers for y correct to one decimal place.

x	-3	-2	-1	0	1	2
y						

(d) Use the graph to solve $2^{-x} = 7$, correct to one decimal place.

7. The charge Q in coulombs (C) on the capacitor in a defibrillator builds up to its final value according to the equation, $Q = 0{\cdot}2(1 - 2{\cdot}7^{-\frac{5}{8}t})$, $0 \leq t \leq 9$, $t \in \mathbb{R}$, where t is the time in seconds after the charging begins.

(a) Find the charge on the capacitor at $t = 0$.

(b) Using the table below, plot a graph of Q against t, giving all values correct to three decimal places.

t	0	1	3	5	7	9
Q						

(c) Use the graph to find:

(i) the final charge towards which the charge on the capacitor approaches,

(ii) the time to charge up to half of the final charge, correct to one decimal place.

(d) Find the average rate of charging over the charging time, correct to three decimal places.

8. When a microwave oven is turned on, the temperature T, in degrees Celsius (°C), after t minutes is given by $T = 520 - 500(0{\cdot}9)^t$.

(a) Find the temperature at $t = 0$ minutes. What does this value mean?

(b) Find the temperature at:

(i) $t = 2$ minutes,

(ii) $t = 10$ minutes, correct to one decimal place,

(iii) $t = 20$ minutes, correct to one decimal place.

(c) Find $\lim_{t \to \infty} (0{\cdot}9)^t$.

(d) Find $\lim_{t \to \infty} T$.

(e) What is the maximum temperature the microwave can reach?

(f) Explain why T cannot exceed 520 °C.

(g) Find the average rate of change of the temperature between 10 and 20 minutes, correct to one decimal place.

22.4 Intersecting exponential functions

To find where two functions intersect, equate their y co-ordinates and solve for x. Alternatively, plot them on the same diagram and read off their points of intersection.

ACTIVITY 15

ACTION
Intersecting exponential functions

OBJECTIVE
To plot two functions (where at least one is exponential) and to find their points of intersection

EXAMPLE 

Two functions f and g are defined as:

$f: x \to 2^x, x \in \mathbb{R}$

$g: x \to 2x + 1, x \in \mathbb{R}$

(a) Complete the table below and use it to draw graphs of f and g for $0 \le x \le 3$ on the same diagram.

x	0	0·5	1	1·5	2	2·5	3
f							
g							

(b) Use the graphs to estimate the values of x for which $2^x - 2x - 1 = 0$, correct to one decimal place.

(c) If $2^k = 5$, use the graphs to estimate k and $g(k)$, correct to one decimal place. Solve $2^k = 5$ algebraically and verify both answers are equal.

Solution

$f(x) = 2^x$

$g(x) = 2x + 1$

(a)

x	0	0·5	1	1·5	2	2·5	3
f	1	1·4	2	2·8	4	5·7	8
g	1	2	3	4	5	6	7

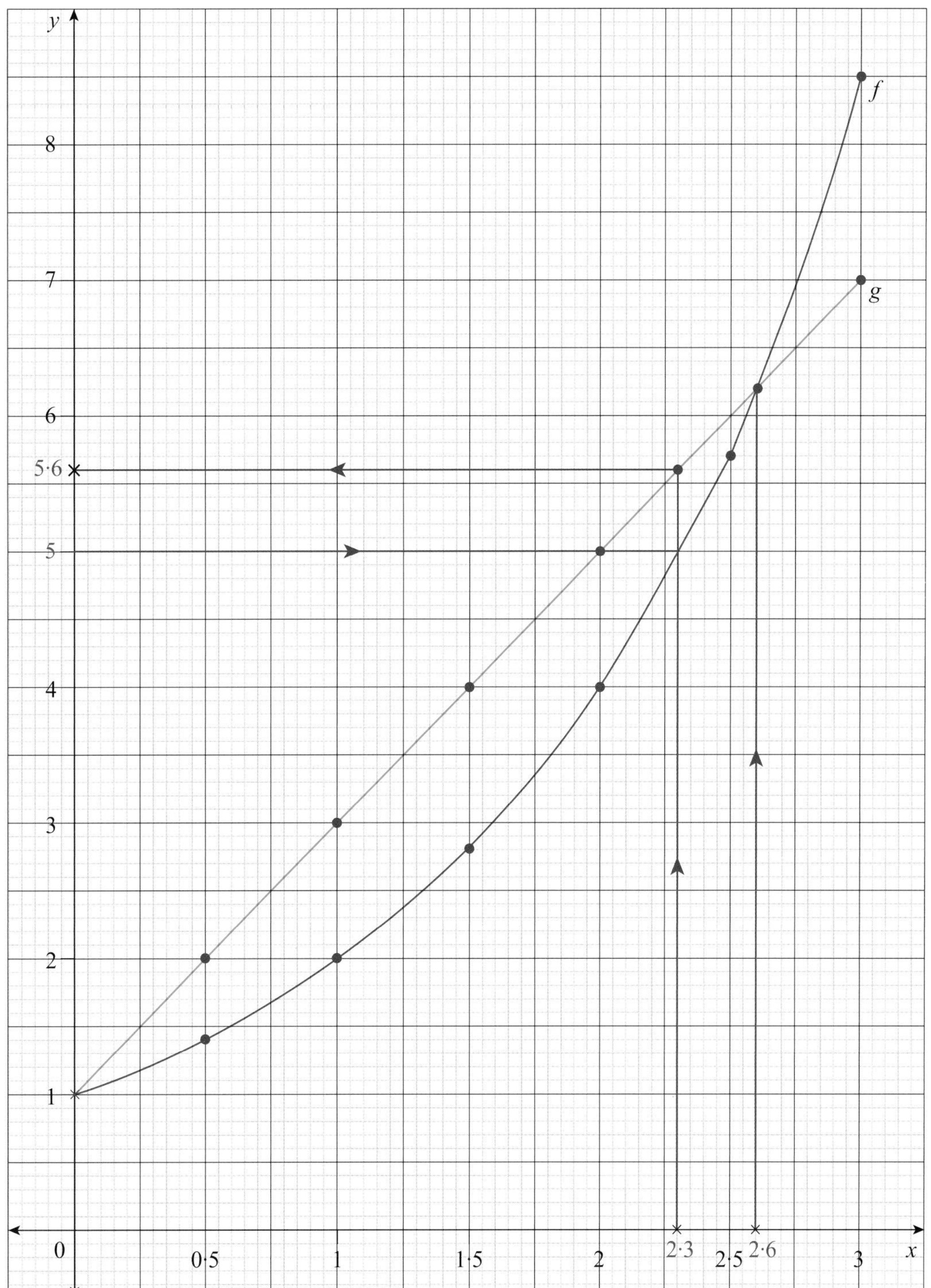

(b) The points of intersection of the curves are the solutions of:

$f(x) = g(x)$

$2^x = 2x + 1$

$2^x - 2x - 1 = 0$

Using the graph, the solutions to $2^x - 2x + 1 = 0$ are $x = 0$ and $x = 2{\cdot}6$.

(c) Graphically: $f(x) = 5$: $2^k = 5 \Rightarrow k = 2{\cdot}3$ and $g(k) = 5{\cdot}6$

Algebraically: $2^k = 5$

$\log_{10} 2^k = \log_{10} 5$

$k \log_{10} 2 = \log_{10} 5$

$$\therefore k = \frac{\log_{10} 5}{\log_{10} 2} = 2{\cdot}3$$

EXAMPLE 7

A missile is fired from a point A. Its height, in tens of metres above the ground, t seconds after being fired, is given by $h_1 = 2^t$, $t \geq 0$. The instant it is fired, another missile is fired from a drone at point B. Its height h_2, in tens of metres above the ground, t seconds after being fired, is given by $h_2 = 10 - t^2$, $t \geq 0$.

(a) Find the initial height of each missile above the ground.

(b) Use the table below to plot graphs of h_1 and h_2 against t on graph paper.

t	0	0·5	1	1·5	2	2·5	3
h_1							
h_2							

(c) Use your graph to estimate when the missiles collide and how high above the ground the collision occurs.

Solution

$h_1 = 2^t$

$h_2 = 10 - t^2$

(a) $t = 0 \Rightarrow h_1 = 1$. The initial height of the first missile is 10 m above the ground.

$t = 0 \Rightarrow h_2 = 10$. The initial height of the second missile is 100 m above the ground.

(b)

t	0	0·5	1	1·5	2	2·5	3
h_1	1	1·4	2	2·8	4	5·7	8
h_2	10	9·8	9	7·8	6	3·8	1

(c) $t = 2{\cdot}3$ s at $h = 48$ m

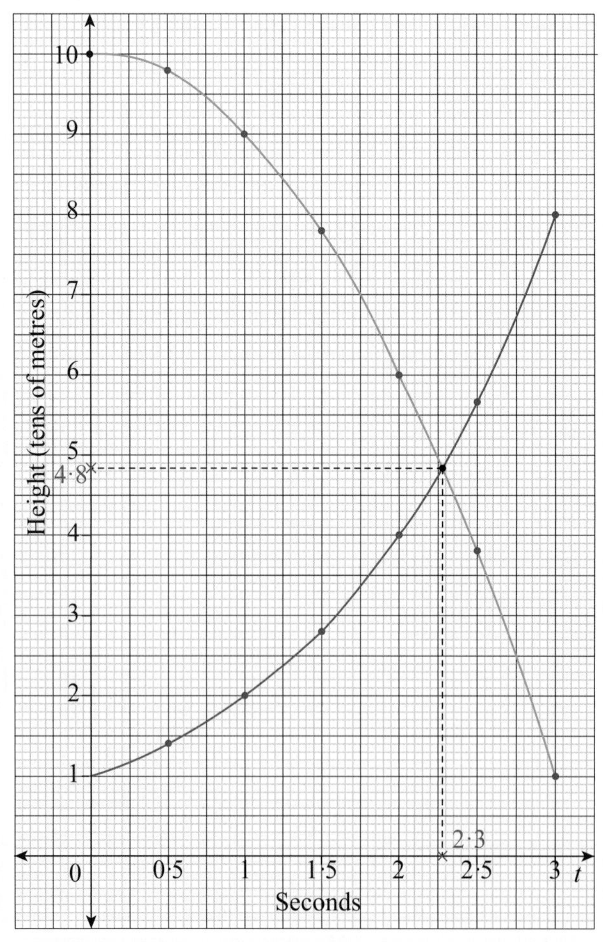

EXERCISE 14

1. A clay pigeon is released from a trap at B. The equation of its path is given by $f(x) = 2^x$, where x is in metres. At the same instant a gun is fired from C and the shot travels along a straight line with equation $g(x) = -x + 4$.

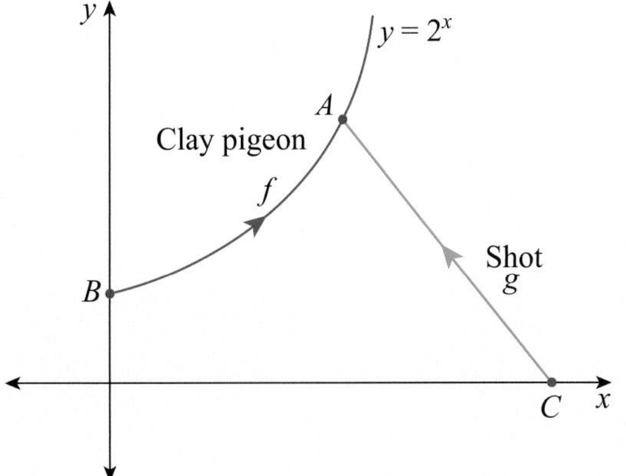

(a) Use the table below to plot f and g on the same diagram. Give all answers in the table correct to one decimal place.

x	0	0·5	1	1·5	2	2·5	3
f							
g							

(b) Use the graphs to find the co-ordinates of the point A at which the shot hits the clay pigeon, correct to one decimal place.

2. Two functions f and g are defined for $x \in \mathbb{R}$ as follows:

$f : x \to x^3 - 4x^2 + x + 6$

$g : x \to \frac{3}{2}(2^x)$

(a) Complete the table below and use it to draw the graphs of f and g for $-1 \leq x \leq 3$.

x	−1	0	1	2	3
$f(x)$					
$g(x)$					

(b) Use your graphs to estimate the values of x for which $x^3 - 4x^2 + x + 6 - \frac{3}{2}(2^x) = 0$, correct to one decimal place.

3. The populations of two colonies of insects vary with time t in days, according to the equations:

Colony 1: $P_1 = 75t - t^3 + 10, 0 \leq t \leq 7$

Colony 2: $P_2 = 30 \times (1{\cdot}5)^t, 0 \leq t \leq 7$

where:

P_1 is the population of colony 1 in thousands.

P_2 is the population of colony 2 in thousands.

(a) By copying and completing the table below, plot graphs of P_1 against t and P_2 against t on the same diagram. Give all answers correct to the nearest whole number.

t	0	1	2	3	4	5	6	7
P_1								
P_2								

(b) Use your graphs to find the times in days at which the two populations are equal, correct to one decimal place.

4. Let $f : x \to 3x$ and $g : x \to \left(\frac{1}{3}\right)^x$.

(a) By copying and completing the table below, draw graphs of f and g on the same diagram for $-2 \leq x \leq 2, x \in \mathbb{R}$.

x	−2	−1	0	1	2

(b) Write down the co-ordinates of their only point of intersection.

(c) Use your graphs to solve:

(i) $3^x = 4{\cdot}5$, correct to one decimal place,

(ii) $2\left(\frac{1}{3}\right)^x = 13$, correct to one decimal place.

(d) Show that $f(x) - g(-x) = 0$.

5. The functions $f(x) = 2^x$ and $g(x) = px^2 + qx + r$ are shown in the diagram. The graphs intersect at A on the y-axis and at B, the point at which $g(x)$ has its maximum value.

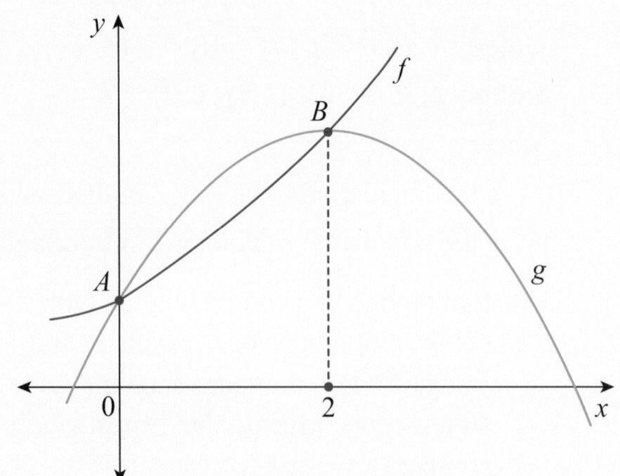

(a) Find the co-ordinates of A.

(b) Find the co-ordinates of B, the vertex of $g(x)$.

(c) Find p, q and r.

6. $f(x) = 2^x - 4$ and $g(x) = px^2 + qx + r$ intersect at A on the x-axis, which is the co-ordinate of the point on g at which g has its minimum value. g crosses the y-axis at $B(0, 2)$.

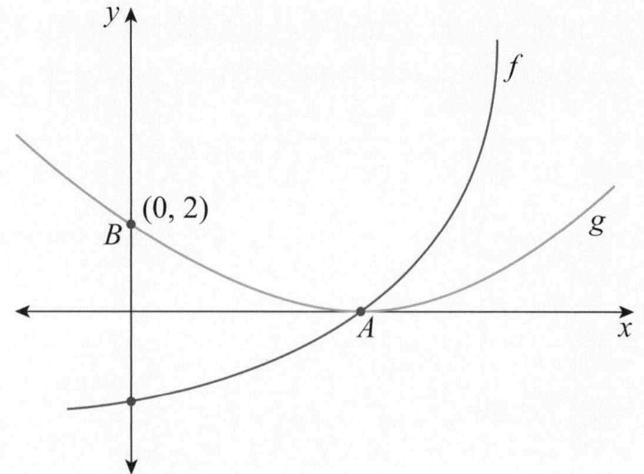

(a) Find the co-ordinates of A.

(b) Find p, q and r.

22.5 What is a log function?

A log function is a function of the form $y = k\log_a(x)$, where $a, k \in \mathbb{R}$, $a > 0$, are constants and x, y are variables with $x > 0$.

- $y = 3\log_2 x$

  $k = 3$, $a = 2$

Exponential functions and log functions are **inverses** of each other.

WORKED EXAMPLE

A log function is the inverse of an exponential function

$y = f(x) = 2^x \Leftrightarrow \log_2 y = x$

$\therefore f^{-1}(x) = \log_2 x$

So a log function can be obtained from an exponential function and vice versa by reflection in the line $y = x$, as shown in the diagram.

- $y = f(x) = -\log_3 x \Leftrightarrow 3^{-y} = x$

  $\therefore f^{-1}(x) = 3^{-x}$

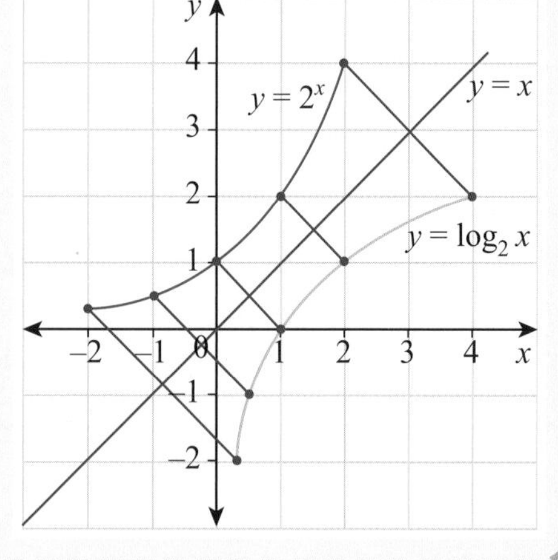

22.6 Plotting graphs of log functions

Method

Substitute the values in the domain for x and calculate the values of y.

ACTIVITY 16

ACTION
Plotting log functions

OBJECTIVE
To draw a number of log functions and intersecting log functions

EXAMPLE 8

Plot $y = \frac{1}{2}\log_3 x$, $\frac{1}{3} \le x \le 9$, $x \in \mathbb{R}$.

Solution

x	$\frac{1}{3}$	1	3	9
y	$-\frac{1}{2}$	0	$\frac{1}{2}$	1

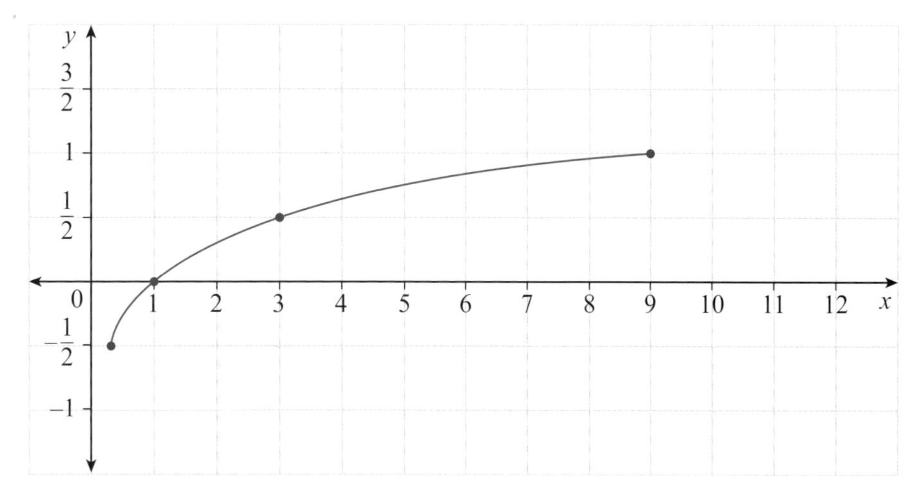

22.7 Properties of log functions

We are dealing with log curves of the form $y = k\log_a x$, where $k, a > 0$, $a \in \mathbb{R}$.

1. A log curve always crosses the x-axis at $x = 1$. It is its only real root.
2. A log curve always increases or decreases. If $k > 0$, it is increasing. If $k < 0$, it is decreasing.

EXAMPLE 9

Plot $y = -\log_2 x$, $\frac{1}{2} \le x \le 8$, $x \in \mathbb{R}$.

Solution

x	$\frac{1}{2}$	1	2	4	8
y	1	0	−1	−2	−3

$a = 2, k = -1$

$k < 0$. Therefore, it is decreasing.

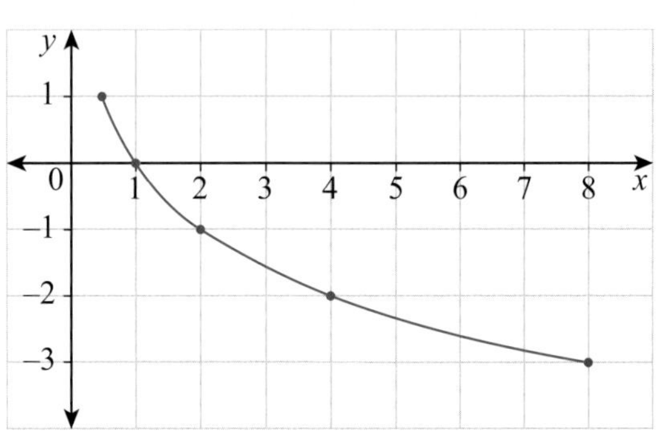

EXAMPLE 10

The average diameter d in mm of the sand particles on a beach is related to the slope s of the beach by the equation $s = 0{\cdot}16 + 0{\cdot}12 \log_{10}(d)$.

(a) Using the table below, plot a graph of s against d on graph paper, giving answers to two decimal places.

***d* (mm)**	0·2	0·4	0·6	0·8	1	1·2
s						

(b) Use the graph to estimate the average diameter of sand particles:

(i) on a beach of slope 0·12,

(ii) on a beach that rises 6 metres for every 100 metres you travel inland.

(c) Calculate algebraically the average diameter of a sand particle on a beach of slope 0·1, giving the answer in mm to three decimal places.

Solution

(a) $s = 0{\cdot}16 + 0{\cdot}12 \log_{10}(d)$

d	0·2	0·4	0·6	0·8	1	1·2
s	0·08	0·11	0·13	0·15	0·16	0·17

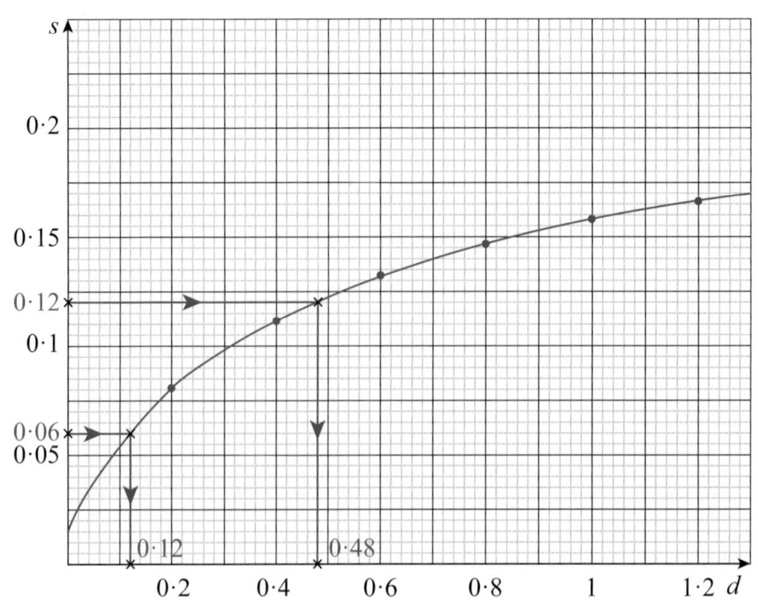

(b) From the graph:

(i) $s = 0{\cdot}12 \Rightarrow d = 0{\cdot}48$ mm

(ii) $s = \frac{6}{100} = 0{\cdot}06 \Rightarrow d = 0{\cdot}12$ mm

(c) $0{\cdot}1 = 0{\cdot}16 + 0{\cdot}12 \log_{10} d$

$\log_{10} d = -\frac{1}{2}$

$d = 10^{-\frac{1}{2}} = 0{\cdot}316$ mm

$\therefore d = 0{\cdot}316$ mm

EXERCISE 15

1. **(a)** Plot the graph of $y = \log_3 x, x > 0, x \in \mathbb{R}$ by copying and completing the table below and using the same scales on the x and y axes. Give all answers correct to two decimal places.

x	0·5	1	1·5	2	2·5	3	3·5	4
y								

(b) On the same diagram, plot $f^{-1}(x), x > 0, x \in \mathbb{R}$.

(c) Use your graphs to estimate the solutions of:

(i) $\log_3 x = 0{\cdot}75$, correct to one decimal place,

(ii) $3^x = 1{\cdot}75$, correct to one decimal place,

(d) Are $f(x)$ and $f^{-1}(x)$ continuous for all $x > 0, x \in \mathbb{R}$?

2. $f(x) = k^x, k > 0$ and $f^{-1}(x)$ are sketched on the right.

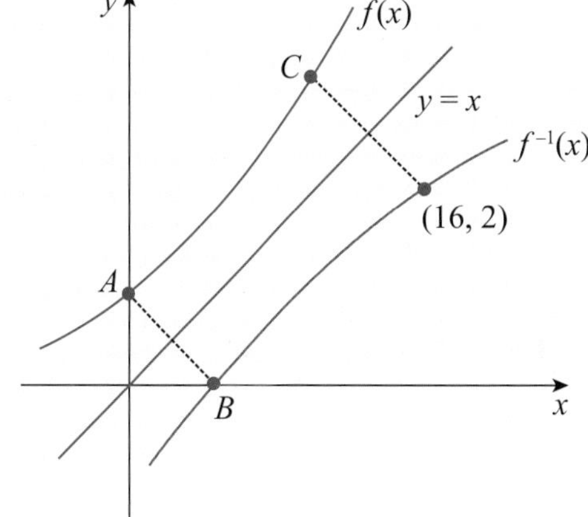

(a) Find the co-ordinates of A.

(b) Find $f^{-1}(x)$.

(c) Find the co-ordinates of B.

(d) If (16, 2) is on $f^{-1}(x)$, find k.

(e) Find C, the image of (16, 2) in the line $y = x$.

3. **(a)** On the same diagram, plot $f(x) = -\log_2 x$ and $g(x) = x^2 - 6x + 5, x \in \mathbb{R}$, using the table below. Give all answers for $f(x)$ correct to one decimal place.

x	−1	0	1	2	3	4	5	6
$f(x)$								
$g(x)$								

(b) Use your graphs to estimate the solutions of:

(i) $-\log_2 x = -1{\cdot}5$, correct to one decimal place,

(ii) $-\log_2 x = x^2 - 6x + 5$, correct to one decimal place.

4. Zipf's law in statistics suggests that the population P of the rth most populous town in a country is given by $P = \frac{k}{r^n}$ where k and n are positive constants.

(a) Show that $\log_2 P = \log_2 k - n\log_2 r$.

(b) Copy and complete the table below for the six most populous towns in a country in 2013. Give the values in each column correct to one decimal place.

r	Town	Population P	$\log_2 P$	$\log_2 r$
1	Pompey	262 144		
2	Fargu	65 536		
3	Gumbo	30 000		
4	Plovdiv	16 384		
5	Wye	10 486		
6	Knot	7281		

(c) Draw a graph with $\log_2 P$ on the y-axis and $\log_2 r$ on the x-axis.

(d) Draw the line of best-fit through these points.

(e) Use the STAT mode on your calculator to find the slope and intercept on the vertical axis of the line of best-fit, correct to the nearest whole number.

(f) Find k and n using the values from part **(e)**.

(g) Use the equation, $P = \frac{k}{r^n}$, with the values of k and n in part **(f)** to estimate the population of Perm, the eighth most populous town in the country.

(h) If the actual population of Perm in 2013 was 5200, calculate the percentage error in Zipf's law estimate, correct to the nearest percentage.

5. The concentration C of serum in mg/ml, t hours after being administered to a patient, is given by $C = a2^{kt}$, where a and k are positive constants.

(a) Show $\log_2 C = \log_2 a + kt$.

(b) Copy and complete the following table, giving the answers in the third column correct to two decimal places.

t	C	$\log_2 C$
0	1·6	
2	1·55	
4	1·5	
6	1·46	
8	1·43	
10	1·38	
12	1·35	

(c) Draw a graph with $\log_2 C$ on the y-axis and t on the x-axis.

(d) Draw the line of best-fit through these points.

(e) Use the STAT mode on the calculator to find the slope and intercept on the vertical axis of the line of best-fit, correct to two decimal places.

(f) Find a and k using the values from part **(e)**, correct to two decimal places.

(g) Use the equation $C = a2^{kt}$ to estimate the concentration after 5 hours, correct to two decimal places.

(h) Using $C = a2^{kt}$, find the time for the concentration to become half its starting level, correct to the nearest hour.

REVISION QUESTIONS

1. Two bodies A and B move along a straight line. At time t, in seconds, the distance s that body A is from the fixed point is given by $s = t^3 - 10t^2 + 24t$. The distance d that body B is from the same fixed point at time t seconds is given by $d = 4 - t$, where s and d are in metres.

(a) Copy and complete the table below.

t	0	1	2	3	4	5	6
s							
d							

(b) Plot graphs of s against t and d against t on the same diagram for $0 \le t \le 6$.

(c) Use your graph to find when body A is 8 m from the fixed point, correct to one decimal place.

(d) Use your graph to find the maximum distance body A is from the fixed point, correct to the nearest metre.

(e) Use your graphs to find the times at which the bodies are the same distance from the fixed point, correct to one decimal place.

(f) Find the times at which:

(i) body A is at the fixed point,

(ii) body B is at the fixed point.

2. The rate R of flow of fluids in a tree over a 24-hour period is given by:

$$R = \begin{cases} 2t^2 - 192, & 0 \le t \le 12 \\ 96, & 12 \le t \le 18 \\ -12t + 312, & 18 \le t \le 24 \end{cases}$$

where R is in cm^3/hour and t is in hours.

(a) Copy and complete the table below.

t	0	3	6	9	12	15	18	21	24
R									

(b) Copy and complete the grid below and use the results in the table to draw a graph of R against t on it.

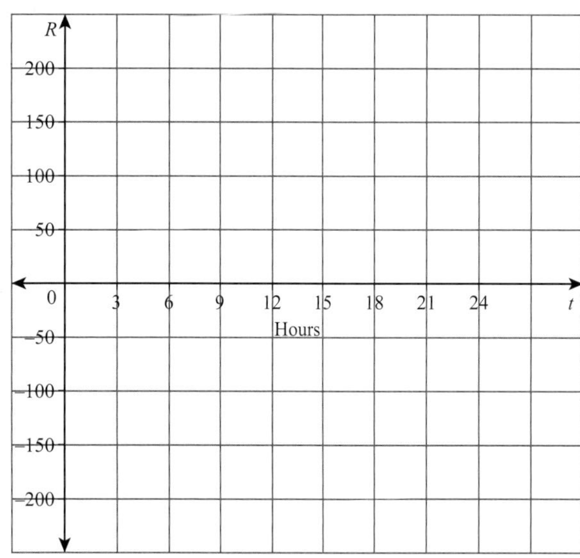

(c) Use your graph to find:

(i) the rate of flow at $t = 16$ hours,

(ii) the rate of flow at $t = 20$ hours, correct to the nearest whole number,

(iii) the times at which the rate of flow is 50 cm^3/hour, correct to the nearest hour,

(iv) the average rate of flow over the 24-hour period.

(d) Is this function continuous? Why?

3. The graphs of $f(x) = -x^2 + 5x + 6$ and $g(x) = -2x + 12$ are sketched below.

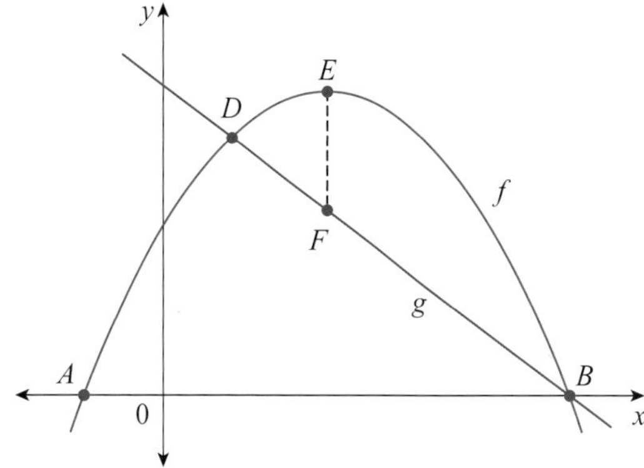

f and g intersect at D and B. A and B are the intercepts of f on the x-axis.

(a) Find the co-ordinates of A and B.

(b) Find the co-ordinates of D.

(c) Find the co-ordinates of E, the maximum point on f.

(d) If EF is parallel to the y-axis, find the co-ordinates of F.

(e) Find $|EF|$.

4. When a games console is switched off, the current I in amps (A) dies away according to the formula $I = 5(0{\cdot}6)^t$, where t is the time in seconds.

(a) Find the current at the instant the console is switched off.

(b) Copy and complete the table below, giving the I values correct to one decimal place.

t (s)	0	1	2	3	4	5
***I* (A)**						

(c) Plot I against t on graph paper.

(d) Use the graph to find:

(i) the current after 2·5 s, correct to one decimal place,

(ii) the time it takes the current to reach 0·5 A, correct to one decimal place.

(e) Evaluate $(0{\cdot}6)^4$ as a rational number and hence calculate the time for the current to become 0·648 A.

5. In a certain country, income tax T, in euro €, is levied as follows. For an income over €20 000, the tax payable is €800 plus 6% of earnings over €20 000.

(a) If a person's income is €x, $x > 20\,000$, write down a linear function connecting T and x.

(b) Use the function to find the tax on an income of €45 000.

(c) Use the function to find the income that will give a tax of €1100.

6. (a) Write 20% as a decimal.

(b) Increase 1000 by 20%.

(c) A population of 1000 organisms increases by 20% every day. Copy and complete the table below for the population P after t days. Give the P values correct to three significant figures.

***t* (days)**	0	1	2	3	4	5	6	7
P	1000							

(d) Draw a graph of P against t on graph paper.

(e) Use your graph to find:

(i) the population after 4·5 days to the nearest hundred,

(ii) the number of days it takes the population to reach 3300, correct to one decimal place.

(f) Find an equation relating P to t.

7. A chessboard has 64 squares. You place a 1-cent coin on the first square, two 1-cent coins on the second square, four 1-cent coins on the third square, always doubling the number of coins on the previous square.

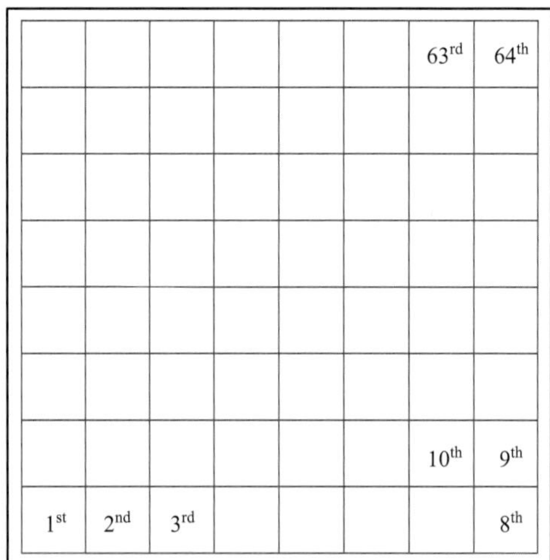

(a) Copy and complete the table.

Square number *R*	1	2	3	4	5	6	7	8
Number *N* of 1-cent coins on the square				2^3				

(b) How many coins are there on:

(i) the 20th square,

(ii) the 64th square?

(c) Write down a formula relating N to R.

(d) If a 1-cent coin is 1 mm thick, how high will the pile of cents on the 64th square be in metres? Give your answer in the form $a \times 10^n$, $1 \leq a \leq 10$, where a is given correct to one decimal place.

(e) The distance from the Earth to the Sun is 150 million km. Express this in metres in the form $a \times 10^n$, $1 \leq a \leq 10$.

(f) Find the ratio of the height of the pile of coins in part **(d)** to the Earth–Sun distance correct to the nearest whole number.

8. **(a)** Express $5 - 10x - x^2$ in the form $p - (x + q)^2$. Hence, write down:

(i) the co-ordinates of the maximum value of the function $y = 5 - 10x - x^2$,

(ii) the equation of the axis of symmetry of $y = 5 - 10x - x^2$.

(b) The curve $s: y = 5 - 10x - x^2$ intersects the line $l : y = 2x + k$, where k is a constant. Show that the x co-ordinates of the points of intersection satisfy the equation $x^2 + 12x + (k - 5) = 0$.

(c) Find the x co-ordinates in terms of k.

(d) Show that $k < 41$ for two points of intersection.

9. A model for the number of people N infected by a disease, t days after the outbreak was discovered, is given by $N = 500 - 400(2^{-\frac{1}{10}t})$, $0 \leq t \leq 50$.

(a) Find the number of people infected on the day the outbreak was discovered.

(b) Copy and complete the table below, giving the N values correct to two significant figures.

***t* (days)**	0	10	20	30	40	50	60
N							

(c) Copy the diagram below and draw a graph of N against t on it.

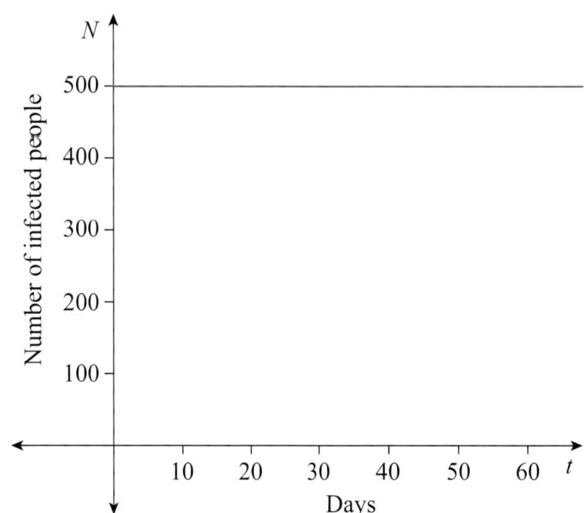

(d) Use the model to predict the number of people infected after 15 days, correct to two significant figures.

(e) If the actual number infected after 15 days is 375, find the percentage error in the model.

(f) What is the maximum value of N predicted by this model?

(g) Use the equation $N = 500 - 400(2^{-\frac{1}{10}t})$, to find t when $N = 250$. Give your answer correct to one decimal place.

10. In a city, the number N of mobile phone subscribers can be modelled by the equation $N = ka^t$, where t is the number of years after 1980.

(a) Show that $\log_3 N = \log_3 k + t \log_3 a$.

(b) Copy and complete the table below, giving all answers in the third column correct to one decimal place.

t	***N***	**$\log_3 N$**
0	300	
5	746	
10	1851	
15	4622	
20	11 501	
25	28 618	
30	71 212	

(c) Copy the diagram below onto your graph paper and plot the points in the table above with $\log_3 N$ on the y-axis and t on the x-axis.

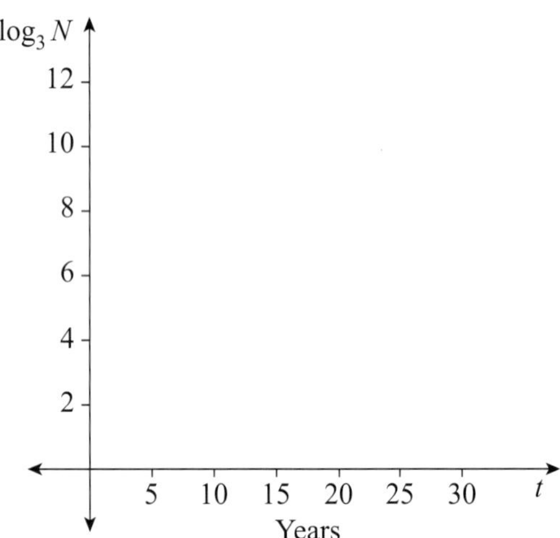

(d) Draw the line of best-fit through these points.

(e) Use the STAT mode on your calculator to find the slope and vertical intercept of the line of best-fit, correct to two decimal places.

(f) Hence, find k to the nearest whole number and a correct to one decimal place.

(g) Use the equation $N = ka^t$ to estimate the number of subscribers after 35 years.

(h) Estimate the average rate of change of the number of subscribers over the 30 years from 1980.

11. A research model for predicting the cumulative number of AIDS cases in thousands, t years after 1980, is given by the equation:

$$N = 150\left(\frac{t+10}{10}\right)^3$$

This model was considered to be a breakthrough as it was originally thought the model would be 'exponential' in nature.

(a) Find the number N predicted by the model described at:

(i) $t = 0$ years,

(ii) $t = 10$ years.

(b) Using the data points in part **(a)**, construct an exponential model of the form $N = ka^t$ by finding k and a. Find a to two decimal places.

(c) Use the first model to find N after 30 years.

(d) Use the exponential model to find N after 30 years.

(e) Find the ratio of the value for N in part **(c)** to that in part **(d)** correct to one decimal place.

(f) Why was the non-exponential model considered a breakthrough?

12. The graph of the function $y = f(x) = x^3$, $x \in \mathbb{R}$, $y \in \mathbb{R}$, is sketched below.

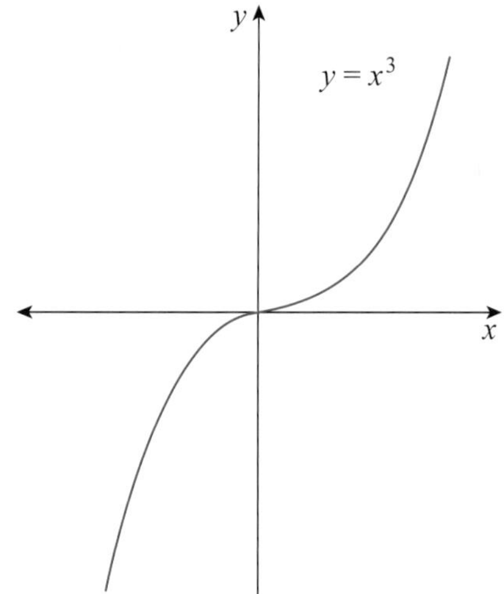

(a) Explain why this function is continuous for all $x \in \mathbb{R}$.

(b) Is this function $f: \mathbb{R} \to \mathbb{R}$

(i) injective? Why?

(ii) surjective? Why?

(iii) bijective? Why?

(c) Describe with the aid of a graph a function that is surjective but not injective.

SUMMARY

1. Function:

   A function $f(x)$ takes values of a variable x from a set called the domain and sends them to values y in a set called the codomain so that each value of x is sent to one and only one value of y.

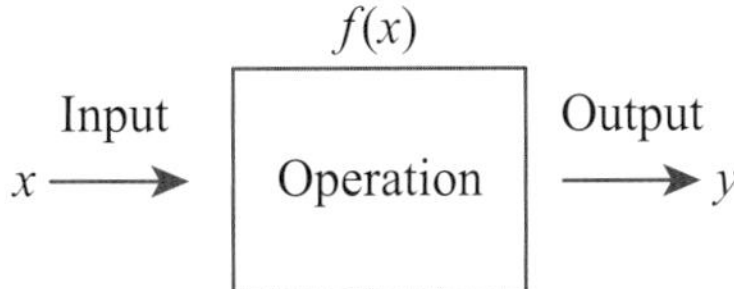

2. Domain and range:

   Domain: The domain of a function is the set of values which is mapped by a function.

   Range: The range of a function is the set of images obtained by mapping the elements of the domain.

   Codomain: The codomain of a function is the set of values into which the elements of the domain are mapped.

3. Test for a function (vertical line test):

   $y = f(x)$ is a function if all lines drawn parallel to the y-axis from all points in the domain of $f(x)$ intersect the graph of $y = f(x)$ **once and only once**.

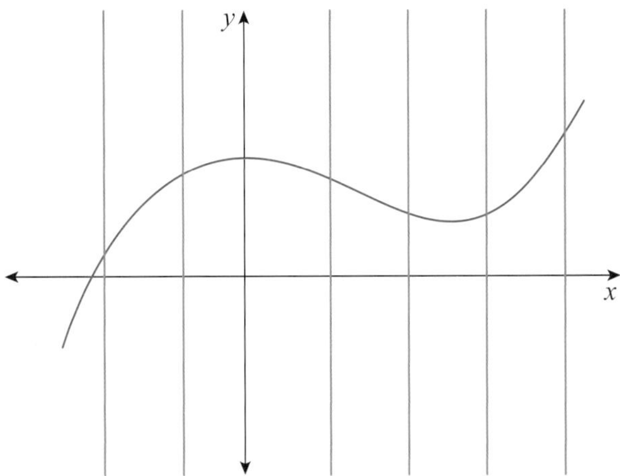

4. Injective, surjective and bijective functions:

   Injective function test: A function $y = f(x)$ is injective if every horizontal line in the codomain cuts the graph of $y = f(x)$ at **most once**.

$f: \mathbb{R} \to \mathbb{R}$

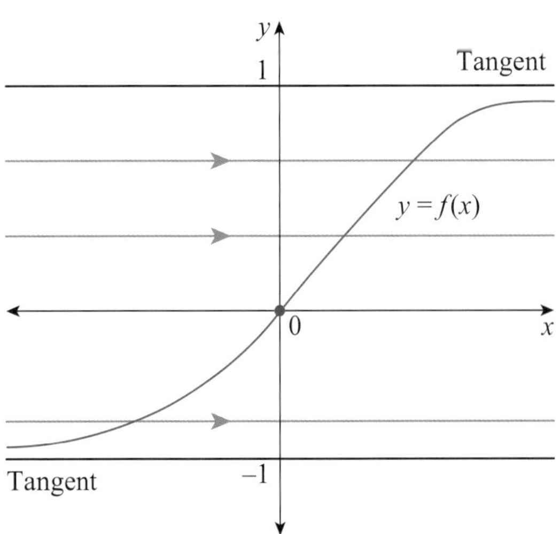

Surjective function test: A function $y = f(x)$ is surjective if every horizontal line in the codomain cuts the graph of $y = f(x)$ at **least once**.

$f: \mathbb{R} \to [-1, 1]$

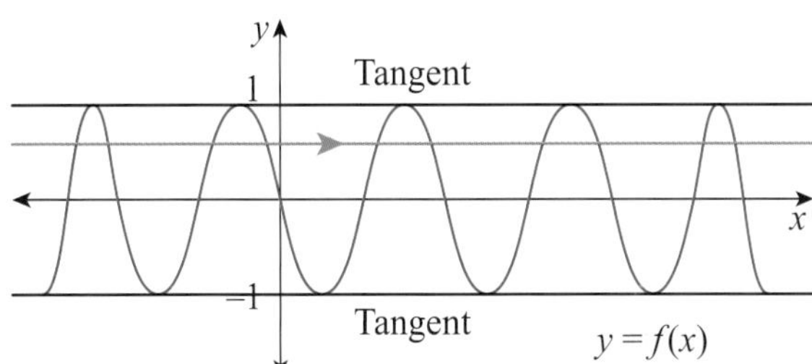

Bijective function test: A function $y = f(x)$ is bijective if every horizontal line in the codomain cuts the graph of $y = f(x)$ **once and only once**.

$f: \mathbb{R} \to \mathbb{R}$

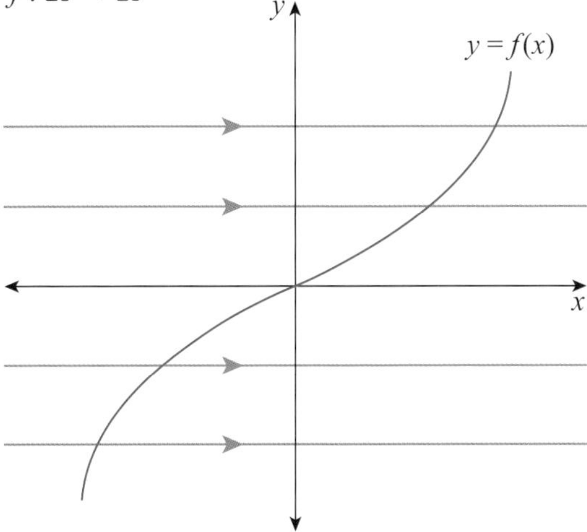

5. The **inverse** of a bijective function $y = f(x)$:

   To find $f^{-1}(x)$:

   (i) Solve for x in terms of y and then replace y by x.

   or

   (ii) Swap the values for x and y in $y = f(x)$ and solve for y.

6. Combining functions:

   $f(g(x)) = (f \circ g)(x)$

   $u = g(x) \Rightarrow f(g(x)) = f(u)$

7. Continuity:

   A function $y = f(x)$ is continuous if $\lim_{x \to a} f(x) = f(a)$.

   A continuous function is a function with no gaps in it.

8. Linear functions:

   (a) Equation: $y = mx + c$ or $y = ax + b$

   (b) Shape:

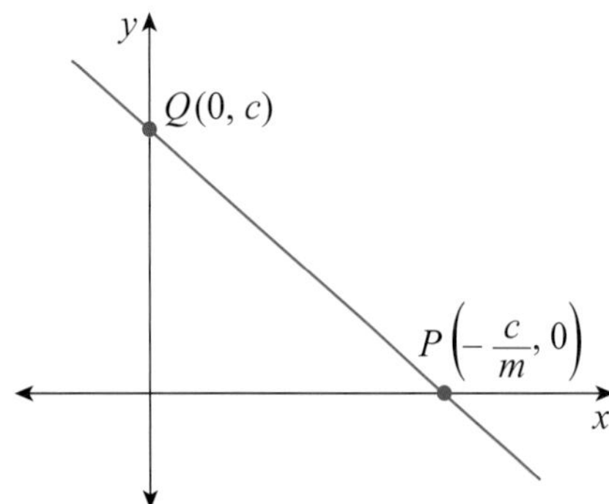

   (c) Forms of the equation of a straight line: $(y - y_1) = m(x - x_1)$ or $y = mx + c$ or $ax + by + c = 0$.

9. Quadratic functions:

   (a) Equation: $y = ax^2 + bx + c$

   (b) Shapes:

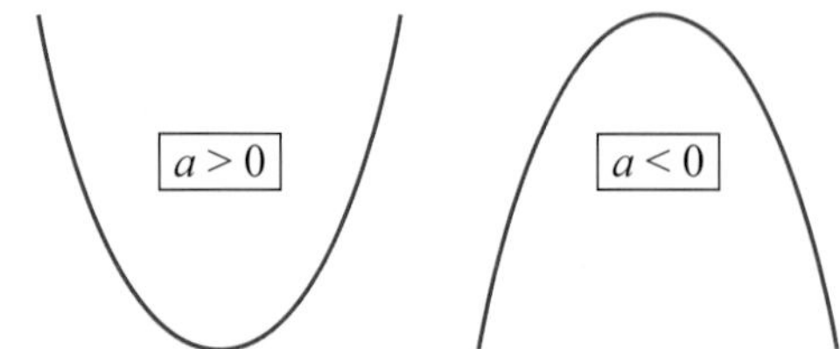

   (c) Roots:

   (i) $b^2 > 4ac \Rightarrow$ 2 different real roots:

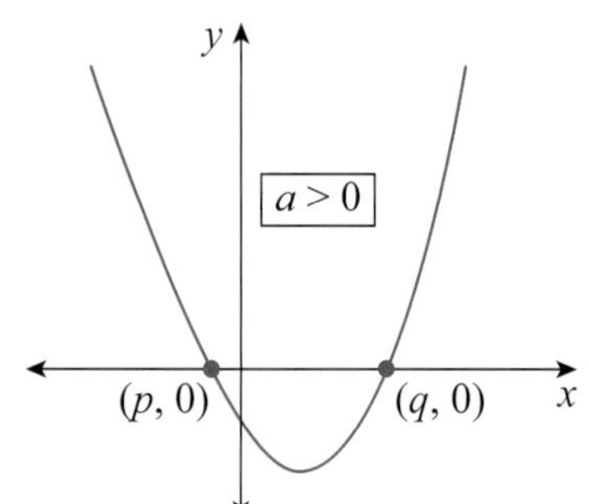

   or

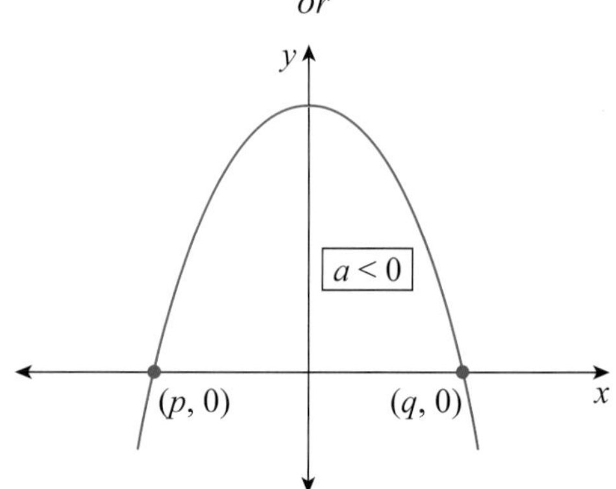

$y = k(x - p)(x - q)$

   (ii) $b^2 = 4ac \Rightarrow$ 2 equal real roots:

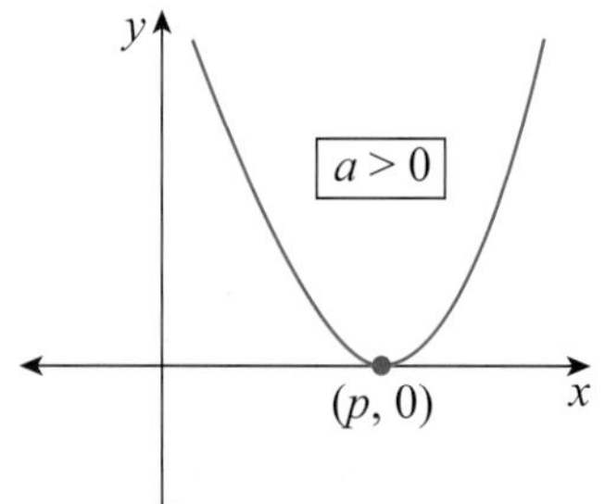

   or

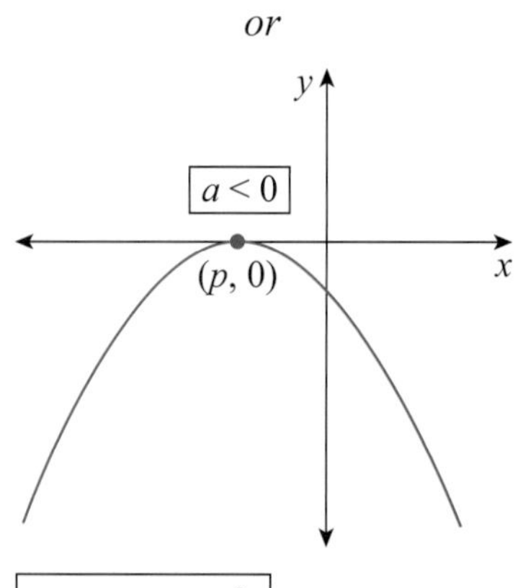

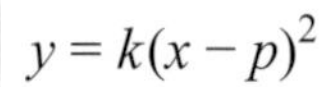

$y = k(x - p)^2$

(iii) $b^2 < 4ac \Rightarrow$ no real roots:

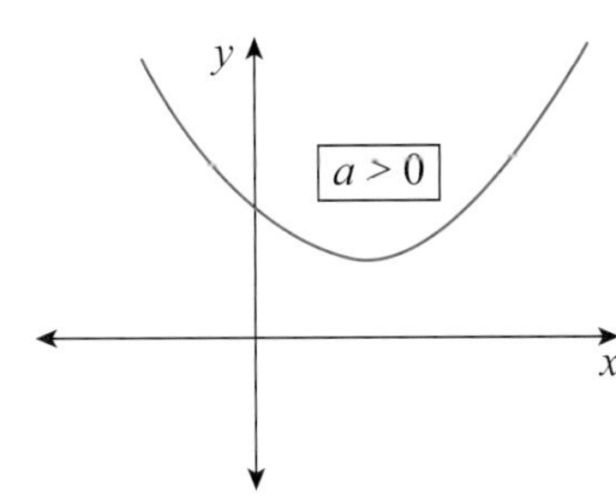

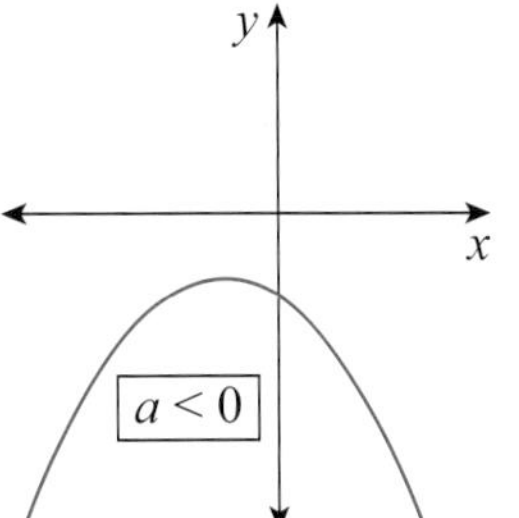

$y = ax^2 + bx + c$

(d) Vertex and axis of symmetry:

(i)

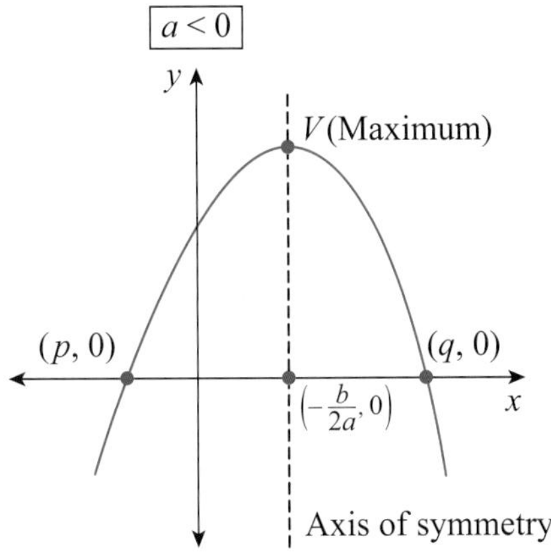

or

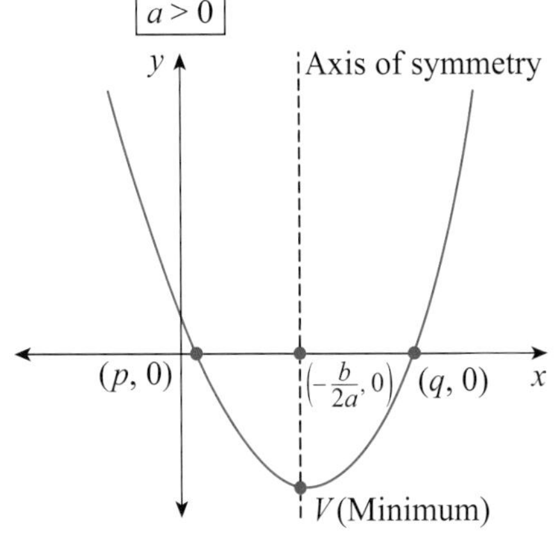

For two different roots:

$\left(-\frac{b}{2a}, 0\right)$ is the midpoint of $(p, 0)$ and $(q, 0)$ and is the x co-ordinate of the vertex.

For two equal roots: $\left(-\frac{b}{2a}, 0\right)$ is the vertex.

(ii) Equation of the axis of symmetry: $x = -\frac{b}{2a}$

(e) Complete the square.

(f) A quadratic function $y = ax^2 + bx + c$ can be written as $y = k(x^2 - Sx + P)$, where S is the sum of the roots and P is the product of the roots.

10. Cubic functions:

(a) Equation: $y = ax^3 + bx^2 + cx + d$

(b) Shapes:

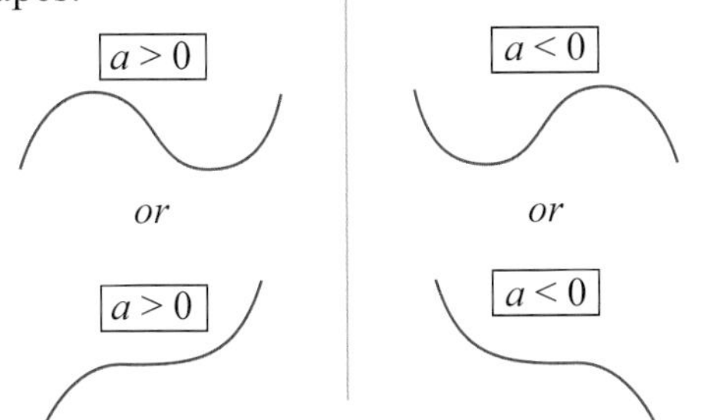

(c) Roots:

(i) Three real different roots:

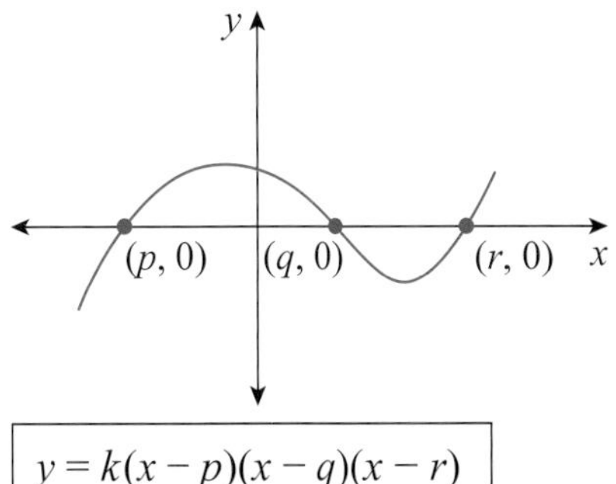

$y = k(x - p)(x - q)(x - r)$

(ii) Three real roots, two of which are the same:

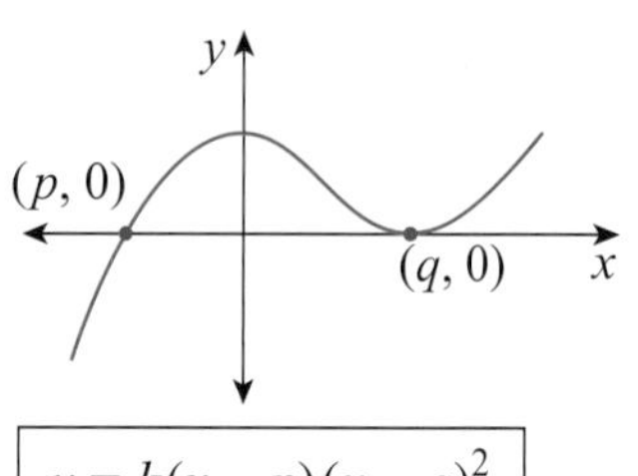

$y = k(x - p)(x - q)^2$

(iii) Only one real root:

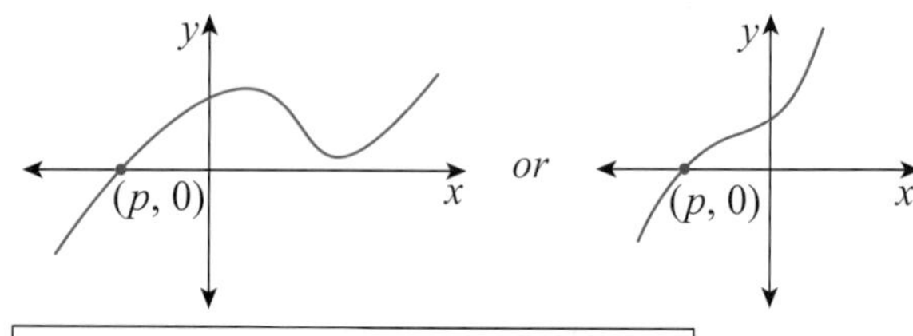

$y = k(x - p)$(Quadratic expression)

11. Transformation of functions:

For $y = f(x)$: $y = f(x + h) + v$ shifts $y = f(x)$ horizontally and vertically.

	> 0	< 0
h	Horizontal left	Horizontal right
v	Vertical up	Vertical down

12. Exponential functions:

(a) Equation: $y = ka^{bx}$, $k, a, b \in \mathbb{R}, a > 0, b > 0$

(b) Shapes:

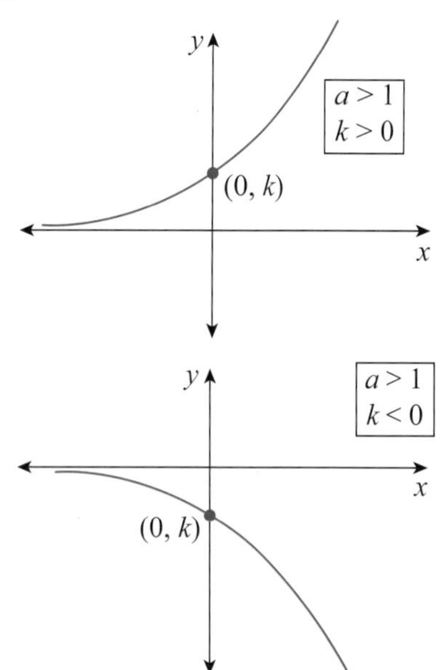

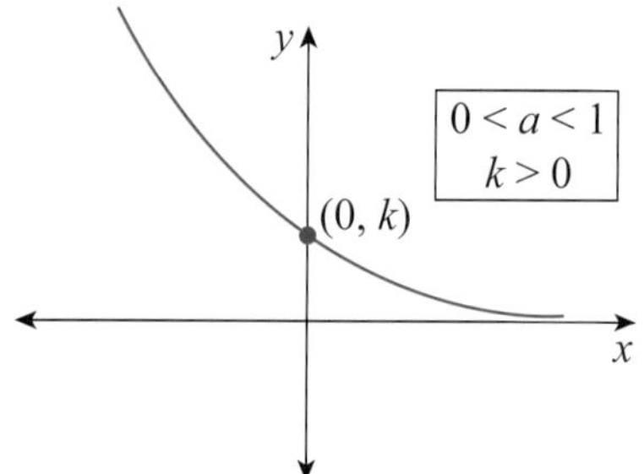

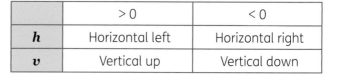

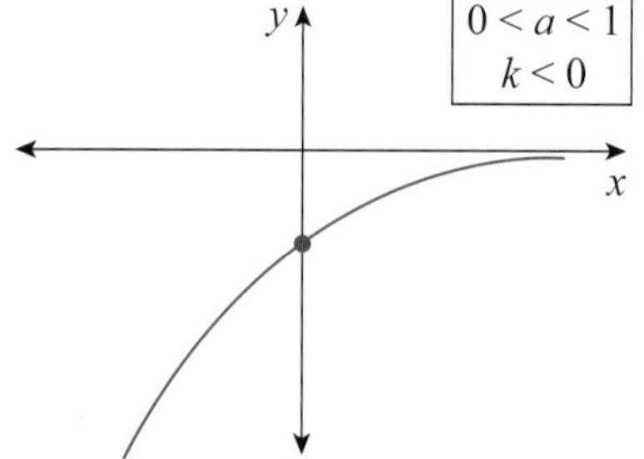

They always cross the y axis at $(0, k)$.

They never cross the x-axis.

They are always increasing or decreasing.

13. Log functions:

(a) Equation: $y = k \log_a x$, $a, k \in \mathbb{R}, a > 0$

(b) Shapes:

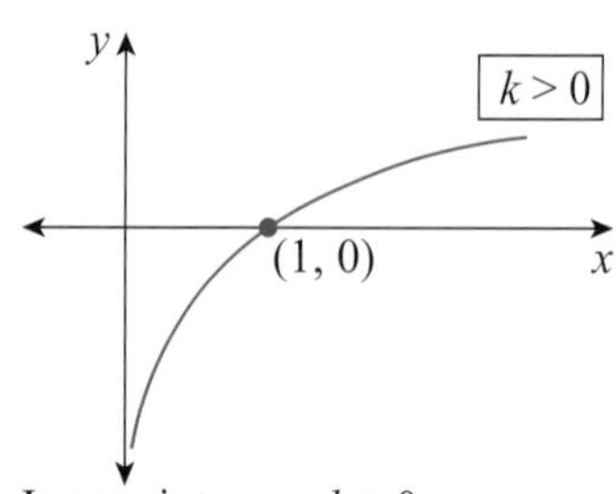

Increasing once $k > 0$.

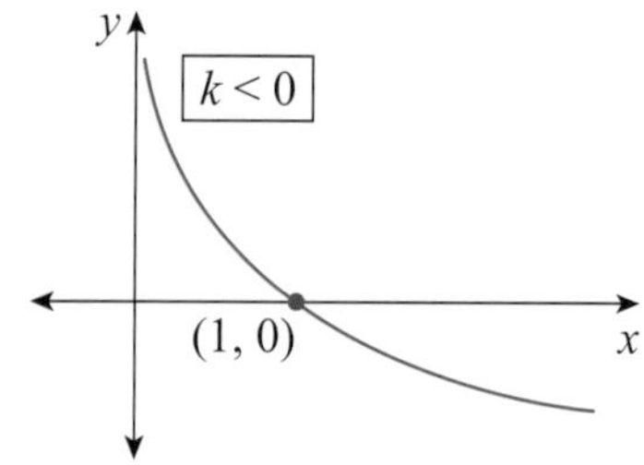

Decreasing once $k < 0$.

They always cross the x-axis at $(1, 0)$.

SECTION 8

Differentiation

Differential calculus is the mathematics of change. Two great mathematicians devised differential calculus:

Newton, who thought of differentiation in terms of the slope of the tangent to a curve and motion, and **Leibniz**, who thought of $\frac{dy}{dx}$ as a limiting sequence of the difference in y values divided by the difference in x values.

Gottfried Wilhelm Leibniz

Sir Isaac Newton

CHAPTER 23 Techniques of Differentiation

Learning Outcomes

- To understand how to obtain an instantaneous rate of change.
- To differentiate from first principles.
- To differentiate functions using the seven rules of differentiation.
- To carry out higher order differentiation.
- To differentiate trigonometric, inverse trigonometric, exponential and log functions.

23.1 Rates of change

The average rate of change of distance s with respect to time t is called average speed.

$$\text{Average speed} = \frac{\text{Distance}}{\text{Time}}$$

WORKED EXAMPLE Average rate of change

The distance s, in metres, a stone falls from rest, t seconds after it is dropped, is given by $s = 4{\cdot}9t^2$.

What is its average speed between $t_1 = 2$ and $t_2 = 5$?

$$\text{Average speed} = \frac{\text{Distance}}{\text{Time}}$$

$t_1 = 2$: $s_1 = 4{\cdot}9 \times 2^2 = 19{\cdot}6$ m

$t_2 = 5$: $s_2 = 4{\cdot}9 \times 5^2 = 122{\cdot}5$ m

Distance $= s_2 - s_1 = 122{\cdot}5 - 19{\cdot}6 = 102{\cdot}9$ m

Time $= t_2 - t_1 = 5 - 2 = 3$

$\therefore$ Average speed $= \dfrac{s_2 - s_1}{t_2 - t_1} = \dfrac{102{\cdot}9}{3} = 34{\cdot}3$ m/s

Average speed $= \dfrac{s_2 - s_1}{t_2 - t_1} =$ Slope of PQ

= Average rate of change of s with respect to t.

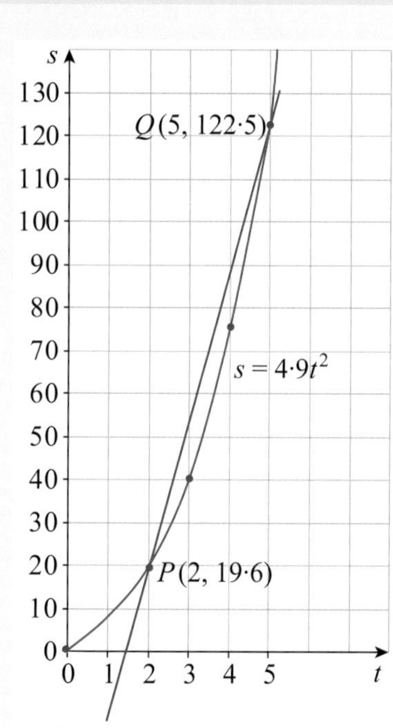

In general, the average rate of change of a function $y = f(x)$ with respect to x from

$P(x_1, y_1)$ to $Q(x_2, y_2) = \dfrac{y_2 - y_1}{x_2 - x_1} = \text{Slope of } PQ = \dfrac{f(x_2) - f(x_1)}{x_2 - x_1}$.

As the stone is dropped, its speed is continuously changing as it moves from point to point. The question arises as to what is the exact speed at any point in its motion. In other words, what is its instantaneous speed?

ACTIVITY 1

ACTION
Investigating instantaneous rates of change

OBJECTIVE
To investigate instantaneous rates of change by sliding a point closer and closer to another point

Instantaneous rate of change

The instantaneous rate of change of distance with time is called instantaneous speed. The instantaneous speed of a body is its speed v at any instant of time t. The instantaneous speed is the slope m of the tangent k to the curve of s against t at any point on the curve.

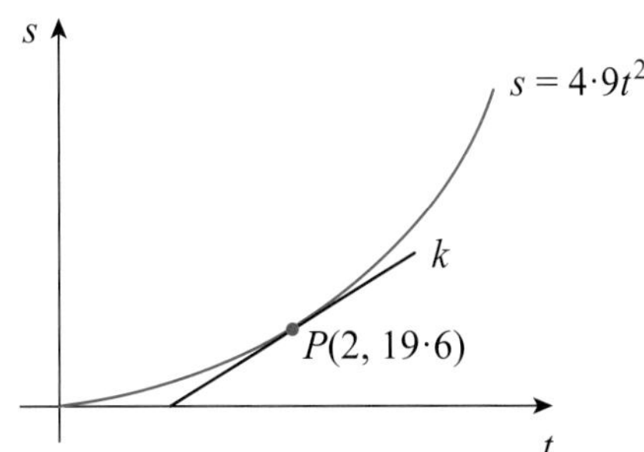

WORKED EXAMPLE Slope of a tangent

Finding the slope of the tangent to a curve at a point on the curve by sliding (limiting process):

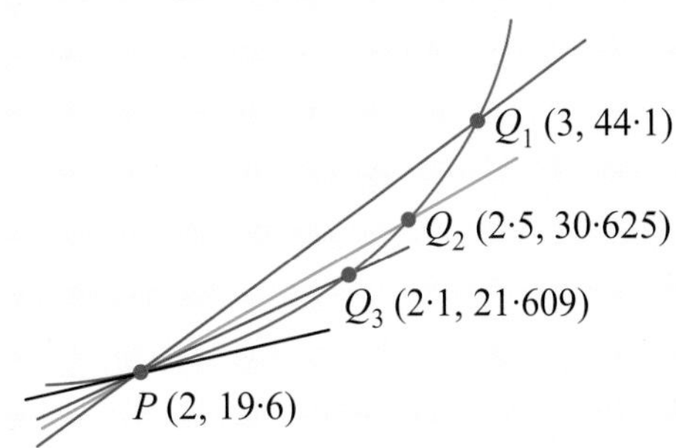

To find the slope of the tangent to the curve $s = 4{\cdot}9t^2$ at $P(2, 19{\cdot}6)$, choose a point $Q_1(3, 44{\cdot}1)$ close to P and work out the slope m_1 of the line PQ_1.

$$m_1 = \frac{\text{difference in } s}{\text{difference in } t} = \frac{s_2 - s_1}{t_2 - t_1} = \frac{44{\cdot}1 - 19{\cdot}6}{3 - 2} = 24{\cdot}5$$

This is not the slope m of the tangent at P. It is a first approximation.

Repeat this process of generating slopes as the point Q moves down the curve, sliding closer and closer to P.

The results are shown in the table below:

Q	Slope of PQ where $P(2, 19{\cdot}6)$
$Q_1(3, 44{\cdot}1)$	$PQ_1 = m_1 = \dfrac{44{\cdot}1 - 19{\cdot}6}{3 - 2} = 24{\cdot}5$
$Q_2(2{\cdot}5, 30{\cdot}625)$	$PQ_2 = m_2 = \dfrac{30{\cdot}625 - 19{\cdot}6}{2{\cdot}5 - 2} = 22{\cdot}05$
$Q_3(2{\cdot}1, 21{\cdot}609)$	$PQ_3 = m_3 = \dfrac{21{\cdot}609 - 19{\cdot}6}{2{\cdot}1 - 2} = 20{\cdot}09$
$Q_4(2{\cdot}01, 19{\cdot}79649)$	$PQ_4 = m_4 = \dfrac{19{\cdot}79649 - 19{\cdot}6}{2{\cdot}01 - 2} = 19{\cdot}649$
$Q_5(2{\cdot}001, 19{\cdot}6196049)$	$PQ_5 = m_5 = \dfrac{19{\cdot}6196049 - 19{\cdot}6}{2{\cdot}001 - 2} = 19{\cdot}6049$
$Q_6(2{\cdot}0001, 19{\cdot}60196005)$	$PQ_6 = m_4 = \dfrac{19{\cdot}60196005 - 19{\cdot}6}{2{\cdot}0001 - 2} = 19{\cdot}60049$
$Q_7(2{\cdot}00001, 19{\cdot}600196)$	$PQ_7 = m_7 = \dfrac{19{\cdot}60196 - 19{\cdot}6}{2{\cdot}00001 - 2} = 19{\cdot}600049$

As the point Q on the curve $s = 4{\cdot}9t^2$ gets closer and closer to $P(2, 19{\cdot}6)$, the slopes of the lines PQ are getting closer and closer to the exact slope of the tangent to the curve at P.

This process of generating slopes, in order to get the slope of the tangent to a curve at a point on a curve, is called **differentiation from first principles**.

The final slope is called $\dfrac{ds}{dt}$ and stands for the final value of $\dfrac{\text{difference } (d) \text{ in } s}{\text{difference } (d) \text{ in } t}$.
It is pronounced as 'Dee s Dee t'.

In the case above, $m = \dfrac{ds}{dt} = 19{\cdot}6$ at $P(2, 19{\cdot}6)$ and is the slope of the tangent to the curve $s = 4{\cdot}9t^2$ at $P(2, 19{\cdot}6)$ on the curve.

Differentiation is the process of finding the slope of the tangent to a curve at a **point** on the curve.

It gives you the change of the dependent variable with respect to the independent variable at a particular point.

EXERCISE 1

1. Find the following from the graph:

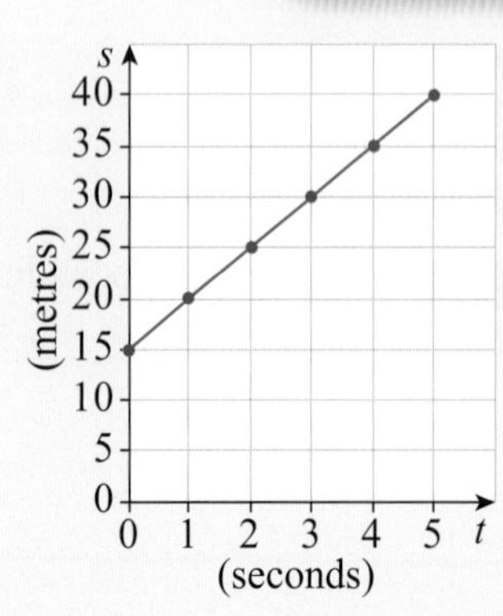

(a) the average rate of change of s with respect to t from $t = 2$ to $t = 5$,

(b) the instantaneous rate of change of s with respect to t at $t = 3$,

(c) why these two results are the same.

2. If k is the tangent to the curve shown at (5, 75), find the following:

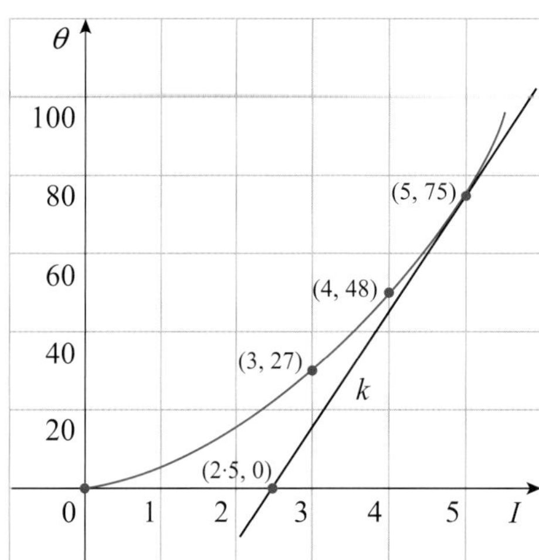

(a) the average rate of change of θ with respect to I from $I = 4$ to $I = 5$,

(b) $\dfrac{d\theta}{dI}$ at $I = 5$.

3. If k is the tangent to the curve shown at (2, 5), find the following:

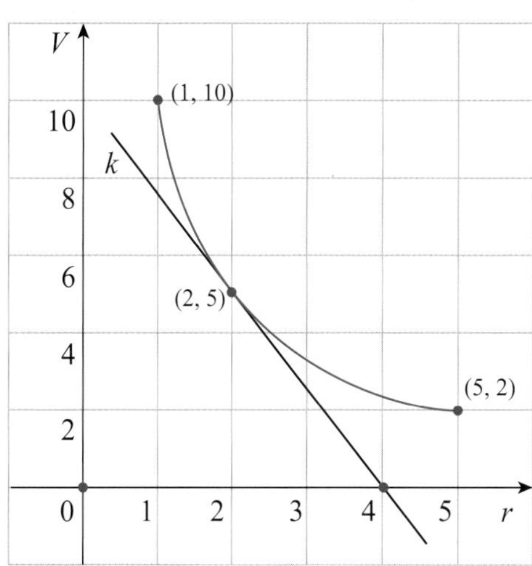

(a) the average rate of change of V with respect to r from $r = 1$ to $r = 5$,

(b) the instantaneous rate of change of V with respect to r at $r = 2$. Why is this negative?

(c) $\dfrac{dV}{dr}$ at $r = 2$.

4. If k is the tangent to the curve at (1, 2), find the following:

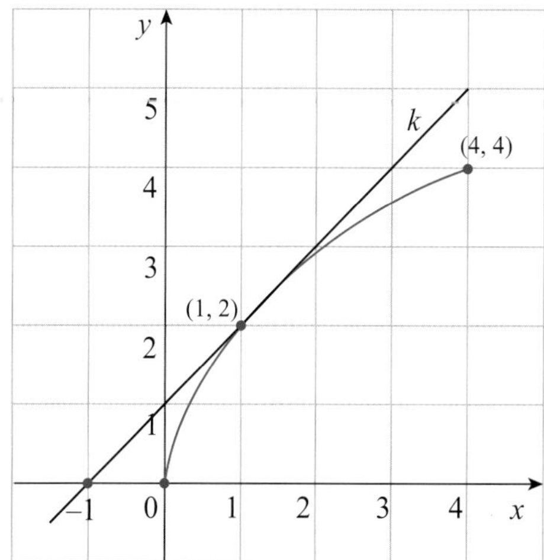

(a) the average rate of change of y with respect to x from $x = 1$ to $x = 4$,

(b) the instantaneous rate of change of y with respect to x at $x = 1$,

(c) the slope of the tangent to the curve at $x = 1$,

(d) $\dfrac{dy}{dx}$ at $x = 1$.

5. The graph of current I in milliamps (mA) against voltage V in Volts (V) in a semiconducting device is shown below.

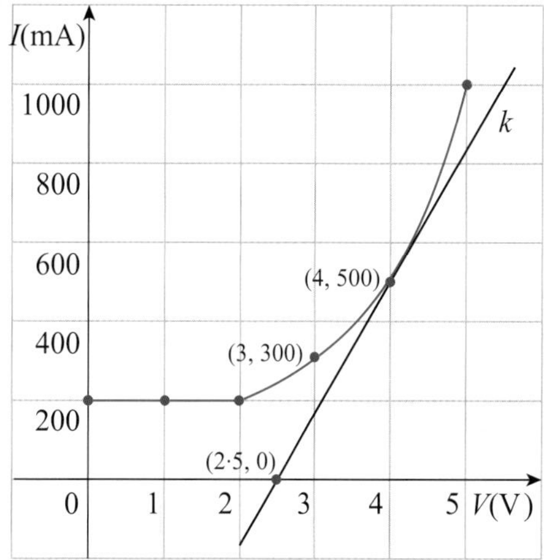

If k is the tangent to the curve at (4, 500), find the following:

(a) the average rate of change of the current with voltage from $V = 3$ V to $V = 4$ V,

(b) the instantaneous rate of change of the current with voltage at $V = 4$ V.

What notation is used to describe the instantaneous rate of change of the current with respect to voltage?

23.2 Differentiation from first principles 

Given any function $y = f(x)$, differentiation from first principles is the process of finding the slope of the tangent to the curve of $y = f(x)$ at a point (x, y) on the curve by successively generating slopes to get the final limiting slope.

$\frac{dy}{dx}$ is the exact slope at any point $(x, y) = (x, f(x))$ on the curve.

These words can be summarised in a simple mathematical formula:

$$\frac{dy}{dx} = \lim_{h \to 0} (\text{Slope of } PQ) \Rightarrow \frac{dy}{dx} = \lim_{h \to 0} \frac{f(x+h) - f(x)}{(x+h) - x}$$

$y = f(x)$

k

$Q(x + h, f(x + h))$

$P(x, f(x))$

$$\frac{dy}{dx} = m = \lim_{h \to 0} \frac{f(x+h) - f(x)}{h}$$

This formula enables you to differentiate any function $y = f(x)$ from first principles.

It is important to note the following:

1. $\frac{dy}{dx} = m =$ slope of the tangent to the curve $y = f(x)$ at any point $(x, f(x))$ on the curve
$=$ (instantaneous) rate of change of y with respect to x.

2. Rate of change with respect to **time** is often just called rate of change.

3. If $y = f(x)$, the slope of the tangent $\frac{dy}{dx}$ is often written as $f'(x)$ [f dash x.]:

$$y = f(x) \Rightarrow \frac{dy}{dx} = m = f'(x)$$

4. The result $\frac{dy}{dx} = m = f'(x)$ of differentiating a function is often called its **derivative**.

5. The equation of the tangent k to a curve at any point $P(x_1, y_1)$ can be found by:

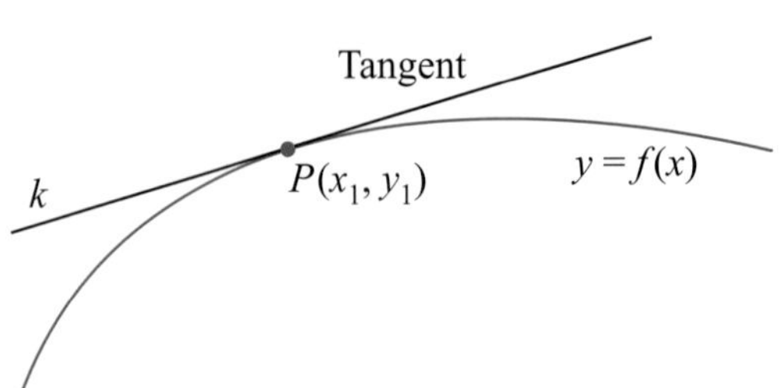

(a) finding the slope m of the tangent to the curve at P:
$m = f'(x)$ at (x_1, y_1) and then,

(b) using the equation of a straight line: $(y - y_1) = m(x - x_1)$

ACTIVITY 2

ACTION
Exploring first principles (1)

OBJECTIVE
To find the slopes of various functions as a first step towards differentiating from first principles

SYLLABUS NOTE

You are only required to differentiate linear and quadratic functions from first principles. In the worked example on the next page the function $y = x^3$ is differentiated from first principles. This is done to show you the development of a pattern to deepen your understanding of the first rule of differentiation.

WORKED EXAMPLE First principles 1

Differentiate $y = x^2$ from first principles.

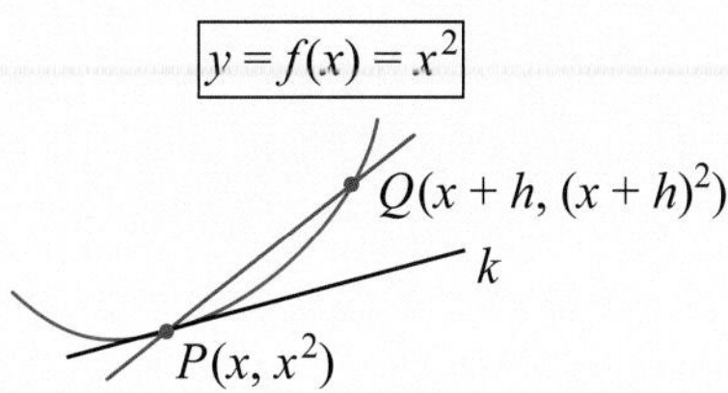

$$\text{Slope of } PQ = \frac{(x+h)^2 - x^2}{(x+h) - x}$$

$$= \frac{x^2 + 2xh + h^2 - x^2}{x + h - x}$$

$$= \frac{h(2x+h)}{h}$$

$$= 2x + h$$

$$\therefore \frac{dy}{dx} = m = \lim_{h \to 0} (2x + h) = 2x$$

$y = x^2 \Rightarrow \frac{dy}{dx} = m = 2x$ is the slope of the tangent to the curve $y = x^2$ at **any** point on the curve.

WORKED EXAMPLE First principles 2

Differentiate $y = x^3$ from first principles.

y = f(x) = x³

Q(x + h, (x + h)³)

k

P(x, x³)

$$\text{Slope of } PQ = \frac{(x+h)^3 - x^3}{(x+h) - x}$$

$$= \frac{x^3 + 3x^2h + 3xh^2 + h^3 - x^3}{h}$$

$$= \frac{h(3x^2 + 3xh + h^2)}{h}$$

$$= 3x^2 + 3xh + h^2$$

$$\frac{dy}{dx} = m = \lim_{h \to 0} (3x^2 + 3xh + h^2)$$

$$\frac{dy}{dx} = 3x^2$$

$y = x^3 \Rightarrow \frac{dy}{dx} = m = 3x^2$ is the slope of the tangent to the curve $y = x^3$ at **any** point on the curve.

ACTIVITY 3

ACTION
Exploring first principles (2)

OBJECTIVE
To find the derivative of some simple functions from first principles

EXAMPLE 1

Use first principles to show that if $y = f(x) = cu(x)$ then $\frac{dy}{dx} = cu'(x)$, where c is a constant and $u(x)$ is any function of x.

Solution

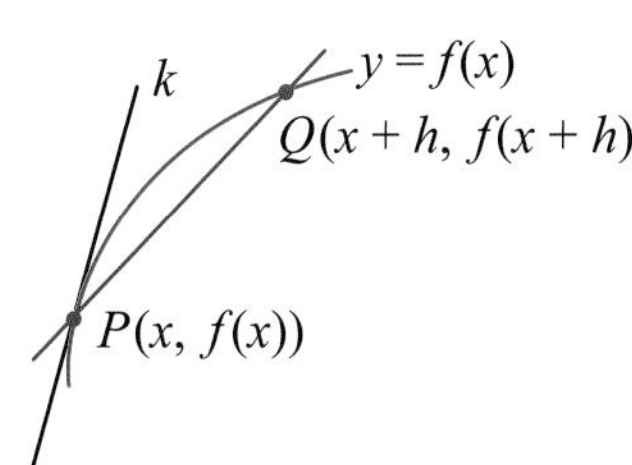

$$\text{Slope of } PQ = \frac{cu(x+h) - cu(x)}{(x+h) - x}$$

$$= c\left(\frac{u(x+h) - u(x)}{h}\right)$$

$$\frac{dy}{dx} = c \lim_{h \to 0} \left(\frac{u(x+h) - u(x)}{h}\right)$$

$\therefore \frac{dy}{dx} = cu'(x)$, where $u'(x)$ is the derivative of $y = u(x)$.

This is a general rule that applies to any function and is known as the **multiplication by a constant rule:** If a function is multiplied by a constant, then its derivative is also multiplied by the constant.

EXAMPLE 2

Find the equation of the tangent to the curve $y = 3x^2$ at $x = -2$.

Solution

$x = -2$: $y = 3(-2)^2 = 12$. Therefore, $(-2, 12)$ is a point on the curve.

$(x_1, y_1) = (-2, 12)$

$y = 3x^2$

$\frac{dy}{dx} = 3(2x) = 6x$

$\left(\frac{dy}{dx}\right)_{x=-2} = 6(-2) = -12 = m$

$\left[\left(\frac{dy}{dx}\right)_{x=-2} = \text{Value of } \frac{dy}{dx} \text{ at } x = -2\right]$

Use $(y - y_1) = m(x - x_1)$ to find the equation of the tangent.

Equation of tangent k: $y - 12 = -12(x - (-2))$

$y - 12 = -12(x + 2)$

$y - 12 = -12x - 24$

$12x + y + 12 = 0$

23.3 Differentiation by rule

First principles differentiation is the basis of all differentiation. However, it is very tedious. Rules of differentiation have been developed from first principles to make the process easier and quicker. In this chapter, these rules will be set out using simple functions and then generalised to all functions.

1. The basic rule

The following derivatives have already been proved from first principles:

$y = x^2 \Rightarrow \frac{dy}{dx} = 2x$

$y = x^3 \Rightarrow \frac{dy}{dx} = 3x^2$

These results seem to suggest that the basic rule of differentiation is:

$$y = x^p \Rightarrow \frac{dy}{dx} = px^{p-1}, p \in \mathbb{R} \quad \textbf{[Rule 1]}$$

The rule in words: For $y = x^p$, slide the power p down in front of the variable and take 1 away from the power.

First principles shows that this rule is true for all $p \in \mathbb{R}$.

- $y = x^1 \Rightarrow \frac{dy}{dx} = 1x^0 = 1$
- $y = x^{\frac{2}{3}} \Rightarrow \frac{dy}{dx} = \frac{2}{3}x^{-\frac{1}{3}} = \frac{2}{3x^{\frac{1}{3}}}$
- $y = x^{32} \Rightarrow \frac{dy}{dx} = 32x^{31}$
- $y = \frac{1}{x^7} = x^{-7} \Rightarrow \frac{dy}{dx} = -7x^{-8} = -\frac{7}{x^8}$

2. Multiplication by a constant rule

It has been shown from first principles that: $y = cu(x) \Rightarrow \frac{dy}{dx} = cu'(x)$.

- $y = 5x^2 \Rightarrow \frac{dy}{dx} = 5(2x) = 10x$
- $y = \frac{x^8}{4} = \frac{1}{4}x^8 \Rightarrow \frac{dy}{dx} = \frac{1}{4}(8x^7) = 2x^7$
- $y = \frac{3}{2\sqrt{x}} = \frac{3}{2}x^{-\frac{1}{2}} \Rightarrow \frac{dy}{dx} = \frac{3}{2}\left(-\frac{1}{2}x^{-\frac{3}{2}}\right) = -\frac{3}{4x^{\frac{3}{2}}}$

In general:

$$y = cu(x) \Rightarrow \frac{dy}{dx} = cu'(x),\ c \text{ a constant} \qquad \textbf{[Rule 2]}$$

The rule in words: To differentiate a function multiplied by a constant, write down the constant again and multiply it by the derivative of the function.

3. The constant rule

This is the rule for differentiating a constant function $y = c$.

$y = c$ (constant) $\Rightarrow \frac{dy}{dx} = 0$ because $y = c$ is a straight line parallel to the x-axis.

Its slope $m = \frac{dy}{dx} = 0$ because it is dead flat.

y
Dead flat
$y = c$
$y = 4$
$y = 2$
x $y = 0$
$y = -2$

ACTIVITY 4

ACTION
Proving the sum rule from first principles

OBJECTIVE
To prove the sum rule from first principles

In general:

$$y = c\,(\text{constant}) \Rightarrow \frac{dy}{dx} = 0 \qquad \textbf{[Rule 3]}$$

The rule in words: The derivative of a constant on its own is zero.

- $y = 3 \Rightarrow \frac{dy}{dx} = 0$
- $y = \frac{1}{2} \Rightarrow \frac{dy}{dx} = 0$
- $y = a^2$ (a a constant) $\Rightarrow \frac{dy}{dx} = 0$

ACTIVITY 5

ACTION
Preparing to differentiate

OBJECTIVE
To manipulate algebraic expressions to get them ready to differentiate and to tidy up afterwards

4. The sum rule

This is the rule for differentiating a sum of functions.

In general:

$$y = u + v \Rightarrow \frac{dy}{dx} = u' + v' = \frac{du}{dx} + \frac{dv}{dx}, \text{ where } u \text{ and } v \text{ are functions of } x. \qquad \textbf{[Rule 4]}$$

The rule in words: If y = a sum of functions, just differentiate each function individually.

EXAMPLE 3

Differentiate $y = x^2 + \frac{2}{x} - 3$ with respect to x.

Solution

$y = x^2 + \frac{2}{x} - 3 = x^2 + 2x^{-1} - 3$

$\frac{dy}{dx} = 2x + 2(-x^{-2}) - 0$

$\frac{dy}{dx} = 2x - \frac{2}{x^2}$

5. The product rule

This is the rule for differentiating **two** functions that are multiplied together.

In general:

$$y = uv \Rightarrow \frac{dy}{dx} = uv' + vu' = u\frac{dv}{dx} + v\frac{du}{dx},$$

where u and v are functions of x. **[Rule 5]**

The rule in words: y = (First)(Second)

$\Rightarrow \frac{dy}{dx}$ = (First)(derivative of Second) + (Second)(derivative of First)

EXAMPLE 4

Differentiate $y = (2x - 1)(x^2 + 4)$ with respect to x.

Solution

$y = (2x - 1)(x^2 + 4)$

$u = (2x - 1) \Rightarrow u' = \frac{du}{dx} = 2$

$v = (x^2 + 4) \Rightarrow v' = \frac{dv}{dx} = 2x$

$\frac{dy}{dx} = uv' + vu' = u\frac{dv}{dx} + v\frac{du}{dx}$

$= (2x - 1)(2x) + (x^2 + 4)(2)$

$= 4x^2 - 2x + 2x^2 + 8$

$= 6x^2 - 2x + 8$

EXAMPLE 5

Differentiate $y = (4x^2 + 1)(1 - x^3)$ with respect to x.

Solution

$y = (4x^2 + 1)(1 - x^3)$

$u = (4x^2 + 1) \Rightarrow u' = \frac{du}{dx} = 8x$

$v = (1 - x^3) \Rightarrow v' = \frac{dv}{dx} = -3x^2$

$\frac{dy}{dx} = uv' + vu' = u\frac{dv}{dx} + v\frac{du}{dx}$

$= (4x^2 + 1)(-3x^2) + (1 - x^3)(8x)$

$= -12x^4 - 3x^2 + 8x - 8x^4$

$= -20x^4 - 3x^2 + 8x$

$= x(-20x^3 - 3x + 8)$

6. The quotient rule

This is the rule for differentiating one function divided by another.

In general:

$$y = \frac{u}{v} \Rightarrow \frac{dy}{dx} = \frac{vu' - uv'}{v^2} = \frac{v\frac{du}{dx} - u\frac{dv}{dx}}{v^2}, \text{ where } u \text{ and } v \text{ are functions of } x.$$ **[Rule 6]**

The rule in words:

$$y = \frac{\text{Top}}{\text{Bottom}} \Rightarrow \frac{dy}{dx} = \frac{(\text{Bottom})(\text{derivative of Top}) - (\text{Top})(\text{derivative of Bottom})}{(\text{Bottom})^2}$$

EXAMPLE 6

Differentiate $y = \frac{2x+1}{3x^2-2}$ with respect to x.

Solution

$$y = \frac{2x+1}{3x^2-2} = \frac{(2x+1)}{(3x^2-2)}$$

$$u = (2x+1) \Rightarrow u' = \frac{du}{dx} = 2$$

$$v = (3x^2-2) \Rightarrow v' = \frac{dv}{dx} = 6x$$

$$\frac{dy}{dx} = \frac{(v)(u') - (u)(v')}{(v)^2} = \frac{(3x^2-2)(2) - (2x+1)(6x)}{(3x^2-2)^2}$$

$$= \frac{6x^2 - 4 - 12x^2 - 6x}{(3x^2-2)^2}$$

$$= \frac{-6x^2 - 6x - 4}{(3x^2-2)^2}$$

$$= \frac{2(-3x^2 - 3x - 2)}{(3x^2-2)^2}$$

EXAMPLE 7

Differentiate $y = \frac{4-x^2}{4+x^2}$ with respect to x.

Solution

$$y = \frac{4-x^2}{4+x^2}$$

$$u = (4-x^2) \Rightarrow u' = \frac{du}{dx} = -2x$$

$$v = (4+x^2) \Rightarrow v' = \frac{dv}{dx} = 2x$$

$$\frac{dy}{dx} = \frac{(4+x^2)(-2x) - (4-x^2)(2x)}{(4+x^2)^2}$$

$$= \frac{2x(-4 - x^2 - 4 + x^2)}{(4+x^2)^2}$$

$$= -\frac{16x}{(4+x^2)^2}$$

7. The chain rule

This is the most powerful rule of differentiation and is used to differentiate complicated (composite) functions by breaking them down into two simpler linked functions.

WORKED EXAMPLE The chain rule

The composite function $y = \sqrt{3x^2 + 1}$ can be written as two linked functions: $y = \sqrt{u}$, where $u = (3x^2 + 1)$.

The chain rule in differentiation comes from the fact that $\frac{dy}{dx}$ = the rate of change of y with respect to x.

If y (Yvonne) runs three times as fast as u (Una) and u (Una) runs four times as fast as x (Xena), then y (Yvonne) runs 12 times as fast as x (Xena).

Mathematically: $\frac{dy}{du} = 3$ and $\frac{du}{dx} = 4 \Rightarrow \frac{dy}{dx} = 3 \times 4 = 12 = \frac{dy}{du} \times \frac{du}{dx}$

This is the chain rule.

In general:

If y is a function of u and u is a function of x then $\frac{dy}{dx} = \frac{dy}{du} \times \frac{du}{dx}$

The rule in words: You can split a hard $\frac{dy}{dx}$ into two easier derivatives multiplied together: $\frac{dy}{dx} = \frac{dy}{du} \times \frac{du}{dx}$.

EXAMPLE 8

Differentiate $y = \sqrt{3x^2 + 1}$ with respect to x.

Solution

$y = \sqrt{3x^2 + 1}$

$u = (3x^2 + 1) \Rightarrow y = u^{\frac{1}{2}}$

Chain rule: $\frac{dy}{dx} = \frac{dy}{du} \times \frac{du}{dx}$

$\frac{dy}{dx} = \frac{1}{2} u^{-\frac{1}{2}} \times 6x = \frac{3x}{\sqrt{u}}$

$\frac{dy}{dx} = \frac{3x}{\sqrt{3x^2 + 1}}$

EXAMPLE 9

Differentiate $y = (5x + 7)^{100}$ with respect to x.

Solution

$y = (5x + 7)^{100}$

$u = (5x + 7) \Rightarrow y = u^{100}$

Chain rule: $\frac{dy}{dx} = \frac{dy}{du} \times \frac{du}{dx}$

$\frac{dy}{dx} = 100\,u^{99} \times 5 = 500\,u^{99}$

$\frac{dy}{dx} = 500\,(5x + 7)^{99}$

The chain rule for any function raised to a power p can be done quickly in your head.

Consider $y = [\,f(x)]^p$, where $f(x)$ is any function of x and $p \in \mathbb{R}$.

$u = f(x) \Rightarrow y = u^p$

Chain rule: $\frac{dy}{dx} = \frac{dy}{du} \times \frac{du}{dx}$

$\frac{dy}{dx} = pu^{p-1} \times f'(x)$

$\frac{dy}{dx} = p[\,f(x)]^{p-1} \times f'(x)$

This is a fantastic result as it enables you to differentiate composite functions very quickly.

In general:

$y = [f(x)]^p \Rightarrow \frac{dy}{dx} = p[f(x)]^{p-1} \times f'(x)$ where $f(x)$ is any function of x, $p \in \mathbb{R}$. **[Rule 7]**

The rule in words: To find the derivative of $y = [f(x)]^p$, slide the power p down in front of the function, subtract 1 from the power p and multiply by the derivative of the function $f(x)$.

- $y = (4x^2 + 3)^7 \Rightarrow \frac{dy}{dx} = 7(4x^2 + 3)^6 \times (8x) = 56x(4x^2 + 3)^6$
- $y = \frac{1}{\sqrt{x^3 + 5}} = (x^3 + 5)^{-\frac{1}{2}} \Rightarrow \frac{dy}{dx} = \left(-\frac{1}{2}\right)(x^3 + 5)^{-\frac{3}{2}}(3x^2)$

$$= -\frac{3x^2}{2(x^3 + 5)^{\frac{3}{2}}}$$

ACTIVITY 6

ACTION
Differentiating algebraic expressions

OBJECTIVE
To differentiate a number of algebraic expressions and to tidy up afterwards, writing them with positive powers

Steps for differentiating functions of the form $y = [f(x)]^p$ using the seven rules

1. Simplify the function, if possible.
2. Select a starting rule (one of the seven).
3. Begin differentiating.
4. Other rules may have to be used as you go along.
5. Tidy up the final expression.
6. Substitute a value if asked.

There are a number of different ways of asking you to differentiate.

EXAMPLE 10

Differentiate $y = 3x^2 + \frac{2}{x} - \frac{1}{x^2}$ with respect to x.

Solution

Starting rule: Sum rule

$y = 3x^2 + \frac{2}{x} - \frac{1}{x^2} = 3x^2 + 2x^{-1} - x^{-2}$

$\frac{dy}{dx} = 6x - 2x^{-2} + 2x^{-3} = 6x - \frac{2}{x^2} + \frac{2}{x^3}$

EXAMPLE 11

Find $\frac{dQ}{dS}$ if $Q = (2s^2 - 1)^5$.

Solution

Starting rule: Chain rule

$Q = (2s^2 - 1)^5$

$\frac{dQ}{dS} = 5(2s^2 - 1)^4(4s) = 20s(2s^2 - 1)^4$

Always differentiate before substituting values for the variable.

EXAMPLE 12

The concentration C of a drug in mg/ml in the bloodstream t hours after injection is given by $C = \dfrac{0 \cdot 14t}{t^2+2}$. Find the **rate of change** of the concentration when $t = 2$ hours.

Solution

$C = \dfrac{0 \cdot 14t}{t^2+2}$

Starting rule: Quotient rule

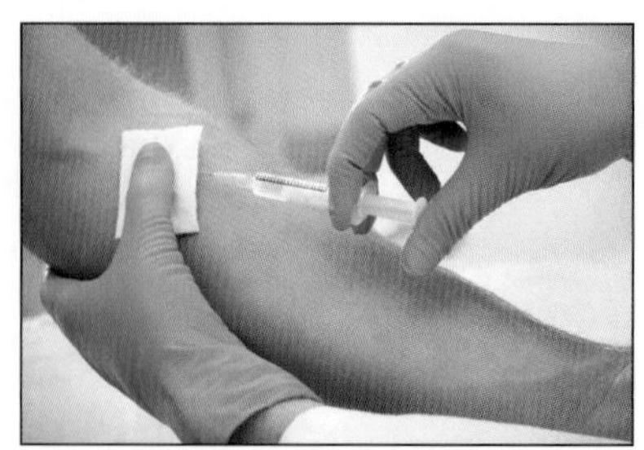

$$\frac{dC}{dt} = \frac{(t^2+2)(0 \cdot 14) - (0 \cdot 14\,t)(2t)}{(t^2+2)^2} = \frac{(0 \cdot 14)(t^2+2-2t^2)}{(t^2+2)^2} = \frac{0 \cdot 14(2-t^2)}{(t^2+2)^2}$$

$$\left(\frac{dC}{dt}\right)_{t=2} = \frac{(0 \cdot 14)(2-4)}{(4+2)^2} = -\frac{7}{900} \text{ mg/ml per hour}$$

You can find the equation of a tangent to a circle using differentiation.

EXAMPLE 13

The equation of a circle s is given by $(x+1)^2 + (y-3)^2 = 13$.

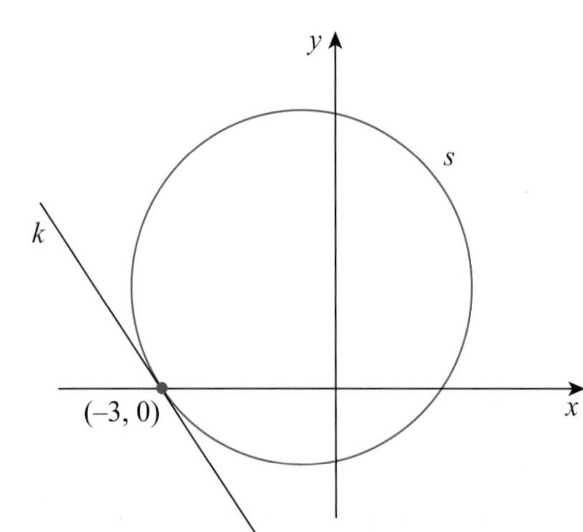

(a) Show that $(-3, 0)$ is on s.

(b) Show that $y = 3 \pm \sqrt{13-(x+1)^2}$.

(c) Find $\dfrac{dy}{dx}$.

(d) Find the equation of the tangent at $(-3, 0)$.

Solution

(a) $s: (x+1)^2 + (y-3)^2 = 13$

$(-3, 0)$:

LHS	RHS
$(-2)^2 + (-3)^2$	13
$= 4 + 9$	
$= 13$	

$\therefore$ LHS = RHS

(b) $(x+1)^2 + (y-3)^2 = 13$

$(y-3)^2 = 13 - (x+1)^2$

$y - 3 = \pm\sqrt{13-(x+1)^2}$

$y = 3 \pm \sqrt{13-(x+1)^2}$

(c) $y = 3 \pm (13-(x+1)^2)^{\frac{1}{2}}$

$\dfrac{dy}{dx} = \pm\dfrac{1}{2}(13-(x+1)^2)^{-\frac{1}{2}} \times [-2(x+1)]$

$= \pm\dfrac{x+1}{\sqrt{13-(x+1)^2}}$

(d) $\left(\dfrac{dy}{dx}\right)_{(-3,\,0)} = \pm\dfrac{(-2)}{\sqrt{9}} = \pm\dfrac{2}{3}$

From the diagram, the slope of tangent k is $-\dfrac{2}{3}$.

Equation of k:

$y - 0 = -\dfrac{2}{3}(x+3)$

$3y = -2x - 6$

$2x + 3y + 6 = 0$

EXAMPLE 14

If $f(x) = \left(\dfrac{5 - x^2}{4 + x^2}\right)^{\frac{1}{3}}$, find $f'(2)$.

Solution

$$f(x) = \left(\frac{5 - x^2}{4 + x^2}\right)^{\frac{1}{3}}$$

Starting rule: Chain rule

$$f'(x) = \frac{1}{3}\left(\frac{5 - x^2}{4 + x^2}\right)^{-\frac{2}{3}} \left\{\frac{(4 + x^2)(-2x) - (5 - x^2)(2x)}{(4 + x^2)^2}\right\}$$

$$= \frac{1}{3}\left(\frac{4 + x^2}{5 - x^2}\right)^{\frac{2}{3}} \left\{\frac{2x(-4 - x^2 - 5 + x^2)}{(4 + x^2)^2}\right\}$$

$$= \frac{1}{3}\left(\frac{4 + x^2}{5 - x^2}\right)^{\frac{2}{3}} \left\{\frac{-18x}{(4 + x^2)^2}\right\}$$

$$= \frac{-6x}{(5 - x^2)^{\frac{2}{3}}(4 + x^2)^{\frac{4}{3}}}$$

$$f'(2) = \frac{-12}{(1)^{\frac{2}{3}}(8)^{\frac{4}{3}}} = -\frac{12}{16} = -\frac{3}{4}$$

EXAMPLE 15

Find the derivative of $y = \dfrac{4x^2 - 1}{2x + 1}$.

Solution

$$y = \frac{4x^2 - 1}{2x + 1}$$

You may be tempted to start with the quotient rule but do not jump in, think of the first step – simplify if possible.

$$y = \frac{4x^2 - 1}{2x + 1} = \frac{(2x - 1)(2x + 1)}{(2x + 1)} = 2x - 1$$

$$\frac{dy}{dx} = 2$$

ACTIVITY 7

ACTION
Tidying up algebraic expressions

OBJECTIVE
To learn to tidy up complex algebraic expressions that are the results of differentiating

Higher order differentiation

A function may be differentiated many times.

Let $y = f(x) = x^7$.

The first derivative $\dfrac{dy}{dx} = m = f'(x) = 7x^6$ is obtained by differentiating $f(x) = x^7$.

The second derivative $\dfrac{d^2y}{dx^2} = \dfrac{dm}{dx} = f''(x) = 42x^5$ is obtained by differentiating $f'(x) = 7x^6$.

The third derivative is $\dfrac{d^3y}{dx^3} = \dfrac{d^2m}{dx^2} = f'''(x) = 210x^4$, and so on.

It is important to note the following:

1. $\dfrac{d^2y}{dx^2}$ is pronounced 'Dee 2 y Dee x squared'.
2. $\dfrac{d^2y}{dx^2} = \dfrac{df'}{dx} = \dfrac{d}{dx}\left(\dfrac{dy}{dx}\right) = \dfrac{dm}{dx}$.
3. Do not confuse $\dfrac{d^2y}{dx^2}$ with $\left(\dfrac{dy}{dx}\right)^2$.
4. $\dfrac{dm}{dx} = \dfrac{d^2y}{dx^2}$ tells you about the shape of a curve around a point (see Chapter 24).

EXAMPLE 16

If $y = 2x^{\frac{3}{2}}$, find:

(a) $\frac{dy}{dx}$

(b) $\frac{d^2y}{dx^2}$

(c) $\left(\frac{dy}{dx}\right)^2$

Solution

$y = 2x^{\frac{3}{2}}$

(a) $\frac{dy}{dx} = 2\left(\frac{3}{2}\right)(x^{\frac{1}{2}}) = 3x^{\frac{1}{2}}$

(b) $\frac{d^2y}{dx^2} = 3\left(\frac{1}{2}\right)(x^{-\frac{1}{2}}) = \frac{3}{2\sqrt{x}}$

(c) $\left(\frac{dy}{dx}\right)^2 = (3x^{\frac{1}{2}})^2 = 9x$

Always do the derivatives before substituting values of the variable.

EXAMPLE 17

If $f(x) = (2x - 1)^3$, find $f'(3)$ and $f''(-1)$.

Solution

$f(x) = (2x - 1)^3$

$f'(x) = 3(2x - 1)^2(2) = 6(2x - 1)^2$

$f''(x) = 6(2(2x - 1))(2) = 24(2x - 1)$

$f'(3) = 6(5)^2 = 150$

$f''(-1) = 24(-3) = -72$

EXERCISE 2

Remember: Once you differentiate, you need to tidy up properly.

1. Differentiate from first principles:

(a) $y = f(x) = x + 2$

(b) $y = f(x) = 3x - 5$

(c) $y = f(x) = ax + b$, a, b constants

(d) $y = 2x^2$

(e) $y = f(x) = x^2 - 1$

(f) $y = f(x) = -3x^2 + 5x - 7$

(g) $y = f(x) = ax^2 + bx + c$, a, b, c constants

2. Differentiate the following with respect to x (use rules 1 to 4). Simplify your answers.

(a) x^7

(b) $-x^5$

(c) $\frac{1}{4}x^8$

(d) $6x^{\frac{3}{2}}$

(e) $-\frac{x^3}{5}$

(f) $\frac{5}{x^3}$

(g) $\frac{1}{5x}$

(h) $\frac{1}{3}x^2 + 2x - \frac{1}{7}$

(i) $5x^2 - \frac{1}{5x}$

(j) $\frac{2 - \sqrt{x}}{\sqrt{x}}$

(k) $2x^3 + 6x^2 - x + 3$

(l) $x^3 - \frac{1}{x^3}$

3. Differentiate the following with respect to x (use rules 1 to 4). Simplify your answers.

(a) $x - \frac{2}{x}$ (f) $\frac{x^3 - x^2 + 2x - 5}{x^{\frac{1}{2}}}$

(b) $\frac{x^2 - 1}{x}$ (g) $(4x^2 - 7)^2$

(c) $\frac{2x^2 + 3}{3x}$ (h) $\sqrt{x}(x^2 - 7x + 9)$

(d) $(2x - 1)(x^2 + 2)$ (i) $\frac{\sqrt{x}}{3} - \frac{3}{\sqrt{x}}$

(e) $(\sqrt{x} - 1)(\sqrt{x} + 1)$ (j) $\frac{x^n - 7}{x^2}$

4. Differentiate the following with respect to x (use rule 5, the product rule). Simplify your answers.

(a) $x(2x - 1)$

(b) $-x^2(2x^2 + 1)$

(c) $(x - 1)(x - 2)$

(d) $(2x^2 + 7)(x^2 - 5x + 1)$

(e) $(\sqrt{x} + 1)(\sqrt{x} + 3)$

(f) $(3x + 2)^2$

(g) $\left(2 - \frac{3}{x}\right)(x - 4)$ (i) $(4x^2 - 1)(2x^3 + 11)$

(h) $(x^3 - 1)(x^2 + 1)$ (j) $(x - 7)(2x^2 + 3x - 9)$

5. Differentiate the following with respect to x (use rule 6, the quotient rule). Simplify your answers.

(a) $\frac{x}{x - 2}$ (e) $\frac{3 - 2x^2}{3 + 2x^2}$

(b) $\frac{3 - x}{2 + x}$ (f) $\frac{3x^2 + 1}{x + 1}$

(c) $\frac{x^2 + 7x - 1}{x - 1}$ (g) $\frac{x^3 + 2}{2x - 1}$

(d) $\frac{a - cx}{c - x}$, a, c constant (h) $\frac{\sqrt{x} - 1}{\sqrt{x} + 1}$

6. Differentiate the following with respect to x (use rule 7, the chain rule). Simplify your answers.

(a) $(x^2 - 1)^7$ (c) $(3x^2 - 1)^{\frac{1}{2}}$

(b) $(3x^2 - 2x + 1)^{50}$ (d) $(4x^2 - 3x + 1)^{-1}$

(e) $(\sqrt{x} + 5)^{17}$ (h) $\frac{1}{(7x^2 - 1)^5}$

(f) $\frac{5}{4}(1 - \sqrt{x})^4$ (i) $\frac{2}{(1 - 3x)^4}$

(g) $\frac{1}{\sqrt{x + 5}}$ (j) $[f(x)]^p$

7. Differentiate the following with respect to x. Simplify your answers.

(a) $x^2(3x - 1)^4$

(b) $x(4x + 2)^3$

(c) $(3x - 1)^2(2x + 1)^3$

(d) $-x\sqrt{x + 3}$

(e) $\frac{2x}{(3 - x)^2}$

(f) $\frac{2x + 5}{(3x - 2)^3}$ (k) $\left(\frac{3 - 2x}{3 + 2x}\right)^{\frac{1}{2}}$

(g) $\frac{x^2 - 1}{x + 1}$ (l) $\left(\frac{ax + b}{cx + d}\right)^n$, a, b, c, d constants

(h) $\frac{8x^3 - 1}{2x - 1}$ (m) $\left(\sqrt{x} + \frac{1}{\sqrt{x}}\right)^2$

(i) $\frac{\sqrt{9 - x^2}}{x}$ (n) $\sqrt{\frac{1 - qx}{1 + qx}}$, q constant

(j) $\left(\frac{5x - 2}{4x + 7}\right)^6$

8. Find $\frac{dy}{dx}$ if:

(a) $y = 5x^{\frac{5}{2}} - 4a^2$, a constant

(b) $y = \frac{ax^2 + bx + c}{x}$, a, b, c constant

(c) $y = \sqrt{5 - 9x}$

(d) $y = \left(a + \frac{b}{x}\right)^7$, a, b constant

(e) $y = x^2\sqrt{a + bx}$, a, b constant

(f) $y = \frac{8 - x^2}{8 + x^2}$

(g) $y = 7^3$

(h) $y = (x + 7)\sqrt{x + 7}$

(i) $y = \frac{2x - 1}{\sqrt{x^2 + 5}}$ (j) $y = \frac{(4x^2 - 1)^2}{7}$

9. **(a)** Find $\frac{dy}{dx}$ at $x = 1$ if $y = \frac{1}{x+1}$.

(b) Find $f'\left(\frac{1}{2}\right)$ if $f(x) = \frac{x-1}{2x+3}$.

(c) Find the derivative of $y = \sqrt{169 - x^2}$ at $x = 12$.

(d) Find the rate of change of y with respect to x at $x = 2$ if $y = (3x - 5)^4$.

(e) Find $\frac{dv}{dq}$ at $q = \frac{1}{2}$ if $v = q^2 + \frac{1}{q^2}$.

(f) Find $\frac{dy}{dx}$ and $\frac{d^2y}{dx^2}$ if $y = \frac{1-x}{1+x}$.

(g) If $f(x) = 2x - \frac{1}{x}$, find $f'(x)$ and $f''(x)$ and show that $xf''(x) + 2f'(x) = 4$.

(h) Find $\frac{dA}{dr}$ if $A = \left(\frac{1-r^2}{1+r^2}\right)^4$.

10. **(a)** Find the slope and hence the equation of the tangent to the curve $y = x + \frac{1}{x}, x > 0$ at $x = -\frac{1}{2}$.

(b) The equation of a circle with centre (0, 0) and radius 5 is given by $x^2 + y^2 = 25$.

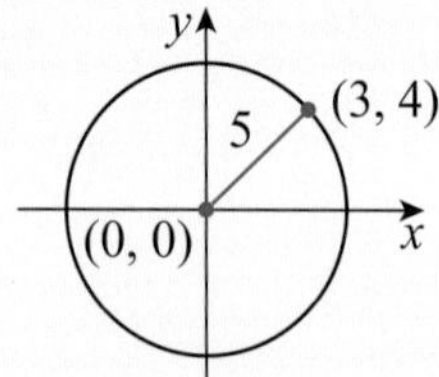

(i) Show that (3, 4) is on the circle.

(ii) Express y in terms of x ($y > 0$).

(iii) Find the equation of the tangent to the circle at (3, 4).

(c) The curve $y = \frac{1}{x^2+1}$ shown is called the 'Witch of Agnesi'.

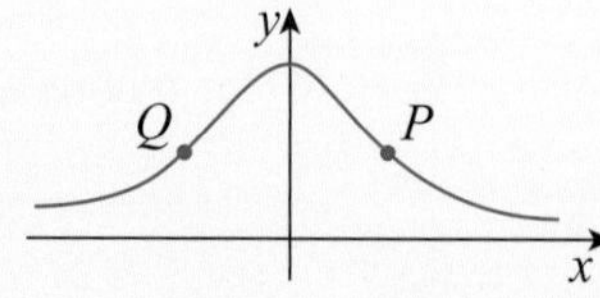

Find the equations of the tangents at $P\left(1, \frac{1}{2}\right)$ and $Q\left(-1, \frac{1}{2}\right)$.

11. The height of a car h(m) above sea level t minutes after starting its journey is given by $h = 5t^3 - 60t^2 + 220t + 105$.

(a) How high is the car above sea level when it starts its journey?

(b) Find the rate of change of its height above sea level 5 minutes after starting its journey.

12. If $c = p^3 + \frac{1}{p^3}$, show that $3c + p\frac{dc}{dp} = 6p^3$.

13. The escape velocity V (m/s) at a distance r (m) from the centre of Earth is given by $V = \frac{2{\cdot}82 \times 10^7}{\sqrt{r}}$.

Find the rate of change of V with respect to r when:

(a) $r = 6{\cdot}4 \times 10^6$ m, correct to three significant figures,

(b) $r = 10^8$ m, correct to three significant figures.

14. The radius of curvature r of a curve at a point on the curve is the radius of the approximating circle at the point and is given by the formula:

$$r = \frac{\left[1 + \left(\frac{dy}{dx}\right)^2\right]^{\frac{3}{2}}}{\left|\frac{d^2y}{dx^2}\right|}$$

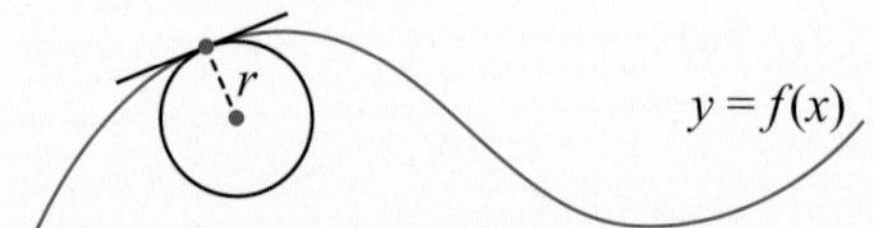

Find the radius of curvature of the curve $y = \sqrt{x}$ at $x = 1$.

15. The stopping distance L in metres of a car is given by $L = 0{\cdot}0056v^2 + 0{\cdot}14v$, where v is its speed in km/h. Find the rate of change of the stopping distance, with respect to speed, when:

(a) $v = 80$ km/h

(b) $v = 120$ km/h

23.4 Differentiating trigonometric functions

Graphs of the functions $y = \sin x$ and $y = \cos x$ are continuous functions for all $x \in \mathbb{R}$. Therefore, it is possible to find the slope of the tangent to these curves at any point on the curve.

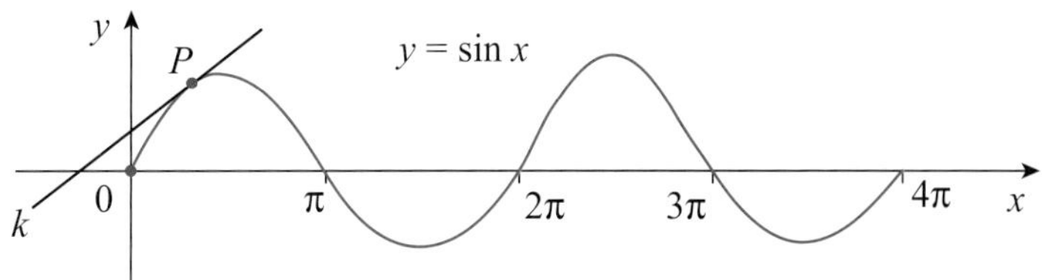

An important limit is required to do this.

Important limit

Consider an angle θ, in radians, that is getting smaller and smaller. If you calculate $\sin\theta$ on your calculator for each value of θ, you will get the following:

θ (rads)	0·1	0·05	0·04	0·03	0·02	0·01	$\to 0$
sin θ	0·1	0·05	0·04	0·03	0·02	0·01	$\to 0$

Therefore: $\sin\theta \to \theta$ as $\theta \to 0$.

or

$\sin\theta \simeq \theta$ for small values of θ if and only if θ **is in radians**.

Differentiating sin x and cos x from first principles

TIP

If $y = \sin x$ and $y = \cos x$ can be differentiated, then any trigonometric function can be differentiated using the rules of differentiation.

SYLLABUS NOTE

The proof of the derivative $y = \sin x$ from first principles is not required.

1. $y = \sin x$

$y = \sin x$

y = sin x

k

$Q(x + h, \sin(x + h))$

$P(x, \sin x)$

$$\text{Slope of } PQ = \frac{\sin(x+h) - \sin x}{(x+h) - h} = \frac{2\cos\left(x + \frac{h}{2}\right)\sin\left(\frac{h}{2}\right)}{h}$$

$$\frac{dy}{dx} = \lim_{h\to 0}\frac{2\cos\left(x+\frac{h}{2}\right)\sin\left(\frac{h}{2}\right)}{h} \quad \left[\sin\left(\frac{h}{2}\right)\simeq\frac{h}{2} \text{ as } h\to 0\right]$$

$$\frac{dy}{dx} = \frac{2\cos x\times\left(\frac{h}{2}\right)}{h} = \cos x$$

$$y=\sin x \Rightarrow \frac{dy}{dx}=\cos x$$

Remember, x must be in radians for this result to hold.

SYLLABUS NOTE

The proof of the derivative $y = \cos x$ from first principles is not required.

2. $y = \cos x$

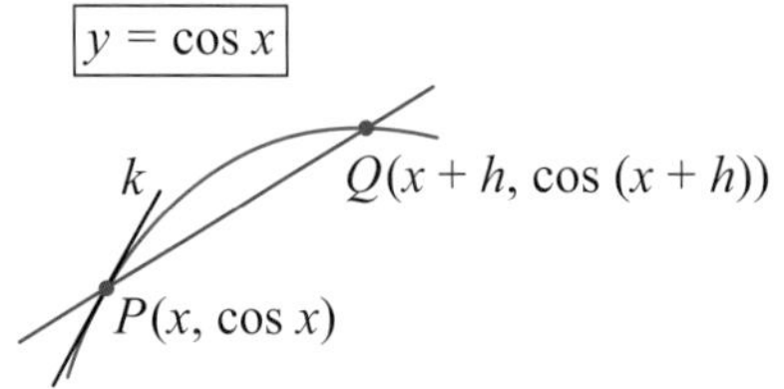

$$\text{Slope of } PQ = \frac{\cos(x+h)-\cos x}{(x+h)-x} = \frac{-2\sin\left(x+\frac{h}{2}\right)\sin\left(\frac{h}{2}\right)}{h}$$

$$\frac{dy}{dx} = \lim_{h\to 0}\frac{-2\sin\left(x+\frac{h}{2}\right)\sin\left(\frac{h}{2}\right)}{h} \quad \left[\sin\left(\frac{h}{2}\right)\simeq\frac{h}{2} \text{ as } h\to 0\right]$$

$$\frac{dy}{dx} = \frac{-2\sin x\times\left(\frac{h}{2}\right)}{h} = -\sin x$$

$$y=\cos x \Rightarrow \frac{dy}{dx}=-\sin x$$

These two results are the basis of trigonometric differentiation and are true only if x is in radians.

Assume all angles are in radians unless otherwise stated.

- $y = 3\sin x \Rightarrow \frac{dy}{dx} = 3(\cos x) = 3\cos x$ [Multiplication by a constant rule]
- $y = \frac{\cos x}{4} + 5\sin x = \frac{1}{4}\cos x + 5\sin x \Rightarrow \frac{dy}{dx} = \frac{1}{4}(-\sin x) + 5(\cos x) = -\frac{\sin x}{4} + 5\cos x$
- $y = x\sin x \Rightarrow \frac{dy}{dx} = x\cos x + \sin x$ [Product rule]
- $y = \cos^2 x = (\cos x)^2 \Rightarrow \frac{dy}{dx} = 2(\cos x)(-\sin x) = -\sin 2x$ [Chain rule]
- $y = \frac{4}{\sin x} = 4(\sin x)^{-1} \Rightarrow \frac{dy}{dx} = 4(-1)(\sin x)^{-2}(\cos x) = -\frac{4\cos x}{\sin^2 x}$
- $y = \sqrt{1-\sin^2 x} = \sqrt{\cos^2 x} = \cos x \Rightarrow \frac{dy}{dx} = -\sin x$

EXAMPLE 18

Differentiate $y = \tan x$ with respect to x.

Solution

$y = \tan x = \dfrac{\sin x}{\cos x}$ [Use the quotient rule.]

$$\frac{dy}{dx} = \frac{\cos x(\cos x) - \sin x(-\sin x)}{(\cos x)^2} = \frac{\cos^2 x + \sin^2 x}{\cos^2 x}$$

$$= \frac{1}{\cos^2 x} \quad \left[\textbf{Note: } \frac{1}{\cos^2 x} = \sec^2 x\right]$$

Harder trigonometric differentiation with complicated angles

Examples: $y = \sin 2x$, $y = \cos(x^2 - 1)$, $y = \sin\sqrt{x}$

These types can be differentiated using the chain rule.

1. $y = \sin f(x)$

$u = f(x) \Rightarrow y = \sin u$

$$\frac{dy}{dx} = \frac{dy}{du} \times \frac{du}{dx} = \cos u \times f'(x)$$

$$= \cos f(x) \times f'(x)$$

2. $y = \cos f(x)$

Similarly: $y = \cos f(x) \Rightarrow \dfrac{dy}{dx} = -\sin f(x) \times f'(x)$

In conclusion:

$$y = \sin f(x) \Rightarrow \frac{dy}{dx} = \cos f(x) \times f'(x)$$

$$y = \cos f(x) \Rightarrow \frac{dy}{dx} = -\sin f(x) \times f'(x)$$

The rule in words:

$y = \sin f(x) \Rightarrow \dfrac{dy}{dx} =$ cos (same angle) × (differentiate the angle)

$y = \cos f(x) \Rightarrow \dfrac{dy}{dx} =$ –sin (same angle) × (differentiate the angle)

- $y = \sin 2x = \sin(2x) \Rightarrow \dfrac{dy}{dx} = \cos 2x \times 2 = 2\cos 2x$
- $y = \cos(x^2 - 1) \Rightarrow \dfrac{dy}{dx} = -\sin(x^2 - 1) \times (2x) = -2x\sin(x^2 - 1)$
- $y = \dfrac{5\sin 3x}{7} = \dfrac{5}{7}\sin 3x \Rightarrow \dfrac{dy}{dx} = \dfrac{5}{7}(\cos 3x) \times (3) = \dfrac{15\cos 3x}{7}$

EXAMPLE 19

Differentiate $y = \sqrt{\cos x^2}$ with respect to x.

Solution

$y = \sqrt{\cos x^2} = [\cos(x^2)]^{\frac{1}{2}}$ [The angle is x^2.]

$$\frac{dy}{dx} = \frac{1}{2}[\cos(x^2)]^{-\frac{1}{2}} \times [\text{differentiate } \cos(x^2)]$$

$$= \frac{1}{2}[\cos x^2]^{-\frac{1}{2}} \times (-\sin x^2) \times (2x) = -\frac{x \sin x^2}{\sqrt{\cos x^2}}$$

ACTIVITY 8

ACTION
Preparing to differentiate trigonometric functions

OBJECTIVE
To manipulate trigonometric expressions to get them ready to differentiate and to tidy up afterwards

Steps for trigonometric differentiation

1. Simplify the trigonometric functions using the formulae in your *Formulae and Tables* book.

   In particular, be aware of the following:

   $\sin^2 A + \cos^2 A = 1$

   $2 \sin A \cos A = \sin 2A$

   $\cos^2 A - \sin^2 A = (\cos A)^2 - (\sin A)^2 = \cos 2A$

   You may also have to use the four formulae for changing products of trigonometric functions into sums:

   $2 \cos A \cos B = \cos(A + B) + \cos(A - B)$

   $2 \sin A \cos B = \sin(A + B) + \sin(A - B)$

   $2 \sin A \sin B = \cos(A - B) - \cos(A + B)$

   $2 \cos A \sin B = \sin(A + B) - \sin(A - B)$

2. Choose a starting differentiation rule.
3. Remember:

$y = \sin f(x)$	$y = \cos f(x)$
$\frac{dy}{dx} = \cos f(x) \times f'(x)$	$\frac{dy}{dx} = -\sin f(x) \times f'(x)$

4. Tidy up your answer.

- $y = \cos^2 5x + \sin^2 5x = 1 \Rightarrow \frac{dy}{dx} = 0$
- $y = 2 \sin 3x \cos 2x = \sin 5x + \sin x$

  $\frac{dy}{dx} = (\cos 5x) \times (5) + \cos x = 5\cos 5x + \cos x$
- $y = \sin^2 x = (\sin x)^2$

  $\frac{dy}{dx} = 2(\sin x) \cos x = \sin 2x$

  $\frac{d^2y}{dx^2} = (\cos 2x) \times (2) = 2\cos 2x$

EXAMPLE 20

Find the equation of the tangent to the curve $y = \cos^2 x$ at $x = \dfrac{\pi}{4}$.

Solution

Point: $x = \dfrac{\pi}{4}: y = \left(\cos\dfrac{\pi}{4}\right)^2 = \left(\dfrac{1}{\sqrt{2}}\right)^2 = \dfrac{1}{2}$.

Therefore, the point P on the curve is $P\left(\dfrac{\pi}{4}, \dfrac{1}{2}\right)$.

Slope: $y = \cos^2 x = (\cos x)^2$

$$\frac{dy}{dx} = 2(\cos x)(-\sin x) - \sin 2x$$

$$\left(\frac{dy}{dx}\right)_{x=\frac{\pi}{4}} = m = -\sin\left(\frac{\pi}{2}\right) = -1$$

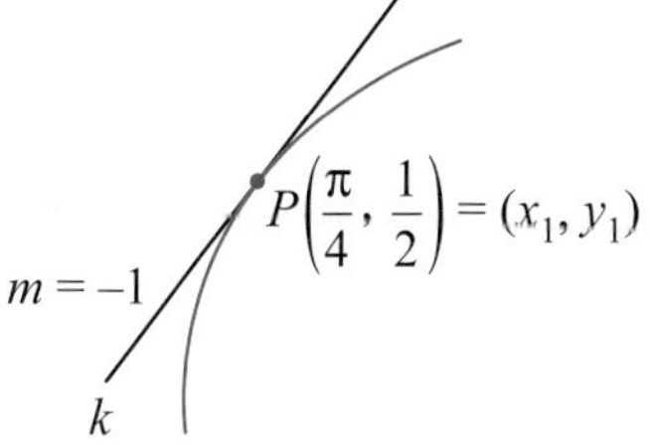

Equation of k: $\left(y - \dfrac{1}{2}\right) = -1\left(x - \dfrac{\pi}{4}\right)$

$$y - \frac{1}{2} = -x + \frac{\pi}{4}$$

$$4y - 2 = -4x + \pi$$

$$\therefore\ 4x + 4y - (2 + \pi) = 0$$

EXAMPLE 21

The height h in metres of water above or below a water line over 24 hours is given by $h = -2 + 5\sin\left(\dfrac{\pi t}{6}\right)$, where t is in hours ($-12 \le t < 12$) and $t = 0$ is noon.

Find:

(a) the rate at which the height is changing at noon,

(b) the rate at which the height is changing at 6 p.m.

Give your answers correct to two decimal places.

Solution

$$h = -2 + 5\sin\left(\frac{\pi t}{6}\right)$$

$$\frac{dh}{dt} = 5\cos\left(\frac{\pi t}{6}\right) \times \left(\frac{\pi}{6}\right)$$

(a) Noon: $\left(\dfrac{dh}{dt}\right)_{t=0} = 5(\cos 0)\left(\dfrac{\pi}{6}\right) = \dfrac{5\pi}{6}$ m/h

Therefore, the height is increasing at 2·62 m/h.

(b) 6 p.m.: $\left(\dfrac{dh}{dt}\right)_{t=6} = 5\cos(\pi) \times \dfrac{\pi}{6} = -\dfrac{5\pi}{6}$ m/h

Therefore, the height is decreasing at 2·62 m/h.

23.5 Inverse trigonometric differentiation

Consider three trigonometric functions defined in the given domain.

The functions $f(x) = \sin x$, $f(x) = \cos x$ and $f(x) = \tan x$ are all bijective and continuous in the given domain.

Their inverse functions can be obtained by reflection in the line $y = x$. These inverse functions $f^{-1}(x) = \sin^{-1}x$, $f^{-1}(x) = \cos^{-1}x$ and $f^{-1}(x) = \tan^{-1}x$ exist and are continuous in these domains. Therefore, the inverse functions can be differentiated at all points in these domains.

ACTIVITY 9

ACTION
Graphing inverse trigonometric functions

OBJECTIVE
To reflect trigonometric functions in the line $y = x$ to obtain their inverse functions

1. Inverse sine

$f: \left[-\frac{\pi}{2}, \frac{\pi}{2}\right] \to [-1, 1]$

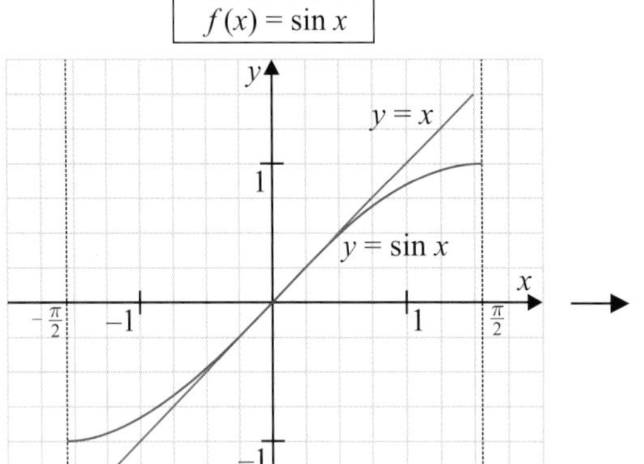

$f: [-1, 1] \to \left[-\frac{\pi}{2}, \frac{\pi}{2}\right]$

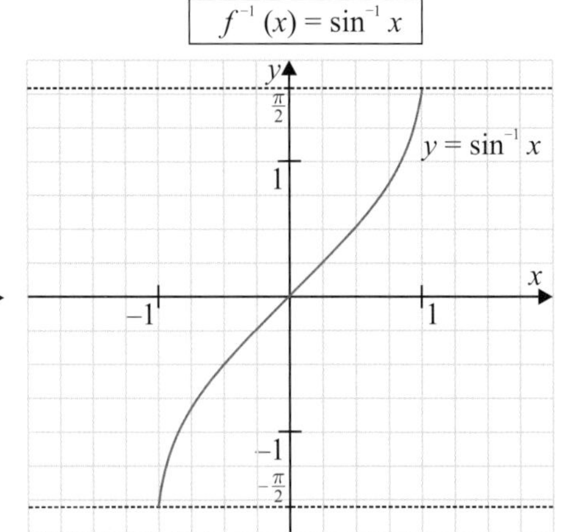

2. Inverse cosine

$f: [0, \pi] \to [-1, 1]$

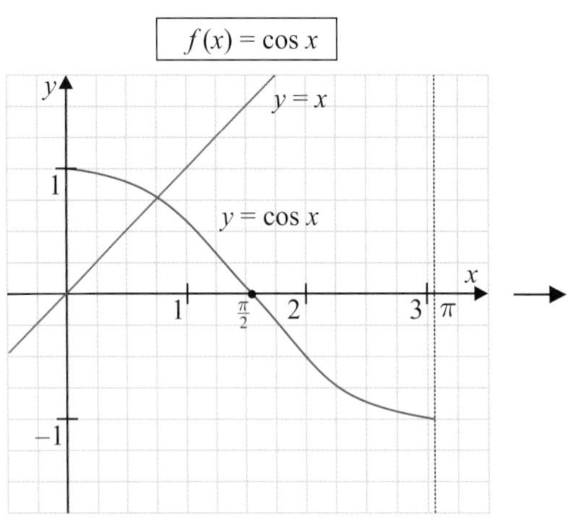

$f: [-1, 1] \to [0, \pi]$

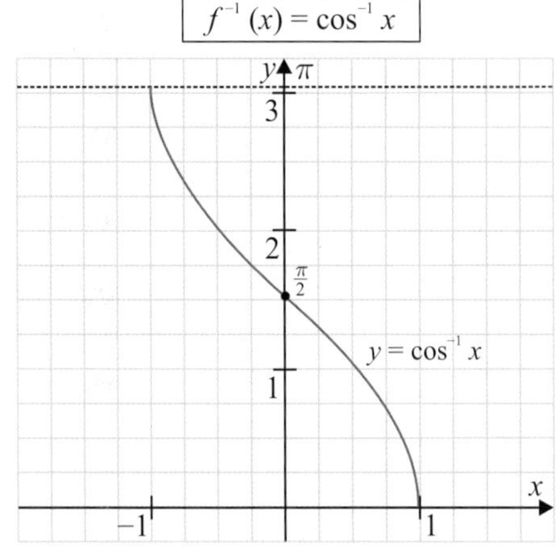

3. Inverse tan

$f: \left[-\frac{\pi}{2}, \frac{\pi}{2}\right] \to [-\infty, \infty]$

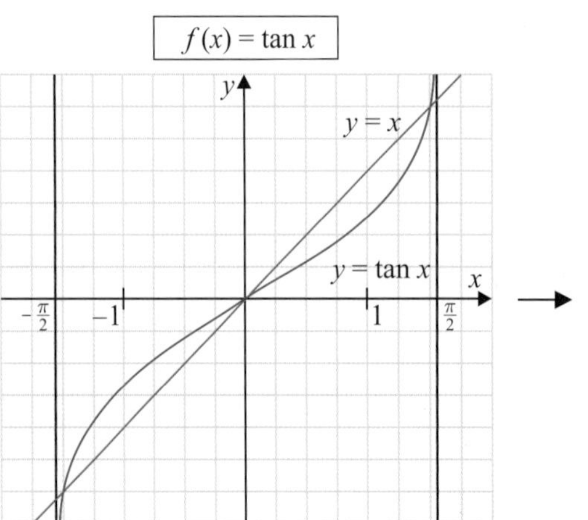

$f: [-\infty, \infty] \to \left[-\frac{\pi}{2}, \frac{\pi}{2}\right]$

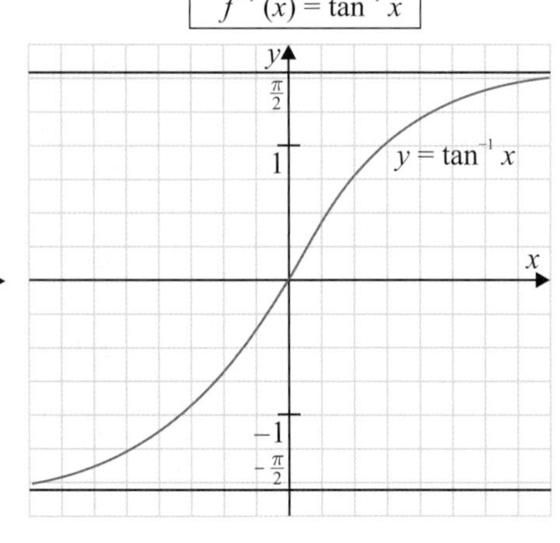

Differentiating the three inverse trigonometric functions

SYLLABUS NOTE
The proof of the derivatives of the inverse trigonometric functions is not required.

$y = \sin^{-1} x$

$\sin y = x$

$x = \sin y$

$\dfrac{dx}{dy} = \cos y$

$\dfrac{dy}{dx} = \dfrac{1}{\cos y}$

$\therefore \dfrac{dy}{dx} = \dfrac{1}{\sqrt{1 - x^2}}$

$\left[\textbf{Note: } \dfrac{dy}{dx} = \dfrac{1}{\left(\dfrac{dx}{dy}\right)}\right]$

This same process can be applied to the other two inverse trigonometry functions.

$$y = \sin^{-1} x \Rightarrow \frac{dy}{dx} = \frac{1}{\sqrt{1 - x^2}}$$

$$y = \cos^{-1} x \Rightarrow \frac{dy}{dx} = -\frac{1}{\sqrt{1 - x^2}}$$

$$y = \tan^{-1} x \Rightarrow \frac{dy}{dx} = \frac{1}{1 + x^2}$$

EXAMPLE 22

Find the equation of the tangent to the curve $y = 2\tan^{-1} x$ at $x = 1$.

Solution

Point P: $x = 1 \Rightarrow y = 2\tan^{-1} 1 = \dfrac{2\pi}{4} = \dfrac{\pi}{2}$

Slope: $y = 2\tan^{-1} x \Rightarrow \dfrac{dy}{dx} = 2 \times \dfrac{1}{1 + x^2}$

$\therefore \left(\dfrac{dy}{dx}\right)_{(1, \frac{\pi}{2})} = \dfrac{2}{1 + 1^2} = \dfrac{1}{1} = 1$

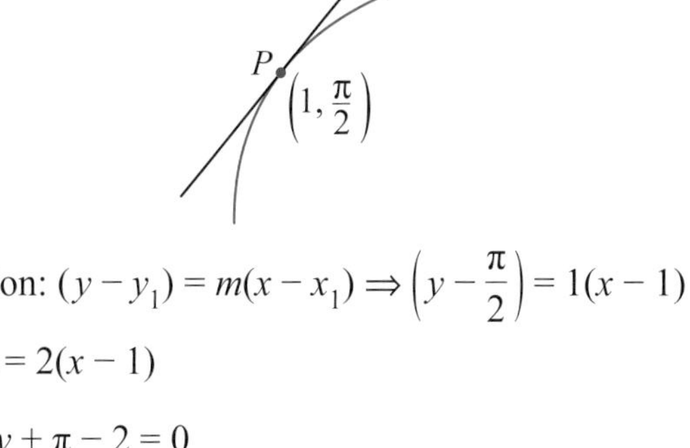

Equation: $(y - y_1) = m(x - x_1) \Rightarrow \left(y - \dfrac{\pi}{2}\right) = 1(x - 1)$

$2y - \pi = 2(x - 1)$

$2x - 2y + \pi - 2 = 0$

Harder inverse trigonometric differentiation

To differentiate $y = \tan^{-1} f(x)$, where $f(x)$ is a function of x:

Let $u = \tan^{-1} f(x)$

$\therefore y = \tan u$

$\dfrac{dy}{dx} = \dfrac{dy}{du} \times \dfrac{du}{dx} = \dfrac{1}{1 + u^2} \times f'(x)$

$\therefore \dfrac{dy}{dx} = \dfrac{1}{1 + f(x)^2} \times f'(x)$

In general:

$$y = \sin^{-1} f(x) \Rightarrow \frac{dy}{dx} = \frac{1}{\sqrt{1 - f(x)^2}} \times f'(x)$$
$$y = \cos^{-1} f(x) \Rightarrow \frac{dy}{dx} = \frac{-1}{\sqrt{1 - f(x)^2}} \times f'(x)$$
$$y = \tan^{-1} f(x) \Rightarrow \frac{dy}{dx} = \frac{1}{1 + f(x)^2} \times f'(x)$$

- $y = \tan^{-1} 3x \Rightarrow \frac{dy}{dx} = \frac{1}{1 + (3x)^2} \times 3 = \frac{3}{1 + 9x^2}$
- $y = \cos^{-1} \sqrt{x} \Rightarrow \frac{dy}{dx} = -\frac{1}{\sqrt{1 - (\sqrt{x})^2}} \times \left(\frac{1}{2} x^{-\frac{1}{2}}\right) = -\frac{1}{2\sqrt{x}\sqrt{1 - x}}$
- $y = x \tan^{-1} 2x \Rightarrow \frac{dy}{dx} = x\left(\frac{1}{1 + (2x)^2} \times 2\right) + \tan^{-1}(2x) \times 1 = \frac{2x}{1 + 4x^2} + \tan^{-1} 2x$

EXERCISE 3

1. Differentiate the following with respect to x:

(a) $y = 2 + \sin x$
(b) $y = 3\cos x - 5x$
(c) $y = x\cos x$
(d) $y = \frac{\cos x}{x}$
(e) $y = \frac{4\cos x}{5}$
(f) $y = \sin^7 x$
(g) $y = 3\cos^5 x$
(h) $y = \sqrt[3]{\sin x}$
(i) $y = \frac{5}{\cos x}$
(j) $y = \sqrt{\sin^3 x}$

2. Differentiate the following with respect to x:

(a) $y = \sin(3x - 7)$
(b) $y = \sin(ax + b)$, a, b constants
(c) $y = \cos(ax + b)$, a, b constants
(d) $y = \sin\left(\frac{5x^2}{3}\right)$
(e) $y = \frac{\cos(7x^3 - 5x + 1)}{11}$
(f) $y = \cos\left(\frac{x}{3} - 2\right)$
(g) $y = \sin\left(\frac{5x}{2}\right)$
(h) $y = 2\sin 3x\cos 3x$
(i) $y = 5\sin x\cos 3x$
(j) $y = \sin\left(\frac{3}{x}\right)$

3. Differentiate the following with respect to x:

(a) $y = \frac{\sin x - \cos x}{\sin x + \cos x}$
(b) $y = \frac{\sin^2 x}{1 - \cos x}$
(c) $y = \cos^2 5x$
(d) $y = \cos^5(4x)$
(e) $y = \sqrt{\frac{1 - \sin x}{1 + \sin x}}$

4. (a) Find $\frac{dy}{dx}$ at $x = \frac{\pi}{6}$ if $y = \sin 3x$.

(b) Find $f'\left(\frac{\pi}{4}\right)$ if $f(x) = \cos^2 x$.

(c) Find the derivative of $y = \sin^2(x + 2)$ at $x = -2$.

(d) Find the rate of change of y with respect to x at $x = \frac{\pi}{4}$ if $y = 5\cos 3x$.

(e) Find $\frac{dp}{dv}$ at $v = \sin^{-1}\left(\frac{3}{5}\right)$ if $p = \cos(2v)$.

(f) Find $\frac{dy}{dx}$ and $\frac{d^2y}{dx^2}$ if $y = 2\sin x\cos x$.

(g) If $f(x) = \frac{\sin x}{1 + \cos x}$, find $f'(x)$ and $f''(x)$ and show that $f''(x) - f(x)f'(x) = 0$.

(h) Find $\frac{dy}{dx}$ if $y = \left(\frac{1 - \cos x}{1 + \cos x}\right)^3$.

5. **(a)** Find the equation of the tangent to the curve $y = \sin 3x$ at $x = \frac{\pi}{9}$.
(b) Find the equation of the tangent to the curve $f(x) = \sin^3 x$ at $x = \frac{\pi}{3}$.
(c) Find the equation of the tangent to the curve $y = \cos^3 2x$ at $x = \frac{\pi}{3}$.

6. A particle oscillates back and forth between two points on the x-axis. Its displacement s(cm) from a fixed point O on the x-axis at time $t(s)$ is given by $s = 3\cos t + 4\sin t$.
(a) Find the rate of change of s with respect to t at **(i)** $t = 0$, **(ii)** $t = \frac{\pi}{2}$.
(b) What did you find in **(i)** and **(ii)**?
(c) Show that $\frac{d^2s}{dt^2} = -s$. What is the meaning of $\frac{d^2s}{dt^2}$?

7. Differentiate the following with respect to x:
(a) $\cos^{-1} 3x$
(b) $\tan^{-1} 4x$
(c) $(\sin^{-1}x)^2$
(d) $\sin^{-1} 4x$
(e) $2\sin^{-1} 4x$
(f) $\frac{\sin^{-1}(4x)}{2}$
(g) $(\sin^{-1} 4x)^2$
(h) $\tan^{-1}(ax)$, a constant
(i) $\cos^{-1}\left(\frac{3}{x}\right)$
(j) $\cos^{-1}(\sin x)$
(k) $\tan^{-1}(x\sqrt{x})$
(l) $y = \frac{\tan^{-1}x}{x}$

8. Show that:
(a) if $y = \cos^{-1} x$, $\frac{dy}{dx} = -\frac{1}{\sqrt{1-x^2}}$,
(b) if $y = \tan^{-1} x$, $\frac{dy}{dx} = \frac{1}{1+x^2}$.

9. If $y = \tan^{-1}\left(\frac{x}{\sqrt{1-x^2}}\right)$, show that $y = \sin^{-1} x$.
Find $\frac{dy}{dx}$.

10. If $y = \frac{\sin^{-1} x}{\sqrt{1-x^2}}$, show that $(1-x^2)\frac{dy}{dx} - xy = 1$.

11. If $y = \sin^{-1}\sqrt{x}$, show that $\frac{dy}{dx} = \frac{1}{\sin 2y}$.

12. Find the equation of the tangent to $y = \sin^{-1}\left(\frac{1}{x}\right)$ at $x = 2$.

23.6 Differentiating exponential functions

To investigate how to differentiate $y = a^x$, $a \in \mathbb{R}$, consider the problem of finding the slope of the tangent to the curve $y = 3^x$ at any point (x, y) on the curve using a calculator.

WORKED EXAMPLE

Differentiating 3^x from first principles

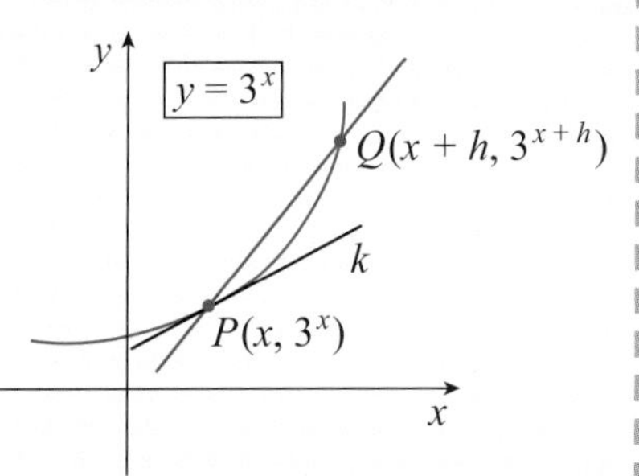

Slope of $PQ = \frac{3^{x+h} - 3^x}{(x+h) - x} = \frac{3^x(3^h - 1)}{h}$

$$\frac{dy}{dx} = \lim_{h \to 0} \frac{3^x(3^h - 1)}{h} = 3^x \lim_{h \to 0} \frac{(3^h - 1)}{h}$$

Now, make $h \to 0$ by giving it a very, very small value of $h = 0{\cdot}0001$.

$$\frac{dy}{dx} = 3^x \times \left(\frac{3^{0\cdot0001} - 1}{0\cdot0001}\right) \simeq 3^x \times 1{\cdot}1 \quad [1{\cdot}1 \text{ on a calculator}]$$

This process can now be generalised for $y = a^x$, where $a \in \mathbb{R}$.

WORKED EXAMPLE

Explaining *e*

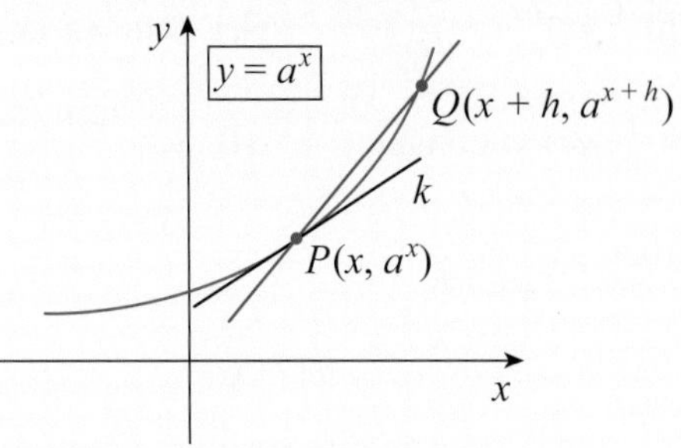

$\frac{dy}{dx} = a^x \lim_{h \to 0} \left(\frac{a^h - 1}{h}\right) = a^x \times \text{constant}$

The constant is the limit $\lim_{h \to 0} \left(\frac{a^h - 1}{h}\right)$ and is a function of ***a* only**.

If this limit was equal to 1, you would have a remarkable function that would be exactly the same when differentiated.

$\frac{a^h - 1}{h} = 1$ as $h \to 0$

$\Rightarrow a^h - 1 \approx h$ for very small values of h

$a^h = h + 1$

$\log_{10} a^h = \log_{10}(h + 1)$

$h \log_{10} a = \log_{10}(h + 1)$

$\log_{10} a = \frac{\log_{10}(h + 1)}{h}$

$a = 10^{\frac{\log_{10}(h+1)}{h}}$

As $h \to 0$: $a \to 10^{\frac{\log_{10}(1\cdot0001)}{0\cdot0001}} \approx 2\cdot718$

(by letting $h = 0\cdot0001$) [calculator]

Therefore: $y = 2\cdot718^x \Rightarrow \frac{dy}{dx} = 2\cdot718^x \times 1 = 2\cdot718^x$

This special number of approximately 2·718 is called e.

In general:

$$y = e^x \Rightarrow \frac{dy}{dx} = e^x, \text{ where } e \approx 2\cdot718.$$

It is important to note the following:

1. $y = e^x$ is called **the exponential function** and obeys all the normal algebraic rules of exponential functions.
2. e^{constant} = constant because e is itself a constant.
3. The inverse function of $y = e^x$:

   $y = e^x \Rightarrow \log_e y = x$

   $\therefore f^{-1}(x) = \log_e x$

   $\log_e x$ is often written as $\ln x$.

The derivative of $y = e^{f(x)}$

$y = e^{f(x)}$

$u = f(x) \Rightarrow y = e^u$

$\frac{dy}{dx} = \frac{dy}{du} \times \frac{du}{dx} = e^u \times f'(x)$

$\frac{dy}{dx} = e^{f(x)} \times f'(x)$

In general:

$$y = e^{f(x)} \Rightarrow \frac{dy}{dx} = e^{f(x)} \times f'(x)$$

The rule in words: $y = e^{f(x)} \Rightarrow \frac{dy}{dx}$ = Repeat $e^{f(x)}$ × (derivative of the power $f(x)$).

- $y = e^{2x} \Rightarrow \frac{dy}{dx} = e^{2x} \times 2 = 2e^{2x}$
- $y = e^{3kx}$, k constant $\Rightarrow \frac{dy}{dx} = e^{3kx} \times 3k = 3k\,e^{3kx}$
- $y = 3e^{2x^2} \Rightarrow \frac{dy}{dx} = 3 \times (e^{2x^2} \times 4x) = 12x\,e^{2x^2}$
- $y = \frac{e^{\sin x}}{4} = \frac{1}{4}e^{\sin x} \Rightarrow \frac{dy}{dx} = \frac{1}{4}(e^{\sin x} \times \cos x) = \frac{e^{\sin x} \cos x}{4}$

SYLLABUS NOTE
The proof of the derivative $y = a^x$ is not required.

The differentiation of $y = a^x$, a constant

$y = a^x$

$\log_e y = x \log_e a$

$\therefore y = e^{x \log_e a}$ [$\log_e a$ is a constant]

$\frac{dy}{dx} = e^{x \log_e a} \times \log_e a$ [Repeat $e^{x \log_e a}$ × derivative of the power]

$\frac{dy}{dx} = \log_e a \times y$

$\frac{dy}{dx} = \log_e a \times a^x$

$\frac{dy}{dx} = a^x \ln a$ [$\ln a = \log_e a$]

In general:

$$y = a^x \Rightarrow \frac{dy}{dx} = a^x \ln a,\ a > 0,\ a \in \mathbb{R}$$

This result can be extended to $y = a^{f(x)}$.

$$y = a^{f(x)} \Rightarrow \frac{dy}{dx} = a^{f(x)} \ln a \times f'(x)$$

The rule in words: $y = a^{f(x)} \Rightarrow \frac{dy}{dx}$ = repeat $a^{f(x)}$ and multiply it by $\ln a$ and $f'(x)$.

- $y = 10^x \Rightarrow \frac{dy}{dx} = 10^x \times \ln 10 = 10^x \ln 10$
- $y = 3^{x^2} \Rightarrow \frac{dy}{dx} = 3^{x^2} \times \ln 3 \times 2x = 2x(3^{x^2}) \ln 3$
- $s = \frac{3}{4^{2t}} \Rightarrow s = 3 \times 4^{-2t}$

  $\frac{ds}{dt} = 3 \times (4^{-2t} \times \ln 4 \times (-2)) = -\frac{6 \ln 4}{4^{2t}}$

ACTIVITY 10

ACTION
Preparing to differentiate exponential functions

OBJECTIVE
To manipulate exponential expressions to get them ready to differentiate and to tidy up afterwards

Steps for differentiating exponential functions

1. Tidy up the exponential functions into a single exponential function using the rules of algebra.
2. Choose one of **seven** starting differentiation rules.
3. Remember:

$y = e^{f(x)}$	$y = a^{f(x)}$
$\frac{dy}{dx} = e^{f(x)} \times f'(x)$	$\frac{dy}{dx} = a^{f(x)} \times \ln a \times f'(x)$ ($\ln a = \log_e a$)

4. Tidy up your answer.

EXAMPLE 23

If $V = \dfrac{p^2 e^p}{e^{3p}}$, find $\dfrac{dV}{dp}$.

Solution

$$V = \frac{p^2 e^p}{e^{3p}} = p^2 e^{-2p}$$

$$\frac{dV}{dp} = p^2(e^{-2p} \times -2) + e^{-2p}(2p) \quad \text{[Product rule]}$$

$$= 2pe^{-2p}(1 - p)$$

EXAMPLE 24

If $s = \dfrac{e^{\cos^2 t}}{e^{\sin^2 t}}$, find $\dfrac{ds}{dt}$ when $t = 0$.

Solution

$$s = \frac{e^{\cos^2 t}}{e^{\sin^2 t}} = e^{\cos^2 t - \sin^2 t} = e^{\cos 2t}$$

$$\frac{ds}{dt} = (e^{\cos 2t} \times -\sin 2t \times 2) = -2 \sin 2t\, e^{\cos 2t}$$

At $t = 0$: $\dfrac{ds}{dt} = -2 \sin 0 \times e^0 = 0$

EXAMPLE 25

The temperature T in °C in a microwave oven t minutes after it is turned on is given by $T = 510 - 490(0{\cdot}9)^t$, $t \geq 0$. Find the rate of change of temperature at $t = 4$.

Solution

$$T = 510 - 490(0{\cdot}9)^t$$

$$\frac{dT}{dt} = -490((0{\cdot}9)^t \times \ln 0{\cdot}9) = -490 \ln 0{\cdot}9 \times (0{\cdot}9)^t$$

$\boldsymbol{t = 4}$: $\dfrac{dT}{dt} = -490 \ln(0{\cdot}9) \times (0{\cdot}9)^4 = 33{\cdot}87$ °C/min

EXAMPLE 26

Differentiate $y = \sqrt{1 - e^x}$ with respect to x.

Solution

$$y = \sqrt{1 - e^x} = (1 - e^x)^{\frac{1}{2}}$$

$$\frac{dy}{dx} = \frac{1}{2}(1 - e^x)^{-\frac{1}{2}}(-e^x) \quad \text{[Chain rule]}$$

$$\therefore \frac{dy}{dx} = \frac{-e^x}{2\sqrt{1 - e^x}}$$

EXAMPLE 27

Find $\dfrac{d^2y}{dx^2}$ if $y = e^{-x^2}$.

Solution

$$y = e^{-x^2}$$

$$\frac{dy}{dx} = e^{-x^2}(-2x) = -2x\, e^{-x^2}$$

$$\frac{d^2y}{dx^2} = (-2x)(e^{-x^2} \times -2x) + e^{-x^2}(-2) \quad \text{[Product rule]}$$

$$= 2e^{-x^2}(2x^2 - 1)$$

$$= \frac{2(2x^2 - 1)}{e^{x^2}}$$

Always remember, when you differentiate, you are finding the slope of the tangent to a curve at a point on the curve.

EXAMPLE 28

Find the equation of the tangent to the curve $y = x^2e^x$ at $x = 1$.

Solution

Point: $x = 1$: $y = 1^2(e^1) = e$

Slope: $y = x^2e^x$

$$\frac{dy}{dx} = x^2(e^x) + e^x(2x) = xe^x(x+2)$$

$$\therefore m = \left(\frac{dy}{dx}\right)_{x=1} = 1 \times e^1(2+1) = 3e$$

$m = 3e$

$(1, e) = (x_1, y_1)$

Equation of the tangent: $y - e = 3e(x-1)$

$y - e = 3ex - 3e$

$3ex - y - 2e = 0$

e-ln tricks

$y = \log_e f(x) \Leftrightarrow e^y = f(x)$ [Escaping from logs]

$$e^{\ln f(x)} = f(x)$$

The trick in words: $e^{\ln(\text{any function})}$ = the function.

In other words, e and ln coming together neutralise each other.

- $e^{\frac{1}{2}\ln x} = e^{\ln x^{\frac{1}{2}}} = \frac{1}{2}$
- $e^{-2\ln x} = e^{\ln x^{-2}} = x^{-2} = \frac{1}{x^2}$

EXAMPLE 29

If $y = e^{\ln \cos x}$, find $\frac{dy}{dx}$ and $\frac{d^2y}{dx^2}$.

Solution

$y = e^{\ln \cos x} = \cos x$

$\frac{dy}{dx} = -\sin x$

$\frac{d^2y}{dx^2} = -\cos x$

EXERCISE 4

1. Find $\frac{dy}{dx}$ of the following:

(a) $y = 5e^x$

(b) $y = \frac{e^x}{5}$

(c) $y = -\frac{3e^x}{5}$

(d) $y = e^{5x}$

(e) $y = e^{5x-7}$

(f) $y = e^{ax+b}$

(g) $y = e^{x^2}$

(h) $y = 3e^{x^2}$

(i) $y = e^{-2x}$

(j) $y = \frac{5}{e^{3x}}$

2. Find $\frac{dy}{dx}$ of the following:

(a) $y = e^{\sqrt{x}}$

(b) $y = e^x e^{x^2}$

(c) $y = \frac{e^{x-1}}{e^{5x-2}}$

(d) $y = e^{e^x}$

(e) $y = e^{\frac{1}{x}}$

(f) $y = \frac{e^x}{\sin x}$

(g) $y = \frac{e^x}{x^2}$

(h) $y = e^{2x}(x^2+1)$

(i) $y = (e^{2x-3})^2$

(j) $y = \sqrt{e^{4x-2}}$

3. Find $\frac{dy}{dx}$ of the following:

(a) $y = 2^x$

(b) $y = 3 \times 4^x$

(c) $y = \frac{4}{2^x}$

(d) $y = 3^x \times 3^{2x}$

(e) $y = 2^{x^2}$

(f) $y = 3^{-2x+1}$

(g) $y = \frac{9^{-x}}{9^{2x}}$

(h) $y = x \times 2^x$

(i) $y = 2^{e^x}$

(j) $y = x^2$

4. Find $\frac{dy}{dx}$ of the following:

(a) $y = \sqrt{\frac{e^{2x}}{e^{4x^2-2}}}$

(b) $y = \frac{1}{\sqrt{e^x}}$

(c) $y = e^{x \sin x}$

(d) $y = e^2$

(e) $y = \sin(e^x)$

5. **(a)** If $y = xe^x$, find $\frac{dy}{dx}$ when $x = 1$.

(b) If $f(x) = e^{\cos x}$, find $f'\left(\frac{\pi}{3}\right)$.

(c) If $y = e^{\frac{1}{x}}$, find the rate of change of y with respect to x at $x = \frac{1}{2}$.

(d) If $y = e^{\ln x}$, find $\frac{dy}{dx}$ and $\frac{d^2y}{dx^2}$.

(e) If $y = e^{\ln(\sin x)}$, find $\frac{dy}{dx}$ when $x = \frac{\pi}{4}$.

6. **(a)** Find the equation of the tangent to the curve $y = xe^x$ at $x = 1$.

(b) Find the equation of the tangent to the curve $y = \frac{x}{e^x}$ at $x = 0$.

(c) Find the equation of the tangent to the curve $y = \frac{1}{2}(e^x + e^{-x})$ at $x = \ln 2$.

7. Nobelium is a radioactive isotope that decays with a short half-life. The mass m, in grams, of radioactive nobelium left in a sample of nobelium after t seconds is given by $m = Me^{-0 \cdot 03t}$.

(a) Find M if $m = 5$ g at $t = 0$.

(b) Find m when $t = 23$, correct to one decimal place.

(c) Find the rate of change of the mass m when $t = 23$, correct to three decimal places.

8. The pressure P in pascals (Pa) at a height h in metres above the surface of the earth is given by $P = Ae^{-\frac{h}{6900}}$, where A is a constant.

Find:

(a) A if $P = 101\,300$ pascals at $h = 0$,

(b) P at the top of Mount Everest, correct to three significant figures, if the height of Mount Everest is 8848 m,

(c) $\frac{dP}{dh}$ at $h = 10\,000$ m, correct to two decimal places.

9. If $y = e^{kx}$, k is a constant and $\frac{d^2y}{dx^2} - 3\frac{dy}{dx} + 2y = 0$, find $k \in \mathbb{R}$.

10. If $f(x) = \frac{1}{2}(e^x - e^{-x})$, show that:

(a) $f''(x) = f(x)$

(b) $[f(x)]^2 = [f'(x)]^2 - 1$

(c) $\frac{f''(2x)}{f(x)} = 2f'(x)$

23.7 Differentiating log functions

The function $y = f(x) = \log_e x$ is known as the 'natural log' because the base e occurs in many natural situations such as radioactive decay and bacterial growth.

As we have seen, it is given a special notation: $y = \log_e x = \ln x$

It is the inverse function of $y = e^x$. This enables us to differentiate it. The graph of $\ln x$ is obtained by reflecting the graph of e^x in the line $y = x$.

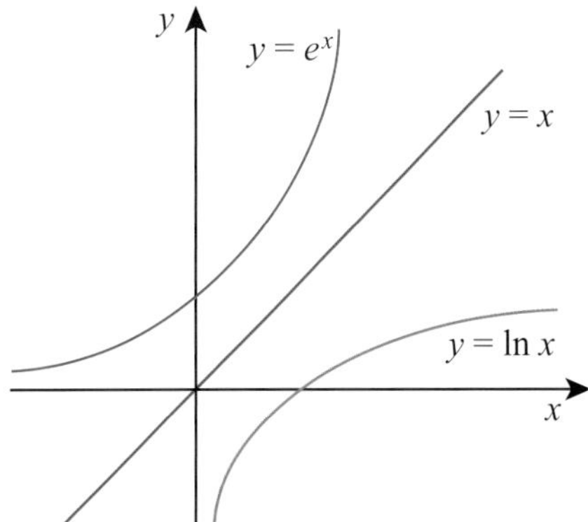

SYLLABUS NOTE

The proof of the derivative $y = \ln x$ is not required.

The derivative of $y = \ln x$

$y = \ln x = \log_e x \Rightarrow e^y = x$ [escaping from logs]

$$x = e^y \Rightarrow \frac{dx}{dy} = e^y$$

$$\Rightarrow \frac{dy}{dx} = \frac{1}{e^y} \qquad \left[\textbf{Note: } \frac{dy}{dx} = \frac{1}{\left(\frac{dx}{dy}\right)}\right]$$

$$\therefore \frac{dy}{dx} = \frac{1}{x}$$

In general:

$$y = \ln x \Rightarrow \frac{dy}{dx} = \frac{1}{x}$$

You can now differentiate more difficult natural log functions by the chain rule.

Consider $y = \ln f(x)$

$u = f(x) \Rightarrow y = \ln u$

$$\frac{dy}{dx} = \frac{dy}{du} \times \frac{du}{dx} = \frac{1}{u} \times f'(x)$$

$$\Rightarrow \frac{dy}{dx} = \frac{1}{f(x)} \times f'(x)$$

In general:

$$y = \ln f(x) \Rightarrow \frac{dy}{dx} = \frac{1}{f(x)} \times f'(x)$$

The rule in words: $y = \ln f(x) \Rightarrow \frac{dy}{dx}$ = one over the function inside the ln multiplied by the derivative of the function inside the ln.

- $y = \ln 3x \Rightarrow \frac{dy}{dx} = \frac{1}{3x} \times 3 = \frac{1}{x}$
- $y = \ln \sin x \Rightarrow \frac{dy}{dx} = \frac{1}{\sin x} \times \cos x = \frac{\cos x}{\sin x}$
- $p = \ln (V^2 + 1) \Rightarrow \frac{dp}{dV} = \frac{1}{V^2+1} \times 2V = \frac{2V}{V^2+1}$

ACTIVITY 11

ACTION
Preparing to differentiate log functions

OBJECTIVE
To manipulate log expressions to get them ready to differentiate and to tidy up afterwards

Steps for log differentiation

1. Simplify the log, if possible, using the rules of logs.
2. Choose one of the **seven** differentiation rules to start.
3. Differentiate each $\ln f(x)$ using $y = \ln f(x) \Rightarrow \frac{dy}{dx} = \frac{1}{f(x)} \times f'(x)$.
4. Tidy up your answer.
5. To differentiate logs in other bases, change the base to ln (natural logs) first.

Always apply the log rules before you differentiate.

- $y = \ln\left(\frac{1}{x}\right) = \ln 1 - \ln x = -\ln x \Rightarrow \frac{dy}{dx} = -\frac{1}{x}$
- $y = \log_2(\sin x) = \frac{\ln(\sin x)}{\ln 2}$

EXAMPLE 30

Differentiate $y = \ln\left(\frac{1-x}{1+x}\right)$ with respect to x.

Solution

$$y = \ln\left(\frac{1-x}{1+x}\right) = \ln(1-x) - \ln(1+x)$$

$$\frac{dy}{dx} = \frac{1}{1-x}(-1) - \frac{1}{1+x}(1) = -\frac{1}{1-x} - \frac{1}{1+x}$$

$$= \frac{-1-x-1+x}{(1-x)(1+x)}$$

$$= -\frac{2}{1-x^2}$$

EXAMPLE 31

Differentiate each of the following with respect to x:

(a) $y = (\ln x)^3$ **(b)** $y = \ln x^3$

Solution

(a) $y = (\ln x)^3$

$$\frac{dy}{dx} = 3(\ln x)^2\left(\frac{1}{x}\right) = \frac{3(\ln x)^2}{x}$$

(b) $y = \ln x^3 = 3\ln x$

$$\frac{dy}{dx} = 3\left(\frac{1}{x}\right) = \frac{3}{x}$$

EXAMPLE 32

Differentiate $y = \ln\sqrt{\frac{2-x^2}{3+x^2}}$ with respect to x.

Solution

$$y = \ln\sqrt{\frac{2-x^2}{3+x^2}} = \frac{1}{2}\ln\left(\frac{2-x^2}{3+x^2}\right)$$

$$= \frac{1}{2}\{\ln(2-x^2) - \ln(3+x^2)\}$$

$$\frac{dy}{dx} = \frac{1}{2}\left\{\frac{1}{2-x^2}(-2x) - \frac{1}{(3+x^2)}(2x)\right\}$$

$$= -x\left\{\frac{1}{2-x^2} + \frac{1}{3+x^2}\right\}$$

$$= -x\left\{\frac{3+x^2+2-x^2}{(2-x^2)(3+x^2)}\right\} = -\frac{5x}{(2-x^2)(3+x^2)}$$

EXAMPLE 33

Differentiate $y = x^2 \ln x$ with respect to x.

Solution

$$y = x^2 \ln x$$

$$\frac{dy}{dx} = x^2\left(\frac{1}{x}\right) + \ln x(2x) \quad \text{[Product rule]}$$

$$= x + 2x \ln x$$

$$= x(1 + 2 \ln x)$$

EXAMPLE 34

The area A in m^2 of a fish farm affected by sea lice increases with time t, in days, according to the equation $A = \ln (2t + 1)^2$. Find the rate of change of the area affected (with respect to time) 5 days after the initial outbreak ($t = 0$).

Solution

$$A = \ln (2t + 1)^2 = 2 \ln (2t + 1)$$

$$\frac{dA}{dt} = 2\left(\frac{1}{2t+1}\right)(2) = \frac{4}{2t+1}$$

$$\left(\frac{dA}{dt}\right)_{t=5} = \frac{4}{11} \text{ m}^2/\text{day}$$

EXAMPLE 35

Differentiate $y = \log_2 (x^2 - 1)$ with respect to x.

Solution

$$y = \log_2 (x^2 - 1) = \frac{\ln (x^2 - 1)}{\ln 2} = \frac{1}{\ln 2} \times \ln(x^2 - 1)$$

$$\frac{dy}{dx} = \frac{1}{\ln 2} \times \frac{1}{(x^2 + 1)} \times 2x = \frac{2x}{(x^2 - 1)\ln 2}$$

EXERCISE 5

1. Differentiate the following with respect to x:

(a) $\ln 5x$
(b) $\ln (3x - 5)$
(c) $\ln (ax + b)$
(d) $\ln x^5$
(e) $\ln 7$
(f) $\ln (3x^5)$
(g) $\ln \left(\frac{4}{x}\right)$
(h) $\ln (4\sqrt{x})$
(i) $\ln \cos x$
(j) $\ln \sin^3 x$

2. Differentiate the following with respect to x:

(a) $\ln (2x - 1)^7$
(b) $\sin (\ln x)$
(c) $(\ln x)^5$
(d) $x \ln x$
(e) $\frac{\ln x}{x}$
(f) $\sin x \ln x$
(g) $e^x \ln x$
(h) $\frac{4 \ln x}{\sqrt{x}}$
(i) $\ln \left(\frac{e^x}{1 + e^x}\right)$
(j) $\ln (x\sqrt{2 + x^2})$
(k) $\ln \left(\frac{3 - x}{3 + x}\right)^{\frac{1}{3}}$
(l) $\ln (\ln x)$
(m) $\ln \sqrt{\sin x \cos x}$
(n) $\frac{\ln (\sin x)}{x}$
(o) $3 \ln (x) - e^x$

3. Differentiate the following with respect to x:

(a) $y = \ln e^x$
(b) $y = \ln \sqrt{e^x}$
(c) $y = \ln e^{\cos^2 x}$
(d) $y = \ln e^{\sqrt{x}}$
(e) $y = \log_{10} x^2$
(f) $y = \ln e^{-x}$

4. **(a)** Find the equation of the tangent to $y = \ln x$ at $x = 1$.

(b) Find the equation of the tangent to $q = \ln \left[\frac{t(t-1)}{2}\right]$ at $t = 2$.

(c) If $v = \frac{1}{4} \ln (s - 2)^2$ and $s > 2$, find the rate of change of v with respect to s at $s = 3$.

(d) The volume V in m^3 of water in a tank after t minutes is given by the formula $V = \ln \left(\frac{2t+1}{t+1}\right)^3, t \geq 0$.
Find the rate of change of the volume when $t = 10$ minutes.

CHAPTER 24 Applications of Differentiation

Learning Outcomes

- To have a knowledge of curves including how to find slopes and tangents, stationary points (local maxima and minima) and how to sketch curves.
- To know the properties of quadratic, cubic, exponential and log curves.
- To carry out rate of change problems. To be able to solve related rate of change problems using the chain rule.
- To solve problems involving modelling and optimisation.

24.1 Curves

ACTIVITY 12

ACTION
Exploring slopes of tangents

OBJECTIVE
To calculate the slopes of a number of tangents to curves

Slopes and tangents

When you draw the curve that describes a function $y = f(x)$, you always read the curve from left to right.

This means that the x co-ordinate is **always** increasing: $x_2 - x_1 = 4 - 2 = +2$.

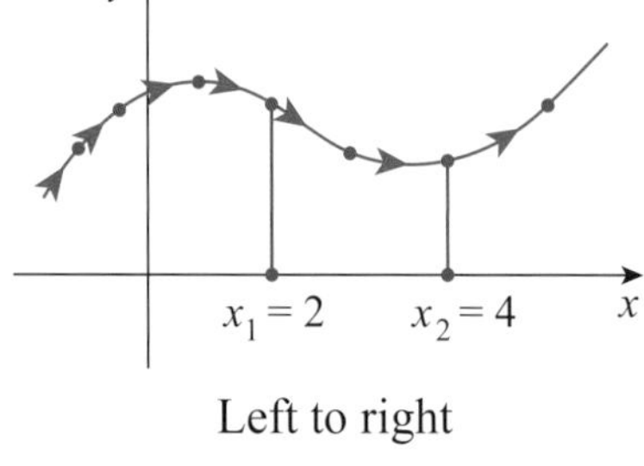

Left to right

Imagine that you go for a walk in the hills, starting at A.

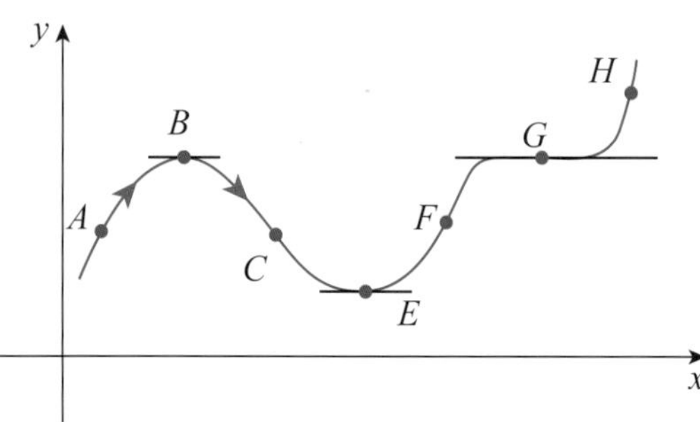

As you climb the hill from A to B, the y co-ordinate is increasing (I). The curve then flattens out at B (stationary point) at the top of the hill. From B to C the y co-ordinate decreases (D) as you go downhill. At C the curvature changes from curving in to curving out. The curve then flattens out again at E (stationary point) at the bottom of the valley. As you continue your walk, the curve rises again (I) until, at F, its curvature changes. Again at G the curve flattens out and from G to H the curve begins to rise (I) again.

Slope of the tangent

$\frac{dy}{dx} = m =$ the slope of the tangent to the curve $y = f(x)$ at **any** point P on the curve $= \tan A$.

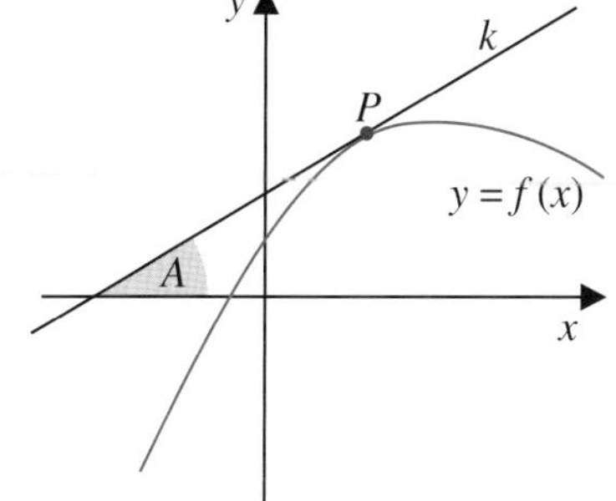

Remember, the point P is the point of contact of the curve and the tangent k and so satisfies the equation of both. To find the equation of a tangent k to a curve you need two things:

1. the slope m of k
2. a point $P(x_1, y_1)$ on k

EXAMPLE 1

Find the equation of the tangent to the curve $f: y = 2x - \frac{1}{x}$ at $x = 2$.

Solution

1. Draw a diagram.
2. Find the point P.

   $\mathbf{x = 2:}\ y = 2(2) - \left(\frac{1}{2}\right) = \frac{7}{2}$

   Since P is on curve f

   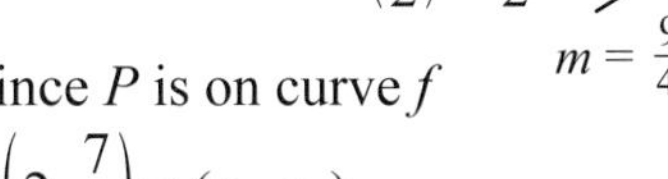

   $P\left(2, \frac{7}{2}\right) = (x_1, y_1)$.
3. Find the slope of k.

   $$y = 2x - \frac{1}{x} = 2x - x^{-1}$$
   $$\frac{dy}{dx} = 2 + x^{-2} = 2 + \frac{1}{x^2}$$
   $$\left(\frac{dy}{dx}\right)_{x=2} = 2 + \frac{1}{4} = \frac{9}{4} = m$$
4. Using $(y - y_1) = m(x - x_1)$, find the equation of k.

   $$\left(y - \frac{7}{2}\right) = \frac{9}{4}(x - 2)$$
   $$4y - 14 = 9x - 18$$

   $k: 9x - 4y - 4 = 0$

EXAMPLE 2

Find the points P and Q on the curve $y = 2x^3 - 3x^2$ shown, at which the slope of the tangent is 12.

Solution

$y = 2x^3 - 3x^2$

$\frac{dy}{dx} = 6x^2 - 6x$

Slope $= 12 \Rightarrow 6x^2 - 6x = 12$

$x^2 - x - 2 = 0$

$(x + 1)(x - 2) = 0$

$\therefore x = -1, 2$

$\mathbf{x = -1:}\ y = -2 - 3 = -5$

$\mathbf{x = 2:}\ y = 16 - 12 = 4$

$\therefore P(-1, -5), Q(2, 4)$

The tangents at P and Q are parallel because they have the same slope.

EXERCISE 6

1. Find the equation of the tangent to the curve at the given point for each of the following:
   (a) $y = 2x^2 + x - 2$ at $x = 1$
   (b) $y = x^3 - 3x + 1$ at $x = 0$
   (c) $y = 3x^4 - 2x^2 + 4$ at $x = 1$
   (d) $y = x^3 - 5x^2 + 7x - 9$ at $(1, -6)$
   (e) $y = \sin^2 x$ at $x = \frac{\pi}{4}$
   (f) $y = \ln \sqrt{x}$ at $x = e$
   (g) $y = 5e^{x-1}$ at $x = 1$
   (h) $y = 3 \times 2^x$ at $x = 0$

2. **(a)** Find the equation of the tangent to the curve $y = f(x) = x^3 - 2x^2 - 3x + 1$ at $(2, -5)$ and find the other point on this curve at which the slope of the tangent is 1.
   (b) Find the co-ordinates of the points on the curve $s = t^2(t - 2)$ at which the tangents have slope 0.
   (c) Find the constant a if the tangent to the curve $y = x(a - x^2)$ at the origin makes an angle of 45° with the $+x$-axis.
   (d) For the function $y = f(x) = x^3 - 4x^2 + 4x - 1$, $x \in \mathbb{R}$,
   (i) show that $f\left(\frac{1}{2}\right) = \frac{1}{8}$,
   (ii) find the equation of the tangent to $y = f(x)$ at $x = \frac{1}{2}$,
   (iii) find c, if this tangent cuts the x-axis at $(c, 0)$.

3. Find the points on the curve $y = \frac{a^2x}{a^2 + x^2}$, a constant, at which the tangents are parallel to the x-axis.

4. The curve $y = ax^3 + bx^2 + cx + d$ passes through $(0, 0)$. The tangent at the origin is the x-axis. The slope of the tangent to the curve at $\left(-\frac{3}{2}, 0\right)$ is 9. Find a, b, c and $d \in \mathbb{R}$.

5. **(a)** $y = ax^2 + bx + c$ passes through $(2, 4)$. If $y = x + 1$ is the equation of the tangent to this curve at $(0, 1)$, find a, b and $c \in \mathbb{R}$.
   (b) The tangent to the curve $f(x) = 2x^3 + ax^2 + bx - 5$ at $x = 1$ has the equation $5x - y - 8 = 0$.
   (i) Show that $(1, -3)$ is the point of contact of the tangent to the curve.
   (ii) Find a and b.

6. The height h (cm) at time t (seconds) of the ripples on a lake are given by $h = 3 \sin 2t$. The graph of this function is shown below.
   (a) Find the times t for which the instantaneous rate of change is 3 cm/s, $0 \leq t \leq \pi$.
   (b) Find the equations of the tangents at the points in part **(a)**.

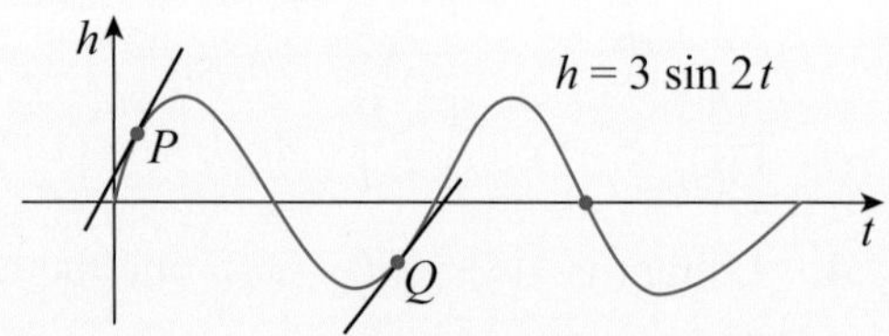

Increasing and decreasing regions of a curve

Increasing (I): As you walk from $O(0, 0)$ to $E(4, 16)$ on the curve shown, the y co-ordinate increases as the x co-ordinate increases. This region from O to E is an increasing region of the curve.

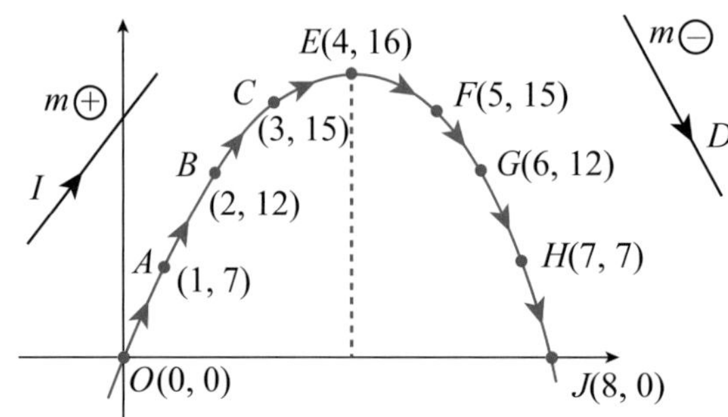

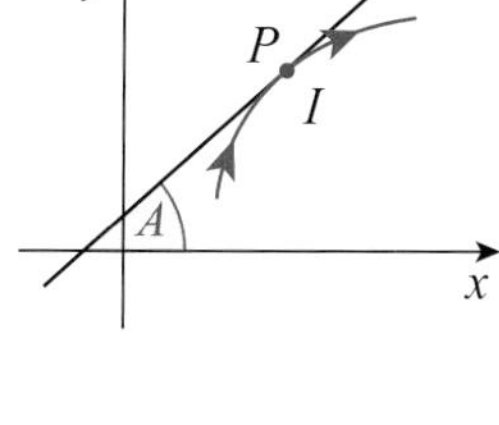

Consider any point P on an increasing part of a curve:

$\frac{dy}{dx}$ = the slope of the tangent at $P = \tan A$.

Since A is acute, $\tan A > 0$.

$\therefore \frac{dy}{dx}$ at $P > 0$

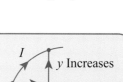

The slope of the tangent is positive at **every point** in an increasing region of a curve.

A curve is increasing at a point P on the curve if $\frac{dy}{dx} > 0$ at this point.

I
y Increases
x Increases

ACTIVITY 13

ACTION
Exploring increasing and decreasing curves

OBJECTIVE
To examine a number of functions to determine where their curves are increasing and decreasing

Decreasing (D): As you walk from $E(4, 16)$ to $J(8, 0)$ on the curve, the y co-ordinate decreases as the x co-ordinate increases. The region from E to J is a decreasing region of the curve.

Consider any point P on a decreasing part of a curve:

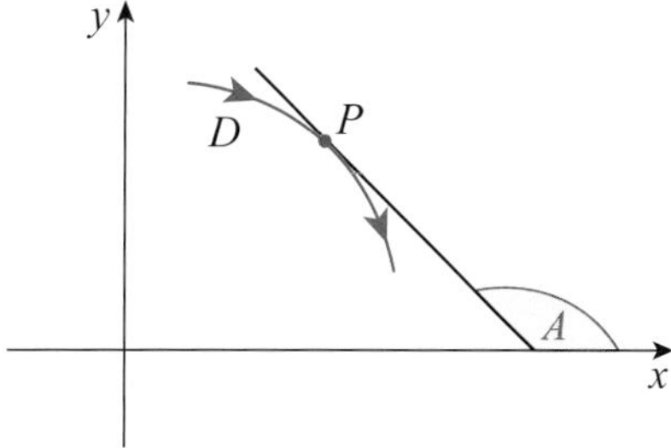

$\frac{dy}{dx}$ = the slope of the tangent at $P = \tan A$.

Since A is obtuse, $\tan A < 0$.

$\therefore \frac{dy}{dx}$ at $P < 0$

The slope of the tangent is negative at **every point** in a decreasing region of a curve.

A curve is decreasing at a point P on the curve if $\frac{dy}{dx} < 0$ at this point.

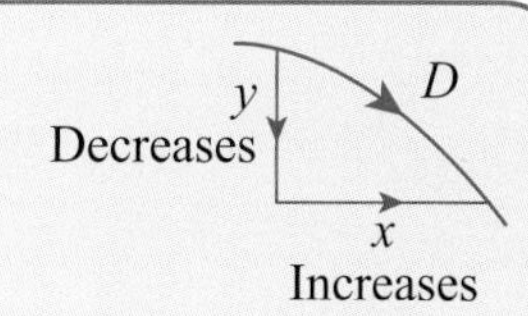

EXAMPLE 3

Investigate if the curve $y = x + \frac{4}{x}$ is increasing or decreasing at $x = 1$.

Solution

$y = x + \frac{4}{x} = x + 4x^{-1}$

$\frac{dy}{dx} = 1 - 4x^{-2} = 1 - \frac{4}{x^2}$

$\left(\frac{dy}{dx}\right)_{x=1} = 1 - \frac{4}{(1)^2} = -3 < 0$

Therefore, the curve is decreasing at $x = 1$.

EXAMPLE 4

The population P of bats in a colony at time t in years is given by $P = \frac{100e^t}{e^t + 1}$. Show that the population is constantly increasing.

Solution

$P = \frac{100e^t}{e^t + 1}$

$\frac{dP}{dt} = \frac{(e^t + 1)(100e^t) - (100e^t)(e^t)}{(e^t + 1)^2}$

$= \frac{100e^t(e^t + 1 - e^t)}{(e^t + 1)^2}$

$= \frac{100e^t}{(e^t + 1)^2} > 0$ for all $t \in \mathbb{R}$, since $e^t > 0$ for all $t \in \mathbb{R}$.

EXERCISE 7

1. Copy the following curves. On each curve shown, find the region where the slope m of the tangent is positive ($m = +$), negative ($m = -$), or zero ($m = 0$). Label the increasing (I) and decreasing (D) regions of each graph.

(a)

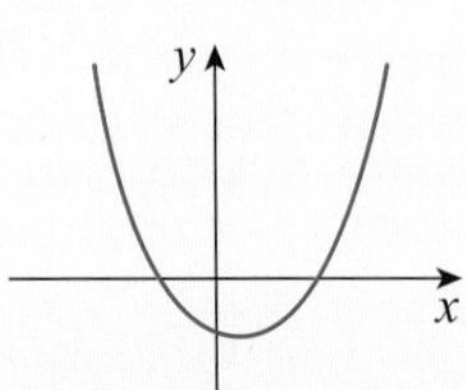

(b)

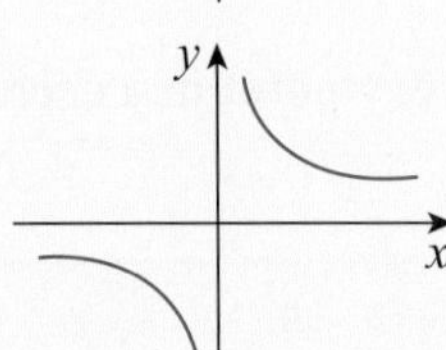

(c)

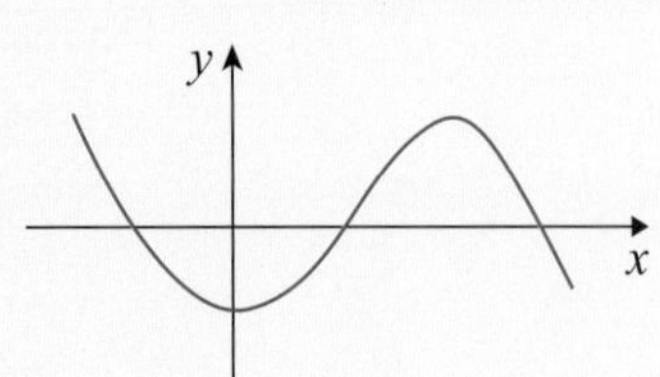

(d)

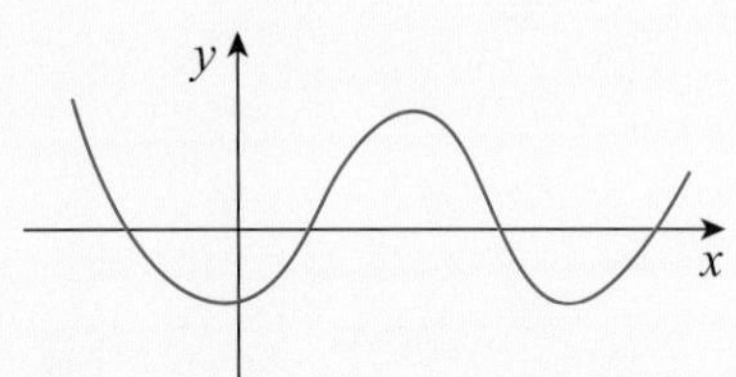

2. Sketch the following curves roughly:

(a) $f'(x) < 0$ for $x < 3$, $f'(3) = 0$, $f'(x) > 0$ for $x > 3$ and $f(3) = 2$

(b) $\frac{dy}{dx} < 0$ for **all** $x \neq 2$ and $\frac{dy}{dx} = 0$ when $x = 2$

(c) $f'(x) > 0$ for $x < -1$ and $x > 4$, $f'(x) = 0$ for $x = -1$ and $x = 4$ and $f'(x) < 0$ for $-1 < x < 4$ and $f(1) = 0$

3. Investigate if the curve $y = f(x)$ is increasing or decreasing at the given point P.

(a) $y = x + \frac{4}{x}$ at $x = 1$

(b) $y = \sin^3\left(\frac{x}{4}\right)$ at $x = \pi$

(c) $y = xe^x$ at $x = \ln 2$

(d) $y = \ln\{(x - 1)(x + 2)\}$ at $x = 3$

(e) $y = 3^{-x}$ at $x = -2$

4. For each of the following, show that:

(a) $y = x^3 + 7x - 1$ is increasing for all $x \in \mathbb{R}$

(b) $y = a^x$, $a > 1$ is increasing for all $x \in \mathbb{R}$

(c) $y = \ln x$ is increasing for all $x > 0$, $x \in \mathbb{R}$

(d) $y = \frac{1}{x}$ is decreasing for $x \in \mathbb{R}$, $x \neq 0$

(e) $y = x^3 - 3x^2 + 27x - 1$ is decreasing for all $x \in \mathbb{R}$

5. Find the range of values of x for which:

   (a) $y = x^2 - 3x + 1$ is decreasing

   (b) $y = x^3 + 12x^2 + 45x - 35$ is increasing

6. The area of the polluted part of a lake is given by $A = 10\sqrt{t} - t, t > 0$ where A is in m^2 and t is in days.

   (a) Show that the area is:

   (i) increasing at $t = 16$

   (ii) decreasing at $t = 36$

   (b) Find the range of values of t for which A is increasing.

Stationary points (critical points)

A stationary or critical point of a curve is a point at which the curve flattens out.

B, E and G are stationary points. They are points at which the slope of the tangent to the curve is zero.

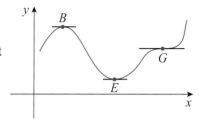

A **stationary point** (SP) of a curve is a point at which $\frac{dy}{dx} = 0$.

B, E and G are stationary points because $\frac{dy}{dx} = 0$ at each of these points.

To find the stationary points of a curve

1. Find $\frac{dy}{dx}$.
2. Put $\frac{dy}{dx} = 0$.
3. Solve for x.
4. Find y.

EXAMPLE 5

Find the stationary points of the curve $y = x^3 - 3x^2 - 9x + 1, x \in \mathbb{R}$.

Solution

$y = x^3 - 3x^2 - 9x + 1$

1. $\frac{dy}{dx} = 3x^2 - 6x - 9$
2. $\frac{dy}{dx} = 0$

   $3x^2 - 6x - 9 = 0$
3. $x^2 - 2x - 3 = 0$

   $(x + 1)(x - 3) = 0$

   $x = -1, 3$
4. $\mathbf{x = -1}$: $y = (-1)^3 - 3(-1)^2 - 9(-1) + 1 = 6$

   $\mathbf{x = 3}$: $y = (3)^3 - 3(3)^2 - 9(3) + 1 = -26$

   The stationary points are $(-1, 6)$ and $(3, -26)$.

EXAMPLE 6

Show that $y = \frac{1}{x + 1}, x \neq -1, x \in \mathbb{R}$ has no stationary points.

Solution

$y = \frac{1}{(x + 1)} = (x + 1)^{-1}$

1. $\frac{dy}{dx} = -(x + 1)^{-2} = -\frac{1}{(x + 1)^2}$
2. $\frac{dy}{dx} = 0$

   $-\frac{1}{(x + 1)^2} = 0$

   $-1 = 0$

This statement is not true. Therefore, there are no solutions and hence no stationary points.

EXAMPLE 7

Show that $f(x) = e^x - 2x + 1, x \in \mathbb{R}$, has only one stationary point. Find this stationary point.

Solution

$f(x) = y = e^x - 2x + 1$

1. $f'(x) = \frac{dy}{dx} = e^x - 2$
2. $\frac{dy}{dx} = 0$

   $e^x - 2 = 0$
3. $e^x = 2$

   $\ln e^x = \ln 2$

   $x = \ln 2$

   Therefore, the function has one stationary point at $x = \ln 2$.
4. $y = e^{\ln 2} - 2\ln 2 + 1 = 2 - \ln 4 + 1 = 3 - \ln 4$

   Therefore, $(\ln 2, 3 - \ln 4)$ is the stationary point.

EXAMPLE 8

The curve $y = \frac{a + bx}{x^2 + 2x}, x \in \mathbb{R}$, has a stationary point at (1, 2). Find the constants a and b.

Solution

$y = \frac{a + bx}{x^2 + 2x}$

Stationary point at $P(1, 2) \Rightarrow \left(\frac{dy}{dx}\right)_{x=1} = 0$

$\frac{dy}{dx} = \frac{(x^2 + 2x)(b) - (a + bx)(2x + 2)}{(x^2 + 2x)^2}$

$\left(\frac{dy}{dx}\right)_{x=1} = \frac{3b - (a + b)4}{9} = 0$

$3b - 4a - 4b = 0$

$b = -4a$

(1, 2) is on the curve $y = \frac{a + bx}{x^2 + 2x}$: $2 = \frac{a + b}{3}$

$a + b = 6$

$b = -4a$

$-3a = 6$

$\therefore a = -2, b = 8$

EXERCISE 8

1. Find the stationary points, if any, for the following curves, $x \in \mathbb{R}$:
   (a) $y = x^2 - 2x + 5$
   (b) $y = -2x^2 + 6x - 3$
   (c) $y = ax^2 + bx + c$
   (d) $y = x^3 - 6x^2 + 9x$
   (e) $y = (x - 2)^3$
   (f) $y = 2x^3 - 9x^2 + 12x - 6$
   (g) $y = \frac{1}{x + 1}$
   (h) $y = \frac{3x - 1}{x + 2}, x \neq -2$
   (i) $y = xe^{-x}$
   (j) $y = x \ln x, x > 0$
   (k) $y = (2x - 1)(x - 2)^4$
   (l) $y = x\sqrt{1 - x}, x \geq 1$
   (m) $P = 2x + \frac{32}{x}, x \neq 0$
2. Show that $y = \sin 2x, x \in \mathbb{R}$, has an infinite number of stationary points and write down a general formula for these points.
3. (a) Find a if $y = 3x^2 - ax - 7$ has a stationary point at $x = \frac{1}{2}$.
   (b) Find a and b if $y = x^3 - ax^2 + bx - 2$ has stationary points at $x = 1$ and $x = -2$.
   (c) The curve $y = x^4 + kx^3 - 5x + 7$ has a stationary point at $x = -\frac{1}{2}$. Find k.

ACTIVITY 14

ACTION
Understanding the nature of slopes

OBJECTIVE
To explore the nature of slopes by finding their first and second derivatives

Curvature

1. Concave up (cup-shaped)

A curve has a concave up shape if the slope m of the tangent increases in value from point to point as you move from left to right along the curve.

This means it is shaped like a cup $\cup$ (fill it up).

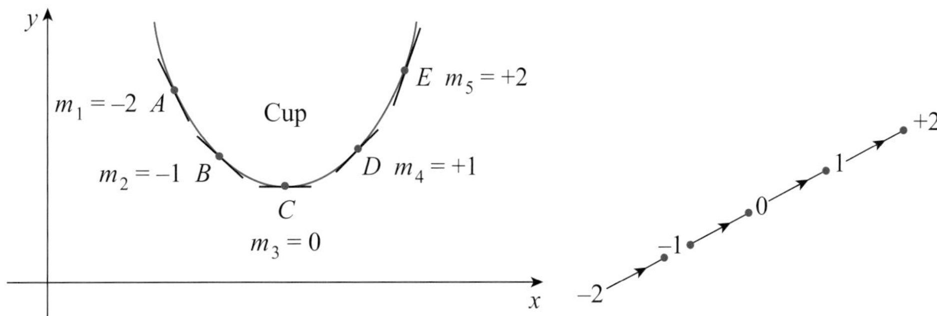

As x increases, the value of the slope m increases.

As you go from $A \to B \to C \to D \to E$, the value of m goes from $-2 \to +2$.

This means $\frac{dm}{dx} > 0$ at all of these points since m increases as x increases.

$$m = \frac{dy}{dx} \Rightarrow \frac{dm}{dx} = \frac{d^2y}{dx^2}$$

$\therefore \frac{dm}{dx} = \frac{d^2y}{dx^2} > 0$ at every point in a cup-shaped region.

> If $\frac{d^2y}{dx^2} > 0$ at a point P, the curve is concave up at this point (cup-shaped).

2. Concave down (cap-shaped)

A curve has a concave down shape if the slope m of the tangent decreases in value from point to point as you move from left to right along the curve.

This means it is shaped like a cap $\cap$ (put it on your head).

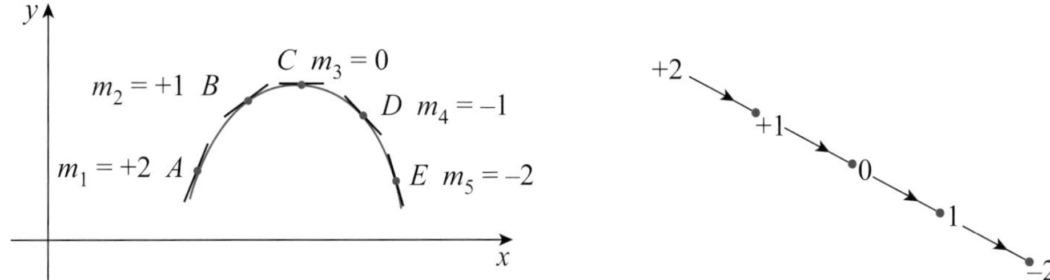

As x increases, the value of the slope m decreases.
As you go from $A \to B \to C \to D \to E$, the value of m goes from $+2 \to -2$.

This means $\frac{dm}{dx} < 0$ at all of these points since m decreases as x increases.

$$m = \frac{dy}{dx} \Rightarrow \frac{dm}{dx} = \frac{d^2y}{dx^2}$$

$\therefore \frac{dm}{dx} = \frac{d^2y}{dx^2} < 0$ at every point in a cap-shaped region.

If $\frac{d^2y}{dx^2} < 0$ at a point P, the curve is concave down at this point (cap-shaped).

3. Point of inflection

A point of inflection (PI) is a point at which a curve changes from concave up (cup) to concave down (cap), or vice versa. It is the point at which its curvature changes from curving in to curving out and vice versa.

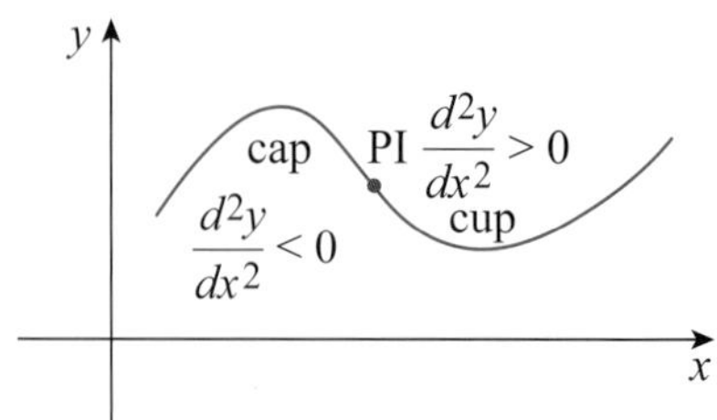

For a continuous curve, a **point of inflection** is a point at which the sign of $\frac{d^2y}{dx^2}$ changes from positive to negative, or vice versa. This means at a point of inflection $\frac{d^2y}{dx^2} = 0$.

EXAMPLE 9

For what values of x is the curve $y = x^3 + x^2 - 2x - 3$ concave down, $x \in \mathbb{R}$.

Solution

$y = x^3 + x^2 - 2x - 3$

$\frac{dy}{dx} = 3x^2 + 2x - 2$

$\frac{d^2y}{dx^2} = 6x + 2$

$\frac{d^2y}{dx^2} < 0 \Rightarrow 6x + 2 < 0$

$6x < -2$

$\therefore x < -\frac{1}{3}, x \in \mathbb{R}$

EXAMPLE 10

Show that the curve $y = e^{2x} + \frac{1}{x^2}$ is concave up for all $x \in \mathbb{R}, x \neq 0$.

Solution

$y = e^{2x} + \frac{1}{x^2} = e^{2x} + x^{-2}$

$\frac{dy}{dx} = 2e^{2x} - 2x^{-3}$

$\frac{d^2y}{dx^2} = 4e^{2x} + 6x^{-4} = 4e^{2x} + \frac{6}{x^4} > 0$ for all $x \in \mathbb{R}, x \neq 0$

$\therefore \frac{d^2y}{dx^2} > 0$ for all $x \in \mathbb{R}, x \neq 0$

Therefore, the curve is concave up for all $x \in \mathbb{R}, x \neq 0$.

To get all the points of inflection of a curve, put $\frac{d^2y}{dx^2} = 0$ and solve for x.

EXAMPLE 11

Find the points of inflection, if any, of the curve $y = x^3 - 6x^2 + 5x - 11$.

Solution

$y = x^3 - 6x^2 + 5x - 11$

$\frac{dy}{dx} = 3x^2 - 12x + 5$

$\frac{d^2y}{dx^2} = 6x - 12$

To find the points of inflection, put $\frac{d^2y}{dx^2} = 0$.

$6x - 12 = 0$

$x = 2$

Therefore, there is only one point of inflection at $x = 2$.

$x = 2$: $y = (2)^3 - 6(2)^2 + 5(2) - 11 = -17$

Therefore, $(2, -17)$ is the only point of inflection.

EXERCISE 9

1. Investigate if the given curve is concave up or concave down at the given point:
   (a) $y = x^2 - \frac{1}{x}$ at $x = 3$
   (b) $y = \sin^2 x$ at $x = \frac{\pi}{3}$
   (c) $y = xe^x$ at $x = 0$
   (d) $y = x \ln x$ at $x = 2$

2. **(a)** For what values of x is the curve $y = x^3 + x^2 - 2x - 7$ concave up?
   (b) Show that $y = 8 - 3x - 2x^2$ is always concave down.
   (c) Show that $y = ax^2 + bx + c$ is concave up if $a > 0$ but concave down if $a < 0$.
   (d) Show that $y = 3e^x - \ln x + 5x - 2$ is always concave up.
   (e) Find the range of values of x for which $f(x) = x^4 + 2x^3 - 12x^2 + 10x - 2$ is concave down.

3. Find the point(s) of inflection, if any, of the curves given for $x \in \mathbb{R}$:
   (a) $y = x^2 - 4x + 1$
   (b) $y = x^3 - 3x^2 - 9x + 2$
   (c) $y = \frac{x}{x+1}, x \neq -1$
   (d) $y = x^4 - 8x^3 + 24x^2 - 6x + 1$

4. **(a)** Find k if $y = kx^3 - 12x^2 + 5x - 1$ has a point of inflection at $x = 1$.
   (b) Find p if $y = x^4 - 3px^2 - 16x + 7$ has a point of inflection at $x = -1$.
   (c) Find p and q if the curve $y = px^4 + 2qx^3 - 72x^2 + 6x - 5$ has points of inflection at $x = -1$ and $x = \frac{1}{2}$.

5. The curve $y = ax^3 + bx^2 + cx + d$ has a stationary point at (0, 2) and a point of inflection at (1, –1). Find a, b, c and d.

6. The standard normal (bell-shaped) probability curve has an equation $y = \frac{1}{\sigma\sqrt{2\pi}} e^{-\frac{x^2}{2\sigma^2}}$, where σ, μ are constants. Show it has points of inflection at $x = \pm\sigma$.

7. **(a)** The graph below shows the decay of the mass M of a radioactive isotope with time.

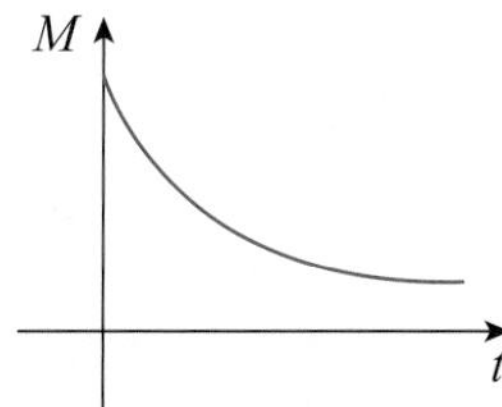

   Describe the signs of **(i)** $\frac{dM}{dt}$, **(ii)** $\frac{d^2M}{dt^2}$.

   (b) The graph below shows the number N of students in a secondary school over time t.

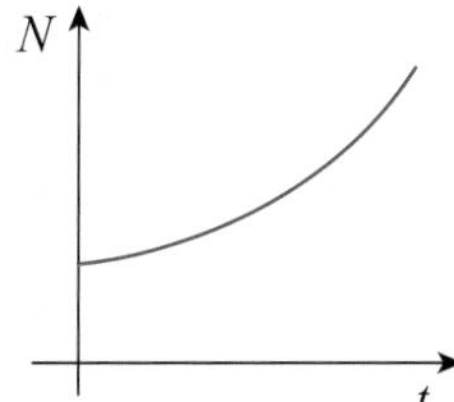

   Describe:
   (i) how the number is changing over time,
   (ii) how the rate of change of the number of students is changing with time.

   (c) The graph below shows the number N of unemployed people over t (months).

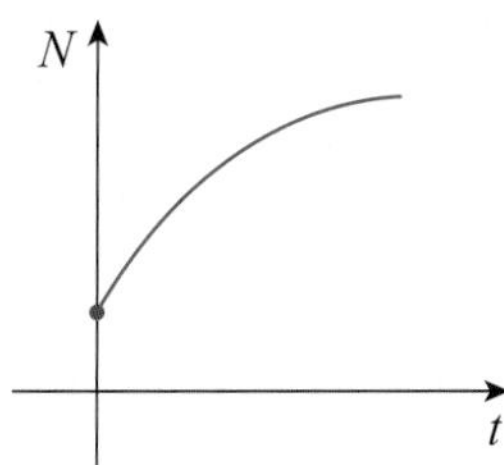

   (i) Describe the signs of $\frac{dN}{dt}$ and $\frac{d^2N_2}{dt}$.
   (ii) How is the number of unemployed people changing over time?
   (iii) How is the rate of unemployment changing?

ACTIVITY 15

ACTION
Sketching graphs of first and second derivatives

OBJECTIVE
To sketch the graphs of the first and second derivative of functions

Maximising and minimising functions

Local maximum (L Max)

The top of a hill is a local maximum and is also known as a turning point.

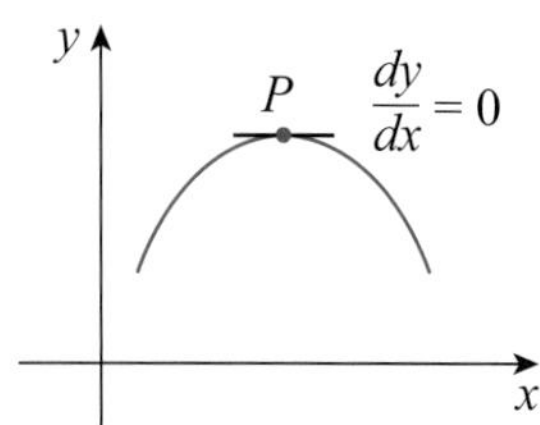

> A **local maximum** is the only point P of a concave down region at which the slope of the tangent is zero (the curve flattens out).

Conditions for a local maximum:

(i) $\frac{dy}{dx} = 0$ (flat)

(ii) $\frac{d^2y}{dx^2} < 0$ (concave down)

Local minimum (L Min)

The bottom of a valley is a local minimum and is also known as a turning point.

> A **local minimum** is the only point Q of a concave up region at which the slope of the tangent is zero (the curve flattens out).

Conditions for a local minimum:

(i) $\frac{dy}{dx} = 0$ (flat)

(ii) $\frac{d^2y}{dx^2} > 0$ (concave up)

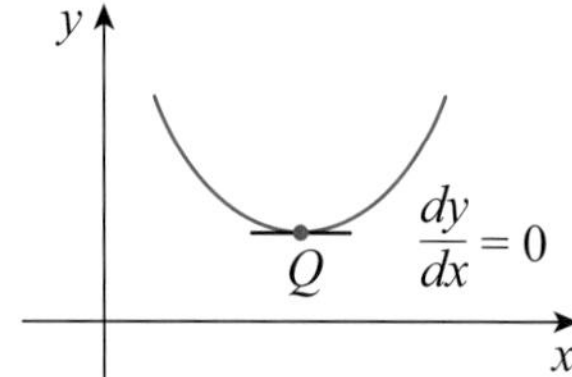

It is important to note the following:

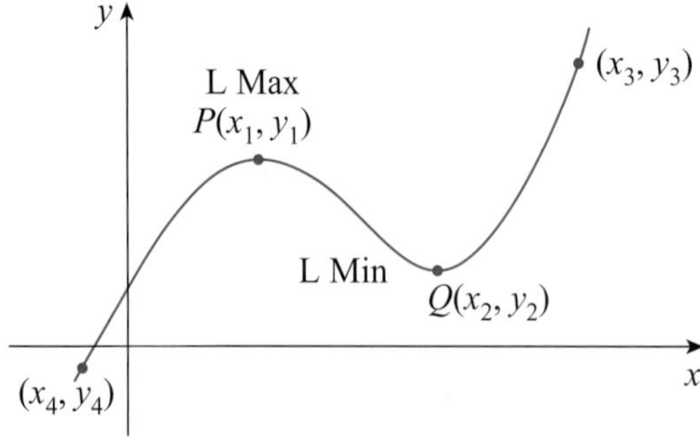

1. The local **maximum value** of a function is the value of the y co-ordinate at the local maximum point (the value of y_1 in the diagram above).
2. The local **minimum value** of a function is the value of the y co-ordinate at the local minimum point (the value of y_2 in the diagram above).
3. They are called **local** maxima and **local** minima because they are only the biggest and smallest values of y in a local region of the curve and not for the whole (global curve). Clearly $y_3 > y_1$ and $y_4 < y_2$.

4. There can be many local maxima and local minima, as shown in this diagram.
5. Local maxima and minima are collectively known as turning points.

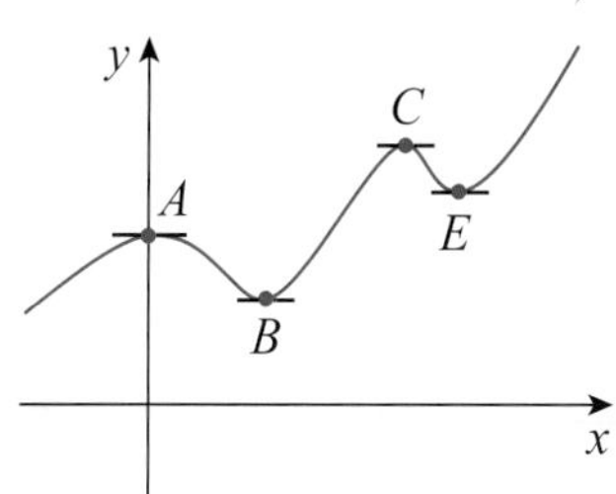

Steps for finding the local maxima and local minima of a function

1. Give the function a suitable symbol (if not already specified in the question) and make sure the function is expressed in terms of a single variable. The symbol used here is y.
2. Find $\frac{dy}{dx}$.
3. Put $\frac{dy}{dx} = 0$ and solve for x to find the stationary points (SP).
4. Find $\frac{d^2y}{dx^2}$.
5. Test the stationary points by substituting them into $\frac{d^2y}{dx^2}$.
6. If $\left(\frac{d^2y}{dx^2}\right)_{SP} < 0$ at a stationary point, the stationary point is a local maximum: ⌒

   If $\left(\frac{d^2y}{dx^2}\right)_{SP} > 0$ at a stationary point, the stationary point is a local minimum: ⌣
7. Substitute the stationary points back into the function to get the local maximum/minimum values.

EXAMPLE 12

Find the local maxima/minima, if any, of the function $y = 3x^4 - 4x^3 - 12x^2 + 2$, $x \in \mathbb{R}$.

Solution

$y = 3x^4 - 4x^3 - 12x^2 + 2$

$\frac{dy}{dx} = 12x^3 - 12x^2 - 24x$

$12x^3 - 12x^2 - 24x = 0$

$12x(x^2 - x - 2) = 0$

$12x(x + 1)(x - 2) = 0$

$x = 0, -1, 2$ [There are three stationary points.]

$\frac{d^2y}{dx^2} = 36x^2 - 24x - 24$

$\left(\frac{d^2y}{dx^2}\right)_{x=0} = -24 < 0$ Local maximum at $x = 0$: ⌒ $x = 0$

$\left(\frac{d^2y}{dx^2}\right)_{x=-1} = 36 + 24 - 24 > 0$

Local minimum at $x = -1$. ⌣ $x = -1$

$\left(\frac{d^2y}{dx^2}\right)_{x=2} = 36(4) - 48 - 24 = 72 > 0$

Local minimum at $x = 2$. ⌣ $x = 2$

$x = 0 : y = 2 \therefore (0, 2)$ is a local maximum.

$x = -1 : y = -3 \therefore (-1, -3)$ is a local minimum.

$x = 2 : y = -30 \therefore (2, -30)$ is a local minimum.

EXAMPLE 13

Find the local maxima/minima, if any, of $y = 2e^x - x + 3,\ x \in \mathbb{R}$.

Solution

$y = 2e^x - x + 3$

$$\frac{dy}{dx} = 2e^x - 1$$

$2e^x - 1 = 0$

$2e^x = 1$

$e^x = \left(\frac{1}{2}\right)$

$\ln e^x = \ln\left(\frac{1}{2}\right)$

$x = \ln\left(\frac{1}{2}\right)$ [This is the only stationary point.]

$\frac{d^2y}{dx^2} = 2e^x$

$\left(\frac{d^2y}{dx^2}\right)_{x=\ln\left(\frac{1}{2}\right)} = 2e^{\ln\left(\frac{1}{2}\right)} = 2 \times \frac{1}{2} = 1 > 0$

Local minimum at $x = \ln\left(\frac{1}{2}\right)$: $x = \ln\frac{1}{2}$

$x = \ln\left(\frac{1}{2}\right)$: $y = 2e^{\ln\left(\frac{1}{2}\right)} - \ln\left(\frac{1}{2}\right) + 3$

$= 1 - \ln 1 + \ln 2 + 3 = 4 + \ln 2$

$\therefore$ $(-\ln 2, 4 + \ln 2)$ is a local minimum. $[\ln 1 = 0]$

EXAMPLE 14

Find the maximum value of $y = \frac{\ln x}{x}$, $x > 0\ x \in \mathbb{R}$, given the function is continuous in this domain.

Solution

$y = \frac{\ln x}{x}$

$$\frac{dy}{dx} = \frac{x\left(\frac{1}{x}\right) - \ln x(1)}{x^2} = \frac{1 - \ln x}{x^2}$$

$\frac{1 - \ln x}{x^2} = 0$

$1 - \ln x = 0$

$\ln x = 1$

$x = e^1$ [There is only one stationary point.]

$\frac{d^2y}{dx^2} = \frac{x^2\left(-\frac{1}{x}\right) - (1 - \ln x)2x}{x^4} = \frac{2\ln x - 3}{x^3}$

$\left(\frac{d^2y}{dx^2}\right)_{x=e} = \frac{2\ln e - 3}{e^3} = -\frac{1}{e^3} < 0$

since $e > 0$.

There is a local maximum at $x = e$. $x = e$

Because there is only a local maximum and no local minimum for this continuous function, no value of y can be greater than the value of y at the local maximum.

Therefore, the maximum value of the function is $y = \frac{\ln e}{e} = \frac{1}{e}$.

Warning!

The maximum/minimum value of a function does not always occur when its first derivative is zero.

It is essential to also examine the values of a continuous function at the end points of the domain for global maxima/minima. Given $y = f(x)$, $a \leq x \leq b$, $x \in \mathbb{R}$, you should examine $f(a)$ and $f(b)$ for $y = f(x)$.

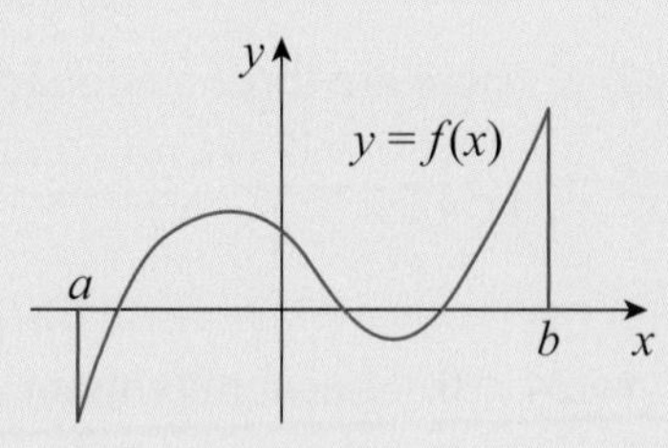

EXERCISE 10

1. Find the local maxima and local minima of the following functions for $x \in \mathbb{R}$:

   (a) $y = 6x - x^2 + 2$

   (b) $y = 12x - x^3$

   (c) $y = 3x^4 + 4x^3 - 12x^2 + 5$

   (d) $y = x + \frac{4}{x^2}, x \neq 0$

   (e) $y = x^2 + \frac{2a^3}{x}, x \neq 0$

   (f) $y = 4x - e^{2x}$

   (g) $y = x \ln x, x > 0$

   (h) $y = 2x + \frac{1}{x} - \ln x, x > 0$

   (i) $y = \frac{x}{2} - \cos x, 0 \leq x \leq 2\pi$

   (j) $y = xe^{-4x}$

2. If $E = te^{-t}$, find the maximum value of E. Why is the local maximum the same as the absolute (global) maximum?

3. Find the local maxima, minima and points of inflection of the curve $y = x^3 - 3x^2 - 9x + 3$, $-4 \leq x \leq 6, x \in \mathbb{R}$. What is the absolute maximum value and absolute (global) minimum value of y in this domain?

Steps for curve sketching

1. Find any local maxima and minima.
2. Find any points of inflection.
3. Find, if possible, where the curve crosses:
   (a) the y-axis
   (b) the x-axis
4. Plot the curve from the points obtained and any other points specified in the domain.

EXAMPLE 15

Find the local maximum and local minimum of $y = -2x^3 - 3x^2 + 12x + 10, x \in \mathbb{R}$. Find the point of inflection and sketch it roughly.

Solution

$y = -2x^3 - 3x^2 + 12x + 10$

Local maximum/minimum: $\frac{dy}{dx} = 0$

$$\boxed{\frac{dy}{dx} = -6x^2 - 6x + 12}$$

$-6x^2 - 6x + 12 = 0$

$x^2 + x - 2 = 0$

$(x - 1)(x + 2) = 0$

$x = 1, -2$

$x = 1 : y = 17$

$x = -2 : y = -10$

$\therefore$ (1, 17) and (–2, –10) are stationary points.

$$\frac{d^2y}{dx^2} = -12x - 6$$

$\left(\frac{d^2y}{dx^2}\right)_{x=1} = -18 < 0$ Local maximum at (1, 17).

$\left(\frac{d^2y}{dx^2}\right)_{-2} = +18 > 0$ Local minimum at (–2, –10).

Point of inflection: $\frac{d^2y}{dx^2} = 0$

$-12x - 6 = 0$

$12x = -6$

$x = -\frac{1}{2}$

$x = -\frac{1}{2} : y = \frac{7}{2}$

$\left(-\frac{1}{2}, \frac{7}{2}\right)$ is a point of inflection.

Cuts the y-axis: $x = 0 \Rightarrow y = 10$

Therefore, the curve crosses the y-axis at (0, 10).

This continuous curve has a local maximum and local minimum on opposite sides of the x-axis. It crosses the x-axis at three different points. This means $y = 0$ has three distinct roots.

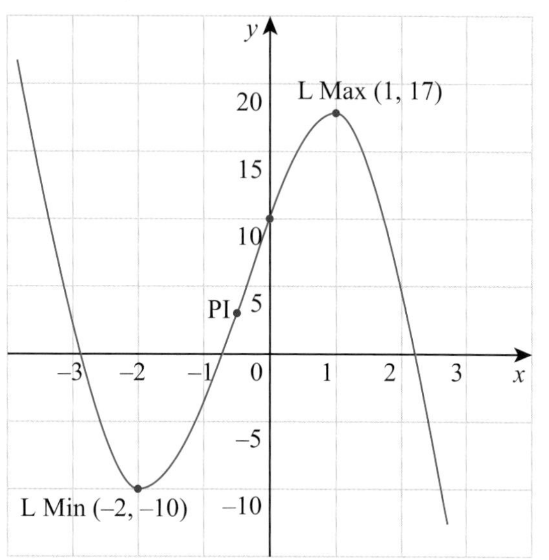

EXAMPLE 16

Find the local maxima, local minima and points of inflection, if any, of the curve $y = x^4 - 2x^2 + 2$, $x \in \mathbb{R}$, and sketch it roughly.

Solution

$y = x^4 - 2x^2 + 2$

Local maximum/minimum: $\frac{dy}{dx} = 0$

$$\boxed{\frac{dy}{dx} = 4x^3 - 4x}$$

$\frac{dy}{dx} = 0$

$4x^3 - 4x = 0$

$4x(x^2 - 1) = 0$

$4x(x - 1)(x + 1) = 0$

$x = 0, 1, -1$

$x = 0 : y = 2$

$x = 1 : y = 1 - 2 + 2 = 1$

$x = -1 : y = 1 - 2 + 2 = 1$

$\therefore$ (0, 2), (1, 1), (–1, 1) are stationary points.

$\frac{d^2y}{dx^2} = 12x^2 - 4$

$\left(\frac{d^2y}{dx^2}\right)_{x=0} = -4 < 0$ Local maximum at (0, 2).

$\left(\frac{d^2y}{dx^2}\right)_{x=1} = 8 > 0$ Local minimum at (1, 1).

$\left(\frac{d^2y}{dx^2}\right)_{x=-1} = 8 > 0$ Local minimum at (–1, 1).

Point of inflection: $\frac{d^2y}{dx^2} = 0$

$12x^2 - 4 = 0$

$12x^2 = 4$

$x^2 = \frac{1}{3}$

$x = \pm\frac{1}{\sqrt{3}}$

$x = \frac{1}{\sqrt{3}} : y = \frac{13}{9}$

$x = -\frac{1}{\sqrt{3}} : y = \frac{13}{9}$

Therefore, $\left(\frac{1}{\sqrt{3}}, \frac{13}{9}\right)$ and $\left(-\frac{1}{\sqrt{3}}, \frac{13}{9}\right)$ are the points of inflection.

Cuts the y-axis: $x = 0 \Rightarrow y = 2$

The curve crosses the y-axis at (0, 2).

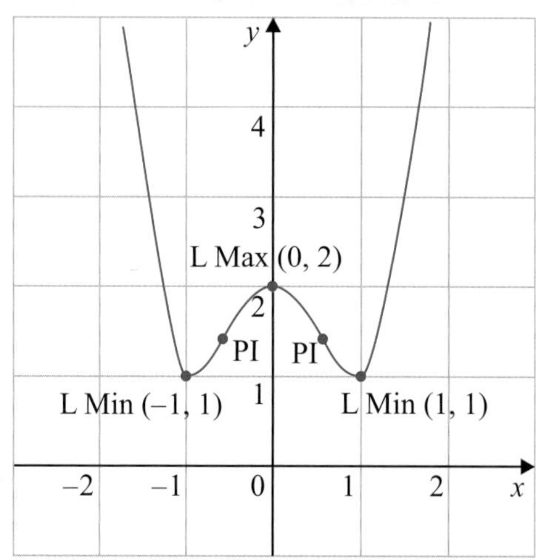

Properties of curves

1. Quadratic curves

The general quadratic curve has the equation $y = ax^2 + bx + c$.

$\therefore \frac{dy}{dx} = 2ax + b$ and $\frac{d^2y}{dx^2} = 2a$.

(a) $\frac{d^2y}{dx^2} = 2a =$ constant means that **all** quadratic curves are either concave up (cup-shaped) or concave down (cap-shaped).

If $a > 0$, the quadratic is concave up (cup).

If $a < 0$, the quadratic is concave down (cap).

(b) $\frac{dy}{dx} = 2ax + b$

$\frac{dy}{dx} = 0 \Rightarrow x = -\frac{b}{2a}$

There is **always one** and **only one** stationary point for a quadratic curve.

It is always at $x = -\frac{b}{2a}$.

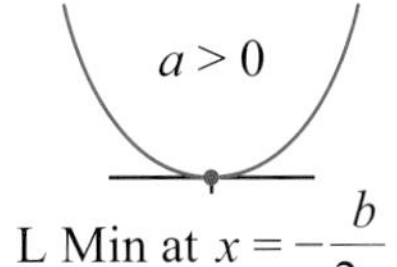

L Max at $x = -\frac{b}{2a}$

$a < 0$

▸ $y = 2x^2 - 5x + 3 \quad [a = 2 > 0, b = -5, c = 3]$

Therefore, the curve has a local minimum at $x = -\frac{(-5)}{4} = \frac{5}{4}$

2. Cubic curves

The general cubic curve has the equation $y = ax^3 + bx^2 + cx + d$.

$\therefore \frac{dy}{dx} = 3ax^2 + 2bx + c$ and $\frac{d^2y}{dx^2} = 6ax + 2b$.

(a) $\frac{d^2y}{dx^2} = 6ax + 2b$

$\frac{d^2y}{dx^2} = 0 \Rightarrow x = -\frac{b}{3a}$

This means that **every cubic curve** has **one** and **only one** point of inflection at $x = -\frac{b}{3a}$.

(b) $\frac{dy}{dx} = 3ax^2 + 2bx + c$ is a quadratic equation.

$\therefore \frac{dy}{dx} = 0$ will have either of the following possibilities:

(i) No solutions or two equal solutions: This means no local maximum and no local minimum, just a point of inflection.

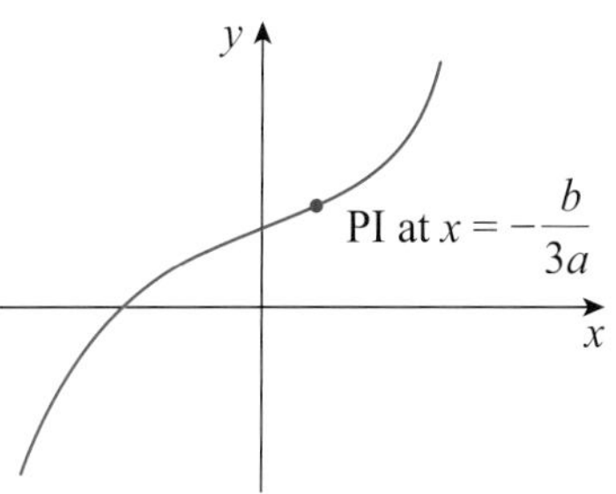

(ii) Two different solutions: This means a local maximum **and** a local minimum.

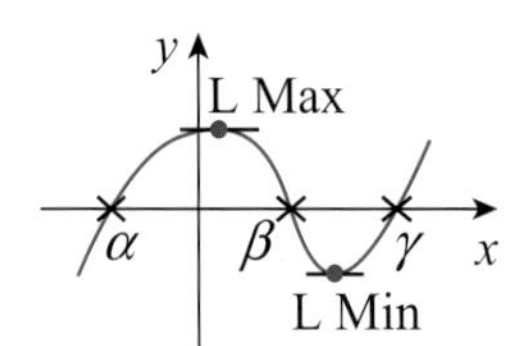	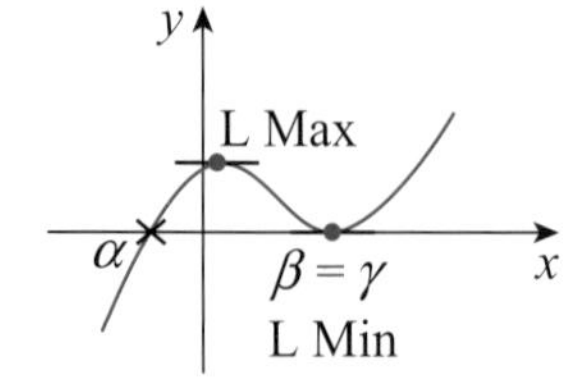	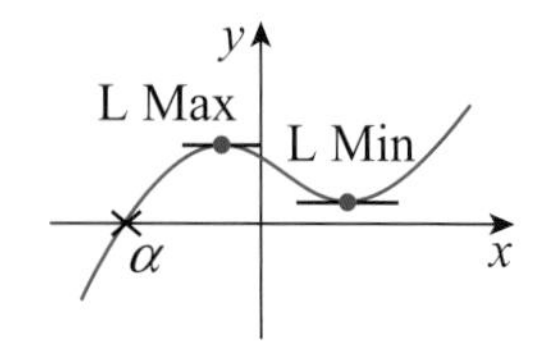
If the local maximum and local minimum are on opposite sides of the x-axis, the curve crosses the x-axis at three different points. Therefore, $y = 0$ has three distinct real roots (α, β and γ).	If either the local maximum or local minimum is on the x-axis, then $y = 0$ has three real roots but two of them are equal ($\alpha, \beta = \gamma$). The double root is at the local maximum or local minimum.	If the local maximum and local minimum are on the same side of the x-axis, the curve crosses the x-axis at one point only. Therefore, $y = 0$ has only one real root (α).

EXAMPLE 17

Find the local maximum, local minimum and point of inflection of the cubic function $y = 2x^3 + 12x^2 + 18x - 3, x \in \mathbb{R}$. Show that $2x^3 + 12x^2 + 18x - 3 = 0$ has only one real root.

Solution

$y = 2x^3 + 12x^2 + 18x - 3$

Local maximum/minimum: $\frac{dy}{dx} = 0$

$\frac{dy}{dx} = 6x^2 + 24x + 18$

$6x^2 + 24x + 18 = 0$

$x^2 + 4x + 3 = 0$

$(x + 3)(x + 1) = 0$

$x = -3, x = -1$

$x = -3 : y = -3$

$x = -1 : y = -11$

$\therefore$ $(-3, -3)$ and $(-1, -11)$ are the stationary points.

$$\frac{d^2y}{dx^2} = 12x + 24$$

$$\left(\frac{d^2y}{dx^2}\right)_{x=-3} = -36 + 24 < 0$$

Local maximum at $(-3, -3)$.

$$\left(\frac{d^2y}{dx^2}\right)_{x=-1} = -12 + 24 > 0$$

Local minimum at $(-1, -11)$.

Point of inflection: $\frac{d^2y}{dx^2} = 0$

$12x + 24 = 0$

$x = -2$

$x = -2: y = -7$

$(-2, -7)$ is a point of inflection.

Since the local maximum $(-3, -3)$ and local minimum $(-1, -11)$ are both below the x-axis, the curve can only cross the x-axis at one point. There is only one real root of $2x^3 + 12x^2 + 18x - 3 = 0$.

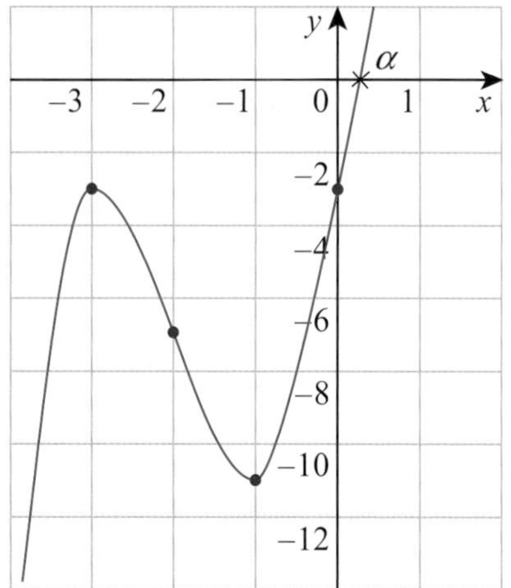

The only root is α.

ACTIVITY 16

ACTION
Sketching exponential curves

OBJECTIVE
To sketch the graphs of exponential functions

3. Exponential curves

Consider exponential curves of the form $y = ka^{bx}$, $k > 0$, $a > 1$, $x \in \mathbb{R}$.

1. The sign: $a^{bx} > 0$ for all $x \in \mathbb{R} \Rightarrow y = ka^{bx} > 0$ for all $x \in \mathbb{R}$, $k > 0$.
Therefore, the graph of $y = ka^{bx}$, $k > 0$, $a > 1$ is always above the x-axis.

2. The first derivative: $y = ka^{bx} \Rightarrow \frac{dy}{dx} = bka^{bx} \ln a$

(a) For $b > 0$: $\frac{dy}{dx} > 0$ [The curve is increasing.]

(b) For $b < 0$: $\frac{dy}{dx} < 0$ [The curve is decreasing.]

(c) $\frac{dy}{dx} = 0$ has no solutions.

> $y = ka^{bx}$, $k > 0$, $a > 1$ has no stationary points and hence no local maxima or minima.

3. The second derivative: $\frac{d^2y}{dx^2} = b^2k(\ln a)^2 a^{bx}$

(a) $\frac{d^2y}{dx^2} = 0$ has no solutions. Therefore, there are no points of inflection.

(b) $\frac{d^2y}{dx^2} = b^2k(\ln a)^2 a^{bx} > 0$ for all $x \in \mathbb{R}$, $k > 0$.

The curve is concave up everywhere.

4. Crossing the axes:

(a) x-axis: $y = 0 \Rightarrow ka^{bx} = 0$ has no solutions. The curve never crosses the x-axis.

(b) y-axis: $x = 0 \Rightarrow y = ka^0 = k$. The curve crosses the y-axis at $(0, k)$.

5. To plot the curve $y = ka^{bx}$, draw up a table of values.

EXAMPLE 18

Show that $y = 3 \times 2^x$ has no local maxima, local minima or points of inflection. Find where it crosses the y-axis and plot it for $-2 \le x \le 3$, $x \in \mathbb{R}$.

Solution

$y = 3 \times 2^x$

$$\frac{dy}{dx} = 3 \times 2^x \ln 2$$

$\frac{dy}{dx} = 0 \Rightarrow 2^x = 0$

There are no solutions. Therefore, there are no local maxima or minima.

$\frac{d^2y}{dx^2} = 3 \ln 2 \times 2^x \ln 2 = 3(\ln 2)^2\, 2^x$

$\frac{d^2y}{dx^2} = 0 \Rightarrow 2^x = 0$

There are no solutions. Therefore, there are no points of inflection.

$\frac{dy}{dx} = 3 \times 2^x \ln 2 > 0$ for all $x \in \mathbb{R}$. Therefore, the curve is increasing for all $x \in \mathbb{R}$.

$\frac{d^2y}{dx^2} = 3(\ln 2)^2\, 2^x > 0$ for all $x \in \mathbb{R}$. Therefore, the curve is concave up for all $x \in \mathbb{R}$.

Crosses the y-axis: $x = 0 : y = 3 \times 2^0 = 3$

y intercept: $(0, 3)$

Draw up a table of values:

x	−2	−1	0	1	2	3
3×2^x	$\frac{3}{4}$	$\frac{3}{2}$	3	6	12	24

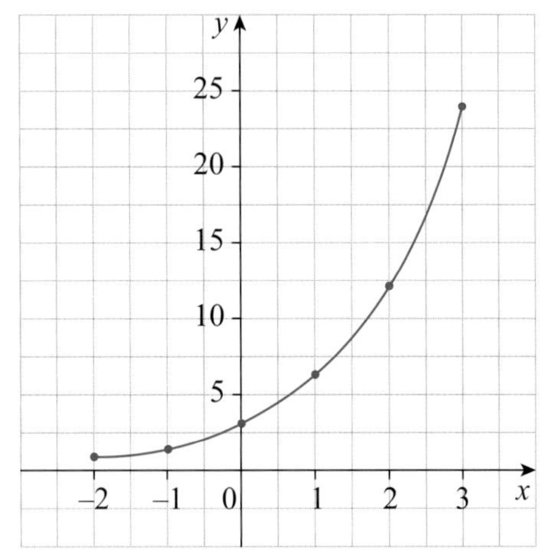

EXAMPLE 19

Show that $y = 2\left(\frac{1}{e^x}\right)$ is decreasing for all $x \in \mathbb{R}$ and has no points of inflection. Sketch the curve for $-2 \le x \le 2, x \in \mathbb{R}$.

Solution

$y = 2\left(\frac{1}{e^x}\right) = 2e^{-x}$

$$\frac{dy}{dx} = 2e^{-x}(-1) = -\frac{2}{e^x}$$

$\frac{dy}{dx} < 0$ for all $x \in \mathbb{R}$. The curve is decreasing for all $x \in \mathbb{R}$.

$\frac{d^2y}{dx^2} = 2e^{-x} = \frac{2}{e^x}$

$\frac{d^2y}{dx^2} > 0$ for all $x \in \mathbb{R}$. The curve has no points of inflection. It is concave up for all $x \in \mathbb{R}$.

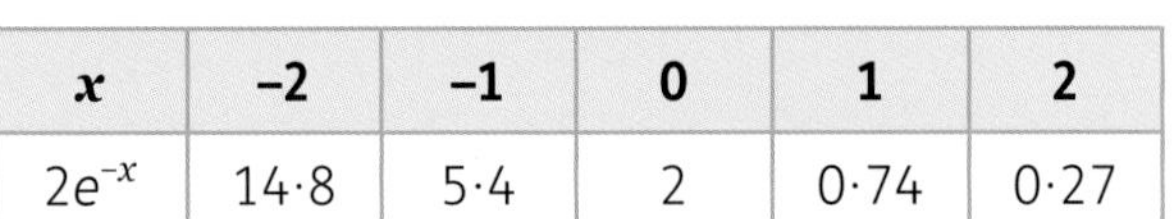

x	−2	−1	0	1	2
$2e^{-x}$	14·8	5·4	2	0·74	0·27

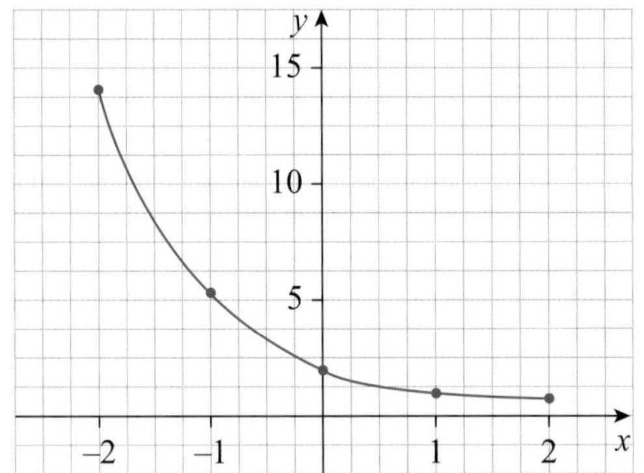

4. Logarithmic curves

Consider functions of the form $y = k \log_a x, a > 1, x > 0, x \in \mathbb{R}$.

$$k \log_a x = k\left(\frac{\log_e x}{\log_e a}\right) = \left(\frac{k}{\log_e a}\right) \ln x$$

1. x must must be positive for $\log_a x$ to be defined. This means the graph of $y = k \log_a x$ is always to the right of the y-axis.
2. The first derivative: $\frac{dy}{dx} = \frac{k}{\log_e a} \times \frac{1}{x}$
   - **(i)** For $k > 0, \frac{dy}{dx} > 0.$ [The curve is increasing.]
   - **(ii)** For $k < 0, \frac{dy}{dx} < 0.$ [The curve is decreasing.]

(iii) $\frac{dy}{dx} = 0$ has no solutions.

$y = k \log_a x, a > 1, x > 0, x \in \mathbb{R}$ has no stationary points and hence has no local maxima or local minima.

ACTIVITY 17

ACTION
Sketching log curves

OBJECTIVE
To sketch the graphs of log functions

3. The second derivative: $\frac{d^2y}{dx^2} = -\frac{k}{\log_e a} \times \frac{1}{x^2}$

(i) For $k > 0$: $\frac{d^2y}{dx^2} < 0$ The curve is concave down (cap).

(ii) For $k < 0$: $\frac{d^2y}{dx^2} > 0$ The curve is concave up (cup).

I Cap

D Cup

(iii) $\frac{d^2y}{dx^2} = 0$ has no solutions. There are no points of inflection.

4. Crossing the axes:

(i) x-axis: $y = 0$

$k \log_a x = 0$

$\log_a x = 0$

$\therefore x = a^0 = 1$. The curve crosses the x-axis at (1, 0).

(ii) y-axis: Since $x > 0$, it never crosses the y-axis.

EXAMPLE 20

Show that $y = 3 \log_2 x$ has no local maxima or minima and no points of inflection. Plot it for $\frac{1}{4} \leq x \leq 8$, $x \in \mathbb{R}$.

Solution

$y = 3 \log_2 x = \frac{3 \log_e x}{\log_e 2} = \frac{3}{\ln 2} \ln x$

$\frac{dy}{dx} = \frac{3}{\ln 2}\left(\frac{1}{x}\right) = 0$ has no solutions.

There are no local maxima or minima.

$\frac{dy}{dx} = \frac{3}{x \ln 2} > 0$ for all $x > 0, x \in \mathbb{R}$.

The curve is increasing for all $x > 0, x \in \mathbb{R}$.

$\frac{d^2y}{dx^2} = -\frac{3}{x^2 \ln 2} = 0$ has no solutions.

Therefore, there are no points of inflection.

$\frac{d^2y}{dx^2} = -\frac{3}{x^2 \ln 2} < 0$ for all $x > 0, x \in \mathbb{R}$.

The curve is concave down for all $x > 0, x \in \mathbb{R}$.

	$\frac{1}{4}$	$\frac{1}{2}$	1	2	4	8
$3 \log_2 x$	-6	-3	0	3	6	9

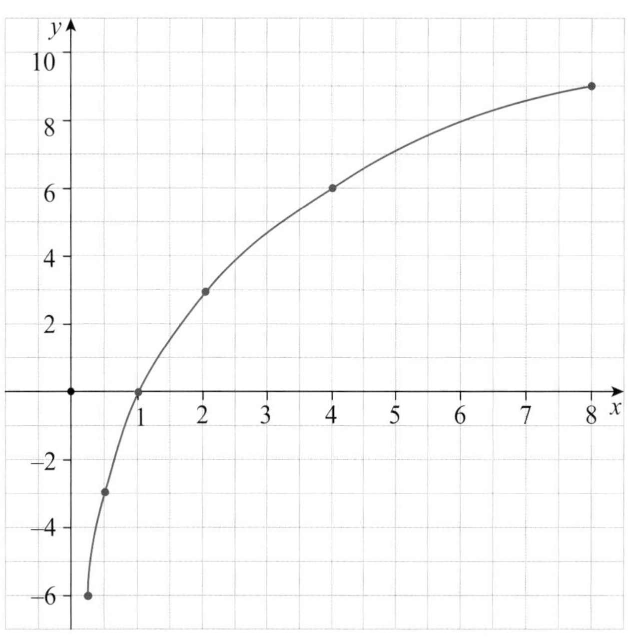

EXERCISE 11

1. Find where the following curves cross the x-axis and y-axis:
   - **(a)** $y = x^2 - 1$
   - **(b)** $y = x^2 - 5x + 6$
   - **(c)** $y = 6x^2 + x - 2$
   - **(d)** $y = x^3 - 3x^2$
   - **(e)** $y = x^3 - 4x$
   - **(f)** $x^2 + y^2 = 25$
   - **(g)** $\frac{x^2}{16} + \frac{y^2}{9} = 1$
   - **(h)** $y = e^x - 1$
   - **(i)** $y = \ln(x + 1) - 1$
   - **(j)** $y = \sin 3x, 0 \leq x \leq 2\pi$

2. For each curve below, defined for $x \in \mathbb{R}$, find the following and sketch the graph roughly:
   - **(i)** the local maximum and local minimum, if any,
   - **(ii)** the points of inflection, if any,
   - **(iii)** the points where it crosses both axes for parts **(a)** and **(b)** and the points where it crosses the y-axis for parts **(c)**, **(d)** and **(e)**.

   - **(a)** $y = x^2 + 2x - 8$
   - **(b)** $y = -2x^2 + x + 3$
   - **(c)** $y = x^3 - 3x^2 - 9x + 10$
   - **(d)** $y = -2x^3 + 3x^2 + 12x - 4$
   - **(e)** $y = \frac{x^4}{4} - \frac{2x^3}{3} - 4x^2 + \frac{32}{3}$

3. **(a)** For the function $y = x^3 + 5x^2 + 3x - 9$, $x \in \mathbb{R}$,
   - **(i)** find the local maximum, local minimum and point of inflection,
   - **(ii)** state why it has three real roots, two of which are the same,
   - **(iii)** solve $x^3 + 5x^2 + 3x - 9 = 0$.

   (b) Find the local maximum and local minimum of the curve $y = 2x^3 - 9x^2 + 12x + 20, x \in \mathbb{R}$. Without sketching it, show that it has only one real root.

4. The monthly profit P of a company in thousands of euros is given by $P = \frac{5}{2}t^3 - 15t^2 + \frac{45}{2}t$, where t is the time in months, $0 \leq t \leq 4$.

   (a) For this function, find the co-ordinates of:
   - **(i)** the local maximum,
   - **(ii)** the local minimum,
   - **(iii)** the point of inflection,
   - **(iv)** the points where the graph of P against t intersects the axes.

   (b) Sketch the graph roughly of P against t. Use your graph to find:
   - **(i)** when the profit was a maximum,
   - **(ii)** the maximum profit,
   - **(iii)** the minimum profit,
   - **(iv)** the time periods for which the profit increased,
   - **(v)** the time period for which the profit decreased.

5. Show that $y = f(x) = e^x, x \in \mathbb{R}$, has no local maxima or minima and no points of inflection. Show that it does not cross the x-axis. Find where it crosses the y-axis. Show the curve is always increasing. Sketch the curve roughly using the table below, using the same scale on both axes:

x	−1	0	1	2
y				

   Find $f^{-1}(x)$ and draw it on the same grid.

6. Show that $y = f(x) = \ln x, x > 0, x \in \mathbb{R}$, has no local maxima or local minima and has no points of inflection. Show it is increasing for all $x \in \mathbb{R}$, $x > 0$. Show it crosses the x-axis but not the y-axis. Sketch the curve roughly using the table below, using the same scale on both axes:

x	$\frac{1}{2}$	1	2	3	4	5
y						

   On the same diagram, draw the graph of $f^{-1}(x)$.

7. Show that $y = 2^x, x \in \mathbb{R}$, and $y = 2^{-x} = \left(\frac{1}{2}\right)^x$, $x \in \mathbb{R}$, have no local maxima or minima or points of inflection. Show that $y = 2^x$ is increasing but $y = 2^{-x}$ is decreasing for all $x \in \mathbb{R}$. Find where the curves cross the axes. Sketch both curves roughly on the same grid using the table below and the same scale on both axes:

x	−2	−1	0	1	2	3
$y = 2^x$						
$y = 2^{-x}$						

24.2 Rate of change applications

We have already learned that $\frac{dy}{dx}$ represents the (instantaneous) rate of change of y with respect to x.

However, when the independent variable is time t, the (instantaneous) rate of change of a quantity with respect to **time** (t) is simply called the **rate of change** of the quantity. There are many quantities in the real world that vary with time.

Examples: populations, share prices, salaries, speed.

WORKED EXAMPLE Rate of change

- A water tank is leaking water at a rate of 20 cm^3 per second at a particular instant. This means at that instant the volume V of water in the tank is decreasing by 20 cm^3 every second at that instant. Mathematically, this is expressed as $\frac{dV}{dt} = -20\ cm^3/s$. This equation states that if the time changes (increases) by 1 second, the volume V changes by –20 cm^3 or decreases by 20 cm^3.
- If V is volume in cm^3 and t is time in seconds, $\frac{dV}{dt}$ = the rate of change of volume. The unit of $\frac{dV}{dt}$ is cm^3/s.
- $\frac{d\theta}{dt} = +5\ °C/h$, where θ is temperature in °C and t is in hours, means the temperature is increasing at 5 °C per hour.
- $\frac{dA}{dt} = -10\ m^2/\text{minute}$, where A is area in m^2, means the area is decreasing at 10 m^2 every minute.

If the rate of change is greater than 0, the quantity is increasing with time.

If the rate of change is less than 0, the quantity is decreasing with time.

If the rate of change is equal to 0, the quantity has reached its maximum or minimum value.

ACTIVITY 18

ACTION
Exploring rates of change

OBJECTIVE
To understand some simple ideas about rate of change

EXAMPLE 21

The height of a flower h in centimetres after growing for t days is given by $h = 120(1 - e^{-0{\cdot}05t})$.

Find the rate of change of the height:

(a) after 5 days **(b)** after 100 days

Solution

$h = 120(1 - e^{-0{\cdot}05t})$

$\frac{dh}{dt} = 120(0{\cdot}05e^{-0{\cdot}05t}) = 6e^{-0{\cdot}05t}$

The height is always increasing as $\frac{dh}{dt} > 0$ for all values of t.

(a) $\left(\frac{dh}{dt}\right)_{t=5} = 6e^{-0{\cdot}25} = 4{\cdot}67$ cm/day **(b)** $\left(\frac{dh}{dt}\right)_{t=100} = 6e^{-5} = 0{\cdot}04$ cm/day

TIP
Remember $e^{f(x)} > 0$ for all $f(x)$.

Distance/speed/acceleration

For motion in a straight line, if s is the distance relative to the origin at time t of a body, then for this body:

$$\text{Velocity } v = \frac{ds}{dt} \text{ and Acceleration } a = \frac{dv}{dt}.$$

Units

Distance s: m, cm, km [s can also be height, position, displacement or depth.]

Time t: seconds, minutes, hours

Velocity v: m/s, km/h, cm/s

Acceleration a: m/s^2, km/h^2, cm/s^2

EXAMPLE 22

The distance s (m) of a body travelling in a straight line from the origin is given by $s = t^3 - 6t^2 + 9t$ after time t (seconds).

Find:

(a) its distance from the origin at $t = 0$,

(b) its initial velocity,

(c) when the body is at rest,

(d) its position after 4 s,

(e) its initial acceleration,

(f) when its acceleration is 0.

Solution

Start by finding v and a from s.

$s = t^3 - 6t^2 + 9t$

$v = \frac{ds}{dt} = 3t^2 - 12t + 9$

$a = \frac{dv}{dt} = 6t - 12$

(a) $t = 0$: $s = 0 - 0 + 0 = 0$

$s = 0$ m

(b) Initial means $t = 0$.

What is v when $t = 0$?

$v = 3t^2 - 12t + 9$

$t = 0$: $v = 9$ m/s

(c) What is t when $v = 0$?

$v = 3t^2 - 12t + 9 = 0$

$t^2 - 4t + 3 = 0$

$(t - 3)(t - 1) = 0$

$t = 1$ s, 3 s

(d) What is s when $t = 4$?

$s = t^3 - 6t^2 + 9t$

$t = 4$: $s = 4^3 - 6 \times 4^2 + 9 \times 4 = 4$ m

(e) What is a when $t = 0$?

$a = 6t - 12$

$t = 0$: $a = -12 \text{ m/s}^2$

(f) What is t when $a = 0$?

$a = 6t - 12 = 0$

$t = 2$ s

Interpretation of signs for s, v, a, t

1. s (+): The body is to the right of the origin.
   s (−): The body is to the left of the origin.
2. v (+): The body is moving to the right.
   v (−): The body is moving to the left.
3. a (+): The body is accelerating.
   a (−): The body is decelerating.
4. t: $t \geq 0$ always (no negative times).
   $t = 0$ is the initial time.

EXAMPLE 23

The distance s in metres of a body relative to the origin O after t seconds is given by $s = 1{\cdot}5t^2 - 48t$.

(a) Find where the body is relative to the origin at:

(i) $t = 0$

(ii) $t = 10$

(iii) $t = 40$

(b) Find the velocity of the body at:

(i) $t = 0$

(ii) $t = 10$

(iii) $t = 40$

(c) Find the acceleration of the body.

Solution

$s = 1{\cdot}5t^2 - 48t$

$v = \dfrac{ds}{dt} = 3t - 48$

$a = \dfrac{dv}{dt} = 3$

(a) $s = 1{\cdot}5t^2 - 48t$

(i) $t = 0 : s = 0$ [It is at the origin.]

(ii) $t = 10 : s = 1{\cdot}5(100) - 48(10) = -330$ [It is 330 m to the left of the origin.]

(iii) $t = 40 : s = 1{\cdot}5(40)^2 - 48(40) = 480$ [It is 480 m to the right of the origin.]

(b) $v = 3t - 48$

(i) $t = 0 : v = -48$ [It is moving to the left at 48 m/s.]

(ii) $t = 10 : v = 30 - 48 = -18$ [It is moving at 18 m/s to the left.]

(iii) $t = 40 : v = 120 - 48 = 72$ [It is moving at 72 m/s to the right.]

(c) $a = 3$ [It is accelerating at 3 m/s^2.]

EXERCISE 12

1. The surface area in m^2 covered by algae in a lake is given by $A = -\frac{1}{3}t^3 + 15t^2, 0 \le t \le 45$ after t days. Find the rate of change of the area when:

(a) $t = 5$ **(b)** $t = 30$ **(c)** $t = 40$

Make a conclusion from each answer.

2. The number P of bacteria in a Petri dish is given by $P = 700(1{\cdot}2)^t$, where t is the time in hours after the experiment has started.

Find:

(a) the number of bacteria in the dish at $t = 0$,

(b) the rate of change of the number of bacteria at time t,

(c) the rate of change of the number of bacteria, correct to the nearest whole number, when:

(i) $t = 0$ **(ii)** $t = 5$

3. The position s (cm) of the piston of a machine in each cycle is given by $s = t\sqrt{8 - 2t}, 0 \le t \le 4$, where t is in seconds. Find:

(a) its velocity at $t = 0$,

(b) its velocity at $t = 2$,

(c) the maximum value of s.

4. A rocket is moving under gravity.
Its velocity v after t seconds is given by
$v = 1500 - 9{\cdot}8t - \ln\left(1 - \frac{3t}{900}\right), 0 \le t < 300.$
Find its acceleration after 290 seconds.

5. A ball is thrown vertically upwards. After t seconds its height h in metres is given by $h = 12 + 14t - 4{\cdot}9t^2$. Find:

 (a) the height when $t = 2$,

 (b) the velocity when $t = 1$,

 (c) the acceleration at $t = 2$.

6. If the velocity time formula for a moving body is given by $v = 4t^2 - 4t - 3$, where v is in metres per second (m/s) and t is in seconds (s), find:

 (a) the acceleration when the velocity is 5 m/s,

 (b) the velocity when the acceleration is 0.

Related rates of change

Given the rate of change of a variable r, the rate of change of a variable A, that is related to r, can be found using the chain rule: $\frac{dA}{dt} = \frac{dA}{dr} \times \frac{dr}{dt}$.

EXAMPLE 24

If $\frac{dx}{dt} = 3$ find $\frac{dV}{dt}$ if $V = x^3$.

Solution

$$\frac{dV}{dt} = \frac{dV}{dx} \times \frac{dx}{dt}$$

$$\frac{dV}{dt} = (3x^2)(3) = 9x^2$$

Steps for finding related rates

1. Write down the rate of change given.
2. Write down the rate of change to be found.
3. Write down a formula (which may be given) connecting the non-time variables.
4. Write down the chain rule for the two variables and time t.
5. Fill in the numbers after the differentiation has been done.

EXAMPLE 25

A balloon contains a given mass of gas with volume V (m^3) at pressure P (Pa) where $P = \frac{10}{V}$. If the volume increases at 5×10^{-5} m^3 per second, find the rate of change of the pressure when $V = 4 \times 10^{-5}$ m^3.

Solution

1. $\frac{dV}{dt} = 5 \times 10^{-5}$
2. $\frac{dP}{dt} = ?$
3. $P = \frac{10}{V} \Rightarrow \frac{dP}{dV} = -\frac{10}{V^2}$
4. $\frac{dP}{dt} = \frac{dP}{dV} \times \frac{dV}{dt} = -\frac{10}{V^2} \times 5 \times 10^{-5}$
5. $V = 4 \times 10^{-5}$: $\frac{dP}{dt} = -\frac{10}{(4 \times 10^{-5})^2} \times 5 \times 10^{-5}$

 $= -312\,500$ Pa/s

EXAMPLE 26

The perimeter of the sector OAB of a circle, centre O and radius r, is 15 cm.

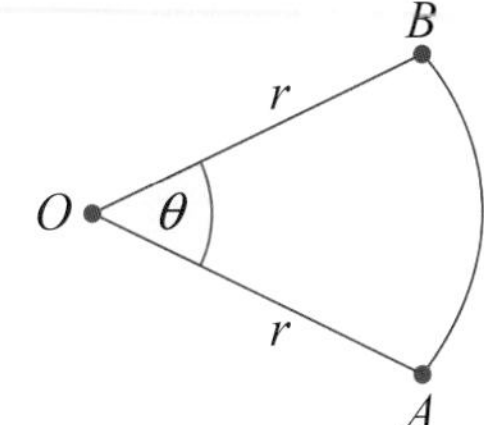

(a) Show that:

(i) $\theta = \frac{15 - 2r}{r}$

(ii) area of $OAB = \frac{15r}{2} - r^2$

(b) If the area of OAB increases at 40 cm^2/s, find the rate of change of the radius when $r = 20$ cm.

Solution

(a) (i) $15 = 2r + r\theta$

$r\theta = 15 - 2r$

$\theta = \frac{(15 - 2r)}{r}$

(ii) $A = \frac{1}{2}r^2\theta$

$= \frac{1}{2}r^2\frac{(15 - 2r)}{r} = \frac{r}{2}(15 - 2r)$

$A = \frac{15r}{2} - r^2$

(b) 1. $\frac{dA}{dt} = +40$

2. $\frac{dr}{dt} = ?$

3. $A = \frac{15r}{2} - r^2 \Rightarrow \frac{dA}{dr} = \left(\frac{15}{2} - 2r\right)$

4. $\frac{dr}{dt} = \frac{dr}{dA} \times \frac{dA}{dt}$

$\frac{dr}{dt} = \frac{1}{\left(\frac{15}{2} - 2r\right)} \times 40$ $\left[\textbf{Note: } \frac{dr}{dA} = \frac{1}{\left(\frac{dA}{dr}\right)}\right]$

5. $r = 20$: $\frac{dr}{dt} = \frac{1}{(7{\cdot}5 - 40)} \times 40$

$= -\frac{80}{65}$

$= -\frac{16}{13}$ cm/s

EXERCISE 13

1. A monkey throws a banana along a path with the equation $y = x^2 - \frac{3}{x}$. If the x co-ordinate is increasing at 2 cm/s, find the rate of change of the y co-ordinate when $x = 7$ cm, correct to one decimal place.

2. The side x (cm) of a square is increasing at 2 cm/s. At what rate is its area increasing when $x = 10$ cm.

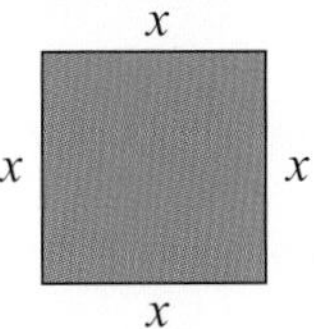

3. Rubbish is being compacted into a cubical volume. Each side x (m) is decreasing at a rate of 0·12 m/s. How fast is the volume changing when $x = 1$ m?

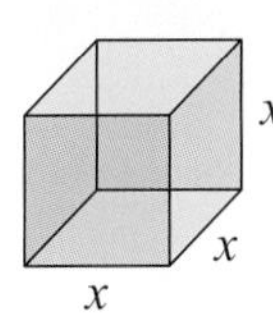
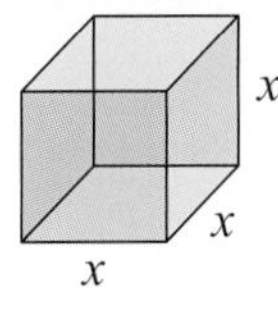

4. A spherical balloon is being inflated at 8 m^3/h.

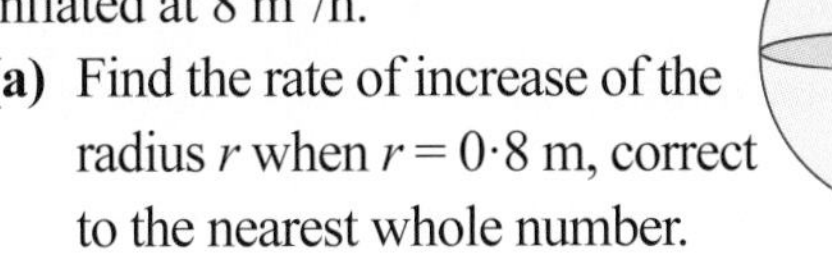

(a) Find the rate of increase of the radius r when $r = 0{\cdot}8$ m, correct to the nearest whole number.

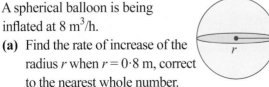

When the radius is 1 m, the inflation is stopped and the air begins to leak out at 2 m^3/h.

(b) Find the rate of decrease of the radius r when $r = 0{\cdot}4$ m, correct to the nearest whole number.

5. Sand is falling on to the ground from a floor above to form a conical pile, as shown.

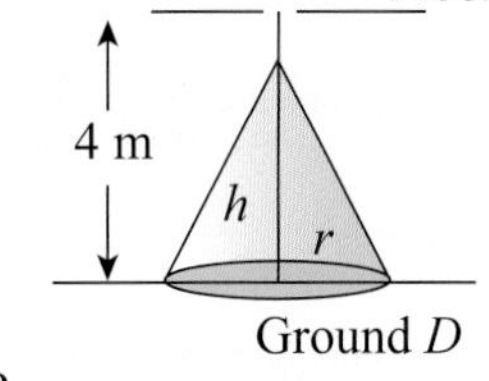

(a) If the height h of the cone is equal to its diameter, show that the volume V of the sand is given by $V = \frac{\pi h^3}{12}$.

(b) If the sand is falling at 600π cm^3/s, find the rate at which the height is increasing when the pile reaches the floor.

(c) How long, in hours, does it take for the sand to reach the floor, correct to two decimal places?

6. The volume V(m^3) of water in a hemispherical pond is given by $V = \frac{\pi h^2}{3}(3 - h)$, where h is the depth in metres.

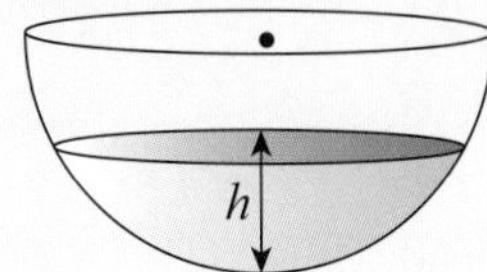

(a) Find $\frac{dV}{dh}$.

(b) If water is poured into the pond at a rate of $0{\cdot}025$ m^3 per minute, find $\frac{dh}{dt}$ when $h = 0{\cdot}5$ m. Give your answer in terms of π.

7. When an object is u cm from a lens of focal length 10 cm, its image is v cm from the lens where $\frac{1}{u} + \frac{1}{v} = \frac{1}{10}$.

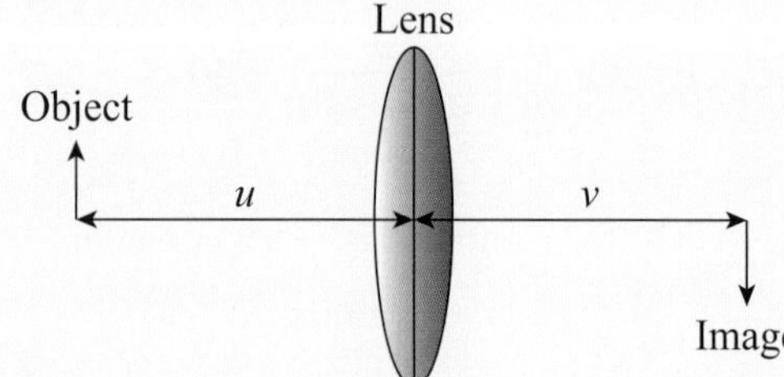

(a) Show that $v = \frac{10u}{u - 10}$.

(b) Find $\frac{dv}{du}$.

(c) If the object is approaching the lens at 5 cm/s, find the rate of change of the distance of the image from the lens when $u = 25$ cm.

8. Water is poured into a conical vessel of semi-vertical angle 45°. After t seconds, the height of the water is h cm and the radius of its surface is r cm.

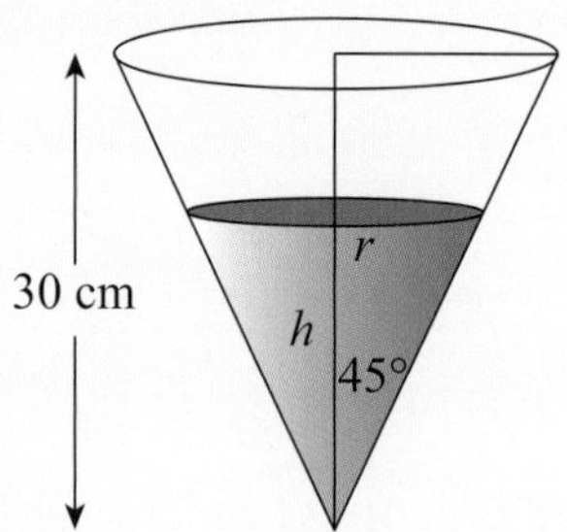

(a) Show that the volume V of water after t seconds is $V = \frac{1}{3}\pi h^3$.

(b) Find $\frac{dV}{dh}$.

(c) If the volume is increasing at 10π cm^3/s, find the rate of change of the height when $h = 4$ cm.

(d) How long does it take to fill the vessel?

24.3 Modelling and optimisation

ACTIVITY 19

ACTION
Exploring modelling and optimisation

OBJECTIVE
To consider some basic ideas about modelling and optimisation

KEY TERMS

Modelling is the process of describing a problem (realistic or otherwise) in mathematical terms. This means writing a quantity in terms of a single variable.

Optimisation is the process of finding the maximum or minimum value of a function.

EXAMPLE 27

The area of rectangle $ABCD$ is 81 m^2.

(a) Express the perimeter P in terms of x.

(b) Find the minimum value of the perimeter.

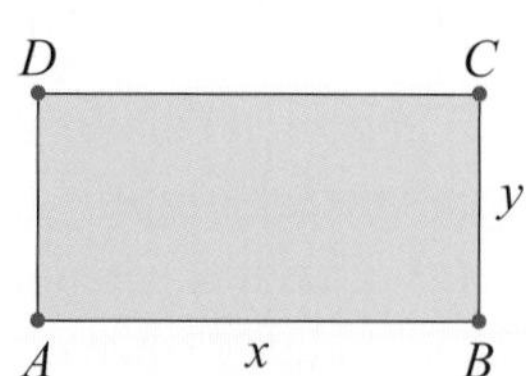

Solution

Modelling entails writing the perimeter P in terms of a single variable.

(a) Area $= xy = 81 \Rightarrow y = \dfrac{81}{x}$

$$P = 2x + 2y = 2x + \frac{162}{x}$$

Optimisation is the process of finding the maximum or minimum value of this function.

(b) $P = 2x + \dfrac{162}{x}$

$$\frac{dP}{dx} = 2 - \frac{162}{x^2}$$

$$\frac{dP}{dx} = 0 \Rightarrow 2x^2 = 162$$

$$x^2 = 81$$

$$x = \pm 9 \quad [-9 \text{ is not allowed.}]$$

$$\therefore x = 9$$

$$\frac{d^2P}{dx^2} = \frac{324}{x^3} \Rightarrow \left(\frac{d^2P}{dx^2}\right)_{x=9} = \frac{324}{9^3} > 0$$

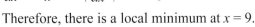

Therefore, there is a local minimum at $x = 9$.

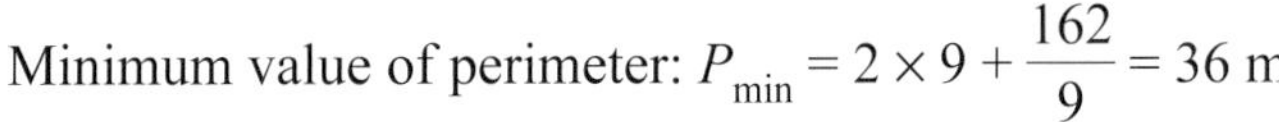

Minimum value of perimeter: $P_{\text{min}} = 2 \times 9 + \dfrac{162}{9} = 36$ m

Steps for modelling and optimising

1. Identify the quantity to be optimised and give it a suitable symbol. For example, A for area.
2. Draw a diagram, if necessary, and put in the variable(s).
3. Write the quantity in terms of the variable(s).
4. If there are two variables, eliminate one of these in terms of the other using some extra information.
5. Hence, write the quantity in terms of a single variable.
6. Differentiate the quantity with respect to the variable. Let it equal 0 and solve.
7. Put the value of the variable back into the quantity to find the optimum value.

You do not have to do the second derivative in most cases as it is obvious from the context whether it is a maximum or a minimum.

Types of optimisation problems

(a) Geometry
(b) Economics
(c) Algebraic
(d) Curves
(e) Motion
(f) Inscribers

(a) Geometry

EXAMPLE 28

A rectangular sheet of metal 80 cm × 50 cm is used to form an open box (no lid) by removing squares of side x cm from each corner, as shown, and folding up the flaps along the dotted lines.

Show that the volume is given by $V = 4x^3 - 260x^2 + 4000x$. Find the maximum volume of the box.

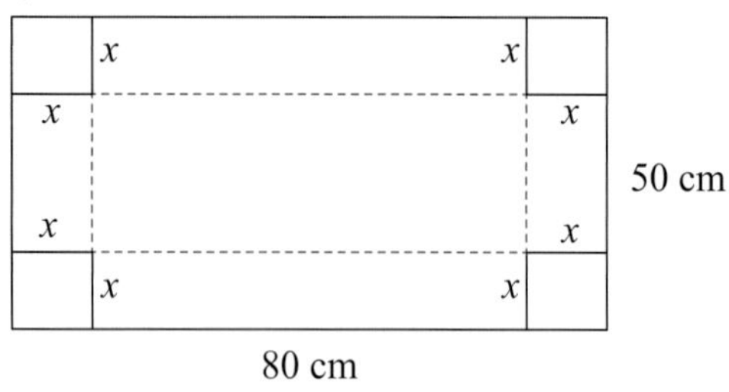

Solution

1. V (volume)

2. Diagram:

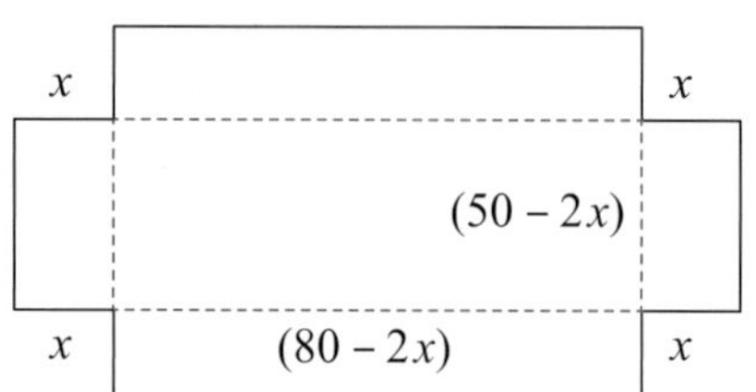

3–5. $V = (80 - 2x)(50 - 2x)x = (4000 - 260x + 4x^2)x$

$V = 4x^3 - 260x^2 + 4000x$

6. $\dfrac{dV}{dx} = 12x^2 - 520x + 4000$

$12x^2 - 520x + 4000 = 0$

$3x^2 - 130x + 1000 = 0$

$(3x - 100)(x - 10) = 0$

$x = \dfrac{100}{3}, 10$ [There are two stationary points.]

Reject $\dfrac{100}{3}$ as it gives $(50 - 2x) < 0$.

7. V_{max} occurs at $x = 10$.

$V_{max} = (80 - 20)(50 - 20)10 = 18\,000 \text{ cm}^3$

EXAMPLE 29

An Olympic running track has two straights and two semicircular ends, as shown. The total perimeter is 400 m. If the area of the shaded region where the field sports are played is to be maximized, find the length of each straight.

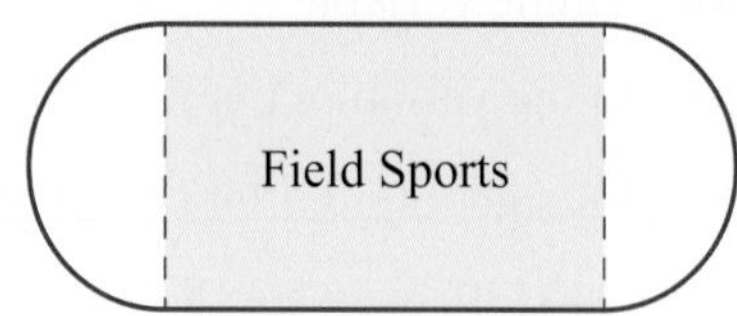

Solution

1. A (area)

2. Diagram:

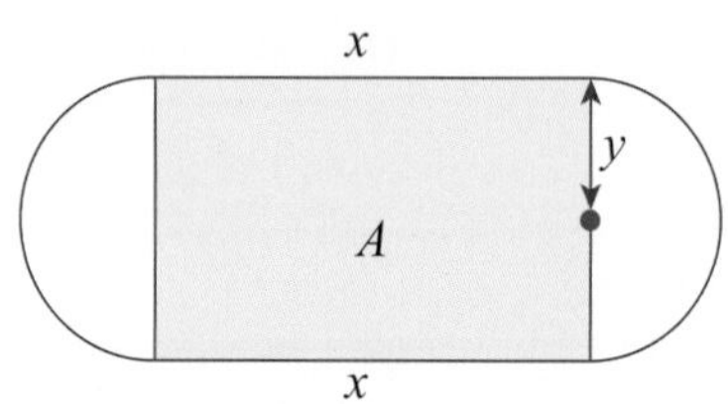

3. $A = x(2y) = 2xy$

4. $400 = 2x + 2\pi y$

$2x = 400 - 2\pi y$

$x = 200 - \pi y$

5. $A = 2y(200 - \pi y) = 400y - 2\pi y^2$

6. $\dfrac{dA}{dy} = 400 - 4\pi y$

$400 - 4\pi y = 0$

$y = \dfrac{100}{\pi}$

7. Maximum area occurs at $y = \dfrac{100}{\pi}$.

$x = 200 - \pi\left(\dfrac{100}{\pi}\right) = 100$

Therefore, the length of each straight is 100 m.

EXAMPLE 30

A satellite is to be constructed in the shape of a cylinder with a hemisphere at each end. The outer surface is to be tiled with heat resistant tiles. The volume of the satellite is $\frac{\pi}{6}$ m^3.

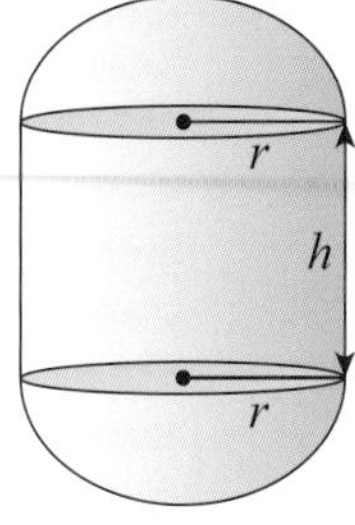

(a) Show that $h = \frac{1 - 8r^3}{6r^2}$.

(b) Show that the surface area A is $\frac{\pi}{3r} + \frac{4}{3}\pi r^3$.

(c) Find the minimum surface area.

Solution

1. A (area)
2. Diagram:

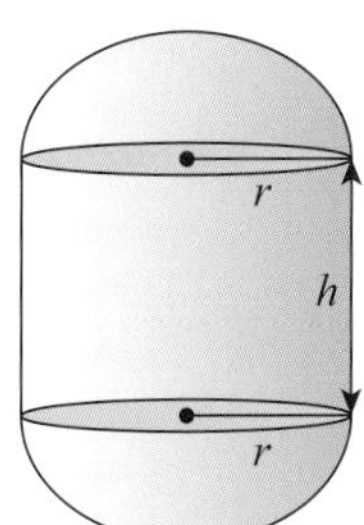

3. $A = 4\pi r^2 + 2\pi rh$ [surface area of sphere and cylinder]

4. $V = \frac{4}{3}\pi r^3 + \pi r^2 h = \frac{\pi}{6}$

$8r^3 + 6r^2 h = 1$

$h = \frac{1 - 8r^3}{6r^2}$

5. $A = 4\pi r^2 + 2\pi r\left(\frac{1 - 8r^3}{6r^2}\right)$

$A = 4\pi r^2 + \frac{\pi}{3r} - \frac{8}{3}\pi r^2$

$A = \frac{\pi}{3r} + \frac{4}{3}\pi r^2$

6. $\frac{dA}{dr} = -\frac{\pi}{3r^2} + \frac{8\pi}{3}r = 0$

$-1 + 8r^3 = 0$

$8r^3 = 1$

$r^3 = \frac{1}{8}$

$r = \frac{1}{2}$

7. $A_{\text{min}} = \frac{2\pi}{3} + \frac{4\pi}{3}\left(\frac{1}{4}\right) = \frac{2\pi}{3} + \frac{\pi}{3} = \pi$ m^2

(b) Economics

Economics insights:

1. Profit (P) = Revenue or income (R) – Costs (C)
2. N objects sold at €x each gives a Revenue (income) R = €Nx

EXAMPLE 31

The fuel economy E (km/l) of an average saloon car is given by $E = -0{\cdot}00375v^2 + 0{\cdot}575v - 2$, where v is the speed of the car in km/h. At what speed, correct to one decimal place, is the fuel economy a maximum?

Solution

1. Fuel economy (E)

3. $E = -0{\cdot}00375v^2 + 0{\cdot}575v - 2$

6. $\frac{dE}{dv} = -0{\cdot}0075v + 0{\cdot}575$

$-0{\cdot}0075v + 0{\cdot}575 = 0$

$v = 76{\cdot}7$ [There is one stationary point.]

Fuel economy is a maximum at a speed of $76{\cdot}7$ km/h.

EXAMPLE 32

A company manufactures and sells shirts. The company's fixed costs are €1500 per week. The production costs are €10 per shirt. The number N of shirts sold per week is given by $N = -10x + 1200$, when the company sells the shirts at €x each.

Find:

(a) the weekly revenue in terms of x,

(b) the weekly costs in terms of x,

(c) the weekly profit in terms of x,

(d) the maximum weekly profit.

Solution

(a) For €x per shirt the number sold is N per week.

Revenue R per week $= Nx = x(-10x + 1200) = 1200x - 10x^2$

(b) Weekly costs:

$C =$ Fixed costs + Cost per shirt × Number of shirts

$C = 1500 + 10(-10x + 1200)$

$C = -100x + 13\,500$

(c) $P = R - C = 1200x - 10x^2 - (13\,500 - 100x)$

$= -10x^2 + 1300x - 13\,500$

Now, for the optimisation of the profit P.

(d) $P = -10x^2 + 1300x - 13\,500$

$\frac{dP}{dx} = -20x + 1300$

$\frac{dP}{dx} = 0$

$-20x + 1300 = 0$

$x = 65$ [There is only one stationary point.]

Maximum profit $P_{max} = -10(65)^2 + 1300(65) - 13\,500 = €28\,750$

(c) Algebraic

EXAMPLE 33

The illumination at a point A is the sum of the illuminations of each light S_1 and S_2 at A. The illumination I at a distance d from a light of candle power P is given by $I = \frac{P}{d^2}$.

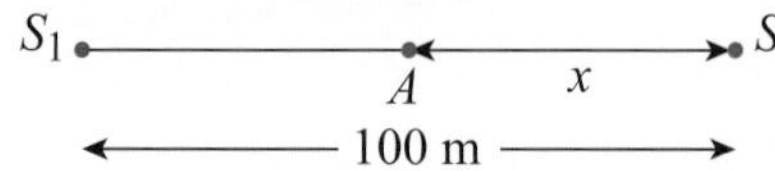

If S_1 has candle power 8 and S_2 has candle power 1, find the point at which the illumination is least.

Solution

1. I (illumination)

2. Diagram:

S_1 $P = 8$ $(100 - x)$ A x $P = 1$ S_2

3. $I = I_1 + I_2 = \frac{8}{(100 - x)^2} + \frac{1}{x^2}$

5. $I = 8(100 - x)^{-2} + x^{-2}$

6. $\frac{dI}{dx} = -16(100-x)^{-3}(-1) - 2x^{-3}$

$= \frac{16}{(100-x)^3} - \frac{2}{x^3}$

$\frac{16}{(100-x)^3} - \frac{2}{x^3} = 0$

$8x^3 = (100-x)^3$

$2x = 100 - x$

$3x = 100$

$x = 33\frac{1}{3}$

Therefore, the illumination is least at $33\frac{1}{3}$ m from S_2.

(d) Curves

Remember, if a point P is on a curve:

(i) to mark it as $P(x, y)$,

(ii) that it satisfies the equation of the curve,

(iii) that you can use co-ordinate geometry.

EXAMPLE 34

Find the point P on the curve $y = \frac{4}{x}$, $x > 0$ that is nearest the origin.

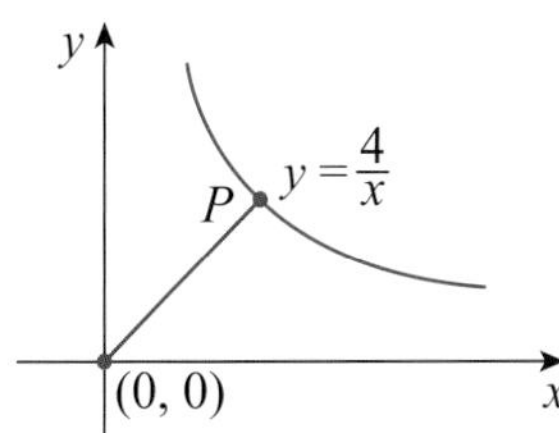

Solution

1. L (distance)
2. Diagram:

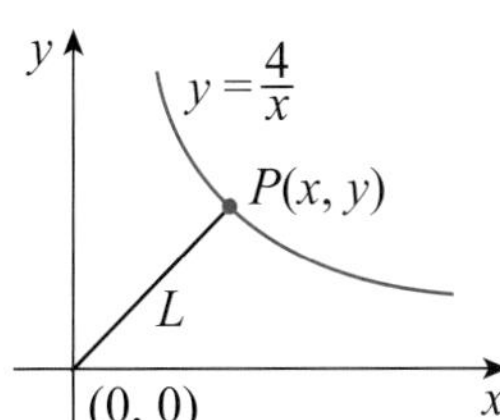

3. $L = \sqrt{x^2 + y^2}$
4. (x, y) is on the curve $y = \frac{4}{x}$.
5. $L = \sqrt{x^2 + \frac{16}{x^2}}$
6. $L = (x^2 + 16x^{-2})^{\frac{1}{2}}$

$\frac{dL}{dx} = \frac{1}{2}(x^2 + 16x^{-2})^{-\frac{1}{2}}\left(2x - \frac{32}{x^3}\right)$

$= \frac{x - \frac{16}{x^3}}{\sqrt{x^2 + \frac{16}{x^2}}}$

$\frac{x - \frac{16}{x^3}}{\sqrt{x^2 + \frac{16}{x^2}}} = 0$

$x - \frac{16}{x^3} = 0$

$x^4 = 16$

$x = \pm 2$ [Reject -2 as $x > 0$.]

7. $x = 2 : y = \frac{4}{2} = 2$

Therefore, (2, 2) is the point nearest to the origin.

(e) Motion

EXAMPLE 35

A body moves in a straight line for 10 seconds with its position s, in metres (m), given by $s = 25t^2 - \frac{5}{3}t^3$, $0 \leq t \leq 10$, where t is in seconds (s). Find its maximum velocity and the position where it achieves this.

Solution

1. v (velocity)

5. $s = 25t^2 - \frac{5}{3}t^3$

$$\Rightarrow v = \frac{ds}{dt} = 50t - 5t^2$$

6. $\frac{dv}{dt} = 50 - 10t$

$50 - 10t = 0$

$t = 5$ s [There is only one stationary point.]

7. $v_{max} = 50(5) - 5(25)$

$= 250 - 125$

$= 125$ m/s

$s = 25(25) - \frac{5}{3}(5)^3$

$= 416\frac{2}{3}$ m

EXAMPLE 36

A fisherman can row at 4 km/h and run at 5 km/h. He is at S, 3 km from the nearest point R on the shore which is 5 km from the fish market Q. How far from Q should the fisherman land to reach Q as quickly as possible.

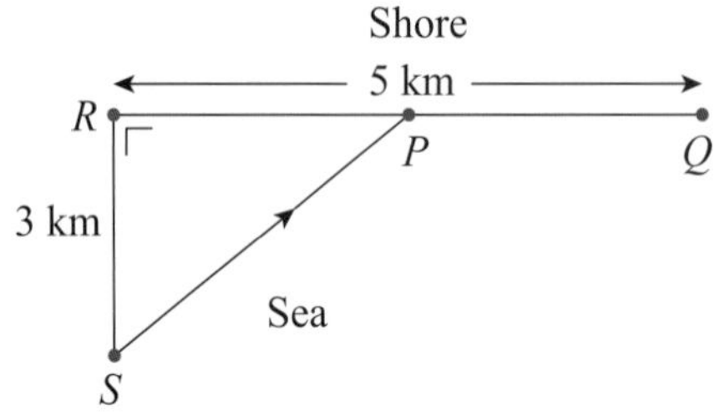

Solution

1. T (time)

2. Diagram:

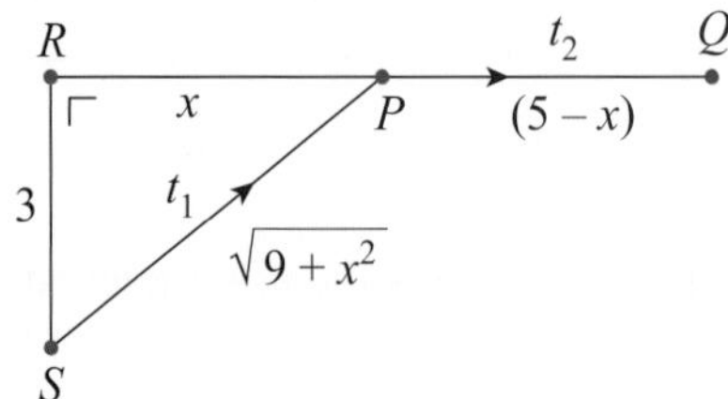

5. $\boldsymbol{S \rightarrow P}$: $4 = \frac{\sqrt{9+x^2}}{t_1}$ $\left[\text{Speed} = \frac{\text{Distance}}{\text{Time}}\right]$

$$t_1 = \frac{\sqrt{9+x^2}}{4}$$

$\boldsymbol{P \rightarrow Q}$: $5 = \frac{5-x}{t_2} \Rightarrow t_2 = \frac{5-x}{5}$

$$\therefore T = \frac{1}{4}(9+x^2)^{\frac{1}{2}} + \frac{1}{5}(5-x)$$

6. $\frac{dT}{dx} = \frac{1}{8}(9+x^2)^{-\frac{1}{2}}(2x) + \frac{1}{5}(-1)$

$$\frac{x}{4\sqrt{9+x^2}} - \frac{1}{5} = 0$$

$$\frac{x}{4\sqrt{9+x^2}} = \frac{1}{5}$$

$$5x = 4\sqrt{9+x^2}$$

$$25x^2 = 144 + 16x^2$$

$$9x^2 = 144$$

$$x^2 = 16$$

$$x = \pm 4 \quad (\text{Reject } -4)$$

Therefore, the fisherman should land 1 km from Q.

(f) Inscribers

KEY TERM

An **inscriber** is one shape inside another shape.

Inscriber insights

1. For a circle or a sphere, always mark the centre O and draw an intelligent radius r.

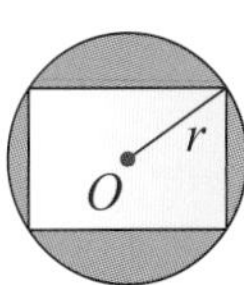

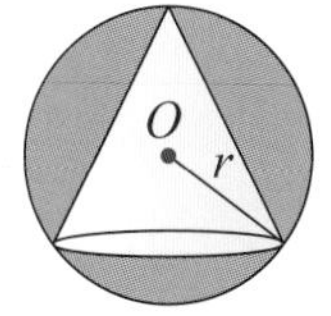

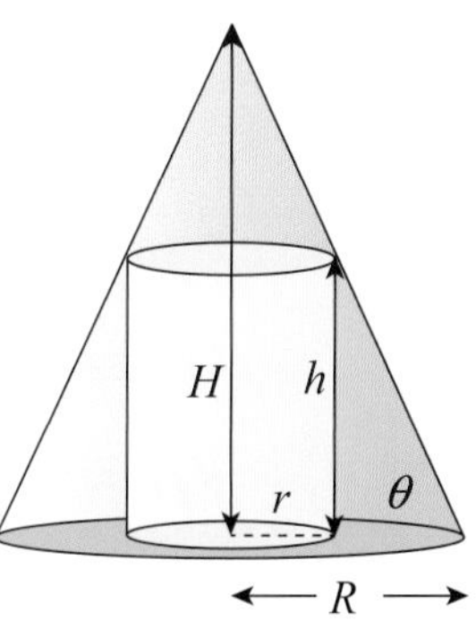

2. Use Pythagoras for right-angled triangles.
3. For a cylinder inside a cone: $\tan\theta = \frac{H}{R} = \frac{h}{(R-r)}$.
4. Always concentrate on the shape that is inside. This is the one to be optimised.

EXAMPLE 37

A rectangular seating arrangement for a concert is to be constructed on a circular cricket pitch.

Find the area of the rectangle of maximum area that can be constructed in a circular pitch of radius 50 m.

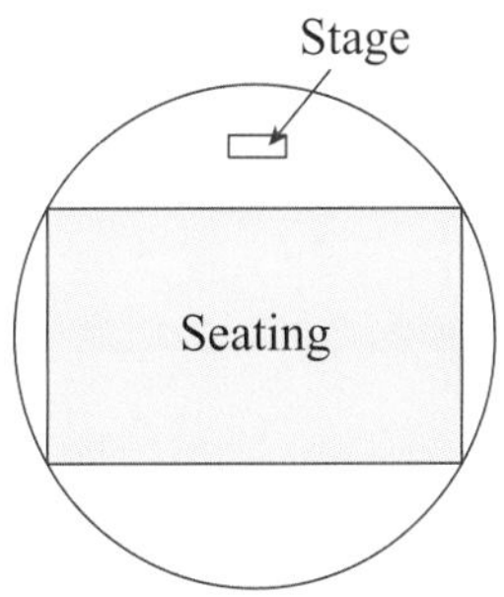

Solution

1. A
2. Diagram:

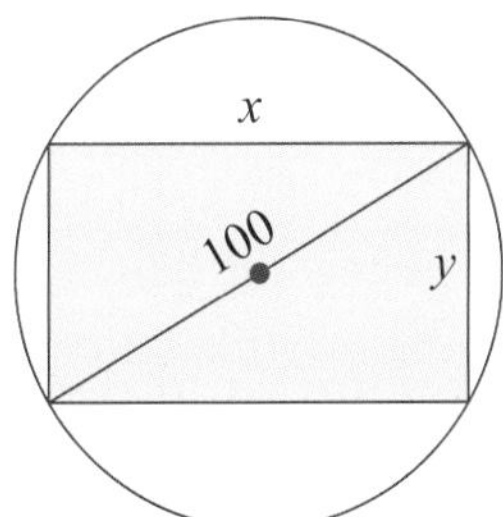

3. $A = xy$
4. Pythagoras: $x^2 + y^2 = 100^2$

   $y = \sqrt{10\,000 - x^2}$
5. $A = x\sqrt{10\,000 - x^2}$
6. $\frac{dA}{dx} = \frac{1}{2}x(10\,000 - x^2)^{-\frac{1}{2}}(-2x) + (10\,000 - x^2)^{\frac{1}{2}}$

   $-x^2(10\,000 - x^2)^{-\frac{1}{2}} + (10\,000 - x^2)^{\frac{1}{2}} = 0$

   Multiply across by $(10\,000 - x^2)^{\frac{1}{2}}$

   $-x^2 + 10\,000 - x^2 = 0$

   $2x^2 = 10\,000$

   $x^2 = 5000$

   $x = 50\sqrt{2}$
7. $A_{max} = 50\sqrt{2}\sqrt{5000} = 5000 \text{ m}^2$

EXAMPLE 38

A cylinder is inscribed in a right circular cone of fixed height 10 cm and fixed radius 5 cm. Prove that the maximum volume of the cylinder is $\frac{4}{9}$ the volume of the cone.

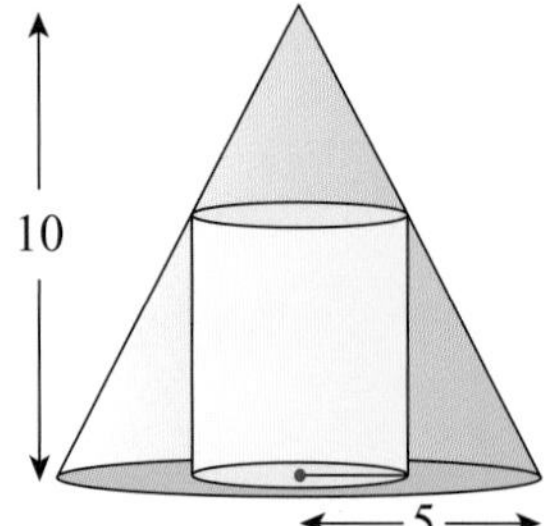

Solution

1. V (volume of the cylinder)
2. Diagram:

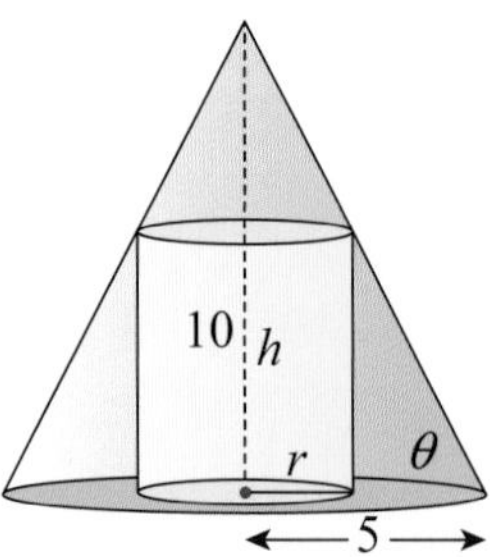

3. $V = \pi r^2 h$
4. $\tan\theta = \dfrac{h}{5-r} = \dfrac{10}{5}$

   $h = 2(5 - r)$
5. $V = 2\pi r^2(5 - r)$

   $= 10\pi r^2 - 2\pi r^3$
6. $\dfrac{dV}{dr} = 20\pi r - 6\pi r^2$

   $20\pi r - 6\pi r^2 = 0$

   $2\pi r(10 - 3r) = 0$

   $r = 0$ [reject], $r = \frac{10}{3}$
7. $V_{max} = 2\pi \dfrac{100}{9} \times \left(\dfrac{5}{3}\right)$

   $= \dfrac{1000\pi}{27}$

   $V_{cone} = \dfrac{1}{3}\pi\,(25)(10)$

   $= \dfrac{250\pi}{3}$

   $\therefore \dfrac{V_{max}}{V_{cone}} = \dfrac{\left(\dfrac{1000\pi}{27}\right)}{\left(\dfrac{250\pi}{3}\right)}$

   $= \dfrac{4}{9}$

EXERCISE 14

Geometry

1. A rectangular box is used to transport pencils. It has a square base of side x cm. If the sum of one side of the square and the height h is 27 cm, express the volume V of the box in terms of x. Find the maximum volume of the box.

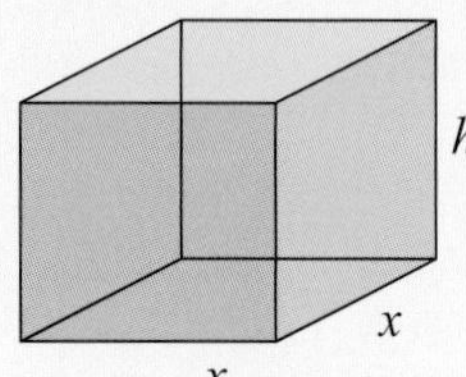

2. A drinking glass, in the shape of a cylinder, can hold 64π cm^3 of liquid when full.

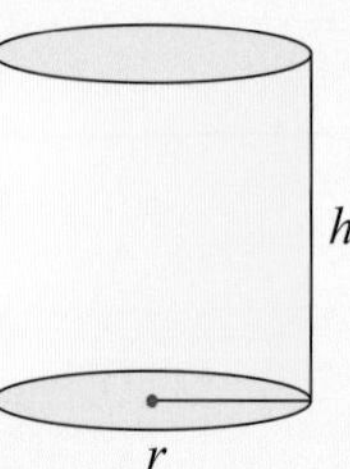

   (a) Show that the height is given by $h = \dfrac{64}{r^2}$.

   (b) Show that the total surface area A is given by $A = \pi r^2 + \dfrac{128\pi}{r}$.

   (c) Find the radius r that minimizes the total surface area of the glass.

3. A farmer has 800 m of fencing and wishes to make an enclosure consisting of four equal area rectangles, as shown.

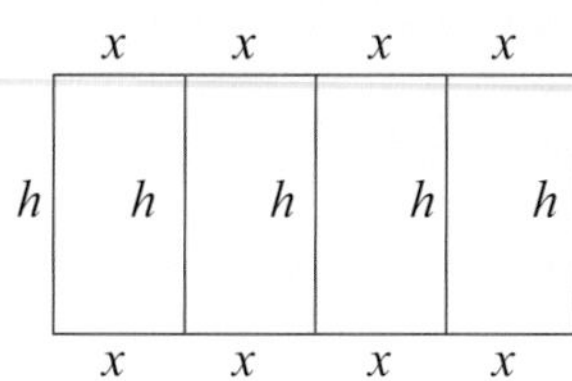

(a) Express h in terms of x.

(b) Express the total area A in terms of x.

(c) Find x if A is to be a maximum.

4. A rectangular page contains 128 cm^2 of printed material with a 1 cm margin at the top and the bottom and 2 cm at each side, as shown.

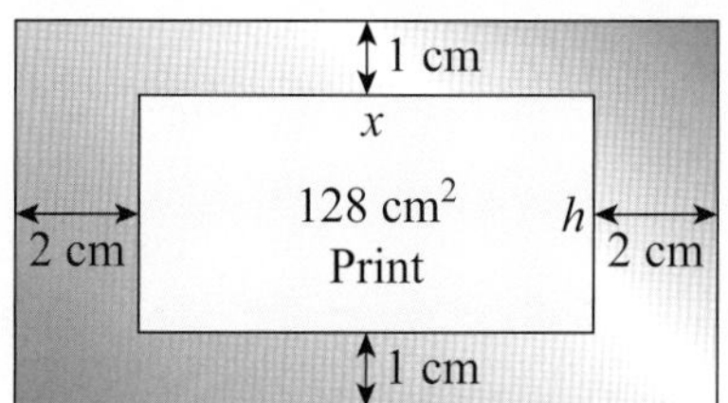

(a) Express h (width of the print) in terms of x (length of the print).

(b) Find an expression for the area A of the whole page in terms of x.

(c) Find the maximum area of the page.

5. A piece of wire of length 21 cm is cut into two parts. One part has length x. This part is bent into a rectangle in which the length of the base y is three times the height h. The other part is bent into a square.

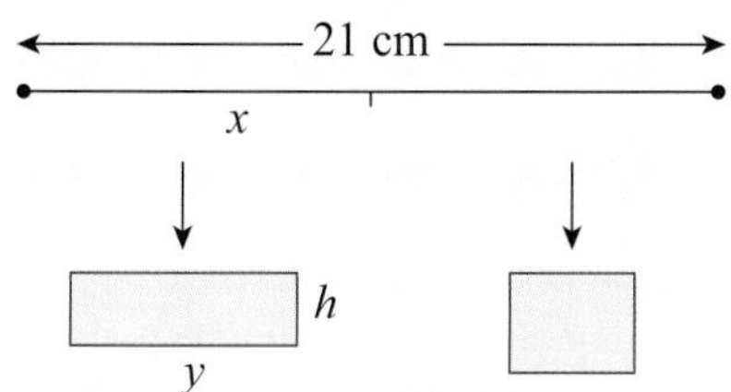

(a) Find the length of a side of the square in terms of x.

(b) Find h and y in terms of x.

(c) Find an expression for the sum S of the areas of the rectangle and the square in terms of x.

(d) Find x to minimize the sum of the areas.

(e) Find this minimum sum.

Economics

6. The total cost C (€) of producing x units of a computer part per week is given by $C = \frac{x^3}{3} - 24x^2 + 560x + 1200$. The total revenue R (€) is given by $R = 400x - 2x^2$.

(a) Express the profit P in terms of x.

(b) Find $\frac{dP}{dx}$ and $\frac{d^2P}{dx^2}$.

(c) Find x to maximize the profit.

7. A lorry is driven from Dublin to Letterkenny at a steady speed of v km/h. The total cost C (€) for the journey is given by $C = \frac{1200}{v} + \frac{3v}{25}$.

(a) Find v for which C is a minimum.

(b) Find $\frac{d^2C}{dv^2}$ and hence verify that the value of v in part **(a)** minimizes C.

(c) Find the minimum value of C.

8. The value of shares €v, after t years, can be modelled by the equation $v = 10 - 2t + 3{\cdot}5t^2 - t^3, 0 \leq t \leq 3$.

(a) Find:

(i) $\frac{dv}{dt}$

(ii) $\frac{d^2v}{dt^2}$

(iii) the local maximum and local minimum turning points

(iv) the maximum value of the shares

(b) Find t when $\frac{d^2v}{dt^2} = 0$. What is the relevance of this result to an investor?

9. A tank with a rectangular base is open at the top. Its width is 4 m and its volume is 64 m^3.

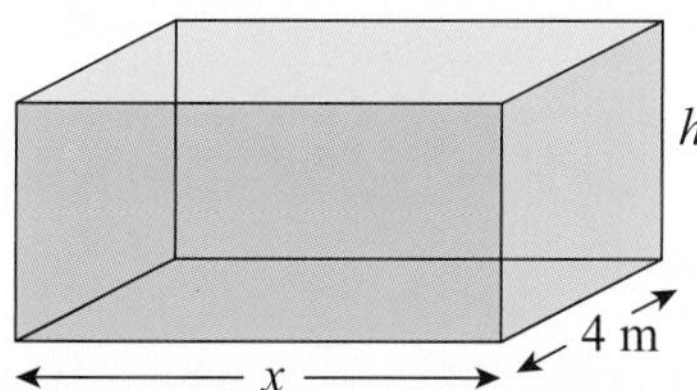

(a) If its length is x m and its height is h, express x in term of h.

The building costs of the tank are €10 per m^2 for the base and €8 per m^2 for the other faces.

(b) Express the total cost to build the tank in terms of h.

(c) Find h to minimize the cost.

(d) Find the minimum cost.

10. A lamp manufacturer finds that she can sell x lamps per week at €p each, where $x = 80 - 2\sqrt{p}$. The total cost C, in euros, of production of all x lamps is given by $C = 300 + 12x + \frac{1}{4}x^2$.

(a) Find an expression in x for the weekly revenue R.

(b) Find an expression in x for the weekly profit.

(c) Find the value of x that will maximize the profit, correct to the nearest whole number.

Algebraic

11. If $xy = 8$ and $A = x^2 + 16y + 9, x > 0$:

(a) express y in terms of x,

(b) express A in terms of x,

(c) find the minimum value of A.

12. The current I (A) in the electric circuit shown is given by $6 = I(R + r)$, where r is a constant and R and r are in ohms.

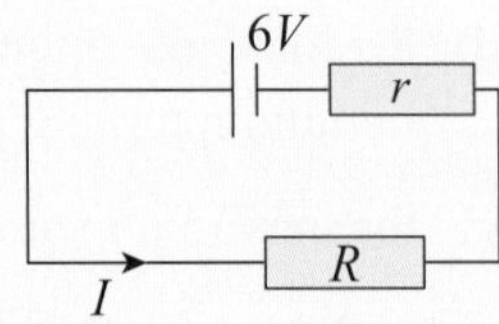

(a) Express I in terms of R and r.

The power P (W) in the resistor R is given by $P = I^2R$.

(b) Express P in term of R and r.

(c) Show that $R = r$ for maximum power P.

13. The number 16 is divided into two parts that add to 16.

(a) If x is one number and y is the other number, express y in terms of x.

If $S = 2y^2 + x^3$:

(b) express S in terms of x,

(c) find x and y to minimize S and the minimum value of S.

Curves

14. The rectangle $OBCD$ has three vertices on the axes and one point $C(x, y)$ on the line k: $2x + y - 6 = 0$.

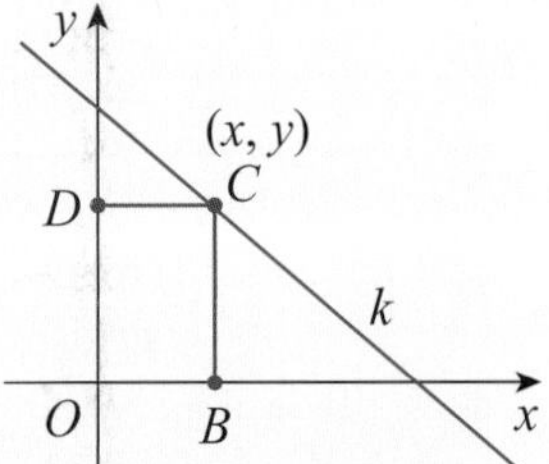

(a) Express y in terms of x.

(b) Express the area A of the rectangle $OBCD$ in terms of x.

(c) Find the maximum area of the rectangle.

15. The equation of an arch is given by $y = e^{-x^2}$.

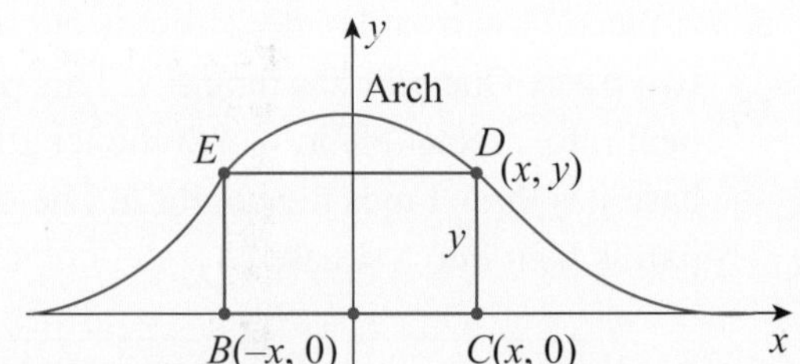

A rectangle $BCDE$ is to be constructed to reinforce the arch, as shown above.

(a) If $D(x, y)$ is on the arch, express y in terms of x.

(b) Express the area A of the rectangle $BCDE$ in terms of x.

(c) Find x to maximize the area A. Find this maximum area.

Motion

16. The distance s in metres (m) of an ant from its nest is given by $s = 3t - (t + 1) \ln (t + 1)$, $0 \leq t \leq 15$, where t is in minutes.

(a) How far is the ant from its nest at $t = 0$?

(b) Find the maximum distance it is from its nest.

(c) How far is the ant from its nest at $t = 1$?

17. Ship P is at A, 20 km due east of port O, at a certain time and is travelling due east at 15 km/h. Ship Q is at B, 20 km due north of port O, at the same time and travelling due south at 30 km/h.

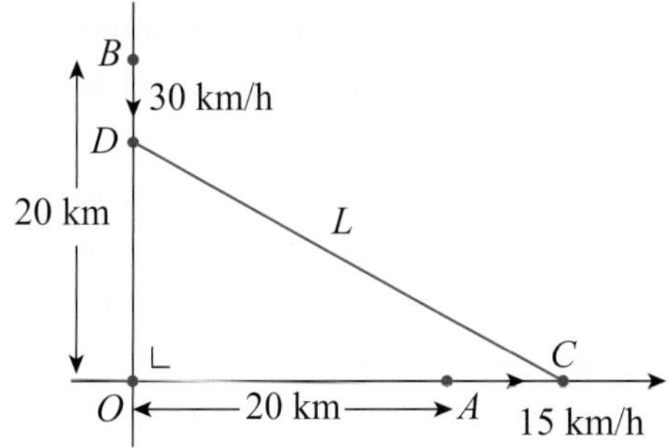

After t hours:

(a) write down how far ship P is from O (find $|OC|$ in terms of t),

(b) write down how far ship Q is from O (find $|OD|$ in terms of t),

(c) find the distance L between the two ships in terms of t,

(d) find the time at which they are closest together,

(e) find their minimum distance apart.

Inscribers

18. A right-circular cone of radius r and height h is inscribed in a sphere, centre O and radius 1. $|OB| = x$ is the distance from the centre of the sphere to the centre of the base of the cone.

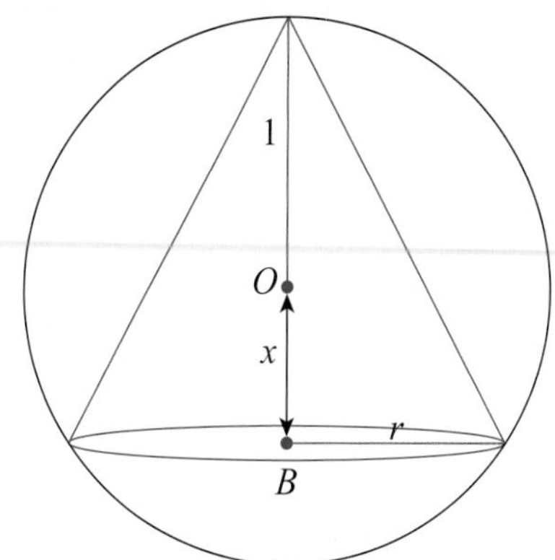

(a) Express h in terms of x.

(b) Express r^2 in terms of x.

(c) Show that the volume V of the cone is given by $V = \frac{\pi}{3}(1 + x - x^2 - x^3)$.

(d) Find the value of x to maximize the volume V of the cone.

(e) Find the maximum volume.

19. A machine part consists of a cylinder inscribed in a sphere with centre O and radius 8 cm.

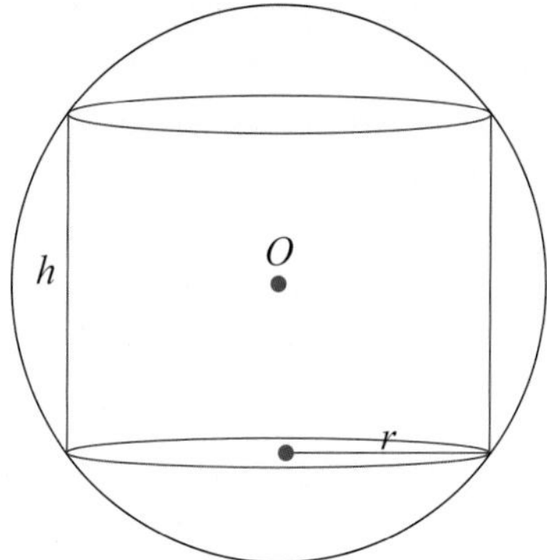

(a) Express r^2 in terms of h, where r is the base radius of the cylinder and h is its height.

(b) Express the volume V of the cylinder in terms of h.

(c) Find h to maximize the volume of the cylinder.

(d) Find the maximum volume of the cylinder.

REVISION QUESTIONS

1. **(a)** What is the equation of the tangent to the curve of the function $y = f(x)$ at $x = 2$ if $f(2) = 6$ and $f'(2) = -1$?

(b) The curve $y = x^3$ is shown. For this curve:

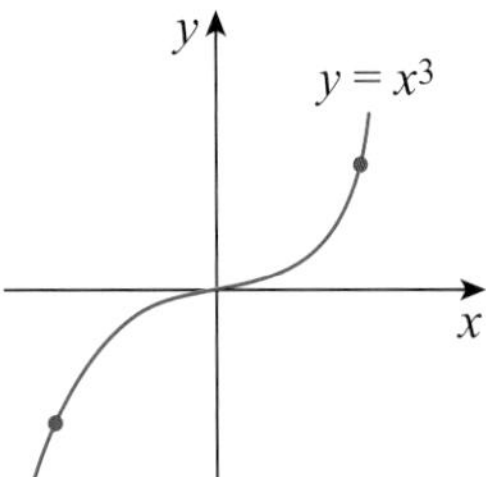

(i) find the average rate of change of y with respect to x from $x = -2$ to $x = 2$,

(ii) find the instantaneous rate of change of y with respect to x at $x = -2$,

(iii) find the equation of the tangent at $x = -2$,

(iv) find the points on the curve at which the slope of the tangent is 27,

(v) find the angle that the tangent to the curve at $x = 1$ makes with the $+x$-axis, correct to two decimal places.

2. **(a)** The equation of a curve is $y = 2^{x^2}$.

(i) Show that $y = e^{x^2 \ln 2}$. Hence, show $\dfrac{dy}{dx} = x(\ln 2)\, 2^{x^2+1}$.

(ii) Find the slope of the tangent to the curve $y = 2^{x^2}$ at $x = 2$.

(b) Show that the tangent to the curve $y = \ln(2x^2 + 3)$ at $x = 0$ is parallel to the x-axis. Find the equation of the tangent.

(c) If $y = \ln \cos^3 x$:

(i) find $\dfrac{dy}{dx}$

(ii) find $\dfrac{d^2y}{dx^2}$

(iii) show that $3\dfrac{d^2y}{dx^2} + \left(\dfrac{dy}{dx}\right)^2 + 9 = 0$

(d) If $y = \dfrac{\sin x}{1 + \cos x}$:

(i) show that $\dfrac{dy}{dx} = \dfrac{1}{1 + \cos x}$

(ii) show that $\dfrac{d^2y}{dx^2} = \dfrac{\sin x}{(1 + \cos x)^2}$

(iii) hence, show that $\dfrac{d^2y}{dx^2} - y\dfrac{dy}{dx} = 0$

3. On a certain day the temperature T in °C in an arid region was given by $T = \dfrac{t(t - 24)(9 - 7t)}{432}$, where t is the time in hours, $0 \le t < 24$ and $t = 0$ corresponds to midnight.

(a) **(i)** Find the temperature at 2 a.m.

(ii) Find the temperature at 3 p.m.

(b) Find the times at which the temperature was 0 °C, correct to the nearest minute.

(c) Find the average rate of change of temperature between 11 a.m. and 1 p.m., correct to one decimal place.

(d) Show that $\dfrac{dT}{dt} = \dfrac{-21t^2 + 354t - 216}{432}$.

(e) Find the instantaneous rate of change of temperature at noon.

(f) Find the times at which the instantaneous rate of change of temperature is 0, correct to the nearest minute.

4. The population P, t years after a species of rhododendrons appeared, is given by $P = \dfrac{3600k\, e^{\frac{1}{2}t}}{1 + k\, e^{\frac{1}{2}t}}$.

(a) If there were 600 rhododendrons initially, find k.

(b) What is the population after 5 years, correct to the nearest whole number?

(c) When is the population 3298 rhododendrons?

(d) Find the rate of change of the population when:

(i) $t = 0$

(ii) $t = 5$, correct to the nearest whole number.

5. The height h in metres above the ground is related to the air temperature T and pressure P by the equation $h = (13T + 3500)\ln\left(\dfrac{760}{P}\right)$, where P is in mm of Hg and T is °C.

(a) How high above Earth is an aeroplane if the temperature outside is 0 °C and the pressure is 300 mm of Hg, correct to one decimal place?

(b) What is the pressure at the summit of a mountain of height 1492·7 m if the temperature at the peak is 5 °C?

(c) For a height of 1000 m, express P in terms of T.

(d) Find the rate of change of P with respect to T at $h = 1000$ m when $T = 10$ °C, correct to two decimal places.

6. In a chemical sample the mass m in grams of radioactive Iodine-131 remaining after t days is given by $m = Me^{-0\cdot087t}$.

(a) At $t = 0$ there is 100 g of Iodine-131 in the sample. Find M.

(b) What mass of Iodine-131 remains after 8 days, correct to two decimal places?

(c) When will 80 grams of Iodine-131 be left? Give your answer correct to two decimal places.

(d) Find an expression for the rate of decay $\frac{dm}{dt}$ of Iodine-131.

In the same sample, the mass m of another radioactive isotope remaining after t days is given by $m = 100 \times 2^{-0\cdot2t}$.

(e) Find the rate of decay of this second isotope.

(f) Find the ratio of the rate of decay of this second isotope to that of Iodine-131 after four days. Give your answer correct to one decimal place.

7. Newton's law of cooling states that the temperature θ (°C) of a hot object time t (minutes) after it starts to cool is given by $\theta = T + (\theta_0 - T)e^{kt}$, $k < 0$, where θ_0 is the initial temperature of the hot object in °C, T is the temperature of the surroundings in °C and k is a constant. An object is heated to 90 °C and is allowed to cool in a room whose air temperature is 25 °C.

(a) If the temperature of the object is 75 °C after 5 minutes, find k, correct to two decimal places.

(b) What will the temperature be after 8 minutes, correct to two decimal places?

(c) When will the temperature be 50 °C, correct to two decimal places?

(d) Find the rate of cooling in terms of t.

(e) Find the ratio of the rate of cooling after 10 minutes with the initial rate of cooling, correct to one decimal place.

8. **(a) (i)** Prove that $\sin^2 A = \frac{1}{2}(1 - \cos 2A)$.

(ii) Write $\sin 2A$ in terms of $\cos A$ and $\sin A$.

A piston P moves back and forth between A and B. Its displacement S, in metres, from A after time t, in seconds, is given by $S = \sin^2 t$.

A | $S = 0$ | P | B

(b) Find $|AB|$.

(c) Find the time it takes for the piston to move from A to B and back again.

(d) Find the velocity $v = \frac{dS}{dt}$ of the piston in terms of t and hence show that $v^2 = 4S(1 - S)$.

(e) Find the piston's acceleration $a = \frac{dv}{dt}$ in terms of t and hence show that $a = 2(1 - 2S)$.

9. Moons, asteroids and other planetary bodies often move in elliptical orbits.

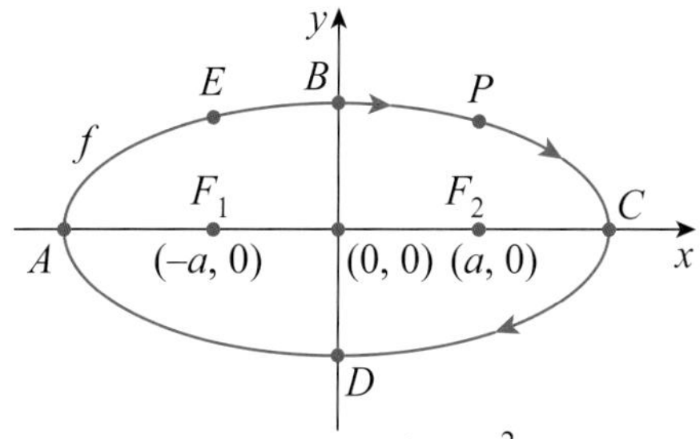

The curve f with equation $\frac{x^2}{25} + \frac{y^2}{16} = 1$ is an ellipse.

(a) Find the points A, B, C, D and E if the x co-ordinate of E is $-a$.

(b) Show that the point $P\left(3, \frac{16}{5}\right)$ is on f.

(c) $F_1(-a, 0)$ and $F_2(a, 0)$ are two points on the x-axis.

(i) Find the sum of distances $d = |CF_2| + |CF_1|$ $(a > 0)$.

(ii) If $|BF_2| + |BF_1| = d$, find a.

(d) Show that $|PF_1| + |PF_2| = d$.

(e) Show that $y = 4\sqrt{1 - \frac{x^2}{25}}, y > 0$.

(f) Find $\frac{dy}{dx}$.

(g) An asteroid moving in the orbit f is struck by a meteor and moves along a tangent to f at P. Find the equation of this tangent line k.

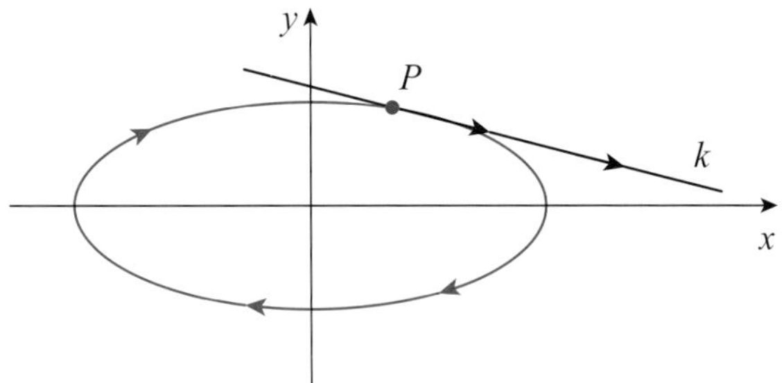

10. (a) (i) Differentiate $\ln(5x^2 - 1)$ with respect to x.

(ii) If $y = \log_{10} f(x)$, show that $y = \log_{10} e \times \ln f(x)$.

(iii) Find $\frac{dy}{dx}$ if $y = \log_{10}(5x^2 - 1)$.

(b) (i) Find the slope of the tangent to the curve $y = \log_{10}\left(\frac{1-x}{1+x}\right)$ at $x = 2$.

(ii) Find the equation of the tangent to the curve $y = \log_2 x$ at $x = 1$.

(c) The height h in cm of a species of grass in a certain region is related to the soil temperature x in °C by the formula $h = 2\log_{10}\{x\sqrt{1+x^2}\}, x > 0$. Find the rate of change of h with respect to x at $x = 20$, correct to three decimal places.

11. The equation of the curve f is $y = x^3 - 13x^2 + 55x - 75, x \in \mathbb{R}$.

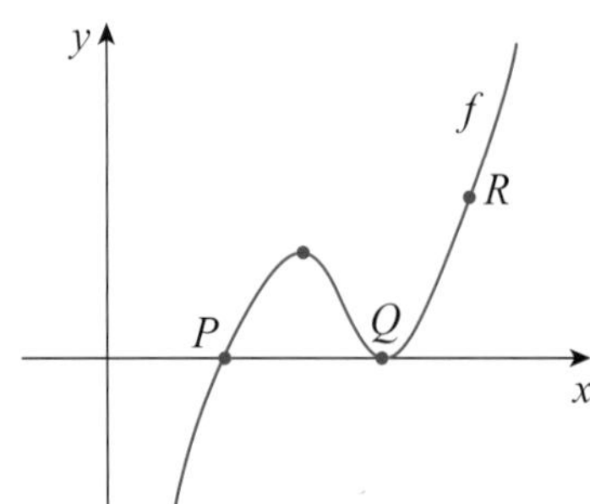

(a) Find the local maximum and local minimum.

(b) Find the point of inflection.

(c) Find the point where f crosses the y-axis.

(d) Find Q where the curve f touches the x-axis.

(e) Find P, the other point where the curve crosses the x-axis by solving $x^3 - 13x^2 + 55x - 75 = 0$.

(f) Find the slope of the tangent to the curve at P.

(g) Find the point R on f at which the tangent is parallel to the tangent at P.

12. A motorcycle trial takes place in a ploughed square field $ABCD$ with a path DC along one side. A motorcyclist can go at 100 km/h along the path and 60 km/h across the field. A motorcyclist starts at D, moves along the path DC and leaves it at P to cross the field from P to B.

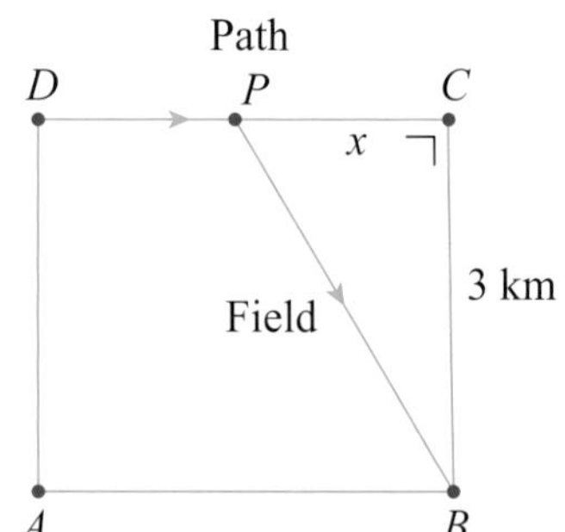

(a) Express $|PB|$ in terms of x, if $|PC| = x$.

(b) Express the time t_1 to go from D to P in terms of x.

(c) Express the time t_2 to go from P to B in terms of x.

(d) Express the total time T from D to B in terms of x.

(e) Find the value of x to minimize the time T.

(f) Find the minimum value of T.

13. The diagram shows a flowerbed consisting of a quarter circle of radius r with centre O with two equal rectangles B and C attached to it along its radii.

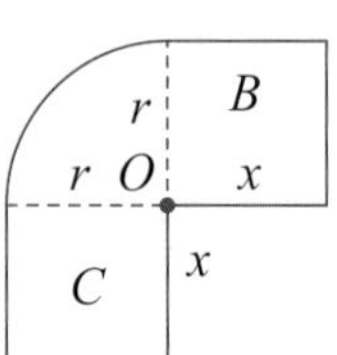

(a) Find the area A of the flowerbed in terms of x and r.

(b) If the area is 8 m^2, show that $x = \dfrac{32 - \pi r^2}{8r}$.

(c) Express the perimeter P in terms of x and r.

(d) Show that $P = 2r + \dfrac{16}{r}$.

(e) Find r to minimize the perimeter.

(f) Find the minimum perimeter length.

14. The cost C (€) of manufacturing x items in a factory every day is given by

$C = 100 \ln x + 10\left(\dfrac{60 - x}{10}\right)^2$.

(a) Find the cost of producing 60 items per day, correct to the nearest cent.

(b) Find $\dfrac{dC}{dx}$, the marginal cost function.

(c) Find $C'(70)$ and $C'(40)$.

(d) Find the cost of making the 71st item, correct to the nearest cent.

(e) Find the value of x to minimize the cost per day.

(f) Find the minimum cost per day that can be achieved, correct to the nearest cent.

15. Two perpendicular roads, AO and OB, intersect at O. A cyclepath AB is to be built so that it passes over a bridge at P where $|QB| = b$ and $|RA| = a$.

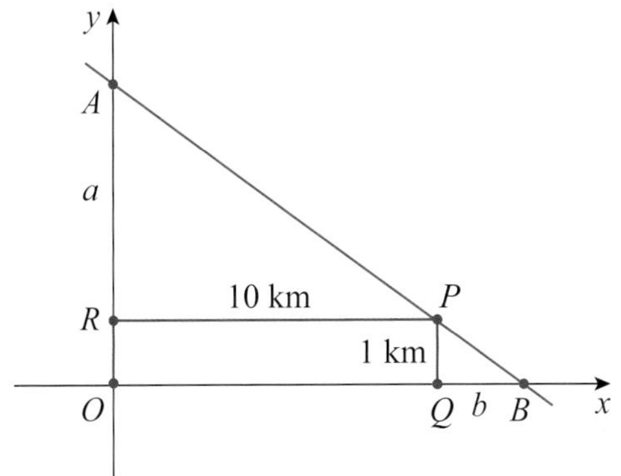

(a) Using similar triangles ΔQBP and ΔRPA, or otherwise, show that $b = \dfrac{10}{a}$.

(b) Find:

(i) $|AP|$ in terms of a,

(ii) $|PB|$ in terms of a.

(c) Show that $|AB| = L = \sqrt{a^2 + 100}\left(1 + \dfrac{1}{a}\right)$.

(d) Find a to minimize L. Give your answer correct to two decimal places.

(e) Find the minimum value of L, correct to one decimal place.

16. In the special theory of relativity, the mass m of a body moving at speed v (m/s) is given by

$m = \dfrac{m_0}{\sqrt{1 - \dfrac{v^2}{c^2}}}$, where m_0 is a constant and

$c = 3 \times 10^8$ m/s is the speed of light.

(a) Find its mass when it is at rest.

(b) If $m_0 = 2 \times 10^4$ kg, find its mass when it is moving at a speed of $\dfrac{c}{10}$, correct to the nearest kilogram.

(c) Find $\dfrac{dm}{dv}$.

(d) Find the instantaneous rate of change of mass in terms of m_0 when $v = \dfrac{3c}{5}$ if the body is accelerating at $0{\cdot}01c$ m/s^2.

(e) Solve for v in terms of m, m_0 and c.

(f) Find the average rate of change in speed with respect to mass m for a 60% increase in mass from m_0 if $m_0 = 2 \times 10^4$ kg. Give your answer correct to one decimal place.

SUMMARY

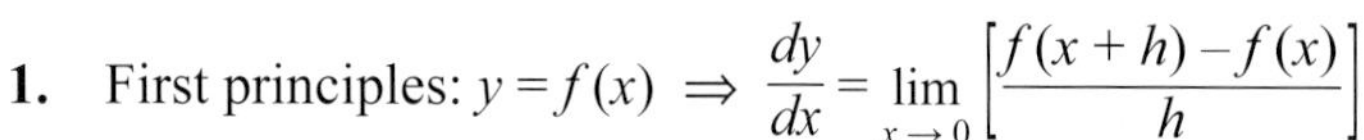

1. First principles: $y = f(x) \Rightarrow \dfrac{dy}{dx} = \lim\limits_{x \to 0}\left[\dfrac{f(x+h) - f(x)}{h}\right]$

2. The rules:

   (a) Basic rule

   $y = x^p \Rightarrow \dfrac{dy}{dx} = px^{p-1}, p \in \mathbb{R}$

   (b) Multiplication by a constant rule

   $y = c \times u(x)$, c a constant $\Rightarrow \dfrac{dy}{dx} = c \times \dfrac{du}{dx}$

   (c) The constant rule

   $y = c$, c a constant (on its own) $\Rightarrow \dfrac{dy}{dx} = 0$

   (d) The sum rule

   $y = u(x) + v(x) \Rightarrow \dfrac{dy}{dx} = \dfrac{du}{dx} + \dfrac{dv}{dx}$

   (e) The product rule

   $y = u(x) \times v(x) \Rightarrow \dfrac{dy}{dx} = u\dfrac{dv}{dx} + v\dfrac{du}{dx}$

   (f) The quotient rule

   $y = \dfrac{u(x)}{v(x)} \Rightarrow \dfrac{dy}{dx} = \dfrac{v\dfrac{du}{dx} - u\dfrac{dv}{dx}}{v^2}$

   (g) The chain rule

   If y is a function of u and u is a function of x:

   $\dfrac{dy}{dx} = \dfrac{dy}{du} \times \dfrac{du}{dx}$

3. Functions:

   (a) Algebraic functions

   (i) $y = x^p \Rightarrow \dfrac{dy}{dx} = px^{p-1}$

   (ii) $y = [f(x)]^p \Rightarrow \dfrac{dy}{dx} = p[f(x)]^{p-1} \times f'(x)$ where $f(x)$ is any function of x.

   (b) Trigonometric functions

   (i) $y = \sin x \Rightarrow \dfrac{dy}{dx} = \cos x$

   (ii) $y = \sin f(x) \Rightarrow \dfrac{dy}{dx} = \cos f(x) \times f'(x)$ where $f(x)$ is any function of x.

   (iii) $y = \cos x \Rightarrow \dfrac{dy}{dx} = -\sin x$

   (iv) $y = \cos\ f(x) \Rightarrow \dfrac{dy}{dx} = -\sin\ f(x) \times f'(x)$ where $f(x)$ is any function of x.

(c) Inverse trigonometric functions

(i) $y = \sin^{-1} x \Rightarrow \dfrac{dy}{dx} = \dfrac{1}{\sqrt{1 - x^2}}$

(ii) $y = \sin^{-1} f(x) \Rightarrow \dfrac{dy}{dx} = \dfrac{1}{\sqrt{1 - f(x)^2}} \times f'(x)$

(iii) $y = \cos^{-1} x \Rightarrow \dfrac{dy}{dx} = -\dfrac{1}{\sqrt{1 - x^2}}$

(iv) $y = \cos^{-1} f(x) \Rightarrow \dfrac{dy}{dx} = -\dfrac{1}{\sqrt{1 - f(x)^2}} \times f'(x)$

(v) $y = \tan^{-1} x \Rightarrow \dfrac{dy}{dx} = \dfrac{1}{1 + x^2}$

(vi) $y = \tan^{-1} f(x) \Rightarrow \dfrac{dy}{dx} = \dfrac{1}{1 + f(x)^2} \times f'(x)$

(d) Exponential functions

(i) $y = e^x \Rightarrow \dfrac{dy}{dx} = e^x$

(ii) $y = e^{f(x)} \Rightarrow \dfrac{dy}{dx} = e^{f(x)} \times f'(x)$ where $f(x)$ is any function of x.

(iii) $y = a^x \Rightarrow \dfrac{dy}{dx} = a^x \times \ln a$

(iv) $y = a^{f(x)} \Rightarrow \dfrac{dy}{dx} = a^{f(x)} \times \ln a \times f'(x)$ where $f(x)$ is any function of x.

(e) Logarithmic functions

(i) $y = \ln x \Rightarrow \dfrac{dy}{dx} = \dfrac{1}{x}$

(ii) $y = \ln f(x) \Rightarrow \dfrac{dy}{dx} = \dfrac{1}{f(x)} \times f'(x)$ where $f(x)$ is any function of x.

(iii) $y = \log_a x = \dfrac{\ln x}{\ln a} \Rightarrow \dfrac{dy}{dx} = \dfrac{1}{x \ln a}$

(iv) $y = \log_a f(x) = \dfrac{\ln f(x)}{\ln a} \Rightarrow \dfrac{dy}{dx} = \dfrac{1}{f(x) \ln a} \times f'(x)$ where $f(x)$ is any function of x.

Always simplify a function before you differentiate it.
Always substitute values into a function **after** you differentiate it.

4. Curves:

(a)

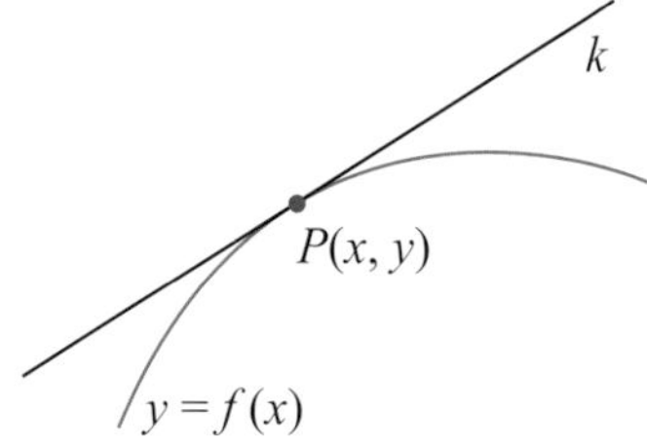

$\frac{dy}{dx}$ = slope of the tangent k to the curve $y = f(x)$ at a point $P(x, y)$ on the curve

(b) A stationary point is a point at which $\frac{dy}{dx} = 0$.

(c)

	> 0	< 0	= 0
$\frac{dy}{dx}$	Increasing (I)	Decreasing (D)	Flat (Flat or Flat)
$\frac{d^2y}{dx^2}$	Concave up	Concave down	Point of inflection

5. Local maxima and minima:

(a) Local maximum at P

$\frac{dy}{dx} = 0$ at P

and

$\frac{d^2y}{dx^2} < 0$ at P

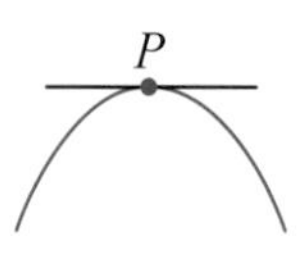

(b) Local minimum at Q

$\frac{dy}{dx} = 0$ at Q

and

$\frac{d^2y}{dx^2} > 0$ at Q

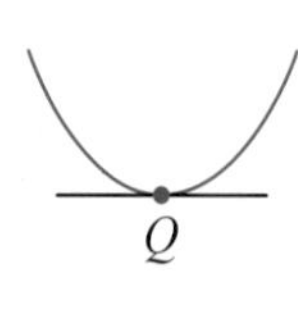

6. Rate of change:

(a) $\frac{dV}{dt}$ = rate of change of V

(b) Velocity: $v = \frac{ds}{dt}$ where s is distance relative to the origin

Acceleration: $a = \frac{dv}{dt}$ where v is velocity

(c) Related rates use the chain rule

$$\frac{dV}{dt} = \frac{dV}{dh} \times \frac{dh}{dt}$$

7. Optimisation:

(a) Model the problem first.

(b) Differentiate to find local maxima/minima.

Integration

Integration deals with two types of problems:

1. Finding a function given its slope or rate of change. This reverse process of differentiation is also known as anti-differentiation.
2. Adding up a very large number of very small (infinitesimal) quantities.

Chapter 25 Techniques of Integration

Learning Outcomes

- To understand the idea of integration.
- To integrate six basic functions whose derivatives you already know.
- To carry out indefinite and definite integration.
- To use three simple rules to carry out integration.
- To integrate different types of functions (functions with rational powers, exponential functions, inverse linear functions and trigonometric functions).

25.1 Explaining integration

When you differentiate a function $f(x)$, in general you get another function $g(x)$.

$f(x) = 4x^2 - 7 \Rightarrow g(x) = f'(x) = 8x$

How do you get back to the original function $f(x)$ from its derivative $g(x)$? This process of getting the original function $f(x)$ from its derivative $g(x)$ is known as anti-differentiation or integration.

KEY TERM

Anti-differentiation or **integration** is the reverse process of differentiation.

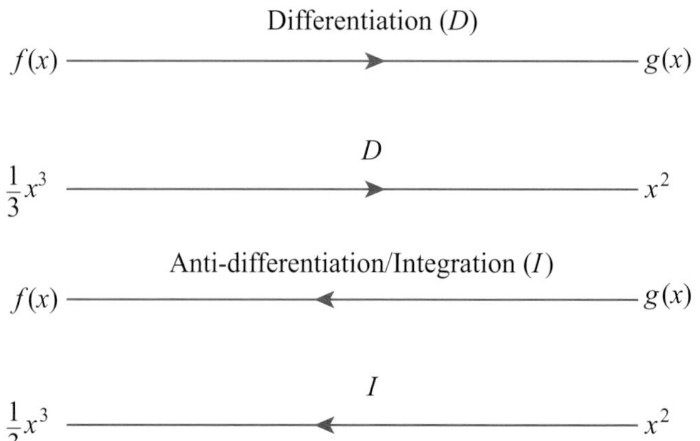

ACTIVITY 1

ACTION
Introducing the idea of integration (anti-differentiation)

OBJECTIVE
To think backwards from the derivative to the original function

Differentiation finds the slope of the tangent k to a curve $y = f(x)$ at any point (x, y) on the curve.

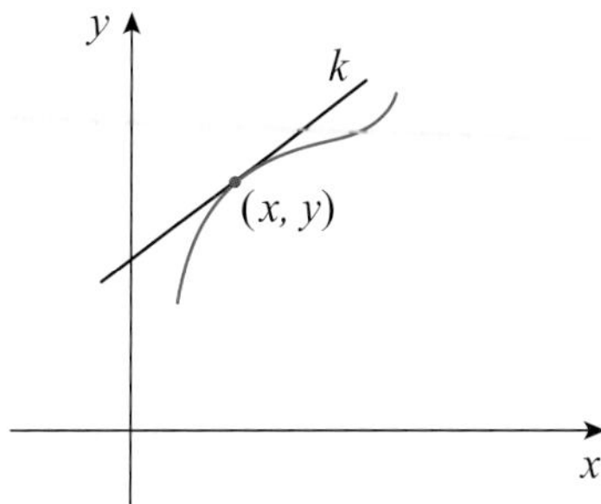

Slope of k at $(x, y) = \frac{dy}{dx} = f'(x)$.

Anti-differentiation finds the area A under a curve $y = g(x)$ by adding up little elements of area. It is just a big sum. That is why it is also known as integration.

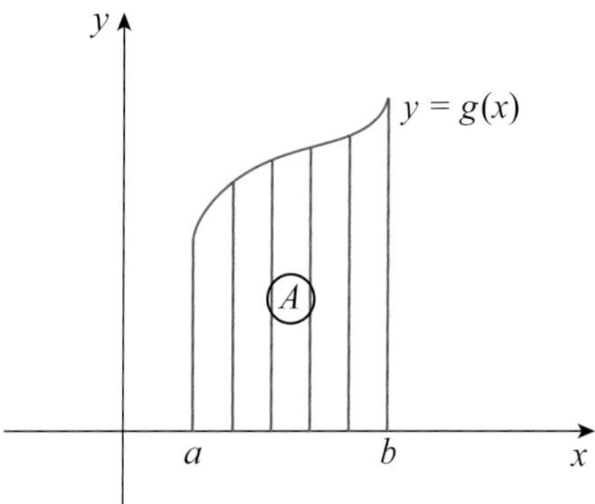

ACTIVITY 2

ACTION
Using rational power integration 1

OBJECTIVE
To think backwards from the derivative to the original function with functions involving rational powers

Notation

The notation for integrating a function $g(x)$ with respect to the variable x is given by: $\int g(x)\,dx$

$\int$ is the integral sign, $g(x)$ is the integrand (the function to be integrated) with respect to x and dx means with respect to x.

> $\int g(x)\,dx$ is shorthand for:
>
> Think of a function $f(x)$ such that when you differentiate it with respect to x, you get $g(x)$.

Integration is the reverse process of **differentiation**.

$\int g(x)\,dx$ is read as: the integral of $g(x)$ with respect to x.

The question	The answer
$\int g(x)\,dx$	$f(x)$, a function that differentiates to give $g(x)$ (Given $\frac{dy}{dx} = f'(x) = g(x)$, integration gives you $y = f(x)$)

The ultimate test for getting the correct answer $f(x)$ to an integral $\int g(x)\,dx$ is that when you differentiate $f(x)$, you get $g(x)$, i.e. $f'(x) = g(x)$.

You already know lots of integrals.

WORKED EXAMPLE The process of integration

Find $\int e^x dx$.

This means can you think of a function $f(x)$ such that when you differentiate it with respect to x you get $g(x) = e^x$. You know the answer because you have already done differentiation. The answer is e^x, of course.

$\therefore \int e^x dx = e^x = f(x)$

Check: $f(x) = e^x \Rightarrow f'(x) = e^x = g(x)$

However, it is not that simple, as some students might suggest other answers.

$\int e^x dx = e^x + 7$

Check: $f(x) = e^x + 7 \Rightarrow f'(x) = e^x = g(x)$

In fact, there are infinitely many answers: $e^x - 2$, $e^x - \frac{1}{3}$, $e^x + 73{\cdot}7$

In general: $f(x) = e^x + c$, where c is any constant, can be given as an answer.

25.2 Integration of six basic functions

ACTIVITY 3

ACTION
Using rational power integration 2

OBJECTIVE
To progress to more complex rational powers (a follow-on activity to Activity 2)

You already know the derivatives of six functions:

1. $y = e^x \Rightarrow \frac{dy}{dx} = e^x$
2. $y = a^x \Rightarrow \frac{dy}{dx} = a^x \ln a$
3. $y = \ln x \Rightarrow \frac{dy}{dx} = \frac{1}{x}$
4. $y = \sin x \Rightarrow \frac{dy}{dx} = \cos x$
5. $y = \cos x \Rightarrow \frac{dy}{dx} = -\sin x$
6. $y = x^{p+1} \Rightarrow \frac{dy}{dx} = (p+1)x^p$

A table of integrals can be drawn up from the above results:

1. $\int e^x \, dx = e^x + c$
2. $\int a^x \, dx = \frac{a^x}{\ln a} + c$
3. $\int \frac{1}{x} \, dx = \ln x + c$
4. $\int \cos x \, dx = \sin x + c$
5. $\int \sin x \, dx = -\cos x + c$
6. $\int x^p \, dx = \frac{1}{p+1} x^{p+1} + c, p \in \mathbb{R}, p \neq -1$

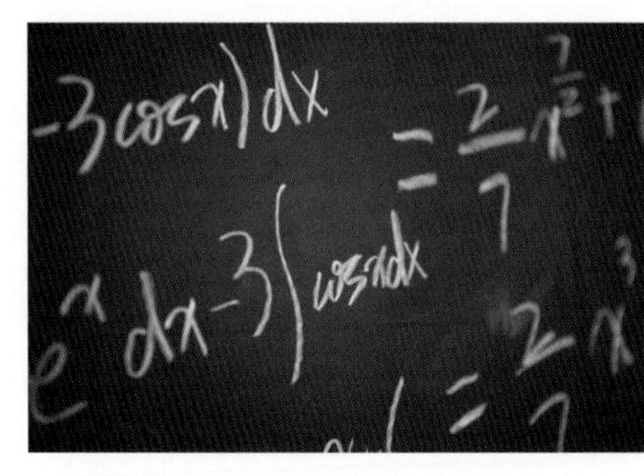

These results make sense because when you differentiate the function on the right-hand side in each case, you must get the function inside the integral sign on the left-hand side.

- $g(x) = x^{\frac{1}{2}}$

  $\int g(x)\,dx = \int x^{\frac{1}{2}}\,dx = \frac{x^{\frac{3}{2}}}{\frac{3}{2}} + c = \frac{2}{3}x^{\frac{3}{2}} + c$ [From integral **6** with $p = \frac{1}{2}$]

  Check: $f(x) = \frac{2}{3}x^{\frac{3}{2}} + c \Rightarrow f'(x) = x^{\frac{1}{2}} = g(x)$

- $g(x) = \frac{1}{x^3}$

  $\int g(x)\,dx = \int \frac{1}{x^3}\,dx = \int x^{-3}\,dx = \frac{x^{-2}}{-2} + c = -\frac{1}{2x^2} + c$ [From integral **6** with $p = -3$]

  Check: $f(x) = -\frac{1}{2x^2} + c = -\frac{1}{2}x^{-2} + c \Rightarrow f'(x) = x^{-3} = \frac{1}{x^3} = g(x)$

- $g(x) = 10^x$

  $\int g(x)\,dx = \int 10^x\,dx = \left(\frac{1}{\ln 10}\right)10^x + c = \frac{10^x}{\ln 10} + c$ [From integral **2** with $a = 10$]

  Check: $f(x) = \left(\frac{1}{\ln 10}\right)10^x + c \Rightarrow f'(x) = \left(\frac{1}{\ln 10}\right)(10^x \ln 10) + 0 = 10^x = g(x)$

Indefinite and definite integration

(a) Indefinite integration

When you integrate a function $g(x)$, you get an infinite number of answers that differ only by a constant.

$\int x^3\,dx = \frac{1}{4}x^4 + c$

Because there is no single definite answer, this process is known as **indefinite** integration.

TIP

Never forget to add a constant c in an indefinite integral.

WORKED EXAMPLE

Finding a value for the constant c

Find $\int \frac{1}{x}\,dx$ means can you think of a function which differentiates to give $\frac{1}{x}$.

$\int \frac{1}{x}\,dx = \ln x + c = f(x)$

You can find c, and hence $f(x)$ exactly, if you are given extra information about the function $f(x)$. This extra information is known as a boundary condition.

For example, find c if $f(1) = 2$.

$f(x) = \ln x + c$

$f(1) = \ln 1 + c = 2$

$\Rightarrow c = 2$

$\therefore f(x) = \ln x + 2$

(b) Definite integration

To eliminate the uncertainty in an integral, you can substitute values (boundary values/limits of integration) in for the variable after you have integrated.

A definite integral is written as: $\int_a^b g(x)\,dx$, where a and b are known as the 'limits of integration'.

It is defined as: $\int_a^b g(x)\,dx = [f(x)]_a^b = f(b) - f(a)$

- $\int_1^2 p\,dp = \left[\frac{p^2}{2}\right]_1^2 = \frac{(2)^2}{2} - \frac{(1)^2}{2} = \frac{3}{2}$

Steps for definite integration

1. Do the integral as normal to get $f(x)$.
2. Do **not** write in the constant c. Why?
3. Put the function $f(x)$ in a box: $[\ ]_a^b$
4. Substitute b for x in $f(x)$ first and then a for x in $f(x)$.
5. Subtract to get $f(b) - f(a)$.

- $\int_0^t e^x\,dx = [e^x]_0^t = e^t - e^0 = e^t - 1$

TIP

You can take constants out as factors from $[\ ]_a^b$

- $\int_2^4 x^2\,dx = \left[\frac{x^3}{3}\right]_2^4 = \frac{1}{3}[x^3]_2^4$

$$= \frac{1}{3}(4^3 - 2^3) = \frac{1}{3}(64 - 8) = \frac{56}{3}$$

Properties of definite integrals

1. $\int_a^a g(x)\,dx = 0$
2. $-\int_a^b g(x)\,dx = \int_b^a g(x)\,dx$
3. $\int_a^b g(x)\,dx = \int_a^c g(x)\,dx + \int_c^b g(x)\,dx$

Try to prove them.

- $\int_3^3 \frac{\sin^4 x}{\sqrt{1+x^2}}\,dx = 0$ [If the limits are the same, the value of the integral is zero.]

- $-\int_{\frac{\pi}{2}}^0 \cos x\,dx = \int_0^{\frac{\pi}{2}} \cos x\,dx = [\sin x]_0^{\frac{\pi}{2}} = \sin\frac{\pi}{2} - \sin 0 = 1$

  [Absorb the negative sign into the integral by switching the limits.]

The rules of integration

There are only three simple rules of integration.

1. The sum rule

$$\int (x^2 + x^3)\,dx = \int x^2\,dx + \int x^3 dx$$
$$= \tfrac{1}{3}x^3 + \tfrac{1}{4}x^4 + c = f(x)$$

Check: $f'(x) = \frac{1}{3} \times 3x^2 + \frac{1}{4} \times 4x^3 + 0 = x^2 + x^3$

You can integrate a sum of functions by integrating each one individually.

So, integrate each function as you go along.

- $\int (e^x + \sin x)\,dx = e^x - \cos x + c$ [Don't forget the c.]

2. Multiplication by a constant rule

$$\int 3x^7\,dx = 3\int x^7\,dx = 3 \times \frac{x^8}{8} + c = \frac{3}{8}x^8 + c = f(x)$$

Check: $f'(x) = \frac{3}{8} \times 8x^7 + 0 = 3x^7$

- $\int 5e^t\,dt = 5\int e^t\,dt = 5e^t + c$

You can take constants (only) outside integrals.

3. The one rule

- $\int dy = \int 1dy = y + c$
- $\int ds = \int 1ds = s + c$
- $\int 3dx = 3\int 1dx = 3 \times x + c = 3x + c$

$\int dx = \int 1dx = \int x^0dx = x^1 + c$

Now put all three rules together.

- $\int (5e^x - 2\sin x + x + 3)\,dx = 5e^x + 2\cos x + \frac{1}{2}x^2 + 3x + c$

EXAMPLE 1

Evaluate $\displaystyle\int_0^1 \left(\frac{2}{\sqrt{x}} - \frac{2^x}{3}\right) dx.$

Solution

Call the integral I.

$$I = \int_0^1 (2x^{-\frac{1}{2}} - \tfrac{1}{3} \times 2^x)\,dx$$

$$= \left[2\left(\frac{x^{\frac{1}{2}}}{\frac{1}{2}}\right) - \frac{1}{3}\left(\frac{2^x}{\ln 2}\right)\right]_0^1 = \left[4\sqrt{x} - \frac{2^x}{3\ln 2}\right]_0^1$$

$$= \left(4(1) - \frac{2^1}{3\ln 2}\right) - \left(0 - \frac{1}{3\ln 2}\right)$$

$$= 4 - \frac{2}{3\ln 2} + \frac{1}{3\ln 2} = 4 - \frac{1}{3\ln 2}$$

EXAMPLE 2

Evaluate $\displaystyle\int_0^{\frac{\pi}{6}} \left(3\cos x + \frac{e^x}{2} - 3\right) dx.$

Solution

Call the integral I.

$$I = \int_0^{\frac{\pi}{6}} \left(3\cos x + \frac{e^x}{2} - 3\right) dx$$

$$= \left[3\sin x + \tfrac{1}{2}e^x - 3x\right]_0^{\frac{\pi}{6}}$$

$$= \left(3\sin\left(\frac{\pi}{6}\right) + \frac{e^{\frac{\pi}{6}}}{2} - \frac{\pi}{2}\right) - \left(3\sin 0 + \frac{e^0}{2} - 0\right)$$

$$= \frac{3}{2} + \frac{e^{\frac{\pi}{6}}}{2} - \frac{\pi}{2} - \frac{1}{2} = 1 - \frac{\pi}{2} + \frac{e^{\frac{\pi}{6}}}{2}$$

EXERCISE 1

Integrate the following:

1. $\int e^x\,dx$
2. $\int 5e^x\,dx$
3. $\int_0^1 x^2\,dx$
4. $\int 3x^2\,dx$
5. $\int_1^2 2^x\,dx$
6. $\int 3 \times 4^x\,dx$
7. $\int_0^2 (e^x + x^2 + 2^x)\,dx$
8. $\int \left(\frac{e^x}{2} - 3x + \frac{2^x}{3}\right)dx$
9. $\int_0^{\frac{\pi}{3}} (3\sin x - 2^x)\,dx$
10. $\int_1^2 \left(\frac{1}{x} + x^2 - e^x\right)dx$
11. $\int \left(2e^x - 3 + \frac{1}{x}\right)dx$
12. $\int \left(\frac{2}{x} - 3e^x + \frac{3x^2}{4}\right)dx$
13. $\int_0^1 \left(\frac{x - e^x}{2}\right)dx$
14. $\int_0^1 \left(\frac{3 \times 10^x}{5}\right)dx$
15. $\int_0^{\frac{\pi}{4}} (\cos x + \sin x)\,dx$
16. $\int_1^2 \left(\frac{3}{x} + x\right)dx$
17. $\int \left(\frac{3e^x}{2} - \frac{1}{x}\right)dx$
18. $\int_1^4 \left(\frac{2}{\sqrt{x}} - \sqrt{x}\right)dx$
19. $\int_0^1 4^t\,dt$
20. $\int (k + 1)\,dp$, k is a constant
21. $\int_1^2 \left(\frac{2}{x^2} + \frac{3}{x} - 4\right)dx$
22. $\int_1^2 \left(x + \frac{1}{x}\right)^2 dx$

25.3 Integrating different types of functions

The central idea in evaluating $\int g(x)\,dx$ is to think of a function which when differentiated gives $g(x)$. However, for certain classes of functions, there are various shortcuts to speed up the process.

1. Rational power integration

This is the integration of functions that can be put in the form x^p.

Developing a shortcut

- $\int x^4\,dx = \frac{x^5}{5} + c = f(x)$

  Check: $f(x) = \frac{1}{5}x^5 + c \Rightarrow f'(x) = \frac{1}{5}(5x^4) + 0 = x^4$

- $\int x^{\frac{3}{5}}dx = \frac{x^{\frac{8}{5}}}{\frac{8}{5}} + c = \frac{5}{8}x^{\frac{8}{5}} + c = f(x)$

  Check: $f'(x) = \frac{5}{8}\left(\frac{8}{5}x^{\frac{3}{5}}\right) + 0 = x^{\frac{3}{5}}$

- $\int \frac{1}{x^{\frac{1}{2}}}\,dx = \int x^{-\frac{1}{2}}\,dx = \frac{x^{\frac{1}{2}}}{\frac{1}{2}} + c = 2x^{\frac{1}{2}} + c = f(x)$

  Check: $f'(x) = 2\left(\frac{1}{2}x^{-\frac{1}{2}}\right) + 0 = x^{-\frac{1}{2}} = \frac{1}{x^{\frac{1}{2}}}$

These results suggest a shortcut for evaluating $\int x^p \, dx, p \in \mathbb{R}$.

$$\int x^p \, dx = \frac{x^{p+1}}{p+1} + c = \frac{1}{p+1} x^{p+1} + c, p \in \mathbb{R}, p \neq -1$$

In words: Add one to the power and divide by **the new power**.

This formula works for all powers $p \in \mathbb{R}$, except $p = -1$.

When $p = -1$: $\int x^{-1} \, dx = \frac{x^0}{0} + c = \infty + c$. The formula fails.

This does not mean that the integral $\int x^{-1} \, dx = \int \frac{dx}{x}$ cannot be evaluated.

It can be done using the basic idea of integration:

'Can you think of a function which when differentiated gives $\frac{1}{x}$?'

This 'odd man out' integral $\int \frac{1}{x} \, dx$ will be dealt with later.

Steps for integrating more difficult rational functions

To integrate functions that can be simplified into sums of functions of the form ax^p, $a \in \mathbb{R}, p \in \mathbb{R}$, use the three steps below.

1. Simplify the integrand by multiplying out brackets and/or dividing and writing each term in the form ax^p, where a is a constant.
2. Integrate out term by term.
3. Simplify the answer, making sure there are no negative powers in it.
4. Substitute in limits of integration if given.

- $\int 3x^{12} \, dx = 3\int x^{12} \, dx = 3 \times \frac{x^{13}}{13} + c = \frac{3x^{13}}{13} + c$
- $\int \frac{3}{2x^2} \, dx = \int \frac{3}{2} x^{-2} \, dx = \frac{3}{2}\left(\frac{x^{-1}}{-1}\right) + c = -\frac{3}{2x} + c$

EXAMPLE 3

Evaluate $\int_1^2 \left(\frac{x^2+1}{x^2}\right) dx$.

Solution

$$I = \int_1^2 \left(\frac{x^2+1}{x^2}\right) dx = \int_1^2 (1 + x^{-2})\, dx$$

$$= \left[x + \frac{x^{-1}}{-1}\right]_1^2 = \left[x - \frac{1}{x}\right]_1^2$$

$$= \left(\left(2 - \frac{1}{2}\right) - \left(1 - \frac{1}{1}\right)\right) = \frac{3}{2}$$

EXAMPLE 4

Evaluate $\int \left(3x^2 - \frac{2}{\sqrt{x}} + 1\right) dx$.

Solution

$$I = \int \left(3x^2 - \frac{2}{\sqrt{x}} + 1\right) dx = \int (3x^2 - 2x^{-\frac{1}{2}} + 1)\, dx$$

$$= 3\left(\frac{x^3}{3}\right) - 2\left(\frac{x^{\frac{1}{2}}}{\frac{1}{2}}\right) + 1(x) + c$$

$$= x^3 - 4\sqrt{x} + x + c$$

EXAMPLE 5

Evaluate $\int_{-3}^{0} (x+1)^2\, dx$.

Solution

$$I = \int_{-3}^{0} (x+1)^2\, dx = \int_{-3}^{0} (x^2 + 2x + 1)\, dx$$

$$= \left[\frac{x^3}{3} + 2\left(\frac{x^2}{2}\right) + 1(x)\right]_{-3}^{0} = \left[\frac{x^3}{3} + x^2 + x\right]_{-3}^{0}$$

$$= \left((0+0+0) - \left(\frac{-27}{3} + 9 - 3\right)\right) = 3$$

ACTIVITY 4

ACTION
Using more difficult rational power integration

OBJECTIVE
To integrate rational powers of brackets with linear expressions

Extending the basic rational power integration rule

Integrals of the form $\int (ax+b)^p\, dx$, where a and b are constants, can also be integrated in your head by noting the following examples.

- $\int (x+1)^7\, dx = \frac{1}{1} \times \frac{(x+1)^8}{8} + c = \frac{(x+1)^8}{8} + c$

Check: $f(x) = \frac{1}{8}(x+1)^8 + c \Rightarrow f'(x) = \frac{8}{8}(x+1)^7(1) = (x+1)^7$

- $\int \frac{1}{(2x+3)^2}\, dx = \int (2x+3)^{-2}\, dx = \frac{1}{2} \times \frac{(2x+3)^{-1}}{-1} + c = -\frac{1}{2(2x+3)} + c$
- $\int \sqrt{3x-7}\, dx = \int (3x-7)^{\frac{1}{2}}\, dx = \frac{1}{3} \times \frac{(3x-7)^{\frac{3}{2}}}{\frac{3}{2}} + c = \frac{2}{9}(3x-7)^{\frac{3}{2}} + c$

$$\int (ax+b)^p\, dx = \frac{1}{a} \times \frac{(ax+b)^{p+1}}{p+1} + c,\ p \in \mathbb{R}, p \neq -1$$

In words: $\frac{1}{a} \times$ (add one to the power and divide by the new power)

EXAMPLE 6

Show that $\int (ax+b)^p\,dx = \frac{1}{a} \times \frac{(ax+b)^{p+1}}{p+1} + c$.

Solution

$$f(x) = \frac{1}{a}\frac{(ax+b)^{p+1}}{p+1} + c.$$

$$f'(x) = \frac{1}{a}\frac{(p+1)(ax+b)^p}{p+1} \times a = (ax+b)^p$$

EXAMPLE 7

Evaluate $\int_{\frac{2}{3}}^{1} (3x-2)^{100}\,dx$.

Solution

$$\int_{\frac{2}{3}}^{1} (3x-2)^{100}\,dx = \left[\frac{1}{3} \times \frac{(3x-2)^{101}}{101}\right]_{\frac{2}{3}}^{1}$$

$$= \frac{1}{303}\left[(3x-2)^{101}\right]_{\frac{2}{3}}^{1} = \frac{1}{303}(1^{101} - 0^{101}) = \frac{1}{303}$$

EXERCISE 2

Evaluate the following:

1. $\int x^{15}\,dx$
2. $\int \sqrt{x}\,dx$
3. $\int \frac{4}{x^3}\,dx$
4. $\int_1^2 \left(x^2 + \frac{1}{x^2}\right)dx$
5. $\int_{-1}^{-2} \left(x + \frac{3}{x}\right)^2 dx$
6. $\int_0^1 (x^2 + 2x - 5)\,dx$
7. $\int (\sqrt{x} - 1)(\sqrt{x} - 1)\,dx$
8. $\int_0^1 (2 - t^2)\sqrt{t}\,dt$
9. $\int \left(\frac{2 - t^2}{\sqrt{t}}\right) dt$
10. $\int_0^2 \left(\frac{x^2 + x - 12}{x+4}\right)dx$
11. $\int \left(\frac{x^3 + 1}{x+1}\right) dx$
12. $\int_1^2 \left(x^2 + \frac{1}{x^2}\right)dx$
13. $\int (x+1)^5\,dx$
14. $\int_1^2 (2x-1)^3\,dx$
15. $\int_0^3 \sqrt{x+1}\,dx$
16. $\int_0^2 \frac{dx}{\sqrt{4x+1}}\,dx$
17. $\int \frac{dx}{(x+1)^2}$
18. $\int_0^1 \frac{4\,dx}{(3x+1)^3}$
19. $\int_0^1 \frac{1}{(2x+1)^{\frac{3}{2}}}\,dx$

ACTIVITY 5

ACTION
Using exponential integration

OBJECTIVE
To think of functions which, when differentiated, give exponential functions

2. Exponential integration

This is the integration of functions of the form e^{px+q} and a^{px+q}, where a, e, p, q are constants.

The basis of integrating all functions of the form e^{px+q} is:

$$\int e^x\,dx = e^x + c$$

Using this result and the rules of differentiation, $\int e^{px+q}\,dx$ can be evaluated.

WORKED EXAMPLE Exponential integration

1. Find $\int e^{2x}\,dx$.

Try e^{2x}. It nearly works. It differentiates to $2e^{2x}$. So, divide it by 2.

$$\int e^{2x}\,dx = \frac{e^{2x}}{2} + c = \tfrac{1}{2}e^{2x} + c = f(x)$$

Check: $f'(x) = \tfrac{1}{2}e^{2x} + c \Rightarrow f'(x) = \tfrac{1}{2}(e^{2x} \times 2) + 0 = e^{2x}$ [It works.]

2. Find $\int e^{3x-7}\,dx$.

Try e^{3x-7}. Again, we are close. It differentiates to $3e^{3x-7}$. So, divide it by 3.

$$\int e^{3x-7}\,dx = \frac{e^{3x-7}}{3} + c = \frac{1}{3}e^{3x-7} + c = f(x)$$

Check: $f(x) = \tfrac{1}{3}e^{3x-7} + c \Rightarrow f'(x) = \tfrac{1}{3}(e^{3x-7} \times 3) + 0 = e^{3x-7}$ [It works.]

$$\int e^{px+q}\,dx = \frac{1}{p}e^{px+q} + c, \text{ where } p, q \text{ are constants.}$$

Steps for integrating functions of the form $\int e^{px+q}\,dx$

1. Tidy up the algebra so that each exponential term is in the form e^{px+q}.
2. Integrate out term by term.

- $\int 2e^{5x}\,dx = 2\left(\frac{e^{5x}}{5}\right) + c = \frac{2}{5}e^{5x} + c$
- $\int \frac{3}{e^{4x}}\,dx = \int 3e^{-4x}\,dx = 3\left(\frac{e^{-4x}}{-4}\right) + c = -\frac{3}{4e^{4x}} + c$

EXAMPLE 8

Evaluate $\int_0^1 \sqrt{e^x}\,dx$.

Solution

$$\int_0^1 \sqrt{e^x}\,dx = \int_0^1 e^{\frac{1}{2}x}\,dx$$

$$= \left[\frac{e^{\frac{1}{2}x}}{\frac{1}{2}}\right]_0^1 = 2\left[e^{\frac{1}{2}x}\right]_0^1$$

$$= 2(e^{\frac{1}{2}} - e^0)$$

$$= 2(\sqrt{e} - 1)$$

EXAMPLE 9

Evaluate $\int_0^{\ln 8} \sqrt[3]{\frac{e^{3x-1}}{e^{2x-1}}}\,dx$.

Solution

$$\int_0^{\ln 8} \sqrt[3]{\frac{e^{3x-1}}{e^{2x-1}}}\,dx = \int_0^{\ln 8} (e^x)^{\frac{1}{3}}\,dx$$

$$= \int_0^{\ln 8} e^{\frac{1}{3}x}\,dx = \left[\frac{e^{\frac{1}{3}x}}{\frac{1}{3}}\right]_0^{\ln 8}$$

$$= 3(e^{\frac{1}{3}\ln 8} - e^0)$$

$$= 3(e^{\ln 2} - e^0)$$

$$= 3(2 - 1) = 3$$

Exponential functions of the form a^{px+q}

The basis of integrating all functions of the form a^{px+q} is:

$$\int a^x \, dx = \frac{a^x}{\ln a} + c$$

Just as for e^{px+q}, this result can be extended to:

$$\int a^{px+q} \, dx = \frac{a^{px+q}}{p \ln a} + c$$

- $\int 7(10^x) \, dx = 7\left(\frac{10^x}{\ln 10}\right) + c = \frac{7 \times 10^x}{\ln 10} + c$
- $\int \frac{3}{2^x} \, dx = 3\int 2^{-x} \, dx = 3\left(\frac{2^{-x}}{-1 \ln 2}\right) + c = -\frac{3}{2^x \ln 2} + c$

EXAMPLE 10

Evaluate:

(a) $\int_0^1 \sqrt{4^x} \, dx$ **(b)** $\int \frac{1}{3^{2x-7}} \, dx$

Solution

(a) $\int_0^1 \sqrt{4^x} \, dx = \int_0^1 4^{\frac{1}{2}x} \, dx$

$= \left[\frac{4^{\frac{1}{2}x}}{\frac{1}{2} \ln 4}\right]_0^1 = \frac{2}{\ln 4}(4^{\frac{1}{2}} - 4^0)$

$= \frac{2}{\ln 4}(2 - 1) = \frac{2}{\ln 4}$

Can you do this integral in a different way?

(b) $\int \frac{1}{3^{2x-7}} \, dx = \int 3^{-2x+7} \, dx$

$= \frac{3^{-2x+7}}{-2 \ln 3} + c$

$= -\frac{1}{2 \ln 3(3^{2x-7})} + c$

EXERCISE 3

Evaluate the following:

1. $\int e^{5x} \, dx$
2. $\int e^{\frac{2}{3}x} \, dx$
3. $\int e^{-2x} \, dx$
4. $\int_{-1}^{0} e^{3x+5} \, dx$
5. $\int_0^1 (e^{x+3})^2 \, dx$
6. $\int_2^3 3e^{4x-7} \, dx$
7. $\int \left(\frac{e^x}{e^{2x-3}}\right) dx$
8. $\int_0^{\ln 2} \left(\frac{1}{e^x} + \frac{2}{e^{2x}}\right) dx$
9. $\int_1^4 e^{\frac{1}{2}\ln x} \, dx$
10. $\int_0^{\ln 2} (e^x + 1)^2 \, dx$
11. $\int 5^x \, dx$
12. $\int_0^1 3(2^{-x}) \, dx$
13. $\int \frac{1}{2^{3x}} \, dx$
14. $\int 2^{kt} \, dt$, k is a constant
15. $\int \left(\frac{10}{3^{kt}}\right) dt$, k is a constant
16. $\int \frac{5^{3x}}{5^{x-1}} \, dx$

ACTIVITY 6

ACTION
Using log integration

OBJECTIVE
To think of functions which, when differentiated, give log functions

3. Inverse linear integration

This is the integration of the inverse linear function. These are functions of the form $\frac{1}{px+q}$ where $p, q \in \mathbb{R}$.

The basis of integrating all functions of the form $\frac{1}{px+q}$ is:

$$\int \frac{1}{x}\,dx = \ln x + c \ (x > 0)$$

This result can be extended to integrate inverse linear functions of the form $\int \frac{dx}{px+q}$.

The integral $\int \frac{1}{x}\,dx$ can also be written as $\int \frac{dx}{x}$ or $\int x^{-1}\,dx$.

WORKED EXAMPLE

Log integration

1. Find $\int \frac{dx}{x+7}$.

Try $\ln(x+7)$. It works. It differentiates to $\frac{1}{x+7}$.

$$\int \frac{dx}{x+7} = \frac{1}{x+7} + c$$

2. Find $\int \frac{dx}{3x+11}$.

Try $\ln(3x+11)$. It nearly works. It differentiates to $\frac{3}{3x+11}$. So, divide it by 3.

$$\int \frac{dx}{3x+11} = \tfrac{1}{3}\ln(3x+11) + c = f(x)$$

Check: $f(x) = \tfrac{1}{3}\ln(3x+11) + c$

$$\Rightarrow f'(x) = \frac{1}{3}\left(\frac{3}{3x+11}\right) + 0 = \frac{1}{3x+11}$$

$$\int \frac{dx}{px+q} = \frac{1}{p}\ln(px+q) + c, \text{ where } p, q \in \mathbb{R}.$$

- $\int \frac{3}{2x}\,dx = \tfrac{3}{2}\int \frac{dx}{x} = \tfrac{3}{2}\ln x + c$
- $\int_0^1 \frac{dx}{x+1} = \left[\ln(x+1)\right]_0^1 = \ln 2 - \ln 1 = \ln 2$
- $\int \left(\frac{3}{5-3x}\right) dx = 3\int \frac{dx}{(-3x+5)} = 3\left(-\frac{1}{3}\ln(-3x+5)\right) + c = -\ln(5-3x) + c$

EXERCISE 4

Evaluate the following:

1. $\int \frac{dx}{3x}$
2. $\int \frac{dx}{x+2}$
3. $\int_4^5 \frac{dx}{x-3}$
4. $\int_1^2 \frac{dx}{2x+1}$
5. $\int_2^3 \frac{dx}{3x-5}$
6. $\int_0^2 \frac{dt}{t+1}$
7. $\int \frac{3\,dx}{\frac{1}{3}x+2}$
8. $\int \frac{5\,dx}{4-3x}$
9. $\int_e^{e^2} \frac{dt}{t}$
10. $\int \frac{dt}{kt+\alpha}$, k, α are constants
11. $\int_3^4 \frac{ds}{2s-5}$
12. $\int_2^3 \frac{x-1}{x^2-1}\,dx$

ACTIVITY 7

ACTION
Using trigonometric integration

OBJECTIVE
To think of functions which, when differentiated, give trigonometric functions

4. Trigonometric integration

This is the integration of trigonometric functions of the form $\sin(px+q)$ and $\cos(px+q)$, $p, q \in \mathbb{R}$. All trigonometric integration is based on two results:

$$\int \sin x\,dx = -\cos x + c$$

$$\int \cos x\,dx = \sin x + c$$

WARNING
It is important to realise that these results are true only if the angle x is in radians.

These results can be extended to integrating functions of the form $\int \cos(px+q)\,dx$ and $\int \sin(px+q)\,dx$.

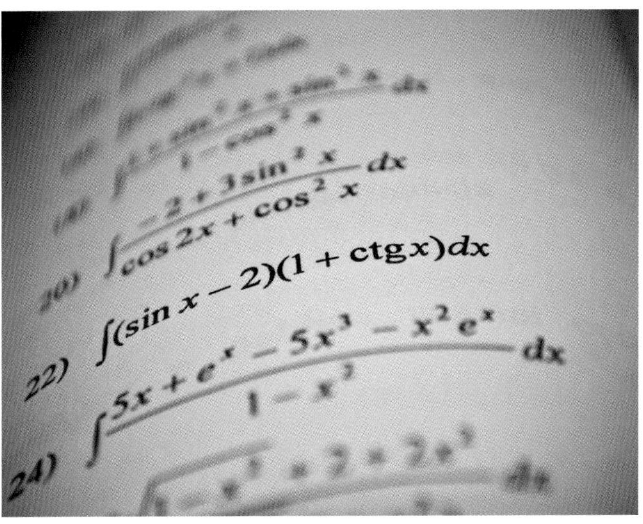

WORKED EXAMPLE Trigonometric integration

1. Find $\int \cos 2x\, dx$.

Try $\sin 2x$. It nearly works. It differentiates to $2\cos 2x$. So, divide it by 2.

$$\int \cos 2x\, dx = \frac{\sin 2x}{2} + c = \tfrac{1}{2}\sin 2x + c = f(x)$$

Check: $f(x) = \tfrac{1}{2}\sin 2x + c \Rightarrow f'(x) = \tfrac{1}{2}\cos 2x \times 2 + 0 = \cos 2x$ [It works.]

2. Find $\int \sin\left(\frac{x}{4}\right) dx$.

Try $-\cos\left(\frac{x}{4}\right)$. Again, it nearly works. It differentiates to $\sin\left(\frac{x}{4}\right) \times \frac{1}{4}$. So, divide it by $\frac{1}{4}$.

$$\int \sin\left(\frac{x}{4}\right) dx = \frac{-\cos\left(\frac{x}{4}\right)}{\frac{1}{4}} + c = -4\cos\left(\frac{x}{4}\right) + c = f(x)$$

Check: $f(x) = -4\cos\left(\frac{x}{4}\right) + c \Rightarrow f'(x) = -4\left(-\sin\left(\frac{x}{4}\right)\right) \times \frac{1}{4} + c = \sin\left(\frac{x}{4}\right)$

3. Find $\int \cos\left(2x - \frac{\pi}{3}\right) dx$.

Try $\sin\left(2x - \frac{\pi}{3}\right)$. It differentiates to $\cos\left(2x - \frac{\pi}{3}\right) \times 2$. So, divide it by 2.

$$\int \cos\left(2x - \frac{\pi}{3}\right) dx = \frac{1}{2}\sin\left(2x - \frac{\pi}{3}\right) + c = f(x)$$

Check: $f(x) = \frac{1}{2}\sin\left(2x - \frac{\pi}{3}\right) \Rightarrow f'(x) = \frac{1}{2}\cos\left(2x - \frac{\pi}{3}\right) \times 2 + 0 = \cos\left(2x - \frac{\pi}{3}\right)$

4. Find $\int \sin(5x - 7)\, dx$.

Try $-\cos(5x - 7)$. It differentiates to $5\sin(5x - 7)$. So, divide by 5.

$$\int \sin(5x - 7)\, dx = -\tfrac{1}{5}\cos(5x - 7) + c = f(x)$$

Check: $f(x) = -\tfrac{1}{5}\cos(5x - 7) + c \Rightarrow f'(x) = -\tfrac{1}{5}(-\sin(5x - 7)) \times 5 = \sin(5x - 7)$

$\int \cos(px + q)\, dx = \frac{1}{p}\sin(px + q) + c$ and

$\int \sin(px + q)\, dx = -\frac{1}{p}\cos(px + q) + c$, where $p, q \in \mathbb{R}$.

EXAMPLE 11

Evaluate:

(a) $\int \sin 5x \, dx$

(b) $\int 3\cos\left(x - \frac{\pi}{2}\right) dx$

(c) $I = \int_0^{\frac{\pi}{3}} \cos 4x \, dx$

Solution

(a) $\int \sin 5x \, dx = -\frac{1}{5}\cos 5x + c$

(b) $\int 3\cos\left(x - \frac{\pi}{2}\right) dx = 3\sin\left(x - \frac{\pi}{2}\right) + c$

(c) $I = \int_0^{\frac{\pi}{3}} \cos 4x \, dx = \left[\frac{1}{4}\sin 4x\right]_0^{\frac{\pi}{3}}$

$= \frac{1}{4}\left(\sin \frac{4\pi}{3} - \sin 0\right)$

$= \frac{1}{4}\left(-\frac{\sqrt{3}}{2}\right) = -\frac{\sqrt{3}}{8}$

More difficult trigonometric integration

Products of two sines or two cosines or products of a sine and a cosine can be integrated by changing them into sums.
Examples: $\sin 2x \cos 3x$, $\sin 4x \sin x$, $\cos 2x \cos 5x$.

To integrate these functions:

1. Change the product into a sum using the following formulae, which are in the *Formulae and Tables* book:

   $2\cos A \cos B = \cos(A + B) + \cos(A - B)$

   $2\sin A \cos B = \sin(A + B) + \sin(A - B)$

   $2\sin A \sin B = \cos(A - B) - \cos(A + B)$

   $2\cos A \sin B = \sin(A + B) - \sin(A - B)$

2. Integrate each trigonometric function.

EXAMPLE 12

Find $\int \sin 2x \cos 3x \, dx$.

Solution

$\int \sin 2x \cos 3x \, dx = \frac{1}{2}\int 2\sin 2x \cos 3x \, dx$ [Change the product to a sum.]

$= \frac{1}{2}\int \sin 5x + \sin(-x) \, dx$ [Deal with the negative sign inside the trigonometric function.]

$= \frac{1}{2}\int (\sin 5x - \sin x) \, dx$

$= \frac{1}{2}\left(\frac{-\cos 5x}{5} + \cos x\right) + c$

$= -\frac{1}{10}\cos 5x + \frac{1}{2}\cos x + c$

EXAMPLE 13

Evaluate $\int_0^{\frac{\pi}{4}} \cos 2x \cos 4x \, dx$.

Solution

$$I = \int_0^{\frac{\pi}{4}} \cos 2x \cos 4x \, dx = \frac{1}{2}\int_0^{\frac{\pi}{4}} 2\cos 2x \cos 4x \, dx$$

$$= \frac{1}{2}\int_0^{\frac{\pi}{4}} (\cos 6x + \cos(-2x))\, dx$$

$$= \frac{1}{2}\int_0^{\frac{\pi}{4}} (\cos 6x + \cos 2x)\, dx$$

$$= \frac{1}{2}\left[\frac{\sin 6x}{6} + \frac{\sin 2x}{2}\right]_0^{\frac{\pi}{4}}$$

$$= \frac{1}{2}\left\{\left(\frac{\sin \frac{3}{2}\pi}{6} + \frac{\sin \frac{1}{2}\pi}{2}\right) - \left(\frac{\sin 0}{6} + \frac{\sin 0}{2}\right)\right\}$$

$$= \frac{1}{2}\left\{\left(\frac{-1}{6} + \frac{1}{2}\right) - 0\right\} = \frac{1}{2}\left(\frac{1}{3}\right) = \frac{1}{6}$$

EXERCISE 5

Evaluate the following:

1. $\int \cos 2x \, dx$
2. $\int_0^{\frac{\pi}{2}} \cos 7x \, dx$
3. $\int_{\frac{3}{2}}^{3} \sin(2x - 3)\, dx$
4. $\int_0^{\frac{\pi}{4}} 3\sin\left(\frac{\pi}{2} - x\right) dx$
5. $\int_0^{\frac{\pi}{8}} \cos 6x \, dx$
6. $\int_0^{\frac{\pi}{2}} \cos 5x \sin 3x \, dx$
7. $\int_0^{\frac{\pi}{2}} \sin 4t \sin 3t \, dt$
8. $\int_0^{\frac{\pi}{2}} 7\sin 2x \sin 3x \, dx$
9. $\int_0^{\frac{\pi}{2}} -5\sin x \cos 2x \, dx$
10. $\int \sin x \cos x \, dx$

5. Miscellaneous integration

When dealing with any integral, follow the steps below.

1. Decide if it is a definite or indefinite integral.
2. Look at the functions inside the integrand (rational/exponential/ inverse linear/trigonometric).
3. Simplify the integrand.
4. Integrate out term by term using the rules of integration.
5. Substitute the limits of integration if required.
6. Tidy up the answer.

EXAMPLE 14

Evaluate $\int_0^{\frac{\pi}{4}} (\cos x + \sin x)^2\, dx$.

Solution

$$I = \int_0^{\frac{\pi}{4}} (\cos x + \sin x)^2\, dx = \int_0^{\frac{\pi}{4}} (\cos^2 x + 2\sin x \cos x + \sin^2 x)\, dx.$$

$$= \int_0^{\frac{\pi}{4}} (1 + \sin 2x)\, dx = \left[x - \frac{1}{2}\cos 2x\right]_0^{\frac{\pi}{4}}$$

$$= \left(\frac{\pi}{4} - \frac{1}{2}\cos\left(\frac{\pi}{2}\right)\right) - \left(0 - \frac{1}{2}\cos 0\right) = \frac{\pi}{4} + \frac{1}{2}$$

EXAMPLE 15

Evaluate $\int_8^{27} e^{\frac{1}{3}\ln x}\, dx$.

Solution

$$I = \int_8^{27} e^{\frac{1}{3}\ln x}\, dx = \int_8^{27} e^{\ln x^{\frac{1}{3}}}\, dx = \int_8^{27} x^{\frac{1}{3}}\, dx$$

$$= \left[\frac{x^{\frac{4}{3}}}{\frac{4}{3}}\right]_8^{27} = \frac{3}{4}\left(27^{\frac{4}{3}} - 8^{\frac{4}{3}}\right) = \frac{3}{4}(81 - 16) = \frac{195}{4}$$

EXERCISE 6

Evaluate the following:

1. $\int \left(x + \frac{1}{\sqrt{x}}\right)^2 dx$

2. $\int \left(\frac{3x^2 - x}{2x}\right) dx$

3. $\int_1^3 dt$

4. $\int (2x - 1)(2x + 1)\, dx$

5. $\int_1^2 \left(x^2 + \frac{1}{x} + e^x\right) dx$

6. $\int \sqrt{\frac{e^{2x-1}}{e^{-4x-5}}}\, dx$

7. $\int (e^x + e^{-x})^2\, dx$

8. $\int_0^{\frac{\pi}{4}} \sin^2 x\, dx$

   (Hint: $\sin^2 A = \frac{1}{2}(1 - \cos 2A)$)

9. $\int_2^3 \ln e^{x^2} dx$

10. $\int_0^{\frac{\pi}{4}} \sin^2 2x\, dx$

11. $\int_{\frac{4}{5}}^1 (5x - 2)^8\, dx$

12. $\int_0^{\frac{\pi}{4}} \frac{2\cos^3 x}{1 + \cos 2x}\, dx$

CHAPTER 26

Applications of Integration

Learning Outcomes

- To realise you are finding the area under a curve when you integrate a function.
- To find the area between curves.
- To solve differential equations.
- To find the average value of a function.

26.1 The area under a curve

In the mensuration section, an **approximate** value for the area under a curve is calculated. The area is split into strips of equal width and the **trapezoidal rule** is applied. This idea can be used to find a formula that gives the exact area under a curve.

The area formula

If you divide the area under the curve $y = g(x)$ into strips of equal width $(x_2 - x_1) = \Delta x$, the approximate area of the highlighted strip $\approx y\Delta x$. Therefore, the approximate area A_1 of the whole region under the curve from $x = a$ to $x = b$ is given by:

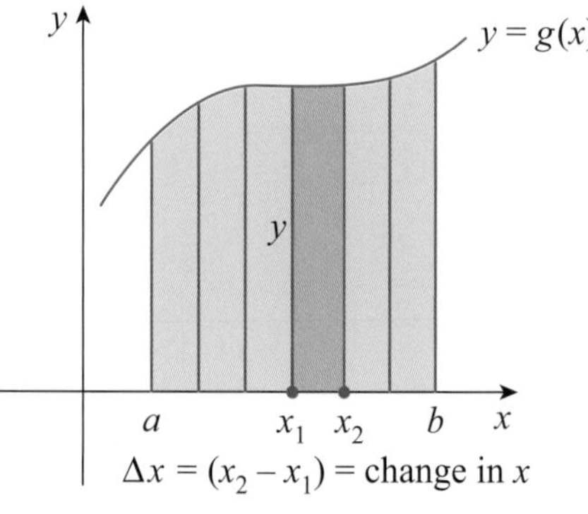

$$A_1 \approx \sum_{x=a}^{x=b} y\Delta x$$

Suppose, for the sake of argument, A_1 turns out to be 4·9. If this procedure is repeated by doubling the number of strips and so making Δx smaller, the second approximation for the area may be $A_2 \approx 4{\cdot}99$. This procedure can be continued by making the width Δx smaller and smaller and generating areas that get closer and closer to the exact area. Therefore, as $\Delta x \to 0$, the area $\to A$ (the exact area).

This limiting procedure can be summarised as:

$A = \lim\limits_{\Delta x \to 0} \sum\limits_{x=a}^{x=b} y\Delta x$ = the exact area under the curve $y = g(x)$ and between the lines $x = a$, $x = b$ and the x-axis.

By an incredibly complicated theorem known as the fundamental theorem of calculus, it can be shown that $\lim_{\Delta x \to 0} \sum_{x=a}^{x=b} y\Delta x = \int_a^b y\,dx$.

The area under the curve $y = g(x)$ and between the lines $x = a$, $x = b$ and the x-axis is given by $A = \int_a^b y\,dx$.

Integration is just a big sum.

Using the area formula

1. The formula $A = \int_a^b y\,dx$, where $y = g(x)$, is the formula for the area under the curve $y = g(x)$ with strips onto the x-axis from $x = a$ to $x = b$.
2. The formula for strips onto the y-axis is $\int_a^b x\,dy$, where $x = g(y)$.
3. The area must be positive.

   If a curve crosses the x-axis between a and b, you have to split the integral into two parts:

   $A_1 = \int_a^c y\,dx > 0$ [positive] and $A_2 = \int_c^b y\,dx < 0$ [negative]

   The total area A is then given by $A = A_1 + |A_2|$.

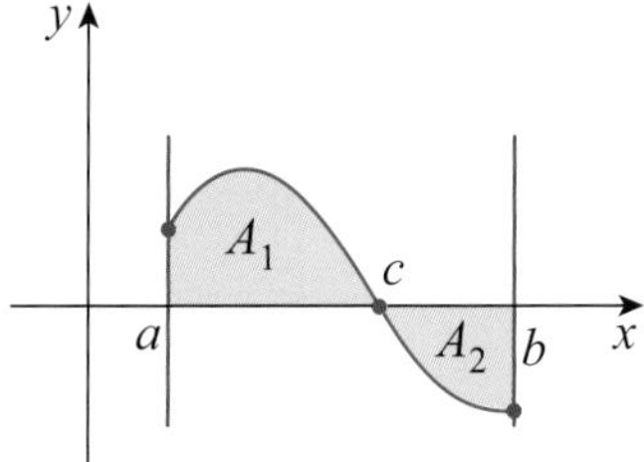

4. Always write the limits of integration in $\int_a^b$ from left (a) to right (b) on the x-axis and from down (a) to up (b) on the y-axis.

Conclusion

1. $A = \int_a^b y\,dx$ = area under the curve $y = g(x)$ and between the lines $x = a$, $x = b$ and the x-axis.

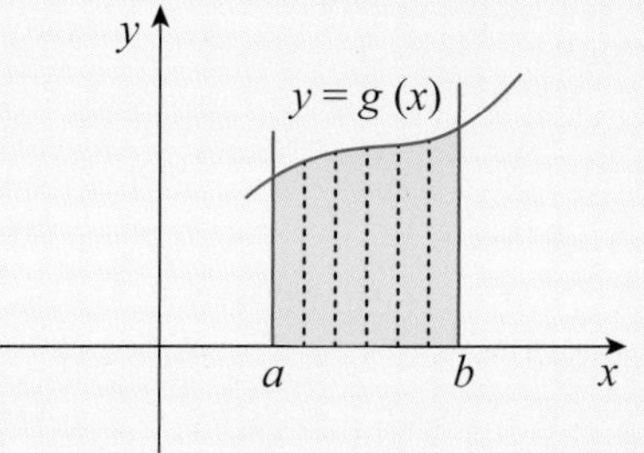

2. $A = \int_a^b x\,dy$ = area under the curve and between the lines $y = a$, $y = b$ and the y-axis.

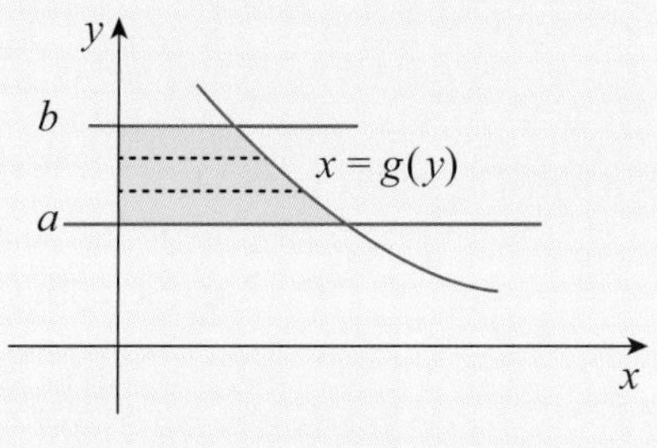

EXAMPLE 1

A swimming pool has a shape described by the equation $y = 5x - x^2$, as shown. Find the area of the pool if it is bounded by the lines $x = 0$ and $x = 4$.

Solution

Limits: $a = 0$, $b = 4$

$$A = \int_0^4 y\,dx = \int_0^4 (5x - x^2)\,dx$$

$$A = \left[\frac{5x^2}{2} - \frac{x^3}{3}\right]_0^4$$

$$= \frac{5 \times 16}{2} - \frac{4^3}{3}$$

$$= 40 - \frac{64}{3}$$

$$= \frac{56}{3} \text{ square units}$$

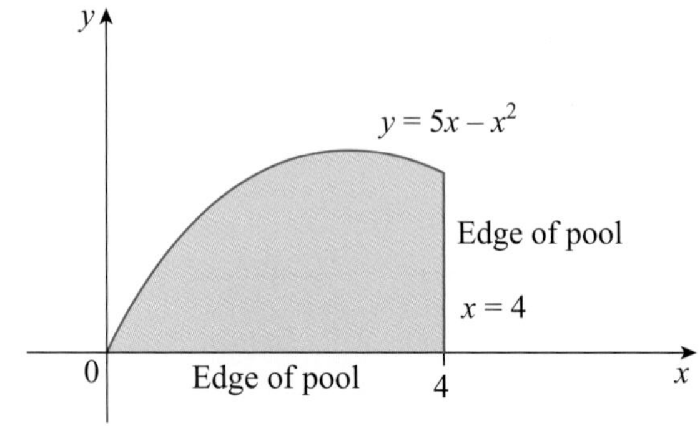

EXAMPLE 2

The area bounded by the curve $y = \dfrac{6}{x+1}$, the x-axis and the lines $x = 2$ and $x = 12$ is shown.

(a) Find an approximation for this area using the trapezoidal rule.

(b) Find the exact area by integration.

(c) Find the percentage error in the true value of the area calculated by the trapezoidal formula.

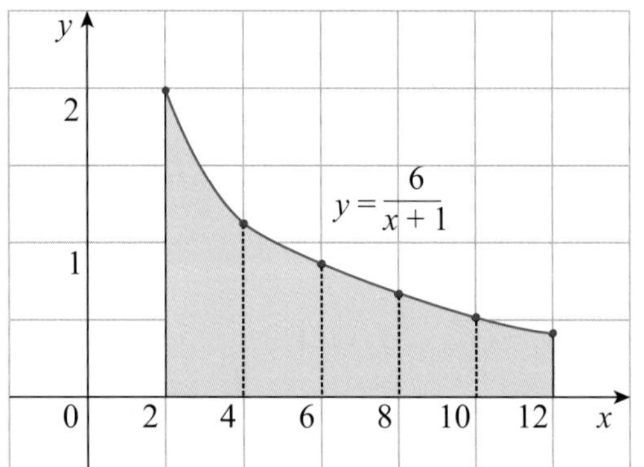

Solution

(a) The area using the trapezoidal rule:

x	2	4	6	8	10	12
y	2	$\frac{6}{5}$	$\frac{6}{7}$	$\frac{6}{9}$	$\frac{6}{11}$	$\frac{6}{13}$

$$A_1 = \frac{2}{2}\left[\left(2 + \frac{6}{13}\right) + 2\left(\frac{6}{5} + \frac{6}{7} + \frac{6}{9} + \frac{6}{11}\right)\right] = 9{\cdot}0$$

(b) The exact area: $A_2 = \displaystyle\int_2^{12} \frac{6\,dx}{x+1}$

$$= 6\,[\ln(x+1)]_2^{12}$$

$$= 6\{\ln 13 - \ln 3\}$$

$$= 6\ln\left(\frac{13}{3}\right)$$

(c) The percentage error in the true value of the area: $\dfrac{|A_2 - A_1|}{A_2} \times 100\% = \dfrac{\left|6\ln\left(\frac{13}{3}\right) - 9\right|}{6\ln\left(\frac{13}{3}\right)} \times 100 = 2{\cdot}3\%$

ACTIVITY 8

ACTION
Finding the area under curves

OBJECTIVE
To use geometric and integration techniques to find the areas under curves

EXAMPLE 3

An underground electricity cable crosses the road AB at C. The shaded area shown is off limits to the public. Find this area if the cable's path is described by the equation $y = \sqrt{x}(x - 4)$.

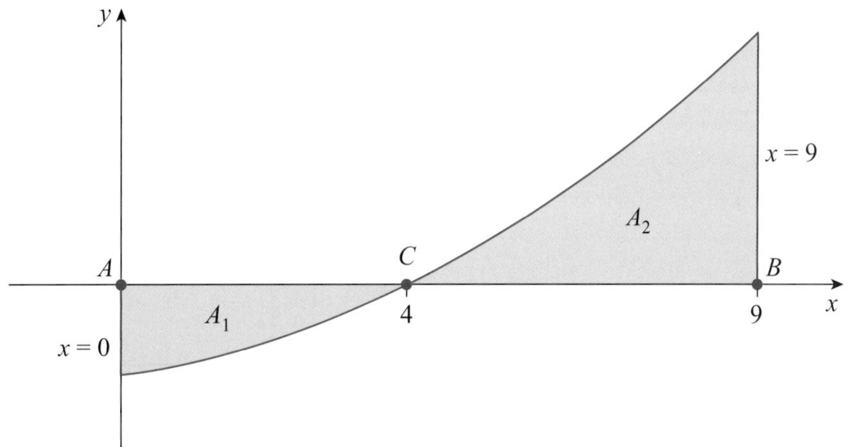

Solution

$$A = |A_1| + A_2$$

$$= \left|\int_0^4 y\,dx\right| + \int_4^9 y\,dx$$

$$= \left|\int_0^4 \left(x^{\frac{3}{2}} - 4x^{\frac{1}{2}}\right)dx\right| + \int_4^9 \left(x^{\frac{3}{2}} - 4x^{\frac{1}{2}}\right)dx$$

$$= \left|\left[\frac{2}{5}x^{\frac{5}{2}} - \frac{8}{3}x^{\frac{3}{2}}\right]_0^4\right| + \left[\frac{2}{5}x^{\frac{5}{2}} - \frac{8}{3}x^{\frac{3}{2}}\right]_4^9$$

$$= \left|\frac{2}{5}(32) - \frac{8}{3}(8)\right| + \left\{\left(\frac{2}{5}(243) - \frac{8}{3}(27)\right) - \left(\frac{2}{5}(32) - \frac{8}{3}(8)\right)\right\}$$

$$= \frac{128}{15} + \frac{126}{5} + \frac{128}{15}$$

$$= \frac{634}{15} \text{ square units}$$

EXERCISE 7

1. Find the area of the following shaded regions:

(a)

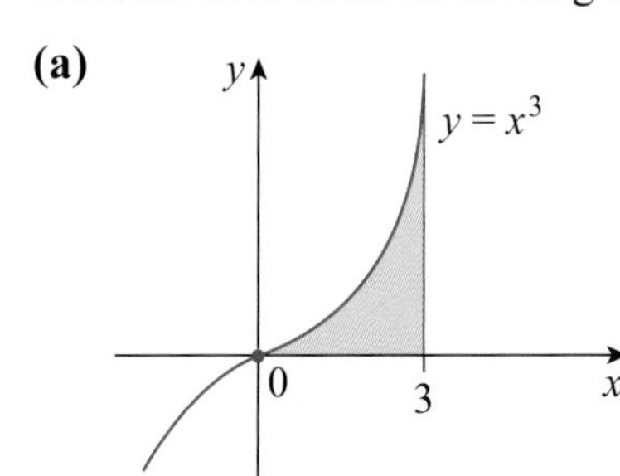

(b)

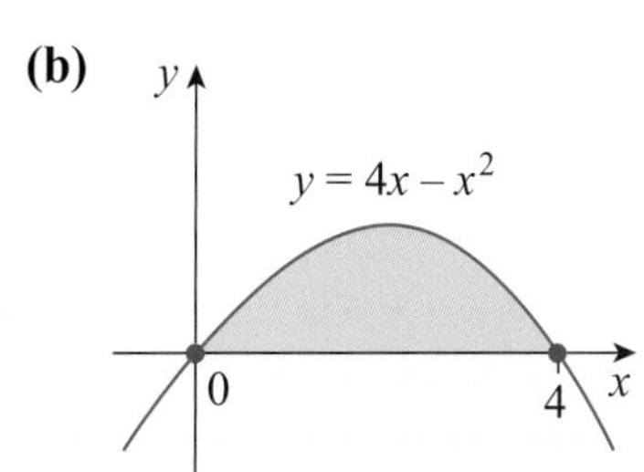

(c)

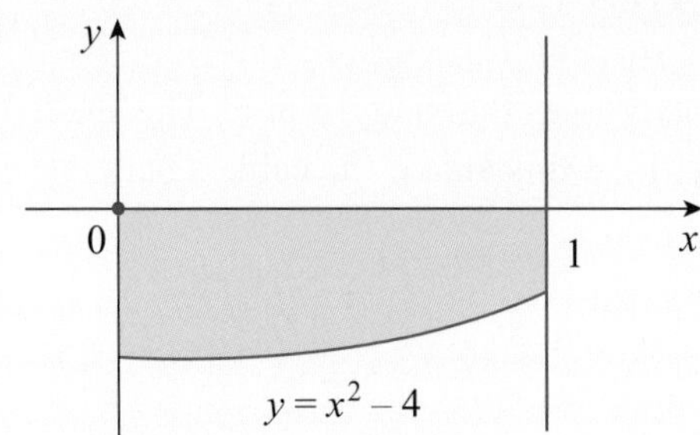

(d)

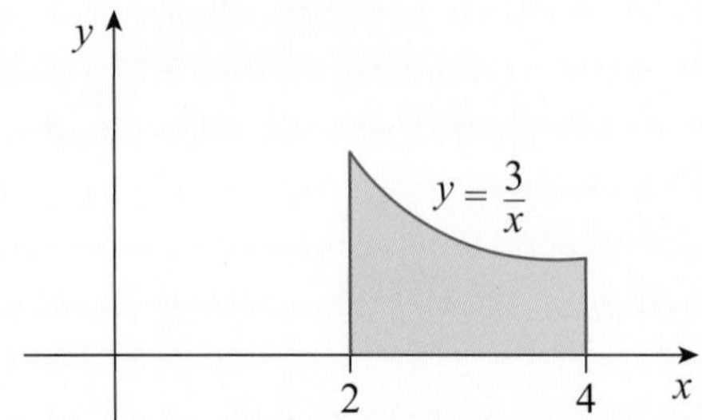

(e)

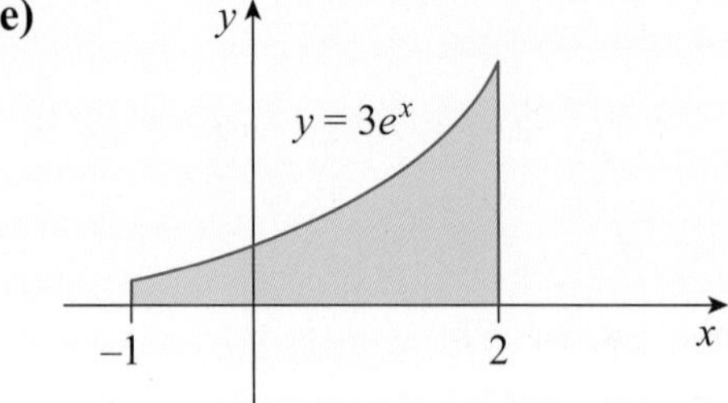

(f)

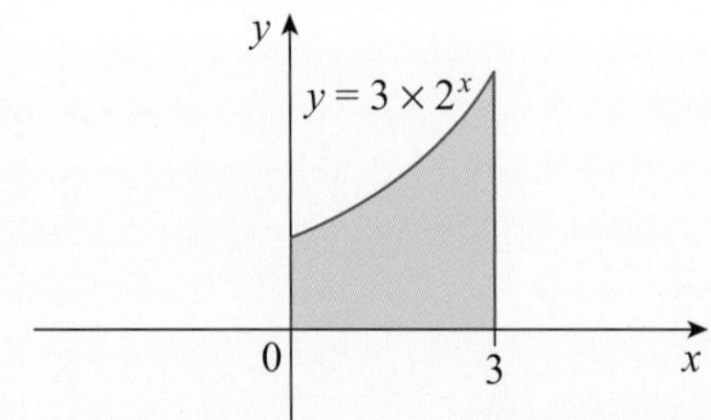

(g)

y

$y = 9 - x^2$

-3 3 x

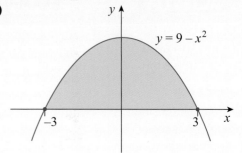

(h)

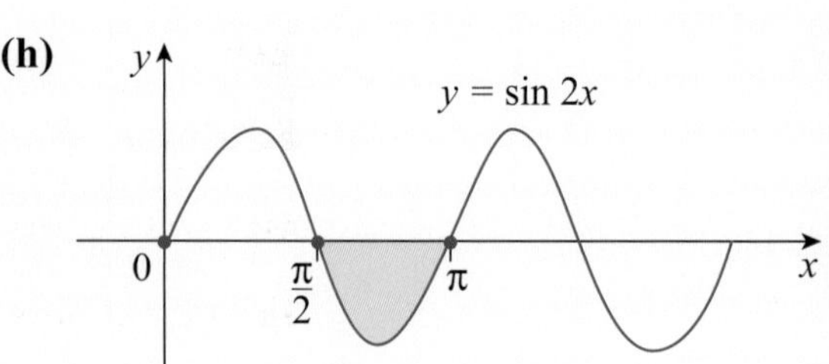

(i)

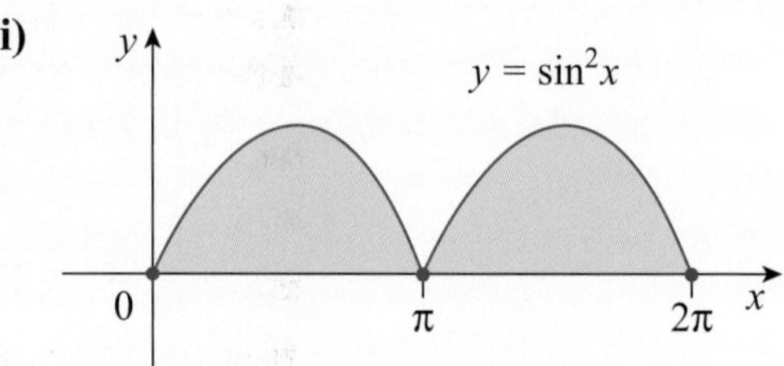

[Hint: $\sin^2 x = \frac{1}{2}(1 - \cos 2x)$]

(j)

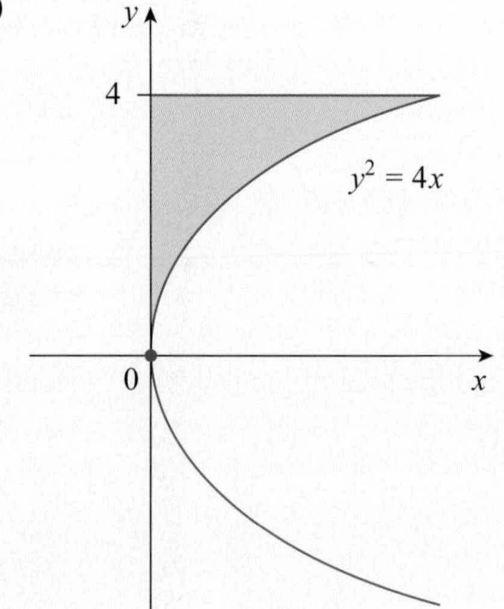

2. Find the shaded area of the following:

(a)

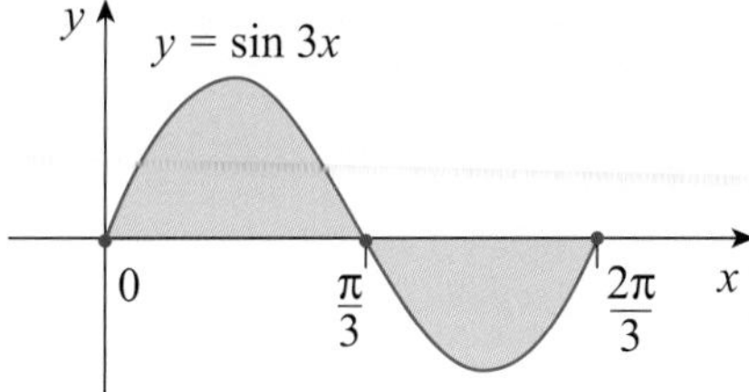

(b)

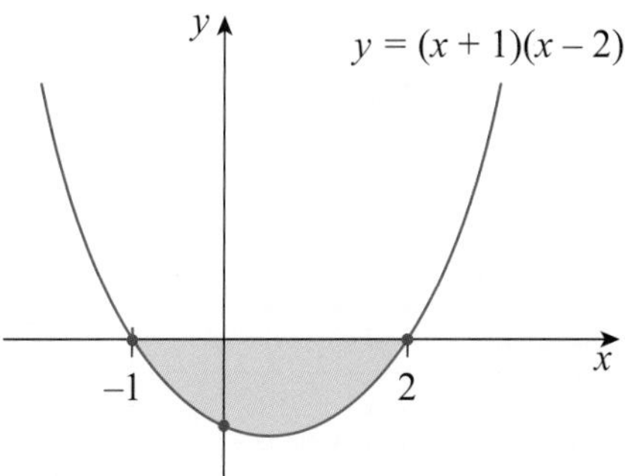

(c)

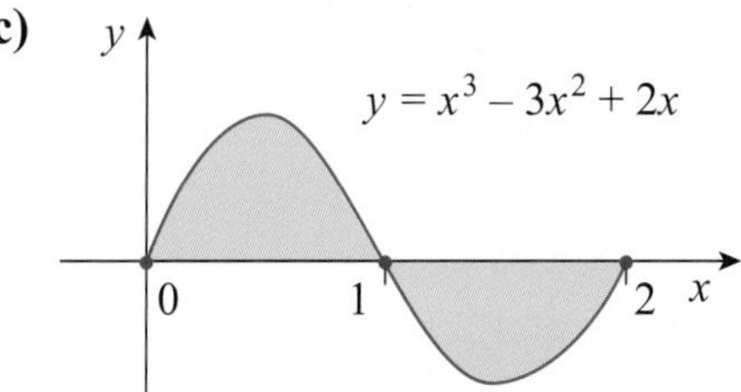

(d)

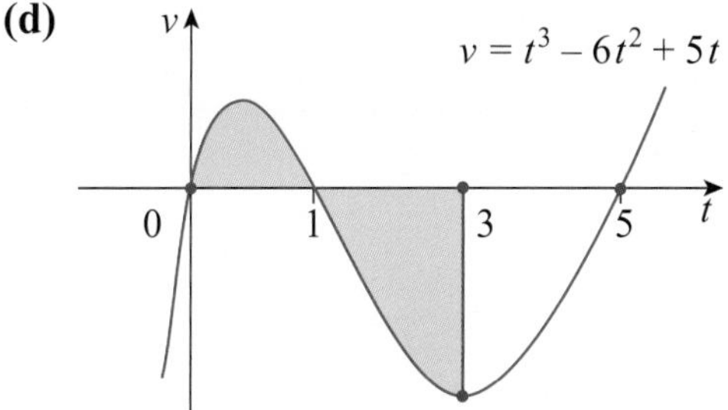

3. (a) (i) Copy and complete the table below for the function $y = 3^x$.

x	−1	0	1	2	3
y					

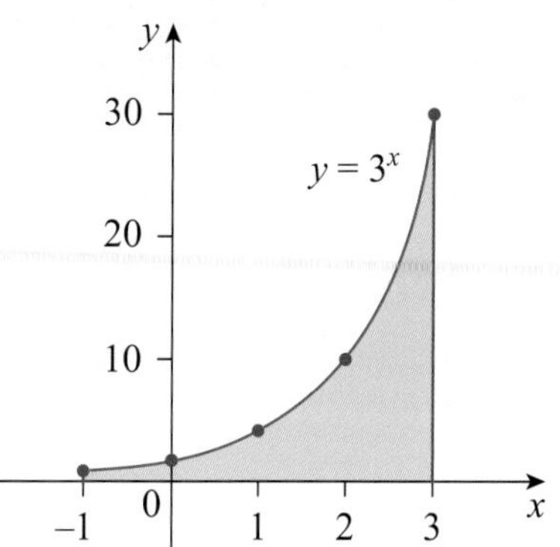

(ii) Use the trapezoidal rule to estimate the shaded area between the curve and the x-axis from $x = -1$ to $x = 3$.

(iii) Find the exact area by integration.

(iv) Find the percentage error in the trapezoidal rule and estimate to the nearest whole number.

(b) A computer generates a graph to show the speed v of a particle in m/s over an 8 second interval.

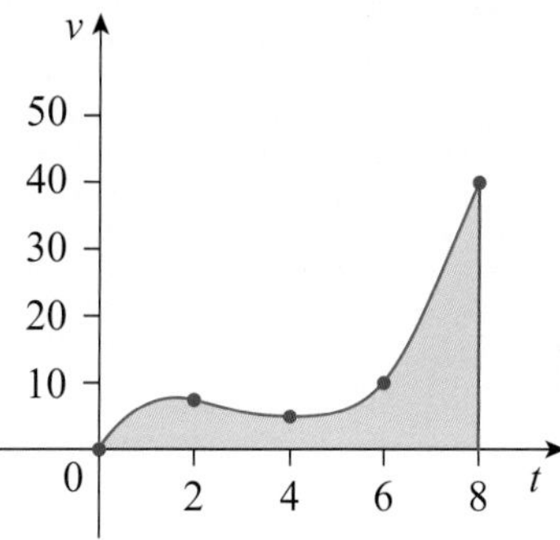

The curve is described by the equation $v = \frac{t^3}{3} - 3t^2 + 8t$. By calculating the area between the curve and the time axis from $t = 0$ to $t = 8$, the distance travelled by the particle during the first 8 seconds can be found.

(i) Find an estimate for the distance using the trapezoidal rule.

(ii) Find the exact distance by integration.

26.2 Area between curves

Consider two functions $f(x)$ and $g(x)$ which are continuous on an interval $[a, b]$ with $f(x) \geq g(x)$ for all $x \in [a, b]$, as shown. Both curves are above the x-axis.

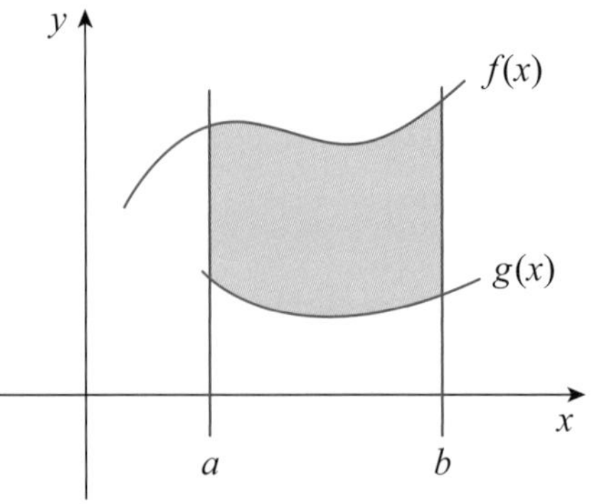

The area under $f(x)$ and between the lines $x = a$ and $x = b$ and the x-axis is given by:

$$A_1 = \int_a^b f(x)\,dx$$

The area under $g(x)$ and between the lines $x = a$, $x = b$ and the x-axis is given by:

$$A_2 = \int_a^b g(x)\,dx$$

The shaded area A between the curves is given by:

$$A = A_1 - A_2 = \int_a^b f(x)\,dx - \int_a^b g(x)\,dx$$

$$A = \int_a^b [f(x) - g(x)]\,dx$$

EXAMPLE 4

Find the area between the curves $f(x) = x^2 - 4x + 10$ and $g(x) = x^2 - 2x + 2$ for $0 \leq x \leq 3, x \in \mathbb{R}$.

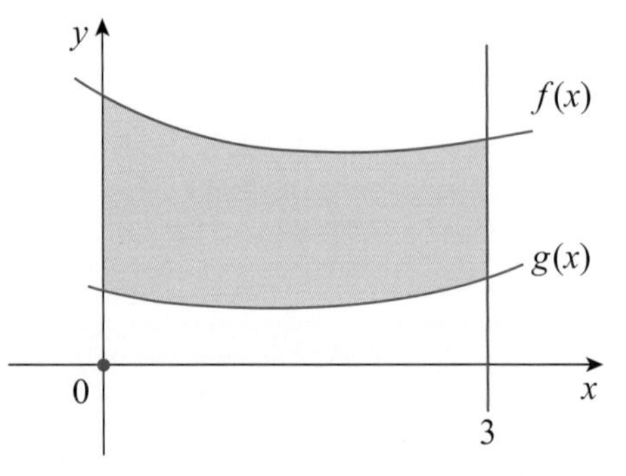

Solution

$$A = \int_0^3 [(x^2 - 4x + 10) - (x^2 - 2x + 2)]\,dx$$

$$= \int_0^3 (-2x + 8)\,dx$$

$$= [-x^2 + 8x]_0^3$$

$$= (-9 + 24) - (0 + 0)$$

$$= 15$$

Formula for area of region between two curves

The analysis above can be extended to any two continuous curves $f(x)$ and $g(x)$, where $f(x) \geq g(x)$ for all x in $[a, b]$ whether or not they are both above the x-axis.

If $f(x)$ and $g(x)$ are continuous on the interval $[a, b]$ and $f(x) \geq g(x)$ for all $x \in [a, b]$, the area A of the region bounded by the curves of f and g and the vertical lines $x = a$ and $x = b$ is given by: $A = \int_a^b [f(x) - g(x)]\,dx$.

EXAMPLE 5

Find the area between the curves $y = \frac{1}{x}$, $x > 0$ and $y = -x^2$, $x \in \mathbb{R}$ and the lines $x = \frac{1}{2}$ and $x = 2$.

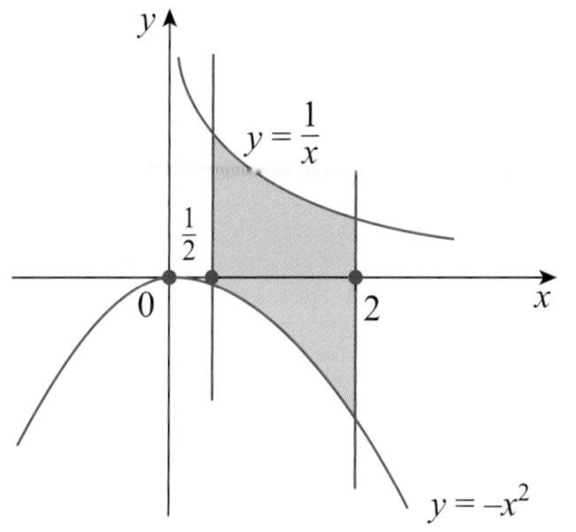

Solution

$$A = \int_{\frac{1}{2}}^{2} \left[\frac{1}{x} - (-x^2)\right] dx$$

$$= \int_{\frac{1}{2}}^{2} \left(\frac{1}{x} + x^2\right) dx$$

$$= \left[\ln x + \frac{x^3}{3}\right]_{\frac{1}{2}}^{2}$$

$$= \left(\ln 2 + \frac{8}{3}\right) - \left(\ln\frac{1}{2} + \frac{1}{24}\right)$$

$$= 2 \ln 2 + \frac{21}{8}$$

Intersecting curves

If the curves intersect at one or more points, these points must be found first by solving the equations of the curves simultaneously to get the limits of integration a and b.

Steps for finding area of region enclosed by two intersecting curves

1. Find the points of intersection of the curves by solving their equations simultaneously to get a and b ($a < b$).
2. Shade in the specified area.

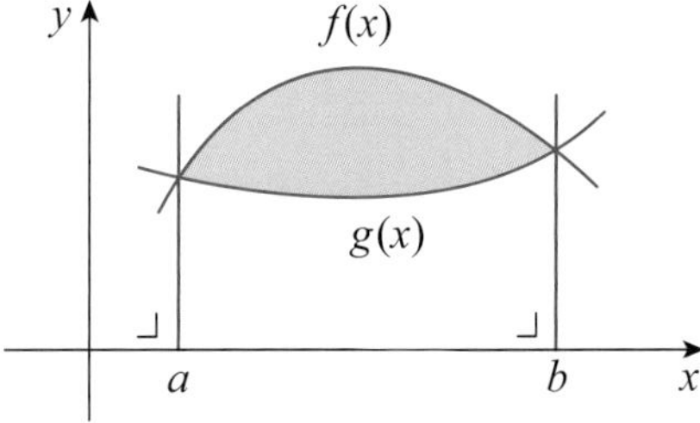

3. Draw lines from the point(s) of intersection perpendicularly onto the x-axis or y-axis.
4. Find the shaded area using:

$$A = \int_{a}^{b} [f(x) - g(x)]\, dx \text{ for the } x\text{-axis, where } f(x) \geq g(x)$$

or

$$A = \int_{a}^{b} [f(y) - g(y)]\, dy \text{ for the } y\text{-axis, where } f(y) \geq g(y).$$

5. Look out for rectangles, triangles and trapeziums. You can simply write down the areas of these shapes.

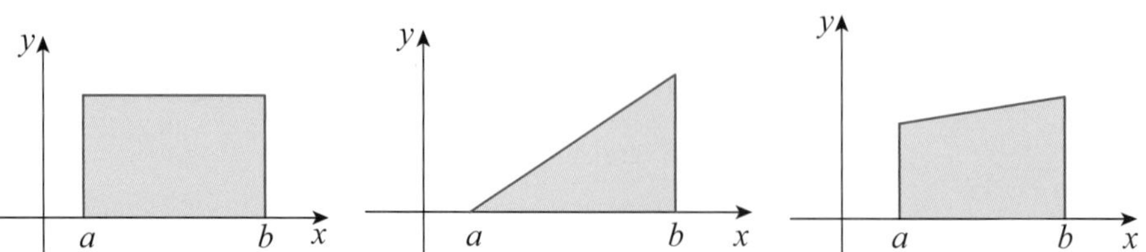

EXAMPLE 6

(a) Find the area between the curves c_1 and c_2.

$c_1: f(x) = y = 8 - x^2$

$c_2: g(x) = x^2$

(b) Hence, find the area of the region shaded green.

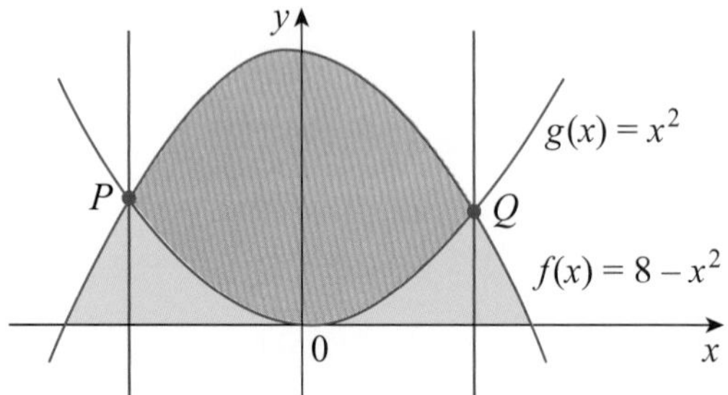

Solution

(a) $f(x) = g(x)$: $\quad x^2 = 8 - x^2$

$$2x^2 = 8$$

$$x^2 = 4$$

$$x = \pm 2$$

The area A_1 between c_1 and c_2:

$$A_1 = \int_{-2}^{2} (8 - x^2 - x^2)\,dx = \int_{-2}^{2} (8 - 2x^2)\,dx$$

$$= \left[8x - \frac{2x^3}{3}\right]_{-2}^{2}$$

$$= \left(16 - \frac{16}{3}\right) - \left(-16 + \frac{16}{3}\right)$$

$$= 32 - \frac{32}{3}$$

$$= \frac{64}{3}$$

(b) Area of region shaded green = area between c_1 and the x-axis – area between the curves

$c_1: f(x) = 0 \Rightarrow 8 - x^2 = 0$

$$x = \pm\sqrt{8}$$

Area A_2 between $f(x)$ and x-axis:

$$A_2 = \int_{-\sqrt{8}}^{\sqrt{8}} (8 - x^2)\,dx$$

$$= \left[8x - \frac{x^3}{3}\right]_{-\sqrt{8}}^{\sqrt{8}}$$

$$= \left(8\sqrt{8} - \frac{8\sqrt{8}}{3}\right) - \left(-8\sqrt{8} + \frac{8\sqrt{8}}{3}\right)$$

$$= 16\sqrt{8} - \frac{16\sqrt{8}}{3}$$

$$= \frac{32\sqrt{8}}{3}$$

$$= \frac{64\sqrt{2}}{3}$$

Area of region shaded green = $A_2 - A_1$

$$= \frac{64\sqrt{2}}{3} - \frac{64}{3}$$

$$= \frac{64}{3}(\sqrt{2} - 1)$$

EXAMPLE 7

Find the area between the curves $f(x) = \sin 2x$ and $g(x) = \cos x$, $0 \le x \le \frac{\pi}{2}$, $x \in \mathbb{R}$.

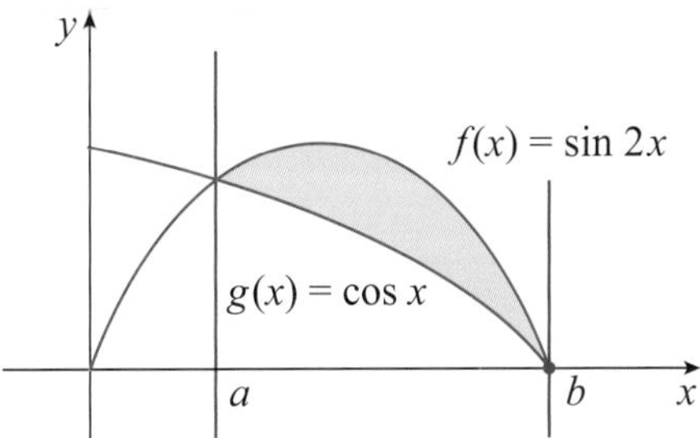

Solution

$f(x) = g(x)$: $\sin 2x = \cos x$

$2 \sin x \cos x - \cos x = 0$

$\cos x(2 \sin x - 1) = 0$

$2 \sin x - 1 = 0 \Rightarrow \sin x = \frac{1}{2}$	$\cos x = 0$
y, $\frac{\pi}{6}$, ✓ ✓, x	y, x
$x = \frac{\pi}{6}$	$x = \frac{\pi}{2}$

$\therefore a = \frac{\pi}{6}, b = \frac{\pi}{2}$

$$A = \int_{\frac{\pi}{6}}^{\frac{\pi}{2}} (\sin 2x - \cos x)\,dx$$

$$= \left[-\frac{1}{2}\cos 2x - \sin x\right]_{\frac{\pi}{6}}^{\frac{\pi}{2}}$$

$$= \left\{\left(-\frac{1}{2}\cos \pi - \sin \frac{\pi}{2}\right) - \left(-\frac{1}{2}\cos \frac{\pi}{3} - \sin \frac{\pi}{6}\right)\right\}$$

$$= \left(\frac{1}{2} - 1\right) + \left(\frac{1}{4} + \frac{1}{2}\right)$$

$$= \frac{1}{4}$$

EXAMPLE 8

(a) Given that the area enclosed by a body's speed–time curve and the time axis between two times is the distance the body travels between these times, find how far the body described by the speed–time curve below travels in the first 2 seconds of its motion.

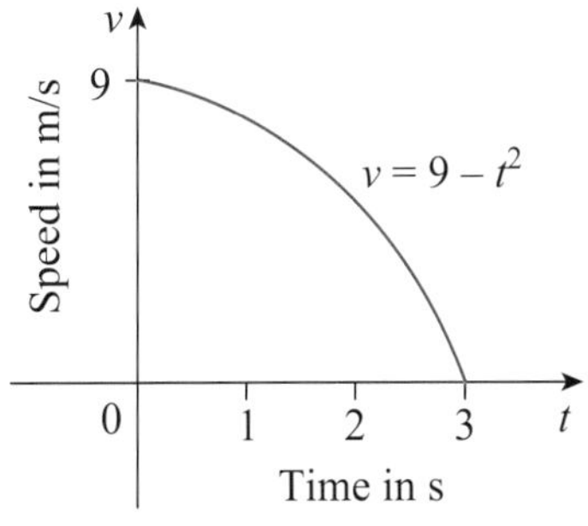

(b) The velocity–time curves of two golf balls A and B, with equations:

A: $v = f(t) = 30t - t^2$

B: $v = g(t) = 18t$

where v is in m/s and t in seconds are shown.

(i) Find the times at which they have the same speed.

(ii) Find how much further A travels than B between these times.

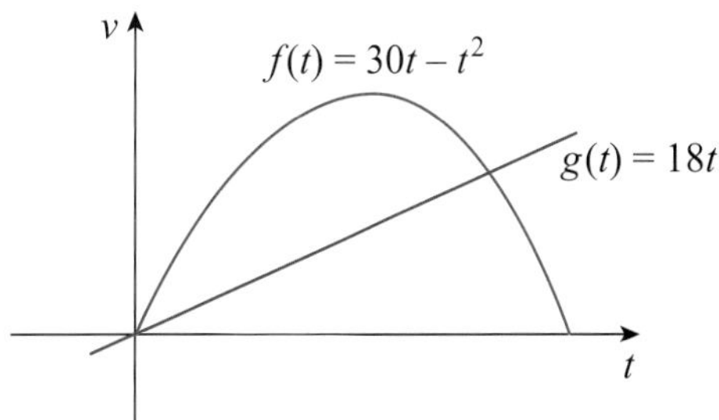

Solution

(a)

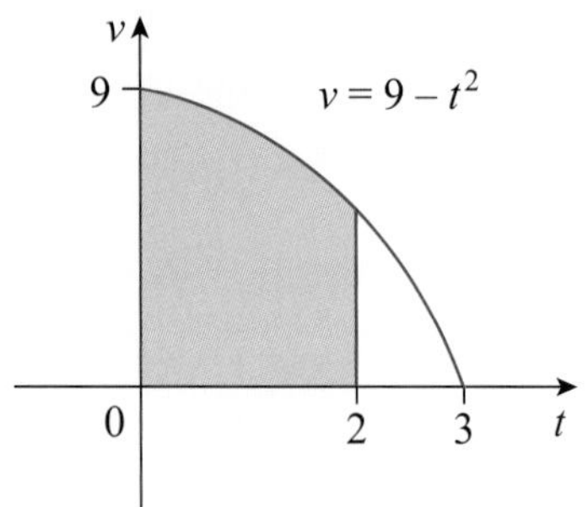

$$s = \int_0^2 v\,dt = \int_0^2 (9 - t^2)\,dt$$

$$= \left[9t - \frac{t^3}{3}\right]_0^2$$

$$= \left(18 - \frac{8}{3}\right) - (0 - 0)$$

$$= \frac{46}{3}\text{ m}$$

(b)

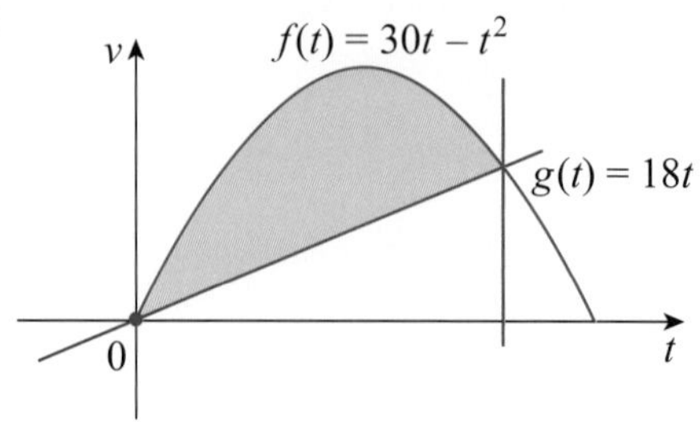

(i) $f(t) = g(t)$: $30t - t^2 = 18t$

$$t^2 - 12t = 0$$

$$t(t - 12) = 0$$

$$t = 0, 12$$

(ii) $s = \int_0^{12} [f(t) - g(t)]\,dt$ [This is the extra distance A has travelled.]

$$= \int_0^{12} (30t - t^2 - 18t)\,dt$$

$$= \int_0^{12} (12t - t^2)\,dt$$

$$= \left[6t^2 - \frac{t^3}{3}\right]_0^{12}$$

$$= 864 - 576$$

$$= 288\text{ m}$$

EXAMPLE 9

A line l meets the curve $y = \sqrt{x}$, $x \geq 0$, at $(0, 0)$ and at a point P whose x co-ordinate is t. If the enclosed area is $\frac{\sqrt{3}}{2}$, find t.

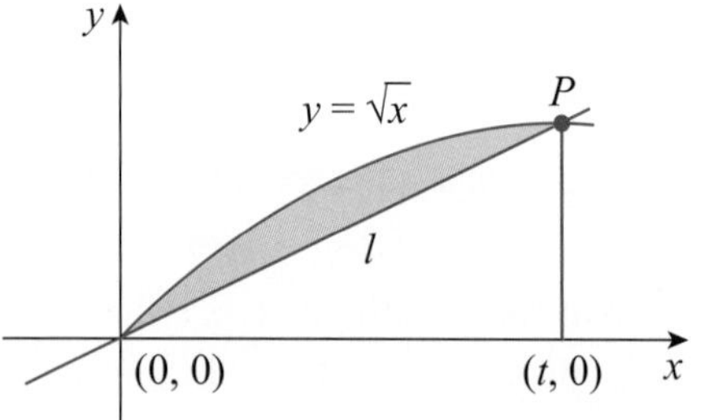

For the curve $y = \sqrt{x}$: $x = t \Rightarrow y = \sqrt{t}$

Therefore, the point P is $(t, \sqrt{t})$.

Slope of $l = \frac{\sqrt{t}}{t} = \frac{1}{\sqrt{t}}$

Equation of l: $y = \frac{1}{\sqrt{t}}x = \frac{x}{\sqrt{t}}$

Shaded area: $A = \int_0^t \left(x^{\frac{1}{2}} - \frac{x}{\sqrt{t}}\right)dx = \frac{\sqrt{3}}{2}$

$$\left[\frac{2}{3}x^{\frac{3}{2}} - \frac{1}{\sqrt{t}}\left(\frac{x^2}{2}\right)\right]_0^t = \frac{\sqrt{3}}{2}$$

$$\frac{2}{3}t^{\frac{3}{2}} - \frac{t^2}{2\sqrt{t}} = \frac{\sqrt{3}}{2}$$

$$4t^{\frac{3}{2}} - 3t^{\frac{3}{2}} = 3\sqrt{3}$$

$$t^{\frac{3}{2}} = 3\sqrt{3}$$

$$t^3 = 27$$

$$t = 3$$

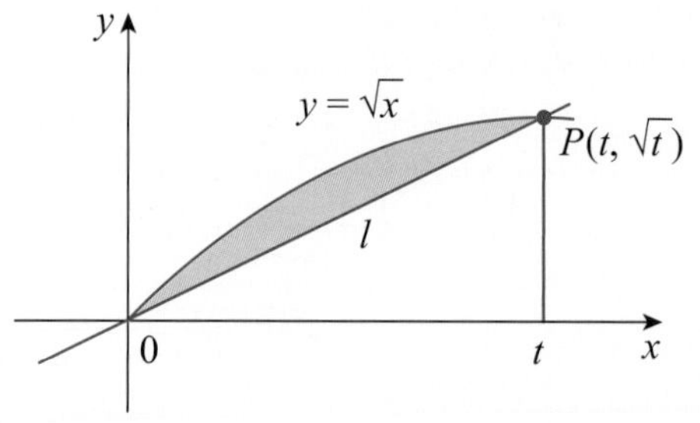

Can you do this question without finding the equation of l?

EXERCISE 8

1. Find the area of the shaded region shown in each diagram:

(a)

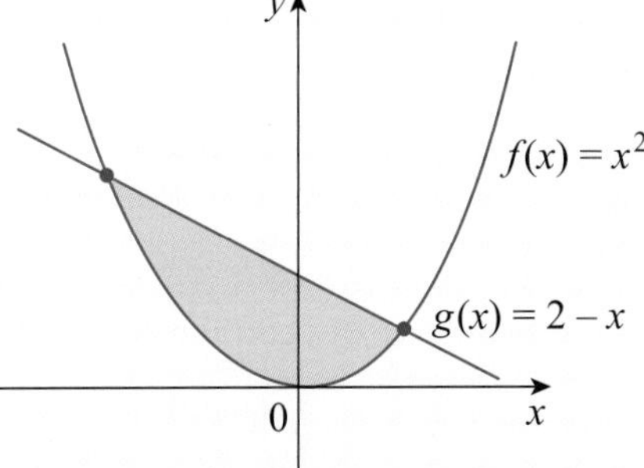

(b)

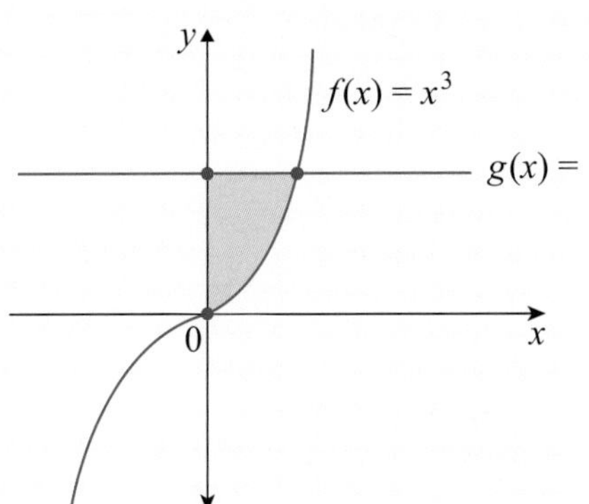

(c)

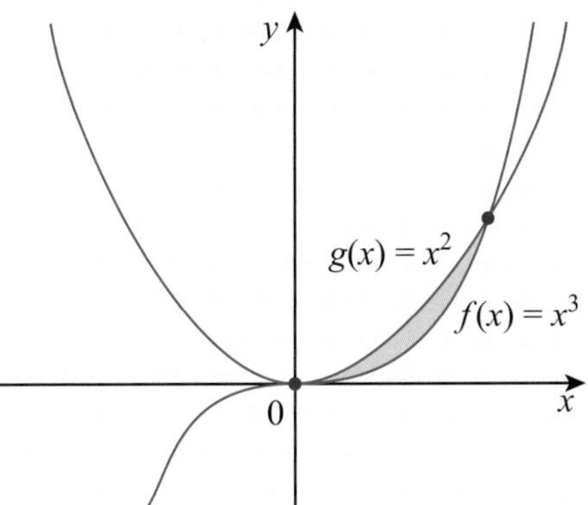

(d)

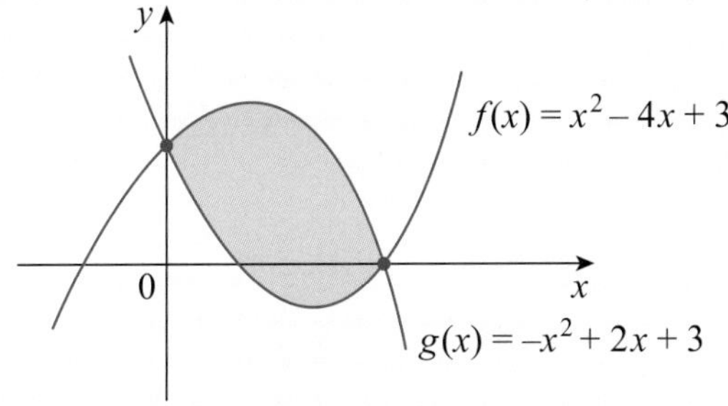

(e)

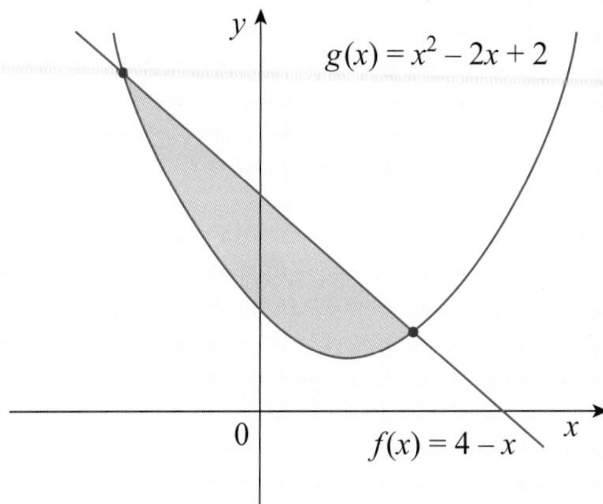

(f)

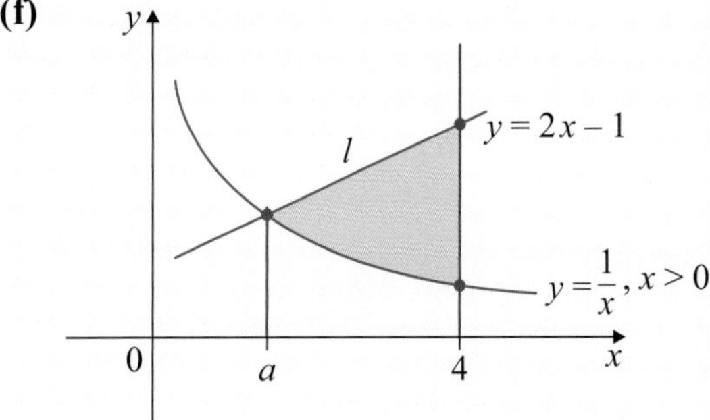

2. A curve c passes through (1, 1). The slope of the tangent at a point (x, y) on the curve is $3x - 5$.

   (a) Find the equation of the curve.

   (b) Find the area enclosed by the curve c and the line l with equation l: $5x - 2y - 3 = 0$.

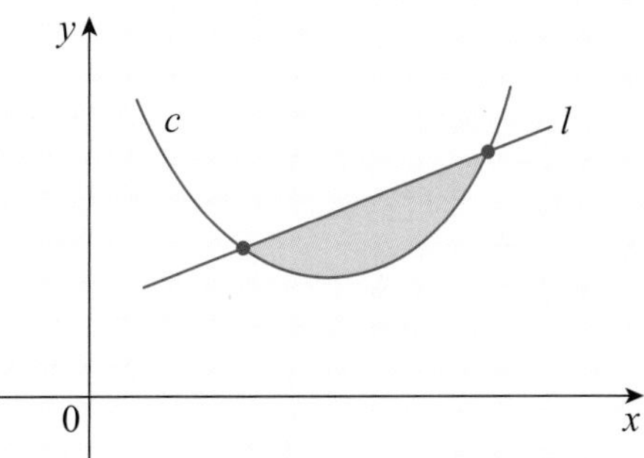

3. A logo for an airline is in the shape of the shaded area as shown. The shaded area is between the curves c_1: $y = x^2$ and c_2: $y = 8 - x^2$. Find the area of the shaded region.

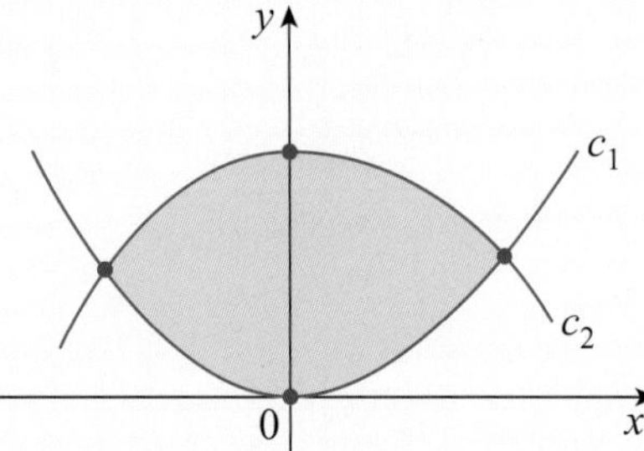

4. The region bounded by the curve $y = x^2$ and the line $y = 4$ is divided into two equal areas by the line $y = a$. Show that $a^3 = 16$.

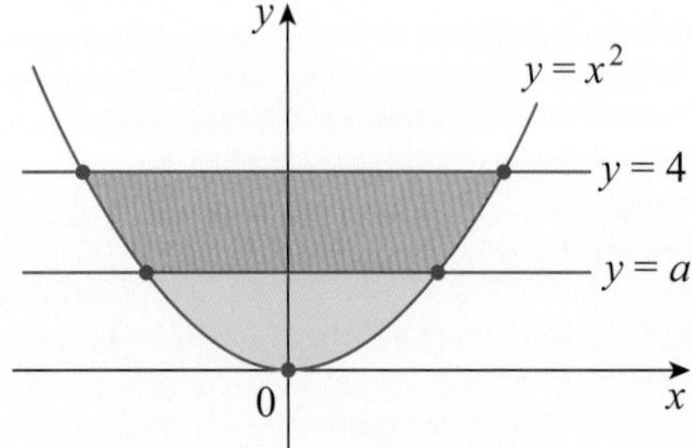

5. Find the shaded area between the line l and the curve $y = e^x$.

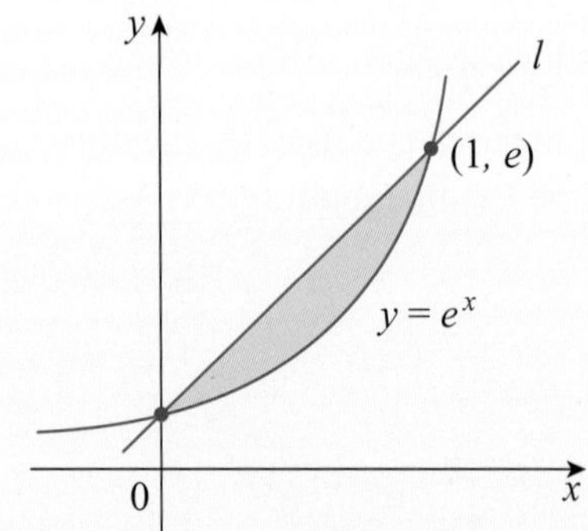

6. Show that the area between the curves c_1: $y = x^n$, $x \geq 0$, $n > 1$ and c_2: $y = x^{\frac{1}{n}}$, $x \geq 0$, $n > 1$ is given by $\frac{n-1}{n+1}$.

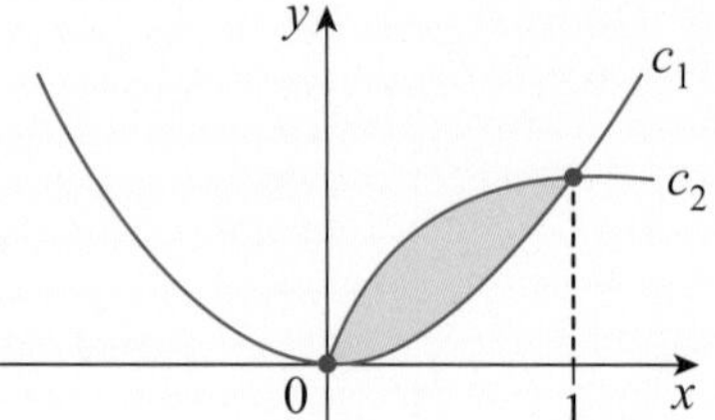

7. Find the area between the curves c_1: $y = f(x) = x(8 - x)$ and c_2: $y = g(x) = x^2 - 8x + 24$.

Hence, find the area of the region shaded green.

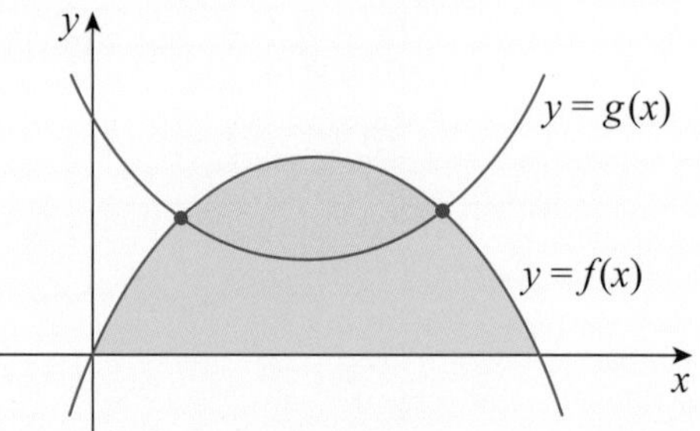

8. Find the area of the region shaded green.

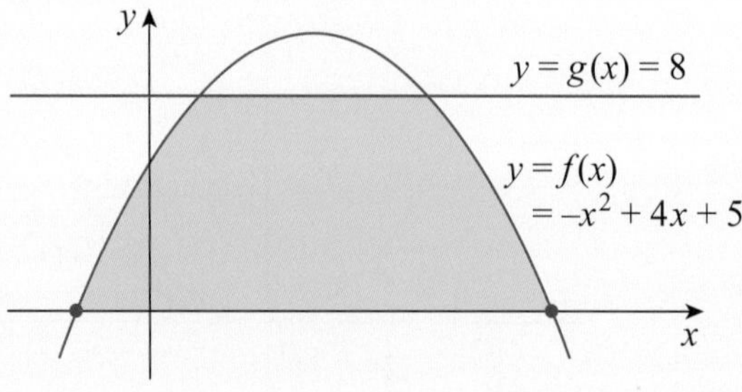

26.3 Differential equations

The derivative of a function given in the form of an equation is known as a **differential equation**.

Examples of differential equations:

$f'(x) = x^2, \ \frac{dv}{dt} = -\frac{2}{t}, \ \frac{dp}{ds} = e^{\frac{1}{2}s}$

Integration is used to obtain the original function from the differential equation.

WORKED EXAMPLE Solving differential equations

If $\frac{dy}{dx} = 3x - 2$, find y in terms of x, if $y = 1$ when $x = -2$.

$\frac{dy}{dx} = (3x - 2)$

1. $dy = (3x - 2)\,dx$ [Separate]
2. $\int dy = \int (3x - 2)\,dx$ [Integrate]

   $y = \frac{3x^2}{2} - 2x + c$
3. To get c, use the extra information called boundary conditions.

   $y = 1$ when $x = -2$: $1 = 6 + 4 + c$

   $c = -9$

The solution of the differential equation is $y = \frac{3x^2}{2} - 2x + 9$.

We have obtained the equation of a curve from the slope $\frac{dy}{dx}$ at a point (x, y) on the curve.

Steps for solving a differential equation

1. Separate the variables so that the dependent variable is on one side and the independent variable is on the other side.
2. Integrate each side with respect to its variable.
3. Put in the boundary condition(s) to determine the constant(s).

EXAMPLE 10

The rate at which the share price p in cents of a certain stock increases over a month is given by $\frac{dp}{dt} = \frac{1}{t+1}$, where t is the number of days after the first day of the month ($t = 0$). If the share price is €9·50 on the first day of the month ($t = 0$), write p as a function of t. Find the price on the 19th day of the month to the nearest cent.

Solution

$\frac{dp}{dt} = \frac{1}{t+1}$

1. $dp = \frac{dt}{t+1}$
2. $\int dp = \int \frac{dt}{t+1}$

   $p = \ln(t + 1) + c$
3. Boundary condition:

   $t = 0, p = 950$: $950 = \ln 1 + c$

   $\therefore c = 950$

   $p = \ln(t + 1) + 950$

   The 19th day means $t = 18$.

   $\therefore p = \ln 19 + 950 = 953$ c

Many of the laws in Physics are in the form of differential equations.
Examples: Newton's law of motion, Newton's law of cooling and the law of radioactive decay.

Terms used in framing differential equations

1. **'Is directly proportional to'**

   The statement: v is directly proportional to t is written as $v \propto t$ or $v = kt$, where k is a constant of proportionality.

2. **'Varies inversely to'**

   The statement: v varies inversely to p^2 is written as $v \propto \frac{1}{p^2}$ or $v = \frac{k}{p^2}$ where k is a constant of proportionality.

3. **'Decreases proportionally to'**

   The statement: a decreases proportionally to t^3 is written as $a \propto -t^3$ or $a = -kt^3$, where $k > 0$ is a constant of proportionality. The negative sign indicates it is decreasing.

4. **'The rate of change of'**

   The statement: The rate of change of Q with respect to Z is 4 is written as: $\frac{dQ}{dZ} = 4$

5. The rate of change with respect to time t is just called the rate of change.

   Rate of change of $w = \frac{dw}{dt}$

   Acceleration a = rate of change of velocity $= \frac{dv}{dt}$

   Velocity v = rate of change of displacement $= \frac{ds}{dt}$

EXAMPLE 11

The acceleration of a rocket in m/s^2 is given by $a = \frac{3t^2}{8} - 2t$, where t is the time in seconds. Find:

(a) the velocity v in terms of t, if $v = 5$ m/s at $t = 0$,

(b) the velocity at $t = 10$ s.

Solution

(a) $a = \frac{3t^2}{8} - 2t$

$$\frac{dv}{dt} = \frac{3t^2}{8} - 2t$$

$$dv = \left(\frac{3t^2}{8} - 2t\right)dt$$

$$\int dv = \int\left(\frac{3t^2}{8} - 2t\right)dt$$

$$v = \frac{3}{8}\left(\frac{t^3}{3}\right) - 2\left(\frac{t^2}{2}\right) + c$$

$$v = \frac{t^3}{8} - t^2 + c$$

Boundary condition: $t = 0, v = 5 \Rightarrow 5 = 0 - 0 + c$

$$\therefore c = 5$$

$$v = \frac{t^3}{8} - t^2 + 5$$

(b) $t = 10$: $v = \frac{(10)^3}{8} - (10)^2 + 5$

$= 125 - 100 + 5$

$= 30$ m/s

EXAMPLE 12

A water tank is filling up. The height of the water after time t in minutes is h metres. The rate of increase of h is directly proportional to the square root of its height.

(a) Write down a differential equation satisfied by h.

(b) If the height is 0 m at $t = 0$, show that $2\sqrt{h} = kt$, where $k > 0$ is the constant of proportionality.

(c) Given the height is $\frac{1}{4}$ m at $t = 4$ minutes, find k and the time it takes to fill the tank if the height of the tank is 1 m.

Solution

(a) $\frac{dh}{dt} \propto \sqrt{h} \Rightarrow \frac{dh}{dt} = kh^{\frac{1}{2}}$

(b) $\frac{dh}{h^{\frac{1}{2}}} = kdt$

$\int h^{-\frac{1}{2}} dh = k \int dt$

$2\sqrt{h} = kt + c$

Boundary condition:

$t = 0, h = 0: \quad 0 = 0 + c$

$c = 0$

$\therefore 2\sqrt{h} = kt$

(c) $h = \frac{1}{4}, t = 4: \ 2\sqrt{\frac{1}{4}} = 4k$

$\therefore k = \frac{1}{4}$

$\therefore 2\sqrt{h} = \frac{1}{4}t$

$h = 1: \ 2\sqrt{1} = \frac{1}{4}t$

$\therefore t = 8$ minutes

EXERCISE 9

1. (a) If $\frac{dy}{dx} = x^2$, find y, if $x = 3$ when $y = 1$.

(b) If $\frac{dy}{dx} = e^x$, find y, if $y = 1$ when $x = 0$.

(c) If $\frac{dy}{dx} = \frac{3}{x}$, find y, if $y = 0$ when $x = 1$.

(d) If $\frac{dv}{dt} = -5$, find v, if $v = 50$ when $t = 0$.

(e) If $\frac{dh}{dt} = 3\cos\left(\frac{\pi}{2} - t\right)$, find h, if $h = 5$ when $t = \frac{\pi}{2}$.

(f) If $f'(x) = e^x + \frac{2}{x}$, find $f(x)$, if $f(1) = 3$.

(g) The slope of the tangent to a curve at any point on the curve is given by $\frac{dy}{dx} = 2x - 1$. If the curve passes through the point (1, 1), find the equation of the curve.

2. (a) The rate of change of Q with respect to Z is $-3Z$. Find Q in terms of Z, if $Q = 10$ when $Z = 4$.

(b) If $v = \frac{ds}{dt}$ and $v = 3t^2$, write s as a function of t, if $s = 0$ when $t = 0$.

(c) The acceleration a of a body in m/s^2 is equal to $\frac{3}{t-2}$, where t is the time in seconds. Find the velocity v in terms of t, if $v = 3$ m/s when $t = 3$.

(d) If the velocity v of a rock is given by $v = u + at$ (u, a are constants), find the displacement s in terms of t, if $s = 0$ when $t = 0$.

(e) A particle starts from rest with acceleration $(30 - 6t)$ m/s^2 at time t. When will it come to rest again?

3. (a) The rate of change of the pressure p in Pascals (Pa) in a gas after t minutes is given by $\frac{dp}{dt} = -3t + 1$. If $p = 10$ Pa at $t = 0$, find the pressure after 2 minutes.

(b) The rate of increase of the strength B in Tesla (T) of a magnetic field is directly proportional to $\frac{t^2}{10}$, where t is the time in minutes.

(i) Write down a differential equation for B.

(ii) If $B = 0$ T at $t = 0$ and $B = 0{\cdot}1$ T at $t = 3$, find an expression for B in terms of t.

(iii) Find B after 6 minutes.

4. A liquid leaks from a hole in a large container. The depth of the water in a container at time t minutes is h metres. The rate of decrease of h is directly proportional to $\sqrt{t}$.

(a) Write down a differential equation satisfied by h, if $k > 0$ is the constant of proportionality.

(b) If the depth of the liquid is 1 m when $t = 0$, show that $h = \frac{3 - 2kt^{\frac{3}{2}}}{3}$.

(c) If the depth is $0{\cdot}5$ m when $t = 4$, find k.

(d) Find the time it takes to empty the tank, correct to two decimal places.

5. An ice cube is melting in warm water. If the rate at which the volume is decreasing is directly proportional to its surface area, show that the rate at which the length of each side is decreasing is a constant.

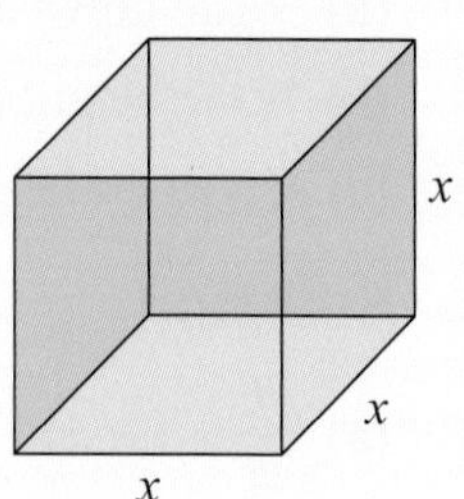

If the initial volume of the cube is 8 cm^3, find the time it takes to melt, if half of it melts after 3 minutes. Give your answer correct to two decimal places.

6. For a gas at low pressure p, the rate of change of the volume V with respect to p equals $-\frac{V}{p}$. If $p = 1$ Pa when $V = 1$ cm^3, show that $pV = 1$.

26.4 The average value of a function

The following two examples will give you the idea of the average value of a function.

EXAMPLE 13

A body moves along a straight line. Its speed v is given by $v = \frac{1}{t^2} + t$, $1 \le t \le 4$, where v is in m/s at time t in seconds. Find its average speed between $t = 1$ and $t = 4$, if $s = 1$ at $t = 1$, where s is its distance in metres from a fixed point O.

Solution

$$v = \frac{ds}{dt} = t + \frac{1}{t^2}$$

$$ds = (t + t^{-2})\,dt$$

$$\int ds = \int (t + t^{-2})\,dt$$

$$s = \frac{t^2}{2} + \frac{t^{-1}}{-1} + c = \frac{t^2}{2} - \frac{1}{t} + c$$

Boundary conditions: $s = 1, t = 1$: $1 = \frac{1}{2} - 1 + c$

$$\therefore c = \frac{3}{2}$$

$$s = \frac{t^2}{2} - \frac{1}{t} + \frac{3}{2}$$

$\boldsymbol{t = 4}$**:** $s_1 = 8 - \frac{1}{4} + \frac{3}{2} = \frac{37}{4}$

$\boldsymbol{t = 1}$**:** $s_2 = \frac{1}{2} - 1 + \frac{3}{2} = 1$

Total distance travelled from $t = 1$ to $t = 4$:

$$s = s_1 - s_2 = \frac{37}{4} - 1 = \frac{33}{4} \text{ m}$$

$$\therefore \text{Average speed} = \frac{\text{Distance}}{\text{Time}} = \frac{\frac{33}{4}}{3} = \frac{11}{4} \text{ m/s}$$

EXAMPLE 14

The velocity–time curve of v against t for $v = \frac{1}{t^2} + t$, $1 \le t \le 4$, where v is in m/s and t is in seconds (s), is shown. Find the area under it and between the lines $t = 1$, $t = 4$ and the t-axis.

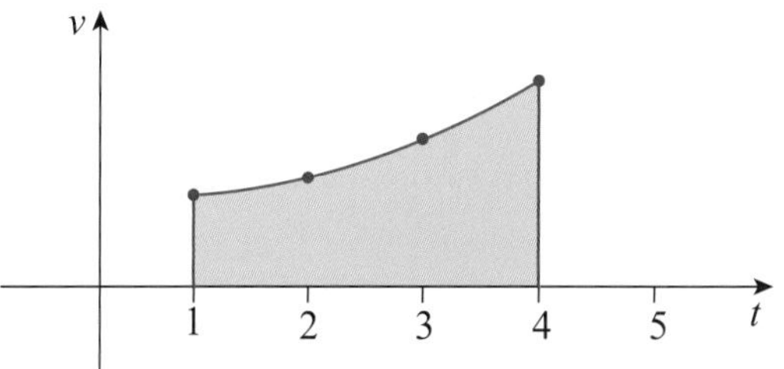

Solution

$$\text{Area } A = \int_1^4 v\,dt$$

$$= \int_1^4 \left(t + \frac{1}{t^2}\right) dt = \int_1^4 (t + t^{-2})\,dt$$

$$= \left[\frac{t^2}{2} + \frac{t^{-1}}{-1}\right]_1^4$$

$$= \left[\frac{t^2}{2} + \frac{1}{t}\right]_1^4$$

$$= \left(8 - \frac{1}{4}\right) - \left(\frac{1}{2} - 1\right)$$

$$= 8 + \frac{1}{4} = \frac{33}{4}$$

$$\frac{\text{Area under the velocity–time curve}}{\text{Time interval}} = \frac{\frac{33}{4}}{4-1} = \frac{11}{4} \text{ m/s}$$

= Average speed $\bar{v}$ for $t = 1$ to $t = 4$ from Example 13

This result can be generalised to find the average value of any continuous function on an interval.

The average value $\bar{y}$ of a continuous function $y = g(x)$ on an interval $[a, b]$ is given by:

$$\bar{y} = \frac{\int_a^b g(x)\,dx}{b-a} = \frac{\int_a^b y\,dx}{b-a}$$

EXAMPLE 15

Find the average value of $y = x^3 - x + 2$ on the interval $[0, 2]$.

Solution

$y = x^3 - x + 2$

Interval $[0, 2]$: $a = 0$, $b = 2$

$$\bar{y} = \frac{\int_0^2 (x^3 - x + 2)\,dx}{2 - 0}$$

$$= \frac{1}{2}\left[\frac{x^4}{4} - \frac{x^2}{2} + 2x\right]_0^2$$

$$= \frac{1}{2}(4 - 2 + 4)$$

$$= 3$$

The above average is an average over the whole interval and cannot be found by finding the average of the values of y at 0 and 2.

Note: $\bar{y} = \dfrac{\int_a^b y\,dx}{(b-a)} = \dfrac{\int_a^b y\,dx}{\int_a^b dx} = \dfrac{\text{Area}}{\text{Width}} = \text{Average height}$

EXAMPLE 16

A 7200 litre water tank takes 12 minutes to drain. After t minutes the volume of water in litres left in the tank is given by $V = 50(144 - t^2)$.

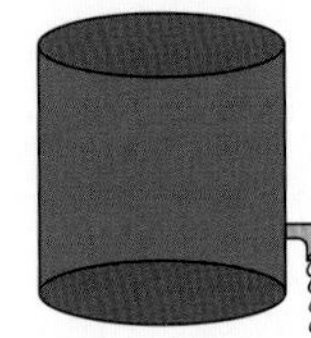

What is the average volume of water in the tank while it is draining?

Solution

$$\overline{V} = \frac{\int_0^{12} V\,dt}{12 - 0} = \frac{1}{12}\int_0^{12} 50(144 - t^2)\,dt$$

$$= \frac{50}{12}\left[144t - \frac{t^3}{3}\right]_0^{12}$$

$$= \frac{25}{6}\left\{144(12) - \frac{(12)^3}{3}\right\} = 4800 \text{ litres}$$

EXAMPLE 17

The output voltage V in volts (V) of an electricity generating company varies periodically with time t in seconds, according to the equation $V = 340\sin(100\pi t)$. A graph of the output voltage is shown below.

(a) Find the average value of V over the interval [0, 0·04].

(b) Find the average value of V^2 over the interval [0, 0·04].

(c) The root mean square voltage V_{RMS} is obtained by getting the square root of the average value of the voltage V squared. Find V_{RMS} over the interval [0, 0·04].

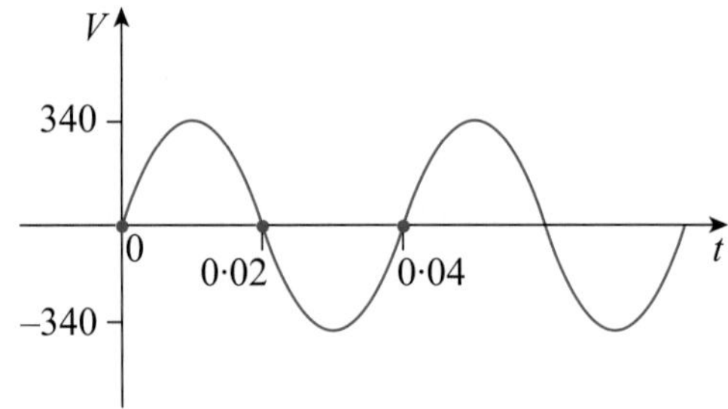

Solution

(a) $$\overline{V} = \frac{\int_0^{0\cdot04} 340\sin(100\pi t)\,dt}{0\cdot04 - 0}$$

$$= \frac{340}{0\cdot04}\int_0^{0\cdot04} \sin(100\pi t)\,dt$$

$$= -8500\frac{1}{100\pi}\left[\cos(100\pi t)\right]_0^{0\cdot04}$$

$$= -\frac{85}{\pi}(\cos 4\pi - \cos 0)$$

$$= -\frac{85}{\pi}(1 - 1) = 0$$

$\therefore V = 0$ V

You cannot pay for 0 volts.

(b) $V^2 = 340^2\sin^2(100\pi t) = 115\,600\sin^2(100\pi t)$

$$\overline{V^2} = \frac{\int_0^{0\cdot04} 115\,600\sin^2(100\pi t)\,dt}{0\cdot04 - 0} \qquad \left[\sin^2 A = \tfrac{1}{2}(1 - \cos 2A)\right]$$

$$= \frac{2\,890\,000}{2}\int_0^{0\cdot04} (1 - \cos(200\pi t))\,dt$$

$$= 1\,445\,000\left[t - \frac{\sin(200\pi t)}{200\pi}\right]_0^{0\cdot04}$$

$$= 1\,445\,000\left(0\cdot04 - \frac{\sin 8\pi}{200\pi}\right)$$

$\therefore \overline{V^2} = 57\,800$

(c) If you take the square root of $\overline{V^2}$, you get what is called the root mean square voltage (V_{RMS}).

$$V_{RMS} = \sqrt{\overline{V^2}} = \sqrt{57\,800} = 170\sqrt{2} = \frac{340}{\sqrt{2}} = 240\cdot4$$

$V_{RMS} = 240$ V is the voltage the company quotes to the public.

EXERCISE 10

1. Find the average value of the given function $y = g(x)$ on the given interval $[a, b]$:
   (a) $y = x^2$ on [2, 5]
   (b) $y = e^x$ on [−2, 3]
   (c) $y = 2x^2 + 3x + 2$ on [1, 3]
   (d) $y = 4\sqrt{x} + 1$ on [1, 4]
   (e) $y = \cos 5x$ on $\left[\frac{\pi}{3}, \frac{4\pi}{3}\right]$

2. **(a)** A bird flies at a velocity given by $v = 2t^2 + 5$ m/s from $t = 1$ to $t = 3$, where t is in seconds. What is its average velocity over this period?

   (b) The temperature in Seville is given by $T = (35 + \sqrt{t})$ degrees Celsius, where t is the number of hours after noon. What is the average temperature over the interval between $t = 4$ and $t = 9$, correct to one decimal place?

   (c) A capacitor in a circuit is charged for 0·5 seconds by a current I measured in amps given by $I = 0{\cdot}3t^3$, at time t in seconds. Find the average value of the current in the circuit over the time.

   (d) A brick falls to the ground. Its speed v in metres/second is given by $v = gt$, where t is the time in seconds after the brick was released. Find its average speed between 3 and 7 seconds after it was released. ($g = 9{\cdot}8$ ms^{-2})

   (e) The mass M in grams of a chemical in a mixture varies with time t in seconds, according to the formula $M = 4{\cdot}7\,e^{-t}$. Find the average mass of the chemical in the mixture over the time interval [0, 3], correct to one decimal place.

   (f) Breathing is a cyclic process. The volume V in litres of air in the lungs varies with time t in seconds, according to the formula $V = 5\sin\left(\frac{2\pi}{5}t\right)$.
   (i) Find the time for a full breathing cycle.
   (ii) Find the average volume of **inhaled** air in the lungs in one breathing cycle, correct to one decimal place.

REVISION QUESTIONS

1. The graph of $y = f'(x)$, where $f(x)$ is a cubic function, is sketched below.

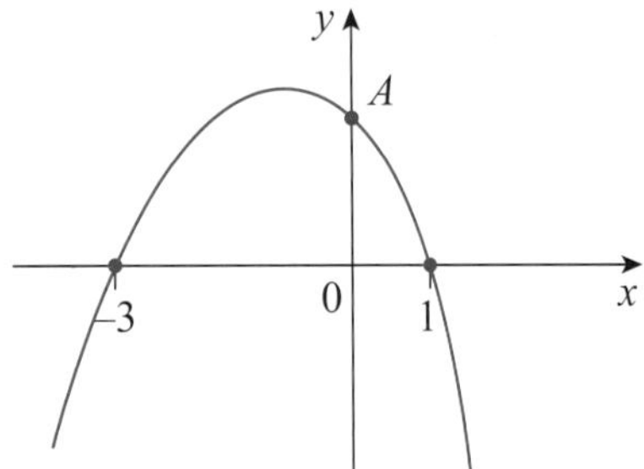

Use the graph to answer the following questions:

(a) What is the x co-ordinate of the maximum value of $f'(x)$?

(b) For what values of x is $f'(x)$ decreasing?

(c) Find the values of x where:

(i) $f(x)$ has a local minimum,

(ii) $f(x)$ has a local maximum.

(d) $A(0, 6)$ is a point on the graph. Find the equation of the curve $y = f'(x)$.

(e) Hence find the equation of the curve $y = f(x)$ if it passes through $(3, -20)$.

2. **(a)** Show that the curve $y = \frac{1}{x}, x > 0$ is always decreasing. If the shaded area is 2, show that $a = e^2$.

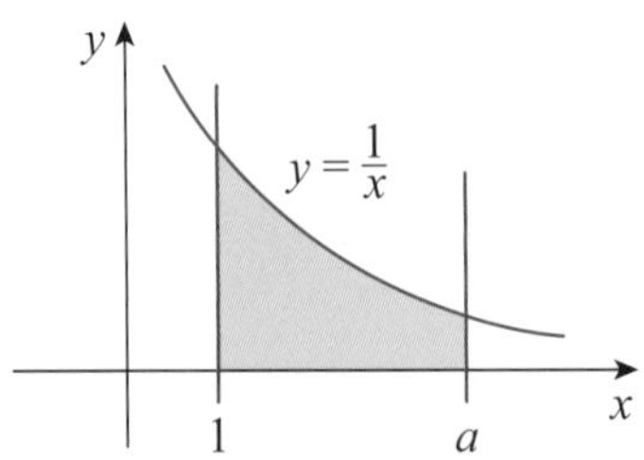

(b) The graph $y = e^{2x} - 4$ is shown below.

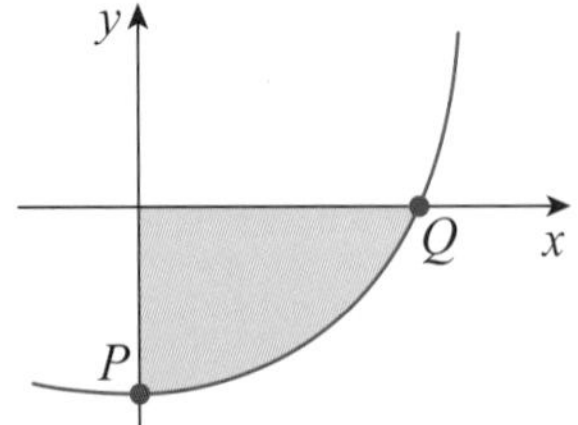

(i) Find P and Q.

(ii) Show that the curve is increasing for all $x \in \mathbb{R}$.

(iii) Find the area of the shaded region.

3. **(a)** Show that the polynomial $P(x) = x^3 - x - 6$ has a root of $x = 2$. By writing $P(x)$ in the form $(x - 2)(x^2 + bx + c)$, show that $P(x) = 0$ has no more real roots.

(b) Find the slope of the tangent to $P(x) = x^3 - x - 6$ at $(2, 0)$.

(c) The graph of $P(x) = x^3 - x - 6 = 0$ is shown below. Find the area of the shaded region.

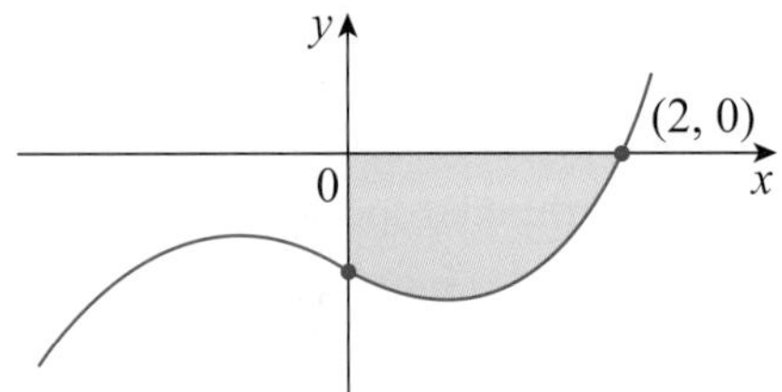

4. The following diagram shows the curve with equation $y = 6x^2 - x^3$ and the line l.

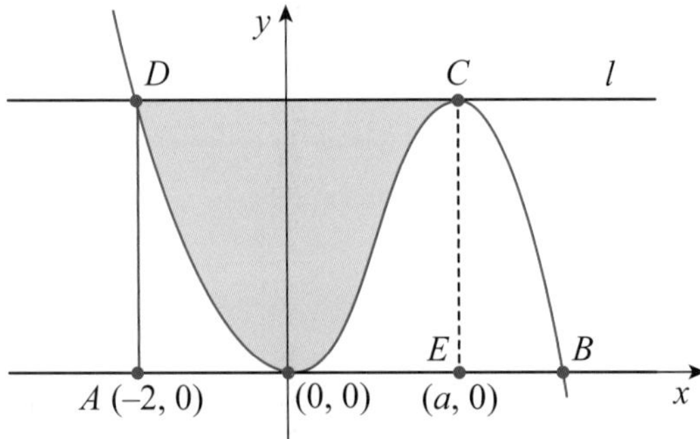

(a) Find the local maximum and the local minimum of the curve $y = 6x^2 - x^3$.

(b) l is a tangent to the curve at C, the local maximum of $y = 6x^2 - x^3$. Find the equation of l.

(c) Find the point B where $y = 6x^2 - x^3$ crosses the x-axis.

(d) Show that D has co-ordinates $(-2, 32)$.

(e) Find the area of the rectangle $AECD$ if $E(a, 0)$, where a is the x co-ordinate of C.

(f) Find $\int_{-2}^{a} y\, dx$.

(g) Find the shaded area.

5. The following diagram shows a sketch of the curve $y = 2(3^x + 1)$. It intersects the y-axis at P.

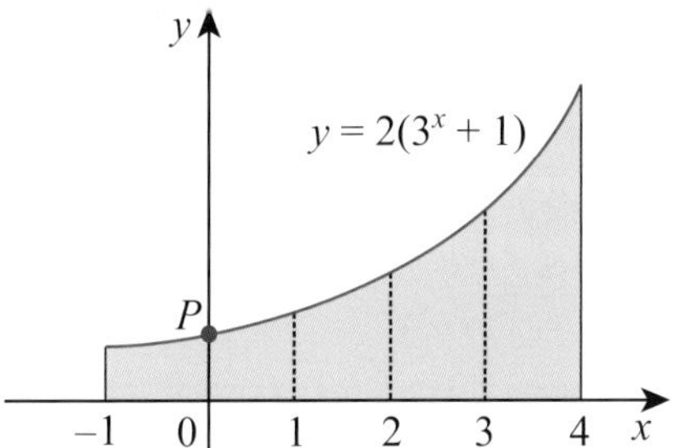

(a) Find the co-ordinates of P.

(b) Use the trapezoidal rule with five strips to find the area under the curve and between the line $x = -1$, $x = 4$ and the x-axis.

(c) Evaluate $\int_{-1}^{4} 2(3^x + 1)\,dx$.

Find the percentage error between the true value of the area and the estimate from part **(b)**, correct to one decimal place.

(d) The line $y = 14$ intersects $y = 2(3^x + 1)$ at Q.

(i) Show that the x co-ordinate of Q satisfies the equation $3^x = 6$.

(ii) Find x to three significant figures.

6. The curve $y = f(x) = 12 - 2x - x^4$ is shown.

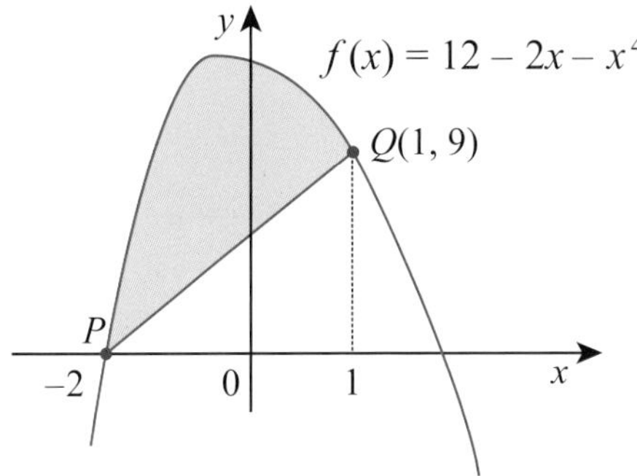

(a) Show that the points $P(-2, 0)$ and $Q(1, 9)$ both lie on the curve $y = f(x)$.

(b) Find the equation of the line PQ.

(c) Find the area between the curve $y = f(x)$ and the straight line PQ.

7. The equation of the curve c is

$y = 4x^{\frac{3}{2}} - 12x + 18, x \geq 0$.

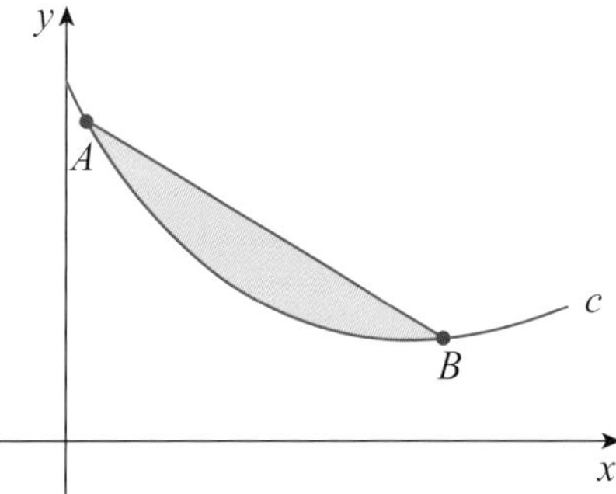

(a) Show that $A(1, 10)$ is on the curve.

(b) Find the minimum turning point B.

(c) Find the equation of the straight line AB.

(d) Find the shaded area between the line AB and the curve c.

8. **(a)** The curve $y = \sin^2 x, 0 \leq x \leq \pi$ is shown in the diagram. Find the shaded area given that $\sin^2 x = \frac{1}{2}(1 - \cos 2x)$.

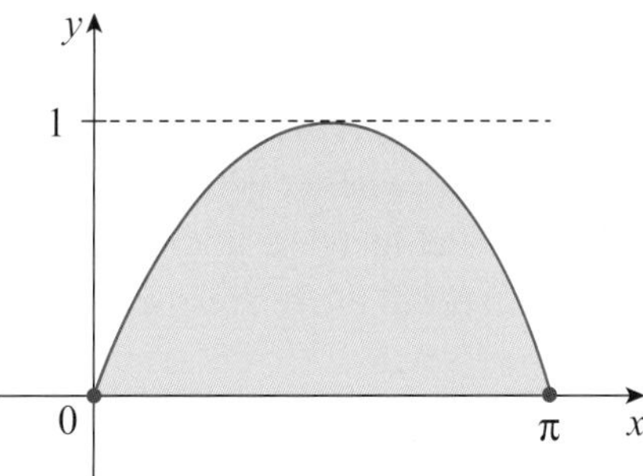

(b) An amount of money, €5000, is compounded continuously according to the law $A = 5000e^{0 \cdot 04t}$, where A is the amount of money in the bank at time t years. What is the average amount of money in the bank over the course of 5 years, correct to the nearest euro?

(c) (i) Find the points of intersection P and Q of the curves $f(x)$ and $g(x)$, $x \geq 0$, $x \in \mathbb{R}$.

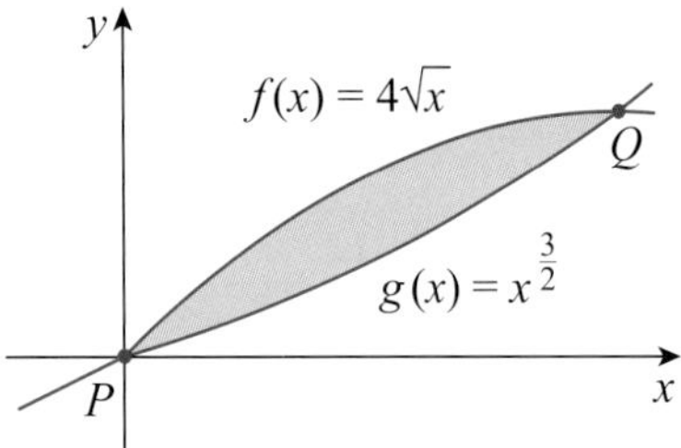

(ii) Find the shaded area.

9. The rate R of oil production in a certain country is given by $R = -5t^2 + 40t + 600$ $(0 \leq t \leq 9)$, where R is in millions of barrels per year and t is the time in years since the start of 2004 $(t = 0)$. During that same period of time, the country exported oil to Europe at a rate of $Q = -2t^2 + 20t + 200$ $(0 \leq t \leq 9)$, where Q is in millions of barrels per year. Find how much oil was not exported by this country to Europe between 2008 and 2012.

10. If the birth rate $f(t)$ of the population of a city is modelled by $f(t) = 2400e^{0\cdot03t}$ per year and the death rate $g(t)$ per year is modelled by $g(t) = 1200e^{0\cdot02t}$, where t is time in years from $t = 0$, find the net increase in the population over 10 years, correct to the nearest whole number.

11. The number of people N per day that ate in a new restaurant t days after its opening can be approximated by $N = \frac{t^3}{120} - \frac{3t^2}{8} + 5t + 40$ for the first 21 days of its existence. During the first 21 days find:

(a) the maximum number of people per day that ate in the restaurant, correct to the nearest whole number,

(b) the average number of people per day over the 21 days that ate in the restaurant.

12. The following diagram shows the graph of $f(x) = \sin x$ from $x = 0$ to $x = \frac{\pi}{2}$. A line $g(x)$ is drawn from a point $Q(0, h)$ on the y-axis to the local maximum P of $f(x) = \sin x$.

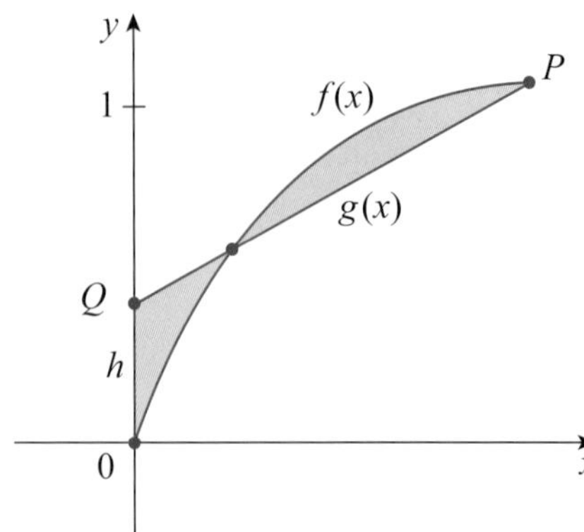

(a) Find the co-ordinates of P.

(b) Using the fact that $\int_a^b y\,dx = \int_a^c y\,dx + \int_c^b y\,dx$, find h if the two shaded areas are equal.

13. (a) The slope of the tangent to a curve $y = f(x)$ at any point (x, y) on the curve is $6x^2 - 2x + 3$. If $(-1, -6)$ is on the curve, find the equation of the curve.

(b) Evaluate $\int_2^3 f'(x)\,dx$, if $f(x) = e^{2x}$.

(c) The following diagram shows a graph of the function $y = (3x - 4)(3x + 4)$.

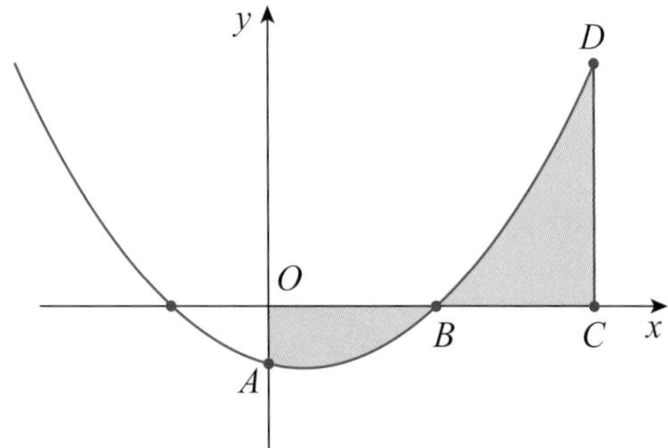

The co-ordinates of C are $(t, 0)$. If area AOB = area BCD, find t, where O is $(0, 0)$.

14. Consider the function $y = x^3 - x^2 - x$.

(a) Show that it has a local maximum at $\left(-\frac{1}{3}, \frac{5}{27}\right)$ and a local minimum at $(1, -1)$.

(b) Show that it crosses the x-axis at $x = 0$.

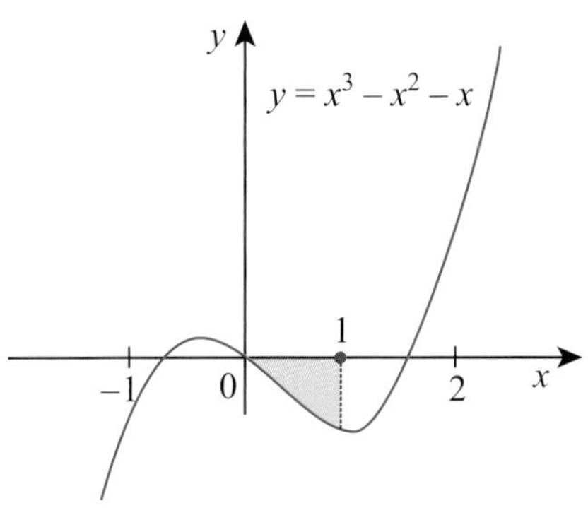

(c) Show that the area enclosed by the curve, the x-axis and the lines $x = 0$ and $x = 1$ is $\frac{7}{12}$.

15. The price €P of a new sun cream varies with time t, according to the formula $P = ae^{0\cdot 2t}$, where t is in years and a is a constant.

(a) Find a, if the initial price is €5.

(b) Find the rate of change of P when **(i)** $t = 0$, **(ii)** $t = 5$.

(c) Find the average price of the sun cream over the first 5 years of its production. Give your answer to the nearest cent.

16. The temperature T (in °C) recorded during a day obeyed the equation $T = 0\cdot 001t^3 - \dfrac{t^2}{10} + 22$, where t is the number of hours from noon ($t = 0$) and $-12 \leq t \leq 12$. Find:

(a) the temperature at noon,

(b) the temperature at 3 p.m., correct to one decimal place,

(c) the rate of change of the temperature at 8 p.m.,

(d) the maximum temperature,

(e) the average temperature during the day (–12 hours to +12 hours).

17. The population P of a town increases steadily from June 1980 ($t = 0$). The rate of increase of the population is directly proportional to the inverse square root of t, where t is the number of years after 1980.

(a) Write down an equation for the rate of change of the population.

(b) In June 1980 ($t = 0$), the population was 42 000 and in June 1989 it was 66 000. Show that $P = 42\,000 + 8000\sqrt{t}$.

(c) If the population continued to rise at the same rate, what was the population in June 1996?

(d) Find how many years it takes the population to become 90 000.

(e) Find the average population in the town from June 1980 to June 1996, correct to the nearest whole number.

18. The cable CD between two pylons has the equation $y = 15\left(e^{-\frac{x}{100}} + e^{\frac{x}{100}}\right)$, where x and y are in metres.

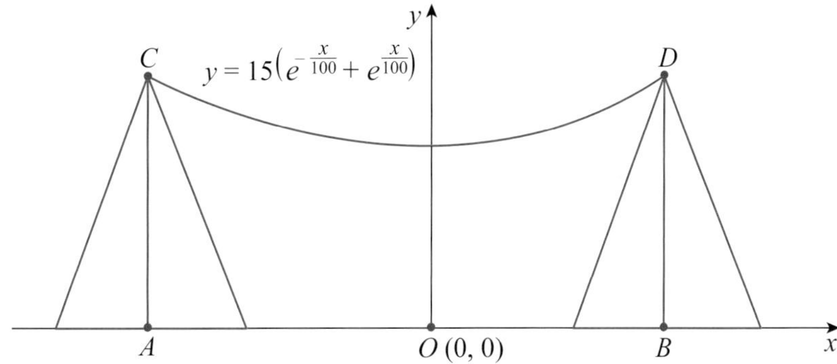

(a) Find the height of the cable above the ground at $x = 0$.

(b) Find the height of each pylon if $|OB| = 100$ m, correct to one decimal place.

(c) Find the area under the cable from A to B, correct to the nearest m^2.

(d) Find the average value of the height of the cable above the ground, correct to the nearest metre.

(e) Show that the local minimum value of y occurs at $x = 0$.

19. (a) Show that $\int_a^b g(x)\,dx = \int_a^c g(x)\,dx + \int_c^b g(x)\,dx$.

(b) The temperature of a hotplate θ varies with the distance from the centre O of the plate.

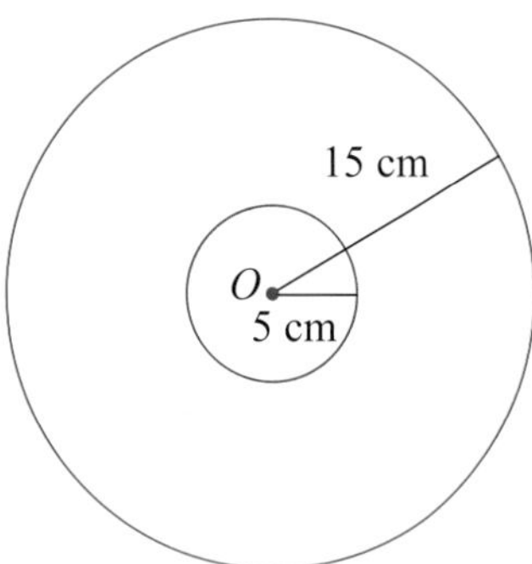

(i) Write down an expression for the average temperature from 0 cm to 5 cm.

(ii) Write down an expression for the average temperature from 5 cm to 15 cm.

(iii) If the average temperature from 0 cm to 5 cm is 102 °C and the average temperature from 5 cm to 15 cm is 87 °C, find the average temperature from 0 cm to 15 cm.

(c) Prove that:

(i) $\int_a^a g(x)\,dx = 0$

(ii) $-\int_a^b g(x)\,dx = \int_b^a g(x)\,dx$

20. The length of daylight varies over the seasons. Over the spring and summer (182 days), the average length l of a day in hours is given by $l = 12 + 4\sin\left(\frac{\pi t}{182}\right)$, where t is the number of days after the start of the spring equinox.

(a) What is the length of the longest day? When does this occur?

(b) What is the length of the day at $t = 0$? Why is this called the equinox?

(c) What is the average length of a day during the spring and summer (182 days), correct to one decimal place?

21. (a) If $f(x) = x\sin x$,

(i) find $f'(x)$,

(ii) evaluate $\int (x\cos x + \sin x)\,dx$.

(b) Use the result in part **(a) (ii)** to evaluate $\int x\cos x\,dx$.

22. (a) Show that $1 + \frac{1}{x+1} = \frac{x+2}{x+1}$. Hence, evaluate $\int \frac{x+2}{x+1}\,dx$.

(b) If $f(x) = x\ln x$, find $f'(x)$. Hence, evaluate $\int \ln x\,dx$. Verify your answer.

SUMMARY

1. Notation:

(a) $\int g(x)\,dx$ = A function $f(x)$ such that when you differentiate it with respect to x, you get $g(x)$.

$\therefore f'(x) = g(x)$

(b) $\frac{dy}{dx} = g(x)$

$dy = g(x)\,dx$

$\int dy = \int g(x)\,dx$

$y = \int g(x)\,dx$

2. Rules:

(a) Sum rule:

$\int (u(x) + v(x))\,dx = \int u(x)\,dx + \int v(x)\,dx$

(b) Multiplication by a constant rule:

$\int c \times u(x)\,dx = c\int u(x)\,dx$, where c is a constant

(c) The one rule:

$\int dx = x + c$

3. Definite integration:

$\int_a^b g(x)\,dx = [f(x)]_a^b = f(b) - f(a)$

4. Functions:

(a) $\int x^p dx = \frac{x^{p+1}}{p+1}, p \in \mathbb{R}, p \neq -1$

$\int (ax+b)^p\,dx = \frac{1}{a} \times \frac{(ax+b)^{p+1}}{p+1}, p \in \mathbb{R}, p \neq -1$

(b) $\int e^x\,dx = e^x + c$

$\int e^{px+q}\,dx = \frac{1}{p}e^{px+q} + c$

(c) $\int a^x\,dx = \frac{a^x}{\ln a} + c$

$\int a^{px+q}\,dx = \frac{a^{px+q}}{p\ln a} + c$

(d) $\int \frac{1}{x}\,dx = \ln x + c\ (x > 0)$

$\int \frac{1}{px+q}\,dx = \frac{1}{p}\ln(px+q) + c$

(e) $\int \sin x\,dx = -\cos x + c$

$\int \sin(px+q)\,dx = -\frac{1}{p}\cos(px+q) + c$

(f) $\int \cos x\,dx = \sin x + c$

$\int \cos(px+q)\,dx = \frac{1}{p}\sin(px+q) + c$

5. Area:

(a) One curve:

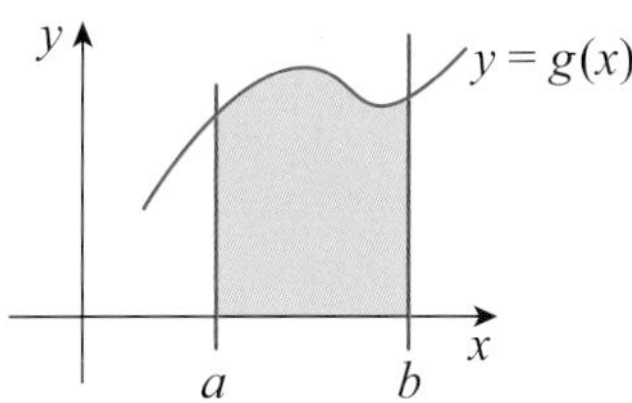

$A = \int_a^b g(x)\,dx$

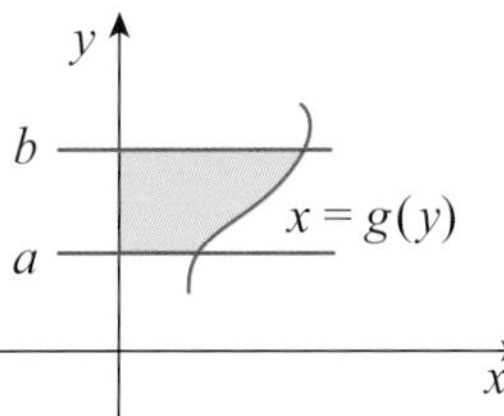

$A = \int_a^b g(y)\,dy$

(b) Two curves:

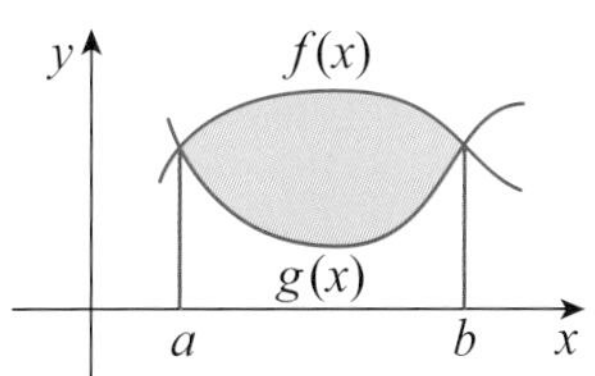

If $f(x) \geq g(x)$ on $[a, b]$:

Shaded area $= \int_a^b [f(x) - g(x)]\,dx$

6. Average value:

The average value $\bar{y}$ of a function $y = g(x)$ on an interval $[a, b]$ is:

$$\bar{y} = \frac{\int_a^b g(x)\,dx}{b-a} = \frac{\int_a^b y\,dx}{b-a}$$

Mathematical Induction

A mathematical proof establishes the validity of a mathematical statement. Mathematical proofs can be subdivided into direct proofs and indirect proofs. Proof by contradiction is an example of an indirect proof. Proof by induction is an example of a direct proof and is a proof of statements involving natural numbers.

Chapter 27 Proof by Induction

Learning Outcomes

- To understand the concept of proof by induction.
- To know the three steps for carrying out mathematical induction.
- To carry out mathematical induction on sums, divisibilities, inequalities and de Moivre's theorem.

27.1 What is proof by induction?

WORKED EXAMPLE Why a proper proof is needed

Consider the following:

$1 + 2 = 3 = \frac{1}{2}(2 \times 3)$

$1 + 2 + 3 = 6 = \frac{1}{2}(3 \times 4)$

$1 + 2 + 3 + 4 = 10 = \frac{1}{2}(4 \times 5)$

$1 + 2 + 3 + 4 + 5 = 15 = \frac{1}{2}(5 \times 6)$

This numerical evidence 'seems' to indicate that $1 + 2 + 3 + \ldots + n = \frac{1}{2}n(n + 1)$, for all $n \in \mathbb{N}$. However, 'seem to' is not an acceptable level of proof. All you need is one example to destroy your 'discovery' completely. Consider the table below.

n	$n^2 + n + 41$	*Total*
1	$1^2 + 1 + 41$	= 43 (a prime number)
2	$2^2 + 2 + 41$	= 47 (a prime number)
3	$3^2 + 3 + 41$	= 53 (a prime number)
4	$4^2 + 4 + 41$	= 61 (a prime number)
5	$5^2 + 5 + 41$	= 71 (a prime number)
6	$6^2 + 6 + 41$	= 83 (a prime number)
7	$7^2 + 7 + 41$	= 97 (a prime number)
8	$8^2 + 8 + 41$	= 113 (a prime number)
9	$9^2 + 9 + 41$	= 131 (a prime number)
10	$10^2 + 10 + 41$	= 151 (a prime number)

Again, from this numerical evidence you might conclude that $n^2 + n + 41 = p$, where p is a prime number for all $n \in \mathbb{N}$. You would be wrong. In fact, for all $n \leq 40$, $n \in \mathbb{N}$, it is true.

However, look at $n = 41$. When $n = 41$:

$n^2 + n + 41 = 41^2 + 41 + 41$

$= 41(41 + 1 + 1) = 41 \times 43$

This number is not prime.

However, discovering general mathematical results from numerical evidence (as in the worked example) is very fruitful if these results can be proved to be true for all values of the variable. This is where proof by induction comes in.

Returning to the result involving the natural numbers n where 'it appears' that $1 + 2 + \ldots + n = \frac{n}{2}(n + 1)$: this can be proved by induction **for all** $n \in \mathbb{N}$.

Proof by induction is a domino effect or chain-reaction proof involving three steps.

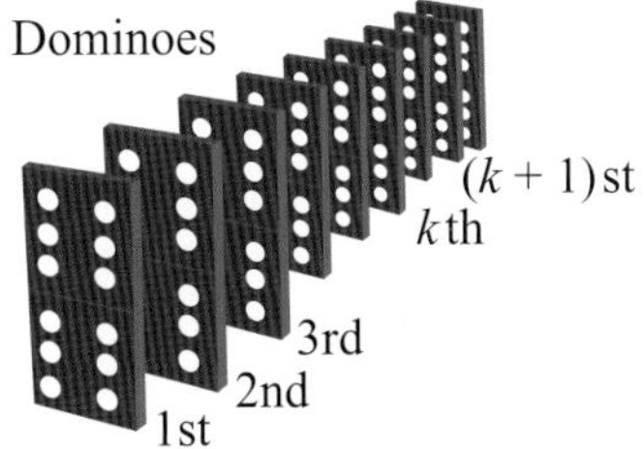

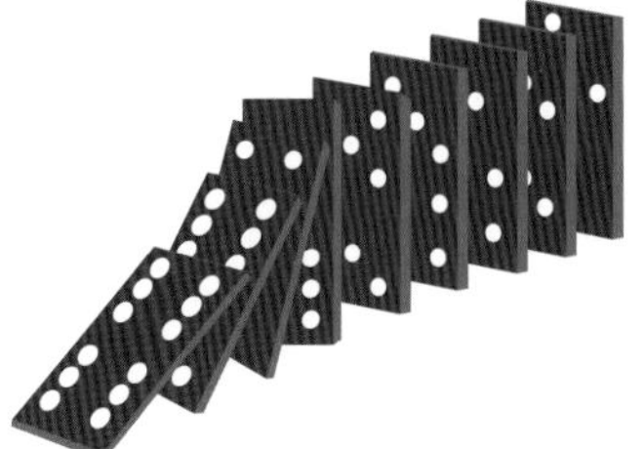

If you can show that for a line of dominoes:

(i) The first one falls and **(ii)** if the kth one falls, ensures that the $(k + 1)$st also falls, then all will fall.

Steps in proof by induction

To prove results involving natural numbers by induction, follow the steps below:

1. Prove that the result is true for some starting value of $n \in \mathbb{N}$ (usually 1 but not always).
2. Assume the result is true for $n = k$.
3. Prove that the result is true for $n = k + 1$, using 2.

TIP

(i) Always do induction in the order of the steps above.
(ii) It is vital that you use **Step 2** in proving **Step 3**.

27.2 Four types of proof by induction

There are four types of mathematical statements that will be proved by induction.

1. Sums ($\sum$)
2. Factorisations (divisibilities)
3. Inequalities
4. De Moivre's theorem

1. Sums

Technique

For $n = k$: $\sum_{n=1}^{k} T_n = (T_1 + T_2 + \ldots + T_k)$ [Write out the series as a list and bracket all terms.]

For $n = k + 1$: $\sum_{n=1}^{k+1} T_n = (T_1 + T_2 + \ldots + T_k) + T_{k+1}$ [Write out the series as a list and isolate the last term T_{k+1}]

ACTIVITY 1

ACTION
Preparing series for mathematical induction

OBJECTIVE
To explore some of the techniques that prove series by induction

EXAMPLE 1

Prove that $\sum_{r=1}^{n} r = \frac{n}{2}(n+1)$ for all $n \in \mathbb{N}$.

Solution

Step 1: $n = 1$: Prove $\sum_{r=1}^{1} r = \frac{1}{2}(1+1)$

Proof: $\sum_{r=1}^{1} r = 1 = \frac{1}{2}(1+1) = 1$. Therefore, it is true for $n = 1$.

Step 2: $n = k$: Assume $\sum_{r=1}^{k} r = \frac{k}{2}(k+1)$

In other words, assume $(1 + 2 + \ldots + k) = \frac{k}{2}(k+1)$

Step 3: $n = k + 1$: Prove $\sum_{r=1}^{k+1} r = \frac{(k+1)(k+2)}{2}$

Proof: $\sum_{r=1}^{k+1} r = \underbrace{(1 + 2 + \ldots + k)} + (k+1) = \frac{(k)(k+1)}{2} + (k+1)$ [By **Step 2**.]

$= \frac{(k+1)(k) + 2(k+1)}{2}$

$= \frac{(k+1)(k+2)}{2}$

Therefore, assuming it is true for $n = k$ means it is true for $n = k + 1$.

So, true for $n = 1$ and true for $n = k$ means it is true for $n = k + 1$ implies it is true for all $n \in \mathbb{N}$.

EXAMPLE 2

Prove that $\sum_{r=1}^{n} x^r = \frac{x(1-x^n)}{(1-x)}$ for all $n \in \mathbb{N}$.

Solution

Step 1: $n = 1$: Prove $\sum_{r=1}^{1} x^r = \frac{x(1-x)}{(1-x)}$

Proof: $\sum_{r=1}^{1} x^r = x^1 = \frac{x(1-x)}{(1-x)} = x$. Therefore, it is true for $n = 1$.

Step 2: $n = k$: Assume $\sum_{r=1}^{k} x^r = \frac{x(1-x^k)}{(1-x)}$

In other words, assume $(x^1 + x^2 + \ldots + x^k) = \frac{x(1-x^k)}{(1-x)}$

Step 3: $n = k + 1$: Prove $\sum_{r=1}^{k+1} x^r = \frac{x(1 - x^{k+1})}{1 - x}$

Proof: $\sum_{r=1}^{k+1} x^r = (x^1 + \ldots + x^k) + x^{k+1} = \frac{x(1 - x^k)}{(1 - x)} + x^{k+1}$

$$= \frac{x(1 - x^k) + x^{k+1}(1 - x)}{(1 - x)}$$

$$= \frac{x - x^{k+1} + x^{k+1} - x^{k+2}}{1 - x}$$

$$= \frac{x - x^{k+2}}{1 - x}$$

$$= \frac{x(1 - x^{k+1})}{1 - x}$$

Therefore, assuming it is true for $n = k$ means it is true for $n = k + 1$. So, true for $n = 1$ and true for $n = k$ means it is true for $n = k + 1$ implies it is true for all $n \in \mathbb{N}$.

2. Factorisations (divisibilities)

Technique

5 is a factor of 15 because it divides into 15 a whole number of times. This means $15 = (\text{whole number}) \times 5$.

b is a factor of $a \Rightarrow a = mb$, where $m \in \mathbb{N}$.

ACTIVITY 2

ACTION
Preparing divisibilities for mathematical induction

OBJECTIVE
To explore some of the techniques that prove divisibilities by induction

EXAMPLE 3

Prove that $7^{2n+1} + 1$ is divisible by 8 for all $n \in \mathbb{N}$.

Solution

Step 1: $n = 1$: Prove $7^3 + 1$ is divisible by 8.

Proof: $\frac{7^3 + 1}{8} = \frac{344}{8} = 43$. Therefore, it is true for $n = 1$.

Step 2: $n = k$: Assume $7^{2k+1} + 1$ is divisible by 8.

In other words, assume $7^{2k+1} + 1 = 8m$, $m \in \mathbb{N}$

$\therefore\ 7^{2k+1} = (8m - 1)$

Step 3: $n = (k + 1)$: Prove $7^{2k+3} + 1$ is divisible by 8. $\left[\begin{array}{l} 2(k+1)+1 \\ = 2k + 2 + 1 = 2k + 3 \end{array}\right]$

Proof: $7^{2k+3} + 1 = 7^2 \times 7^{2k+1} + 1$ [Break it up.]

$= 49(8m - 1) + 1$ [By **Step 2**.]

$= 8 \times 49 \times m - 48$

$= 8(49m - 6)$

$= 8 \times (\text{whole number})$

$\therefore\ 7^{2k+3} + 1$ is divisible by 8.

Therefore, assuming it is true for $n = k$ means it is true for $n = k + 1$. So, true for $n = 1$ and true for $n = k$ means it is true for $n = k + 1$ implies it is true for all $n \in \mathbb{N}$.

EXAMPLE 4

Prove that 2 is a factor of $n^2 + n$ for all $n \in \mathbb{N}$.

Solution

Step 1: $n = 1$: Prove $1^2 + 1$ is divisible by 2.

Proof: $\frac{1^2+1}{2} = \frac{2}{2} = 1$. Therefore, it is true for $n = 1$.

Step 2: $n = k$: Assume $k^2 + k$ is divisible by 2.

In other words, assume $k^2 + k = 2m$.

$$k^2 = (2m - k)$$

Step 3: $n = (k + 1)$: Prove $(k + 1)^2 + (k + 1)$ is divisible by 2.

Proof: $(k + 1)^2 + (k + 1) = k^2 + 2k + 1 + k + 1$

$= (2m - k) + 3k + 2$

$= 2m + 2k + 2$

$= 2(m + k + 1)$

$= 2 \times$ (whole number)

Therefore, assuming it is true for $n = k$ means it is true for $n = k + 1$. So, true for $n = 1$ and true for $n = k$ means it is true for $n = k + 1$ implies it is true for all $n \in \mathbb{N}$.

ACTIVITY 3

ACTION
Preparing inequalities for mathematical induction

OBJECTIVE
To explore some of the techniques that prove inequalities by induction

3. Inequalities

(a) Technique for inequalities with factorial and exponential expressions

When a factorial occurs in an inequality, put it on the left-hand side of the inequality and break it up into factors.

$(k + 1)! = (k + 1)(k)(k - 1) \dots 1$

$= (k + 1)\{k(k - 1)(k - 2) \dots 1\}$

$= (k + 1) \times k!$

TIP

1. We are dealing only with natural numbers. This means the smallest value of $(k + 1)$, $k \in \mathbb{N}$ is 2.
   $\therefore k + 1 \geq 2$
2. $a = b$ and $s > t \Rightarrow as > bt$ for natural numbers a, b, s, t.

EXAMPLE 5

Prove that $3^n < n!$ for all $n \geq 7$, $n \in \mathbb{N}$.

Solution

First turn it around: $n! > 3^n$ [So that the factorial is on the left.]

Step 1: $n = 7$: Prove $7! > 3^7$. [7 is the smallest natural number in this question.]

Proof: $7! = 5040$

$3^7 = 2187$

$\therefore 7! > 3^7$. Therefore, it is true for $n = 7$.

Step 2: $n = k$: Assume $k! > 3^k$.

Step 3: $n = k + 1$: Prove $(k + 1)! > 3^{k+1}$.

Proof: $(k + 1)! = (k + 1) \times k!$

$(k + 1)! > (k + 1) \times 3^k$ [From **Step 2**.]

$(k + 1)! > 8 \times 3^k$ [The smallest value $(k + 1)$ can have is $8 \Rightarrow k + 1 \geq 8$]

$\therefore (k + 1)! > 3 \times 3^k$

$(k + 1)! > 3^{k+1}$

Therefore, assuming it is true for $n = k$ means it is true for $n = k + 1$. So, true for $n = 7$ and true for $n = k$ means it is true for $n = k + 1$ implies it is true for all $n \geq 7, n \in \mathbb{N}$.

(b) Techniques for inequalities with exponential and polynomial expressions

(i) Polynomial expressions of degree 1 (n^1)

In **Step 1** put the exponential expression on the left-hand side of the inequality and in **Step 3** break up the exponential expression.

EXAMPLE 6

Prove by induction that $(1 + x)^n \geq 1 + nx$ for all $n \in \mathbb{N}$ $(x \geq -1)$.

Solution

Step 1: $n = 1$: Prove $(1 + x)^1 \geq 1 + 1x$.

Proof: $(1 + x)^1 = 1 + x$

$\therefore (1 + x)^1 \geq 1 + 1x$. Therefore, it is true for $n = 1$.

Step 2: $n = k$: Assume $(1 + x)^k \geq 1 + kx$.

Step 3: $n = k + 1$: Prove $(1 + x)^{k+1} \geq 1 + (k + 1)x$.

Proof: $(1 + x)^{k+1} = (1 + x)^k(1 + x)$

$(1 + x)^{k+1} \geq (1 + kx)(1 + x)$ [From **Step 2**.]

$(1 + x)^{k+1} \geq 1 + kx + x + kx^2$

$(1 + x)^{k+1} \geq 1 + (k + 1)x + kx^2$

$\therefore (1 + x)^{k+1} \geq 1 + (k + 1)x$ [Since $kx^2 > 0$]

Therefore, assuming it is true for $n = k$ means it is true for $n = k + 1$. So, true for $n = 1$ and true for $n = k$ means it is true for $n = k + 1$ implies it is true for all $n \in \mathbb{N}$.

(ii) Polynomial expressions of degree two or higher $(n^2, n^3, n^4, \ldots)$

In **Step 1** put the polynomial expression on the left-hand side of the inequality and then in **Step 3** factorise the polynomial expression so that what appears on the left-hand side in **Step 2** is a factor of the polynomial.

TIP

(i) $3 > 2 \Rightarrow \frac{1}{2} > \frac{1}{3}$ [By dividing by 6]

(ii) $k > 7 \Rightarrow \frac{1}{7} > \frac{1}{k}$ $(k > 0)$ [By dividing by $7k$]

EXAMPLE 7

Prove that $2^n > n^2$ for all $n \geq 4$, $n \in \mathbb{N}$.

Solution

First of all turn it around: $n^2 < 2^n$

Step 1: $n = 1$: Prove $1^2 < 2^1$.

Proof: $1^2 < 2^1 \Leftrightarrow 1 < 2$. Therefore, it is true for $n = 1$.

Step 2: $n = k$: Assume $k^2 < 2^k$.

Step 3: $n = k + 1$: Prove $(k + 1)^2 < 2^{k+1}$.

Proof: $(k+1)^2 = k^2\left(1 + \frac{1}{k}\right)^2$

$(k+1)^2 < 2^k\left(1 + \frac{1}{k}\right)^2$ [From **Step 2**.]

$(k+1)^2 < 2^k\left(1 + \frac{1}{4}\right)^2$ $\left[k \geq 4 \Rightarrow \frac{1}{k} \leq \frac{1}{4}\right]$

$(k+1)^2 < 2^k\left(\frac{5}{4}\right)^2$

$(k+1)^2 < 2^k\left(\frac{25}{16}\right)$ [**Note:** $\frac{25}{16} < 2$]

$(k+1)^2 < 2^k \times 2$

$\therefore (k+1)^2 < 2^{k+1}$

Therefore, assuming it is true for $n = k$ means it is true for $n = k + 1$. So, true for $n = 4$ and true for $n = k$ means it is true for $n = k + 1$ implies it is true for all $n \geq 4$, $n \in \mathbb{N}$.

4. De Moivre's theorem

EXAMPLE 8

Prove that $[r(\cos\theta + i\sin\theta)]^n = r^n(\cos n\theta + i\sin n\theta)$, $n \in \mathbb{N}$.

Solution

Step 1: $n = 1$: Prove $[r(\cos\theta + i\sin\theta)]^1 = r^1(\cos 1\theta + i\sin 1\theta)$.

$r(\cos\theta + i\sin\theta) = r(\cos\theta + i\sin\theta)$

It is true for $n = 1$.

Step 2: $n = k$: Assume $[r(\cos\theta + i\sin\theta)]^k = r^k(\cos k\theta + i\sin k\theta)$.

Step 3: $n = k + 1$: Prove

$[r(\cos\theta + i\sin\theta)]^{k+1} = r^{k+1}[(\cos(k+1)\theta + i\sin(k+1)\theta)]$

Proof: $[r(\cos\theta + i\sin\theta)]^{k+1} = [r(\cos\theta + i\sin\theta)]^k[r(\cos\theta + i\sin\theta)]$

$= r^k(\cos k\theta + i\sin k\theta)r(\cos\theta + i\sin\theta)$ [From **Step 2**.]

$= r^{k+1}[(\cos k\theta\cos\theta - \sin k\theta\sin\theta) + i(\sin k\theta\cos\theta + \cos k\theta\sin\theta)]$

$= r^{k+1}[\cos(k+1)\theta + i\sin(k+1)\theta]$

Therefore, assuming it is true for $n = k$ means it is true for $n = k + 1$. So, true for $n = 1$ and true for $n = k$ means it is true for $n = k + 1$ implies it is true for all $n \in \mathbb{N}$.

EXERCISE 1

1. Prove the following by induction (series):

   (a) $\sum_{r=1}^{n} r^2 = \frac{n}{6}(n+1)(2n+1)$

   (b) $\sum_{r=1}^{n} r^3 = \left(\frac{n}{2}(n+1)\right)^2$

   (c) $\sum_{r=1}^{n} (3r-2) = \frac{n(3n-1)}{2}$

   (d) $\sum_{p=1}^{n} ar^{p-1} = \frac{a(1-r^n)}{1-r}$

   (e) $\sum_{r=1}^{n} 2^r = 2(2^n - 1)$

2. Prove the following by induction (factors):

   (a) $7^n - 4^n$ is divisible by 3 for all $n \in \mathbb{N}$

   (b) 8 is a factor of $9^n + 7$ for all $n \in \mathbb{N}$

   (c) $n^3 - n + 3$ is divisible by 3 for all $n \geq 2$, $n \in \mathbb{N}$

   (d) $11^{n+2} + 12^{2n+1}$ is divisible by 133 for all $n \in \mathbb{N}$

   (e) $x^n - y^n$ is divisible by $x - y$ for all $n \in \mathbb{N}$, $x, y \in \mathbb{N}, x > y$

3. Prove the following by induction (inequalities):

   (a) $n < 2^n$ for all $n \in \mathbb{N}$

   (b) $n! > 4^n$ for all $n \geq 9$, $n \in \mathbb{N}$

   (c) $n^3 < 3^n$ for all $n \geq 4$, $n \in \mathbb{N}$

   (d) $(1+a)^n > 1 + na$ for all $n \geq 2$, $n \in \mathbb{N}, a > 0$

SUMMARY

1. Steps for proving by induction:
   (a) Prove that the result is true for a starting value of $n \in \mathbb{N}$.
   (b) Assume the result is true for $n = k$.
   (c) Prove that the result is true for $n = k + 1$ using **(b)**.

2. Types:
   (a) Sums (Σ):

   Technique: $\sum_{n=1}^{k+1} T_r = (T_1 + T_2 + \cdots + T_k) + T_{k+1}$

   (b) Factorisation (divisibilities):

   Technique: b is a factor of $a \Rightarrow a = mb,\ m \in \mathbb{N}$

   (c) Inequalities:

   (i) Factorial/Exponential:
   - Put factorial on the left and break it up.
   - $a = b$ and $s > t \Rightarrow as > bt$
   - $(k + 1)! = (k + 1) \times k!$

   (ii) Polynomial/Exponential:

   (1) Linear polynomials (polynomials in which the power of the variable n is 1):
   In **Step 1** put the exponential expression on the left-hand side of the inequality and in **Step 3** break up the exponential expression.

   (2) Polynomials in which the power of the variable is greater than 1 (e.g. n^2, n^3, n^4, etc.):
   In **Step 1** put the polynomial expression on the left-hand side of the inequality and in **Step 3** factorise the polynomial expression so that what appears on the left-hand side in **Step 2** is a factor of the polynomial.

   Note: If $k \geq a$ and a and k are both positive,

   then dividing by $ak \Rightarrow \frac{1}{a} \geq \frac{1}{k} \Rightarrow \frac{1}{a^2} \geq \frac{1}{k^2}$

   (d) De Moivre's theorem

Answers

Section 1

Chapter 1

Exercise 1

1. (a) Composite; $2 \times 3 \times 3$ (b) Composite; $3 \times 3 \times 5$ (c) Prime (d) Composite; $2 \times 2 \times 7$ (e) Composite; $3 \times 3 \times 2 \times 5$ (f) Composite; 5×17 (g) Composite; 2×31 (h) Prime (i) Composite; 3×17 (j) Prime **2.** 47, 91 **3.** No; Even **4.** No; Divisible by 3 **5.** (a) No; Even (b) No; Divisible by 5 **7.** 17 girls, 19 boys **8.** $3 = 2 + 1$ **9.** (a) 2, 4, 6, 8, 10, 12, 14, 16, 18, 20 (b) $2n$ (c) Yes **10.** (a) 1, 3, 5, 7, 9, 11, 13, 15, 17, 19 (b) $2n - 1$ (c) Yes **11.** (a) 3 453 389 167 (b) $p = 2111$, $q = 1783$ **12.** 3, 7, 31, 127, 2047, 8191, 131 071, 524 287 **13.** 13, 17 are prime; Predators hatching every 2, 3, 4, 5, 6, 7, 8, 9, 10, 11, 12 years will not coincide with cicadas

Exercise 2

1. 75 °C **2.** –27, –26, –25 **3.** 503 years **4.** –1 °C **5.** €26 000 **6.** 125 °C **7.** 180 °F **8.** 100 **9.** (a) –1 (b) –1 (c) 1 (d) 1 (e) 0 (f) –1 **10.** –9, –8, –7 **11.** (a) {…, –3, –2, –1, 0} (b) {1, 2, 3, 4, …}; Yes

Exercise 3

1. (b) (i) Yes; Because $\mathbb{Z} \subset \mathbb{Q}$ (ii) Yes; Because $\mathbb{N} \subset \mathbb{Q}$ **2.** (a) Infinite number (b) $0 < x < 1, x \in \mathbb{Q}$ **3.** (a) 2 (b) $\frac{35}{18}$ (c) $-\frac{4}{7}$ (d) $\frac{1}{4}$ **4.** (a) $\frac{2}{9}$ (b) $\frac{37}{99}$ (c) $\frac{409}{99}$ (d) $\frac{407}{90}$ **5.** (a) $x = 2$; $\mathbb{N}$ (b) $x = -5$; $\mathbb{Z}$ (c) $x = -\frac{2}{5}$; $\mathbb{Q}$

Exercise 4

1. (a) 72 (b) $\frac{69}{4}$ (c) 1·72 (d) $\frac{1}{\sqrt{2}}$ (e) $\frac{3\sqrt{2}}{4}$ (f) 0 (g) π (h) $\frac{5}{6}$ **2.** (a) 2 (b) 2 (c) $\sqrt{2} - 1$ (d) $\pi - 3$ (e) $\pi - 3$ (f) $\sqrt{3} - \sqrt{2}$ (g) $a - b$ (h) $b - a$

Chapter 2

Exercise 5

1. (a) 90% (b) 36% (c) 40% (d) 92·6% (e) 75% **2.** (a) 32 (b) 47 (c) €22·80 (d) 9920 (e) €320 **3.** (a) €2820·95 (b) €413·40 (c) 1 692 561 sq miles (d) 18 (e) €28·80 **4.** (a) €42 (b) 212 (c) 248·67 million (d) €560 (e) 51

Exercise 6

1. (a) 0·03 (b) 0·000412 (c) 357 000 (d) 2 000 000 (e) 0·00000056 (f) 0·00006 (g) 0·0001 (h) 100 000 (i) 3·3 (j) 780 000 000 **2.** (a) 15 (b) 100 **3.** (a) –9 (b) 15 (c) 15 **4.** (a) (i) 1000 (ii) 3 (iii) 5 (b) (i) It is 100 times too big (ii) 2701·34; She multiplied by 62 (iii) 2701·34 miles **5.** –6 **6.** 10^7 notes

Exercise 7

1. (a) €13·65 (b) (3·7 ± 0·2) Ω (c) (4 ± 0·2) mm (d) (3·8 ± 0·2) cm (e) (5·85 ± 1·44) cm^2 (f) (i) 560 ml (ii) 540 ml **2.** (a) (13 600 ± 544) kg/m^3 (b) (i) 80 g (ii) 20% (c) 7·5%; 67 kg

Exercise 8

1. (a) 43·0 cm^2 (b) 50·24 (c) 173·96 (d) $y = 3·012$ (e) 459·7 **2.** (a) 479 400 (b) 1·33 (c) 57·32 (d) 6·0 (e) 0·000573 **3.** 2·4 **4.** 0·37%

Exercise 9

1. 0·69 m/s **2.** 10 900 per year **3.** –3 °C/h **4.** (a) 6·92 m/s (b) 12·05 m/s (c) 10·44 m/s **5.** (a) –4000 l/h (b) –800 l/h (c) –2400 l/h **6.** 6 cm^3/s

Exercise 10

1. 360 km **2.** $y = 2·5x$ (a) 62·5 (b) 12 **3.** $F = 4a$; 140 **4.** $I = \frac{1}{3}V$; $\frac{10}{3}$ **5.** (a) $y = \frac{2}{3}x$ (b) $\frac{2}{3}$ (c) 600 **6.** (a) $F \propto x$ (b) $F = kx$ (c) 800 (d) 29·6 N **7.** 5; 14·4 **8.** (a) $w = 18$ (b) $u = 3$, $w = 5$ (c) $w = 45$, $u = 15$, $v = 85$ **9.** (a) Yes; $\frac{y}{x} = 7·5$ = constant (b) 7·5 (c) $y = 7·5x$ (e) 7·5 **10.** (a) Yes; $\frac{y}{x} = 2$ = constant (b) Yes; $\frac{y}{x} = 3$ = constant (c) No; Graph of y against x is not a straight line through the origin (d) Yes; $\frac{y}{x} = \frac{1}{2}$ = constant (e) No; Graph of y against x is not a straight line

Exercise 11

1. 100 (a) 4 (b) 2·5 **2.** (a) $t = \frac{k}{N}$ (b) 300 (c) 25 minutes **3.** (a) Inversely (b) $t = \frac{2400}{v}$ (c) 80 km/h **4.** (a) As P increases V decreases (b) $P = \frac{k}{V}$ (d) 0·0156 m^3 **5.** $x = \frac{k}{t}$; 600; 25 men

6. 16 pumps **7.** 8·4 days **8.** 650·24 Hz **9.** (a) 5 (b) $v = \frac{5}{m}$; 25 km/h **10.** (a) $g = \frac{k}{r^2}$ (b) 0·392 m/s^2

Revision Questions

1. (a) 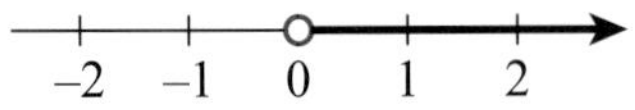

(c) $\mathbb{N}$ (d) Set of negative, real numbers $\mathbb{R}^-$
2. (a) All even numbers are divisible by 2
3. (c) (i) 1001 (ii) 579 579 **4.** (a) $3{\cdot}2 \times 10^3, 2{\cdot}157 \times 10^4, 2{\cdot}25 \times 10^4, 2{\cdot}5 \times 10^4$ (b) (i) 13 (ii) 15·8
(c) (i) 343·4 cm (ii) 342·6 cm;
Maximum area = 8·726 m^2, minimum area = 8·699 m^3
5. (a) $1{\cdot}6 \times 10^{-6}$ (b) 0·9 N (c) (i) 8 (ii) 7·4 (iii) 8·1%
6. (a) $1{\cdot}74 \times 10^8$ km (b) (i) 9 (ii) 7·96 (c) (i) 1005 ml (ii) 975 ml; Maximum amount of sugar = 110·55 g
7. (a) $6{\cdot}2 \times 10^{-2}$ (b) (i) (1·4 ± 0·1) cm (ii) 1·95 cm^2
(c) (i) €43 (ii) €43·15 (iii) 0·35%
8. (a) (i) $2{\cdot}4 \times 10^{-3}, 2{\cdot}4, 10^3, 2200, 2{\cdot}4 \times 10^3$
(ii) $1{\cdot}68 \times 10^{12}$ (b) 3·8% (c) (i) 87·5 km (ii) 156·25 km
(d) (i) $I = \frac{k}{R}$ (ii) 6·4 amps **9.** (a) (i) Straight line through the origin (ii) $\frac{2}{5}$ (iii) $y = \frac{2}{5}x$ (iv) 81·25
(b) 24 m/s (c) (i) $r = \frac{k}{t}$ (ii) 2·65 hours
10. (a) (i) 23·08% (ii) 25% (iii) 30·77% (b) 0·0189
(c) (i) –5 (ii) $\frac{1}{3}$ miles/gallon/mph (d) 2·5 metres

Section 2

Chapter 3

Exercise 1

1. (a) $x^2 + 7x + 10$ (b) $6x^2 + 23x + 21$ (c) $y^2 + 13y + 40$
(d) $6x^2 - 13x + 5$ (e) $2x^3 - 2x^2 - 12x$ (f) $2x^3 + 3x^2 + 2x + 1$
(g) $x^3 - 4x^2 + 8x - 15$ (h) $3x^3 + 2x^2 - 12x + 7$
(i) $2x^3 - 7x^2 + 11x - 6$ **2.** (a) $x^2 - 4$ (b) $4x^2 - 1$
(c) $16x^2 - 1$ (d) $x^4 - 1$ (e) $9x^2 - 4$ (f) $16x^2 - 9y^2$
(g) $x^4 - 25$ (h) $x^{2n} - 9$ **3.** (a) $x^2 + 4x + 4$
(b) $9x^2 + 12x + 4$ (c) $x^2 - 8x + 16$ (d) $25x^2 - 40x + 16$
(e) $x^4 - 22x^2 + 121$ (f) $16y^2 - 40y + 25$
(g) $a^2x^2 - 2abx + b^2$ (h) $4a$ **4.** (a) $x^3 + x^2 - 4x - 4$
(b) $4x^3 + 12x^2 - x - 3$ (c) $12x^3 - 4x^2 - 27x + 9$
(d) $x^3 + 3x^2 + 3x + 1$ (e) $8x^3 - 12x^2 + 6x - 1$
(f) $2x^3 - 9x^2 + 7x + 6$ **5.** (a) (i) $3x + 2$ (ii) $-x - 8$
(iii) $x^2 - 6x + 9$ (iv) $4x^2 + 20x + 25$ (v) $2x^2 - x - 15$
(vi) $2x^3 - 7x^2 - 12x + 45$ (b) (i) $3x^2 + 2x - 1$
(ii) $-x^2 - 4x + 3$ (iii) $5x^2 + 5x - 3$ (iv) $x^2 + 9x - 7$
(c) (i) $4x^3 + 10x - 2$ (ii) $4x^3 - 4x^2$ (iii) $-8x^3 + 10x^2 + 5x - 1$
(iv) $2x^3 - 7x^2 + 6x - 1$ **6.** (a) 32·5 (b) 22 (c) 45
(d) –45 (e) 225 (f) –3 (g) 68 (h) –37 (i) 36 (j) –79
(k) 56·75

Exercise 2

1. 1, 1, 1, 1, 1; 1 **2.** 1, 1, 1, 1, 1; 1
3. (a–d) ${}^nC_r = {}^nC_{n-r}$ **4.** (a) $x^4 + 4x^3 + 6x^2 + 4x + 1$
(b) $p^8 + 8p^7q + 28p^6q^2 + 56p^5q^3 + 70p^4q^4 + 56p^3q^5 + 28p^2q^6 + 8pq^7 + q^8$
(c) $q^5 + 5q^4p + 10q^3p^2 + 10q^2p^3 + 5qp^4 + p^5$
(d) $x^4 - 8x^3y + 24x^2y^2 - 32xy^3 + 16y^4$
(e) $8x^3 + 36x^2y + 54xy^2 + 27y^3$
(f) $(0{\cdot}6)^6 - 6(0{\cdot}6)^5(0{\cdot}4) + 15(0{\cdot}6)^4(0{\cdot}4)^2 + 20(0{\cdot}6)^3(0{\cdot}4)^3 + 15(0{\cdot}6)^2(0{\cdot}4)^4 + 6(0{\cdot}6)^1(0{\cdot}4)^5 + (0{\cdot}4)^6 = 1$
(g) $(0{\cdot}8)^4 + 4(0{\cdot}8)^3(0{\cdot}2) + 6(0{\cdot}8)^2(0{\cdot}2)^2 + 4(0{\cdot}8)(0{\cdot}2)^3 + (0{\cdot}2)^4 = 1$ **5.** (a) $70p^4q^4$ (b) $35x^4y^3$
(c) $240x^4y^2$ (d) $21p^2q^4$ **6.** (a) $35p^3q^4$ (b) $56p^3q^5$
(c) $495(0{\cdot}4)^8(0{\cdot}6)^4 = 0{\cdot}042$
(d) $126(0{\cdot}85)^5(0{\cdot}15)^4 = 0{\cdot}028$ (e) $210p^6q^4$
(f) $56p^5q^3$

Exercise 3

1. (a) $3(x^2 + 3x - 6)$ (b) $8a^2(1 - 2b^2)$ (c) $7x^2y(y - 2)$
(d) $(x - 2y)(3 - 5x)$ (e) $(a + b)(m - 3n)$
2. (a) $(x + 2)(ax + 1)$ (b) $(a - b)(x + y)$ (c) $(x - 3)(2 - b)$
(d) $(z - 2)(x^2 + y^2)$ (e) $(3x - 2)(1 + 4y)$
(f) $(3 - 2by^2)(7 - ax^2)$ **3.** (a) $(x - 2y)(x + 7y)$
(b) $(5x - 1)(2x + 3)$ (c) $(7x - y)(x - 3y)$ (d) $(2a + 3b)(a - b)$
(e) $(a - 4)(a + 4)$ (f) $(5x - 2)(6x - 1)$ (g) $(bx + c)(bx + c)$
(h) $(2p - 1)(2p - 1)$ **4.** (a) $(2x - 1)(2x + 1)$
(b) $(5x - y)(5x + y)$ (c) $(x - ab)(x + ab)$
(d) $(2m - 9n)(2m + 9n)$ (e) $(x + y - z)(x + y + z)$
(f) $3x(x - 2y)$ (g) $(x - z + 1)(x + z + 1)$
(h) (Yoke – Thing)(Yoke + Thing)
(i) $(a + 5b)(5a - b)$ (j) 8000 **5.** (a) $(x + 4)(x^2 - 4x + 16)$
(b) $(x + 3y)(x^2 - 3xy + 9y^2)$ (c) $(2x - 3)(4x^2 + 6x + 9)$
(d) $(10 - 3y)(100 + 30y + 9y^2)$ (e) $(ab + c)(a^2b^2 - abc + c^2)$
(f) $(5x - 4ab)(25x^2 + 20abx + 16a^2b^2)$
(g) $x(x^2 - 6x + 12)$ (h) $2x(x^2 + 12)$
(i) $(x + y - 1)(x^2 + y^2 - xy + x - 2y + 1)$
(j) (Thing – Yoke)((Thing)^2 + (Thing)(Yoke) + (Yoke)^2)
6. (a) $2(x - 2)(x + 2)$ (b) $2(3a - 2b)(3a + 2b)$
(c) $3(4x + 3y)(3x - y)$ (d) $(y + 2)(x - 1)(x + 1)$
(e) $7(2 - x)(2 + x)$ (f) $4(x - 3y)^2$ (g) $-2(x - y)^2$
(h) $(a - 2)(a + 4)$ (i) $4(2x - 3)(2x - 1)$
(j) $2(a - 17)(a + 17)$ (k) $3(x - 2)(x^2 + 2x + 4)$
(l) $x^2(y - 3)(y^2 + 3y + 9)$ (m) $a^2b(b - 2)(b^2 + 2b + 4)$

(n) $-2(x+3)(x^2-3x+9)$
(o) $(\cos\theta+\sin\theta)(1-\sin\theta\cos\theta)$
7. (a) $(x+y-9)(x+y+9)$ (b) $(a-b+3)(a+b+3)$
(c) $(a+4b-c)(a+4b+c)$ (d) $(a-b-4c)(a-b+4c)$
(e) $(x^2+y^2)(x-y)(x+y)$
(f) $(x-y)(x+y)(x^2+xy+y^2)(x^2-xy+y^2)$
(g) $(a-b)(a-b-1)$ (h) $x(x-1)^2$
(i) $(x^2+1)^2$ (j) $(a+b)(a-1)(a^2+a+1)$ **8.** (b) a^2-4b^2, $(a-2b)(a+2b)$ (c) $5x^2-12x+4$, $(5x-2)(x-2)$

Exercise 4

1. €$(98y-30x)$ **2.** (a) $P=(2x+4y+6)$ m
(b) $A=(xy+2y+2)$ m^2 **3.** $P=xy^2-x^2y=xy(y-x)$
4. $(2005x+4000y+2000)$ c **5.** (a) (i) $P=(2x+2y)$ m
(ii) $A=(xy)$ m^2 (b) 100 m, 600 m^2
6. (a) $L=(2x+4y+6)$ m (b) $A=(2xy+4y)$ m^2
(c) $y=1{\cdot}5$ **7.** (a) (i) $x+1$ (ii) $2x+1$
8. (a) $2\pi r$ (b) $8r$ (c) πr^2 (d) $4r^2$ (e) $4r^2-\pi r^2$
9. (a) $(2x+1{\cdot}5y)$ m (b) $(1{\cdot}8x+1{\cdot}3y+41)$ m
10. (a) $x(x+2)$ m^2 (b) $x(x-2)$ m^2 (c) $4x$ m^2

Chapter 4

Exercise 5

1. (a) $3x-7$ (b) $4x^2-7x-5$ (c) $9x^3-2x^2-5x+1$
(d) $-8x^3+5x^2+4x-1$ (e) $2x^3+3x^2+5x$
2. (a) $x^2+(k+1)x+k$ (b) $2kx^2+(k+2)x+1$
(c) $kx^2+(2-k)x-2$ (d) $-2x^2+(1+2k)x-k$
(e) $x^3+(k+1)x^2+kx$ (f) $x^3+(-k-1)x^2+(k+1)x-k$
(g) $2kx^3-10x^2-kx+5$
(h) $3x^3+(3k-1)x^2+(-k-6)x+2$
(i) $6x^3+(2k+3)x^2+(k-6)x-3$
(j) $x^3+(k-c)x^2+(d-kc)x-cd$
3. (a) $k=4$ (b) $k=2$ (c) $a=6, b=1, c=-2$ (d) $2x+1$
(e) $(2x-7)$, $k=-30$ (f) $k=8$, $a=15$, $b=-29$
(g) (i) $10x^2-17x+3$ (ii) $20x^2-34x+6$
(iii) $20x^2-34x+6$ (h) (i) x^2-2 (ii) $x^2+2\sqrt{3}-4$
(iii) $2x^2-3\sqrt{3}\,x-6$ **4.** (a) $(x+1)$, $k=2$, $l=3$
(b) $(x-2)$, $b=3$, $k=-11$ (c) $k=-6$, $a=6$, $(3x-1)$
(d) $k=7$, $(x-1)$, $(x+4)$ (e) $k=-6$, x^2-3 (f) $k=4$, $b=-16$, $(4x+2)$ **5.** (b) 3 (d) (ii) $f(x)=(x^2-a^2)(x+1)$
(e) $(3-x)$, $(x+1)$, $(2-x)$ (h) $a=2$, $b=-3$

Exercise 6

1. (a) -1 (b) $-x$ (c) $x+3$ (d) x (e) x^2 (f) $5x+7$
(g) x^2+2x+4 (h) $x+1$ (i) $2x^2-3x$ (j) $-4x-12$
2. (a) x^2+5x+4 (b) x^2-5x+5 (c) $2x^2+3x-1$
(d) $5x^2-3x+6$ (e) x^2+5x (f) $-2x-3$ (g) x^2-1
(h) $3x^2+2x$ (i) $9x^2+3x+1$ (j) $(x-2)$ **3.** (a) $x+2$
(b) $10x^2+22x+10$

Exercise 7

1. (a) -2 (b) $\dfrac{x^2-2}{x}$ (c) $\dfrac{1-2x}{(x-1)(x-2)}$ (d) $\dfrac{(\alpha-\beta)(\alpha+\beta)}{\alpha\beta}$
(e) $-\dfrac{1}{8x}$ (f) $\dfrac{(m-1)(m+1)}{m}$ (g) 0 (h) $\dfrac{a+1}{20(a+2)}$
(i) $\dfrac{x+2}{x(x-1)(x+1)}$ (j) $\dfrac{8}{(x+10)(x+2)}$ **2.** (a) $\dfrac{2a}{5b}$
(b) $-\frac{1}{3}$ (c) $-\dfrac{b}{4a}$ (d) $\dfrac{a}{b}$ (e) 1 (f) 1 (g) $\dfrac{y^2-3y+9}{y-3}$
(h) $\dfrac{(3+2a)(3-2a)}{a^2}$ (i) $\dfrac{(2a-3b)^2}{36}$
(j) $\dfrac{(2y+3x)(x-8y)}{2xy}$ (k) $(x-2)^2(x+2)$ **3.** (a) $2x$
(b) $\frac{1}{2x}$ (c) $-\frac{6}{5}$ (d) 2 (e) $5a-2$ (f) $3(2b+1)$ (g) $\dfrac{x+1}{x-1}$
(h) x^2+y^2 (i) $x+y$ (j) $3x-2$ **4.** (a) $\dfrac{6}{x^2}$ (b) $\dfrac{3x^2}{2}$ (c) $\frac{1}{6}$
(d) $x+1$ (e) $\dfrac{2x+1}{2x-1}$ (f) $-\dfrac{x+2}{x+3}$ (g) $-t^3$

Chapter 5

Exercise 8

1. (a) 27 (b) 32 (c) 625 (d) 100 000 000 (e) 1 (f) 1
(g) -1 (h) 16 (i) -243 (j) $\frac{1}{4}$ (k) $\frac{4}{9}$ (l) $-\frac{1}{8}$ (m) $\frac{16}{25}$ (n) $\frac{49}{4}$
(o) $\frac{121}{16}$ (p) $-\frac{125}{8}$ **2.** (a) $\frac{1}{2}$ (b) $\frac{1}{9}$ (c) $\frac{1}{64}$ (d) $\frac{1}{25}$ (e) $\frac{1}{16}$
(f) $\frac{5}{18}$ (g) $\frac{4}{3}$ (h) $\frac{3}{2}$ (i) $\frac{2}{3}$ (j) 6 (k) $\frac{1}{6}$ (l) 6 (m) $\frac{1}{64}$ (n) $-\frac{1}{27}$
(o) $\frac{8}{27}$ **3.** (a) 27 (b) 5 (c) 125 (d) 16 (e) $\frac{1}{6}$ (f) $\frac{1}{4}$ (g) 1
(h) 8 (i) $\frac{3}{500}$ (j) 28 (k) $\frac{3}{2}$ (l) $\frac{1}{3}$ (m) 1 000 000 (n) -32
(o) $\frac{1}{10}$ (p) $\frac{3}{2}$ (q) $\frac{2}{3}$ (r) $-\frac{2}{3}$ (s) $-\frac{3}{2}$ (t) 1 (u) 3 (v) -3 (w) $\frac{2}{3}$
(x) $\frac{9}{5}$ (y) $\frac{27}{64}$ **4.** (a) $2^{\frac{7}{2}}$ (b) $3^{\frac{5}{2}}$ (c) $\dfrac{1}{2^{\frac{5}{2}}}$ (d) $7^{\frac{13}{6}}$ (e) $5^{\frac{3}{2}}$
(f) 10^{27} (g) $\dfrac{3^6}{2^3}$ (h) 2^3 (i) $3^{\frac{3}{2}}$ (j) 5^3 **5.** (a) a^9 (b) a^{21}
(c) a^4 (d) a^4 (e) $a^{\frac{1}{3}}$ (f) $a^{\frac{3}{2}}$ (g) a^4 (h) a^{12} (i) $\dfrac{1}{a^2}$ (j) $a^{\frac{3}{2}}$
(k) a^5 (l) $a^{\frac{2}{3}}$ (m) $a^{\frac{23}{2}}$ (n) $\dfrac{1}{a^3}$ (o) $a^{\frac{7}{2}}$ **6.** (a) x^4y (b) $2x^5$
(c) $4x$ (d) $\dfrac{1}{2x^2}$ (e) 2 (f) $2x^5y$ (g) 2^{2x} (h) $x\times 2^{4x}$ (i) $\dfrac{2}{x^3}$
(j) $\dfrac{x^8y^4}{81z^{12}}$ (k) $\dfrac{5}{2x^2}$ (l) $(a+3b)^5$ (m) $\dfrac{b}{xy}$ (n) $\dfrac{3^{2x-1}}{2}$

(o) $\frac{1}{2a^2y^2}$ (p) $2a^2y^2$ (q) $2x$ (r) $\frac{5}{y}$ (s) xy (t) $2x^2y$

7. (a) 121 500 (b) 88 573 500 (c) 729 **8.** (b) $\frac{1}{16}$

9. (b) 2·5 mg (c) 87·5% **10.** (a) 1·2597 (b) €7347 (c) €9255

Exercise 9

1. (a) $2\sqrt{3}$ (b) $3\sqrt{3}$ (c) $11\sqrt{10}$ (d) $16\sqrt{2}$ (e) $\frac{2\sqrt{2}}{3}$
(f) $\frac{3\sqrt{2}}{5}$ (g) $\frac{7\sqrt{3}}{10}$ (h) $2x\sqrt{x}$ (i) $2xy\sqrt{2y}$ (j) $\frac{2x\sqrt{3x}}{y}$
(k) $\frac{4z^{30}\sqrt{z}}{3xy}$ **2.** (a) $3\sqrt{11}$ (b) $-4+15\sqrt{3}$ (c) $3x-7\sqrt{y}$
(d) 0 (e) 0 (f) $5\sqrt{2}+5\sqrt{3}$ (g) 0 (h) $\sqrt{x}$ (i) $3ay\sqrt{ay}$
(j) $-4\sqrt{x-3}$ **3.** (a) $2\sqrt{2}$ (b) $\sqrt{6}$ (c) $60\sqrt{3}$
(d) $6(1+\sqrt{2}+\sqrt{3})$ (e) $4+2\sqrt{3}$ (f) 2 (g) $ab(\sqrt{a}+\sqrt{b})$
(h) $20+2\sqrt{91}$ (i) -6 (j) $4x+9y+12\sqrt{xy}$ (k) 1
(l) $-3x+2\sqrt{x}$ (m) $a-\sqrt{a^2-x^2}$ (n) x^3-x^2-2x+2
(o) $x-1$ (p) $\frac{1}{x}-1$ (q) $16y-\frac{9}{y}$ (r) $x+\frac{4}{x}+4$
(s) $\frac{x}{y^2}+\frac{y^2}{x}-2$ **4.** (a) $\frac{\sqrt{5}}{5}$ (b) $-\frac{\sqrt{2}}{2}$ (c) $\frac{2\sqrt{3}}{3}$ (d) $\frac{2\sqrt{2}}{5}$
(e) $-\frac{\sqrt{3}}{2}$ (f) $\frac{\sqrt{42}}{14}$ (g) $\frac{x\sqrt{y}}{y}$ (h) $\frac{\sqrt{xy}}{y}$ (i) $\sqrt{2}-1$ (j) $3+2\sqrt{2}$
(k) $3\sqrt{2}+2\sqrt{3}$ (l) $\frac{3+\sqrt{5}}{2}$ (m) $\frac{10x+15\sqrt{x}}{9-4x}$
(n) $5+2\sqrt{6}$ (o) $\sqrt{a}+\sqrt{a-x}$ **5.** 0 **6.** (a) $4x$
(b) $4x(4-x^2)$ **7.** 11 **10.** (a) (i) $P_1=2\pi\sqrt{\frac{R^3}{GM}}$
(ii) $P_2=16\pi\sqrt{\frac{R^3}{GM}}$ **13.** (a) $T_1=2\pi\sqrt{\frac{d}{g}}$
(b) $T_2=\pi\sqrt{\frac{d}{g}}$

Exercise 10

1. (a) 2 (b) -5 (c) -1 (d) $\frac{1}{2}$ (e) -1 (f) -2 (g) $\frac{2}{3}$ (h) -4
(i) 4 (j) $-\frac{3}{2}$ **2.** (a) $289=17^2$ (b) $16=4^2$ (c) $\frac{1}{16}=4^{-2}$
(d) $4=16^{\frac{1}{2}}$ (e) $\frac{1}{4}=16^{-\frac{1}{2}}$ (f) $3=3^1$ (g) $1=a^0$ (h) $a=b^c$
(i) $16=8^{\frac{4}{3}}$ (j) $8=16^{\frac{3}{4}}$ **3.** (a) $\log_2 15$ (b) $\log_3 4a^2$
(c) $\log_e(1-x^2)$ (d) 0 (e) $\log_5 y$ (f) $\log_4(x^3-1)$
(g) $\log_3 e^{3x-1}$ (h) 1 (i) $\log_k(x-1)$ (j) 0 **4.** (a) 1
(b) 1 (c) $\log_e(x-1)$ (d) $\log_5 49$ (e) $\log_4(x-1)$ (f) $\log_3 e^2$
(g) $\log_9 3=\frac{1}{2}$ (h) 1 (i) 1 (j) $\log_a x^2$ **5.** (a) $\log_2 125$
(b) $\log_3\left(\frac{1}{49}\right)$ (c) $\log_4 5$ (d) $\log_2\left(\frac{1}{216}\right)$ (e) $\log_k y^2$
(f) $\log_5(1+x^2)$ (g) $\log_3\left(\frac{1}{zy}\right)$ (h) $\log_7 4y$ (i) $\log_e 2^x$
(j) $\log_5\left(\frac{1}{y}\right)$ **6.** (a) $\frac{\log_2 5}{\log_2 3}$ (b) $\frac{\log_5 4}{\log_5 7}$ (c) $\frac{\log_b y}{\log_b a}$
(d) $\frac{\log_7(x-2)}{\log_7 5}$ (e) $\frac{\log_e a}{\log_e 10}$ (f) $\frac{1}{\log_3 5}$ (g) $\frac{1}{\log_x 4}$
(h) $\frac{1}{\log_5 x}$ (i) $\log_x 2$ (j) $\log_x e$

7. (a) (i) $2\log_a x+\frac{1}{2}\log_a y$ (ii) $2\log_2 u+3\log_2 v$
(iii) $\log_5 3+\frac{1}{2}\log_5 x-2\log_5 p-3\log_5 q$
(iv) $2+3\log_3 x-6\log_3 y$ (v) -2
(vi) $2\log_k(x+3)+3\log_k(2x-1)$
(vii) $7\log_2(x+7)-2-\frac{1}{2}\log_2(2x-3)$
(viii) $\frac{1}{2}\log_5(x-1)-\frac{1}{2}\log_5(x+1)$ (b) (i) $a+b$
(ii) $3a+b$ (iii) $2b-3a$ (iv) $a+b+1$ (v) $b+1$
(vi) $4b$ (vii) $4a-3b$ (viii) $2a+2-3b$ (ix) $4a+b$
(x) $\frac{2a+b}{b}$ **8.** (a) (i) 2 (ii) 1 (iii) 1 (iv) 0
(b) (i) $\log_5 x^2y$ (ii) $\log_k\left(\frac{x^3y^2}{z^{\frac{1}{4}}}\right)$ (iii) $\log_3\left(\frac{\sqrt{x-1}}{\sqrt{(x+1)^3}}\right)$
(iv) $\log_3\left\{\frac{2(x+5)}{(4x-1)^3}\right\}^7$ (v) $\log_4 a^{\frac{3}{2}}$ (vi) $\log_a\sqrt{x+1}$
(vii) $\log_e\left\{\frac{3(3x+2)}{(x^2+1)^{\frac{3}{2}}}\right\}$ (viii) $\log_e x^{x+e-\frac{1}{2}}$ **14.** (a) 7
(b) 4 (c) $\frac{1}{2}$ (d) 3 (e) 8 (f) $\sqrt{x}$
15. (a) 3 (b) $n(n-1)(n-2)\ldots1=n!$ **17.** (a) (i) 50 dB
(ii) 110 dB **19.** (a) 54 (b) $\frac{5}{2}$ (c) 50 (d) 2

Revision Questions

1. (a) $\frac{7-3\sqrt{5}}{2}$ (b) $k=-13$, $(x-2)$, $(x+3)$
(c) $(2x-1)$ **2.** (a) $-\sqrt{3}$ (b) $\frac{1}{(x+2)(x+4)}$
3. (a) $a=5$, $b=-2$, $c=-12$ (c) $x^4+\frac{1}{x^4}$ **4.** (a) 3
(b) $\frac{2x}{x-1}$ (c) (i) $a=2$, $b=1$, $c=3$ (ii) $a=-1$,
$b=-3$ **5.** (a) $p^3+3p^2q+3pq^2+q^3$ (b) $35p^4q^3$
6. (a) 3 (b) (i) $-\frac{3}{2(x+4y)}$ (ii) $2x-1$, $k=2+2\sqrt{3}$
(c) $a=2$, $b=3$ **7.** (a) 1 000 000 000 001
(b) (i) $\frac{10}{99}$ (ii) $1+2x^2$ **8.** (a) 172 800 (b) 491 520
9. (c) 1·26 **11.** (a) $\frac{1}{x}$ (b) $-\frac{1}{x+2}$ (c) $\frac{2}{x(x+2)}$
(d) $\frac{8}{5}\text{ m}^{-1}$, $\frac{5}{8}$ m **12.** (a) $\frac{2}{x-2}$ hours (b) $\frac{2}{x+2}$ hours
(c) The man, bigger speed (d) $\frac{8}{x^2-2^2}$ (e) 3 min 26 s
13. (a) 3200×2^t; 3200 (b) 100×2^{2t}; 100 (c) 2^{t-5}
(i) $\frac{1}{8}$ (ii) 1 (iii) 32 (d) The number in sample *B* is less than the number in sample *A* for the first 5 minutes but after that it is always bigger

Section 3

Chapter 6

Exercise 1

1. (a) 5 (b) $\frac{14}{3}$ (c) 8 (d) 1 (e) $\frac{9}{4}$ **2.** (a) 2 (b) $-\frac{1}{4}$ (c) 14 (d) 7 (e) 7 (f) 3 (g) 4 **3.** (a) 5 (b) 5 (c) $-\frac{23}{7}$ (d) $-\frac{7}{4}$ **4.** (d) –5 **5.** (a) 69 cm, 23 cm (b) 13·75 m, 8·25 m, 113·4375 m^2 (c) 15 cm, 20 cm, 25 cm (d) 8, 12 (e) 14, 16, 18 (f) Sandra 14, Anna 12 (g) 21, 24, 27 (h) 15 (i) 16 @ €1·50, 9 @ €1 (j) 360 units (k) 7, 8, 9, 10, 11 (l) 80 km (m) 120 weeks (n) 414 (o) Man 40, son 20

Exercise 2

1. (a) –2, 1 (b) 3, $-\frac{1}{2}$ (c) $\frac{7}{2}$ (d) 0, 3 (e) 0, $\frac{7}{3}$ (f) 0, 2 (g) 0, 3 (h) 0, $\frac{1}{9}$ (i) –3, 3 (j) 0, $\frac{1}{4}$ **2.** (a) –5, 5 (b) –2, 2 (c) –3, 5 (d) –11, 3 (e) $-\frac{1}{2}$, –1 (f) $\frac{5}{4}$, $\frac{2}{3}$ (g) $\frac{2}{3}$, –6 (h) $-\frac{8}{7}$, 1 (i) 2, 3 (j) $-\frac{1}{32}$, $\frac{1}{32}$ **3.** (a) $x^2 + 24x - 25 = 0$, –25, 1 (b) $x^2 + 7x + 12 = 0$, –4, –3 (c) $x^2 - x - 2 = 0$, –1, 2 (d) $7x^2 + 3x - 4 = 0$, –1, $\frac{4}{7}$ (e) $3x^2 - 8x - 3 = 0$, $-\frac{1}{3}$, 3 **4.** (a) $k = -\frac{3}{2}$ (c) Yes (d) $p = 3, q = 3$ (e) $p = 5$, $q = 15$ **5.** (a) $2 \pm \sqrt{2}$ (b) $1 \pm 2\sqrt{2}$ (c) $-1 \pm \sqrt{5}$ (d) $\frac{1}{2} \pm \frac{\sqrt{3}}{2}$ (e) $-1 \pm \frac{\sqrt{5}}{2}$ (f) $\frac{7 \pm \sqrt{61}}{6}$ (g) $\frac{5 \pm \sqrt{17}}{2}$ (h) $\frac{3}{2}, \frac{1}{2}$ (i) 2, 3 (j) $\frac{3 \pm \sqrt{65}}{4}$ **6.** (a) $1 \pm \sqrt{31}$, –4·57, 6·57 (b) $1 \pm \sqrt{10}$, –2·16, 4·16 (c) $\frac{19 \pm \sqrt{345}}{8}$, 0·05, 4·70 (d) $-\frac{2}{3}, \frac{1}{2}$, –0·67, 0·5 (e) $\frac{5 \pm \sqrt{73}}{4}$, –0·89, 3·39 (f) $\frac{4 \pm \sqrt{22}}{3}$, –0·23, 2·90 (g) $\frac{-4 \pm \sqrt{30}}{7}$, –1·35, 0·21 (h) $\frac{-4 \pm \sqrt{22}}{2}$, –4·35, 0·35 (i) $\pm\sqrt{3}$, –1·73, 1·73 (j) $\pm 2\sqrt{2}$, –2·83 2·83 **7.** (a) (i) Real, different, rational (ii) Real, equal (iii) Real, equal (iv) Real, different, irrational (v) Complex (vi) Complex (vii) Real, equal (viii) Real, different, irrational (b) (i) $k = 4$ (ii) $k = -11$ (c) (i) –1, $1 - k$ (Different once $k \neq 2$) **8.** $a = 2$ **9.** $a = -1, b = 2$ **10.** $a = -1$, $b = 2$ **11.** (a) $x^2 - 3x + 2 = 0$ (b) $x^2 - 6x + 9 = 0$ (c) $x^2 + 3x + 2 = 0$ (d) $x^2 + x - 30 = 0$ (e) $x^2 - 2 = 0$ (f) $4x^2 - 8x + 3 = 0$ (g) $15x^2 - 7x - 2 = 0$ (h) $x^2 - 4x + 1 = 0$ (i) $x^2 + 8x - 29 = 0$ (j) $x^2 - (\alpha + \beta)x + \alpha\beta = 0$ **12.** (a) $-\frac{1}{3}, \frac{5}{2}$ (b) –1, 3 (c) $-\frac{40}{7}$, –4 (d) $-\frac{3}{4}, -\frac{1}{2}$ (e) –3, $\frac{1}{2}$ (f) 3, 5 (g) 2, $\frac{7}{3}$ (h) –3·3, 0·3 (i) –1, 6 (j) 1 **13.** (a) $x = 2, 5; y = 4, 7$ (b) $x = -\frac{2}{3}, \frac{5}{2}; t = \frac{1}{3}, \frac{7}{2}$ (c) $x = 1, \frac{4}{3}; y = 6, 7$ (d) $x = 3, 7; x = -3, -2, 6, 9$ (e) $x = \frac{3}{5}, 4; y = \frac{13}{5}, 6$ (f) $x = \frac{4}{3}, 5; x = \frac{16}{9}, 25$ (g) $x = -5, 4; t = 2$ (h) $x = 5, 6, t = 2, -3, \frac{-1 \pm \sqrt{21}}{2}$ **14.** (a) 12 teams (b) 4, 6, 8 (c) €5 *or* €45 (d) 4 (e) 50, 190 (f) 3 Ω (g) Bill: 4 hours, Ben: 6 hours (h) 2 s, 14 s (i) 90 km/h, 80 km/h (j) 20 km, 30 km (k) 11·1 m, 24·1 m (l) 0·8 m (m) 2 m (n) 5 cm (o) $w + 3$, 10·8 m, 7·8 m (p) 8 m, 15 m

Exercise 3

1. (a) Yes (b) No (c) Yes (d) 2 (e) 8 (f) 2 (g) $a = -12$, $b = 22$ (h) $a = -24, b = 20$ **2.** (a) –1, $\frac{5}{2}$ (b) –7, 0 (c) –2, 1 (d) –1, 1 (e) –1, $\frac{1}{3}$ **3.** (a) –3, $\frac{1}{2}$, 2 (b) $-\frac{1}{3}$, $\frac{1}{4}$, 1 (c) –2, $-\frac{2}{3}$, $-\frac{3}{2}$, (d) $-\frac{1}{2}$, $\frac{3}{2}$, 3 (e) $-\frac{7}{4}$, 1, 3 **4.** (a) –5, –2, 3 (b) $-\frac{1}{2}$, $1 \pm \sqrt{2}$ (c) 4, $6 \pm \sqrt{5}$ (d) $k = 9$; 3, $3 \pm \sqrt{6}$ (e) 2, $\frac{-1 \pm \sqrt{13}}{2}$ **5.** (a) $U\left(-\frac{3}{2}, 0\right)$, $V\left(\frac{1}{2}, 0\right)$, $W\left(\frac{7}{2}, 0\right)$, $Z(0, 21)$ (b) $U(2, 0)$, $V\left(\frac{5}{2}, 0\right)$, $W(0, -20)$ (c) $U(1 - \sqrt{2}, 0)$, $V(1 + \sqrt{2}, 0)$, $W(3, 0)$, $Z(0, 3)$ (d) $U\left(-\frac{1}{3}, 0\right)$, $V(0, 0)$, $W(1, 0)$ (e) $U\left(\frac{1}{2}, 0\right)$, $V(2, 0)$, $W(0, 2)$ (f) $U\left(\frac{1 - \sqrt{5}}{2}, 0\right)$, $V\left(\frac{1 + \sqrt{5}}{2}, 0\right)$, $W(0, 1)$ **6.** (a) $x^3 - x^2 - 10x - 8 = 0$ (b) $(x - 2)^3 = 0$ (c) $2x^3 + x^2 - 13x + 6 = 0$ (d) $x^3 - cx^2 - a^2x + a^2c = 0$ (e) $x^3 - 9x^2 + 21x - 5 = 0$ (f) $x^3 - 7x^2 - 3x + 21 = 0$ **7.** 3 **8.** 2 m **9.** 2, $\sqrt{5}$, 3 **10.** $\frac{2}{3}$ s, 1 s **11.** 3 m **12.** 3 cm, 18·88 cm

Chapter 7

Exercise 4

1. (a) $\frac{1}{100}$ (b) $2·5 \times 10^9$ (c) 23 (d) $\frac{103}{2}$ (e) $\frac{4}{5}$ (f) –4, $\frac{9}{2}$ (g) 8 (h) 6 (i) 4 (j) 5 (k) 8 (l) 5 **3.** $-\frac{9}{2}$, 4 **4.** 24·8 cm **5.** $\frac{144}{25} = 5·76$ **6.** 8, 3 cm, 4 cm **7.** 3·2 cm × 2·4 cm **8.** (a) $3 + 2\sqrt{2}$ (b) $A(3 + 2\sqrt{2}, 2 + 2\sqrt{2})$ **9.** (a) ±1024 (b) –3, 1 (c) $\frac{3}{2}$ (d) ±243 (e) 27 (f) ±32

Exercise 5

1. (a) $\frac{h}{1+st}$ (b) $\sqrt{\frac{mv^2-2E}{m}}$ (c) $\frac{P_1V_1T_2}{P_2V_2}$ (d) $\frac{m_2a}{g-a}$ (e) $\frac{2sT}{t-T}$ (f) $\frac{aW}{W-2PE}$ (g) $\pm D\sqrt{\frac{f+P}{f-P}}$ (h) $-\frac{1}{Lq^2+Rq}$ (i) $\frac{A-\pi r^2}{2\pi r}$ (j) $\pm\sqrt{\frac{p^2-2pq-2q^2}{5}}$

3. $A=\frac{(C-s)^2}{6400\,d^2}$; 2500 m^2 **4.** $2{\cdot}6\times10^8$ m/s

Exercise 6

1. (a) 2^2 (b) 2^2 (c) 2^4 (d) 2^0 (e) $2^{-\frac{7}{2}}$ (f) 2^{-4} (g) $2^{-\frac{1}{2}}$ (h) $2^{-\frac{5}{3}}$ (i) $2^{\frac{2}{3}}$ **2.** (a) 3^2 (b) 3^8 (c) 3^{-2} (d) 3^6 (e) 3^3 (f) 3^6 (g) $3^{\frac{3}{2}}$ (h) 3^1 (i) $3^{\frac{11}{12}}$ **3.** (a) 2^{2x} (b) 2^{3x+3} (c) 2^{-x} (d) 2^{3x+1} (e) 2^{3x-1} (f) 2^{1-3x} (g) 2^{4-4x} (h) 2^{4-x} (i) 2^{5x-1} (j) 2^{4x} (k) 2^{x+6} (l) 2^{3x+4} (m) 2^{8x-1} (n) 2^{-2x} (o) 2^{2x}

4. (a) 3^{2x} (b) 3^{-2x} (c) 3^{-x} (d) 3^{x+7} (e) 3^{3x} (f) 3^{2x+1} (g) 3^{3-3x} (h) 3^{-x} (i) 3^{3x+1} (j) 3^{2x+1} (k) 3^{2x-4} (l) 3^{3x+2} (m) $3^{\frac{3}{2}-2x}$ (n) 3^{-2x+2} (o) 3^{3x} **5.** (a) 2 (b) –2 (c) 4 (d) –2 (e) $\frac{4}{3}$ (f) $\frac{3}{2}$ (g) $\frac{3}{2}$ (h) $-\frac{3}{2}$ (i) 3 (j) –8 (k) $\frac{3}{2}$ (l) 4 (m) –2 (n) 1 (o) $-\frac{1}{3}$ (p) 1, –3 (q) –1, 5 (r) 3, 4 (s) $\frac{7}{4}$

6. (a) $2^{-\frac{7}{2}}$; $-\frac{15}{2}$ (b) $3^{\frac{13}{3}}$; $-\frac{1}{6}$ (c) $2^{\frac{7}{2}}$; $\frac{5}{8}$ (d) $5^{\frac{11}{2}}$; 4

8. (a) 17 (b) 1·5 years **9.** (a) 51 (b) 2 years

10. 1 min **11.** (a) 100% (b) 6·25% (c) 7

12. (a) 1, 2 (c) Yes, $\log_5 3$ (f) 23 years

Exercise 7

1. (a) 8 (b) ±3 (c) 10^8 (d) 50 (e) –1, 6 (f) 302 (g) $-\frac{4}{3}, \frac{1}{2}$ (h) k^b (i) $1+e^{-2\cdot8}$ (j) 3·6 **2.** (a) 16 (b) 8 (c) $-\frac{1}{4}$ (d) 5 (e) $\frac{301}{195}$ (f) $\sqrt{5}$ (g) 3, 6 (h) $\frac{5}{2}$ (i) 1 (j) 5 (k) 3 (l) 0, 6 (m) 18 **3.** (a) 4, 8 (b) $4^{\frac{2}{3}}$, 8 (c) $\sqrt{3}$, 9 (d) 9 (e) 1 (f) $\frac{1}{2}$, 4 **4.** (i) $A=1$ **5.** (a) $F=2^{15}$, $b=2$ (b) 128 (c) $p=128\sqrt{\frac{2}{N}}$ (d) $2\sqrt{2}$ **6.** (a) 3 (b) $A=10^{\frac{M+5}{2}}-4000$ (c) 96 000 km^2 **7.** (b) 18·1 kg (c) 1·51 m

Exercise 8

1. (a) 5 (b) 5 (c) $\sqrt{5}$ (d) $\frac{1}{\sqrt{5}}$ (e) e (f) $3-\sqrt{3}$ (g) $2-\sqrt{2}$ (h) $7-2\pi$ (i) t^2+1 (j) e^x+1 (k) 2^x (l) $b-a$

2. (a) ±7 (b) 1, –15 (c) –2, $\frac{5}{2}$ (d) $-\frac{7}{3}$, 1 (e) 4, $-\frac{2}{5}$ (f) 24 (g) 4 (h) $\pm\frac{1}{2}$ **4.** (a) –1, 7 (b) $\frac{1}{3}$, 1 **6.** (a) Yes (b) Yes (c) No (d) No **7.** $|x-2|=3$; –1, 5 **8.** Yes; $x^2>0$ for all $x\in\mathbb{R}$

Chapter 8

Exercise 9A

1. (4, 1) **2.** (8, –4) **3.** (6, –4) **4.** (4, 10) **5.** (–5, –3) **6.** (3, 4) **7.** $\left(2, \frac{1}{2}\right)$ **8.** (2, 5) **9.** (2, 1) **10.** (3, 4) **11.** $\left(\frac{1}{2}, 1\right)$ **12.** $\left(4, -\frac{1}{2}\right)$

13. (a) $x=\frac{2}{3}$, $y=-\frac{16}{3}$ (b) $x=21$, $y=6$ (c) $x=\frac{1}{2}$, $y=1$ (d) $x=3$, $y=4$ (e) $x=\frac{7}{4}$, $y=-\frac{1}{4}$ (f) $x=25$, $y=-\frac{1}{2}$ (g) $x=1$, $y=2$ **14.** (1, 4) **15.** (27, 16) **16.** $\left(27, \frac{1}{3}\right)$

Exercise 9B

1. 71, 64 **2.** 7, 4 **3.** 3, –5 **4.** 17, 12 **5.** 72, 24 **6.** 6, 6 **7.** 25 m, 32 m, 800 m^2 **8.** (a) $x=5$, $y=1$ (b) 24 cm, 35 cm^2 **9.** (a) $x=12$, $y=8$ (b) 60 cm, $100\sqrt{3}$ cm^2 **10.** 7 cm, 7 cm, 3 cm **11.** €15 000 @ 2%, €5000 @ 3% **12.** Bankwin shares cost €4·80, Academic Enterprise shares cost €6·20

13. 37 @ 5 c and 4 @ 10 c **14.** 8 @ 5 marks, 5 @ 12 marks **15.** 108 spaces for cars; 54 spaces for trucks **16.** 10 l of the 30% solution and 10 l of the 50% solution **17.** 37·17 g of 90% gold and 15·93 g of 80% gold **18.** Speed of current = 3 km/h, speed of boat = 27 km/h

19. Aeroplane's speed = 864 km/h, wind speed = 96 km/h

20. Speed of the current = 4 km/h, speed of boat = 20 km/h

21. A = 1 000 000 computations/s, B = 6 000 000 computations/s **22.** 180 g, 150 g

23. 46 cm, 25 cm, 1150 cm^2

Exercise 10A

1. (3, 4), (4, 3) **2.** (7, 6), (–6, –7) **3.** (1, 2), (2, 1) **4.** (–2, –3), (3, 2) **5.** (2, 6), (6, 2) **6.** (a) (4, 2) (b) It is a tangent **7.** (3, 1), $\left(\frac{27}{11}, \frac{29}{11}\right)$

8. $\left(\frac{3}{2}, -4\right)$, (–2, 3) **9.** (0, –5), $\left(\frac{5}{2}, 0\right)$ **10.** (–1, 3), (3, –5) **11.** $\left(-\frac{56}{13}, \frac{33}{13}\right)$, (4, –3) **12.** $\left(3, -\frac{2}{3}\right)$, (5, –2) **13.** $\left(-\frac{22}{17}, -\frac{31}{17}\right)$, (1, 2) **14.** (1, 1), $\left(-\frac{19}{13}, -\frac{35}{13}\right)$ **15.** $\left(-\frac{13}{25}, \frac{16}{25}\right)$, (3, –2) **16.** $\left(\frac{3}{2}, \frac{3}{2}\right)$, (1, 2)

Exercise 10B

1. $x=11$, $y=8$; $x=-11$, $y=-8$ **2.** $x=23$, $y=19$

3. $x=15$, $y=8$ **4.** $x=\frac{3+\sqrt{5}}{2}$, $y=\frac{3-\sqrt{5}}{2}$

5. 45 m, 80 m **6.** (–3, –5), $\left(\frac{11}{5}, \frac{27}{5}\right)$
7. $x = 4$, $y = 3$, length = 9 cm, breadth = 4 cm, area = 36 cm^2 **8.** 0·6 m, 0·8 m, 0·24 m^3
9. *Ulysses* 74 km/h, *Jonathan Swift* 40 km/h
10. (3, 0), $\left(\frac{12}{5}, -\frac{3}{5}\right)$

Exercise 11A

1. (1, 2, 3) **2.** $\left(2, -1, \frac{1}{2}\right)$ **3.** (2, 3, 1) **4.** (1, 2, –1)
5. (3, –3, 2) **6.** (3, 3, 3) **7.** (2, 2, –2)
8. (1, 3, 6) **9.** $\left(\frac{3}{2}, 1, -\frac{3}{2}\right)$ **10.** $\left(\frac{4}{5}, \frac{12}{13}, \frac{6}{7}\right)$
11. (5, 3, –4) **12.** (5, 0, –2)

Exercise 11B

1. $x = 1$ A, $y = 3$ A, $z = 2$ A **2.** $a = 2$, $b = -3$, $c = 7$
3. $A + B + C = 42\,000$; $2A - B = 0$; $B - 4C = 0$

A	B	C
12000	24000	6000

4. 50 one-person tents, 110 two-person tents, 200 four-person tents

Chapter 9

Exercise 12

1. (a) $x > -2, x \in \mathbb{R}$ (b) $x \leq 6, x \in \mathbb{R}$ (c) $x \geq \frac{5}{3}$, $x \in \mathbb{R}$ (d) $x \geq 3, x \in \mathbb{R}$ (e) $x \geq 15, x \in \mathbb{R}$
(f) $x > -11, x \in \mathbb{R}$ **2.** (a) $x < -5, x > 2, x \in \mathbb{R}$
(b) $-7 < x < 11, x \in \mathbb{R}$ (c) $x \leq -3, x \geq \frac{1}{2}, x \in \mathbb{R}$
(d) $-2 \leq x \leq -\frac{1}{3}, x \in \mathbb{R}$ (e) $\frac{3}{2} \leq x \leq 2, x \in \mathbb{R}$
(f) $x < -\frac{1}{2}, x > \frac{1}{2}, x \in \mathbb{R}$ **3.** (a) $-\frac{5}{2} < x < -1, x \in \mathbb{R}$
(b) $x < -9, x > -2, x \in \mathbb{R}$ (c) $x > 0, x \in \mathbb{R}$ (d) $-2 < x < 3$, $x \in \mathbb{R}$ (e) $1 < x < \frac{4}{3}, x \in \mathbb{R}$ **4.** (a) $-4 < x < 4, x \in \mathbb{R}$
(b) $x < -4, x > 6, x \in \mathbb{R}$ (c) $-4 \leq x \leq 3, x \in \mathbb{R}$
(d) $x \leq \frac{1}{3}, x \geq 7, x \in \mathbb{R}$ (e) $\frac{2}{3} < x < 4, x \in \mathbb{R}$
(f) $x \leq -\frac{5}{2}, x \geq \frac{15}{2}, x \in \mathbb{R}$ **5.** (a) $-3 < x < 5, x \in \mathbb{R}$
(b) $-5 \leq x \leq 2, x \in \mathbb{R}$ (c) $x \leq -3, x \geq \frac{9}{2}, x \in \mathbb{R}$
(d) $x < -2, x > 6, x \in \mathbb{R}$ **6.** (a) $|x - 220| \leq 8$, $212 \leq x \leq 228$ (i) 215 V is in this range (ii) 208 V is not in this range (b) $x < 99, x > 125, x \in \mathbb{R}$ (c) $63° \leq x \leq 77°$, $x \in \mathbb{R}$; Yes (d) $13 < x < 19, x \in \mathbb{N}$ **7.** (a) $k \leq -2, k \geq 2$, $k \in \mathbb{R}$ (b) $k \leq \frac{1}{9}, k \geq 1, k \in \mathbb{R}$

Revision Questions

1. (a) $-\frac{1}{2}$ (b) (i) 0, 4 (ii) $\frac{1}{2}$ (c) $2 < x < \frac{5}{2}, x \in \mathbb{R}$
2. (a) (3, –2, 4) (b) (2, –1), $\left(\frac{50}{17}, \frac{31}{17}\right)$ (c) (i) $x < 1, x > 5$, $x \in \mathbb{R}$ **3.** (a) (ii) 2, 6 (b) $P(x) = (x-1)(x-2)(x+4)$
(c) $2k, 3k$ **4.** (a) $\left(-10, \frac{5}{3}\right)$ (b) $b = -2$, $c = -3$, $E(3, 0)$ (c) $\frac{d \pm \sqrt{d^2 - 12S^2}}{2}$, 3, 1 **5.** (a) (i) 6 years
(ii) 13 years (b) 2s, 6s; 28 m (c) 40% **6.** (a) $\frac{5}{4}$
(b) $\sqrt{2}$, (1, 2) **7.** (a) 6 days 16 hrs
(b) (i) $1 - \sqrt{5} < x < 1 + \sqrt{5}, x \in \mathbb{R}$
(ii) $x < -2, x > 2, x \in \mathbb{R}$ (iii) $x < 74, x > 90, x \in \mathbb{N}$
(d) 160 @ €40, 120 @ €60, 140 @ €90
8. (a) –5, –9 (b) (–4, –3), (4, 3); x: $(-4\sqrt{2}, 0)$, $(4\sqrt{2}, 0)$, y: $(0, -3\sqrt{2})$, $(0, 3\sqrt{2})$ (c) (i) –ln 4 (ii) 4
(iii) $a^2u^2 + au - 1 = 0$; $\frac{-1 \pm \sqrt{5}}{2a}$ **9.** (a) $-\frac{3b}{a}, \frac{2b}{a}$
(b) $x = 3$; 4 $t = 8$, 16 **10.** (a) $a = -1$, $b = 1$
(b) $b = -6$, $c = 11$; $x = 1, 2, 3$ (c) (i) 16, 8
(ii) $x = \frac{4}{3}$, $y = -\frac{11}{3}$

Section 4

Chapter 10

Exercise 1

1. (a) –8 (b) 5 (c) Start at –8 and jump by 5
(d) 22, 27, 32, 37 (f) $T_n = -8 + (n-1)5$ (g) 157
(h) Infinite **2.** (b) $3n + 8$ (c) (i) 119 (ii) 308 (iii) 311
3. (b) $T_n = n^3$ (c) 10 648 **4.** (a) A constant equal to 3
(c) $T_n = 2 \times 3^n$ (d) 3 **5.** (a) (i) 1 (ii) 4 (iii) 19 (iv) 31
(b) 32nd **6.** (a) 3, 8, 15, 24, 35 (b) 10th (c) $2n + 3$
7. (a) $\frac{1}{3}, \frac{2}{5}, \frac{3}{7}, \frac{4}{9}, \frac{5}{11}$ (b) 25th **8.** (a) 2, 1, $\frac{1}{2}, \frac{1}{4}, \frac{1}{8}$ (b) 9th
9. (a) (i) 0 (ii) 2 (iii) $\log_{10}(n+1)$ (b) $\log_{10}\left(\frac{n+1}{n}\right)$
10. (a) (i) 4 (ii) $\frac{4}{125}$ (iii) $\frac{100}{5^{3n+2}}$ **11.** (b) 5, 9, 13, 17
(d) $T_n = 4n + 1$ (e) 41 (f) 15th
12. (a) (iii) $T_n = 180° \times (n-2)$ (b) 1440° (c) 23
13. (a) (i) 2 (ii) 5 (iii) 9 (b) 2, 5, 9, 14, 20 (d) 90
(e) 18 **14.** (b) $T_n = n^2 + 3n + 1$ (c) 6, 8, 10
(d) The difference between consecutive terms is a constant = 2

Chapter 11

Exercise 2

1. (a) 0, convergent (b) ∞, divergent
(c) $\frac{1}{3}$, convergent (d) 0, convergent (e) ∞, divergent
(f) $\frac{2}{3}$, convergent (g) 1, convergent
(h) Undefined, divergent (i) 2, convergent
(j) $\frac{1}{10}$, convergent **2.** (a) 22 (b) 54 (c) $\frac{1}{2}$ (d) –1
(e) ∞ (f) 0 (g) 0 (h) ∞ (i) 7 (j) 0 **3.** (a) $\frac{1}{3}$ (b) $\frac{2}{3}$ (c) 1

(d) –2 (e) 0 (f) 0 (g) ∞ (h) 0 (i) 0 (j) $\frac{3}{8}$
4. (a) Convergent to 0 (b) Convergent to 0 (c) Convergent to 0 (d) Convergent to 1 (e) Convergent to $-\frac{3}{5}$ (f) Convergent to 0 (g) Convergent to $-\frac{1}{2}$ (h) Convergent to 0

Exercise 3

1. (a) (i) 1 + 3 + 5 + 7 + 9 + … (ii) 25, 16
(b) (i) $\frac{2}{5}+\frac{3}{7}+\frac{4}{9}+\frac{5}{11}+\frac{6}{13}+\frac{7}{15}+\dots$ (ii) $\frac{5986}{3465}, \frac{401}{315}, \frac{29}{35}$
(c) (i) $\frac{1}{2}+\frac{5}{4}+\frac{5}{2}+\frac{17}{4}+\frac{13}{2}+\frac{37}{4}+\frac{25}{2}+\dots$
(d) (i) $\frac{3}{2}, 1, \frac{3}{4}, \frac{3}{5}, \frac{1}{2}$ (ii) $\frac{3}{2}, \frac{5}{2}, \frac{13}{4}, \frac{77}{20}, \frac{87}{20}$ **2.** (a) (i) 6 (ii) 14 (iii) 24 (iv) 6 (v) 8 (vi) 10 (vii) 6, 8, 10 (b) (i) 2 (ii) 8 (iii) 26 (iv) 80 (v) 2 (vi) 6 (vii) 18 (viii) 54 (ix) 2 + 6 + 18 + 54 + … (c) (i) 1 (ii) 9 (iii) 36 (iv) 100 (v) 225 (vi) 1 (vii) 8 (viii) 27 (ix) 64 (x) 125 (xi) 1 + 8 + 27 + 64 + 125 + … (xii) $T_n = n^3$
3. (a) 25 (b) –134 (c) 4 (d) 4334
(e) $S_{n-1} = n^2 - 3n + 2, T_n = 2n - 2, T_1 = 0, T_{20} = 38$
(f) $S_{n-1} = \frac{n(n-1)}{2}, T_n = n, T_1 = 1, T_{38} = 38$
(g) $S_{n-1} = \frac{(n-1)(n)(2n-1)}{6}, T_n = n^2, T_1 = 1, T_{20} = 400$
4. (a) $(-1)^2 + (0)^2 + (1)^2 + (2)^2 + (3)^2 + (4)^2 + (5)^2 + (6)^2 + (7)^2 + (8)^2$ (b) 7 + 9 + 11 + 13 + 15 + 17 + 19
(c) $\left(\frac{3}{2}\right)^1 + \left(\frac{3}{2}\right)^2 + \left(\frac{3}{2}\right)^3 + \dots$
(d) $0 + \frac{1}{4} + \frac{2}{5} + \frac{1}{2} + \frac{4}{7} + \frac{5}{8} + \frac{2}{3} + \frac{7}{10}$
(e) $\left(\frac{1}{2} - 2\right) + \left(\frac{1}{4} - 4\right) + \left(\frac{1}{8} - 6\right) + \left(\frac{1}{16} - 8\right) + \left(\frac{1}{32} - 10\right)$
(f) $\left(\frac{3}{4}\right)^1 + \left(\frac{3}{4}\right)^2 + \dots + \left(\frac{3}{4}\right)^{n-1} + \left(\frac{3}{4}\right)^n$
(g) $(1) + \left(\frac{1}{2}\right) + \dots + \frac{1}{2^{n+2}} + \frac{1}{2^{n+3}}$
(h) $\frac{1}{1} + \frac{1}{2} + \dots + \frac{1}{n+2} + \frac{1}{n+3}$
(i) 4 + 11 + 22 + 37 + 56 + 79 + 137
(j) 1! + 2! + … + (n – 1)! + n! **5.** (a) $T_n = (n-2)^2$, 10
(b) $T_r = 2r + 5$, 7 (c) $T_r = \left(\frac{3}{2}\right)^r$, ∞ (d) $T_n = \frac{n-1}{n+2}$, 8
(e) $T_r = \left(\frac{1}{2}\right)^r - 2r$, 5 (f) $T_l = \left(\frac{3}{4}\right)^l$, n (g) $T_n = \frac{1}{2^{n-1}}$, n + 4
(h) $T_n = \frac{1}{n}$, n + 3 (i) $T_r = 2r^2 + r + 1$, 8 (j) $T_n = n!$, n
6. (a) $T_n = n^2, \sum_{n=1}^{20} n^2$ (b) $T_n = \frac{1}{n}, \sum_{n=1}^{35} \frac{1}{n}$
(c) $T_n = 2n, \sum_{n=1}^{50} 2n$ (d) $T_r = 2r + 1, \sum_{r=1}^{17} (2r+1)$
(e) $T_n = \frac{1}{2 \times 3^n}, \sum_{n=1}^{\infty} \frac{1}{2 \times 3^n}$
(f) $T_n = \frac{1}{(n+2)(n+4)}, \sum_{n=1}^{18} \frac{1}{(n+2)(n+4)}$
(g) $T_r = r + 3, \sum_{r=1}^{45} (r+3)$ (h) $T_n = \frac{1}{2^{n+1}}, \sum_{n=1}^{\infty} \frac{1}{2^{n+1}}$

Chapter 12

Exercise 4

1. (a) $T_1 = 4, T_2 = 9, T_3 = 14, T_5 = 24, T_{11} = 54, T_{122} = 609$ (b) $T_1 = 4, T_2 = 2, T_3 = 0, T_{55} = -104, T_{105} = -204$ (c) $T_1 = 5, T_7 = 8, T_9 = 9, T_{50} = 29{\cdot}5, T_{73} = 41$ (d) $T_5 = 15, T_8 = 24, T_{22} = 66$ (e) 180 kg (f) 9·15 km (g) 108 sweets (h) (i) €24 000, €27 000, €30 000, €33 000, €36 000 (ii) Yes, common difference = €3000 = constant (iii) €24 000, €3000 (iv) €141 000 **2.** (a) 128 (b) 1, 4, 7, 10 (c) –5, 2, 9, 16, 23 (d) a = 15, d = 3 (e) 6, 2, –2, –6 (f) a = 100, d = –4 (g) –3, 4, 11, 18, … (h) a = 11, d = 6 (i) a = 5, d = 6 (j) 26 steps/min (k) 28 kg, 840 kg (l) 54
3. (a) $a = 2, d = 2, T_n = 2n, T_{20} = 40$ (b) $a = -1, d = 3, T_n = 3n - 4, T_{15} = 41$ (c) $a = \frac{3}{2}, d = \frac{1}{2}, T_n = \frac{n+2}{2}, T_{11} = \frac{13}{2}$ (d) $a = -3, d = -2, T_n = -2n - 1, T_{27} = -55$ (e) $a = 1, d = -\frac{1}{2}, T_n = \frac{3-n}{2}, T_{30} = -\frac{27}{2}$
(f) $a = p, d = -1, T_n = p - n + 1, T_9 = p - 8$
(g) $a = 2b - 3, d = 4, T_n = 4n + 2b - 7, T_{14} = 49 + 2b$
(h) $a = \log_3 2, d = 2 \log_3 2, T_n = (2n - 1) \log_3 2, T_9 = 17 \log_3 2$ (i) $a = \sqrt{3}, d = \sqrt{2}, T_n = \sqrt{3} + \sqrt{2}\,(n-1), T_{20} = \sqrt{3} + 19\sqrt{2}$ (j) $a = \sin 15°, d = -x, T_n = \sin 15° - (n-1)x, T_{10} = \sin 15° - 9x$ **4.** (a) 4·8 km (b) $T_n = 4 + \frac{n}{10}$ **5.** (a) a = 3, d = 3; 3, 6, 9, 12, 15 (b) a = 2, d = 1; 2, 3, 4, 5, 6 (c) a = 1, d = 2; 1, 3, 5, 7, 9 (d) a = 7, d = 5; 7, 12, 17, 22, 27 (e) a = –5, d = 8; –5, 3, 11, 19, 27 (f) a = 3, d = –3; 3, 0, –3, –6, –9
(g) $a = 2, d = \frac{5}{2}; 2, \frac{9}{2}, 7, \frac{19}{2}, 12$ (h) $a = -\frac{4}{3}, d = -\frac{5}{3}; -\frac{4}{3}, -3, -\frac{14}{3}, -\frac{19}{3}, -8$ **6.** (a) 7th (b) 20th (c) 10th (d) $T_n = 16 - 4n$, 28 (e) No (f) Yes, it is the 11th term (g) 27 June (h) 10 (i) 13; €2250
7. (a) (i) Arithmetic; The slope is constant, T_n is increasing at a uniform rate with respect to n (ii) 10 (iii) 5 (iv) $T_n = 10n - 5$ (v) $T_4 = 35, T_5 = 45$ (b) (i) Decreasing; The slope is negative (ii) –4 (iii) a = 17, d = –4 (iv) $T_n = 21 - 4n$ (v) $T_{33} = -111$
8. (a) a = 8, d = 3 (b) $a = -\frac{29}{4}, d = \frac{3}{4}$ **9.** (a) x = –8, y = –20 (b) $x = 7\frac{3}{4}, y = 10\frac{1}{4}$ (c) $k = 5, T_{12} = 147$ (d) $x = -2, y = 12, T_{18} = 117$ (e) x = 2, y = –3 (f) a = –12; –23, –38, –53 (g) x = 3; 4, 7, 10 (h) $a = \frac{1}{3}$ **10.** (a) –5, –2, 1 (b) 3, 8, 13 (c) 5, 7, 9

(d) –2, 2, 6 **11.** (a) (i) 5 (ii) $\frac{11}{2}$ (iii) $\frac{5x+6}{2}$ (iv) x (v) $\frac{9}{20}$ (vi) $\frac{a^2+b^2}{2}$ (b) (i) 7, 3 (ii) 7, –1

Exercise 5

1. (a) $S_n = n(n+2)$, $S_{12} = 168$ (b) $S_n = n(8-n)$, $S_{15} = -105$ (c) $S_n = \frac{n(13-n)}{4}$, $S_{20} = -35$ (d) $S_n = \frac{3n(1-n)}{8}$, $S_{26} = -\frac{975}{4}$ (e) $S_n = \frac{n(3n-19)}{2}$, $S_{54} = 3861$ (f) $S_n = \frac{n\sqrt{2}(n+1)}{2}$, $S_{16} = 55\sqrt{2}$ (g) $S_n = \frac{n(2n+1)}{12}$, $S_{40} = 270$ **2.** (a) €2250 (b) €1 904 000, €63 200 (c) €377 500 (d) 63, 1020 (e) 14, 1225 (f) 4092
3. (a) 22 (b) 21 (c) 13 (d) 10 (e) 11 days
4. (a) 15 252 (b) 14 094 (c) 12 480 (d) 9996
5. (a) $\frac{14}{19}$ (b) $a = -18$, $d = 2$; –18, –16, –14 (c) $a = -3$, $d = 6$ (d) $a = -100$, $d = 10$; –100, –90, –80 (e) $a = \frac{3}{2}$, $d = \frac{5}{2}$ (f) $a = 76$, $d = -20$ (g) €1200, €60
6. (a) $a = 10$, $d = 3$, $S_n = \frac{n(3n+17)}{2}$ (b) $-\frac{441a}{10}$ (d) $S_{25} = 125$ (e) (i) $S_1 = -15$, $T_1 = -15$, $S_2 = -28$, $T_2 = -13$ (ii) $a = -15$, $d = 2$ (iii) $T_n = 2n - 17$ (iv) $n = 7, 9$ (g) 21

Exercise 6

1. (a) (i) $T_n = n + 1$ (ii) $T_1 = 2$, $T_2 = 3$ (iii) $a = 2$, $d = 1$ (iv) 12, $S_{12} = 90$ (b) (i) $T_n = 3 - n$ (ii) $T_1 = 2$, $T_2 = 1$ (iii) $a = 2$, $d = -1$ (iv) Infinite number (c) (i) $T_n = 2 + 3n$ (ii) $T_1 = 5$, $T_2 = 8$ (iii) $a = 5$, $d = 3$ (iv) n, $S_n = \frac{n(3n+7)}{2}$ (d) (i) $T_n = 5 - n$ (ii) $T_1 = 4$, $T_2 = 3$ (iii) $a = 4$, $d = -1$ (iv) 25, $S_{25} = -200$ (e) (i) $T_n = 3 - \frac{n}{2}$ (ii) $T_1 = \frac{5}{2}$, $T_2 = 2$ (iii) $a = \frac{5}{2}$, $d = -\frac{1}{2}$ (iv) n, $S_n = \frac{n(11-n)}{4}$
2. (a) $S_{30} = -345$ (b) $S_n = \frac{n(5n+9)}{2}$ (c) $S_{58} = \frac{8497}{2}$ (d) $S_{15} = \frac{375}{2}$ (e) $S_{36} = 804$ **3.** (a) 12 (b) 11 (c) 31 (d) 23

Chapter 13

Exercise 7

1. (a) (i) $a = 16$, $r = \frac{1}{2}$, $T_n = 2^{5-n}$ (ii) $a = 8$, $r = \frac{3}{2}$, $T_n = 8\left(\frac{3}{2}\right)^{n-1}$ (iii) $a = 48$, $r = \frac{3}{4}$, $T_n = 48\left(\frac{3}{4}\right)^{n-1}$ (iv) $a = 2$, $r = -3$, $T_n = 2(-3)^{n-1}$ (v) $a = 1$, $r = \frac{1}{3}$, $T_n = \left(\frac{1}{3}\right)^{n-1}$ (vi) $a = xy$, $r = x$, $T_n = x^n y$ (b) $T_n = 6(3)^{n-1}$ (c) $a = 1$, $r = -7$, $T_{10} = -40\,353\,607$, $T_n = (-7)^{n-1}$ (d) (i) $T_n = 2^{n-1}$, $T_6 = 32$ (ii) $T_n = \frac{3}{4}(2)^{n-1}$, $T_{18} = 98\,304$ (iii) $T_n = (5)^{n-1}$, $T_{31} = 5^{30}$ (iv) $T_n = 7\left(\frac{\sqrt{42}}{7}\right)^{n-1}$, $T_{21} = \frac{6^{10}}{7^9}$ (v) $T_n = 2 \times 3^{n-1} \tan^n x$, $T_{15} = 9\,565\,938 \tan^{15} x$ (vi) $T_n = 2^n (\log_2 3)^n$, $T_{17} = 2^{17} (\log_2 3)^{17}$ (vii) $T_n = b^5 (c)^{n-1}$, $T_{51} = b^5 c^{50}$ (viii) $T_n = \frac{c}{2}\left(\frac{b}{3}\right)^{n-1}$, $T_{12} = \frac{cb^{11}}{2 \times 3^{11}}$
2. (a) $T_1 = 2$, $r = 2$; 2, 4, 8, 16, 32, … (b) $T_1 = \frac{3}{2}$, $r = 2$; $\frac{3}{2}$, 3, 6, 12, 24, … (c) $T_1 = x$, $r = xy$; $x, x^2y, x^3y^2, x^4y^3, x^5y^4, \ldots$ (d) $T_1 = \frac{a^2}{b^2}$, $r = \frac{a}{b}$; $\frac{a^2}{b^2}, \frac{a^3}{b^3}, \frac{a^4}{b^4}, \frac{a^5}{b^5}, \frac{a^6}{b^6}, \ldots$ (e) $T_1 = 5$, $r = 5$; $5^1, 5^2, 5^3, 5^4, 5^5, \ldots$ (f) $T_1 = \frac{1}{32}$, $r = 4$; $\frac{1}{32}, \frac{1}{8}, \frac{1}{2}$, 2, 8, ... (g) $T_1 = 2\sin x$, $r = \sin x$; $2\sin x, 2\sin^2 x, 2\sin^3 x, 2\sin^4 x, 2\sin^5 x, \ldots$ (h) $T_1 = 9\sqrt{3}$, $r = \sqrt{3}$; $9\sqrt{3}, 27, 27\sqrt{3}, 81, 81\sqrt{3}, \ldots$
3. (a) 2 (b) 4 (c) $a = 2$, $r = 2$ (d) $T_n = 2^n$ (e) 2^{20}
4. (a) 27 (b) 8 (c) 6 (d) Yes, the 11th term (e) No (f) 7th day (g) 2022 **5.** (a) 6 (b) 11 (c) 8 (d) 7 (e) $p + 1$ (f) $p + 1$ (g) 5 (h) 8 **6.** (a) Not a geometric sequence (b) A geometric sequence, $a = 1$, $r = \frac{3}{2}$ (c) A geometric sequence, $a = \frac{1}{2}$, $r = \frac{1}{2}$ (d) A geometric sequence, $a = 1$, $r = \frac{1}{7}$ (e) A geometric sequence, $a = \frac{1}{6}$, $r = 3$ (f) A geometric sequence, $a = \frac{25}{3}$, $r = -5$
7. 8 m, 4 m, 2 m, 1 m, 0·5 m **8.** (b) Year 1 €1030, Year 2 €1060·9; Year 3 €1092·727, Year 4 €1125·50881 (c) $a =$ €1030, $r = 1{\cdot}03$ (d) €1344
9. (d) Yes, common ratio of 2 between terms, 2^{14}
10. (a) 6 (b) 36 (c) $6^{10} = 60\,466\,176$ (d) $\frac{1}{36}$ **11.** 226
12. (a) (i) €20 240 (ii) €13 340 (b) 46 875 (c) $\frac{9}{16}$ cm (d) 16 (e) (i) 300 (ii) 14 700 (iii) 13 022 **13.** (a) -2^{19} (b) $r = 3$, $a = \frac{4}{27}$; $\frac{4}{27}, \frac{4}{9}, \frac{4}{3}$, 4. $r = -3$, $a = -\frac{4}{27}$; $-\frac{4}{27}, \frac{4}{9}, -\frac{4}{3}$, 4 (c) $r = 2$, $a = \frac{1}{2^{29}}$; $\frac{1}{2^{29}}, \frac{1}{2^{28}}, \frac{1}{2^{27}}, \frac{1}{2^{26}}$ (d) $a = \frac{2}{5}$, $r = \frac{3}{2}$, $T_7 = \frac{729}{160}$ (e) 5%; €40 841 (f) 20%, 46·875 °C **14.** (a) $x = \pm 6$, $y = 18$, $z = \pm 54$ (b) $x = -20$, $y = -80$ (c) €33 800, €43 940
15. (a) 3, 6, 12 (b) 6, 18, 54 **16.** (a) $x = 0$ or 16; 9, –6, 4 or 25, 10, 4 (b) $x = 0$ or 3; 1, –3, 9 or $\frac{1}{4}, \frac{3}{8}, \frac{9}{16}$ (c) $b = 5$; $T_8 = 640$ **17.** (a) (i) 18 (ii) 1·1 (iii) ar^2 (iv) $x^2 - y^2$ (b) (i) 3 (ii) 8, 2 (iii) 9, 3

Exercise 8

1. (a) $S_n = 8\left(\left(\frac{3}{2}\right)^n - 1\right)$, $S_{12} = 8\left(\left(\frac{3}{2}\right)^{12} - 1\right)$
(b) $S_n = 2\left(1 - \left(\frac{1}{2}\right)^n\right)$, $S_6 = \frac{63}{32}$ (c) $S_n = 1-(-2)^n, S_8 = -255$
(d) $S_n = \frac{x(1-x^n)}{1-x}$, $S_{15} = \frac{x(1-x^{15})}{1-x}$
(e) $S_n = \frac{4\left(1 - \left(-\frac{\sqrt{2}}{2}\right)^n\right)}{2+\sqrt{2}}$, $S_{22} = \frac{4\left(1 - \frac{1}{2^{11}}\right)}{2+\sqrt{2}}$
(f) $S_n = \frac{1 - \frac{1}{b^{2n}}}{b^2 - 1}$, $S_{20} = \frac{1 - \frac{1}{b^{40}}}{b^2 - 1}$ (g) $S_n = \frac{2\left((\sqrt{3})^n - 1\right)}{\sqrt{3} - 1}$,
$S_{40} = \frac{2(3^{20} - 1)}{\sqrt{3} - 1}$ (h) $S_n = \frac{3}{4}(2^n - 1)$, $S_{11} = \frac{6141}{4}$
2. (a) (i) 62 (ii) 2046 (iii) 1984 (b) $\frac{255}{256}$ (c) 13; $\frac{8191}{16}$
(d) (i) €231·85 (ii) €1093·68 (e) €17 852·52
(f) (i) 14 071 (ii) 95 491 (g) Multiply left above and below by –1 (h) (i) 2^{63} (ii) $(2^{64} - 1)$ cent (i) $\frac{85D}{64}$ mg
3. (a) 5 (b) 107 (c) 5 (d) 6 (e) 6 (f) 7·2 mins
4. (a) 211 (b) 7 (c) $r = \frac{1}{2}$; $S_7 = 31\frac{3}{4}$ (d) $r = 7, -8$
(e) $S_{12} = \frac{4095 \log_3 x}{2048}$ **5.** (a) $S_n = 3(2^n - 1)$ (b) $a = \frac{2}{3}$, $r = \frac{1}{3}$, $S_n = 1 - \left(\frac{1}{3}\right)^n$ **6.** (a) $\frac{7}{5}$ (b) 10 (c) $\frac{2}{3}$ (d) $\frac{32}{3}$
(e) $\frac{1}{x-1}$ (f) 2 (g) 32 (h) $\frac{3}{2}$ **7.** (a) $\frac{125}{2}$ or $\frac{125}{3}$
(b) 96, 24, 6, $\frac{3}{2}$ (c) 20 or $\frac{20}{3}$, $\frac{1}{4}$ or $\frac{3}{4}$ (d) 24
8. (a) $\frac{1}{1+\tan^2 x}$, $\frac{3}{4}$ (b) 11 (c) 4000 cm^2 (d) $b = 2, p = \frac{2}{3}$
9. (a) $\frac{1}{6}$ (b) $\frac{23}{99}$ (c) $\frac{19}{3}$ (d) $\frac{118}{99}$ (e) $\frac{80}{33}$ (f) $\frac{139}{330}$
10. (a) 363 (b) 1365 (c) $\frac{381}{128}$ (d) 1 (e) $\frac{1}{\cos^2 x}$

Revision Questions

1. (a) $r = \frac{\sqrt{3}}{6}$; $S_\infty = \frac{2}{11}(6 + \sqrt{3})$
(b) 11; $\frac{1}{3072}\left(1 - \left(\frac{1}{4}\right)^{11}\right)$ (c) 57 (d) 6 (e) $\frac{37}{99}$
(f) (i) $a = 8$ (ii) $T_{20} = -\frac{1}{2^{16}}$ (iii) $S_{20} = \frac{16}{3}\left(1 - \frac{1}{2^{20}}\right)$
2. (a) (i) $T_n = 3^{4-n}$ (ii) $r = \frac{1}{3} < 1$ (iii) $S_n = \frac{81}{2}\left(1 - \frac{1}{3^n}\right)$
(iv) $S_\infty = \frac{81}{2}$ (v) 8 (b) Yes, because the total volume held by the other 19 is less than the volume of the first tank **3.** (a) $N = 3n + 1$ (b) 175 (c) 40
4. (a) 150 cm (b) $1 + x$ (c) (i) 25·6 mm (ii) 15 (iii) 32
5. (a) 21 (b) 10 (c) $a = 9, r = \frac{1}{3}$ **6.** (a) $\frac{8}{45}$ (b) $a = 16$
(c) 6 cm, 9 cm, 13·5 cm **7.** (a) 10 (b) 7
(c) $3l, \frac{15l}{7}, \frac{9l}{7}$ **8.** (a) €5904 (b) $\frac{4D}{3}\left(1 - \frac{1}{4^n}\right)$,
451·76 mg (c) (i) $S_{2n} = \frac{a(1 - r^{2n})}{1 - r}$, (ii) $S_n = \frac{b(1 - r^{2n})}{1 - r^2}$
9. (a) 10 (b) –2, 1, 4 (c) $x = 8, y = 12$
10. (a) 32 (b) $0 < k < 2, k \in \mathbb{R}$; $S_\infty = 2$
(c) The difference between consecutive terms is a constant = $2a$

Section 5

Chapter 14

Exercise 1

1. (a) 62·8 km/h (b) €5·40; 90c per can (c) No
(d) 160-page refill pad (e) 870 ml bottle (f) 416 m^2
(g) 36·25% (h) $\frac{2}{3}$ **2.** (a) 5×10^{-2} m (b) $2{\cdot}7 \times 10^{-3}$ km
(c) $5{\cdot}4 \times 10^6$ m^2 (d) $2{\cdot}6 \times 10^{-4}$ m^2 (e) $6{\cdot}8 \times 10^{-4}$ m^3
(f) 5×10^3 kg (g) $5{\cdot}6 \times 10^{-6}$ m^3 (h) 5×10^3 cm^3
(i) 5×10^{-3} m^3 **3.** (a) 20 m/s (b) 30 m/s
(c) $27\frac{7}{9}$ m/s = 27·8 m/s (d) 12·5 m/s (e) 36 km/h
(f) 56·16 km/h (g) 10·8 km/h (h) 90 km/h
(i) $20\frac{5}{6}$ m/s = 20·8 m/s (j) 32·4 km/h **4.** 13 gallons
5. 6697·6 km **6.** 8847·6 m **7.** 4·16 **8.** 2·44 m; 1·62 feet
9. (a) 52 500 m^2 (b) $5{\cdot}25 \times 10^{-2}$ km^2 (c) 5·25 hectares
(d) 13 acres **10.** 120 yards **11.** (a) $1{\cdot}08 \times 10^9$ km/h
(b) $6{\cdot}7 \times 10^8$ mph

Exercise 2

1. (a) £659·36 (b) \$1091·20 (c) CAD\$1216·80
(d) R12 248 **2.** (a) €366·57 (b) €788·64
(c) €1457·42 (d) \$5406·13 (e) £120·85
(f) 1783·70 rupees **3.** (a) \$1620·43 (b) €513·75
4. (a) (i) €66·73 (ii) 707·30 HKD (b) 2248 THB
(c) 2544·91 THB **5.** (a) €645·21 (b) €678·43
(c) €33·22 **6.** (a) $\frac{5}{4}$ (b) $y = \frac{5}{4}x$ (c) €250 (d) £240; Exchange rate from £ to € is constant over this period

Exercise 3

1. €270·60 **2.** £346·80 **3.** €219·56 **4.** €357
5. €378·51 **6.** €62·39 **7.** €60·86 **8.** (a) €38 610 in Luxembourg (b) €40 920 in Finland
9. €35 593·22; €42 711·86 **10.** €21 049

11. €6000; €2700 **12.** (a) €37 (b) €13·91 (c) €20 (d) €70·91 (e) €429·09 **13.** (a) €2240 (b) €2373·06 (c) €12 270 (d) €39 116·94 yearly; €3259·75 monthly **14.** €48 000; €1933·06 **15.** €57 490 **16.** (a) €68 644 (b) €2745·76 (c) €45 432·16

Exercise 4

1. (a)

CP (€)	SP (€)	Profit (€)	% Profit	Profit margin
100	150	50	50	$33\frac{1}{3}\%$
180	300	120	$66\frac{2}{3}$	40%
250	312·50	62·50	25	20%
50·40	72	21·60	42·86	30%
72	160	88	122·2	55%

(b)

CP (€)	SP (€)	Loss	% Loss
100	75	25	25
172	87	85	49·4
170	100	70	41·2

2. (a) 20% (b) €1073·52 **3.** 14·3% **4.** €446·25
5. (a) €6210 (b) 76·2% (c) 43·2% **6.** 20%
7. (a) €30 000 (b) €19 755·09

Chapter 15

Exercise 5

1. (a) €2131·25 (b) €206·72 (c) 4·2% (d) 9·3% (e) €277·28 **2.** (a) €420 (b) €3780 (c) €1209·60 (d) €4989·60 (e) €103·95 **3.** (a) €1350 (b) €13 425·84 (c) €14 775·84 (d) €1275·84 (e) 9·45% **4.** (a) €4650 (b) €1046·25 (c) €158·23 (d) €7196·25 **5.** €405 **6.** (a) (i) €10 300 (ii) €10 609 (iii) €10 927·27 (b) (i) €25 625 (ii) €26 265·63 (iii) €26 922·27 **7.** (a) €10 302·25 (b) €23 622·32 **8.** (a) €8700 (b) €8654 (c) Paula's investment is more profitable by €46 **9.** (a) €20 665·13 (b) €14 111·17 (c) €20 000 **10.** (a) 1·57% (b) 2·4% **11.** (a) 4 years (b) 7·5 years **12.** (a) €10 250 (b) €16 120 (c) 4% (d) €28 295·79 (e) 1·32% **13.** 41·4% **14.** €26 520; €2·50 **15.** 5%, €2500 **16.** (a) €11 411·66 (b) €10 710; Option 2 is better **17.** 3·16%

18. Monthly interest rate = 0·347%; Weekly interest rate = 0·080%; €3172·39, €3171·88, €3172·02 **19.** €2125 **20.** €45 999 **21.** 20% **22.** (a) €13 500 (b) €12 150 **23.** 43·75%

24.

Time	Reducing balance method	Straight line method
0	€25 000·00	€25 000·00
1	€19 650·00	€21 500·00
2	€15 444·90	€18 000·00
3	€12 139·69	€14 500·00
4	€9541·80	€11 000·00
5	€7499·85	€7500·00

25. (a) €5800 (b) 36% **26.** 13 years **27.** 31·9%

Exercise 6

1. (a) €20 664·18; €5664·18 (b) €13 340·20; €2340·20 (c) €8512·66; €412·66 (d) €6519·27; €279·27 (e) €1895·57; €95·87 **2.** €15 307·68 **3.** €7947·45 **4.** €14 402·02; €1202·02 **5.** €14 026·22 **6.** €16 374·76 **7.** €130·17 **8.** €208·52; €48·18 **9.** €182·64 **10.** €224·07 **11.** €239·36; €204·83; €386·16 **12.** €280·99; €64·75; €24·40 **13.** €2072·44 **14.** €2025·40

15.

Year	Annual repayment	Present values of repayments
1	€3799·67	€3544·47
2	€3799·67	€3306·41
3	€3799·67	€3084·33
4	€3799·67	€2877·18
5	€3799·67	€2683·93
6	€3799·67	€2503·67
Total	€22 798·02	€18 000

16. (a) €866 605·40 (b) €1396·53 **17.** (a) €540 512·68 (b) €649·74 (c) €1119·42 **18.** €5430·86 **19.** €2202·66 **20.** €428 556·80; €903 556·80 **21.** €5003·09 **22.** €561·49 **23.** (a) €11 705·73 (b) €11 732·61 (c) €11 735·11

Revision Questions

1. (a) €4200 (b) €23 800 (c) 6%, 7·5% (d) €35 140, €42 280 (e) €585·67, €440·42 **2.** (a) €10 506 (b) 2·5% **3.** (a) $\frac{A}{1{\cdot}062} + \frac{A}{1{\cdot}062^2} + \frac{A}{1{\cdot}062^3} + \dots + \frac{A}{1{\cdot}062^7}$

(b) €4059·24 (d) 0·5025% (e) €329·02 (f) €777 **4.** (a) €1560 (b) 192% (c) €38 768·06 (d) €51 660 (e) 25% **5.** (a) (i) 4 hrs (ii) €475·20 (iii) €21·30 (b) €852 (c) €210·80 (d) €147·80 (e) €34·08 (f) €33·27 (g) €636·85
6. (a) $\frac{A}{(1+i)} + \frac{A}{(1+i)^2} + \frac{A}{(1+i)^3} + ... + \frac{A}{(1+i)^t}$
7. (a) €336 866·63 (b) (i) 266 (ii) €26 600 (iii) 38·7% (iv) €7140 **8.** (a) 34·6 (b) 28·74 (c) 17% (d) Mass = 183·12 pounds, height = 66·93 inches **9.** (a) €1 = £0·8394 (b) €655·23 (c) €1 = £0·7983 (d) £534·86
10. (a) €571·34 (b) 6·5% (c) €2432
11. (a) (i) €50 000 (ii) €20 000 (b) –7500 euro/year (c) $V = 50000 - 7500t$ (d) 1 August 2016 (e) 20·5% **12.** (a) 8·208 m^2 (b) 377 tiles (c) 3·2% (d) 10 boxes (e) 23 (f) €1045·50

13. (a) €39 308·30

(b)

Repayment number	Fixed repayment	Interest	Debt repayment	Balance
0	€0			€250 000
1	€39 308·30	€13 500	€25 808·30	€224 191·70
2	€39 308·30	€12 106·35	€27 201·95	€196 989·75
3	€39 308·30	€10 637·45	€28 670·85	€168 318·90
4	€39 308·30	€9089·22	€30 219·08	€138 099·82
5	€39 308·30	€7457·39	€31 850·91	€106 248·91
6	€39 308·30	€5737·44	€33 570·86	€72 678·05
7	€39 308·30	€3924·61	€35 383·69	€37 294·36
8	€39 308·30	€2013·90	€37 294·40	€0

14. (a) $1 178 485; $1 783 285 (b) $16·7 million

Section 6

Chapter 16

Exercise 1

1. (a) 4 Re (b) –7 Re (c) $-3\sqrt{2}$ Re (d) $4i$ Im (e) $7i$ Im (f) $-5i$ Im (g) $\sqrt{3}i$ Im (h) $\sqrt{2}i$ Im (i) $\frac{3}{4}i$ Im (j) $40i$ Im (k) $-36i$ Im **2.** (a) 7 Re (b) –9 Re (c) $7i$ Im (d) $-9i$ Im (e) $28i$ Im (f) $-5\sqrt{2}i$ Im (g) $5\sqrt{2}i$ Im (h) $1i$ Im **3.** (a) $-i$ (b) 1 (c) i (d) –1 (e) 3 (f) $2i$ (g) $3i$ (h) $4i$ (i) –1 (j) $-11i$ (k) $-18i$ (l) i (m) $2i$ (n) $32i$ (o) –64 (p) –8 (q) –2187 (r) $2\sqrt{2}$ (s) 1 (t) $-i$ **4.** (a) Yes (b) No (c) No

Exercise 2

1. Re = 5, Im = 2 **2.** Re = 5, Im = –2 **3.** Re = $\sqrt{2}$, Im = 1 **4.** Re = –6, Im = 0 **5.** Re = 0, Im = 3 **6.** Re = $-\frac{2}{3}$, Im = $\frac{1}{2}$ **7.** Re = $\frac{\sqrt{2}}{7}$, Im = –7 **8.** Re = $\frac{7}{2}$, Im = $-\frac{1}{\sqrt{3}}$ **9.** Re = $x + y + 7$, Im = –1 **10.** Re = $3x + 3q$, Im = $5y - 2p$ **11.** Re = –2, Im = $2 - k$ **12.** Re = $2 + k$, Im = $3 - 5k$

Exercise 3

1. (a) (2, 7) (b) (3, 18) (c) (17, 52) (d) (11, –5) (e) (–3, 7) (f) (–7, –6) (g) $\left(\frac{1}{2}, \frac{3}{2}\right)$ (h) $\left(\sqrt{2}, -\frac{7}{2}\right)$ (i) (6, –5) (j) (–8, –11) (k) $(x + 1, -2)$ (l) $(-2, y + 3)$
2. (a) $1 + 0i$ (b) $-3 + 0i$ (c) $0 + 5i$ (d) $-5 + 6i$ (e) $-7 - 2i$ (f) $\frac{1}{2} + \sqrt{2}i$ (g) $-\frac{2}{3} + i$ (h) $5 - \frac{11}{3}i$ (i) $4 + \frac{3}{\sqrt{2}}i$ (j) $\frac{1}{\sqrt{2}} + \frac{1}{\sqrt{2}}i$ (k) $(y - 1) + 2i$ (l) $-3 + (a - 2)i$
4. (a) (3, 4) (b) $\frac{4}{3}$ (c) 5 **5.** (a) (i) $3 + 3i$ (ii) 1 (iii) 1 (iv) $3\sqrt{2}$ (b) 5, $\sqrt{41}$ (c) 4, $-\frac{4}{3}$ (d) –5 (e) 7, 3
6. (a) $\frac{y}{x}$, $\sqrt{x^2 + y^2}$ (b) $-\frac{y}{x}$, $\sqrt{x^2 + y^2}$; $180° - \tan^{-1}\theta$ (c) $\frac{y}{x}$, $180° + \tan^{-1}\theta$; $-\frac{y}{x}$, $360° - \tan^{-1}\theta$

Exercise 4

1. (a) $9 + 9i$ (b) $14 + 12i$ (c) $14 + 8i$ (d) $13 + 20i$ (e) $3 + 12i$ (f) $8 + 18i$ (g) $19 + 17i$ (h) $13 + 3i$ (i) $2 + 14i$ (j) $(a + b) + 5i$ **2.** (a) $9 + 8i$, $-3 - 6i$

(b) $4 + 5i, 4 - 5i$ (c) $7 - 8i, 3 - 6i$ (d) $23 + 6i, -1 + 2i$ (e) $\frac{1}{2} + 7i, -\frac{1}{2} + 3i$ (f) $2\sqrt{3} + 4i, 0 + 0i$ (g) $2x - 2i, 0 + 6i$ (h) $9 + 4xi, 1 - 2xi$ (i) $3x + 4yi, -x - 2yi$ (j) $(x - 3y) + (y + 2x)i, (x + 3y) + (y - 2x)i$ **3.** (a) $10 + 7i$ (b) $11 - 1i$ (c) $-\frac{21}{2} - 6i$ (d) $12 - 2i$ (e) $y + 5i$ **4.** (a) 4 (b) $12 - 3\sqrt{2}i$ (c) $2 - 13i$ (d) $7\sqrt{2} + 3i$ (e) $3\sqrt{5} - 4\sqrt{5}i$ **5.** (a) $13 + 4i$ (b) $(0, 0) \to (-2, 8), -2 + 8i$ (c) $(0, 0) \to (7, -13), -7 + 13i$ (d) $-9 - 4i$ **6.** $5 + 3i$ **7.** (a) $2 + 1i$ (b) $2 + 4i$ (c) $4 + 5i$ **8.** $2 + 0i, 0 + 4i$

Exercise 5

1. (a) $12 + 8i$ (b) $42 + 14i$ (c) $24 - 6i$ (d) $20 + 10i$ (e) $-1 - 4i$ (f) $\frac{10}{3} + 12i$ (g) $2 + 3i$ (h) $5a + 5bi$ (i) $ka + kbi$ (j) $1 - 10i$ (k) $3 - 7i$ (l) $-32 - 50i$ (m) $(3k + 4l) + (2k + 2l)i$ (n) $(ka + lc) + (kb + ld)i$ **2.** (a) $-6 + 0i$ (b) $13 + 15i$ (c) $2 + 12i$ (d) $1 - 3i$ (e) $-28 - 24i$ (f) $17 + 12i$ (g) $-\frac{9}{2} - \frac{9}{2}i$ (h) $17 + 21i$ (i) $1 + 6i$ (j) $3 + 3i$ **3.** (a) 13 (b) $-10 + 24i$, 26 (c) $20 - 48i$, 52 (d) $\frac{5}{2} - 6i, \frac{13}{2}$ (e) $-\frac{5}{13} + \frac{12}{13}i$, 1 **4.** (b) $(-4, -2), (4, 2), (-8, -4), (-2, -1), (-10, -5)$ (c) $\frac{1}{2}, \frac{1}{2}, \frac{1}{2}, \frac{1}{2}, \frac{1}{2}$; $2\sqrt{5}, 2\sqrt{5}, 4\sqrt{5}, \sqrt{5}, 5\sqrt{5}$ **6.** (a) $\sqrt{a^2 + b^2}$ (b) $ka + kbi$ **7.** (a) (i) $6 - 9i$ (ii) $-6 + 2i$ (iii) $-7i$

Exercise 6

1. (a) 5 (b) $\sqrt{5}$ (c) $\sqrt{41}$ (d) $\sqrt{29}$ (e) $2\sqrt{10}$ (f) $\sqrt{2}$ (g) $\sqrt{577}$ (h) $\sqrt{13}$ (i) 2 (j) $\frac{\sqrt{5}}{3}$ (k) 1 (l) $\frac{\sqrt{5}}{4}$ **3.** 5, 13 (a) $8\sqrt{2}$, 18 (b) $2\sqrt{65}, -8$ (c) 10, 10 (d) $2\sqrt{13}$, 8 (e) $\sqrt{146}$, 14 (f) $\sqrt{401}, -3$ (g) 1, 1 (h) 1, 1 **4.** (b) $5\sqrt{2}$, 12·5 **6.** $2\sqrt{5}$ **7.** (b) $4\sqrt{5}$ (c) 128 **9.** (a) $\sqrt{(y + 7)^2 + (3 - x)^2}$ (b) $\sqrt{(x + 3)^2 + (y - 2)^2}$ (c) $x^2 + y^2 = 25$, centre (0, 0) (d) $(x + 7)^2 + (y + 5)^2 = 6$, centre $(-7, -5)$ **10.** (a) ± 24 (b) ± 3 (c) ± 3 (d) $\pm\frac{5}{3}$

Exercise 7

1. (a) $2, \frac{\pi}{6}$ (b) $2, \frac{5\pi}{6}$ (c) $2, \frac{7\pi}{6}$ (d) $2, \frac{11\pi}{6}$ (e) $1, \frac{5\pi}{3}$ (f) $1, \frac{5\pi}{4}$ (g) $1, \frac{\pi}{2}$ (h) $4, \pi$ (i) $8, \frac{3\pi}{2}$ (j) $4\sqrt{2}, \frac{5\pi}{4}$ **3.** (a) $\sqrt{x^2 + y^2}, \tan^{-1}\left(\frac{y}{x}\right)$ (b) $\sqrt{(x + 3)^2 + (2 - y)^2}, \tan^{-1}\left(\frac{2 - y}{x + 3}\right)$ (c) $\sqrt{(x + 3)^2 + (y + 1)^2}, \tan^{-1}\left(\frac{-y - 1}{x + 3}\right)$ (d) $\sqrt{(x + c)^2 + y^2}, \tan^{-1}\left(\frac{-y}{x + c}\right)$ (e) $\sqrt{(3x - 3)^2 + 9y^2}, \tan^{-1}\left(\frac{-y}{x - 1}\right)$ (f) $\sqrt{(2 - x)^2 + (1 + y)^2}, \tan^{-1}\left(\frac{-1 - y}{2 - x}\right)$ (g) $\sqrt{(x + a)^2 + (y - b)^2}, \tan^{-1}\left(\frac{y - b}{x + a}\right)$

5. (a) $x = 2, y = 2\sqrt{3}, z = 2 + 2\sqrt{3}i$ (b) $x = -\frac{1}{\sqrt{2}}, y = -\frac{1}{\sqrt{2}}, z = -\frac{1}{\sqrt{2}} + \frac{1}{\sqrt{2}}i$ (c) $x = -1, y = -\sqrt{3}, z = -1 - \sqrt{3}i$ **6.** (a) $|z| = 1$, $\arg z = 45°$ (b) $|z| = 1$, $\arg z = 0°$ **7.** It is the straight line with equation: $x - y - 5 = 0$

Exercise 8

1. (a) $3 + 0i$ (b) $-2 + 0i$ (c) $0 - 5i$ (d) $0 + 7i$ (e) $-2 - 3i$ (f) $-1 - 5i$ (g) $\sqrt{3} + 6i$ (h) $8 + 3i$ (i) $(x - 7) - 2i$ (j) $(3 + x) + yi$ (k) $(4x + y - 2) + 3i$ **2.** (a) $15 - 21i$ (b) $-8 + 32i$ (c) $7 + 11i$ (d) $12 - 22i$ (e) $4 - 3i$ (f) $8 - 22i$ (g) $3 - 15i$ (h) $17 + 29i$ (i) $26 + 0i$ (j) $13 + 29i$ **4.** (d) $5 - 12i, -5 - 12i, 5 + 12i$

Exercise 9

1. (a) $-4 + 6i$ (b) $5 + 5i$ (c) $6 + 17i$ (d) $-13 + 13i$ (e) $-5 + 0i$ (f) $19 - 9i$ (g) $2 + 8i$ (h) $\frac{11}{4} + \frac{1}{2}i$ (i) $1 + 7\sqrt{2}i$ (j) $0 - 2i$ (k) $11 - 2i$ (l) $0 - 2i$ (m) $2 - 4i$ **2.** (a) $26 - 2i$ (b) $0 - 34i$ (c) $-14 - 22i$ (d) $26 + 2i$ (e) $26 + 2i$ (f) $0 + 34i$ (g) $-22 - 14i$ (h) $-136 - 68i$ (i) $4 + 152i$ (j) $-124 + 88i$ **3.** (a) 2 (b) 13 (c) 29 (d) 45 (e) 5 (f) $\frac{1}{2}$ (g) 19 (h) 10 (i) $x^2 + 4$ (j) $x^2 + y^2$ **4.** (a) 25 (b) $10 - 10i$ (c) $13 + 13i$ (d) -3 **5.** (a) $-11 + 60i$ (b) $-2 - 2i$ (c) -4 (d) $8i$ (e) $12i$ (f) 0 **6.** (a) $-6 - 8i$ (c) 10, 10 (d) Anticlockwise rotation by 90° **7.** (b) $4 - 2i$ (d) $2\sqrt{5}, 2\sqrt{5}$ (e) Anticlockwise rotation by 270° **8.** (a) 0°, 3 (b) Anticlockwise, 90°, 1 (c) Anticlockwise, 180°, $\frac{1}{2}$ (d) Anticlockwise, 270°, 3 **9.** (a) 2, 60° (b) 2, 30° (c) 4, 90° **10.** (b) $3\sqrt{5}$, 116·57° (c) $\sqrt{5}$, 296·57° (d) $9 + 12i$ (e) 15, 53·13° **11.** Anticlockwise; the angle w makes with the + Re axis; multiplied by the modulus of w **12.** (b) $\sqrt{2}$ (c) 45° (e) $2i$ (f) $2i$ **13.** (b) 0° (c) 13 (e) The + Re axis, $|z|^2$

Exercise 10

1. (a) $0 - 3i$ (b) $0 + 7i$ (c) $0 + 5i$ (d) $0 - \frac{2}{3}i$ (e) $\frac{6}{5} + \frac{3}{5}i$ (f) $\frac{14}{29} - \frac{6}{29}i$ (g) $-\frac{10}{13} - \frac{15}{13}i$ (h) $\frac{3}{5} + \frac{1}{5}i$ (i) $\frac{3}{5} - \frac{1}{5}i$ (j) $\frac{7}{13} - \frac{4}{13}i$ (k) $\frac{11}{5} - \frac{2}{5}i$ (l) $-\frac{3}{25} + \frac{29}{25}i$ (m) $-2 + 3i$ (n) $-4 + 2i$ (o) $b - ai$ (p) $-\frac{1}{2} + \frac{\sqrt{3}}{2}i$ **2.** (a) $-\frac{14}{25} + \frac{23}{25}i$ (b) $-\frac{14}{29} - \frac{23}{29}i$ (c) $\frac{2}{29} - \frac{5}{29}i$ (d) $-\frac{21}{29} + \frac{20}{29}i$ (e) $-\frac{7}{25} - \frac{24}{25}i$ (f) $\frac{26}{25} + \frac{7}{25}i$ (g) $\frac{26}{29} + \frac{7}{29}i$ (h) $-\frac{14}{25} - \frac{23}{25}i$ (i) $-\frac{14}{29} + \frac{23}{29}i$

(j) $\frac{26}{25} - \frac{7}{25}i$ (k) $\frac{\sqrt{29}}{5}$ (l) $\frac{\sqrt{29}}{5}$ (m) $\frac{\sqrt{29}}{29}$
3. (a) $-\frac{1}{5} + \frac{3}{5}i$ (b) $\frac{62}{5} - \frac{16}{5}i$ (c) $7 + 3i$ (d) $\frac{17}{29} - \frac{1}{29}i$ (e) $\frac{1}{2} + 0i$ (f) $0 + 4i$ (g) $0 + \frac{8}{5}i$ **4.** (a) 3, 0°; 3, 270° (b) 9, 270°; 9, 0° (c) 8, 180°; 4, 0° (d) 12, 0°; 4, 90° (e) $\sqrt{2}$, 315°; 1, 225° (f) 5, 323°; 1, 53°
5. (a) $0 + 4i$, 4, 90° (b) 8, 300° (c) 2, 210° (e) Rotate it clockwise by 210° and divide its modulus by 2
6. (a) 2, 30° (b) $\sqrt{2}$, 45° (c) $\frac{\sqrt{3}+1}{2} + \frac{(1-\sqrt{3})}{2}i$, $\sqrt{2}$, 345° **7.** (a) (i) 9, 165° (ii) 4, 75° (b) arg $w^2 = 90°$, this means it is on the Im axis, $w^2 = \frac{9}{4}i$

Chapter 17

Exercise 11

1. (a) 2, 3 (b) –3, 3 (c) –4, 3 (d) 1, –6 (e) $\frac{3}{2}$, –2 (f) 3, –8 (g) –8, –2 (h) 2, –1 (i) 4, 3 (j) 4, 8
2. (a) 1, 2 (b) 4, 6 (c) 2, 0 (d) 1, –2 (e) –2, 2
3. (a) $\frac{2}{5}, \frac{1}{5}$ (b) $\frac{3}{2}, -\frac{3}{2}$ (c) $\frac{1}{10}, -\frac{3}{10}$ (d) $\frac{7}{5}, -\frac{4}{5}$

Exercise 12

1. (a) $z^2 - 9z + 20 = 0$ (b) $z^2 + 9z + 20 = 0$ (c) $12z^2 + 5z - 2 = 0$ (d) $z^2 - 4z + 1 = 0$ (e) $mz^2 - (m^2 + 1)z + m = 0$ (f) $z^2 + 4z + 29 = 0$ (g) $z^2 + 2\sqrt{3}z + 7 = 0$ (h) $z^2 - 2az + a^2 + b^2 = 0$ (i) $z^2 + \sqrt{3}z + 1 = 0$ (j) $z^2 + 25 = 0$ **2.** (a) ± 3 (b) $\pm 3i$ (c) $-2 \pm 5i$ (d) $1 \pm \sqrt{6}i$ (e) $4 \pm 3i$ (f) $-\frac{5}{2} \pm \frac{1}{2}i$ (g) –8, –3 (h) $-\frac{5}{4}, \frac{1}{3}$ (i) $\frac{1}{2} \pm \frac{1}{3}i$ (j) $-\frac{1}{2} \pm \frac{\sqrt{3}i}{2}$
3. (a) $z^2 - 2z + 5 = 0$ (b) $z^2 + 6z + 13 = 0$ (c) $4z^2 - 8z + 13 = 0$ (d) $z^2 + 6z + 11 = 0$ (e) $z^2 + 5 = 0$ (f) $z^2 + 14z + 53 = 0$ (g) $5z^2 - 6z + 2 = 0$ (h) $2z^2 + 2z + 25 = 0$ **4.** (a) Real and different (b) Real and equal (c) Complex (d) Real and different (e) Complex (f) Complex (g) Real and different (h) Real and equal (i) Real and different (j) Complex **5.** (a) $a = 0$, $b = 1$ (b) $b = -6$, $c = 10$ (c) $z^2 + 10z + 29 = 0$ (d) $k = 4$, $c = 7$ (e) $a = 1$, $b = 5$ (f) $a = 2$, $b = \pm 3$ (g) $k = 2 + 5i$
8. (a) $z^3 - 3z^2 - 13z + 15 = 0$ (b) $z^3 - 5z^2 + 8z - 6 = 0$ (c) $z^3 + (1 - 2i)z^2 + (-6 - 2i)z + 12i = 0$ (d) $z^3 - z^2 + 2z + 4 = 0$ (e) $z^3 - 4z^2 + 13z + 50 = 0$ (f) $z^3 - 8z^2 + 29z - 52 = 0$ **9.** (a) Roots: $1 - i$, $1 + i$, 3 (b) Roots: $2 + 3i$, $2 - 3i$, –4 (c) Roots: $-3i$, $3i$, 3 (d) Roots: $1 + 2i$, $1 - 2i$, i (e) Roots: i, $-3i$, $3i$ (f) Roots: $a + bi$, $a - bi$, 1 **10.** (a) 52 (b) 1 (c) 18 (d) 3

Exercise 13

1. (a) $\sqrt{3} + i$ (b) $1 - i$ (c) $\frac{1}{2} - \frac{\sqrt{3}}{2}i$ (d) $-3\sqrt{2} - 3\sqrt{2}i$ (e) $\frac{\sqrt{3}}{2} - \frac{3}{2}i$ (f) 4 (g) $-1 - \sqrt{3}i$ (h) $5 - 5\sqrt{3}i$ (i) $0 - 8i$ (j) $0{\cdot}743 + 0{\cdot}669i$ **3.** (a) $\frac{3}{2} + \frac{3\sqrt{3}}{2}i$ (b) $-\frac{1}{\sqrt{2}} + \frac{1}{\sqrt{2}}i$ (c) $\frac{\sqrt{3}}{4} - \frac{1}{4}i$ (d) $\sqrt{2} - \sqrt{2}i$ (e) $-\frac{3\sqrt{3}}{2} - \frac{3}{2}i$ (f) $-\sqrt{3} - i$
4. (a) $3\sqrt{2}\left\{\cos\frac{\pi}{4} + i\sin\frac{\pi}{4}\right\}$ (b) $2\left\{\cos\frac{3\pi}{4} + i\sin\frac{3\pi}{4}\right\}$ (c) $1\left\{\cos\frac{2\pi}{3} + i\sin\frac{2\pi}{3}\right\}$ (d) $16\left\{\cos\frac{2\pi}{3} + i\sin\frac{2\pi}{3}\right\}$ (e) $4\sqrt{2}\left\{\cos\frac{\pi}{4} + i\sin\frac{\pi}{4}\right\}$ (f) $2\left\{\cos\frac{7\pi}{6} + i\sin\frac{7\pi}{6}\right\}$ (g) $\frac{5\sqrt{2}}{3}\left\{\cos\frac{7\pi}{4} + i\sin\frac{7\pi}{4}\right\}$ (h) $1\left\{\cos\frac{3\pi}{2} + i\sin\frac{3\pi}{2}\right\}$ (i) $\sqrt{13}\{\cos 3{\cdot}73 + i\sin 3{\cdot}73\}$ (j) $2\sqrt{3}\left\{\cos\frac{5\pi}{4} + i\sin\frac{5\pi}{4}\right\}$
5. (a) $3\{\cos 2n\pi + i\sin 2n\pi\}$, $n \in \mathbb{N}_0$
(b) $2\left\{\cos\left(\frac{\pi + 4n\pi}{2}\right) + i\sin\left(\frac{\pi + 4n\pi}{2}\right)\right\}$, $n \in \mathbb{N}_0$
(c) $2\sqrt{2}\left\{\cos\left(\frac{\pi + 8n\pi}{4}\right) + i\sin\left(\frac{\pi + 8n\pi}{4}\right)\right\}$, $n \in \mathbb{N}_0$
(d) $2\sqrt{3}\left\{\cos\left(\frac{5\pi + 12n\pi}{6}\right) + i\sin\left(\frac{5\pi + 12n\pi}{6}\right)\right\}$, $n \in \mathbb{N}_0$
(e) $1\left\{\cos\left(\frac{7\pi + 8n\pi}{4}\right) + i\sin\left(\frac{7\pi + 8n\pi}{4}\right)\right\}$, $n \in \mathbb{N}_0$
(f) $16\left\{\cos\left(\frac{5\pi + 6n\pi}{3}\right) + i\sin\left(\frac{5\pi + 6n\pi}{3}\right)\right\}$, $n \in \mathbb{N}_0$
(g) $\frac{\sqrt{2}}{2}\left\{\cos\left(\frac{\pi + 8n\pi}{4}\right) + i\sin\left(\frac{\pi + 8n\pi}{4}\right)\right\}$, $n \in \mathbb{N}_0$
(h) $5\{\cos(\pi + 2n\pi) + i\sin(\pi + 2n\pi)\}$, $n \in \mathbb{N}_0$
(i) $6\left\{\cos\left(\frac{3\pi + 4n\pi}{2}\right) + i\sin\left(\frac{3\pi + 4n\pi}{2}\right)\right\}$, $n \in \mathbb{N}_0$
(j) $2\left\{\cos\left(\frac{\pi + 4n\pi}{2}\right) + i\sin\left(\frac{\pi + 4n\pi}{2}\right)\right\}$, $n \in \mathbb{N}_0$
6. W 83° N

Exercise 14

2. (a) 1 (b) $\frac{1}{2} - \frac{\sqrt{3}}{2}i$ (c) $-\frac{81}{2} - \frac{81\sqrt{3}}{2}i$ (d) $4 - 4\sqrt{3}i$ (e) –1024 **3.** (a) $-1 + 0i$ (b) $\sqrt{3} + i$ (c) $1 + \sqrt{3}i$ (d) $0 + 2i$ (e) $-\frac{\sqrt{2}}{4} + \frac{\sqrt{2}}{4}i$ **4.** (a) $\frac{1}{2} - \frac{\sqrt{3}}{2}i$ (b) $\frac{\sqrt{3}}{2} + \frac{1}{2}i$ (c) $-\frac{\sqrt{2}}{2} - \frac{\sqrt{2}}{2}i$ (d) $\frac{\pi}{12}$ (e) $\frac{\sqrt{2}}{2} + \frac{\sqrt{2}}{2}i$
5. (a) $\cos 2A + i\sin 2A$ (b) $\cos 5A + i\sin 5A$ (c) $\cos 8A - i\sin 8A$ (d) $\cos 4A + i\sin 4A$ (e) $\cos 6A + i\sin 6A$ **6.** (a) (i) 2^{16} (ii) $-2^{13}i$

(iii) $-\frac{1}{2}+\frac{\sqrt{3}}{2}i$ (iv) $-128-128i$ (v) $-\frac{1}{2^{21}}-\frac{\sqrt{3}}{2^{21}}i$

(vi) 1 (b) (i) $1, -\frac{1}{2}+\frac{\sqrt{3}}{2}i, -\frac{1}{2}-\frac{\sqrt{3}}{2}i$

(ii) $\sqrt{2}+\sqrt{2}i, -\sqrt{2}+\sqrt{2}i, -\sqrt{2}-\sqrt{2}i, \sqrt{2}-\sqrt{2}i$

(iii) $i, -\frac{\sqrt{3}}{2}-\frac{1}{2}i, \frac{\sqrt{3}}{2}-\frac{1}{2}i$

(iv) $(\sqrt{2})^{\frac{1}{4}}\left\{\cos\frac{7\pi}{16}+i\sin\frac{7\pi}{16}\right\}$,

$(\sqrt{2})^{\frac{1}{4}}\left\{\cos\frac{15\pi}{16}+i\sin\frac{15\pi}{6}\right\}$,

$(\sqrt{2})^{\frac{1}{4}}\left\{\cos\frac{23\pi}{6}+i\sin\frac{23\pi}{6}\right\}$,

$(\sqrt{2})^{\frac{1}{4}}\left\{\cos\frac{31\pi}{16}+i\sin\frac{31\pi}{16}\right\}$ (v) $\cos\left(\frac{5\pi}{12}\right)+i\sin\left(\frac{5\pi}{12}\right)$,

$\cos\left(\frac{17\pi}{12}\right)+i\sin\left(\frac{17\pi}{12}\right)$

(vi) $(2\sqrt{3})^{\frac{1}{3}}\left\{\cos\frac{4\pi}{9}+i\sin\frac{4\pi}{9}\right\}$,

$(2\sqrt{3})^{\frac{1}{3}}\left\{\cos\frac{10\pi}{9}+i\sin\frac{10\pi}{9}\right\}$,

$(2\sqrt{3})^{\frac{1}{3}}\left\{\cos\frac{16\pi}{9}+i\sin\frac{16\pi}{9}\right\}$,

(c) (i) $\sqrt{2}+\sqrt{2}i, 2\left\{\cos\frac{7\pi}{12}+i\sin\frac{7\pi}{12}\right\}$,

$2\left\{\cos\frac{11\pi}{12}+i\sin\frac{11\pi}{12}\right\}, -\sqrt{2}-\sqrt{2}i$,

$2\left\{\cos\frac{19\pi}{12}+i\sin\frac{19\pi}{12}\right\}, 2\left\{\cos\frac{23\pi}{12}+i\sin\frac{23\pi}{12}\right\}$

(ii) $\cos\frac{\pi}{10}+i\sin\frac{\pi}{10}, i, \cos\frac{9\pi}{10}+i\sin\frac{9\pi}{10}$,

$\cos\frac{13\pi}{10}+i\sin\frac{13\pi}{10}, \cos\frac{17\pi}{10}+i\sin\frac{17\pi}{10}$

(iii) $\cos\frac{\pi}{18}+i\sin\frac{\pi}{18}, \cos\frac{13\pi}{18}+i\sin\frac{13\pi}{18}$,

$\cos\frac{25\pi}{18}+i\sin\frac{25\pi}{18}$ (iv) $-\frac{1}{2}+\frac{\sqrt{3}}{2}, i, \frac{1}{2}-\frac{\sqrt{3}}{2}i$

Revision Questions

1. (b) 2, 2, 1 (c) 150°, 210°, 300°
(e) $z^2+2\sqrt{3}z+4=0$; All are real because roots are complex conjugates **2.** (a) $i, -i, i, -i, i$ (b) (i) 5
(ii) 5 km/h (iv) $-2+11i$, $5\sqrt{5}$ km **3.** (a) (i) $-i$
(ii) i (iii) $-i$ (b) (i) $1+\sqrt{3}i$ (ii) $-2\sqrt{3}+2i$
(iii) $-4\sqrt{3}-4i$ (iv) $2i$ **4.** (a) $\frac{75}{26}+\frac{11}{26}i$
5. (a) $-2-2\sqrt{3}i, k=-2$ (b) (i) $-8+4i$ (ii) $2-i$
(c) $6\sqrt{2}\left\{\cos\frac{5\pi}{3}+i\sin\frac{5\pi}{3}\right\}, 6^{10}\times 2^4\{-1+\sqrt{3}i\}$
6. (a) $1+2i, 1-2i$ (b) $p=1, q=-7, 2+3i, 5$
(c) $13\{\cos(1{\cdot}176+2n\pi)+i\sin(1{\cdot}176+2n\pi)\}$,
$3+2i, -3-2i$ **7.** (a) (i) $\sqrt{2}\left\{\cos\frac{\pi}{4}+i\sin\frac{\pi}{4}\right\}$
(ii) $2\left\{\cos\frac{\pi}{6}+i\sin\frac{\pi}{6}\right\}$ (iii) $\frac{\sqrt{2}}{2}\left\{\cos\frac{\pi}{12}+i\sin\frac{\pi}{12}\right\}$,
$\left(\frac{\sqrt{2}}{2}\right)^n\left\{\cos\frac{n\pi}{12}+i\sin\frac{n\pi}{12}\right\}$; 12
(b) $(1, \sqrt{5}), (1, -\sqrt{5})$ **8.** (a) $2+23i$ (i) $2-23i$
(ii) 41, 13 (b) $a=-4-4i, b=-3+4i$ (c) $p=-3, q=-1$
9. (a) (i) x^2+y^2 (ii) $x=3, y=-1$, 3 (b) (i) 24 (ii) 285°
(iii) $\frac{3}{2}$ (iv) 195° (c) arg $w^2=90°$, $w^2=16i$
(d) Real, 216 **10.** (a) $1, -\frac{1}{2}+\frac{\sqrt{3}i}{2}, -\frac{1}{2}-\frac{\sqrt{3}i}{2}$
(b) $\cos 2n\pi+i\sin 2n\pi, n\in\mathbb{N}_0$ 1,
$\cos\frac{2\pi}{3}+i\sin\frac{2\pi}{3}=-\frac{1}{2}+\frac{i\sqrt{3}}{2}$
$\cos\frac{4\pi}{3}+i\sin\frac{4\pi}{3}=-\frac{1}{2}-\frac{i\sqrt{3}}{2}$
11. (a) $\sqrt{3}$, (b) (i) $-\frac{1}{\sqrt{2}}+\frac{1}{\sqrt{2}}i$
(ii) $\cos 2A+i\sin 2A, \cos 14A+i\sin 14A$
(iii) $\cos 7A+i\sin 7A$

Section 7

Chapter 18

Exercise 1

1. (i) (a) $S=\{(2,1),(4,5),(6,7),(8,3)\}$
(b) $D=\{2,4,6,8\}, I=\{1,3,5,7\}$ (c) Yes, it is a function (ii) (a) $S=\{(3,a),(3,b),(2,c)\}$
(b) $D=\{3,2\}, I=\{a,b,c\}$ (c) It is not a function
(iii) (a) $S=\{(1,5),(2,5)\}$ (b) $D=\{1,2\}, I=\{5\}$
(c) Yes, it is a function (iv) (a) $S=\{(1,a),(1,b)\}$
(b) $D=\{1\}, I=\{a,b\}$ (c) It is not a function
(v) (a) $S=\{(a,b),(b,e),(c,f)\}$ (b) $D=\{a,b,c\}$, $I=\{d,e,f\}$ (c) Yes, it is a function **2.** (a) Yes, it is a function as each element of the domain has one and only one image; $D=\{a,b,c\}, I=\{1\}$
(b) It is not a function as 1 has two images; $D=\{1,2\}, I=\{a,b\}$ (c) Yes, it is a function as each element of the domain has one and only one image; $D=\{1,2,3,4\}, I=\{1,4,9,16\}$ (d) It is not a function as 1 has two images and 4 has two images; $D=\{1,4\}, I=\{-2,-1,1,2\}$ (e) Yes, it is a function as each element of the domain has one and only one image; $D=\{1,2,3,4\}, I=\{0\}$ **3.** (a) Yes, it is a function; Range: $0\le y\le 2, y\in\mathbb{R}$ (b) Yes, it is a function; Range: $y\ge 0, y\in\mathbb{R}$ (c) It is not a function; Range: $-3\le y\le 3, y\in\mathbb{R}$ (d) It is not a function;

Range: $y \in \mathbb{R}$ (e) Yes, it is a function; Range: $0 \le y \le 1$, $y \in \mathbb{R}$ (f) Yes, it is a function; Range: $y > 0$, $y \in \mathbb{R}$.

Exercise 2

1. (a) 17 (b) –4 (c) $\frac{3}{2}$ (d) 3 (e) $\frac{11}{2}$ (f) –3 (g) 2·5 (h) 1 **2.** (a) 5, 9, –4 (b) 1, $\frac{1}{2}$, 2, –3 (c) 8, $\frac{1}{2}$, $\frac{17}{8}$ (d) (i) 44 (ii) 9 (e) 0, 0, 4 (f) $\frac{1}{54}$, –4 (g) 5, 5, 5, 5 (h) 1, 3 **3.** (a) 11, $2x + 9$, $13 - 4x$ (b) 0, $4 - 4t^2$ (c) 1, $\frac{3}{x+4}$ (d) 13, $s + 4$, $s^2 - 2s + 5$ (e) $\frac{3}{4}$, $12p^2 - 8p + 2$ (f) 12, $3 \times 2^{3x-1}$ (g) $\frac{1}{4}$, $\sin^2 4x$ (h) 1, 0, $\sin p$ (i) 2, $-\log_2 x$ (j) 2, $\log_{10} x$ **4.** (a) $x = 1$ (b) $t = 15$ (c) $x = 1, 6$ (d) $n = 4$ (e) $k = 4$ (f) $x = 4$ (g) $x = -4, 2$ (h) $t = -2, 0, 1$ (i) $x = \frac{1}{4}$ (j) $x = 10\,000$ **5.** (a) $k = -20$ (b) $t = -3$ (c) $x = 4$ (d) $x = -3, 1$ (e) $a = -1, k = -2$ (f) $a = 5, b = 2$

Exercise 3

1. (a) None (b) None (c) Bijective (d) Bijective
2. (a) None (b) Surjective (c) None
3. (a) Injective (b) Injective (c) None **4.** (a) Not injective, surjective (b) Bijective because each pigeon hole in B has a different pigeon in A
5. (a) Bijective (b) Not injective, not surjective (c) Not injective, not surjective (d) Not injective, surjective (e) Injective, not surjective (f) Injective, surjective, bijective **7.** 1, –1, does not exist; Every value of x in the domain $\mathbb{R}$ has a different image in the codomain $\mathbb{R}$ and so it is injective. However, not every value of y in the codomain $\mathbb{R}$ has at least one corresponding value in the domain, so $y = f(x)$ is not surjective. Therefore, the function is not bijective.

Exercise 4

1. (a) 5 (b) 9 (c) 2 (d) 4 **2.** (a) 9 (b) 4 (c) 1 (d) 0 (e) 9 (f) 4: $f^{-1}(x)$ is not a function from $\mathbb{R} \to \mathbb{R}^+$ **3.** (a) $\frac{x-2}{3}$, $\mathbb{R}$, $\mathbb{R}$ (b) $2x - 1$, $\mathbb{R}$, $\mathbb{R}$ (c) $\frac{1}{x}$, $\mathbb{R}^+$, $\mathbb{R}^+$ (d) $-\log_2 x$, $\mathbb{R}^+$, $\mathbb{R}$ (e) 5^x, $\mathbb{R}$, $\mathbb{R}^+$ (f) $x^{\frac{1}{3}} - 1$, $\mathbb{R}$, $\mathbb{R}$ **4.** (a) Yes, as $f(x)$ is bijective (b) Yes, as $f(x)$ is bijective (c) Yes, as $f(x)$ is bijective (d) No, $f(x)$ is not injective and so it is not bijective

Exercise 5

1. (a) 15 (b) –7 (c) –1 (d) 2

2. (a) $-4x^2 - 12x - 8$, $-2x^2 + 5$ (b) $4\sqrt{2x+4}$, $2\sqrt{2x+1}$ (c) $\frac{1}{2x+5}$, $\frac{2}{x} + 5$ (d) $3^{\sqrt{x}}$, $3^{\frac{x}{2}}$ (e) $\frac{x^2-1}{3}$, $\frac{x^2-2x+1}{9}$ (f) $\sin 3x$, $3\sin x$ (g) $\frac{1}{x^3}$, $\frac{1}{x^3}$ (h) x, x **3.** (a) $\frac{11}{3}$ (b) $k = 2$, $b = 3$ (c) (i) $\frac{x-2}{3}$, (ii) x (iii) x
4. (a) 3^{x-2} (b) $-1 - x^2$ (c) 3^{1-x^2} (d) $-x^2 + 4x - 3$ (e) $3^x - 2$ (f) $-x^4 + 2x^2$ (g) $x - 4$ (h) 3^{-x^2-1} (i) 3^{-1-x^2} (j) 3^{-x^2-1}

Exercise 6

1. (a) Discontinuous at $x = 2$ (b) Continuous (c) Discontinuous at $x = 0$ (d) Discontinuous at $x = 6$ (e) Discontinuous at $x = 2$

2. $f(x) = \begin{cases} x + 1, & x \in \mathbb{R}, \quad x \neq 1 \\ 3, & x = 1 \end{cases}$

3. (a) Discontinuous (b) Continuous (c) Discontinuous (d) Continuous
4. (a) Discontinuous (b) $a = \frac{4}{3}$, –1 (c) $k = \frac{3}{4}$, $l = -\frac{1}{4}$

Chapter 19

Exercise 7

2. (a) $y = -x + \frac{7}{3}$ (b) $y = \frac{4}{3}x - 3$ (c) $y = 7x - \frac{1}{2}$ (d) $y = 0x + 5$ (e) $y = -x + 8$
3. (a) Yes, linear: $y = -\frac{2}{3}x - \frac{1}{3}$ (b) Yes, linear: $y = \frac{3}{5}x + 4$ (c) Yes, linear: $y = 2\pi x + 0$ (d) No, quadratic (e) Yes, linear: $y = -\frac{1}{64}x + 13$
4. (a) $y = 3x - 2$ (b) $y = -2x + 10$ (c) $y = -\frac{2}{5}x + \frac{19}{5}$ (d) $y = -\frac{1}{3}x + \frac{7}{3}$ (e) $y = -7x + 11$
5. (a) $V = -180t + 500$ (b) $\theta = \frac{9}{5}T + 32$ (c) $y = -\frac{3}{2}x + 6$ (d) $P = 1{\cdot}5t + 5$ **6.** (a) $x = \frac{3}{2}$ (b) $x = 0{\cdot}5$ (c) $x = 2$ (d) $x = -3$

Exercise 8

1. (a) $V = -4000t + 50\,000$ (b) $t = 7{\cdot}5$ years (c) $t = 12{\cdot}5$ years **2.** $s = -300t + 6000$; 20 mins
3. Linear, $y = \frac{1}{8}x + 1$ **4.** (a) B, the slope is constant (b) (i) $P = 0{\cdot}24t + 7{\cdot}6$ (ii) 24·4 million (c) 0·334 million per year **5.** (a) Membership fee = €250; Cost per round = €30 (b) $C = 30n + 250$ (c) €1750 (d) 25 **6.** (b) 500 (c) $n = -5t + 200$; 40 days

Chapter 20

Exercise 9

2. (a) y: (0, –1); x: (–1, 0), (0, 1) (b) y: (0, 1); x: does not cross (c) y = (0, 6); x: (3, 0), (2, 0) (d) y: (0, –2), x: (2, 0), (1, 0) (e) y: (0, 2); x: $\left(\frac{1}{2}, 0\right)$ (f) y: (0, –4); x: $\left(\frac{2}{3}, 0\right)$, (2, 0) (g) y: (0, 3); x: (3, 0), (–1, 0) (h) y: (0, 7); x: $\left(\frac{7}{2}, 0\right)$, $\left(\frac{1}{2}, 0\right)$ (i) y: (0, 7); x: does not cross (j) y: (0, –11); x: $\left(\frac{-7+\sqrt{137}}{4}, 0\right)$, $\left(\frac{-7-\sqrt{137}}{4}, 0\right)$
3. (a) Min (0, –1); x = 0 (b) Min (0, 1); x = 0 (c) Min $\left(\frac{5}{2}, -\frac{1}{4}\right)$, $x = \frac{5}{2}$ (d) Max $\left(\frac{3}{2}, \frac{1}{4}\right)$; $x = \frac{3}{2}$ (e) Max $\left(\frac{1}{2}, 0\right)$; $x = \frac{1}{2}$ (f) Max $\left(\frac{4}{3}, \frac{4}{3}\right)$; $x = \frac{4}{3}$ (g) Max (1, 4); x = 1 (h) Min (2, –9); x = 2 (i) Max $\left(\frac{5}{2}, \frac{3}{4}\right)$; $x = \frac{5}{2}$ (j) Min $\left(-\frac{7}{4}, -\frac{137}{8}\right)$; $x = -\frac{7}{4}$ **4.** (a) Two different points (b) No points (c) Two different points (d) No points (e) Two different points (f) One point (g) Two different points (h) Two different points (i) Two different points (j) One point **5.** (a) V = (–1, –12) min (b) V(–2, –11) min (c) $V = \left(-\frac{5}{2}, \frac{37}{4}\right)$ max (d) $V = \left(\frac{7}{6}, -\frac{59}{12}\right)$ max **6.** (a) b = 8, c = –1 (b) b = 12, c = 12 (c) b = 2 (d) b = 4, c = 10
7. (a) $y = -\frac{7}{4}x^2 + 7x$ (b) $y = \frac{3}{8}x^2 - \frac{3}{4}x - 3$ (c) $y = -\frac{1}{2}x^2 + 2x - 2$ (d) $y = \frac{1}{4}x^2 - x + 3$ (e) $y = \frac{3}{4}x^2 - 3x + 1$ (f) $y = -\frac{1}{3}x^2 + 2x + 4$ (g) $y = -\frac{1}{3}x^2 - 2x + 3$ (h) $y = -\frac{1}{2}x^2 - 2x - 3$
8. (a) $y = -\frac{3}{10}x^2 - \frac{9}{10}x + 3$ (b) $y = \frac{2}{9}x^2 + \frac{4}{3}x + 2$ (c) $y = \frac{1}{3}x^2 + 2x - 1$ (d) $y = -\frac{7}{25}x^2 - \frac{28}{25}x + \frac{97}{25}$

Exercise 10

1. (a) –2·4, 0·9 (b) –1·6, 3·6 (c) 0·3, –3·3 (d) –0·6, 2·3 (e) –1·6 (f) –1, 1·5
2. (a) (i) (0, –3) (ii) $\left(\frac{1}{2}, 0\right)$, (–3, 0) (iii) $\left(-\frac{5}{4}, -\frac{49}{8}\right)$ **3.** (b) (i) –1·8 °C (ii) 9 °C (iii) 1·8 hours (iv) After 1·6 hours and 4·4 hours (c) a = 1, b = –6, c = 7 **4.** (b) (i) 48 cm (ii) 6 cm, 34 cm (iii) 50 cm **5.** (b) (i) 24 m (ii) 0·9 s, 3·9 s (iii) 30 m (c) $\frac{1489}{49}$ m (d) 1·3%
6. (c) (i) 600 m (ii) 150 m **7.** (a) 2 years, 10 years (b) $2 < x < 10, x \in \mathbb{R}$ **8.** (a) $x < 25, x \in \mathbb{R}$ (c) (i) €780 (ii) €12·50 (iii) €6, €19 (iv) 25, 100 (d) €781·25
9. (–1, 8), (4, 18) **10.** (3, 11) **11.** (a) a = 1, b = –10, c = 25 (b) p = 0, q = 1 (d) 9 m (e) t < 5, s is decreasing; The athlete is getting closer to B; t > 5, s is increasing; The athlete is getting further away from B **12.** (a) (i) $(x-2)^2 + 7$ (ii) (2, 7) (iii) Min $a > 0$ (b) (–1, 16), (7, 32) **13.** (a) B(3, 0) (b) C(0, 6) (c) A(–1, 0) (d) p = –3, q = 6, r = 9 (e) D(0, 9) (f) $P\left(-\frac{1}{3}, \frac{20}{3}\right)$

Chapter 21

Exercise 11

1. (a) –1·9, –0·3, 2·1; (0, –1) (b) –4·3, –1·7, 1·1; (0, 8) (c) –1·0, 2·0; (0, –2) (d) –3·0, 1·0; (0, –3) (e) 2·7; (0, –2) (f) 1·0; (0, –1) (g) –1·0; (0, –1)
2. (a) One (b) Three, two equal (c) Three (d) One
3. (a) x: (–2, 0), (1, 0), (2, 0), y: (0, 4) (b) x: (0, 0), $\left(\frac{1}{2}, 0\right)$, (–2, 0); y: (0, 0) (c) x: (0, 0), (1, 0); y: (0, 0) (d) x: (0, 0); y: (0, 0) (e) x: (2, 0), $\left(\frac{3-\sqrt{13}}{2}, 0\right)$, $\left(\frac{3+\sqrt{13}}{2}, 0\right)$; y: (0, 4) (f) x: (2, 0), (3, 0), (4, 0); y: (0, 24) (g) x: (–1, 0), $\left(-\sqrt{\frac{2}{3}}, 0\right)$, $\left(\sqrt{\frac{2}{3}}, 0\right)$; y: (0, –2) (h) x: (0, 0), $\left(\frac{2}{3}, 0\right)$; y: (0, 0) (i) x: (–1, 0), $\left(\frac{3}{4}, 0\right)$, $\left(\frac{2}{5}, 0\right)$; y: (0, 6) (j) x: (–5, 0); y: (0, –10)
4. (a) $y = x^3 - 6x^2 + 5x + 12$ (b) $y = -x^3 + x^2 + 14x - 24$ (c) $y = x^3 - x^2 - x + 1$ (d) $y = \frac{1}{2}x^3 + x^2 - \frac{15}{2}x - 18$ (e) $y = -\frac{1}{3}x^3 - \frac{5}{2}x^2 - \frac{31}{6}x - 2$ (f) $y = -\frac{1}{4}x^3 - x^2 + x + 4$
5. (a) $y = -\frac{2}{3}x^3 + \frac{4}{3}x^2 + \frac{10}{3}x - 4$ (b) $y = \frac{1}{5}x^3 - \frac{6}{5}x^2 - \frac{1}{5}x + 6$ (c) $y = \frac{1}{2}x^3 + \frac{3}{2}x^2 - 2$ (d) $y = \frac{5}{18}x^3 - \frac{10}{9}x^2 - \frac{5}{6}x + 5$

6. (b) (i) 1999–2000, 2007–2008 (ii) 330 (iii) 280, 490 **7.** (a) $d = 800$ (c) (i) 1600 (ii) 2004 (iii) 2007 **8.** (a) –2·2, –1, 0·7 (b) 3·6 (c) –1·2, 0, 3·2 (d) –0·9, 0·5, 4·4 (e) –2·6, –0·4, 2 (f) 0·8 (g) –2·6, 0·3, 2·3 **9.** (a) (2, 0) (b) $p = 1, q = -3$ (c) $B(-2, -4)$ **10.** (c) 1·5, 3, 4·5 **11.** (b) –0·6, 1, 1·6 **12.** (b) –1·3, 0·9 (c) 3

Exercise 12

1. (a) $y = f(x+2) = (x+2)^2$ (b) $y = f(x-4)$ (c) $y = x^2 + 3$ (d) $y = f(x-3) - 2$ **2.** (i) (5, 4) (ii) (–3, 4) (iii) (2, 7), (2, –1) (iv) (2, –1) (v) (–3, –2)

Chapter 22

Exercise 13

1. (b) $x = 1{\cdot}6$ (c) 1·4 **2.** $k = 0{\cdot}5, a = 3$ **3.** (a) 20 000 (b) (i) 80 900 (ii) 327 000 (d) 13 days **4.** (a) 60 (b) 68 (d) 11·6 (e) 4% **5.** (a) 1280 (b) €40 (c) $t = 8$ **6.** (a) (–2, 0) (b) (0, –3) (d) –2·8 **7.** (a) 0 C (c) (i) 0·2 C (ii) 1·1 s (d) 0·022 C/s **8.** (a) 20 °C, room temperature (b) (i) 115 °C (ii) 345·7 °C (iii) 459·2 °C (c) 0 (d) 520 °C (e) 520 °C (f) As $t \to \infty$, $500(0{\cdot}9)^t$ decreases continuously from 500 to 0. So T increases continuously from 20 °C to 520 °C (g) 11·4 °C/min

Exercise 14

1. (b) (1·4, 2·6) **2.** (b) –0·9, 1·2 **3.** (b) 0·3 days, 5·3 days **4.** (b) (0, 1) (c) (i) 1·4 (ii) –1·7 **5.** (a) $A(0, 1)$ (b) $B(2, 4)$ (c) $p = -\frac{3}{4}, q = 3, r = 1$ **6.** (a) (2, 0) (b) $p = \frac{1}{2}$, $q = -2, r = 2$

Exercise 15

1. (c) (i) 2·3 (ii) 0·5 (d) Yes **2.** (a) $A(0, 1)$ (b) $y = \log_k x = f^{-1}(x)$ (c) $B(1, 0)$ (d) $k = 4$ (e) (2, 16) **3.** (b) (i) 2·8 (ii) 1, 4·4 **4.** (e) Slope = –2, intercept = 18 (f) $k = 262\,144, n = 2$ (g) 4096 (h) 21% **5.** (e) Slope = –0·02, intercept = 0·67 (f) $a = 1{\cdot}59, k = -0{\cdot}02$ (g) 1·48 mg (h) 50 hours

Revision Questions

1. (c) 0·4 s, 3·1 s (d) 17 m (e) 0·2 s, 4 s, 5·8 s (f) (i) 0 s, 4 s, 6 s (ii) 4 s **2.** (c) (i) 96 cm³/h (ii) 72 cm³/h (iii) 11 hours, 22 hours (iv) 9 cm³/h/h (d) Yes; There are no breaks in the graph **3.** (a) $A(-1, 0)$, $B(6, 0)$ (b) $D(1, 10)$ (c) $E\left(\frac{5}{2}, \frac{49}{4}\right)$ (d) $F\left(\frac{5}{2}, 7\right)$ (e) 5·25 **4.** (a) 5 A (d) (i) 1·4 A (ii) 4·5 s (e) $\frac{81}{625}$, 4 s **5.** (a) $T = 0{\cdot}06x - 400$ (b) €2300 (c) €25 000 **6.** (a) 0·2 (b) 1200 (e) (i) 2300 (ii) 6·5 days (f) $P = 1000 \times (1{\cdot}2)^t$ **7.** (b) (i) 2^{19} (ii) 2^{63} (c) $N = 2^{R-1}$ (d) $9{\cdot}2 \times 10^{15}$ m (e) $1{\cdot}5 \times 10^{11}$ m (f) 61 333 **8.** (a) (i) (–5, 30) (ii) $x = -5$ (c) $x = -6 \pm \sqrt{41 - k}$ **9.** (a) 100 (d) 360 (e) 4% (f) 500 (g) 6·8 days **10.** (e) Slope = 0·17, intercept = 5·18 (f) $k = 296, a = 1{\cdot}2$ (g) 174 837 (h) 2332 per year **11.** (a) (i) 150 (ii) 1200 (b) $k = 150, a = 1{\cdot}23$ (c) 9600 (d) 74 686 (e) 7·8 (f) Because the exponential alternative would have put huge pressure on medical services **12.** (a) There are no breaks in the function (b) (i) Yes, each value of x in the domain has a different image in the codomain (ii) Yes, each value of y in the codomain has at least one image in the domain (iii) Yes, because it is injective and surjective

(c)

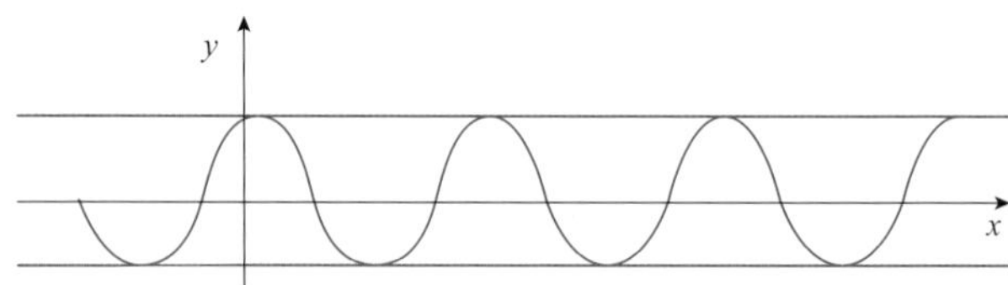

$f: R \to [-1, 1]$

$f(x) = \cos x$

Section 8

Chapter 23

Exercise 1

1. (a) 5 (b) 5 (c) The slope is a constant **2.** (a) 27 (b) 30 **3.** (a) –2 (b) –2·5 (c) –2·5 **4.** (a) $\frac{2}{3}$ (b) 1 (c) 1 (d) 1 **5.** (a) 200 mA/V (b) $\frac{1000}{3}$ mA/V; $\frac{dI}{dV}$

Exercise 2

1. (a) 1 (b) 3 (c) a (d) $4x$ (e) $2x$ (f) $-6x + 5$ (g) $2ax + b$

2. (a) $7x^6$ (b) $-5x^4$ (c) $2x^7$ (d) $9\sqrt{x}$ (e) $-\frac{3x^2}{5}$ (f) $-\frac{15}{x^4}$ (g) $-\frac{1}{5x^2}$ (h) $\frac{2}{3}x + 2$ (i) $10x + \frac{1}{5x^2}$ (j) $-\frac{1}{x^{\frac{3}{2}}}$

(k) $6x^2 + 12x - 1$ (l) $3x^2 + \frac{3}{x^4}$ **3.** (a) $1 + \frac{2}{x^2}$ (b) $1 + \frac{1}{x^2}$ (c) $\frac{2}{3} - \frac{1}{x^2}$ (d) $2(3x^2 - x + 2)$ (e) 1 (f) $\frac{5}{2}x^{\frac{3}{2}} - \frac{3\sqrt{x}}{2} + \frac{1}{\sqrt{x}} + \frac{5}{x^{\frac{3}{2}}}$ (g) $16x(4x^2 - 7)$ (h) $\frac{5}{2}x^{\frac{3}{2}} - \frac{21}{2}x^{\frac{1}{2}} + \frac{9}{2\sqrt{x}}$ (i) $\frac{1}{6\sqrt{x}} + \frac{3}{2x^{\frac{3}{2}}}$ (j) $(n-2)x^{n-3} + \frac{14}{x^3}$ **4.** (a) $4x - 1$ (b) $-2x(4x^2 + 1)$ (c) $2x - 3$ (d) $8x^3 - 30x^2 + 18x - 35$ (e) $1 + \frac{2}{\sqrt{x}}$ (f) $6(3x + 2)$ (g) $2 - \frac{12}{x^2}$ (h) $x(5x^3 + 3x - 2)$ (i) $2x(20x^3 - 3x + 44)$ (j) $2(3x^2 - 11x - 15)$ **5.** (a) $-\frac{2}{(x-2)^2}$ (b) $-\frac{5}{(2+x)^2}$ (c) $\frac{x^2 - 2x - 6}{(x-1)^2}$ (d) $\frac{a - c^2}{(c - x)^2}$ (e) $-\frac{24x}{(3 + 2x^2)^2}$ (f) $\frac{3x^2 + 6x - 1}{(x+1)^2}$ (g) $\frac{4x^3 - 3x^2 - 4}{(2x-1)^2}$ (h) $\frac{1}{\sqrt{x}(\sqrt{x} + 1)^2}$ **6.** (a) $14x(x^2 - 1)^6$ (b) $100(3x - 1)(3x^2 - 2x + 1)^{49}$ (c) $\frac{3x}{\sqrt{3x^2 - 1}}$ (d) $\frac{3 - 8x}{(4x^2 - 3x + 1)^2}$ (e) $\frac{17(\sqrt{x} + 5)^{16}}{2\sqrt{x}}$ (f) $-\frac{5(1 + \sqrt{x})^3}{2\sqrt{x}}$ (g) $-\frac{1}{2(x+5)^{\frac{3}{2}}}$ (h) $-\frac{70x}{(7x^2 - 1)^6}$ (i) $\frac{24}{(1 - 3x)^5}$ (j) $p[f(x)]^{p-1} \times f'(x)$ **7.** (a) $2x(9x - 1)(3x - 1)^3$ (b) $2(8x + 1)(4x + 2)^2$ (c) $30x(3x - 1)(2x + 1)^2$ (d) $-\frac{3(x+2)}{2\sqrt{x+3}}$ (e) $\frac{2(3+x)}{(3-x)^3}$ (f) $-\frac{(12x + 49)}{(3x - 2)^4}$ (g) 1 (h) $2(4x + 1)$ (i) $-\frac{9}{x^2\sqrt{9 - x^2}}$ (j) $\frac{258(5x - 2)^5}{(4x + 7)^7}$ (k) $-\frac{6}{(3 - 2x)^{\frac{1}{2}}(3 + 2x)^{\frac{3}{2}}}$ (l) $\frac{n(ad - bc)(ax + b)^{n-1}}{(cx + d)^{n+1}}$ (m) $1 - \frac{1}{x^2}$ (n) $-\frac{q}{(1 - qx)^{\frac{1}{2}}(1 + qx)^{\frac{3}{2}}}$ **8.** (a) $\frac{25}{2}x^{\frac{3}{2}}$ (b) $a - \frac{c}{x^2}$ (c) $-\frac{9}{2\sqrt{5 - 9x}}$ (d) $-\frac{7b}{x^2}\left(a + \frac{b}{x}\right)^6$ (e) $\frac{x(4a + 5bx)}{2\sqrt{a + bx}}$ (f) $-\frac{32x}{(8 + x^2)^2}$ (g) 0 (h) $\frac{3\sqrt{x + 7}}{2}$ (i) $\frac{x + 10}{(x^2 + 5)^{\frac{3}{2}}}$ (j) $\frac{16x(4x^2 - 1)}{7}$ **9.** (a) $-\frac{1}{4}$ (b) $\frac{5}{16}$ (c) $-\frac{12}{5}$ (d) 12 (e) -15 (f) $-\frac{2}{(1+x)^2}, \frac{4}{(1+x)^3}$ (g) $2 + \frac{1}{x^2}, -\frac{2}{x^3}$ (h) $\frac{-16r(1 - r^2)^3}{(1 + r^2)^5}$ **10.** (a) -3, $3x + y + 4 = 0$ (b) (ii) $y = \sqrt{25 - x^2}$ (iii) $3x + 4y - 25 = 0$ (c) $P: x + 2y - 2 = 0$, $Q: x - 2y + 2 = 0$ **11.** (a) 105 m (b) -5 m/min **13.** (a) $-8{\cdot}71 \times 10^{-4}$ m/s/m (b) $-1{\cdot}41 \times 10^{-5}$ m/s/m **14.** $\frac{5\sqrt{5}}{2}$ **15.** (a) $1{\cdot}036$ m/km/h (b) $1{\cdot}484$ m/km/h

Exercise 3

1. (a) $\cos x$ (b) $-3\sin x - 5$ (c) $\cos x - x\sin x$ (d) $\frac{-x\sin x - \cos x}{x^2}$ (e) $-\frac{4\sin x}{5}$ (f) $7\sin^6 x\cos x$ (g) $-15\cos^4 x\sin x$ (h) $\frac{\cos x}{3(\sin x)^{\frac{2}{3}}}$ (i) $\frac{5\sin x}{\cos^2 x}$ (j) $\frac{3\sqrt{\sin x}\cos x}{2}$ **2.** (a) $3\cos(3x - 7)$ (b) $a\cos(ax + b)$ (c) $-a\sin(ax + b)$ (d) $\frac{10x}{3}\cos\left(\frac{5x^2}{3}\right)$ (e) $-\frac{(21x^2 - 5)\sin(7x^3 - 5x + 1)}{11}$ (f) $-\frac{1}{3}\sin\left(\frac{x}{3} - 2\right)$ (g) $\frac{5}{2}\cos\left(\frac{5x}{2}\right)$ (h) $6\cos 6x$ (i) $5(2\cos 4x - \cos 2x)$ (j) $-\frac{3\cos\left(\frac{3}{x}\right)}{x^2}$ **3.** (a) $\frac{2}{(\sin x + \cos x)^2}$ (b) $-\sin x$ (c) $-5\sin 10x$ (d) $-20\sin 4x\cos^4 4x$ (e) $-\frac{\cos x}{(1 - \sin x)^{\frac{1}{2}}(1 + \sin x)^{\frac{3}{2}}}$ **4.** (a) 0 (b) -1 (c) 0 (d) $-\frac{15}{\sqrt{2}}$ (e) $-\frac{48}{25}$ (f) $2\cos 2x, -4\sin 2x$ (g) $\frac{1}{1 + \cos x}, \frac{\sin x}{(1 + \cos x)^2}$ (h) $\frac{6\sin x(1 - \cos x)^2}{(1 + \cos x)^4}$ **5.** (a) $9x - 6y + 3\sqrt{3} - \pi = 0$ (b) $9x - 8y + 3\sqrt{3} - 3\pi = 0$ (c) $6\sqrt{3}x + 8y + 1 - 2\sqrt{3}\pi = 0$ **6.** (a) (i) 4 cm/s (ii) -3 cm/s (b) (i) At $t = 0$ the particle is moving to the right (ii) At $t = \frac{\pi}{2}$ it is moving to the left (c) The acceleration of the particle **7.** (a) $-\frac{3}{\sqrt{1 - 9x^2}}$ (b) $\frac{4}{1 + 16x^2}$ (c) $\frac{2\sin^{-1}x}{\sqrt{1 - x^2}}$ (d) $\frac{4}{\sqrt{1 - 16x^2}}$ (e) $\frac{8}{\sqrt{1 - 16x^2}}$ (f) $\frac{2}{\sqrt{1 - 16x^2}}$ (g) $\frac{8\sin^{-1}(4x)}{\sqrt{1 - 16x^2}}$ (h) $\frac{a}{1 + a^2x^2}$ (i) $\frac{3}{x\sqrt{x^2 - 9}}$ (j) -1 (k) $\frac{3\sqrt{x}}{2(1 + x^3)}$ (l) $\frac{x - (1 + x^2)\tan^{-1}x}{x^2(1 + x^2)}$ **9.** $\frac{1}{\sqrt{1 - x^2}}$ **12.** $3x + 6\sqrt{3}y - 6 - \sqrt{3}\pi = 0$

Exercise 4

1. (a) $5e^x$ (b) $\frac{1}{5}e^x$ (c) $-\frac{3}{5}e^x$ (d) $5e^{5x}$ (e) $5e^{5x-7}$ (f) ae^{ax+b} (g) $2xe^{x^2}$ (h) $6xe^{x^2}$ (i) $-\dfrac{2}{e^{2x}}$ (j) $-\dfrac{15}{e^{3x}}$ **2.** (a) $\dfrac{e^{\sqrt{x}}}{2\sqrt{x}}$ (b) $(2x+1)e^{x+x^2}$ (c) $-4e^{-4x+1}$ (d) e^{e^x+x} (e) $-\dfrac{e^{\frac{1}{x}}}{x^2}$ (f) $\dfrac{e^x(\sin x - \cos x)}{\sin^2 x}$ (g) $\dfrac{e^x(x-2)}{x^3}$ (h) $2(x^2+x+1)e^{2x}$ (i) $4e^{4x-6}$ (j) $2e^{2x-1}$ **3.** (a) $2^x \ln 2$ (b) $4^x \ln 64$ (c) $-\dfrac{\ln 16}{2^x}$ (d) $3^{3x+1}\ln 3$ (e) $x2^{x^2}\ln 4$ (f) $-\dfrac{6\ln 3}{3^{2x}}$ (g) $-\dfrac{3\ln 9}{9^{3x}}$ (h) $2^x(x\ln 2 + 1)$ (i) $2^{e^x} \times e^x \ln 2$ (j) $2x$

4. (a) $(1-4x)e^{-2x^2+x-1}$ (b) $-\dfrac{1}{2\sqrt{e^x}}$ (c) $(x\cos x + \sin x)e^{x\sin x}$ (d) 0 (e) $e^x \cos(e^x)$ **5.** (a) $2e$ (b) $\dfrac{\sqrt{3e}}{2}$ (c) $-4e^2$ (d) 1, 0 (e) $\dfrac{1}{\sqrt{2}}$ **6.** (a) $2ex - y - e = 0$ (b) $x - y = 0$ (c) $3x - 4y + 5 - \ln 8 = 0$ **7.** (a) 5 g (b) 2·5 g (c) –0·075 g/s **8.** (a) A = 101 300 Pa (b) 28 100 Pa (c) –3·45 Pa/m **9.** k = 1, 2

Exercise 5

1. (a) $\dfrac{1}{x}$ (b) $\dfrac{3}{3x-5}$ (c) $\dfrac{a}{ax+b}$ (d) $\dfrac{5}{x}$ (e) 0 (f) $\dfrac{5}{x}$ (g) $-\dfrac{1}{x}$ (h) $\dfrac{1}{2x}$ (i) $-\tan x$ (j) $\dfrac{3\cos x}{\sin x} = \dfrac{3}{\tan x}$ **2.** (a) $\dfrac{14}{2x-1}$ (b) $\dfrac{\cos(\ln x)}{x}$ (c) $\dfrac{5(\ln x)^4}{x}$ (d) $1 + \ln x$ (e) $\dfrac{1-\ln x}{x^2}$ (f) $\dfrac{\sin x}{x} + \cos x \ln x$ (g) $e^x\left(\dfrac{1}{x} + \ln x\right)$ (h) $\dfrac{2(2-\ln x)}{x^{\frac{3}{2}}}$ (i) $\dfrac{1}{1+e^x}$ (j) $\dfrac{2(1+x^2)}{x(2+x^2)}$ (k) $-\dfrac{2}{9-x^2}$ (l) $\dfrac{1}{x\ln x}$ (m) $\dfrac{\cos 2x}{\sin 2x} = \dfrac{1}{\tan 2x}$ (n) $\dfrac{x\cos x - \sin x \ln(\sin x)}{x^2 \sin x}$ (o) $\dfrac{3}{x} - e^x$ **3.** (a) 1 (b) $\frac{1}{2}$ (c) $-\sin 2x$ (d) $\dfrac{1}{2\sqrt{x}}$ (e) $\dfrac{2}{x\ln 10}$ (f) –1 **4.** (a) $x - y - 1 = 0$ (b) $3t - 2q - 6 = 0$ (c) $\frac{1}{2}$ (d) $\frac{1}{77}$ m^3/min

Chapter 24

Exercise 6

1. (a) $5x - y - 4 = 0$ (b) $3x + y - 1 = 0$ (c) $8x - y - 3 = 0$ (d) $y + 6 = 0$ (e) $4x - 4y + 2 - \pi = 0$ (f) $x - 2ey = 0$ (g) $5x - y = 0$ (h) $3x\ln 2 - y + 3 = 0$

2. (a) $x - y - 7 = 0$, $\left(-\dfrac{2}{3}, \dfrac{49}{27}\right)$, (2, –5) (b) (0, 0), $\left(\dfrac{4}{3}, -\dfrac{32}{27}\right)$ (c) $a = 1$ (d) (ii) $3x - 4y - 1 = 0$ (iii) $c = \frac{1}{3}$ **3.** $\left(-a, -\dfrac{a}{2}\right), \left(a, \dfrac{a}{2}\right)$ **4.** $a = 4, b = 6, c = 0, d = 0$ **5.** (a) $a = \frac{1}{4}, b = 1, c = 1$ (b) (ii) $a = -1, b = 1$ **6.** (a) $\dfrac{\pi}{6}$ s, $\dfrac{5\pi}{6}$ s (b) $6t - 2h + 3\sqrt{3} - \pi = 0$, $6t - 2h - 3\sqrt{3} - 5\pi = 0$

Exercise 7

2. (a)

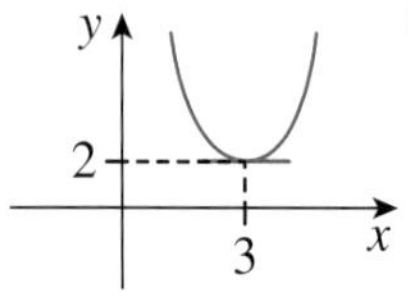

(b)

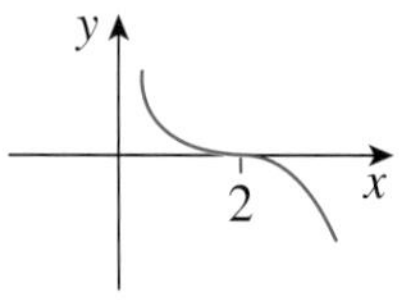

(c)

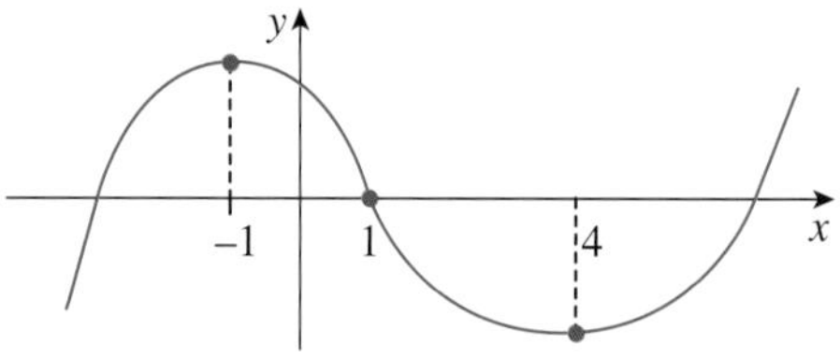

3. (a) Decreasing (b) Increasing (c) Increasing (d) Increasing (e) Decreasing **5.** (a) $x < \frac{3}{2}, x \in \mathbb{R}$ (b) $x < -5, x > -3, x \in \mathbb{R}$ **6.** (b) $0 < t < 25$

Exercise 8

1. (a) (1, 4) (b) $\left(\dfrac{3}{2}, \dfrac{3}{2}\right)$ (c) $\left(-\dfrac{b}{2a}, -\dfrac{b^2}{4a} + c\right)$ (d) (1, 4) (3, 0) (e) (2, 0) (f) (1, –1), (2, –2) (g) No stationary points (h) No stationary points (i) $\left(1, \dfrac{1}{e}\right)$ (j) $\left(\dfrac{1}{e}, -\dfrac{1}{e}\right)$ (k) $\left(\dfrac{4}{5}, \dfrac{3888}{3125}\right)$, (2, 0) (l) $\left(\dfrac{2}{3}, \dfrac{2\sqrt{3}}{9}\right)$ (m) (–4, –16), (4, 16)

2. $x = \dfrac{(2n-1)\pi}{4}, n \in \mathbb{Z}$ **3.** (a) $a = 3$ (b) $a = -\frac{3}{2}, b = -6$ (c) $k = \frac{22}{3}$

Exercise 9

1. (a) Concave up (b) Concave down (c) Concave up (d) Concave up **2.** (a) $x > -\frac{1}{3}, x \in \mathbb{R}$ (e) $-2 < x < 1, x \in \mathbb{R}$ **3.** (a) No point of inflection (b) (1, –9) (c) No point of inflection (d) (2, 37) **4.** (a) $k = 4$ (b) $p = 2$ (c) $p = 24, q = 12$

5. $a = \frac{3}{2}, b = -\frac{9}{2}, c = 0, d = 2$

7. (a) (i) $\dfrac{dM}{dt} < 0$ (negative) (ii) $\dfrac{d^2M}{dt^2} > 0$ (positive) (b) (i) Increasing $\dfrac{dN}{dt} > 0$ (ii) Increasing

(concave up), $\frac{d^2N}{dt^2} > 0$ (c) (i) $\frac{dN}{dt} > 0$, $\frac{d^2N}{dt^2} < 0$
(ii) Increasing (iii) Unemployment rate decreasing

Exercise 10

1. (a) L Max (3, 11) (b) L Min (–2, –16), L Max (2, 16) (c) L Min (–2, –27), L Max (0, 5) L Min (1, 0) (d) L Min (2, 3) (e) L Min $(a, 3a^2)$ (f) L Max $\left(\frac{1}{2}\ln 2, \ln 4 - 2\right)$ (g) L Min $\left(\frac{1}{e}, -\frac{1}{e}\right)$ (h) L Min (1, 3) (i) L Max $\left(\frac{7\pi}{6}, \frac{7\pi}{12} + \frac{\sqrt{3}}{2}\right)$ L Min $\left(\frac{11\pi}{6}, \frac{11\pi}{12} - \frac{\sqrt{3}}{2}\right)$ (j) L Max $\left(\frac{1}{4}, \frac{1}{4e}\right)$
2. $\left(1, \frac{1}{e}\right)$; It is an absolute maximum as it is the only maximum of a continuous function **3.** L Max (–1, 8), L Min (3, –24), point of inflection (1, –8); Absolute maximum = 57, absolute minimum = –73

Exercise 11

1. (a) (–1, 0), (1, 0); (0, –1) (b) (2, 0), (3, 0); (0, 6) (c) $\left(\frac{1}{2}, 0\right), \left(-\frac{2}{3}, 0\right)$; (0, –2) (d) (0, 0), (3, 0); (0, 0) (e) (0, 0), (–2, 0), (2, 0); (0, 0) (f) (–5, 0), (5, 0); (0, –5), (0, 5) (g) (–4, 0), (4, 0); (0, –3), (0, 3) (h) (0, 0); (0, 0) (i) $(e - 1, 0)$; (0, –1) (j) (0, 0), $\left(\frac{\pi}{3}, 0\right), \left(\frac{2\pi}{3}, 0\right)$, $(\pi, 0)$, $\left(\frac{4\pi}{3}, 0\right), \left(\frac{5\pi}{3}, 0\right)$, $(2\pi, 0)$; (0, 0) **2.** (a) (i) L Min (–1, –9) (ii) No points of inflection (iii) x: (–4, 0), (2, 0); y: (0, –8) (b) (i) L Max $\left(\frac{1}{4}, \frac{25}{8}\right)$ (iii) x: (–1, 0), $\left(\frac{3}{2}, 0\right)$; y : (0, 3) (c) (i) L Max (–1, 15), L Min (3, –17) (ii) Point of inflection (1, –1) (iii) y: (0, 10) (d) (i) L Max (2, 16), L Min (–1, –11) (ii) Point of inflection $\left(\frac{1}{2}, \frac{5}{2}\right)$ (iii) y: (0, –4) (e) (i) L Max $\left(0, \frac{32}{3}\right)$, L Min (–2, 4), L Min (4, –32) (ii) Point of inflection (2·4, –13·3), (–1·1, 7·1) (iii) y-axis $\left(0, \frac{32}{3}\right)$ **3.** (a) (i) L Max (–3, 0), double root; L Min $\left(-\frac{1}{3}, -\frac{256}{27}\right)$; point of inflection $\left(-\frac{5}{3}, -\frac{128}{27}\right)$ (iii) Roots –3, –3, 1 (b) L Max (1, 25), L Min (2, 24); Since L Max and L Min are both above x-axis there is only 1 real root
4. (a) (i) (1, 10) (ii) (3, 0) (iii) (2, 5) (iv) (0, 0) (3, 0) (b) (i) 1 month, 4 months (ii) €10 000 (iii) €0 (iv) In the first month, in the last month (v) During the second and third months
5. Crosses y-axis at (0, 1), $\frac{dy}{dx} = e^x > 0$ for all $x \in \mathbb{R}$
7. $y = 2^x$; crosses y-axis at (0, 1); $y = 2^{-x}$, crosses y-axis at (0, 1)

Exercise 12

1. (a) 125 m^2/day (b) 0 m^2/day (c) –400 m^2/day
2. (a) 700 (b) 700 ln1·2 × $(1{\cdot}2)^t$ per hour (c) (i) 128 per hour (ii) 317 per hour **3.** (a) $2\sqrt{2}$ cm/s (b) 1 cm/s (c) $\frac{8}{3}\sqrt{\frac{8}{3}}$ cm **4.** –9·7 m/s^2
5. (a) 20·4 m (b) 4·2 m/s (c) –9·8 m/s^2
6. (a) 12 m/s^2 (b) –4 m/s

Exercise 13

1. 28·1 cm/s **2.** 40 cm^2/s **3.** – 0·36 m^3/s
4. (a) 1 m/h (b) –1 m/h **5.** (b) $1{\cdot}5 \times 10^{-4}$ m/s (c) 2·47 hours **6.** (a) $\pi h(2 - h)$ (b) $\frac{1}{30\pi}$ m/min
7. (b) $-\frac{100}{(u - 10)^2}$ (c) $\frac{20}{9}$ cm/s **8.** (b) πh^2 (c) $\frac{5}{8}$ cm/s (d) 900 s

Exercise 14

1. $V = 27x^2 - x^3$, 2916 cm^3 **2.** (c) 4 cm
3. (a) $h = \frac{800 - 8x}{5}$ (b) $A = 640x - \frac{32x^2}{5}$ (c) $x = 50$ m
4. (a) $h = \frac{128}{x}$ (b) $A = 136 + 2x + \frac{512}{x}$ (c) 200 cm^2
5. (a) $\left(\frac{21 - x}{4}\right)$ (b) $h = \frac{x}{8}$, $y = \frac{3x}{8}$ (c) $\frac{3x^2}{64} + \frac{(21 - x)^2}{16}$ (d) $x = 12$ cm (e) 11·8125 cm^2
6. (a) $P = -\frac{x^3}{3} + 22x^2 - 160x - 1200$ (b) $\frac{dP}{dx} = -x^2 + 44x - 160$, $\frac{d^2P}{dx^2} = -2x + 44$ (c) 40
7. (a) 100 km/h (b) $\frac{d^2C}{dv^2} = \frac{2400}{v^3} > 0$ for $v = 100$ (c) €24 **8.** (a) (i) $\frac{dv}{dt} = -2 + 7t - 3t^2$ (ii) $\frac{d^2v}{dt^2} = 7 - 6t$ (iii) L Max (2, 12), L Min $\left(\frac{1}{3}, \frac{523}{54}\right)$ (iv) €12 (b) $t = \frac{7}{6}$; After $\frac{7}{6}$ years the rate of increase of the shares has stopped and will start to slow down
9. (a) $x = \frac{16}{h}$ (b) $C = €660{\cdot}77$ (c) $h = \sqrt{10}$ m (d) $€128(2 + \sqrt{10})$
10. (a) $R = \frac{x}{4}(80 - x)^2$ (b) $P = \frac{x^3}{4} - \frac{161}{4}x^2 + 1588x - 300$ (c) 26 units
11. (a) $y = \frac{8}{x}$ (b) $A = x^2 + \frac{128}{x} + 9$ (c) 57

12. (a) $I = \dfrac{6}{R+r}$ (b) $P = \dfrac{36R}{(R+r)^2}$ **13.** (a) $y = 16 - x$ (b) $S = x^3 + 2(16 - x)^2$ (c) $x = 4, y = 12, S_{MIN} = 352$

14. (a) $y = (6 - 2x)$ (b) $A = 6x - 2x^2$ (c) $\frac{9}{2}$

15. (a) $y = e^{-x^2}$ (b) $A = 2xe^{-x^2}$ (c) $x = \dfrac{1}{\sqrt{2}}, A_{MAX} = \sqrt{\dfrac{2}{e}}$

16. (a) 0 m (b) $(e^2 - 3)$ m (c) $(3 - 2\ln 2)$ m

17. (a) $|OC| = (20 + 15t)$ km (b) $|OD| = (20 - 30t)$ km (c) $L = \sqrt{(20+15t)^2 + (20-30t)^2}$ km (d) $t = 16$ minutes (e) $12\sqrt{5}$ km **18.** (a) $h = 1 + x$ (b) $r^2 = 1 - x^2$ (d) $x = \frac{1}{3}$ (e) $V_{Max} = \dfrac{32\pi}{81}$

19. (a) $r^2 = 64 - \dfrac{h^2}{4}$ (b) $V = 64\pi h - \dfrac{\pi h^3}{4}$ (c) $h = \dfrac{16}{\sqrt{3}}$ cm (d) $V_{Max} = \dfrac{2048}{3\sqrt{3}}$ cm^3

Revision Questions

1. (a) $x + y - 8 = 0$ (b) (i) 4 (ii) 12 (iii) $12x - y + 16 = 0$ (iv) $(-3, -27)$, $(3, 27)$ (v) 71·57° **2.** (a) (ii) 64 ln 2 (b) $y = \ln 3$ (c) (i) $-3\tan x$ (ii) $-\dfrac{3}{\cos^2 x}$ **3.** (a) (i) 0·51 °C (ii) 30 °C (b) Midnight, 1:17 a.m. (c) 2·3 °C/h (e) $\frac{7}{3}$ °C/h (f) 4:13 p.m., 0:38 a.m. **4.** (a) $k = \frac{1}{5} = 0{\cdot}2$ (b) 2552 (c) After 8 years (d) (i) 250 per year (ii) 371 per year **5.** (a) 3253·4 m (b) 500 mm Hg (c) $P = 760\, e^{-\left(\frac{1000}{137T + 3500}\right)}$ (d) 0·57 mm of Hg per °C

6. (a) $M = 100$ g (b) 49·86 g (c) 2·56 days (d) $-8{\cdot}7e^{-0{\cdot}087t}$ g/day (e) $-20 \ln 2e^{-0{\cdot}2t}$ g/day (f) 1·3

7. (a) $k = \dfrac{1}{5}\ln\left(\dfrac{10}{13}\right) = -0\cdot05$ (b) 68·57 °C (c) 19·11 minutes (d) $-\frac{13}{4}e^{-0{\cdot}05t}$ (e) 0·6 **8.** (b) 1 m (c) π s (d) $v = \sin 2t$ (e) $a = 2\cos 2t$

9. (a) $A(-5, 0)$, $B(0, 4)$, $C(5, 0)$, $D(0, -4)$, $E\left(-a, \dfrac{4\sqrt{25 - a^2}}{5}\right)$ (c) (i) $d = 10$ (ii) $a = 3$ (f) $\dfrac{dy}{dx} = -\dfrac{4x}{5\sqrt{25 - x^2}}$ (g) $3x + 5y - 25 = 0$

10. (a) (i) $\dfrac{10x}{5x^2 - 1}$ (iii) $\dfrac{10x}{(5x^2 - 1)\ln 10}$ (b) (i) $\dfrac{2}{3\ln 10}$ (ii) $x \log_2 e - y - \log_2 e = 0$ (c) 0·087 cm/°C

11. (a) L Max $\left(\dfrac{11}{3}, \dfrac{32}{27}\right)$, L Min (5, 0) (b) $\left(\dfrac{13}{3}, \dfrac{16}{27}\right)$ (c) (0, –75) (d) $Q(5, 0)$ (e) $P(3, 0)$ (f) 4 (g) $R\left(\dfrac{17}{3}, \dfrac{32}{27}\right)$

12. (a) $|PB| = \sqrt{x^2 + 9}$ (b) $\dfrac{3 - x}{100}$ (c) $\dfrac{\sqrt{x^2 + 9}}{60}$ (d) $T = \dfrac{3 - x}{100} + \dfrac{\sqrt{x^2 + 9}}{60}$ (e) 2·25 km (f) 4·2 minutes

13. (a) $\dfrac{\pi r^2}{4} + 2xr$ (c) $4x + 2r + \dfrac{\pi r}{2}$ (e) $r = \sqrt{8}$ m $= 2\sqrt{2}$ m (f) $8\sqrt{2}$ m **14.** (a) €409·43 (b) $\dfrac{100}{x} - \dfrac{(60 - x)}{5}$ (c) $C'(70) = \frac{24}{7}$, $C'(40) = -\frac{3}{2}$ (d) €3·52 (e) 50 (f) €401·20 **15.** (b) (i) $\sqrt{100 + a^2}$ (ii) $\sqrt{1 + \dfrac{100}{a^2}}$ (d) $a = \sqrt[3]{100} = 4{\cdot}64$ km (e) 13·4 km

16. (a) m_0 (b) 20 101 kg (c) $\dfrac{dm}{dv} = \dfrac{m_0 v}{c^2\left(1 - \dfrac{v^2}{c^2}\right)^{\frac{3}{2}}}$ (d) $\dfrac{3m_0}{256}$ kg/s (e) $v = \dfrac{c\sqrt{m^2 - m_0^2}}{m}$ (f) 19 515·6 m/s/kg

Section 9

Chapter 25

Exercise 1

1. $e^x + c$ **2.** $5e^x + c$ **3.** $\frac{1}{3}$ **4.** $x^3 + c$ **5.** $\dfrac{2}{\ln 2}$ **6.** $\dfrac{3 \times 4^x}{\ln 4} + c$ **7.** $e^2 + \dfrac{5}{3} + \dfrac{3}{\ln 2}$ **8.** $\dfrac{e^x}{2} - \dfrac{3x^2}{2} + \dfrac{2^x}{3\ln 2} + c$ **9.** $\dfrac{1 - 2^{\frac{\pi}{3}}}{\ln 2} - \dfrac{3}{2}$ **10.** $\ln 2 + \frac{7}{3} - e^2 + e$ **11.** $2e^x - 3x + \ln x + c$ **12.** $2\ln x - 3e^x + \dfrac{x^3}{4} + c$ **13.** $\dfrac{3}{4} - \dfrac{e}{2}$ **14.** $\dfrac{27}{5\ln 10}$ **15.** 1 **16.** $3\ln 2 + \frac{3}{2}$ **17.** $\frac{3}{2}e^x - \ln x + c$ **18.** $-\frac{2}{3}$ **19.** $\dfrac{3}{\ln 4}$ **20.** $(k + 1)p + c$ **21.** $3\ln 2 - 3$ **22.** $\frac{29}{6}$

Exercise 2

1. $\dfrac{x^{16}}{16} + c$ **2.** $\frac{2}{3}x^{\frac{3}{2}} + c$ **3.** $-\dfrac{2}{x^2} + c$ **4.** $\frac{17}{6}$ **5.** $-\frac{77}{6}$ **6.** $-\frac{11}{3}$ **7.** $\frac{1}{3}x^2 - x + c$ **8.** $\frac{22}{21}$ **9.** $4\sqrt{t} - \frac{2}{5}t^{\frac{5}{2}} + c$ **10.** –4 **11.** $\frac{1}{2}x^3 - \frac{1}{2}x^2 + x + c$ **12.** $\frac{17}{6}$ **13.** $\dfrac{(x+1)^6}{6} + c$ **14.** 10 **15.** $\frac{14}{3}$ **16.** 1 **17.** $-\dfrac{1}{x+1} + c$ **18.** $-\dfrac{2}{3(3x+1)^2} + c$ **19.** $1 - \dfrac{1}{\sqrt{3}}$

Exercise 3

1. $\frac{1}{5}e^{5x} + c$ **2.** $\frac{3}{2}e^{\frac{2}{3}x} + c$ **3.** $-\dfrac{1}{2e^{2x}} + c$ **4.** $\frac{1}{3}e^2(e^3 - 1)$ **5.** $\frac{1}{2}e^6(e^2 - 1)$ **6.** $\frac{3}{4}e(e^4 - 1)$ **7.** $-e^{-x+3} + c$ **8.** $\frac{5}{4}$

9. $\frac{14}{3}$ **10.** $\frac{7}{2} + \ln 2$ **11.** $\frac{5^x}{\ln 5} + c$ **12.** $\frac{3}{2\ln 2}$

13. $-\frac{1}{3\ln 2 \times 2^{3x}}$ **14.** $\frac{2^{kt}}{k\ln 2} + c$ **15.** $-\frac{10}{k\ln 3 \times 3^{kt}} + c$

16. $\frac{5^{2x+1}}{2\ln 5} + c$

Exercise 4

1. $\frac{1}{3}\ln x + c$ **2.** $\ln(x+2) + c$ **3.** $\ln 2$ **4.** $\frac{1}{2}\ln\left(\frac{5}{3}\right)$

5. $\frac{1}{3}\ln 4$ **6.** $\ln 3$ **7.** $9\ln\left(\frac{x}{3} + 2\right) + c$

8. $-\frac{5}{3}\ln(4 - 3x) + c$ **9.** 1 **10.** $\frac{1}{k}\ln(kt + \alpha) + c$

11. $\frac{1}{2}\ln 3$ **12.** $\ln\frac{4}{3}$

Exercise 5

1. $\frac{\sin 2x}{2} + c$ **2.** $-\frac{1}{7}$ **3.** $\frac{1 - \cos 3}{2}$ **4.** $\frac{3\sqrt{2}}{2}$ **5.** $\frac{\sqrt{2}}{12}$

6. $-\frac{1}{2}$ **7.** $\frac{4}{7}$ **8.** $\frac{14}{5}$ **9.** $\frac{5}{3}$ **10.** $-\frac{1}{4}\cos 2x + c$

Exercise 6

1. $\frac{1}{3}x^3 + \frac{4}{3}x^{\frac{3}{2}} + \ln x + c$ **2.** $\frac{3}{4}x^2 - \frac{1}{2}x + c$ **3.** 2

4. $\frac{4}{3}x^3 - x + c$ **5.** $\frac{7}{3} + \ln 2 + e(e - 1)$ **6.** $\frac{1}{3}e^{3x+2} + c$

7. $\frac{e^{2x}}{2} + 2x - \frac{1}{2e^{2x}} + c$ **8.** $\frac{\pi}{8} - \frac{1}{4}$ **9.** $\frac{19}{3}$ **10.** $\frac{\pi}{8}$

11. $\frac{19171}{45}$ **12.** $\frac{\sqrt{2}}{2}$

Chapter 26

Exercise 7

1. (a) $\frac{81}{4}$ (b) $\frac{32}{3}$ (c) $\frac{11}{3}$ (d) $3\ln 2$ (e) $3\left(e^2 - \frac{1}{e}\right)$ (f) $\frac{21}{\ln 2}$

(g) 36 (h) 1 (i) π (j) $\frac{16}{3}$ **2.** (a) $\frac{4}{3}$ (b) $\frac{9}{2}$ (c) $\frac{1}{2}$ (d) $\frac{51}{4}$

3. (a) (ii) $\frac{80}{3}$ (iii) $\frac{80}{3\ln 3}$ (iv) $100(\ln 3 - 1)\% \approx 10\%$

(b) (i) $90\frac{2}{3}$ m (ii) $85\frac{1}{3}$ m

Exercise 8

1. (a) $\frac{9}{2}$ (b) $\frac{3}{4}$ (c) $\frac{1}{12}$ (d) 9 (e) $\frac{9}{2}$ (f) $12 - \ln 4$

2. (a) $y = \frac{3}{2}x^2 - 5x + \frac{9}{2}$ (b) $\frac{27}{4}$ **3.** $\frac{64}{3}$ **5.** $\frac{3 - e}{2}$

7. $\frac{64}{3}$; 64 **8.** $\frac{104}{3}$

Exercise 9

1. (a) $y = \frac{1}{3}x^3 - 8$ (b) $y = e^x$ (c) $y = 3\ln x$
(d) $v = -5t + 50$ (e) $h = 5 - 3\sin\left(\frac{\pi}{2} - t\right)$
(f) $f(x) = e^x + 2\ln x + 3 - e$ (g) $y = x^2 - x + 1$

2. (a) $Q = 34 - \frac{3}{2}Z^2$ (b) $s = t^3$ (c) $v = 3\ln(t - 2) + 3$
(d) $s = ut + \frac{1}{2}at^2$ (e) 10 s **3.** (a) $p = 6$ Pa
(b) (i) $\frac{dB}{dt} = \frac{kt^2}{10}$ (ii) $B = \frac{t^3}{270}$ (iii) $\frac{4}{5}$ T **4.** (a) $\frac{dh}{dt} = -kt^{\frac{1}{2}}$
(c) $k = \frac{3}{32}$ (d) 6·35 mins **5.** 14·54 mins

Exercise 10

1. (a) 13 (b) $\frac{e^5 - 1}{5e^2}$ (c) $\frac{50}{3}$ (d) $\frac{65}{9}$ (e) $\frac{\sqrt{3}}{5\pi}$ **2.** (a) $\frac{41}{3}$ m/s
(b) 37·5 °C (c) $9{\cdot}375 \times 10^{-3}$ amps (d) 49 m/s
(e) 1·5 g (f) (i) 5 s (ii) 3·2 litres

Revision Questions

1. (a) $x = -1$ (b) $x > -1, x \in \mathbb{R}$ (c) (i) $x = -3$
(ii) $x = 1$ (d) $f'(x) = -2x^2 - 4x + 6$
(e) $y = f(x) = -\frac{2}{3}x^3 - 2x^2 + 6x - 2$
2. (b) (i) $P(0, -3)$, $Q(\ln 2, 0)$
(iii) $4\ln 2 - \frac{3}{2}$ **3.** (a) $P(x) = (x - 2)(x^2 + 2x + 3)$ (b) 11
(c) 10 **4.** (a) L min (0, 0), L max (4, 32) (b) $y = 32$
(c) $B(6, 0)$ (e) 192 (f) 84 (g) 108 **5.** (a) $P(0, 4)$
(b) $\frac{514}{3}$ (c) $\frac{484}{3\ln 3} + 10$; 9·2% (d) (ii) 1·63
6. (b) $y = 3x + 6$ (c) $\frac{189}{10}$ **7.** (b) $B(4, 2)$
(c) $y = -\frac{8}{3}x + \frac{38}{3}$ (d) $\frac{22}{5}$ **8.** (a) $\frac{\pi}{2}$ (b) €5535
(c) (i) $P(0, 0)$, $Q(4, 8)$ (ii) $\frac{128}{15}$ **9.** 1632 million barrels
10. 14 705 **11.** (a) 61 (b) 57 **12.** (a) $P\left(\frac{\pi}{2}, 1\right)$
(b) $h = \frac{4}{\pi} - 1$ **13.** (a) $y = 2x^3 - x^2 + 3x$ (b) $e^4(e^2 - 1)$
(c) $t = \frac{4\sqrt{3}}{3}$ **15.** (a) $a = 5$ (b) (i) €1 per year
(ii) €e per year (c) €$5(e - 1)$ = €8·59
16. (a) 22 °C (b) 21·1 °C (c) –1·408 °C/h (d) 22 °C
(e) 17·2 °C **17.** (a) $\frac{dP}{dt} = \frac{k}{\sqrt{t}}$ (c) 74 000 (d) 36 years
(e) 63 333 **18.** (a) 30 m (b) 46·3 m (c) 7051 m^2
(d) 35 m **19.** (b) (i) $\frac{\int_0^5 \theta\, dr}{5}$ (ii) $\frac{\int_5^{15} \theta\, dr}{10}$
(iii) 92 °C **20.** (a) 16 hours; 91 days after the spring equinox (b) 12 hours; Because there are equal number of hours per day and night (c) 14·5 hours
21. (a) (i) $x\cos x + \sin x$ (ii) $x\sin x + c$
(b) $x\sin x + \cos x + c$ **22.** (a) $x + \ln(x + 1)$
(b) $1 + \ln x$, $x\ln x - x + c$